AMERICAN BUSINESS ABROAD

Origins and Development
of the Multinational Corporation

AMERICAN BUSINESS ABROAD

Origins and Development
of the Multinational Corporation

*See last pages of this volume for
a complete list of titles*

STATISTICS ON AMERICAN
BUSINESS ABROAD
1950-1975

ARNO PRESS
A New York Times Company
1976

Editorial Supervision: SHEILA MEHLMAN

———◆———

Reprint Edition 1976 by Arno Press Inc.

Copyright © 1976 by Arno Press Inc.

AMERICAN BUSINESS ABROAD: Origins and
Development of the Multinational Corporation
ISBN for complete set: 0-405-09261-X
See last pages of this volume for titles.

Manufactured in the United States of America

Publisher's Note: This work has been reprinted
from the best available copies.

———◆———

Library of Congress Cataloging in Publication Data

Main entry under title:

Statistics on American business abroad, 1950-1975.

    (American business abroad)
    Reprinted from the Survey of current busines, 1950-
1975.
    1. Investments, Americqn--Addresses, essays,
lectures. I. Survey of current business. II. Series.
HG4538.S74 1976   332.6'7373   76-5035
ISBN 0-405-09301-2

CONTENTS

Pizer, Samuel and Frederick Cutler
PRIVATE FOREIGN INVESTMENTS NEAR $37 BILLION.
(Reprinted from Vol. 38, No. 9, September, 1958)

Pizer, Samuel and Frederick Cutler
U.S. INDUSTRY EXPANDS INVESTMENT ABROAD.
(Reprinted from Vol. 39, No. 10, October, 1959)

Pizer, Samuel and Frederick Cutler
UNITED STATES FOREIGN INVESTMENTS: Measures of
Growth and Economic Effects. (Reprinted from Vol. 40,
No. 9, September 1960)

Pizer, Samuel and Frederick Cutler
CAPITAL OUTLAYS ABROAD BY U.S. COMPANIES: Rising
Plant Expansion in Manufacturing. (Reprinted from Vol. 40,
No. 10, October, 1960)

Pizer, Samuel and Frederick Cutler
UNITED STATES ASSETS AND INVESTMENTS ABROAD.
(Reprinted from Vol. 41, No. 8, August, 1961)

Pizer, Samuel and Frederick Cutler
EXPANSION IN U.S. INVESTMENTS ABROAD. (Reprinted
from Vol. 42, No. 8, August, 1962)

Cutler, Frederick
FINANCING U.S. DIRECT FOREIGN INVESTMENT.
(Reprinted from Vol. 42, No. 9, September, 1962)

Cutler, Fred[erick] and Samuel Pizer
FOREIGN OPERATIONS OF U.S. INDUSTRY: Capital
Expenditures, Sales and Financing. (Reprinted from Vol. 43,
No. 10, October, 1963)

Cutler, Fred[erick] and Samuel Pizer
U.S. FIRMS ACCELERATE CAPITAL EXPENDITURES
ABROAD. (Reprinted from Vol. 44, No. 10, October, 1964)

Pizer, Samuel and Frederick Cutler
FOREIGN INVESTMENTS, 1964-65. (Reprinted from Vol. 45,
No. 9, September, 1965)

Pizer, Samuel and Frederick Cutler
FOREIGN INVESTMENTS, 1965-66. (Reprinted from Vol. 46,
No. 9, September, 1966)

Lederer, Walther and Frederick Cutler
INTERNATIONAL INVESTMENTS OF THE UNITED STATES
IN 1966. (Reprinted from Vol. 47, No. 9, September, 1967)

PLANT AND EQUIPMENT EXPENDITURES BY FOREIGN
AFFILIATES OF U.S. CORPORATIONS, 1967-69. (Reprinted
from Vol. 48, No. 9, September, 1968)

Nelson, Emil L. and Frederick Cutler
THE INTERNATIONAL INVESTMENT POSITION OF THE
UNITED STATES IN 1967. (Reprinted from Vol. 48, No. 10,
October 1968)

Devlin, David T. and Frederick Cutler
THE INTERNATIONAL INVESTMENT POSITION OF THE
UNITED STATES: Developments in 1968. (Reprinted from
Vol. 49, No. 10, October, 1969)

Devlin, David T. and George R. Kruer
THE INTERNATIONAL INVESTMENT POSITION OF THE
UNITED STATES: Developments in 1969. (Reprinted from
Vol. 50, No. 10, October, 1970)

Murad, Howard
PLANT AND EQUIPMENT EXPENDITURES BY FOREIGN
AFFILIATES OF U.S. CORPORATIONS: Revised Estimates
for 1970 and 1971. (Reprinted from Vol. 51, No. 3,
March, 1971)

Murad, Howard
PLANT AND EQUIPMENT EXPENDITURES BY FOREIGN
AFFILIATES OF U.S. CORPORATIONS, 1970-72. (Reprinted
from Vol. 51, No. 9, September, 1971)

Freidlin, Julius N. and Leonard A. Lupo
U.S. DIRECT INVESTMENTS ABROAD IN 1971. (Reprinted
from Vol. 52, No. 11, November, 1972)

Lupo, Leonard A.
U.S. DIRECT INVESTMENT ABROAD IN 1972. (Reprinted
from Vol. 53, No. 9, September, 1973)

Kraseman, Thomas W. and Betty L. Barker
EMPLOYMENT AND PAYROLL COSTS OF U.S.
MULTINATIONAL COMPANIES. (Reprinted from Vol. 53,
No. 10, October, 1973)

Belli, R. David, Smith W. Allnutt and Howard Murad
PROPERTY, PLANT, AND EQUIPMENT EXPENDITURES BY
MAJORITY-OWNED FOREIGN AFFILIATES OF U.S.
COMPANIES: Revised Estimates for 1966-72 and Projections
for 1973 and 1974. (Reprinted from Vol. 53, No. 12,
December, 1973)

Freidlin, J[ulius] N. and L[eonard] A. Lupo
U.S. DIRECT INVESTMENT ABROAD IN 1973. (Reprinted
from Vol. 54, No. 8, Part II, August, 1974)

Lupo, Leonard A. and Julius N. Freidlin
U.S. DIRECT INVESTMENT ABROAD IN 1974. (Reprinted
from Vol. 55, No. 10, October, 1975)

INCOME ON INTERNATIONAL INVESTMENTS
OF THE UNITED STATES

Samuel Pizer

by Samuel Pizer

Income on International Investments of the United States

THE amount of income received from United States investments abroad rose in 1950, continuing the strong expansion which began in 1946. Income received from abroad in 1950 amounted to $1,743 million, exclusive of undistributed earnings of $443 million by United States-controlled foreign companies. The income received by foreigners from investments in this country was $437 million, exclusive of undistributed earnings of about $170 million by foreign controlled enterprises in the United States.[1]

Growth of Income Receipts

Income receipts from investments abroad in 1950 were 24 percent above 1949 and were nearly double the prewar high for 1929. However, this comparison makes no allowance for large increases in price levels and changes in other international accounts in the last two decades. For instance, in 1929 foreign countries used about 17 percent of the dollar proceeds of their exports of goods and services to the United States to cover income remittances to the United States, while in 1950 such remittances used only about 15 percent.

By far the largest part of the growth in income receipts since 1946 has come from the expansion of American direct investments abroad (chart 1). These foreign operations produced increasing quantities of vitally necessary materials in a period when, except for a temporary setback in 1949, world demand was pushing prices of commodities steadily upward. Both increasing output and rising prices were important in 1950, although there was also in that year a tendency to pay out a larger proportion of earnings, and, in a few important cases, to pay dividends out of earnings of prior years.

Direct investments accounted for 84 percent of the 1950 income receipts while the return on private portfolio investments was only $165 million, or less than 10 percent of the total, with United States Government income making up the remainder. This compares with a proportion of about 50 percent for portfolio income in 1929.

Although the value of direct investments has moved up to 70 percent of private long-term foreign investments, this fact was of lesser importance in accounting for the larger share of direct-investment income than the higher rates of return realized on these investments since 1946. From about 6 percent of book value in 1929, the earnings on direct investments went to about 15 percent in 1950. This latter figure is much closer to earnings rates in the United States than was the case in 1929.[2] On the other hand, the return

on private portfolio investments, which was about the same as for direct investments in 1929, about 6 percent, was down to about 3 percent in 1950. This, in part, reflects the lower interest rate structure today, but also the results of defaults, retirements, and refunding operations which scaled down the interest rates on outstanding obligations.

In 1950 the rate of return on all United States-controlled manufacturing investments abroad was about 16 percent, which was about the same as the rate of return for domestic manufacturing enterprises, excluding petroleum and automotive products.[3] Of course, the industrial composition of

Table 1.—United States Income on International Investments, by Type, 1946–50

[Millions of dollars]

Type	1946	1947	1948	1949	1950
Receipts					
Total balance-of-payments income receipts	810	1,146	1,375	1,405	1,743
Private	789	1,080	1,273	1,307	1,634
Long-term	784	1,070	1,260	1,296	1,624
Direct investments	636	924	1,111	1,148	1,469
Dividends	268	379	420	505	656
Interest	38	34	32	35	35
Branch profits	330	511	659	608	778
Dollar bonds	65	58	61	60	69
Other long-term investments	83	88	88	88	86
Short-term investments	5	10	13	11	10
United States Government	21	66	102	98	109
Undistributed earnings of direct-investment subsidiaries	303	387	581	436	443
Total earnings on United States investments abroad	1,113	1,533	1,956	1,841	2,186
Payments					
Total balance-of-payments income payments	216	249	284	353	437
Private	201	233	267	328	406
Long-term [1]	201	233	267	328	406
Direct investments	76	84	109	159	196
Dividends	51	45	56	76	110
Interest	1	1	1	2	12
Branch profits	24	38	52	81	74
Other long-term investments	125	149	158	169	210
Dividends	103	116	138	148	190
Interest	22	33	20	21	20
United States Government	15	16	17	25	31
Undistributed earnings of direct-investment subsidiaries	37	90	156	143	172
Total earnings on foreign investments in the United States	253	339	440	496	609

[1] Payments on private short-term obligations were negligible.
Source: U. S. Department of Commerce, Office of Business Economics.

manufacturing companies in the United States and abroad differs greatly, but nearly half of the industry subgroups under manufacturing in the United States had higher rates of return than the average rate on all United States-controlled manufacturing enterprises abroad.

NOTE: MR. PIZER IS A MEMBER OF THE BALANCE OF PAYMENTS DIVISION, OFFICE OF BUSINESS ECONOMICS. MR. FREDERICK CUTLER OF THAT DIVISION CONTRIBUTED MATERIALLY TO THE SECTIONS ON DIRECT INVESTMENTS.

[1] For definitions of terms see the technical note at the end of the article.
[2] Such calculated rates of return are subject to some statistical and conceptual difficulties, but the figures cited can be taken as illustrative of the change which has occurred.

[3] Source for data on rates of return for United States industry is the National City Bank of New York monthly letter for April 1951.

An important factor in the increased earnings of direct investments was the shift in industrial composition from a high proportion, about 22 percent, of public utility holdings in the 1920's to a heavy concentration of investments in petroleum and manufacturing enterprises. These latter industries, in contrast to public utilities whose rates are closely regulated, shared more prominently both here and abroad in the world-wide expansion of demand for their products.

Government income due to increase

Interest received by the United States Government on foreign credits mounted from $15 million in 1946 to $109 million in 1950, and is scheduled to become considerably greater as interest payments come due on some of the larger postwar credits. The annual average amount of interest due to the United States Government on foreign credits now outstanding is about $170 million for the 1950 decade, or about $40 million more than the annual average received during the 1920's on the World War I loans.

Most direct-investment earnings plowed back

Over the five-year period 1946–50, American direct investments abroad earned $7.5 billion (including interest payments to parent companies of $174 million), but about half of this was retained abroad for investment. As shown in chart 2, earnings exceeded additions to investment in every year, and in 1950 capital additions actually fell off although earnings rose to record heights. The disposition of earnings can be accounted for as follows: (a) foreign-incorporated subsidiaries of United States companies earned $4.6 billion in the 1946–50 period, of which $2.4 billion was paid out as dividends and interest to parent companies and the remainder reinvested, and (b) branch profits totaled $2.9 billion, of which more than 55 percent was retained abroad, in the aggregate. Thus, out of total additions of $5.2 billion to direct investments abroad in 1946–50, about $3.8 billion came out of retained earnings and the remainder represented new investments of United States funds.

Results by industries

Most of the sharp rise in income receipts in 1950, as shown in table 3, was the result of very high income in the petroleum industry. However, income receipts from petroleum enterprises rose more sharply than earnings, indicating a decline in capital investment abroad from reinvested earnings by this industry. Moreover, capital outflows from the parent companies in the United States declined by an even larger amount.

Income from direct investments in other industries in 1950 did not gain so much as income in the petroleum industry; however, for these industries earnings rose more than income remittances to the United States. American investments in manufacturing enterprises abroad are about as important as petroleum enterprises so far as earnings are concerned. In 1946–50, earnings of manufacturing enterprises amounted to $2.5 billion as compared with $2.6 billion for petroleum. The earnings of manufacturing enterprises were more stable in this period than those of other direct investments abroad, as shown in chart 2, and did not decline in 1949, in contrast to earnings of the petroleum and mining industries. More than half the earnings and income receipts from manufacturing enterprises abroad originated in Canada, with the countries of Western Europe and Latin America accounting for most of the remainder.

Earnings of mining and smelting enterprises fell off sharply in 1949 and then recovered to a record amount in 1950, reflecting extreme sensitivity to developments in the United States market. These enterprises are largely centered in the Western Hemisphere and showed very little tendency to expand after the war until 1950. The proportion of earnings

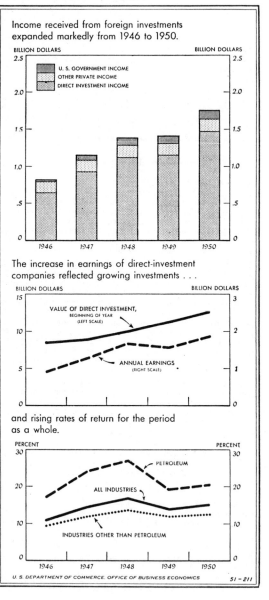

Chart 1

Income received from foreign investments expanded markedly from 1946 to 1950.

BILLION DOLLARS   BILLION DOLLARS

U. S. GOVERNMENT INCOME
OTHER PRIVATE INCOME
DIRECT INVESTMENT INCOME

The increase in earnings of direct-investment companies reflected growing investments . . .

BILLION DOLLARS   BILLION DOLLARS

VALUE OF DIRECT INVESTMENT, BEGINNING OF YEAR (LEFT SCALE)

ANNUAL EARNINGS (RIGHT SCALE)

and rising rates of return for the period as a whole.

PERCENT   PERCENT

PETROLEUM

ALL INDUSTRIES

INDUSTRIES OTHER THAN PETROLEUM

U. S. DEPARTMENT OF COMMERCE, OFFICE OF BUSINESS ECONOMICS   51 – 211

reinvested by subsidiaries in Canada was quite low prior to 1950 and then moved upward, when as shown in chart 2, an increase in capital investment in mining got under way. However some of the principal projects being developed are not yet in the income-producing stage. Earnings from foreign direct investments in other industries have not been very large and have increased only gradually.

Income on Investments by Area

Nearly 40 percent of the income received from abroad in the 1946–50 period originated in the Latin American Republics, very largely from direct investments (table 2). Increased income from Latin America was responsible for about one-third of the total rise in income receipts in this period. However, while income from every other area increased in each year after the war, income from Latin America showed a severe setback in 1949 as metal and petroleum earnings fell off. In 1950 there was a striking reversal of this situation and of the increase of about $340 million in income received from all areas in 1950, $240 million came from Latin America, chiefly from additional earnings of the petroleum industry. As shown in table 4, Venezuela has accounted for an increasing share of income from Latin America.

Second in importance in income receipts was Canada, accounting for 26 percent of the total received in the 1946–50 period. Although direct investments also dominated income receipts from that country, there were substantial amounts of income received on American holdings of Canadian securities denominated in both United States and Canadian dollars. However, income from these portfolio investments remained stable while direct-investment income, largely from manufacturing, more than doubled from 1946 to 1950.

Income receipts from the countries grouped under "other foreign countries" and from the dependencies of the ERP countries are derived very largely from petroleum invest-

ments. Income from these areas rose sharply, therefore, as the petroleum industry utilized large postwar additions to its capacity and output moved upward. Present indications are that petroleum earnings in these areas, largely the Middle East, will rise further as the demand for petroleum in areas serviced by the Middle East fields continues to press against the available output, although requirements to pay larger local royalties and taxes will cut into the increase.

Government income large from ERP countries

A leading feature of income receipts from the ERP countries in 1946–50 was the expansion of interest payments on United States Government credits. Interest receipts on such credits rose from $14 million in 1946 to $78 million in 1950 (table 2), while the increase in direct-investment income was comparatively small. The United Kingdom was the source of most of the direct-investment income, which consisted largely of returns on investments in manufacturing enterprises. By far the largest amounts of interest on United States Government credits were paid by France on credits extended soon after the war's end. However, beginning with 1951, when interest on loans to Britain becomes due, the total interest obligation of ERP countries will rise to $160–$165 million annually for the next few years.

Income Payments on Foreign Investments in the United States

The amount of income paid on foreign investments here is, of course, far less than the amount received, and has been less since the first World War. As shown in table 1, the excess of receipts rose from about $600 million in 1946 to over $1.3 billion in 1950, although the increase in payments was proportionally about the same as the increase in receipts.

Table 2.—Investment Income Receipts and Payments, by Area, 1946–50

Area and type	1946 Receipts	1946 Payments	1946 Net	1947 Receipts	1947 Payments	1947 Net	1948 Receipts	1948 Payments	1948 Net	1949 Receipts	1949 Payments	1949 Net	1950 Receipts	1950 Payments	1950 Net
Total, all areas	810	216	+594	1,146	249	+897	1,375	284	+1,091	1,405	353	+1,052	1,743	437	+1,306
Direct	636	76	+560	924	84	+840	1,111	109	+1,002	1,148	159	+989	1,469	196	+1,273
Other private	153	125	+28	156	149	+7	162	158	+4	159	169	−10	165	210	−45
U. S. Government	21	15	+6	66	16	+50	102	17	+85	98	25	+73	109	31	+78
Canada	248	44	+204	302	32	+270	319	54	+265	387	66	+321	406	76	+330
Direct	148	25	+123	203	11	+192	223	25	+198	295	39	+256	365	39	+266
Other private	100	15	+85	99	19	+80	94	25	+69	92	20	+72	101	27	+74
U. S. Government	(1)	4	−4	(1)	2	−2	2	4	−2	(1)	7	−7	(1)	10	−10
Latin American Republics	334	10	+324	477	11	+466	556	12	+544	455	11	+444	696	14	+682
Direct	314	1	+313	451	1	+450	525	1	+524	425	(1)	+425	664		+664
Other private	15	8	+7	17	9	+8	19	10	+9	18	9	+9	18	12	+6
U. S. Government	5	1	+4	9	1	+8	12	1	+11	12	2	+10	14	2	+12
ERP countries	107	146	−39	153	183	−30	195	196	−1	202	252	−50	216	322	−106
Direct	64	49	+15	80	71	+9	93	82	+11	97	118	−21	108	155	−47
Other private	29	94	−65	30	110	−80	32	111	−79	32	130	−98	30	160	−130
U. S. Government	14	3	+11	43	2	+41	70	3	+67	73	4	+69	78	7	+71
ERP dependencies	20	2	+18	32	3	+29	75	2	+73	78	2	+76	90	3	+87
Direct	20		+20	32		+32	73		+73	77		+77	90		+90
Other private		2	−2		2	−2		2	−2		2	−2		2	−2
U. S. Government				(1)	1	−1	2	(1)	+2	1	(1)	+1		1	−1
Other Europe	4	(1)	+4	11	1	+10	10	2	+8	11	2	+9	13	1	+12
Direct	1	(1)	+1	(1)	(1)		(1)	(1)		(1)	1	−1	(1)	1	−1
Other private	3	(1)	+3	3	1	+2	2	2		2	1	+1	2	(1)	+2
U. S. Government				8	(1)	+8	8	(1)	+8	9	(1)	+9	11	(1)	+11
Other foreign countries	97	14	+83	171	15	+156	213	13	+200	265	14	+251	316	14	+302
Direct	89	1	+88	158	1	+157	197	1	+196	254	1	+253	302	1	+301
Other private	6	6		7	8	−1	8	8		8	7	+1	8	9	−1
U. S. Government	2	7	−5	6	6		8	4	+4	3	6	−3	6	4	+2
International institutions					4	−4	7	5	+2	7	6	+1	6	7	−1
Direct															
Other private					4	−4	7		+7	7		+7	6		+6
U. S. Government								5	−5		6	−6		7	−7

1 Less than $500,000.   Source: U. S. Department of Commerce, Office of Business Economics.

Moreover, the gap will probably continue to grow as United States investments abroad continue in much larger amounts than foreign investments in the United States.

Chart 2

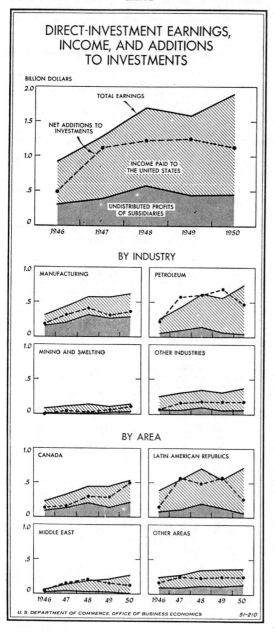

DIRECT-INVESTMENT EARNINGS, INCOME, AND ADDITIONS TO INVESTMENTS

BILLION DOLLARS

TOTAL EARNINGS

NET ADDITIONS TO INVESTMENTS

INCOME PAID TO THE UNITED STATES

UNDISTRIBUTED PROFITS OF SUBSIDIARIES

BY INDUSTRY

MANUFACTURING   PETROLEUM

MINING AND SMELTING   OTHER INDUSTRIES

BY AREA

CANADA   LATIN AMERICAN REPUBLICS

MIDDLE EAST   OTHER AREAS

U. S. DEPARTMENT OF COMMERCE, OFFICE OF BUSINESS ECONOMICS   51-210

Income payments mostly on portfolio investments

In contrast with United States investments abroad, foreign investors in the United States have concentrated on portfolio investments, so that of total payments abroad in the 1946–50 period of $1.5 billion, over $800 million was on private portfolio investments, about $100 million was paid on long- and short-term United States Government obligations, and somewhat over $600 million was derived from American enterprises controlled abroad.

Dividends paid abroad on foreign portfolio investments in United States corporate stocks accounted for nearly half of all income payments from 1946 to 1950 (table 1). Fluctuations in these payments are closely related to the dividend policies followed by American corporations. Much of the explanation for the continued increase in income payments to foreigners since 1946, and particularly the sharp rise in 1950, rests on this factor. Tabulations of dividends paid to foreigners in the 1946–50 period have shown that in each year payments abroad have risen at a somewhat higher rate than all United States dividend payments in spite of some reduction in foreign holdings of United States corporate stocks. This suggests that foreign holdings are centered in stock issues on which dividend rates have risen relatively sharply in recent years.

Interest payments by the United States Government are comparatively minor and result from a tendency by foreign governments and central banks to invest dollar reserves in interest-bearing securities rather than to hold them in the form of demand deposits or gold, which yield no income. Interest payments on foreign holdings of United States corporate bonds jumped for a year or two after the war as payments in arrears were made up, but then settled down to small annual amounts.

Expansion of foreign direct investments financed by earnings

Foreign-controlled companies operating in the United States depended almost entirely on earnings in the United States as a source of funds for expansion in the 1946–50 period. Total earnings of these companies for the period are estimated at $1.2 billion. About half of this amount was paid out as dividends and branch profits, while $600 million was retained here by the American subsidiaries of foreign companies. In addition, about $150 million of the branch profits was added to the value of United States branches of foreign companies, primarily insurance companies, by the retention of these earnings in the United States. There were only a few minor instances of new foreign capital flowing to the United States; what appears in the United States balance of payments as capital movements to the United States from foreign parent companies was largely the branch earnings mentioned above. These are reflected in the balance of payments as current income payments, and as capital inflows to the extent they are not actually transferred abroad.

Insurance companies lead in branch profits

The insurance field is one of the few segments of American business in which foreign companies have a position of some significance. The largest operations of these companies are through United States branches rather than subsidiaries, primarily in the field of fire and marine underwriting. In this field foreign insurance companies accounted for about 15 percent of net premiums written in recent years. Out of total estimated branch profits of $270 million for 1946–50, insurance companies were responsible for considerably more than half. In addition, United States subsidiaries of foreign insurance companies earned about $65 million in 1946–50, of which less than half was paid out in dividends.

In the aggregate, foreign-controlled insurance enterprises earned about $255 million in 1946–50, more than enough to finance an increase in their value of $205 million for the period. However, British companies, which are preeminent in this field, accounted for about $200 million of the earnings but only about $125 million of the increase in value. Most of the difference between these figures is accounted for by payments of $46 million out of earnings in this period to the Reconstruction Finance Corporation as repayments on an outstanding loan to the British Government. However, in addition, British companies withdrew a sizable proportion of their earnings, while other insurance companies, principally Continental European and Canadian, added to their investment an amount equal to their earnings plus about $30 million of new funds.

Table 3.—Direct-Investment Income Receipts by Area and Industry, 1946–1950

[In millions of dollars]

Area	Year	Manufacturing	Distribution	Agriculture	Mining and smelting	Petroleum	Public utilities	Miscellaneous	Total
Total, all areas	1946	156	48	74	68	204	45	41	636
	1947	230	84	94	107	323	43	43	924
	1948	248	84	89	129	472	31	58	1,111
	1949	301	93	80	88	487	39	60	1,148
	1950	328	97	98	112	705	45	84	1,469
Canada	1946	80	9	(¹)	23	5	15	16	148
	1947	106	23	(¹)	26	6	21	21	203
	1948	123	16	(¹)	34	8	12	30	223
	1949	179	29	2	29	11	18	27	295
	1950	181	27	2	33	12	11	39	305
Latin American Republics	1946	33	21	61	43	115	30	11	314
	1947	60	32	80	74	172	22	11	451
	1948	50	33	80	84	243	19	16	525
	1949	35	24	68	44	217	21	16	425
	1950	54	36	90	64	362	33	25	664
ERP countries	1946	37	12	------	(¹)	7	------	8	64
	1947	47	17	------	(¹)	10	------	6	80
	1948	51	18	------	1	8	------	5	93
	1949	60	19	------	(¹)	8	------	10	97
	1950	68	21	------	1	7	(¹)	11	108
ERP dependencies	1946	(¹)	1	1	1	17	(¹)	(¹)	20
	1947	(¹)	2	1	6	22	(¹)	1	32
	1948	1	5	1	7	58	(¹)	1	73
	1949	2	7	1	12	54	(¹)	1	77
	1950	2	3	5	9	68	(¹)	3	90
Other foreign countries	1946	6	5	12	1	60	(¹)	6	90
	1947	17	10	13	1	113	(¹)	4	158
	1948	23	12	8	3	145	(¹)	6	197
	1949	25	14	9	3	197	(¹)	6	254
	1950	23	10	1	5	256	1	6	302

¹ Less than $500,000.

Source: U. S. Department of Commerce, Office of Business Economics.

Insurance earnings are affected not only by returns on underwriting and investments, but also by unrealized gains and losses on their holdings of securities. The generally rising security market in the United States since 1945 is, therefore, partly responsible for substantial insurance company earnings.

Direct investments concentrated

Foreign-controlled enterprises operating in the United States, other than insurance companies, had earnings of about $940 million in the 1946–50 period, out of which was derived nearly all of the $570 million added to the foreign equity in these enterprises. Over this period United States subsidiaries of foreign companies, except insurance com-

panies, reinvested 63 percent of their earnings, or nearly the same proportion as all United States corporations, which retained about 60 percent of earnings. About 40 percent of the additions to investment were in enterprises in the petroleum industry in the United States, and a somewhat smaller proportion went into companies producing alcoholic beverages. A few large companies, mainly in these industries, accounted for a very large part of the total earnings and income payments of foreign direct investments in the United States. For example, 64 percent of all dividend payments abroad by direct-investment companies in the years 1946–50 were made by eight companies.

Most income payments go to Western Europe

Foreign investments in the United States at present represent largely a remainder of the past foreign investment activities of Western European countries, principally England, Switzerland, and the Netherlands. Only in the case of the ERP countries, as shown in table 2, do outpayments from the United States exceed receipts by any substantial margin. However, this favorable balance for ERP countries will be reduced with the assumption of the full interest burden on United States Government credits and the increased earnings to be expected from growing United States direct investments in those countries.

Next in importance to the ERP countries, which received over 70 percent of all income payments from the United States, was Canada with about 18 percent. Most of the income paid to Canada was by Canadian-controlled companies in the United States. However, although payments to Canada are fairly substantial, they were equal to only about 16 percent of United States income receipts from Canada in the 1946–50 period.

Investment Income in the United States Balance of International Payments

In the preceding discussion investment income receipts and payments have been almost entirely abstracted from the general pattern of the United States balance of payments, but a few of the interrelationships between investment income and other items in the balance of payments can be examined with the data now available.

On a quantitative basis, income receipts have accounted for 7.7 percent of all United States balance-of-payments receipts on current account for the 1946–50 period as a whole. However, the amount of income received has increased in each year while total current account receipts fell off after 1947, so that the proportion of income receipts to total receipts rose from 5.4 percent in 1946 to 11.8 percent in 1950. In the years since 1947 income receipts have been the largest receipts item in the current account of the United States except merchandise exports.

The earnings of American direct investments abroad followed the course of United States imports quite closely in 1946–50, especially from 1947 on. Earnings were more quickly influenced by changes in United States imports than income payments, since the latter are also affected by decisions as to the amount to be retained for reinvestment and by exchange controls. This was particularly evident in 1949 when both imports and earnings fell off from the previous year but income receipts rose somewhat as dividends paid out went up.

Concurrent movements in earnings and United States imports from abroad are partly the direct outcome of the fact that a considerable part of the output of direct investments abroad is sold in the United States. The exact amount of

United States imports derived from these specific companies cannot be determined, but imports of certain important commodities from certain countries can be identified, with reasonable accuracy, as coming from direct-investment companies. On the basis of a necessarily rough calculation of this kind, covering 21 important primary products, it appears that about 25 percent of United States imports in the 1946–50 period were derived from United States-controlled companies abroad.

However, although these sales to the United States were very large, amounting to about $2.5 billion in 1950, they probably accounted for only about 30 percent of the earnings of United States-controlled companies in that year. This conclusion is derived from a limited analysis of the industrial composition of 1950 earnings of $1.9 billion along the following lines.

Table 4.—Income Received From American Direct Investments in Selected Countries, 1946–50

[In millions of dollars]

Area and country	1946	1947	1948	1949	1950
All areas	636	924	1,111	1,148	1,469
Canada and Newfoundland	148	203	223	295	305
Latin American Republics, total	314	451	525	425	664
Argentina	21	37	20	7	8
Brazil	30	38	38	49	76
Chile	31	44	56	35	43
Colombia	4	6	10	18	18
Cuba	33	52	55	44	69
Mexico	21	42	38	13	34
Peru	8	9	12	13	14
Uruguay	2	4	3	3	4
Venezuela	102	153	228	161	324
Other Latin American Republics	60	63	62	77	69
Undistributed	2	3	3	5	5
ERP countries, total	64	80	93	97	108
Belgium	3	3	10	9	16
Denmark	2	4	4	2	2
France	7	4	4	4	8
Portugal	2	4	5	2	3
Sweden	1	3	3	2	2
Switzerland	2	2	5	3	5
United Kingdom	46	58	58	70	62
Other ERP countries	1	2	4	4	8
Undistributed				1	2
ERP dependencies, total	20	32	73	77	90
British West Indies	1	1	1	1	1
Malaya and Hong Kong	2	6	8	11	14
Netherlands East Indies [1]	(²)	(²)	5	16	(¹)
Netherlands West Indies and Surinam	8	4	7	12	10
Other ERP dependencies	9	21	52	37	65
Other foreign countries, total	90	158	197	254	302
Australia	7	8	10	9	15
China	11	10	8	−1	−1
Egypt	2	3	3	3	2
India (including Burma, Ceylon, and Pakistan)	8	14	16	19	17
Republic of the Philippines	5	13	20	20	18
Indonesia [1]	(¹)	(¹)	(¹)	(¹)	27
Union of South Africa	6	12	18	22	23
Other foreign countries	51	97	120	179	196
Undistributed			1	2	5

[1] Netherlands East Indies entered under Indonesia in 1950.
[2] Less than $500,000.

Source: U. S. Department of Commerce, Office of Business Economics.

Mining and smelting companies earned about $150 million abroad in 1950. These companies produce nonferrous metals primarily, and sell so large a part of their output in the United States that it might be assumed for this purpose that they derive their whole income from the United States market. Similarly, the earnings of agricultural enterprises, $105 million in 1950, may be assumed for this purpose to derive entirely from sales of their products, largely sugar and bananas, to the United States. Certain other industries can be assumed to earn practically nothing from sales to the United States. These would include public utilities, distribution facilities abroad, motion picture companies, insurance companies, banks, etc. The total earnings of these enterprises in 1950 amounted to about $270 million.

Since United States-controlled manufacturing companies abroad produce a great variety of products, it is not possible

to identify them with any degree of accuracy among United States imports. However, aside from large amounts of newsprint and other forest products shipped here by direct-investment companies in Canada, most of the output of these companies is undoubtedly sold in foreign markets. Out of earnings in 1950 of about $625 million by this industry, it is not likely that more than $150 million resulted from sales in the United States.

Direct investment companies in the petroleum industry earned about $750 million in 1950, partly from sales t the United States and partly from sales in foreign markets. The oil sold in the United States was largely from Latin-American fields, where costs of operation were somewhat higher than in the Middle East fields which supplied chiefly foreign markets. When an average rate of earnings per barrel of output for the major American producers in Latin America is applied to United States imports, the conclusion is that these sales to the United States accounted for a relatively small proportion of the $750 million of earnings, say about $175 million.

If the assumptions above are reasonable, only about $600 million out of total direct-investment earnings of $1.9 billion in 1950 were related directly to sales to the United States. The fact that the remaining 70 percent of earnings also responds to changes in United States imports reflects the powerful impact of the United States economy on economic activity in foreign countries.

An example of the interaction of earnings of foreign investments and the general balance of payments position of the United States is the experience of the petroleum industry in 1949. In that year petroleum earnings abroad were cut by 10 percent, although there was an increase of about 15 percent in United States imports of petroleum, largely from United States companies abroad. Foreign countries, particularly Britain, experienced deep cuts in their gold and dollar reserves resulting from large deficits with the United States in 1948 and the first half of 1949. To stop these losses they restricted dollar imports, including oil which is sold for dollars, and substituted nondollar sources of supply as far as possible. Consequently, American companies abroad were forced to reduce output, and the earnings of the companies were seriously affected.

Dollar flows originating in direct investments abroad

Another aspect of the foreign operations of direct investment companies which can be explored to some extent is whether such operations produced more dollars through sales to the United States and capital flows from the United States than were required by the companies to finance their purchases in the United States and to transfer their earnings to the United States. This question must be limited to the dollar flows which actually occurred in 1950, insofar as they can be measured, leaving largely out of account the indirect and longer-run effects on international transactions of the activities of these companies, which cannot be handled statistically. Also, for simplicity, all earnings and capital movements are aggregated in the following discussion, although it would be desirable to examine the companies or industries separately since there are great differences among them.

The relevant data for 1950 are as follows: the companies produced about $2.5 billion in dollar exchange through sales to the United States, as discussed above, and an additional $400 million was provided by the outflow of new direct-investment capital from the United States, i. e., capital investment not stemming from undistributed earnings. Out of this $2.9 billion, the companies remitted $1.1 billion in income to the United States (derived by subtracting from total earnings of $1.9 billion about $800 million retained

Table 5.—Reinvested Earnings of Foreign-Incorporated Subsidiaries as a Ratio of Earnings on Common Stock, 1946–50, by Area and Industry

[In millions of dollars]

Area and industry	1946			1947			1948			1949			1950		
	Rein-vested earnings	Earn-ings on common stock	Ratio	Rein-vested earnings	Earn-ings on common stock	Ratio	Rein-vested earnings	Earn-ings on common stock	Ratio	Rein-vested earnings	Earn-ings on common stock	Ratio	Rein-vested earnings [1]	Earn-ings on common stock	Ratio
All areas	303	584	51.9	387	774	50.1	581	1,032	56.3	436	972	44.9	443	1,132	39.1
Manufacturing	161	291	55.4	213	404	52.8	320	538	59.5	269	545	49.3	291	591	49.2
Petroleum	60	102	59.1	102	143	70.9	153	233	65.9	78	186	41.8	45	244	18.4
All other	82	191	42.9	72	227	31.7	108	261	41.4	89	241	36.9	107	297	36.0
Canada	98	216	45.1	131	308	42.5	213	403	52.7	144	407	35.3	225	487	46.1
Manufacturing	67	136	49.5	103	203	50.9	170	289	58.9	108	284	37.7	158	338	46.8
Petroleum	5	10	46.1	11	16	66.5	22	30	71.2	12	24	51.3	21	32	64.2
All other	26	70	37.1	17	89	19.1	21	84	25.0	24	99	24.2	46	117	39.3
Latin American Republics	89	169	52.7	117	223	52.7	209	303	69.0	147	232	63.6	76	277	27.4
Manufacturing	37	60	62.4	50	85	59.5	72	99	72.4	71	89	79.6	55	100	54.8
Petroleum	20	36	55.5	36	53	66.7	83	93	88.7	37	69	53.6	-5	81	
All other	32	73	43.8	31	85	36.5	54	111	48.6	39	74	52.7	26	96	27.1
ERP countries	61	118	51.6	72	139	51.9	84	168	49.7	83	170	48.9	75	162	46.4
Manufacturing	48	81	58.5	51	92	54.9	60	109	55.0	66	122	54.5	55	107	51.0
Petroleum	3	7	38.4	8	13	59.7	6	23	25.8	6	13	43.5	11	18	64.4
All other	10	30	33.3	13	34	38.2	18	36	50.0	11	35	31.4	9	37	24.3
ERP dependencies	21	30	71.9	48	53	89.8	38	72	53.6	36	73	49.1	-10	37	
Manufacturing	(1)	(1)	100.0	1	1	75.0	2	3	92.3	3	4	73.2	1	1	57.1
Petroleum	20	28	71.4	47	52	90.6	37	64	58.4	35	61	56.8	-8	30	
All other	1	2	50.0				-1	5		-2	8		-3	6	
Other foreign countries	34	51	66.7	19	51	37.2	37	86	43.0	26	90	28.8	77	169	45.5
Manufacturing	9	14	64.2	8	23	37.8	16	38	42.1	21	46	45.6	22	45	48.8
Petroleum	13	21	61.9		9		5	23	21.7	-12	19		26	83	31.3
All other	12	16	75.0	11	19	57.9	16	25	64.0	17	25	68.0	29	41	70.7

[1] Less than $500,000.

NOTE: Ratios are derived from unrounded data.

Source: U. S. Department of Commerce, Office of Business Economics.

abroad by branches and subsidiaries) and paid somewhat under $100 million in fees and royalties to the parent companies. This would leave a margin of about $1.7 billion for purchases of capital goods, raw materials, etc., in the United States.

The difficulty of identifying those exports from the United States which were purchased by specific foreign companies is so great as to preclude any categorical statement as to whether such exports were less than $1.7 billion. However, an examination of the export data by country for a large number of commodities, particularly metal manufactures and various types of machinery, equipment and parts, indicates that exports to direct-investment companies were probably not more than $1.5 billion. It seems likely, therefore, that direct investments provided somewhat more dollars to foreign countries in 1950 than were required to service them.

Although direct investments abroad probably represented a dollar gain for foreign countries in 1950 measured in this limited way, there are other aspects of the growth of direct investments which have an important effect on the balance of payments position of the United States and foreign countries but are not readily measurable. For instance, the contribution to industrial activity abroad by direct investments would be of basic importance even if the dollar costs were large. Furthermore, the dollars contributed to foreign countries by direct investments can be measured only in part by the sales of those enterprises to the United States; in addition, exports to the United States of other foreign enterprises may depend on the existence of direct investments, or the products of direct-investment companies may substitute for imports from the United States and thus save dollars.

Transfer difficulties vary by area

For individual countries or areas, there are considerable differences in the importance of the problem of transferring income. In the case of Canada, for instance, more than enough United States dollars are realized from the sale in the United States of newsprint, other forest products and nonferrous metals produced by American-controlled companies to cover all direct-investment income and other pay-ments to the United States from that country. The same would be true of Latin America as a whole, where dollars are realized not only from the sale to the United States of petroleum, nonferrous metals, sugar, and other products by United States controlled companies, but also from the sale of petroleum and possibly other products to third countries for United States dollars. Of course, some Latin American countries are much better situated in this regard than others.

On the other hand, the ERP countries make large net dollar payments as a result of the operations of United States direct-investment companies. These companies in Europe probably produce few products which are sold in the United States, although they may export to other areas against dollar payment. In 1950 ERP countries had to finance about $100 million of direct-investment income payments to the United States, but also had to pay out much larger amounts of dollars to buy oil, metals, and other products of direct-investment enterprises located in other areas.

However, although the ERP countries paid out dollars, on balance, to United States direct-investment companies in 1950, the factors of increased industrial productivity and dollar savings mentioned above must also be taken into account. For instance, the fact that Venezuela earns dollars from oil shipped to the United Kingdom means also that the United Kingdom can earn dollars by selling to Venezuela goods in which it has a competitive advantage over the United States. If the United Kingdom had to purchase the same amount of oil in the United States, it is doubtful if as large an amount of dollars could be recovered through exports to the United States.

TECHNICAL NOTE

The definitions of some terms used in this article are as follows:

Direct investments.—Enterprises in one country controlled by investors in another country or in the management of which foreign investors have an important voice; these are usually branch establishments or corporations in which a foreign parent company owns 25 percent or more of the voting stock. Holdings of United States residents other than those of the controlling interest are also included in the value of direct investments abroad; similarly all foreign interests in foreign direct investments in the United States are counted as part of the direct investment.

Portfolio investments.—All other private long-term investments, including, for convenience, miscellaneous holdings such as interests in trusts and estates or bank loans.

Earnings.—Net income of direct-investment branches and subsidiaries after payment of all taxes (except withholding taxes on dividends) in the country of operation.

Income.—The amount entered in the balance-of-payments current account, which is the sum of interest and dividends for portfolio investments and dividends, interest, and branch profits for direct investments. Income from direct-investment companies excludes undistributed profits of subsidiaries which are included in earnings, and all income is taken after the payment of any foreign taxes thereon.

Rate of return.—On direct investments, the ratio of earnings during a year to the book value of investment as reflected on the books of the foreign enterprise at the beginning of the same year. The rate of return on portfolio investments is the ratio of income received to the market value of securities and face or stated value of other components.

Additions to value of direct investments.—The estimated net addition to capital investment through capital movements primarily from the parent company, and through the reinvestment of earnings. In the case of branches the net addition cannot be allocated between these two sources as accurately as for subsidiaries, due to the nature of the accounts for branches, which reflect only the net change in book value without indicating specifically the source of the funds employed. It is assumed that for branches the funds

used to increase investment are from branch earnings up to the amount of branch earnings, and any difference is assumed to result from capital movements with the home office. However, the data have been developed only for aggregate branch earnings and capital movements. An estimate derived by calculating the "reinvested earnings" for each enterprise separately and then adding these individual figures might yield quite different results.

Reinvested earnings.—In the case of subsidiaries, the amount of earnings which is retained in the business, after payment of taxes in the country of operation and of gross dividends and interest, i. e., before any taxes on such distributions. However, to some extent this is a convention since it is a common practice for dividends to be credited to the intercompany books and not actually transferred in the period in which declared, so that they are reinvested as effectively as that part of earnings not paid out. In the case of branches the designation "reinvested earnings" is less clear cut since, as noted above, increases in book value in any particular time period are considered to be derived from earnings up to the total of earnings in that period only; increases in value in excess of earnings are considered to be capital outflows from the home office and an increase in value of less than the amount of earnings would be considered to indicate a remittance of earnings to the home office to the extent of the difference, but not greater than the earnings for the period.

Data collected in the field of international investments are not accurate enough to justify drawing conclusions from changes of only a few million dollars in any of the components shown in the tables, although the data are carried to millions of dollars for arithmetic convenience.

PRIVATE CAPITAL OUTFLOWS TO FOREIGN COUNTRIES

Private Capital Outflows to Foreign Countries

The net outflow of private long-term capital to foreign countries in the first 9 months of 1951 was $583 million, or $525 million less than for the same period in 1950, a year in which a postwar record outflow of almost $1.2 billion was reached. As shown in table 8, there was a considerable slump in the outflow of direct investment capital in 1950 which was further accentuated this year. However, reinvested earnings of direct-investment companies, which are not counted as part of capital outflows, did not decline in 1950 and possibly increased in 1951.[1]

Offsetting the fall in direct-investment activity was a greatly increased outflow of portfolio capital, which reached a peak in the third quarter of 1950 and kept up in substantial volume through 1951. The following discussion covers in detail data for 1950 which were published first in summary in the SURVEY OF CURRENT BUSINESS for June 1951. Estimates for the first three quarters of 1951 have been prepared but, for direct investments, only the general trends are apparent from the data now available, and individual country and industry estimates are not possible at this time.

Table 8.—Net Outflow of Private Long-Term Capital and Reinvested Earnings, 1946 to September 1951

[In millions of dollars; inflow (−)]

Item	1946	1947	1948	1949	1950	1951 January–September ᵖ
Capital outflows from the United States	59	810	748	796	1,108	583
Direct investments	183	724	684	786	702	440
Portfolio investments	−124	86	64	10	466	143
Reinvested earnings	303	387	581	436	413	(na)

ᵖ Preliminary.
na = not available.
Source: U. S. Department of Commerce, Office of Business Economics.

[1] For a discussion of reinvested earnings see the SURVEY OF CURRENT BUSINESS for October 951, p. 7 et seq.

The resurgence of "portfolio" investments (all long-term private investments other than direct investments) raised net private long-term capital outflows to a postwar high in 1950, but a large part of this investment was related to special circumstances rather than a resumption of the private lending characteristic of the 1920's. Of net portfolio investments amounting to $466 million, about $325 million went to Canada. The outflow to Canada was massed in the third quarter of 1950 and was concentrated largely in outstanding issues of the Canadian Government payable in Canadian dollars. Canadian securities such as these ordinarily have a wide market among United States individual and institutional investors because they have a relatively high yield and are considered sound investments, but the sudden rise in United States purchases in 1950 was undoubtedly the result of the speculative possibilities introduced by rumors of an upward revaluation of the Canadian dollar. An official Canadian source[2] described this development as follows: "During the third quarter of 1950 it became apparent that private capital was flowing into Canada at an excessive rate and was exercising an inflationary influence in Canada at a time when inflationary pressures were already causing concern. Moreover, the inflows were bringing about a substantial and involuntary increase in Canada's gross foreign debt and annual service charge without any corresponding increase in its productive resources or ability to export."

The exchange rate of the Canadian dollar rose in October 1950 when the existing official rate was abandoned, but a return flow of capital to the United States did not occur. Instead, there has been in 1951 a larger volume of new Canadian bonds denominated in United States dollars sold in the United States than in any year since 1930. In that year the total sold here was slightly higher but it included a larger amount for refunding purposes. Through November of this year there were 20 major Canadian new issues sold in the United States (not including issues of direct-investment companies) of which the amount taken by United States investors was about $280 million. The issues were by various

[2] Canadian Foreign Exchange Control Board, Annual Report to Minister of Finance for the Year 1950, p. 14.

Table 9.—Value of Private American Direct Investments Abroad, by Area and Industry, 1946–50

[In millions of dollars]

Area and year end	Manufacturing	Distribution	Agriculture	Mining and smelting	Petroleum	Public utilities	Miscellaneous	Total
All areas:								
1946	2,854	740	545	1,062	1,769	1,277	607	8,854
1947	3,171	818	585	1,109	2,346	1,268	668	9,965
1948	3,551	921	641	1,140	2,981	1,288	684	11,206
1949	3,831	977	651	1,218	3,664	1,308	769	12,418
1950	4,242	1,065	654	1,324	4,072	1,338	855	13,550
Canada:								
1946	1,202	153	14	463	178	378	275	2,663
1947	1,328	160	14	481	208	344	271	2,806
1948	1,532	186	13	488	274	345	258	3,096
1949	1,642	196	14	519	349	313	206	3,350
1950	1,853	216	15	580	518	343	325	3,850
Latin American republics:								
1946	488	165	445	398	768	821	61	3,146
1947	595	209	480	425	1,048	846	102	3,705
1948	685	258	531	441	1,337	864	117	4,233
1949	756	284	535	487	1,721	883	132	4,798
1950	844	329	536	516	1,772	907	161	5,065
ERP countries:								
1946	885	281	4	64	310	20	204	1,768
1947	946	293	4	64	345	20	214	1,887
1948	1,010	309	4	64	390	20	222	2,019
1949	1,079	321	4	64	403	20	242	2,133
1950	1,155	321	4	64	453	20	255	2,272
ERP dependencies:								
1946	13	19	55	39	153	5	7	291
1947	15	18	56	38	253	5	7	392
1948	18	20	56	40	351	5	9	499
1949	22	22	57	39	410	5	9	564
1950	23	27	56	42	398	5	10	561
Other Europe:								
1946	108	39	2	85	64	10	25	333
1947	111	40	2	83	66	10	25	337
1948	106	39	2	81	63	8	25	324
1949	109	40	2	81	76	8	25	341
1950	114	41	2	81	78	8	25	349
All other countries:								
1946	158	83	25	13	296	43	35	653
1947	176	98	29	18	425	43	49	838
1948	200	109	35	26	566	46	53	1,035
1949	223	114	39	28	705	49	65	1,223
1950	253	131	41	41	853	55	79	1,453

Source: U. S. Department of Commerce, Office of Business Economics.

Canadian provinces and municipalities, and only about $15 million of the total was to refund issuers outstanding in the United States. The remainder was new American capital going to Canada, although the issuers used some of the funds to retire internal obligations rather than for new works programs.

The principal reason for the large amount of borrowing in the United States by Canadian issues this year appears to be that credit controls had a greater effect on bond yields in Canada than similar restraints had in the United States. Canadian issuers found they could borrow more cheaply in the United States than at home. Other considerations which may have influenced borrowing here were the comparative ease of marketing large amounts in the United States and the possibility of a gain by the borrowers if the Canadian dollar should rise to parity with the United States dollar.

In addition to the large Canadian borrowing in the United States in 1951, the International Bank sold two issues totaling $150 million, nearly all taken by United States investors, and there was a relatively small volume of sales starting in May of Government of Israel issues.

About $190 million of the net outflow of portfolio capital in 1950 was to France and was the result of a credit arrangement between United States financial institutions and the French Government under which all the dollar funds advanced to France were reinvested in United States Government securities. This transaction facilitated certain domestic operations of the French Government but did not constitute, on balance, a real capital outflow from the United States.

Although net portfolio capital outflows were large in 1950 and continue to be substantial in 1951, these outflows were still confined almost entirely to Canada and the International Bank, and there has been no apparent revival of interest in large-scale private lending to other foreign borrowers. Much of the potential lending to these countries is now being channeled through the International Bank for Reconstruction and Development. The bonds of this institution are fully guaranteed, in effect, by the United States subscription to its capital. Most foreign borrowers can secure a loan from the IBRD on better terms than could be found in the private United States capital market. This will continue to be the case except for those borrowers whose credit rating is sufficiently good that they can borrow on terms less than one percent higher than the terms paid by the IBRD, the difference representing charges to the borrower by the Bank over and above the Bank's cost of borrowing in the United States.

The experience of the IBRD has shown that an important limiting factor on the volume of private lending, either direct or through the IRBD, is the lack of well conceived and planned projects on the part of the borrowers. Another factor undoubtedly operating to hold down the demand for loans is the unwillingness of foreign debtors to incur fixed dollar expenditures if their individual balances of payments have proven susceptible to severe setbacks in the depression years and since the war.

Rate of direct investment declines

The amount added to the United States equity in direct-investment companies abroad (derived from table 9) amounted to more than $1 billion in 1950 for the fourth successive year, and will probably be near that amount in 1951 in spite of severe cutbacks in capital outflows. Capital outflows from the United States were reduced from $786 million in 1949 to $702 million in 1950 and about $600 million in 1951, but undistributed profits of foreign-incorporated subsidiaries continued at about the 1949 level.

Table 10.—Net Direct-Investment Capital Outflows, 1949–50, by Area and Industry

[In millions of dollars, inflow (−)]

Area	Manufacturing	Distribution	Mining and smelting	Petroleum	Public utilities	Agriculture and miscellaneous	Total
All areas:							
1949	10	17	54	616	10	79	786
1950	119	59	68	364	16	76	702
Canada:							
1949	2	3	15	63	−2	38	119
1950	53	16	26	148	−4	26	265
Latin American republics:							
1949	(1)	14	36	358	12	9	429
1950	33	32	24	56	20	26	191
ERP countries:							
1949	2	1	(1)	7	(1)	21	31
1950	21	1	(1)	39	(1)	14	75
ERP dependencies:							
1949	1	1	3	23	(1)	(1)	28
1950	(1)	4	7	−3		1	9
Other Europe:							
1949	1	(1)		13	(1)	−1	13
1950	(1)	(1)		1	(1)	(1)	1
Other foreign countries:							
1949	4	−2	(1)	152	(1)	12	166
1950	12	6	11	123	(1)	9	161

[1] Less than $500,000.

Source: U. S. Department of Commerce, Office of Business Economics.

For the first time since the war the amount added to the value of manufacturing enterprises was larger in 1950 than additions to petroleum investments. Additions to United States-owned manufacturing facilities abroad were quite substantial from 1945 on, amounting to $1.6 billion from 1945 through 1950 as compared with $2.5 billion in the same period for petroleum properties. Most of the increased investment in manufacturing enterprises has been financed out of undistributed earnings which do not appear in the United States balance of international payments. On the other hand, petroleum operations abroad were largely through branches whose reinvested earnings are reflected in the balance of payments as capital outflows. Aside from this technical distinction, it was true that the petroleum expansion was financed to a much greater extent out of new United States capital funds than was the case for older established manufacturing facilities. There was a spurt in capital outflows in manufacturing in 1950, particularly to the Western Hemisphere and Europe, and there was also an increase in the amount of reinvested earnings.[3] It is not yet clear whether the total for 1951 will approach the 1950 amount.

Nearly $400 million was added to the value of foreign petroleum properties in 1950. This was a decline from the record $700 million of the previous year, but available data for 1951 indicate further steep reductions this year. Capital expenditures by this industry are relatively low at present because the facilities necessary to meet requirements, as projected in the immediate postwar period, have now been completed. However, the heavy demand for petroleum products generated by the present world situation, further complicated by the shutting off of Iranian oil in July 1951, has again put existing American-owned producing facilities abroad under supply pressure. In 1951 the capital outflow has been reversed in some cases as foreign enterprises have turned over to their parent companies the cash proceeds of their sales which they no longer require for investment.

Investments in mining and smelting enterprises are gradually rising, although additions to value in 1950 of $105 million were still relatively small. There are several major development projects, however, which are already under-way or firmly committed, and which will probably raise the annual outlays in this industry considerably. Most of the recent investments were in Canada, and were intended to increase the supply of a wide range of metals and minerals including iron ore, titanium, copper, zinc, and asbestos.

Direct investments shift by area

The changing industrial distribution of investments abroad caused some large changes in the country and area distribution. The declining amounts of petroleum investment displaced Latin America as the area receiving the largest amounts of investment. Only about $50 million was added to petroleum investments in that area in 1950 and there may be no additions, on balance, in 1951. The country chiefly affected was Venezuela (table 11), although a considerable amount of the reduction in the net outflow to that country resulted from shifts of liquid funds to the United States as mentioned above. Investments in the ERP dependencies, which had been quite substantial as petroleum installations were being expanded, resulted in a small net return flow to the United States in 1950 after taking account of dividends in excess of current earnings. On the other hand, investments in Canada were greatly accelerated as new petroleum and mining ventures were undertaken and manufacturing and distribution facilities were augmented. About $490 million was added to United States direct investments in Canada in 1950, nearly 45 percent of the world total, and a like amount is expected in 1951. Capital outflows (table 11) were more than doubled in 1950 and the amount added from undistributed profits also increased greatly. There was also some expansion of investment in England and a few other European countries as some major additions were made to petroleum refining installations and manufacturing facilities in 1950, and capital outflows to this area have kept up to a similar volume in 1951.

Table 11.—Net Direct-Investment Capital Movements to Selected Countries by Industry, 1949, and Total 1950

[In millions of dollars; inflow (−)]

Country and area	1949 Manufacturing and distribution	Mining and smelting	Petroleum	Other[1]	Total	1950 Total[9]
All countries	27	54	616	89	786	702
Canada	5	15	63	36	119	265
Latin American republics	14	36	358	21	429	191
Argentina	−2	1	−2	4	1	22
Brazil	13	1	18	−1	31	24
Chile	(*)	21	(*)	3	24	23
Colombia	1	(*)	6	3	10	14
Costa Rica	(*)		(*)	−1	−1	3
Cuba		1	(*)	−2	−1	16
Dominican Republic	(*)			−5	−5	−1
Guatemala	1	(*)	(*)	2	3	2
Honduras	(*)	(*)	10	6	16	6
Mexico	−7	−4		2	−8	17
Panama	(*)		[3]124	(3)	[3]124	[3]87
Peru	2	1	(3)	−20	−17	−31
Uruguay	−2		−1	4	1	1
Venezuela	7	15	218	5	245	7
Other	1	(*)	4	1	6	1
ERP countries	3	(*)	7	21	31	75
United Kingdom	1		−1	20	20	42
Belgium	(*)		(*)	(*)	(*)	3
France	3		2	−1	4	7
Germany	(*)		−1	(*)	−1	5
Italy	−1		7	(*)	6	12
Netherlands	(*)		6	(*)	6	4
Switzerland	(*)		−1	(*)	−1	−4
Turkey	(*)		(3)	2	2	1
Other	(*)	(*)	−7	2	−5	5
ERP dependencies	2	3	23	(*)	28	9
British West Indies	(*)	1	1	(*)	2	1
Netherlands East Indies	(*)		4	(*)	4	(4)
Hong Kong	(*)		2	(*)	2	−2
Malaya	−1		1	(*)	(*)	1
Dependencies in Africa	2	(*)	−4	(*)	−2	11
Other	1	2	19		22	−2
Other Europe	1		13	−1	13	1
Spain	1		13	(*)	14	1
Other	(*)		(*)	−1	−1	(*)
All other countries	2	(*)	152	12	166	161
Australia	(*)	(*)	10	4	14	13
China	1		−5	(*)	−4	1
Egypt	1		−2	(*)	−1	−16
India, Ceylon, and Pakistan	(*)		2	1	3	13
Indonesia	(5)	(5)	(5)	(5)	(5)	−9
Japan, Korea and Siam	1		2	(*)	3	5
Middle Eastern countries[6]	11		106	2	113	117
New Zealand	−2	(*)	(*)	1	−1	1
Philippine Republic	−8	−1	2	1	−6	−4
Union of South Africa	−2	(*)	−4	1	−5	19
Other	(3)	1	[7]47	2	[7]50	[7]21

[1] Includes agriculture, public utilities and miscellaneous.
[2] Includes ship sales to United States-controlled Panamanian operators amounting to $64 million in 1949 and $61 million in 1950.
[3] Included in "Other."
[4] See all other countries—Indonesia.
[5] See ERP dependencies—Netherlands East Indies.
[6] Includes Iran, Iraq, Israel, Jordan, Lebanon, Oman, Saudi Arabia, Syria, Trucial Oman and Yemen; excludes Bahrein and Kuwait.
[7] Consists almost entirely of ship sales to United States-controlled Liberian operators.
* Less than $500,000.
[9] Preliminary.

Source: U. S. Department of Commerce, Office of Business Economics.

[3]See SURVEY OF CURRENT BUSINESS, October 1951, p. 13, table 5.

UNITED STATES DIRECT INVESTMENTS IN FOREIGN COUNTRIES

Joseph A. Zettler
and
Frederick Cutler

by Joseph A. Zettler and Frederick Cutler ☆

United States Direct Investments
in Foreign Countries

THE United States equity in direct investments in foreign countries at the end of 1950 amounted to $11.8 billion, based on tabulations of reports submitted in the Census of American Direct Investments in Foreign Countries undertaken by the Department of Commerce in 1951. This compares with a valuation for such investments of $7.9 billion in 1943, $6.7 billion at the end of 1936, and $7.5 billion at the end of 1929.

The 1950 census data were tabulated from returns of more than 2,800 reporters covering more than 8,000 foreign organizations. The value of the American investments is given as reflected on the books of the foreign organizations, converted into dollars according to the exchange rates used by the United States parent companies. This is discussed in greater detail in the technical notes appended. The book values of these properties are generally much lower than either of two alternative methods of valuation—market value or replacement value—would have been in recent years. However, there is no practical way to obtain either of the other valuations, since necessary data are not available.

A principal feature of book values is that fixed assets appear at their depreciated original cost, which in the aggregate is much less than their replacement cost at present price levels.

Market values cannot be established for most foreign investments because there is no open market for such aggregates of plant and equipment. The substitute of using current quotations of prices of publicly traded security issues as a yardstick for valuation is not available either, since most foreign enterprises are owned either entirely by their parent companies, or jointly with foreign companies.

Investments in Western Hemisphere predominant

For the period 1929 to 1950, covered in table 1, United States direct investments in the Western Hemisphere consistently accounted for about 70 percent of all direct investments abroad.

The preponderance of American direct investments in this area reflects the development of nearby sources of raw materials for use in the expanding economy of the United States, and also the American participation in the industrial development of countries such as Canada, Venezuela, and Brazil, which have been growing at a comparatively rapid rate.

Direct investments in the Latin American republics increased by more than two-thirds from 1943 to 1950 and accounted for almost 40 percent of the total at the end of 1950. Investments in these countries in the petroleum and manufacturing industries more than doubled in the seven-year period and accounted for $1.3 billion of the total increase of $2.0 billion.

In Canada, direct investments increased by 50 percent from 1943 to 1950, mainly in manufacturing enterprises and, to a lesser extent, in petroleum. Much of this increase was based on the reinvested earnings of the very large investments already established in Canada in 1943.

Although there was very little change in the valuation of direct investments in Western Europe between 1943 and 1950

NOTE.—MR. ZETTLER AND MR. CUTLER ARE MEMBERS OF THE BALANCE OF PAYMENTS DIVISION, OFFICE OF BUSINESS ECONOMICS.

Direct Foreign Investment of the United States

The value at the end of 1950 was about fifty percent higher than 1943

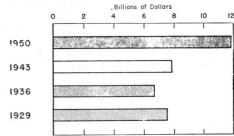

Major increase was for development of Western Hemisphere resources

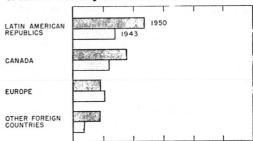

Investments flowed mainly to expand manufacturing and extractive industries

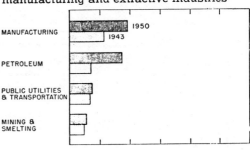

Table 1.—Value of United States direct investments in foreign countries, by country and type of industry for 1950, and country totals for 1943, 1936, and 1929

[Millions of dollars]

Areas and countries	Agriculture	Mining and smelting	Petroleum	Manufacturing	Transportation, communication and public utilities	Trade	Finance and insurance	Miscellaneous	1950 total	Totals only [1] 1943	1936	1929
Canada	20.5	334.3	418.1	1,881.4	284.4	240.1	313.2	72.1	3,564.1	2,377.6	1,951.6	2,010.3
Latin American republics:												
Argentina	(²)	(²)	48.5	146.0	77.0	34.9	22.0	7.6	354.6	380.1	348.3	331.8
Boliva		6.1			(²)	2.0	(²)	(²)	11.4	13.2	18.3	61.6
Brazil	(²)	(²)	112.4	270.2	137.6	70.1	21.7	7.0	627.0	232.7	194.3	193.6
Chile		340.6	(²)	29.4	137.0	14.5	1.5	(²)	529.9	328.3	483.7	422.6
Columbia	(²)	(²)	111.7	24.8	29.1	8.9	3.9	3.0	193.5	117.0	107.5	124.0
Costa Rica	(²)		3.8	(²)	10.8	2.8		(²)	62.1	30.4	13.3	22.2
Cuba	239.0	(²)	20.4	71.8	270.5	18.7	(²)	9.8	638.4	526.3	666.3	919.0
Dominican Republic	(²)		(²)	29.2	10.7	.9	(²)	2.3	105.7	70.5	40.7	69.3
Ecuador	(²)		(²)	.6	5.3	1.7	3.6	(²)	14.2	10.8	4.9	11.8
El Salvador		(²)	2.3	(²)	16.8	.5	(²)	(²)	18.4	14.9	17.2	29.5
Guatemala	(²)	(²)	3.6	(²)	72.2	3.3	(²)		105.9	86.9	50.4	70.0
Haiti	7.9		(²)	(²)	2.3	(²)		(²)	12.7	14.1	9.7	14.2
Honduras	(²)	(²)	(²)	(²)	8.8	(²)		(²)	61.9	37.0	36.4	71.5
Mexico	3.0	119.4	12.7	118.1	107.2	29.7	2.3	6.2	398.6	286.3	479.5	682.5
Panama	(²)		174.7	1.7	139.1	10.6	4.8	(²)	348.7	110.3	26.7	28.5
Peru	(²)	55.1	(²)	15.5	4.6	12.9	(²)	.8	140.0	70.8	96.1	123.8
Uruguay			3.3	33.1	1.6	4.3	12.4	.5	55.3	5.5	13.9	27.9
Venezuela	(²)	(²)	845.6	23.8	10.0	23.6	13.1	6.7	981.4	372.8	186.3	232.5
Other Latin American republics	(²)	(²)	4.7	5.6	1.1	.6		(²)	55.6	13.3	13.3	25.6
Total	475.6	617.4	1,390.0	774.1	1,044.1	240.3	85.3	48.2	4,675.0	2,721.2	2,803.1	3,461.9
Western Europe:												
Belgium			17.0	34.8	.4	10.6	.3	1.8	64.9	62.9	⁴ 34.9	⁴ 64.3
Denmark			19.7	7.9	(²)	3.7	(²)	(²)	31.6	21.9	13.8	15.8
France		3.3	92.5	161.2	5.4	5.9	11.2	5.6	285.1	167.4	145.7	145.0
Germany	(²)	(²)	37.8	121.0	3.6	18.8	2.6	17.3	202.1	512.8	227.8	216.5
Italy and Trieste	(²)		36.6	19.0	(²)	1.4	3.5	1.5	62.6	85.0	70.2	113.2
Netherlands	(²)	(²)	42.8	22.7	.5	13.2	2.5	2.3	84.4	59.6	18.8	43.2
Norway		(²)	6.4	5.1	1.0	1.4	(²)	.6	24.3	30.1	26.7	23.0
Portugal		(²)	5.6	2.2	1.8	5.4	(²)	.3	16.0	13.9	5.7	11.5
Spain	(²)	(²)	5.6	15.3	(²)	2.3	(²)	5.0	30.7	124.1	80.5	72.2
Sweden			24.8	25.9	(²)	5.0	(²)	1.8	57.8	32.8	25.5	19.?
Switzerland			5.8	10.1	(²)	5.7	.9	(²)	24.5	43.7	8.6	16.8
United Kingdom		3.2	122.7	535.2	10.6	102.0	16.0	50.0	839.7	518.8	⁴ 474.1	⁴ 485.2
Other Western European countries		.1	23.5	10.1	1.2	10.6	.9	3.8	50.2	112.5	33.0	37.¹
Total	.8	17.7	440.8	970.5	28.0	186.0	38.1	92.0	1,773.9	1,785.5	1,165.3	1,263.8
Eastern Europe	⁵ n. a.	n. a.	n. a.	n. a.	n. a.	n. a.	n. a.	n. a.	n. a.	259.0	93.2	88.7
Western European dependencies:												
Belgium, Portuguese. and Spanish dependencies	(²)	.4	6.2	(²)	.1	2.0		.2	9.6	5.8	⁶ 10.5	⁶ 9.0
British dependencies in Africa	.4	25.2	11.4	.7	.2	3.0			40.9	26.9	n. s. s.	n. s. s.
British dependencies in Western Hemisphere	3.0	31.9	12.0	1.4	14.7	2.7	.4	.7	66.8	36.6	⁷ 44.0	⁷ 57.0
Other British dependencies	5.7	23.4	148.6	5.0	.6	3.0	(²)	.2	186.5	29.5	⁸ 27.0	⁸ 27.1
French North Africa		(²)	11.0		2.0	.9	(²)	.1	14.5	8.3	n. s. s.	n. s. s.
Other French dependencies	(²)	(²)	15.9		.2	1.2			17.5	4.6	⁹ 18.8	⁹ 9.9
Netherlands dependencies		6.3	87.3	(²)	.3	.3		−.2	94.0	¹⁰ 120.1	¹⁰ 69.8	¹⁰ 66.0
Total	9.3	87.7	292.4	7.8	18.1	13.1	.2	1.2	429.8	231.8	170.1	169.0
Other:												
Australia		(²)	(²)	94.8	(²)	13.9	.2	7.8	197.9	114.1	89.0	¹¹ 149.2
Burma, Ceylon, Iran, and Thailand			5.1		.2	1.6	−.5	1.6	8.0	3.3	n. s. s.	n. s. s.
China	n. a.	n. a.	n. a.	n. a.	n. a.	n. a.	n. a.	n. a.	n. a.	40.7	90.6	113.8
Egypt and Anglo-Egyptian Sudan			26.2	8.0	.5	2.8	.1	2.1	39.7	16.8	8.3	6.5
Ethiopia, Eritrea, Libya, and Tangier			5.1		(²)	(²)		(²)	5.6	1.1	n. s. s.	n. s. s.
India		(²)	13.0	16.0	2.0	6.0		−.5	37.7	¹² 41.3	¹² 29.7	¹² 32.7
Indochina			(²)					(²)	4.5	n. s. s.	n. s. s.	n. s. s.
Indonesia	13.5		30.7	9.7	(²)	1.7	(²)	2.6	58.2	(¹³)	(¹³)	(¹³)
Israel	(²)		6.8	.9	.5	−2.1	(²)	3.7	12.4	¹⁴ 6.3	¹⁴ 29.6	¹⁴ 13.3
Japan, Korea, and Formosa			12.5	4.7	.8	.4		.7	19.0	32.9	46.7	60.7
Liberia	(²)	(²)	(²)		(²)	(²)	(²)		82.0	17.5	n. s. s.	n. s. s.
New Zealand		(²)	(²)	9.2	(²)	4.4	(²)	.6	24.8	13.7	22.0	n. s. s.
Pakistan			(²)		(²)	4.9		.1	7.8	n. s. s.	n. s. s.	n. s. s.
Philippine Republic	15.3	(²)	27.4	23.3	47.1	29.6	(²)	1.4	149.2	94.6	92.2	79.9
Saudi Arabia, Iraq, Jordan, Lebanon, and Syria		(²)	569.9	(²)	1.1	1.7		.2	574.5	¹⁶ 54.3	¹⁷ 17.8	¹⁷ 1.1
Union of South Africa		32.9	44.8	44.0	(²)	13.5	(²)	2.1	139.9	49.9	¹⁸ 55.1	¹⁸ 76.8
Total	38.7	56.4	895.6	210.7	53.6	79.0	2.9	24.4	1,361.3	486.5	481.0	534.0
Total, all areas	544.9	1,113.5	3,436.9	3,844.5	1,428.2	758.5	439.7	237.9	11,804.1	7,861.6	¹⁹ 6,690.5	7,527.?

n. s. s. Not separately shown.
n. a. Valuations for properties in Eastern Europe and China were not generally available for the end of 1950.
1. Sources for the data shown for 1929, 1936, and 1943 are as follows:
   1929—American Direct Investments in Foreign Countries, Trade Information Bulletin No. 731, U. S. Government Printing Office, Washington: 1930
   1936—American Direct Investments in Foreign Countries—1936, Economic Series No. 1, U. S. Government Printing Office, Washington: 1938
   1943—Census of American-Owned Assets in Foreign Countries, U. S. Treasury Department, Office of the Secretary, U. S. Government Printing Office, Washington: 1947
   The total reported in the Treasury publication was adjusted to exclude non-profit organizations and is adjusted upward by $653 million, entirely in Canada, to make it comparable with estimates for prior years and the census totals for 1950. This addition adds back into the 1943 data the United States equity in certain Canadian companies in which American stockholders owned more than 50 percent of the voting securities.
2. Included in totals.
3. Less than $50,000.
4. Includes Luxembourg.

5. Includes Gibraltar and Malta.
6. Portuguese Africa only.
7. Includes French and Netherlands West Indies.
8. Includes French Indo-China, French Oceania, and Thailand.
9. Includes all of French Africa, Belgian Congo, Italian Africa, Spanish Africa, Ethiopia, Liberia, and Tangier.
10. Includes Netherlands East Indies which appears as Indonesia in 1950.
11. Includes New Zealand.
12. Includes Ceylon and Pakistan.
13. Included in Netherlands dependencies.
14. Includes Jordan.
15. Includes Cyprus, Iraq, and Syria.
16. Includes British Arabia, Iraq, and Syria.
17. Includes Bahrein and Iran.
18. Includes all other British Africa.
19. Includes $26.2 million shown as "International."

Source: U. S. Department of Commerce, Office of Business Economics.

This article gives the first tabulations made in the Census of American Direct Investments in Foreign Countries, conducted by the Office of Business Economics. Complete tabulations of the data will be published in a bulletin, including such information as total assets and liabilities, income, capital movements, reinvested earnings, and foreign income taxes paid.

These are the first comprehensive statistics collected in this field since the 1943 census conducted by the Treasury Department, and provide a much-needed new benchmark for current estimates of the value of direct investments abroad as well as for related income and capital movements. Some of the new information, particularly the more detailed data for individual countries and industrial subdivisions, will be especially useful in studies related to the role of private foreign investments in the development of foreign countries.

as shown in table 1, there were net capital outflows from the United States and reinvested earnings of over $600 million in this period which were offset mainly by the effects of currency devaluations and war losses. Investments in France and the United Kingdom increased in value by over $400 million, and the increase would appear larger were it not for the depreciation of the dollar value of assets as a result of currency devaluations. Thus, in spite of the uncertainties in the European economic situation, American direct investments in the two principal countries of that area have increased proportionately as much as in the rest of the world as a whole. A substantial amount of this postwar investment in Europe has been in manufacturing and petroleum refineries, which helped to reduce Europe's demand for dollar exchange.

Investments in the Persian Gulf area increased by nearly $700 million from 1943 to 1950, reflecting the development of petroleum resources. Other large increases occurred in the Union of South Africa, Australia, Liberia, and the Philippine Republic.

Investments spread to new countries

Although table 2 shows that over 80 percent of total outstanding investments in 1950 are concentrated in relatively few countries, American investments may be found in nearly all parts of the world. Furthermore, a comparison of the figures for 1929 and 1950 indicate that there was some change in the countries attracting United States investments. In the former year about 60 percent of the total investments were in 5 countries: Canada, Cuba, Mexico, the United Kingdom and Chile. By 1950 Brazil, Venezuela and Saudi Arabia ranked among those with the most investment. Some of the smaller countries, while not in the top group as to total investment, nevertheless showed a more than the average rise.

Manufacturing leads in foreign investments

Despite the postwar spurt in petroleum investments, the manufacturing industry maintained its position as the most important single industry in the field of American direct investments in foreign countries. In addition, much of the investment in the petroleum industry is in refineries, which are usually considered a manufacturing operation.

Table 3 on page 10 shows that most of the investment in manufacturing has gone to countries which were either well developed industrially or were making rapid strides in that direction. This reflects the fact that a major prerequisite for the establishment for manufacturing branches or subsidiaries is a sufficiently large market to permit the operation of facilities of an efficient size. In the case of many countries, notably in the British Commonwealth, there was also the desire to preserve or enlarge markets which could not be

reached by goods exported from the United States because of tariff barriers or exchange restrictions.

In less-developed countries investments in manufacturing appear to follow the development of more basic resources, after the latter have raised incomes sufficiently to create the necessary demand. Our investments in some of the major countries in Latin America as well as in the Philippines and some of the British dominions are examples of this process.

Apparently the relatively low cost of unskilled labor in undeveloped countries is a less important factor in attracting American investments than a large market for finished products and a supply of skilled or semi-skilled labor.

Table 2.—Investment in specified countries, 1943 and 1950

[Millions of dollars]

Country	1950	1943	Increase
Canada	3,564	2,378	1,186
Persian Gulf Area [1]	726	61	665
Venezuela	981	373	608
Brazil	627	233	394
United Kingdom	840	519	321
Panama [1]	349	110	239
Chile	530	328	202
France	285	167	118
Mexico	399	286	113
Cuba	638	526	112
Union of South Africa	140	50	90
Australia	198	114	84
Colombia	194	117	...
Peru	140	71	69
Liberia [2]	82	18	64
Philippine Republic	149	95	54
Total for specified countries	**9,842**	**5,446**	**4,396**

1. Includes Saudi Arabia, Iraq, Jordan, Lebanon, Syria, Aden, Bahrein, Kuwait, and Qatar.
2. Increases represent mainly ships registered under foreign flags and owned mainly by subsidiaries of United States corporations.

Source: U. S. Department of Commerce, Office of Business Economics.

One of the more important results of this new census is the breakdown of broad industry groups into the major component sub-groups; the last information of this type was in the previous Commerce survey of 1940.[1] For the manufacturing industry, table 4 shows a rather even distribution of investment in 1950 over a wide range of manufactured products.

Total investment in manufacturing abroad changed very little from 1929 to 1943, but from 1943 to 1950 it nearly doubled. In 1929 investments in food processing, electrical machinery and paper and pulp producers accounted for 40 percent of the manufacturing total. In 1950 the share of these industries was reduced to about 33 percent, although each had grown in total value.

Between 1929 and 1940 other industry groups, such as automotive products, chemicals, and primary and fabricated

1. American Direct Investments in Foreign Countries—1940, United States Government Printing Office, Washington, 1942.

metals were growing in importance. Between 1940 and 1950 there was an increase of approximately $2.0 billion in all manufacturing enterprises, and of this total the largest increases were in chemicals ($300 million), food products ($250 million), machinery ($225 million), automotive products ($210 million), electrical equipment ($175 million), and rubber products ($120 million). In addition, major investments were made in "other industries", such as textiles, building materials, abrasives, photographic equipment, leather, printing, precision equipment and tobacco products which were not important fields for investment prior to 1940.

Extractive industries show fastest growth

Aside from the development of foreign markets for products manufactured by American companies, the second major stimulus to foreign investment has been the need to develop new sources of supply for raw materials.

The greatly expanded output of American industry as well as the increased requirements abroad has made it necessary to look more and more toward foreign sources for certain raw materials for which the United States was formerly a major source of supply. In particular the need for petroleum and its products has resulted in a large increase in investments in Venezuela and in the Persian Gulf Area. Along with these investments in raw materials production, there have been additional investments in refining, processing and distributing these raw materials.

Table 3.—Rise in manufacturing investments in principal countries, 1943 to 1950

[Millions of dollars]

Country	1950	1943	Increase
Canada	1,881	941	940
United Kingdom	535	307	228
Brazil	270	66	204
Mexico	118	22	96
France	161	75	86
Australia	95	48	47
Argentina	146	101	45
Union of South Africa	44	11	33
Total for 8 countries	3,250	1,571	1,679
Total for world [1]	3,721	1,884	1,837

1. Excluding investments in Germany, Austria, Yugoslavia, Eastern Europe and China, which were seriously affected by war damage and nationalization.

Source: U. S. Department of Commerce, Office of Business Economics.

The mining and smelting and petroleum industries, as defined in this Census, are not exclusively extractive industries. Because some of the major corporations operating in extractive industries combine several stages of production, transportation and distribution, the financial reports used in this census do not permit a segregation of the various activities. A partial breakdown of the investments in the petroleum industry may be obtained, however, by separating the investments in those countries in which crude petroleum is not produced. At the end of 1950, the investments in the latter countries amounted to $1.1 billion.

With these adjustments, the remaining United States investments in mining and smelting and petroleum increased from $1.7 billion in 1943 to $3.4 billion in 1950. Of this increase 88 percent was distributed among three countries and the Persian Gulf Area.

Public utilities attract less capital

Investment in public utilities and transportation, while maintaining its third ranking position, showed an increase of

only $37 million over the 1943 figure. Almost 75 percent of the total investment in public utilities and transportation at the end of 1950 was located in Latin American countries, and 20 percent was in Canada.

About one-half of the investment in this industry was in electric light, power and gas, about 10 percent in communications and about 40 percent in transportation excluding facilities for the movement of petroleum products. In all these industrial subdivisions about 95 percent was invested in the Western Hemisphere. In 1929, almost 90 percent was in the Western Hemisphere.

Investments in public utilities in recent years have been deterred because in many foreign countries this industry has

Table 4.—Value of United States direct investments in foreign countries by area and industry groups, 1950

[Millions of dollars]

Industry	Total, all areas	Canada	Latin American republics	Western Europe	Western European dependencies	Other countries
Agriculture, total	544.9	20.5	475.6	0.8	9.3	38.7
Fruit	154.5		147.7	.1	.8	5.9
Sugar	312.8		302.4		1.5	8.9
Rubber	28.1		1.1		5.7	21.3
All other agriculture	49.5	20.5	24.4	.7	1.3	2.6
Mining and smelting, total	1,113.5	334.3	617.4	17.7	87.7	56.4
Iron	88.3	20.6	63.7	(1)		4.0
Gold, silver, and platinum	74.3	24.9	21.8	2.2	(1)	25.4
Other metals	862.4	276.1	475.9	6.4	77.1	26.9
Nonmetallic minerals	88.5	12.7	56.0	9.1	10.6	.1
Petroleum, total [2]	3,436.9	418.1	1,390.0	440.8	292.4	895.6
Crude extraction	n. s. s.	n. s. s.	990.1	16.9	232.9	474.6
Refining and processing	2,951.8	352.7	n. s. s.	237.3	n. s. s.	n. s. s.
Distribution	n. s. s.	n. s. s.	213.5	175.0	58.4	200.4
Tankers	292.8	35.7	177.5	11.6	1.1	66.9
Pipelines	192.3	29.7	8.9			153.7
Manufacturing, total	3,844.5	1,881.4	774.1	970.5	7.8	210.7
Food	496.3	213.8	181.9	66.5	.9	33.2
Paper and allied products	378.2	347.6	4.5	5.3		.8
Chemicals and allied products	518.3	198.3	179.9	105.5	.1	34.5
Rubber products	181.6	59.0	60.3	30.7	2.8	28.8
Primary and fabricated metals	383.8	248.6	19.3	112.2	.8	2.9
Machinery	419.9	203.8	12.2	176.9	.3	26.7
Electrical machinery, equipment, and supplies	390.6	140.5	79.4	156.5	1.2	13.0
Motor vehicles and their equipment	484.9	160.0	82.9	191.2	.3	50.5
All other manufacturing	590.9	289.8	153.7	125.7	1.4	20.3
Transportation, communication and public utilities, total	1,428.2	284.4	1,044.1	28.0	18.1	53.6
Railroads	286.6	91.3	186.4			8.9
Water transportation	189.3	11.7	152.4	10.2	13.4	1.6
All other transportation	62.9	15.8	31.7	9.5	1.9	4.0
Communication	151.1	11.2	127.4	6.1	2.4	4.0
Electric light, power, and gas	738.3	154.4	546.2	2.2	.4	35.1
Trade, total	758.5	240.1	240.3	186.0	13.1	79.0
Wholesale trade	538.1	179.2	189.2	102.2	5.1	62.4
Retail trade	220.4	60.9	51.1	83.8	8.0	16.6
Finance and insurance, total	439.7	313.2	85.3	38.1	.2	2.9
Banking and other finance	170.5	105.9	37.8	22.2	.4	4.2
Holding companies	70.4	12.4	42.8	12.8		2.4
Insurance	198.8	194.9	4.7	3.1	−.2	−3.7
Miscellaneous, total	237.9	72.1	48.2	92.0	1.2	24.4
Real estate	37.3	9.5	7.5	16.5	.5	3.3
Motion pictures	111.6	22.9	16.4	56.4	.4	15.5
All other	89.0	39.7	24.3	19.1	.3	5.6

n. s. s. Not shown separately.
1. Less than $50,000.
2. The classification of petroleum investment into the major branches of the industry is based on the major activity of each reported foreign enterprise; the effect of this is to understate the investment in distribution, tankers, and pipelines and to overstate the investment in producing and refining, the latter being the major activities of most large integrated foreign enterprises.

Source: U. S. Department of Commerce, Office of Business Economics.

become increasingly regarded as a field for local private or government development. Also, in many countries rates of return on these investments have been low because of restrictions imposed by foreign governments. To a large extent postwar investments in this field were financed through foreign loans from the International Bank and the Export-

Import Bank. Thus, United States capital is still instrumental in increasing such investments, although not much is done through private direct investments. In Eastern Europe and China such investments were actually or virtually confiscated and in a few other countries, such as Spain and Argentina, some properties were sold to local governments.

Subsidiaries predominate in manufacturing

The form of organization most frequently adopted by American corporations for their foreign operations is the

Table 5.—Direct investments in mining and smelting and petroleum,[1] 1943 and 1950

[Millions of dollars]

Country	1950	1943	Increase
Persian Gulf Area [2]	722	55	667
Venezuela [3]	905	344	561
Canada	752	545	207
Chile	341	219	122
Total for selected countries	2,720	1,163	1,557
Total for world	3,412	1,716	1,696

1. Adjusted to exclude petroleum investments in countries in which crude petroleum is not produced.
2. Includes Saudi Arabia, Iraq, Jordan, Lebanon, Syria, Aden, Bahrein, Kuwait and Qatar.
3. Includes agriculture.

Source: U. S. Department of Commerce, Office of Business Economics.

foreign-incorporated subsidiary. Of the approximately 8,000 foreign organizations reported in the Census, about 5,600 were foreign-incorporated enterprises. In both Canada and Western Europe 90 percent of the direct investment is in subsidiaries; about 58 percent of the value of all foreign subsidiaries and 64 percent of the number is in these areas. The principle reason for the adoption of this form in these countries is that most of the investments are in manufacturing enterprises, and local incorporation gives a degree of local consumer acceptance frequently withheld from foreign organizations. There are other important reasons for incorporating abroad, including certain advantages with respect to United States and foreign taxes.

Direct branches of American companies are concentrated in industries producing raw materials destined to a large extent for the United States market. Two-thirds of the branch investment is in these industries. Thus, 40 percent of the amount invested in Latin American republics and the "all other countries" area of table 6, which produce many of the raw materials imported into the United States, is in branch operations, and 75 percent of the investments in these branches are in the petroleum, mining, and agriculture industries.

About half the number of all branches established abroad is located in these areas, but they account for about 80 percent of the amount invested in branches. This is because the operations in these areas include the largest branch units, such as oil companies, metal producers, and fruit or sugar plantations.

In other areas, a relatively small investment by branches of United States corporations is accounted for by a relatively large number of units. This is reflected in an average size of $2¼ million per branch in the Latin American Republics, and "all other countries" areas, and an average size of about $0.5 million in the rest of the world. The establishment of branches in Canada and Latin America is encouraged by provisions of the United States tax laws which reduce the tax rates applicable to Western Hemisphere Trade Corporations, i. e., United States corporations operating entirely

within the Western Hemisphere but outside of the United States.

Comparison with previous estimates

The new valuation of American direct investments abroad in 1950 is $1.7 billion lower than estimates in use up to now. These estimates were based on the wartime Treasury census and brought up to date with annual adjustments for estimated capital movements and reinvested earnings. However, there are many factors affecting the foreign book valuations of these investments which could not be measured accurately until reports based upon the books of the foreign enterprises became available. The census was necessary to determine these changes, and the results indicate the need for periodic enumerations to permit the compilation of current data.

Major factors accounting for the downward revision of the value of foreign investments include the elimination, from

Table 6.—Value of United States direct investments in foreign countries, by area and industry, and by foreign subsidiaries and branches, 1950

[Millions of dollars]

	Total, all areas	Canada	Latin American republics	Western Europe	Western European dependencies	All other countries
All industries:						
Subsidiaries	8,463.6	3,143.1	2,584.1	1,656.6	338.4	741.4
Branches	3,340.5	421.0	2,090.9	117.3	91.4	619.9
Total	11,804.1	3,564.1	4,675.0	1,773.9	429.8	1,361.3
Agriculture:						
Subsidiaries	318.2	17.6	257.1	.8	6.2	36.5
Branches	226.7	2.9	218.5		3.1	2.2
Total	544.9	20.5	475.6	.8	9.3	38.7
Mining and smelting:						
Subsidiaries	642.2	302.2	195.4	16.9	71.4	56.3
Branches	471.3	32.1	422.0	.8	16.3	.1
Total	1,113.5	334.3	617.4	17.7	87.7	56.4
Petroleum:						
Subsidiaries	1,915.6	360.4	542.7	416.7	242.6	353.2
Branches	1,521.3	57.7	847.3	24.1	49.8	542.4
Total	3,436.9	418.1	1,390.0	440.8	292.4	895.6
Manufacturing:						
Subsidiaries	3,581.2	1,797.3	642.5	948.9	6.3	186.2
Branches	263.3	84.1	131.6	21.6	1.5	24.5
Total	3,844.5	1,881.4	774.1	970.5	7.8	210.7
Transportation, communication and public utilities:						
Subsidiaries	1,038.7	260.9	720.8	12.4	6.9	37.7
Branches	389.5	23.5	323.3	15.6	11.2	15.9
Total	1,428.2	284.4	1,044.1	28.0	18.1	53.6
Trade:						
Subsidiaries	574.2	211.5	145.3	164.7	4.0	48.7
Branches	184.3	28.6	95.0	21.3	9.1	30.3
Total	758.5	240.1	240.3	186.0	13.1	79.0
Finance and insurance:						
Subsidiaries	210.1	127.1	49.7	27.5	.3	5.5
Branches	229.6	186.1	35.6	10.6	−.1	−2.6
Total	439.7	313.2	85.3	38.1	.2	2.9
Miscellaneous:						
Subsidiaries	183.4	66.1	30.6	68.7	.7	17.3
Branches	54.5	6.0	17.6	23.3	.5	7.1
Total	237.9	72.1	48.2	92.0	1.2	24.4

Source: U. S. Department of Commerce, Office of Business Economics.

the present census, of enterprises now within Communist territories ($300 million), the effects of war damage in Germany, Austria, and the Far East ($200 million) and the reduction in the dollar value of foreign enterprises resulting from the devaluation of the currencies of the countries in which they are located. This item can not be accurately evaluated but may be well in excess of $500 million.

Other reductions have been made to eliminate certain companies no longer considered United States direct investments, such as foreign branches and subsidiaries of enterprises incorporated here but owned by foreigners ($240 million) and foreign corporations whose stock is widely held in the United States but without American-controlling participation in management ($140 million).

Finally, certain items such as exploration losses and depletion charges, which appear as capital outflows in the balance of payments, are not included as capital investments in the books of the reporting companies; these items amounted to approximately $200 million by the end of 1950. To some extent these reductions in the former estimates were offset by investments made since the war which were not previously recorded, as well as various upward adjustments on the foreign books.

Technical Notes

Census definitions and methods of compilation:

Definitions: As used for the purpose of this census, the term foreign direct investments includes the following:

1. The value of the United States equity in foreign business organizations owned to the extent of 25 percent or more of the voting securities of the foreign corporations, by persons, or groups of affiliated persons, ordinarily resident of the United States, and analogous interests in partnerships and other organizations.

2. The United States equity in foreign corporations whose voting stock is publicly held within the United States to an aggregate extent of 50 percent or more but distributed among stockholders so that no one investor or affiliated group of investors owns as much as 25 percent.

3. Outright ownership of real property, other than property held solely for the personal use of the owner, or of a sole proprietor type of business enterprise.

4. The net assets of foreign branches of United States companies. A branch is defined as a business enterprise conducted abroad by a United States corporation in its own right and not through a subsidiary foreign company.

The United States equity in these types of controlled foreign enterprises includes the book value of all capital stock held in the United States, whether by the parent company or others, the equity of these stockholders in surplus and surplus reserves, the net balance of intercompany accounts between the foreign enterprise and its parent organization or United States affiliates of the parent organization, and long-term indebtedness payable to the parent company or nonaffiliated United States persons, to the extent that information regarding the latter indebtedness was available.

Since information was not specifically requested regarding the extent of the foreign organizations' liabilities to United States interests other than the reporter, or regarding the assets held in the United States by the foreign organizations aside from accounts payable by the parent company, the data may in some cases overstate or understate the equity in net foreign assets controlled by United States interests in direct-investment enterprises abroad.

Scope: Replies in the census were mandatory under authority granted in the Bretton Woods Agreements Act. Forms and instructions were mailed to all known holders of reportable investments. Foreign direct investments not included in the census are probably relatively insignificant in relation to the total value reported, although they may be large in number.

Reports for investments located in countries with Communist governments were incomplete, and, when reported, the information was generally applicable to an earlier date and was unreliable. Consequently, investments in these countries except Yugoslavia have been omitted entirely from the 1950 data.

Values: The dollar values represent the amounts carried on the books of the foreign organization converted into United States dollars. Where these conversions were ordinarily made on their own books by reporters they were required to submit their reports in both foreign currency and United States dollars.

If the reporter did not ordinarily convert the foreign currency into United States dollars, the report was submitted in foreign currency only. Reports submitted in foreign currencies only were converted to United States dollars by using the average rate of conversion derived from reports employing both currencies. Reporters that submitted statements in both currencies usually converted to United States dollars by using the exchange rate current at the date of the report to convert current assets and liabilities

Fixed assets and related depreciation reserves were generally converted at the rate current at the time the assets were acquired. To the extent that fixed assets were acquired at exchange rates higher than the rate of exchange current at the date of the report, this method of converting to United States dollars resulted in average conversion rates somewhat higher than the rates current at the end of 1950.

This method is different from that employed in previous surveys where, generally, all amounts were converted at the then current rates of exchange. The values arrived at conform as nearly as possible to standard accounting practices but, as mentioned in the text, they are generally lower than market values or replacement costs at current price levels.

Industry classification: The reports submitted were financial reports consolidating all the activities of a foreign corporation or branch operation. No breakdown based on type of activity was required. The reports were therefore classified on the basis of what was considered to be the major field of activity.

In a few instances, foreign corporations have established subsidiary companies to handle incidental functions which might ordinarily have been the responsibility of a division within the foreign parent company. These organizations were classified in the category of the foreign parent organization when located in the country of the parent.

The industry groups used in the census compare with similar groups of the *Standard Industrial Classification* except in mining and smelting, and petroleum. Smelting operations are classified in the manufacturing group in the Standard Industrial Classification but not in the present census, because smelting facilities are considered a subsidiary operation to mining.

The petroleum group as used in the census combines extractive and exploratory activities, refining, tankers and pipelines owned by petroleum companies and distribution facilities. These activities are classified by the Standard Industrial Classification as mining, manufacturing, transportation and wholesale or retail trade, respectively.

Geographic and industrial allocation: In those cases where the "controlled" foreign corporation owned 50 percent or more of the voting securities of another foreign corporation operating in a different foreign country or in another industry in the same country, a report was required covering the second corporation as a "secondary foreign corporation." Included in the category of "secondary foreign corporation" were the branch operations of "controlled" foreign corporations in countries other than the country in which the first or "primary" corporation was located.

In such cases, the total equity of the primary corporation in the secondary corporation as it appeared on the books of the latter was included in computing the United States equity in the primary corporation. The United States equity in the secondary corporation was deducted from the United States direct investment in the country or industry of the primary and allocated to the country or industry of the secondary corporation. The United States equity in the secondary corporation was computed by allocating the equity of the primary organization in the secondary organization according to the proportional investment of United States and foreign stockholders and creditors in the primary organization.

INCOME ON UNITED STATES FOREIGN INVESTMENTS

Samuel Pizer
and
Frederick Cutler

by Samuel Pizer and Frederick Cutler ☆

Income on United States Foreign Investments

EARNINGS on United States private and Government foreign investments and credits, including earnings retained abroad, reached $2.7 billion in 1952, an increase of about $70 million over the previous year. This increase was much less than in other postwar years, excepting 1949, and compares with an increase of over a half billion dollars in 1951.

This article brings up to date the summary facts on income from direct private investments abroad. *Foreign Investments of the United States* gave detailed results of the 1950 census of foreign investments, presenting complete data on value, location, industry distribution, and other essential characteristics of direct investments. The data on income flows from foreign investment in this article supersede previously published estimates for 1951 and 1952. Statistics in extension of the 1950 census on capital movements and the value of direct investments for these years are scheduled to appear in our January 1954 issue.

Income on private portfolio investments and interest received on United States Government credits, which account for a relatively small part of foreign earnings, rose by very small amounts in 1952.

Earnings of direct investments abroad, which account for about 85 percent of total earnings on foreign investments, amounted to $2.3 billion. The petroleum industry, which currently has about 30 percent of the total value of direct investments abroad and over 40 percent of the earnings, showed substantially higher 1952 earnings. Agricultural, manufacturing, and mining and smelting enterprises had lower earnings than in 1951. Developments which affected the latter industries included price declines of some basic commodities, higher taxes and other costs, a moderate setback in industrial production in some countries, and large exploratory expenses charged to income. But an important factor is that much of the recent investment has been in enterprises which have not yet reached the production and earnings stage.

Partial data available for the first 9 months of 1953 indicate little change in direct investment earnings from the 1952 amount. Prices of many mineral and agricultural commodities produced abroad by the United States-controlled enterprises were again lower in 1953, but there was no major change in petroleum production or prices. Industrial activity in many foreign countries turned up late in 1952 and continued to rise in 1953, so that manufacturing earnings are expected to be up.

An important development in 1952 was an increase to $875 million in the amount retained abroad by foreign-incorporated subsidiary companies. As a result there was a decline in the income from these enterprises as shown in the balance of payments. Such income consists of dividends, interest and branch profits, after payment of all foreign

NOTE.—MR. PIZER AND MR. CUTLER ARE MEMBERS OF THE STAFF OF THE BALANCE OF PAYMENTS DIVISION, OFFICE OF BUSINESS ECONOMICS.

8

taxes. Data so far available for 1953 indicate a similar distribution, with earnings, retained earnings and dividends each remaining close to the 1952 amount.

Data are not currently available on the amount of foreign income taxes paid by the direct investment enterprises abroad. The recent census of direct foreign investments showed that in 1950 the companies, in the aggregate, paid foreign taxes of about 30 percent on their foreign earnings. The percentage was undoubtedly considerably higher in 1951 and 1952 as many foreign countries increased their income tax rates. The earnings data reported in this article are measured after payment of such foreign taxes.

Petroleum earnings up—other industries decline

Foreign earnings on petroleum investments reached a total of $1 billion in 1952—13 percent larger than in 1951. The continued high earnings of the petroleum industry are based primarily on its ability to raise output from the properties which were developed after the war. With an output of about 1 billion barrels in 1952, the production of American companies abroad was equal to about 55 percent of world production outside the United States and Russia. World oil output outside the United States, Iran, and Russia, increased by 555 million barrels per year from 1950 to 1952. Over half of this increase was contributed by the American

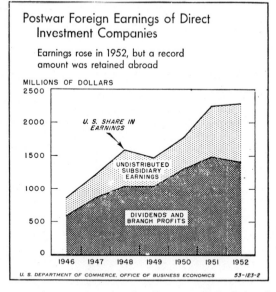

Postwar Foreign Earnings of Direct Investment Companies

Earnings rose in 1952, but a record amount was retained abroad

MILLIONS OF DOLLARS

U. S. SHARE IN EARNINGS

UNDISTRIBUTED SUBSIDIARY EARNINGS

DIVIDENDS AND BRANCH PROFITS

1946 1947 1948 1949 1950 1951 1952

U. S. DEPARTMENT OF COMMERCE, OFFICE OF BUSINESS ECONOMICS   53-123-2

companies operating abroad. About one-third of the oil produced by the United States companies abroad entered the United States market in the 1949–52 period.

Whereas earnings of other industries were reduced by higher foreign taxes in 1951 and 1952, the oil producers had already experienced the bulk of such tax increases in 1949 and 1950. Moreover the prices of oil products were quite stable in 1952 while prices of other raw materials declined. Another factor bolstering the earnings of petroleum companies was the growth of their tanker operations, which by 1952 were accounting for about 10 percent of their foreign earnings.

Despite their larger earnings the petroleum companies remitted smaller amounts to the United States than in 1951. Out of their branch profits of about $550 million, about 40 percent in the aggregate was retained abroad in 1952, as against a negligible amount in the previous year. Out of subsidiary earnings of $465 million, only about $130 million was paid out as dividends in 1952, although some of the remainder was remitted as intercompany advances.

Table 1.—United States Income Receipts From and Earnings on Foreign Investments, by Type, 1950–52

[Millions of dollars]

Item	Type	1950	1951	1952
	Direct foreign investments:			
1	Income receipts, after all foreign taxes	1,294	1,492	1,419
2	Common dividends	614	608	504
3	Preferred dividends	8	8	9
4	Interest	48	42	44
5	Branch profits	624	834	863
6	Plus: U. S. equity in undistributed subsidiary profits	475	752	876
7	Foreign withholding taxes on dividends	53	42	37
8	Less: Preferred dividends and interest	56	50	53
9	U. S. equity in earnings of direct-investment companies	1,766	2,236	2,280
10	Private portfolio income receipts	181	185	196
11	United States Government income receipts	109	192	204
12	Total balance of payments income receipts from foreign investments (item 1+10+11)	1,584	1,869	1,819
13	Total earnings on foreign investments (item 9+10+11)	2,056	2,613	2,680

Source: U. S. Department of Commerce, Office of Business Economics.

About one-third of the 1952 increase in petroleum earnings was derived from increased output in the Middle East, another third resulted from the recent expansion in refining and other facilities to serve the needs of Western Europe, and the remainder was mainly based on continued high levels of activity in the Western Hemisphere. Charges against income on account of exploration expenses were quite large for Canada, virtually offsetting the income from operations.

Petroleum earnings in the first half of 1953 were approximately at the 1952 rate. Moderately higher prices in the second half of the year and a continued large output to meet market demands are expected to raise the annual total slightly above the previous year.

Manufacturing industries

Earnings from manufacturing in 1952 were $640 million, $50 million below the 1951 total. Lower earnings were reported in all areas where manufacturing investments were important.

In Canada, the course of business was similar to that in the United States, with manufacturing companies showing smaller profits before taxes. However, nearly all the reduction in direct-investment manufacturing earnings resulted from lower earnings of companies in the paper and pulp industry, with other lines of manufacturing apparently virtually unchanged from 1951.

Lower manufacturing earnings in Europe coincided with a moderate downturn in industrial production in the second and third quarters of 1952, although in most countries industrial activity was on the increase from the latter part of 1952 and continued up in 1953. All the European coun-

281300°—53——2

tries where United States manufacturing investments are substantial were similarly affected. The decline in production was particularly noticeable in the United Kingdom, which accounts for more than half of the manufacturing earnings in this area, with the great majority of companies reporting substantially lower earnings. Some of the decline in the United Kingdom is probably attributable to an excess profits tax which went into effect in 1952 and extended through 1953, although profits declined also before taxes.

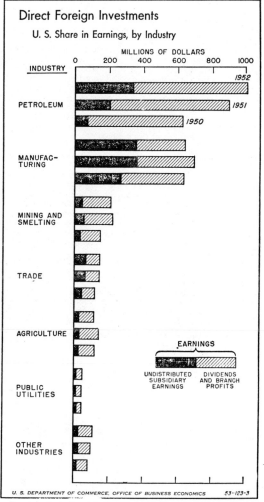

Direct Foreign Investments
U. S. Share in Earnings, by Industry

U. S. DEPARTMENT OF COMMERCE, OFFICE OF BUSINESS ECONOMICS   53-123-3

On the whole the falling off in manufacturing earnings was quite moderate, about 7 percent, but it represented the first interruption of regular annual postwar gains. However, the general improvement in the economic situation of foreign countries in 1953, plus the continued additions to manufacturing plant and equipment, should result in some improvement in earnings this year.

Earnings of mining and smelting companies were also moderately lower in 1952. For this industry the course of prices of various minerals is an important influence in earnings. These rose sharply from 1950 to a peak in 1951, as prices of nonferrous metals rose, and declined with the downturn of prices for many of these metals in 1952. The downward movement of earnings, reinforced by the interruption of Chilean copper production and sales, apparently continued in 1953. The only exceptions to this downturn were in some areas, such as Africa, where recent investments have brought about considerable increases in the production of some metals. A large part of the more recent mining investments, particularly in the development of iron ore, is in facilities which are not yet completed, so that earnings of mining enterprises should reflect this added investment in the future.

Among other industries, the greatest decline in earnings—20 percent—took place in agriculture. Most of the investments in this industry are in the production of sugar and bananas in the Caribbean area, and to a lesser extent in the production of rubber, fibres, fats and oils, cork, etc. Prices of most of these commodities fell very sharply in 1952 and continued to decline in 1953, and there was also costly damage from storms and other natural causes. The recent seizure of agricultural properties in Guatemala will tend to reduce future earnings of the industry.

Income receipts from many countries lower

The revised data for earnings and income receipts from individual countries for the 1950–52 period are given in table 4. Income receipts from a large number of countries were reduced in 1952 because of reduced earnings for some industries, as well as the higher proportion of subsidiary earnings retained abroad. Only in the European dependencies in the Middle East, where oil production was greatly expanded, did both earnings and income receipts increase significantly.

Earnings of direct-investment enterprises in Latin America were unchanged from 1951, and with about 40 percent of the total continued to exceed earnings in any other area. However, there was a drop of $50 million in direct-investment income receipts from Latin America resulting from reduced dividends. Earnings were somewhat lower in Chile and Peru, where the effects of falling metal prices and rising costs

Table 2.—United States Income Receipts on International Investments, by Area and Type, 1950–52

[Millions of dollars]

Year and type	Total	Canada	Latin American Republics	Western Europe	Western European dependencies	Other countries	International institutions
1952							
Private	1,615	348	619	159	127	353	10
Direct	1,419	222	599	129	127	343	
Portfolio	196	126	20	30		10	10
United States Government	204	(1)	18	167		19	
Total	1,819	348	637	326	127	372	10
1951							
Private	1,677	362	669	145	109	386	6
Direct	1,492	236	652	119	109	376	
Portfolio	185	126	17	26		10	6
United States Government	192	(1)	16	158		18	
Total	1,869	362	685	303	109	404	6
1950							
Private	1,475	411	540	141	98	279	6
Direct	1,294	294	522	111	98	269	
Portfolio	181	117	18	30		10	6
United States Government	109	(1)	14	78		17	
Total	1,584	411	554	219	98	296	6

1. Less than $500,000.

Source: U. S. Department of Commerce, Office of Business Economics.

were important, and for the Caribbean countries such as Cuba and the Dominican Republic where declining earnings of agriculture were primarily responsible. Petroleum earnings in Venezuela increased sufficiently to offset most of the reductions elsewhere. Income receipts from most countries in Latin America were reduced in 1952 from peaks established in 1951. In most cases lower income receipts resulted from lower earnings, but in some countries, such as Brazil and Venezuela, earnings were up while dividend distributions were reduced.

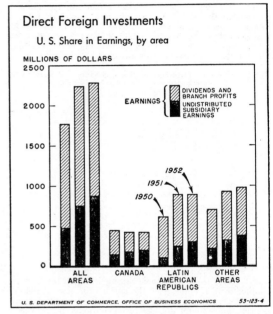

Direct Foreign Investments

U. S. Share in Earnings, by area

MILLIONS OF DOLLARS

EARNINGS { DIVIDENDS AND BRANCH PROFITS / UNDISTRIBUTED SUBSIDIARY EARNINGS

ALL AREAS — CANADA — LATIN AMERICAN REPUBLICS — OTHER AREAS

U. S. DEPARTMENT OF COMMERCE, OFFICE OF BUSINESS ECONOMICS　　53-123-4

Earnings in Canada of direct-investment companies were about the same in 1952 as in the previous year, but were under the 1950 amount, principally because of higher tax rates. However, income receipts were down moderately from 1952 as manufacturing companies paid lower dividends and branches of petroleum companies continued to show substantial losses because of the expanded exploratory activity and the resultant expenses charged to income.

There was very little change in either earnings or income receipts from Western European countries. A decline in manufacturing earnings in this area was offset by a continued rise in the earnings of expanding investments in petroleum refineries and distribution facilities.

In the rest of the world earnings were increased by a small amount because of higher petroleum earnings but there was a marked reduction in income receipts as dividend payments fell off.

Growing importance of retained earnings

In each year since the war the foreign-incorporated subsidiaries of American companies have increased the amount which they have retained abroad out of their foreign earnings. On the average about 50 percent of their earnings were retained abroad, but in 1952 this proportion rose to 62 percent.

On the basis of the census of direct private foreign investment, the foreign subsidiaries had on their books at the end of 1950 a little over $3 billion of undistributed profits. In the following 2 years, as shown in table 5, undistributed profits of over $1.6 billion were added to this total, illustrating the cumulative growth of this source of funds.

In general, these additional sums could be utilized in three principal ways: (1) the expansion of plant and equipment or necessary working balances; which has been by far the most important, (2) as intercompany loans or advances to parent companies, or (3) as more or less idle or unproductive funds in countries where neither local permanent investment or remittance to the United States was feasible. The data currently collected on direct investments abroad do not provide a good basis for determining the relative amounts utilized for these purposes, but some generalizations are possible.

For Canada and the United Kingdom, which together accounted for about $300 million out of $875 million of undistributed profits in 1952, retained earnings were probably largely for the expansion of existing investments. There are no restrictions on income remittances from these countries, and there is no indication of large intercompany advances. Another $200 million of undistributed profits was in various dependencies or countries in Asia and Africa. A check of the companies active in these countries, particularly petroleum companies, indicates that in the main the retained earnings were utilized for permanent investment. In many noteworthy cases the companies were not only retaining profits abroad but were adding substantial funds for new investment.

The situation in the Latin American countries with respect to undistributed subsidiary profits is less clear. In Mexico and Panama, accounting for about $90 million of the total, the data indicate that a large part of the undistributed profits was remitted back to the parent companies through the intercompany accounts. On the other hand a large part of the undistributed profits in Venezuela probably went into the continuing growth of the petroleum industry. In Brazil there were large undistributed profits, and for most companies additional funds were also provided by the United States parent companies. However, both types of investment were made involuntarily, at least in part, because of the severe restrictions on dollar remittances for income or other payments.

On the whole, the available data indicate that the greater part of undistributed profits in 1952 was retained abroad to facilitate the long-term development of the foreign enterprises.

A similar segregation of earnings as between distributed earnings and retained earnings is not made on the books of branch enterprises. Nevertheless, an approximation of this segregation which is sufficiently accurate for purposes of comparison can be obtained by assuming that branch profits were retained abroad to the extent they did not exceed the net additions to branch assets in a given year. (See table 6.)

According to this criterion, applied country by country and industry by industry, about 40 percent of all branch profits were retained abroad in 1952, much more than in the preceding two years. Most important in this connection was a sharp upturn in the investment activity of branches of mining and petroleum companies. Although the branch

Table 3.—U. S. Equity in Direct Investment Earnings and Income Receipts by Type, Area and Industry, 1950–52

[Millions of dollars]

Industry	Total			Canada			Latin American Republics			Western Europe			Western European dependencies			Other countries		
	1950	1951	1952	1950	1951	1952	1950	1951	1952	1950	1951	1952	1950	1951	1952	1950	1951	1952
All industries:																		
Earnings	1,766	2,236	2,280	445	420	419	616	888	888	265	302	305	100	120	154	340	506	513
Income receipts	1,294	1,492	1,419	294	236	222	522	652	599	111	119	129	98	109	127	269	377	343
Branch profits	624	834	863	12	−2	−3	360	473	472	22	30	26	51	68	98	179	265	270
Dividends and interest	670	658	556	282	238	226	162	179	127	89	90	103	46	41	28	91	111	73
Agriculture:																		
Earnings	115	140	113	1	1	1	89	107	84	(¹)	(¹)	(¹)	4	3	3	20	29	24
Income receipts	91	110	86	1	1	(¹)	76	92	73	(¹)	(¹)	(¹)	4	3	1	11	15	11
Branch profits	56	66	58	(¹)	(¹)	(¹)	55	65	57				(¹)	(¹)	(¹)	(¹)	1	(¹)
Dividends and interest	36	44	28	(¹)	(¹)	(¹)	21	27	16	(¹)	(¹)	(¹)	4	3	1	11	14	11
Mining and smelting:																		
Earnings	148	220	209	52	68	54	69	104	96	3	4	5	15	30	31	10	14	23
Income receipts	112	159	159	31	34	36	64	87	81	1	1	1	12	25	27	3	12	14
Branch profits	58	87	83	(¹)	(¹)	(¹)	51	76	70	(¹)	(¹)	(¹)	8	10	13	(¹)	(¹)	
Dividends and interest	54	73	77	31	34	36	14	11	11	1	1	1	5	15	15	3	12	14
Petroleum:																		
Earnings	627	896	1,013	17	3	12	274	409	438	42	49	79	74	76	112	220	360	371
Income receipts	555	696	677	−3	−17	−20	262	327	303	9	15	33	75	73	93	212	298	268
Branch profits	384	512	548	−16	−31	−40	201	250	259	3	3	1	39	52	82	156	238	245
Dividends and interest	171	184	129	13	14	20	61	77	44	6	12	32	36	21	11	56	60	22
Manufacturing:																		
Earnings	637	696	643	301	268	257	106	170	156	172	194	169	1	2	2	57	63	59
Income receipts	357	331	287	211	164	139	55	72	64	69	71	56	1	1	1	22	23	26
Branch profits	40	68	61	6	5	4	21	46	43	6	10	7	(¹)	(¹)	(¹)	7	6	6
Dividends and interest	317	263	225	204	159	135	34	26	21	63	61	49	1	1	1	15	17	20
Public utilities:																		
Earnings	41	43	43	9	9	9	26	27	32	(¹)	(¹)	(¹)	(¹)	(¹)	(¹)	6	6	7
Income receipts	44	45	49	9	11	11	31	33	35	(¹)	(¹)	(¹)	(¹)	(¹)	(¹)	1	4	3
Branch profits	8	5	9	−1	(¹)		8	5	9	(¹)			(¹)			(¹)		
Dividends and interest	36	40	40	10	11	11	25	26	26	(¹)	(¹)	(¹)	(¹)	(¹)	(¹)	1	4	3
Trade:																		
Earnings	117	143	146	29	28	34	29	49	55	35	34	33	4	6	4	20	26	21
Income receipts	72	79	79	17	13	14	17	26	25	21	20	24	3	4	3	14	16	14
Branch profits	35	42	43	5	3	5	12	17	18	6	6	7	3	4	2	10	12	12
Dividends and interest	37	36	36	12	10	9	5	8	7	16	14	16	(¹)	1	1	4	4	3
Miscellaneous:																		
Earnings	81	98	109	37	43	53	22	23	26	13	20	20	2	3	2	7	10	8
Income receipts	63	71	83	29	31	41	15	16	18	10	12	14	2	2	2	6	9	7
Branch profits	43	53	61	17	20	27	12	13	16	7	10	10	2	2	2	5	8	7
Dividends and interest	19	17	22	12	11	15	3	3	2	3	2	4	(¹)	(¹)	(¹)	1	1	1

1. Less than $500,000.

Note.—Negative entries for Canada largely reflect exploratory expenses charged against branch profits.

Source: U. S. Department of Commerce, Office of Business Economics.

profits of these industries were only about $30 million greater in 1952 than in the previous year, they increased their rate of branch investments from $60 million in 1951 to over $350 million in 1952, so that a greater proportion of earnings was clearly used abroad.

Foreign earnings and domestic industry

The extension of American enterprises into foreign countries, which began about 50 years ago and has proceeded on an unprecedented scale since 1945, is largely an outgrowth of the search for wider and more diversified markets for the products which American manufacturers can mass produce efficiently, and the need for raw materials necessary to higher production levels in the United States and other countries. These enterprises, valued at nearly $15 billion at the end of 1952, are increasingly important adjuncts to the domestic business of the United States parent companies and to the United States economy as a whole. An important aspect of the considerable reliance on the activities of the foreign enterprises is the role of direct investments abroad in supplying various materials essential for our domestic economy.

In an earlier article [1] the proportion of United States imports which was derived from American-owned productive facilities abroad was estimated to be about 25 percent in 1950. A more detailed study covering 19 major import commodities in 1952 has now been completed and the principal results are shown in tables 7 and 8.

Many sources were used in deriving the data for imports of the selected commodities. In some cases it was known that the sole producer of a given commodity in a given country was a United States-controlled enterprise. Where production was from several sources, or facilities were jointly owned, there were data sometimes available regarding shipments to the United States by the United States enterprise. In still other cases where there were several producers of a given basic commodity within a country, it was necessary to assume that United States imports could be attributed to United States producers in proportion to their share in the output of the commodity in the country. Alternatively, it could have been assumed that United States imports were derived first from the output of the United States-controlled companies. On this basis the share of imports attributable

1. SURVEY OF CURRENT BUSINESS, October 1951.

Table 4.—U. S. Equity in Direct-investment Earnings and

[Millions of dollars]

Areas and countries	Total						Manufacturing			
	1950		1951		1952		1950		1951	
	Earnings	Income receipts	Earnings	Income receipts	Earnings	Income receipts	Earnings	Income receipts	Earnings	Income receipts
All areas, total	1,766	1,294	2,236	1,492	2,280	1,419	637	357	696	331
Canada	445	291	420	236	419	222	301	211	268	164
Latin American Republics	616	522	888	652	888	599	106	55	170	72
Argentina	17	6	28	11	29	12	14	4	19	5
Brazil	96	61	143	75	148	65	47	22	89	39
Chile	37	41	56	54	53	51	(1)	(1)	(1)	(1)
Colombia	16	10	15	12	19	13	4	2	4	3
Costa Rica	13	13	12	11	14	14	(2)	(2)	(2)	(2)
Cuba	56	43	60	49	50	44	7	5	6	4
Dominican Republic	17	14	31	25	21	14	(1)	(1)	(1)	(1)
Ecuador	2	2	2	3	4	4	(1)	(1)	(1)	(1)
Guatemala	11	10	7	7	4	3	(1)	(1)	(1)	(1)
Honduras	16	15	17	16	16	15	(1)	(1)	(1)	(1)
Mexico	43	29	63	31	59	32	17	8	29	8
Panama	25	18	103	37	98	43	(2)	(2)	(2)	(2)
Peru	21	15	37	33	32	25	(1)	(1)	(1)	(1)
Uruguay	6	4	11	6	7	4	4	3	4	3
Venezuela	232	236	297	278	329	256	5	4	6	5
Other countries	8	5	7	4	5	3	1	1	1	(2)
Western Europe	265	111	302	119	305	129	172	69	194	71
Belgium	15	6	17	6	17	6	10	3	12	4
Denmark	2	2	3	1	3	2	1	1	1	1
France	31	6	41	10	37	10	21	4	28	6
Germany	27	3	21	4	19	4	18	1	12	3
Italy	8	2	13	5	10	7	5	1	7	2
Netherlands	15	5	14	5	13	5	2	1	2	1
Portugal	3	3	3	2	4	2	(2)	(2)	(2)	(2)
Sweden	7	2	8	3	7	4	4	1	5	2
Switzerland	5	4	6	4	5	4	5	3	5	3
United Kingdom	141	73	163	74	174	78	103	53	118	49
Other countries	12	6	12	4	17	6	4	1	4	(2)
Western European dependencies	100	98	120	109	154	127	1	1	2	1
Western Hemisphere	13	10	15	12	12	12	(2)	(2)	----	----
Africa	14	11	29	21	27	15	(2)	(2)	(2)	(2)
Asia and Oceania	74	76	76	75	115	99	1	1	2	1
Other countries	340	269	507	376	513	343	57	22	63	23
Africa:										
Egypt	4	2	5	2	8	5	2	1	3	1
Liberia	15	12	35	13	46	12	----	----	----	----
Union of South Africa	28	13	33	23	35	23	12	4	13	8
Asia:										
India	14	12	15	10	16	10	6	4	7	3
Indonesia	36	27	38	34	28	4	6	1	4	1
Japan	2	2	8	3	3	3	(1)	(1)	(1)	(1)
Philippine Republic	39	28	36	26	36	27	(1)	(1)	(1)	(1)
Other Asia	171	161	296	250	303	248	(2)	(2)	(2)	(2)
Other areas:										
Australia	28	11	36	11	34	8	22	6	28	4
New Zealand	3	2	4	3	4	2	2	1	2	1

1. Included in totals.   2. Less than $500,000.   Source: U. S. Department of Commerce, Office of Business Economics.

to United States-controlled companies would have been somewhat higher.

No attempt was made to make estimates for nonspecified commodities, particularly manufactures, which are imported from United States-owned foreign enterprises. The estimate for imports derived from American-owned facilities abroad is therefore probably an understatement of the total.

Imports of selected commodities from United States-controlled sources in 1952 may be estimated at about $2.2 billion or 21 percent of total imports, nearly the same ratio as in 1950, although total imports were $1.8 billion higher in 1952.

Among the commodities listed in table 7 are many which are of crucial importance in the United States economy. Some of them, such as petroleum, copper, nickel, and aluminum, are derived almost entirely from foreign enterprises in which Americans are the principal investors. For others, such as crude rubber and iron ore, a smaller share comes from United States-controlled sources. In the case of iron ore, however, the supply from United States-developed sources abroad will soon be greatly expanded, and this will also be true of such commodities as manganese and titanium.

Income received on United States portfolio investments abroad—holdings of foreign securities, claims or miscellaneous assets not connected with foreign affiliated companies—was at a postwar high of nearly $200 million in 1952. Income from this source was small relative to the income from direct investments, in contrast with its primary importance in the 1920's. Nevertheless it has increased slowly since the war as Americans added to their investments in Canadian bonds and stocks and began to purchase substantial quantities of the obligations of the International Bank for Reconstruction and Development. However, income from Canadian securities will probably decline in 1953 as a result of a liquidation of some internal issues acquired mainly in 1950.

A new development affecting the income from portfolio securities, as well as their future market in the United States, was the signing of agreements with Germany and Japan which will result in the resumption of interest payments on their debts to American bondholders. In the case of Germany, the interest payments will depend partly upon the extent to which the outstanding bonds are still held in the United States and presented for validation. At a minimum these payments were estimated to be about $5 million annually. A further $5 million of interest will also be paid by Japan under the new agreement.

Income Receipts by Countries and Major Industries, 1950–52

[Millions of dollars]

Manufacturing—Con.		Petroleum						Other industries					
1952		1950		1951		1952		1950		1951		1952	
Earnings	Income receipts	Earnings	Income receipts	Earnings	Income receipts	Earnings	Income receipts	Earnings	Income receipts	Earnings	Income receipts	Earnings	Income receipts
643	287	627	555	896	696	1,013	677	502	382	643	465	624	456
257	139	17	−3	3	−17	12	−20	128	86	149	89	150	102
156	64	274	262	409	327	438	303	235	206	309	252	293	232
18	4	(¹)	(¹)	4	3	4	2	3	2	5	4	7	6
88	32	28	25	26	23	24	18	22	15	28	14	36	15
(¹)	(¹)	(¹)	4	(¹)	2	(¹)	(¹)	34	38	51	51	48	49
4	3	(¹)	(²)	2		5	2	8	8	9	7	10	8
(²)	(²)	(²)	(²)	(²)	(²)	(²)	(²)	13	13	12	11	14	14
5	5	2	2	1	1	2	1	47	36	53	44	42	39
(¹)	(¹)	(¹)	(¹)	(¹)	(¹)	(¹)	(¹)	15	14	29	25	20	14
(¹)	(¹)	(¹)	(¹)	(¹)	(¹)	(¹)	(¹)	2	2	2	2	4	4
(¹)	(¹)	(¹)	(¹)	(¹)	(¹)	(¹)	(¹)	11	10	7	7	3	3
(¹)	(¹)	(¹)	(¹)	(¹)	(¹)	(¹)	(¹)	15	15	16	16	15	15
23	7	(¹)	5	(²)	22	1	30	25	20	33	21	35	24
(²)		11		85		81		14	13	17	14	17	13
(¹)	(¹)	(¹)	(¹)	(¹)	1	(¹)	(²)	11	10	26	·23	18	14
1	2	(²)	226	282	266	308	239	2	1	6	2	6	2
7	5	219						8	6	9	7	14	11
1	1	1	(²)	1	(²)	1	(²)	6	4	5	3	3	2
169	56	42	9	49	15	79	33	51	33	59	33	58	39
13	3	2	1	2	1	2	1	3	2	2	2	2	2
1	1	(²)	(²)	2	(²)	1	(²)	(²)	(²)	(²)	(²)	(²)	(²)
25	6	8	1	10	3	8	3	2	1	3	1	4	1
12	4	5	(²)	7	(²)	5	(²)	3	1	2	1	2	(²)
6	2	2		4	2	2	3	2	1	2	1	2	1
1	1	6	2	7	1	8	1	6	3	5	3	4	3
(²)	(²)	2	2	2	2	2	2	1	1	1	1	2	1
4	2	(²)	(²)	(²)	(²)	(²)	(²)	1	1	2	1	2	2
4	4	(²)		(²)		(²)		(²)	1	1	1	1	
98	33	12	1	13	6	44	22	27	20	33	19	32	24
4	1	3	2	2	1	6	6	5	3	7	3	7	.3
2	1	74	75	76	73	112	93	25	21	42	35	40	33
		8	8	10	8	8	8	5	2	5	4	5	4
(²)	(²)	10	8	10	9	10	3	4	3	18	12	17	12
2	1	56	59	55	56	95	82	16	16	19	18	19	16
59	26	220	212	360	298	371	268	63	35	84	55	83	49
2	2	1	1	1	1	6	3	1	1	1	(²)	(²)	(²)
		3	2	13	2	28	1	12	10	22	11	18	10
12	9	6	7	6	4	2	1	9	2	14	12	21	13
10	4	(¹)	(¹)	(¹)	(¹)	(¹)	(¹)	(¹)	(¹)	(¹)	(¹)	(¹)	(¹)
3	1	(¹)	(¹)	(¹)	(¹)	(¹)	(¹)	(¹)	(¹)	(¹)	(¹)	(¹)	1
(¹)	(¹)	(¹)	(¹)	(¹)	(¹)	(¹)	(¹)	(²)	(²)	2	2	1	1
(²)	(²)	167	159	293	248	300	246	32	14	25	16	23	14
								4	3	3	2	2	2
24	4	(¹)	(¹)	(¹)	(¹)	(¹)	(¹)	(¹)	(¹)	(¹)	(¹)	(¹)	(¹)
2	1	(¹)	(¹)	(¹)	(¹)	(¹)	(¹)	(¹)	(¹)	(¹)	(¹)	(¹)	(¹)

Interest on Government credits

Interest payments by foreign countries on credits from the United States Government were about $200 million in 1952, and were scheduled to reach a peak of about $230 million in 1954.[2] Of course, any large new credits by the United States

Government would increase these interest receipts in the future. About 80 percent of the interest is paid by countries in Western Europe, largely the United Kingdom and France. Payments of interest on these Government credits by Western European countries were about $40 million higher than the income received from direct investments in these countries in 1952. Income payments by Western Europe to the United States on both private and Government investments are currently about equal to the income received by Europe on its accumulated investments in the United States.

Table 5.—United States Equity in Undistributed Profits of Foreign Subsidiaries, 1950–52, by Industry and Specified Countries

[Millions of dollars]

	1950	1951	1952
Total	475	752	876
Industries			
Agriculture	24	29	28
Mining and smelting	33	56	45
Petroleum	74	204	338
Manufacturing	266	359	357
Public utilities	16	14	15
Trade	44	63	66
Other	18	27	27
Countries			
Canada	146	181	199
Latin American Republics	109	249	303
Argentina	12	18	18
Brazil	36	67	85
Chile	(1)	3	3
Colombia	6	3	7
Cuba	16	15	9
Dominican Republic	3	6	7
Mexico	15	33	29
Panama	12	70	58
Peru	6	3	6
Uruguay	2	5	3
Venezuela	−4	19	73
Other	5	7	4
Western Europe	151	181	174
Belgium	7	9	10
France	23	30	25
Germany	24	17	14
Italy	7	9	3
Netherlands	9	9	8
Spain	2	3	3
Sweden	5	4	3
United Kingdom	69	90	98
Other	5	10	10
Western European dependencies	−3	9	27
Western Hemisphere	2	2	−2
Africa	3	8	12
Asia	−8	−1	16
Other countries	71	132	172
Australia	16	25	25
Egypt	2	3	2
India	1	4	5
Indonesia	9	4	25
Liberia	3	22	36
Philippine Republic	11	9	6
Union of South Africa	12	10	12
Other	17	55	60

1 Less than $500,000.
Note.—Negative amounts reflect the payment of dividends in excess of earnings for the year.
Source: U. S. Department of Commerce, Office of Business Economics.

Table 6.—Branch Profits and Capital Movements, 1950–52, by Industry

[Millions of dollars]

Industries	1950 Branch profit	1950 Branch capital outflows	1951 Branch profits	1951 Branch capital outflows	1952 Branch profits	1952 Branch capital outflows
Total	624	191	834	143	863	424
Agriculture	56	1	66	27	58	−10
Mining and smelting	58	54	87	55	83	136
Petroleum	384	62	512	5	548	220
Manufacturing	40	21	68	29	61	29
Public utilities	8	10	5	−12	9	7
Trade	35	20	42	33	43	33
Other	44	24	53	5	61	8

Source: U. S. Department of Commerce, Office of Business Economics

2. For detailed projections see the SURVEY OF CURRENT BUSINESS, October 1953, page 19. The projections are based on credits outstanding as of June 30, 1953.

Table 7.—Selected United States Imports, 1952, Total and Estimated Portion Attributable to United States Direct-Investment Companies, by Specified Areas

[Millions of dollars]

Selected commodities	Total — Total imports	Total — Percent from direct-investment companies	Canada — Total imports	Canada — Percent from direct-investment companies	Latin American Republics — Total imports	Latin American Republics — Percent from direct-investment companies	Other — Total imports	Other — Percent from direct-investment companies
Crude rubber	619	15			2	(1)	617	15
Newsprint	571	35	552	40			19	
Crude oil	434	95	3	70	329	90	102	95
Sugar	415	45			324	50	91	20
Copper	397	85	52	75	288	95	57	35
Paper base stocks	325	75	278	90			47	
Refined oil products	257	70	5	75	64	70	188	65
Sawmill products	222	10	194	10	16	20	12	20
Lead	202	55	38	15	101	90	63	20
Bananas	158	75			158	75		
Vegetable oils and oil seeds	137	10			59	5	78	15
Fertilizers	114	40	45	35	30	90	39	(1)
Nickel	113	90	98	90	8	100	7	50
Zinc	112	25	50	15	47	40	15	10
Iron ore	83	50	14	90	39	60	30	10
Aluminum, including bauxite	78	90	43	100			35	75
Silver	67	50	17	30	36	70	14	30
Asbestos	62	30	54	35			8	
Chrome	38	40			2	50	36	40
Total	4,404	51	1,443	50	1,503	73	1,458	29

1 Less than 5 percent.
NOTE.—The percentages of imports of specified commodities attributable to United States direct-investment companies are estimates based on a number of sources, and, although they are believed to be reasonably accurate, they are not to be considered literally accurate. The list of commodities does not include all commodities which are produced abroad by United States direct-investment companies for sale in the United States.
Source: U. S. Department of Commerce, Office of Business Economics.

Table 8.—United States General Imports of Specified Commodities, Total and Portion Attributable to United States Direct Investments Abroad, Compared to Total United States Imports, 1952

[Amounts in millions of dollars]

Item	Areas — Total	Areas — Canada	Areas — Latin American Republics	Areas — Other
Total census imports, adjusted [1]	10,885	2,400	3,547	4,938
Imports of commodities listed in table 7	4,404	1,443	1,503	1,458
Ratio of selected imports to total imports	40	60	42	30
Selected imports—ratio of United States produced imports to total	51	50	74	29
Total imports—ratio of imports of United States produced selected commodities to imports of all commodities	21	30	31	9

1. The adjustments consist of the addition of silver to the census totals and a revaluation of banana imports.
Source: U. S. Department of Commerce, Office of Business Economics.

GROWTH IN PRIVATE FOREIGN INVESTMENTS

Samuel Pizer
and
Frederick Cutler

by Samuel Pizer and Frederick Cutler ☆

Growth in Private Foreign Investments

AMERICAN private investors added a record $1.8 billion to direct investments abroad in 1952, raising the book value of these investments to $14.8 billion at the end of that year. Partial data for 1953 indicate that the additions were somewhat smaller but probably brought the total value to well over $16 billion. This was an increase of more than 30 percent over the value at the end of 1950 reported in the recent census published in *Foreign Investments of the United States*, a 1953 Supplement to the SURVEY OF CURRENT BUSINESS.

A considerable part of the continued large amounts added to direct investments abroad in the postwar years is attributable to ploughing back current earnings of foreign subsidiaries.[1] Capital flows from the United States and reinvestment of current earnings increased sharply in 1952, with the latter accounting for more than half of the additions to investment in that year.

Gross and net capital outflows

The data on capital outflows for 1951 and 1952 given in detail in the accompanying tables are revisions of previous estimates and are based on the census data for 1950. Similarly detailed data for 1953 are not yet available.

In addition to the customary data on net capital outflows for direct investment, it is helpful in analyzing changes in

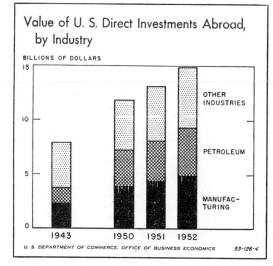

Value of U. S. Direct Investments Abroad, by Industry

BILLIONS OF DOLLARS

OTHER INDUSTRIES

PETROLEUM

MANUFAC-TURING

1943   1950   1951   1952

U. S. DEPARTMENT OF COMMERCE. OFFICE OF BUSINESS ECONOMICS   53-126-4

these flows to obtain information on the amount of capital moving in each direction. This can be done to some extent, as in table 4, from the data available by separating those enterprises receiving capital from the United States parent company from those returning capital to the United States

parent in the same year. On this basis, the overall increase in net capital outflows from 1951 to 1952 was due to rising gross capital outflows, with gross inflows practically stable, but there was considerable variety in the experience of different industries and areas.

In manufacturing, the flow in both directions increased, with the net outflow rising slightly. However, the gross movement abroad for this industry was down in every area but Canada, where new investments in aluminum production

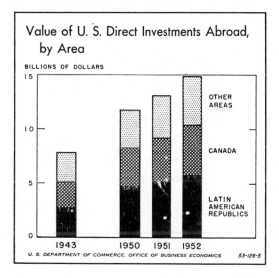

Value of U. S. Direct Investments Abroad, by Area

BILLIONS OF DOLLARS

OTHER AREAS

CANADA

LATIN AMERICAN REPUBLICS

1943   1950   1951   1952

U. S. DEPARTMENT OF COMMERCE. OFFICE OF BUSINESS ECONOMICS   53-126-5

dominated the picture. In the other areas net capital outflows for manufacturing were also reduced by larger gross inflows. This was particularly true in Latin America.

The gross flow of capital for mining investments was expanded to record amounts in Canada and Latin America as investments in iron ore and other properties reached a peak. Capital outflows in the petroleum industry were up by about $200 million in 1952, but the inflow to the United States also remained high, except for Canada, where there was practically no inward movement.

A large part of the shift in public utility investments from 1951 to 1952 is connected with the liquidation of an investment in Mexico in 1951, which resulted in an abnormally large return flow in that year.

Largest expansion in manufacturing

In the 2 years 1951 and 1952 about $1.1 billion was invested by American manufacturing companies in their foreign plants. This was certainly a record amount for such a short period and reflected the growing interest in expanded foreign markets. With this added investment the book

---

1. See SURVEY OF CURRENT BUSINESS, December 1953, pp. 8-14.

NOTE.—MR. PIZER AND MR. CUTLER ARE MEMBERS OF THE BALANCE OF PAYMENTS DIVISION OF THE OFFICE OF BUSINESS ECONOMICS.

value of the foreign enterprises was raised to $4.9 billion at the end of 1952.

About two-thirds of the investments in 1951–52 was financed out of plowed-back foreign earnings, and the remainder represented additional capital provided from the United States. Reinvested earnings were particularly important in Canada and Western Europe, where manufacturing plants have been long established. Net capital flowing across the border to Canada to manufacturing industries increased sharply in 1952, reflecting the financing of hydroelectric power and other facilities needed for developing new aluminum capacity. There was also a larger capital flow to Canadian enterprises producing chemicals, paper and allied products, and various kinds of machinery.

Among the countries of Latin America, there was a particularly sharp change in manufacturing investments in Mexico, with a number of important enterprises withdrawing funds in 1952 and also in 1953, possibly reflecting a slackened rate of increase in industrial production in Mexico in this period. In Brazil, on the other hand, manufacturing capital entered at a high rate in 1951 and 1952 as industrial production mounted. To some extent this new investment may have resulted from the blocking of dollar payments due to the parent companies by Brazil, and 1953 investments in this country appear to be substantially smaller. The reduction in the capital flowing to Latin America in 1952 occurred in nearly every major line of manufacturing, with only food products and fabricated metals moderately higher.

Petroleum investments expanding

Petroleum investments, after reaching an annual rate of about $550 million in the 1947–49 period, including over $50 million annually for oil tankers, were reduced to about $320 million annually in 1950 and 1951. In 1952, however, there was a sharp upturn, raising the figure for this year to about $600 million, and bringing the total book value of investments in the petroleum industry abroad at the end of 1952 to $4.3 billion. Additions to petroleum investments in 1953 were probably even greater, with capital outflows in the first 9 months exceeding the 1952 total and retained earnings also high.

As shown in table 1, there were differences in the area distribution of the investments. Petroleum investments in Canada, including reinvested earnings, remained at $140–$150 million in each year of the 1950–52 period. In Latin America, on the other hand, there was a sharp change from a reduction in investments of $60 million in 1950–51, to an increase of $170 million in 1952. Some of the increase resulted from higher undistributed earnings of tanker subsidiaries, and did not go into fixed investment within the area. To the extent these funds were remitted to the United States through intercompany accounts, they appear in table 3 as capital inflows, mainly from Panama. However, a significant development in 1952 was a resumption of investment activity in Venezuela in many phases of the industry, including exploration, pipeline construction and refinery expansion.

Table 1.—Value of United States Direct Private Investments Abroad, Capital Movements and Undistributed Subsidiary Earnings, by Area and Industry, 1949–52

[Millions of dollars; reduction of investment (−)]

Area and additions to value	All industries 1950	All industries 1951	All industries 1952	Agriculture 1950	Agriculture 1951	Agriculture 1952	Mining and smelting 1950	Mining and smelting 1951	Mining and smelting 1952	Petroleum 1950	Petroleum 1951	Petroleum 1952	Manufacturing 1950	Manufacturing 1951	Manufacturing 1952	Public utilities 1950	Public utilities 1951	Public utilities 1952	Trade 1950	Trade 1951	Trade 1952	Miscellaneous 1950	Miscellaneous 1951	Miscellaneous 1952
All areas:																								
Value at beginning of year	10,700	11,788	13,089	574	589	642	1,011	1,129	1,317	3,074	3,390	3,703	3,373	3,831	4,352	1,411	1,425	1,431	650	762	883	607	662	762
Net capital movements	621	528	850	−9	24	−8	87	100	278	248	93	248	192	190	211	−2	−8	23	68	58	17	37	70	80
Undistributed subsidiary earnings	475	752	876	24	29	28	33	56	45	74	204	338	266	359	357	16	14	15	44	63	66	18	28	27
Other changes	−8	22	4				−2	32	2	−6	16	2		−28				2					2	
Value at end of year	11,788	13,089	14,819	589	642	662	1,129	1,317	1,642	3,390	3,703	4,291	3,831	4,352	4,920	1,425	1,431	1,469	762	883	966	662	762	869
Canada:																								
Value at beginning of year	3,146	3,579	3,972	18	21	22	287	334	400	276	418	562	1,724	1,897	2,000	287	284	285	196	240	262	357	385	440
Net capital movements	287	240	420	2	(1)	−1	29	36	134	122	124	122	88	30	121	−6	−1	1	32	6	2	21	44	42
Undistributed subsidiary earnings	146	181	199	1	1	(1)	18	30	14	20	20	31	85	101	120	3	2	1	12	16	20	7	11	12
Other changes		−28	2						2					−28										
Value at end of year	3,579	3,972	4,593	21	22	21	334	400	550	418	562	715	1,897	2,000	2,241	284	285	287	240	262	284	385	440	494
Latin American Republics:																								
Value at beginning of year	4,590	4,735	5,176	513	520	557	595	628	736	1,467	1,408	1,408	667	780	992	1,035	1,041	1,044	212	242	303	102	116	136
Net capital movements	40	165	277	−7	22	−4	29	60	120	−69	−75	32	64	116	80	−3	−7	21	18	38	11	7	11	18
Undistributed subsidiary earnings	109	249	303	14	15	11	4	16	15	14	82	135	49	96	94	9	10	11	12	23	30	7	7	8
Other changes	−4	27	2					32		−4	−7	2											2	
Value at end of year	4,735	5,176	5,758	520	557	564	628	736	871	1,408	1,408	1,577	780	992	1,166	1,041	1,044	1,076	242	303	344	116	136	162
Western Europe:																								
Value at beginning of year	1,450	1,720	1,979	1	1	1	19	21	23	319	424	511	799	932	1,070	23	27	27	166	186	207	123	129	138
Net capital movements	119	62	−8	(1)	(1)	(1)	(1)	(1)	(1)	73	37	−24	32	17	6	4	(1)	(1)	7	7	2	3	1	8
Undistributed subsidiary earnings	151	181	174	(1)	(1)	(1)	2	3	3	32	33	45	101	121	111	(1)	(1)	(1)	13	14	9	3	8	6
Other changes		16						−1			17													
Value at end of year	1,720	1,979	2,145	1	1	1	21	23	26	424	511	532	932	1,070	1,187	27	27	28	186	207	218	129	138	152
Western European dependencies:																								
Value at beginning of year	427	435	445	8	9	10	75	88	95	311	296	295	6	9	8	16	18	18	10	13	16	1	1	1
Net capital movements	14	1	−5	(1)	1	(1)	13	2	18	−6	−2	−23	3	−2	(1)	2	(1)	(1)	2	2	1	(1)	(1)	(1)
Undistributed subsidiary earnings	−3	9	27	1	(1)	2	2	5	4	−7	1	18	(1)	1	1	(1)	(1)	(1)	1	1	1	(1)	(1)	(1)
Other changes	−3						−2			−2														
Value at end of year	435	445	467	9	10	12	88	95	117	296	295	290	9	8	9	18	18	18	13	16	18	1		1
All other countries:																								
Value at beginning of year	1,086	1,318	1,516	35	39	53	33	56	61	702	844	926	177	214	281	49	54	56	67	81	95	22	30	45
Net capital movements	161	59	166	−4	1	−2	16	2	6	127	8	142	6	29	4			2	9	5	2	6	14	13
Undistributed subsidiary earnings	71	132	172	8	13	13	7	2	9	15	68	109	31	38	31	4	2	3	5	9	6	2	1	1
Other changes		7						1			6													
Value at end of year	1,318	1,516	1,854	39	53	64	56	61	76	844	926	1,177	214	281	316	54	56	61	81	95	103	30	45	59

1. Less than $500,000.

Source: U. S. Department of Commerce, Office of Business Economics.

NOTE.—"Other changes" consist of adjustments to the value of direct investments abroad caused by the revaluation of foreign properties, the transfer of assets from one country to another, adjustments for loss or profit on liquidations and other technical adjustments.

Table 2.—Value of United States Direct Private Investments Abroad, Capital Movements and Undistributed Subsidiary Earnings, by Selected Countries, 1949–52

[Millions of dollars; reduction of investment (−)]

Country	Value end of 1949	Changes 1950				Changes 1951				Changes 1952			
		Net capital outflows	Undistributed subsidiary earnings	Other changes	Value end of 1950	Net capital outflows	Undistributed subsidiary earnings	Other changes	Value end of 1951	Net capital outflows	Undistributed subsidiary earnings	Other changes	Value end of 1952
All area, total	10,700	621	475	−8	11,788	528	752	22	13,089	850	876	4	14,819
Canada	3,146	287	146		3,579	240	181	−28	3,972	420	199	2	4,593
Latin American Republics, total	4,590	40	109	−4	4,735	165	249	27	5,176	277	303	2	5,758
Argentina	329	15	12		356	−9	18		365	8	18	2	393
Brazil	588	20	36		644	92	67		803	125	85		1,013
Chile	518	22	(¹)		540	40	3		583	37	3		623
Colombia	194	−7	6		193	11	3		207	20	7		234
Costa Rica	57	2	1		60	(¹)	1		61	(¹)	(¹)		61
Cuba	619	7	16		642	13	15	2	672	5	9		686
Dominican Republic	102	1	3		106	11	6		123	−7	7		123
Ecuador	16	2	(¹)		14	(¹)	(¹)		14	(¹)	(¹)		14
Guatemala	104	1	1	−4	106	−1	1		106	1	1		108
Honduras	60	1	1		62	14	2		78	2	1		81
Mexico	374	25	15		414	24	33		471	−10	29		490
Panama	337	−1	12		348	−38	70	−7	373	−48	58		383
Peru	148	−9	6		145	17	3	33	197	28	6		230
Uruguay	51	3	2		56	6	5		67	1	3		71
Venezuela	1,036	−39	−4		993	−16	19		996	115	73		1,184
Other countries	57	−3	2		56	2	3		61	(¹)	3		64
Western Europe, total	1,450	119	151		1,720	62	181	16	1,979	−8	174		2,145
Belgium	55	3	7		65	13	9		87	−2	10		95
Denmark	30	2	(¹)		32	3	2		37	(¹)	1		38
France	185	9	23		217	2	30		249	2	25		276
Germany	173	7	24		204	3	17	10	234	3	14		251
Italy	37	19	7		63	(¹)	9		72	5	3		80
Netherlands	57	18	9		84	7	9		100	(¹)	8		108
Norway	22	(¹)	2		24	1	3		28	1	4		33
Portugal	14	2	(¹)		16	3	(¹)		19	(¹)	2		21
Spain	27	2	2		31	2	3		36	1	3		40
Sweden	51	2	5		58	3	4		65	2	3		70
Switzerland	22	2	1		25	2	1		28	(¹)	(¹)		28
Turkey	17	−1	(¹)		16	1	(¹)		17	(¹)	1		18
United Kingdom	729	49	69		847	18	90	6	961	−21	98		1,038
Other countries	31	5	2		38	4	4		46	2	2		50
Western European dependencies, total	427	14	−3	−3	435	1	9		445	−5	27		467
Western Hemisphere:													
British	61	5	3	−3	66	1	4		71	15	2		88
Other European	65	1	−1		65	5	−2		68	5	−3		70
Africa:													
British	37	3	1		41	6	7		54	6	6		66
French	27	2	2		31	(¹)	1		32	−1	5		36
Other European	10	2	(¹)		12	(¹)	(¹)		12	1	1		14
Other areas:													
British	201	−3	−8		190	−12	−1		177	−39	16		154
Other European	26	4	(¹)		30	2	(¹)		32	7	(¹)		39
Other countries, total	1,086	161	71		1,318	59	132	7	1,516	166	172		1,854
Africa:													
Egypt	38	−1	2		39	2	3		44	(¹)	2		46
Liberia	47	32	3		82	(¹)	22		104	(¹)	36		140
Union of South Africa	105	23	12		140	7	10		157	25	12		194
Other countries	5	2	(¹)		7	(¹)	(¹)		7	1	(¹)		8
Other areas:													
India	27	10	1		38	7	4		49	9	5		63
Indonesia	62	−13	9		58	4	4	6	72	−23	25		74
Israel	13	2	(¹)		15	19	(¹)		34	7	(¹)		41
Japan	12	7	(¹)		19	21	5		45	23	1		69
Philippine Republic	132	6	11		149	5	9		163	9	6		178
Other countries in Asia	467	62	16		545	−39	48		554	81	58		693
Australia	161	24	16		201	29	25	1	256	29	25		310
New Zealand	17	7	1		25	4	2		31	4	2		37

1. Less than $500,000.

Source: U. S. Department of Commerce, Office of Business Economics.

Note. "Other changes" consist of adjustments to the value of direct investments abroad caused by the revaluation of foreign properties, the transfer of assets from one country to another, adjustments for loss or profit on liquidations and other technical adjustments.

Investments in Western Europe, notably the United Kingdom, were affected by a reversal of the capital flow in 1952 after two years of substantial capital additions. The small further increase in investments which took place in 1952 resulted entirely from larger reinvested earnings. A major expansion in refinery capacity was carried out in Western Europe in 1950 and 1951 by the petroleum companies, and some projects were continuing in 1952 and 1953. However,

by 1952 the principal expenditures had been made, and as the facilities went into operation the foreign enterprises were able to begin reducing their indebtedness to the United States parent companies.

Somewhat the same situation prevailed in the Western European dependencies in the Middle East, where petroleum investments were reduced by small amounts in 1950–52 in contrast to the sizable capital outflows in the earlier post-

Table 3.—Net Direct Private Investments—Capital Movements to Selected Countries by Major Industries, 1950–52

[Millions of dollars]

Country	All industries			Mining and smelting			Petroleum			Manufacturing			Trade			Other		
	1950	1951	1952	1950	1951	1952	1950	1951	1952	1950	1951	1952	1950	1951	1952	1950	1951	1952
Total	621	528	850	87	100	278	248	93	248	192	190	211	68	58	17	26	87	96
Canada	287	240	420	29	36	134	122	124	122	88	30	121	32	6	2	17	43	41
Latin American Republics, total	40	165	277	29	60	120	69	75	32	64	116	80	18	38	11	−3	26	35
Argentina	15	−9	8	(1)	(1)	(1)	(1)	(1)	(1)	1	−5	12	−4	5	4	−4	−3	5
Brazil	20	92	125	(1)	(1)	(1)	4		17	34	17	61	65	1	8	9	(1)	(1)	(1)
Chile	22	40	37	17	30	35	(1)	(1)	(1)	(2)	3	−2	4	1	−3	(1)	(1)	(1)
Colombia	−7	11	20	(1)	(1)	(1)	−13	4	5	7	2	8	−2	2	7	(1)	(1)	(1)
Costa Rica	2	(2)	(2)				(2)	(2)	(2)	(2)	(2)	(2)	(2)	(2)	(2)	(2)	(2)	(2)
Cuba	7	13	5	(1)	(1)	(1)	(1)	(1)	(1)	4	5	1	3	2	−3	(2)	3	10
Dominican Republic	1	11	−7				(1)	(1)	(1)	(1)	−1	(1)	(1)	(1)	(1)	(2)	12	−7
Honduras	1	14	2	(1)	(1)	(1)	(1)	(1)	(1)	(1)	(1)	(1)	(1)	(1)	(1)	(2)	13	2
Mexico	25	24	−10	−8	−5	−4	5	−2	1	23	42	−3	5	8	−6	(2)	−19	2
Panama	−1	−38	−48				−7	−44	−47	(2)	1	(2)	1	1	−3	4	4	1
Peru	−9	17	28	3	24	29	(1)	(1)	(1)	3	3	−6	2	2	3	(1)	(1)	(1)
Uruguay	3	6	1				(2)	(2)	1	(2)	3	1	(2)	3	(2)	−1	(2)	(2)
Venezuela	−39	−16	115	(1)	(1)	(1)	−68	−39	48	4	3	4	7	5	3	(1)	(1)	(1)
Other countries	(2)	(2)	(2)	(2)	(2)	1	1	(2)	(2)	1	(2)	−2	(2)	1	(2)	−2	−1	(2)
Western Europe, total	119	62	−8	(2)	(2)	(2)	73	37	−24	32	17	6	7	7	2	7	1	9
Belgium	3	13	−2				2	3	2	(2)	8	−3	1	1	(2)	(2)	(2)	(2)
France	9	2	2				3	(2)	−4	5	1	1	(2)	(2)	(2)	1	1	5
Germany	7	3	3	(1)	(1)	(1)	3	−1	−3	(2)	3	4	(1)	(1)	(1)	5	1	2
Italy	19	(2)	5	(1)	(1)	(1)	20	(2)	4	(2)	(2)	1	1	(2)	(2)	−1	(2)	(2)
Netherlands	18	7	(2)	(1)	(1)	(1)	16	6	(2)	(2)	(2)	(2)	1	1	(2)	(1)	(1)	(1)
Portugal	2	3	(2)	(2)	(2)	(2)	1	2	(2)	(2)	(2)	(2)	1	(2)	(2)	(2)	(2)	(2)
Spain	2	2	1	(1)	(1)	(1)	1	3	1	(2)	−1	(2)	(1)	(2)	(2)	(1)	(1)	(1)
Sweden	2	3	2				3	1	2	−1	1	(2)	2	(2)	−1	−1	1	1
United Kingdom	49	18	−21	(2)	(2)	(2)	21	18	−24	24	1	5	2	3	−2	2	−3	1
Other countries	9	11	2	(2)			4	6	−1	4	4	−1	(2)	1	3	(2)	(2)	1
Western European dependencies, total	14	1	−5	13	2	18	−6	−2	−23	3	−2	(2)	2	2	1	2	1	(2)
Western Hemisphere:																		
British	5	1	15	(1)	(1)	(1)	2	−1	2	1		(1)	(1)	(1)	(1)	2	(2)	(2)
Other European	1	5	5	(1)	(1)	(1)	(1)	(1)	(1)	(1)		(1)	(1)	(1)	(1)	(2)	(2)	(2)
Africa:																		
British	3	6	6	(2)	1	2	2	5	5	(1)	(1)	(1)	(1)	(1)	(1)	(2)		(2)
French	2	(2)	−1			(2)	2	−1	−2	−1		1	1	(2)	(2)	(2)	(2)	(2)
Other European	2	(2)	1	(1)	(1)	(1)	2	(2)	1	(1)	(1)	(1)	(2)	(2)	(2)	(2)	(2)	(2)
Other areas:																		
British	−3	−12	−39	10			−16	−12	−38	2	−2	(2)	(2)	1	(2)	(2)	1	(2)
Other European	4	2	7				(1)	(1)	(1)				(1)	(1)	(1)			
Other countries, total	161	59	166	16	2	6	127	8	142	6	29	4	9	5	2	3	15	12
Africa:																		
Liberia	32	(2)	(2)	(1)	(1)	(1)	30	−1	−2				(1)	(1)	(1)	(1)	(1)	(1)
Union of South Africa	23	7	25	14	1	6	10	−1	21	−1	5	−3	(2)	2	(2)	(2)	(2)	1
Other countries	1	3	1				(1)	(1)	(1)	−1	(2)	(2)	1	(2)	(2)	(1)	(1)	(1)
Other areas:																		
Australia	24	29	29	(1)	(1)	(1)	(1)	(1)	(1)	6	7	4	3	1	(2)	(2)	1	2
India	10	7	9	(2)			(1)	(1)	(1)	3	(2)	−3	(2)	1	(2)	(1)	(1)	(1)
Indonesia	−13	4	−23				(1)	(1)	(1)	−1	2	(2)	(2)	(2)	1	(1)	(1)	(1)
Israel	2	19	7				(2)	3	−4	1	12	7	(2)	(2)	(2)	1	4	4
Japan	7	21	23				(1)	(1)	(1)	(2)	1	1	(2)	(2)	(2)	(2)	2	4
Philippine Republic	6	5	9	(1)	(1)	(1)	(1)	(1)	(1)	−1	1	(2)	2	−1	(2)	2	4	−1
Other countries	69	−35	85	(2)		(2)	65	−38	88	1	1	−1	3	1	−1	1	(2)	(2)

1. Included in totals.   2. Less than $500,000.   Source: U. S. Department of Commerce, Office of Business Economics.

war years when the various properties were being brought into production. However, petroleum investments in the independent Middle Eastern countries and in the Far East increased substantially in 1952. In the Middle East the intensification of investments raised oil production to record levels.

The major activity in the Far East was the further expansion of refining capacity, but exploration for new oil resources also required a considerable amount of capital. One of the results of these expenditures was the recent discovery of new oil reserves in Australia.

The far-sighted postwar foreign investment by United States petroleum companies has undoubtedly been a major factor in facilitating the recovery and expansion of economic activity in Europe and nearly every other part of the world. Not only did the United States companies abroad increase their output of crude oil from nearly 400 million barrels in 1946 to about 1 billion barrels in 1952, but they also provided for moving the oil to the consuming areas by pipeline and tanker, and erected the required refining, storage and distribution facilities. In addition, by spending very large sums for exploration and development the companies are locating new reserves which will provide for consumption for many years.

Mining investments higher

Capital outflows for mining investments abroad in 1952 were about $280 million, far higher than in any previous year. This investment was mainly connected with a few large projects, although much activity was carried out on a smaller scale to develop new sources of essential raw materials. The amount of reinvested earnings was down from 1951 as earnings were reduced by price declines of some metals and minerals.

Table 4.—Gross Movements of Direct Private Capital, by Areas and Industries, 1951–52 [1]

[Millions of dollars; net inflows (−)]

Industries and years	All areas			Canada			Latin American Republics			Western Europe			Western European dependencies			Other countries		
	Out-flows	In-flows	Net	Out-flows	In-flows	Net	Out-flows	In-flows	Net	Out-flows	In-flows	Net	Out-flows	In-flows	Net	Out-flows	In-flows	Net
All industries:																		
1951	1,003	476	528	330	91	240	414	249	165	97	35	62	30	29	1	132	73	59
1952	1,381	531	850	518	98	420	469	192	277	68	76	−8	55	60	−5	272	106	166
Agriculture:																		
1951	42	18	24	1	1	(²)	39	17	22						1	1	......	1
1952	12	19	−8	(²)	2	−1	11	15	−4				(²)	(²)		1	3	−2
Mining and Smelting:																		
1951	125	25	100	36	1	36	84	24	60	(²)	......	(²)	3	(²)	2	2	(²)	2
1952	299	21	278	135	(²)	134	140	20	120	(²)	(²)	(²)	18	......	18	6	(²)	6
Petroleum:																		
1951	329	237	93	128	4	124	54	129	−75	50	13	37	23	25	−2	74	66	8
1952	526	279	248	124	2	122	112	81	32	27	51	−24	35	58	−23	228	86	142
Manufacturing:																		
1951	300	110	190	103	73	30	136	20	116	30	13	17	(²)	2	−2	31	2	29
1952	359	148	211	203	82	121	120	40	80	21	15	6	(²)	(²)	(²)	15	11	4
Public Utilities:																		
1951	25	33	−8	1	2	−1	24	31	−7	(²)	(²)	(²)	(²)	......	(²)	......		
1952	31	7	23	1	(²)	1	27	7	21	(²)	(²)	(²)	......	(²)	(²)	2		2
Trade:																		
1951	91	33	58	13	7	6	56	18	38	10	3	7	3	1	2	9	5	5
1952	65	47	17	9	7	2	39	28	11	9	7	2	2	1	1	6	5	2
Other:																		
1951	91	21	70	48	4	44	21	10	11	8	6	1	(²)	(²)	(²)	14	1	14
1952	90	10	80	46	4	42	20	2	18	11	3	8	(²)	(²)	(²)	14	1	13

1. The gross capital outflow shown in each area-industry cell of this table represents the sum of the net capital outflows to those foreign subsidiaries and branches for which net outflows were reported for each of the years covered. Conversely, the gross inflows shown for each cell represent the sum of the net inflows from those foreign subsidiaries and branches for which inflows were reported in each year. The totals for "all areas" are the sums of the figures shown in the area-industry cells. It should be noted that the gross totals, but not the net amounts, would change if the compilation were done on a quarterly basis.

2. Less than $500,000.

Source: U. S. Department of Commerce, Office of Business Economics.

Some of the largest investments were in Canada, including the well-known projects for developing the iron ore resources of Labrador. Another large investment in 1952 was the development of Venezuelan iron ore resources. Capital outflows for these projects were at a peak in 1952, but a part of this capital was not utilized until the following year.

Capital sent abroad to finance trade and distribution enterprises declined in 1952, particularly in Latin America, while reinvested earnings remained about the same as in 1951. However, these capital items are essentially short-term and show considerable annual variation.

Table 5.—Private Long-Term Portfolio Investments Abroad, by Area and Type, 1950–52

[Millions of dollars; capital inflows to United States (−)]

Type	Total	Canada	Latin American Republics	Western Europe	Other countries	International institutions
1952—Total	143	30	−34	19	10	118
New foreign security issues	287	158			47	83
Amortizations and redemptions	−66	−38	−10	−9	−10	......
Transactions in outstanding foreign securities	−129	−100	−16	−7	−40	35
Banking and commercial loans	51	10	−8	35	13	......
1951—Total	361	220	−29	−24	40	153
New foreign security issues	491	302			50	139
Amortizations and redemptions	−113	−88	−11	−3	−11	......
Transactions in outstanding foreign securities	−37	8	−22	−15	−22	14
Banking and commercial loans	20	−2	4	−6	23	......
1950—Total	467	324	−27	157	10	2
New foreign security issues	254	163	10	......	......	80
Amortizations and redemptions	−297	−167	−19	−3	−8	−100
Transactions in outstanding foreign securities	324	332	−21	−8	−2	23
Banking and commercial loans	186	−4	3	168	20	−1

Source: U. S. Department of Commerce, Office of Business Economics.

284297°—54——2

Investments in other industries continued to show moderate gains in 1952. In agriculture, capital flowing back to the United States in 1952 exceeded the movement abroad, with reinvested earnings accounting for the small increase in investment. Continued price declines in 1952 and 1953 for some of the more important products produced abroad by United States-owned agricultural facilities, as well as unsettled political situations in some areas, were deterrents to any sizable new investments. Public utility companies have been investing moderate amounts in Latin America to meet the growing need for electric power. The net capital inflow shown for this industry in 1951 was connected with the sale of one property in Mexico.

Two-thirds invested in Western Hemisphere

In the 1950–52 period, as in earlier periods of American direct investment abroad, the proportion invested in Western Hemisphere countries was maintained at about two-thirds of the total. In 1951 and 1952 about $2 billion was added to direct investments in these countries out of total additions of a little over $3 billion. By the end of 1950 the value of investments in this area alone exceeded the value of all direct investments abroad in 1943.

Direct investments in Canada reached a record rate of over $600 million in 1952. It appears that there will be some reduction in capital flowing to Canada as the financing of some of the very large mining and petroleum ventures has been largely accomplished, while much of the manufacturing investment is financed out of earnings.

The rate of direct investment in Latin America was also very high in 1952, particularly for mining and petroleum enterprises. The largest increases in investment in that year were in Brazil and Venezuela. By the end of 1952 the book value of United States direct investments in each of these countries was over $1 billion.

Additions to direct investments in Western Europe were reduced in each year from 1950 through 1952, mainly because of the decreasing need for United States funds for the construction of petroleum refineries. There was a marked change in capital flows from 1951 to 1952, with a large increase in the amount sent back to the United States by companies reducing their investments and a drop in the amount being invested in Europe by those companies carrying out further investments. Investments out of retained earnings remained high, however, so that by the end of 1952 United States direct investments in the United Kingdom were also valued at over $1 billion.

Investment activity by United States companies in other areas was considerably higher in 1952 than in the previous two years. The renewed investment in Middle Eastern

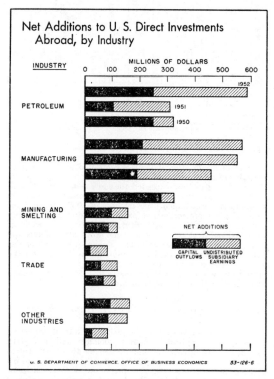

Net Additions to U. S. Direct Investments Abroad, by Industry

U. S. DEPARTMENT OF COMMERCE, OFFICE OF BUSINESS ECONOMICS   53-126-6

petroleum has already been discussed above. Other countries where investments are going forward, as shown in table 2, include India, Japan, the Philippine Republic, the Union of South Africa and Australia.

Portfolio investments remain low

Private investments in foreign bonds and stocks and various types of claims or assets with a maturity of more than one year, have had a minor attraction for American investors in the postwar years. The rate of portfolio capital outflows declined in each year from 1950 through 1952 and

in 1953 changed into a net return of capital from abroad.

Much of this portfolio lending in the 1950–52 period has been directed to Canada which received about 60 percent of the nearly $1 billion net new investment. In this period a substantial number of bond issues have been sold in the United States by Canadian provinces and municipalities to finance a wide variety of projects, and Canadian corporations have also sold their common stock in the United States in sizable amounts. However, a large part of the recent capital movement to and from Canada has been associated with the short-term fluctuations of exchange rates and bond yields rather than with more permanent investments.

American private investors have also provided a sizable amount of financing for the International Bank for Reconstruction and Development by buying the bonds of that institution. The International Bank is also finding that foreign governments and other investors in recent years have increased their participation in the Bank's financing by purchasing both foreign currency and U. S. dollar bonds.

Aside from the portfolio capital going to Canada and the International Bank the outflow has been sporadic and for rather special purposes, including sales of bonds of the Government of Israel and a fully secured special bank loan to France in 1950. There are no indications as yet that port-

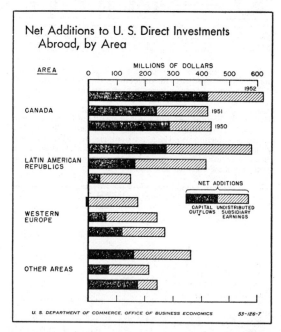

Net Additions to U. S. Direct Investments Abroad, by Area

U. S. DEPARTMENT OF COMMERCE, OFFICE OF BUSINESS ECONOMICS   53-126-7

folio capital outflows can be expected to increase materially, although there have been a number of favorable developments in the position of outstanding dollar bonds. Dollar bonds held in the United States in default and not now covered by agreements had a par value of $103 million out of a total par value for foreign bonds held in the United States of $2.6 billion at the end of 1952.

FOREIGN INVESTMENTS AND INCOME

Samuel Pizer
and
Frederick Cutler

by Samuel Pizer and Frederick Cutler ☆

Foreign Investments and Income

UNITED STATES corporations added about $1.5 billion to their direct investments in foreign subsidiaries and branches in 1953, and continued to increase the total at about the same rate in the first half of 1954. This rate is below the 1952 peak, but maintains the high volume of direct private foreign investments which has characterized the entire postwar period.

Additions to Direct Investments Abroad
By Industry

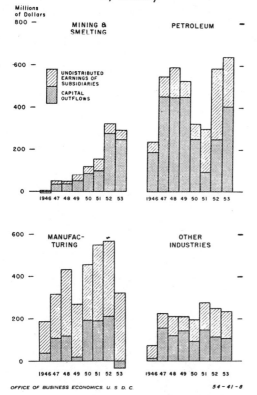

OFFICE OF BUSINESS ECONOMICS. U. S. D. C.
54-41-8

Nearly $10 billion were added to United States direct foreign investments from 1946 through the middle of 1954, raising their present book value to some $17 billion as compared with about $7 billion at the end of 1946. The great productive facilities represented by these sums have con-

tributed much to the postwar recovery and development of foreign countries. With this greater productive capacity these countries are able to supply more of their own needs and also to participate in an increased amount and variety of foreign trade.

Earnings of the direct investments abroad have been steady at about $2.2 billion annually since 1950, after payment of foreign taxes of some $1 billion a year. Nearly $800 million a year out of the net earnings in this period has been retained abroad by foreign subsidiaries, mainly to finance the expansion and modernization of foreign operations. The remaining $1.5 billion of dividends, interest and branch profits has been an important part of the total annual earnings of many United States companies.

Private portfolio investments, which consist mainly of purchases of foreign government and corporate securities and loans by United States financial institutions, have tended to fluctuate widely from year to year. This contrasts with the more steady flow of direct investments. In 1953 portfolio investments were liquidated, on balance, but late in 1953 and in 1954 a sizable outflow was resumed.

Direct Investments

Both the flow of direct investment capital from the United States and the reinvestment of earnings of foreign subsidiary companies remained high in 1953. Each contributed about equally to the total increase of $1.5 billion in the value of direct investments abroad. Partial information for the first half of 1954, as given in table 1, shows that capital outflows are being well maintained. Aiding this movement is the growing strength of foreign economies and increased freedom in trade and foreign exchange transactions, which, in turn, are in part the result of productive capacity added by the direct investment projects.

Although the aggregate capital outflow for direct investment abroad has been relatively stable in the postwar period, marked fluctuations have occurred from year to year in the area and industry distribution of the total. Such fluctuations have resulted from various causes, including the discovery and development of new sources for raw materials, the completion of scheduled investment programs, and relatively short-term flows connected with such factors as exchange restrictions or changes in exchange rates, or the timing of new financing and tax payments.

Direct foreign investments are quite diverse, comprising a combined investment of some $17 billion by more than 2,000 leading United States corporations, but the net capital flow in most postwar years has been dominated by a relatively few large projects or areas of intense development. While such projects are under way the capital outflow may be very large, but when the particular project is completed and the new facilities are put into operation, a return flow of capital to the United States is often set in motion to repay advances by the parent company and to set aside reserves against depreciation and depletion. Fluctuations due to this factor, and the others mentioned above, sometimes

NOTE.—MR. PIZER AND MR. CUTLER ARE MEMBERS OF THE BALANCE OF PAYMENTS DIVISION. OFFICE OF BUSINESS ECONOMICS.

tend to obscure the consistent flow of United States invest-ments abroad to finance new ventures during the postwar period.

Manufacturing down in 1953

One of these major fluctuations occurred in 1953, when capital flows connected with manufacturing enterprises changed from a net outflow of over $200 million in 1952 to a net inflow of about $30 million in 1953. The reversal was most marked in Latin America where the flow changed from an outward movement of $80 million in 1952 to an inward movement of about the same amount in 1953. Brazil ac-counted for over 80 percent of these totals. It is clear that United States parent companies financed a large amount of equipment and materials required to carry on manufacturing in that country in 1952 while dollar exchange was not avail-able. In 1953 they were repaid, in part from the proceeds of an Export-Import Bank loan and in part by remitting dollars at less than the official rate though free markets.

Earnings of manufacturing enterprises were also down in Latin America in 1953, particularly in Argentina and Brazil. Lower industrial activity was apparently the principal fac-tor in Argentina. Earnings in terms of local currency were higher in Brazil because of rising output and prices, but in converting to dollars an exchange rate of about 20 cruzeiros to the dollar was used in 1952 while a rate of about 50 cru-zeiros to the dollar was used in 1953, so that the dollar equivalent of the earnings was considerably reduced. Brazil accounts for over half of the earnings of United States-owned manufacturing companies in Latin America.

Table 1.—Direct Investment Capital Movements, by Area and Industry, January–June 1954

[In millions of dollars; inflows to the United States (−)]

Areas	Total	Mining	Petro-leum	Manufac-turing	Other in-dustries
All areas, total	406	55	144	58	149
Canada	243	44	97	41	61
Latin American Republics	79	1	32	2	44
Western Europe	25		−3	7	21
Western European depend-encies	−14	3	−18	1	
Other countries	73	7	36	7	23

Note: Based on partial information.

Source: U. S. Department of Commerce, Office of Business Economics.

Capital flows for manufacturing in Canada were greatly reduced in 1953 from the 1952 peak because of the comple-tion of United States financing for the development of facilities for processing aluminum. However, the expansion of other manufacturing facilities in Canada continued at a rapid rate, and improved earnings in 1953 permitted larger reinvestments.

Manufacturing activities outside of the Western Hemis-phere did not involve significant amounts of capital flows in the aggregate. Reinvested earnings continued to be the major source of funds for expansion, especially in Western Europe, and moderately higher earnings were available in 1953 for this purpose.

Note.—Detailed data for 1946–49 given in this article are based on the complete 1950 Census published in FOREIGN INVESTMENTS OF THE UNITED STATES, a special supplement to the SURVEY OF CURRENT BUSINESS, and are revisions of previously published estimates.

Record petroleum investment

American petroleum companies were very active abroad in all phases of the industry in 1953 and invested a record amount of $640 million. About $400 million of this total represented capital flows, the highest since the rapid growth of the 1947–49 period. Reinvested earnings of foreign subsidiaries amounting to about $240 million were substan-tially less than in 1952 but higher than in any other year. Total earnings abroad of the industry were cut back some-what in 1953, in spite of higher prices and sustained output, because of large exploration costs and a sharp drop in earnings from tanker operations.

About half of the capital flow for this industry went to Canada as the companies intensively explored and developed the petroleum resources of Western Canada, and continued the construction of pipelines and refinery capacity. More-over, the capital flows do not include additional exploration and development costs, totalling over $50 million which were charged against earnings in 1953.

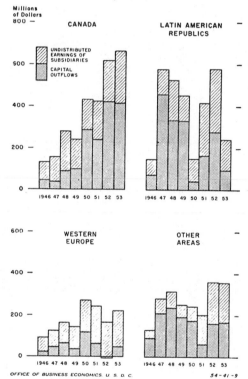

Additions to Direct Investments Abroad By Area

Millions of Dollars

OFFICE OF BUSINESS ECONOMICS. U. S. D. C.   54-41-9

Petroleum investments in Latin America continued small in comparison with the earlier postwar years. About $100 million was invested in 1953, divided about equally between capital flows and reinvested earnings. Venezuela received half of the total as the companies continued to expand their productive facilities in that country. About $30 million was invested in Brazil, but this represented primarily the value of imports of petroleum products from the parent companies for which payment was not made.

Petroleum investments attributed to Panama consist mainly of ocean tankers operated under the Panamanian flag. Because of the very low tanker rates prevailing in 1953 earnings from such investments were reduced, and, because these earnings flow back to the United States through intercompany accounts, there was also a reduction in the net return capital flow to the United States.

Foreign Earnings of Direct Investment Companies

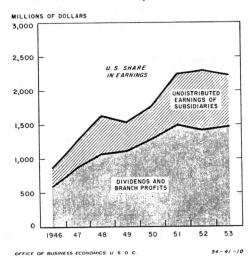

MILLIONS OF DOLLARS

U. S. SHARE IN EARNINGS

UNDISTRIBUTED EARNINGS OF SUBSIDIARIES

DIVIDENDS AND BRANCH PROFITS

1946   47   48   49   50   51   52   53

OFFICE OF BUSINESS ECONOMICS. U. S. D. C.   54-41-10

Considerable amounts were invested in Western Europe in 1953 by the petroleum companies, both to improve and enlarge the refinery facilities which have contributed significantly to the economic strength of Europe and to find and develop new indigenous sources of oil, especially in France, Germany and Italy.

American petroleum companies also continued to spend large sums for further expansion of production in the Middle East, and to build and enlarge refineries in the Far East. Additional large amounts are scheduled to go to Iran as the result of an agreement under which oil production has been resumed in that country.

Mining investments high

Direct investments abroad in mining which have grown faster since 1949 than in the case of any other major industry, reached nearly $2 billion by the end of 1953. The amount added was lower in 1953 than in 1952 because some large projects in Canada, Venezuela, Chile, and Peru were nearing completion. Capital outflows for mining will probably be further reduced in 1954, especially so since there is likely to be a return flow as large-scale shipments begin from some of the mines. This will also be reinforced to the extent that some enterprises are operating under provisions for rapid de-

preciation. However, the outlook for this industry includes a wide range of new developments so that investments are expected to continue at a substantial rate.

Earnings of the mining enterprises were severely cut in 1953 by reduced output and prices. This was particularly marked in Chile.

Other industries little changed

Both capital flows from the United States and earnings abroad of most other industries were relatively stable in 1953. The principal development was a sharp drop in the earnings of agricultural enterprises to the lowest point since 1949. Sugar producers experienced most of the decline because of lower world market prices for their products and restrictions on the size of the crop.

Table 2.—Direct Investment Capital Movements, by Major Areas and Industries, 1946–53

[Millions of dollars; inflows to the United States (−)]

Area and year	Total	Agriculture	Mining and smelting	Petroleum	Manufacturing	Public utilities	Trade	Other industries
All areas, total:								
1953	722	−17	247	404	−34	13	26	83
1952	850	−8	278	248	211	23	17	80
1951	528	24	100	93	190	−8	58	70
1950	621	−9	87	248	192	−2	68	37
1949	660	10	51	448	16	20	26	89
1948	721	23	37	448	118	30	30	24
1947	749	15	36	451	107	55	58	27
1946	230	4	−6	186	36	−71	27	54
Canada:								
1953	413	(1)	115	181	49	2	25	41
1952	420	−1	134	122	121	1	2	42
1951	240	(1)	36	124	30	−1	6	44
1950	287	2	29	122	88	−6	32	21
1949	100	1	13	33	7	−3	4	44
1948	88	−4	8	43	43	1	8	−11
1947	39	(1)	1	36	13	−4	−1	−4
1946	47	(1)	1	13	−9	−2	1	43
Latin American Republics:								
1953	93	−18	119	57	−83	5	−5	18
1952	277	−4	120	32	80	21	11	18
1951	166	22	60	−75	116	−7	38	11
1950	40	−7	29	−69	64	−3	18	7
1949	332	9	32	234	−7	23	28	14
1948	333	20	16	174	59	26	25	13
1947	457	10	36	232	65	60	34	19
1946	71	4	−7	104	23	−71	13	5
Western Europe:								
1953	48	......	(1)	32	−3	(1)	7	12
1952	−8	......	(1)	−21	6	(1)	2	5
1951	62	......	(1)	37	17	......	7	1
1950	119	(1)	(1)	73	32	4	−1	3
1949	36	......	(1)	12	6	(1)	−1	19
1948	64	......	(1)	41	5	(1)	2	16
1947	46	......	1	17	15	(1)	9	4
1946	23	......		8	7	(1)	4	3
Western European dependencies:								
1953	79	(1)	3	73	(1)	(1)	1	1
1952	−5	(1)	18	−23	(1)	(1)	1	(1)
1951	1	1	2	−2	−2	......	2	(1)
1950	14	(1)	13	−6	3	2	2	(1)
1949	29	1	3	25	1	(1)	(1)	(1)
1948	71	(1)	1	61	2	2	2	(1)
1947	55	−1	−1	49	(1)		4	(1)
1946	5	−1	−1	5	(1)	(1)	1	1
Other countries:								
1953	89	1	9	62	3	5	−3	11
1952	166	−2	6	142	4	2	2	13
1951	59	1	2	8	29	......	5	14
1950	161	−4	16	127	6	1	9	6
1949	163	(1)	2	145	9	(1)	−6	12
1948	165	7	8	128	9	2	4	6
1947	152	4	2	117	12	−2	12	7
1946	84	1	......	56	15	2	7	3

1. Less than $500,000.

Source: U. S. Department of Commerce, Office of Business Economics.

Overall capital outflows for trade and distribution were somewhat higher, mainly because of a large increase in Canada. There were sizable inflows from Brazil, however, as remittances were made on earlier advances.

Investment in Canada leads

Out of a total increase of $1.5 billion in direct investments abroad in 1953, Canada accounted for $650 million—a record amount. Capital flows to Canada were over $400 million, as in 1952, with increased investments in petroleum and trade offsetting reductions in manufacturing and mining. Reinvested earnings rose to $250 million, as earnings improved somewhat, mainly in manufacturing, while dividends were cut below the 1952 amount.

A feature in 1954 was the organization in the United States of a number of investment funds to be incorporated in Canada for the specific purpose of acquiring Canadian securities, especially corporate stocks. Total capital issues offered by the funds through October totaled $100 million. Of this about $30 million is included in direct investment outflows in the second quarter of 1954.

Additions to direct investments in Latin America were less than half of the 1952 total, with both capital flows and reinvestment of earnings reduced. However, the reduction in net capital flows was not connected with changes in basic trends but was associated very largely with inflows of relatively short-term capital from Brazil, as noted above. Reinvestments were lower partly because of a reduction in

Table 3.—Net Direct Investment Capital Movements by Selected Countries, 1946–53

[Millions of dollars; net inflows to the United States (−)]

Country	1946	1947	1948	1949	1950	1951	1952 Total	Mining and smelting	Petroleum	Manufacturing	Trade	Other industries	1953 Total	Mining and smelting	Petroleum	Manufacturing	Trade	Other industries
All areas, total	230	749	721	660	621	528	850	278	248	211	17	96	722	247	404	−34	26	78
Canada	47	39	88	100	287	240	420	134	122	121	2	41	413	115	181	49	25	43
Latin American Republics, total	71	457	333	332	40	166	277	120	32	80	11	35	93	119	57	−83	−5	5
Argentina	−86	44	29	7	15	−9	8	(1)	(1)	12	4	5	4	(1)	(1)	−4	2	5
Brazil	30	83	48	40	20	92	125	(1)	34	65	9	(1)	−50	(1)	28	−71	−11	(1)
Chile	3	9	−4	21	22	40	37	35	(1)	−2	−3	(1)	35	31	(1)	1	−2	(1)
Colombia	17	−3	6	10	−7	11	20	(1)	5	8	7	(1)	1	(1)	−5	3	2	(1)
Costa Rica	5	8	5	−1	2	(2)	(2)		(2)	(2)	(2)	(2)	(2)		(2)		(2)	(2)
Cuba	−8	(2)	5	−2	7	13	5	(1)	(1)		−3	10	−5	(1)	(1)	−6	2	(1)
Dominican Republic	3	4	13	4	1	11	−7		(1)	(1)	(1)	−7	−6		(1)	(1)		−6
Honduras	5	9	3	5	1	14	2	(1)	(1)	(1)	(1)	2	(2)	(1)	(1)	(1)	(1)	(2)
Mexico	4	31	23	−13	25	24	−10	−4		1	−3	−6	3	7	(2)	−6	−1	3
Panama	16	119	33	98	−1	−38	−48		−47	(2)	−3	1	−15		−11	1	1	−5
Peru	9	20	−2	−15	−9	17	28	29	(1)	−6	3	(1)	30	16	(1)	−1	2	(1)
Uruguay	1	1	1	1	3	6	1		1	1	(2)	(2)	−3		(2)	−2	−1	1
Venezuela	63	129	166	168	−39	−16	115	(1)	48	4	3	(2)	93	(1)	27	1	2	(1)
Other countries	8	2	7	9	(2)	(2)	1	(1)		(2)	−2	(2)	5	2	1	(2)		1
Western Europe, total	23	46	64	36	119	62	−8	(2)	−24	6	2	9	48	(2)	32	−3	7	12
Belgium	3	7	3	(2)	3	13	−2		2	−3	(2)	(2)	9		4	3	1	(1)
France	2	3	16	3	9	2	−2		−4	1	(2)	5	11		7	3	(2)	(1)
Germany	1	2	5	1	7	3	3	(1)	−3	1	(2)	2	7	(1)	6	−1	(1)	2
Italy	1	2	4	4	19	(2)	5		4	1	(2)	(2)	13		8	1	(2)	4
Netherlands	4	1	6	5	18	7	(2)	(1)	(2)	(2)	(2)	(1)	7	(1)	4	2	(2)	(1)
Portugal	1	3	(2)	−2	2	3	(2)	(2)	(2)	(2)	(2)	(2)	(2)	(2)	(2)	(2)	(2)	(2)
Spain	1	2	2	14	2	2	1	(1)	1	(2)	(2)	(2)	3	(1)	2	(2)	(2)	(2)
Sweden	4	6	−1	(2)	2	3	2		2	(2)	−1		(2)		(2)	(2)	(2)	1
United Kingdom	1	13	24	14	49	18	−21	(2)	−24	5	−2	1	−11	(2)	−4	−13	4	2
Other countries	5	6	6	−3	9	11	2		−1	−1	3	1	9		6	1	1	1
Western European dependencies, total	5	55	71	29	14	1	−5	18	−23	(2)	1	(2)	79	3	73	(2)	1	1
Western Hemisphere:																		
British	1	5	3	2	5	1	15	(1)	2		(1)	(2)	2	(1)	(2)	(1)	(1)	(2)
Other European	−11	−7	11	10	1	5	5	(1)	(1)	(1)	(1)	(2)	2	(1)	(1)	(1)	(1)	(2)
Africa:																		
British	2	2	4	1	3	6	6	2	5	(1)	(1)	(2)	−2	(2)	−3	(1)	(1)	(2)
French	(2)	2	2	−1	2	(2)	−1	(2)	−2		1		−1		−2		(1)	(2)
Other European	1	1	2	(2)	2	(2)	1	(1)	(1)	(1)	(2)	(2)	(2)	(1)	(1)	(1)	(1)	(2)
Other areas:																		
British	7	21	50	13	−3	−12	−39	(1)	(1)	(1)	(1)	(2)	72	(1)	(1)	(1)	(1)	(1)
Other European[3]	5	30	(2)	5	4	2	7		(1)	(1)	(1)	(1)	5		(1)		(1)	(1)
Other countries, total	84	152	165	163	161	59	166	6	142	4	2	12	89	9	62	3	−3	17
Africa:																		
Liberia	(2)		(2)	38	32	(2)	(2)	(1)	(1)			(1)	14	(1)	(1)		(1)	(1)
Union of South Africa	6	15	11	−1	23	7	25	6	21	−3	(2)	1	4	8	−6	2	−1	1
Other countries	5	9	15	1	1	3	1		(1)	(2)	(2)	(1)	3		(1)	(2)	1	(1)
Other areas:																		
Australia	3	19	8	11	24	29	29	(1)		4	(2)	2	−19	(1)	(1)	−3	(2)	2
India	4	−1	−1	3	10	7	9		(1)	−3	(2)	(1)	2		(1)	−1	(2)	(1)
Indonesia	(2)	(2)	(2)	(2)	−13	4	−23		(1)		1	(1)	14		(1)		(2)	(1)
Israel	(2)	1	1	12	2	19	7		−4	7	(1)	4	14		(1)	3	(2)	4
Japan	1	4	2	5	7	21	23		(1)	1	(1)	4	16		3	7	(2)	
Philippine Republic	17	19	13	−5	6	5	9	(1)	(1)	−1		−1	5	(1)	(1)	−1	(1)	−1
Other countries	47	87	112	98	69	−35	85	(2)	88	−1	−1	(2)	35	(2)	34	(1)	−2	(2)

1. Included in totals.   2. Less than $500,000.

3. Indonesia is included in "other European" dependencies in the years 1946–49 and is shown separately under "other areas" in the years 1950–53.

Source: U. S. Department of Commerce, Office of Business Economics.

earnings in agriculture and mining and reduced earnings of tanker companies. The use of lower exchange rates to convert local currency earnings retained in Brazil also reduced the estimated dollar value of reinvested earnings.

Capital outflows to Western Europe picked up in 1953, although, as usual, most of the increase of over $200 million in the value of direct investments in that area came out of reinvested earnings. The outstanding development in 1953 was a rise in net capital outflows of petroleum companies to about $30 million. This was in sharp contrast to 1952 when there were net flows back to the United States from several countries as earlier loans by parent companies for investments in refineries were partly repaid.

Overall additions to direct investments in countries outside the Western Hemisphere and Europe were about equal to the 1952 amount and well above the postwar average. There was practically no change in the industry distribution of these investments, with petroleum continuing to account for about 70 percent of the current additions. However, sizeable shifts occurred in capital flows to the various countries in Africa and Asia. Middle East petroleum investments did not change greatly in total, for instance, but heavy expenditures shifted from one part of the area to another. Reduced flows to the Union of South Africa and Australia were connected with the completion of programs for increasing petroleum refining capacity.

Direct Investment Earnings

Foreign earnings of direct investment companies were unfavorably affected by weaknesses in some world markets in 1953, and were also retarded by growing charges against income. Price weaknesses for nonferrous metals and sugar, together with reduced output, caused a drop in earnings from mining and agriculture. Charges against the earnings of mining and petroleum companies for exploration and development expenses, and allowances for accelerated depreciation, also increased. Petroleum earnings were further affected by much lower earnings of tanker operations and other distribution facilities. Earnings from the production and refinery operations of this industry were higher, however, reflecting sustained output at somewhat higher prices and the use of expanded refinery capacity.

Earnings of other industries changed comparatively little from the prior year, although manufacturing earnings increased substantially outside of Brazil, where there was a special situation resulting from the shift in exchange valuation.

Income receipts in 1953, i. e., dividends, interest, and branch profits, were also close to the 1952 amount. The principal change was an increase in branch profits from the production of petroleum in Latin America.

Gains from direct investments

American direct investments abroad constitute an important segment of the world economy, not only contributing directly to world output and welfare but also providing in many countries an example of the gains from modern industrial methods. Quantitative measures of the overall importance of the direct investment enterprises to the foreign countries and the United States economy would be inadequate at best, partly because of the heterogeneity of the enterprises and the relatively greater concentration in some countries and industries, and partly because some of the

Table 4.—Gross Movements ¹ of Direct Investment Capital, by Areas and Industries, 1951–53

[Millions of dollars; net inflows (−)]

Industry and year	All areas			Canada			Latin American Republics			Western Europe			Western European dependencies			Other countries		
	Out-flows	Inflows	Net	Out-flows	Inflows	Net	Out-flows	Inflows	Net	Out-flows	Inflows	Net	Out-flows	Inflows	Net	Out-flows	Inflows	Net
All industries:																		
1951	1,003	476	528	330	91	240	414	249	166	97	35	62	30	29	1	132	73	59
1952	1,381	531	850	518	98	420	469	192	277	68	76	−8	55	60	−5	272	106	166
1953	1,236	515	722	497	84	413	355	262	93	111	66	48	90	12	79	180	91	89
Agriculture:																		
1951	42	18	24	1	1	(²)	39	17	22				1		1	1		1
1952	12	19	−8	(²)	2	−1	11	15	−4					(²)	(²)	1	3	−2
1953	6	23	−17	(²)	(²)	(²)	3	21	−18				(²)	(²)	(²)	2	1	1
Mining and smelting:																		
1951	125	25	100	36		36	84	24	60	(²)		(²)	3	(²)	2	2	(²)	2
1952	299	21	278	135	(²)	134	140	20	120	(²)	(²)	(²)	18		18	6	(²)	6
1953	268	22	247	118	3	115	137	18	119	(²)	(²)	(²)	3		3	9	(²)	9
Petroleum:																		
1951	329	237	93	128	4	124	54	129	−75	50	13	37	23	25	−2	74	66	8
1952	526	279	248	124	2	122	112	81	32	27	51	−24	35	58	−23	228	86	142
1953	559	154	404	190	9	181	100	44	57	57	24	32	83	11	73	129	68	62
Manufacturing:																		
1951	300	110	190	103	73	30	136	20	116	30	13	17	(²)	2	−2	31	15	29
1952	359	148	211	203	82	121	120	40	80	21	15	6	(²)	(²)	(²)	15	11	4
1953	187	220	−34	105	56	49	37	119	−83	28	32	−3	(²)	(²)	(²)	16	13	3
Public utilities:																		
1951	25	33	−8	1	2	−1	24	31	−7	(²)	(²)	(²)	(²)			2		2
1952	31	7	23	1	(²)	1	27	7	21	(²)	(²)	(²)		(²)	(²)	5		5
1953	32	19	13	4	2	2	22	17	5	(²)	(²)	(²)		(²)	(²)			
Trade:																		
1951	91	33	58	13	7	6	56	18	38	10	3	7	3	1	2	9	5	5
1952	65	47	17	9	7	2	39	28	11	9	7	2	2	1	1	6	5	2
1953	73	47	26	32	7	25	22	27	−5	11	4	7	2	1	1	5	8	−3
Other industries:																		
1951	91	21	70	48	4	44	21	10	11	8	1	8	(²)	(²)	(²)	14	1	14
1952	90	10	80	46	4	42	20	2	18	11	3	8	(²)	(²)	(²)	14	1	13
1953	112	29	83	47	6	41	34	16	18	18	5	12	2	(²)	(²)	12	1	11

1. The gross capital outflow shown in each area-industry cell of this table represents the sum of the net capital outflows to those foreign subsidiaries and branches for which net outflows were reported for each of the years covered. Conversely, the gross inflows shown for each cell represent the sum of the net inflows from those foreign subsidiaries and branches for which inflows were reported in each year. The totals for "all areas" are the sums of the figures shown in the area-industry cells. It should be noted that the gross totals, but not the net amounts, would change if the compilation were done on a quarterly basis.

2. Less than $500,000.

Source: U. S. Department of Commerce, Office of Business Economics.

Table 5.—Value of Direct Investments Abroad, by Area and Industry, 1950–53

[Millions of dollars]

Area and year	All industries	Agriculture	Mining and smelting	Petroleum	Manufacturing	Public utilities	Trade	Other industries
All areas:								
1953	16,304	658	1,934	4,931	5,242	1,499	1,046	994
1952	14,819	662	1,642	4,291	4,920	1,469	966	869
1951	13,089	642	1,317	3,703	4,352	1,431	883	762
1950	11,788	589	1,129	3,390	3,831	1,425	762	662
Canada:								
1953	5,257	21	681	932	2,436	294	331	562
1952	4,593	21	550	715	2,241	287	284	494
1951	3,972	22	400	562	2,000	285	262	440
1950	3,579	21	334	418	1,897	284	240	385
Latin American Republics:								
1953	6,001	548	1,002	1,683	1,139	1,091	352	187
1952	5,758	564	871	1,577	1,166	1,076	344	162
1951	5,176	557	736	1,408	992	1,044	303	136
1950	4,735	520	628	1,408	780	1,041	242	116
Western Europe:								
1953	2,367	1	30	608	1,299	28	231	170
1952	2,145	1	26	532	1,187	28	218	152
1951	1,979	1	23	511	1,070	27	207	138
1950	1,720	1	21	424	932	27	186	129
Western European dependencies:								
1953	593	13	128	392	11	18	27	3
1952	468	12	118	290	9	18	18	1
1951	446	10	96	295	9	18	16	1
1950	435	9	88	296	9	18	13	1
Other countries:								
1953	2,085	75	93	1,316	357	68	105	72
1952	1,854	64	76	1,177	316	61	103	59
1951	1,516	53	61	926	281	56	95	45
1950	1,318	39	56	844	214	54	81	30

Source: U. S. Department of Commerce, Office of Business Economics.

Table 6.—Value of Direct Investments Abroad, by Selected Countries, 1949–53—Continued

[Millions of dollars]

Country	1949	1950	1951	1952	1953
Western European dependencies, total	427	435	446	468	593
Western Hemisphere:					
British	61	66	71	88	98
Other European	65	65	68	70	76
Africa:					
British West Africa	8	11	14	21	28
Other British	29	30	40	45	45
French North Africa	13	14	18	24	25
Other French	14	17	14	12	13
Other European	10	12	12	14	16
Other areas:					
Malaya	18	18	21	24	24
Other British	183	172	156	130	223
Other European	26	30	32	39	45
Other countries, total	1,086	1,318	1,516	1,854	2,085
Africa:					
Egypt	38	39	44	46	47
Liberia	47	82	104	140	187
Union of South Africa	105	140	157	194	213
Other countries	5	7	7	8	10
Other areas:					
Australia	161	201	256	310	328
India	27	38	49	63	68
Indonesia	62	58	72	74	88
Israel	13	15	34	41	56
Japan	12	19	45	69	88
New Zealand	17	25	31	37	34
Pakistan	6	8	8	9	8
Philippine Republic	132	149	163	178	188
Other countries	461	537	546	684	769

Source: U. S. Department of Commerce, Office of Business Economics.

Table 6.—Value of Direct Investments Abroad, by Selected Countries, 1949–53

[Millions of dollars]

Country	1949	1950	1951	1952	1953
All areas, total	10,700	11,788	13,089	14,819	16,304
Canada	3,146	3,579	3,972	4,593	5,257
Latin American Republics, total	4,590	4,735	5,176	5,758	6,001
Argentina	329	356	365	393	406
Bolivia	10	11	11	11	15
Brazil	588	644	803	1,013	1,003
Chile	518	540	583	623	666
Colombia	194	193	207	234	235
Costa Rica	57	60	61	61	61
Cuba	619	642	672	686	686
Dominican Republic	102	106	123	123	121
Ecuador	16	14	14	14	17
El Salvador	19	19	20	21	22
Guatemala	104	106	106	108	107
Haiti	14	13	14	15	16
Honduras	60	62	78	81	82
Mexico	374	414	471	490	509
Nicaragua	9	9	9	10	9
Panama	337	348	373	383	398
Peru	148	145	197	230	259
Uruguay and Paraguay	55	61	74	77	82
Venezuela	1,036	993	996	1,184	1,308
Western Europe, total	4,450	1,720	1,979	2,145	2,367
Austria	11	13	16	18	20
Belgium	55	65	87	95	111
Denmark	30	32	37	38	37
Finland	8	9	8	9	10
France	185	217	249	276	307
Germany	173	204	234	251	276
Greece	5	6	8	9	9
Italy	37	63	72	80	97
Netherlands	57	84	100	108	124
Norway	22	24	28	33	37
Portugal	14	16	19	21	25
Spain	27	31	36	40	45
Sweden	51	58	65	70	74
Switzerland	22	25	28	28	32
Turkey	17	16	17	18	25
United Kingdom	729	847	961	1,038	1,125
Other countries	7	11	14	14	15

Table 7.—Private Long-Term Portfolio Capital Movements, by Type and Area, 1946–June 1954

[Millions of dollars; capital outflows (−)]

	1946–49, annual average	1950	1951	1952	1953	1954, first half
All areas, total	−18	−495	−437	−214	178	−224
New foreign securities	−187	−254	−491	−286	−276	−254
Amortizations and redemptions	192	301	113	66	139	71
Transactions in outstanding foreign issues, net	9	−322	25	131	222	−54
Banking and commercial loans, net	−32	−220	−84	−125	93	13
Canada, total	23	−324	−232	−30	−8	−144
New foreign securities	−98	−163	−302	−158	−209	−154
Amortizations and redemptions	148	172	88	38	108	47
Transactions in outstanding foreign issues, net	−27	−337	−20	100	113	−48
Banking and commercial loans, net	(¹)	4	2	−10	−20	11
Latin American Republics, total	61	27	30	34	33	1
New foreign securities		−10				
Amortizations and redemptions	25	19	11	10	9	5
Transactions in outstanding foreign issues, net	44	21	22	16	25	10
Banking and commercial loans, net	−5	−3	−3	8	−1	−14
Europe, total	−47	−196	−35	−90	207	76
New foreign securities	−9					
Amortizations and redemptions	11	6	12	9	7	7
Transactions in outstanding foreign issues, net	−25	40	16	11	89	−12
Banking and commercial loans, net	−24	−212	−63	−110	111	81
Other countries, total	5	(¹)	−47	−10	7	−66
New foreign securities	−19		−50	−46	−36	−16
Amortizations and redemptions	8	4	2	9	7	4
Transactions in outstanding foreign issues, net	17	7	21	40	33	11
Banking and commercial loans, net	−1	−11	−20	−13	3	−65
International institutions, total	−63	−2	−153	−118	−61	−91
New foreign securities	−61	−81	−139	−82	−31	−84
Amortizations and redemptions		100			8	8
Transactions in outstanding foreign issues, net		−23	−14	−36	−38	−15
Banking and commercial loans, net	−2	2				

¹ Net movement less than $500,000.

Source: U. S. Department of Commerce, Office of Business Economics.

greatest effects are intangible. Nevertheless, a few scattered comparisons may help to indicate the role of these enterprises.

From the standpoint of foreign countries, the gains from direct investments could be measured partly from their contribution to overall output, both for export and local consumption. The data required to compute such a measure on a careful and comprehensive basis have never been assembled. However, rough calculations made for Latin America indicate that as much as one-tenth of the value of goods and services produced in the area may be accounted for by United States-owned enterprises. The proportion would be much higher for such industries as mining or petroleum, but even in manufacturing the ratio seems to be about 15 percent. Similarly, the ratios would be higher for a number of individual countries in the area.

Some 25 percent of total exports to the United States by foreign countries is produced by United States direct invest-

ment companies abroad which have developed and made possible this large trade with the United States.

Foreign direct investments also have a sizeable effect on the United States economy, not only providing essential imports but also accounting for a significant share of the earnings and investments of many companies. For instance, foreign earnings account for about 10 percent of the total earnings of United States companies in manufacturing industries operating both domestically and abroad. Almost the same percentage of the net book assets of these companies is located abroad. Over one-third of the total earnings of the United States petroleum industry is derived from producing abroad and supplying crude and refined products to the United States and the expanding economies of foreign countries. Nearly one quarter of the net book assets of the industry is devoted to these activities in foreign countries.

Table 8.—Direct Investment Earnings by Areas and Industries, 1946–53

[Millions of dollars]

Area and year	Total	Agriculture	Mining and smelting	Petroleum	Manufacturing	Public utilities	Trade	Other industries
All areas:								
1953	2,216	87	142	1,003	667	48	141	129
1952	2,280	113	209	1,013	643	48	146	109
1951	2,236	140	220	896	696	43	143	98
1950	1,766	115	148	627	637	41	117	81
1949	1,519	75	112	562	566	23	106	75
1948	1,607	109	135	606	553	20	112	72
1947	1,239	108	111	404	434	24	96	62
1946	832	84	72	234	305	21	72	44
Canada:								
1953	443	1	44	16	274	10	33	65
1952	419	1	54	12	257	9	34	53
1951	420	1	68	3	268	9	28	43
1950	445	1	52	17	301	9	29	37
1949	393	1	37	6	277	7	30	35
1948	395	(1)	30	22	279	5	19	40
1947	298	(1)	36	11	197	6	18	30
1946	210	(1)	28	9	133	5	13	22
Latin American Republics:								
1953	747	64	45	409	122	30	45	32
1952	888	84	96	438	156	32	55	26
1951	888	107	104	409	170	27	49	23
1950	616	89	69	274	106	26	29	22
1949	475	64	51	203	96	12	30	19
1948	672	99	85	301	113	12	45	17
1947	521	94	64	188	106	15	42	12
1946	347	72	39	112	67	15	32	10
Western Europe:								
1953	324	(1)	4	76	193	(1)	30	21
1952	305	(1)	5	79	169	(1)	33	20
1951	302	(1)	4	49	194	(1)	34	20
1950	265	(1)	3	42	172	(1)	35	13
1949	203	(1)	2	25	142	(1)	23	11
1948	193		1	38	121	(1)	23	10
1947	160		1	25	105	(1)	17	12
1946	129		1	15	92	(1)	14	7
Western European dependencies:								
1953	169	2	29	120	2	(1)	13	2
1952	154	3	31	112	2	(1)	4	2
1951	120	3	30	76	2	(1)	6	3
1950	100	4	15	74	1	(1)	4	2
1949	132	1	10	109	6	(1)	3	2
1948	115	1	7	98	3	(1)	5	1
1947	78	1	3	69	1	(1)	2	2
1946	42	1	2	38	(1)	(1)	1	(1)
Other countries:								
1953	534	20	19	382	77	7	19	9
1952	513	24	23	371	59	7	21	8
1951	507	29	14	360	63	6	26	10
1950	340	20	10	220	57	6	20	7
1949	315	9	11	218	45	4	21	7
1948	232	9	12	147	37	3	20	4
1947	182	13	7	111	25	3	17	6
1946	104	11	2	60	13	1	12	5

1. Less than $500,000.

Source: U. S. Department of Commerce, Office of Business Economics.

Table 9.—Direct Investment Income Receipts, by Areas and Industries, 1946–53

[Millions of dollars]

Area and year	Total	Agriculture	Mining and smelting	Petroleum	Manufacturing	Public utilities	Trade	Other industries
All areas:								
1953	1,463	70	96	765	309	49	85	90
1952	1,419	86	159	677	287	49	79	83
1951	1,492	110	159	696	331	45	79	71
1950	1,294	91	112	555	357	44	72	63
1949	1,112	65	80	490	307	36	68	65
1948	1,064	76	121	453	251	33	66	64
1947	869	79	99	302	234	40	65	51
1946	589	61	64	182	157	46	38	42
Canada:								
1953	199	1	26	−20	132	10	12	39
1952	222	(1)	36	−20	139	11	14	11
1951	236	1	34	−17	164	11	13	31
1950	294	1	31	−3	211	9	17	29
1949	254	1	22	−3	171	10	16	35
1948	201	(1)	26	3	118	8	9	37
1947	178	(1)	20	2	104	13	13	29
1946	134	(1)	17	5	76	10	5	20
Latin American Republics:								
1953	608	58	35	356	68	35	32	25
1952	599	73	81	303	64	35	25	18
1951	652	92	87	327	72	31	26	16
1950	522	76	64	262	55	33	17	15
1949	377	59	42	177	43	26	15	15
1948	488	69	83	218	57	25	22	14
1947	414	68	71	149	67	27	22	10
1946	281	49	43	92	37	3	14	10
Western Europe:								
1953	147		1	30	75	(1)	24	17
1952	129	(1)	1	33	56	(1)	24	14
1951	119	(1)	1	15	71	(1)	20	12
1950	111	(1)	1	9	69	(1)	21	10
1949	93	(1)	1	4	60		20	8
1948	93	(1)	1	18	50		19	5
1947	81	(1)	1	10	48		17	5
1946	64	(1)	1	7	37		12	7
Western European dependencies:								
1953	122	2	22	91	(1)	(1)	5	2
1952	127	1	27	93	1	(1)	3	2
1951	109	3	25	73	1	(1)	4	2
1950	98	1	12	75	1	(1)	3	2
1949	98	(1)	12	77	5	(1)	2	2
1948	70	(1)	8	55	2	(1)	4	1
1947	31	(1)	6	22	−1	(1)	3	1
1946	20	(1)	2	17		(1)	1	(1)
Other countries:								
1953	386	9	12	308	33	4	13	7
1952	343	11	14	268	26	3	14	7
1951	377	15	12	298	23	4	16	9
1950	269	11	3	212	22	4	14	6
1949	292	5	3	235	20	(1)	14	6
1948	212	7	3	159	24	(1)	12	7
1947	165	11	1	119	19	(1)	10	5
1946	91	12	1	61	7	(1)	6	5

1. Less than $500,000.

Note: Income receipts consist of dividends, interest and branch profits, after payment of foreign taxes but before United States income taxes.

Source: U. S. Department of Commerce, Office of Business Economics.

INTERNATIONAL INVESTMENTS AND EARNINGS

Samuel Pizer
and
Frederick Cutler

by Samuel Pizer and Frederick Cutler ☆ ────────────────────────────

International Investments

and Earnings

UNITED STATES private investments abroad increased by a record of nearly $3 billion in 1954 to reach a total of more than $26½ billion at the end of the year. Half of the increase was in direct investments, as United States corporations continued to expand their foreign enterprises at a rapid rate.

Well over $10 billion has been invested abroad by United States corporations since the war. The great expansion of foreign productive facilities represented by this investment has been of great importance in the improvement in economic conditions abroad. New industries and greater supplies of essential raw materials have generated increased employment, higher standards of living, and much greater capacity to produce goods for rising local consumption and for export to the rapidly expanding United States market. As the enterprises established abroad enter into production, the effect of their aggregate current output on foreign

Table 1.—International Investment Position of the United States in Selected Years, 1914–54

[Billions of dollars]

	1914 [1]	1919	1930	1939	1946	1953 r	1954 p
United States investments abroad	3.5	7.0	17.2	11.4	18.7	39.6	42.2
Private	3.5	7.0	17.2	11.4	13.5	23.8	26.6
Long-term	3.5	6.5	15.2	10.8	12.3	22.3	24.4
Direct	2.6	3.9	8.0	7.0	7.2	16.3	17.7
Portfolio	.9	2.6	7.2	3.8	5.1	6.0	6.7
Short-term	na	.5	2.0	.6	1.3	1.6	2.2
United States Government [2]					5.2	15.7	15.6
Foreign investments in the United States	7.2	4.0	8.4	9.6	15.9	23.6	26.8
Long-term	6.7	3.2	5.7	6.3	7.0	9.2	11.0
Direct	1.3	.9	1.4	2.0	2.5	3.8	4.0
Portfolio	5.4	2.3	4.3	4.3	4.5	5.4	7.0
Short-term assets [3]	.5	.8	2.7	3.3	8.9	14.4	15.7
United States net creditor position	−3.7	3.0	8.8	1.8	2.8	16.0	15.4
Net long-term	−3.2	3.3	9.5	4.5	10.5	28.5	28.6
Net short-term	−.5	−.3	−.7	−2.7	−7.6	−12.6	−13.1

na—Not available.   r Revised.   p Preliminary.
1. At June 30.
2. Excludes World War I loans; includes some short-term assets.
3. Includes United States Government obligations in 1946, 1953, and 1954.
NOTE.—Data for various years are not wholly comparable because of different sources and methods, but the data are adequate to show main trends over the period.
Source.—U. S. Department of Commerce, Office of Business Economics.

economies is very much greater than the net investment from the United States which may take place in any given year.

Major developments in United States direct investments abroad in 1954 included reductions in the rate of investment in petroleum and mining properties, largely resulting from the completion of several large projects, accompanied by rising investments in manufacturing and scattered increases

NOTE.—MR. PIZER AND MR. CUTLER ARE MEMBERS OF THE BALANCE OF PAYMENTS DIVISION, OFFICE OF BUSINESS ECONOMICS.

in other industries. Direct investments in Canada during 1954 continued to be much higher than in any other area, and there was some falling off in Latin America and the Middle East.

A striking development in 1954 was an increase of $1.4 billion in the value of United States private investments in foreign securities and short-and-medium-term credits and assets abroad. Some $860 million of this increase resulted from net capital flows from the United States, and the remainder reflected improved market values for the dollar bonds and local-currency bonds and equity securities of foreign countries.

The value of foreign-owned investments and assets in the United States also increased by about $3 billion during 1954, but the composition of these investments and the nature of the increase, was much different from that of United States investments abroad. Foreign-owned short-term dollar assets, including obligations of the United States Government, are the largest component of foreign holdings in the United States. Such assets rose by $1.3 billion during the year.

In addition foreign countries purchased about $300 million of gold from the United States, although gold holdings are not included in the tabulations of international investments as given in table 2. The major factors accounting for this improvement in reserves have been discussed regularly in the SURVEY OF CURRENT BUSINESS in quarterly reviews of the United States balance of payments, most recently in the issue for June 1955.

Foreign long-term direct and portfolio investments in the United States increased in value by $1.8 billion in 1954, but of this increase about $1½ billion represented the sharp rise in the market value of United States corporate stocks. The remainder, although relatively small, represents a considerable increase in foreign purchases of United States corporate stocks as well as continued moderate additions to foreign direct investments in the United States.

Though earnings on United States investments abroad were a record $2.8 billion in 1954, the increase since 1951 has been quite modest when compared with the rapidly growing value of the investments. Out of this total nearly $650 million was left abroad by direct-investment subsidiaries, mainly to finance continued expansion.

Earnings on foreign assets in the United States are smaller than earnings on United States investments abroad, partly because foreign holdings in the United States are primarily in the form of liquid assets, and the earnings total has risen more slowly since the war. Nevertheless, earnings on investments in the United States still constitute an important source of dollars for some countries.[1]

1. Data for earlier years for many of the series contained in this article may be found in the SURVEY OF CURRENT BUSINESS for December 1953, January 1954, and May 1954, and in FOREIGN INVESTMENTS OF THE UNITED STATES, a special 1953 supplement to the SURVEY OF CURRENT BUSINESS.

United States Investments Abroad

United States direct investment abroad have been built up at a very regular rate since 1946, reaching a total of $17.7 billion by the end of 1954.

Although the rate of progress has been steady, there have been changes from year to year in the emphasis on various areas of the world and on different industries. In 1954, unlike other recent years, there were no large individual projects which absorbed great amounts of capital. The only single development of special significance in the total was the establishment of United States-owned investment funds in Canada with a paid-up capital in 1954 of some $100 million.

United States Investments Abroad

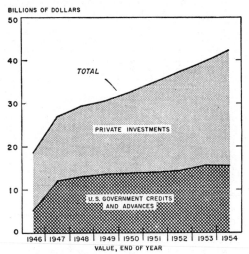

BILLIONS OF DOLLARS

TOTAL

PRIVATE INVESTMENTS

U. S. GOVERNMENT CREDITS AND ADVANCES

VALUE, END OF YEAR

U. S. DEPARTMENT OF COMMERCE, OFFICE OF BUSINESS ECONOMICS   55-44-8

The proportion of additions to direct investment going to Canada rose to 50 percent in 1954. The proportion going to Latin America was about 14 percent, about the same as in 1953 but much lower than in most earlier years. Europe's share of total 1954 investments was also 14 percent, about the same as in 1953, and there was some reduction in investments in other areas, mainly because petroleum investments in the Middle East were not as high.

Out of a total book value for direct investments of $17.7 billion at the end of 1954, $5.9 billion was in Canada and $6.3 billion in Latin America. The increase in Canada since 1949, amounting to $2.8 billion, has been far greater than in any other area. Developments in major industries in 1954 were as follows:

Petroleum

Net additions to petroleum investments abroad were down from $645 million in 1953 to $420 million in 1954. Net capital outflows and undistributed subsidiary earnings were each reduced by a little over $100 million. Investments in Canada were $225 million, slightly higher than in 1953, and reflected continued activity in the exploration and develop-

ment of Canadian oil reserves. Expenditures for pipelines were much lower than in 1953, although large expenditures for such facilities will have to be made in the future.

The reduction in net investment in other areas is the result of a considerable number of varying types of transactions. In Latin America, petroleum investments have been comparatively small in recent years, and they dropped by $100 million to less than $10 million in 1954. However, practically the entire change was the result of large liquidations of accounts receivable for oil products delivered in 1953. A considerable amount of investment activity being carried out in the area is not reflected in these figures since it is either financed out of current charges for depreciation and amortization, or, in the case of exploration expenses, is charged against income.

Net additions to petroleum investments in Europe were down slightly, partly because of the sale of some properties to European interests, and also because of somewhat lower earnings available for reinvestment and the completion of some refineries. However, there was considerable interest in the development of oil reserves in various European countries.

Elsewhere, additions to petroleum investments in India, Australia, and Iran, as well as for additions to tanker fleets operating under the Liberian flag were larger than in 1953, but these increases were more than offset by the sale of certain properties to foreign interests, some withdrawals of surplus funds and a reduction of new Middle East investments, outside of Iran, to a relatively small amount. Investment in Iran will be much higher in 1955 as the United States companies participating in the new group organized to bring about a resumption of oil production in that country will be called on for substantial amounts of capital.

The great diversity of capital flows in the petroleum industry in 1954 is illustrated, in part, by table 6 showing the composition of the gross flows. Gross outflows were higher than in 1953 by nearly $200 million, but gross inflows rose by $300 million. Gross outflows were higher in every area except dependencies in the Middle East, but they were more than matched by rising inflows in Latin America, Western Europe, and various other countries.

Manufacturing

Investments in manufacturing were quite substantial in 1954, reaching $425 million and raising the total for this industry group to $5.7 billion. As usual, a large part of earnings was ploughed back into the local economies; the companies reinvested $350 million out of total earnings of $700 million. Net capital outflows were $75 million, in contrast to net inflows of $50 million in 1953.

Additions to manufacturing investments in Europe were unusually high, the $136 million total reflecting larger reinvestments of earnings as total earnings rose sharply in line with heightened economic acitivity in the area. There was also a small net increase in capital flows to Europe. Most of the increased reinvestment was in the United Kingdom, while capital flows were higher to Belgium, the Netherlands and Sweden.

In Latin America the net investment in manufacturing was $100 million in 1954 after a reverse flow of small proportions in 1953. Much of the change occurred in Brazil, where a heavy liquidation of overdue accounts in 1953 was followed by a relatively modest resumption of new credits in 1954. About 60 percent of subsidiary profits were left in this country, probably partly for investment and partly because of difficulties in making remittances. Virtually all of the earnings of manufacturing companies in Argentina were retained in that country, largely because they could not be transferred into dollars.

There were sizeable capital outflows for manufacturing to Colombia and Venezuela, but there was a continuation of net inflows from Cuba, Mexico and Uruguay.

Manufacturing investments in Canada were adversely affected by a minor decline in economic activity through most of 1954. Earnings were reduced by $56 million and undistributed profits were cut back nearly as much, as dividend payments changed little. Net capital flows to Canada normally finance only a small part of additions to investments and they were off by only a minor amount in 1954. In the rest of the world there was a small increase in manufacturing investments to a total of $54 million. Australia accounted for $23 million of the total, and the Union of South Africa for $10 million.

Mining and other industries

New investments in mining and smelting properties were sharply reduced in 1954 from the levels prevailing in the past few years. Most major projects in Canada and Latin America, primarily to develop iron ore and copper and nickel resources, were virtually completed. Although other large projects are in view they have not yet begun to absorb funds. Earnings of the mining enterprises were somewhat improved in 1954, as discussed below, but the amount reinvested did not increase proportionately.

To some extent, the 1954 drop in the rate of mining investments is not indicative of the position of permanent investments because of the experience of copper companies. These companies provided funds to finance mounting inventories in 1953 but recovered their outlays in 1954 when inventories were shipped to the United States and sold.

The turnabout in mining investments from 1953 to 1954 is clearly reflected in table 6, showing gross capital flows. Mining and smelting is the only industry in which gross outflows were reduced while gross inflows climbed sharply.

Direct investments in trade and distribution facilities (other than those which are direct adjuncts of petroleum or manufacturing enterprises) continued to increase in 1954. There was some decline in Canada from the unusually high rate of additions in 1953, partly because there were no large new investments as in the previous year. An increased capital flow to Latin America was connected in part with a resumption of outflows to Brazil, and also resulted from sizable new investments in Colombia. In Europe there was a net inflow of capital derived from the sale of a large establishment in Germany, but investments out of earnings were higher. Additions to investments in public utilities remained quite small, but there was an increased capital flow to Latin America. There was also a trend in that area toward financing new capital expenditures through securities issued in local capital markets.

Net investment in "other" industries during 1954 was over $250 million, bringing the total outstanding to $1.3 billion. About $185 million of the increase was in Canada, and of this about $100 million represented the stock of investment funds newly established in Canada. These investment funds placed their capital primarily in the stocks and bonds of Canadian corporations, so that in their effect on the Canadian economy they resemble large-scale portfolio investments. Another large field for recent investment in Canada has been in finance companies, including consumer credit, and this accounted for a sizeable capital outflow in 1954. Other capital outflows were connected with such diverse fields as real estate, engineering and construction, and motion pictures.

Table 2.—International Investment Position of the United States, by Area, 1953–54

[Millions of dollars]

	Total		Western Europe		Western European dependencies		Other Europe		Canada		Latin American Republics		Other foreign countries		International institutions	
	1953 r	1954 p	1953 r	1954 p	1953 r	1954 p	1953 r	1954 p	1953 r	1954 p	1953 r	1954 p	1953 r	1954 p	1953 r	1954 p
United States investments abroad, total	39,567	42,229	13,974	14,372	710	683	334	331	8,790	9,721	7,981	8,670	3,907	4,503	3,871	3,949
Private investments	23,847	26,609	4,207	4,809	647	648	14	15	8,771	9,706	7,051	7,710	2,732	3,217	425	504
Long-term	22,259	24,385	3,731	4,093	624	622	12	14	8,568	9,480	6,399	6,747	2,500	2,925	425	504
Direct	16,329	17,748	2,369	2,605	603	600			5,242	5,939	6,034	6,256	2,081	2,348		
Foreign dollar bonds	2,383	2,720	82	160			1	3	1,477	1,604	136	143	262	306		
Foreign currency securities	2,048	2,304	328	465					1,630	1,727	30	33	60	79		
Other	1,499	1,613	952	863	21	22	11	11	219	210	199	315	97	192		
Short-term	1,588	2,224	476	716	23	26	2	1	203	226	652	963	232	292		
Deposits	371	502	193	296	7	7	1	1	93	111	51	57	26	30		
Other	1,217	1,722	283	420	16	19	1		110	115	601	906	206	262		
United States Government credits and claims	15,720	15,620	9,767	9,563	63	35	320	316	19	15	930	960	1,175	1,286	3,446	3,445
Long-term	15,415	15,208	9,541	9,311	62	33	312	308	18	14	927	954	1,109	1,143	3,446	3,445
Short-term	305	412	226	252	1	2	8	8	1	1	3	6	66	143		
Foreign assets and investments in the United States, total	23,628	26,768	11,541	13,781	501	477	69	60	3,657	4,078	2,687	3,035	2,379	2,339	1,955	2,160
Long-term investments	9,172	11,025	6,020	7,340	188	228	29	34	2,019	2,332	684	822	210	239	22	30
Direct	3,776	3,981	2,386	2,533	19	20			1,188	1,246	138	136	45	46		
Corporate stocks	3,650	5,254	2,525	3,660	80	118	12	17	675	935	285	417	68	95	5	12
Corporate, State, and municipal bonds	269	304	178	209	5	6			16	11	43	49	10	11	17	18
Other	1,477	1,486	931	938	84	84	17	17	140	140	218	220	87	87		
Short-term assets and United States Government obligations	14,456	15,743	5,521	6,441	313	249	40	26	1,638	1,746	2,003	2,213	2,169	2,100	1,933	2,130
Private obligations	7,637	8,459	3,146	3,561	218	210	33	19	642	721	1,689	1,941	1,826	1,912	83	95
Deposits	6,530	7,437	2,434	2,856	188	195	16	17	571	654	1,522	1,829	1,716	1,798	83	88
Other	1,107	1,022	712	705	30	15	17	2	71	67	167	112	110	114		7
United States Government obligations	6,819	7,284	2,375	2,880	95	39	7	7	996	1,025	314	272	343	188	1,850	2,035
Long-term	1,019	1,059	420	428	22	23	5	5	141	7	125	215	20	21	286	360
Short-term [1]	5,800	6,225	1,955	2,452	73	16	2	2	855	1,018	189	57	323	167	1,564	1,675

r Revised.   p Preliminary.
1. Total includes estimated United States currency not distributed by areas [in millions]: 1953, $839; 1954, $838. Also included are miscellaneous liabilities of various United States Government agencies amounting to $177 million at the end of 1954.

NOTE.—For 1946–52 data see the SURVEY OF CURRENT BUSINESS, May 1954.

Source: U. S. Department of Commerce, Office of Business Economics.

Investments in foreign securities

Investors in the United States owned foreign stocks and bonds with a market value of slightly more than $5.0 billion at the end of 1954, an increase of $500 million for the year. The increase resulted from net purchases of foreign securities of a little over $100 million, with improvements in the market prices of foreign corporate stocks accounting for most of the remainder.

About $2.7 billion of the total holdings were in foreign bond issues payable in United States dollars, $0.5 billion was in bonds payable in foreign currencies, and $1.8 billion was in equity securities of foreign corporations (other than those controlled in the United States).

Securities issued in Canada accounted for the largest part of each category, including $1.6 billion of United States dollar bonds, $450 million of bonds payable in Canadian dollars, and $1.3 billion of equity securities of Canadian corporations. Other sizeable holdings include about $500 million of IBRD bonds, smaller holdings of dollar bonds of Germany, Israel, Australia, Japan, Italy, and Brazil, as shown in table 7, and about $400 million of equity securities of European enterprises.

There was a heavy liquidation of Canadian internal issues in 1954 as long-term interest rates in Canada were reduced much more than those in the United States, wiping out nearly all of the interest rate differential that is normally one of the strong inducements for United States investment in these securities. Canadian exchange rate fluctuations were also important in earlier years but were not a noticeable factor in 1954.

United States holdings of Canadian bonds denominated in United States dollars were similarly affected by 1954 trends in interest rates. New issues sold in the United States were relatively low at $167 million, and over $130 million of the total was sold in the first quarter of the year when there was still a substantial interest rate differential.

United States investors are taking a much greater interest in dollar bonds of other countries than at any time since the war, making possible the successful flotation of a $25 million new issue by Australia late in 1954, followed in early 1955 by the sale of a $30 million issue of Belgium and a $15 million issue of Norway.

About $84 million was added to the market value of United States holdings of foreign dollar bonds in 1954 as German issues were validated under the terms of the London agreement of 1953. This validation procedure is still in process and an estimated additional $20 million of United States holdings may enter the market in 1955.

In 1954 United States investors purchased $88 million of a $100 million new issue of the International Bank offered in the United States and participations by United States financial institutions in new loans and purchases of outstanding loans of the Bank amounted to about $28 million, of which some $15 million was paid out. In the first half of 1955, participations and purchases totalled $29 million, and about $8 million was paid out. Thus, as of June 30, 1955, there was a backlog of some $34 million which United States financial institutions had agreed to lend.

Greatly increased purchases by Americans of the equity securities of Canadian and European enterprises were also an important feature of United States investment abroad in 1954 and the first half of 1955. Net purchases of foreign equity securities in 1954 were a record $160 million, not including some $100 million of the shares of newly-organized Canadian investment funds mentioned above. Of the $160 million, about $100 million was invested in Europe and over $50 million in Canada. Some $90 million of the European total consisted of purchases of stock of companies organized

in the Netherlands, probably largely in securities recently listed on United States stock exchanges.

Purchases of Canadian stocks are a more common feature of United States investments abroad, although the 1954 total was unusually large.

Prices of corporate stocks rose in Western Europe and Canada, as they did in the United States, so that in addition to increases in holdings resulting from net purchases, nearly $300 million was added to the market value of United States holdings through price increases.

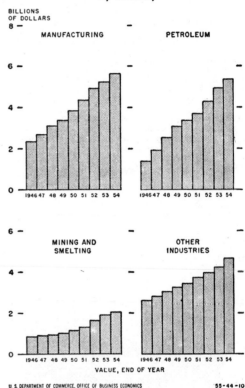

Value of U. S. Direct Investments Abroad By Industry

BILLINGS OF DOLLARS

MANUFACTURING   PETROLEUM

MINING AND SMELTING   OTHER INDUSTRIES

VALUE, END OF YEAR

U. S. DEPARTMENT OF COMMERCE, OFFICE OF BUSINESS ECONOMICS   55-44-10

These trends continued in the early months of 1955, with reported net purchases by Americans of foreign stocks totaling $60 million through April, including over $30 million in Europe and a somewhat smaller amount in Canada.

The largest outflow of capital from the United States in 1954 was in the form of short- and medium-term credits to foreign borrowers by United States banks and commercial concerns. Short-term funds employed abroad increased nearly $650 million, to reach a total of $2.2 billion, while medium-term loans by financial institutions and commercial concerns rose by $115 million to about $750 million.

At present more than half of the short-term claims reported by banks are against Latin America, as well as substantial amounts of medium-term bank credits and commercial credits, as shown in table 9. The increase of over $400 million in such credits to Latin America in 1954 was sufficient to finance over half of United States exports to Brazil and about 5 percent of United States exports to all other countries in the area combined.

The net outflow of nearly $500 million in short-term banking credits includes $120 million of net disbursements of Federal Reserve loans on gold collateral to central banks and an increase of about $100 million in deposits and other claims payable in foreign currencies. Nearly all of the latter increase represented sterling deposits and claims, as United States banks placed funds in the London market when interest rates there provided a sufficient margin over domestic rates, after taking account of other costs. However, in the early months of 1955 there was a withdrawal of funds from the United Kingdom of about the same amount, despite an even wider differential in interest rate, indicating the continued strength of other considerations, especially the weakness of the forward sterling exchange rate and the rapidly growing domestic demand for bank loans.

Other short-term outflows reported by commercial banks included about $120 million in loans to foreign official institutions, banks and others, an increase of about $60 million in collections outstanding (mainly for the account of domestic customers), and about $80 million of other short-term financing. In 1954 short-term credits by commercial concerns rose by nearly $100 million, spread over many countries but with the largest increases reported for the United Kingdom and Brazil. Longer-term commercial credits expanded by about $20 million.

Foreign Assets and Investments in the United States

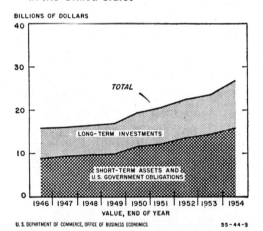

BILLIONS OF DOLLARS

TOTAL

LONG-TERM INVESTMENTS

SHORT-TERM ASSETS AND U.S. GOVERNMENT OBLIGATIONS

1946 | 1947 | 1948 | 1949 | 1950 | 1951 | 1952 | 1953 | 1954

VALUE, END OF YEAR

U. S. DEPARTMENT OF COMMERCE, OFFICE OF BUSINESS ECONOMICS 55-44-9

A very large part of the medium-term financing by banks as of the end of 1954 represented loans against which they held collateral in the form of gold or United States Government bonds, or which were guaranteed by the Export-Import Bank. The last category accounts for some $118 million at the end of 1954, including about $80 million to Japan to finance exports of cotton, about $27 million to Brazil, and $10 million to Uruguay.

The net outflow of short-and-medium-term credits by banks and commercial concerns in the first half of 1955, based on partial data, appears to have been about $50

million, although the total was brought down by the liquidation of about $80 million of sterling balances as well as the repayment of nearly $100 million outstanding on a loan by commercial banks to the French Government.

Outstanding long-term credits to foreign countries and subscriptions to the International Bank and International Monetary Fund by the United States Government topped $15.2 billion at the end of 1954, but was slightly less than at the end of 1953. Repayments of $500 million exceeded new loan disbursements of $300 million, leading to the first annual postwar reduction in the amount outstanding.[1] Net repayments continued in the first quarter of 1955.

Of the $11.8 billion of long-term credits to foreign countries outstanding at the end of 1954, Western Europe and dependent areas had $9.1 billion, Latin American Republics had $900 million, and the largest amount elsewhere was $361 million to India, of which $161 million represents silver returnable in kind in 1957. Repayments in the year were mainly on the loans to Europe made soon after the war.

The United States Government also held short-term foreign assets valued at $412 million at the end of 1954. Most of these holdings are in the form of foreign-currency deposits arising out of the counterpart fund provisions of aid programs and deposits and claims arising from the sale of agricultural commodities abroad. These currencies are used for grants and loans to foreign countries and to defray certain United States expenses abroad. The net increase of about $100 million in 1954, and a further increase of a like amount in the first quarter of 1955, were a consequence of large sales of agricultural products which began late in 1953 and considerably exceeded disbursements.

Foreign Investments in the United States

A record amount of just over $3 billion was added in 1954 to the value of foreign long-term investments and liquid dollar assets in the United States, raising the total to $26.8 billion. The largest gains were made in holdings of corporate stocks and short-term dollar assets. However, of the $1.6 billion increase in the value of corporate stocks only $135 million represented net capital flows to the United States; the remainder reflected the rise in market prices during the year. In the case of liquid assets, on the other hand, the increase of $1.3 billion reflects the net result of transactions between the United States and other countries during 1954.

The rate of increase in foreign dollar assets appears to be somewhat lower in 1955, although still substantial.

Countries in Western Europe held over half of the total investments in the United States at the end of 1954 and accounted for two-thirds of the increase in the year. These countries hold the bulk of the corporate stocks, which scored sharp price increases, and also accounted for $900 million out of a total increase of $1.3 billion in short-term assets. Investors in these countries were also making sizeable new investments in United States corporate stocks and controlled enterprises.

Canadian investments in the United States increased $400 million in 1954, although only about $50 million resulted from net flows to the United States of Canadian capital, the remainder being reinvested earnings and price increases.

Latin American holdings in the United States are primarily short-term assets, which increased about $200 million in the year. For some countries in the area, however, the gains resulted primarily from short- or medium-term credits received in the United States. In the case of Mexico there was a very substantial increase in dollar holdings beginning in June 1954 and still under way in the first quarter of 1955.

Dollar assets of the international institutions also rose about $200 million in the year. Repayments to the Inter-

1. For a detailed discussion of United States Government grants and credits in 1954 see the SURVEY OF CURRENT BUSINESS, April 1955.

national Monetary Fund by a number of countries greatly exceeded drawings by members, and the International Bank received more funds from new subscriptions, earnings, new bond issues, repayments of principal, etc., than were disbursed on new loans.

Long-term investments

Foreign holdings of United States corporate stocks have increased by about $2,750 million since 1949, reaching a total of over $5 billion at the end of 1954. However, only some $300 million of the increase has resulted from net purchases in the United States market—over $2.4 billion was added by the generally rising market values of United States corporate stocks.

Sharply rising stock prices in the United States and increased freedom for international capital movements in 1954 brought forth a postwar record amount of $135 million of net foreign purchases of these securities. Purchases were especially heavy at the end of the year and continued to be fairly substantial in the early months of 1955. As shown in table 10, the bulk of the 1954 purchases were for Western Europe, especially the United Kingdom and Switzerland, and Latin America, but there were sizeable net sales by investors in Canada and the Netherlands. The same pattern continued in 1955. Apparently Canadian and Dutch investors were attracted by the favorable prospects for corporate stocks of their own countries, as were United States investors.

Additions to foreign direct investments in the United States in 1954 were about $200 million, somewhat lower than the 1953 amount but not much different from the average for the last few years. As in other postwar years, except 1953, most of the added investment came out of undistributed earnings of the United States enterprises. Although several large enterprises have been established in the United States in the last few years by British investors, the capital required has been largely derived from United States sources.

Dollar and gold reserves

Foreign countries have been able to add very great amounts to their reserves of gold and dollars since the war, in spite of some temporary periods when losses were heavy. By the end of 1954 foreign holdings of short-term dollar assets and United States Government obligations totalled $15.7 billion and foreign gold holdings were almost equal at $15.6 billion. These holdings are by far the greatest ever reached and reflect a gain of about $9 billion since 1946 and $5 billion since 1952.

Since gold reserves are not included in the tabulation of the international investment position of the United States, that statement does not fully reflect the improvement in the situation of foreign countries. However, after purchasing $1.2 billion of gold from the United States in 1953, foreign countries reduced their purchases to about $300 million in 1954 and they were further reduced in 1955. The falling off of purchases here partly reflects a decline in the overall gain in reserves by foreign countries, but there is also a decided tendency for monetary authorities to cut down their gold acquisitions when a certain level has been reached, and to place additional amounts into interest-bearing dollar assets.

Out of $15.7 billion of foreign-owned short-term dollar assets and United States Government obligations at the end of 1954, over $9.6 billion was held by foreign official accounts and international institutions. Virtually the whole increase of $1.3 billion in 1954 went into such accounts, rather than into private foreign accounts. In 1953, official accounts rose nearly $1 billion while private accounts changed very little. The current tendency for private accounts to remain stable while official accounts grow, is associated with such factors as the increase in foreign purchases of United States corporate stocks, the growth of investment opportunities abroad, and the increasing ease with which dollar funds for working balances can be obtained as needed from official reserves.

Value of U. S. Direct Investments Abroad
By Area

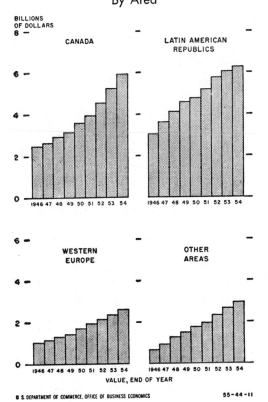

BILLIONS OF DOLLARS

CANADA | LATIN AMERICAN REPUBLICS

1946 47 48 49 50 51 52 53 54

WESTERN EUROPE | OTHER AREAS

1946 47 48 49 50 51 52 53 54

VALUE, END OF YEAR

U. S. DEPARTMENT OF COMMERCE, OFFICE OF BUSINESS ECONOMICS   55-44-11

Earnings on International Investments

United States investments abroad earned about $2.8 billion in 1954, including the undistributed portion of the earnings of direct-investment subsidiary companies. This total was about $160 million higher than the 1953 amount, but there has been very little variation in the total since 1950 despite an increase of $9.4 billion in United States investments abroad in the 4-year period.

Direct-investment enterprises abroad continue to produce the greater part of earnings, accounting for $2.3 billion in 1954 out of the $2.8 billion total. This is about the same as the 1951 amount as various factors have tended to hold down total earnings relative to investment. Such factors include (1) a large amount of investment since 1950, particularly in petroleum and mining, had not yet reached the production stage by the end of 1954 or was not yet fully productive, (2) the intensive search for new sources of raw materials, together with development expenses, has been extremely costly and has either been reflected as operating losses of new enterprises or lowered earnings of long-established enterprises, (3) some important properties are subject to accelerated depreciation, keeping earnings low even though output may increase sharply, (4) currency depreciation in a few countries in Latin America has drastically cut the dollar value of local-currency earnings, and (5) higher direct and indirect taxes, including discriminatory exchange rates, have also cut into earnings abroad.

Petroleum investments abroad, which currently account for some 42 percent of total direct-investment earnings, have been subject to most of the depressing factors mentioned above. In addition, earnings of the tanker fleets operated by the companies were very much reduced in the past few years by lower shipping rates. Thus, 1954 petroleum earnings of $960 million were lower than in 1952–53, and only $60 million higher than in 1951.

Table 3.—Value of Direct Investments Abroad, by Selected Countries, 1949–54, and Major Industries, 1953–54

[Millions of dollars]

Countries	1949	1950	1951	1952	1953 r							1954 p						
					Total	Mining and smelting	Petroleum	Manufacturing	Public utilities	Trade	Other industries	Total	Mining and smelting	Petroleum	Manufacturing	Public utilities	Trade	Other industries
All areas, total	10,700	11,788	13,089	14,819	16,329	1,933	4,935	5,226	1,508	1,049	1,678	17,748	2,071	5,353	5,655	1,545	1,148	1,976
Canada	3,146	3,579	3,972	4,593	5,242	677	933	2,418	300	330	584	5,939	783	1,160	2,553	301	358	784
Latin American Republics, total	4,590	4,735	5,176	5,758	6,034	999	1,684	1,149	1,093	354	755	6,256	1,003	1,688	1,248	1,120	402	795
Argentina	329	356	365	393	406	(¹)	(¹)	200	70	48	28	125	(¹)	(¹)	218	69	46	28
Bolivia	10	11	11	11	10	3	1	(¹)	1	4	(¹)	3	(¹)	1	(¹)	2	4	(¹)
Brazil	588	644	803	1,013	1,017	(¹)	206	483	149	119	(¹)	1,050	(¹)	178	534	150	128	(¹)
Chile	518	540	583	623	657	445	(¹)	34	(¹)	9	4	633	407	(¹)	35	(¹)	10	7
Colombia	194	193	207	234	235	(¹)	117	41	32	22	(¹)	263	(¹)	109	51	35	34	(¹)
Cuba	619	642	672	686	686	(¹)	(¹)	58	297	24	279	713	(¹)	(¹)	55	303	35	288
Dominican Republic	102	106	123	123	120		(¹)	11	16	(¹)	89	133	5	(¹)	11	17	(¹)	92
Ecuador	16	14	14	14	17		(¹)	(¹)	6	2	7	20		(¹)	(¹)	6	2	8
El Salvador	19	19	20	21	22	(¹)	4	(¹)	17	1	−1	23	(¹)	5	(¹)	17	1	
Haiti	14	13	14	15	15	(²)	(¹)	(¹)	3	(¹)	10	16	(²)	(¹)	(¹)	3	(¹)	9
Mexico	374	414	471	490	514	144	10	214	90	41	15	523	142	12	217	90	45	17
Panama	337	348	373	383	407		209	4	138	14	43	433		218	4	146	17	48
Peru	148	145	197	230	268	170	(¹)	17	(¹)	21	22	255	172	(¹)	19	(¹)	22	24
Uruguay	5ı	56	67	71	74		4	38	2	9	21	73		3	37	2	9	22
Venezuela	1,036	993	996	1,184	1,308	(¹)	1,006	37	13	38	(¹)	1,399	(¹)	1,038	53	15	44	(¹)
Other countries	235	241	260	267	278	11	17	12	96	(¹)	(¹)	287	9	20	13	97	(¹)	(¹)
Western Europe, total	1,450	1,720	1,979	2,145	2,369	30	609	1,295	29	232	174	2,605	35	671	1,432	29	235	203
Austria	11	13	16	18	20	(¹)	(¹)	5	(¹)	2	3	24	(¹)	(¹)	6	(¹)	2	11
Belgium	55	65	87	95	108		29	63	(²)	14	3	117		27	72	(²)	15	3
Denmark	30	32	37	38	36		24	8	(¹)	4	(¹)	38		24	9	(¹)	4	(¹)
Finland	8	9	8	9	10		6	(¹)	(¹)	3	1	14		10	(¹)	(¹)	3	2
France	185	217	249	276	304	4	90	173	5	11	21	333	5	96	188	5	12	27
Germany	173	204	234	251	276	(¹)	67	155	(¹)	23	26	278	(¹)	69	165	(¹)	10	28
Italy	37	63	72	80	95		49	33	1	2	11	121		64	36	1	3	18
Netherlands	57	84	100	108	125	(¹)	72	28	(¹)	18	7	140	(¹)	78	33	(¹)	21	9
Norway	22	24	28	33	37	(¹)	11	9	2	2	21	40	(¹)	10	11	2	2	(¹)
Portugal	14	16	19	21	23	1	(¹)	(¹)	2	7	(²)	23	1	(¹)	(¹)	2	7	1
Spain	27	31	36	40	45	(¹)	14	18	(¹)	3	7	49	(¹)	14	20	(¹)	4	9
Sweden	51	58	65	70	74		31	33	(¹)	5	(¹)	84		32	41	(¹)	6	(¹)
Switzerland	22	25	28	28	31		8	13	(²)	5	(¹)	35		10	14	(²)	6	4
United Kingdom	729	847	961	1,038	1,131	3	170	745	11	119	84	1,245	3	185	824	11	130	92
Other countries	29	33	39	41	54	(²)	25	10	1	10	1	64	(²)	40	10	1	10	3
Western European dependencies, total	427	435	446	468	603	136	395	11	18	27	16	600	105	412	-14	20	31	18
Western Hemisphere, total	126	131	139	158	178	61	84	(¹)	15	12	(¹)	172	61	73	(¹)	17	15	(¹)
Africa:																		
British ³	37	41	54	66	77	45	26	(¹)	(¹)	4	(¹)	45	15	23	(¹)	(¹)	5	(¹)
French	27	31	32	36	37	(¹)	29	(¹)	2	4	(¹)	42	(¹)	35	(¹)	2	4	(¹)
Other European	10	12	12	14	16	(¹)	(¹)	2	(¹)	(¹)	1	19	(¹)	(¹)	3	(¹)	(¹)	1
Other areas:																		
British	201	190	177	154	250	24	205	7	1	4	9	276	24	226	10	1	6	10
Other European	26	30	32	39	45		(¹)	(¹)	(¹)	(¹)		47		(¹)	(¹)	(¹)	(¹)	
Other countries, total	1,086	1,318	1,516	1,854	2,081	92	1,314	353	68	105	149	2,348	146	1,421	407	75	122	177
Africa:																		
Egypt	38	39	44	46	46		27	10	(¹)	4	(¹)	54		33	12	(¹)	4	(¹)
Liberia	47	82	104	140	186	(¹)	135	(¹)	8	(¹)	(¹)	236	(¹)	178	(¹)	9	(¹)	(¹)
Union of South Africa	105	140	157	194	212	59	65	61	(¹)	20	(¹)	216	69	44	73	(¹)	23	(¹)
Other countries ³	5	7	7	8	10			(¹)	(¹)	(¹)	(¹)	52	39	(¹)	(²)	(¹)	(¹)	(¹)
Other areas:																		
Australia	161	201	256	310	326	15	(¹)	172	(¹)	19	14	387	20	(¹)	195	(¹)	21	16
India	27	38	49	63	68	(²)	(¹)	23	2	9	(¹)	92	(²)	(¹)	28	2	10	(¹)
Indonesia	62	58	72	74	88		(¹)	17	(¹)	3	(¹)	66		(¹)	19	(¹)	4	(¹)
Israel	13	15	34	41	56		10	24	1	(²)	20	63		11	27	1	1	23
Japan	12	19	45	69	92	(¹)	(¹)	8	1	2	(¹)	106	(¹)	(¹)	10	1	2	(¹)
New Zealand	17	25	31	37	34	(¹)	(¹)	12	(¹)	7	1	40	(¹)	(¹)	15	(¹)	9	1
Philippine Republic	132	149	163	178	188	(¹)	(¹)	25	53	33	24	216	(¹)	(¹)	29	58	36	27
Other countries	467	545	554	693	776	(¹)	758	(²)	2	7	(¹)	820	(¹)	799	(²)	2	10	(¹)

r Revised.   p Preliminary.
1. Included in total.   2. Less than $500,000.
3. Thru 1953, Northern and Southern Rhodesia and Nyasaland are included in British Dependencies in Africa; in 1954, they are included in other countries in Africa.

Source: U. S. Department of Commerce, Office of Business Economics.

Earnings in Latin America were cut from 1951 to 1954 by a drop of some $70 million in the return on tanker operations, although tanker rates are now moving upward. The United States share of production in the area increased by 150,000 barrels per day from 1951 to 1954, yielding somewhat greater revenues from this source, but higher costs

Earnings on International Investments

BILLIONS OF DOLLARS

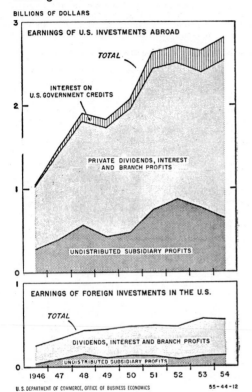

U. S. DEPARTMENT OF COMMERCE, OFFICE OF BUSINESS ECONOMICS   55-44-12

including rising exploration expenditures have held down net earnings. Earnings from Venezuelan operations continue to have the greatest importance, accounting for $340 million out of the $380 million total for Latin America in 1954.

Petroleum companies have raised their investment in Canada from about $400 million in 1950 to about $1.2 billion at present, but consolidated earnings of the companies remain at only $10 million in 1954 because of large exploration costs. Earnings in Western Europe were reduced in 1954, possibly because of rising costs and also because the companies are also spending large amounts in this area to develop new oil fields.

Middle East earnings have scored the greatest rise since 1951, from $343 million in 1951 to $413 million in 1954, reflecting an increase of nearly 900 thousand barrels per day in the amount of oil produced by United States owned companies.

353028°– 55——3

Manufacturing earnings abroad rose moderately in 1954 to a total of $705 million. In the year there were divergent trends in different areas; in Canada there was a very sharp drop of some $50 million as economic activity in the country went through a downturn similar to that in the United States, but this was approximately offset by increased earnings in Western Europe, as output in these countries rose to unprecedented levels.

Earnings of mining properties rose in 1954, but in this industry also the total was still lower than in 1951 and 1952. Over $30 million of the $50 million increase was in Latin

Table 4.—Direct Investment Capital Outflows, by Major Areas and Industries, 1950–54

[Millions of dollars; inflows to the United States (−)]

Area and year	Total	Agriculture	Mining and smelting	Petroleum	Manufacturing	Public utilities	Trade	Other industries
All areas, total:								
1954 ᴾ	761	21	110	302	75	16	28	209
1953 ʳ	721	−11	243	408	−53	16	29	89
1952	850	−8	278	248	211	23	17	80
1951	528	24	100	93	190	−8	58	70
1950	621	−9	87	248	192	−2	68	37
Canada:								
1954 ᴾ	469	1	85	202	24	(¹)	(¹)	157
1953 ʳ	387	(¹)	110	181	27	2	25	41
1952	420	−1	134	122	121	1	2	42
1951	240	(¹)	36	124	30	−1	6	44
1950	287	2	29	122	86	−6	32	21
Latin American Republics:								
1954 ᴾ	102	18	18	−22	32	16	33	6
1953 ʳ	117	−11	120	58	−73	8	−3	18
1952	277	−4	120	32	80	21	11	18
1951	166	22	60	−75	116	−7	38	11
1950	40	−7	29	−69	64	−3	18	7
Western Europe:								
1954 ᴾ	36		(¹)	23	3	(¹)	−13	23
1953 ʳ	51		(¹)	33	−7	(¹)	8	16
1952	−8		(¹)	−24	6	(¹)	2	8
1951	62		(¹)	37	17	(¹)	7	1
1950	119	(¹)	(¹)	73	32	4	7	3
Western European dependencies: ²								
1954 ᴾ	−6	(¹)	−5	−4	1	(¹)	1	2
1953 ʳ	82	(¹)	5	76	(¹)	(¹)	1	1
1952	−5	(¹)	18	−23	(¹)	(¹)	2	(¹)
1951	1	1	2	−2	−2	(¹)	2	(¹)
1950	14	(¹)	13	−6	3	2	2	(¹)
Other countries: ²								
1954 ᴾ	160	2	12	102	15		8	21
1953 ʳ	84	(¹)	7	60	−1	6	−3	15
1952	166	−2	6	142	4	2	2	13
1951	59	1	2	8	29		5	14
1950	161	−4	16	127	6	1	9	6

ʳ Revised.   ᴾ Preliminary.   1. Less than $500,000. •
2. Through 1953, Northern and Southern Rhodesia and Nyasaland are included in Western European dependencies; in 1954, they are included in Other countries.

Source: U. S. Department of Commerce, Office of Business Economics.

America, reflecting the improved price and market situation for copper and other metals and the beginning of large scale production of iron ore. New legislation in Chile with respect to the copper companies should have the effect of reducing the arbitrarily high local-currency costs of operation.

Mining properties in Canada and other countries also experienced somewhat higher returns in 1954, reflecting rising prices and a strong demand for metals and minerals. Continued low earnings for agricultural properties abroad resulted from lower prices and output for sugar producers and considerable losses from floods and strikes in parts of Central America. • There was some improvement in public utility earnings in the year, although they remained comparatively low.

Earnings of foreign subsidiary companies were slightly lower in 1954 than in the preceding year. The disposition of the earnings differed, with relatively more being distributed in dividends. The undistributed portion was $641 million, compared with $776 million in 1953.

Manufacturing companies in Canada sharply reduced their reinvestment of earnings, as their overall earnings were reduced, but larger amounts were reinvested in Europe and Latin America. In the case of mining enterprises, a few unusually large dividend payments out of accumulated funds resulted in a smaller total of reinvested earnings. Although total petroleum earnings were higher than in 1953 a smaller proportion of the earnings of the companies was retained abroad.

Dividends and interest received on foreign securities and loans held by private investors in the United States have been rising slowly since the war, reaching $229 million in 1954. This total includes $75 million of dividends, $93 million of interest on foreign dollar bonds, and about $20 million each of interest on foreign-currency bonds, medium-term banking and commercial loans, and short-term credits.

About 60 percent of the interest received on United States holdings of dollar bonds comes from Canada and 15 percent from the International Bank. Holdings in most other countries have been so reduced, or the terms have been so modified, that interest payments on these debts have become a minor item in their balances of payments.

A very large part of the dividends and interest received on foreign-currency stocks and bonds comes from Canada and the United Kingdom, but dividends from the Netherlands and other countries will rise somewhat as a result of recent

Table 5.—Direct Investment Capital Flows and Undistributed Subsidiary Earnings, by Specified Countries and Industries, 1953–54

[Millions of dollars]

| Country | Net capital outflow | | | | | | | | | | Undistributed subsidiary earnings | | | | | | | | | |
| | 1953 r | | | | | 1954 p | | | | | 1953 r | | | | | 1954 p | | | | |
	Total	Mining and smelting	Petroleum	Manufacturing	Other industries	Total	Mining and smelting	Petroleum	Manufacturing	Other industries	Total	Mining and smelting	Petroleum	Manufacturing	Other industries	Total	Mining and smelting	Petroleum	Manufacturing	Other industries
All areas, total	721	243	408	−53	123	761	110	302	75	274	776	48	238	361	129	641	28	116	353	144
Canada	387	110	181	27	69	469	85	202	24	158	259	16	36	153	54	215	21	25	111	58
Latin American Republics, total	117	120	58	−73	12	102	18	−22	32	74	152	11	51	54	36	121	−15	29	67	40
Argentina	4	(1)	(1)	−4	8	−3	(1)	(1)	(2)	−3	9	(1)	(1)	6	3	22	(1)	(1)	18	4
Brazil	−35	(1)	28	−59	−4	−8	(1)	−32	23	1	38	(1)	6	26	6	40	(1)	4	28	8
Chile	26	23	(1)	1	2	−28	(1)	−38	(1)	9	8	2	(1)	(2)	6	4	(1)	(2)	4	4
Colombia	1	(1)	−5	(1)	4	33	(1)		4	7	1	(1)	−2	2	1	−3	(1)	−9	4	2
Costa Rica	−1		(2)	(1)	−1	2			1	(1)	1	(1)		(2)	(1)	1		(2)	(1)	1
Cuba	−5	(1)	−1	−6	2	26	(1)		1	−3	3	(1)	1	1	1	1	(1)	1	1	−1
Dominican Republic	−6		(1)		−6	8	5	(1)		3	5		(1)	(2)	5	5		(1)	(2)	5
Honduras	7	(1)	(1)	(1)	7	1	(1)		(1)	1	1		(2)		1	2	(1)		(1)	2
Mexico	7	8	(2)	−7	6	15		18	1	−7	17	4	(2)	10	3	−6	−20	(1)	10	3
Panama	−11		−12	1	(2)	13			2	(2)	29		22	1	6	13		7	(2)	6
Peru	39	24	(1)	−1	16	−13	(2)	(1)	−1	−14	−1	3	(1)	1	−5	(2)	2	(1)	1	−3
Uruguay	−3		(2)	−2	−1	−2			−2	1	6		(2)	4	2	2		(2)	(2)	2
Venezuela	93	(1)	28	(2)	65	53	(1)		7	34	34	(1)	26	4	4	37	(1)	24	4	9
Other countries	1	1	(2)	(2)	(2)	5	−2		5	(2)	2	(2)	(2)	(2)	2	3	(2)	1	(2)	2
Western Europe, total	51	(2)	33	−7	25	36	(2)		23	3	173	2	45	115	11	197	5	36	133	23
Belgium	6		4	1	1	4			−4	6	7		1	6	(2)	5		2	3	(2)
France	8	(1)	6	1	1	4	(1)		−1	5	20	(1)	2	15	3	25	(1)	7	16	2
Germany	7	(1)	6	−1	2	−12	(1)		−1	1	18	(1)	6	10	2	14	(1)	3	9	2
Italy	13		8	1	4	19			12	1	4		(2)	3	1	8		3	3	2
Netherlands	7	(1)	4	2	1	7	(1)		2	4	9		1	6	1	2	8	(1)	4	2	2
Portugal	(2)		(1)	(2)	(2)	−2	(2)	(1)	(2)	−2	2		(1)	(2)	2	2	(1)	(1)	(2)	2
Spain	3	(1)	(1)	(2)	3	2	(1)	(1)		−1	3	(2)	(1)	1	2	2	(1)	(1)		2
Sweden	(2)		(1)	(2)	(2)	4			1	2	4		1	2	1	7		(1)	6	1
United Kingdom	−4	(1)	−4	−10	10	2	(1)		4	−8	97	(2)	24	71	2	112	(1)	11	87	14
Other countries	11	(1)	9	−1	3	8	(1)		10	−2	10	(1)	4	4	2	14	(1)	3	5	6
Western European dependencies, total	82	5	76	(2)	1	−6	−5		−4	1	49	10	29	2	8	41	8	25	3	5
Western Hemisphere:																				
British	3	(1)	(2)	(2)	3	1	(1)	(2)	(2)	1	9	(1)	(2)		9	6	(1)	(2)		6
Other European	2	(1)	(1)	(2)	2	−18	(1)			−18	5	(1)	(1)		5	5	(1)	(1)		5
Africa:																				
British [3]	−2	(2)	−3	(2)	1	−2			−2	(2)	9	6	3		(2)	8	4	4		(2)
French	−2	1	−3	(2)	(2)	3	(2)		3		3		3		(2)	3		3		(2)
Other European	1	(2)	(1)	(2)	1	2			(1)	(2)	2	1	(1)	(2)	1	1	(1)	(2)	(2)	1
Other areas:																				
British	75	1	(1)	(2)	74	6	(2)	(1)	(1)	1	5		(1)	2	19	19		(2)	3	16
Other European	5		5			2			2		1		1		−1	−1		(1)	−1	
Other countries, total	84	87	60	−1	17	160	12	102	15	31	143	8	77	38	20	67	9	1	39	18
Africa:																				
Liberia	12	(1)	(1)		12	56	(1)	(1)		56	33	(1)	(1)		33	−5	(1)	(1)		−5
Union of South Africa	3	7	−7	2	1	−12	9	−24	1	2	15	5	4	4	2	16	1	2	10	3
Other countries [3]	2		1	(2)	1	10	2	5	2	1	(2)	(2)	−1	1	(2)	3	3	1	−1	(2)
Other areas:																				
Australia	−22	(1)	(1)	−6	−16	33	(1)	(1)	(1)	5	28	38	(1)	26	12	28	(1)	(1)	18	10
India	3		(1)	−1	4	18		(1)	(1)	1	17	3	(1)	2	1	6		(1)	4	2
Indonesia	14		(1)	(1)	14	−4		(1)	(1)	−4	(2)		(1)	(2)	(2)	−17		(1)	(1)	−17
Israel	13		(1)	(1)	13	7			(1)	7	1		(1)	(1)	1	(2)		(1)	(1)	(2)
Japan	20		(1)	(2)	20	9		(1)	(2)	9	3		(1)	1	2	5		(1)	2	3
Philippine Republic	5	(1)	(1)	(2)	5	18	(1)	(1)		2	16	(1)	(1)	1	4	8	(1)	(2)	2	6
Other countries	34	(1)	34	(2)	(2)	25	(1)		20	4	45	(1)	43	1	1	23	(1)	19	2	2

r Revised.   p Preliminary.   1. Included in "other industries."   2. Less than $500,000.   3. In 1953, Northern and Southern Rhodesia and Nyasaland are included in British dependencies in Africa; in 1954 they are included in other countries in Africa.   Source: U. S. Department of Commerce, Office of Business Economics.

Table 6.—Gross Movements [1] of Direct-Investment Capital by Major Industries, 1952–54

[Millions of dollars; net inflows (—)]

Year	Total	Mining and smelting	Petro-leum	Manu-facturing	Trade	Other indus-tries
1954 ᴾ						
Outflows	1,758	228	757	341	119	313
Inflows	997	118	455	266	91	67
Net	761	110	302	75	28	246
1953 ʳ						
Outflows	1,273	271	565	196	75	166
Inflows	553	28	157	250	47	71
Net	721	243	408	—53	29	94
1952						
Outflows	1,381	299	526	359	65	132
Inflows	531	21	279	148	47	36
Net	850	278	248	211	17	95

ʳ Revised.   ᴾ Preliminary.

1. The gross capital outflow shown in each industry cell of this table represents the sum of the net capital outflows to those foreign subsidiaries and branches for which net outflows were reported for each of the years covered. Conversely, the gross inflows shown for each cell represent the sum of the net inflows from those foreign subsidiaries and branches for which inflows were reported in each year. It should be noted that the gross totals, but not the net amounts, would change if the compilation were done on a quarterly basis.

Source: U. S. Department of Commerce, Office of Business Economics.

Table 7.—United States Holdings of Dollar Bonds of Specified Countries, Market and Par Values, 1952–54

[Millions of dollars]

	1952		1953 ʳ		1954 ᴾ	
	Market Value	Par Value	Market Value	Par Value	Market Value	Par Value
All areas	2,244	2,620	2,383	2,751	2,720	2,916
Western Europe	84	231	82	223	160	218
Belgium	17	17	17	17	15	15
Denmark	18	20	16	16	8	8
Germany		104		104	84	112
Italy	26	50	27	49	31	48
Norway	13	13	12	12	11	11
Other	10	27	10	25	11	24
Canada	1,384	1,390	1,477	1,492	1,604	1,573
Latin American Republics	147	306	136	289	143	279
Bolivia	6	38	5	38	6	38
Brazil	40	64	37	58	37	54
Chile	26	61	22	56	22	54
Colombia	25	47	21	42	25	40
Other	50	96	51	95	53	93
Other foreign countries	229	274	263	305	309	347
Australia	86	93	86	87	94	94
Israel	97	97	136	136	173	173
Japan	44	40	38	38	38	36
Other [1]	2	44	3	44	4	44
International Bank for Reconstruction and Development	400	419	425	442	504	499

ʳ Revised.   ᴾ Preliminary.

1. Includes Eastern Europe, China, and the Philippine Republic.

Source: United States Department of Commerce, Office of Business Economics.

Table 10.—Earnings on International Investments, by Type, 1950–54.

[Millions of dollars]

Type of earnings	1950	1951	1952	1953 ʳ	1954 ᴾ
Earnings on United States investments abroad, total	2,068	2,634	2,704	2,642	2,807
Direct investments, total	1,769	2,244	2,295	2,174	2,306
Dividends, interest and branch profits	1,294	1,492	1,419	1,398	1,665
Undistributed profits of subsidiaries	475	752	876	776	641
Portfolio investments	190	192	205	216	229
Interest on United States Government credits	109	198	204	252	272
Earnings on foreign investments in the United States, total	478	481	472	571	549
Direct investments, total	281	255	234	306	305
Dividends, interest and branch profits	148	129	152	185	175
Undistributed profits of subsidiaries	133	126	82	121	130
Portfolio investments	166	179	174	179	185
Interest on United States Government obligations	31	47	64	86	59

ʳ Revised.   ᴾ Preliminary.

Source: United States Department of Commerce, Office of Business Economics.

Table 8.—Banking and Commercial Claims on Foreigners, by Selected Countries [1] 1953–54

[Millions of dollars]

Countries	December 31, 1953 ʳ				December 31, 1954 ᴾ			
	Total	Banking claims		Com-mercial claims [2]	Total	Banking claims		Com-mercial claims [2]
		Short-term	Medium-term			Short-term	Medium-term	
Total	1,723	905	325	493	2,394	1,384	423	587
Western Europe, total	597	236	207	154	726	396	121	209
United Kingdom	124	71	(³)	53	246	169	(³)	77
France	178	11	151	16	125	14	96	15
Turkey	26	16	(³)	10	57	41	(³)	16
Germany	39	31	(³)	8	81	68	2	11
Belgium	58	13	36	9	29	20	(³)	9
Canada	169	56	22	91	175	76	13	86
Latin America, total	687	470	62	155	1,097	732	167	198
Brazil	165	125	12	28	404	278	76	50
Colombia	80	57	10	13	137	107	12	18
Cuba	63	51	(³)	12	122	71	35	16
Mexico	125	93	8	24	161	116	18	27
Venezuela	62	42	1	19	87	63	3	21
All other countries, total	270	143	34	93	396	180	122	94
Israel	43	23	8	12	37	11	20	6
Japan	42	26	1	15	140	50	74	16
Union of South Africa	28	2	20	6	30	6	18	6

ʳ Revised.   ᴾ Preliminary.

1. Includes major categories of claims as reported to the Treasury Department regularly by banks and commercial concerns, but does not include estimates for other types of claims included in table 2 as short-term or "other" long-term private investments.

2. Not including medium-term claims totaling $84 million at the end of 1953 and $102 million at the end of 1954.

3. Less than $500,000.

Source: *Treasury Bulletin,* March and July 1955.

Table 9.—Foreign Holdings of Domestic Stocks, by Selected Countries, 1946–54

[Market values; millions of dollars]

	Value, year end			Change in 1954		Value, year-end 1954 ᴾ
	1946	1949	1953 ʳ	Net foreign purchases	Price change	
Total [1]	2,440	2,240	3,400	135	1,469	5,004
Western Europe [1]	1,690	1,490	2,350	116	1,019	3,485
Belgium	62	68	103	3	44	150
France	193	57	100	11	46	157
Netherlands	430	312	374	—34	151	491
Switzerland	505	522	903	56	394	1,353
United Kingdom	418	450	744	79	330	1,153
Other countries	82	81	126	1	54	181
Western European dependencies	50	52	80	4	34	118
Canada [1]	460	480	650	—15	275	910
Latin American Republics [1]	174	173	245	25	107	377
All other [1]	66	45	75	5	34	114

ʳ Revised.   ᴾ Preliminary.

1. Grand total and area totals exclude the following holdings by United States citizens resident abroad approximately as given for 1941 in the Treasury Census, TFR 300: Total, $250 million; Canada, $25 million; Latin American, $40 million; Western Europe, $175 million; other countries, $10 million. These amounts are included in table 2.

Source: U. S. Department of Commerce, Office of Business Economics.

Table 11.—Direct Investment Earnings by Industry, 1950–54

[Millions of dollars]

Industry	1950	1951	1952	1953 ʳ	1954 ᴾ
All industries	1,769	2,244	2,295	2,174	2,306
Agriculture	115	139	114	76	73
Mining and smelting	145	215	204	149	204
Petroleum	629	900	1,015	952	964
Manufacturing	623	690	644	676	698
Public utilities	60	59	64	63	75
Trade	116	142	145	133	149
Other industries	81	98	110	125	143

ʳ Revised.   ᴾ Preliminary.

Source: United States Department of Commerce, Office of Business Economics.

United States purchases of corporate stocks. Most of the interest on medium- and short-term loans is received on amounts outstanding in Latin America, which have grown considerably in recent years. A small amount of interest is also earned on loans to United Kingdom entities and short-term funds held in London.

Interest received on United States Government credits to foreign countries rose to $272 million in 1954. About $200 million of this amount came from Europe, largely the United Kingdom, France and Germany, and about $30 million from Latin America.

Earnings of foreigners on their investments in the United States fell slightly to about $550 million in 1954, primarily because of a lower return on United States Government obligations.

About 60 percent of foreign earnings in the United States are derived from direct investments. Major direct investments are in insurance and finance, petroleum, food and beverages, and a wide variety of manufacturing concerns. United States branches of foreign insurance companies earned about $45 million in 1954, and the bulk of this was added to reserves in the United States. A major portion of the earnings of other enterprises is also reinvested here, resulting in a steady growth of foreign-owned enterprises since the war.

Most of the income on foreign portfolio investments here is derived from holdings of corporate stocks, which have been increasing sharply in value. However, the total amount of dividends paid has not expanded rapidly—since 1950 the increase has been about 10 percent, which is the same as the increase in all United States dividend payments.

Table 12.—Direct Investment Earnings [1] and Income by Selected Countries, 1950–54, with Major Industries for 1954

[Millions of dollars]

Country	Earnings									Income								
	1950	1951	1952	1953 r	1954 p Total	Mining and smelting	Petroleum	Manufacturing	Other industries	1950	1951	1952	1953 r	1954 p Total	Mining and smelting	Petroleum	Manufacturing	Other industries
All areas, total	1,769	2,244	2,295	2,174	2,306	204	964	698	440	1,294	1,492	1,419	1,398	1,665	175	849	345	296
Canada	440	417	421	467	451	60	15	249	128	294	236	222	208	236	39	−10	138	69
Latin American Republics, total	631	901	902	722	751	73	380	123	175	522	652	599	570	630	88	351	56	135
Argentina	18	29	30	20	32	(2)	(2)	21	10	6	11	12	11	10	(2)	(2)	3	7
Brazil	97	142	150	112	85	(2)	11	50	24	61	75	65	74	45	(2)	7	22	16
Chile	41	57	54	34	42	31	(2)	3	7	41	54	51	26	38	31	(2)	3	4
Colombia	16	15	20	13	16	(2)	−6	8	14	10	12	13	12	19	(2)	3	4	12
Costa Rica	13	12	14	12	13	----	(2)	(2)	13	13	11	14	12	12	----	(2)	(2)	12
Cuba	59	64	53	30	36	(2)	3	5	27	43	49	44	28	35	(2)	2	5	28
Dominican Republic	17	31	21	8	9	----	(2)	(2)	8	14	25	14	4	4	----	(2)	(2)	4
Honduras	16	18	16	17	11	(2)	(2)	(2)	11	15	16	15	16	9	(2)	(2)	(2)	9
Mexico	44	64	61	47	45	13	1	21	10	29	31	32	30	50	(3)	33	11	6
Panama	30	107	101	49	45	----	17	(2)	27	18	37	43	19	31	----	10	(2)	21
Peru	21	36	31	21	28	15	(2)	4	9	15	33	25	22	28	13	(2)	3	12
Uruguay	6	11	7	9	6	----	1	2	3	4	6	4	3	4	----	(2)	2	2
Venezuela	232	297	329	334	372	(2)	342	7	24	236	278	256	300	335	(2)	317	3	15
Other countries	21	18	14	15	12	1	2	2	8	17	14	10	13	10	(2)	1	1	8
Western Europe, total	262	300	303	316	381	7	68	239	67	111	119	129	143	185	2	32	106	45
Belgium	12	15	15	14	16	----	3	11	3	6	6	6	7	11	----	1	8	2
France	29	40	36	31	42	(2)	11	27	4	6	10	10	11	17	(2)	4	11	2
Germany	27	21	18	22	26	(2)	4	18	4	4	4	4	4	13	(2)	1	9	3
Italy	9	14	10	9	13	----	3	7	3	2	5	7	6	6	----	(2)	4	2
Netherlands	14	14	13	15	14	(2)	5	4	6	5	5	5	5	6	(2)	1	2	3
Portugal	3	2	4	4	5	(2)	(2)	(2)	3	5	3	2	2	3	(2)	(2)	(2)	3
Spain	3	4	4	3	5	(2)	(2)	3	2	(2)	1	1	1	3	(2)	(2)	1	2
Sweden	7	7	7	9	11	----	1	8	2	2	3	4	5	4	----	(2)	2	2
United Kingdom	142	164	176	187	221	(2)	34	150	37	73	74	78	90	109	(2)	23	63	23
Other countries	16	18	20	22	27	(2)	4	12	11	12	8	11	12	13	(2)	1	6	6
Western European dependencies, total	95	118	154	180	184	35	130	3	16	98	109	127	131	143	27	105	(3)	11
Western Hemisphere.																		
British	4	4	3	14	16	(2)	(3)	----	16	(3)	(3)	1	5	10	(2)	−1	----	11
Other European	9	10	9	13	13	(2)	(2)	----	13	10	12	11	8	8	(2)	(2)	----	8
Africa:																		
British [4]	5	21	20	27	15	10	----	4	1	4	14	13	17	7	6	----	1	(2)
French	7	6	5	4	6	----	----	5	1	5	4	1	1	4	----	----	3	1
Other European	2	2	2	1	3	(2)	(2)	(2)	1	3	2	3	1	2	(2)	(2)	(2)	2
Other areas:																		
British	68	74	115	122	131	10	(2)	----	3	76	75	99	101	112	10	(2)	(2)	102
Other European	(3)	(3)	(3)	(3)	−1	----	−1	----	----	(3)	(3)	(3)						
Other countries, total	340	508	515	489	538	29	372	84	54	269	376	343	346	471	19	371	45	36
Africa:																		
Liberia	15	35	48	35	21	(2)	(2)	----	21	12	13	12	1	26	(2)	(2)	----	26
Union of South Africa	25	33	35	40	42	11	8	19	5	13	23	23	24	26	10	6	9	1
Other countries [5]	4	5	8	5	16	11	2	1	1	2	2	5	6	13	9	1	2	1
Other areas:																		
Australia	27	36	33	51	53	(2)	(2)	38	5	15	12	10	8	25	(2)	(2)	20	5
India	13	14	15	12	18	----	(2)	6		11	10	10	9	12	----	(2)	2	10
Indonesia	36	38	29	32	26	----	(2)	(2)	2	25	34	4	32	43	----	(2)	(2)	43
Israel	1	2	1	1	2					1	2	1	(3)	1				
Japan	2	8	4	8	15	----	(2)	4		10	2	3	4	9	----	(2)	2	7
Philippine Republic	39	35	33	29	34	(2)	(2)	7		28	26	27	24	26	(2)	(2)	5	21
Other countries	178	302	308	277	312	(2)	303	4	5	162	251	219	233	290	(2)	283	2	5

r Revised.   p Preliminary.
1. Income is the sum of dividends, interest, and branch profits; earnings is the sum of income and undistributed subsidiary earnings.
2. Combined with "other industries."   3. Less than $500,000.
4. Includes Northern and Southern Rhodesia and Nyasaland in 1950-53.
5. Include Northern and Southern Rhodesia and Nyasaland in 1954.

Source: U. S. Department of Commerce, Office of Business Economics.

GROWTH OF FOREIGN INVESTMENTS IN THE UNITED STATES AND ABROAD

Samuel Pizer
and
Frederick Cutler

by Samuel Pizer and Frederick Cutler ☆

Growth of Foreign Investments in the United States and Abroad

UNITED STATES private investments abroad continued to grow at a rapid rate in 1955, increasing by $2.4 billion to a year-end total of $29 billion. Long-term investments were expanded by the record amount of $2.2 billion, while private short-term assets abroad rose much less than in 1954.

Contributing to the worldwide upsurge in economic activity in 1955, United States companies added nearly $1.6 billion to their net investments in foreign branches and subsidiaries through capital outflows from the United States and the reinvestment of foreign earnings. Since this figure excludes most expenditures for exploration and development, and funds derived from depreciation charges, it understates actual capital expenditures abroad by the companies. Major expansions in 1955 were in the manufacturing and petroleum industries.

Based on partial data for the first half of 1956, and announced plans for the rest of this year, it appears that United States companies are further accelerating their investments abroad.

Net purchases of foreign securities by Americans were quite small in 1955; acquisitions of about $190 million of European and Canadian corporate stocks were nearly offset by reductions in holdings of foreign bonds. However, price increases added about $300 million to the market value of United States holdings of foreign securities.

Foreign investments and assets in the United States increased in value by nearly $2.8 billion in 1955, to a year-end total of $29.6 billion. This increase differed in character from the growth of United States investments abroad. Nearly $1.2 billion of the increases resulted from the appreciation of the market value of foreign holdings of United States corporate stocks, and about $1.1 billion represented increases in foreign holdings of liquid dollar resources, such as bank deposits or obligations of the United States Government. Net inflows of foreign capital for long-term investment in foreign-controlled enterprises or corporate securities were about $350 million, and reinvested earnings of direct investments were about $125 million.

Earnings on United States investments abroad in 1955 rose over the preceding year by $500 million to a record of $3.4 billion, reflecting both the growing volume of investment and expanding output to meet world demands for manufactures and raw materials. Reinvested earnings of foreign subsidiaries, included in these totals, were $870 million and absorbed over 40 percent of the additional earnings.

Foreigners earned $100 million more on their holdings in the United States than in 1954, mainly reflecting higher dividend payments by United States corporations and an increase of over $1 billion in foreign holdings of interest-bearing United States Government obligations. Total earnings on these foreign assets were $640 million in 1955.

Changes in net creditor position

As the international investment position of the United States has developed, especially since 1946, there has been a widening difference between the character of United States investments abroad and foreign investments in the United States. Over 90 percent of the increase in United States private investments abroad, as shown in table 1, was in long-term investments, while most of the increase in foreign holdings in the United States has been in the form of liquid assets. Moreover, because of the different methods of valuation applied to different types of investments, the debtor-creditor statement has tended to understate the relative significance of United States private long-term investments abroad as compared with foreign long-term investments in the United States.

The principal valuation difference is that direct investments are carried at book values, while portfolio holdings of marketable securities are included at market values. United States direct investments abroad make up two-thirds of our total private investments abroad, and accounted for $12 billion of the total $15½ billion increase in these investments from 1946 through 1955. Under present circumstances the book value of these direct investments is much lower than their replacement or market value. A review of the limited

Annual Additions to U. S. Direct Investments Abroad, by Area

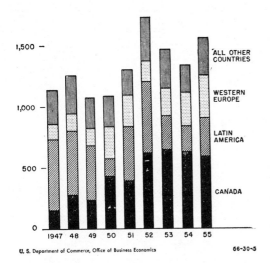

MILLIONS OF DOLLARS
2,000 —

1,500 —

ALL OTHER COUNTRIES

WESTERN EUROPE

1,000 —

LATIN AMERICA

500 —

CANADA

0 —

1947 48 49 50 51 52 53 54 55

U. S. Department of Commerce, Office of Business Economics   66-30-5

NOTE.—MR. PIZER AND MR. CUTLER ARE MEMBERS OF THE BALANCE OF PAYMENTS DIVISION, OFFICE OF BUSINESS ECONOMICS.

number of enterprises for which both a market and book value can be established indicates that the market value of direct investments could well be more than double their book value. Of course, either method of valuation has only limited validity, although the market value would more nearly reflect the great productivity and earning power of these enterprises.

On the other hand, the market value of foreign direct investments in the United States would not exceed their book value by any similar proportion, nor would use of market values actually affect the total value of foreign investment in the United States by any great amount since only about 15 percent of the total are direct investments. The lesser difference between market and book values of foreign direct investments here results partly from the industry distribution of the total, since enterprises in the insurance and finance category account for nearly one-fourth of the investment and do not have a large spread between book value and market value.

In the case of portfolio investments in securities, the value of United States holdings of foreign securities increased by $1.4 billion from 1946 through 1955, very largely through net capital outflows, while in the same period foreign holdings of United States corporate stocks and bonds increased in value by $3.9 billion, but almost entirely through the appreciation of market values and with very small net capital inflows for the period as a whole.

Table 1.—International Investment Position of the United States In Selected Years, 1914–55

[Billions of dollars]

	1914[1]	1919	1930	1939	1946	1953	1955[p]
United States investments abroad	3.5	7.0	17.2	11.4	18.7	39.6	44.9
Private	3.5	7.0	17.2	11.4	13.5	23.8	29.0
Long-term	3.5	6.5	15.2	10.8	12.3	22.3	26.6
Direct	2.6	3.9	8.0	7.0	7.2	16.3	19.2
Portfolio	.9	2.6	7.2	3.8	5.1	6.0	7.4
Short-term	na	.5	2.0	.6	1.3	1.6	2.4
United States Government[2]					5.2	15.7	15.9
Long-term					5.0	15.4	15.2
Short-term					.2	.3	.7
Foreign investments in the United States	7.2	4.0	8.4	9.6	15.9	23.6	29.6
Long-term	6.7	3.2	5.7	6.3	7.0	9.2	12.6
Direct	1.3	.9	1.4	2.0	2.5	3.8	4.3
Portfolio	5.4	2.3	4.3	4.3	4.5	5.4	8.3
Short-term assets[3]	.5	.8	2.7	3.3	8.9	14.4	17.0
United States net creditor position	−3.7	3.0	8.8	1.8	2.8	16.0	15.3
Net long-term	−3.2	3.3	9.5	4.5	10.3	28.5	29.2
Net short-term	−.5	−.3	−.7	−2.7	−7.4	−12.5	−13.9

na—Not available.　p Preliminary.　1. At June 30.　2. Excludes World War I loans.
3. Includes U. S. Government obligations in 1946, 1953, and 1955.

NOTE.—Data for various years are not wholly comparable because of different sources and methods, but the data are adequate to show main trends over the period.

Source: U. S. Department of Commerce, Office of Business Economics.

Of the increase of $13.7 billion in the value of foreign investments and assets in the United States from 1946 through 1955, about $8.1 billion consisted of liquid dollar assets. Over 80 percent of the gain in liquid dollars was in foreign official accounts and in the accounts of international institutions, and the remainder represented to a considerable extent the rebuilding of private working balances required for the larger volume of foreign trade.

The accumulation of these dollar reserves reflects the overall transactions of the United States with foreign countries as measured in the balance of payments statements. Over the 1946–55 period foreign countries received very large amounts of dollars from the United States through massive aid programs, various United States Government expenditures abroad, and the increased imports required by the expanding United States economy. As a group, they used part of these dollar receipts to add to their reserves rather than increase their purchases from the United States. The growth of these foreign assets in the United States is in sharp contrast to the growth of United States foreign investments, which have resulted primarily from long-term private and Government programs to develop additional production abroad.

United States Investments Abroad

The great postwar expansion of United States enterprise abroad through foreign branches and subsidiaries, with the total investment now reaching nearly three times the investment at the end of the war, has been one of the most dynamic aspects of postwar international economic relationships. As

Annual Additions to U. S. Direct Investments Abroad, by Industry

MILLIONS OF DOLLARS
2,000 —

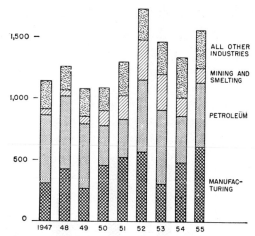

U. S. Department of Commerce, Office of Business Economics　　56-30-8

these enterprises have gone into production they have greatly augmented the domestic output, income, and government revenues of foreign countries. They have enabled foreign countries to increase their foreign trade and domestic consumption, and have become a major source of supply for the raw materials which are a prerequisite of expansion in the United States and abroad.

Through the postwar years, as shown in the first two charts, there have been shifts in investment among areas and industries, and after reaching a peak in 1952 there appeared to be a tendency for the total outflow of capital to decline or level off. In 1955, however, there was a definite upward turn, spurred by increased activity in manufacturing and petroleum particularly, and extending to a large number of countries. Information available up to now for 1956 indicates an even greater rate of expansion of United States enterprises abroad this year.

Western Europe investments higher

Mounting industrial output in Western Europe since 1952 has been accompanied by an accelerated pace of United States investments in the area, both in direct investments, which increased by a record $350 million in 1955, and through the purchase of securities of leading European corporations.

European affiliates of United States petroleum companies added nearly $100 million to their investment in 1955. Petroleum investments rose in nearly all countries in the area, notably in the United Kingdom and France.

Manufacturing investments in Europe rose by nearly $200 million, mainly through the reinvestment of earnings. The United Kingdom accounted for over half of the increase, and France and Germany also showed considerable gains.

Latin American investments show large gain

Direct investments in Latin America of more than $300 million in 1955 were the largest since 1952. Moreover, this enlarged rate of investment has continued in 1956.

Much of the 1955 increase resulted from greatly expanded manufacturing investments, with petroleum and mining also up substantially. In the case of petroleum, in this and other areas, the available data greatly understate the total capital expenditures by the companies since they exclude exploration and development expenses charged to earnings, as well as expenditures out of current depreciation charges. This is especially important for Latin America in recent years when exploration activities have widened and much actual expansion is financed out of depreciation charges against the large investment made in the early postwar years.

Petroleum investments in 1955 were especially large in Venezuela and will expand greatly in the near future when new areas are opened to development. Large investments attributed to Panama are a special case, reflecting primarily the expansion of tanker fleets registered under the Panamanian flag. In Brazil a moderate addition was made to investments in distributing facilities following the repayment in 1954 of large amounts owing to the companies for earlier deliveries of petroleum.

United States investments in manufacturing in Latin America have been expanding faster than those in any other industry since 1953. In 1955 about $125 million was added to these investments, including a record amount of over $50 million in Mexico and sizable amounts in Brazil, Argentina, Colombia, and Venezuela. As in other recent years, a large part of the investment in Argentina and Brazil was financed by the use of undistributed earnings of long-established subsidiary companies.

After rising to a peak in 1952–53, the amount of net addition to mining facilities in Latin America fell off sharply, not only because of the limited expansion of older properties but also because of rapid amortization of new properties producing iron ore and other metals and minerals. Beginning in 1955, however, new expansion plans were developed in Peru, Mexico, and Chile, and a number of large projects in these and other countries are scheduled to be carried out in the next few years.

New investment survey

Further information on United States investments in Latin America in 1955, including many types of data never before available, such as total output, employment, expenditures on plant and equipment, etc., is being compiled by the

Growth of U. S. Manufacturing Investments Abroad, by Major Products *

Value at end of year

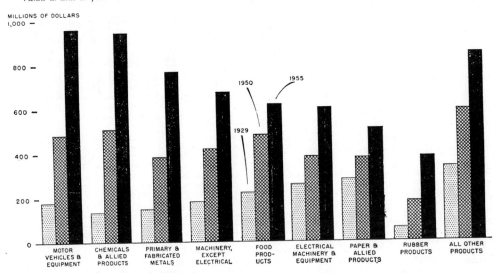

*Excludes manufacturing operations of petroleum and mining companies

U. S. Department of Commerce, Office of Business Economics

Office of Business Economics on the basis of a recent comprehensive survey of companies in the area. The results of this analysis are scheduled for publication in the SURVEY OF CURRENT BUSINESS for January 1957.

Canada leads other areas

Direct investments in Canada increased in 1955 by a greater amount than those in any other area, although there was a moderate decline from the rate of increase in 1954, mainly in the mining and petroleum industries. Mining investments were very large in the 1952–54 period when new sources of iron ore were being developed, and although since declining from that peak they continue to be very substantial. The moderate decline from the record high of 1954 in petroleum investments will probably be reversed in 1956 because of the large amounts required to finance new pipelines as well as the continued outlays for exploration and development. Manufacturing investments underwent a rapid expansion in Canada, as in other areas in 1955, financed mainly by the reinvestment of earnings.

It should be noted that United States investments in certain Canadian investment funds, which were previously included in direct investments, have been shifted from this category and are combined with other portfolio investments.

There was a considerable rise in 1955 in direct investments in a number of other countries, notably in Australia, the Union of South Africa, Egypt, Indonesia, Iran, and Japan. In all of these countries the most important factor was an increase in petroleum investments, reflecting the expansion of refineries and producing and distributing facilities. In Australia and the Union of South Africa there was also a substantial increase in manufacturing investments.

Autos and chemicals top manufacturing

A special analysis of the $2.5 billion increase in manufacturing investments since 1950 shows that the largest growth has been in the manufacture of motor vehicles and chemicals. (See table 6.) Investments in motor vehicles expanded at an average rate of about $100 million annually, following the overall course of manufacturing investments with a marked decline in 1953 followed by a sharp rise in 1954 and 1955. These investments were widely spread geographically.

Enterprises producing chemicals have been developed at only a slightly lower rate but with much greater concentration in the Western Hemisphere, constituting by far the largest component of manufacturing investments in Latin America. Important investments in the production of various chemicals have also been made by petroleum companies, but separate data on this part of their investment are not available.

The large investment in primary and fabricated metals includes the production of aluminum, accounting for the heavy concentration in Canada, and a great number of implements and other metal products. Investments in the production of electrical and other machinery, are also growing at a rapid rate, especially in Canada and Europe. The rate of growth of rubber manufactures has been outstanding since 1950, especially in Latin America, and these investments are comparatively widespread.

Production of paper and allied products is highly concentrated in Canada where the necessary raw materials are easily accessible, and the rate of growth has been relatively slow. Investments in food products have also developed slowly, partly reflecting the difficulties of meatpacking plants in Latin America where this industry is comparatively large.

392868°—56——3

Other private investments reach $10 billion

Although direct private investments have been the principal form of private investment since the war, other investments in the form of holdings of foreign securities or banking and commercial claims of various maturities have risen by $3.5 billion since 1946, to a total value of nearly $10 billion at the end of 1955.

Earnings on International Investments

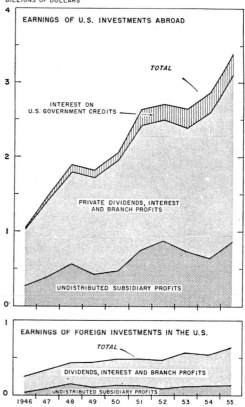

BILLIONS OF DOLLARS

EARNINGS OF U.S. INVESTMENTS ABROAD

TOTAL

INTEREST ON U.S. GOVERNMENT CREDITS

PRIVATE DIVIDENDS, INTEREST AND BRANCH PROFITS

UNDISTRIBUTED SUBSIDIARY PROFITS

EARNINGS OF FOREIGN INVESTMENTS IN THE U.S.

TOTAL

DIVIDENDS, INTEREST AND BRANCH PROFITS

UNDISTRIBUTED SUBSIDIARY PROFITS

1946 47 48 49 50 51 52 53 54 55

U. S. Department of Commerce, Office of Business Economics   56-30-8

United States holdings of foreign dollar bonds increased from $1.5 billion at the end of 1946 to $2.6 billion at the end of 1955. Purchases by Americans of new issues of foreign dollar bonds totaled $2.4 billion from 1946 through 1955 redemptions and amortizations totaled $1.4 billion, and there has been some improvement in market values. Of the new issues, $1.4 billion were by Canada, nearly $600 million were by the International Bank, and about $200 million were by Israel. In the past two years Belgium, Cuba, Norway, Australia and the Union of South Africa have successfully floated loans here.

At the end of 1946 foreign currency securities were about evenly divided between stocks and bonds, but of the $2.9

billion held at the end of 1955 nearly $2.5 billion were corporate stocks. Over 90 percent of the holdings of foreign-currency bonds were Canadian obligations. These holdings were expanded until 1950, but large amounts were liquidated in the following years. By the latter part of 1955 these sales were diminishing, partly because holdings had by then been greatly reduced and also as a result of comparative trends in interest and exchange rates which made liquidation less attractive.

In contrast to this movement, United States investors began to purchase substantial amounts of Canadian corporate stocks in 1954, and have continued to do so through the early months of 1956. An important factor in this development was the formation of special types of investment funds in Canada which offered certain tax advantages to United States investors. The value of United States holdings of Canadian corporate stocks has also increased by some $500 million since 1953 through price appreciation.

United States investments in European corporate stocks have also increased rapidly since 1953. Net purchases totaled about $100 million in 1954, about $70 million in 1955, and $25 million in the first five months of 1956. Over this period net purchases were $77 million from the United Kingdom and $132 million from the Netherlands. European stocks have risen sharply in market value since 1953, partly because of the intensified demand from the United States for selected issues.

United States banks and commercial concerns have an important role in financing United States exports and providing financial assistance to foreign countries through short- and medium-term credits At the end of 1955 the amount of such private claims outstanding as reported to the Treasury was $2.8 billion (see table 11). The increase during 1954 and 1955 was $1.1 billion, with most of the increase coming in 1954. In 1955 the rise of over $400 million resulted mainly from the increasing trade debt of Turkey, Colombia, Venezuela, and some countries in Asia, together with increased investments of short-term bank funds in Germany, Canada, and Mexico and medium-term bank loans to Cuba, Norway, and some Asiatic countries. Offsetting these increases in claims were a sharp drop in holdings of sterling in the United Kingdom and large debt repayments by France and Brazil. In the case of Brazil the reduction in short-term debt was largely financed by drawing on medium-term bank loans.

The increase in United States Government credits and claims against foreign countries in 1955 was concentrated in the short-term category. A detailed discussion of these transactions is contained in the SURVEY OF CURRENT BUSINESS for April 1956. In brief, the increase in short-term claims resulted mainly from sales of agricultural commodities for foreign currencies in the amount of over $550 million, out of which the United States Government used over $200 million for grants, credits and expenditures abroad. For the second successive year repayments on outstanding long-term credits exceeded new disbursements. However, the debt reduction was largely in Western Europe and there were increases in loans outstanding to many countries in other areas.

Foreign Investments in the United States

The flow of foreign capital to the United States for long-term investments in corporate securities and foreign-controlled enterprises has been on the rise since 1952, and reached a postwar high of $344 million in 1955.

Table 2.—International Investment Position of the United States, by Area, 1954–55

[Millions of dollars]

	Total		Western Europe		Western European dependencies		Other Europe		Canada		Latin-American Republics		Other foreign countries		International institutions	
	1954 r	1955 p	1954 r	1955 p	1954 r	1955 p	1954 r	1955 p	1954 r	1955 p	1954 r	1955 p	1954 r	1955 p	1954 r	1955 p
United States investments abroad, total	42,209	44,888	14,407	14,953	682	710	331	325	9,754	10,655	8,658	9,237	4,428	5,089	3,949	3,919
Private investments	26,589	28,994	4,843	5,362	647	680	15	14	9,739	10,648	7,698	8,224	3,143	3,590	504	476
Long-term	24,365	26,605	4,127	4,623	621	658	14	13	9,513	10,344	6,735	7,293	2,851	3,198	504	476
Direct[1]	17,626	19,185	2,639	2,986	599	636			5,871	6,464	6,244	6,556	2,273	2,543		
Foreign dollar bonds	2,720	2,646	160	194			3	2	1,604	1,476	143	148	306	350	504	476
Other foreign securities	2,406	2,900	465	598					1,828	2,153	33	39	80	110		
Other	1,613	1,874	863	845	22	22	11	11	210	251	315	550	192	195		
Short-term	2,224	2,389	716	739	26	22	1	1	226	304	963	931	292	392		
Deposits	502	447	296	229	7	7	1		111	127	57	53	30	31		
Other	1,722	1,942	420	510	19	15		1	115	177	906	878	262	361		
United States Government credits and claims	15,620	15,894	9,564	9,591	35	30	316	311	15	7	960	1,013	1,285	1,499	3,445	3,443
Long-term	15,208	15,162	9,311	9,128	33	29	308	303	14	5	954	983	1,143	1,271	3,445	3,443
Short-term	412	732	253	463	2	1	8	8	1	2	6	30	142	228		
Foreign assets and investments in the United States, total	26,804	29,575	13,746	15,643	476	500	60	65	4,096	4,137	3,026	3,289	2,402	2,850	2,160	2,252
Long-term investments	10,947	12,606	7,257	8,468	227	263	34	39	2,350	2,601	813	924	236	267	30	44
Direct	3,995	4,274	2,526	2,707	19	19			1,266	1,365	136	134	48	49		
Corporate stocks	5,254	6,575	3,660	4,643	118	154	17	22	935	1,091	417	524	95	123	12	18
Corporate, State and municipal bonds	212	259	133	165	6	6			9	6	40	48	6	8	18	26
Other	1,486	1,498	938	953	84	84	17	17	140	139	220	218	87	87		
Short-term assets and United States Government obligations	15,857	16,969	6,489	7,175	249	237	26	26	1,746	1,536	2,213	2,365	2,166	2,583	2,130	2,208
Private obligations	8,525	8,471	3,561	3,359	210	198	19	19	721	687	1,941	2,023	1,978	2,078	95	107
Deposits	7,437	7,402	2,856	2,657	195	181	17	18	654	623	1,829	1,885	1,798	1,939	88	99
Other	1,088	1,069	705	702	15	17	2	1	67	64	112	138	180	139	7	8
United States Government obligations	7,332	8,498	2,928	3,816	39	39	7	7	1,025	849	272	342	188	505	2,035	2,101
Long-term	1,107	1,636	476	623	23	23	5	5	7	351	215	264	21	43	360	327
Short-term	2 6,225	2 6,862	2,452	3,193	16	16	2	2	1,018	498	57	78	167	462	1,675	1,774

r Revised.   p Preliminary.
1. Direct investments at book value, securities at market value, other investments and claims at stated value.
2. Includes United States currency not distributed by area as follows: 1954, $838 million; 1955, $839 million.

NOTE.—For earlier years see the SURVEY OF CURRENT BUSINESS, May 1954 and August 1955.

Source: U. S. Department of Commerce, Office of Business Economics.

Most of the capital inflow has been for the purchase of publicly traded stock in United States corporations, amounting to $135 million in 1954, $127 million in 1955, and about $75 million in the first 5 months of 1956. Information is not available as to the actual purchasers of these securities, since the basic reports identify only the country from which the orders originate. Thus, reported net purchases in 1955 were $112 million for Switzerland and $32 million for the United Kingdom, but some of these transactions were probably for the account of investors residing in other coun-

tries. Canadian investors were net sellers of United States corporate stocks in 1954 and 1955, presumably in order to place their funds in the very active Canadian market.

In addition to increases from capital inflows, the rising market value of United States stocks added some $1.1 billion to foreign holdings. At the end of 1955 such holdings had a record value of $6.6 billion; according to earlier studies by the Office of Business Economics, some 85 percent of foreign holdings are listed on the New York Stock Exchange, accounting for about 2.7 percent of the market

Table 3.—Value of Direct Investments Abroad, by Selected Countries, 1950–55, and Major Industries, 1954–55

[Millions of dollars]

Countries	1950	1951	1952	1953 r	1954 r Total	Mining and smelting	Petroleum	Manufacturing	Public utilities	Trade	Other industries	1955 p Total	Mining and smelting	Petroleum	Manufacturing	Public utilities	Trade	Other industries
All areas, total	11,788	13,089	14,819	16,286	17,626	2,078	5,270	5,711	1,547	1,166	1,855	19,185	2,195	5,792	6,322	1,588	1,289	2,000
Canada	3,579	3,972	4,593	5,242	5,871	792	1,152	2,592	302	358	676	6,464	862	1,329	2,834	318	384	738
Latin American Republics, total	4,735	5,176	5,758	6,034	6,244	1,001	1,689	1,240	1,120	405	789	6,556	1,022	1,779	1,366	1,132	440	817
Argentina	356	365	393	406	424	(1)	(1)	218	69	46	25	446	(1)	(1)	230	69	45	28
Bolivia	11	11	11	10	10	3		3	(1)	1	3	11	3	4	(1)	1	3	(1)
Brazil	644	803	1,013	1,017	1,049	(1)	176	533	150	(1)	(1)	1,107	(1)	186	563	158	137	(1)
Chile	540	583	623	657	633	407		35	(1)	10	7	636	404	(1)	37	(1)	11	8
Colombia	193	r205	r232	r233	260	(1)		108	51	35	36	272	(1)	105	60	35	40	(1)
Costa Rica	60	61	61	62	60		6	(1)	11	(1)	(1)	61	6	(1)	11	(1)	(1)
Cuba	642	672	686	686	713		(1)	55	303	35	288	723	(1)	54	305	31	293
Dominican Republic	106	123	123	120	136	5	(1)	11	17		96	134	6	13	5	(1)	103
Ecuador	14	14	14	17	20	(1)	(1)	6	2	8	25	(1)	6	2	8
El Salvador	19	20	21	22	23	(1)	5	17	1	-1	21	(1)	6	17	1	-1
Guatemala	106	106	108	102	100	(1)	4	(1)	73	(1)	(1)	103	(1)	6	73	(1)	(1)
Haiti	13	14	15	15	16	(2)	(1)	(1)	3	(1)	9	18	(2)	3	(1)	9
Honduras	62	78	81	98	101	(1)	(1)	12	(1)	(1)	101	(1)	12	(1)	(1)
Mexico	414	471	490	514	524	142	12	217	90	45	18	599	153	13	269	91	55	18
Panama	348	373	383	407	436		219	4	146	18	49	479	251	5	151	17	52
Peru	145	r203	r212	r287	283	171	(1)	19	22	26	301	193	(1)	23	27	30
Uruguay	56	67	71	74	73	3	36	2	10	22	74	4	36	2	10	22
Venezuela	993	r992	r1,174	r1,291	1,366	(1)	1,012	46	15	45	(1)	1,424	(1)	1,056	59	18	55	(1)
Other countries	13	15	17	16	18	(1)	7	7	1	1	1	19	(1)	7	7	1	1	(1)
Western Europe, total	1,720	1,979	2,145	2,369	2,639	35	668	1,451	30	253	202	2,986	40	761	1,630	35	292	229
Austria	13	16	18	20	24	(1)	(1)	6	(1)	2	3	28	(1)	6	(1)	3	3
Belgium	65	87	95	108	116		27	71	(1)	15	3	133	(2)	32	76	(2)	21	3
Denmark	32	37	38	36	39		24	10	(1)	4	(1)	39	24	10	(1)	5	(1)
Finland	9	8	9	10	15		11	(1)	(1)	3	1	18	12	(1)	(1)	3	2
France	217	249	276	304	334	5	96	189	5	12	27	378	6	113	212	5	17	26
Germany	204	234	251	276	293	(1)	69	167	(1)	25	27	330	(1)	74	188	(1)	34	28
Italy	63	72	80	95	126		64	41	1	3	18	154	80	45	1	4	24
Netherlands	84	100	108	125	140	(1)	78	34	(1)	20	9	159	(1)	86	37	(1)	24	11
Norway	24	28	33	37	40	(1)	10	11	2	2	(1)	43	(1)	10	12	2	2	(1)
Portugal	16	19	21	23	23	1	(1)	(1)	2	7	1	26	1	(1)	(1)	2	6	1
Spain	31	36	40	45	50	(1)	15	20	(1)	4	9	56	(1)	18	21	(1)	4	11
Sweden	58	65	70	74	83		32	40	(1)	6	(1)	95	36	44	(1)	7	(1)
Switzerland	25	28	28	31	37		10	15	(2)	8	4	40	10	18	(2)	9	4
United Kingdom	847	961	1,038	1,131	1,257	3	184	835	12	132	92	1,420	3	216	941	16	141	103
Other countries	33	39	41	54	63	(2)	37	11	1	10	3	68	(2)	35	16	1	12	3
Western European dependencies, total	435	446	468	r601	599	103	411	15	20	32	18	636	110	429	15	25	38	19
Western Hemisphere, total	131	139	158	178	172	61	73	(1)	17	15	(1)	181	61	74	(1)	21	18	(1)
Africa:																		
British	41	54	66	77	45	15	23	(1)	(1)	5	(1)	56	21	27	(1)	(1)	6	(1)
French	31	32	36	37	44	(1)	36	(1)	2	4	(1)	45	(1)	38	(1)	2	4	(1)
Other European	12	12	14	16	19	(1)	(1)	3	(1)	(1)	1	21	(1)	(1)	3	(1)	(1)	1
Other areas:																		
British	190	177	154	r248	272	24	221	11	1	6	10	280	26	224	11	1	7	10
Other European	30	32	39	45	47		(1)		(1)	(1)		54	(1)		(1)	(1)	
Other countries, total	1,318	1,516	1,854	r2,040	2,273	147	1,350	413	75	117	171	2,543	161	1,495	476	78	135	197
Africa:																		
Egypt	39	44	46	46	54		33	12	(1)	4	(1)	72		49	13	(1)	4	(1)
Liberia	82	104	140	186	230	(1)	178	9	(1)	9	(1)	261	(1)	205		9	(1)	(1)
Union of South Africa	140	157	194	212	216	69	44	73	(1)	23	(1)	257	73	60	87	(1)	29	(1)
Other countries	7	7	8	10	54	39	(1)	(2)	(1)	(1)	62	43	(1)	(2)	(1)	(1)
Other areas:																		
Australia	201	256	310	326	393	20	201	(1)	21	17	494	25	237	(1)	26	21
India	38	49	63	68	92	(2)	27	2	10	(1)	96	(2)	30	2	10	(1)
Indonesia	58	72	74	88	65	(1)	19	(1)	3	(1)	86	(1)	21	(1)	3	(1)
Japan	19	45	69	92	106	(1)	10	1	2	(1)	126	(1)	13	1	4	(1)
New Zealand	25	31	37	34	40	(1)	(1)	15	(1)	9	1	42	(1)	(1)	18	(1)	9	1
Philippine Republic	149	163	178	188	217	(1)	29	58	37	27	226	(1)	31	61	39	28
Other countries	560	588	734	r791	807	(1)	736	27	3	8	(1)	820	(1)	748	27	3	(1)

NOTE.—The following area changes apply to all tables: Through 1953, Northern and Southern Rhodesia and Nyasaland are included in British dependencies in Africa; in 1954 and 1955 they are included in other countries in Africa.

r Revised.   p Preliminary.   1. Included in total.   2. Less than $500,000.

Source: U. S. Department of Commerce, Office of Business Economics.

value of stocks listed on that Exchange at the end of 1955. The proportion of foreign holdings of these stocks is about the same now as in 1949 and lower than the proportion in 1946. Foreign holdings of the large aggregate of corporate stocks not listed on the New York Stock Exchange are less than 1 percent.

European investors have also been purchasing growing amounts of United States corporate bonds since 1952, including about $35 million of new corporate bonds sold in Switzerland.

Canadian and European investors have also been adding to their direct investments in United States enterprises, both through the expansion of old-established firms and establishment or purchase of additional enterprises. This expansion is financed not only by capital inflows and reinvested earnings but also by loans obtained in the United States.

Foreign holdings of liquid dollar assets in the United States increased by $1.1 billion in 1955, reflecting the results of overall foreign transactions with the United States as given in the balance of payments statements.[1] Although gold transactions with the United States were minor in 1955, foreign countries added over $600 million to their official reserves, mainly out of current gold production.

The gain in foreign dollar holdings cannot be exactly divided between official and other accounts, but the bulk of the increase in 1955, as in 1953 and 1954, was in official accounts.

1. See the SURVEY OF CURRENT BUSINESS for June 1956, p. 21 ff.

Table 4.—Direct Investment Capital Flows and Undistributed Earnings, by Specified Countries and Industries, 1954–55

[Millions of dollars]

| | Net capital outflow | | | | | | | | | | Undistributed subsidiary earnings | | | | | | | | | |
| | 1954 r | | | | | 1955 p | | | | | 1954 r | | | | | 1955 p | | | | |
	Total	Mining and smelting	Petroleum	Manufacturing	Other industries	Total	Mining and smelting	Petroleum	Manufacturing	Other industries	Total	Mining and smelting	Petroleum	Manufacturing	Other industries	Total	Mining and smelting	Petroleum	Manufacturing	Other industries
All areas, total	664	109	277	111	168	679	43	320	160	156	644	29	94	376	145	868	74	200	423	171
Canada	385	85	190	51	59	279	32	132	54	61	232	21	25	123	63	298	38	40	158	61
Latin American Republics, total	88	17	−22	24	68	141	6	49	60	26	125	−15	29	69	41	175	15	44	67	49
Argentina	−5	(¹)	(¹)	(²)	−5	8	(¹)	(¹)	(¹)	3	22	(¹)	(¹)	18	4	15	(¹)	(¹)	10	5
Brazil	−6	(¹)	−34	25	−3	22	(¹)	(¹)	7	6	40	(¹)	4	28	9	36	(¹)	3	25	8
Chile	−28	−38	(¹)	1	9	−2	−3	(¹)	1	1	4	(²)	(¹)	(²)	4	4	(¹)	(¹)	1	2
Colombia	33	(¹)	5	7	21	14	(¹)	6	4	4	−3	(¹)	−9	4	2	1	(¹)	−5	4	2
Costa Rica	−3		1	(¹)	−4	(²)		(²)	(¹)	(²)	1		(²)	(¹)	(²)	(²)		(²)	(¹)	(²)
Cuba	27	(¹)	2	−3	28	2	(¹)	(¹)	7	−1	1	(¹)	1	1	−1	8	(¹)	3	1	4
Dominican Republic	10	5	(¹)		6	−4	2	(¹)	(¹)	1	5		(¹)	(²)	4	3		(¹)	(²)	3
Honduras	−1	(¹)	(¹)	(¹)	−1	−2	(¹)	(¹)	(¹)	−2	2	(¹)	(¹)	1	2	1	(¹)	(¹)	1	1
Mexico	14	18	1	−9	3	43	5	(²)	33	5	−4	−20	1	12	3	32	7	1	19	6
Panama	13		2	(²)	11	20		17	1	2	15		7	(²)	8	24		15	(²)	8
Peru	−13	−1	(¹)	1	−12	4	19	(¹)	4	−19	8	2	(¹)	1	5	14	4	(¹)	(²)	10
Uruguay	−2		−1	−2	(²)	−1		(²)	(²)	−1	1		(²)	−1	2	2		(²)	1	1
Venezuela	46	(¹)	7	5	34	27	(¹)	24	8	−5	29	(¹)	16	4	9	31	(¹)	20	5	7
Other countries	2	(²)	5	(²)	−3	9	(²)	8	1	(²)	3		1	1	1	3	(²)	1	(²)	2
Western Europe, total	50	(²)	20	21	9	129	(²)	53	36	41	198	5	36	134	24	218	5	40	144	30
Belgium	3		−4	5	1	7		1	(²)	6	5		2	3	(²)	9		4	5	(²)
France	5	(¹)	−1	1	6	11	(¹)	5	6	−1	25	(¹)	7	16	2	34	(¹)	12	18	4
Germany	−16	(¹)	−1	2	−17	23	(¹)	15	6	2	15	(¹)	3	10	2	13	(¹)	−10	15	8
Italy	24		12	5	6	21		15	2	5	8		3	3	2	7		1	3	3
Netherlands	6	(¹)	2	4	1	12	(¹)	5	1	5	8	(¹)	4	2	2	8	(¹)	3	2	2
Portugal	−2	(²)	(¹)	(²)	−2	2	(²)	(¹)	(²)	2	2		(¹)	(²)	2	1		(¹)	(²)	1
Spain	3	(¹)	(¹)	−1	3	3	(¹)	(¹)	(²)	3	2	(¹)	2	(²)	4	3	(¹)	1	(²)	3
Sweden	4		1	2	2	12		5	3	4	6		(²)	5	(²)	−1		−1	(²)	(²)
Switzerland	4		2	(²)	2	2		1	(²)	1	2		−1	2	(²)	2		−1	2	(²)
United Kingdom	14	(¹)	3	3	8	34	(¹)	6	14	13	112	(¹)	11	86	14	129	(¹)	25	92	11
Other countries	6	(¹)	8	(²)	−2	3	(¹)	(¹)	−5	4	14	(¹)	4	5	4	13	(¹)	4	5	5
Western European dependencies, total	−4	−5	−3	1	4	−3	−1	−3	−1	3	39	8	22	3	6	40	9	22	2	8
Western Hemisphere:																				
British	1	(¹)	(²)	(²)	1	4	(¹)	(¹)	3	(²)	6	(¹)	(²)			6	7	(¹)	−1		8
Other European	−18	(¹)	(¹)		−18	−7	(¹)	(¹)		−7	5	(¹)	(¹)			5	5	(¹)	(¹)		5
Africa:																				
British	−2		−2	(²)	(²)	3	1	1	(²)	(²)	8	4	4		1	8	5	3		(²)
French	4	(²)	4	(²)	(²)	−2	(²)	−1	(¹)	(²)	3		2		(²)	3		(¹)		(²)
Other European	1		(¹)	(²)	1	1		(²)	(²)	1	1	(¹)	(¹)	(²)	1	1	(¹)	(²)	(²)	1
Other areas:																				
British	7	(²)	(¹)	1	6	−9	1	(¹)	−1	−10	17	(²)	(¹)	2	14	16	(²)	(¹)	1	15
Other European	2		2			8		8			−1		−1			(²)		(²)		
Other countries, total	145	12	92	13	28	133	7	89	11	25	50	10	−18	47	12	137	7	55	52	23
Africa:																				
Egypt	8		6	2	(²)	15		14	(²)	1	1		(¹)	1	(²)	3		1	2	(¹)
Liberia	56	(¹)	(¹)		56	14	(¹)	(¹)		14	−11	(¹)	(¹)		−11	17	(¹)	(¹)		17
Union of South Africa	−13	9	−24	1	1	23	5	14	2	3	17	1	2	11	3	18	(¹)	3	12	4
Other countries	2	2	−1	(²)	1	5	1	3	(²)	1	2	2	1	−1	(²)	3	3	(²)	(¹)	(²)
Other areas:																				
Australia	32	(¹)	(¹)	5	27	62	(¹)	(¹)	(¹)	6	35	(¹)	(¹)	24	11	39	(¹)	(¹)	29	10
India	18		(¹)	(¹)	17	−1		(¹)	(¹)	1	6		(¹)	4	2	5		(¹)	2	3
Indonesia	−5		(¹)	(¹)	−5	7		(¹)	(¹)	7	−17		(¹)	(¹)	−17	14		(¹)	(¹)	14
Israel	7		(¹)	(¹)	7	1		(¹)	(¹)	1	(¹)		(¹)	(¹)	(²)	(¹)		(¹)	(¹)	(¹)
Japan	8		(¹)	(²)	9	13		(¹)	(¹)	13	5		(¹)	2	3	6		(¹)	3	5
New Zealand	4	(¹)	(¹)	1	3	−1	(¹)	(¹)	(²)	−1	2	(¹)	(¹)	(¹)	2	3	(¹)	(¹)	1	1
Philippine Republic	19	(¹)	(¹)	2	17	−4	(¹)	(¹)	(²)	−4	8	(¹)	(¹)	2	6	14	(¹)	(¹)	1	12
Other countries	8		8	(²)	(²)	−1	(¹)	(¹)	(¹)	−1	1	(¹)	(¹)	(²)	(²)	13	(¹)	13	(²)	(²)

r Revised.   p Preliminary.   1. Combined in "Other Industries."   2. Less than $500,000.   Source: U. S. Department of Commerce, Office of Business Economics.

Earnings on International Investments

Nearly all the increase of $500 million in the 1955 earnings of United States foreign investments was derived from the heightened activity of direct investment enterprises. Increased earnings were reported for all industries and areas.

Petroleum earnings advanced by $200 million to a record of over $1.2 billion. More than $100 million of the gain was in Latin America, mainly in Venezuela, and $50 million in Western Europe, largely in the United Kingdom. Output of crude petroleum by United States companies abroad rose 15 percent from 3.4 million barrels per day in 1954 to 3.9 million barrels per day in 1955. Refining capacity and other facilities, including plants for petrochemicals, have been greatly expanded in recent years in many countries.

Earnings of manufacturing enterprises were up by about $100 million in 1955 to over $800 million, also a record. Most of the increase was in Canada and Western Europe, reflecting high levels of economic activity. Most European countries showed increases, with the largest gains in Germany and the United Kingdom. Earnings of manufacturing companies in Latin America were somewhat lower than in 1954, however, partly as a result of depreciating exchange rates, and also because local currency earnings were down in Brazil as severely restricted imports slowed production.

Mining and smelting operations earned nearly $300 million in 1955, well above any previous year. Sharply rising prices for copper and other nonferrous metals were largely responsible for greater earnings by this industry in Canada, Chile, Mexico, Peru, and Africa. The beginning of full-scale shipments of iron ore also improved earnings.

All other industry groups also enlarged their earnings in 1955, but by much smaller amounts. Earnings of agricultural enterprises were still far below earlier years, reflecting the reduction in sugar and other prices and the effects of damage to many properties in Central America. Although earnings of the public utilities abroad remain low relative to the amount invested, they have advanced steadily since 1953 to new postwar highs.

Of the increase in direct-investment earnings in 1955, about $170 million was in foreign branches and a little over $300 million in foreign-incorporated subsidiary companies. It is not possible to calculate at present the extent to which branch earnings were retained abroad, but in the case of foreign subsidiary companies over two-thirds of the increase in earnings was reinvested in foreign countries. On an overall basis, reinvested earnings of subsidiaries accounted for over half of the net addition to direct foreign investments in 1955, and were a much larger proportion of the net addition in manufacturing and several other industries.

Table 5.—Net and Gross Movements [1] of Direct Investment Capital, by Areas and Industries, 1951–55

[Millions of dollars; net inflows (−)]

Industry and year	All areas			Canada			Latin American Republics			Western Europe			Western European dependencies			Other countries		
	Outflows	Inflows	Net	Outflows	Inflows	Net	Outflows	Inflows	Net	Outflows	Inflows	Net	Outflows	Inflows	Net	Outflows	Inflows	Net
All Industries:																		
1951	1,003	476	528	330	91	240	414	249	166	97	35	62	30	29	1	132	73	59
1952	1,381	531	850	518	98	420	469	192	277	68	76	−8	55	60	−5	272	106	166
1953	1,273	553	721	496	110	387	379	262	117	118	69	51	96	13	82	184	99	84
1954	1,262	598	664	504	119	385	309	221	88	166	116	50	28	32	−4	254	109	145
1955	1,247	568	679	464	185	279	332	191	141	204	75	129	28	30	−3	219	86	133
Agriculture:																		
1951	42	18	24		1	(²)	39	17	22					1	1	1		1
1952	12	19	−8	(²)	2	−1	11	15	−4				(²)	(²)	(²)	1	3	−2
1953	12	23	−11	(²)	(²)	(²)	10	21	−11				(²)	(²)	(²)	2	2	(²)
1954	27	11	16	1	(²)	1	23	10	13				(²)	(²)	(²)	3	(²)	3
1955	13	11	2	(²)	(²)	(²)	11	9	2				(²)	(²)	(²)	1	1	(²)
Mining and smelting:																		
1951	125	25	100	36	1	36	84	24	60	(²)		(²)	3	(²)	2	2	(²)	2
1952	299	21	278	135	(²)	134	140	20	120	(²)	(²)	(²)	18		18	6	(²)	6
1953	271	28	243	118	8	110	138	18	120	(²)	(²)	(²)	6	1	5	8	1	7
1954	178	69	109	89	4	85	74	57	17	(²)		(²)	1	6	−5	14	2	12
1955	116	73	43	57	25	32	45	39	6	(²)		(²)	3	4	−1	11	4	7
Petroleum:																		
1951	329	237	93	128	4	124	54	129	−75	50	13	37	23	25	−2	74	66	8
1952	526	279	248	124	2	122	112	81	32	27	51	−24	35	58	−23	228	86	142
1953	565	157	408	190	9	181	101	43	58	58	25	33	87	11	76	129	69	60
1954	549	272	277	215	25	190	58	80	−22	68	48	20	21	24	−3	186	94	92
1955	525	205	320	140	8	132	117	68	49	90	37	53	21	24	−3	157	68	89
Manufacturing:																		
1951	300	110	190	103	73	30	136	20	116	30	13	17	(²)	(²)	−2	31	2	29
1952	359	148	211	203	82	121	120	40	80	21	15	6	(²)	(²)	(²)	15	11	4
1953	196	250	−53	105	78	27	47	120	−73	28	35	−7	(²)	(²)	(²)	16	17	−1
1954	256	145	111	116	65	51	62	38	24	56	35	21	1	(²)	1	20	7	13
1955	355	195	160	188	134	54	87	27	60	61	25	36	(²)		1	20	9	11
Public utilities:																		
1951	25	33	−8	1	2	−1	24	31	−7	(²)	(²)	(²)	(²)			2		2
1952	31	7	23	1	(²)	1	27	7	21	(²)	(²)	(²)		(²)	(²)	2		2
1953	35	19	16	4	2	2	25	17	8	(²)	(²)	(²)	(²)	(²)	(²)	6	(²)	6
1954	30	13	17	7	7	(²)	22	7	15	1	(²)	1	(²)	(²)	(²)			
1955	33	19	14	10	(²)	9	19	18	1	4	(²)	4	(²)	(²)	(²)			
Trade:																		
1951	91	33	58	13	7	6	56	18	38	10	3	7	3	1	2	9	5	5
1952	65	47	17	9	7	2	39	28	11	9	7	2	2	1	1	6	8	−3
1953	75	47	29	32	7	25	24	27	−3	12	4	8	2	1	1	5	8	−3
1954	85	59	26	10	10	(²)	51	16	35	13	27	−14	3	1	2	9	5	4
1955	81	39	42	7	4	3	41	25	16	20	5	15	2	(²)	2	11	4	6
Other industries:																		
1951	91	21	70	48	4	44	21	10	11	8	6	1	(²)	(²)	(²)	14	1	14
1952	90	10	80	46	4	42	20	2	18	11	3	8	(²)	(²)	(−)	14	1	13
1953	120	29	89	47	6	41	34	16	18	21	5	16	1	(²)	1	17	2	14
1954	137	29	108	66	8	58	19	13	6	28	6	22	2	(²)	2	22	1	21
1955	124	26	98	62	13	49	12	4	8	29	7	22	1	(²)	1	19	1	18

1. The gross capital outflow shown in each area-industry cell of this table represents the sum of the net capital outflows to those foreign subsidiaries and branches for which net outflows were reported for each of the years covered. Conversely, the gross inflows shown for each cell represent the sum of the net inflows from those foreign subsidiaries and branches for which inflows were reported in each year. The totals for "all areas" are the sums of the figures shown in the area-industry cells. It should be noted that the gross totals, but not the net, would change if the compilations were done on a quarterly basis.

2. Less than $500,000.

Source: U. S. Department of Commerce, Office of Business Economics.

Table 6.—Value of Direct Investments in Manufacturing [1] Enterprises Abroad, 1950–55, by Major Products

[Millions of dollars; year-end]

	All areas total	Canada	Latin American Republics	United Kingdom	Other Western Europe	Other areas
All manufacturing:						
1950	3,831	1,897	780	542	390	222
1953	5,224	2,418	1,149	745	549	363
1955	6,322	2,834	1,366	942	688	491
Food products:						
1950	483	227	158	36	28	34
1953	553	246	186	44	35	42
1955	622	275	197	59	41	50
Paper and allied products:						
1950	378	367	5	1	4	1
1953	486	463	13	2	4	4
1955	511	477	22	3	4	5
Chemicals and allied products:						
1950	512	198	205	54	21	34
1953	768	275	326	84	30	53
1955	945	311	407	109	48	70
Rubber products:						
1950	182	59	60	21	10	32
1953	306	87	120	33	13	53
1955	386	102	156	41	16	71
Primary and fabricated metals:						
1950	385	249	22	66	44	4
1953	627	431	42	87	58	9
1955	771	526	52	109	70	14
Machinery (except electrical):						
1950	420	204	13	108	67	28
1953	567	231	29	155	109	43
1955	673	253	38	185	134	63
Electrical machinery, equipment and supplies:						
1950	387	141	79	79	74	14
1953	528	194	111	98	99	26
1955	602	228	128	106	112	28
Motor vehicles and equipment:						
1950	485	160	83	103	88	51
1953	709	207	130	144	129	99
1955	963	285	153	209	173	143
All other manufacturing:						
1950	599	292	155	74	54	24
1953	680	284	192	98	72	34
1955	848	377	213	121	90	47

1. Excludes manufacturing operations of petroleum and mining companies.

Source: U. S. Department of Commerce, Office of Business Economics.

Table 7.—Foreign Holdings of United States Corporate Stocks, by Selected Countries, 1946–55

[Market values; millions of dollars]

	Value, year-end				Change in 1955		Value year-end p 1955
	1946	1949	1953	1954 r	Net foreign purchases	Price change	
Total [1]	2,440	2,240	3,400	5,004	129	1,192	6,325
Western Europe [1]	1,690	1,490	2,350	3,485	146	837	4,468
Belgium	62	68	103	150	10	37	197
France	193	57	100	157	10	38	205
Netherlands	430	312	374	491	-22	112	581
Switzerland	505	522	903	1,353	112	331	1,796
United Kingdom	418	450	744	1,153	32	276	1,461
Other countries	82	81	126	181	4	43	228
Western European dependencies	50	52	80	118	6	29	154
Canada [1]	460	480	650	910	-51	207	1,066
Latin American Republics [1]	174	173	245	377	17	91	484
All other [1]	66	45	75	114	11	28	153

r Revised.   p Preliminary.

1. Holdings by United States citizens resident abroad, approximately as given for 1941 in the Treasury Census, TFR 300: Total, $250 million; Canada, $25 million; Western Europe, $175 million; Latin America, $40 million; other countries, $10 million, are included in table 2 but are excluded from this table.

NOTE.—Data for individual countries are derived from reports which do not identify the residence of beneficial owners. Thus, amounts reported for Switzerland may include securities purchased in the United States market through Swiss banks by residents of other countries.

Source: U. S. Department of Commerce, Office of Business Economics.

Table 8.—Earnings on International Investments, by Type, 1950–55

[Millions of dollars]

	1950	1951	1952	1953	1954 r	1955 p
Earnings on United States investments abroad, total	2,068	2,634	2,704	2,643	2,871	3,380
Direct investments, total	1,769	2,244	2,295	2,171	2,369	2,846
Dividends, interest, and branch profits	1,294	1,492	1,419	1,419	1,725	1,978
Undistributed profits of subsidiaries	475	752	876	753	644	868
Portfolio investments	190	192	205	216	230	260
Interest on United States Government credits	109	198	204	252	272	274
Earnings on foreign investments in the United States, total	478	481	472	571	511	641
Direct investments, total	281	255	234	306	300	331
Dividends, interest, and branch profits	148	129	152	185	175	202
Undistributed profits of subsidiaries	133	126	82	121	125	129
Portfolio investments	166	179	174	179	185	216
Interest on United States Government obligations	31	47	64	86	59	94

r Revised.   p Preliminary.

Source: U. S. Department of Commerce, Office of Business Economics.

Table 9.—Direct Investment Earnings by Industry, 1950–55

[Millions of dollars]

Industry	1950	1951	1952	1953	1954 r	1955 p
All industries	1,769	2,244	2,295	2,174	2,369	2,846
Agriculture	115	139	114	76	65	76
Mining and smelting	145	215	204	149	182	288
Petroleum	629	900	1,015	952	1,029	1,239
Manufacturing	623	690	644	676	722	821
Public utilities	60	59	64	63	74	86
Trade	116	142	145	133	148	180
Other industries	81	98	110	125	149	155

r Revised.   p Preliminary.

Source: U. S. Department of Commerce, Office of Business Economics.

Dividends and interest received from United States portfolio investments abroad continued their steady postwar rise in 1955, increasing by 15 percent to $260 million. The gains since the war reflect the mounting volume of United States holdings of foreign securities and bank loans outstanding. About half of the 1955 income is derived from Canada, and much smaller amounts from the United Kingdom, continental Europe, and Latin America.

Imports from direct investments

The shift of United States investment toward a much greater proportion of direct investments since the war has greatly increased the overall total of earnings, since producing enterprises all over the world during this period have experienced high output and earnings, but the shift has also directly and indirectly increased the supply of dollars to foreign countries.

A considerable part of the increased dollar supply has resulted from sales to the United States of goods produced by United States direct investments abroad. Out of $11.5 billion of nonmilitary merchandise imports in 1955, about $2.6 billion was produced by United States-owned companies. Similarly, of the $6.4 billion rise in United States imports from 1946 to 1955, about $1.2 billion can be accounted for by imports of goods produced by these companies. Thus, the increase of $1.4 billion in income remitted from direct investments over the period was to a large extent financed by the increase in direct dollar earnings of the enterprises.

A new computation of the proportion of total 1955 imports derived from direct-investment companies by product and area is given in table 12. The results show that nearly one-quarter of United States imports last year were produced by United States companies abroad. Such imports accounted for about one-third of total imports from Canada and Latin America and about one-tenth of total imports from the rest of the world. Comparisons with similar computations for earlier postwar years show that the overall percentage of United States imports produced by direct investment companies has risen sharply from about 16 percent in 1946. The proportion for Canada has not changed significantly over the period, but the percentage for Latin America has risen from about 22 percent in 1946, largely because much of the increase in imports over the period has been in such products as petroleum, copper, iron ore, and sugar, which are primarily imported from direct investment companies.

More than half of United States direct investments abroad are in manufacturing, public utilities, and service industries which contribute to the overall economic strength of many foreign countries by saving dollars through local production of necessary goods, and providing a capital base for further expansion.

Earnings by foreigners on their investments in the United States rose 20 percent in 1955 to a record $640 million, nearly twice the prewar high of 1929. Most of the increase resulted from higher dividend payments on both direct investments and rising portfolio holdings of United States

Table 10.—Direct Investment Earnings and Income [1] by Selected Countries, 1950–55, With Major Industries for 1955

[Millions of dollars]

Country	Earnings										Income									
						1955ᵖ										1955ᵖ				
	1950	1951	1952	1953	1954ʳ	Total	Mining and smelting	Petroleum	Manufacturing	Other industries	1950	1951	1952	1953	1954ʳ	Total	Mining and smelting	Petroleum	Manufacturing	Other industries
All areas, total	1,769	2,244	2,295	2,174	2,369	2,846	288	1,239	821	497	1,294	1,492	1,419	1,442	1,725	1,978	214	1,039	398	327
Canada	440	417	421	467	470	596	84	44	330	138	294	236	222	208	237	298	45	4	172	77
Latin American Republics, total	631	901	902	722	715	910	121	483	119	187	522	652	599	570	589	735	106	438	52	139
Argentina	18	29	30	20	31	26	(²)	(²)	14	12	6	11	12	11	9	11	(²)	(²)	4	7
Brazil	97	142	150	112	83	75	(²)	14	36	25	61	75	65	74	43	39	(²)	11	12	16
Chile	41	57	54	34	41	84	73	(²)	4	7	41	54	51	26	37	80	72	(²)	3	5
Colombia	16	15	20	13	15	24	(²)	2	8	14	10	12	13	12	18	23	(²)	7	4	12
Costa Rica	13	12	14	12	11	11		(²)	(²)	11	13	11	14	12	12	10		(²)	(²)	10
Cuba	59	64	53	30	35	45	(²)	3	6	36	43	49	44	28	33	37	(²)	1	5	31
Dominican Republic	17	31	21	8	9	9	(²)	(²)	1	8	14	25	14	4	4	6	(²)	(²)	(²)	6
Guatemala	11	8	4	6	1	5	(²)	(²)	(²)	5	10	7	3	6	(³)	4	(²)	(²)	(²)	4
Honduras	16	18	16	17	9	4	(²)	(²)	(²)	4	15	16	15	16	7	3	(²)	(²)	(²)	3
Mexico	44	64	61	47	45	67	22	1	30	14	29	31	32	30	49	35	15	(³)	11	9
Panama	30	107	101	49	43	49		21	1	27	18	37	43	19	28	25		6	(²)	19
Peru	21	36	31	21	29	41	20	(²)	4	17	15	33	25	22	20	26	16	(²)	3	7
Uruguay	6	11	7	9	5	6		1	2	3	4	6	4	3	3	4		(²)	1	3
Venezuela	232	297	329	334	346	452	(²)	426	10	16	236	278	256	300	318	421	(²)	406	6	9
Other countries	10	10	10	9	11	12	1	2	2	7	7	7	7	7	7	11	(³)	2	1	8
Western Europe, total	262	300	303	316	384	480	6	114	274	86	111	119	129	143	186	262	2	74	130	56
Belgium	12	15	15	14	16	20		5	12	3	6	6	6	7	11	10		1	6	3
France	29	40	36	31	41	53	(²)	16	31	6	6	10	10	11	17	20	(²)	4	13	3
Germany	27	21	18	22	27	51	(²)	4	35	12	3	4	4	4	13	38	(²)	15	20	3
Italy	9	14	10	9	13	13		1	8	4	2	5	7	6	5	6		(³)	5	1
Netherlands	14	14	13	15	14	15	(²)		5	4	5	5	5	5	6	8	(²)	2	2	4
Portugal	3	2	4	4	5	6	(³)	(²)	1	5	3	2	2	2	3	4	(³)	(²)	(²)	4
Spain	3	4	4	3	5	6	(²)	(²)	2	4	(²)	1	1	1	2	2	(²)	(²)	1	1
Sweden	7	7	7	9	10	6		−1	4	3	2	3	4	5	4	7		(³)	4	3
Switzerland	5	5	5	6	7	10		(³)	8	2	4	4	4	4	5	8		(³)	6	2
United Kingdom	142	164	176	187	226	278		75	163	40	73	74	78	90	113	149		50	71	28
Other countries	11	13	15	16	21	22	5	3	8	6	8	4	7	8	7	9	(²)	1	3	5
Western European dependencies, total	95	118	154	180	179	206	41	141	2	22	98	109	127	133	141	166	32	120	1	13
Western Hemisphere:																				
British	4	4	3	14	16	19	(²)	−2		21	(³)	(³)	1	5	10	11	(²)	−2		13
Other European	9	10	9	13	13	16	(²)	(²)		16	10	12	11	8	8	11	(²)	(²)		11
Africa:																				
British [4]	5	21	20	27	15	14	(²)	3		11	4	14	13	17	7	6	(²)	(²)		6
French	7	6	5	4	5	6		4	(³)	2	2	4	1	1	2	3		1	(³)	2
Other European	2	2	2	1	1	2	(³)	(²)	(³)	2	2	3	1	(³)	(³)	2	(²)	(²)	(³)	2
Other areas:																				
British	68	74	115	121	129	149	(²)	(²)	2	147	76	75	99	103	113	132	(²)	(²)	1	131
Other European	(²)	(²)	(²)	(²)	−1	(²)		(²)			(²)	(²)	(²)	(²)	(²)	(²)	(²)	(²)		
Other countries, total	340	508	515	489	621	654	36	457	96	65	269	376	343	387	572	517	29	402	44	42
Africa:																				
Egypt	4	5	8	5	6	3		(²)	(²)	3	2	2	5	5	6	1		(²)	(²)	1
Liberia	15	35	48	35	18	31	(²)	(²)		31	12	13	12	1	29	15	(²)	(²)		15
Union of South Africa	25	33	35	40	43	56	16	10	23	7	13	23	23	24	26	38	17	7	12	2
Other countries [3]	4	5	8	5	16	17	14	(³)	2	1	2	2	5	6	13	11	11	−2	1	1
Other areas:																				
Australia	27	36	33	51	60	64	(²)	(²)	48	16	11	11	8	13	25	24	(²)	(²)	19	5
India	13	14	15	12	18	16		(²)	3	13	12	10	9	11	(²)	(²)	1	10
Indonesia	36	38	29	32	26	37		(²)	(²)	37	27	34	4	32	43	23		(²)	1	22
Japan	2	8	4	8	15	20	(²)	5	15	2	3	3	4	10	12	(²)	2	10
Philippine Republic	39	35	33	29	34	37	(²)	(²)	8	29	28	26	27	24	26	23	(²)	6	17
Other countries	175	299	301	273	385	373	(²)	363	3	7	161	251	245	269	382	359	(²)	351	2	6

ʳ Revised.　　ᵖ Preliminary.
1. Income is the sum of dividends, interest, and branch profits; earnings is the sum of income and undistributed subsidiary earnings.
2. Combined with other industries.　　3. Less than $500,000.

4. Includes Northern and Southern Rhodesia and Nyasaland in 1950–53.
5. Includes Northern and Southern Rhodesia and Nyasaland in 1954–55.

Source: U. S. Department of Commerce, Office of Business Economics.

corporate stocks. Interest paid on United States Government obligations owned abroad also rose by over $30 million, as over $1 billion was added to holdings. The countries of Western Europe account for two-thirds of the earnings by foreigners, and Canada accounts for one-fourth.

Table 11.—Banking and Commercial Claims on Foreigners, by Selected Countries,[1] 1953–55

[Millions of dollars]

Countries	Dec. 31, 1953	Dec. 31, 1954				Dec. 31, 1955			
			Banking claims		Com-mer-cial claims[2]		Banking claims		Com-mer-cial claims[2]
	Total[2]	Total[2]	Short term	Medi-um term		Total[2]	Short term	Medi-um term	
Total	1,723	2,400	1,387	426	587	2,817	1,549	649	619
Western Europe, total	597	734	402	122	210	733	423	93	217
United Kingdom	124	250	173	(³)	77	172	109	3	60
France	177	125	14	96	15	30	12	---------	18
Turkey	26	56	41	(³)	15	113	78	15	20
Germany	39	82	70	1	11	110	88	2	20
Belgium	58	30	20	1	9	29	16	2	11
Norway	15	19	2	15	2	58	9	45	4
Canada	169	175	76	13	86	258	144	16	98
Latin America, total	686	1,094	727	170	197	1,306	703	410	193
Brazil	165	400	273	77	50	314	69	208	37
Colombia	80	137	107	12	18	172	143	10	19
Cuba	63	121	71	35	15	209	92	101	16
Mexico	123	161	116	18	27	206	154	24	28
Venezuela	62	88	63	4	21	173	105	46	22
Asia, total	189	300	143	94	63	410	233	101	76
Israel	43	38	11	20	7	42	10	25	7
Japan	42	139	50	74	15	149	103	30	16
Other Asia	104	123	82	(³)	41	219	120	46	53
All other countries, total	82	97	39	27	31	110	46	29	35

1. Includes major categories of claims as reported to the Treasury Department regularly by banks and commercial concerns, but does not include estimates for other types of claims included in table 2 as short-term or "other" long-term private investments.
2. Not including medium-term commercial claims as follows: 1953, $84 million; 1954, $102 million; 1955, $106 million.
3. Less than $500,000.

Source: U. S. Department of Commerce, Office of Business Economics.

Table 12.—United States Imports From United States Direct-Investment Companies Abroad, 1955, by Selected Commodities and Areas

[Millions of dollars]

Commodities	All areas		Canada		Latin American Republics		Other areas	
	Total im-ports	From U. S. com-panies abroad	Total im-ports	From U. S. com-panies abroad	Total im-ports	From U. S. com-panies abroad	Total im-ports	From U. S. com-panies abroad
Total imports	11,516	2,645	2,675	940	3,468	1,135	5,373	570
Imports of selected commodities, total	4,664	2,645	1,751	940	1,502	1,135	1,411	570
Crude oil	662	580	42	30	409	350	211	200
Newsprint	613	240	597	210	--------	--------	16	--------
Crude rubber	443	80	--------	--------	1	--------	442	80
Sugar	415	180	--------	--------	305	150	110	30
Copper	414	300	67	50	236	225	111	25
Refined oil products	368	230	(¹)	(¹)	147	90	221	140
Sawmill products	323	35	286	30	16	(¹)	21	5
Paper base stocks	319	250	276	250	--------	--------	43	--------
Nickel	183	160	144	135	17	15	22	10
Iron ore	177	150	79	70	78	70	20	10
Bananas	159	140	--------	--------	159	140	--------	--------
Aluminum, including bauxite	114	110	71	70	--------	--------	43	40
Lead	111	55	20	5	47	40	44	10
Fertilizers	110	40	51	20	24	20	35	(¹)
Zinc	86	30	46	10	27	15	13	5
Silver	71	25	19	5	34	20	18	(¹)
Asbestos	59	25	53	25	--------	--------	6	(¹)
Chrome	37	15	--------	--------	2	(¹)	35	15
Total imports and percent from U. S. companies	$11,516	23%	$2,675	35%	$3,468	33%	$5,373	11%
Selected commodities and percent from U. S. companies	4,664	58	1,751	54	1,502	76	1,411	40

1. Amount believed to be insignificant.   NOTE.—The amounts of imports of specified commodities attributable to United States direct-investment companies are estimates based on a number of sources, and are believed to be reasonably accurate, although they cannot be precise. The list of commodities includes only major commodities which are produced abroad by United States direct-investment companies for sale in the United States. For earlier data, see Survey of Current Business December 1953, p. 14.

Source: U. S. Department of Commerce, Office of Business Economics.

RECORD GROWTH
OF FOREIGN INVESTMENTS

Samuel Pizer
and
Frederick Cutler

by Samuel Pizer and Frederick Cutler☆

Record Growth of Foreign Investments

UNITED STATES private investments abroad rose by the unprecedented amount of nearly $4 billion in 1956 to a year-end total of $33 billion. American parent companies added $2.8 billion to their direct investments abroad as a result of the sustained rise in world demand for manufactures and raw materials and to provide for anticipated future demands. At the same time, United States financial institutions and other private investors supplied short- and long-term loans and credits totaling over $1 billion.

The increase in direct investments was more than $1 billion greater than the previous record increase in 1952, and the outflow of other private capital was somewhat larger than the previous highs in 1927 and 1928. The combined total exceeded any prewar year, even in real terms.

In the first half of this year the value of direct investments rose by about $1.5 billion, and extensive further investments are planned by the parent companies. Other types of private capital movements are subject to more fluctuation, but the continued relatively high yields on capital employed in foreign countries suggest that the net outflow of about $0.7 billion during the first half of this year will be well sustained in the second half. Thus, the 1957 expansion of foreign investments is expected to be of the same general magnitude as last year's high.

The remarkable rise in capital outflows from the United States in 1956 and 1957 has been a major source of financing for our record exports, which in turn have bolstered the United States economy. Some of the direct investment outflows covered the export of capital goods and other materials to United States-owned foreign enterprises. An unusually large part of the direct investments, however, together with the other private capital outflows, provided liquid dollar resources for the use of foreign countries. The increased capital outflow to foreign countries, despite the persistent demand for capital in the United States, suggests that investors regard foreign investments more favorably than in the earlier postwar period.

While private foreign investments increased last year, earnings also were growing, but at a much slower rate. Total earnings on private investments were $3.4 billion in 1956, compared with $3.1 billion in 1955. Direct investments earned $3.1 billion, an increase of nearly $300 million over the previous year. About one-third of the increase represented larger undistributed profits of foreign subsidiaries, which totaled $1 billion in 1956 and were a major factor in financing the expansion of the investments.

Direct Investments

Last year's upsurge of United States direct investments abroad extended into nearly every part of the free world, and across a broad range of industries. Most noteworthy, however, was the sharp rise in petroleum investments, which increased by $1.4 billion in the year to a total book value of $7.2 billion at the end of 1956. Manufacturing investments also increased by a record $740 million, while other industries such as mining and smelting and public utilities tended

NOTE: MR. PIZER AND MR. CUTLER ARE MEMBERS OF THE BALANCE OF PAYMENTS DIVISION, OFFICE OF BUSINESS ECONOMICS.

upward from their relatively slow rate of growth in the past few years.

The figures given here for increases in book values, which are the sums of net capital outflows, undistributed subsidiary earnings, and relatively minor accounting adjustments, fall considerably short of the total gross capital expenditures being carried out by United States companies abroad. Such expenditures would consist of outlays for plant and equipment, increases in inventories, and exploration and development expenses. A substantial part of these outlays is financed out of charges against the income of the foreign enterprises, primarily representing depreciation allowances or development expenditures which are accounted for as operating costs. Neither these amounts, nor expenditures financed by borrowing or equity financing in foreign capital markets, are counted as part of the increase in book values. Moreover, book valuations themselves are in present conditions much lower than alternative valuations of the foreign properties, such as replacement cost or market values, where these can be determined.

Data on gross investments have been compiled for Latin America for the year 1955 on the basis of a special survey covering that area,[1] but similar data for all countries would require a world-wide survey.

1. *Survey of Current Business,* January 1957, "The Role of United States Investments in the Latin American Economy."

Annual Additions to U. S. Direct Investments Abroad, by Industry

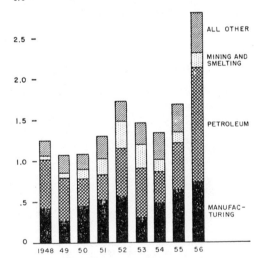

BILLIONS OF DOLLARS

ALL OTHER

MINING AND SMELTING

PETROLEUM

MANUFACTURING

1948 49 50 51 52 53 54 55 56

U. S. Department of Commerce, Office of Business Economics

57-24-5

Petroleum leads

As indicated above, about half of the entire increase in direct investments abroad in 1956 was accounted for by the petroleum industry. Acquisitions of new leases on potential producing areas, mainly in Venezuela, made up over one-fifth of the total amount added to these investments. The purchase of an existing foreign company from British owners required a cash payment of about $180 million, and the financing of gas and oil pipelines in Canada required about $100 million. In addition to these large expenditures, the companies were expanding refining and distribution facilities, modernizing producing properties to improve their recovery rates, and developing the utilization of byproducts of the industry. It should be noted that much of this investment is manufacturing in character rather than extractive.

Current activities of petroleum companies, including many companies which are entering the foreign field for the first time on a substantial scale, are primarily related to the projected increase in world consumption in the next few years. The search for new resources abroad is probably more intensive than ever before, and is encouraged both by the relatively high costs of discovery relative to potential output in the United States, and the growing recognition on the part of foreign countries that they require rapid development of their petroleum and other resources to facilitate their economic progress. Therefore, the outlook for this industry is a continuation of very large investments abroad.

In 1956 petroleum investments in Latin America expanded by about $425 million, with Venezuela accounting for about $350 million, largely because of payments for leases on new areas. This factor is also important in 1957. Elsewhere in Latin America sizable investments were made in petroleum refining and marketing facilities in Brazil and Cuba, and in producing properties in Peru. Additions to tanker fleets also raised the total for Panama, where these vessels are registered. Exploration activities in a number of Latin American countries also require substantial expenditures which are not reflected as capital investments. In 1956 such expenditures in the area may have approached $100 million.

Petroleum investments in Canada proceeded at a record rate in 1956, and in addition, holdings in that country were increased to the extent that properties of the petroleum company purchased from British investors are located in Canada. All branches of the oil and gas industry were being expanded, with particular emphasis on pipelines and the continued development and exploration of producing fields.

A considerable expansion of petroleum investments in Western Europe was also underway in 1956, mainly to increase refinery capacity, but also in the search for producing areas on the continent. The largest investments were made in the United Kingdom, not counting the existing company purchased from British holders, but sizable investments were in progress in Germany and France and many other countries in the area.

Table 1.—International Investment Position of the United States, by Area, 1955–56

[Millions of dollars]

	Total		Western Europe		Western European dependencies		Other Europe		Canada		Latin American Republics		Other foreign countries		International institutions	
	1955 r	1956 p	1955 r	1956 p	1955 r	1956 p	1955 r	1956 p	1955 r	1956 p	1955 r	1956 p	1955 r	1956 p	1955 r	1956 p
United States investments abroad, total	44,947	49,462	14,952	15,728	711	895	318	327	10,632	12,073	9,292	10,410	5,123	6,133	3,919	3,896
Private investments	29,054	32,977	5,360	6,103	681	874	14	29	10,625	12,070	8,282	9,306	3,616	4,175	476	420
Long-term	26,668	30,055	4,624	5,195	659	843	13	14	10,320	11,733	7,348	8,214	3,228	3,636	476	420
Direct	19,313	22,118	3,004	3,493	637	821			6,494	7,480	6,608	7,408	2,570	2,916		
Foreign dollar bonds	2,660	2,863	193	184			2	3	1,489	1,710	150	135	360	411	476	420
Other foreign securities 1	2,821	3,011	580	572					2,086	2,266	39	52	116	121		
Other	1,874	2,063	848	946	22	22	11	11	251	277	550	619	192	188		
Short-term	2,386	2,922	736	908	22	31	1	15	305	337	934	1,092	388	539		
Deposits	447	416	225	217	7	10	1	1	128	111	55	46	31	31		
Other	1,939	2,506	511	691	16	21		14	177	226	879	1,046	357	508		
United States Government credits and claims	15,893	16,485	9,592	9,625	30	21	304	298	7	3	1,010	1,104	1,507	1,958	3,443	3,476
Long-term	15,170	15,219	9,128	8,929	29	21	303	297	5	1	983	973	1,279	1,522	3,443	3,476
Short-term	723	1,266	464	696	1		1	1	2	2	27	131	228	436		
Foreign assets and investments in the United States, total	2 29,557	2 31,624	15,648	16,898	501	560	66	57	4,115	4,645	3,287	3,645	2,846	3,066	2,253	1,904
Long-term investments	12,587	13,356	8,472	9,034	264	275	39	39	2,579	2,712	924	965	265	277	44	54
Direct	4,255	4,540	2,711	2,873	20	20			1,343	1,475	134	134	47	47		
Corporate stocks	6,575	6,961	4,643	4,965	154	165	22	22	1,091	1,093	524	560	123	136	18	20
Corporate, State and municipal bonds	259	309	165	204	6	6			6	5	48	53	8	7	26	34
Other	1,498	1,537	953	992	84	84	17	17	139	139	218	218	87	87		
Short-term assets and United States Government obligations	16,970	18,268	7,176	7,864	237	285	27	18	1,536	1,933	2,363	2,680	2,581	2,789	2,209	1,850
Private obligations	8,471	9,503	3,360	3,624	108	231	20	11	686	1,031	2,024	2,300	2,076	2,209	107	97
Deposits	7,416	8,073	2,659	2,619	175	194	18	10	623	935	1,888	2,146	1,954	2,072	99	97
Other	1,055	1,430	701	1,005	23	37	2	1	63	96	136	154	122	137	8	
United States Government obligations	8,499	8,765	3,816	4,240	39	54	7	7	850	902	339	380	505	580	2,102	1,753
Long-term	1,636	1,501	623	504	23	23	5	5	351	281	264	260	43	31	327	397
Short-term	2 6,863	2 7,264	3,193	3,736	16	31	2	2	499	621	75	120	462	549	1,775	1,356

r Revised.   p Preliminary.

1. Consists primarily of securities payable in foreign currencies, but includes some dollar obligations, including participations in loans made by the International Bank for Reconstruction and Development.

2. Includes United States currency not distributed by area as follows: 1955, $841 million; 1956, $849 million.

Note.—For earlier years, see the SURVEY OF CURRENT BUSINESS, May 1954, August 1955, and August 1956.

Source: U. S. Department of Commerce, Office of Business Economics.

Table 2.—Value of Direct Investments Abroad, by Selected Countries and Years, and Major Industries, 1955–56

[Millions of dollars]

Line	Countries	1950	1952	1953	1954	1955 Total	1955 Mining and smelting	1955 Petroleum	1955 Manufacturing	1955 Public utilities	1955 Trade	1955 Other industries	1956 Total	1956 Mining and smelting	1956 Petroleum	1956 Manufacturing	1956 Public utilities	1956 Trade	1956 Other industries
1	All areas total	11,788	14,819	16,286	17,626	19,313	2,209	5,849	6,349	1,614	1,282	2,010	22,118	2,391	7,244	7,088	1,694	1,444	2,257
2	Canada	3,579	4,593	5,242	5,871	6,494	862	1,350	2,841	326	383	732	7,480	938	1,752	3,186	338	426	840
3	Latin American Republics, total	4,735	5,758	6,034	6,244	6,608	1,024	1,801	1,372	1,143	442	826	7,408	1,090	2,227	1,515	1,192	495	889
4	Argentina	356	393	406	424	447	(1)	(1)	230	69	45	28	470	(1)	(1)	242	69	44	34
5	Brazil	644	1,013	1,017	1,049	1,115	(1)	194	565	156	137	(1)	1,209	(1)	213	610	180	138	(1)
6	Chile	540	623	657	633	639	406	(1)	37	11		7	677	434	(1)	40	(1)	12	9
7	Colombia	193	232	233	260	274	(1)	107	58	37	42	(1)	289	(1)	103	70	40	44	(1)
8	Cuba	642	686	686	713	736	(1)	(1)	55	312	30	298	774	(1)	(1)	65	316	35	302
9	Mexico	414	490	514	524	607	154	15	274	91	56	17	675	165	18	309	94	71	18
10	Peru	145	242	287	283	305	191	(1)	24	(1)	27	30	354	221	(1)	26	(1)	29	35
11	Venezuela	993	1,174	1,291	1,366	1,428	(1)	1,058	60	18	57	(1)	1,817	(1)	1,411	77	21	76	(1)
12	Central America, Dominican Republic and Haiti	722	802	835	881	938	16	291	27	279	21	304	1,010	19	318	33	285	23	332
13	Other countries	86	103	108	111	119	(1)	17	43	9	15	(1)	133	(1)	19	43	10	24	(1)
14	Western Europe, total	1,720	2,145	2,369	2,639	3,004	40	764	1,640	42	286	233	3,493	44	994	1,835	45	311	264
15	Belgium	65	95	108	116	134		32	78	(2)	20	3	150		38	88	(2)	21	3
16	Denmark	32	38	36	39	39		24	10	(1)	5	(1)	44		26	12	(1)	5	(1)
17	France	217	276	304	334	376	6	113	210	5	17	26	426	6	136	230	5	19	30
18	Germany	204	251	276	293	332	(1)	74	191	(1)	33	28	424	(1)	111	231	(1)	12	30
19	Italy	63	80	95	126	157		80	47	1	4	26	204		107	56	1	7	33
20	Netherlands	84	108	125	140	162	(1)	87	38	(1)	25	11	182	(1)	102	41	(1)	25	13
21	Norway	24	33	37	40	43	(1)	10	12	2	2	(1)	61	(1)	25	13	2	2	(1)
22	Spain	31	40	45	50	58	(1)	18	21	(1)	4	12	62	(1)	20	21	(1)	5	14
23	Sweden	58	70	74	83	96		36	45	(1)	7	(1)	117		52	47	(1)	7	(1)
24	Switzerland	25	28	31	37	41		10	17	(2)	10	4	47		10	21	(2)	12	4
25	United Kingdom	847	1,038	1,131	1,257	1,426	3	217	946	24	133	104	1,599	3	279	1,039	25	140	113
26	Other countries	70	88	107	124	140	14	63	25	3	25	9	177	17	88	33	3	27	10
27	Western European dependencies, total	435	468	601	599	637	111	431	15	25	36	20	821	122	573	17	32	45	32
28	Western Hemisphere	131	158	178	172	179	61	71	(1)	22	18	(1)	324	71	181	(1)	31	25	(1)
29	Other areas	304	309	423	427	458	50	360	(1)	3	18	(1)	498	51	393	(1)	1	20	(1)
30	Other countries, total	1,318	1,854	2,040	2,273	2,570	173	1,504	480	79	136	199	2,916	197	1,699	536	87	165	232
31	Australia	201	310	326	393	498	25	(1)	240	(1)	26	21	551	29	(1)	264	(1)	28	27
32	India	38	63	68	92	95		(1)	29	2	10	(1)	109		(1)	34	2	10	(1)
33	Indonesia	58	74	88	65	86		(1)	21	(1)	3	(1)	119		(1)	24	(1)	3	(1)
34	Japan	19	69	92	106	128		(1)	13	1	5	(1)	144		(1)	20	1	7	(1)
35	Liberia	82	140	186	230	277	(1)	215		9	(1)	41	338	(1)	263		11	(1)	45
36	New Zealand	25	37	34	40	42	(1)	(1)	18	(1)	9	1	48	(1)	(1)	20	(1)	11	1
37	Philippine Republic	149	178	188	217	229	(1)	(1)	31	62	39	28	266	(1)	(1)	36	67	52	31
38	Union of South Africa	140	194	212	216	259	77	60	86	(1)	28	(1)	289	81	69	95	(1)	31	(1)
39	Other countries	606	788	847	914	957	47	814	41	(1)	(1)	36	1,053	54	893	44	(1)	(1)	39

r Revised.
ᵖ Preliminary.
1. Included in total.   2. Less than $500,000.
Source: U. S. Department of Commerce, Office of Business Economics.

NOTE: The following area changes apply to all tables: Through 1953, Northern and Southern Rhodesia and Nyasaland are included in "other areas" dependencies, line 29; in 1954 and later years they are included in "other countries," line 39. Through 1955, Morocco is included in "other areas" dependencies, line 29; in 1956 it is included in "other countries," line 39.

Petroleum investments in the Middle East were being increased at a somewhat more rapid rate in 1956 than in other recent years, including activities in new areas as well as continuing expansion of existing properties.

Outstanding in the rest of the world were investments in Australia and Indonesia, and the expansion of tanker fleets registered in Liberia. Investments in Trinidad became sizable with the acquisition of the British-owned company mentioned above.

Manufacturing sets record

United States manufacturing companies are turning increasingly to the establishment of factories abroad in order to maintain and enlarge their foreign sales. In 1956 these activities required an investment of nearly $750 million, of which about two-thirds was derived from undistributed foreign earnings.

Expansion was largest in Canada, contributing substantially to the unprecedented rate of industrial expansion in that country. Manufacturing investments in Latin America were also higher than in 1955, with Brazil, Mexico, and Venezuela receiving the principal amounts. In this area high local interest rates caused foreign subsidiaries to call increasingly on the parent companies for working capital requirements.

In Western Europe direct investments in manufacturing continued to increase by an annual amount of nearly $200 million. Nearly half of the additional investment was in the United Kingdom, as in 1955, but a striking development was the increase of nearly $45 million in Germany, about twice the 1955 amount. Expansion was also sizable in France, Italy, and Belgium. In the rest of the world, there was a significant increase in manufacturing investments in Australia, and smaller increases in South Africa, Japan, India, and the Philippines.

Table 3.—Direct Investment Capital Flows and Undistributed Earnings, by Selected Countries, 1955–56, With Major Industries for 1956

Table 4.—Direct Investment Earnings and Income,[1] by Selected Countries, 1955–56, With Major Industries for 1956

[Millions of dollars]

Table 3												Table 4												Line
Net capital outflow						Undistributed subsidiary earnings						Earnings						Income						
1955 r total	1956 P					1955 r total	1956 P					1955 r	1956 P					1955 r	1956 P					
	Total	Mining and smelting	Petroleum	Manufacturing	Other industries		Total	Mining and smelting	Petroleum	Manufacturing	Other industries		Total	Mining and smelting	Petroleum	Manufacturing	Other industries		Total	Mining and smelting	Petroleum	Manufacturing	Other industries	
779	1,838	95	1,139	268	336	898	974	89	258	468	159	2,811	3,134	350	1,406	858	521	1,912	2,160	262	1,148	390	361	1
3C0	544	34	280	101	129	298	360	40	48	237	36	591	701	95	75	393	139	293	341	55	27	156	103	2
193	612	50	365	76	121	192	212	20	67	72	53	870	1,052	140	597	125	190	678	840	120	530	53	137	3
9	10	(1)	(1)	4	6	18	12	(1)	(1)	8	4	27	25	(2)	(2)	14	11	9	13	(2)	(2)	6	7	4
30	45	(1)	8	20	17	38	50	(1)	10	27	13	71	79	(2)	16	38	25	33	29	(2)	6	11	5	5
1	34	27	(1)	2	5	7	4	4	1	(1)	2	74	100	88	(2)	3	9	67	96	87	(2)	2	7	6
16	24	(1)	5	9	10	2	2	(2)	(1)	−7	3	23	22	(2)	(3)	5	17	21	22	(2)	7	2	13	7
15	31	(1)	11	9	11	8	10	(1)	4	2	4	42	51	(2)	3	5	44	34	41	(2)	−2	3	40	8
51	28	−3	2	15	14	34	46	14	1	24	7	66	80	24	4	37	16	32	34	10	3	13	9	9
7	40	30	(1)	1	9	15	9	(2)	(1)	1	8	40	34	14	(2)	4	16	25	25	14	(2)	3	8	10
31	357	(1)	333	13	11	32	32	(1)	20	4	8	434	566	(2)	526	15	25	402	534	(2)	506	11	17	11
27	30	3	−2	5	24	35	47	(1)	32	1	14	81	83	1	36	2	44	46	36	1	4	1	30	12
5	12	...	3	−1	10	3	3	(1)	(1)	1	2	13	13	(3)	(3)	3	11	9	10	(3)	(2)	2	9	13
140	456	(2)	344	83	29	219	208	4	63	111	30	474	485	6	139	246	94	255	277	2	76	135	64	14
8	7	...	2	5	(2)	9	9	...	3	5	(2)	18	19	...	5	11	4	9	11	...	1	6	3	15
(2)	4	...	(1)	2	2	1	1	...	(2)	(2)	(2)	3	3	...	(3)	2	1	2	3	...	(2)	2	1	16
11	16	...	9	4	3	32	33	(1)	14	17	3	50	51	(2)	17	30	4	18	18	(2)	3	13	2	17
24	60	(1)	29	28	3	15	30	(1)	8	14	8	51	53	(2)	9	33	11	36	23	(2)	1	19	3	18
23	32	...	21	6	6	7	14	...	6	4	4	12	22	...	8	9	5	5	8	...	1	5	2	19
13	9	(1)	8	2	−1	9	10	(1)	7	1	2	16	19	(2)	9	3	7	7	8	(2)	2	2	5	20
(2)	15	(1)	14	1	1	4	3	(1)	(2)	1	2	5	5	(2)	1	2	1	1	2	(2)	(3)	1	1	21
4	1	(1)	1	−2	2	4	3	(1)	(1)	1	1	5	3	(2)	(3)	2	1	1	1	(2)	(3)	1	(2)	22
13	19	...	17	(2)	2	(2)	2	...	(2)	2	(2)	7	8	...	(3)	5	3	7	5	...	(3)	2	3	23
2	3	...	(2)	1	3	3	3	...	(2)	1	1	10	11	...	(3)	7	4	7	8	...	(3)	5	2	24
37	261(3)	...	221	31	9	127	90	...	19	61	10	280	273	...	86	139	48	153	183	...	67	78	38	25
4	29	...	20	5	4	10	10	2	5	1	1	18	18	4	5	3	6	8	7	2	(3)	1	5	26
−4	35	4	12	1	18	42	45	7	24	1	13	206	220	45	150	2	23	164	175	38	126	1	10	27
−5	14	6	−6	1	13	12	20	3	6	(2)	11	34	45	21	11	(2)	13	22	25	18	5	...	2	28
1	21	−2	19	(2)	4	30	25	4	18	1	3	172	175	24	139	2	22	142	150	20	121	1	8	29
150	192	7	137	9	39	147	149	18	56	47	28	669	676	64	445	92	75	522	527	46	389	45	47	30
65	16	(1)	(1)	4	12	40	37	(1)	(1)	20	16	64	67	(2)	(2)	41	27	24	30	(2)	(2)	20	10	31
−2	7	...	(1)	2	5	5	6	...	(1)	3	4	16	13	...	(2)	4	9	11	6	...	(2)	1	5	32
7	29	...	(1)	1	28	14	4	(1)	(1)	2	2	37	35	...	(2)	2	33	23	31	...	(2)	(3)	31	33
14	3	...	(1)	(2)	3	9	13	...	(1)	7	6	21	23	...	(2)	...	10	13	12	...	(2)	2	8	34
24	39	(1)	(1)	...	39	22	23	(1)	(1)	...	23	37	37	(2)	(2)	...	37	15	14	(2)	(2)	...	14	35
(2)	3	(1)	(1)	1	2	3	3	...	(1)	1	2	7	8	(2)	(2)	4	4	4	5	(2)	(2)	3	2	36
−3	15	(1)	(1)	1	14	15	23	(1)	(1)	4	4	38	45	(2)	(2)	10	35	24	22	(2)	(2)	6	16	37
23	10	4	2	1	2	20	20	3	6	8	3	58	66	32	9	18	7	38	46	29	3	10	4	38
22	70	1	66	(2)	4	19	21	6	12	2	1	391	382	21	351	3	7	372	362	14	340	2	6	39

r Revised.
P Preliminary.
1. Combined in "Other industries."
2. Less than $500,000.
3. Includes the purchase for $180 million from British owners of a petroleum company with assets located in the West Indies, Canada, and the United Kingdom. The necessary adjustments have been made in the value table to show the investment in the countries where the assets are located.

Source: U. S. Department of Commerce, Office of Business Economics.

r Revised.
P Preliminary.
1. Income is the sum of dividends, interest, and branch profits; earnings is the sum of income and undistributed subsidiary earnings.
2. Combined with "Other industries."
3. Less than $500,000.

Within the broad category of manufacturing, the largest increases in foreign investments in 1956 were in chemicals, automotive products, and machinery, with each of these commodity groups accounting for about 20 percent of the total increase. Automotive investments were largest in Canada and Western Europe, while investments in chemical-producing facilities were outstanding in Latin America and Canada.

Investments in foodstuffs, paper and pulp, fabricated metals, and rubber products, each accounted for about 10 percent of the addition to manufacturing investments abroad in 1956. This investment was more widely dispersed geographically, although the investment in pulp and paper was concentrated in Canada, as was a large part of the invest-

ment in fabricated metals, which mainly represented facilities for the production of aluminum.

Other industries rise

Investments in mining and smelting enterprises abroad were also rising in 1956, although the increase of about $180 million was not so great as in the 1952–53 expansion, when very large projects were under construction. In 1956 the principal additions to mining investments were in Canada, where a wide range of metals and minerals is produced, in copper properties in Chile and Peru, and in various metals and minerals in Mexico and Africa. As in the case of petroleum, the renewal of sizable mining investments is primarily related to projected future demands. Very large ad-

.ditional expenditures are being considered to increase copper production in Latin America and elsewhere, to develop new sources of iron ore and other metals in Canada, and to expand bauxite reserves and facilities for producing aluminum in several countries.

United States public utility enterprises abroad noted some improvement in their rate structure and operating conditions in 1956, especially in a few Latin American countries. Consequently, additions to investments were double the 1955 rate, and were particularly large in Brazil.

Expansion of investments in a wide variety of trade and service enterprises abroad was also notable in 1956, totaling about $360 million. About $150 million of the increase was in Canada, including about $50 million in insurance branches, and large outflows to consumer finance organizations. In Latin America the increase was over $90 million, with sizable investments in distribution facilities in Mexico, Venezuela, and Panama. Investments in these industries were also substantial during the year in the United Kingdom, Germany, Australia, and the Philippines.

Canada leads other areas

Nearly $1 billion was added to the book value of United States direct investments in Canada in 1956, a jump of $400 million over the 1955 addition. The major increase was in petroleum and manufacturing, but other industries also gained. Although the 1956 volume of new investment was far higher than in any previous year, the developments which are in progress are expected to require a comparable level of financing in 1957, and will continue to be important in the continued rapid development of Canada's economy.

Direct investments in Latin America rose by a record $800 million in 1956, compared with less than $400 million in 1955. Nearly half of the investment was in Venezuela, largely in the petroleum industry but with growing investments in manufacturing, trade and service industries. Brazil also continued to attract a large share of United States investments in Latin America, about $95 million in 1956, and the increase in Mexico was nearly $70 million. Manufacturing investments were most important in both of these countries. Investments in Chile, Peru, Cuba, and Panama rose by about $40–$50 million each.

Almost $500 million was added to direct investments in Western Europe in 1956, primarily by petroleum and manufacturing companies. The increase in the United Kingdom was $175 million, over $90 million was invested in Germany, and there were substantial increases in most other countries of the area.

The increase of about $185 million in the Western European dependencies reflected primarily the acquisition from British holders of a petroleum enterprise in the West Indies. Middle East investments were up considerably in 1956, but the increase was less rapid than in earlier postwar years.

In the Far East substantial additions were made to direct investments in India, Indonesia, Japan, and the Philippines. Investments in Australia increased by over $50 million indicating the sustained interest of many United States' companies. The Union of South Africa also continued to receive a considerable amount of investment from the United States in a number of industries. In Liberia the principal increase in investments was in shipping operations, but investments in other industries were also of some importance.

Other Private Investments

United States financial institutions and other private investors provided $1.1 billion of new capital to foreign countries in 1956. This total includes an increase of $575 million in short- and medium-term loans reported by American banks, about $150 million added to credits by exporters and manufacturers, and net purchases of about $420 million of foreign bonds and corporate stocks.

Credit extended by United States banks to foreign governments and private borrowers in foreign countries has been mounting at a rapid rate since 1953. The total of bank credits outstanding at the end of 1953 was $1.2 billion, and by the end of 1956 it had risen to nearly $2.8 billion. Further substantial increases were reported in the first half of 1957. In many instances these credits have been a significant factor in alleviating temporary shortages of dollar exchange. However, much of the outflow in 1956 was to countries not experiencing foreign exchange difficulties but rather offering higher yields than were available in the United States.

Short-term bank credits expanded by nearly $400 million in 1956, as shown in table 5, with particularly large increases in amounts outstanding for Canada, Germany, Mexico, Venezuela, and Japan. Medium-term bank credits rose about $175 million, and included substantial loans to Canada, Norway, the United Kingdom, and Cuba. Direct credits by nonfinancial concerns were extended to many countries, notably Canada, Germany, Brazil, and Japan.

The combined total of banking and commercial credits outstanding at the end of 1956 was about $3.6 billion, of which $2.7 billion had an original maturity of 1 year or less. A relatively small amount of other short-term assets, such as brokerage balances, was also held abroad. Over $1.5 billion of these credits was outstanding in Latin America at the end of 1956, about $1 billion in Western Europe, and $300 million in Canada.

The other principal component of private capital outflows is the purchase of foreign securities. In 1956 foreign countries sold over $450 million of new issues of dollar bonds to

Annual Additions to U. S. Direct Investments Abroad, by Area

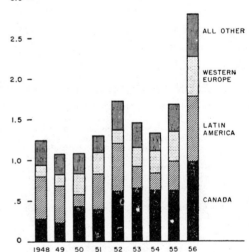

BILLIONS OF DOLLARS

U. S. Department of Commerce, Office of Business Economics

57-24-6

United States investors. This was the highest amount for a postwar year, except for 1951, and included about $380 million for Canada, and much smaller amounts for Australia and Israel.

In the first half of 1957 new issues sold in the United States totaled over $350 million, indicating that the intense demand for capital abroad and the still relatively moderate interest costs in the United States continued to be strong factors in the capital markets. However, new issues were still mainly for the account of Canada and the International Bank, and in the case of Canada the sustained premium on the Canadian dollar was a deterrent to Canadian borrowers. Market values of outstanding dollar bonds, as shown in table 6, were somewhat depressed as world interest rates rose.

Amortizations of outstanding dollar bonds amounted to about $170 million in 1956, mainly relating to Canadian issues and an issue of the International Bank.

Net purchases of foreign corporate stocks by United States investors were about $110 million in 1956, substantially less than in 1955. Purchases of Canadian stocks were about $90 million, only slightly less than in the previous year, but purchases of European issues were greatly reduced in 1956, partly because of the Suez crisis, and amounted to only about $20 million. The appreciation of the market values of Canadian stocks in the year was partly offset by reduced prices of European issues. Transactions in foreign-currency bonds were relatively minor.

Outstanding United States Government credits and short-term assets in foreign countries rose by nearly $600 million in 1956, considerably more than in other recent years. Over $500 million of the increase represented the growth of holdings of foreign currencies or equivalent short-term claims arising primarily out of the sale of agricultural commodities under Government disposal programs. Gross disbursements of United States Government loans to foreign countries rose to almost $500 million but were almost entirely offset by large repayments. The Government also invested $35 million in the International Finance Corporation and increased its investments in certain producing facilities abroad. Details of these Government transactions are given in the *Survey of Current Business* for April 1957.

Earnings of United States Investments

As indicated above, of the $3.4 billion earned by private United States investments abroad in 1956, $3.1 billion was accounted for by direct investments. The rate of increase for direct-investment earnings was considerably lower than in 1955, despite greatly increased investment activity, partly because of developments in certain industries, as discussed below. However, important factors tending to hold down earnings were the still incomplete stage of certain projects, mounting depreciation and amortization charges, and charges against income for exploration and development of natural resources which are estimated at roughly $300 million for 1956.

Earnings of petroleum companies were about $1.4 billion in 1956, nearly $200 million more than in 1955. Almost half of the gain was in Latin America, mainly in Venezuela, reflecting an increase in output from 595 million barrels in 1955 to 665 million barrels in 1956, as well as some price increase late in the year. On the other hand, Middle East earnings were about the same as in 1955, reflecting the reduction in output late in the year resulting from the Suez crisis. Petroleum earnings in Canada increased, although they were still small relative to the amount invested because of continued large development expenditures. Earnings of petroleum enterprises in Western Europe were also higher than in the previous year.

Earnings of United States manufacturing companies abroad increased 4 percent in 1956 and totaled about $860 million. There was a substantial increase in Canada, where economic activity continued to rise, and small increases occurred in Latin America. Elsewhere, however, the leveling off of production and rising costs reduced manufacturing earnings below the 1955 levels in many countries. The reduction was especially large in the United Kingdom. A somewhat larger proportion of manufacturing earnings was reinvested than in 1955, but this was attributable almost wholly to the Canadian enterprises, which were expanding rapidly. In most other countries reinvested earnings of manufacturing companies were lower.

Earnings of mining companies reached about $350 million in 1956, a substantial gain over 1955 and much higher than in earlier years. The gain was attributed largely to improved prices for copper and other nonferrous metals, as well as greater output of a variety of metals and minerals. Greater earnings were experienced in all areas, with major gains in Canada and Chile, and in the Union of South Africa and other African countries.

Increases in earnings of most other industries were relatively minor, although generally earnings were above those in any other postwar year. The principal exception was a drop in agricultural earnings to about $65 million, despite a relatively strong market for sugar. Lower earnings of fruit-producing properties in Central America and elsewhere were a major factor in the decline for this industry.

On an area basis, the greatest increase in earnings of direct investments was in Latin America, where the total rose by $180 million from the 1955 amount to over $1 billion. This gain reflected largely the higher petroleum and mining earnings discussed above. Most of the rise was in Venezuela, but there were also sizable increases in a number of

Earnings of U. S. Investments Abroad

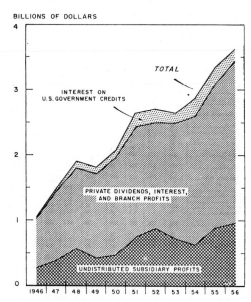

BILLIONS OF DOLLARS

TOTAL

INTEREST ON U. S. GOVERNMENT CREDITS

PRIVATE DIVIDENDS, INTEREST, AND BRANCH PROFITS

UNDISTRIBUTED SUBSIDIARY PROFITS

1946 47 48 49 50 51 52 53 54 55 56

U. S. Department of Commerce, Office of Business Economics   57 - 24 - 7

other countries in the area. Earnings in Canada improved by a little over $100 million in 1956, with the largest gain in manufacturing. In Western Europe 1956 earnings were about the same as in the previous year, as higher petroleum earnings were offset by a drop in manufacturing earnings. For countries in the rest of the world, 1956 earnings were generally close to the 1955 amounts.

Earnings of United States direct investment companies abroad are derived from their sales in local foreign markets and also to a considerable extent from their exports to the United States. Part of the increases in their earnings in 1956, therefore, were connected with the rise in United States imports. Of the overall increase of $1.3 billion in United States merchandise imports in 1956, it is estimated that about one-third represented larger imports from foreign affiliates of United States companies. For some commodities showing large year-to-year gains, such as crude and refined oil, copper, iron ore, aluminum, lead, and zinc, the share of United States companies was substantially higher.

Income from other private investments abroad, mainly interest on dollar bonds and dividends on portfolio holdings of foreign stocks, rose by $45 million to about $300 million in 1956, as shown in table 7. About half of this income is derived from investments in Canada, and about $65 million is from Western Europe. The 1956 increase reflected the continued growth of United States holdings of foreign securities, as well as the general rise in interest rates on bonds and other short- and long-term credits extended by United States investors.

Earnings on foreign investments and assets in the United States increased by about $100 million to $732 million in 1956. Earnings on foreign direct investments in the United States and on foreign portfolio holdings of securities of United States corporations each increased by about $20 million. The largest gain in foreign earnings resulted from en-

Table 5.—Banking and Commercial Claims on Foreigners, by Selected Countries,[1] 1954–56

[Million of dollars]

Countries	Dec. 31, 1954 Total [2]	Dec. 31, 1955 Total [2]	Dec. 31, 1955 Banking claims Short term	Dec. 31, 1955 Banking claims Medium term	Dec. 31, 1955 Commercial claims [2]	Dec. 31, 1956 Total [2]	Dec. 31, 1956 Banking claims Short term	Dec. 31, 1956 Banking claims Medium term	Dec. 31, 1956 Commercial claims [2]
Total	2,400	2,825	1,549	660	616	3,515	1,942	831	742
Western Europe, total	734	744	423	104	217	1,013	567	201	245
Belgium	30	29	16	2	11	49	28	8	13
France	125	30	12		18	39	18	1	20
Germany	82	110	88	2	20	190	157	3	30
Norway	19	58	9	45	4	97	23	71	3
Turkey	56	113	78	15	20	106	88		18
United Kingdom	250	171	109	3	59	215	104	57	54
Canada	175	258	144	16	98	304	157	38	109
Latin America, total	1,094	1,306	703	410	193	1,549	836	477	236
Brazil	400	314	69	208	37	339	72	208	59
Colombia	137	172	143	10	19	176	145	12	19
Cuba	121	209	92	101	16	232	90	120	22
Mexico	161	206	154	24	28	284	213	42	29
Venezuela	88	173	105	46	22	213	144	40	29
Asia, total	300	407	233	101	73	511	334	77	100
Israel	38	42	10	25	7	42	16	16	10
Japan	139	149	103	30	16	198	167	3	28
Other Asia	123	216	120	46	50	271	151	58	62
All other countries, total	97	110	46	29	35	138	48	38	52

1. Includes major categories of claims as reported to the Treasury Department regularly by banks and commercial concerns, but does not include estimates for other types of claims included in table 1 as short-term or "other" long-term private investments.
2. Not including medium-term commercial claims as follows: 1954, $102 million; 1955, $97 million; 1956, $120 million.

Source: *Treasury Bulletin*, March, June, and July, 1957.

Table 6.—United States Holdings of Dollar Bonds of Specified Countries, Market and Par Values, 1950, 1955, and 1956

[Millions of dollars, year-ends]

Country	1950 Market Value	1950 Par Value	1955 Market Value	1955 Par Value	1956 Market Value	1956 Par Value
Total	1,693	2,049	2,660	2,851	2,863	3,151
Western Europe	85	234	193	240	184	232
Belgium	19	18	35	35	33	34
Germany		104	96	112	97	112
Italy	10	33	31	47	28	45
Other	56	79	31	46	26	41
Canada	1,106	1,065	1,489	1,466	1,710	1,763
Latin American Republics	159	336	150	274	135	260
Bolivia	5	38	6	38	5	38
Brazil	46	75	36	48	31	43
Chile	29	66	25	53	24	52
Colombia	28	54	24	39	21	37
Other	51	103	59	96	54	90
Other foreign countries	117	189	352	393	414	457
Australia	87	95	91	93	99	103
Israel			213	213	267	267
Japan			36	34	36	34
Other	10	53	12	53	12	53
International Bank for Reconstruction and Development	226	225	476	478	420	439

Source: U. S. Department of Commerce, Office of Business Economics.

larged holdings of obligations of the United States Government and rising yields on these obligations.

Foreign Investments in the United States

Foreign investors have been adding to their long-term investments in the United States at an increasing rate since 1952, and in 1956 long-term capital inflows from abroad rose sharply to a postwar high of about $540 million. Although part of the 1956 inflow may have been spurred by unsettled conditions in some countries, the recorded transactions indicate a fairly steady rate of investment throughout the year, reflecting the attractiveness of investment opportunities in the United States.

Net foreign purchases of publicly traded stock in United States corporations reached a peak of over $250 million in 1956, about twice the amount purchased in the previous year. Most of the transactions continued to be recorded for British and Swiss accounts, as shown in table 8, although these countries are not necessarily the countries of residence of the actual purchasers. Canadian holders of United States corporate stocks have been liquidating these investments in the past 2 years, however, in response to the strong local demand for capital, and liquidations recorded for the Netherlands may also have reflected similar conditions in that country.

Rising market quotations resulted in a further increase of about $130 million in the market value of foreign holdings of corporate stocks. This was much less than the price gain of over $1 billion in 1955. By the end of 1956 the aggregate market value of foreign holdings of United States corporate stocks reached about $7 billion, and foreign purchases were continuing at a substantial rate in the early months of 1957.

Although foreign holdings of bonds of United States corporations and local governmental authorities are now much smaller than holdings of corporate stocks, rising bond yields in recent years have attracted substantial amounts of foreign capital. In 1956 net foreign acquisitions of such bonds were about $65 million, including nearly $50 million by European purchasers and about $10 million by international institutions.

Foreign investments in foreign-controlled enterprises in the United States rose by nearly $300 million in 1956, more than in any previous postwar year. European investments increased by $160 million and Canadian investments by $130 million. The increase in investments was financed

Table 7.—Earnings on International Investments, by Type, 1950–56

[Millions of dollars]

	1950	1951	1952	1953	1954	1955 r	1956 p
Earnings on United States investments abroad, total	2,068	2,634	2,704	2,686	2,871	3,343	3,632
Direct investments, total	1,769	2,244	2,295	2,218	2,369	2,811	3,134
Dividends, interest, and branch profits	1,294	1,492	1,419	1,442	1,724	1,912	2,160
Undistributed profits of subsidiaries	475	752	876	776	644	898	974
Portfolio investments	190	192	205	216	230	258	304
Interest on United States Government credits	109	198	204	252	272	274	194
Earnings on foreign investments in the United States, total	478	481	472	571	544	631	732
Direct investments, total	281	255	234	306	300	320	341
Dividends, interest, and branch profits	148	129	152	185	175	191	227
Undistributed profits of subsidiaries	138	126	82	121	125	129	114
Portfolio investments	166	179	174	179	185	217	237
Interest on United States Government obligations	31	47	64	86	59	94	154

r Revised.   p Preliminary.

Source: U. S. Department of Commerce, Office of Business Economics.

by $180 million of capital inflows and about $115 million of undistributed profits of United States subsidiaries of foreign parent companies.

Most of the capital inflow was from Canada, as Canadian companies continued to build up their manufacturing facilities and distribution establishments here. European investments increased mainly out of reinvested earnings of established petroleum and other enterprises. The largest part of the capital inflow from Europe represented additions to the net assets of United States branches of foreign insurance companies.

Gains in reserves

Holdings of liquid dollar assets by foreign countries and international institutions rose by $1.3 billion in 1956 to a total of $18.3 billion, as shown in table 1. These holdings include deposits in United States banks, other short-term claims against banks and other private persons and businesses in the United States, and United States Government long- and short-term obligations, made up largely of Treasury notes, certificates and bills. Approximately $11 billion of the total was held for foreign official accounts and the international institutions.

The gain in liquid dollar assets was somewhat offset by net sales of $280 million of gold to the United States in 1956.

Changes in the gold and dollar reserves of foreign countries as a whole reflect partly the purchase of newly mined gold, but mainly transactions with the United States.[2] These transactions resulted in a continuous gain in foreign reserves from early in 1952 through the third quarter of 1956, totaling about $7½ billion for the period. Beginning in the fourth quarter of 1956, however, foreign reserves declined, partly because of pressures connected with the Suez crisis, and the declines continued in the early part of 1957.

2. See the *Survey of Current Business* for June 1957, p. 23 ff.

Large changes in the liquid dollar reserves of a few countries were responsible for much of the overall change in reserves in 1956. Canada gained about $400 million, mainly in nonofficial accounts, reflecting the capital outflows described above. Venezuela's gain of nearly $200 million in dollar holdings and a like amount in gold also was connected with record capital inflows from the United States. German dollar holdings increased by nearly $400 million, together with an increase in gold holdings of about $575 million, but these gains were primarily related to Germany's transactions with countries other than the United States. A number of other countries, including Italy, Brazil, and Japan, increased their dollar holdings by sizable amounts.

Losses of reserves during the year were most striking for France. French dollar holdings fell by $600 million in 1956, and continued to decline in 1957 despite large drawings on the International Monetary Fund. The United Kingdom's position was also weakened, although changes in United Kingdom dollar reserves reflect transactions of other countries in the sterling area. Dollar reserves of the United Kingdom rose by nearly $400 million in 1956, but this was largely a reflection of drawings of $562 million from the International Monetary Fund, about $180 million realized from the sale of a petroleum enterprise to United States investors, and the sale of $100 million of gold to the United States.

The $360 million decline in liquid dollar assets of international institutions shown in table 1 resulted primarily from the large disbursement to the United Kingdom mentioned above, offset by sales of $200 million of gold to the United States by the International Monetary Fund. Further sales of gold by the IMF were necessary in the first half of 1957 to meet large drawings of dollars by France, India, and others.

Foreign holdings in the United States differ greatly in their character and purpose from United States investments in foreign countries. United States investments abroad are very largely long-term, or represent extensions of credit to foreign borrowers seeking funds in the United States. By contrast, about 60 percent of foreign assets here are not held primarily for the income they produce, but rather as readily available reserves required for the monetary systems of foreign countries and to finance international payments.

Table 8.—Foreign Holdings of United States Corporate Stocks, by Selected Countries, 1946–56

[Market values; millions of dollars]

Country	Value, year end				Change in 1956		Value year end 1956 p
	1946	1953	1954	1955	Net foreign purchases	Price change	
Total [1]	2,440	3,400	5,004	6,325	256	130	6,711
Western Europe [1]	1,690	2,350	3,485	4,468	231	91	4,790
Netherlands	430	374	491	581	−10	12	583
Switzerland	505	903	1,353	1,796	118	36	1,950
United Kingdom	418	744	1,153	1,461	75	29	1,565
Other countries	337	329	488	630	48	14	692
Canada [1]	460	650	910	1,066	−21	23	1,068
Latin American Republics [1]	174	245	377	484	26	10	520
All other [1]	116	155	232	307	20	7	334

p Preliminary.

1. Holdings by United States citizens resident abroad, approximately as given for 1941 in the Treasury Census, TFR 300: Total, $250 million; Canada, $25 million; Latin America, $40 million; Western Europe, $175 million; other countries, $10 million, are included in table I but are excluded from this table.

NOTE.—Data for individual countries are derived from reports which do not identify the residence of beneficial owners. Thus, amounts reported for Switzerland may include securities purchased in the United States market through Swiss banks by residents of other countries.

Source: U. S. Department of Commerce, Office of Business Economics.

Shifts in these international reserves are of critical importance for many countries, and very large changes have taken place in the postwar years which can be reviewed briefly in the context of the overall debtor-creditor position of the United States.

In the 10 years from 1946 through 1956 the value of foreign dollar assets and investments in the United States doubled, rising from $15.9 billion to $31.6 billion. Nearly $9½ billion of the increase was in relatively liquid dollar holdings, such as bank deposits or United States Government securities. Foreign gold reserves also rose by over $4 billion, although net gold sales to the United States over the 10-year period were about $1.4 billion. By the end of 1956, gold and liquid dollar resources of foreign countries and their residents aggregated nearly $34 billion. Of this total, $26½ billion was held in official accounts and by the international institutions, and thus was readily available for monetary and other purposes.

These gains in monetary reserves have greatly facilitated the growth of international transactions, especially by making possible a gradual reduction in restrictions on international payments. However, the uneven distribution of gains in reserves has reduced the effectiveness of the overall accumulation.

Of the total gain of $13.6 billion in gold and liquid dollar reserves, countries in Western Europe accounted for over $7½ billion. Germany was by far the largest gainer, adding $3.3 billion to reserves in the 10-year period. Italy added nearly $1 billion and Swiss holdings were up by $0.7 billion, not including the very substantial additions to holdings of United States corporate securities. Holdings of other countries of Western Europe were also generally higher

than in 1946, but the increases were not commensurate with the much greater increase in their international trade and payments. Moreover, especially in the case of France and the United Kingdom, very large dollar obligations to the United States Government and others were incurred in the period.

Canadian international reserves rose by $1.4 billion from 1946 through 1956, whereas other countries in the midst of very rapid expansions of their domestic economies, with attendant large deficits in their foreign trade balances, were not able to add to their reserves. However, much of Canada's expansion was financed by inflows of United States and other foreign capital.

Reserves of the Latin American Republics increased by only $0.8 billion in the period under review, and only Venezuela and Mexico, with increases of $0.7 billion and $0.3 billion, respectively, showed substantial improvement. Argentina's reserves were down by $0.8 billion, mainly reflecting losses in 1947, and other countries in the area made little progress in their reserve positions. Few countries in other areas made significant gains, with the exception of Japan, which accumulated about $1 billion of liquid dollar holdings.

A considerable gain in world reserves, however, resulted from the net addition of $3 billion to the gold and dollar holdings of the international institutions, largely reflecting the capital subscribed by the United States Government and bond sales to United States investors. The contribution made by the International Monetary Fund to world liquidity was especially evident in the period from November 1956 to mid-July 1957, when dollar drawings by foreign countries amounted to $1.3 billion.

PRIVATE FOREIGN INVESTMENTS NEAR $37 BILLION

Samuel Pizer
and
Frederick Cutler

by Samuel Pizer and Frederick Cutler ☆

Private Foreign Investments
Near $37 Billion

IN 1957, for the second successive year, private United States foreign investments were nearly $4 billion. Direct investments by United States companies in their foreign branches and subsidiaries increased more than $3 billion reaching a total book value of over $25 billion by the end of 1957.

Part of the expansion in direct investments in both 1956 and 1957 was attributable to large cash payments for newly acquired properties or oil leases, but most of the stepped-up outflow reflected continued expectations of strong long-run demand for basic materials here and abroad, coupled with a tendency to establish production facilities abroad to supply foreign markets.

Other private capital investment in 1957 totaled $1.1 billion, mainly representing purchases of foreign dollar bonds and long- and short-term bank loans. The outflow was greatest in the first half of the year, and was offset to some extent by reduced market values of Canadian and other foreign-currency securities.

Annual Additions to U. S. Direct Foreign Investments, By Area

Billion Dollars

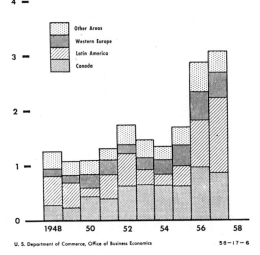

U. S. Department of Commerce, Office of Business Economics   58—17—6

In the first half of 1958 the net outflow of private capital was about $1,750 million, nearly as high as the record amount of 1957 if extraordinary items are omitted. Direct investment flows, lacking any especially large transactions, were much lower than in the first half of 1957, but new issues of foreign dollar bonds and foreign stocks reached record proportions in the first half of this year, and foreign lending by United States commercial banks is also continuing on a large scale. Although rising interest rates in the United States may discourage some foreign borrowing, the demand for short- and long-term financing by many countries remains high.

Large-scale private foreign investments supplied, directly and indirectly, an important part of the increase in the total demand for United States products in 1956 and the first half of 1957, when export shipments reached a peak. Although exports have since declined, the sustained outflow of capital has been a supporting element and may have contributed to the stabilization in United States export trade which has occurred since the first quarter of this year.

Earnings on private foreign investments advanced to a high of $3.7 billion in 1957, nearly $300 million more than the 1956 amount, reflecting the rapidly growing amount of capital invested. Over two-thirds of the gain was accounted for by direct investments, even though much of the investment outlay in the past 2 years has been in properties which are not yet fully productive. Interest and dividend receipts from portfolio and short-term investments rose considerably as these investments expanded.

Direct Investment

The geographic distribution of direct investment in 1957 showed as usual a concentration in the Western Hemisphere and Europe, which accounted for seven-eighths of the total. As shown in table 5, investments in less developed countries since 1950 have been largely in petroleum and mining, with the notable exception of some Latin American countries where both local and foreign capital are now developing the industrial and market potential.

Resource development with the aid of foreign capital is often the most effective initial stimulus to rising national incomes, especially since it is usually accompanied by the construction of transportation and other public utilities. In this connection, it is significant that a number of investment projects just beginning or under consideration involve large outlays for resource development in areas where private United States investment has previously not been large.

NOTE.—MR. PIZER AND MR. CUTLER ARE MEMBERS OF THE BALANCE OF PAYMENTS DIVISION, OFFICE OF BUSINESS ECONOMICS.

Considerable amounts are being invested in certain areas, despite the economic and political instability which are major deterrents to investment activity.

New high for Latin America

Over 40 percent of United States direct foreign investment during 1957 was in Latin America, far exceeding the record outlays of the previous year and raising the total investment in that area to $8.8 billion. More than $900 million was added to petroleum investments, with Venezuela accounting for about $770 million, including some $360 million paid for oil leases. By the end of 1957, United States direct investments in Venezuela had a book value of about $2.7 billion, nearly one-third of the total for the area.

Petroleum investments in other Latin American countries were also rising in 1957, but were sizable in only a few where imports were being financed or exploration and development work was underway on a considerable scale. Undistributed earnings of Panamanian-flag tanker fleets, although showing as book investments in Panama, were probably utilized for investment elsewhere.

Mining investments in Latin America also spurted upward in 1957, largely reflecting increased activity in Mexico and Peru, while outlays in Chile remained steady. Although the market softened for most metals and minerals during 1957, bringing a sharp reduction in earnings—especially for Chile— the outlook is for continued and perhaps rising investments in this industry in Latin America.

Investment in public utilities in Latin America was also stepped up in 1957, especially for installations in Cuba and Venezuela and shipping operating under the Panamanian flag. Earnings of public utilities were somewhat improved, in a few countries, allowing for larger reinvestments.

Additions to capital invested in manufacturing establishments in Latin America were $150 million in 1957, slightly reduced from the 1956 amount as funds available out of earnings were lower. In Mexico, manufacturing investments rose by $63 million, continuing the rapid growth of recent years, and in Brazil, an increase of $45 million also carried forward a significant expansion of manufacturing capacity. A number of other countries in the area received a regular, though smaller, inflow of manufacturing investments from the United States.

Agricultural investments did not expand for the area as a whole in 1957, largely because of the sale of sizable existing properties and some short-term withdrawals of funds. Earnings were improved as the price of sugar continued strong. Investments in the trade and service industries were also lower than in 1956.

Large investment in Canada

An addition of $870 million was made to United States direct investments in Canada last year, where a large expansion of industrial facilities has been carried out in recent years. This total was under the 1956 record because earnings and reinvestments were reduced as economic activity declined.

Table 1.—International Investment Position of the United States by Area, 1956–1957

[Millions of dollars]

	Total		Western Europe		Western European Dependencies		Other Europe		Canada		Latin American Republics		Other foreign countries		International institutions	
	1956 r	1957 p	1956 r	1957 p	1956 r	1957 p	1956 r	1957 p	1956 r	1957 p	1956 r	1957 p	1956 r	1957 p	1956 r	1957 p
United States investments abroad, total	49,476	54,215	15,759	16,758	879	973	327	382	12,032	12,873	10,453	12,252	6,130	6,926	3,896	4,051
Private investments	33,000	36,812	6,137	6,793	858	955	29	27	12,029	12,867	9,355	11,013	4,172	4,586	420	571
Long-term	30,082	33,588	5,224	5,778	827	928	14	22	11,693	12,542	8,251	9,743	3,653	4,404	420	571
Direct	22,177	25,252	3,520	3,993	805	906			7,460	8,332	7,459	8,805	2,933	3,216		
Foreign dollar bonds	2,826	3,255	185	193			3	3	1,672	1,907	135	123	411	458	420	571
Other foreign securities [1]	3,022	2,663	573	516					2,289	1,987	39	37	121	123		
Other	2,057	2,418	946	1,076	22	22	11	19	272	316	618	778	188	207		
Short-term	2,918	3,224	913	1,015	31	27	15	5	336	325	1,104	1,270	519	582		
Deposits	417	421	218	222	10	8	1	1	111	112	46	47	31	31		
Other	2,501	2,803	695	793	21	19	14	4	225	213	1,058	1,223	488	551		
United States Government credits and claims	16,476	17,403	9,622	9,965	21	18	298	355	3	6	1,098	1,239	1,958	2,340	3,476	3,480
Long-term	15,219	15,548	8,929	9,077	21	18	297	305	1		973	1,119	1,522	1,555	3,476	3,474
Short-term	1,257	1,855	693	888			1	50	2	6	125	120	436	785		6
Foreign assets and investments in the United States, total	31,607	31,351	16,874	16,895	545	530	57	57	4,668	4,786	3,644	3,808	3,068	2,618	1,904	1,810
Long-term investments	13,354	12,840	9,008	8,682	275	253	39	36	2,735	2,619	965	910	278	276	54	64
Direct	4,547	4,788	2,847	2,984	20	20			1,498	1,590	134	135	48	59		
Corporate stocks	6,961	6,091	4,965	4,415	165	139	22	19	1,093	884	560	493	136	122	20	19
Corporate, State and municipal bonds	309	417	204	284	6	10			5	6	53	64	7	8	34	45
Other	1,537	1,544	992	999	84	84	17	17	139	139	218	218	87	87		
Short-term assets and United States Government obligations	18,253	18,511	7,866	8,213	270	277	18	21	1,933	2,167	2,679	2,898	2,790	2,342	1,850	1,746
Private obligations	9,488	9,877	3,626	3,896	216	221	11	14	1,031	1,348	2,299	2,558	2,208	1,759	97	81
Deposits	8,056	8,052	2,621	2,651	180	170	10	9	935	1,200	2,146	2,371	2,067	1,572	97	79
Other	1,432	1,825	1,005	1,245	36	51	1	5	96	148	153	187	141	187		2
United States Government obligations	8,765	8,634	4,240	4,317	54	56	7	7	902	819	380	340	582	583	1,753	1,665
Long-term	1,501	1,449	504	541	23	23	5	5	281	371	260	215	31	36	397	397
Short-term	r 7,264	r 7,185	3,736	3,776	31	33	2	2	621	448	120	95	551	547	1,356	1,437

1. Consists primarily of securities payable in foreign currencies, but includes some dollar obligations, including participations in loans made by the International Bank for Reconstruction and Development.
2. Includes United States currency not distributed by area estimated at $847 million at end of 1956 and 1957.

Source: U. S. Department of Commerce, Office of Business Economics.
r Revised.   p Preliminary.

The outflow to Canada for most industries was again large, but only in petroleum was the 1956 total exceeded. In this industry, capital from the United States going into the development of Canadian resources rose to over $300 million. Operations in all phases of the industry were expanded and some existing properties were acquired to further future operations. Investment activity may lessen in 1958, however, as production and earnings are affected by trade restrictions and ample world supplies. However, even some slackening would leave an outflow of major significance.

Manufacturing investments in Canada, although not growing quite so steeply as petroleum investments, are still much larger, accounting for over 40 percent of the outstanding United States direct investment in that country. In 1957, the increase in manufacturing investments was less than in the prior year, but this reflected a sizable reduction in retained earnings as profits declined. Capital outflows from the United States were up substantially, indicating the strength of the expansion drive despite reduced internal sources of funds.

Increases in mining investments were lower than in recent years, although in this industry also the slackened investment growth resulted from reduced reinvestment of earnings, with capital continuing to move from the United States at a slightly higher rate. While generally reduced prices for mineral products may have currently a dampening influence, further large investments in this industry, especially for iron ore, are anticipated.

United States trade, finance and service investments are large in Canada, totaling over $1.3 billion at the end of 1957, and these continued to expand in line with the needs of the Canadian economy.

Steady growth in Europe

Nearly $500 million was added to direct investments in Western Europe in 1957, about 10 percent less than the 1956 amount, omitting the purchase from United Kingdom investors in 1956 of large petroleum properties in Trinidad and elsewhere. Manufacturing is the principal field for United States business capital in Europe, and these investments continued to grow at an annual rate of over $200 million. The share of the United Kingdom in this increase was larger than usual in 1957, accounting for two-thirds of the rise.

Manufacturing investments in Germany were substantial, though less than in 1956; the flow to Italy was up considerably, but most countries showed reductions. Investment in the United Kingdom benefited from higher earnings which were a major source of funds for expansion of manufacturing plants.

Data for 1957 do not appear to show, as yet, an augmented flow of United States capital to continental Europe in anticipation of the Common Market arrangements. However, there are many indications that this flow could be substantial..

Another major field for United States investment in Europe is the petroleum industry, principally in refineries and distribution systems. Overall investment in this industry in 1957 was nearly $200 million, which was not much less than the 1956 amount if the special transaction mentioned above is omitted. However, the share of the United Kingdom was up sharply to more than half of the total, and the continental countries, except Germany and the Netherlands, showed a reduced rate of investment, with the decline for Italy particularly severe. In view of scheduled expansions of refineries and other petroleum facilities, however, investment by this industry in a number of European countries is likely to continue in substantial amounts.

477726°—58 —3

Middle East

Despite recurring crises, the flow of United States direct investment capital to the Middle East area held at an annual rate of about $100 million in 1956 and 1957. There were sharp fluctuations in the flow of funds to individual parts of the area, but these often reflected temporary variations in cash positions rather than trends in fixed investment or exploration and development. The latter activity is going forward extensively, and in addition to the sums accounted for as capital expenditures, roughly $25 million was spent in essentially non-producing countries in the Middle East and North Africa in the search for additional reserves.

The current rate of capital outflow to this area is less than in earlier postwar years, when production was being rapidly expanded. Crude oil produced in the Middle East by United States operators, or as their share of joint operations, fluctuated widely as a result of the Suez crisis and later developments, but averaged 2 million barrels per day in 1957, about 50 percent of the total produced in the free world outside the Western Hemisphere. Major expenditures are in prospect for the area to develop new reserves in North Africa, in offshore locations, and in Iran, and in unproven areas.

Investments in Africa south of the Sahara increased by about $40 million in 1957, exclusive of shipping companies in Liberia. This was less than the 1956 rate, as there were sharp reductions in the outflow of capital for petroleum investment, especially for the Union of South Africa.

Distribution of
U. S. Direct Foreign Investments, 1957

Book Values, $25.3 Billion

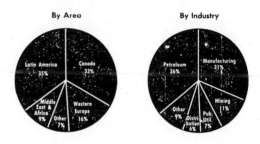

By Area

Latin America 35%
Canada 33%
Middle East & Africa 9%
Western Europe 16%
Other 7%

By Industry

Petroleum 36%
Manufacturing 31%
Mining 11%
Other 9%
Distribution 6%
Pub. Util. 7%

Earnings, $3.3 Billion

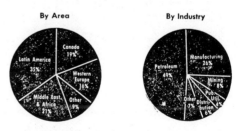

By Area

Canada 19%
Latin America 35%
Western Europe 16%
Middle East & Africa 21%
Other 9%

By Industry

Manufacturing 26%
Petroleum 49%
Mining 8%
Other 7%
Pub. Util. 4%
Distribution 6%

U. S. Department of Commerce, Office of Business Economics   58-17-8

In the past year there has been a notable rise in interest by United States business concerns in the possible development of the mineral resources of parts of the African continent in which United States investment has been small or nonexistent. Some of the contemplated investments are comparatively large and could be significant steps in the economic development of this area.

A steady rate of investment was maintained in the Far East, yielding an increase in direct investments of about $175 million for 1957. Additions to investments in Australia were about $50 million, mainly for manufacturing plants. The rise in Indonesia largely reflected petroleum activities, and in Japan the principal industry showing increases was manufacturing, with petroleum also higher than in 1956.

Increases in the Philippine Republic were spread over several industries. Elsewhere in the Far East there was little growth of United States direct investments in 1957, and the total invested to the end of 1957, outside of the countries mentioned above, was comparatively small.

Petroleum investment

On an industry basis, investments in the petroleum industry dominated the growth of direct investments in 1957, increasing by $1.7 billion to a total book value of about $9 billion. Over half of the rise was in Latin America, with Venezuela far in the lead. Output by United States companies in Venezuela reached a high of a little over 2 million

Table 2.—Value of Direct Investments Abroad, by Selected Countries and Years, and Major Industries, 1956–57

[Millions of dollars]

Line	Countries	1950	1953	1954	1955	1956 r Total	1956 Mining and smelting	1956 Petroleum	1956 Manufacturing	1956 Public utilities	1956 Trade	1956 Other industries	1957 p Total	1957 Mining and smelting	1957 Petroleum	1957 Manufacturing	1957 Public utilities	1957 Trade	1957 Other industries
1	All areas, total	11,788	16,286	17,626	19,313	22,177	2,399	7,280	7,152	1,702	1,447	2,197	25,252	2,634	8,981	7,918	1,817	1,589	2,312
2	Canada	3,579	5,242	5,871	6,494	7,460	940	1,768	3,196	340	424	793	8,332	996	2,154	3,512	351	472	847
3	Latin American Republics, total	4,735	6,034	6,244	6,608	7,459	1,096	2,232	1,543	504	28	875	8,805	1,238	3,161	1,693	536	1,291	886
4	Argentina	356	406	424	447	466	(¹)	(¹)	249	68	44	28	501	(¹)	(¹)	256	67	45	30
5	Brazil	644	1,017	1,049	1,115	1,218	(¹)	211	614	171	148	(¹)	1,301	(¹)	227	659	179	159	(¹)
6	Chile	540	657	633	639	676	434	(¹)	39	(²)	12	9	702	457	(²)	39	(¹)	12	10
7	Colombia	193	233	260	274	298	(¹)	107	67	43	45	(¹)	297	(¹)	106	62	43	46	(¹)
8	Cuba	642	686	713	736	777	(¹)	(¹)	66	322	36	290	850	(¹)	(¹)	80	344	35	292
9	Mexico	414	514	524	607	690	166	17	321	93	74	19	787	191	18	384	97	76	22
10	Peru	145	287	283	305	343	221	(¹)	26	(¹)	30	33	400	258	(¹)	33	(¹)	31	33
11	Venezuela	993	1,291	1,366	1,428	1,829	(¹)	1,411	78	37	74	(¹)	2,683	(¹)	2,179	97	55	80	(¹)
12	Central America, Dominican Republic and Haiti	722	835	881	938	1,030	22	325	36	289	24	335	1,132	27	392	39	315	31	328
13	Other countries	86	108	111	119	132	(¹)	20	46	11	18	(¹)	151	(¹)	34	44	12	22	(¹)
14	Western Europe, total	1,720	2,369	2,639	3,004	3,520	45	992	1,861	47	310	264	3,993	50	1,184	2,077	54	337	291
15	Belgium	65	108	116	134	150		38	88	(²)	21	3	156		43	89	(²)	21	3
16	Denmark	32	36	39	39	45		26	13	(¹)	5	(¹)	45		26	13	(¹)	6	(¹)
17	France	217	304	334	376	427	6	136	232	5	19	30	457	7	147	243	6	23	33
18	Germany	204	276	293	332	429	(¹)	111	239	(¹)	42	30	496	(¹)	151	268	(¹)	48	29
19	Italy	63	95	126	157	207		108	57	1	8	33	233	(²)	108	73	1	10	42
20	Netherlands	84	125	140	162	186	(¹)	102	43	(¹)	25	13	213	(¹)	119	44	(¹)	24	14
21	Norway	24	37	40	43	61	(¹)	25	14	2	2	(¹)	62	(¹)	23	15	2	2	(¹)
22	Spain	31	45	50	58	62	(¹)	19	21	(¹)	4	14	65	(¹)	18	28	(¹)	6	15
23	Sweden	58	74	83	96	115		50	48	(¹)	7	(¹)	118		49	51	(¹)	7	(¹)
24	Switzerland	25	31	37	41	48	(²)	10	22	(²)	(²)	5	55	(²)	11	25	(²)	4	5
25	United Kingdom	847	1,131	1,257	1,426	1,612	3	279	1,052	25	140	114	1,899	3	394	1,201	26	150	126
26	Other countries	70	107	124	140	177	17	88	33	3	26	10	194	23	95	34	3	28	10
27	Western European dependencies, total	435	601	599	637	805	121	569	17	18	43	37	906	132	644	18	21	51	40
28	Western Hemisphere	131	178	172	179	314	70	181	(¹)	17	21	(¹)	339	76	190	(¹)	20	30	(¹)
29	Other areas	304	423	427	458	491	51	389	(¹)	1	19	(¹)	567	56	454	(¹)	1	21	(¹)
30	Other countries, total	1,318	2,040	2,273	2,570	2,933	197	1,718	536	87	166	228	3,216	218	1,839	618	100	193	217
31	Australia	201	326	393	498	552	29	(¹)	266	(¹)	28	27	601	32	(¹)	302	(¹)	32	30
32	India	38	68	92	95	108		(¹)	33	2	(¹)	(¹)	110		(¹)	36	2	10	(¹)
33	Indonesia	58	88	65	86	118		(¹)	24	(¹)	3	(¹)	150		(¹)	24	(¹)	3	(¹)
34	Japan	19	92	106	128	145		(¹)	21	1	8	(¹)	181		(¹)	36	1	12	(¹)
35	Liberia	82	186	230	277	334	(¹)	263		11	(¹)	41	380	(¹)	296		18	(¹)	42
36	New Zealand	25	34	40	42	47	(¹)	(¹)	19	(¹)	11	1	51	(¹)	20	(¹)	9	11	2
37	Philippine Republic	149	188	217	229	267	(¹)	(¹)	35	67	53	32	307	(¹)	(¹)	41	73	61	37
38	Union of South Africa	140	212	216	259	288	84	69	94	(¹)	32	(¹)	305	92	108	(¹)	38	(¹)	40
39	Other countries	606	847	914	957	1,073	54	912	44	(¹)	(¹)	38	1,131	59	954	51	(¹)	(¹)	40

r Revised.
p Preliminary.
1. Included in total.
2. Less than $500,000.

Source: U. S. Department of Commerce, Office of Business Economics.

NOTE: The following area changes apply to all tables: Through 1953, Northern and Southern Rhodesia and Nyasaland are included in "other areas" dependencies, line 29; in 1954 and later years they are included in "other countries," line 39. Through 1955, Morocco is included in "other areas" dependencies, line 29; in 1956 it is included in "other countries," line 39. Through 1956, Ghana and Tunisia are included in "other countries," line 29; in 1957 they are included in "other countries," line 39.

barrels per day during the Suez crisis, when Middle East production was cut back, and averaged 1.9 million barrels per day in 1957, up about 9 percent over 1956 putput.

Most of the Latin American increase was financed by larger capital outflows from the United States, and reinvested earnings were also higher. Parent companies in the United States were under considerable pressure to raise the funds required for expansion in this and other areas, and placed several large security issues in the United States capital market.

Petroleum investments in Canada were again large in 1957, and in Europe also the flow was maintained in substantial amounts, particularly to the United Kingdom and Germany. In the Middle East and North Africa, petroleum accounted for practically all United States investment, with the outflow of somewhat over $100 million about the same as in 1956. The rate of investment was considerably cut back elsewhere in Africa, and was also off in the Far East.

Manfacturing sustained

Manufacturing currently ranks next to petroleum as a field for United States direct foreign investments, with additional investments of over $750 million in 1957 raising the total value of such investments to $7.9 billion. Investment in this industry was slightly less than in 1956 because of smaller reinvestments of earnings. The outflow of capital, on the other hand, rose substantially.

Table 3.—Direct Investment Capital Flows and Undistributed Earnings, by Selected Countries, 1956–57, With Major Industries for 1957

Table 4.—Direct Investment Earnings and Income,[1] by Selected Countries, 1956–57, With Major Industries for 1957

[Millions of dollars]

| Table 3 — Net capital outflow | | | | | | Table 3 — Undistributed subsidiary earnings | | | | | | Table 4 — Earnings | | | | | | Table 4 — Income | | | | | | Line |
1956 r total	1957 p Total	Mining and smelting	Petroleum	Manufacturing	Other industries	1956 r total	1957 p Total	Mining and smelting	Petroleum	Manufacturing	Other industries	1956 r	1957 p Total	Mining and smelting	Petroleum	Manufacturing	Other industries	1956 r	1957 p Total	Mining and smelting	Petroleum	Manufacturing	Other industries	
1,859	2,072	177	1,332	370	192	1,000	1,017	61	364	391	201	3,120	3,330	281	1,623	852	574	2,120	2,313	220	1,259	461	373	1
542	584	39	322	160	63	367	274	17	56	151	50	720	641	71	95	348	127	353	367	54	39	197	77	2
592	1,104	130	828	91	55	241	251	12	101	60	78	1,041	1,166	102	701	124	238	800	915	90	600	64	160	3
[2]	15	[1]	[1]	-3	18	10	21	[1]	[1]	10	10	22	31	[2]	[2]	15	15	12	10	[2]	[2]	5	5	4
55	48	[1]	7	28	13	48	35	[1]	9	17	8	75	75	[2]	17	34	24	27	40	[2]	8	16	16	5
33	24	25	[1]	-1	[2]	3	2	-2	[1]	1	2	93	50	42	[2]	2	6	90	48	44	[2]	1	3	6
24	9	[1]	10	-4	4	1	-9	[1]	-11	[2]	3	23	17	[2]	-4	7	14	22	26	[2]	7	8	11	7
28	61	[1]	27	11	23	11	10	[1]	1	2	7	51	66	[2]	1	7	58	40	56	[2]	2	5	51	8
33	61	15	[2]	43	3	49	36	10	1	20	6	82	77	17	3	40	18	33	41	7	2	20	12	9
27	47	37	[1]	8	4	11	10	1	[1]	[2]	9	34	37	14	[2]	4	19	23	27	13	[2]	4	10	10
350	795	[1]	736	13	46	45	58	[1]	32	5	21	550	675	[2]	613	8	53	505	617	[2]	581	3	32	11
34	25	5	14	-2	9	58	86	[2]	53	4	28	99	131	....	55	6	71	40	45	....	1	2	43	12
10	17	[1]	14	-1	4	5	1	[1]	[2]	[2]	2	12	7	....	-2	1	8	8	6	....	-2	1	6	13
486	254	1	120	94	40	204	236	7	70	124	34	483	547	9	163	269	106	280	311	2	92	145	72	14
7	[2]	....	1	-1	[2]	9	6	....	4	2	1	20	21	....	5	11	15	11	15	....	1	10	4	15
5	-1	....	[1]	[2]	-1	1	[2]	....	[1]	[2]	[2]	3	3	....	[2]	2	3	1	3	....	[2]	2	1	16
18	5	[1]	[1]	-1	3	33	23	[1]	11	7	4	52	46	[2]	17	22	8	18	23	[2]	6	14	3	17
66	58	[1]	34	21	3	29	30	[1]	6	12	12	53	61	[2]	8	36	17	24	31	[2]	2	24	5	18
35	15	[2]	-2	10	7	15	11	....	2	6	4	22	25	....	7	11	6	7	14	....	5	5	3	19
14	14	[1]	4	1	8	10	14	[1]	12	1	1	19	22	[2]	13	2	6	9	9	[2]	1	5		20
15	-2	[1]	[1]	[2]	-2	3	3	[1]	[1]	1	1	5	5	[2]	1	2	2	2	2	[2]	[2]	1	1	21
1	-1	[1]	-2	-1	1	2	4	[1]	[1]	1	3	3	5	[2]	1	3	1	[2]	-1	[2]	[2]		1	22
16	-1	....	-2	[2]	1	2	4	....	1	3	[2]	7	12	....	1	7	4	5	8	....	[3]	4	4	23
3	4	[2]	2	1	1	4	3	....	-1	2	2	12	11	....	[2]	7	4	8	8	....	[3]	5	3	24
278	157	5	86	59	13	85	128	[2]	29	88	10	271	326	[3]	111	165	50	186	198	1	82	77	39	25
28	5	1	3	[2]	2	11	10	5	3	1	[2]	16	11	7	-2	....	5	5	[3]	1	-6	1	4	26
38	66	5	57	[2]	4	37	34	6	18	1	9	219	239	52	164	2	21	182	205	46	147	1	12	27
19	13	3	8	[2]	1	12	12	2	1	....	9	40	50	31	7	....	11	28	38	30	6	....	2	28
20	53	1	49	[2]	1	25	22	4	17	1	[2]	179	189	21	157	2		154	167	16	141	1	10	29
201	64	3	6	25	30	151	222	18	118	56	29	656	737	47	499	109	82	505	515	28	381	53	52	30
17	2	[1]	[1]	8	-6	47	[1]	[1]	28	18		62	83	[2]	53	30	26	36	[2]	25	12			31
7	-4		[1]	-1	-4	6	6		[1]	3	2	12	15		[2]	3	11	6	9		[2]	1	8	32
28	-13		[1]	-1	-12	4	44	[1]	[1]	1	43	35	52		[2]	2	49	31	7		[2]	1	6	33
4	19	....	[1]	6	13	13	17	....	[1]	[1]	9	21	27	....	[2]	10	18	8	11	....	[1]	1	10	34
39	15	[1]	[1]	[2]	15	13	30	[1]	[1]	[1]	31	38	48	[2]	[2]	4	48	19	18	[2]	[2]	3	18	35
2	2	[1]	[1]	[2]	2	3	2	[1]	[1]	[2]	2	7	8	[2]	[2]	4	4	4	4	[2]	[2]	4		36
16	16	[1]	[1]	1	15	22	24	[1]	[1]	[2]	6	44	47	[2]	[2]	10	10	22	23	[2]	[2]	5	18	37
9	-15	2	-21	4	[2]	20	31	6	9	10		63	65	23	10	24	8	43	33	17	1	14	2	38
78	41	[2]	29	9	3	29	21	5	16	[2]	1	374	392	13	369	3	8	346	371	9	353	2	7	39

r Revised.
p Preliminary.
1. Combined in "other industries."
2. Less than $500,000.
3. Includes the purchase for $180 million from British owners of a petroleum company with assets located in the West Indies, Canada, and the United Kingdom. The necessary adjustments have been made in the value table to show the investment in the countries where the assets are located.

Source: U. S. Department of Commerce, Office of Business Economics.

r Revised.
p Preliminary.
1. Income is the sum of dividends, interest, and branch profits; earnings is the sum of income and undistributed subsidiary earnings.
2. Combined in "other industries."
3. Less than $500,000.

Source: U. S. Department of Commerce, Office of Business Economics.

Canada has received about 40 percent of United States direct manufacturing investments abroad in the past 2 years. Although manufacturing earnings in Canada were down sharply in 1957, additional capital supplied by parent companies was sufficient to offset most of the decline in investment funds available out of earnings.

In Western Europe, additions to manufacturing investments were maintained at an annual rate of over $200 million. Investment in manufacturing in the United Kingdom predominates, with Germany and Italy receiving sizable, though lesser, amounts. In the rest of the world, manufacturing investments continued to rise significantly in Australia, the Union of South Africa, and Japan.

Other industries vary

Among other industries, mining and smelting investments showed a sizable increase in 1957, despite a sharp decline in earnings resulting from lower prices for metals and minerals. Capital moving to Latin America for mining investments rose steeply, with substantial amounts going to Chile, Peru and Mexico. A number of large new projects are in prospect for South America and the Caribbean area. Mining investments in Canada were substantial in 1957, though reinvested earnings were smaller. Sizable new projects are also underway in that country.

Public utility investments rose somewhat in 1957, although remaining comparatively low. Most of the investment went to Latin America, largely to Cuba, Venezuela and Brazil. Panamanian shipping companies reinvested substantial amounts and received additional sums from parent companies. It is particularly difficult to trace the investments of the shipping subsidiaries, and sizable amounts shown for Panama or Liberia may actually be utilized elsewhere to meet the requirements of the parent companies. The growing number

of holding company arrangements also increases the difficulty of determining the countries in which actual investments are occurring.

Direct investments in agricultural enterprises resulted in a net reduction on balance because of the sale of sizable properties. Investments in trade, finance and service establishments abroad form a sizable portion of all direct investments, having an aggregate book value of $3.2 billion at the end of 1957. The increase of $300 million in 1957 was less than in 1956, largely because of reduced capital outflows to finance organizations in Canada. There were also reductions in these investments in several Latin American countries.

Other Private Investments

Private United States capital for long-term portfolio investments abroad amounted to more than $800 million in 1957, and about $300 million of short-term private credits were extended to foreign borrowers. The combined total of $1.1 billion was about equal to the 1956 amount, but the proportion of short-term capital was lower in 1957.

New issues of foreign dollar bonds sold in the United States totaled about $600 million in 1957. The greater part of the offerings came in the first half of the year, falling off in the second half as the relative interest rates and exchange rate differential discouraged Canadian borrowers, that accounted for over half of the new issues sold in the year. Nearly $200 million was also raised by the International Bank for Reconstruction and Development, and small amounts were obtained by a growing list of other borrowers.

In the first half of 1958, conditions were again conducive to foreign borrowing in the United States, and by the end of June, total sales of new foreign securities exceeded the full amount sold in the previous year. Moreover, there was a further extension of the list of borrowers, that included, besides Canada and the International Bank, the Netherlands, Norway, the European Coal and Steel Community, the Belgian Congo, Australia, Northern Rhodesia, Israel, and the Union of South Africa. Also sold in the United States market in early 1958 were large issues of stock by European petroleum companies. As in other postwar years, however, a large part of some of the issues was purchased by foreign investors rather than United States residents. In the period since June of this year, foreign bond issues have been minor, with recent increases in interest costs acting as a deterrent.

Net purchases by United States investors of outstanding foreign corporate stocks amounted to only $33 million in 1957, compared with over $100 million in 1956. Purchases of such securities, principally issues of Canadian and large European corporations, had been substantial from 1953 to the time of the Suez crisis in 1956. Thereafter, purchases of Canadian issues continued in considerable volume, but there was a net liquidation of European stocks through 1957. In the first half of 1958, purchases of European stocks were resumed, reflecting generally prosperous conditions in these countries. Net purchases of outstanding foreign bonds continued in 1957 and 1958 on a modest scale.

Loans extended to foreigners, both short-term and those with maturities of up to about 5 years, increased by a net amount of nearly $600 million in 1957. As shown in table 7, the total of these claims and loans outstanding at the end of 1957 was $4.1 billion. Principal recipients of this financing in 1957 were France, the United Kingdom (partly to finance purchases of oil leases), Brazil, Mexico, Venezuela, and a few Asian countries.

The availability of bank financing has been important for these countries, and has helped to reduce the severity of

Annual Additions to U. S. Direct Foreign Investments, By Industry

Billion Dollars

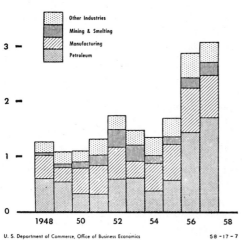

- Other Industries
- Mining & Smelting
- Manufacturing
- Petroleum

1948   50   52   54   56   58

U. S. Department of Commerce, Office of Business Economics

58 -17 - 7

fluctuations in United States and world trade. Such credits are expanding at an even more rapid rate in 1958, and announcements of large bank loans to foreign governments in need of financing have been appearing with increasing frequency in recent months. Direct financing of exports by United States manufacturers and exporters provided an additional $80 million in 1957, very largely to Latin American countries.

United States Government claims and credits

Long-term United States Government credits and loans to foreign countries outstanding at the end of 1957 were about $330 million higher than a year earlier, with gross disbursements during the year of nearly $1 billion the highest since 1948, while repayments of about $660 million were a record high. Over 40 percent of the net outflow, or about $145 million, was to Latin America, mainly as Export-Import Bank loans. The net outflow to Western Europe was about the same, although both disbursements and repayments were larger than for Latin America. The outflow to Europe included a $250 million drawing against the $500 million Export-Import Bank loan to the United Kingdom, which was provided at the time of the Suez crisis to support sterling area reserves. For most other European countries, repayments exceeded new loans. Although the net outflow to the rest of the world was small, this was the result of large repayments by India and Pakistan of silver loaned under lend-lease arrangements, while disbursements were as large as in the previous year.

Beginning in 1954, the fastest growing component of United States Government foreign assets has been the accumulation of foreign currencies, or equivalent claims, derived from the sale of surplus agricultural commodities. In 1957, the net short-term capital outflow associated with these assets was $635 million, but the increase in the value of these holdings recorded in table 1 is somewhat less because of declining exchange values of some of the foreign currencies. Detailed information regarding these Government transactions was given in the SURVEY OF CURRENT BUSINESS for April 1958.

Earnings of United States Investments

Earnings of direct private foreign investments, which account for about seven-eighths of total earnings on foreign investments, increased by nearly 7 percent in 1957 to over $3.3 billion. Virtually the whole increase flowed from the petroleum industry, reflecting generally maintained production—although declines in the Middle East early in the year were offset by increased output in Latin America—and a strong demand situation.

Petroleum earnings in 1957 accounted for nearly half of the direct investment total. Earnings of this industry in Latin America were $700 million, rising substantially from the previous year's record as output in Venezuela was pushed upward early in the year to meet demands normally supplied from the Middle East. Earnings in Western Europe rose considerably, especially in the United Kingdom, reflecting intensified refinery operations. In other areas, principally the Middle East, earnings were up moderately over the 1956 figures, showing the recovery from the effects of the shutdowns during the Suez crisis.

Most other industries did not fare so well. Agriculture, public utilities, and trade, finance and service enterprises reported marginal gains over the 1956 results. In agriculture, profits of sugar properties were better with the improved sugar market, but other branches of the industry earned about the same amount as in 1956.

Earnings of U. S. Direct Foreign Investments, By Industry

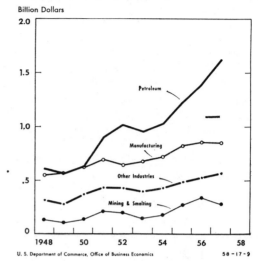

Billion Dollars

Petroleum

Manufacturing

Other Industries

Mining & Smelting

1948   50   52   54   56   58

U. S. Department of Commerce, Office of Business Economics   58-17-9

Earnings of mining and smelting enterprises fell by nearly 20 percent in 1957, as metal and mineral prices reacted from earlier highs. Latin America experienced a reduction, and Canada and the Union of South Africa were also down considerably. In only a few countries where new properties were entering production was there an upturn in earnings of this industry.

Aggregate earnings of United States owned manufacturing plants abroad were about $850 million in 1957, only slightly lower than in 1956. However, earnings in Canada were cut substantially by the business recession in that country, while earnings in Europe were up considerably. Earnings in the United Kingdom were particularly strong, reflecting sustained high levels of production from expanded facilities, and there were sizable increases in Australia and the Union of South Africa.

The reinvestment of foreign earnings of United States corporations, amounting to about $1 billion annually in 1956 and 1957, continued to be a major source of financing for expanding their foreign enterprises. Over half of the earnings of foreign subsidiary companies remained undistributed in 1957. A similar figure is not available for foreign branch operations, but since these are most prevalent in the petroleum industry, it is likely that the extraordinary expansion of this industry in 1957 relied heavily on current earnings for financing.[1]

Dividends and interest received from private portfolio and short-term investments abroad rose substantially in 1957 to a total of over $360 million. About one-third of this income is earned on United States holdings of foreign dollar bonds, which have been expanding steadily and generally under conditions of rising yields. Rapidly growing long- and short-term bank loans outstanding, at rising interest rates, have also resulted in larger interest receipts.

---

[1] A study of the sources and uses of funds of foreign branch and subsidiary investments is now being prepared, and will be published in the SURVEY. It is expected that this study will develop new data on the extent to which internal sources of funds and foreign capital, in addition to parent company funds, supply the financing of plant and equipment expenditures and other capital outlays abroad.

Canada accounts for nearly half of these income receipts, reflecting the concentration of long-term portfolio investments in Canada shown in table 1. A large part of the interest on bank loans and commercial credits is derived from Latin America.

Foreign Investments in the United States

The flow of foreign capital to the United States for long-term investment fell off sharply in 1957 from the high of the previous year. Net foreign purchases of United States corporate stocks declined to about $145 million from a postwar high of $256 million in 1956. Such purchases, mainly for European investors, reached a peak in the first half of 1957, but tightening of British exchange controls and declining prices of United States corporate stocks after July resulted in a net liquidation of sizable proportions, beginning in September and continuing in the early months of this year

Table 5.—United States Direct Investments in Selected Areas, 1950 and 1957

[Book values; Millions of dollars]

Area	1950				1957			
	Total	Petroleum	Mining and smelting	Other	Total	Petroleum	Mining and smelting	Other
Middle East............	731	692	11	28	1,284	1,177	9	98
Africa [1]............	107	52	31	24	319	134	111	74
Far East [2]............	320	120	11	189	716	307	19	390
Latin American Republics [3].........	4,445	1,233	628	2,584	8,308	2,861	1,238	4,209
European dependencies in the Western Hemisphere.....	131	70	38	23	339	190	75	74
Total............	5,734	2,167	719	2,848	10,966	4,669	1,452	4,845

[1] Excludes the estimated value of ships registered in Liberia; excludes the Union of South Africa.
[2] Excludes Japan, Australia, and New Zealand.
[3] Excludes the estimated value of ships registered in Panama.

Table 6.—United States Holdings of Dollar Bonds of Specified Countries, Market and Par Values, 1950, 1956, 1957

[Millions of dollars, year-ends]

Countries	1950		1956		1957	
	Market value	Par value	Market value	Par value	Market value	Par value
Total..............	1,693	2,049	2,826	3,110	3,255	3,533
Western Europe, total...............	85	234	185	233	193	237
Belgium..............	19	18	33	34	36	36
Germany..............		104	98	113	95	109
Italy.................	10	33	28	45	27	43
Other...............	56	79	26	41	35	49
Canada..............	1,106	1,065	1,672	1,721	1,907	1,934
Latin American Republics, total.....	159	336	135	260	123	245
Bolivia...............	5	38	5	38	6	38
Brazil................	46	75	31	43	29	38
Chile.................	29	66	24	52	21	50
Colombia.............	28	54	21	37	18	35
Other...............	51	103	54	90	49	84
Other foreign countries, total........	117	189	414	457	461	503
Australia..............	87	95	99	103	100	103
Israel.................			267	267	314	314
Japan.................	20	41	36	34	35	33
Other...............	10	53	12	53	12	53
International Bank for Reconstruction and Development.............	226	225	420	439	571	614

Source: U. S. Department of Commerce, Office of Business Economics.

This was offset to some extent by continued foreign purchases of United States corporate bonds.

Foreign direct-investment capital flows to the United States also declined in 1957 from the 1956 high, primarily reflecting a sharp drop in the inflow from Canada, which had been much larger than usual in 1956 because of the acquisition of interests in existing United States companies. In addition to increases financed by capital inflows of about $120 million, United States subsidiaries of foreign companies reinvested nearly $125 million out of earnings of a little more than $200 million. Of the combined rise in book values of some $240 million, the United Kingdom accounted for over $100 million and Canada for about $90 million.

Earnings of foreign investors on their holdings in the United States rose slightly in 1957, reaching a total of $776 million, as shown in table 8. Direct investments of foreigners in the United States earned about $325 million, including about $125 million of undistributed profits. Foreign investments in United States corporate stocks earned dividends, after withholding taxes, of over $230 million. The largest increase in foreign earnings here, however, resulted from greater holdings of United States Government obligations at generally higher interest rates.

Gains in reserves

Aggregate foreign holdings of gold (excluding Soviet bloc holdings) and liquid dollar assets were up by less then $200 million for the year 1957 as a whole. Liquid dollar assets, as shown in table 1, increased by over $250 million, but during the year foreign countries sold $770 million of gold to the United States. Offsetting the sale of gold to the United States were receipts into foreign official reserves of about $700 million of newly mined gold and sales of Soviet-bloc gold to the West. Thus, foreign official gold holdings declined by about $70 million in 1957

Table 7.—Banking and Commercial Claims on Foreigners, by Selected Countries, 1953-57

[Millions of dollars]

Countries	1953	1954	1955	1956	1957			
					Total	Banking claims		Commercial claims
						Short term	Medium term	
Total..........	1,723	2,400	2,825	3,523	4,131	2,229	1,120	782
Western Europe, total.........	597	734	744	1,017	1,257	670	342	245
Belgium..........	58	30	29	48	57	33	11	13
France..........	177	125	30	40	138	114	3	21
Germany..........	39	82	110	190	178	140	13	25
Norway..........	15	19	58	97	125	23	97	5
Turkey..........	26	56	113	106	98	76	....	22
United Kingdom......	124	250	171	215	285	109	121	55
Canada............	169	175	258	303	335	154	69	112
Latin America, total.........	686	1,094	1,306	1,549	1,812	963	575	274
Brazil..........	165	400	314	339	379	100	211	68
Colombia........	80	137	172	177	135	107	18	10
Cuba............	63	121	209	232	239	113	101	25
Mexico..........	123	161	206	285	362	229	100	33
Venezuela.......	62	88	173	213	274	173	55	46
Asia, total.........	189	300	407	517	580	386	87	107
Israel............	43	38	42	43	55	24	23	8
Japan............	42	139	149	201	196	145	9	42
Other Asia......	104	123	216	273	329	217	55	57
All other countries, total.........	82	97	110	137	147	56	47	44

Source: Treasury Bulletin, various issues.

The year 1957 was marked by wide fluctuations in the reserve positions of foreign countries. Losses of gold and dollars began toward the end of 1956, at the time of the Suez crisis, and intensified in the first quarter of 1957. In the second quarter, reserves gained considerably, partly because of extraordinary private capital outflows from the United States and also as a result of seasonal factors in other balance of payments transactions. Sizable losses reappeared in the third quarter, featured by speculative pressures against sterling and certain other European currencies. These pressures were alleviated after September by the strong measures taken by the British authorities, aided by the extension of a large Export-Import Bank loan. The overall balance of payments situation subsequently resulted in a sizable gain in foreign reserves.

The manner in which foreign countries came through the various pressures of events in 1956 and 1957 reflected in large part the quick action taken by the International Monetary Fund in supplying financial resources, particularly to the United Kingdom in 1956 and to France, India and many other countries in 1957. Most of the gold sales to the United States in both of these years came from holdings of the Fund, enabling aggregate dollar holdings of foreign countries to remain relatively stable.

In the first half of 1958, the accumulation of foreign reserves accelerated, as discussed in the Balance of Payments report beginning on page 9 of this issue. However, though the aggregate gain was very large, and is apparently continuing to the present, there are many countries that are

not sharing in these gains, for various reasons, and for them the continued availability of private and Government funds from the United States, as well as capital from the international institutions and some foreign countries is extremely important.

Table 8.—Earnings on International Investments, by Type, 1950–57

[Millions of dollars]

	1950	1952	1953	1954	1955	1956 r	1957 p
Earnings on United States investments abroad, total	2,068	2,704	2,686	2,871	3,343	3,611	3,898
Direct investments, total	1,769	2,295	2,218	2,369	2,811	3,120	3,330
Dividends, interest, and branch profits	1,294	1,419	1,442	1,724	1,912	2,120	2,313
Undistributed profits of subsidiaries	475	876	776	644	898	1,000	1,017
Portfolio and short-term investments	190	205	216	230	258	297	363
Interest on United States Government credits	109	204	252	272	274	194	205
Earnings on foreign investments in the United States, total	478	472	571	544	631	699	776
Direct investments, total	281	234	306	300	320	309	325
Dividends, interest and branch profits	148	152	185	175	191	190	202
Undistributed profits of subsidiaries	138	82	121	125	129	119	123
Portfolio investments	166	174	179	185	217	236	250
Interest on United States Government obligations	31	64	86	59	94	154	201

r Revised.   p Preliminary.

Source: U. S. Department of Commerce, Office of Business Economics.

U.S. INDUSTRY EXPANDS INVESTMENT ABROAD

Samuel Pizer
and
Frederick Cutler

by Samuel Pizer and Frederick Cutler ☆

U.S. Industry Expands
Investment Abroad

CAPITAL expenditures by U.S. companies to expand and modernize their productive facilities in foreign countries were reduced by about 14 percent in 1958 from the peak established in 1957. The contraction in 1958 was accounted for largely by the absence of large cash payments for petroleum leases such as occurred in 1957, and by the general leveling off of industrial activity abroad. Slower economic expansion was also reflected in a shift in inventories of the foreign enterprises from a substantial accumulation in 1957 to a net reduction in 1958.

U. S. Foreign Investments in Plant and Equipment Expenditures

1957 [ ]   1958 [ ]

Million Dollars

MANUFACTURING

PETROLEUM

MINING, AGRICULTURE, AND UTILITIES

Canada   Latin America   Europe   Other

U. S. Department of Commerce, Office of Business Economics   59-10-11

The decline in foreign capital expenditures by U.S. companies in 1958 was considerably less than the decline in such domestic expenditures, especially for the manufacturing, mining, and petroleum industries. Expenditures by these industries for plant and equipment, both domestic and foreign, were about $20 billion in 1957 and $15 billion in 1958, with the proportion of foreign expenditures up from some 15 percent in 1957 to 17 percent in 1958. These percentages would be somewhat higher if allowance were made for foreign expenditures not covered in these annual surveys.[1]

For 1959 a rise in capital outlays abroad by U.S. business is indicated by larger capital flows from the United States and by a tendency to reinvest a larger proportion of foreign earnings. This increase is in line with the upturn in industrial production in major foreign countries as well as in the United States. Sources of funds to finance additional expansion appear to be adequate, as earnings in the United States and abroad have recovered, and credit conditions in Europe are relatively favorable.

Comparison with balance-of-payments data

Data collected in this second annual survey of the financing and capital expenditures of foreign enterprises controlled by U.S. companies continue to show that their gross investments abroad are much larger than the amount reflected in balance-of-payments data on net capital outflows from the United States and undistributed profits. In 1958, for instance, the book value of the U.S. interest in direct-investment enterprises abroad in the manufacturing, mining, and petroleum industries increased by $1.5 billion, while expenditures for fixed capital abroad reported by the smaller group of companies covered in this report in these industries were $2.7 billion.

Annual variations in plant and equipment expenditures abroad are much smaller than the combined changes in net capital outflows from the United States and undistributed profits from foreign operations, which represents the amount added to the U.S. interest in the book value of the foreign enterprises each year. While the latter amount for the mining, petroleum, and manufacturing industries declined from $2.7 billion in 1957 to $1.5 billion in 1958, the change in expenditures for fixed capital abroad for the survey companies was from $3.2 billion to $2.7 billion.

---

[1] See the SURVEY OF CURRENT BUSINESS of Jan., 1959, pp. 20-24, for a description of the coverage and procedures used in these surveys. Data for 1957 have been revised and adjusted to a minor extent to correspond to the coverage for 1958. Based on ratios of earnings, reporting companies account for about three quarters of U.S. direct foreign investments, but coverage varies from nearly complete coverage in petroleum to about 60 percent in manufacturing. Data in this article cover only companies reporting in the annual survey, unless otherwise noted.

NOTE.—MR. PIZER AND MR. CUTLER ARE MEMBERS OF THE BALANCE OF PAYMENTS DIVISION, OFFICE OF BUSINESS ECONOMICS.

Of course, each set of statistics is designed for a specific purpose; the capital outflow series relates primarily to the international transactions of the United States, while the data on sources and uses of funds relate primarily to the scope and impact of the investment activities of these enterprises in the countries in which they operate.

Supply of Funds Reduced

Funds available to the foreign enterprises controlled by reporting companies fell from about $6.3 billion in 1957 to $5.2 billion in 1958. Net income was sharply reduced in the mining and petroleum industries but held up well in manufacturing and service industries.[2] At the same time income paid out to parent companies and other owners rose somewhat over the previous year, so that funds retained abroad out of earnings for this survey group were cut by some $550 million. A similar sharp drop in retained profits also occurred for domestic corporations.

Most of the drop in retained earnings abroad was in the petroleum industry, which utilized less funds as a result of lower investment activity and reductions in inventories. Income in this industry was down from the 1957 amount in most areas except the Middle East, but income paid out was not reduced to the same extent. Retained earnings were also lower in the mining industry, primarily because of lesser income receipts. In the manufacturing and service industries the amount and proportion of earnings retained abroad were about the same in 1958 as in 1957.

Financing provided by parent companies and other sources in the United States was about 40 percent lower in 1958, dropping from $1.3 billion in 1957 to $0.8 billion. This figure does not correspond closely to the net direct-investment capital outflow included in the balance-of-payments accounts because of differences in recording the flow of funds between U.S. companies and their foreign branches, as well as differences in the industries and companies covered, and in the treatment of certain capital flows. For the three major industry groups—mining, petroleum, and manufacturing—the balance-of-payments accounts, after adjustments for comparability, show a drop of $1.2 billion from 1957 to 1958 in the amount of funds provided by parent companies and undistributed profits. Reports for the group of companies in these industries covered in this survey show a drop of $1 billion.

In addition to funds supplied by parent companies, the foreign enterprises obtained sizable amounts from U.S. capital markets and, in a few cases, from the U.S. Government. About $185 million was obtained from these sources in 1958, compared with $290 million in 1957. Nearly all of the public financing went to manufacturing, petroleum pipeline, and other enterprises in Canada. U.S. Government financing by the Export-Import Bank, amounting to $57 million in 1958, was provided to mining and public utility operations in Latin America.

Funds obtained abroad

The other major sources of funds available to the direct-investment enterprises abroad are charges for depreciation and depletion, and financing provided by capital markets or creditors, including foreign governments, in the countries in which they operate.

Depreciation charges on existing fixed assets continued to mount in 1958, rising by 14 percent from 1957 to a total of $1.3 billion for the survey companies. This rate of increase is similar to the annual average rate of increase in the book

[2] Earnings of direct foreign investments in 1958 are discussed in the Survey of Current Business for August 1959, pp. 25–32.

525103°—59——3

value of U.S. direct investments abroad since 1950. Relative to other sources of funds depreciation was rising in 1958, and accounted for 29 percent of all funds available.

Most of the rise in depreciation charges in 1958 was reported for manufacturing and petroleum companies. In the petroleum industry depreciation charges increased mainly in Latin America, where major expansions in investments have been carried out in the past few years. Such charges also increased substantially in Canada and the Middle East. For manufacturing, the greater part of the rise in depreciation charges was in Canada and Europe, also reflecting rapidly mounting investments.

Included in these figures for depreciation charges is about $60 million of depletion charges, nearly all for petroleum companies and about equally divided between Canada and Latin America.

Foreign branches and subsidiaries of U.S. companies covered in this report obtained about three quarters of a billion dollars from foreign sources in 1958, compared with a little over $1 billion in 1957. However, companies reduced their borrowing abroad proportionately less than they reduced

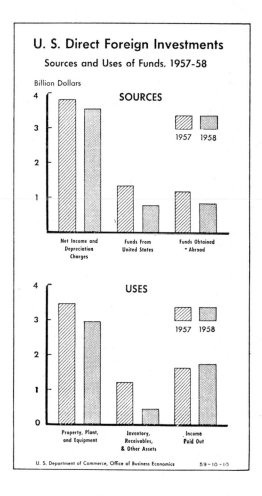

U. S. Direct Foreign Investments

Sources and Uses of Funds, 1957-58

U. S. Department of Commerce, Office of Business Economics   59-10-10

Table 1.—Sources and Uses of Funds of U.S. Direct Foreign

[Millions of dollars]

Areas and industries	Sources of funds											
	1957						1958					
	Total	Net income	Funds from United States	Funds obtained abroad	Depreciation and depletion	Other	Total	Net income	Funds from United States	Funds obtained abroad	Depreciation and depletion	Other
All areas, total	6,290	2,632	1,325	1,056	1,171	106	5,151	2,188	763	734	1,342	124
Mining and smelting	446	216	128	10	89	3	445	169	182	13	79	2
Petroleum	3,886	1,607	857	695	653	74	2,966	1,222	450	415	753	96
Manufacturing	1,371	563	259	220	315	14	1,292	558	97	176	382	19
Trade	310	160	23	73	53	1	230	173	-4	50	66	5
Agriculture and public utilities	277	87	57	58	61	14	219	65	39	50	63	2
Canada, total	1,506	551	432	141	354	28	1,248	387	326	84	397	54
Mining and smelting	172	121	30	-4	25	(1)	132	62	57	-7	20	(1)
Petroleum	705	146	251	135	152	21	578	61	247	57	170	43
Manufacturing	550	249	141	-1	158	3	463	221	42	9	183	5
Trade	51	29	7	2	13	(1)	42	33	-16	4	18	3
Agriculture and public utilities	27	7	2	9	5	4	32	7	-4	22	5	2
Latin American Republics, total	2,239	866	724	279	344	26	1,395	567	219	176	393	40
Mining and smelting	241	70	100	15	56	(1)	234	64	107	7	55	1
Petroleum	1,478	621	513	128	205	11	738	371	31	63	248	25
Manufacturing	183	66	45	46	23	1	179	44	26	69	29	11
Trade	102	38	14	39	8	3	78	41	15	11	9	2
Agriculture and public utilities	234	71	52	49	52	10	166	46	40	27	53	(1)
Europe, total	1,241	432	186	351	253	19	1,211	395	72	425	288	31
Mining and smelting	1			-1	(1)		-2	(1)	(1)	-2	(1)	
Petroleum	570	104	122	162	111	11	619	90	61	328	111	29
Manufacturing	539	189	64	164	113	9	455	221	17	74	141	2
Trade	130	77	-1	26	29	-1	138	84	-5	24	35	(1)
Agriculture and public utilities	(1)	(1)	(1)	(1)	(1)		(1)	(1)	(1)	(1)	(1)	
Other areas, total	1,304	784	-18	285	220	33	1,296	839	145	49	264	-1
Mining and smelting	32	24	-3	1	8	2	80	43	18	15	3	1
Petroleum	1,133	677	-29	270	185	30	1,030	700	112	-3	223	-2
Manufacturing	98	59	10	8	21	(1)	134	68	12	24	29	1
Trade	27	16	2	6	3	(1)	32	15	2	11	4	(1)
Agriculture and public utilities	15	8	3	(1)	3	1	20	12	2	2	1	(1)

drawings of funds from U.S. sources. Requirements for foreign financing are related largely to changes in working capital needs of the companies, and requirements for such financing were much reduced from 1957 to 1958, as receivables increased more slowly and inventories were sharply cut back. In fact, despite a reduction in foreign borrowing, there appears to have been a decrease in net working capital abroad for the survey companies as a whole, in contrast to an increase in 1957.

Reduced borrowing abroad was particularly notable in the petroleum industry, and was also significant for manufacturing enterprises. Most of the change for the petroleum companies occurred in the Middle East and Far East, reflecting a large increase in funds supplied from the United States, a much lower rate of accumulation of receivables, and a liquidation of inventories abroad. In Western Europe, however, the petroleum industry utilized over $300 million of foreign financing, double the amount obtained in 1957.

Large amounts of funds were needed by this industry for accelerated fixed investment in Europe, largely in refineries and marketing facilities, and the increase in borrowing abroad reflected the growing ability of European financial centers to supply funds for industrial expansion.

Although manufacturing enterprises abroad reduced their local borrowing in the aggregate, this resulted entirely from a sharp decline in Europe, in contrast with the experience of the petroleum companies. Manufacturing companies in Europe reduced their outlays for plant and equipment as part of a general slowdown of industrial expansion in this area, and also required less funds to finance inventories and receivables. At the same time, larger amounts were provided by retained earnings and depreciation charges, so that sizable amounts of cash were probably accumulated.

Of the $¾ billion of financing obtained abroad in 1958, about $70 million was raised by the sale of capital stock and the remainder represented increased liabilities, including accrued taxes. Equity financing, therefore, continued to be a relatively small part of the total. Most of the equity financing was obtained by Canadian enterprises, with only minor amounts reported in Europe or Latin America.

Plant Expansion Abroad

The continued modernization and expansion of productive facilities established abroad by U.S. companies is a major factor affecting the rate of economic progress in many countries as well as the size and character of world trade. New ventures are being developed or are under consideration in many countries to serve growing markets and utilize untapped reserves of raw material. However, most of the capital expenditures by U.S. industry abroad are

Table 2.—Exploration and Development Expenditures Abroad by U.S. Petroleum Companies, 1957–58

[Millions of dollars]

	Total	Canada	Latin American Republics	Europe	Other areas
1958—Total	780	227	338	49	166
Charged against income	375	133	118	31	93
Other	405	94	220	18	73
1957—Total	1,046	248	609	40	149
Charged against income	326	129	98	24	75
Other	720	119	511	16	74

NOTE.—Data for reporting companies only.

Source: U.S. Department of Commerce, Office of Business Economics.

Investments in 1957 and 1958, by Area and Industry

[Millions of dollars]

Areas and industries	Uses of funds											
	1957						1958					
	Total	Property, plant, and equipment	Inventories	Receivables	Other assets	Income paid out	Total	Property, plant, and equipment	Inventories	Receivables	Other assets	Income paid out
All areas, total	6,290	3,468	593	402	209	1,618	5,151	2,993	−109	195	347	1,725
Mining and smelting	446	300	33	3	−29	139	445	348	−29	−6	7	125
Petroleum	3,886	2,059	347	276	144	1,060	2,966	1,693	−88	109	99	1,153
Manufacturing	1,371	805	148	58	55	305	1,232	626	−10	64	235	317
Trade	310	134	53	53	17	53	290	132	26	20	34	78
Agriculture and public utilities	277	170	11	12	23	61	219	195	−7	7	−27	51
Canada, total	1,506	1,115	115	−16	2	290	1,248	914	−87	44	105	272
Mining and smelting	172	110	19	3	−28	68	132	119	−5	−13	−15	46
Petroleum	705	564	52	10	10	69	578	480	−20	30	23	65
Manufacturing	550	395	33	11	11	140	463	272	−64	24	88	143
Trade	51	32	9	(¹)	5	5	42	19	2	2	4	15
Agriculture and public utilities	27	15	2	−1	3	8	32	25	−1	1	5	2
Latin American Republics, total	2,239	1,218	201	149	112	559	1,395	869	−37	33	36	494
Mining and smelting	241	171	14	2	3	51	234	183	−19	5	23	42
Petroleum	1,478	822	138	50	49	419	738	425	−40	−5	1	357
Manufacturing	183	65	18	40	31	30	179	83	21	22	26	27
Trade	102	13	22	45	11	11	78	22	5	5	20	26
Agriculture and public utilities	234	147	8	12	19	48	166	156	−5	6	−34	43
Europe, total	1,241	673	185	133	−2	252	1,211	707	13	107	133	251
Mining and smelting	1	1	(¹)	(¹)	(¹)	1	−2	(¹)	(¹)	(¹)	−2	......
Petroleum	570	284	82	91	−5	118	619	395	−15	85	43	111
Manufacturing	539	306	85	38	−8	102	455	230	19	9	89	108
Trade	130	81	18	4	−5	32	138	82	9	12	3	32
Agriculture and public utilities	(¹)	(¹)	(¹)	(¹)	(¹)	(¹)	(¹)	(¹)	(¹)	(¹)	(¹)	(¹)
Other areas, total	1,301	462	92	136	97	517	1,296	502	3	11	73	707
Mining and smelting	32	19	1	−2	−5		80	46	−6	2	1	37
Petroleum	1,133	389	75	125	90	454	1,030	393	−14	−2	32	621
Manufacturing	98	39	12	8	5	34	134	41	13	9	32	39
Trade	27	8	3	4	7	5	32	9	9	1	7	6
Agriculture and public utilities	15	8	(¹)	1	1	5	20	14	(¹)	(¹)	1	5

¹ Less than $500,000.

Note.—Detail may not add to totals because of rounding. Data for reporting companies only.

Source: U.S. Department of Commerce, Office of Business Economics.

associated not with entirely new enterprises, but with the steady expansion of existing businesses. Of the $3 billion of expenditures for plant and equipment reported for 1958, only about 15 percent related to enterprises established since 1950. The proportion for new enterprises would probably be somewhat higher, however, if all direct investments were covered, since newer enterprises are not as well represented in the survey.

About 88 percent of the funds available to the foreign enterprises (after income distributions) was expended for plant and equipment in 1958, compared with about 75 percent in 1957. In 1959, it seems likely that the amount of funds available from all sources and the amount spent for plant and equipment are both increasing.

Petroleum investment slowed

Most of the reduction in capital expenditures abroad by U.S. companies from 1957 to 1958 took place in the petroleum industry. However, nearly all of the overall drop in outlays by this industry, amounting to $365 million, represented the elimination of large payments for leases in Venezuela, so that other expenditures for plant and equipment were well maintained. Moderate reductions in capital expenditures were reported for Canada and a number of countries in Latin America, probably related to the adverse market conditions in 1958 for petroleum produced in these countries. In the Middle East, on the other hand, rising production encouraged a small rise in capital expenditures, and there were substantially higher outlays in several European countries where refinery expansions were in progress.

Capital expenditures abroad by manufacturing enterprises covered in these surveys fell 22 percent in 1958. Decreases were substantial in Canada, the United Kingdom, and some other European countries. In most of these countries the reduction in capital expenditures was part of a general slowdown in the rate of industrial expansion, although industrial production was again rising in the final months of the year. Small gains in capital outlays were reported for a number of Latin American countries.

Companies covered in this survey in the manufacturing category probably account for less than two-thirds of capital expenditures abroad by United States manufacturing enterprises. Since expenditures by the reporting companies totalled $626 million, the overall total may have approached $1 billion in 1958.

Mining companies raised their capital outlays abroad slightly in 1958, with gains reported in Canada and Latin America. Sustained expansion abroad in this industry contrasted with a sharp contraction in the United States. In other industries covered in the survey, the major change in 1958 was an increase in capital investment in Latin America for public utilities.

Expenditures in 1958 for the exploration and development of resources abroad by the petroleum enterprises covered in the survey totalled about $780 million, somewhat higher than the amount for the previous year when the large lease payments in Venezuela are excluded. The gain was primarily in Latin America; a moderately lower rate of expenditure was reported for Canada. Over 40 percent of the total expenditures were in Latin America and about 30 percent in Canada.

Of the total of such expenditures, about $400 million is included as part of the total for property, plant and equipment expenditures, while the remaining $375 million was accounted for by charges against income and therefore does not appear in table 1. The combined total of capital expenditures and exploration and development outlays abroad for the petroleum companies in 1958 was over $2 billion. However, this total does not include the activities of some of the newer exploration ventures, or of most of the foreign tanker operations conducted by U.S. companies.

Inventories cut back

In contrast to an expansion of some $600 million in 1957, inventories of the foreign enterprises controlled by U.S. companies were reduced in nearly all industries and areas in 1958. Inventories of petroleum companies accounted for most of the change in both years, with the general cutbacks in 1958 representing largely an adjustment of the unusual expansion in inventories stemming from the Suez crisis.

Manufacturing inventories were reduced only slightly overall, as moderate increases in most areas were more than offset by a sharp decline in Canada associated with the slowdown in business activity in that country until mid-year. Inventories of mining companies were liquidated in most areas as demand and prices were generally weak.

Inventories and receivables taken together absorbed less than $100 million of the total funds available to the foreign enterprises in 1958, compared with about $1 billion in 1959. One result of this change, as well as of other changes in the overall flow of funds, was a sizable accumulation of cash and securities reported under the heading of "other assets." This accumulation was largest in manufacturing enterprises operating in Canada and Europe, providing a readily available source of funds for continued expansion.

Income distribution high

Remittances of dividends and branch profits rose somewhat in 1958, but there was considerable variation among industries. For the petroleum companies, income paid out in most areas exceeded or was close to total income. However, the proportion of income paid out by this industry tends to be somewhat overstated relative to other industries because a number of enterprises are still in the exploration stage and report sizable losses which offset the earnings of other enterprises. Also, companies often report remittances from branches as income distributions which, in the case of foreign subsidiaries, would be regarded as repayments of capital. Adjustments were made to some reports to show remittances in excess of current earnings as repayments of capital funds to the parent company. The general picture for the year in this industry, however, was one of sustained or slightly increased income distributions as the need for funds for other purposes declined.

The amount of income paid out by other major industry groups changed little between 1957 and 1958 although earnings were generally somewhat reduced.

Table 3.—Plant and Equipment Expenditures Abroad by U.S. Companies, 1957 and 1958

[Millions of dollars]

	1957	1958
All areas, total	3,468	2,993
Canada	1,115	914
Latin American Republics	1,218	869
Argentina	14	23
Brazil	70	70
Chile	50	54
Cuba	81	119
Mexico	36	36
Peru	115	96
Venezuela	741	384
Other countries	111	87
Europe	673	707
Belgium	23	26
France	81	116
Germany	122	146
Italy	45	42
Netherlands	25	31
United Kingdom	331	300
Other countries	43	46
Other areas	462	502
Australia	64	62
Japan	30	15
Philippine Republic	20	21
Union of South Africa	18	21
Middle East	130	155
Other countries and International	200	225

NOTE.—Data for reporting companies only.

Source: U.S. Department of Commerce, Office of Business Economics.

UNITED STATES FOREIGN INVESTMENTS:

Measures of Growth and Economic Effects

Samuel Pizer
and
Frederick Cutler

BY SAMUEL PIZER AND FREDERICK CUTLER

United States Foreign Investments:
Measures of Growth and Economic Effects

THIS article analyzing recent trends and major features of the foreign investments of the United States summarizes the results of the worldwide Office of Business Economics census, containing a broad range of new data, soon to be published in the complete volume: *U.S. Business Investments in Foreign Countries.* For a number of basic series, including values, capital flows, and earnings of direct foreign investments, the comprehensive benchmark data obtained by the new census are carried up-to-date on the basis of sample data supplied regularly by companies which have a large part of the total. New data on sales of the foreign enterprises are also carried forward by a sampling procedure, as

are data on sources and uses of funds which will appear in a following article in the October SURVEY OF CURRENT BUSINESS.

Other comprehensive data obtained in the census, including the outlays of the enterprises abroad for wages, materials, taxes, and services, numbers of employees, structure and ownership of assets, and international shipments are not so significant as time series and the information is presented for the census year 1957.

These data add greatly to knowledge here and in foreign countries of the contributions to economic development and well-being flowing from the operations of these enterprises.

Growth of Direct Investments

UNITED STATES firms added $2½ billion to their investments in foreign subsidiaries and branches in 1959, a larger increase than in 1958 but substantially less than that of the peak year 1957. Reports for the first half of 1960 indicate a moderate reduction in direct-investment outflows, although the rate is close to $1 billion a year, and a like amount is being invested abroad each year out of undistributed profits of foreign subsidiaries.

The flow in 1959 included some $160 million spent to acquire additional stock of existing subsidiaries or other companies already established abroad, and there have been no sizable transactions of this type so far this year.

As shown in the accompanying charts, the pace at which U.S. firms have raised

NOTE.—Substantial portions of the basic data contained in this article were prepared by Julius N. Freidlin, Bertil Renborg, Christopher M. Douty, James Lopes, and Edmund L. Auchter.

their foreign investments since 1950, and especially since 1955, has greatly exceeded that of any extended prior period. The current investment programs of the companies indicate some stabilization of the overall rate of flow, but with considerable divergences among the various industries and countries.

European investments spurt

U.S. firms intensified their build-up of production facilities in Europe in 1959, adding nearly $¾ billion through capital outflows and retained earnings. About $80 million of the capital flow resulted from the purchases of securities of existing companies. A similar investment pace is indicated for the current year.

The share of the United Kingdom in the additions being made to direct investments in Europe was about 45 per-

cent in 1959 and the first half of 1960. Although there has been some reduction in the United Kingdom's share of new investments since 1950, that country's share of the total direct investment in Europe is still considerably larger than it was before World War II.

Much of the increase in the recent flow to Europe has gone to Germany and France, with Italy and the Netherlands also showing large gains.

Rapid expansion of manufacturing plants accounts for most of the U.S. investment in Europe; since 1950 some $2 billion has been added in this industry. As shown in Table 4, the increases have been spread over many product groups, with especially large gains in non-electrical machinery, transportation equipment and chemicals.

Substantial investments are also continuing by petroleum companies to enlarge refining capacity and distribution facilities. Since 1957, however, earnings of these facilities have been very low, except for those in the United Kingdom.

Variable flow to Latin America

Year-to-year changes in the flow of investment by U.S. companies are frequently wider in Latin America than in other major areas. The flow to Latin America (including European dependencies) is largely connected with the petroleum industry's investments in Venezuela, which were at a peak in 1956–57, and then dropped sharply, although these still are larger than any other single element in the investment picture.

Aside from Venezuela, the flow to other countries in the area recovered sharply in 1959 from the reduction of 1958. In the first half of 1960, however, data available up to now indicate a decline in the overall outflow to the area, but with countries other than

15

Venezuela continuing to receive a substantial capital flow.

Capital flows and undistributed profits in Latin America amounted to $615 million in 1959, but the U.S. dollar valuation of underlying assets was reduced by further depreciations of some local currencies in terms of U.S. dollars. The book values for 1957 derived from the new census were much lower than previous estimates for some countries, particularly Argentina and Brazil, because of the restatement of net current assets at current exchange rates.

Among the countries receiving sizable flows from the United States in 1959 were Cuba, Argentina, Brazil, and Chile. The flow to Cuba represented the continuation of large expansion programs of mining and utility companies, and extensions of credit to subsidiaries of petroleum companies. This investment activity was brought to a stop when nearly all U.S. investments in Cuba were seized earlier this year.

Argentina is now receiving a substantial investment flow into petroleum development and manufacturing ventures; Brazil's inflow is mainly for further expansion of manufacturing plants, and manufacturing investments are also sizable in Mexico and Venezuela.

Large Canadian investments

U.S. firms added another $800 million to their Canadian investments in 1959, about evenly divided between capital flows and retained earnings. The capital flow was about equal to the 1958 amount, but included a sharp drop in petroleum investments counterbalanced by increased amounts in the mining and manufacturing categories.

Earnings of the Canadian subsidiaries and branches were at a record of over $700 million in 1959, but since remittances of income were held to less than half of this amount, nearly $400 million was available for reinvestment. About 60 percent of the reinvested earnings went into manufacturing plants.

Manufacturing continues to be the leading industry for U.S. investments in Canada, with $635 million added in 1958-59. Expansion was largest in

the transportation equipment, chemicals, and primary metals categories.

Petroleum investments are restrained currently by marketing difficulties, although the construction of new pipelines for natural gas will require considerable outlays. In mining there is a continuation of sizable investments, notably in further development of iron ore reserves.

Africa and Asia

Investment by U.S. companies in Africa and Asia is proceeding at a relatively modest rate and concentrated in a few countries. On the African continent there is considerable investment by petroleum companies in developing reserves in Northern Africa,

GROWTH OF DIRECT FOREIGN INVESTMENTS, BY AREA

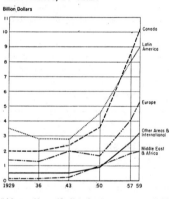

Billion Dollars

U. S. Department of Commerce, Office of Business Economics   60-9-8

especially in Libya. A large part of the outlay required is not reflected in increased capital values (Table 1) because it is charged against income (Table 3).

Elsewhere in Africa there are major iron ore and other mining ventures in progress along the West coast although some proposed investments may develop less rapidly than anticipated because of the unrest in certain parts of that area. Investments in Central and South Africa have been increased by only minor amounts since 1958.

Growth of investments in the Middle East, very largely in petroleum resources, has slowed down greatly since 1957. Activity necessary to expand or improve existing facilities, or establish

the potentialities of new fields, is financed largely out of funds generated by the foreign enterprises, so that there is little or no increase in the book value of the U.S. investment.

In the Far East investment activity by U.S. companies is reflected in sizable expansion in the Philippine Republic and Japan in 1959, and an increased but still relatively small flow to India. There have been some return flows from Indonesia as financing of earlier expansions is repaid.

Australia received further large U.S. investments in 1959, mainly in the manufacturing category. Most of the growth is coming out of reinvested earnings.

Record Manufacturing Investments

In 1959, the growth in manufacturing investments abroad for the first time exceeded $1 billion, accounting for two-fifths of the overall increase in direct investments. The rate of investment was $300 million higher than in 1958, and reflected strong upturns in business activity in Canada and Europe coupled with some large special transactions in Canada and the United Kingdom.

Nearly $450 million of the increase in manufacturing investments was in Europe. The United Kingdom received more than half of this amount, with France and Germany also showing large gains. Manufacturing investments in Canada were also stepped up, largely out of reinvested earnings.

Investments in foreign mining properties in 1959 were at the highest rate since 1952-53. Canada accounted for about half of the $300 million invested in the year, substantially more than in 1958, and the flow to Chile, Peru, Western Hemisphere dependencies and West Africa was sizable.

Capital flows and reinvested earnings in the petroleum industry aggregated over $600 million in 1959, but this amount, while still very large, reflected reductions for many countries from the levels of the past few years. Although world productive capacity is in excess of current demand, a considerable amount of investment activity is still being devoted to developing new reserves, and expanding refining, marketing and transportation facilities.

Among the other industries sizable amounts were being invested in 1959 in trade and distribution establishments, especially in parts of Latin America and Europe, as well as in public utilities in Canada and some Latin American countries, and in the shipping enterprises classified as "International."

Production Abroad by Direct Investment Enterprises

AN IMPORTANT feature of the comprehensive 1957 census is the new data gathered on the participation by U.S. firms in economic growth abroad through the output of the foreign subsidiaries and branches for domestic use and export.

Aggregate sales of commodities by the foreign enterprises were $32 billion in 1957, after eliminating intercorporate sales as far as possible. Over $3½ billion of these sales were exported to the United States, accounting for more than one quarter of all U.S. imports in that year. An additional $5 billion entered into international trade among foreign countries, but except for raw materials most production abroad was for consumption in home markets.

The bulk of the exports to the United States consisted of crude and processed raw materials such as petroleum, food stuffs and metals. Imports of manufactures and semi-manufactures from U.S.-owned factories abroad totalled about $1 billion, somewhat less than one quarter of all imports of such items. Nearly 80 percent of the shipments of manufactures to the United States from direct investments abroad came from Canada, and were comprised mainly of newsprint, wood pulp, and aluminum. Imports from European plants were about $200 million, with automobiles and parts the largest single item.

Manufacturing sales accelerate

Total sales of the manufacturing enterprises abroad were over $18 billion in 1957, so that sales to the United States were only about 5 percent of the total. Data for overall manufacturing sales have been updated to 1959 and show a rise to about $21 billion (Table 5). Among the major commodity group, foreign sales are largest for auto-

561165°—60——3

motive products, chemicals, food products, and machinery.

The major impact of manufacturing sales from foreign plants is currently in foreign markets rather than in shipment to the United States. Sales of the foreign plants are 50 percent greater in the aggregate than shipments of comparable items from the United States, exceeding such shipments for

GROWTH OF DIRECT FOREIGN INVESTMENTS, BY INDUSTRY

Billion Dollars

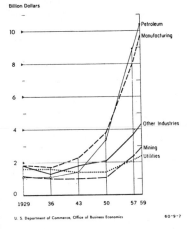

U. S. Department of Commerce, Office of Business Economics   60-9-7

many types of manufactures and in many countries.

As the expansion of manufacturing output abroad by U.S. companies speeds the industrial development of foreign countries, and to a considerable extent of those countries already industrially strong, additional marketing difficulties are met for comparable U.S. exports. In the longer run, expanding markets abroad and the development of new products might be expected to give support to export sales, but at least temporarily the accelerated growth of manufacturing facilities abroad by U.S. companies, especially in the advanced countries, adds to the problem of adjustment in the U.S. balance of international payments.

Growing petroleum production

Sales of petroleum enterprises abroad are difficult to state on a comparable basis because of the prevalence of intercorporate sales, differences in accounting practice, and vertically integrated operations from raw materials production to retail distribution. For 1957, consolidated sales of this industry were tabulated at $11 billion, after eliminating more than $3½ billion of intercorporate sales and shipping revenues.

This consolidated sales figure cannot be carried forward since the necessary detailed reports are not available, but the progress of the industry is indicated by the fact that production of crude oil by U.S. companies abroad (including their share of joint operations) rose from 4.8 million barrels per day in 1957 to about 5.6 million in 1959, while their foreign refinery capacity advanced from 3.4 million barrels per day in 1957 to about 4.2 million at present. Offsetting these gains in physical capacity, however, have been reductions in prices.

Mining companies produced $2 billion of metals and minerals abroad in 1957, of which some 45 percent was exported to the United States. Production in Latin America accounted for nearly half of the total, Canada for about 35 percent, and Africa for over 10 percent. Of the various metals produced abroad, copper, lead and zinc led in sales with about 40 percent, while sales of iron ore and nickel were each about 15 percent.

Sales of mining enterprises dropped off in 1958 as world demand slackened, but by 1959 had recovered to somewhat more than the 1957 total.

Agricultural production by direct-investment enterprises was valued at $850 million in 1957, mainly in Central America and the West Indies. Sales of properties in Cuba were about $300 million, including $250 million exported to the United States and other countries.

In addition to sales of commodities produced abroad, gross revenues of $1.2

billion resulted from the operations of utility companies, other service industries had revenues of $1.2 billion, and sales by retail and wholesale trading establishments were $5.6 billion.

Expenditures in Foreign Countries

Operations of the direct-investment enterprises generate a substantial flow of incomes abroad and provide a large volume of employment. Aggregate production outlays abroad and foreign taxes paid by the direct-investment companies were $30 billion in 1957. This total excludes goods purchased by trading companies, intercorporate petroleum sales, imports from the United States, and depreciation charges, but includes both service industries and commodity producers.

Wages paid and employment provided

Wages and salaries paid in foreign countries were nearly $7 billion, with manufacturing enterprises accounting for over half of the total and petroleum firms for about one-sixth. Employee compensation was highest in Canada, at $2.6 billion, followed by $2 billion in Western Europe and $1.4 billion in Latin America.

Data on the number of persons employed abroad by the companies were supplied on a voluntary basis, and the partial data have been expanded to estimated totals by using the complete data obtained on employee compensation. Total foreign employment by the firms was over 3 million persons in 1957, with over 1 million in Europe, nearly 1 million in Latin America, and 670 thousand in Canada. The largest number of employees, 1.7 million, were in manufacturing enterprises, and petroleum ranked next with 370 thousand.

The data indicate that persons sent from the United States comprised about one percent of the foreign employment total. Of the more specialized supervisory, professional, or technical positions, about 10 percent were filled by U.S. personnel, with the proportion lower in Canada and Europe and higher mainly in those areas where petroleum operations required U.S. technicians.

Materials and services purchased

The largest outlays by the companies abroad were for materials and services, which totaled about $17 billion after eliminating estimated duplications and imports from the United States. Manufacturing firms spent about $10 billion for this purpose, plus over $1 billion for non-capital goods imported from the United States.

Similar outlays abroad by the petroleum enterprises are more difficult to determine, but are estimated at $4–5 billion in 1957. This total excludes some $3½ billion of intercorporate sales and tanker revenues and about $¾ billion of imports from the United States.

Imports by the direct-investment firms from the United States were reported on a partial, voluntary basis at over $2½ billion in 1957, including about $0.7 billion of capital equipment. The total for all imports would be substantially higher, and for capital equipment would probably exceed $1 billion. These amounts do not include transactions of trading companies.

Over $1 billion of the imports from the United States were by manufacturing companies, indicating that a sizable portion of the foreign sales total represented assembly or further processing of U.S. components and materials.

Tax payments to foreign governments

Overall taxes paid abroad by the direct investment enterprises were $4½ billion, comprised of $2.4 billion classified as taxes on income, and $2.1 billion of indirect taxes, including some production royalties as well as excise taxes and import duties.

Income taxes of $500–$600 million were paid in Canada, Europe, Latin America, and Asia. Petroleum companies paid over $1 billion of income taxes and manufacturing companies about $0.8 billion.

The total for other taxes is a mixture of many types of tax, and $1.6 billion of the aggregate is paid by petroleum companies. In this industry the tax and sales figures include large amounts of import duties; manufacturing companies accounted for the most of the other payments of indirect taxes.

In some countries or areas the direct investment companies account for a

substantial portion of total government revenues. In the Latin American Republics, the enterprises contribute some 20 percent of total revenues, with considerably higher percentages in some countries in the area. For Canada, the proportion of overall government revenue was about 16 percent in 1957, and the proportion of corporate income taxes paid by companies classified as direct investments was about 50 percent.

Other operating costs, including amounts not allocated by the foreign enterprises, amounted to $1.7 billion in 1957, and an additional $0.4 billion was paid as interest charges. In addition to these cash outlays, charges against income for depreciation and depletion totaled $1.7 billion.

These operating outlays represent a substantial overall support to incomes abroad, and contribute a significant share of income flows in countries where the investments are concentrated.

Further income flows are generated by the companies through foreign capital outlays wh'ch amount currently to some $4 billion annually, exclusive of imports from the United States. These expenditures will be discussed in detail in the next issue of the SURVEY OF CURRENT BUSINESS.

Earnings Reflect Growth

The U.S. share in the earnings of direct investment enterprises reached a peak of over $3½ billion in 1957, largely on the basis of a surge in the petroleum industry. Earnings of this industry dropped sharply in 1958 and declined further in 1959 as the extraordinary conditions of 1957 subsided, tax and other costs rose, and prices weakened. On the other hand, earnings of the manufacturing companies, which had advanced relatively slowly to 1957, jumped over 20 percent in 1959 to $1.1 billion.

Reflecting these offsetting movements, overall earnings dropped to about $3 billion in 1958 and then recovered to $3.3 billion in 1959.

Recent declines in petroleum earnings have centered largely in Venezuela and the Middle East, the major producing areas. Earnings in most other countries, and from tanker operations, remained low in 1959 compared to the 1957 amounts. Net losses were reported in a number of countries, although in some, notably North Africa, these represented costs of developing new properties rather than current operating results.

Improvement in manufacturing earnings was widespread in 1959, with Canada, Germany, and the United Kingdom responsible for large gains. In part the increase in earnings reflects the mounting investment in manufacturing facilities abroad, as well as the general upturn in economic activity in these and other countries in 1959.

Mining companies also reported a sharp recovery in earnings in 1959—some 50 percent—as prices rose and output of some metals, particularly copper, iron ore and nickel, was increased. Canada and Chile each accounted for about $30 million of the gain from the depressed earnings level of 1958.

Trade and distribution enterprises accounted for $300 million of earnings in 1959, as this industry steadily grows in importance. Earnings of public utilities were about $110 million, slightly reduced from 1958, while earnings of agricultural properties at $50 million remained low compared to earlier years.

In addition to the U.S. share in earnings discussed above, foreign shareholders had an equity of about $400 million in earnings as tabulated in the new census. Half of this amount was for Canadian companies, and foreign shares were also sizable in manufacturing enterprises in Europe and Latin America, and in mining companies in Africa.

Income receipts stable

Payments to the United States from the direct investments of dividends, interest and branch profits totaled $2.2 billion in 1959, about the same as in 1957 and slightly above the 1958 amount. Income receipts have been comparatively stable in recent years as variations in earnings have affected mainly the amount retained abroad as undistributed profits of subsidiaries.

As shown in Table 3, the petroleum industry now accounts for about half of the income receipts and manufactur-

ing for about one quarter. Since 1957 the share of petroleum has fallen and that of manufacturing is rising.

On an area basis the Latin American Republics and the Middle East each

EARNINGS OF DIRECT FOREIGN INVESTMENTS, BY INDUSTRY

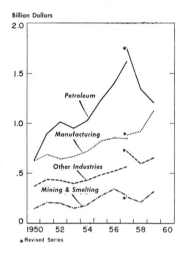

Billion Dollars

Petroleum

Manufacturing

Other Industries

Mining & Smelting

1950   52   54   56   58   60

★ Revised Series

U. S. Department of Commerce, Office of Business Economics   60-9-9

accounted for $600 million of income receipts in 1959, substantially less than in 1958. Higher receipts from mining

operations in Latin America offset some of the drop in petroleum.

Substantially higher receipts from Europe, and a moderate increase from Canada, resulted from the advance in manufacturing earnings.

Reinvested earnings finance growth

Over $1 billion of the earnings of foreign subsidiaries was retained abroad for investment in 1959, providing a large share of the financing available for expansion. Increased investment activity and improved earnings in most industries raised the amount reinvested as compared with 1958; the total amount reinvested would have exceeded the record $1.4 billion of 1957 if it were not for sharp declines in the petroleum and shipping categories from their 1957 highs.

Manufacturing enterprises accounted for over half of total reinvested earnings in 1959, as they continued to retain abroad about half of their earnings. About 80 percent of the gain in Canadian manufacturing earnings in 1959 was retained abroad, but only 30 percent of the gain in Europe.

Of the other industries, the trade and distribution firms showed a large increase in the amount retained abroad, absorbing most of their increased earnings. For petroleum companies the overall decline in undistributed subsidiary profits showed up primarily in international tanker operations.

Balance-of-Payments Effects

IN THE course of establishing a complex aggregate of productive facilities abroad, and setting in motion new streams of goods and services, many direct and indirect changes are made in the existing structure of international transactions and of domestic economies. The full effects of these changes can not be measured, but the data collected in the new census give some dimensions which can assist in understanding and analyzing these effects.

Transactions with the United States

Transactions of the foreign enterprises which were directly reflected in the balance of international payments of the United States for 1957 were (1) exports to the United States of $3.7 billion, (2) capital flows from the United States of $2.5 billion, (3) remittances of income and fees to the United States of $2.5 billion, (4) reported imports from the United States of $2.6 billion. These transactions, allowing for some understatement

Table 1.—Value of direct investments abroad, by selected

Table 2.—Direct-investment capital flow and undistributed subsidiary

Table 3.—Direct-investment earnings and income,[1] by selected

[Millions of dollars]

Line		Table 1										Table 2						
					1959 p							Net capital outflows						
														1959 p				
		1950	1957 r	1958 r	Total	Mining and smelting	Petroleum	Manufacturing	Public utilities	Trade	Other	1957 r	1958 r	Total	Mining and smelting	Petroleum	Manufacturing	Other
1	All areas, total	11,788	25,262	27,255	29,735	2,858	10,423	9,692	2,413	2,039	2,310	2,482	1,181	1,439	239	511	460	230
2	Canada, total	3,579	8,637	9,338	10,171	1,090	2,465	4,558	636	564	858	718	421	409	120	113	139	37
3	Latin American Republics, total	4,445	7,434	7,751	8,218	1,258	2,963	1,405	1,101	641	850	1,163	299	338	75	129	63	71
4	Mexico, Central America and West Indies, total	1,488	2,234	2,355	2,515	254	268	498	581	262	652	159	54	80	24	19	8	28
5	- Cuba	642	819	879	955	(*)	143	115	313	44	341	88	20	62	(*)	14	(*)	43
6	Dominican Republic	106	88	93	87	(*)	5	(*)	5	2	80	-16	5	-7	(*)	(*)	(*)	-7
7	Guatemala	106	106	116	131	(*)	20	(*)	63	5	42	13	9	13	(*)	2	(*)	11
8	Honduras	62	108	114	110	(*)	(*)	(*)	22	1	86	-10	4	-5	(*)	(*)	(*)	-5
9	- Mexico	415	739	745	759	137	30	355	118	83	36	65	-10	-6	-4	-2	3	-2
10	Panama	58	201	268	328	16	29	8	21	117	136	15	31	19	7	1	2	9
11	Other countries	100	143	140	145	14	23	11	38	9	50	3	-5	3	1	2	(**)	(**)
12	South America, total	2,957	5,200	5,396	5,702	1,004	2,696	907	520	378	198	1,004	245	257	50	110	55	42
13	Argentina	356	333	330	361	(*)	(*)	158	(*)	16	187	21	8	45	(*)	(*)	12	33
14	- Brazil	644	835	795	839	5	82	438	192	101	21	53	32	45	(**)	-2	35	12
15	Chile	510	666	687	729	526	(*)	21	(*)	10	172	28	23	35	29	(*)	(**)	6
16	Colombia	193	396	383	399	(*)	225	77	28	39	31	12	-8	10	(*)	(**)	8	2
17	Peru	145	383	409	427	242	79	31	19	36	19	50	30	17	24	-9	2	(**)
18	- Venezuela	993	2,465	2,658	2,808	(*)	2,164	160	29	166	289	826	140	97	(*)	82	-2	17
19	Other countries	86	121	135	139	2	53	22	16	11	36	3	20	7	(**)	8	-1	(**)
20	Western Hemisphere dependencies	131	618	696	772	158	349	21	49	47	149	57	30	51	17	29	3	3
21	Europe, total	1,733	4,151	4,573	5,300	50	1,453	2,927	44	581	245	287	190	466	(**)	148	231	87
22	Common Market, total	637	1,680	1,908	2,194	9	732	1,135	28	209	81	96	106	171	(**)	68	72	31
23	Belgium and Luxembourg	69	192	208	210		53	129	1	22	4	3	2	-3		-2	-2	(**)
24	France	217	464	546	632	8	201	334	10	61	18	15	37	45		9	28	8
25	Germany	204	581	666	795	(*)	201	489	2	74	29	75	24	77	(*)	35	25	17
26	Italy	63	252	280	313	(*)	142	126	1	23	21	-2	25	21	(*)	2	14	5
27	Netherlands	84	191	207	244		135	58	14	29	8	6	18	32		23	8	1
28	Other Europe, total	1,096	2,471	2,666	3,106	41	721	1,792	16	372	165	191	84	295	(**)	80	159	56
29	Denmark	32	42	49	48		23	15	(**)	8	2	1	5	1		(**)	(**)	1
30	Norway	24	51	53	62	(*)	25	18	(**)	4	15	-1	-1	9	(*)	8	(**)	1
31	Spain	31	44	48	53	(*)	16	25	3	7	3	(**)	(**)	2	(*)	1	1	(**)
32	Sweden	58	109	107	125	(*)	55	38	(**)	26	5	4	1	21		11	8	3
33	Switzerland	25	69	82	158	(**)	11	69	(**)	53	24	4	5	63		1	23	39
34	- United Kingdom	847	1,974	2,147	2,475	(**)	492	1,607	9	240	126	172	63	190	(*)	53	127	9
35	Other countries	79	182	181	186	28	99	20	3	34	3	11	10	10	(**)	6	(**)	4
36	Africa, total	287	664	746	843	255	338	120	5	45	80	9	38	48	27	23	-1	-1
37	North Africa	56	106	121	148	2	126	8	4	5	3	16	12	25	1	26	1	-2
38	East Africa	12	30	35	43	1	39	(**)		3	(**)	4	3	6	(**)	6		(**)
39	West Africa	42	147	183	225	102	64	1	1	4	62	13	17	30	25	4	1	(**)
40	Central and South Africa, total	177	381	407	417	150	109	112		32	14	-24	7	-13	1	-12	-3	1
41	Rhodesia and Nyasaland	26	59	65	72	63	(*)	(*)		2	8	-4	1	(**)	(**)	(*)	(*)	(**)
42	Union of South Africa	140	301	321	323	87	(*)	109	(**)	28	98	-21	5	-12	1	(*)	-3	-10
43	Other countries	12	21	22	21	(**)	19	(*)		2	1	1	1	-1		(*)	(*)	-1
44	Asia, total	1,001	2,019	2,178	2,236	20	1,662	248	95	114	96	141	95	2	(**)	-28	12	17
45	Middle East	692	1,138	1,224	1,208		1,170	23	3	7	5	71	99	-8		-16	5	3
46	Far East, total	309	881	954	1,028	20	492	225	92	107	92	70	-4	9	(**)	-12	7	14
47	India	38	113	120	136		(*)	43	2	10	82	4	-2	5		(*)	3	2
48	Indonesia	58	169	196	163		(*)	9	(**)	9	153	25	-3	-44		(*)	(**)	-44
49	Japan	19	185	181	210		(*)	71	1	21	117	16	-11	15		(*)	3	12
50	Philippine Republic	149	306	341	385	(*)	(*)	86	85	45	169	24	6	21	(*)	(*)	1	20
51	Other countries	46	108	116	134	1	(*)	16	3	30	75	1	5	12	(*)	(*)	1	11
52	Oceania	256	698	786	876	28	355	412	1	48	33	-1	35	26	(**)	5	14	8
53	Australia	201	583	655	739	27	(*)	396	(*)	33	282	-3	21	24	(**)	(*)	14	10
54	New Zealand	25	48	50	54		(*)	15	(*)	14	24	-1	(**)	1		(*)	(**)	1
55	Other countries	30	66	81	83	(**)	(*)	(*)	(**)	(*)	83	3	13	1		(*)	(**)	1
56	International	356	1,041	1,188	1,320		838		482			108	73	98		91		7

*Combined in other industries.
**Less than $500,000.
r Revised.   p Preliminary.

NOTE.—Book values in 1958 and 1959 have been adjusted downward by $142 million and $88 million, respectively, to reflect declining exchange rates for some currencies. The major reductions were in Argentina ($42 million) and Brazil ($126 million). Adjustments made for other reasons have increased values by $40 million in the 2 years, primarily in Canada.

countries and years, and major industries, 1959

earnings, by selected countries, 1957–58, and major industries, 1959

countries, 1957–59, with major industries for 1959

[Millions of dollars]

Table 2—Continued							Table 3														
Undistributed subsidiary earnings							Earnings							Income							
1957 r	1958 r	1959 p					1957 r	1958 r	1959 p					1957 r	1958 r	1959 p					Line
		Total	Mining and smelting	Petroleum	Manufacturing	Other			Total	Mining and smelting	Petroleum	Manufacturing	Other			Total	Mining and smelting	Petroleum	Manufacturing	Other	
1,363	945	1,081	68	109	574	329	3,561	3,034	3,255	315	1,185	1,129	626	2,249	2,140	2,228	249	1,100	549	330	1
357	279	393	32	44	240	78	653	569	713	67	74	438	134	335	315	345	32	41	206	66	2
239	143	202	10	31	71	90	1,096	760	774	141	321	120	191	880	641	600	135	292	50	123	3
89	67	80	3	12	20	44	213	167	156	14	8	44	91	134	111	90	11	-4	15	45	4
30	10	14	(*)	8	3	3	73	46	28	(*)	6	7	15	48	42	22	(*)	-1	3	19	5
1	1	1	(*)	(*)	(*)	1	9	3	5	(*)	(*)	(*)	5	2	5	5	(*)	(*)	(*)	5	6
2	2	2	(*)	(**)	(*)	2	2	-3	-1	(*)	-4	(*)	3	(**)	-5	-2	(*)	-5	(*)	3	7
1	1	1	(*)	(*)	(*)	1	5	8	6	(*)	(*)	(*)	6	4	7	5	(*)	5	(*)	5	8
15	15	20	2		16	2	54	54	52	8	2	33	9	42	42	35	6	2	17	10	9
38	36	41	1		3	36	54	51	59	1	2	1	54	17	15	19	(**)	-1	1	20	10
2	2	2	(**)	1	(**)	1	17	9	8	1	2	1	5	15	7	7	1	(**)	(**)	5	11
150	76	122	7	19	50	47	883	593	617	127	313	76	100	746	530	509	124	296	26	64	12
12	1	14	(*)		10	4	29	12	24	(*)	(*)	15	9	17	11	11	(*)	(*)	5	6	13
33	19	34	1	1	27	6	69	40	54	2	63	3	11	42	27	25	1	63	12	9	14
5	8	10	3	(*)	2	5	47	42	77	(*)		3	10	46	38	71	(*)		6	1	7	15
(**)	-5	6	(*)	(**)	1	5	20	-3	17	(*)		5	2	6	20	3	11	(*)		1	1	4	16
12	-1	4	(**)	2	1	1	34	17	26		12	2	6	24	19	23		13	1	4	17
86	53	53	(*)	11	11	31	679	483	425	(*)	312	14	99	593	431	373	(*)	302	3	69	18
2	1	(**)	(**)	(**)	-1	1	5	2	-6	(**)	1	(**)	9	4	1	-5	(**)	-15	2	7	19
91	48	24	4	-3	(**)	22	123	95	95	51	19	1	25	31	47	71	47	21	1	3	20
294	238	258	-1	-7	207	60	582	582	709	10	114	444	142	281	339	443	11	125	226	80	21
116	113	99	(**)	-1	76	23	207	201	241	(**)	17	171	52	83	81	134		22	84	27	22
21	13	5		2	2	1	32	25	22			13	6	9	10	13		1	8	4	23
34	39	23	(**)	5	10	8	59	62	46	(*)	8	25	13	20	20	20		3	12	4	24
39	57	52	(*)	-8	54	6	65	91	131	(*)	-1	113	19	24	30	71	(*)		53	11	25
10	5	12	(*)	(**)	8	4	20	17	29	(*)		7	7	11	12	22	(*)		11	8	26
12	-2	6		(**)		1	31	6	13		(**)		4	8	18	8	8			(**)	3	27
178	125	160	-2	-6	131	37	376	381	469	10	97	272	90	199	257	309	11	102	142	53	28
1	2	-2		-4	1	1	4	4	4		-4	3	2	4	3	3		(**)	2	1	29
1	2	1	(*)	-1	1	1	2	4	2	(*)		2	2	1	1	1	(*)		(**)	1	30
3	4	4	(*)	1	3	(**)	2	4	4	(**)		3	1	-1	(**)	(**)	(*)	-1	1	1	31
2	-3	-3		-2		-1	8	6	7		-1	2	6	6	9	9			1	7	32
3	8	13		-2	5	10	13	18	23		-2	11	13	9	10	10			6	4	33
160	109	138		-4	119	23	332	340	418		112	248	59	173	232	281		115	130	36	34
7	3	9	-2		7	2	15	6	13	9	-6	3	8	7	2	4	11	-13	1	4	35
47	44	49	16	16	4	13	94	51	56	38	-27	17	28	41	8	7	23	-43	13	14	36
-1	2	2	(**)	2	1	(**)	-24	-28	-33	1	-36	1	(**)	-23	-31	-36	1	-38	(**)	(**)	37
1	2	3		3	(**)	(**)	-1	3	3	(**)	3	(**)	(**)	-2	1	(**)	(**)	(**)		(**)	38
22	19	22	9	1		12	37	27	32	12	-2		23	15	7	10	3	-4		11	39
25	20	22	6	10	4	2	81	50	53	25	8	16	4	51	30	32	19	-2	13	2	40
1	5	7	5	(*)	(*)	2	15	7	12	10	(*)		1	9	5	9	5	(*)	(*)		41
24	15	15	(*)		3	11	64	42	43	15	(*)	16	13	40	27	29	14	(*)	13	2	42
1	(**)	(**)	(**)	(*)	(*)	(**)	2	(**)	-2	(*)	(*)		-2	2	(**)	-2	(*)	(*)		-2	43
122	67	56	2	12	19	23	751	800	757	3	663	37	55	630	738	704	(**)	656	16	32	44
39	-13	-9		-10	1	(**)	607	656	591		587	1	2	568	670	601		599	(**)	2	45
83	79	65	2	22	19	23	144	144	166	3	76	36	52	63	68	102	(**)	57	16	29	46
7	9	11		(*)	3	8	13	17	17		7	9		6	8	5		(*)	3	1	47
44	32	12		(*)	1	11	52	52	54		2	52		11	25	46		(**)		46	48
8	7	14		(*)	5	9	22	10	24		6	18		15	4	10		1	9	49
21	29	22	(*)	(**)	7	15	42	55	58	(*)		17	9	19	25	33	(*)		9	24	50
2	3	5	(*)	8	2	-5	14	10	13	(*)		4	9	12	6	8	(*)		5	3	51
50	53	64	6	21	32	5	91	100	111	6	21	72	12	37	42	43	1	(**)	36	7	52
47	50	60	5	(*)	33	22	81	90	101	6	(*)	68	26	30	35	37	1	(**)	32	5	53
1	2	2	(**)	(*)		2	8	9	9		(*)		5	7	7	6		(*)	4	2	54
2	2	2				2	2	2	2	(**)	(*)		2	(**)	(**)	6		(**)	(*)		55
163	74	34		-5		39	170	76	41		1		40	14	9	14		8		6	56

*Combined in other industries.
**Less than $500,000.
r Revised. p Preliminary.
¹ Income is the sum of dividends, interest, and branch profits; earnings is the sum of the U.S. share in net earnings of subsidiaries and branch profits.
r Revised. p Preliminary.
*Included in total.
**Less than $500,000.

of imports from the United States, yield a large direct dollar return to foreign countries in the aggregate, and are particularly important in the cases of many individual countries.

Far outweighing this particular though beneficial result, however, is the gain in foreign incomes resulting from production abroad of goods or services which otherwise would not have been available, and from the capital formation originating with the companies' activities.

The full amount of production costs and other payments abroad cannot be taken as a measure of the net gain to foreign countries, since the foreign factors of production employed would have been utilized to some extent in any case, yet a substantial part of this total represents a net gain in production abroad. In the relatively undeveloped countries, where resources would have been inefficiently utilized without the benefit of outside capital, a very large part of the incomes generated by the U.S. investment can be regarded as a net gain to local economies.

Operations in Latin America

Direct investment enterprises are a major element in international and domestic economic developments in most countries of Latin America. Gross production by the companies had a sales value of nearly $8 billion in 1957, and after deducting imports and profit remittances is equivalent to roughly 10 percent of the economic product of the area. Nearly $3 billion of these sales represents exports from Latin America, and these exports amounted to one-third of all exports from Latin America; Venezuela, Chile, and Mexico, account for the larger part of this export activity.

Direct transactions with the United States resulted in a net dollar gain of about $1 billion for Latin America in 1957 and a like gain of foreign exchange resulted from transactions with countries in the rest of the world.

Production of manufactures, fuels, and other commodities for Latin American consumption resulted in a saving of foreign exchange no less important

than the gains resulting from actual international transactions. Local sales by the companies aggregated $4½ billion in 1957, and are rising steadily.

Total operating costs of the direct investments in Latin America (after eliminating imports and noncash charges) were about $6 billion in 1957, including about $300 million in European dependencies in the area. In addition, local outlays on capital account, after making an allowance for imported equipment, were approximately $1 billion.

Manufacturing and petroleum enterprises each accounted for about a third of the current outlays, and petroleum companies were responsible for a major part of the capital expenditures. It appears that about 70 percent of the value of commodities produced by the companies in the area consisted of local outlays for labor, materials, other costs, and taxes.

Canada

U.S. direct investments in Canada have contributed extensively to that country's industrial development and to the expansion of its international trade. The sales value of commodities and utility services furnished by the companies exceeded $11 billion in 1957. Export sales amounted to $2 billion, about 60 percent of which was manufactures and 30 percent was metals and minerals other than petroleum. Two-thirds of these exports from Canada went to the United States.

Production by the firms in Canada immediately affects the balance of payments of that country by reducing imports of certain goods and augmenting exports. For a wide range of manufactured items, production within Canada greatly exceeds imports from the United States and similar results have come from the development of mineral resources. Of course, the gross value of local sales is not a measure of net exchange savings to Canada, since imported components and materials, mainly from the United States, were well over $1 billion, alternative uses of the resources could be expected to yield some foreign exchange income, and some of the earnings are remitted to the United States.

Table 4.—Direct Investments in Manufacturing Enterprises Abroad, 1950, 1957, and 1959, by Commodity

[Millions of dollars]

Area and year	Manu-factur-ing, total	Food prod-ucts	Paper and allied prod-ucts	Chem-icals and allied prod-ucts	Rubber prod-ucts	Primary and fabri-cated metals	Machin-ery (ex-cept elec-trical)	Elec-trical machin-ery	Trans-porta-tion equip-ment	Other prod-ucts
All areas, total										
1950	3,831	483	378	512	182	385	420	387	485	599
1957	8,009	723	722	1,378	401	941	927	731	1,204	983
1959	9,693	821	811	1,657	460	1,161	1,200	834	1,602	1,147
Canada										
1950	1,897	227	308	198	59	249	204	141	160	292
1957	3,924	320	626	647	133	671	327	330	398	471
1959	4,559	366	687	742	142	772	391	366	550	534
Latin America [1]										
1950	781	158	5	205	60	23	13	79	83	155
1957	1,280	201	39	334	133	60	52	136	134	190
1959	1,426	185	50	361	150	71	57	137	210	205
Europe										
1950	932	64	5	74	31	111	175	153	192	128
1957	2,195	149	42	319	59	178	488	214	475	272
1959	2,927	197	54	440	70	276	674	270	603	343
Africa										
1950	55	6		9	11	1	2	3	17	6
1957	106	10	3	12	21	5	17	5	27	6
1959	120	14	3	15	24	5	20	5	26	8
Asia										
1950	60	9		12	14	(**)	5	2	8	10
1957	190	15	9	40	38	20	15	12	23	18
1959	249	19	13	59	49	27	16	15	28	23
Oceania										
1950	107	18	1	13	8	2	22	9	26	8
1957	314	28	3	27	17	8	26	34	146	26
1959	412	40	4	40	25	10	42	41	176	34

1. Includes minor amounts in the Western Hemisphere dependencies.
** Less than $500,000.

Europe

Direct investments in the industrialized countries of Europe differ substantially in nature and effect from those established in less developed countries. The investments are primarily in manufacturing and distribution, with only minor investments in natural resource development.

Manufacturing operations by U.S. companies in Europe are significant to many countries through their production of items formerly imported, while in others they also have a sizable share in the development of export markets. Total manufacturing production by the companies in Europe had a sales value of $6.3 billion in 1957, compared with imports from the United States of similar manufactures of less than $2 billion. Some of the imports from the United States are brought in by the companies. For most of the manufactured goods, production in the area far exceeded imports from the United States.

Production by the companies for export is large in only a few countries, notably the United Kingdom, Germany, Belgium and Switzerland. Export sales totalled $1.4 billion in 1957, including about $200 million to the United States. Exports from the United Kingdom accounted for more than half of each of these amounts, and contributed more than 10 percent of all United Kingdom exports of manufactures, with much higher percentages for many specific commodities.

For other European countries, the share of the U.S. enterprises in exports was relatively minor, amounting to about 3 percent in Germany, for instance.

Considering the very substantial scale of operations of the direct-investment companies in Europe, their transactions with the United States are quite small. In 1957, the capital flow from the United States and remittances of income to the United States were each about $0.3 billion, while imports and exports of the United States related to the activities of these companies were only a minor part of total United States trade with Europe. Capital flows to Europe and income remitted have each risen to over $0.4 billion in 1959.

Private Portfolio Investments Abroad

PURCHASES of foreign securities and long- and short-term loans by banks amounted to a further private capital outflow of nearly $1 billion in 1959, and are proceeding at a somewhat higher rate in the current year.

Sales of new foreign security issues in the U.S. market were at a peak in 1958, but diminished in 1959 as interest rate differentials were reduced, and have been quite small since the early months of this year. Most of the change from 1958 to 1959 resulted from a shift by the International Bank which borrows funds in Europe to a greater extent than previously.

Acquisitions of foreign corporate stocks, which had been sizable in 1958 and the first half of 1959, were resumed again on a substantial scale this year. Market values of these securities advanced sharply in 1959 and continue to rise but at a slower rate.

Medium and short-term loans and liquid foreign assets held by banks for their own account and for customers were increased by about $¼ billion in the first half of 1960, approximately

Table 5.—Sales of Direct-Investment Enterprises, by Areas and Selected Industries, 1957 and 1959

[Millions of dollars]

	All areas		Canada		Latin America [1]		Europe		Other	
	1957	1959	1957	1959	1957	1959	1957	1959	1957	1959
Selected Industries, total	21,219	23,960	8,823	9,760	3,956	4,230	6,385	7,740	2,055	2,230
Manufacturing, total	18,331	21,030	7,897	8,770	2,435	2,680	6,313	7,670	1,685	1,910
Food products	2,457	2,590	928	950	608	650	734	750	188	240
Chemicals and allied products	2,411	2,940	897	1,060	499	590	822	1,030	193	260
Primary and fabricated metals	1,548	1,560	927	950	111	90	435	450	75	70
Machinery, except electrical	1,903	2,180	695	750	66	80	1,009	1,200	133	140
Electrical machinery	2,047	2,050	1,080	1,030	190	200	678	720	99	110
Transportation equipment	4,228	5,360	1,488	1,850	375	400	1,700	2,370	665	740
Other	3,738	4,340	1,883	2,170	586	670	935	1,150	334	350
Agriculture	856	810	186	200	602	540	(2)	(2)	67	70
Mining and smelting	2,032	2,120	740	790	919	1,010	70	70	303	250

1. Includes Western Hemisphere dependencies.
2. Negligible.

Table 6.—Current Expenditures of Direct Investments, 1957, by Type, Area, and Industry

[Millions of dollars]

Area and industry	Total costs	Materials and services [1]	Wages and salaries	Depreciation and depletion	Interest	Other taxes (indirect)	Income taxes	Other and unallocated [2]
Total	37,274	22,025	6,878	1,708	426	2,106	2,395	1,736
Areas								
Canada	11,777	7,001	2,654	586	161	218	582	574
Latin American Republics	6,951	3,580	1,374	426	96	508	575	392
Western Hemisphere dependencies	438	267	99	33	2	8	28	1
Europe	11,379	6,947	1,950	355	97	1,031	512	485
Africa	1,119	750	123	44	9	56	71	66
Asia	3,231	1,732	425	160	39	226	550	99
Oceania	1,390	916	219	49	9	61	71	64
International	991	834	33	51	12	(**)	7	54
Industries								
Agriculture	764	439	197	47	4	27	37	13
Mining and smelting	1,751	803	394	174	21	34	248	77
Petroleum	12,908	7,976	1,187	705	91	1,613	1,035	302
Manufacturing	17,477	11,243	3,652	561	127	326	779	789
Public utilities	1,070	478	264	112	56	19	42	99
Trade	1,317	(1)	741	64	21	56	163	272
Other industries	1,985	1,086	442	46	106	31	91	183

1. Excludes cost of goods sold by trading organizations.
2. Excludes claims paid by insurance companies.
** Less than $500,000.

equal to the gain for the year 1959. Preliminary data show a marked increase in short-term flows after the middle of 1960, leading to more rapid foreign accumulations of dollars and gold than would otherwise occur. The recent outflows reflect a widening of effective yields, especially in favor of United Kingdom bills, and a continuation of credit extensions to Venezuela and Japan.

As a result of these capital outflows and improved market prices, private long-term foreign investments, other than direct investments, reached a total of nearly $11½ billion by the end of 1959, and short-term assets were in excess of $3½ billion.

Foreign Investments and Assets in the United States

Investments by foreigners in long-term assets in the United States were at a postwar high in 1959, with capital inflows reaching nearly $550 million and reinvested earnings approaching $200 million. After taking into account some gains in security prices, the value of these investments neared $17 billion at the end of 1959, as shown in table 7.

The inflow of funds for investment, which mitigated to some extent foreign acquisitions of liquid dollar assets and gold, continued high in the first quarter of 1960 but has since fallen off.

Purchases of U.S. corporate securities by European investors were the principal feature of the inflow in 1959 and the first quarter of 1960. This flow appears to be diminishing.

The inflow of foreign funds for direct investment has not been large in recent years, with most of the funds required for expansion coming out of earnings, or from borrowing in the United States.

Reinvested earnings in 1959 and probably also in 1960 have increased sharply as dividend distributions have been stable while earnings rose considerably.

Although not requiring large inflows of capital, there has been some increase in activity by foreign companies establishing affiliates in the United States.

Table 7.—International Investment Position of the United States, by Area, 1958–59

[Millions of dollars]

	Total		Western Europe		Canada		Latin American Republics		Other foreign countries		International institutions and unallocated	
	1958	1959	1958	1959	1958	1959	1958	1959	1958	1959	1958	1959
U.S. investments abroad, total	59,335	64,779	17,928	18,478	14,662	15,779	11,853	12,778	9,288	10,643	5,604	7,101
Private investments	11,004	44,775	7,959	9,100	14,658	15,769	10,154	10,838	6,105	6,812	2,128	2,256
Long-term	37,516	41,152	6,905	8,206	14,251	15,333	8,790	9,431	5,442	5,926	2,128	2,256
Direct	27,255	29,735	4,573	5,300	9,338	10,171	7,751	8,218	4,405	4,726	1,188 [1]	1,320 [1]
Foreign dollar bonds	3,931	4,314	244	327	2,094	2,310	139	140	517	634	907	903
Other foreign securities	3,690	4,229	974	1,473	2,474	2,508	40	40	169	175	33 [2]	33 [2]
Other	2,640	2,874	1,114	1,106	345	344	860	1,033	321	391	----	----
Short-term	3,488	3,623	1,054	894	407	436	1,364	1,407	663	886	----	----
U.S. Government credits and claims	18,331	20,004	9,969	9,378	4	10	1,699	1,940	3,183	3,831	3,476	4,845
Long-term	16,192	17,586	9,074	8,528	----	----	1,559	1,781	2,087	2,432	3,472	4,845
Short-term	2,139	2,418	895	850	4	10	140	159	1,096	1,399	4	----
Foreign assets and investments in the United States, total	34,931	40,658	19,313	21,924	5,351	5,790	3,730	3,794	3,521	4,317	2,126	3,927
Long-term	15,219	16,652	10,399	11,503	2,943	3,079	1,080	1,164	716	803	81	103
Direct	4,940	5,220	3,080	3,280	1,631	1,688	135	139	94	113	----	----
Corporate stocks	8,305	9,363	6,030	6,856	1,171	1,250	663	743	409	476	32	38
Corporate, State and municipal bonds	455	520	316	364	1	1	64	64	25	26	49	65
Other	1,519	1,549	973	1,003	140	140	218	218	188	188	----	----
Short-term assets and U.S. Government obligations	19,712	24,006	8,914	10,421	2,408	2,711	2,650	2,630	2,805	3,514	2,045	3,824
Private obligations	10,931	10,868	4,675	4,455	1,447	1,698	2,367	2,357	2,198	2,214	244	144
U.S. Government obligations	8,781	13,138	4,239	5,966	961	1,013	283	273	607	1,300	1,801	3,680
Long-term	1,480	2,149	473	838	252	363	187	187	67	95	501	666
Short-term [3]	7,301	10,989	3,766	5,128	709	650	96	86	540	1,205	1,300	3,014

1. Represents the estimated investment in shipping companies registered in Panama and Liberia.
2. Consists primarily of securities payable in foreign currencies, but includes some dollar obligations, including participations in loan made by the International Bank for Reconstruction and Development.
3. Includes U.S. currency not distributed by area estimated at $890 million at the end of 1958 and $906 million at the end of 1959.

Source: U.S. Department of Commerce, Office of Business Economics.

CAPITAL OUTLAYS ABROAD
BY U.S. COMPANIES:

Rising Plant Expansion in Manufacturing

Samuel Pizer
and
Frederick Cutler

BY SAMUEL PIZER AND FREDERICK CUTLER

Capital Outlays Abroad by U.S. Companies:

Rising Plant Expansion in Manufacturing

CAPITAL outlays abroad by U.S. manufacturing companies are being stepped up to a rate of $1.3 billion this year, from an annual rate of under $1.2 billion in 1958 and 1959. The current rate is nearly equal to the amount reported for 1957, the first

Comparison of Domestic and Foreign Plant and Equipment Expenditures By U. S. Companies – 1957-60

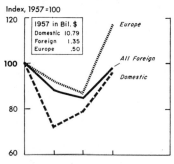

MANUFACTURING*- More Moderate Swing Abroad: Upsurge in Europe in 1960

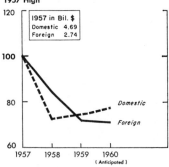

PETROLEUM AND MINING – Foreign Expenditures Continue Decline From 1957 High

* Excludes primary iron and steel and petroleum and coal products

U. S. Department of Commerce, Office of Business Economics 60-10-13

18

year for which such information was collected. Related information for capital flows from the United States and reinvested earnings, which is available over a long period, indicates that 1957 was a peak year for foreign capital expenditures.

In contrast to the upturn in the manufacturing industry, capital expenditures abroad by petroleum companies have declined from $2.3 billion in 1957 to $1.6 billion in 1959 and a like amount in 1960. Mining investments held steady at a little over $400 million in the 1957–59 period, but are expected to be moderately lower in 1960 because of the completion of a few large projects.

Information for other industries is not collected currently in the same detail— in the aggregate they amounted to about $0.7 billion in 1957 and are estimated at $0.6 billion in 1959 and 1960.

For all industries combined, foreign expenditures for plant and equipment were $4.9 billion in 1957, and at a rate of about $3.7 billion in 1959 and $3.9 billion in 1960.

Comparison With Domestic Outlays

For some U.S. manufacturing industries, foreign plant and equipment expenditures now form a sizable part of their overall capital expenditure programs. As shown in the following tabulation, the proportion of foreign expenditures to total ranges from 10 to 25 percent in several major industries. There is an overstatement in the foreign figures for specific industries, since they include acquisitions of existing assets as well as new plant and equipment, but this is not believed to be significant. Also, the foreign figure includes the share of foreign investors as well as of the U.S. controlling interests.

Variations in the direction of domestic and foreign capital expenditures, depicted in the first chart, reflect a number of influences, both short-run and longer term, although the period for which comparable data are available is too brief to establish consistent relationships. For manufacturing investment, both domestic and foreign outlays reflected, and in turn reacted

Expenditures for Plant and Equipment in Selected Manufacturing Industries, 1959

[Amounts in billions of dollars]

Industries	Expenditures			Percent of total, foreign
	Total	Domestic	Foreign	
Primary and fabricated metals [1]	1.13	1.00	.13	12
Electrical machinery and equipment	.61	.52	.09	15
Machinery, except electrical	1.02	.91	.11	11
Transportation equipment	1.29	1.03	.26	20
Paper and allied products	.72	.63	.09	13
Chemicals and allied products	1.45	1.23	.22	15
Rubber products	.26	.19	.07	27
Food and beverages	.91	.83	.08	9
Total, selected industries	7.39	6.34	1.05	14

1. Excludes primary iron and steel producers.

upon, the downturn in industrial activity from 1957 to 1958, with foreign expenditures declining less partly because economic activity in major countries abroad, except for Canada, did not weaken significantly.

In 1959, on the other hand, domestic expenditures were raised along with the general level of economic activity, while foreign outlays fell off slightly in the face of strongly advancing economic activitity in major industrial countries. The explanation for this lies primarily in continued declines in Canada, where industrial production was recovering slowly, and a sharp but temporary drop in the transportation equipment sector in the United Kingdom. Manufacturing outlays elsewhere were generally higher in 1959 than in 1958.

Outlays anticipated by manufacturing companies for 1960 turned strongly upward both at home and abroad. The notable feature of the foreign situation, however, is the striking rise projected for Europe. This rise is probably in part influenced by the continued upward movement of industrial production in Europe, even though the curve is not so steep as in 1959. Also important for this area, however, is a longer run expectation of expanding demand, and growing competition, as well as some lag in implementing plans formed last year.

The situation is considerably different in the petroleum and mining industries.

Capital outlays abroad by the petroleum companies in 1959 and projected for 1960 are larger than those of any other industry, but have been declining since 1957 as available supplies are ample to meet expected demands. Mining investments abroad have also, at least temporarily, established adequate supplies of a number of metals and minerals. However, domestic petroleum outlays, although turning upward since 1958, are still below the level of the early 1950's, while foreign expenditures by this industry are currently larger than in periods prior to 1956.

Upturn in Manufacturing Investment

U.S. manufacturing companies anticipate an increase of some 15 percent in plant and equipment expenditures abroad in 1960 as compared to 1959, following a sharp dip in such outlays in 1958 and a further moderate decline in 1959. The 1960 upturn is broadly based, as shown in the second chart, affecting all major areas and industry groups, though in varying degrees.

European plants expanding rapidly

Outlays in Europe—over 40 percent of the total—are rising sharply, both in the Common Market countries and in the United Kingdom. In the latter country, scheduled outlays in manufacturing of about $300 million for 1960 are about the same as the level attained in 1957, both in total and for major commodities. About one-third of the outlays are in the transportation equipment group, with the chemical and primary and fabricated metals industries also reporting substantial amounts.

In the Common Market countries capital expenditures by U.S. manufacturing companies are now well above the 1957 amounts, and are probably at a record rate. Transportation equipment and chemicals are also major fields for investment in this area, together with various types of machinery. About two-thirds of the outlays in the Common Market countries are in Germany, and nearly one-fifth in France.

Canadian expenditures steady

Capital outlays in manufacturing in Canada have been maintained at about $400 million annually beginning in 1958. In 1957 the total was much higher, but this reflected exceptionally large outlays by a few companies in the paper and pulp and primary metals categories.

U.S. direct investments are a large element in manufacturing in Canada, accounting for about 40 percent of capital outlays in these industries in that country in 1959 and in 1960, when both series are adjusted to a comparable basis. However, outlays by these U.S. direct-investment enterprises have not been rising recently while outlays for Canadian manufacturing as a whole have increased moderately since 1958.

> The basic data on sources and uses of funds of foreign subsidiaries and branches of U.S. companies contained in this article, and related data on the assets, liabilities, and ownership of these enterprises, were collected in the comprehensive Office of Business Economic census, the complete results of which will soon be available in a supplement to the SURVEY OF CURRENT BUSINESS entitled *U.S. Business Investments in Foreign Countries*, now at the printer.
>
> The census benchmark data for 1957 have been carried forward by the use of data made available currently covering a large proportion of the foreign investment activity.

Continued rise in Latin America

Since 1957 U.S. manufacturing companies have increased substantially their plant and equipment investments in Latin America, reaching an anticipated total of $234 million in 1960. Among the products for which large outlays are in progress are chemicals, transportation equipment, and electrical machinery.

Outlays are largest in Brazil, amounting to nearly $75 million in 1960. In Argentina, expenditures rose, amounting to nearly $70 million in 1960, more than double the 1957–59 average. A sharp rise is reported for most industries in Argentina, especially in transportation equipment.

In Mexico, capital outlays have held steady at a little under $50 million annually since 1957, and Venezuela has also received a steady though smaller

PLANT AND EQUIPMENT EXPENDITURES ABROAD

U. S. Companies Expand Foreign Manufacturing Facilities

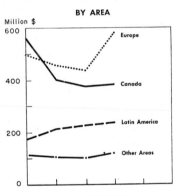

BY AREA

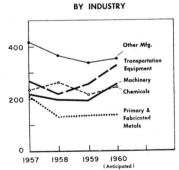

BY INDUSTRY

U. S. Department of Commerce, Office of Business Economics　60-10-14

amount of investment. For these countries, and for Latin America as a whole, the sums invested annually for plant and equipment are much larger than capital flows from the United States, since the companies utilize other sources of funds, especially retained earnings, depreciation charges, and local financing.

Other countries

Expansion of manufacturing facilities in the rest of the world is concentrated primarily in such industrialized countries as Australia, Japan, and the Union of South Africa, with steady expenditures in India and the Philippine Republic. These countries together account for all but about $10 million of total manufacturing outlays by U.S. companies in Africa and Asia.

Australia has been a leading field for U.S. manufacturing investments for many years, with 1960 expenditures for plant and equipment expected to be nearly $60 million, spread over many commodity groups. Expenditures in Japan, scheduled at about $25 million in 1960, are especially large in chemicals, while in the Philippine Republic the emphasis is on food products.

Large Petroleum Outlays Abroad

Nearly $2 billion is being spent abroad by U.S. petroleum companies in 1960 to add to plant and equipment and for development in all phases of the industry. This total includes $1.6 billion classified as capital outlays and some $400 million of exploration and development expenditure charged against income. The latter outlays are relatively stable, and are based on the long-term expectation of rising world demand. Despite cutbacks since 1957, therefore, this industry continues to account for a major portion of foreign investment activity by U.S. business.

Exploration and Development Expenditures of Petroleum Companies Charged Against Income

[Millions of dollars]

	1957	1958	1959
Total	386	444	402
Canada	153	158	123
Latin America	113	136	131
Europe	45	57	51
Africa	29	47	49
Asia	46	46	48

In some areas investments in the petroleum industry are rising in 1960; refinery expansion and other outlays increased in a number of European countries and in Australia, and development of new resources required larger investments in North Africa. Capital outlays were considerably lower in 1960 in Latin America, with the reduction centered in Venezuela.. Although plant and equipment expenditures in Canada have also declined, they remain at an annual rate of nearly $400 million annually, accounting for about one quarter of the industry's foreign capital expenditures.

Mining outlays lower

Reduced capital expenditures by mining enterprises abroad in 1960 reflect primarily the completion of a few large projects. These reductions occurred largely in Chile, Peru and Cuba; in the last named country the existing properties have recently been seized.

Mining investments in Canada account for two-thirds of the industry total in 1960, and are expected to continue on a large scale. New projects are also expected to bring an upturn

Table 1.—Plant and Equipment Expenditures of Direct Foreign Investments, by Country and Major Industry, 1957–1960

[Millions of dollars]

	1957			1958			1959			1960		
	Mining and smelting	Petroleum	Manufacturing	Mining and smelting	Petroleum	Manufacturing	Mining and smelting	Petroleum	Manufacturing	Mining and smelting	Petroleum	Manufacturing
All areas, total	421	2,322	1,347	421	1,875	1,180	430	1,574	1,141	358	1,575	1,314
Canada	163	584	561	172	510	404	240	378	379	240	390	382
Latin American Republics, total	196	993	173	202	533	210	125	412	226	48	346	232
Mexico, Central America and West Indies, total	32	43	53	46	19	66	31	24	55	12	27	56
Cuba	(*)	32	17	(*)	6	19	(*)	11	10	(*)	10	9
Mexico	13	(**)	36	7	1	47	8	-1	45	6	1	47
Other countries	(*)	11		(*)	12		(*)	12		(*)	16	
South America, total	164	950	120	156	514	144	96	388	171	39	319	176
Argentina	(*)	(*)	21	(*)	8	28	(*)	30	29	(*)	28	67
Brazil	1	8	63	3	8	83	1	8	114	1	10	74
Chile	52	(*)	3	66	(*)	2	41	1	3	21	(*)	2
Colombia	(*)	40	7	(*)	30	7	(*)	25	7	(*)	20	8
Peru	74	39	8	73	25	6	46	25	5	9	27	5
Venezuela	(*)	849	17	(*)	430	17	(*)	290	12	(*)	230	19
Other countries	(**)	8	1	(*)	12	1	(*)	9	1	(*)	3	1
Western Hemisphere dependencies	20	46	1	16	50	1	26	50	2	30	46	2
Europe, total	2	275	497	(**)	422	459	(**)	339	433	2	369	580
Common Market, total	1	159	179	(**)	254	166	(**)	174	213	(**)	176	269
Belgium and Luxembourg	(**)	10	10	(**)	17	10	(**)	11	8	(**)	22	11
France	1	46	44	(**)	84	42	(**)	41	47	(**)	41	48
Germany	(**)	49	100	(**)	84	95	(**)	59	139	(**)	60	183
Italy	(**)	29	18	(**)	39	14	(**)	19	10	(**)	27	15
Netherlands		25	7	(**)	39	5	(**)	44	9	(**)	26	12
Other Europe, total	(*)	116	319	(**)	168	293	(**)	165	220	2	193	311
Denmark		6	2		11	1		11	1		11	1
Norway	(*)	2	3		6	3		18	3	(**)	25	3
Spain	(*)	(**)	5	(**)	1	3	(**)	(**)	2	(**)	1	4
Sweden		8	3		12	2		12	2		18	3
Switzerland	(*)	4	4	(**)	3	4	(**)	3	3	(**)	6	3
United Kingdom		94	299		124	277		99	204		99	293
Other countries	(**)	4	3	(**)	11	3	(**)	22	4	2	33	4
Africa, total	26	47	12	21	48	10	25	65	6	24	121	7
North Africa	(**)	13	(**)	1	18	1	1	36	1	1	90	1
East Africa	(**)	10	(**)	(**)	9	(**)	(**)	9	(**)	(**)	10	(**)
West Africa	3	10	(**)	4	7	(**)	4	9	(**)	5	10	(**)
Central and South Africa, total	12	12	11	16	14	9	20	11	5	18	11	6
Union of South Africa	9	(*)	11	6	(*)	9	6	(*)	5	6	(*)	6
Other countries	14	(*)	(**)	10	(*)	(**)	14	(*)	(**)	12	(*)	(**)
Asia, total	1	264	57	2	261	42	2	226	41	2	228	52
Middle East	(**)	144	3		189	3		129	3		124	4
Far East, total	1	119	54	2	72	39	2	97	38	2	104	48
India		(*)	6		(*)	7		(*)	9		(*)	9
Japan		(*)	28		(*)	16		(*)	14		(*)	25
Philippine Republic	(*)	(*)	18	(*)	(*)	14	(*)	(*)	13	(*)	(*)	12
Other countries	(*)	(*)	2	(*)	(*)	2	(*)	(*)	2	(*)	(*)	2
Oceania	13	26	46	8	36	54	12	49	54	12	65	59
Australia	13	(*)	44	8	(*)	53	12	(*)	53	12	(*)	57
International		87			15			55			10	

*Included in area total. **Less than $500,000.

for the industry in Latin America and some parts of Africa.

Other industries

Investment by other industries, excluding construction abroad by some shipping companies, is estimated at at about $0.6 billion in 1960. About half of these outlays are by firms in trade and distribution, which have increased their investment programs each year since 1957, and reported a sharp increase in Europe in 1960.

Outlays by the public utilities have dropped very sharply from the 1957 amount. In Canada, where pipelines are an important part of this industry, some increase in expenditures is expected. For Latin America the aggregate of capital outlays by the utility firms is declining rapidly, though not in every country. Agricultural investments, also important in Latin America, continue to drop, with large properties in Cuba seized by the government, and operating problems remaining to be solved in other countries.

Increase in other assets

After reducing inventories on balance in 1958, the foreign enterprises resumed a sizable inventory accumulation in 1959, amounting to $0.4 billion. Receivables also increased $0.5 billion in the year, and about $0.8 billion was used to acquire other assets. These figures cover only the manufacturing, petroleum and mining companies. Enterprises in other industries, especially

in trade and distribution, also added moderate amounts to inventories and receivables in 1959.

Inventory accumulation was largest in manufacturing, paralleling the general experience of industrial companies in the 1959 business upturn. This industry also accounted for most of the expansion in receivables and miscellaneous assets, notably in European operations.

Sources of Financing

IN order to carry out the additions to fixed and other assets described above, the companies in the manufacturing, petroleum and mining industries required $4.8 billion of funds in 1959. Over half of these resources were provided by the foreign enterprises out of retained earnings of $0.9 billion and depreciation and depletion charges of $1.8 billion. External financing of $1.2 billion was supplied by

parent companies and others in the United States, and $0.9 billion by foreign creditors and investors.

The volume of financing utilized in 1959 was $0.4 billion larger than in 1958, mainly because of the step up in inventory accumulations. In 1957 a peak amount of nearly $6 billion was necessary to pay for large expansions of both fixed and current assets.

Enterprises in other industries obtained about $1 billion in 1959, of which nearly two-thirds was provided out of retained earnings and depreciation charges.

Internal Fund Sources

The largest and most consistent source of funds for financing foreign operations is the annual charge for depreciation and amortization of existing fixed assets, including small amounts of depletion charges. These charges for the three major industries amounted to $1.8 billion in 1959, and are growing by some $150–200 million annually. About $300 million a year is also charged to depreciation by enterprises in other industries.

At current levels depreciation charges are equal to about 60 percent of foreign plant and equipment expenditures. In comparable domestic industries the proportion is much higher.

About $0.9 billion of the depreciation charges originate in the petroleum industry, including about $100 million of depletion charges. Latin America accounted for one-third of the total. In the aggregate, these charges were equal to over half of this industry's capital expenditures, with the

Table 2.—Plant and Equipment Expenditures Abroad by U.S. Manufacturing Companies, by Major Commodities and Areas, 1957–60

[Millions of dollars]

	Manufacturing, total	Food products	Paper and allied products	Chemicals and allied products	Rubber products	Primary and fabricated metals	Machinery (except electrical)	Electrical machinery	Transportation equipment	Other manufacturing
All areas, total										
1957	1,347	78	144	234	80	208	120	99	268	117
1958	1,180	87	102	261	67	130	116	83	221	113
1959	1,141	76	90	216	69	132	106	88	259	105
1960	1,314	110	78	245	55	135	127	129	327	108
Canada										
1957	561	20	120	95	17	148	28	32	56	45
1958	404	25	82	96	10	58	11	22	59	41
1959	379	22	75	76	14	61	8	22	61	40
1960	382	38	60	68	14	60	16	33	53	40
Latin America [1]										
1957	174	16	11	49	17	15	3	22	20	21
1958	211	22	8	51	18	17	4	15	50	26
1959	228	14	5	56	17	17	3	15	83	18
1960	234	28	7	71	15	9	2	36	51	15
Europe:										
Common market										
1957	179	10	4	26	3	11	37	14	61	13
1958	166	6	4	22	5	7	53	18	36	15
1959	213	17	3	22	5	7	64	20	59	16
1960	269	14	3	36	4	12	66	24	93	17
Other Europe										
1957	319	20	4	48	19	26	44	20	110	28
1958	293	19	5	71	23	40	41	12	61	21
1959	220	11	4	49	25	37	25	15	36	18
1960	311	17	5	50	15	39	34	20	107	24
Other areas										
1957	115	12	5	16	24	8	8	11	21	10
1958	106	15	3	21	11	8	7	16	15	10
1959	101	12	3	13	8	10	6	16	20	13
1960	118	13	3	20	7	15	9	16	23	12

1. Includes minor amounts in European dependencies.

Note: Data for 1960 are based on anticipations of reporting companies.

Table 3.—Plant and Equipment Expenditures Abroad in Selected Industries, by Area, 1957-60

[Millions of dollars]

Areas and industries	1957	1958	1959	1960
Selected industries, total	729	643	572	605
Agriculture	103	57	53	48
Public utilities ¹	335	309	212	177
Trade	186	191	224	296
Miscellaneous	105	86	83	84
Canada, total	285	225	202	217
Public utilities	136	110	75	80
Trade	47	55	65	75
Agriculture and miscellaneous	102	60	62	62
Latin America, total	258	269	203	170
Agriculture	48	40	34	29
Public utilities	164	182	122	82
Trade	20	31	33	45
Miscellaneous	26	16	14	14
Europe, total	125	94	109	148
Trade	107	87	102	141
Public utilities and miscellaneous	18	7	7	7
Other areas	61	55	58	70
Agriculture	9	7	7	7
Public utilities ¹	24	16	14	14
Trade	12	18	24	35
Miscellaneous	16	14	13	14

1. Excludes expenditures of international shipping companies.

ratio higher in Latin America and Asia, but lower in Canada where such expenditures were considerably larger.

Depreciation charges in the manufacturing enterprises at about $0.7 billion are growing rapidly in line with the expansion of the industry. In 1959, as in the previous 2 years, this was the largest source of funds for manufacturing, exceeding reinvested earnings and capital flows from the United States. Most of the depreciation charges are in Canada and Europe, where manufacturing assets are largest.

In the mining and smelting industry, these depreciation and depletion charges are comparatively small in the aggregate, although in 1959 they were about 40 percent as large as capital expenditures.

Retained earnings

For the manufacturing, petroleum and mining enterprises, retained earnings amounted to $0.9 billion in 1959. This was somewhat larger than the 1958 amount, but much smaller than the record $1.4 billion of 1957, when a large part of peak earnings in petroleum was retained abroad for investment.

Over $0.6 billion of the 1959 amount was retained abroad by the manufacturing companies. Earnings in this industry reached a new high in that year, and 60 percent of the increase, in the aggregate, was reinvested. The

increased availability of funds from this source was especially important in Canada.

For the petroleum enterprises, the amount of income considered to have been remitted has remained fairly steady in the 1957-59 period. Earnings of the industry were much higher in 1957 than in subsequent years, and about half of the total was retained abroad to finance peak foreign outlays. With investments considerably lower thereafter, the companies have relied primarily on other sources of funds.

Earnings of mining companies rose sharply in 1959, with most of the increase retained abroad for investment.

External Financing

The three major industries, mining, petroleum and manufacturing, obtained about $1.2 billion of financing from U.S. investors and creditors in 1959. As shown in table 4, this was a small increase over the 1958 amount, with manufacturing enterprises in Europe responsible for most of the rise.

This category of the sources of funds accounts corresponds, with some modifications, to the data for capital outflows included in the balance-of-payments accounts. In both 1958 and 1959 these capital outflows were substantial, but were only about one-third as large as outlays abroad for plant and equipment. Increased cash flows from other sources tend to reduce reliance on transfers of funds from parent companies except when major projects are undertaken, or there is a sharp fluctuation in working capital requirements. Of course, new enterprises are financed largely by parent companies. In the aggregate, the increase in funds supplied from the United States between 1958 and 1959 provided about 30 percent of the overall increase in funds required.

In addition to the increased financing from the United States of manufacturing operations in Europe, the flow to this industry in Canada was also raised in 1959. The aggregate flow to petroleum enterprises was unchanged; the amount provided for Canadian operations was lower, in line with reduced investment activity, while somewhat larger amounts flowed to Europe and Latin America.

SOURCES AND USES OF FUNDS
Direct Foreign Investments

SOURCES: Operations of the Foreign Affiliates a Major Factor in Financing

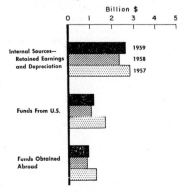

USES: Resources Are Used Principally To Enlarge and Improve Productive Facilities

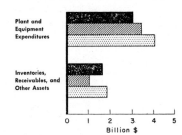

NOTE.—Includes only the manufacturing mining and petroleum industries.

U. S. Department of Commerce, Office of Business Economics   60-10-15

Funds obtained abroad

Foreign creditors and investors provided about $0.9 billion in 1959, slightly less than in 1958. Petroleum companies sharply reduced their use of local financing; in Canada and Europe the reduction reflected a lower rate of investment in fixed and other assets, while in Latin America part of the shift from 1958 was related to payments of tax liabilities accrued in 1958.

A large increase in external foreign funds employed in the manufacturing enterprises was reported in Europe, and a smaller increase occurred in Canada. In both cases the financing appeared to be related largely to mounting working capital needs.

Assets and Financial Structure

A MAJOR objective of the Office of Business Economics census of foreign business investments was to obtain new data on the assets employed by the direct-investment enterprises, and to examine their financial structure.

Total assets employed by U.S. direct-investment enterprises abroad were nearly $42 billion in 1957, excluding assets of financial organizations and after consolidating investments in affiliated foreign enterprises.

Financing of these resources was divided between U.S. parent companies and other U.S. residents, that had $24 billion invested, and local investors abroad that provided $18 billion. The U.S. ownership was mainly in the form of equity interests in stock, surplus, and branch accounts, while foreign investors financed most of the debt of the enterprises.

Assets employed in 1957 were $23 billion larger than the 1950 total of $19 billion. The U.S. investment in these enterprises (excluding finance) rose $13 billion in the period, and the firms utilized $10 billion of financing obtained abroad. The latter figure includes the share of foreign investors in undistributed earnings.

Fixed assets

About half of the assets employed abroad consisted of fixed assets, after deducting reserves for depreciation and amortization; current assets accounted for 43 percent, and miscellaneous assets, for 7 percent. Gross fixed assets, before deducting reserves, were over $32 billion.

About 40 percent of the gross assets were utilized by petroleum companies and 30 percent in manufacturing. Mining and public utility enterprises each accounted for somewhat over 10 percent.

Depreciation

About 36 percent of the value of fixed assets was set aside in reserves for depreciation, amortization and depletion of the underlying plant, property and equipment. The ratio was somewhat higher than this average in manufacturing and mining, and, as usual, much lower in public utilities.

In general, the ratio of reserves to fixed assets is lower in the foreign direct-investment enterprises than in comparable industries in the United States.

Current assets

Nearly $18 billion of current assets were held by direct-investment enterprises in 1957, including cash, receivables, and inventories. About 45 percent was held by manufacturing companies, and nearly 30 percent by the petroleum industry.

Current assets made up 30–34 percent of total assets in the extractive industries, around 55 percent in manufacturing, and about 70 percent for the trading companies. These ratios tended to be higher than those in comparable U.S. industry groups, although the general pattern was quite similar. In domestic firms holdings of government and other securities tend to be much larger proportionately than equivalent assets on the foreign books. If

Table 4.—Sources and Uses of Funds of Direct Investment Enterprises, by Area and Selected Industry, 1957–59

[Millions of dollars]

SOURCES OF FUNDS

Area and industry	Total			Net income			Funds from United States			Funds obtained abroad [1]			Depreciation and depletion		
	1957	1958	1959	1957	1958	1959	1957	1958	1959	1957	1958	1959	1957	1958	1959
All areas, total	7,584	6,273	6,732	3,063	2,611	2,843	1,702	1,065	1,181	1,429	982	937	1,390	1,615	1,771
Mining and smelting	746	657	854	329	242	372	234	227	184	19	43	136	163	145	162
Petroleum	4,301	3,278	2,886	1,738	1,325	1,196	1,043	529	528	832	594	248	688	830	914
Manufacturing	2,537	2,338	2,992	996	1,044	1,275	425	309	469	578	345	553	539	640	695
Canada, total	1,863	1,603	1,833	662	541	717	480	423	376	234	131	184	487	508	556
Mining and smelting	269	225	395	117	62	112	77	78	121	11	35	95	64	50	67
Petroleum	764	616	439	150	76	99	213	234	112	231	128	39	170	178	189
Manufacturing	830	762	999	395	403	509	190	111	143	−8	−32	50	253	280	300
Latin America, total	2,472	1,655	1,470	930	653	655	864	272	238	330	295	106	348	435	471
Mining and smelting	387	342	343	125	127	187	159	130	36	24	10	46	79	75	74
Petroleum	1,625	919	702	660	409	333	582	75	132	159	135	−90	224	300	327
Manufacturing	460	394	425	145	117	135	123	67	70	147	150	150	45	60	70
Europe, total	1,560	1,547	1,875	507	503	620	238	162	381	513	519	445	300	363	429
Mining and smelting	10	10	10	10	8	8	1	1	(*)	−3	(*)	1	1	1	1
Petroleum	574	648	578	155	105	116	162	65	150	149	356	144	107	122	168
Manufacturing	976	889	1,287	342	390	496	75	96	231	367	163	300	192	240	260
Other areas, total	1,691	1,468	1,554	964	914	851	120	208	186	352	37	202	255	309	315
Mining and smelting	80	80	106	77	45	65	−3	18	27	−13	−2	−6	19	19	20
Petroleum	1,339	1,095	1,167	773	735	648	86	155	134	293	−25	155	187	230	230
Manufacturing	272	293	281	114	134	138	37	35	25	72	64	53	49	60	65

USES OF FUNDS

[Millions of dollars]

Area and industry	Total			Property, plant, and equipment			Inventories			Receivables			Other assets			Income paid out		
	1957	1958	1959	1957	1958	1959	1957	1958	1959	1957	1958	1959	1957	1958	1959	1957	1958	1959
All areas, total	7,584	6,273	6,732	4,090	3,454	3,091	637	−36	378	705	362	500	508	622	814	1,645	1,871	1,949
Mining and smelting	746	657	854	421	420	417	45	−30	37	24	20	70	34	37	77	222	210	253
Petroleum	4,301	3,278	2,886	2,322	1,854	1,554	265	−58	−8	467	166	65	296	178	189	952	1,138	1,086
Manufacturing	2,537	2,338	2,992	1,347	1,180	1,120	327	52	349	214	176	365	178	407	548	471	523	610
Canada, total	1,863	1,603	1,833	1,308	1,086	997	124	−92	164	13	92	118	85	196	202	333	321	352
Mining and smelting	269	225	395	163	172	240	22	−5	18	5	1	26	9	−2	50	70	59	61
Petroleum	764	616	439	581	510	378	49	−22	−4	24	56	12	41	25	−5	66	47	58
Manufacturing	830	762	999	561	404	379	53	−65	150	−16	35	80	35	173	157	197	215	233
Latin America, total	2,472	1,655	1,470	1,429	1,000	825	147	9	89	292	51	95	187	84	−19	417	511	480
Mining and smelting	387	342	343	216	221	151	21	−20	18	18	10	10	25	57	30	84	101	134
Petroleum	1,625	919	702	1,039	577	462	59	−20	−30	196	−10	30	54	16	−48	277	356	288
Manufacturing	460	394	425	174	202	212	67	49	101	86	51	40	76	38	14	56	54	58
Europe, total	1,560	1,547	1,875	774	882	759	243	18	94	198	169	247	61	187	392	283	291	383
Mining and smelting	10	10	10	2	....	(*)	(*)	(*)	1	−1	−1	−1	1	(*)	1	8	10	11
Petroleum	574	648	578	275	422	339	90	−20	5	86	110	23	16	41	86	107	95	125
Manufacturing	976	889	1,287	497	460	420	152	38	89	113	60	225	46	145	306	168	180	247
Other areas, total	1,691	1,468	1,554	579	486	510	123	29	31	202	50	40	175	155	239	612	748	734
Mining and smelting	80	80	106	40	27	26	1	−5	1	10	10	20	−31	8	12	60	40	47
Petroleum	1,339	1,095	1,167	424	345	375	67	4	21	161	10	(*)	185	96	156	502	640	615
Manufacturing	272	293	281	115	114	109	55	30	9	31	30	20	21	51	71	50	68	72

1. Includes miscellaneous and unidentified sources.
*Less than $500,000.

all nonfixed assets are combined, the ratios for domestic firms and foreign investments in the same industries are fairly similar.

Financial Structure

The financial structure of the ownership of the foreign enterprises is unlike that of domestic industry because of the importance of intercompany accounts and branch accounts with parent companies in the United States. Of total foreign assets of nearly $42 billion, some $18 billion represented debt (including debt to parent companies) and $24 billion represented equity investments, counting branch-head office accounts as the equivalent of equity interests.

Liabilities—About 55 percent of the liabilities were short-term, although this ratio was considerably lower in Canada and higher in Europe. Among the industries, the ratio of current to total liabilities was relatively high in agriculture, manufacturing, and trade, and low in public utilities and mining.

Long-term debt of $5.4 billion was concentrated in Canada, where subsidiaries in several industries were able to obtain a relatively large proportion of their capital from local and U.S. capital markets. In Canada, and a few other countries with sizable capital markets, there is a substantial demand for marketable debt of these enterprises at interest rates comparable to those in the United States.

Equity—Of the $24 billion of equity ownership of the foreign enterprises, about one-fourth is represented by branch accounts, and the remainder by capital stock and accumulated surplus accounts. About 60 percent of the combined total of stock and surplus is in the latter, indicating the importance of retained earnings as a source of financing. In addition, reductions in asset values resulting from currency depreciations, as well as occasional capitalizations of surplus accounts, tend to result in an understatement of the contribution of retained earnings to the accumulated equity position.

Technical Note

The basic data on sources and uses of funds contained in this article are derived from the complete Office of Business Economics census for 1957, to be published in *U.S. Business Investments in Foreign Countries*, and annual reports prepared by about 200 U.S. companies covering each of their foreign subsidiaries and branches, supplemented by published reports for certain foreign corporations. In addition, quarterly reports supplied by a larger group of companies for use in the balance-of-payments accounts were used to broaden the coverage of data on earnings and capital flows from the United States.

Plant and equipment expenditures

A measure of the coverage of total capital expenditures provided by annual reports to the Office of Business Economics and supplementary data is given in the following tabulation:

Ratio of Plant and Equipment Expenditures of Reporting Companies to Estimated Totals for Specified Industries, 1959

[Percent]

Area	Mining and smelting	Petroleum	Manufacturing
All areas	77	80	48
Canada	85	72	49
Latin America	69	81	40
Europe	(1)	89	54
Other areas	50	77	40

1. Absolute amount not significant.

Other assets

Increases or decreases in inventories, receivables, or other assets held by the foreign enterprises are estimated by relating the changes reported by the sample companies to total changes reported in the 1957 census. As for other uses and sources of funds, the foreign enterprises are sorted into industry-country cells, and within these cells are further stratified by size where a few large enterprises predominate.

Sources of funds

Data for earnings, income paid out, and the residual amount of retained earnings, are related to the estimates prepared for the balance of payments accounts, but differ in the following respects: (1) the share of foreign investors as well as U.S. owners is included in the earnings data in the sources and uses series, (2) the balance of payments series includes interest in income receipts, but withholding taxes abroad are deducted, and (3) in the balance of payments series all branch earnings are deemed to be paid out, but in the sources and uses series, earnings are deemed to be paid out only to the extent they exceed the increase in net foreign assets of the branches. This treatment of branches results in a lower figure for income paid out in the sources and uses series, a larger figure for retained earnings, and a correspondingly lower figure for funds obtained from the United States.

The data for funds obtained from the United States, as given in the sources and uses series, differ from the balance of payments series mainly because of the treatment of branch earnings described above, and because certain funds supplied by U.S. residents other than parent companies are included.

Financing obtained abroad is a mixture of accrued liabilities of various kinds, as well as increased current accounts payable and long-term debt or equity financing. Into this category also fall any discrepancies between the estimates of the various other sources and uses of funds.

Table 5.—Assets, Liabilities and Net Worth of Direct Investments by Area and Industry,[1] 1957

[Millions of dollars]

Area and industry	Assets						Liabilities				Net worth			
	Current assets	Investments in affiliates	Fixed assets, at cost	Less: Related reserves	Other assets	Total assets	Current liabilities	Long-term debt	Other liabilities	Total liabilities	Capital stock	Surplus and surplus reserves	Branch accounts	Total net worth
All areas, total	17,870	778	32,278	11,522	3,066	12,470	10,237	5,437	2,450	18,123	7,737	10,455	6,156	24,348
Agriculture	307	16	1,090	433	145	1,036	162	47	28	237	190	271	338	799
Mining and smelting	1,285	38	3,498	1,307	548	3,862	524	483	187	1,193	518	1,087	1,064	2,669
Petroleum	4,962	222	12,823	4,623	1,366	14,750	3,332	1,696	1,160	6,187	2,116	2,754	3,692	8,563
Manufacturing	8,207	322	9,643	3,826	651	14,997	4,288	1,660	676	6,624	3,275	4,763	335	8,374
Public utilities	570	46	3,616	818	218	3,632	451	1,212	170	1,833	918	507	374	1,799
Trade	1,980	96	987	283	165	2,945	1,070	139	117	1,356	521	787	281	1,589
Miscellaneous	558	38	712	232	174	1,249	410	201	83	693	200	286	70	556
Canada, total	5,518	307	11,330	3,997	886	14,044	2,340	2,840	557	5,737	2,477	4,974	856	8,307
Agriculture	60	(**)	212	62	3	214	40	25	6	70	31	112	(**)	144
Mining and smelting	539	22	1,208	462	217	1,525	199	191	87	477	234	636	177	1,047
Petroleum	804	65	3,109	827	205	3,446	385	812	131	1,329	716	888	514	2,117
Manufacturing	3,151	184	4,971	2,175	263	6,395	1,274	1,090	242	2,607	972	2,736	80	3,788
Public utilities	142	6	1,216	279	105	1,191	87	533	34	653	337	177	23	537
Trade	551	16	356	109	37	851	253	83	46	381	124	295	51	470
Miscellaneous	181	12	258	83	56	424	102	105	13	220	62	131	11	204
Latin America, total	4,142	157	10,627	3,843	784	11,866	2,610	993	695	4,298	2,040	1,681	3,848	7,568
Agriculture	213	16	709	330	140	748	108	20	21	149	139	126	334	599
Mining and smelting	455	1	1,801	678	75	1,654	168	195	35	398	101	283	871	1,255
Petroleum	1,149	57	4,673	1,886	261	4,254	849	123	350	1,323	320	607	2,005	2,932
Manufacturing	1,283	14	1,266	410	147	2,301	765	127	117	1,010	800	335	156	1,291
Public utilities	226	3	1,842	422	60	1,709	267	477	93	837	470	85	316	871
Trade	679	53	202	73	68	928	347	20	58	425	156	210	131	503
Miscellaneous	138	12	134	43	32	273	104	31	21	155	54	30	33	117
Europe, total	5,127	174	5,221	1,892	609	9,239	3,356	725	673	4,753	2,258	2,053	175	4,486
Agriculture	1			(**)		2	(**)	1			(**)	(**)	(**)	1
Mining and smelting	39	1	70	30	8	87	21	9	3	33	33	13	8	54
Petroleum	1,343	26	1,795	694	302	2,772	1,016	296	340	1,652	684	386	50	1,120
Manufacturing	3,029	113	2,729	1,004	193	5,060	1,811	353	277	2,441	1,263	1,319	37	2,619
Public utilities	22		38	8	3	55	9	14	2	24	14	-1	18	31
Trade	528	21	366	78	50	888	366	25	32	423	192	226	47	464
Miscellaneous	162	13	223	77	53	374	131	29	18	178	71	111	15	197
Other areas, total	3,083	142	5,101	1,792	788	7,321	1,932	878	525	3,336	963	1,745	1,277	3,985
Agriculture	33		78	41	1	71	13	2	1	16	19	33	3	55
Mining and smelting	252	14	420	136	47	596	136	87	61	284	150	154	7	311
Petroleum	1,576	72	3,246	1,216	599	4,278	1,081	464	338	1,883	396	874	1,123	2,393
Manufacturing	742	11	678	238	48	1,241	437	90	38	566	240	374	63	677
Public utilities	180	37	519	108	50	679	89	188	42	319	96	246	18	359
Trade	222	6	63	22	10	279	103	12	13	127	50	49	53	152
Miscellaneous	76	2	96	30	32	178	73	36	30	140	13	15	11	38

1. Excludes finance and insurance.   **Less than $500,000.

Note: Investment in affiliates appears in the accounts of the primary foreign enterprises, and represents a duplication of assets (and liabilities and net worth) of this amount.

UNITED STATES ASSETS AND INVESTMENTS ABROAD

Samuel Pizer
and
Frederick Cutler

BY SAMUEL PIZER AND FREDERICK CUTLER

United States Assets and Investments Abroad

Private Capital Outflow at Peak in 1960
Earnings Score Broad Advance

UNITED STATES business concerns and other private investors, responding to continued economic growth in many countries and to possibilities for invest-

Private Capital Outflows
Reached a Postwar High in 1960

Reinvested Earnings Continued Strong

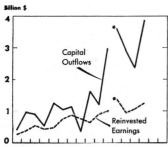

Short-Term Capital Outflows Accounted for Most of 1959 to 1960 Upturn

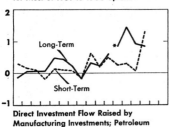

Direct Investment Flow Raised by Manufacturing Investments; Petroleum Dips Sharply

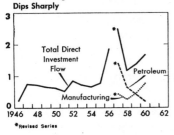

*Revised Series

U. S. Department of Commerce, Office of Business Economics   61-8-10

20

ing liquid funds profitably abroad, added over $5 billion to their assets and investments abroad in 1960, raising their total holdings to more than $50 billion.

Direct investments in subsidiaries and branches were pushed forward in most areas at a more rapid pace in 1960 than in 1959, though there were sharp reductions in certain situations, notably in resource development in some Latin American countries. In total, direct investment capital flows increased from $1.4 billion to $1.7 billion. About $200 million of this rise in direct investment capital outflows reflected increased cash outlays to purchase minority interests held by foreigners in existing subsidiaries abroad.

Although only limited data on direct investment capital flows in 1961 are now available, it appears that the total is likely to remain near the 1960 amount. Companies reporting on their expected outlays abroad for plant and equipment this year indicate substantial gains in both the manufacturing and petroleum industries, with little or no reduction projected for 1962. These data will be given in detail in the SURVEY OF CURRENT BUSINESS for September as part of a report on sources and uses of funds of direct-investment enterprises abroad.

Earnings of the direct investment enterprises improved in all major indus-

tries in 1960, and in nearly all countries. Aggregate earnings rose by 8 percent to about $3.5 billion, nearly equal to the peak reached in 1957. Of this total, foreign subsidiaries retained abroad about $1¼ billion, up from $1.1 billion in 1959.

The principal element in the overall rise in capital outflows in 1960 was the sharp rise in the flow of short-term funds to capital markets abroad. In contrast to the experience of earlier postwar years, when there were moderate outflows in most years corresponding in large part to the need for working balances to finance larger volumes of international transactions, the 1960 outflow appeared to result primarily from higher interest rates abroad, and to some extent from apprehensions about economic and political developments in the United States. These outflows have been greatly reduced since the first quarter of 1961, as discussed below.

Other private capital outflows dropped slightly in 1960, though remaining at a substantial rate of $850 million annually. Sales of new issues of foreign securities in the United States, especially Canadian issues, were lower, and continue to decline, and medium-term lending by U.S. banks has also been reduced. However, there was a resumption in the first half of 1961 of substantial purchases of foreign equity securities.

Direct Investments Abroad

WITH both capital outflows and reinvested earnings high in 1960, the value of direct investments abroad rose by $2.9 billion in the year to an accumulated total of $32.7 billion. Nearly half of the expansion represented the growth

of manufacturing investments in many countries, bringing the total invested in this industry to $11.2 billion.

The buildup of petroleum investments has now fallen considerably behind manufacturing investments, accounting

Table 1.—Factors Affecting U.S. Private Investments Abroad, 1959 and 1960

[Millions of dollars]

Type of investment	1959	1960
Direct investments		
Value, beginning of year	27,387	29,805
Add: Capital outflow [1]	1,372	1,694
Reinvested earnings	1,089	1,254
Other adjustments [2]	−43	−9
Value, end of year	29,805	32,744
Other long-term private investments		
Value, beginning of year	10,261	11,417
Add: Capital outflow [1]	926	850
Price changes	230	365
Value, end of year	11,417	12,632
Short-term assets		
Value, beginning of year	3,488	3,596
Add: Capital outflow [1]	77	1,312
Adjustments [2]	31	1
Value, end of year	3,596	4,909
Combined change	3,682	5,467
Capital outflow	2,375	3,856
Reinvested earnings	1,089	1,254
Other factors	218	357

[1] Included in the balance-of-payments accounts.
[2] Mainly changes in coverage, reclassifications, or revaluations.

for only about 20 percent of the 1960 combined total of capital outflows and reinvested earnings. Of the other industries, trade continues to grow in importance, mining investments were at a reduced rate in 1960, agricultural enterprises were not expanding in the aggregate, and growth in utilities was largely in the operation of ocean shipping and pipelines.

Mixed trends in Latin America

Because of the comparatively small overall capital flow for direct investment in Latin America—about $100 million in 1960—there has been some concern that political instability and losses in Cuba have stifled investor interest. However, the more detailed figures now available do not appear to support this view.

The sharp decline in capital outflows to this area reflected primarily a return to the United States of funds from mining properties in a few countries as expansion was completed and production began, together with continued relatively low activity in the petroleum industry resulting in a net capital inflow from Venezuela. These developments affected primarily Venezuela, Chile and Peru. Part of the

overall decline was also attributable to Cuba, where capital flows exceeded $60 million in 1959 and have now virtually ceased. Nearly all of the U.S. investments in Cuba have now been seized, but they have not been written off in these tabulations.

In contrast to these developments, manufacturing ventures by U.S. companies in Latin America were expanded at a record rate in 1960, and appear likely to continue at a high rate in 1961. Most of the increase over 1959 was in capital flows from the United States, augmented by larger amounts of retained earnings as profits in the area rose. Capital outflows for manufacturing were increased in 1960 to most countries in Latin America, especially to Mexico, Brazil, Argentina and Venezuela.

Increased flows to Canada

Capital flows for direct investment in Canada rose to nearly $500 million in 1960, with most of the rise in the mining and petroleum industries. The capital flow for manufacturing was the lowest in many years, and was about $100 million less than in 1959, when it included a special outflow to purchase minority interests.

Projected plant and equipment expenditures for Canada indicate only minor changes in manufacturing and petroleum in 1961 and 1962 from the 1960 amounts, but a considerable reduction in mining. However, the flow of funds from parent companies in the United States will also be affected by differential interest costs in the two countries and expectations about the exchange rate.

European investment at peak

Over $1¼ billion was added to U.S. direct investments in Europe in 1960, raising the accumulated value to $6.6 billion. The previous high was the $725 million added in 1959, and about $300 million of the difference represented larger cash outlays by U.S. companies in 1960 to acquire minority interests in existing manufacturing companies. There remained, however, a broad upturn in investments in most countries and industries.

Common Market countries received capital outflows of $280 million from U.S. companies in 1960, plus over $150 million of reinvested earnings. Of the combined total, nearly $300 million went into manufacturing—double the 1959 amount—and petroleum investments were also raised. Nearly half of the amount added to direct investments in this area in 1960 went to Germany, and there were also substantial gains in the other Common Market countries.

The capital flow to the United Kingdom was extraordinarily high in 1960 because of the special transaction mentioned above—without this transaction there would still have been a moderate increase over the 1959

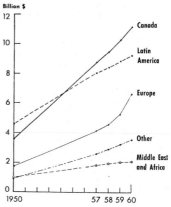

GROWTH OF DIRECT FOREIGN INVESTMENTS, BY AREA

European Share Rises

Billion $

Canada
Latin America
Europe
Other
Middle East and Africa

1950　　57 58 59 60

U. S. Department of Commerce, Office of Business Economics　　61-8-11

amount, mainly for larger petroleum investments. In the case of Sweden, there was a reduction in manufacturing investments as an old-established interest in a Swedish company was sold out.

A continued and perhaps increased flow of investment capital to Europe may be required to finance the steep rise in plant expansion by U.S. companies under way in 1961 and scheduled to remain large in 1962.

Table 2.—Value of Direct Investments Abroad, by
Table 3.—Direct-Investment Capital Flow and Undistributed Subsidiary
Table 4.—Direct-Investment Earnings and Income, [1]

[Millions of dollars]

Line	Area and country	Table 2 1950	1957 ʳ	1958 ʳ	1959 ʳ	1960 ᵖ Total	Mining and smelting	Petroleum	Manufacturing	Public utilities	Trade	Other	Table 3 Net capital outflows 1959 ʳ	1960 ᵖ Total	Mining and smelting	Petroleum	Manufacturing	Other
1	All areas, total	11,788	25,394	27,387	29,805	32,744	3,013	10,944	11,152	2,546	2,397	2,692	1,372	1,694	158	455	802	278
2	Canada ¹	3,579	8,769	9,470	10,310	11,198	1,329	2,667	4,827	645	630	1,100	417	471	202	138	31	99
3	Latin American Republics, total	4,445	7,434	7,751	8,098	8,365	1,155	2,882	1,610	1,131	718	870	218	95	−73	−7	125	50
4	Mexico, Central America and West Indies, total	1,488	2,234	2,355	2,516	2,620	245	306	530	586	292	661	81	68	26	24	27	−8
5	Cuba ²	642	849	879	956	956	(*)	147	111	313	44	341	63					
6	Dominican Republic	106	88	93	87	88	(*)	(*)	(*)	6	2	80	−7	(**)	(*)	(*)	(*)	(**)
7	Guatemala	106	106	116	132	131	(*)	26	(*)	66	5	34	14	−3	(*)	2	(*)	−4
8	Honduras	62	108	114	110	100	(*)	(*)	(*)	23	1	76	4	−11	(*)	(*)	(*)	−11
9	Mexico	415	739	745	758	795	130	32	391	119	85	39	−7	56	26	1	28	2
10	Panama	58	201	268	327	405	17	56	9	22	145	156	18	30		23	−1	7
11	Other countries	100	143	140	146	145	15	22	11	37	10	50	4	−4	1	−2	−1	−3
12	South America, total	2,957	5,200	5,396	5,582	5,745	910	2,576	1,079	545	426	208	137	27	−99	−31	99	58
13	Argentina	356	333	330	366	472	(*)	(*)	213	(*)	21	239	50	70	(*)	(*)	24	47
14	Brazil	644	835	795	828	953	10	76	515	200	130	23	31	83	2	−9	52	38
15	Chile	540	666	687	729	738	517	(*)	22	(*)	12	188	35	2	−10	(*)	(**)	12
16	Colombia	193	396	383	401	424	(*)	233	92	28	46	26	11	15	(*)	7	11	−2
17	Peru	145	383	409	428	446	251	79	35	19	42	20	18	7	9	−5	2	2
18	Uruguay	55	57	51	45	47	(*)	15	20	(*)	4	23	−2	(**)	(*)	(*)	(**)	(**)
19	Venezuela	993	2,465	2,658	2,690	2,569	(*)	1,995	180	32	165	197	−22	−150	(*)	−60	11	−101
20	Other countries	31	64	84	96	97	3	49	3	14	7	21	12	−1	(**)	−1	(**)	(**)
21	Western Hemisphere dependencies	131	618	696	768	884	176	382	21	49	64	192	48	54	13	31	(**)	10
22	Europe, total	1,733	4,151	4,573	5,323	6,645	49	1,726	3,797	45	736	291	484	962	(**)	273	607	81
23	Common Market, total	637	1,680	1,908	2,208	2,644	9	827	1,436	29	254	90	180	282	(**)	73	182	27
24	Belgium and Luxembourg	69	192	208	211	231		52	146	1	29	4	−3	10		(**)	6	4
25	France	217	464	546	640	741	9	223	402	10	76	21	51	53		2	43	8
26	Germany	204	581	666	796	1,006	(*)	248	638	2	85	32	78	133	(*)	45	82	7
27	Italy	63	252	280	315	384	(*)	160	170	1	28	23	21	55	(*)	20	32	3
28	Netherlands	84	191	207	245	283		143	80	15	36	9	32	31		6	19	5
29	Other Europe, total	1,096	2,471	2,666	3,116	4,001	40	899	2,361	17	482	201	304	680	(**)	200	425	54
30	Denmark	32	42	49	48	67		40	16	(**)	9	2	4	19		18	(**)	1
31	Norway	24	51	53	62	83	(*)	42	21	(**)	5	16	9	18	(*)	17	(**)	1
32	Spain	31	44	48	53	59	(*)	17	27	3	8	4	1	2	(*)	2	(**)	1
33	Sweden	58	109	107	125	116	(**)	64	18	(**)	29	5	21	−7		11	−22	4
34	Switzerland	25	69	82	164	254	(**)	7	91	(**)	104	53	68	27		−2	12	17
35	Turkey	16	63	54	44	65	(*)	55	2	(**)	4	4	1	19	(*)	22	(**)	−4
36	United Kingdom	847	1,974	2,147	2,477	3,194	(**)	600	2,164	(**)	288	133	190	589		129	432	28
37	Other countries	63	119	127	143	162	24	75	22	3	35	3	9	12	(**)	3	2	6
38	Africa, total	287	664	746	833	925	247	407	118	5	53	94	39	81	14	62	−5	9
39	North Africa	56	106	121	145	195	2	172	7	4	6	4	22	51		49	(**)	1
40	East Africa	12	30	35	43	46	1	42	(**)		4	(**)	6	1	(**)	1		(**)
41	West Africa	42	147	183	228	290	125	80	1	1	9	74	23	42	18	19		5
42	Central and South Africa, total	177	381	407	416	394	119	114	110	1	31	16	−12	−13	−4	(*)	−5	2
43	Rhodesia and Nyasaland	26	59	65	72	82	72	(*)	(*)		2	9	(**)	1	1	(*)	(*)	(**)
44	Union of South Africa	140	301	321	323	286	46	(*)	108	(**)	31	100	−11	−18	−6	(*)	−5	−7
45	Other countries	12	21	22	21	26	2	(*)	(*)	(**)	2	22	−1	4	2	(*)	(*)	4
46	Asia, total	1,001	2,019	2,178	2,237	2,315	24	1,655	286	103	137	110	2	−20	2	−57	14	20
47	Middle East	692	1,138	1,224	1,213	1,163	(**)	1,119	26	3	7	7	−3	−72	(**)	−76	2	2
48	Far East, total	309	881	954	1,024	1,152	24	536	259	99	130	103	5	52	2	20	12	18
49	India	38	113	120	134	159	(*)	(*)	51	2	12	93	3	13	(*)	(*)	4	9
50	Indonesia	58	169	196	163	178		(*)	11	(**)	1	166	−44	2		(*)	(**)	2
51	Japan	19	185	181	209	254		(*)	91	1	27	135	14	18		(*)	7	12
52	Philippine Republic	149	306	341	387	414	(*)	(*)	91	92	50	181	22	6	(*)	(**)	1	6
53	Other countries	46	108	116	131	147	(*)	(*)	16	3	40	88	10	13	(*)	(*)	1	12
54	Oceania, total	256	698	786	879	994	33	372	494	1	58	36	28	41	(**)	2	29	10
55	Australia	201	583	655	742	856	33	(*)	476	(*)	42	305	26	46	(**)	(*)	29	17
56	New Zealand	25	48	50	54	53		(*)	18	(*)	16	19	1	−5		(*)	(**)	−5
57	Other countries	30	66	81	83	85	(**)	(*)		(*)	(**)	85	1	(**)		(*)		(**)
58	International	356	1,041	1,188	1,357	1,418		851		567			135	12		12		(**)

ʳ Revised.   ᵖ Preliminary.   *Combined in other industries.   **Less than $500,000.

NOTE.—Detail may not add to totals because of rounding.

1 The value for U.S. direct investments in Canada for 1957 and subsequent years has been raised by $132 million to include certain liabilities of Canadian financial institutions to U.S. sources previously omitted.
2 The estimated value of U.S. direct investments in Cuba in 1960 is carried forward from 1959 without change. No estimates have been made for net capital flows, reinvestment of subsidiary earnings, net earnings, or income receipts for Cuba for 1960.

Selected Countries and Years, and Major Industries, 1960
Earnings, by Countries with Major Industries for 1960
by Selected Countries, 1959–60, with Major Industries for 1960

[Millions of dollars]

| Table 3—Continued | | | | | | Table 4 | | | | | | | | | | | | |
| Undistributed subsidiary earnings | | | | | | Earnings | | | | | | Income | | | | | | |
1959 r	Total	Mining and smelting	Petroleum	Manufacturing	Other	1959 r	Total	Mining and smelting	Petroleum	Manufacturing	Other	1959 r	Total	Mining and smelting	Petroleum	Manufacturing	Other	Line
1,089	1,254	56	157	627	414	3,241	3,546	394	1,282	1,176	693	2,206	2,348	337	1,143	550	319	1
393	389	38	46	234	72	713	718	88	97	398	134	345	361	47	60	176	78	2
202	215	-13	33	86	108	774	829	164	345	146	174	600	641	180	311	63	87	3
80	52	-17	7	12	50	156	126	17	2	32	74	90	85	33	-4	26	31	4
14	----	(*)	(*)	(*)	1	28	----	(*)	(*)	(*)	8	22	----	(*)	(*)	(*)	7	5
1	1	(*)	(*)	(*)	1	5	8	(*)	(*)	(*)	8	5	7	(*)	(*)	(*)	7	6
1	1	(*)	(**)	(*)	1	-1	-4	(*)	(*)	(*)	-4	-2	-5	(*)	(*)	(*)	-4	7
1	1	(*)	(*)	10	1	6	1	(*)	(*)	(*)	1	5	(**)	(*)	(*)	(*)	-1	8
20	-3	-17	1	1	4	52	54	10	3	29	12	35	65	26	2	24	(**)	9
41	48	1	5	1	42	59	62	1	4	2	56	19	16	(**)	-1	1	16	10
2	3		(**)	(**)	2	8	4	2	-2	(**)	3	7	1	2	-2	(**)	2	11
122	163	4	27	74	58	617	703	147	342	114	100	509	556	147	316	38	56	12
14	36	(*)	(*)	29	7	24	46	(*)	(*)	35	11	11	10	(*)	(*)	6	4	13
34	39	2	(**)	29	8	54	80	3	(*)	57	16	25	45	1	3	26	15	14
10	7	(**)	(*)	1	6	77	72	56	(*)	3	13	71	72	58	(*)	2	12	15
6	8	(*)	1	3	3	17	26	(*)	18	4	4	11	19	(*)	16	1	2	16
4	11	(**)	5	2	(**)	26	58	36	10	3	9	23	48	37	4	1	6	17
-1	2	(*)	(**)	1	(**)	1	4	(*)	(*)	3	2	2	3	(*)	(*)	2	1	18
53	59	(*)	12	8	40	425	428	(**)	321	9	98	373	371	(*)	309	2	60	19
2	1	(**)	(**)	(**)	(**)	-7	-11	(**)	-15	(**)	4	-8	-11	(**)	-15	(**)	4	20
24	63	5	5	(**)	52	95	141	60	25	1	55	71	78	55	20	1	3	21
266	526	-1	1	237	89	667	762	10	85	487	180	393	427	11	85	241	90	22
103	154	(**)	22	104	28	245	310	(**)	42	205	63	134	144	----	21	90	33	23
6	10		-1	10	2	22	35		1	28	7	13	21	----	2	14	5	24
26	48	(**)	20	17	10	48	72	(**)	26	31	16	20	22	----	6	11	5	25
52	76	(*)	3	66	8	131	148	(*)	7	120	21	71	66	(*)	5	49	12	26
14	14	(*)	1	10	4	31	36	(*)	7	21	8	24	24	(*)	8	12	4	27
6	7		1	1	4	13	19		2	6	11	8	11	(**)		4	7	28
163	172	-1	-21	133	61	421	452	10	43	282	117	259	282	11	64	150	56	29
-2	(**)	-1	(**)	1		4	-1		3	2		8	4		(**)	3	1	30
1	3	(*)	3	(**)		2	5	(*)	(**)	3	1	2	(*)	1	1	1		31
4	4	(*)	1	-1		7	7	(*)		3	2	9	(**)	(*)	-1	1	1	32
-3	-3		-2	1	-1	7	7		-2	3	2	7	9	(**)		1	7	33
13	35		-3	10	28	23	48		-3	17	34	10	14			1	8	34
3	2	(*)	1	(**)	(**)	-12	-9	(*)	-10	(**)	1	-14	-10	(*)	-11	(**)	1	35
140	123		-21	116	29	370	369		51	53	251	65	231	247	(*)	74	136	36
6	7	-2	5	(**)	3	25	24	9	6	2	7	18	17	11	1	1	3	37
48	50	20	13	3	14	55	33	61	-77	19	30	7	-17	41	-90	16	17	38
2	2	(**)	2	-1	(**)	-33	-69	1	-71	(**)	1	-36	-71	1	-74	1	(**)	39
3	2		2	(**)	(**)	3	-2	(**)	-3	(**)	(**)	(**)	-5	(**)	-5	(**)		40
22	19	11	-3		11	32	37	24	-13		25	10	18	14	-10		14	41
21	27	9	11	4	2	52	68	35	9	19	1	32	41	26	-2	15	2	42
7	10	8	(*)	(*)	1	12	19	18	(*)	(*)	1	5	10	10	(*)	(*)	(**)	43
14	17	1	(*)	4	12	42	50	17	(*)	19	14	34	16	(*)	15	2	4	44
(**)	(**)		(*)	(*)	(**)	-2	-2		(*)	(*)	-2	-2		(*)	(*)	-2		45
56	88	2	45	17	21	785	901	3	799	42	58	732	816	1	759	23	33	46
-9	21		20	1	1	619	721		717	2	2	629	701		698	1	2	47
65	67	2	25	16	23	166	181	3	82	10	56	102	114	1	60	22	32	48
10	12	(*)	(*)	6	6	16	14	(*)	(*)	10	4	5	1	(*)	(*)	4	-2	49
12	13		(*)	2	11	51	70		(*)	2	68	46	60		(*)	60		50
13	17		(*)	5	12	23	32		(*)	8	24	10	15		(*)	4	11	51
21	21	(*)	(*)	3	18	60	52	(*)	(*)	17	36	33	28	(*)	(*)	12	16	52
5	3	(*)	(*)	1	2	13	13	(*)	(*)	4	9	8	10	(*)	(*)	2	7	53
65	74	5	15	50	4	112	115	8	14	82	11	43	37	2	-1	29	7	54
61	68	5	(*)	48	15	102	101	8	(*)	75	19	37	30	2	(*)	24	4	55
2	4		(*)	2	2	9	11		(*)	(*)	7	4	7		(*)	(*)	6	2	56
2	2	(**)	(*)		2	2	2	(**)	(*)		2	6	(**)	(**)	(**)		(**)	57
34	49		-2		51	41	47			-5		52	14	5		(**)		5	58

[1] Income is the sum of dividends, interest, and branch profits; earnings is the sum of the U.S. share in net earnings of subsidiaries and branch profits.

Other areas

Africa.—Petroleum companies considerably stepped up their expenditures to develop North African production in 1960. Part of this was reflected in a capital outflow of about $50 million, but an even larger amount was accounted for as exploration and development expenses and is reflected in large operating losses in the area. There was a net inflow to the United States of capital from mining and manufacturing investments in the Union of South Africa.

Asia.—In the Middle East capital outlays in petroleum were still being financed largely by the operating companies or their affiliates abroad, resulting on balance in a net capital inflow to the United States. Production of oil in the area increased substantially in 1960, and earnings also turned upward.

Most of the increased capital flow to Far Eastern countries in 1960 was accounted for by the petroleum industry, which had been withdrawing funds in 1958 and 1959.

Oceania—Direct investments in manufacturing in Australia rose considerably in 1960, with capital flows and reinvested earnings both larger than in 1959. There were minor inflows from New Zealand. Earnings in the area changed little.

International—In this category, representing shipping subsidiaries utilizing the flags of Panama, Liberia and Honduras, there was a sharp reduction in capital outflows in 1960 as compared with 1959. Most of this represented a decline in the financing of tanker subsidiaries of petroleum companies as ship mortgages were paid off. Earnings of the tanker fleets were further depressed, but other shipping enterprises reported some improved earnings.

Industry Developments

Manufacturing—Responding to various attractions and pressures, United States manufacturing companies raised further in 1960 the amount invested abroad through capital outflows and

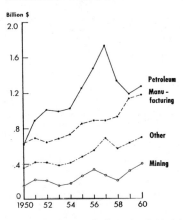

EARNINGS OF DIRECT FOREIGN INVESTMENTS, BY INDUSTRY

U. S. Department of Commerce, Office of Business Economics   61-8-13

reinvested profits. Europe was the area receiving the largest amount of these funds—over $800 million out of a world total of $1.4 billion for the manufacturing industry in 1960. Common Market countries received nearly $300 million and the United Kingdom about $550 million, but the latter included about $370 million for purchases of minority interests.

Manufacturing investments by United States firms in Canada continued to grow at a substantial rate, mainly out of reinvested earnings.

In Latin America, and in some others of the less developed countries, manufacturing investments are being carried out at a somewhat accelerated rate partly because of promising future markets, but also under the threat of exclusion from such markets unless local manufacture is undertaken.

Although this industry is now very actively expanding abroad, the sums being invested in Africa and Asia are still relatively small, amounting to $30 million for both continents in 1960, about the same as in 1959.

Among the major commodity groups in the manufacturing category, the fastest growing in 1960 were transportation equipment (largely automobiles), chemicals, food products, and machinery. Other commodity groups also expanded substantially abroad, as shown in table 5.

Table 5.—Direct Investments in Manufacturing Enterprises Abroad, 1950, 1957, 1959, and 1960, by Commodity

[Millions of dollars]

Area and year	Manufacturing, total	Food products	Paper and allied products	Chemicals and allied products	Rubber products	Primary and fabricated metals	Machinery (except electrical)	Electrical machinery	Transportation equipment	Other products
All areas, total										
1950	3,831	483	378	512	182	385	420	387	485	599
1957	8,009	723	722	1,378	401	941	927	731	1,204	983
1959	9,707	823	813	1,661	461	1,163	1,202	833	1,603	1,148
1960	11,152	913	861	1,902	570	1,256	1,333	918	2,118	1,301
Canada										
1950	1,897	227	368	198	59	249	204	141	160	292
1957	3,924	320	626	647	133	671	327	330	398	471
1959	4,565	367	687	743	142	773	391	367	540	535
1960	4,827	399	723	817	161	803	394	393	558	580
Latin America [1]										
1950	781	158	5	205	60	23	13	79	83	155
1957	1,280	201	39	334	133	60	52	136	134	190
1959	1,417	184	50	358	149	71	57	136	209	204
1960	1,631	228	52	408	165	82	70	169	231	227
Europe										
1950	932	64	5	74	31	111	175	153	192	128
1957	2,195	149	42	319	59	178	488	214	475	272
1959	2,947	198	55	447	75	277	677	270	604	344
1960	3,797	224	63	537	90	324	782	288	1,074	415
Africa										
1950	55	6	--------	9	11	1	2	3	17	6
1957	106	10	3	12	21	5	17	5	27	6
1959	120	14	3	15	23	5	20	5	26	8
1960	118	14	3	16	23	6	20	6	22	8
Asia										
1950	60	9	--------	12	14	**	5	2	8	10
1957	190	15	9	40	38	20	15	12	23	18
1959	244	19	13	58	48	27	15	14	27	23
1960	286	20	15	76	54	30	19	16	29	27
Oceania										
1950	107	18	1	13	8	2	22	9	26	8
1957	314	28	3	27	17	8	26	34	146	26
1959	415	41	5	40	25	10	42	41	177	34
1960	494	58	5	47	28	12	48	43	204	44

Note: Detail may not add to totals because of rounding.
[1] Includes minor amounts in the Western Hemisphere dependencies.
**Less than $500,000.

Investments in automotive plants overseas were raised by about $½ billion in the year, of which $370 million resulted from the special outlay in the United Kingdom discussed above. Automotive investments also increased substantially in other European countries and in Australia.

About $¼ billion was added to U.S. investments in the chemical industry abroad in 1960, not including petrochemical plants owned by petroleum companies. Expansion by this industry was significant in Canada, Latin America, and Europe.

More than half of the $215 million increase in investments in enterprises producing machinery was in Europe. Manufacturers of food products accelerated their rate of investment in most areas.

Petroleum—About $600 million was added by U.S. petroleum companies to their foreign investments in 1960, raising the total stake to $11 billion. This rate of investment was moderately higher than that of 1959, with most of the gain showing up in refinery construction in Europe and the Far East, and in distribution facilities in Canada and Europe. There was also heightened development activity in North Africa, as noted above, and in Argentina.

The industry remains moderately active in exploring throughout the world and is carrying out a large scale expansion in refineries, petrochemicals, transmission systems, and other phases of the industry.

Trade—Investments in enterprises whose major activity is trading or distribution are now growing at an accelerated rate—about $360 million was invested in such operations abroad in 1960. Many of these enterprises also perform additional functions including licensing, management and research services, and activity as financial intermediaries.

Earnings generally higher

With increased demand abroad for petroleum, metals, and manufactures, earnings of the direct investments continued a steady advance. However, the total was still under the 1957 record despite additional investments of nearly $7½ billion since that time.

601431—61——4

Petroleum earnings rose most notably in the Middle East, where oil production by the companies increased 14 percent. There were moderate gains in earnings in other producing areas and from increased refinery output in Europe and elsewhere.

Earnings of the mining companies were much higher than in recent years as prices firmed and more properties reached the producing stage.

Improved earnings for manufacturing enterprises in most countries reflected general business expansion. An exception was Canada, where earnings were depressed as business activity remained low, and there was scarcely any change in manufacturing earnings in the United Kingdom.

Of the total direct-investment earnings of $3.5 billion in 1960, about $1.1 billion was branch profits and $2.4 billion represented the U.S. share in the profits of foreign subsidiary companies. Of the latter amount, about $1.25 billion, or 52 percent, was retained abroad, a proportion generally characteristic of the postwar experience.

Income receipts from abroad, as entered into the balance-of-payments accounts, included all branch profits, common dividends, preferred dividends ($10 million in 1960) and interest ($109 million), less any taxes withheld abroad. The income total for 1960 on this basis was $2.3 billion, about 5 percent more than the 1959 amount. More than half

of the increase in earnings for the year was retained abroad.

Other Private Foreign Investments

A significant part of the pressure on the balance of payments in 1960, offsetting gains made in the trade accounts, came from accelerated outflows of short-term funds beginning about midyear. The accompanying chart, using the relationship between yields on United States Treasury bills and comparable bills in Canada and the United Kingdom as representative of broader changes in world money markets, shows the incentive for investing liquid funds abroad as it developed during 1960.

Table 6.—Selected Short-term Banking and Commercial Claims on Foreigners, by Type and Area

[Millions of dollars]

Area and type	December 1959	June 1960	December 1960	May 1961
Banking claims, total	2,624	2,764	3,590	4,088
Loans	1,308	1,113	1,296	1,394
Acceptances and other	1,099	1,371	1,814	2,188
Payable in foreign currencies	217	280	480	506
By area and country				
Europe	534	575	717	695
United Kingdom	121	181	245	171
Canada	272	272	409	478
Latin America	1,176	1,111	1,354	1,336
Other countries	642	806	1,110	1,579
Japan	323	497	⁻96	1,204
Claims by non-financial concerns, total	730	843	¹ 1,450	n.a.

¹ Includes temporary holdings of sterling ($370 million) intended for direct investment in the United Kingdom.
n.a.—not available.

Source: Treasury Bulletin.

Interest Rate Differentials, With Forward Exchange Cover, Between Three-Month U.S. Treasury Bills and Comparable Canadian and U.K. Bills

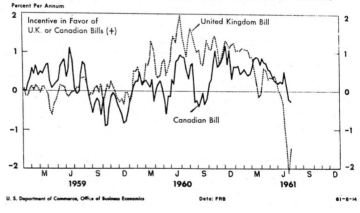

Percent Per Annum

Incentive in Favor of U.K. or Canadian Bills (+)

United Kingdom Bill

Canadian Bill

U. S. Department of Commerce, Office of Business Economics   Data: FRB   61-8-14

Table 7.—International Investment Position of the United States, by Area, 1959–60

[Millions of dollars]

Type of investment	Total		Western Europe		Canada		Latin American Republics		Other foreign countries		International institutions and unallocated	
	1959 r	1960 p	1959 r	1960 p	1959 r	1960 p	1959 r	1960 p	1959 r	1960 p	1959 r	1960 p
U.S. assets and investments abroad, total	64,830	71,407	18,488	20,412	15,917	17,238	12,675	13,537	10,612	12,759	7,138	7,431
Private investments	44,818	50,285	9,128	11,231	15,907	17,235	10,749	11,473	6,741	7,835	2,293	2,508
Long-term	41,222	45,376	8,229	9,922	15,472	16,600	9,311	9,850	5,917	6,496	2,293	2,508
Direct	29,805	32,741	5,323	6,645	10,310	11,198	8,098	8,365	4,717	5,118	1,357	1,418
Foreign dollar bonds	4,314	4,941	327	357	2,310	2,573	140	240	634	747	903	1,024
Other foreign securities [2]	4,229	4,617	1,473	1,798	2,508	2,517	40	53	175	183	33	66
Other	2,874	3,074	1,106	1,122	344	312	1,033	1,192	391	448		
Short-term	3,596	4,909	899	1,312	435	635	1,438	1,623	824	1,339		
U.S. Government credits and claims	20,012	21,122	9,360	9,208	10	3	1,926	2,064	3,871	4,924	4,845	4,923
Long-term	17,605	18,230	8,522	8,458			1,767	1,889	2,471	2,967	4,845	4,916
Short-term	2,407	2,892	838	750	10	3	159	175	1,400	1,957		7
Foreign assets and investments in the United States, total	42,146	44,682	23,120	24,048	5,997	6,196	3,794	3,726	4,402	4,837	3,927	4,965
Long-term	18,050	18,438	12,675	13,004	3,301	3,303	1,154	1,153	817	858	103	120
Direct [2]	6,604	6,931	4,452	4,713	1,896	1,949	129	130	127	139		
Corporate stocks	9,363	9,302	6,856	6,836	1,250	1,209	743	728	476	490	38	39
Corporate, state and municipal bonds	534	648	364	449	15	5	64	75	26	38	65	81
Other	1,549	1,557	1,003	1,006	140	140	218	220	188	191		
Short-term assets and U.S. Government obligations	24,096	26,244	10,445	11,044	2,696	2,893	2,640	2,573	3,585	3,979	3,824	4,845
Private obligations	10,893	12,113	4,451	4,893	1,704	1,981	2,358	2,211	2,236	2,709	144	319
U.S. Government obligations	13,203	14,131	5,994	6,151	992	912	282	362	1,349	1,270	3,680	4,526
Long-term	2,149	2,276	838	803	363	327	187	141	95	114	666	891
Short-term [3]	11,054	11,855	5,156	5,348	629	585	95	221	1,254	1,156	3,014	3,635

r Revised.
p Preliminary.
[1] Represents the estimated investment in shipping companies registered in Panama and Liberia.
[2] Consists primarily of securities payable in foreign currencies, but includes some dollar obligations, including participation in loan made by the International Bank for Reconstruction and Development.
[3] Total includes estimated foreign holdings of U.S. currency: 1959, $906 million; 1960, $910 million; not distributed by area.

Basic factors underlying the behavior of interest rates were sagging economic activity in the United States, which was accompanied by a fall in short-term interest rates from a peak at the beginning of the year to a low of a little over 2 percent at mid-year, and the booming economies of other industrial countries, leading to attempts by their monetary authorities to restrain credit. The flow of liquid funds toward the latter countries tended to frustrate their monetary policies, and eventually, as the loss of gold and dollars by the United States became very large, and fears of devaluation grew, flights of capital developed. In some countries this led to a shift from primary emphasis on monetary measures of restraint to increased reliance on measures other than high short-term interest rates. Short-term rates in the United Kingdom and Germany were consequently sharply reduced in the last quarter of the year, and, in the case of Germany, have

continued to decline this year. Germany also appreciated the value of its currency in March 1961.

Short-term interest rates in the United Kingdom nevertheless remained well above the United States rates, but the incentive to move funds to that market was wiped out early in the year by a widening discount on forward sterling. Recent announcement of a sharp boost in the discount rate in the United Kingdom has altered this relationship. In the case of Canada, short-term interest rates remained attractive through the first five months of 1961, and then were offset by depreciation of the Canadian dollar and lower interest rates there.

By far the largest outflow of funds, however, was recorded for Japan, as shown in table 6. Interest rates in that country persist well above those in other industrial countries, attracting both United States funds and dollars owned by residents of other countries.

Monetary authorities here and abroad are now better prepared to mitigate the disturbing effects of such capital flows, cooperating in lending short-term support to currencies coming under pressure from this source.

Private portfolio investments

Long-term private portfolio investments abroad were increased by $1.2 billion in 1960—about the same amount as in 1959—reaching a total value of $12.6 billion. About $850 billion of the 1960 gain resulted from capital outflows, and the remainer consisted of improved market values for foreign stocks and dollar bonds.

U.S. purchases of new foreign securities offered here have fallen since the 1958 peak, when interest rates here were comparatively low. The total for 1960 was $573 million, with the volume reduced after the first half and continuing at a low level this year. Canadian borrowers have lately raised a much higher proportion of their needs in their own capital market, and the other major issuer here, the International Bank, has not entered this market to any extent in this period of balance-of-payments problems. There was a considerable variety of other issues offered here in 1960, led by a $100 million issue sold privately by a Mexican institution.

Investors in the United States added nearly $100 million to their holdings of other foreign bonds, purchasing sizable amounts of European issues and participating in loans originated by the International Bank.

Americans reduced their acquisitions of foreign corporate stocks in 1960, but accelerated their purchases again in the first half of 1961. Most of the stocks were issues of companies on the European continent; there were net liquidations of Canadian and United Kingdom equities in 1960, reflecting a downward drift of prices in those countries.

Medium term foreign loans by U.S. banks increased by $160 million in 1960 to a total of $1.7 billion. Most of the increase went to Argentina and Venezuela. There was a general but moderate reduction of outstanding bank loans in the first five months of 1961. Credits extended by non-financial concerns rose moderately in most areas in 1960.

EXPANSION IN U.S. INVESTMENTS ABROAD

Samuel Pizer
and
Frederick Cutler

By SAMUEL BIZER and FREDERICK CUTLER

Expansion in U.S. Investments Abroad

Record capital flow and earnings in 1961—Total value $56 billion—

Reduced outflows indicated for 1962

THE outflow of U.S. private capital to foreign countries reached a high of nearly $4.0 billion in 1961, about $100 million above the mark of the previous year. Direct investments accounted for $1½ billion, net purchases of foreign securities and medium-term loans for about $1.0 billion, and short-term loans and acquisitions of liquid assets abroad for $1½ billion.

In broad outline, foreign investments in 1961 resembled the 1960 pattern. For direct investments the flow was still strong to Europe, but the total and the European sector were not pushed up, as in 1960, by any large single investment; the principal changes in direct investments from year-to-year were a reduced flow to Canada and a sharp upturn to enterprises in the Middle East, some parts of Africa, and Australia.

Purchases of foreign securities rose slightly to $750 million (net), with the share of Canada less than in earlier postwar years, and a rising share for Europe and other countries. Outflows of short-term capital reached a new high in 1961, led by large investments of banking and other short-term capital in Canada and Japan, while the flow to Europe lessened considerably from the 1960 amount.

By the end of 1961 private U.S. assets and investments abroad were valued at nearly $56 billion, a gain of over $5 billion in the year. Most of the change came from the investment of additional U.S. capital outlined above, but other increases resulted from the reinvestment of $1.0 billion of direct investment earnings and some revaluations of assets.

Developments in 1962

Since the turn of the year the limited data available indicate some slowing down in the rate of foreign investment,

18

although the total remains well above all but a few postwar years. Direct investments are affected by the much reduced rate of growth of industrial production in Europe, by unsettled conditions in some countries of Latin America, economic difficulties in Canada, and more than adequate productive capabilities for raw materials at current levels of demand. On the other hand, the companies have ample funds for investment which are not being committed to domestic expansion, and are continuing to invest large sums abroad where opportunities exist.

Investments in foreign equity securities have tended to taper off as markets in most financial centers abroad have been weak, and a realignment of prices and yields appear to be taking place both here and abroad. Overall sales of foreign bonds in the United States have been relatively low so far this year, but there has been a significant increase in issues offered by European borrowers.

Short-term capital outflows in the first half of 1962 were moderate, and were largely connected with loans negotiated earlier for Japan. On balance, there were reductions in short-term foreign loans of U.S. banks in Canada and Europe.

For both portfolio and short-term investments abroad, the United States remains the most accessible and lowest cost capital market. Interest rates here may tend to harden somewhat, but short-term rates have also been rising recently in other financial centers, so that the basic incentives for capital outflows remain. Some large borrowers, however, have possibly reached a ceiling on the amount of indebtedness considered justified by their ability to repay, while others, notably Canada, may now have become more attractive than in the first half of the year.

Income receipts higher

Income received from private foreign investments advanced by over $400 million to $3.3 billion in 1961. Three quarters of the increase came from direct investments and reflected not only higher earnings but also for some countries a larger proportion of earnings paid out as dividends.

Interest and dividends received on short-term and portfolio investments rose by over $100 million in 1961, offsetting to some degree the large capital outflows of these types in the past few years.

Foreign Direct Investments

U.S. business added another $2½ billion to investments in foreign subsidiaries, branches, and affiliated companies in 1961, made up of capital outflows of $1½ billion and about $1.0 billion of undistributed profits. The total added from these sources was about $½ billion less than in 1960, with capital flows and undistributed profits each lower by about $¼ billion. Since the 1960 capital flow included $370 million for a single investment in the United Kingdom, there was some increase in other flows. Undistributed profits were reduced mainly because dividends were raised substantially by manufacturing companies while earnings were only slightly higher.

The 1961 annual rate of additions to investment was exceeded only in 1960, and in the postwar peaks of 1956–57. In the latter period the rate of investment was especially high in the petroleum industry as new producing properties were acquired and developed, and there were also substantial investments by other industries. In 1960, manufacturing investments in Europe were the leading feature. The advance in 1961 was more evenly distributed among the principal industries, with investments in petroleum and manufacturing each being increased by about $0.9 billion, while in other industries a slower but relatively steady rate of increase was maintained.

Some sizable adjustments were made to the valuations of direct investments as of the end of 1961, which had the net effect of reducing the aggregate book value by about $0.6 billion. The largest change resulted from eliminating from these tabulations Cuban investments with a book value of $956 million at the end of 1960. No information on these investments has been available since they were expropriated, for the most part during 1960. There was also some reduction in book values of enterprises in other countries particularly in Latin America. Offsetting these adjustments, there were upward revaluations of $586 million, of which the largest was a $406 million increase in the book value of the next fixed assets of a large enterprise in the petroleum industry in Venezuela.

After giving effect to the additional investments and adjustments just noted, the book value of U.S. direct foreign investments reached a peak of $34.7 billion at the end of 1961.

Regional Developments

Nearly $1.0 billion was added to the European investments of U.S. companies in 1961 (40 percent of the total increment in the year) raising their accumulated book value to $7.7 billion. Capital flows to Europe amounted to nearly $0.7 billion, and undistributed profits were about $0.3 billion.

Though down from the 1960 peak, aggregate capital flows to Europe are shown in the first chart to be far above

the average of earlier years. However, the chart also shows some recent diminution of the capital flow to manufacturing, while petroleum companies have been raising their outlays for several years, mainly to add to refining and distributing capacity. Undistributed profits have been slowly increasing over the postwar period, but were cut back in 1961.

Investments in the Common Market countries were raised by $0.4 billion last year, about the same amount as in 1960. France, Germany, and Italy each received substantial capital inflows with petroleum investments especially large in Italy and manufacturing in the others. The rate of investment in the United Kingdom by U.S. companies

was reduced in 1961, even after eliminating the special 1960 transaction mentioned above, but the $0.3 billion added in 1961 ranked second only to the amount for Canada. Nearly one-half of the 1961 investment was added to manufacturing investments and most of the remainder to petroleum.

Switzerland stands out among the other European countries, as U.S. direct investments mounted by $150 million. More than half of this increase was in trading and financial organizations, and a considerable part of these investments is ultimately invested in other countries.[1] However, there is also an impressive rate of growth in enterprises operating mainly within Switzerland.

1. New information on investment flows among foreign affiliates is now being collected and tabulated.

DIRECT FOREIGN INVESTMENT EARNINGS CONTINUE UP IN 1961
With Larger Proportion Distributed as Dividends

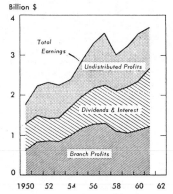

Major Gains in Europe and Other Eastern Hemisphere

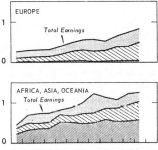

Earnings in Western Hemisphere Lagging Since 1956-57

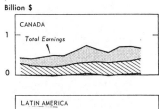
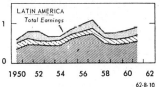

U.S. Department of Commerce, Office of Business Economics

62-8-10

Slow pace in Latin America

Capital flows to Latin America registered some improvement in 1961 over the low point of 1960, amounting to $141 million. However, nearly all of this investment flow occurred in the first half of the year. After mid-year, net outflows of capital ceased as continued investments to Argentina, Mexico, and Chile for manufacturing and mining investments were offset by net inflows from Venezuela (petroleum) and Brazil (manufacturing), and to a lesser extent, from various of the smaller Caribbean countries. In other countries no strong changes were discernible.

DIRECT INVESTMENT CAPITAL OUTFLOWS, 1950-61

Europe Shows Strong Uptrend Since 1955; Petroleum Investments Up in 1961

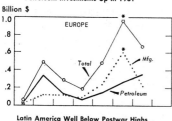

Latin America Well Below Postwar Highs

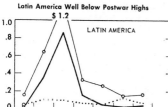

Canadian Flow Has Tended Downward

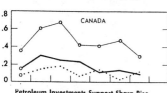

Petroleum Investments Support Sharp Rise In Africa and Asia

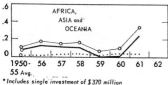

1950- 56 57 58 59 60 61 62
55 Avg.

*Includes single investment of $370 million

U.S. Department of Commerce, Office of Business Economics   62-8-11

Notable shifts in 1961 were an increase in capital flows into mining operations, and a decline in the volume going into manufacturing enterprises. In the mining industry, there were relatively small investments in Venezuela, Peru, and in other countries in 1961, contrasting with a sizable return to the United States of funds from some of these mining properties in 1960, resulting in a swing of about $100 million in this industry over the 2-year period. In the manufacturing industry, outflows to Argentina increased for the fourth successive year, reaching a widening range of industrial and consumer commodities, while the flow of new capital to Brazil dwindled to less than $1 million from $52 million in 1960.

Reinvestment of subsidiary earnings in the area remained stable at a little over $200 million in 1961, showing little change in individual industries or in the area totals despite a moderate increase in earnings. However, on a country basis, Argentina, Mexico, and Panama showed a larger volume of reinvestment, while Venezuela's total was off by about $20 million, as some holding companies with sizable earnings were shifted from Venezuela to Switzerland.

Flow to Canada lower

Both capital flows and reinvested earnings in Canada were reduced in 1961, with the combined total amounting to less than $0.6 billion compared with nearly $0.9 billion in 1960. The average annual increase in direct investments in Canada since 1950 has been about $750 million.

Funds going into manufacturing operations amounted to $260 million, about the same total as in the past few years. However, a higher proportion in 1961 took the form of capital flows, compensating for a drop in retained earnings. A considerable flow of funds went into Canadian mining ventures, although the overall total was reduced below the experience of other recent years by an inflow connected with the refinancing of a major project. Petroleum investments also tended downward, to the lowest rate since 1949, reflecting the

completion of major phases of the industry's development. Among the other industry sectors, there was only a minor addition to the amount invested in trade and distribution enterprises, which had been growing relatively fast for some years.

Other areas receive larger flows

Africa.—American companies considerably stepped up investment operations in Africa, adding about $175 million to their investment in 1961 compared with $130 million in 1960. Reinvestment remained steady at about $50 million, but capital flows continued to increase and exceeded $100 million, nearly all in North Africa.

With oil companies approaching large-scale production in Libya and adjoining North African areas, a continuation of considerable investment activity will be needed to provide the necessary production, transportation, storage and service facilities. Since 1954, the U.S. companies have invested over $½ billion to develop the oil resources of this area. Much of the investment is not reflected in the book value figures, since it was accounted for as operating expenses. A small but significant increase in flows for mining operations occurred in 1961, as a number of companies entered the early stages of major mining developments in West Africa.

Asia.—With continued increases in oil production in the Middle East, a renewed flow of capital was recorded to the area, both for fixed investment to increase production facilities and to finance increased receivables from affiliates and customers. In the Far East, a continued but modest increase in manufacturing investments was more than offset by a declining volume of new investments in petroleum operations.

Oceania.—Direct investments in Australia continued to grow at a rate of about $100 million per year. A decline in reinvestment of earnings of manufacturing companies by $40 million was due to declining profits and a higher proportion of pay-out of dividends, but oil companies increased their investment in refining and other product lines, and in distribution facilities.

Completion of some phases of current development work on mining and petroleum in the Western Hemisphere dependencies sharply reduced capital flows and reinvested earnings in this area.

Developments by Industry

Domestic manufacturing companies invested an additional $0.9 billion in manufacturing facilities abroad in 1961, bringing the accumulated total invested in foreign plants to nearly $12.0 billion. This was substantially less than the record increases of 1959–60, but about the same as the annual rate of investment since 1955.

Large share of manufacturing to Europe

Europe received over 40 percent of the manufacturing investment in 1961, rising from about 30 percent of the total in 1953–57. Data collected on actual and projected expenditures for plant and equipment by U.S.-owned plants in the area [2] show a substantial rise in 1961–62 from the 1960 amount, but there appears to have been some cutback from the earlier expectations. As a result, the need for capital from the United States may stabilize or be reduced.

Manufacturing investments in Canada appear to be holding steady, with additions amounting to about $0.3 billion annually. Projected plant and equipment expenditures show a similar lack of movement. For Latin America, the principal manufacturing activity is now in Argentina and Mexico, with investments in Brazil much reduced from earlier levels. In the rest of the world there was some increase in manufacturing investments in Japan, but the flow to Australia diminished in 1961.

In most of the major commodity groupings of manufacturing shown in table 5, the rate of growth in investments was either lower than in 1960,

2. *Survey of Current Business* for September 1961 and forthcoming issue of September 1962.

or showed only small advances. Investments in chemical plants registered the largest increase in 1961 ($130 million), but this was not much more than half the 1960 amount. Moreover, the 1961 figure includes a sizable jump in investments by oil companies in affiliates producing petrochemicals.

Increases of over $100 million each were scored by the transportation equipment, machinery, and primary metals groups, but only the latter had a larger gain than in 1960.

Petroleum.—Capital flows and reinvested earnings of the petroleum industry in 1961 were in excess of $900 million, making this the highest year since 1957. An additional $430 million was added to the book value of investments in this industry because of various adjustments, the largest being a revaluation by a large company of net fixed assets in Venezuela amounting to $406 million.

More than 40 percent of the investment in 1961 went to Europe to expand refining and distribution facilities, excluding investments in petrochemical plants mentioned above. Projections of plant and equipment expenditures show a continuation of outlays at a high level in Europe, underlining the present need of the petroleum industry to develop refining and distribution facilities in European and other markets. In earlier periods of high investment activity by this industry, such as 1947–49 and 1956–57, the main portion of oil investments went for the acquisition and exploration of producing areas, mainly in Latin America and the Middle East.

North Africa remains the most active area for the development of new oil fields, and about $100 million was spent here in 1961 to find and develop new oil resources and to prepare them for large scale production. Sizable amounts were also spent for this purpose in Canada, Argentina, the Middle East, Australia, and, to a lesser extent, in a number of other countries.

Trade and distribution.—Substantial investments in trading and distribution facilities abroad continued in 1961, with $0.3 billion added in the year.

About a third of the increase was in Panama and Switzerland.

In 1961, the book value shown under the heading of public utilities was reduced by about $375 million. This reflects in part the elimination of Cuban properties ($313 million) and the transfer to "miscellaneous" of utility investments in Argentina and Mexico which were acquired by those countries in 1961, with the sales proceeds to be reinvested locally over a period of years. Offsetting these reductions, there were sizable additions to investments in international shipping out of undistributed profits.

Limited Gain in Foreign Earnings

Earnings of direct foreign investments advanced by a little over 4 percent in 1961 to a record $3.7 billion. Petroleum companies earned $1.4 billion, with higher earnings reflecting a 4 percent increase in their output of crude oil.

As in the past, earnings in the petroleum industry show up mainly in the producing areas, with 1961 increases large in Canada, Venezuela, and the

Table 1.—Factors Affecting U.S. Private Investments Abroad, 1960 and 1961.

[Millions of dollars]

Type of investment	1960	1961
Direct investments		
Value, beginning of year	29,827	32,778
Add: Capital outflow [1]	1,694	1,467
Reinvested earnings	1,266	1,046
Other adjustments [2]	−9	−607
Value, end of year	32,778	34,684
Other long-term private investments		
Value, beginning of year	11,417	12,632
Add: Capital outflow [1]	850	1,006
Price changes	365	745
Value, end of year	12,632	14,383
Short-term assets		
Value, beginning of year	3,596	4,983
Add: Capital outflow [1]	1,338	1,472
Adjustments [2]	49	135
Value, end of year	4,983	6,590
Combined change	5,553	5,264
Capital outflow [1]	3,882	3,945
Reinvested earnings	1,266	1,046
Other factors	405	273

1. Included in the balance of payments accounts.
2. Mainly changes in coverage, reclassifications, or revaluations (see note to Table 2).

Table 2.—Value of Direct Investments Abroad by
Table 3.—Direct-Investment Capital Flow and Undistributed Subsidiary
Table 4.—Direct-Investment Earnings and Income,[1]

[Millions of dollars]

Line	Area and country	Table 2				1961 p							Table 3 Net capital outflows 1960 r	1961 p				
		1950	1957	1959	1960 r	Total	Mining and smelting	Petroleum	Manufacturing	Public utilities	Trade	Other		Total	Mining and smelting	Petroleum	Manufacturing	Other
1	All areas, total	11,788	25,394	29,827	32,778	34,684	3,061	12,151	11,936	2,166	2,648	2,722	1,694	1,467	72	747	460	188
2	Canada	3,579	8,769	10,310	11,198	11,804	1,380	2,841	5,093	687	639	1,164	471	297	12	99	122	65
3	Latin American Republics, total[1]	4,445	7,434	8,120	8,387	8,166	1,105	3,247	1,655	664	763	732	95	141	34	26	73	8
4	Mexico, Central America and West Indies, total[1]	1,488	2,234	2,538	2,642	1,773	181	193	449	186	306	459	68	42	-2	22	20	1
5	Cuba[1]	642	849	956	956	(1)	(1)	(1)	(1)	(1)	(1)	(1)	(1)	(1)	(1)	(1)	(1)	(1)
6	Dominican Republic	106	88	104	105	105	(*)	(*)	(*)	6	2	97	(**)	-2	(*)	(*)	(*)	-2
7	Guatemala	106	106	132	131	126	(*)	28	(*)	66	6	26	-3	-6	(*)	2	(*)	-9
8	Honduras	62	108	110	100	95	(*)	(*)	(*)	23	1	71	-11	-6	(*)	(*)	(*)	-5
9	Mexico	415	739	758	795	822	130	48	414	29	97	104	56	45	1	16	16	12
10	Panama	58	201	327	405	468	17	64	12	21	189	165	30	8	------	4	2	2
11	Other countries	100	143	151	150	156	12	28	13	40	11	52	-3	2	(**)	(**)	1	(**)
12	South America, total	2,957	5,200	5,582	5,745	6,394	924	3,055	1,207	478	458	273	27	99	36	4	53	7
13	Argentina	356	333	360	472	635	(*)	(*)	283	(*)	28	324	70	96	(*)	(*)	38	58
14	Brazil	644	835	828	953	1,000	14	92	543	198	127	26	83	-8	1	16	1	-9
15	Chile	540	666	729	738	725	503	(*)	27	(*)	13	183	2	-15	-14	(*)	4	-5
16	Colombia	193	396	401	424	425	(*)	229	94	28	50	24	15	-6	(*)	-7	(**)	1
17	Peru	145	383	428	446	437	242	71	37	20	43	25	7	12	18	(*)	(**)	5
18	Uruguay	55	57	45	47	49	(*)	(*)	22	(*)	5	23	(**)	(**)	(*)	(*)	(**)	(**)
19	Venezuela[1]	993	2,465	2,690	2,569	3,017	(*)	2,371	196	33	186	231	-150	4	(*)	-42	11	35
20	Other countries	31	64	96	97	106	7	56	4	14	7	19	-1	-1	5	-2	(**)	-3
21	Western Hemisphere dependencies	131	618	768	884	942	179	401	23	49	77	212	54	27	1	15	1	10
22	Europe, total	1,733	4,151	5,323	6,681	7,655	48	2,131	4,212	47	889	328	962	676	(**)	360	227	89
23	Common Market, total	637	1,680	2,208	2,644	3,041	9	946	1,659	29	299	99	282	270	(*)	109	132	29
24	Belgium and Luxembourg	69	192	211	231	256	------	50	169	1	32	5	10	15	------	2	10	3
25	France	217	464	640	741	840	(*)	244	460	10	92	25	53	71	------	10	49	12
26	Germany	204	581	796	1,006	1,170	(*)	292	747	2	93	35	133	94	(*)	45	45	4
27	Italy	63	252	315	384	467	(*)	215	187	1	38	25	55	79	(*)	59	14	5
28	Netherlands	84	191	245	283	308	------	144	95	15	44	10	31	11	------	-7	14	4
29	Other Europe, total	1,096	2,471	3,116	4,037	4,614	39	1,185	2,553	17	591	229	680	405	(**)	251	95	60
30	Denmark	33	42	48	67	95	------	61	21	(**)	11	2	19	27	------	25	1	1
31	Norway	24	51	62	83	92	(*)	46	23	(**)	7	16	18	6	(*)	5	(**)	1
32	Spain	31	44	53	59	68	(*)	21	29	4	11	4	2	6	(*)	3	(**)	2
33	Sweden	58	109	125	116	140	(**)	77	21	(**)	36	5	-7	30	------	16	8	6
34	Switzerland	25	69	164	254	408	(**)	42	123	(**)	163	80	27	102	------	41	25	35
35	Turkey	16	63	44	65	98	(*)	83	3	(**)	7	4	19	32	(*)	29	1	3
36	United Kingdom	847	1,974	2,477	3,231	3,523	190	761	2,305	10	316	131	589	188	------	120	58	9
37	Other countries	63	119	143	162	190	22	93	18	3	41	4	12	16	------	11	3	3
38	Africa, total	287	664	833	925	1,070	285	491	113	6	62	112	81	122	27	96	-3	2
39	North Africa	56	106	145	195	260	3	238	6	4	5	5	51	91	------	93	-1	-1
40	East Africa	12	30	43	46	56	1	51	(**)	------	4	(**)	1	8	(**)	8	------	(**)
41	West Africa	42	147	228	290	341	155	82	2	2	10	90	42	30	25	1	1	3
42	Central and South Africa, total	177	381	416	394	413	127	120	106	(**)	42	17	-13	-7	1	-6	-3	1
43	Rhodesia and Nyasaland	26	59	72	82	87	75	(*)	(*)	------	2	10	1	(*)	-1	(*)	(*)	1
44	Union of South Africa[3]	140	301	323	286	304	50	(*)	103	(**)	39	113	-18	-2	2	(*)	-3	-1
45	Other countries	12	21	21	26	21	2	(*)	(*)	(**)	2	17	4	-5	------	(*)	(*)	-5
46	Asia, total	1,001	2,019	2,237	2,291	2,482	27	1,750	321	115	152	117	-20	132	(*)	108	19	5
47	Middle East	692	1,138	1,213	1,139	1,240	(**)	1,191	28	4	8	9	-72	108	(*)	104	1	3
48	Far East, total	309	881	1,024	1,152	1,241	27	558	293	111	144	109	52	24	(**)	4	17	3
49	India	38	113	134	159	189	(*)	(*)	63	2	18	105	13	15	(*)	(*)	4	10
50	Indonesia	58	169	163	178	147	(*)	(*)	12	(**)	1	133	2	-31	------	(*)	(**)	-31
51	Japan	19	185	209	254	310	------	(*)	110	1	30	169	18	37	------	(*)	14	22
52	Philippine Republic	149	306	387	414	439	(*)	(*)	89	104	55	191	6	-1	(*)	(*)	-1	(**)
53	Other countries	46	108	131	147	156	(*)	(*)	18	4	39	96	13	6	(*)	(**)	(**)	5
54	Oceania, total	256	698	879	994	1,101	36	423	518	1	66	57	41	88	(**)	44	22	22
55	Australia	201	583	742	856	951	36	(*)	501	(*)	47	368	46	80	(**)	(*)	22	22
56	New Zealand	25	48	54	53	63	------	(*)	17	(*)	19	27	-5	7	------	(*)	(**)	7
57	Other countries	30	66	83	85	87	(**)	(*)	(*)	(*)	(**)	87	(*)	(**)	------	(*)	------	(**)
58	International	356	1,041	1,357	1,418	1,463	------	866	------	597	------	------	12	-15	------	-1	------	-14

r Revised.   p Preliminary.   *Combined in other industries.   **Less than $500,000.
NOTE.—Detail may not add to totals because of rounding.
1. Data for table 2 for 1961 exclude Cuba which was carried for the year 1960 at $956 million. The tables on net capital outflows, reinvested subsidiary earnings, earnings and income, exclude Cuba for both years.

2. The value of direct investments in Venezuela in 1961 has been raised by $406 million because of the revaluation of plant and equipment of a major oil company.
3. The value of direct investments in the Union of South Africa has been adjusted downward by $36 million because of the loss suffered by an American mining company on the liquidation of their South African operations.

Selected Countries and Years, and Major Industries, 1961
Earnings, by Selected Countries, with Major Industries for 1961
by Selected Countries, with Major Industries for 1961

[Millions of dollars]

Table 3—Continued						Table 4												Line
Undistributed subsidiary earnings						Earnings						Income						
1960 r	1961 p					1960 r	1961 p					1960 r	1961 p					
	Total	Mining and smelting	Petroleum	Manufacturing	Other		Total	Mining and smelting	Petroleum	Manufacturing	Other		Total	Mining and smelting	Petroleum	Manufacturing	Other	
1,266	1,046	63	159	437	387	3,566	3,700	359	1,449	1,180	711	2,355	2,672	296	1,303	710	364	1
389	284	37	51	141	55	718	684	90	121	360	113	361	409	48	74	212	75	2
215	221	6	39	83	92	829	910	141	436	152	181	641	711	139	397	67	108	3
52	71	(**)	7	9	55	126	151	16	12	33	90	85	87	16	5	23	43	4
(1)	(1)	(1)	(1)	(1)	(1)	(1)	(1)	*(1)	(1)	(1)	(1)	(1)	(1)	(1)	(1)	(1)	(1)	5
1	2	(*)	(*)	(*)	2	8	12	(*)	(*)		12	7	10	(*)	(*)	(*)	10	6
1	2	(*)	(**)	(*)	1	-4	-2	(*)	-2	(*)	-1	-5	-3	(*)	-2	(*)	-1	7
1	1	(*)	(*)	(*)	1	1	9	(*)		(*)	9	(**)	8	(*)	(*)	(*)	8	8
-3	8	-1	(**)		2	54	50	8	3	28	11	65	45	8	2	21	13	9
48	55	1	4	7	1	62	72	1	5	2	64	16	20	(**)	2	1	17	10
3	4		2	(**)	2	4	11	2	3	(**)	5	1	7	2	1	(**)	4	11
163	150	6	31	75	37	703	759	125	424	119	91	556	624	123	392	43	65	12
36	52	(*)	33	19		46	86	(*)	(*)	48	38	10	34	(*)	(*)	14	20	13
39	39	3	28	1	7	80	71	4	9	43	15	45	35	1	8	14	11	14
7	1	(**)	(*)	1	(**)	72	53	41	(*)	3	9	72	59	43	(*)	2	15	15
8	8	(*)	3	3	2	26	29	(*)	17	4	8	19	22	(*)	15	1	6	16
11	7	(**)	4	2	2	58	65	41	7	5	13	48	58	43	2	2	17	17
2	2	(*)	(**)	2	(**)	4	4	(*)	41	4	(**)	3	2	(*)	43	2	(**)	18
59	38	(*)	12	5	21	428	459	(*)	377	12	70	371	422	(*)	365	7	50	19
1	2	(**)	(**)	(**)	1	-11	-7	(**)	-11	(**)	3	-11	-9	-11	(**)	2		20
63	30	3	4	1	23	141	122	64	29	1	28	78	94	61	26	(**)	7	21
363	314	-1	8	194	113	769	841	8	84	532	217	397	511	9	75	324	102	22
154	127	(*)	10	91	25	310	341	(*)	40	235	65	144	197	(*)	29	130	37	23
10	10		-4	13	1	35	43		-1	37	7	21	27		2	19	6	24
48	28	(**)	11	10	7	72	58	(**)	17	29	11	22	27		6	16	4	25
76	70	(*)	-2	64	7	148	183	(*)	9	151	23	66	104	(*)	11	78	15	26
14	5	(*)	-4	3	6	36	27	(*)	3	14	9	24	23	(*)	8	13	3	27
7	14		8	1	5	19	30		12	5	14	11	16		3	4	9	28
208	188	-1	-2	102	88	459	501	8	43	297	152	252	314	9	46	195	64	29
(**)	1		-4	4	1	4	6		-4	8	2	4	5		(**)	4	1	30
3	3	(*)	(**)	2	1	5	5	(*)	(**)	3	2	5	3	(*)	1	1	1	31
4	5	(*)	1	2	1	5	7	(*)	(**)	4	4	3	3	(*)	-1	1	3	32
-3	-1		-3	1	1	7	10		-3	2	11	11	11		(**)	2	9	33
35	52		-6	7	51	48	78		-6	23	61	14	25		-7	15	10	34
2	1	(*)	(**)	(**)	(**)	-9	-5	(*)	-7	1	1	-10	-6	(*)	-7	(**)	1	35
160	116		4	83	29	375	372		58	252	63	217	258		53	171	34	36
7	12	-2	7	3	4	24	27	7		5	9	17	15	9	-1	2	5	37
50	51	11	17	-2	24	33	28	44	-84	19	50	-17	-23	33	-101	20	25	38
2	3	(**)	2	(**)	1	-69	-71	1	-75	(**)	3	-71	-74	1	-77	(**)	2	39
2	1		1	(**)	(**)	-2	-2	(**)	-3	(**)	(**)	-5	-3	(**)	-3		(*	40
19	21	5	1		16	37	28	18	-24		34	18	7	14	-25			41
27	26	6	13	-1	8	68	73	24	17	19	13	41	47	18	4	20	(* \	42
10	6	5	(*)	(*)	1	19	14	13	(*)	(*)	1	10	8	8	(*)	(*)	9	43
17	20	2	(*)	-2	20	50	59	12	(*)		18	34	39	10	(*)	20	(**)	44
(**)	(**)		(*)	(*)	(**)	-2	(**)		(*)	(*)	(**)	-2	(**)		(*)	(*)	(**)	45
64	66	3	18	17	28	914	958	4	840	50	64	853	893	1	826	30	36	46
-3	-6		-8	1	1	734	751		745	3	3	738	760		755	2	2	47
67	72	3	25	17	28	181	207	4	95	47	61	114	133	1	71	28	34	48
12	15	(*)	(*)	8	7	14	23	(*)	(*)	13	10	13	7	(*)	(*)	4	3	49
13	7		(*)	2	5	70	65		(*)	3	63	60	61		(*)	1	60	50
17	19		(*)	6	14	32	34		(*)	10	23	15	15		(*)	5	10	51
21	27	(*)	(*)	(**)	27	52	63	(*)	(*)	16	47	28	32	(*)	(*)	13	19	52
3	3		(*)	1	2	13	22	(*)	(*)	6	16	10	18	(*)	(*)	5	14	53
74	20	3	7	3	7	115	91	8	4	66	13	37	65	4	-3	57	6	54
68	15	3	(*)	4	9	101	77	8	(*)	59	10	30	55	4	(*)	50	1	55
4	3		(*)	-1	3	11	12		(*)		6	7	9		(*)		2	56
2	2	(**)	(*)		2	2	2	(**)	(*)		2	(**)	(**)	(**)	(*)		(**)	57
49	60		16		45	47	65		20		45	5	13		9		5	58

1. Income is the sum of dividends, interest and branch profits; earnings is the sum of the U.S. share in the net earnings of subsidiaries and branch profits.

Table 5.—Direct Investments in Manufacturing Enterprises Abroad, 1959, 1960 and 1961, by commodity group

[Millions of dollars]

	1959	1960	1961 [1]
Manufacturing, total	9,707	11,152	11,936
Food products	823	943	1,019
Paper and allied products	813	861	918
Chemicals and allied products	1,661	1,902	2,030
Rubber products	461	520	528
Primary and fabricated metals	1,163	1,256	1,373
Machinery (except electrical)	1,202	1,333	1,439
Electrical machinery	833	918	1,008
Transportation equipment	1,603	2,118	2,237
Other products	1,148	1,301	1,385

NOTE: Detail may not add to totals because of rounding.

1. 1961 data excludes Cuba. These investments were estimated at year-end 1960 at $111 million, and included $21 million for food products, $28 million for chemicals and allied products, $28 million for the "other products" group and $34 million for all other manufacturing industries.

Middle East. Earnings on the rapidly growing refinery and distribution installations showed very little gain in 1961. As the newly developed areas in North Africa come into production, earnings will gain both from increased sales and reduced expenses connected with initial exploration and development.

Manufacturing earnings amounting to $1,180 million were unchanged in 1961 from the 1960 total. A moderate increase in European earnings, mainly in Germany, the Benelux countries and Switzerland, was offset by reduced earnings in Canada, Australia, and Brazil. This interruption of a steady growth in manufacturing earnings reflected lagging economic activity in several countries, and probably also some situations where costs were rising rapidly. Earnings of mining companies which had risen in 1960, dropped back to $359 million in 1961 as prices for most minerals and metals weakened. Few changes were noted in other industries.

Income receipts from direct investments (dividends, interest, and branch profits) rose to $2.7 billion in 1961, more than $300 million above the 1960 figure. Most of the gain reflected an increase of $220 million in dividend receipts, largely from manufacturing firms. Subsidiary earnings did not materially improve, so that the rate of dividend pay-out in 1961 was the highest since 1950. The rate of reinvestment for all subsidiary earnings was 46 percent in 1961 and for manufacturing operations it was 44 percent. By comparison, the average rate of rein-

vestment for the 1951–60 period was about 56 percent.

Fees and royalties increase rapidly

In addition to receipts in the form of dividends, interest, and branch profits, U.S. parent companies are receiving from their foreign affiliates substantial amounts in payment for management services of various kinds or for the use of patents, copyrights, and similar intangible property. By 1961, this flow was approaching $0.4 billion annually, and was continuing to rise more rapidly than amounts labelled "income."

Other Private Investments

Outflows of private U.S. capital other than those connected with direct investments have become important factors in our balance of payments in the past 2 years. Such flows include purchases of foreign securities, bank loans of varying maturities, financing of foreign trade and other international transactions, and transfers of cash funds into higher-yielding liquid assets abroad. Taken together, recorded outflows of these types averaged $0.3 billion in the 1950–55 period, $1.3 billion in the years 1956–59, and then rose sharply to $2.2 billion in 1960 and a record $2.5 billion in 1961.

The leading feature of the upsurge in 1960–61 was the rise in lending by banks, and, to a lesser extent, by industrial corporations. As shown in table 6, a major share of this lending was directed to Japan, and represented primarily acceptance credits at substantially higher interest rates than prevail domestically. The enlarged flow to Europe in 1960, and the sharp drop to that area in 1961, were largely related to fluctuations in the relative attractiveness of interest rates in the United Kingdom, although the recorded flows were not very great. Canada received a sizable amount of corporate cash funds in 1961 and again in the early part of 1962, reflecting higher interest rates paid on deposits in Canadian banks and certain tax advantages. Increases in short-term financing to Latin America in these 2 years were fairly typical of experience since 1950.

U.S. banks, and to a lesser extent nonfinancial corporations, have been expanding their longer-term foreign loans or credits at an annual rate of over $200 million since 1955. Banks added $1.4 billion to their foreign credits during these years, of which about half went to Latin America, mainly Brazil, Venezuela, and Mexico, and about $350 million to Europe, including substantial amounts to finance Norway's shipping industry.

Sizable purchases of foreign securities have also been a consistent feature of the U.S. balance of payments beginning in 1956, averaging nearly $0.8 billion a year since then. In most years purchases of foreign bonds have predominated, reaching a high of about $1 billion in 1958, when our interest rate structure was exceptionally low. In 1961 net purchases of foreign bonds were reduced to about $0.4 billion, featured by a growing share of issues of European countries, Japan, and other relatively new borrowers.

In the first half of 1962 a marked rise in foreign bond issues in the United

Table 6.—Portfolio and Short-Term Private Capital Outflows, 1960 and 1961

[Millions of dollars; inflow to U.S. (−)]

Area and country	Total	Net purchases of foreign securities		Other medium-term loans (net)	Short-term capital (net)	
		Bonds	Stocks		Banks	Corporate and other
Total						
1961	2,478	399	354	253	1,063	409
1960	2,188	552	98	200	990	348
Europe						
1961	424	14	241	117	49	3
1960	557	35	86	16	180	240
United Kingdom						
1961	−87	−6	58	−3	−65	−71
1960	308	37	−42	−31	125	219
Canada						
1961	700	180	71	−11	116	344
1960	370	202	−8	−32	149	59
Latin American Republics						
1961	256	17	5	97	121	16
1960	439	86	9	159	175	10
Other countries						
1961	1,118	208	37	50	777	46
1960	704	111	11	57	486	39
Japan						
1961	727	50		14	639	24
1960	498	−1	1	2	482	14
International Institutions						
1961	−20	−20				
1960	118	118				

States occurred, including nearly $200 million offered by European borrowers, of which about half was purchased by U.S. residents, the remainder being purchased by European and other foreign investors. It is noteworthy that the interest cost on new European bonds offered in 1961 and 1962 has ranged from about 5½–6 percent for government issues to well over 6 percent for corporate issues, and interest costs on Japanese issues have ranged from 6½ percent to over 7½ percent. These interest costs compare with a yield of a little over 5 percent for lower grade domestic corporate bonds. This gap indicates both the relative attractiveness of foreign issues for U.S. investors and the relatively high cost of alternative financing in foreign capital markets.

Foreign equity securities, particularly European corporate stocks, have also attracted substantial amounts of U.S. capital. In 1961 such purchases amounted to over $350 million, of which three-quarters went to Europe. This flow diminished quickly in the first half of 1962, as stock prices tumbled in all principal markets, but major European companies offered large blocks of stock in the U.S. market in June and August.

Foreign Investments in the United States

Although small by comparison with U.S. investments abroad, the flow of foreign capital to the United States for direct investments and purchases of U.S. securities has been of some importance, averaging over $0.4 billion annually beginning in 1955.

Foreign direct investments in the United States accounted for about 35 percent of these inflows, and undistributed profits of these enterprises currently amount to over $0.2 billion annually. Detailed data on these investments, with a book value of $7.4 billion at the end of 1961, are given in a new Office of Business Economics publication soon to be issued entitled *Foreign Business Investments in the United States.*[3]

The flow of foreign capital into U.S. corporate stocks has been large but irregular since the middle 1950's, with net liquidations taking place at times of market instability in the United States such as 1957–58, the last half of 1960, and in June 1962. In 1961, there were net foreign purchases of U.S. corporate stocks of over $0.3 billion, but the major factor in the rise of foreign holdings of U.S. corporate stocks to a value of $11.8 billion at the end of the year was a market appreciation which added over $2.1 billion. Nearly all of this market gain was wiped out in the first half of 1962.

[3] Summary results were published in the *Survey of Current Business* for October 1961.

Table 7.—**International Investment Position of the United States, by Area, 1960–61**

[Millions of dollars]

Type of investment	Total		Western Europe		Canada		Latin American Republics		Other foreign countries		International institutions and unallocated	
	1960 r	1961 p	1960 r	1961 p	1960 r	1961 p	1960 r	1961 p	1960 r	1961 p	1960 r	1961 p
U.S. assets and investments abroad, total	71,497	77,331	20,487	21,189	17,274	19,229	13,565	14,274	12,740	15,111	7,431	7,528
Private investments	50,393	55,517	11,279	12,737	17,271	19,224	11,501	11,579	7,834	9,445	2,508	2,532
Long-term	45,410	48,927	9,958	11,340	16,600	18,010	9,872	9,765	6,472	7,251	2,508	2,531
Direct	32,778	34,684	6,681	7,655	11,198	11,801	8,387	8,166	5,094	5,596	1,418	1,463
Foreign dollar bonds	4,891	5,300	357	406	2,523	2,701	240	215	747	927	1,024	1,018
Other foreign securities [2]	4,667	5,615	1,798	2,040	2,567	3,230	53	65	183	230	66	50
Other	3,074	3,328	1,122	1,239	312	302	1,192	1,289	448	498		
Short-term	4,983	6,590	1,321	1,397	671	1,184	1,629	1,814	1,362	2,194		1
U.S. Government credits and claims	21,104	21,814	9,208	8,452	3	5	2,064	2,695	4,906	5,666	4,923	4,996
Long-term	18,212	18,874	8,458	7,819			1,889	2,521	2,949	3,559	4,916	4,975
Foreign currencies and short-term claims	2,892	2,940	750	633	3	5	175	174	1,957	2,107	7	21
Foreign assets and investments in the United States, total [4]	44,670	50,018	24,044	28,252	6,184	6,784	3,723	4,039	4,843	4,844	4,966	5,186
Long-term	18,418	21,451	12,998	15,279	3,288	3,638	1,153	1,353	859	1,039	120	142
Direct	6,910	7,392	4,707	5,129	1,934	1,989	130	130	139	144		
Corporate stocks	9,302	11,808	6,836	8,706	1,209	1,461	728	927	490	664	39	50
Corporate, state and municipal bonds	649	645	449	435	5	2	75	76	39	40	81	92
Other	1,557	1,606	1,006	1,009	140	186	220	220	191	191		
Short-term assets and U.S. Government obligations	26,252	28,567	11,046	12,973	2,896	3,146	2,570	2,686	3,984	3,805	4,846	5,044
Private obligations	12,127	14,114	4,896	6,418	1,984	2,079	2,208	2,235	2,719	2,974	320	408
U.S. Government obligations	14,125	14,453	6,150	6,555	912	1,067	362	451	1,265	831	4,526	4,636
Long-term	2,276	2,781	803	798	327	340	141	333	114	79	891	1,231
Short-term [4]	11,849	11,672	5,347	5,757	585	727	221	118	1,151	752	3,635	3,405

r Revised.
p Preliminary.
1. Data for Cuba are omitted in 1961; the 1960 total for U.S. direct investment in Cuba was $956 million (book value). See notes to table 2 for other adjustments.
2. Represents the estimated investment in shipping companies registered in Panama and Liberia.
3. Consists primarily of securities payable in foreign currencies, but includes some dollar obligations, including participation in loan made by the International Bank for Reconstruction and Development.
4. Total includes estimated foreign holdings of U.S. currency: 1960, $910 million; 1961, $913 million; not distributed by area.

FINANCING U.S. DIRECT FOREIGN INVESTMENT

Frederick Cutler

BY FREDERICK CUTLER

Financing U.S. Direct Foreign Investment

1962 Capital Outlays Near $5 Billion

More Than Half of Funds Used Generated Internally—Foreign Production Outstrips Exports

This report covers the fifth annual survey of the sources and uses of funds of foreign subsidiaries and branches of U.S. companies, giving the structure of these accounts for 1961, plus projections of plant and equipment expenditures through 1963 and data on sales of the foreign manufacturing enter- prises as they have developed in the 1957–61 period.

These data provide measures of the scope and some of the effects of the rapidly growing foreign component of U.S. industry which supplement the data entering the balance-of-payments accounts. Foreign capital outlays and working capital in mining, manufac- turing and petroleum required total financing of $5.6 billion in 1961, after income distributions, of which the cap- ital flow from the United States sup- plied only a little over $1.2 billion. The remaining $4.4 billion came from internal funds generated by the opera- tions of the companies abroad, or was obtained from foreign external sources.

Stepped up expenditures by U.S. in- dustry for plant and equipment abroad, especially in the manufacturing indus- tries, are directly responsible for sub- stantial gains in foreign production of a wide range of commodities.

Foreign Capital Outlays Rising

U.S. companies with direct foreign investments report that they expect to spend $4.8 billion to expand or improve their plant and equipment abroad in 1962, compared to $4.2 billion spent in 1961. This outcome would be only slightly under the record amount spent in 1957, when outlays by the petroleum industry were at a peak.

Current projections by the companies raise their previous anticipation for 1962 by about 6 percent, with most of the upward revision in the manufacturing facilities in Europe. Looking further ahead to 1963, the totals projected show little change for most industries and areas, although there is a tendency for reported amounts to become lower as they are projected further ahead

because plans are less firm. There is, however, relatively strong indication that outlays in Europe by the trans- portation equipment industry will be reduced.

Manufacturing Investments at Peak

In 1962, U.S. manufacturing compa- nies for the third successive year spent, or anticipated spending, larger sums for plant and equipment abroad. There is, however, a considerable selectivity in both industries and areas of invest- ment. Projected capital outlays of $1.9 billion were $180 million more than the year before. Two thirds of this increase is being channeled into the Common Market area, with little change in the volume flowing into the rest of Europe (including the United Kingdom).

Investment activity by this industry in Latin America and Canada rose slightly, but declined in the rest of the world. On a commodity basis, nearly all of the additional capital outlays occurred in the transportation and chemical industries, while other indus- tries, on balance, showed little net change.

Europe.—For the first time, Germany ranks highest in capital outlays with expected expenditures of $432 million in 1962 ($318 million in 1961). In comparison, the rate of capital expen- ditures in Canada was $391 million and the United Kingdom was in third position with $331 million. Plant in- vestments by American companies in the rest of the Common Market area were $164 million, only moderately above the level of earlier years. In addition to heavy investments in the transportation industry, large amounts went into machinery and chemical industries.

CAPITAL EXPENDITURES ABROAD BY U.S. MANUFACTURING COMPANIES

1962 Gains Mainly in Common Market Countries

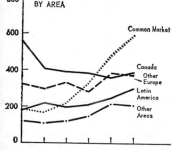

Increased Outlays Centered in Transportation Equipment and Chemicals

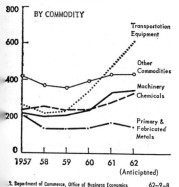

.S. Department of Commerce, Office of Business Economics   62–9–8

654959—62——3

The $331 million being invested in the United Kingdom is 90 percent of the total invested. In the rest of Europe, there was little change in the relatively small amounts spent in Scandinavia. The same industries important in the Common Market Countries, also play the major role in investments in the United Kingdom and the rest of Europe.

For 1963, the projected decline in expenditures in the Common Market, and the increase of expenditures in the rest of Europe, is mainly connected with changes in the planned build-up of automotive and related facilities. Investments in chemicals are also rising strongly, influenced by activities of oil companies in the petrochemical field.

Canada.—Affected by a lagging rate of economic expansion in Canada in the last few years, investment activities of U.S.-controlled manufacturing companies in Canada have changed little. After a small reduction of capital outlays in 1961, the former level is expected to be regained in 1962, with 1963 totals expected to hold at the 1962 amount. Modest gains in 1962 in most industries (except for primary and fabricated metals) amount to $30 million, bringing total outlays to $391 million. Current investment expenditures are considerably below the 1957 total of $561 million, when major additions were made to the primary metals and paper industries.

Latin America.—Manufacturing outlays for Latin America are the highest reported since the beginning of these surveys in 1957, amounting to an anticipated $300 million, 20 percent above the 1961 total. In this area, as in Europe, the new investment programs are concentrated in the chemical and transportation industries. Expansion is largely limited to three countries— Argentina, Brazil, and Mexico.

As in 1961, anticipated investments were largest in Argentina, with Brazil being next in importance. These two countries account for more than two-thirds of all such investments in the area. In Mexico and Venezuela, capital expenditures for manufacturing have held relatively steady since 1957.

The stability of planned capital outlays in Latin America contrasts with wider fluctuations in capital flows from the United States. Within the aggregate of all industries these fluctuations in capital flows reflect largely net inflows to the United States from petroleum investments which offset outflows for manufacturing. For manufacturing alone, however, it should be noted that these outflows from the United States accounted for about one fifth of the funds available to the enterprises (table 5) in 1961, and only about one third of their plant and equipment expenditures.

Investment in manufacturing facilities elsewhere is confined primarily to a few of the industrially more advanced countries—Australia, Japan, the Union of South Africa, and a few others. These countries account for nearly all of the capital expenditures by American manufacturing companies in Africa, Asia and Oceania. Reduced outlays were reported for India, where the 1961 amount was unusually high, but the total for Australia increased to $103 million ($90 million in 1961), while expenditures in Japan were expected to remain unchanged at $49 million.

Petroleum and Mining Expansion

American oil companies are currently investing abroad at an annual rate o

Table 1.—Plant and Equipment Expenditures of Direct Foreign Investments, by Country and Major Industry, 1960–63

(Millions of dollars)

Area and country	1960			1961 r			1962 e			1963 e		
	Mining and smelting	Petroleum	Manufacturing	Mining and smelting	Petroleum	Manufacturing	Mining and smelting	Petroleum	Manufacturing	Mining and smelting	Petroleum	Manufacturing
All areas, total	426	1,467	1,337	320	1,572	1,681	395	1,829	1,866	343	1,811	1,735
Canada	290	360	384	165	340	361	200	345	391	175	360	390
Latin American Republics, total	53	297	206	72	270	248	75	305	298	59	283	277
Mexico, Central America and West Indies, total	10	20	39	8	21	47	6	27	49	7	24	45
Mexico	8	1	37	7	2	44	5	2	46	6	2	42
Other countries	2	19	2	1	19	3	1	25	3	1	23	3
South America, total	44	277	167	64	249	201	69	278	249	52	259	232
Argentina	(*)	63	51	(*)	60	89	(*)	60	128	(*)	45	118
Brazil	2	5	63	2	5	62	1	5	72	1	5	69
Chile	25	(*)	3	28	(*)	6	30	(*)	6	24	(*)	5
Colombia	(*)	25	21	(*)	22	15	(*)	21	14	(*)	18	12
Peru	11	17	9	27	28	10	29	31	7	18	21	7
Venezuela	(*)	160	17	(*)	128	17	1	150	19	(*)	160	18
Other countries	(**)	(*)	3	2	(*)	2	(*)	1	4	(*)	(*)	3
Other Western Hemisphere	24	44	1	23	39	1	33	57	1	31	61	1
Europe, total	2	345	608	1	438	856	3	597	968	1	549	864
Common Market, total	(**)	145	328	(**)	186	475	(**)	285	596	(**)	313	464
Belgium and Luxembourg	(**)	20	15	(**)	7	21	(**)	9	22	(**)	10	26
France	(**)	32	66	(**)	31	68	(**)	48	73	(**)	51	76
Germany	(**)	55	205	(**)	70	318	(**)	140	432	(**)	128	284
Italy	(**)	18	20	(**)	64	40	(**)	38	50	(**)	64	51
Netherlands		20	22		14	28		50	20		60	28
Other Europe, total	2	200	280	1	252	381	3	312	372	1	237	400
Denmark		17	2		19	2		32	2		22	2
Norway	(**)	21	5	(**)	7	5	(**)	9	7	(**)	9	8
Spain	(**)	3	4	(**)	3	6	(**)	8	9		25	8
Sweden		17	4		18	10		34	9		8	16
Switzerland		4	8		3	19		6	12		5	16
United Kingdom		100	252		170	335		200	331		150	355
Other countries	2	39	5	1	32	4	3	24	7	1	18	5
Africa, total	44	115	10	47	171	10	67	188	12	56	169	12
North Africa	(**)	75	(**)	(**)	111	(**)	(**)	134	(**)	(**)	116	(**)
East Africa	(**)	7	(**)	(**)	9	(**)	(**)	12	(**)	(**)	13	(**)
West Africa	16	23	(**)	22	34	(**)	37	30	(**)	26	29	(**)
Central and South Africa, total	28	10	10	25	17	10	30	11	12	30	12	12
Union of South Africa	15	(*)	8	10	8	8	10	10	11	10	(*)	11
Other countries	13	(*)	2	15	(*)	2	20	(*)	1	20	(*)	1
Asia, total	(**)	176	72	(**)	195	114	1	243	92	1	310	83
Middle East		76	13		87	12		111	6		102	6
Far East, total	(**)	101	60	(**)	108	102	1	132	86	1	148	77
India	(*)	(*)	16			39	(*)	22		(*)	(*)	16
Japan	(*)	(*)	30			48	(*)	49		(*)	(*)	40
Philippine Republic	(*)	11	(*)	(**)	(*)	9	(*)	9	5	(*)	(*)	16
Other countries	(**)	(*)	4	(**)	(*)	6	(*)	1		(*)	1	
Oceania, total	12	66	56	12	64	92	16	35	105	20	39	109
Australia	12	(*)	55	12	(*)	90	16	(*)	103	(*)	(*)	106
Other countries		(*)	2		(*)	2	(**)	(*)	2	(**)	(*)	4
International shipping		65			55			60			40	

*Included in area total.   **Less than $500,000.   r Revised.   e Estimated on the basis of company projections.

NOTE.—Detail may not add to totals because of rounding.

$2¼ billion to develop new producing and refining capacity. This includes exploration and development costs charged against income of $.4 billion, and capital expenditures of over $1.8 billion.

Capital outlays of this industry are expected to rise in all areas in 1962 and are currently projected by the companies to remain stable for 1963. The most pronounced growth is seen for Europe, where outlays are now anticipated at close to $600 million for 1962, an increase of $160 million from the prior year.

Nearly all of this capital is intended for new refinery capacity, as well as the related facilities to transport, store and market the additional output. Most of these outlays are going to the United

ACTUAL AND PROJECTED* PLANT AND EQUIPMENT EXPENDITURES ABROAD

MANUFACTURING—Current Anticipation for 1962 Raised Over Previous Figure, but 1961 Actual Fell Short of Forecast

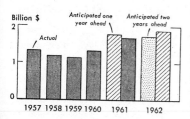

PETROLEUM—Projection for 1962 Stable Rise Projected for 1961 Was Not Realized

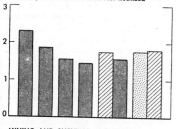

MINING AND SMELTING—Little Variation in Anticipations

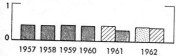

*Projections are based on reports supplied by a sample group of companies

U.S. Department of Commerce, Office of Business Economics   62-9-9

Kingdom ($200 million) and Germany ($140 million), but significant amounts are also being invested in the Scandinavian countries, the Netherlands and, to a lesser extent, in France and Italy.

Plant and equipment expenditures are still on the increase in North Africa where new oil fields have been brought to production (Libya), or are being explored and tested (Algeria and other North African countries). In the Middle East and Far East, capital expenditures are scheduled to rise substantially in 1962 and advance further in 1963.

Capital outlays in Latin America are higher in 1962 due to active development work carried out by oil companies in Argentina, and a somewhat higher volume of investment in Venezuela and Trinidad. Exclusive of activity in Venezuela, 1962 is expected to show a peak of oil investment activity in Latin America, with capital spending amounting to $212 million. Aside from Argentina and Trinidad, substantial operations are carried on in Bolivia, Colombia, Peru, and Central America.

Expenditures in Canada were little changed from the 1961 volume, but companies report a moderate improvement in spending levels for 1963.

Mining investments are also expected to be generally higher in 1962. Increases are reported mainly in Canada, Surinam and Jamaica, Central and West Africa, and, to a more limited extent, in Australia.

In Canada, new capital outlays are connected with the development of additional iron ore resources, largely in association with foreign concerns. Even though these investment programs carry over into 1963, reports received indicate reduced capital spending in that year. In other parts of Western Hemisphere, facilities connected with the production of bauxite and its reduction to alumina, and renewed investment in copper mine properties, result in a projected rise of 15 percent in 1962. Elsewhere, the growth of mining outlays is largely restricted to Central and West Africa and is based on the development of iron ore mines and of bauxite.

Other industries

Investments in other industries, excluding shipping companies and con-

struction and engineering firms, are scheduled to rise in 1962 to $672 million. Companies in the trade and distribution field continue to expand capital outlays, which are at a peak in 1962 and are projected to be higher in 1963. The growth in capital spending by this industry is largely centered in Europe, where it is rising by $50 million to $225 million for 1962.

Plant and equipment expenditures

Comparison of Domestic and Foreign Plant And Equipment Expenditures by U.S. Companies, 1957-62

MANUFACTURING*—Foreign Expenditures Show Stronger Growth Than Domestic Expenditures

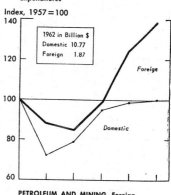

PETROLEUM AND MINING—Foreign Expenditures Turn Upward in 1962

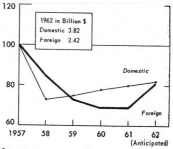

*Excludes primary iron and steel and petroleum products.

U.S. Department of Commerce, Office of Business Economics   62-9-10

of the public utility and agriculture industries have tended downward and in 1962 are the lowest since 1957. These investments are located principally in Latin America, and the investment programs have been strongly influenced by major liquidations and expropriations in that area.

Table 2.—Plant and Equipment Expenditures Abroad by U.S. Manufacturing Companies, by Area and Major Commodity, 1959–63

(Millions of dollars)

Areas and years	Total	Food products	Paper and allied products	Chemicals	Rubber products	Primary and fabricated metals	Machinery, except electrical	Electrical machinery	Transportation equipment	Other manufacturing
All areas, total										
1959	1,147	82	83	232	76	127	109	96	228	114
1960	1,337	97	78	237	68	133	132	104	336	152
1961 r	1,681	116	71	277	91	169	190	141	473	153
1962 ᵉ	1,866	113	70	329	87	142	185	158	618	166
1963 ᵉ	1,735	104	67	383	72	140	208	153	477	131
Canada										
1959	389	22	65	78	15	65	10	27	65	43
1960	384	30	55	75	05	49	17	30	63	50
1961 r	361	20	54	55	18	55	16	31	60	52
1962 ᵉ	391	24	58	65	25	40	15	35	69	60
1963 ᵉ	390	20	55	75	15	40	14	36	75	60
Latin America [1]										
1959	193	20	8	52	16	16	6	15	41	20
1960	207	24	7	49	12	11	8	18	47	31
1961 r	249	37	5	47	19	23	9	27	52	30
1962 ᵉ	299	30	2	85	19	12	10	25	87	29
1963 ᵉ	278	30	2	98	18	11	12	23	58	24
Europe:										
Common Market										
1959	214	16	2	20	4	9	61	21	62	19
1960	328	17	2	44	11	10	72	21	128	23
1961 r	475	30	3	63	11	19	105	36	181	27
1962 ᵉ	596	29	3	62	12	32	95	44	283	37
1963 ᵉ	464	26	3	87	16	34	118	37	111	33
Other Europe										
1959	236	13	5	60	23	30	26	17	40	22
1960	280	18	3	42	15	50	24	18	74	35
1961 r	381	17	4	49	15	46	47	30	141	31
1962 ᵉ	372	20	4	65	17	37	50	42	109	29
1963 ᵉ	400	19	4	73	12	35	51	44	158	4
Other areas										
1959	115	11	3	22	19	7	6	16	20	11
1960	138	8	12	28	16	13	10	16	23	12
1961 r	216	12	5	63	28	26	13	17	39	13
1962 ᵉ	208	10	3	52	14	21	15	12	70	11
1963 ᵉ	204	9	3	50	11	20	13	13	75	10

r Revised.
ᵉ Estimated on the basis of company projections.
NOTE.—Detail may not add to totals because of rounding.
1. Includes other Western Hemisphere.

Table 3.—Plant and Equipment Expenditures of Direct Foreign Investments, Major Industries, 1957–63

(Millions of dollars)

Area and industry	1957	1958	1959	1960	1961 r	1962 ᵉ	1963 ᵉ
All areas, total	4,819	4,097	3,705	3,789	4,176	4,762	4,565
Mining and smelting	421	420	437	426	320	395	343
Petroleum	2,322	1,854	1,558	1,467	1,572	1,829	1,811
Manufacturing	1,347	1,180	1,147	1,337	1,681	1,866	1,735
Trade	186	191	198	256	331	402	413
Other industries	543	452	365	303	272	270	262
Canada, total	1,593	1,311	1,179	1,259	1,041	1,102	1,097
Mining and smelting	163	172	240	290	165	200	175
Petroleum	584	510	380	360	340	345	360
Manufacturing	561	404	389	384	361	391	390
Trade	47	55	45	60	63	58	65
Other industries	238	170	125	165	112	108	107
Latin America, total [1]	1,687	1,269	1,003	750	805	928	869
Mining and smelting	216	221	147	78	95	108	90
Petroleum	1,039	577	449	340	309	362	344
Manufacturing	174	202	193	207	249	299	278
Trade	20	31	31	35	45	55	50
Other industries	238	238	183	90	107	104	107
Europe, total	899	976	906	1,092	1,483	1,810	1,660
Mining and smelting	2	--------	2	2	1	3	1
Petroleum	275	422	339	345	438	597	549
Manufacturing	497	460	450	608	856	968	864
Trade	107	87	101	125	175	225	230
Other industries	18	7	14	12	13	17	16
Other areas, total	640	541	617	688	847	922	939
Mining and smelting	40	27	48	56	59	84	77
Petroleum	424	345	390	422	485	525	558
Manufacturing	115	114	115	138	216	208	204
Trade	12	18	21	36	48	64	68
Other industries [2]	49	37	43	36	40	41	32

r Revised.
ᵉ Estimated on the basis of company projections.
NOTE.—Detail may not add to totals because of rounding.
1. Includes other Western Hemisphere.
2. Excludes international shipping.

Share of foreign outlays

As the relative increase of foreign plant and equipment expenditures continues to exceed the domestic rate, foreign outlays have tended for some time to take a larger share of total plant expansions by U.S. manufacturing companies. The anticipated 1962 rise in foreign outlays is 14 percent, compared to a domestic increase of 8 percent, as reviewed in an analysis in this issue.

For major segments of the manufacturing industry foreign capital investments range from 9 percent to 34 percent of total outlays, as shown in table 4. The overall ratio for the industries shown is 18 percent in 1962. This proportion has risen from 13–14 percent in 1959–60.

Foreign capital outlays now account for well over one third of the combined total for petroleum and mining, and have been growing somewhat faster recently than domestic expenditures.

Working Capital Requirements

About $2 billion was used by foreign affiliates in the mining, oil and manufacturing industries to add to working capital and other assets in 1961, about $¼ billion more than in 1960. Inventory accumulation has been relatively volatile, tending to increase sharply as the rate of economic activity is stepped up in various areas. Thus, in 1961 the rate of inventory accumulation was much reduced for manufacturing companies in Europe from the extraordinary rate of 1960, and there were also lower accumulations for this industry in Latin America and the Far East, while accumulations in Canada were somewhat larger.

Additions to inventories by mining and petroleum companies were relatively minor.

Receivables on the books of the foreign affiliates continued to rise in 1961, at a somewhat faster rate than in 1960. Most of these receivables accumulated on the books of manufacturing companies and are related to the build up of production facilities abroad and the ever larger volume of foreign sales. Petroleum companies have substantially increased the growth of receivables, partly owing to larger sales and partly related to the lengthening of payment terms.

Nearly $800 million was added to "other" assets in 1961, compared with $330 million in 1960, the smallest amount since 1957.

The 1960 increase in these assets appears to have been unusually low because of the need to finance the increase in manufacturing inventories in Europe, whereas in 1961 these companies used less funds for this purpose and also increased their external financing abroad. On the other hand, petroleum affiliates in the producing areas reported substantial increases in "other" assets in 1961, possibly representing longer-term financing extended to affiliates and other customers or to local governments.

Sources of Financing

In order to finance fixed capital outlays and the accumulation of inventories and other assets, U.S. companies abroad rely principally on internally generated funds. Of the $5.6 billion needed in the major industries to cover these requirements in 1961, about $3.0 billion came from the companies' own resources, mainly cash flows from depreciation and depletion charges, and from retained earnings. This was not greatly different from the amount generated the year before, though a larger volume of funds available from depreciation and depletion accounts counterbalanced a decline in retained earnings.

Depreciation and related items amounted to $2.2 billion in 1961, up from $1.9 billion in 1960. As in earlier years, depreciation charges were large relative to plant and equipment expenditures abroad, amounting to 70 percent for oil companies, 53 percent for manufacturing companies, and 65 percent for mining firms.

Oil companies charged about $1.1 billion to depreciation and depletion accounts abroad, including about $.4 billion in Latin America. This provided ample funds for capital outlays by a number of companies in the oil industry in that area, but elsewhere, particularly in Europe and the other areas, this source of funds was inadequate and had to be supplemented by

external sources of funds. These contrasting situations are related to the reduced flows of direct investment capital to Latin America for this industry, while there were sizable outflows from the United States to Europe, North Africa, and the rest of the Eastern Hemisphere.

The manufacturing industry reported depreciation charges in 1961 of $.9 billion, about $100 million more than the year before, with about 80 percent in Europe and Canada. Although capital outlays in Canada declined slightly, requirements for working capital increased as well as income distributions so that somewhat larger amounts of external funds were used by the Canadian organizations. In Europe, capital needs were heavy and internally generated funds did not increase in the year as retained earnings were cut back. Accordingly, manufacturing firms in Europe raised larger amounts from outside sources. Foreign investors and creditors together with U.S. parent companies, invested $820 million to add to fixed assets or finance working balances. This was the highest amount raised from external sources in the 1957–61 period.

A slightly larger volume of internal sources of funds, together with lower needs in 1961 for investment in fixed and current assets, made it possible for mining firms to decrease reliance on

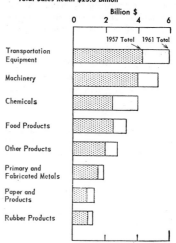

SALES OF MANUFACTURES BY DIRECT INVESTMENT ENTERPRISES ABROAD

Machinery, Chemicals, and Transportation Equipment Show Largest Gains
Total Sales Reach $25.6 Billion

U.S. Department of Commerce, Office of Business Economics   62-9-11

external sources of funds. These external sources accounted for only $130 million of the $450 million used in this industry.

Retained earnings have also long been an important source of internal funds for United States direct investment enterprises abroad, usually accounting for about one fifth of the funds

Table 4.—Domestic and Foreign Expenditures for Plant and Equipment in Selected Industries 1960–62

(Amounts in millions of dollars)

Industry	Expenditures—1960				Expenditures—1961				Expenditures—1962 [*]			
	Total	Domestic	Foreign	Percent of foreign total	Total	Domestic	Foreign	Percent of foreign total	Total	Domestic	Foreign	Percent of foreign total
Manufacturing												
Food products	1,017	920	97	10	1,096	980	·116	11	1,143	1,030	113	10
Paper and allied products	828	750	78	9	751	680	71	9	780	710	70	9
Chemicals	1,837	1,600	237	13	1,897	1,620	277	15	1,979	1,650	329	17
Rubber products	298	230	68	23	311	220	91	29	337	250	87	26
Primary and fabricated metals [1]	1,143	1,010	133	12	1,089	920	169	16	1,202	1,060	142	12
Machinery, except electrical	1,232	1,100	132	11	1,290	1,100	190	15	1,425	1,240	185	13
Electrical machinery	784	680	104	13	831	690	141	17	848	690	158	19
Transportation equipment	1,646	1,310	336	20	1,603	1,130	473	30	1,828	1,210	618	34
Selected industries, total	8,785	7,600	1,185	13	8,868	7,340	1,528	17	9,542	7,840	1,702	18
Mining and petroleum	5,523	3,630	1,893	34	5,632	3,740	1,892	34	6,044	3,820	2,224	37

[*] Estimated on the basis of company projections.
[1.] Excludes primary iron and steel producers.

NOTE.—Foreign expenditures include acquisitions of existing fixed assets, which are excluded from the domestic series.

utilized. However, in 1961 the amount of these reinvested earnings in manufacturing, petroleum and mining was reduced to $768 million, nearly two-thirds accounted for by manufacturing companies. While petroleum and mining reinvestment was not much changed from 1960, the amount for manufacturing was sharply reduced to $485 million from $744 million the year before. Most of the decline was in Canada, where dividends rose though earnings were reduced.

External financing

Funds from external sources amounting to $2.6 billion in 1961 were about evenly divided between funds obtained from the U.S. parent companies and other U.S. sources, and funds obtained abroad by the foreign companies. These external sources rose by nearly $600 million in 1961, with foreign sources providing most of the increase. Where internal sources of funds were adequate to finance needs for investment outlays and for working capital,

funds drawn from the United States were at a minimum. However in industries and areas where heavy investment activity was taking place, funds from parents and other U.S. investors tended to rise significantly. In particular, increased investments in manufacturing and petroleum in Europe and the rest of the Eastern Hemisphere required accelerated capital flows from United States owners, and accounted for nearly three-quarters of the total outflow from the United States.

As mentioned above foreign investors and creditors provided American-owned foreign enterprises with sizable amounts of funds to supplement internal sources and parent company financing. The rapidly advancing investments of manufacturing companies in Europe used about $600 million of such financing accounting for 40 percent of the funds used in these European affiliates. Petroleum companies in Europe also increased their use of foreign financing. In Canada larger amounts of foreign funds were used to refinance mining ventures and also to finance larger working capital requirements in manufacturing.

Growth of Manufacturing Production Abroad

In 1961 sales by U.S.-owned manufacturing companies abroad reached $25½ billion, a rise of $2 billion in the year and some 40 percent over the amount reported in 1957, when the collection of these data began.

Supported by the heavy investment activity of recent years, output has gained rapidly in Europe and reached $10.7 billion in 1961. Growth since 1957 was about 70 percent, and more than 15 percent in 1961. Gains over 1960 were large in the chemicals, food and machinery groups, but automobile sales slowed compared to earlier years, with 1961 totals only 3 percent above 1960. Sales increased substantially in France, Germany and the United Kingdom.

Manufacturing production in Latin America grew more rapidly than in any other area in 1961, gaining nearly 20 percent. Argentina, where companies for a number of years have added

Table 5.—Sources and Uses of Funds of Direct-Investment Enterprises by Area and Selected Industry, 1959–61

(Millions of dollars)

SOURCES OF FUNDS

Area and industry	Total sources			Net income			Funds from United States			Funds obtained abroad [1]			Depreciation and depletion		
	1959	1960ʳ	1961	1959	1960ʳ	1961	1959	1960ʳ	1961	1959	1960ʳ	1961	1959	1960ʳ	1961
All areas, total	6,774	7,245	8,217	2,837	3,255	3,381	1,181	1,046	1,249	985	1,017	1,391	1,771	1,927	2,196
Mining and smelting	873	1,015	813	372	519	476	184	158	16	155	147	113	162	191	208
Petroleum	2,893	2,930	3,696	1,196	1,366	1,553	528	454	743	255	153	301	914	957	1,099
Manufacturing	3,008	3,300	3,708	1,269	1,370	1,352	469	434	490	575	717	977	695	779	889
Canada, total	1,845	1,737	1,852	711	786	760	376	371	235	202	−22	220	556	602	637
Mining and smelting	395	447	390	112	157	161	121	202	9	95	13	140	67	75	80
Petroleum	441	549	535	99	159	199	112	138	99	41	45	20	189	207	217
Manufacturing	1,009	741	927	500	470	400	143	31	127	66	−80	60	300	320	340
Latin America, total [2]	1,470	1,714	1,781	655	789	874	238	89	110	106	314	186	471	522	611
Mining and smelting	343	332	291	187	239	219	36	−60	−20	46	61	−10	74	92	102
Petroleum	702	730	915	333	380	477	132	24	44	−90	−24	−10	327	350	404
Manufacturing	425	652	575	135	170	178	70	125	86	150	277	206	70	80	105
Europe, total	1,877	2,001	2,315	620	658	709	381	513	587	447	373	723	429	457	559
Mining and smelting	12	11	8	8	10	8	(**)	(**)	(**)	3	−1	−2	1	2	2
Petroleum	578	493	770	116	87	87	150	273	360	144	−12	130	168	145	193
Manufacturing	1,287	1,497	1,800	496	561	614	231	240	227	300	386	595	260	310	364
Other areas, total	1,582	1,793	2,006	851	1,022	1,038	186	73	317	230	352	262	315	346	389
Mining and smelting	123	225	124	65	113	88	27	16	27	11	74	−15	20	22	24
Petroleum	1,172	1,158	1,476	648	740	790	134	19	240	160	144	161	230	255	285
Manufacturing	287	410	406	138	169	160	25	38	50	59	134	116	65	69	80

USES OF FUNDS

Area and industry	Total uses			Property, plant, and equipment			Inventories			Receivables			Other assets [3]			Income paid out		
	1959	1960ʳ	1961	1959	1960ʳ	1961	1959	1960ʳ	1961	1959	1960ʳ	1961	1959	1960ʳ	1961	1959	1960ʳ	1961
All areas, total	6,774	7,245	8,217	3,142	3,230	3,574	378	793	482	487	630	766	818	330	782	1,949	2,260	2,613
Mining and smelting	873	1,015	813	437	426	320	37	96	27	67	37	18	79	41	79	253	413	369
Petroleum	2,893	2,930	3,696	1,558	1,467	1,572	−8	20	85	65	164	274	192	58	388	1,086	1,221	1,377
Manufacturing	3,008	3,300	3,708	1,147	1,337	1,681	349	677	370	355	429	474	547	231	315	610	626	867
Canada, total	1,845	1,737	1,852	1,009	1,034	866	164	93	121	118	60	193	202	160	184	352	390	488
Mining and smelting	395	447	390	240	290	165	18	58	51	26	−10	40	50	25	48	61	84	86
Petroleum	441	549	535	380	360	340	−4	5	10	12	25	27	−5	60	36	58	99	122
Manufacturing	1,009	741	927	389	384	361	150	30	60	80	45	126	157	75	100	233	207	280
Latin America, total [2]	1,470	1,714	1,781	789	625	653	89	124	37	95	256	220	17	25	137	480	684	734
Mining and smelting	343	332	291	147	78	95	18	22	−18	25	31	−17	19	−50	17	134	251	213
Petroleum	702	730	915	449	340	309	−30	−24	−5	30	105	107	−35	−50	70	288	359	434
Manufacturing	425	652	575	193	207	249	101	126	60	40	120	130	33	125	50	58	74	86
Europe, total	1,877	2,001	2,578	791	955	1,295	94	453	315	237	220	264	372	10	241	383	361	463
Mining and smelting	12	11	8	2	2		(**)	(**)	(**)	−3	−1	(**)	1	−1		11	9	9
Petroleum	578	493	770	339	345	438	5	29	75	23	3	95	86	29	82	125	87	80
Manufacturing	1,287	1,497	1,800	450	608	856	89	424	240	215	220	170	286	−20	160	247	265	374
Other areas, total	1,582	1,793	2,006	553	616	760	31	123	9	37	94	89	227	135	220	734	825	928
Mining and smelting	123	225	124	48	56	59	1	16	−6	17	19	−4	10	65	15	47	69	60
Petroleum	1,172	1,158	1,476	390	422	485	21	10	5	(**)	31	45	146	19	200	615	676	741
Manufacturing	287	410	406	115	138	216	9	97	10	20	44	48	71	51	5	72	80	127

(**) Less than $500,000.
ʳ Revised.
1. Includes miscellaneous sources.
2. Includes other Western Hemisphere.
3. Includes miscellaneous uses.

Note: Detail may not add to totals because of rounding.

Table 6.—Production Abroad by Direct-Investment Enterprises, Principal Commodities by Areas, 1957, 1959-61

(Millions of dollars)

Area and year	Manufacturing total	Food products	Paper and allied products	Chemicals	Rubber products	Primary and fabricated metals	Machinery excluding electrical	Electrical machinery	Transportation equipment	Other products
All areas, total:										
1957	18,331	2,457	881	2,411	968	1,548	1,903	2,047	4,228	1,889
1959	21,100	2,810	1,170	2,950	1,040	1,590	2,200	2,100	5,140	2,100
1960	23,570	2,920	1,260	3,290	1,170	1,680	2,490	2,280	6,170	2,310
1961	25,580	3,270	1,310	3,975	1,215	1,875	2,735	2,470	6,000	2,730
Canada:										
1957	7,897	928	769	897	272	927	695	1,080	1,488	842
1959	8,670	1,060	1,030	1,070	290	950	760	1,030	1,600	880
1960	8,920	1,020	1,100	1,150	310	920	780	1,040	1,650	950
1961	8,920	1,095	1,115	1,300	295	940	760	1,000	1,450	965
Latin America¹										
1957	2,435	608	55	499	239	111	66	190	375	292
1959	2,830	740	60	590	260	100	80	190	470	340
1960	3,180	750	70	620	280	100	100	240	710	310
1961	3,770	780	85	820	300	160	115	300	770	440
Europe:										
1957	6,313	734	34	822	262	435	1,009	678	1,700	639
1959	7,690	760	50	1,050	290	470	1,210	770	2,350	740
1960	9,310	900	60	1,240	360	590	1,420	890	2,970	880
1961	10,670	1,120	70	1,510	400	690	1,635	1,050	3,070	1,125
Other areas:										
1957	1,685	188	23	193	195	75	133	99	665	116
1959	1,910	250	30	240	200	70	150	110	720	140
1960	2,160	250	30	280	220	70	190	110	840	170
1961	2,220	275	40	345	220	85	225	120	710	200

1. Includes other Western Hemisphere.

sizable amounts to their plant facilities, showed gains of about 30 percent. Sales grew strongly in chemicals, in primary and fabricated metals, and electrical machinery.

No increase in sales was reported for Canada, with total production remaining stable at $8.9 billion. Decreases in sales in the transportation industry, in machinery, and in rubber products, offset gains in other commodity groups, notably a rise of output in the chemical industry of nearly 15 percent. Sales in other areas were moderately improved overall, despite reduced sales of transportation equipment.

Comparison with U.S. exports

In the period since 1957, production in selected industries in United States-owned manufacturing plants abroad rose by more than 40 percent, while in the same period exports from the United States of the same commodities advanced by less than 10 percent (see table 8). These selected industries had sales in 1961 of $17.7 billion, out of production by all manufacturing groups abroad totaling $25.6 billion.

While the figures show a strong rise of foreign production, considerable variations exist between areas and industry groups. Production in Canada by United States manufacturing subsidiaries advanced by less than 15 percent since 1957, and remained at a standstill in 1961. In the same period exports to Canada of these products declined slightly.

On the other hand, production in Europe rose by nearly 70 percent since 1957 (15 percent in 1961 alone), and U.S. exports to Europe of the same commodity groups also increased by about 70 percent since 1957, and by about 14 percent in 1961. For both Canada and Europe, the absolute size of production abroad for these items is much greater than exports from the United States.

For the "Other Area" group, which includes Australia, Japan, and other countries in the Middle East and Far

Table 7.—Production Abroad by Direct-Investment Manufacturing Enterprises, by Selected Countries 1957, 1959-61

(Millions of dollars)

Area and country	1957	1959	1960	1961
All areas total	18,331	21,100	23,570	25,580
Canada	7,897	8,670	8,920	8,920
Latin American, total¹	2,435	2,830	3,180	3,770
Argentina	385	426	696	895
Brazil	659	764	879	940
Mexico	643	751	770	850
Venezuela	268	364	360	390
Other countries	480	525	475	695
Europe, total	6,313	7,690	9,310	10,670
Belgium, Netherlands and Luxembourg	416	461	602	740
France	763	789	965	1,195
Germany	1,116	1,572	1,835	2,265
Italy	230	244	350	475
United Kingdom	3,303	4,070	4,715	5,070
Other countries	485	574	843	925
Other areas, total	1,685	1,910	2,160	2,220
Australia	787	933	1,085	1,045
Japan	217	240	290	380
Philippine Republic	118	141	140	160
Union of South Africa	300	292	305	335
Other countries	263	304	340	300

1. Includes other Western Hemisphere.

Table 8.—Exports From the United States and Production by Direct Investments Abroad of Selected Manufactures, by Area, 1957, 1960-61

(Millions of dollars)

Commodities	All areas, total			Canada			Latin America¹			Europe			Other areas		
	1957	1960	1961	1957	1960	1961	1957	1960	1961	1957	1960	1961	1957	1960	1961
Selected manufactures:															
Foreign production	12,438	16,660	17,705	5,201	6,030	5,920	1,424	2,020	2,390	4,505	6,940	7,735	1,308	1,670	1,660
U.S. exports	7,536	7,941	8,235	1,869	1,871	1,769	2,633	2,121	2,055	1,326	2,008	2,285	1,709	1,941	2,126
Paper and allied products:															
Foreign production	881	1,260	1,310	769	1,100	1,115	55	70	85	34	60	70	23	30	40
U.S. exports	324	419	453	65	72	78	97	24	22	91	163	179	71	160	171
Chemicals:															
Foreign production	2,411	3,290	3,975	897	1,150	1,300	499	620	820	822	1,240	1,510	193	280	345
U.S. exports	1,376	1,661	1,709	246	277	285	457	420	379	353	561	574	320	403	471
Rubber products:															
Foreign production	968	1,170	1,215	272	310	295	239	280	300	262	360	400	195	220	220
U.S. exports	300	372	330	43	62	48	62	74	63	97	153	121	98	83	98
Machinery, except electrical:															
Foreign production	1,903	2,490	2,735	695	780	760	66	100	115	1,009	1,420	1,635	133	190	225
U.S. exports	3,160	3,295	3,595	876	824	766	1,007	833	859	567	806	1,047	710	832	923
Electrical machinery:															
Foreign production	2,047	2,280	2,470	1,080	1,010	1,000	190	240	300	678	800	1,050	99	110	120
U.S. exports	810	793	867	246	230	223	291	235	264	114	171	212	160	157	168
Transportation equipment:															
Foreign production	4,228	6,170	6,000	1,488	1,650	1,450	375	710	770	1,700	2,970	3,070	665	840	710
U.S. exports²	1,566	1,401	1,281	393	406	369	719	535	468	104	154	152	350	306	292

1. Includes other Western Hemisphere.
2. Excludes civilian aircraft.

NOTE.—Detail may not add to totals, due to rounding.

East, both foreign production by U.S. enterprises and exports from the United States rose by about 25 percent in the period. Exports to these areas are still larger than local production by United States-owned plants for most major commodities and include, of course, shipments financed by Government grants and credits.

Production by U.S. companies of these manufacturing commodities in Latin America has made considerable gains since 1957, increasing by $1 billion to a total of $2.4 billion. In the same period, exports from the United States have declined, so that local production in the area of such items as chemicals, electrical machinery, and transportation equipment now exceeds U.S. exports.

The comparative volumes of exports and local sales are influenced by many factors, including overall demand conditions in individual foreign markets, the degree of interchangeability between specific products, special foreign exchange or trading restrictions enforced in some countries, the technical conditions of production and shipment, and many others.

FOREIGN OPERATIONS OF U.S. INDUSTRY:

Capital Expenditures, Sales
and Financing

Fred[erick] Cutler
and
Samuel Pizer

by FRED CUTLER and SAMUEL PIZER

Foreign Operations of U.S. Industry

Capital Expenditures, Sales, and Financing

THE latest survey of the foreign operations of U.S. industrial firms,[1] conducted in the summer months by the Office of Business Economics shows the following principal developments:

(1) An increase of 8 percent in plant and equipment expenditures abroad from 1962 to 1963, to a total of $4.9 billion, with the largest gain in the petroleum industry. For 1964, the company projections indicate some reductions in outlays, but a continued high rate of growth in foreign productive capacity.

(2) Sales of the foreign manufacturing units reached $28.1 billion in 1962, an increase of $2.5 billion from the previous year. Outstanding increases were reported for chemicals, electrical machinery and automobiles. Of the total sales, $1.4 billion were exports to the United States and $3.2 billion were export sales to third countries (i.e, were sold to foreign countries other than the country of production).

(3) Financing of the foreign affiliates shifted increasingly to non-U.S. sources. A total of $5.8 billion was required to finance mining, petroleum and manufacturing operations abroad in 1962 (apart from dividends and branch profits paid out). Of this total, 16 percent was supplied directly from parent companies and other U.S. sources, by far the lowest proportion since the collection of these data began in 1957. About 60 percent of the financing required was supplied from internal sources of the foreign affiliates

(earnings and depreciation charges), and about 25 percent from external capital sources abroad.

In the following article these major aspects of the foreign operations of U.S. companies are examined in some detail.

CAPITAL EXPENDITURES ABROAD BY U.S. MANUFACTURING COMPANIES

● Outlays Are Projected to Rise in Most Areas
● Planned Common Market Expenditures Dip From High Level

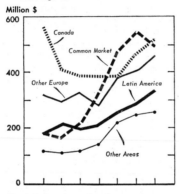

Chemicals Show Strong Growth

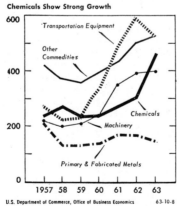

U.S. Department of Commerce, Office of Business Economics   63-10-8

---

1. A representative sample of large U.S. firms (except those in finance or shipping abroad) having foreign branches and subsidiaries is covered, and the results are expanded to universe totals for certain key categories. Data for plant and equipment expenditures are expanded for all industries by area, but country detail is developed only for the three major industries, manufacturing, mining and smelting, and petroleum; data for sales are given only for the manufacturing sector; data for sources and uses of funds are derived only as area aggregates for the three major industries.

detail. This discussion is closely related to the article on international investments published in the August SURVEY OF CURRENT BUSINESS, which gave data on net capital flows, book value, and income as used in the balance of payments accounts. To round out the information necessary to evaluate the overall effects of the expansion of producing units operated by foreign subsidiaries and branches of U.S. firms, a new annual survey is being initiated giving data on exports from the United States to these foreign affiliates.

Plant Expansion Abroad

At midyear, U.S. firms estimated that expenditures for property, plant and equipment by their foreign affiliates would exceed $4.9 billion during 1963, about 8 percent more than in 1962. This would represent a high volume of capital outlays and compares with $4.8 billion in 1957, when these surveys began. At the same time, companies projected a decline for 1964 to $4.5 billion. Actual expenditures in 1962 were $4.6 billion, slightly less than the $4.8 billion previously projected for that year. Manufacturing investments exceeded projections, while petroleum outlays fell short.

In the past few years projected expenditures for manufacturing companies have been on the low side; this suggests that final totals for this industry in 1963, as well as in 1964, may turn out to be higher than now projected. On the other hand, projections of future capital outlays by oil companies have consistently exceeded actual investment experience. For mining companies, little divergence has been observed between actual and projected capital outlays. It is not yet possible to derive correction factors for these projections of foreign outlays.

Actual and Projected Plant and Equipment Expenditures Abroad, 1960–64

[Millions of dollars]

	1960	1961	1962	1963	1964
Manufacturing					
Actual expenditures.....	1,337	1,697	1,949	-----	-----
Expenditures as projected 1 year ahead....	1,314	1,755	1,866	2,057	-----
Expenditures as projected 2 years ahead..	na	na	1,706	1,735	1,971
Petroleum					
Actual expenditures.....	1,467	1,534	1,633	-----	-----
Expenditures as projected 1 year ahead.....	1,575	1,776	1,829	1,950	-----
Expenditures as projected 2 years ahead..	na	na	1,794	1,811	1,653
Mining and smelting					
Actual expenditures.....	426	312	371	-----	-----
Expenditures as projected 1 year ahead.....	358	438	395	321	-----
Expenditures as projected 2 years ahead..	na	na	407	343	258

na = Not available.

Manufacturing investments still rising

In 1963, for the first time, capital outlays by U.S. controlled foreign manufacturing companies are expected to exceed $2 billion despite a leveling in investments by European affiliates, which are barely topping 1962 outlays. In other areas, however, investment activity appears to be stronger, particularly in Canada and Latin America, since 1963 outlays are expected to exceed the previous year's total by about $50 million each.

The chemical industry which is raising capital investments by more than $150 million this year, accounts for the major change in the manufacturing total. Outlays by other manufacturing industries are currently running near or below the 1962 levels. Capital investments in the transportation equipment industry, which had been rising rapidly in earlier years, are now $60 million below the 1962 amounts with Common Market countries showing a drop of more than $80 million, now that major expansion aims appear to have been met. However, these figures do not include purchases by U.S. companies of existing enterprises or minority interests.

New investment in Europe, which had risen by about $100 million in 1962, remains practically unchanged at better than $950 million in 1963, a little under half of the world total. A decline in Common Market countries caused by a drop of investments in the transportation equipment industry is being balanced by higher outlays in other European countries, primarily in the United Kingdom. Plant and equipment expenditures by chemical companies (including sizable amounts for petrochemical firms largely financed by oil companies) are rising by more than 50 percent.

New capital investments in the United Kingdom and in Germany will account for over two-thirds of the funds now being invested by U.S. controlled companies in Europe. Higher outlays in 1963 were reported for other Common Market countries, except France, with investments for new chemical and other manufacturing facilities rising by more than 50 percent.

Not much change is foreseen by companies in projecting 1964 capital spending for Europe; chemical companies expect to raise investments further, but companies in the transportation equipment industry (primarily automobiles) predict another cut in their capital investment programs.

U.S. companies reported spending for new plant in Canada at the rate of $520 million in 1963, 10 percent more than expenditures in 1962. This relative increase is in line with projections for all of Canadian industry. For U.S. companies there is a strong rise in outlays by chemical companies, which accounted for 25 percent of all U.S. manufacturing expenditures.

In Latin America, as in Canada, renewed highs for capital spending are tied to the rapidly expanding chemical companies, which expect to show a rise of 60 percent over 1962, to account for one-third of all manufacturing spending by U.S. companies in Latin America.

Most of the increase in manufacturing investment in Latin America is centered on Mexico, where expenditures for plant and equipment are rising rapidly; the total for 1964 now predicted is double 1962 outlays. Investments in other countries in South America and the Caribbean area, bolstered by a few major projects for fertilizer and other chemical plants in Argentina and Trinidad, showed little change for the year. The decline in 1964 totals is caused primarily by the completion of some of these major projects, rather than by a widespread decrease of investment activity, and remains well above the average of the 1957–62 period despite the disturbed political and economic conditions in some of these countries. Projected expenditures in Argentina are particularly affected by project terminations, and are dropping by 40 percent between 1962 and 1964. Outlays in Brazil in 1964 are expected at the 1962 level, somewhat down from the $80 million for 1963.

In the rest of the world (Africa, Asia and Oceania), a sustained growth of manufacturing investments continues, with an increasing volume of investments going into the automotive and machinery industries, and into petrochemical and other chemical plants. About one-half of these outlays are being made in Australia, and investment spending is substantial in Japan and India.

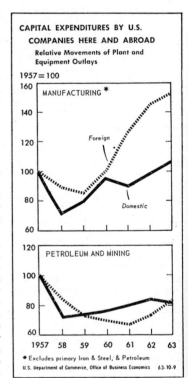

CAPITAL EXPENDITURES BY U.S. COMPANIES HERE AND ABROAD
Relative Movements of Plant and Equipment Outlays
1957 = 100

MANUFACTURING *

Foreign

Domestic

PETROLEUM AND MINING

1957 58 59 60 61 62 63

* Excludes primary Iron & Steel, & Petroleum

U.S. Department of Commerce, Office of Business Economics   63-10-9

Petroleum investments expanding

Oil companies report current spending for plant and equipment of $2 billion for 1963 and project expenditures of $1.7 billion for 1964, not greatly different from the 1958–62 average. In addition to these capitalized expenditures and investments, companies also charged against income certain exploration and development costs. Figures for 1962 are shown below.

Exploration and Development Expenditures Charged Against Income, 1962

[Millions of dollars]

	Total	Petroleum	Mining
All areas	411	371	40
Canada	157	127	30
Latin America	93	87	6
Europe	20	20	(x)
Other areas	141	137	4

(x) Less than $500,000.

Most of these investments and expenditures are being made in the Eastern Hemisphere, reflecting the continued construction and expansion of oil refining facilities in Europe and other areas, particularly the Far East, and the buildup of related transportation and marketing operations. Investment and expenditures made for new producing fields are particularly heavy in North Africa, but active search in other areas ranges from the North Sea to Australia.

Mining investments decline

Mining and smelting companies in Canada reported sharp drops from 1962 in projected capital investments for 1963 and 1964. Major mining projects for the development of iron ore deposits have either been completed, or are nearly complete, and few new ventures are taking their place. There is little prospect now of large scale mining developments in other minerals or metals in the near future.

In Latin America, little change is seen in the 1962–64 period in capital outlays for mining operations, with expenditures ranging between $90 million and $100 million annually. Major investment activities continue to center on Chile and Peru in the development of copper and iron ore properties, Jamaica (bauxite), and Venezuela (iron ore).

As for other areas, the development of bauxite and iron ore deposits is important in West Africa, and manganese and copper projects are being developed in Central and South Africa.

Trade and other industries

Plant and equipment expenditures of companies in trade and distribution are continuing the rising trend observed in earlier surveys. More than half of these expenditures are being made or projected for Europe.

Capital investments in the "other industries" group are being made at the rate of $255 million in 1963, and are projected downward to $235 million for 1964. The 1963 total is about equally divided among three groups: agricultural enterprises, public utility companies, and engineering firms and other service industries.

Most of the agricultural expenditures are being made in Latin America ($40 million), but capital outlays in Canada are also important, particularly for forest operations. The bulk of the public utility investments are also located in Latin America, where they now total about $50 million. In Canada, public utility operations are frequently related to mining operations

Table 1.—Plant and Equipment Expenditures of Direct Foreign Investments, by Country and Major Industry, 1961–64

[Millions of dollars]

Area and country	1961 r Mining and smelting	1961 r Petroleum	1961 r Manufacturing	1962 r Mining and smelting	1962 r Petroleum	1962 r Manufacturing	1963 * Mining and smelting	1963 * Petroleum	1963 * Manufacturing	1964 * Mining and smelting	1964 * Petroleum	1964 * Manufacturing
All areas, total	312	1,534	1,697	371	1,633	1,949	321	1,950	2,057	258	1,653	1,971
Canada	165	315	385	193	325	473	155	350	520	115	315	434
Latin American Republics, total	64	267	249	63	257	274	70	276	314	52	272	286
Mexico, Central America and West Indies, total	8	21	47	5	24	51	5	27	82	5	23	100
Mexico	7	2	44	5	2	50	4	4	82	3	2	100
Other countries	1	19	3	(**)	22	1	1	23	(**)	2	21	(**)
South America, total	56	246	202	58	233	223	65	249	232	47	249	186
Argentina	(*)	60	94	(*)	38	115	(*)	24	102	(*)	27	71
Brazil	2	5	62	3	4	63	3	5	80	1	2	63
Chile	20	(*)	6	20	(*)	4	32	(*)	8	25	(*)	8
Colombia	(*)	30	11	(*)	32	7	(*)	31	9	(*)	19	14
Peru	27	10	10	27	9	6	18	10	5	9	10	8
Venezuela	(*)	135	17	(*)	145	25	(*)	173	26	(*)	184	20
Other countries	2	(*)	2	(*)	(*)	3	(*)	(*)	1	(*)	(*)	2
Other Western Hemisphere	23	39	1	32	62	7	30	39	16	38	38	2
Europe, total	1	438	847	4	494	949	4	643	953	2	486	952
Common Market, total	(**)	186	475	(**)	269	547	(**)	386	497	(**)	303	482
Belgium and Luxembourg	(**)	7	21	(**)	9	26	(**)	15	47	(**)	17	61
France	(**)	31	68	(**)	74	100	(**)	50	* 99	(**)	64	95
Germany	(**)	70	318	(**)	115	360	(**)	155	265	(**)	77	240
Italy	(**)	64	40	(**)	29	39	(**)	110	56	(**)	104	53
Netherlands		14	28		42	22		56	30		41	33
Other Europe, total	1	252	372	4	225	402	4	257	456	2	183	470
Denmark		19	2		30	2		45	2		15	1
Norway	(**)	7	5	(**)	7	8	(**)	8	12	(**)	8	10
Spain	(**)	3	6	(**)	7	11	(**)	40	15	(**)	15	13
Sweden		18	10		30	14		28	15		16	9
Switzerland		3	10		4	10		4	11		10	15
United Kingdom	1	170	335		125	347		110	394		95	414
Other countries	1	32	4	4	22	4	1	22	7	2	24	8
Africa, total	47	171	10	69	176	12	50	202	20	38	186	17
North Africa	(**)	111	(**)	(**)	137	(**)	(**)	161	(**)	(**)	134	(**)
East Africa	(**)	9	(**)	(**)	15	(**)	(**)	19	6	(**)	20	5
West Africa	22	34	(**)	43	11	1	32	9	1	14	24	8	1
Central and South Africa, total	25	17	10	26	13	11	18	13	13	11	24	11
Union of South Africa	10	(*)	8	14	(*)	11	15	(*)	13	6	(*)	11
Other countries	15	(*)	2	12	(*)		3	(*)		5	(*)	
Asia, total	(**)	195	114	1	178	112	1	331	103	(**)	280	130
Middle East		87	12		72	6		162	2		109	3
Far East, total	(**)	108	102	1	106	106	1	169	101	(**)	171	127
India		(*)	39		(*)	26		(*)	32		(*)	36
Japan		(*)	48		(*)	59		(*)	52		(*)	66
Philippine Republic	(**)	(*)	9	(**)	(*)	12	(**)	(*)	11	(**)	(*)	15
Other countries	(**)	(*)	6	1	(*)	9	1	(*)	6	(**)	(*)	10
Oceania, total	12	64	92	9	76	122	11	68	131	16	45	150
Australia	12	(*)	90	9	(*)	119	11	(*)	125	16	(*)	141
Other countries		(*)	2		(*)	3		(*)	6		(*)	9
International shipping		45			65			41			31	

*Included in area total. **Less than $500,000. r Revised. * Estimated on the basis of company projections.

Note.—Detail may not add to totals because of rounding.

Table 2.—Plant and Equipment Expenditures Abroad by U.S. Manufacturing Companies, by Area and Major Commodity, 1960–64

[Millions of dollars]

Areas and years	Total	Food products	Paper and allied products	Chemicals	Rubber products	Primary and fabricated metals	Machinery, excluding electrical	Electrical machinery	Transportation equipment	Other manufacturing
All areas, total										
1960	1,337	97	78	237	68	133	132	104	336	152
1961 r	1,697	116	71	278	91	169	205	141	473	153
1962 r	1,949	128	110	307	85	167	214	176	585	177
1963 *	2,057	141	115	463	88	141	213	185	526	185
1964 *	1,971	142	85	464	82	143	229	176	488	162
Canada										
1960	384	30	55	75	15	49	17	30	63	50
1961 r	385	20	54	55	18	55	40	31	60	52
1962 r	473	28	90	75	19	57	38	50	65	51
1963 *	520	22	92	125	19	55	42	40	80	45
1964 *	434	18	65	115	16	50	45	30	70	25
Latin America 1										
1960	207	24	7	49	12	11	8	18	47	31
1961 r	250	37	5	48	19	23	9	27	52	30
1962 r	281	35	6	52	12	20	10	25	81	40
1963 *	330	35	8	111	16	15	20	27	54	44
1964 *	288	36	7	77	14	16	13	29	51	45
Europe										
Common Market										
1960	328	17	2	44	11	10	72	21	128	23
1961 r	475	30	3	63	11	19	105	36	181	27
1962 r	547	35	4	54	20	25	85	44	245	35
1963 *	497	40	2	83	20	26	90	40	160	36
1964 *	482	41	1	95	24	26	96	38	125	36
Other Europe										
1960	280	18	3	42	15	50	24	18	74	35
1961 r	372	17	4	49	15	46	38	30	141	31
1962 r	402	18	6	51	12	50	65	41	123	36
1963 *	456	32	8	78	10	32	46	54	155	41
1964 *	470	35	8	81	15	33	57	48	152	41
Other areas										
1960	138	8	12	28	16	13	10	16	23	12
1961 r	216	12	5	63	28	26	13	17	39	13
1962 r	246	12	4	75	22	15	16	16	71	15
1963 *	254	12	5	66	23	13	15	24	77	19
1964 *	297	12	4	96	13	18	18	31	90	15

r Revised.   * Estimated on the basis of company projections.   1 Includes other Western Hemisphere.

NOTE.—Detail may not add to totals because of rounding.

Table 3.—Plant and Equipment Expenditures of Direct Foreign Investments, Major Industries, 1957–64

[Millions of dollars]

Area and industry	1957	1958	1959	1960	1961 r	1962 r	1963 *	1964 *
All areas, total	4,819	4,097	3,705	3,789	4,122	4,564	4,929	4,527
Mining and smelting	421	420	437	426	312	371	321	258
Petroleum	2,322	1,854	1,558	1,467	1,534	1,633	1,950	1,653
Manufacturing	1,347	1,180	1,147	1,337	1,697	1,949	2,057	1,971
Trade	186	191	198	256	307	354	346	411
Other industries	543	452	365	303	272	257	255	234
Canada, total	1,593	1,311	1,179	1,259	1,016	1,151	1,181	1,022
Mining and smelting	163	172	240	290	165	193	155	115
Petroleum	584	510	380	360	315	325	350	315
Manufacturing	561	404	389	384	385	473	520	434
Trade	47	55	45	60	39	55	64	63
Other industries	238	170	125	165	112	105	92	95
Latin America, total 1	1,687	1,269	1,003	750	795	840	900	834
Mining and smelting	216	221	147	78	87	95	100	90
Petroleum	1,039	577	449	340	306	319	315	310
Manufacturing	174	202	193	207	250	281	330	288
Trade	20	31	31	35	45	46	48	58
Other industries	238	238	183	90	107	99	107	88
Europe, total	899	976	906	1,092	1,474	1,670	1,808	1,688
Mining and smelting	2	--------	2	2	1	4	4	2
Petroleum	275	422	339	345	438	494	643	486
Manufacturing	497	460	450	608	847	949	953	952
Trade	107	87	101	125	175	200	181	225
Other industries	18	7	14	12	13	23	27	23
Other areas, total	640	541	617	688	837	903	1,040	983
Mining and smelting	40	27	48	56	59	79	62	51
Petroleum	424	345	390	422	475	495	642	542
Manufacturing	115	114	115	138	216	246	254	297
Trade	12	18	21	36	48	53	53	65
Other industries	49	37	43	36	40	30	29	28

r Revised.   * Estimated on the basis of company projections.   1 Includes other Western Hemisphere.

NOTE.—Detail may not add to totals because of rounding.

(railroads), or oil company activities (pipelines), but are classified as public utilities because they are common carriers.

Domestic and foreign capital outlays

With the rate of increase of foreign capital outlays for manufacturing plants and equipment by U.S. companies slowing somewhat in 1963, to a rate about equal to the rising domestic rate, the proportion of foreign to total capital outlays held steady at nearly 20 percent. In the mining and petroleum industries, the foreign segment of investment activity by U.S. companies has moved upward in the past two years, to about 37 percent in 1963.

Among the principal types of manufactures, the foreign rate of expansion significantly exceeded the domestic rate in 1962 for chemicals, and was slightly higher for a number of others, but was considerably lower for transportation equipment.

Sources and Uses of Funds in 1962

Aggregate financing required by affiliates in the mining, petroleum and manufacturing industries totaled $5.8 billion in 1962, after deducting $2.8 billion used to pay out dividends and branch profits to the owners. The major requirement was for plant and equipment expenditures of nearly $4.0 billion, which was about $0.4 billion more than in 1961. In addition, $1.8 billion was used to add to working capital (inventories, cash, and receivables) and to other assets. This amount was about $0.2 billion less than in 1961, reflecting mainly a cutback by the petroleum companies.

Manufacturing affiliates abroad added substantially to their inventories in Canada in 1962, where business activity was strong, but reduced the rate of accumulation in Europe while there was a sharp gain in sales volume. Accounts receivable rose by $0.7 billion, lower in most instances than the unusually large increases registered in 1961. Most of the falling off of capital requirements other than those for fixed investments was reported under the heading of "other assets," which includes not only cash but also acquisitions of other assets. Petroleum affiliates in oil producing countries in the Middle East and Far East accounted for much of this decline, since they had reported abnormally large amounts under this heading in 1961.

Sources of financing

The financing of foreign affiliates has shown a fairly steady trend toward a greater share of internal and foreign external sources of financing as compared with funds coming from the United States. The latter provided 24 percent of the financing required in the three major industries in the 1957–61 period, but only 16 percent in 1962. This trend reduces the capital outflow from the United States and therefore benefits the balance of payments accounts.

As used in the context of the sources and uses of funds the "funds from United States" tends to be lower than

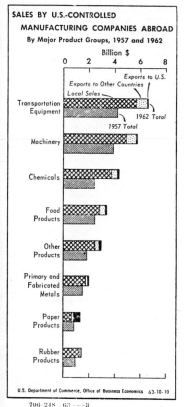

SALES BY U.S.-CONTROLLED MANUFACTURING COMPANIES ABROAD
By Major Product Groups, 1957 and 1962

U.S. Department of Commerce, Office of Business Economics   63-10-10

706-248   63——3

the net capital outflow for direct investments shown in the balance of payments accounts. This is because the latter includes acquisitions of the stock of existing ventures or purchases of outstanding stock (neither of which supplies new funds to the foreign operating affiliates), and also counts as capital flows the entire increase in net foreign assets of branches; some of the increase in net branch assets is attributed to reinvested earnings in table 5. On the other hand, funds from the United States shown in table 5 include banking and commercial loans included as short-term or portfolio investments in the balance of payments accounts, and also some U.S. Government financing. The following table illustrates these relationships for 1962:

Reconciliation of Data on Capital Flows and Earnings, 1962

[Millions of dollars]

	Total, speci- fied indus- tries	Min- ing and smelt- ing	Petro- leum	Manu- factur- ing
Net capital outflow appearing in balance of payments accounts	1,310	91	538	681
Less:				
Purchase of existing enterprises and minority interests	252	(x)	92	160
Retained branch profits	196	51	145	(x)
Plus:				
U.S. financing, other than parent	152	77	47	28
Other adjustments and residual	−91	−23	−73	5
Equals:				
Net funds from U.S. (table 5)	923	94	275	554
Undistributed earnings of subsidiaries consistent with balance of payments accounting [1]	724	55	148	521
Plus:				
Undistributed earnings of minority interests	195	45	12	138
Retained branch profits	196	51	145	(x)
Other adjustments and residual	−39	7	−47	1
Equals:				
Retained earnings as derived from table 5	1,076	158	258	660

[1] Not actually included in U.S. balance of payments statement.
(x) Negligible.

The data for earnings retained abroad also differ, in part because of the change in treatment of branch earnings mentioned above, and also because in the sources and uses context the foreign subsidiaries are treated as if they were wholly owned, so that retained earnings include a sizable portion accruing to foreign minority stockholders.

Funds obtained from external sources abroad are related more to working capital requirements than to plant and equipment expenditures, though there

is no necessary or direct link between specific sources and uses of funds. In 1962, as noted above, there was a reduction of about $0.2 billion in the amount required for working balances, but there was a small increase of about $50 million in foreign external financing. The differential movement was notable for the petroleum companies, which required $300 million less for working capital, but increased their financing abroad by $165 million. This net switch of $465 million made possible a very considerable reduction in pressures on the U.S. balance of payments, since this industry reduced the use of funds for these foreign affiliates from the United States by a like amount.

For manufacturing companies the experience varied among areas, and in the aggregate foreign financing was reduced while working capital increased. In Europe a sizable decline in working capital needs was about matched by a drop in the amount obtained from foreign source financing, and in Canada a large increase in working capital was financed largely from local sources.

A partial breakdown of the types of financing from external sources abroad was obtained for the first time for 1962, and can be summarized as follows:

[Millions of dollars]

	Total	Min- ing and smelt- ing	Pe- tro- leum	Man- ufac- tur- ing
Total	1,447	47	466	934
Borrowing from financial institutions	253	4	102	147
Other increases in foreign liabilities	780	−1	226	555
Funds obtained from foreign affiliates	21	23	9	−11
Issues of equity securities	256	14	42	200
Other foreign sources	137	7	87	43

The largest external source abroad, other increases in foreign liabilities, represents trade credits, accruing tax and other liabilities, and probably some long-term debt sold to the public. Borrowing from foreign financial institutions and issues of equity securities were also large, however, aggregating over $0.5 billion. Europe accounted for about $0.2 billion of this total and Canada for about $150 million.

Internal sources largest

Funds generated by the earnings and depreciation charges of the foreign affiliates accounted for about 60 percent

Table 4.—Domestic and Foreign Expenditures for Plant and Equipment in Selected Industries, 1961–63

[Millions of dollars]

Industry	Expenditures 1961				Expenditures 1962				Expenditures 1963			
	Total	Domestic	Foreign	Percent of foreign to total	Total	Domestic	Foreign	Percent of foreign to total	Total	Domestic	Foreign	Percent of foreign to total
Manufacturing												
Food products	1,096	980	116	11	1,118	990	128	11	1,161	1,020	141	12
Paper and allied products	751	680	71	9	830	720	110	13	835	720	115	14
Chemicals	1,898	1,620	278	15	1,867	1,560	307	16	2,123	1,660	463	22
Rubber products	311	220	91	29	315	230	85	27	318	230	88	28
Primary and fabricated metals	1,089	920	169	16	1,097	930	167	15	1,241	1,100	141	11
Machinery, except electrical	1,305	1,100	205	16	1,484	1,270	214	14	1,383	1,170	213	15
Electrical machinery	831	690	141	17	856	680	176	21	915	730	185	20
Transportation equipment	1,603	1,130	473	30	1,885	1,300	585	31	2,026	1,500	526	26
Selected industries, total	8,884	7,340	1,544	17	9,452	7,680	1,772	19	10,002	8,130	1,872	19
Mining and petroleum	5,586	3,740	1,846	33	5,964	3,960	2,004	34	6,091	3,820	2,271	37

* Estimated on basis of company projections.   † Excludes primary iron and steel producers.

NOTE.—Foreign expenditures include acquisitions of existing fixed assets, which are excluded from the domestic series.

Table 5.—Sources and Uses of Funds of Direct Foreign Investments, by Area and Selected Industry, 1960–1962

[Millions of dollars]

SOURCES OF FUNDS

Area and industry	Total sources			Net income			Funds from United States			Funds obtained abroad			Depreciation and depletion		
	1960	1961 r	1962	1960	1961 r	1962	1960	1961 r	1962	1960	1961 r	1962	1960	1961 r	1962
All areas, total	7,245	8,217	8,537	3,255	3,381	3,833	1,046	1,249	923	1,017	1,391	1,447	1,927	2,196	2,334
Mining and smelting	1,015	813	821	519	476	478	158	16	94	147	113	47	191	208	202
Petroleum	2,930	3,696	3,675	1,366	1,553	1,824	454	743	275	153	301	466	957	1,099	1,110
Manufacturing	3,390	3,708	4,041	1,370	1,352	1,531	434	490	554	717	977	934	779	889	1,022
Canada, total	1,737	1,852	2,048	786	760	905	371	235	164	-22	220	294	602	637	685
Mining and smelting	447	396	328	157	161	163	202	9	95	13	140	-25	75	80	95
Petroleum	549	535	533	189	199	189	138	99	50	45	20	74	207	217	210
Manufacturing	741	927	1,187	470	400	543	31	127	19	-80	60	245	320	340	380
Latin America, total	1,714	1,781	1,794	789	874	1,015	89	110	-23	314	186	222	522	611	580
Mining and smelting	332	291	329	239	219	246	-60	-20	-28	61	-10	31	92	102	80
Petroleum	730	915	854	380	477	567	24	44	152	-24	-10	44	350	404	390
Manufacturing	652	575	611	170	178	202	125	86	152	277	206	147	80	105	110
Europe, total	2,001	2,578	2,426	709	658	618	513	587	526	373	723	594	157	559	658
Mining and smelting	11	8	8	10	8	5	(*)	(*)	1	-1	-2	1	2	2	1
Petroleum	493	770	727	87	87	74	273	360	235	-12	130	198	145	193	220
Manufacturing	1,497	1,800	1,691	561	614	569	240	227	290	386	595	395	310	364	437
Other areas, total	1,793	2,006	2,269	1,022	1,038	1,265	73	317	256	352	262	337	646	389	411
Mining and smelting	225	124	156	113	88	64	16	27	26	74	-15	40	22	24	26
Petroleum	1,158	1,476	1,561	740	790	984	19	240	137	144	161	150	255	285	290
Manufacturing	410	406	552	168	160	217	38	50	93	134	116	147	69	80	95

USES OF FUNDS

Area and industry	Total uses			Property, plant and equipment			Inventories			Receivables			Other assets [2]			Income paid out		
	1960	1961 r	1962	1960	1961 r	1962	1960	1961 r	1962	1960	1961 r	1962	1960	1961 r	1962	1960	1961 r	1962
All areas, total	7,245	8,217	8,537	3,230	3,544	3,953	793	491	644	630	780	699	330	779	484	2,260	2,623	2,757
Mining and smelting	1,015	813	821	426	312	371	96	27	41	37	18	45	41	87	44	413	369	320
Petroleum	2,930	3,696	3,675	1,467	1,534	1,632	20	85	50	164	292	264	58	398	162	1,221	1,387	1,506
Manufacturing	3,300	3,708	4,041	1,387	1,697	1,949	677	379	553	429	470	390	231	294	278	626	867	871
Canada, total	1,737	1,852	2,269	1,034	865	991	93	121	216	60	204	166	160	174	173	390	488	502
Mining and smelting	447	390	329	290	165	193	58	51	19	-16	40	6	25	48	15	84	86	95
Petroleum	549	535	533	360	315	325	5	10	5	25	42	30	60	46	25	99	122	148
Manufacturing	741	927	1,187	384	385	473	30	60	192	45	122	130	75	80	133	207	280	259
Latin America, total	1,714	1,781	1,794	625	643	695	124	37	85	256	223	100	25	144	184	684	734	739
Mining and smelting	332	291	329	78	87	95	22	-18	5	31	-17	25	-50	25	34	251	214	170
Petroleum	730	915	854	340	306	319	-21	-5	-15	105	-110	10	-50	70	65	359	434	475
Manufacturing	652	575	611	207	250	281	126	60	95	120	130	65	125	49	85	74	86	85
Europe, total	2,001	2,578	2,426	955	1,286	1,147	453	324	244	220	264	212	10	211	68	361	463	455
Mining and smelting	11	8	8	2	1	4	(*)	(*)	-3	-1	1	-1	-1	-2	9	9	5
Petroleum	493	770	727	345	438	494	20	75	44	3	95	71	20	82	50	87	80	68
Manufacturing	1,497	1,800	1,691	608	847	919	424	249	200	220	170	140	-20	160	20	265	374	382
Other areas, total	1,793	2,006	2,269	616	750	820	123	9	99	94	89	221	135	220	59	825	938	1,070
Mining and smelting	225	124	156	56	59	79	16	-6	17	19	-4	13	65	15	-3	69	69	50
Petroleum	1,158	1,476	1,561	422	475	495	10	5	16	31	45	153	19	200	22	676	751	875
Manufacturing	410	406	552	138	216	246	97	10	66	44	48	55	51	5	40	80	117	145

*Less than $500,000.   r Revised.   [1] Includes miscellaneous sources.   [2] Includes other Western Hemisphere.
[3] Includes miscellaneous uses.

NOTE.—Detail may not add to totals because of rounding.

of all their financing in 1962, compared with about 53 percent of a smaller total in 1961. Depreciation charges increased by only a minor amount in 1962, mainly in the manufacturing sector. In the extractive enterprises there may have been a reduction in accelerated depreciation rates stemming from the Korean and Suez emergencies.

Retained earnings turned up sharply in all industries in 1962, accounting for about 19 percent of the funds used rather than the unusually small 14 percent reported in 1961. The increase in earnings retained abroad was about $0.3 billion, out of a $450 million increase in earnings. The ratio of earnings retained abroad to total earnings rose to about 28 percent.

Sales from Foreign Plants

Production in foreign plants operated as direct investments of U.S. companies rose by $2½ billion, or 10 percent, in 1962. This was the largest increase since the sharp expansion in 1960, and brought the total sales of these plants to $28.1 billion.

Sales in Europe accounted for $1.1 billion of the rise, with the increase spread rather evenly over a number of lines of manufacturing. For the individual countries, shown in table 7, strong advances were reported in Germany, France, Italy and the United Kingdom, with the overall rate of increase of about 10 percent exceeding the 6 percent rate of increase for European manufacturing production as a whole (including petroleum refining).

For Canada the companies reported a marked upturn in sales after a relatively slow rate of growth in the 1959–61 period, reflecting a broad expansion of the Canadian economy. Gains were largest in the automotive products group.

Sales in Latin America showed continued steady growth, with chemical production up by a considerable amount. Substantially expanded sales were reported for Brazil and Mexico; but sales in Argentina lagged reflecting generally depressed conditions in that country.

Most of the increase in manufacturing sales in the rest of the world was concentrated in Australia, with smaller increases in Japan and the Republic of South Africa.

Comparisons of the sales data with the figures for net income show a slight improvement in the overall income/sales ratio to 5.44 percent in 1962 from 5.28 percent in 1961. The gain was primarily in Canadian operations; in Europe the ratio dropped sharply to 4.83 percent from 5.75 percent; rising costs were a significant factor in the European economy in 1962.

Destination of sales

Over 80 percent of the output from the foreign manufacturing plants in 1962 was sold in the domestic markets of the countries where the plants were located. The breakdown in table 8 shows that out of total foreign sales of $28.1 billion, about $1.4 billion came to the United States and $3.2 billion were exported from the producing countries to other foreign countries.

Most of the sales to the United States originate in Canada, and consist primarily of such traditional items as food products, paper and other wood products, chemicals and metals. Imports from the European plants amounted to $175 million, mainly chemicals and non-electrical machinery. For Latin America and other countries food products were the only sizable manufactured export to the United States.

These figures are comparable to those collected by a complete survey covering 1957, and show that in the 6-year period the increase in exports from U.S.-controlled plants abroad to the United States was only about $250 million, and this was almost entirely for Canada. However, there was an increase of about $1.5 billion in export sales among foreign countries, of which $1.1 billion was reported for European countries and about $0.3 billion for Latin America, mainly in foodstuffs. This indicates that the main impact on U.S. trade is on export trade rather than in the U.S. domestic market.

Exports and foreign production

For the group of major manufactured items included in table 9, sales from foreign plants of U.S. companies continued to grow considerably faster than exports from the United States in 1962. Since 1957, the value of foreign production has risen by over $7 billion, while exports increased by a little over $1 billion.

Table 6.—Sales by Direct Foreign Investments, Principal Commodities by Areas, 1957 and 1959–62

[Millions of dollars]

Areas and Years	Manufacturing, total	Food products	Paper and allied products	Chemicals	Rubber products	Primary and fabricated metals	Machinery excluding electrical	Electrical machinery	Transportation equipment	Other products
All areas, total:										
1957	18,331	2,457	881	2,411	968	1,518	1,903	2,017	4,228	1,889
1959	21,100	2,810	1,170	2,250	1,010	1,590	2,200	2,100	5,140	2,100
1960	23,570	2,920	1,260	3,290	1,170	1,680	2,490	2,280	6,170	2,310
1961	25,580	3,270	1,310	3,975	1,215	1,875	2,735	2,470	6,000	2,730
1962	28,120	3,385	1,420	4,400	1,365	2,025	3,015	2,835	6,665	3,010
Canada:										
1957	7,897	928	769	897	272	927	695	1,080	1,488	842
1959	8,670	1,060	1,030	1,070	290	950	760	1,050	1,600	880
1960	8,920	1,020	1,100	1,150	310	920	780	1,040	1,650	950
1961	8,920	1,095	1,115	1,300	295	910	760	1,000	1,450	965
1962	9,610	1,115	1,160	1,245	369	1,065	790	1,115	1,730	1,030
Latin America:[1]										
1957	2,435	608	55	499	239	111	66	190	375	292
1959	2,830	710	60	550	260	100	80	190	470	310
1960	3,180	750	70	620	280	100	100	210	470	310
1961	3,770	780	85	820	300	160	115	300	710	440
1962	4,190	820	120	1,000	300	180	100	375	770	520
Europe:										
1957	6,313	734	34	822	262	435	1,000	678	1,700	639
1959	7,690	760	50	1,650	290	470	1,210	770	2,350	740
1960	9,310	900	60	1,210	360	590	1,420	890	2,970	880
1961	10,670	1,120	70	1,510	400	690	1,635	1,050	3,070	1,125
1962	11,780	1,185	80	1,760	460	715	1,850	1,220	3,280	1,230
Other areas:										
1957	1,685	188	23	193	195	75	133	99	665	116
1959	1,910	250	30	240	200	70	150	110	720	140
1960	2,160	250	30	280	220	70	190	110	840	170
1961	2,220	275	40	315	220	85	225	120	710	200
1962	2,540	265	60	395	245	85	265	125	870	230

[1] Includes other Western Hemisphere.

Source: U.S. Department of Commerce, Office of Business Economics.

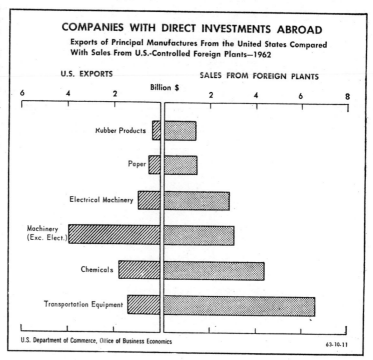

COMPANIES WITH DIRECT INVESTMENTS ABROAD

Exports of Principal Manufactures From the United States Compared With Sales From U.S.-Controlled Foreign Plants—1962

U.S. EXPORTS   SALES FROM FOREIGN PLANTS

Billion $

Rubber Products
Paper
Electrical Machinery
Machinery (Exc. Elect.)
Chemicals
Transportation Equipment

U.S. Department of Commerce, Office of Business Economics   63-10-11

During 1962, foreign production grew four times as much as exports, with only non-electrical machinery showing greater gains in exports than production abroad. The greatest contrast in sales patterns was in chemicals and transportation equipment, both of which were produced in much greater volume in foreign plants in 1962, but showed only minor export increases.

Of course, production in foreign plants requires a considerable exportation from the United States of materials and parts, as well as capital equipment. Data for these related exports will be available from a recently initiated annual survey, making it possible to evaluate more accurately the changes in trading patterns connected with the establishment of foreign producing units.

Table 7.—Sales by Direct Investment Manufacturing Enterprises Abroad by Selected Countries and Years

[Millions of dollars]

Area and country	1957	1959	1960	1961	1962
All areas, total	18,331	21,100	23,570	25,580	28,120
Canada	7,897	8,670	8,920	8,920	9,610
Latin America, total	2,435	2,830	3,180	3,770	4,190
Argentina	385	426	696	805	865
Brazil	659	764	879	940	1,125
Mexico	643	754	770	850	1,020
Venezuela	268	364	360	390	400
Other countries	480	525	475	695	780
Europe, total	6,313	7,690	9,310	10,670	11,780
Belgium, Netherlands and Luxembourg	416	461	602	740	800
France	763	789	965	1,195	1,440
Germany	1,116	1,572	1,835	2,265	2,690
Italy	230	244	350	475	575
United Kingdom	3,303	4,050	4,715	5,070	5,265
Other countries	485	574	843	925	1,100
Other areas, total	1,685	1,910	2,160	2,220	2,540
Australia	787	933	985	1,045	1,290
Japan	217	240	290	380	440
Philippine Republic	118	141	140	160	165
Republic of South Africa	300	292	305	235	365
Other countries	263	304	340	300	280

Table 8.—Local Sales and Exports by Direct Investment Manufacturing Enterprises Abroad, Principal Commodities by Areas, 1962

[Millions of dollars]

Areas and industry	Total sales	Local sales	Exported to U.S.	Exported to other countries
All areas, total	28,120	23,550	1,350	3,226
Food products	3,385	2,870	105	110
Paper and allied products	1,420	715	580	125
Chemicals	4,400	3,795	160	445
Rubber products	1,365	1,270	10	85
Primary and fabricated metals	2,025	1,755	125	145
Machinery, excluding electrical	3,015	2,385	100	536
Electrical machinery	2,835	2,545	15	275
Transportation equipment	6,665	5,715	85	865
Other products	3,010	2,500	170	340
Canada, total	9,610	8,095	1,080	435
Food products	1,115	1,035	30	50
Paper and allied products	1,160	480	580	100
Chemicals	1,245	1,115	100	30
Rubber products	360	350	5	5
Primary and fabricated metals	1,065	905	120	40
Machinery, excluding electrical	790	680	50	60
Electrical machinery	1,085	1,085	5	25
Transportation equipment	1,730	1,630	45	55
Other products	1,030	815	145	70
Latin America, total [1]	4,190	3,795	40	355
Food products	820	545	25	250
Paper and allied products	120	110		10
Chemicals	1,000	940	10	50
Rubber products	300	295		5
Primary and fabricated metals	160	155		5
Machinery, excluding electrical	110	105		5
Electrical machinery	375	355		20
Transportation equipment	785	786		
Other products	520	505	5	10
Europe, total	11,780	9,295	175	2,310
Food products	1,185	1,130	5	50
Paper and allied products	80	70		10
Chemicals	1,760	1,360	50	350
Rubber products	460	385	5	70
Primary and fabricated metals	715	610	5	100
Machinery, excluding electrical	1,850	1,340	50	460
Electrical machinery	1,220	990	10	220
Transportation equipment	3,280	2,440	40	800
Other products	1,230	970	10	250
Other areas, total	2,540	2,365	55	120
Food products	265	160	45	60
Paper and allied products	60	55		5
Chemicals	395	380		15
Rubber products	245	240		5
Primary and fabricated metals	85	85		
Machinery, excluding electrical	265	260		5
Electrical machinery	125	115		10
Transportation equipment	870	860		10
Other products	230	210	10	10

[1] Includes other Western Hemisphere.

Table 9.—Exports from the United States and Sales by Direct Investment Enterprises Abroad of Selected Manufactures, by Area, 1957, 1961–62

[Millions of dollars]

Commodities	All areas, total			Canada			Latin America [1]			Europe			Other Areas		
	1957	1961	1962	1957	1961	1962	1957	1961	1962	1957	1961	1962	1957	1961	1962
Selected manufactures:															
Foreign sales	12,438	17,705	19,700	5,201	5,920	6,400	1,424	2,390	2,690	4,505	7,735	8,650	1,308	1,660	1,960
U.S. exports	7,536	8,235	8,781	1,869	1,769	1,977	2,633	2,123	2,109	1,326	2,285	2,439	1,709	2,058	2,256
Paper and allied products:															
Foreign sales	881	1,310	1,420	769	1,115	1,160	55	85	93	23	40	60			
U.S. exports	324	453	457	65	78	76	97	90	93	91	179	173	71	106	115
Chemicals:															
Foreign sales	2,411	3,975	4,400	897	1,300	1,245	499	820	1,000	822	1,510	1,760	193	345	395
U.S. exports	1,376	1,709	1,771	246	285	287	457	379	419	353	574	600	320	471	465
Rubber products:															
Foreign sales	968	1,215	1,365	272	295	360	239	300	300	262	400	460	195	220	245
U.S. exports	300	330	332	43	48	54	62	63	65	97	121	119	98	98	94
Machinery, except electrical:															
Foreign sales	1,903	2,735	3,015	695	760	790	66	115	110	1,009	1,635	1,850	133	225	265
U.S. exports	3,160	3,595	3,927	876	766	847	1,007	859	844	567	1,047	1,145	710	923	1,091
Electrical machinery:															
Foreign sales	2,047	2,470	2,835	1,080	1,000	1,115	190	300	375	678	1,050	1,220	99	120	125
U.S. exports	810	867	916	246	223	250	291	264	225	114	212	253	160	168	188
Transportation equipment:															
Foreign sales	4,228	6,000	6,665	1,488	1,450	1,730	375	770	785	1,700	3,070	3,280	665	710	870
U.S. exports [2]	1,566	1,281	1,378	393	369	463	719	468	463	104	152	149	350	292	303

[1] Includes other Western Hemisphere.   [2] Excludes civilian aircraft.

NOTE.—Detail may not add to totals because of rounding.

U.S. FIRMS ACCELERATE CAPITAL EXPENDITURES ABROAD

Fred[erick] Cutler
and
Samuel Pizer

by FRED CUTLER and SAMUEL PIZER

U.S. Firms Accelerate Capital Expenditures Abroad

A notable expansion in foreign invest-ment by U.S. firms is now underway, and a sustained high level is indicated for 1965, according to the latest OBE survey of foreign investment plans.[1] For 1964, companies have projected expenditures of $5.9 billion on plant and equipment abroad—a 16-percent gain over 1963 and more than in any year since these surveys began in 1957. For 1963, these expenditures are now reported at $5.1 billion, slightly higher than was anticipated in the reports submitted last year.

The projections made for the period two years ahead have usually been quite low for manufacturing operations. Although the 1965 level as reported is somewhat below the 1964 amount, an upward correction of the size indicated for 1963–64 (see chart on page 6) would more than offset the apparent decline. For other major industries there is not so clear cut a tendency in the 2-year ahead projections, but in any case the reports indicate a strong rate of investment in 1965.

This heightened investment activity in manufacturing came as sales of foreign manufacturing affiliates are also scoring significant gains. Total sales for 1963 reached $31.3 billion, a 13-percent increase over 1962 and the most rapid upswing yet reported.[2] Higher sales were experienced in all product lines and nearly all foreign areas; the greatest gains were in the trans-portation equipment industry (largely automobiles) and in European opera-tions. Virtually none of the increase in sales of the foreign affiliates repre-sented higher exports back to the United States.

Another significant feature of the foreign operations of U.S. companies in 1963 was the sharp rise in the funds used.[3] The increase of $1.6 billion, about 28 percent, came from a $0.6-billion gain in internal cash flows (re-tained earnings and depreciation), a major increase of $0.6 billion in ex-ternal financing from foreign sources, and a rise of $0.4 billion in funds from U.S. sources. Increased plant and equipment expenditures in 1963 for the three major industries absorbed $0.4 billion of the increased flow of funds, but the major part of the in-crease was used to finance working capital and the acquisition of other assets.

If, in addition to the projected sharp increase in fixed investment, the flow of working capital required by the foreign affiliates should rise further in 1964, a severe strain on their financial re-sources would result. With tighter monetary policies in many foreign countries limiting the availability of external financing abroad, which was so large a factor in 1963, an enlarged flow of funds from the United States is indicated. Data available on direct investment capital outflows for the first half of 1964, however, do not yet show any significant change in the rate compared to 1963.

Plant and Equipment Expenditures

American industry is now engaged in raising both domestic and foreign capi-tal expenditures by very large amounts. For all industries the 16-percent in-crease in foreign outlays projected for 1964 may be compared with an ex-pected domestic increase of 13 percent. For manufacturing operations alone (excluding petroleum refining) there is a marked difference in investment

[1] For a description of the survey and its coverage see the methodology note at the end of the article.

[2] A small part of the increase in sales represented the inclusion of 1963 figures and the exclusion of 1962 data of previously existing foreign firms acquired by U.S. companies.

[3] Data for sources and uses of funds are tabulated only for the manufacturing, petroleum and mining industries, which are the major sectors for U.S. foreign investments.

Capital Expenditures Abroad by U.S. Manufacturing Companies

Major advances indicated for developed countries, notably Canada

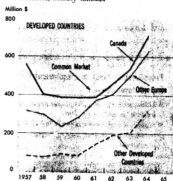

Moderate increases for less developed areas

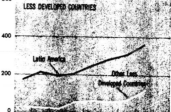

Transport equipment and chemicals lead upturn

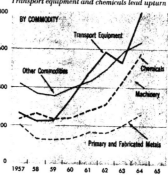

U.S. Department of Commerce, Office of Business Economics   64-10-4

5

rates: foreign expenditures are scheduled to rise 26 percent while domestic plant and equipment expenditures are expected to advance 16 percent this year.

Strong rise in Europe

A further substantial step-up in European investment of U.S. firms is already evident in 1964, continuing the path of rapid expansion begun in the late 1950's. Not only are expenditures of affiliates for new plant and equipment greater, but in the past few years large sums have also been spent to acquire

Projections of Plant and Equipment Expenditures Abroad

- *Manufacturing affiliates project major increase in outlays for 1964*
- *Sustained high level suggested for 1965, based on past performance of 2-year projections*

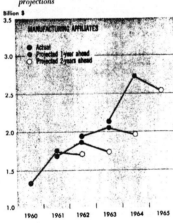

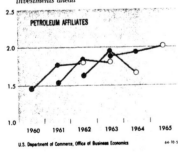

Petroleum projections also show strong investments ahead

U.S. Department of Commerce, Office of Business Economics   64-10-5

stock in existing enterprises. The latter type of investment appears immediately as a capital outflow in the balance of payments accounts, and the capital outlays of the newly-acquired firms subsequently become part of the series on plant and equipment expenditures of foreign affiliates.

While many factors affect the individual investment decisions of the firms, the principal considerations influencing the European expansion are probably the expectation of a strong rate of economic growth—without too much concern with temporary setbacks in one country or another—and great financial strength of both the parent companies and many of the European affiliates themselves.

Most of the increase in capital expenditures in Europe in 1964 is scheduled for manufacturing operations, especially for motor vehicles, machinery, and chemicals. Petroleum companies had raised their European investments to a peak rate in 1963, constructing the refineries and distribution facilities needed for rapidly expanding demand and also developing some local gas and oil resources. A similar pace is being maintained in 1964, though there is considerable shifting among countries, and no significant change from this relatively high level is indicated for 1965. However, a new development as yet reflected only to a minor extent in these figures is the exploration and development of oil reserves that may be found under the North Sea. This search will be very active in 1965, and will cause sizable increases in either plant and equipment expenditures or charges against earnings for the costs of exploration. Affiliates in the trade and distribution industries are also making substantial capital expenditures in Europe, and they have scheduled substantially higher rates of investment in 1964 and 1965.

Among the countries of Europe, the United Kingdom is slated for the largest rise in 1964 capital expenditures, led by expansions in motor vehicles and chemicals; outlays are expected to continue high in 1965. Germany is receiving most of the increase in manufacturing investment in the Common Market, but German petroleum investment is less than in the past few years.

Canadian outlays high

This year U.S. firms expect capital outlays for manufacturing in Canada to reach $710 million, a striking upward revision from last year's projection of $434 million for 1964. The new estimate would represent a one-third gain over 1963 outlays. The revision of plans cut across several major industries and was much greater than in prior years; it suggests stronger expectations of continued growth in the Canadian economy and in foreign markets for some of these manufactures. Recent actions of the Canadian government rescinding proposed tax increases and providing credit against certain import duties when exports of automotive components are increased, may also have induced some investments. This is also indicated by the high projection of relatively high investment in the transportation equipment industry for 1965.

Petroleum and mining investments are also important in Canada. The projections for the former show a small dip in 1964 and a recovery in 1965 to a substantial level, though not so high as was experienced when new fields were being opened up in the 1950's. Some new mineral deposits are now under development in Canada, and capital expenditures in the mining industry are likely to be well sustained.

Rising outlays in other developed countries

In each of the other major developed countries—Australia, Japan, and the Union of South Africa—there is considerably heightened investment activity by U.S. companies in 1964 and a similar scale of activity has been projected for 1965. Manufacturing investments in Australia are at a record rate, owing largely to the expansion of the auto industry, and to the increase in manufacturing facilities of aluminum producers. The automobile industry is also responsible for much of the recent investment advance in South Africa.

Outlays by petroleum companies for refinery construction are high and rising in Japan; in Australia also the industry is spending considerable amounts, including some to develop reserves. Mining investments in the

Union of South Africa and Australia are fairly sizable and are showing moderate increases.

Scattered gains in less-developed countries

Capital expenditures by U.S. companies in the less-developed countries of the world are projected to move somewhat higher in 1964, but their share of the total would remain at nearly 30 percent. Sizable gains, are limited to relatively few countries.

In the Latin American Republics, manufacturing investments are up considerably, centered on a record expansion in Mexico with small improvements in most other countries. Larger automotive investments were induced by measures in Mexico and other countries to restrict imports, and investments in chemicals were also raised considerably. Reductions now projected for 1965 may be moderated, given a greater degree of political stability in the larger countries of the area. Petroleum investments

appear to have stabilized in the range of $250–300 million annually. It also appears that mining investments will be held at their current relatively low levels, unless there is a significant change in policy in some countries.

Other areas in the Western Hemisphere, primarily dependencies or former dependencies of European countries, have been attracting substantial investments in recent years. Mining in Surinam and Jamaica, petroleum in Trinidad, and manufacturing in Trinidad and the Bahamas, all involve large capital outlays by U.S. firms.

For the less-developed countries of Africa, by far the most important investment by U.S. companies is in the petroleum industry in North Africa, mainly in Libya. Petroleum investments also predominate among U.S. investments in the less-developed countries of Asia. In the Middle East there has been a steady though moderate increase in capital outlays for some time, for the extension and development of existing and new fields and the rising level of output needed to meet world demand. A sizable volume of investment in Far Eastern countries, especially India and the Philippine Republic, has been required to construct oil refineries and distribution facilities.

There are a few instances of gains in manufacturing investments in these less-developed areas; they include the construction of aluminum producing facilities in West Africa, and somewhat higher capital expenditures in India and the Philippine Republic.

Exploration and development expenditures

An important part of investment activity for the extractive industries is accounted for by charges against earnings. In 1963 these charges were

$480 million, about $70 million more than was spent in 1962. Most of the expenditures were by petroleum companies, who carried out substantial development programs in Canada and Latin America, and who raised their expenditures in Europe, Africa and the Middle East. Details are shown in the preceding table.

Foreign Plants Raise Output

Reflecting the rapid buildup of production facilities, and the acquisition of some existing companies, sales of the foreign manufacturing affiliates of U.S. firms grew vigorously in 1963, advancing 13 percent to a total of $31.3 billion. The absolute increase over 1962 was a record $3.6 billion, of which $1.3 billion

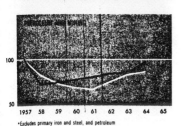

Capital Expenditures by U.S. Companies Here and Abroad

1957 = 100

* Excludes primary iron and steel, and petroleum

U.S. Department of Commerce, Office of Business Economics　64-10-6

Exploration and Development Expenditures Charged Against Incomes, 1962 and 1963

(Millions of dollars)

	Total		Petroleum		Mining	
	1962	1963	1962	1963	1962	1963
All areas	411	483	371	451	40	32
Canada	157	172	127	150	30	22
Latin America	93	100	87	94	6	6
Europe	20	28	20	28	(*)	(*)
Other areas	141	183	137	179	4	4

*Less than $500,000.

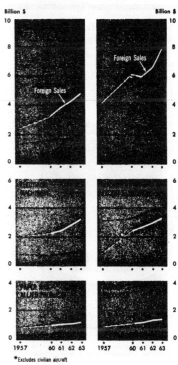

Exports and Foreign Sales

For most major manufactures, sales by foreign plants are larger and faster growing than exports from the U.S.

Billion $

*Excludes civilian aircraft

U.S. Department of Commerce, Office of Business Economics　64-10-7

was accounted for by the fast-growing transportation equipment industry. Sales of each of the other manufacturing industries also rose substantially in 1963.

Half of the sales increase in 1963 was registered by European plants, led by a 25 percent jump in sales of automobiles and parts and sizable gains in chemicals and electrical machinery. The rate of increase in manufacturing sales accelerated in most of the European countries, and was outstanding in Italy, France and Germany. The largest absolute gains were nearly $500 million for Germany and $700 million for the United Kingdom. In all cases, the sales of U.S. affiliates increased very much faster than overall industrial production, which also registered strong gains in most countries of the area.

Sales of Canadian plants also turned up sharply, sharing in the rise in Canadian industrial production, and exceeded $10 billion in 1963. Here, as in other areas, a considerable part of

Sources and Uses of Funds of Foreign Affiliates of U.S. Companies

U.S. funds a minor factor as financing rises sharply

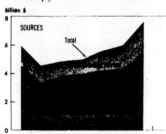

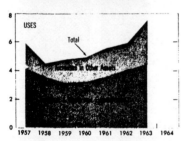

Note: Includes only foreign affiliates in the mining, petroleum, and manufacturing industries. Total sources and uses are after deducting income paid out.

U.S. Department of Commerce, Office of Business Economics　　　64-10-8

the sales gain was in the transportation equipment industry.

Among the other developed countries the largest increases were in Australia and Japan, reflecting the intensive investment activity of recent years.

In the less-developed countries, there was comparatively little expansion of output by U.S. manufacturing plants. In Latin America the increase was about 7 percent, mainly in food products and chemicals, and in some categories sales were lower. Mexico and Venezuela showed substantial improvement. and Argentina recovered from the dip in 1962. Only minimal increases in the dollar value of sales occurred in Brazil. but the change in volume of sales is not clear because of the very sharp change in exchange rates and general price indexes.

Since 1957 the rate of increase in sales of manufacturing affiliates has been about the same in less-developed countries as in the industrialized countries—about 70 percent. In dollar terms they have accounted for only about $2 billion of the $13-billion rise in sales over the period. Moreover, three-fourths of the sales gain in the less-developed countries has been in a few larger countries in Latin America.

Participation in foreign trade

Most sales of manufactures by foreign affiliates—82 percent—are made in the same countries in which the plants are located. Of the $5.5 billion exported in 1963, $1 billion came to the United States and $4.5 billion was exported to third countries abroad. Export sales by these firms now account for approximately 10 percent of all exports of manufactured goods by countries other than the United States. For some goods, including chemicals, paper and related products, food items, and rubber products, the proportion is somewhat higher than this, and for transportation equipment the foreign affiliates account for about 15 percent of all foreign exports.

Exports to the United States did not rise materially in 1963 (table 7), and are not much different from the 1957 amounts. Imports from Canada now account for 75 percent of the sales into the U.S. market; imports from Europe remain small and consist mainly of non-

electrical machinery and automobiles, and only food products and chemicals enter in sizable amounts from other areas.

Exports lag behind foreign production

Continuing the pattern of recent years, sales from foreign plants grew faster than exports from the United States in 1963 for major categories of manufactures. For the products shown in table 8. sales of foreign affiliates increased 14 percent while U.S. exports rose about 6 percent. For some items, especially chemicals and electrical machinery, exports performed well in 1963 compared to the experience since 1957, but did not match the growth of foreign sales in U.S.-owned plants abroad.

The disparity in growth rates is notable in Latin America, where U.S. exports of these manufactures declined during the 1957–63 period while local sales by affiliates rose. In Europe, both U.S. exports and sales of U.S. affiliates have been gaining as these countries have expanded their economies, but sales by affiliates have increased much faster. In the rest of the world the growth paths of exports and foreign sales since 1957 have shown similar upward trends.

Sales of mining affiliates

In contrast to the rapid increase in sales of manufacturing affiliates abroad from 1957 to 1963, the sales of mining affiliates have advanced only 20 percent. Since the prices of the major metals produced—copper, lead, zinc, iron ore, and bauxite—declined by approximately 10 percent in the period, the

Sales of Mining Affiliates Abroad, Total and Exports, 1957 and 1963

(Millions of dollars)

	Total sales		Exported to U.S.		Exported to other countries	
	1957	1963	1957	1963	1957	1963
All areas, total	2,032	2,402	898	962	809	1,008
Canada	740	1,000	400	465	216	300
Latin America, total. Mexico, Central America and West Indies [1]	920	963	403	452	413	389
	223	223	112	123	20	20
South America	586	620	228	227	321	352
Other Western Hemisphere	111	120	63	102	48	17
Europe	70	50	4	2	48	38
Africa	238	285	77	37	112	244
Asia and Oceania	65	104	14	6	20	37

[1] West Indies includes Cuba, Haiti and Dominican Republic in 1957, but excludes Cuba in 1963.

gain of output in physical quantities was roughly one-third.

Most of the increase in mining sales has been in Canada, accounted for largely by new iron ore producers. In Africa there have been increases in iron ore, and in Latin America sales of the copper-lead-zinc group, and of bauxite, have risen. With new production facilities being installed abroad by U.S. companies, and an upward movement of prices since 1963, sales of these affiliates should move ahead at a somewhat faster pace.

Sources and Uses of Funds

Last year foreign affiliates of U.S. companies raised their use of funds by over $1.6 billion, far more than in any other year since. 1957, as they utilized nearly $7.6 billion of financing. These figures cover firms in the mining, petroleum and manufacturing industries, and are after deducting $2.8 billion of income distributions. Manufacturing affiliates stepped up their financing to record amounts and petroleum affiliates approached their 1957 peak.

Of the $1.6 billion increase in funds utilized, $.4 billion came from retained earnings, $.2 billion from depreciation charges, nearly $.4 billion from U.S. sources, including both parent companies and others, and over $.6 billion from external sources abroad.

Manufacturing affiliates in Canada and Europe accounted for the rise in retained earnings, as their incomes rose substantially while dividends were reduced. Petroleum affiliates were responsible for the rise in U.S.-source financing; some of these funds were needed to finance larger outlays connected with acquisitions of existing firms in Canada and reductions of tax and other liabilities of Latin American affiliates.

Intensified use of foreign-source external financing was a major factor in the financing of manufacturing and petroleum affiliates in 1963. In both cases the external financing occurred primarily in Europe.

The increase in foreign-source funds used in 1963 consisted very largely of higher liabilities in the form of accounts payable, tax and other accrued liabil-

744-465 O—64——2

Table 1.—Plant and Equipment Expenditures of Direct Foreign Investments, Major Industries, 1957–65

(Millions of dollars)

Area and industry	1957	1958	1959	1960	1961	1962 [r]	1963	1964 [e]	1965 [e]
All areas, total	4,819	4,097	3,705	3,789	4,122	4,618	5,058	5,864	5,687
Mining and smelting	421	420	437	426	312	438	398	431	416
Petroleum	2,322	1,854	1,558	1,467	1,534	1,628	1,889	1,940	2,005
Manufacturing	1,347	1,180	1,147	1,337	1,697	1,941	2,153	2,730	2,533
Trade	186	191	198	256	307	354	354	446	456
Other industries	543	452	365	303	272	257	264	317	277
Canada, total	1,593	1,311	1,179	1,259	1,016	1,163	1,279	1,457	1,407
Mining and smelting	163	172	240	290	165	245	195	224	202
Petroleum	584	510	380	360	315	300	375	300	360
Manufacturing	561	404	389	384	385	458	535	710	657
Trade	47	55	45	60	39	55	71	78	70
Other industries	238	170	125	165	112	105	103	145	118
Latin America, total ¹	1,687	1,269	1,003	750	795	860	870	870	860
Mining and smelting	216	221	147	78	87	95	109	120	124
Petroleum	1,039	577	449	340	306	339	307	321	313
Manufacturing	174	202	193	207	250	281	305	360	266
Trade	20	31	31	35	45	46	46	60	58
Other industries	238	238	183	90	107	99	103	118	99
Europe, total	899	976	906	1,092	1,474	1,674	1,895	2,102	2,045
Mining and smelting	2		2	2	1	4	5	4	4
Petroleum	275	422	339	345	438	494	642	628	576
Manufacturing	497	460	450	608	847	953	1,034	1,214	1,188
Trade	107	87	101	125	175	200	183	229	248
Other industries	18	7	14	12	13	23	31	27	29
Other areas, total	640	541	617	688	837	921	1,014	1,326	1,375
Mining and smelting	40	27	48	56	59	94	89	83	86
Petroleum	424	345	390	422	475	495	565	691	756
Manufacturing	115	114	115	138	216	249	279	446	422
Trade	12	18	21	36	48	53	54	79	80
Other industries	49	37	43	36	40	30	27	27	31

[r] Revised.   [e] Estimated on the basis of company projections.   ¹ Includes "other Western Hemisphere."

NOTE.—Detail may not add to totals because of rounding in this and the following tables.

Table 2.—Plant and Equipment Expenditures Abroad by U.S. Manufacturing Companies, by Area and Major Commodity, 1960–65

(Millions of dollars)

Areas and Years	Total	Food products	Paper and allied products	Chemicals	Rubber products	Primary and fabricated metals	Machinery excluding electrical	Electrical machinery	Transportation equipment	Other manufacturing
All areas, total:										
1960	1,337	97	78	237	68	133	132	104	336	152
1961	1,697	116	71	278	91	169	205	141	473	153
1962 [r]	1,941	126	95	308	91	162	214	177	585	183
1963	2,153	132	134	436	98	204	232	164	530	223
1964 [e]	2,730	154	142	571	102	262	282	188	790	239
1965 [e]	2,533	127	132	440	94	224	298	167	809	242
Canada:										
1960	384	30	55	75	15	49	17	30	63	50
1961	385	20	54	55	18	55	40	31	60	52
1962 [r]	458	28	75	75	19	57	38	30	65	51
1963	535	30	100	110	16	60	39	40	94	46
1964 [e]	710	26	103	102	22	100	47	49	145	56
1965 [e]	657	23	90	130	20	50	60	43	193	48
Latin America: ¹										
1960	207	24	7	49	12	11	8	18	47	31
1961	250	37	5	48	19	23	9	27	52	30
1962 [r]	281	35	6	52	12	20	10	25	81	40
1963	305	32	9	94	17	16	16	19	50	52
1964 [e]	360	32	13	111	19	15	20	27	92	31
1965 [e]	266	19	11	70	17	13	18	20	69	29
Europe:										
Common Market:										
1960	328	17	2	44	11	10	72	21	128	23
1961	475	30	3	63	11	19	105	36	181	27
1962 [r]	548	30	4	54	26	25	85	44	245	35
1963	534	29	7	82	26	45	100	39	155	51
1964 [e]	584	32	5	83	22	41	104	37	214	46
1965 [e]	592	33	6	70	20	34	128	40	217	44
Other Europe:										
1960	280	18	3	42	.5	50	24	18	74	35
1961	372	17	4	49	15	46	38	30	141	31
1962 [r]	405	21	6	51	12	45	65	41	123	41
1963	500	24	10	71	18	46	60	51	166	54
1964 [e]	630	42	6	97	12	14	92	50	201	86
1965 [e]	596	27	6	66	12	15	74	42	220	104
Other areas:										
1960	138	8	12	28	16	13	10	16	23	12
1961	216	12	5	63	28	26	13	17	39	13
1962 [r]	249	12	4	76	22	15	16	17	71	16
1963	279	17	8	79	21	37	17	15	65	20
1964 [e]	446	22	15	118	27	62	19	25	138	20
1965 [e]	422	25	19	104	25	82	18	22	110	17

[r] Revised.   [e] Estimated on the basis of company projections.   ¹ Includes "other Western Hemisphere."

ities, and possibly some long-term borrowing. There was some increase in the use of foreign financial institutions, which provided about $400 million in 1963, but the sale of equity securities to foreign investors was down a little at $334 million.

Financing of Affiliates from External Sources Abroad

(Millions of dollars)

	Total	Mining and smelting	Petroleum	Manufacturing
Total:				
1962	1,521	107	506	908
1963	2,146	102	777	1,267
Borrowing from financial institutions:				
1962	307	12	144	151
1963	404	12	212	180
Funds from foreign affiliates:				
1962	25	18	14	−7
1963	18	18	−90	90
Other increases in foreign liabilities:				
1962	696	4	218	474
1963	1,294	62	389	843
Issues of equity securities:				
1962	353	65	51	237
1963	334	10	149	175
Other foreign sources:				
1962	140	8	79	53
1963	96	(*)	117	−21

*Less than $500,000.

Uses of funds

While plant and equipment expenditures in 1963 continued to absorb the major portion of available funds—$4.4 billion out of total resources (less income distributions) of $7.6 billion—funds required to add to inventories, receivables and other assets jumped to a record $3.1 billion. Thus, out of the total increase of $1.6 billion in financing in 1963, fixed investments used $.4 billion and additions to current and other assets used $1.2 billion.

Inventories of manufacturing affiliates expanded considerably in 1963, but the increase was less in relation to the sales gain than in recent years. Petroleum inventories increased very little. Receivables were considerably increased relative to sales, however, by manufacturing affiliates operating in Canada and Europe, and receivables of petroleum companies increased by smaller but still substantial amounts in Europe and Asia.

Much of the upsurge in financing requirements in 1963 resulted from the addition of $1.2 billion to "other" assets of the foreign affiliates. The nature of these assets is not identified in the reports supplied by the companies; they range from investments in the stock of existing companies—or their outright acquisition—to accumulations of liquid assets in the form of deposits or government obligations. Investments in other enterprises were sizable for the petroleum industry in Canada.

Methodological Note

Basic data used in this article are supplied by a sample of 450 U.S. firms reporting on Form BE-133, Sources and Uses of Funds of U.S. Direct Investments Abroad. The reports are completed by most firms in the early summer months of the current year, giving data on sources and uses of funds, and sales of each foreign affiliate for the preceding calendar year, and providing projections of plant and equipment expenditures for the current year (referred to as the 1-year ahead projection) and for the following year. Thus, reports filed by mid-year 1964 gave an actual plant and equipment figure for 1963, together with projections for 1964 and 1965.

The benchmark data for all of the series are provided in the comprehensive survey covering 1957, published in *U.S. Business Investments in Foreign Countries* in 1960. The sample has been gradually expanded over the years; the coverage and blow-up procedures for each major series are as follows:

Plant and equipment expenditures

Reported and expanded estimates of plant and equipment expenditures for 1963 are as follows:

(In millions of dollars)

	Reported data	Estimated total	Percent reported
All industries	3,817	5,058	75
Mining and smelting	306	398	77
Petroleum	1,642	1,889	87
Manufacturing	1,491	2,153	69
Trade	242	354	68
Other industries	136	264	52

Table 3.—Plant and Equipment Expenditures of Direct Foreign Investments, by Country and Major Industry, 1962-65

(Millions of dollars)

	1962 r			1963			1964 e			1965 e		
	Mining and smelting	Petroleum	Manufacturing	Mining and smelting	Petroleum	Manufacturing	Mining and smelting	Petroleum	Manufacturing	Mining and smelting	Petroleum	Manufacturing
All areas, total	438	1,628	1,941	398	1,889	2,153	431	1,940	2,730	416	2,005	2,533
Canada	245	300	458	195	375	535	224	300	710	202	360	657
Latin American Republics, total	63	277	274	75	245	268	66	269	346	78	269	249
Mexico, Central America and West Indies, total	5	44	51	7	42	65	12	27	113	10	26	65
Mexico	5	2	50	5	10	60	10	2	108	8	2	59
Other countries	(**)	42	1	2	32	5	2	25	5	2	24	6
South America, total	58	233	223	68	203	203	54	242	233	68	243	184
Argentina	(*)	38	115	(*)	12	86	(*)	14	93	(*)	13	64
Brazil	3	4	63	2	3	57	4	2	63	4	3	54
Chile	20	(*)	4	25	(*)	4	24	(*)	8	26	(*)	6
Colombia	(*)	32	7	(*)	30	23	(*)	42	26	(*)	35	24
Peru	27	9	6	18	10	13	10	12	20	26	11	15
Venezuela	(*)	145	25	(*)	142	16	(*)	167	18	(*)	175	16
Other countries	2	(*)	3	1	(*)	4	1	(*)	5	2	(*)	5
Other Western Hemisphere	32	62	7	34	62	37	54	52	14	46	44	17
Europe, total	4	494	953	5	642	1,034	4	628	1,214	4	576	1,188
Common Market, total	(**)	269	548	1	386	534	1	363	584	1	278	592
Belgium and Luxembourg	(**)	9	26		11	38		24	48		21	35
France	(**)	74	100	(**)	56	110	(**)	78	121	(**)	60	133
Germany	(**)	115	391	(**)	184	261	(**)	85	319	(**)	80	335
Italy	(**)	29	39	(**)	85	89	(**)	130	61	(**)	82	52
Netherlands		42	22		50	36		46	35		35	37
Other Europe, total	4	225	405	4	256	500	3	265	630	3	298	596
Denmark		30	2		37	5		22	6		28	4
Norway	(**)	7	8	(**)	8	12	(**)	9	12	(**)	11	13
Spain	(**)	7	11	(**)	20	23	(**)	13	30	(**)	10	11
Sweden		30	14		25	17		27	14		28	14
Switzerland		4	10		4	10		13	11		12	13
United Kingdom		125	350	1	140	399		138	528		175	512
Other countries	4	22	10	3	22	34	3	43	29	3	34	29
Africa, total	69	176	12	58	164	24	55	250	75	54	242	97
North Africa	(**)	137	(**)		129	1		183	1		166	1
East Africa	(**)	15	(**)		14	(**)		14	1		19	(**)
West Africa	43	11	1	38	8	3	25	16	22	30	20	52
Central and South Africa, total	26	13	11	20	13	20	30	37	51	24	37	44
Union of South Africa	14	(*)	11	15	(*)	19	25	(*)	50	20	(*)	44
Other countries	12	(*)		5	(*)	1	5	(*)	1	4	(*)	(**)
Asia, total	1	178	115	2	297	116	2	346	162	2	433	157
Middle East		72	6		125	5		137	5		170	5
Far East, total	1	106	109	2	172	111	2	209	157	2	263	152
India		(*)	26		(*)	17		(*)	28		(*)	26
Japan		(*)	59		(*)	49		(*)	65		(*)	73
Philippine Republic	(**)	(*)	15	1	(*)	20	1	(*)	44	1	(*)	34
Other countries	1	(*)	9	1	(*)	25	1	(*)	20	1	(*)	19
Oceania, total	24	76	122	29	64	139	26	50	209	30	61	168
Australia	24	(*)	119	29	(*)	136	26	(*)	200	30	(*)	159
Other countries		(*)	3		(*)	3		(*)	9		(*)	9
International shipping		65			40			45			20	

*Included in area total. **Less than $500,000. r Revised. e Estimated on the basis of company projections.

For the three major industries, mining, petroleum and manufacturing, estimates are made by linking back each country/industry cell to the last year for which the estimate is considered final, and supplementing the percentage change indicated by matching samples of foreign affiliates with data on newly reported affiliates and from other relevant sources. For manufacturing affiliates the stratification is carried to a two-digit SIC level. Data for the smaller industries are expanded in a similar way, but no attempt is made to obtain a sample large enough to warrant derivation of country data.

Sales of Foreign Affiliates

Although most of the firms reporting on Form BE–133 include data for sales, no attempt has been made since the 1957 survey to develop a total for all industries. For some industries—trade and distribution, finance and insurance, and contractual services—coverage has been small and data on sales or revenues are not very significant for economic analysis. For the petroleum industry data on physical production or refinery capacity can be developed, but the computation of an unduplicated dollar value of sales is so complex that it cannot be done annually with available resources. Consequently, sales data have been developed and published annually in detail only for the manufacturing affiliates, with occasional estimates of the sales of foreign mining affiliates.

For manufacturing affiliates the reported sample and the expanded estimates of total sales for 1963 are as follows:

(Millions of dollars)

	Reported data	Estimated total	Percent reported
All areas	21,411	31,317	68
Canada	6,443	10,387	62
Latin America	2,736	4,285	64
Europe	9,978	13,610	73
Other areas	2,254	3,035	74

Sources and Uses of Funds

The computation of universe estimates for sources and uses of funds of foreign affiliates from the sample returns is done only for the three major industries for which sample coverage is adequate, and is benchmarked on complete reports for 1957. Certain of the items—net income, funds from the United States, income paid out and retained earnings—are related to data reported by a much larger group of companies on quarterly reports (BE–577 and BE–578) required for the compilation of the balance of payments accounts. This relationship is illustrated in the following table:

Reconciliation of Data on Capital Flows and Earnings, 1963

(Millions of dollars)

	Total, specified industries	Mining and smelting	Petroleum	Manufacturing
Net capital outflow appearing in balance of payments accounts	1,591	65	810	716
Less:				
Purchase of existing enterprises and minority interests	253		71	182
Retained branch profits	–52	–2	–51	1
Plus:				
U.S. financing, other than parent	(*)	–35	(*)	35
Other adjustments and residual	–1	9	–1	–9
Equals:				
Net funds from U.S. (table 9)	1,389	41	789	559
Undistributed earnings of subsidiaries consistent with balance of payments accounting [1]	1,100	66	182	852
Plus:				
Undistributed earnings of minority interests	241	62	52	127
Retained branch profits	–52	–2	–51	1
Other adjustments and residual	169	13	73	83
Equals:				
Retained earnings as derived from table 9	1,458	139	256	1,063

[1] Not actually included in U.S. balance of payments statement.
*Negligible.

With these more broadly based estimates, and the estimate for plant and equipment expenditures established, the principal remaining items requiring estimation are funds obtained abroad, depreciation and depletion charges, inventories, receivables, and "other" assets. Of these, the annual change in depreciation charges is relatively regular; for the others the changes indicated by the sample reported are used as a base, but a balancing of individual items is required to effect a reconciliation of total sources and uses. Because the changes in working capital items are often erratic, the estimates for these items are subject to a considerable range of error, though it is believed the principal trends are correctly indicated.

Definition of Foreign Affiliates

As used in this article the term "foreign affiliate" applies to unincorporated foreign branches of U.S. firms, or foreign corporations in which U.S. companies have a directly held voting interest of 25 percent or more. In practice, the voting interest is predominantly in the range of 75 percent or more. The data used for each affiliate are taken for its entire operation—no reduction is made to allow for the interest of foreign stockholders in the operations of the affiliates. This tends to inflate somewhat the U.S. interest in these firms, but no practical way exists, in this context, for other procedures to be used. Also, the reports do not cover operations of secondary foreign affiliates (i.e., affiliates owned through a foreign corporation itself directly owned in the United States) when they are not consolidated by the reporter.

Table 4.—Domestic and Foreign Expenditures for Plant and Equipment in Selected Industries, 1962–64

(Millions of dollars)

Industry	Expenditures 1962 ʳ				Expenditures 1963				Expenditures 1964 ᵉ			
	Total	Domestic	Foreign	Percent of foreign to total	Total	Domestic	Foreign	Percent of foreign to total	Total	Domestic	Foreign	Percent of foreign to total
Manufacturing, total for selected industries	9,438	7,680	1,758	18.6	10,090	8,160	1,930	19.1	11,941	9,450	2,491	20.9
Food products	1,116	990	126	11.3	1,102	970	132	12.0	1,174	1,020	154	13.1
Paper and allied products	815	720	95	11.7	854	720	134	15.7	1,102	960	142	12.9
Chemicals	1,868	1,560	308	16.5	2,046	1,610	436	21.3	2,321	1,750	571	24.6
Rubber products	321	230	91	28.3	338	240	98	29.0	372	270	102	27.4
Primary and fabricated metals [1]	1,092	930	162	14.8	1,304	1,100	204	15.6	1,622	1,360	262	16.2
Machinery, except electrical	1,484	1,270	214	14.4	1,472	1,240	232	15.8	1,812	1,530	282	15.6
Electrical machinery	857	680	177	20.7	854	690	164	19.2	858	670	188	21.9
Transportation equipment	1,885	1,300	585	31.0	2,120	1,590	530	25.0	2,680	1,890	790	29.5
Mining and petroleum	6,026	3,960	2,066	34.3	6,247	3,960	2,287	36.6	6,931	4,560	2,371	34.2

ʳ Revised. ᵉ Estimated on basis of company projections. [1] Excludes primary iron and steel producers.

NOTE.—Foreign expenditures include acquisitions of existing fixed assets, which are excluded from the domestic series.

Table 5.—Sales by Direct Foreign Investments, Principal Commodities by Areas, 1957 and 1959–63

(Millions of dollars)

Areas and years	Manufacturing total	Food products	Paper and allied products	Chemicals	Rubber products	Primary and fabricated metals	Machinery excluding electrical	Electrical machinery	Transportation equipment	Other products
All areas, total:										
1957	18,331	2,457	881	2,411	968	1,548	1,903	2,047	4,228	1,889
1959	20,870	2,810	940	2,950	1,040	1,590	2,200	2,100	5,140	2,100
1960	23,315	2,920	1,005	3,290	1,170	1,680	2,490	2,280	6,170	2,310
1961	25,195	3,270	1,055	3,845	1,215	1,875	2,735	2,470	6,000	2,730
1962	27,714	3,385	1,160	4,245	1,367	2,033	3,019	2,850	6,665	2,990
1963	31,317	3,667	1,269	4,832	1,415	2,333	3,311	3,220	7,960	3,310
Canada:										
1957	7,897	928	769	897	272	927	695	1,080	1,488	842
1959	8,440	1,060	800	1,070	290	950	760	1,030	1,600	880
1960	8,665	1,020	845	1,150	310	920	780	1,040	1,650	950
1961	8,665	1,095	860	1,300	295	940	760	1,000	1,450	965
1962	9,375	1,115	920	1,250	360	1,065	790	1,115	1,730	1,030
1963	10,387	1,142	969	1,352	385	1,148	881	1,300	2,090	1,120
Latin America: [1]										
1957	2,435	608	55	499	239	111	66	190	375	292
1959	2,830	740	60	590	260	100	80	190	470	340
1960	3,180	750	70	620	280	100	100	240	710	310
1961	3,640	780	85	690	300	160	115	300	770	440
1962	3,999	820	100	840	302	163	114	375	785	500
1963	4,285	940	130	1,000	310	195	120	300	750	540
Europe:										
1957	6,313	734	34	822	262	435	1,009	678	1,700	639
1959	7,690	760	50	1,050	290	470	1,210	770	2,350	740
1960	9,310	900	60	1,240	360	590	1,420	890	2,970	880
1961	10,670	1,120	70	1,510	400	690	1,635	1,050	3,070	1,125
1962	11,780	1,185	80	1,760	460	715	1,850	1,220	3,280	1,230
1963	13,610	1,265	95	2,040	430	840	1,990	1,470	4,100	1,380
Other areas:										
1957	1,685	188	23	193	195	75	133	99	665	116
1959	1,910	250	30	240	200	70	150	110	720	140
1960	2,160	250	30	280	220	70	190	110	840	170
1961	2,220	275	40	345	220	85	225	120	710	200
1962	2,560	265	60	395	245	90	265	140	870	230
1963	3,045	320	75	440	290	150	320	150	1,020	270

[1] Includes "other Western Hemisphere."

Table 6.—Sales by Direct Investment Manufacturing Enterprises Abroad

(Millions of dollars)

Area and country	1957	1959	1960	1961 r	1962 r	1963
All areas, total	**18,331**	**20,870**	**23,315**	**25,195**	**27,714**	**31,317**
Canada	**7,897**	**8,440**	**8,665**	**8,665**	**9,375**	**10,387**
Latin America, total [1]	**2,435**	**2,830**	**3,180**	**3,640**	**3,999**	**4,285**
Argentina	385	426	696	865	825	855
Brazil	659	764	879	910	1,075	1,095
Mexico	643	751	770	825	975	1,075
Venezuela	268	364	360	375	380	450
Other countries	480	525	475	665	744	810
Europe, total	**6,313**	**7,690**	**9,310**	**10,670**	**11,780**	**13,610**
Belgium, Netherlands, and Luxembourg	416	461	602	740	800	900
France	763	789	965	1,195	1,440	1,700
Germany	1,116	1,572	1,835	2,265	2,600	3,090
Italy	230	244	350	475	575	730
United Kingdom	3,303	4,050	4,715	5,070	5,265	5,960
Other countries	485	574	843	925	1,100	1,230
Other areas, total	**1,685**	**1,910**	**2,160**	**2,220**	**2,560**	**3,035**
Australia	787	933	1,085	1,045	1,305	1,550
Japan	217	240	290	380	440	530
Philippine Republic	118	141	140	160	165	190
Republic of South Africa	300	292	305	335	365	425
Other countries	263	304	340	300	285	340

r Revised. [1] Includes "other Western Hemisphere."

Table 7.—Exports by Foreign Manufacturing Affiliates, 1962 r and 1963

(Millions of dollars)

Areas and industry	Exports to U.S.		Exports to other countries	
	1962r	1963	1962r	1963
All areas, total	**1,069**	**1,092**	**3,738**	**4,494**
Food products	125	127	350	454
Paper and allied products	354	283	340	375
Chemicals	115	136	465	591
Rubber products	10	8	83	89
Primary and fabricated metals	105	153	355	415
Machinery, excluding electrical	90	97	540	659
Electrical machinery	15	20	243	302
Transportation equipment	90	78	872	1,144
Other products	165	190	490	465
Canada, total	**814**	**819**	**875**	**962**
Food products	30	20	50	54
Paper and allied products	354	283	315	355
Chemicals	80	91	60	61
Rubber products	5	8	5	2
Primary and fabricated metals	100	142	235	230
Machinery, excluding electrical	50	53	60	73
Electrical machinery	5	9	25	60
Transportation equipment	45	48	55	72
Other products	145	165	70	55
Latin America, total [1]	70	75	322	393
Food products	50	50	225	290
Paper and allied products	(*)	(*)	10	10
Chemicals	15	20	45	50
Rubber products	----	----	5	(*)
Primary and fabricated metals	----	1	10	20
Machinery, excluding electrical	(*)	3	5	7
Electrical machinery	(*)	1	10	9
Transportation equipment	(*)	(*)	2	2
Other products	5	(*)	10	5
Europe, total	**130**	**115**	**2,450**	**3,000**
Food products	5	10	50	75
Paper and allied products	----	----	10	5
Chemicals	15	10	350	450
Rubber products	5	(*)	70	85
Primary and fabricated metals	5	10	100	150
Machinery, excluding electrical	40	40	470	570
Electrical machinery	10	10	200	225
Transportation equipment	45	30	800	1,050
Other products	5	5	400	390
Other areas, total	**55**	**83**	**91**	**139**
Food products	40	47	25	35
Paper and allied products	----	----	5	5
Chemicals	5	15	10	30
Rubber products	----	----	3	2
Primary and fabricated metals	----	----	10	15
Machinery, excluding electrical	----	1	5	9
Electrical machinery	(*)	(*)	8	8
Transportation equipment	----	(*)	15	20
Other products	10	20	10	15

r Revised. *Less than $500,000. [1] Includes "other Western Hemisphere"

Table 8.—Exports from the United States and Sales by Direct Investment Enterprises Abroad of Selected Manufactures, by Area, 1957, 1962–63

(Millions of dollars)

Commodities	All areas, total			Canada			Latin America [1]			Europe			Other Areas		
	1957	1962	1963	1957	1962	1963	1957	1962	1963	1957	1962	1963	1957	1962	1963
Selected manufactures:															
Foreign sales	**12,438**	**19,306**	**22,007**	**5,201**	**6,165**	**6,977**	**1,424**	**2,516**	**2,610**	**4,505**	**8,650**	**10,125**	**1,308**	**1,975**	**2,295**
U.S. exports	**7,536**	**8,781**	**9,334**	**1,869**	**1,977**	**2,110**	**2,633**	**2,109**	**2,056**	**1,326**	**2,439**	**2,684**	**1,709**	**2,256**	**2,484**
Paper and allied products:															
Foreign sales	881	1,160	1,269	769	920	969	55	100	130	34	80	95	23	60	75
U.S. exports	324	457	507	65	76	73	97	93	106	91	173	194	71	115	134
Chemicals:															
Foreign sales	2,411	2,445	4,832	897	1,250	1,352	499	840	1,000	822	1,760	2,040	193	395	440
U.S. exports	1,376	1,771	1,943	246	287	301	457	419	476	353	600	656	320	465	510
Rubber products:															
Foreign sales	968	1,367	1,415	272	360	385	239	302	310	262	460	430	195	245	290
U.S. exports	300	332	318	43	54	53	62	65	59	97	119	115	98	94	91
Machinery, except electrical:															
Foreign sales	1,903	3,019	3,311	695	790	881	66	114	120	1,009	1,850	1,990	133	265	320
U.S. exports	3,160	3,927	3,982	876	847	911	1,007	844	773	567	1,145	1,200	710	1,091	1,098
Electrical machinery:															
Foreign sales	2,047	2,850	3,220	1,080	1,115	1,300	190	375	300	678	1,220	1,470	99	140	150
U.S. exports	810	916	1,084	246	250	262	291	225	221	114	253	350	160	188	251
Transportation equipment:															
Foreign sales	4,228	6,665	7,960	1,488	1,730	2,090	375	785	750	1,700	3,280	4,100	665	870	1,020
U.S. exports [2]	1,566	1,378	1,500	393	463	510	719	463	421	104	149	169	350	303	400

[1] Includes "other Western Hemisphere." [2] Excludes civilian aircraft.

Table 9.—Sources and Uses of Funds of Direct Foreign Investments, by Area and Selected Industry, 1961–63

(Millions of dollars)

SOURCES OF FUNDS

Area and industry	Total sources			Net income			Funds from United States			Funds obtained abroad [1]			Depreciation and depletion		
	1961	1962 r	1963	1961	1962 r	1963	1961	1962 r	1963	1961	1962 r	1963	1961	1962 r	1963
All areas, total	**8,217**	**8,677**	**10,306**	**3,381**	**3,833**	**4,214**	**1,249**	**1,009**	**1,389**	**1,391**	**1,521**	**2,146**	**2,196**	**2,314**	**2,557**
Mining and smelting	813	906	875	476	494	493	16	98	41	113	107	102	208	207	239
Petroleum	3,696	3,765	4,667	1,553	1,824	1,953	743	340	789	301	506	777	1,099	1,095	1,148
Manufacturing	3,708	4,006	4,764	1,352	1,515	1,768	490	571	559	977	908	1,267	889	1,012	1,170
Canada, total	**1,852**	**2,106**	**2,363**	**760**	**905**	**1,055**	**235**	**201**	**192**	**220**	**320**	**332**	**637**	**680**	**784**
Mining and smelting	390	389	347	161	179	187	9	95	−24	140	15	70	80	100	114
Petroleum	535	570	768	199	199	245	99	77	148	20	84	100	217	210	275
Manufacturing	927	1,147	1,248	400	527	623	127	29	68	60	221	162	340	370	395
Latin America, total [2]	**1,781**	**1,794**	**1,903**	**874**	**1,015**	**978**	**110**	**−23**	**204**	**186**	**222**	**146**	**611**	**580**	**575**
Mining and smelting	291	329	364	219	246	234	−20	−28	14	−10	31	15	102	80	101
Petroleum	915	854	886	477	567	545	44	−147	34	−10	44	−44	404	390	351
Manufacturing	575	611	653	178	202	199	86	152	156	206	147	175	105	110	123
Europe, total	**2,578**	**2,447**	**3,220**	**709**	**648**	**770**	**587**	**548**	**573**	**723**	**593**	**1,109**	**559**	**658**	**768**
Mining and smelting	8	9	12	8	5	4	(*)	3	7	−2	(*)	−1	2	1	2
Petroleum	770	747	1,068	87	74	69	360	255	331	130	198	431	193	220	237
Manufacturing	1,800	1,691	2,140	614	569	697	227	290	235	595	395	679	364	437	529
Other areas, total	**2,006**	**2,330**	**2,820**	**1,038**	**1,265**	**1,411**	**317**	**283**	**420**	**262**	**386**	**559**	**389**	**396**	**430**
Mining and smelting	124	179	152	88	64	68	27	28	44	−15	61	18	24	26	22
Petroleum	1,476	1,594	1,945	790	984	1,094	240	155	276	161	180	290	285	275	285
Manufacturing	406	557	723	160	217	249	50	100	100	116	145	251	80	95	123

USES OF FUNDS

Area and industry	Total uses			Property, plant and equipment			Inventories			Receivables			Other assets [3]			Income paid out		
	1961	1962 r	1963	1961	1962 r	1963	1961	1962 r	1963	1961	1962 r	1963	1961	1962 r	1963	1961	1962 r	1963
All areas, total	**8,217**	**8,677**	**10,306**	**3,544**	**4,007**	**4,440**	**491**	**652**	**742**	**780**	**728**	**1,202**	**779**	**530**	**1,166**	**2,623**	**2,760**	**2,756**
Mining and smelting	813	906	875	312	438	398	27	45	−3	18	42	45	87	58	81	369	323	354
Petroleum	3,696	3,765	4,667	1,534	1,628	1,889	85	54	119	292	296	439	398	221	523	1,387	1,566	1,697
Manufacturing	3,708	4,006	4,764	1,698	1,941	2,153	379	553	626	470	390	7182	94	251	562	867	871	705
Canada, total	**1,852**	**2,106**	**2,363**	**865**	**1,003**	**1,105**	**121**	**215**	**122**	**204**	**175**	**293**	**174**	**208**	**432**	**488**	**505**	**411**
Mining and smelting	390	389	347	165	245	195	51	20	−12	40	(*)	19	48	26	60	86	98	85
Petroleum	535	570	768	315	300	375	10	5	24	42	45	59	46	72	192	122	148	118
Manufacturing	927	1,147	1,248	385	458	535	60	190	110	122	130	215	80	110	180	280	259	208
Latin America, total [2]	**1,781**	**1,794**	**1,903**	**643**	**715**	**721**	**37**	**75**	**135**	**223**	**95**	**105**	**144**	**179**	**92**	**734**	**730**	**850**
Mining and smelting	291	329	364	87	95	109	−18	5	5	−17	25	10	25	34	16	214	170	224
Petroleum	915	854	886	306	339	307	−5	−25	15	110	5	10	70	60	1	434	475	553
Manufacturing	575	611	653	250	281	305	60	95	115	130	65	85	49	85	75	86	85	73
Europe, total	**2,578**	**2,447**	**3,220**	**1,286**	**1,451**	**1,681**	**324**	**249**	**340**	**264**	**218**	**484**	**241**	**74**	**319**	**463**	**455**	**396**
Mining and smelting	8	9	12	1	4	5	(*)	(*)	−1	−1	2	1	−1	−2	(*)	9	5	7
Petroleum	770	747	1,068	438	494	642	75	49	60	95	76	145	82	60	155	80	68	66
Manufacturing	1,800	1,691	2,140	847	953	1,034	249	200	281	170	140	338	160	16	164	374	382	323
Other areas, total	**2,006**	**2,330**	**2,820**	**750**	**838**	**933**	**9**	**113**	**145**	**89**	**240**	**320**	**220**	**69**	**323**	**938**	**1,070**	**1,099**
Mining and smelting	124	179	152	59	94	89	−6	20	5	−4	15	15	15	(*)	5	60	50	38
Petroleum	1,476	1,594	1,945	475	495	565	5	25	20	45	170	225	200	29	175	751	875	961
Manufacturing	406	557	723	216	249	279	10	68	120	48	55	80	5	40	143	127	145	100

*Less than $500,000. r Revised.
[1] Includes miscellaneous sources.
[2] Includes "other Western Hemisphere."
[3] Includes miscellaneous uses.

FOREIGN INVESTMENTS, 1964-65

Samuel Pizer
and
Frederick Cutler

by SAMUEL PIZER and FRED CUTLER

Foreign Investments, 1964-65

THE very sharp rise of private capital outflows to nearly $6.5 billion, by far the largest amount on record, was a major feature of the U.S. balance of payments in 1964. This development has already been discussed in connection with the President's program to improve the balance of payments. This article provides more complete statistics on private foreign investments than have been available up to now, together with some indications of current and prospective developments as reflected in projections of plant and equipment expenditures abroad in 1965 and 1966.

Return on Manufacturing Investments

⌐ *Domestic return above overall foreign rate since 1961*

⌐ *Following a sharp drop, return in Europe is now comparable to U.S. rate*

Percent

NOTE.—Return on domestic manufacturing represents net income applied to net worth at the beginning of the year (First National City Bank of N.Y.). Return on direct manufacturing investments abroad and in Europe represents the U.S. share of net earnings for the year (see table 4) applied to book value of these investments at the beginning of the year. (See table 2.)

U.S. Department of Commerce, Office of Business Economics   65-9-9

22

All components of private capital outflows except purchases of foreign securities moved upward last year: Direct investments were up $0.4 billion to $2.4 billion; net lending by banks (including assets held for customers) rose by about $1.0 billion to $2.5 billion, and loans and acquisitions of short-term assets abroad by nonfinancial concerns increased very sharply to $0.9 billion. Purchases of foreign securities were inhibited by the Interest Equalization Tax (IET) and were reduced to a net of $0.7 billion. These outflows, together with reinvested direct investment earnings of $1.4 billion, gains in market prices of foreign securities, and sizable additions to foreign assets resulting from improved reporting by some banks and nonfinancial concerns, raised the accumulated total of private U.S. foreign investments to more than $75 billion by the beginning of this year.

Capital outflows picked up throughout 1964 and reached a peak of $2.2 billion (seasonally adjusted) in the last quarter. New issues of foreign securities were temporarily inflated when passage of the IET, first proposed in July 1963, clarified the conditions under which foreign securities could be purchased. These issues have since returned to a more normal level. However, the further increases in bank lending and in direct investment flows that showed up late in 1964 were still evident in early 1965, and could not be assumed to be merely temporary. As is by now well known, major components of the program to improve the balance of payments are the reduction of bank lending to about $0.5 billion for the year and a strenuous effort by firms with direct investments abroad to conduct their international operations so as to raise

considerably their net contribution to the balance of payments.

The data on capital flows for the first half of 1965, given in the article beginning on page 11, show that after the announcement of the program in February, banks acted quickly to cut back their foreign lending and industrial firms promptly repatriated a large part of their liquid funds held outside the United States. However, from the projections of foreign plant and equipment expenditures presented later in this report, it is clear that industrial companies reporting in May and June planned to carry out an extraordinary amount of investment abroad this year and next. Such plans cannot be altered rapidly or without considerable loss, nor can alternative foreign sources of financing be arranged readily, especially when many countries are carrying out relatively tight domestic monetary policies. Consequently, direct-investment capital outflows in the first half of the year were $2.1 billion, double the amount for the first 6 months of last year, and the total for all of 1965 will probably be higher than in 1964. However, the first-half total includes sizable flows, especially to Canada and the Middle East, connected with special developments not likely to be repeated in the second half. Also, the first-half flow probably included some anticipatory placing of funds abroad for later use.

Direct Foreign Investments

Capital outflows for direct investment abroad have been moving up to successively higher rates since the end of World War II. They reached $2.4 billion in 1964 and have shown a further increase so far this year. At the same time, increased income derived from foreign affiliates has been one of the major elements of strength in the balance of payments. Last year, earnings of the affiliates rose by over $½ billion and reached $5.1 billion. Out of that total, $3.7 billion was returned to the United States—compared to $3.1 billion in 1963—and $1.4 billion was retained abroad. The aggregate increase in the value of the U.S. investment in the foreign affiliates—derived

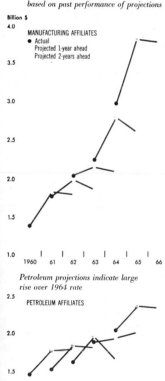

CHART 10

Projections of Plant and Equipment Expenditures Abroad

- *Manufacturing affiliates report major expansion in 1965*
- *Further step-up suggested for 1966, based on past performance of projections*

Billion $

MANUFACTURING AFFILIATES
- Actual
  Projected 1-year ahead
  Projected 2-years ahead

Petroleum projections indicate large rise over 1964 rate

PETROLEUM AFFILIATES

U.S. Department of Commerce, Office of Business Economics   65-9-10

from net capital flows plus retained earnings—was $3.8 billion.

This article also presents figures for 1965 and 1966 on gross expenditures for plant and equipment abroad projected by companies with foreign affiliates. Such expenditures are considerably larger than the sum of capital outflows from the United States plus retained earnings, since they can also be financed from depreciation reserves accumulated by the foreign companies or through external financing obtained abroad. In 1964, capital outlays for fixed assets abroad amounted to $6.1 billion. The company projections for the current year show a rise of 20 percent to $7.4 billion, and taking account of the experience in previous years, which shows that projections made nearly 2 years ahead have been lower than actual outlays (see chart 10), another gain seems likely in 1966.

Increases in capital expenditures abroad for 1965 are fairly widespread, and some areas show outstanding gains. A particularly strong growth is projected for European capital outlays, with an overall advance of 25 percent and a 34 percent rise in manufacturing. In Canada, the rate of capital expenditures by all affiliates of U.S. firms is projected to be up by nearly 20 percent, and the rise for manufacturing affiliates is 34 percent, quite close to the increase reported in surveys of Canadian manufacturing as a whole. Substantial upturns in investment activity by U.S. companies are also reported for mining in Australia, manufacturing in Japan, and petroleum in the Middle East and Far East. (See table 11.)

These reports on foreign plant and equipment expenditures give some indication of prospective capital outflows from the United States, though the link between the two series is indirect. Capital outflows represent the net amount invested in the period by parent companies, to increase stock ownership in, or provide credits of all maturities to, new or existing foreign affiliates, or to acquire existing enterprises from their foreign owners. Capital transfers by the U.S. parent companies provide only a portion of the funds currently available a to the foreign affiliates. While expenditures on plant and equip-

ment by these affiliates account for a major portion of the funds that they use, they also need funds to finance working capital requirements.

Information on the overall sources and uses of the funds of the foreign affiliates, including changes in working capital requirements, will be published in the SURVEY as soon as possible.

In the period since 1957, capital outflows for direct investment have amounted to 35–40 percent of the plant and equipment expenditures of foreign affiliates. If this relationship persists, and if no major changes occur in foreign financing or amounts spent to acquire existing foreign enterprises, the rate of capital outflow could be expected to rise from 1964 to 1965 by $½ billion to $3 billion.

The persistent and rapid extension of U.S. industry into expanded production facilities abroad has been an important feature of recent economic developments, and much more research is

Table 1.—Factors Affecting the U.S. Private Investment Position, 1963 and 1964

(Millions of dollars)

Type of investment	1963 r	1964
U.S. private investments abroad:		
Total, beginning of year	60,025	66,513
Add: Capital outflow [1]	4,456	6,462
Reinvested earnings	1,507	1,417
Price changes and other adjustments	525	1,027
Total, end of year	66,513	75,419
Direct investments:		
Value, beginning of year	37,226	40,686
Add: Capital outflow [1]	1,976	2,377
Reinvested earnings	1,507	1,417
Other adjustments [2]	−23	−137
Value, end of year	40,686	44,343
Other long-term private investments abroad:		
Value, beginning of year	15,506	17,644
Add: Capital outflow [1]	1,695	1,975
Price changes	459	325
Other adjustments	−16	444
Value, end of year	17,644	20,388
Short-term assets and claims:		
Value, beginning of year	7,293	8,183
Add: Capital outflow [1]	785	2,111
Enlarged coverage of reports	105	394
Value, end of year	8,183	10,688
Foreign long-term investments in the United States:		
Direct investments:		
Value, beginning of year	7,612	7,944
Add: Capital inflow [1]	−5	−5
Reinvested earnings	236	327
Other adjustments [3]	101	97
Value, end of year	7,944	8,363
Other long-term investments:		
Value, beginning of year	12,604	14,847
Add: Capital inflow	331	115
Price changes	1,902	1,641
Other adjustments	10	13
Value, end of year	14,847	16,616

r Revised.
[1] Included in the balance of payments accounts.
[2] For detail see note to table 2.
[3] Mainly revaluations of securities held by affiliates of foreign insurance companies.

needed to determine its causes and effects. Decisions by manufacturing firms to meet foreign demand by producing abroad rather than producing here and exporting result from the interplay of such factors as (a) lower costs and expected higher rates of return abroad, (b) prospective market growth abroad in general and for specific products, (c) tariffs, quotas, local preferences, or competition abroad that threaten markets for exports, and (d) the availability of funds for financing domestic and foreign plants.

Rates of return are notoriously difficult to derive and compare meaningfully. However, chart 9 suggests that until 1961 rates of return on European manufacturing investments (but not on foreign manufacturing investments in general), although declining, were still

Table 2.—Value of Direct Investments Abroad [1] by Selected Countries and Industries, at Yearend 1963 and 1964

Table 3.—Direct-Investment Earnings, by Selected

[Millions of dollars]

Line	Area and country	Table 2 — 1963ʳ — Total	Mining and smelting	Petroleum	Manufacturing	Public utilities	Trade	Other	Table 2 — 1964ᵖ — Total	Mining and smelting	Petroleum	Manufacturing	Public utilities	Trade	Other	Table 3 — Net capital outflows — 1963ʳ	1964ᵖ Total	Mining and smelting	Petroleum	Manufacturing	Other
1	All areas, total	40,686	3,369	13,652	14,937	2,061	3,307	3,359	44,343	3,564	14,350	16,861	2,023	3,736	3,808	1,976	2,376	88	739	997	552
2	Canada	13,044	1,549	3,134	5,761	457	747	1,396	13,820	1,671	3,228	6,191	467	805	1,458	365	250	45	30	138	38
3	Latin American Republics, total	8,662	1,093	3,095	2,102	715	882	775	8,932	1,098	3,142	2,340	568	951	832	69	156	-8	4	93	68
4	Mexico	907	116	65	502	25	93	105	1,035	128	56	607	27	111	106	24	94	5	-7	79	16
5	Panama	616	19	94	12	26	273	193	663	19		23	29	282	206	31	25		2	16	7
6	Other Central America and West Indies	539	26	125	32	141	23	192	594	31	145	45	142	26	205	29	41	5	20	5	12
7	Argentina	829	(*)	(*)	454	(*)	38	336	883	(*)	(*)	497	(*)	42	344	20	16	(*)	(*)	9	7
8	Brazil	1,132	30	60	664	193	148	38	994	34	51	673	41	153	42	-8	-44	(*)	-13	-35	5
9	Chile	768	503	(*)	27	(*)	15	223	788	499	(*)	30	(*)	20	239	14	9	-5		(**)	13
10	Colombia	465	(*)	246	120	27	52	19	530	(*)	270	145	30	53	22	-1	39	(*)	20	15	3
11	Peru	448	240	56	64	21	41	27	460	241	56	65	22	46	31	-5	10	1	4	1	4
12	Venezuela	2,808	(*)	2,166	202	36	185	218	2,808	(*)	2,162	219	18	200	209	-35	-50	(*)	-25	-3	-22
13	Other countries	150	6	48	25	21	15	35	186	7	67	35	21	18	38	(**)	17	(**)	6	7	3
14	Other Western Hemisphere	1,229	210	541	111	47	82	238	1,386	250	569	166	49	89	263	167	134	38	31	40	25
15	Europe, total	10,340	55	2,776	5,634	44	1,237	595	12,067	56	3,086	6,547	53	1,472	854	930	1,342	2	389	601	349
16	Common Market, total	4,490	10	1,330	2,528	34	438	150	5,398	13	1,511	3,098	45	551	180	588	787	(*)	227	444	115
17	Belgium and Luxembourg	356		63	229	1	51	12	452	(**)	66	296	1	73	16	35	73		5	57	10
18	France	1,240	9	261	764	11	158	38	1,437	9	281	893	22	189	43	164	132	(*)	4	86	43
19	Germany	1,780	(*)	496	1,121	5	109	49	2,077	(*)	576	1,315	5	119	63	216	273	(*)	123	131	19
20	Italy	668	(*)	309	259	2	65	34	845	(*)	350	382	2	74	37	120	203	(*)	56	143	4
21	Netherlands	446		201	155	16	56	19	587	(**)	238	212	16	96	25		106		40	28	38
22	Other Europe, total	5,850	45	1,447	3,106	9	799	445	6,669	43	1,575	3,449	8	921	674	341	555	(*)	162	157	236
23	Denmark	133	1	88	26	(**)	16	2	165	1	116	28	(**)	18	2	18	33	(**)	30	1	1
24	Norway	123	(*)	67	(*)	(**)	11	17	193	(*)	68	29	(**)	14	17	14	17	(*)	11	2	4
25	Spain	155	(*)	40	83	4	21	7	258	(**)	51	96	(**)	41	7	28	33	(**)	10	11	11
26	Sweden	221	(**)	136	36	(**)	41	7	128	(**)	157	44	(**)	49	8	43	31	(**)	2	11	18
27	Switzerland	672	(**)	30	131	(**)	271	240	944	(**)	52	158	1	345	389	97	215	1	9	53	162
28	United Kingdom	4,172	2	886	2,739	6	369	171	4,550	2	905	3,015	4	384	239	124	207	(**)	32	122	9
29	Other countries	374	28	200	64	-1	69	15	431	26	226	79	-2	79	22	79	22	(*)	17	9	8
30	Africa, total	1,426	349	702	177	12	80	106	1,629	356	830	225	2	93	122	109	135	2	97	18	18
31	Liberia	197	(*)	(*)	(*)	(*)	(*)	(*)	197	(*)	(*)	(*)	(*)	(*)	(*)	11	-7	(*)	(*)	(*)	-7
32	Libya	304	(*)	(*)	(*)	(*)	(*)	(*)	382	(*)	(*)	(*)	(*)	(*)	(*)	38	73	(*)	73	(*)	(*)
33	Republic of South Africa	411	63	(*)	158	(**)	47	142	467	68	(*)	192	(**)	51	157	12	17	1	(*)	4	12
34	Other countries	513	192	272	17	6	18	8	593	197	325	32	6	24	9	48	51	2	30	14	4
35	Asia, total	2,793	32	1,920	430	40	199	171	3,062	34	2,014	535	55	238	186	213	188	(**)	98	50	40
36	Middle East	1,277	2	1,206	35	4	10	21	1,331	2	1,238	39	4	11	36	65	42	1	25	3	14
37	Far East, total	1,515	30	714	396	36	189	150	1,731	31	775	496	52	227	150	148	146	(**)	74	48	25
38	India	206	(*)	(*)	77	2	22	104	234	(*)	(*)	94	2	30	109	8	20	(*)	(*)	10	10
39	Japan	472		(*)	145	2	53	272	591		(*)	191	2	72	326	68	73		(*)	15	58
40	Philippine Republic	415	(*)	(*)	110	27	64	214	469	(*)	(*)	130	43	68	227	21	37	(*)	(*)	17	20
41	Other countries	423	(*)	(*)	64	5	50	304	438	(*)	(*)	81	5	57	294	52	16	(*)	(*)	6	11
42	Oceania, total	1,460	82	496	723	1	80	77	1,582	100	444	856	2	87	93	97	115	10	30	56	19
43	Australia	1,274	82	(*)	687	(*)	57	448	1,465	100	(*)	806	(*)	62	497	96	121	10	(*)	57	54
44	Other countries	186	(**)	(*)	36	(*)	23	126	118	(**)	(*)	50	(*)	26	42	1	-6	(**)	(*)	-1	-5
45	International	1,733		988				745	1,865		1,038				827		27		56		60

1. The value of direct investments abroad was reduced in 1963 by $23 million, and in 1964 by $137 million, owing to valuation adjustments on companies books, profits and losses on liquidations, or transfers to other investment categories. In particular, the value of direct investments in the public utilities industry in Brazil was reduced by $153 million as of the end of 1964 by a settlement with the Brazilian Government. The equivalent value was added to the total for U.S. private portfolio investments included in table 15. The value of investments in specific industries and countries is also affected by capital flows among foreign affiliates as shown in table 6.

higher than those obtained on manufacturing investments in the United States. Since then, returns in the United States and in Europe have been similar, and both have turned sharply upward.

The fact that growth rates in Europe (and in a few other developed countries) have surpassed the U.S. rate since the 1950's may also have encouraged production abroad. In this connection, there may now be some shift in favor of the United States, since several industrialized foreign countries have experienced a slowdown in growth—though they have taken measures to correct this—at a time when the United States has enjoyed a very strong growth rate. These changes, including the relative shift in rates of return, would tend to strengthen the comparative

Capital Flows and Undistributed Subsidiary Countries, With Major Industries for 1964

Table 4.—Direct-Investment Earnings and Income,[2] by Selected Countries, With Major Industries for 1964

[Millions of dollars]

Table 3—Continued						Table 4												
Undistributed subsidiary earnings						Earnings						Income						
1963 r	1964 p					1963 r	1964 p					1963 r	1964 p					Line
	Total	Mining and smelting	Petroleum	Manufacturing	Other		Total	Mining and smelting	Petroleum	Manufacturing	Other		Total	Mining and smelting	Petroleum	Manufacturing	Other	
1,507	1,417	102	−49	914	450	4,587	5,118	505	1,860	1,816	936	3,134	3,741	399	1,922	876	543	1
533	498	77	54	289	78	948	1,104	191	170	565	177	455	634	114	118	269	133	2
173	219	10	3	140	66	964	1,104	184	510	229	181	801	900	172	503	92	133	3
13	34	(**)	−2	30	3	61	92	17	(**)	2	55	49	61	12	(**)	27	18	4
63	31	(**)	9	4	18	85	73	(**)	9	8	55	23	43	(**)	9	5	38	5
3	9	-----	(**)	4	5	32	36		3	5	20	31	28	(**)	9	1	16	6
−3	29	(*)	(*)	26	3	52	91	(*)	(*)	60	31	57	64	(*)	(*)	34	30	7
57	58	(*)	(*)	44	11	65	58	(*)	1	45	11	13	5	(*)	−2	3	3	8
−2	12		(*)	3	8	62	80		61	5	15	66	73		60	1	12	9
8	11	(*)	−1	9	3	33	33	(*)		9	14	25	22	(*)	9	5	7	10
1	2	(**)	−4	1	6	70	83		53	10	13	65	77		54	5	8	11
32	27	(*)	−1	17	11	510	552	(*)	(*)	460	27	526	480	(*)	(*)	461	55	12
1	6	(**)	(**)	3	3	−6	6		1	−4	3	−7	2		1	−3	3	13
10	34	3	−1	16	16	161	149		76	34	17	155	116	73	33	4	7	14
513	410	−1	−87	327	172	996	1,112	3	8	754	348	507	654	5	64	412	173	15
145	102	(*)	−60	129	33	398	399	(*)	−38	344	94	232	275	(*)	24	196	56	16
28	13	(**)	−3	11	6	48	53	(**)	−1	42	12	15	34	(**)	2	26	6	17
40	56	(*)	11	36	9	72	86	(*)	11	56	19	27	27	(*)	(**)	17	10	18
63	16	(*)	−46	56	7	215	209	(*)	−21	198	32	140	178	(*)	27	130	21	19
5	−5	(*)	−17	7	6	31	19	(*)	−18	23	13	24	23	(*)	−1	16	7	20
9	21		−4	19	5	33	33		−10	25	18	25	13		−5	6	12	21
368	309	(*)	−27	198	138	598	713	(*)	46	410	257	275	379	(*)	41	216	122	22
−1	−1		−2	−1	2	3	5		−3	5	3	6	8		1	5	2	23
8	3	(*)	(**)	2	1	11	7	(*)	(**)	3	5	3	5	(*)	(**)	1	4	24
6	2	(*)		1	1	12	10	(*)		4	6	4	6	(*)		2	5	25
4	4		−6	6	4	18	20		−6	8	18	14	16	(**)	(**)	2	14	26
125	113		−4	17	100	153	151		−4	20	134	30	40			4	36	27
219	170		−20	164	25	376	476		44	360	72	199	276		28	200	48	28
8	18	(*)		9	5	25	44	(*)	14	11	19	11	26	(*)		14	11	29
42	40	6	4	30	(**)	166	343	38	227	43	35	123	301	32	223	13	34	30
(**)	−4	(*)	(*)	(*)	−4	13	18	(*)	(*)	(*)	18	15	22	(*)	(*)	(*)	22	31
1	4	(*)	(*)	4	4	85	256	(*)	(*)	256	(*)	83	252	(*)	(*)	252	(*)	32
39	38	(*)	(*)	29	6	82	87	(*)	(*)	67	20	40	46	(*)	15	12	19	33
2	1		2	−3	1	−13	−19	(*)	(*)	−39	20	−16	−19	(*)	15	−36	11	34
72	57	1	−12	41	26	1,116	1,067	3	912	82	70	1,017	1,046	1	960	34	50	35
11	11	-----	8	1	2	935	876	-----	867	5	5	893	899	-----	893	3	3	36
60	47	1	−20	40	25	182	191	3	45	78	65	124	148	1	68	32	47	37
5	7	(*)	(*)	5	2	14	23	(*)	(*)	14	9	7	12	(*)	(*)	6	6	38
29	35		(*)	24	10	49	54		(*)	32	21	26	31		(*)	8	23	39
16	13	(*)	(*)	1	12	38	46	(*)	(*)	16	30	20	28	(*)	(*)	12	16	40
9	−8	(*)	(*)	10	−18	81	69	(*)	(*)	16	53	16	77	(*)	(*)	5	72	41
83	80	7		71	3	145	143	10	−6	126	14	57	59	3	−6	53	10	42
71	65	7	(*)	61	−3	127	122	10	(*)	114	−1	51	54	3	(*)	50	1	43
12	15	-----	(*)	10	5	18	21	(*)	(*)	13	9	6	6	(*)	(*)	3	3	44
82	79	-----	−9	-----	88	90	96	-----	6	-----	90		19	-----	30	-----	26	45

2. Income is the sum of dividends, interest and branch profits; earnings is the sum of the U.S. share in the net earnings of subsidiaries and branch profits.
r Revised.
p Preliminary.

*Combined in "other industries."
**Less than $500,000.
NOTE.—In this and subsequent tables, detail may not add to totals because of rounding.

attractiveness of capital investments in the United States.

Barriers to export sales and the advantages of being close to varied demands in local markets no doubt continue to be prime factors in the location of production facilities abroad. Efforts to bring about reductions in trade barriers that tend to discourage exportation from the United States in favor of production abroad, and to maintain competitive cost and price conditions at home, would also tend to favor production in the United States relative to production abroad.

An additional factor affecting investments in the natural resource industries has been the discovery of new sources of supply that can be operated competitively. Since the war, there

have been several instances of discovery and very rapid growth in such investments. A number of new major projects that will involve very sizable capital expenditures are now planned or underway, such as the development of Australian iron ore and bauxite and offshore petroleum or gas reserves in the North Sea and the Persian Gulf area.

Currently, U.S. manufacturing firms are sharply raising both their domestic and foreign plant and equipment expenditures (chart 11), especially foreign. This worldwide expansion is being facilitated by a growth of funds internally generated out of U.S. operations (retained profits and depreciation charges) which has been even faster than the growth of domestic outlays on plant and equipment. Thus, in general, foreign expansion has not been limited by the availability of investment funds or the pressure of requirements for domestic capital expenditures.

Developed areas preferred

The recent experience with direct investments abroad represents an intensification of the patterns of the past few years. European investments predominate, accounting for nearly half of the additions to direct investments in 1964 (capital outflows plus retained earnings) and about the same proportion so far this year. In 1964, the European investment flow included over $300 million to acquire existing foreign interests. The European share in foreign plant and equipment expenditures by U.S. firms was about 35 percent (table 9), but is projected to rise to about 40 percent of total foreign outlays in 1966.

Of the $1.7 billion added to the value of European direct investments in 1964, the largest share—$0.9 billion—went to the Common Market countries; $0.4 billion went to the United Kingdom, and $0.4 billion to the rest of Europe. The $1.7 billion total included a sharp rise to $1.3 billion in capital flows from the United States; this was offset, in part, by a decline in undistributed profits in the petroleum industry. Preliminary data for the first half of 1965 show capital outflows to Europe well ahead of the first half of 1964.

Manufacturing is the largest activity of U.S. firms in Europe and accounted for $6.5 billion out of $12.1 billion invested there at the end of 1964. Of the $0.9 billion added to these investments during 1964, nearly two-thirds went to the Common Market and most of the remainder to the United Kingdom. Investments are widely dispersed over the major manufacturing industries (table 5) and are growing most rapidly in transportation equipment and machinery. This is demonstrated also by the figures for plant and equipment expenditures (table 10), which show capital outlays in these sectors rising through 1966.

American petroleum companies are also very actively expanding their European investments, not only in refining, transportation, and marketing facilities but also in the development of potentially important reserves of gas and oil. Part of the costs of developing new resources are charged against income, and this contributed to the decline in earnings in this industry in Europe, as may be seen in table 4. However, the decline in petroleum earnings in 1964 also reflected competitive pressures. Nevertheless, the industry has scheduled a continuous rise in European capital expenditures to keep up with increasing demand and to provide refining and distribution facilities for the additional output of affiliated producing companies. As shown in table 11, petroleum investments in the United Kingdom and in several continental countries are expected to rise this year and next.

Investments in other industries in Europe have been growing by smaller amounts, though capital flows to financial affiliates in Switzerland and the United Kingdom, including a sizable investment in a British insurance firm increased by about $100 million in 1964 over 1963.

Canada

The strong growth trend in the Canadian economy is attracting a great deal of investment by U.S. firms. This is shown most clearly in plant and equipment expenditures, which rose by $0. billion in 1964 and will probably ris

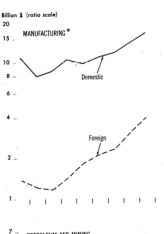

CHART 11

Capital Expenditures by U.S. Companies Domestic and Foreign

Billion $ (ratio scale)

MANUFACTURING*

Domestic

Foreign

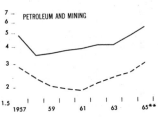

PETROLEUM AND MINING

1957   59   61   63   65**

* Excludes primary iron and steel, and petroleum.
** Anticipated. Domestic investment includes actual outlays for 1st half.
U.S. Department of Commerce, Office of Business Economics   65-9-11

by a like amount in 1965. Outstanding increases are reported for manufacturing, and a higher rate of investment in mining is also indicated.

Most of the growth in U.S. investments in Canada, especially in the manufacturing sector, is financed out of retained earnings. These were down slightly in 1964 because dividend distributions were raised very substantially and outpaced the considerable rise in earnings. Net capital outflows to Canada were reduced to the unusually low figure of $250 million in 1964 because of sales of interests in Canadian affiliates amounting to about $140 million. This year, the capital flow rose sharply to $370 million in the first half alone, and included about $100 million of parent company refinancing of outstanding debt of a Canadian affiliate.

Other developed countries

U.S. companies raised their rate of investment in Australia and Japan by relatively modest amounts in 1964, but held to the relatively low level of recent years for the Republic of South Africa. In Australia, where manufacturing investments have been growing quite vigorously, projections of plant and equipment expenditures indicate some acceleration. Mining investments in Australia are also reaching significant dimensions. The rate of manufacturing investments in Japan has also increased recently. In both countries, substantial amounts are being invested by petroleum companies.

Less developed countries

Direct investments in less developed countries (capital flows and reinvested earnings) rose by $100 million in 1964 to $0.8 billion, about one-fifth of the worldwide total. Nearly 70 percent of the 1964 investment was in the Western Hemisphere, but the increase for the year occurred largely in a few Latin American countries. There was a notable rise in capital flows to Mexico, especially for manufacturing, and smaller increases occurred in investments in Colombia and Peru. The amount invested in Argentina also rose in 1964, but this represented largely the reinvestment of substantially higher earnings of manufacturing affiliates rather than a flow of new capital. On balance, return flows from existing enterprises in Venezuela and Brazil exceeded new outflows.

Among the other less developed countries, there was a substantial rise in investment flows for the petroleum industry in Libya, and some increase occurred in flows to India and the Philippine Republic. A sizable capital flow was maintained by the petroleum industry to other African locations and to the Middle East.

Table 11 gives some indications of near-term trends in plant and equipment expenditures by U.S. companies

---

Table 6.—Net Capital Flows Between Primary and Secondary Foreign Affiliates, 1961–64

[Millions of dollars; net inflows (—)]

	1961	1962	1963	1964
Canada	4		−4	3
Latin America	2	16	−1	1
Panama	10	13	14	11
Argentina	−6	−11	−14	−14
Mexico	−4	11	−5	(**)
Europe		−22	24	20
France	−15	−14	−5	−1
Germany	−8	−4	−20	−6
Italy	−25	−21	−9	−5
Switzerland	29	48	105	60
United Kingdom	−6	−9	−4	1
Other Europe	−6	−22	−43	−29
Other countries	−6	6	−19	−24

**Less than $500,000.

Table 5.—Direct Investments in Manufacturing Enterprises Abroad, 1950, 1957, and 1961–64, by Industry

[Millions of dollars]

Area and year	Manufacturing total	Food products	Paper and allied products	Chemicals and allied products	Rubber products	Primary and fabricated metals	Machinery (except electrical)	Electrical machinery	Transportation equipment	Other products
All areas, total:										
1950	3,831	483	378	512	182	385	420	387	485	599
1957	8,009	723	722	1,378	401	941	927	731	1,204	983
1961	11,997	1,018	923	2,059	531	1,373	1,463	1,004	2,240	1,386
1962	13,250	1,105	967	2,260	583	1,495	1,626	1,106	2,500	1,548
1963	14,937	1,234	1,055	2,605	625	1,664	1,809	1,196	2,946	1,803
1964	16,861	1,393	1,126	3,068	674	1,830	2,027	1,316	3,351	2,076
Canada:										
1950	1,897	227	368	198	59	249	204	141	160	292
1957	3,924	320	626	647	133	671	327	330	398	471
1961	5,076	422	775	848	162	847	402	406	593	621
1962	5,312	435	817	857	159	882	455	436	613	658
1963	5,761	467	880	936	173	939	508	467	681	710
1964	6,191	519	917	1,012	176	986	549	501	758	773
Latin America: [1]										
1950	781	158	5	205	60	23	13	79	83	155
1957	1,280	201	39	334	133	60	52	136	134	190
1961	1,707	237	50	438	149	96	83	189	248	217
1962	1,944	254	51	504	155	119	96	197	315	253
1963	2,212	300	59	576	161	132	116	199	360	309
1964	2,507	315	66	682	180	150	131	203	428	352
Europe:										
1950	932	64	5	74	31	111	175	153	192	128
1957	2,195	149	42	319	59	178	488	214	475	272
1961	4,255	259	70	614	110	375	885	336	1,144	462
1962	4,883	297	72	711	147	416	975	392	1,338	535
1963	5,634	326	81	855	158	488	1,060	442	1,565	659
1964	6,547	389	102	1,073	168	544	1,186	506	1,783	796
Africa:										
1950	55	6		9	11	1	2	3	17	6
1957	106	10	3	12	21	5	17	5	27	6
1961	122	15	4	16	24	6	19	8	21	9
1962	144	17	3	19	26	9	24	7	27	12
1963	177	21	3	24	30	12	33	10	28	15
1964	225	27	5	31	34	25	42	13	29	19
Asia:										
1950	60	9		12	14	(**)	5	2	8	10
1957	190	15	9	40	38	20	15	12	23	18
1961	315	22	17	88	57	33	22	17	29	30
1962	354	23	18	102	63	36	24	21	30	37
1963	430	31	24	134	67	42	28	25	34	46
1964	535	39	27	173	74	50	39	33	40	60
Oceania:										
1950	107	18	1	13	8	2	22	9	26	8
1957	314	28	3	27	17	8	26	34	146	26
1961	523	63	7	55	29	16	52	48	205	48
1962	613	79	6	67	33	33	52	53	237	53
1963	723	89	8	80	36	51	64	53	278	64
1964	856	104	9	97	42	75	80	60	313	76

1. Includes $166 million in "other Western Hemisphere." Excludes investments in Cuba since 1961. These Cuban investments were estimated at yearend 1960 at $111 million, and included $21 million for food products, $28 million for chemicals and allied products, $28 million for the "other products" group and $34 million for all other manufacturing industries.
**Less than $500,000.

Source: U.S. Department of Commerce, Office of Business Economics.

in the less developed countries. Some moderate increase is suggested in Latin America, in Africa (especially in the petroleum resources of North Africa), and in Middle Eastern oil, but major gains in U.S. investments in these areas are not indicated. However, capital flows to these developing areas in the first half of 1965 were far ahead of the

1964 amounts, partly because of such temporary factors as tax settlements and payments for development concessions.

Trends in major industries

In 1964, a record $1.9 billion was invested in foreign manufacturing affiliates, financed by $1.0 billion of capital supplied by U.S. parent firms (including $260 million to acquire foreign enterprises or to buy out minority holders) and $900 million reinvested from foreign earnings. In the first half of 1965, there was no slackening of these investments, and as noted above, projections of plant and equipment expenditures of foreign manufacturing affiliates show a 28 percent rise for 1965.

Manufacturing investments expanded in all industry sectors during 1964. (See table 5.) The chemical industry, which is carrying out a major expansion program for fertilizer and petrochemical plants, increased its investment by over $450 million, and the transportation industry (including automobile producers) raised its investment by $400 million. Most of these manufacturing investments were in the developed countries; under $400 million went to the less developed countries for all branches of manufacturing.

Net new investments of petroleum companies abroad declined in 1964, partly because of negative undistributed earnings in European subsidiaries and partly because of lower capital outflows to Canada and the Middle East. In the Middle East, settlements of oil companies with some of the oil-producing countries resulted in temporary accumulations in the United States of funds that were paid out in 1965. Though a major part of oil investment is still being used to increase refining capacity and marketing facilities around the world, renewed attention is being given to developing new production and to exploring for new sources of oil and natural gas in North Africa, the Persian Gulf area, Northwestern Europe, and adjoining continental shelf areas.

Companies engaged in mineral operations other than petroleum were somewhat more active in 1964 than in recent years. Activity centered on the development of bauxite properties in Australia and the Caribbean, and iron ore properties in Canada and Australia.

Investments in trade and miscel-

Table 7.—Acquisitions and Sales by American Companies of Foreign Enterprises,[1] by Area and Industry, 1963–64

[Millions of dollars]

Area and industry	1963 Acquisitions	1963 Sales	1963 Net	1964 Acquisitions	1964 Sales	1964 Net
All areas, total	228	52	176	429	166	263
Petroleum	30	4	26	10	29	−19
Manufacturing	171	39	132	336	76	260
Other industries	27	9	18	83	61	22
Canada, total	71	32	39	84	140	−56
Petroleum	30	4	26	2	29	−27
Manufacturing	23	18	5	79	73	6
Other industries	18	9	9	3	37	−34
Europe, total	147	7	140	321	3	318
Petroleum				8		8
Manufacturing	140	7	133	244	1	243
Other industries	7		7	70	2	68
Other areas, total	9	13	−4	24	23	1
Petroleum	(**)		(**)	1		1
Manufacturing	7	13	−6	13	1	12
Other industries	2		2	10	22	−12

[1] Includes acquisitions and sales of minority interests.
**Less than $500,000.

Table 8.—Direct-Investment Receipts of Royalties and Fees,[1] by Areas and Major Industries, 1963–64

[Millions of dollars]

Area and industry	1963 [r]	1964 [p] Total	1964 [p] Royalties, license fees and rentals	1964 [p] Management fees and service charges
All areas, total	660	754	264	490
Petroleum	120	114	13	101
Manufacturing	371	461	193	269
Trade	65	76	40	36
Other industries	105	104	19	85
Canada, total	134	162	41	121
Petroleum	16	15	(**)	15
Manufacturing	96	124	35	89
Trade	6	9	3	6
Other industries	16	14	3	11
Latin America, total	124	134	35	99
Petroleum	29	26	2	24
Manufacturing	47	62	25	37
Trade	17	16	6	10
Other industries	31	30	2	28
Europe, total	272	306	147	159
Petroleum	22	17	1	16
Manufacturing	186	219	112	107
Trade	32	37	26	11
Other industries	32	33	7	26
Other areas, total	130	151	41	110
Petroleum	53	56	10	46
Manufacturing	42	57	21	36
Trade	9	13	5	8
Other Industries	25	26	6	20

[r] Revised.
[p] Preliminary.
[1] Excludes foreign film rentals.
**Less than $500,000.

Table 9.—Plant and Equipment Expenditures of Direct Foreign Investments, Major Industries, 1957–66

[Millions of dollars]

Area and industry	1957	1958	1959	1960	1961	1962	1963	1964	1965 [*]	1966 [*]
All areas, total	4,819	4,097	3,705	3,789	4,122	4,618	5,068	6,118	7,372	7,323
Mining and smelting	421	420	437	426	312	438	398	420	584	493
Petroleum	2,322	1,854	1,558	1,467	1,534	1,628	1,889	2,066	2,350	2,330
Manufacturing	1,347	1,180	1,147	1,397	1,782	2,042	2,251	2,983	3,821	3,809
Trade	186	191	198	196	222	253	266	328	340	396
Other industries	543	452	365	303	272	257	264	321	277	295
Canada, total	1,593	1,311	1,179	1,259	1,016	1,163	1,279	1,559	1,843	1,696
Mining and smelting	163	172	240	290	165	245	195	220	248	190
Petroleum	584	510	380	360	315	300	375	385	377	358
Manufacturing	561	404	389	384	385	458	535	769	1,031	964
Trade	47	55	45	60	39	55	71	80	82	72
Other industries	238	170	125	165	112	105	103	105	105	112
Latin America, total [1]	1,687	1,269	1,003	750	795	860	870	1,023	1,097	932
Mining and smelting	216	221	147	78	87	95	95	126	156	109
Petroleum	1,039	577	449	340	306	339	307	327	368	334
Manufacturing	174	202	193	211	254	286	308	402	420	336
Trade	20	31	31	31	41	41	43	50	58	54
Other industries	238	238	183	90	107	99	103	118	94	99
Europe, total	899	976	906	1,092	1,474	1,674	1,903	2,142	2,659	2,893
Mining and smelting	2		2	2	1	4	5	3	7	8
Petroleum	275	422	339	345	438	494	642	643	728	776
Manufacturing	497	460	450	650	906	1,024	1,107	1,293	1,737	1,855
Trade	107	87	101	83	116	129	118	160	155	221
Other industries	18	7	14	12	13	23	31	43	32	33
Other areas, total	640	541	617	688	837	921	1,016	1,394	1,773	1,502
Mining and smelting	40	27	48	56	59	94	89	71	173	186
Petroleum	424	345	390	422	475	495	565	711	877	862
Manufacturing	115	114	115	152	238	274	301	519	632	654
Trade	12	18	21	22	26	28	34	38	45	49
Other industries	49	37	43	36	40	30	27	55	46	51

[*] Estimated on the basis of company projections.
[1] Includes "other Western Hemisphere."

laneous service industries (including financial and holding companies) were each increased by about $0.4 billion in 1964. About three-quarters of the new investment in trade and service industries was made in the developed countries, mostly in Europe, and smaller amounts went to Canada.

Earnings and Income

Last year, earnings of foreign affiliates of U.S. firms rose by a record $530 million to reach $5.1 billion. Manufacturing operations accounted for $0.3 billion of the increase, scoring large gains in most areas and particularly in Europe. Some of the upward movement of earnings was the result of the enlarged investment base, but in manufacturing industries, earnings also rose relative to the book value of outstanding investments. This suggests, among other things, that plant facilities were better utilized or that current costs of production were reduced. Data on sales of the foreign affiliates will appear in a later issue of the SURVEY.

Earnings of mining operations abroad also registered a substantial gain of more than $0.1 billion, mainly in Canada and Latin America. This industry benefited from generally rising prices for metals and minerals last year.

Foreign earnings of the petroleum industry advanced very little in 1964. There was a gain of well over $0.1 billion from rising production in North Africa, and earnings on Latin American production also improved, but these changes were partly offset by lower earnings of European operations, especially in the Common Market countries.

Income returned from these direct foreign investments—in the form of dividends, branch profits, and interest— rose even more rapidly than total earnings. These receipts amounted to $3.7 billion in 1964, a gain of $0.6 billion over the 1963 amount. Over two-thirds of the gain in manufacturing earnings was paid out as dividends. Income of the petroleum affiliates rose by $0.2 billion even though underlying earnings rose only slightly.

Some of the spurt in dividend remittances was probably related to the scheduled drop in the U.S. corporate tax rate at the beginning of 1964, which caused dividends to be held back in 1963. A further sharp rise of 15 percent over 1964 in income received is estimated for the first half of 1965. This may reflect the second step of the reduction in corporate tax rates as well as rising foreign earnings. Remittances may also be increasing in response to the voluntary balance of payments program.

Because dividend remittances rose faster last year than the earnings of foreign subsidiaries, undistributed profits fell slightly from the record $1.5 billion of 1963. The principal reductions in undistributed profits were in European petroleum affiliates and in Canadian manufacturing affiliates. These reductions were offset in part by larger reinvested earnings of manufacturing affiliates in Latin America and Europe and by those of mining affiliates in Canada.

Returns from foreign affiliates in the form of royalties and fees are also important elements in the balance of payments. These increased by $0.1 billion in 1964 (table 8), mainly from manufacturing operations in developed countries. Of the $¾ billion of royalties and fees received in 1964, about two-thirds represented charges for management services and the rest were payments of royalties, license fees, and rentals.

Portfolio and Short-Term Investments

American investors have severely limited their purchases of foreign securities since the proposal of the Interest

Table 10.—Plant and Equipment Expenditures Abroad by U.S. Manufacturing Companies, by Area and Major Commodity, 1960–66

[Millions of dollars]

Areas and years	Total	Food products	Paper and allied products	Chemicals	Rubber products	Primary and fabricated metals	Machinery, excluding electrical	Electrical machinery	Transportation equipment	Other manufacturing
All areas, total:										
1960	1,397	97	78	237	68	133	192	104	336	152
1961	1,782	116	71	278	91	169	290	141	473	153
1962	2,042	126	95	308	91	162	315	177	585	183
1963 ʳ	2,251	132	134	436	98	204	330	164	530	223
1964	2,983	157	166	621	109	299	415	212	733	270
1965 ᵉ	3,821	182	213	870	164	356	594	218	957	267
1966 ᵉ	3,809	143	136	835	147	368	693	202	1,067	217
Canada:										
1960	384	30	55	75	15	49	17	30	63	50
1961	385	20	54	55	18	55	40	31	60	52
1962	458	28	75	75	19	57	38	50	65	51
1963 ʳ	535	30	100	110	16	60	39	40	94	46
1964	769	29	116	177	30	110	47	46	167	47
1965 ᵉ	1,031	50	132	290	30	119	60	56	229	65
1966 ᵉ	964	36	83	300	25	80	90	52	238	60
Latin America: [1]										
1960	211	24	7	49	12	11	12	18	47	31
1961	254	37	5	48	19	23	13	27	52	30
1962	286	35	6	52	12	20	15	25	81	40
1963 ʳ	308	32	9	94	17	16	19	19	50	52
1964	402	42	15	124	16	23	23	34	75	50
1965 ᵉ	420	45	19	140	23	34	36	28	54	42
1966 ᵉ	336	35	13	101	20	27	17	23	69	30
Europe:										
Common Market:										
1960	370	17	2	44	11	10	114	21	128	23
1961	534	30	3	63	11	19	164	36	181	27
1962	619	30	4	54	26	25	156	44	245	35
1963 ʳ	607	29	7	82	26	45	173	39	155	51
1964	682	26	11	123	26	64	184	46	151	52
1965 ᵉ	993	25	19	153	35	52	289	53	314	54
1966 ᵉ	1,100	25	19	180	30	38	353	63	362	38
Other Europe:										
1960	280	18	3	42	15	50	24	18	74	35
1961	372	17	4	49	15	46	38	30	141	31
1962	405	21	6	51	12	45	65	41	123	41
1963 ʳ	500	24	10	71	18	46	60	51	166	54
1964	611	41	11	92	14	40	82	62	177	93
1965 ᵉ	744	35	18	142	31	53	106	55	225	79
1966 ᵉ	755	24	9	140	39	51	127	42	256	68
Other areas:										
1960	152	8	12	28	16	13	24	16	23	12
1961	238	12	5	63	28	26	35	17	39	13
1962	274	12	4	76	22	15	41	17	71	16
1963 ʳ	301	17	8	79	21	37	39	15	65	20
1964	519	19	14	105	23	63	80	24	163	28
1965 ᵉ	632	27	26	145	45	98	103	26	136	27
1966 ᵉ	654	24	18	114	34	172	106	22	142	22

ʳ Revised.
ᵉ Estimated on the basis of company projections.
[1] Includes "other Western Hemisphere."

Table 11.—Plant and Equipment Expenditures of Direct Foreign Investments, by Country and Major Industry, 1963–66

[Millions of dollars]

	1963 r			1964			1965 e			1966 e		
	Mining and smelting	Petroleum	Manufacturing	Mining and smelting	Petroleum	Manufacturing	Mining and smelting	Petroleum	Manufacturing	Mining and smelting	Petroleum	Manufacturing
All areas, total	398	1,889	2,251	420	2,066	2,983	584	2,350	3,821	493	2,330	3,809
Canada	195	375	535	220	385	769	248	377	1,031	190	358	964
Latin American Republics, total	75	245	271	72	272	363	102	309	399	70	282	329
Mexico	5	10	60	9	5	112	11	4	122	8	4	70
Other countries in Central America and West Indies	2	32	5	2	30	5	2	41	9	2	29	6
Argentina	(*)	12	89	(*)	12	90	(*)	14	100	(*)	16	85
Brazil	2	3	57	3	4	61	4	3	64	5	3	70
Chile	25	(*)	4	27	(*)	8	38	(*)	8	(*)	2	6
Colombia	(*)	30	23	(*)	58	24	(*)	29	31	(*)	25	32
Peru	18	10	13	22	9	22	38	12	26	24	13	21
Venezuela	(*)	142	16	(*)	134	24	(*)	172	31	(*)	166	33
Other countries in South America	1	(*)	4	1	(*)	17	2	(*)	8	1	(*)	6
Other Western Hemisphere	34	62	37	54	55	39	54	59	21	39	52	7
Europe, total	5	642	1,107	3	643	1,293	7	728	1,737	8	776	1,855
Common Market, total	1	386	607	1	395	682	1	376	963	1	406	1,100
Belgium and Luxembourg		11	38		29	67		30	112		20	118
France	(**)	56	160	(**)	68	176	(**)	105	238	(**)	99	225
Germany	(**)	184	261	(**)	121	279	(**)	124	478	(**)	98	535
Italy	(**)	85	107	(**)	124	105	(**)	82	92	(**)	77	110
Netherlands		50	41		53	55		35	73		112	112
Other Europe, total	4	256	500	2	248	611	5	352	744	7	370	755
Denmark		37	5		20	6		4			26	3
Norway	(**)	8	12	(**)	10	13	(**)	13	19	(**)	12	12
Spain	(**)	20	23	(**)	25	42	(**)	7	36	(**)	8	31
Sweden		25	17		23	12		26	16		32	16
Switzerland		4	10		6	15		18	20		16	13
United Kingdom	1	140	399	(**)	126	501	(**)	214	607	(**)	235	651
Other countries	3	22	34	2	38	22	5	50	42	7	41	29
Africa, total	58	164	24	41	268	63	46	287	92	31	350	97
North Africa		129	1		188	1		195	3		254	8
East Africa		14	(**)		8	1		10	1		7	1
West Africa	38	8	3	19	47	16	22	51	40	7	68	52
Republic of South Africa	15	(*)	19	5	(*)	45	8	(*)	48	8	(*)	36
Other countries in Central and South Africa	5	(*)	1	17	(*)	(**)	16	(*)	(**)	16	(*)	(**)
Asia, total	2	297	136	1	278	214	1	441	267	1	377	218
Middle East		125	5		114	9		203	9		146	24
Far East, total	2	172	131	1	164	205	1	238	258	1	231	194
India		(*)	17		(*)	36		(*)	47		(*)	31
Japan		(*)	69		(*)	113		(*)	160		(*)	123
Philippine Republic	1	(*)	20	1	(*)	40	(**)	(*)	34	(**)	(*)	19
Other countries	1	(*)	25	(**)	(*)	16	(**)	(*)	17	(**)	(*)	21
Oceania, total	29	64	141	29	65	242	126	83	274	154	75	339
Australia	29	(*)	138	29	(*)	235	126	(*)	263	154	(*)	327
Other Countries		(*)	3		(*)	7		(*)	11		(*)	12
International shipping		40			100			66			60	

*Included in area total.
**Less than $500,000.
r Revised.
e Estimated on the basis of company projections.

Table 12.—Domestic and Foreign Expenditures for Plant and Equipment in Selected Industries, 1963–65

[Millions of dollars]

Industry	Expenditures 1963 r				Expenditures 1964				Expenditures 1965 e			
	Total	Domestic	Foreign	Percent of foreign to total	Total	Domestic	Foreign	Percent of foreign to total	Total	Domestic	Foreign	Percent of foreign to total
Manufacturing, total for selected industries	10,188	8,160	2,028	19.9	12,652	9,940	2,712	21.4	15,624	12,070	3,554	22.7
Food products	1,102	970	132	12.0	1,217	1,060	157	12.9	1,352	1,170	182	13.5
Paper and allied products	854	720	134	15.7	1,106	940	166	15.0	1,343	1,130	213	15.9
Chemicals	2,046	1,610	436	21.3	2,591	1,970	621	24.0	3,340	2,470	870	26.0
Rubber products	338	240	98	29.0	379	270	109	28.8	514	350	164	31.9
Primary and fabricated metals ¹	1,304	1,100	204	15.6	1,709	1,410	299	17.5	2,016	1,660	356	17.7
Machinery, except electrical	1,570	1,240	330	21.0	2,055	1,640	415	20.2	2,584	1,990	594	23.0
Electrical machinery	854	690	164	19.2	872	660	212	24.3	1,018	880	218	21.4
Transportation equipment	2,120	1,590	530	25.0	2,723	1,990	733	26.9	3,457	2,500	957	27.7
Mining and petroleum	6,247	3,960	2,287	36.6	7,036	4,550	2,486	35.3	8,074	5,140	2,934	36.3

r Revised. e Estimated on basis of company projections.
¹ Excludes primary iron and steel producers.
NOTE.—Foreign expenditures include acquisitions of existing fixed assets, which are excluded from the domestic series.

Equalization Tax in mid–1963. Purchases of new issues still provide a considerable amount of capital to Canada and some other borrowers exempt from the IET, but issues by European and other countries that were making extensive use of the U.S. market prior to mid–1963 have become inconsequential. (See table 13.) Some of the demand has shifted to European markets—although these have been open only on a limited basis and mainly for European borrowers—or may have been replaced by other forms of U.S. capital outflows. U.S. investment firms have been active in placing new foreign securities in European markets, and a number of such issues have been sold in the U.S. market entirely to foreign investors.

On balance, U.S. investors have been liquidating their existing holdings of foreign securities since the IET was proposed. This has affected mainly European issues and may reflect weaknesses in most European equity markets, but there has also been net selling of Canadian issues despite the comparative strength of the Canadian market.

At the beginning of this year, U.S. holdings of foreign securities had an estimated market value of $14.5 billion (table 15), about $10.0 billion more than at the end of 1950. Some $9.0 billion of the total was in the form of bonds or other debt securities, and $5.3 billion was in corporate stocks. By far the largest amount, $8.1 billion, was invested in Canadian securities, and $2.9 billion in European securities. Though there were large holdings of bonds of international institutions, only a few less developed countries have been able to sell significant amounts of their securities in the U.S. market since the 1920's.

Since 1950, American banks have steadily expanded their foreign loans and other assets (including some assets held for their customers), which reached a peak net capital outflow of $2.5 billion in 1964. This raised the total outstanding at the end of 1964 to nearly $12 billion, including $0.7 billion reported for the first time as banks reviewed their records more closely in connection with the voluntary program. During 1964, the net capital outflow by banks to developing countries was unusually high, but the most rapid growth was in loans to European countries, which may have substituted, directly or indirectly, for sales of securities or longer term loans that would have been subject to the IET.

Nonfinancial firms accounted for an outflow of $0.9 billion in 1964. This included the acquisition of liquid assets, such as time deposits or financial paper in Canada and the United Kingdom, as well as a $250 million loan to finance a power project in Canada. In accordance with the guidelines of the voluntary balance of payments program, a substantial portion of the liquid assets held abroad by industrial firms was withdrawn after Febraury 1965.

Foreign Investments in the United States

Capital inflows from foreign investors for direct investments or purchases of U.S. securities or other assets (other than short-term assets or special Government issues) have been relatively small in recent years and amounted to only $110 million in 1964. In the first half of 1965, there was a negligible net inflow.

The largest negative factor has been a liquidation of foreign holdings of U.S. securities, other than Treasury public debt issues. This has been largely, but not entirely, for United Kingdom account, and reach $250 million in the second quarter of 1965. Despite the net liquidation, the improvement in market prices raised the estimated value of foreign holdings of U.S. corporate stocks to $13.8 billion by the end of 1964. Over $10 billion of that amount was in European holdings.

Part of the "long-term" capital inflow in 1964 and the first half of 1965, $236 million and $195 million, respectively, represented increases in foreign funds held in long-term time deposits in the United States. Much of this was the temporary investment of the proceeds of sales of securities in the United States, including $235 million, net, by international and interregional organizations.

There has also been a small net outward flow of direct investment capital in the last few years, however, as shown in table 14. This was the balance of a moderate inflow for new investments and slightly higher net transfers abroad through intercompany accounts or liquidations. Most of the annual increase in the value of foreign direct investments in the United States resulted from undistributed profits, which rose to more than $300 million in 1964. This reflected a considerable gain in earnings of the U.S. affiliates, especially in the manufacturing sector, while income distributed abroad was slightly reduced.

Table 13.—New Foreign Issues Placed in the United States, 1963–June 1965

[Millions of dollars; before deducting discounts and commissions]

Areas	Gross amount sold			U.S. portion		
	Total	Publicly offered	Privately offered	Total	Publicly offered	Privately offered
1965 (January–June) ᵖ						
Total	754	462	292	632	345	287
Canada	334	54	280	328	53	275
Europe	65	65		12	12	
Australia, Republic of South Africa, New Zealand, and Japan	68	68		37	37	
Other countries	106	94	12	82	82	12
International Bank	181	181		161	161	
1964 (July–December)						
Total	705	198	507	670	171	499
Canada	443		443	434		434
Europe	32	15	17	27	10	17
Australia, Republic of South Africa, New Zealand, and Japan						
Other countries ¹	¹ 230	¹ 183	47	¹ 209	¹ 161	48
International Bank						
1964 (January–June)						
Total	450	149	301	415	123	292
Canada	282		282	282		275
Europe	19	15	4	11	7	4
Australia, Republic of South Africa, New Zealand, and Japan						
Other countries ²	² 144	² 129	15	² 124	² 111	13
International Bank	5	5		5	5	
1963 (July–December)						
Total	295	142	153	257	105	152
Canada	86		86	86		86
Europe	69	20	49	53	5	48
Australia, Republic of South Africa, New Zealand, and Japan	66	48	18	60	42	18
Other countries	74	74		58	58	
1963 (January–June) ʳ						
Total	1,124	269	855	995	173	822
Canada	623	(*)	623	594	(*)	594
Europe ³	³ 285	108	³ 177	³ 222	45	³ 177
Australia, Republic of South Africa, New Zealand, and Japan	164	125	39	130	93	37
Other countries	52	36	16	49	35	14

ᵖ Preliminary.
*Less than $500,000.
ʳ Revised.
¹ Includes $100 million offering of Inter-American Development Bank bonds.
² Includes $50 million offering of Inter-American Development Bank bonds.
³ Includes $115 million of bonds of Shell Funding Corporation.

NOTE.—The amounts shown for U.S. purchases exceed the figures used in the balance of payments because the latter exclude discounts and commissions. The International Bank for Reconstruction and Development issues are reduced by the amount of delayed deliveries included in subsequent years. A detailed listing of foreign issues placed in the U.S. in the years 1952–64 is available on request.

Table 14.—Foreign Direct Investments in the United States, Selected Data, 1963 and 1964, by Country and Industry

[Millions of dollars]

	Value			Capital flow						Earnings ¹		
	December 1950	December 1963	December 1964 ᵖ	1963			1964			1964		
				Total	New investments ²	Other	Total	New investments ²	Other	Earnings	Income ¹	Undistributed profits
Total	3,391	7,944	8,363	−5	151	−156	−5	71	−76	596	294	327
By Area												
Canada	1,029	2,183	2,284	44	32	11	26	8	18	177	132	61
United Kingdom	1,168	2,665	2,796	44	36	7	−36	33	−69	169	75	95
Other Europe	1,059	2,826	3,023	−61	62	−123	24	26	−2	220	64	161
Belgium	nss	161	175	−2		−2	8		8	6	3	6
France	nss	182	197	−5	1	−6	3	5	12	5	7
Germany	nss	149	156	−9	1	−10	−5	5	−10	14	3	11
Italy	nss	102	82	−5	25	−6	−9	2	−11	−11	1	−11
Netherlands	334	1,134	1,231	−35	15	−50	−6	4	−10	121	20	102
Sweden	nss	185	199	(*)		(*)	7	10	−3	9	2	7
Switzerland	348	825	896	−32	20	−52	24	2	22	67	30	37
Other	377	89	88	3		3	−3	(*)	−3	2	(*)	2
Other countries	134	269	259	−31	21	−52	−19	4	−23	30	23	10
By Industry												
Petroleum	405	1,513	1,612	−44	20	−65	−55	1	−56	172	18	154
Manufacturing	1,138	3,018	3,213	42	63	−22	59	14	45	235	105	136
Trade	nss	706	675	−51	3	−53	−65	4	−1	38	3	34
Insurance	³ 1,065	³ 2,045	³ 2,181	−37		−37	−1		−1	38	38	
Other finance	(⁴)	(⁴)	(⁴)	37	30	8	34	5	29	105	105	6
Other industries	784	663	683	48	35	12	23	16	7	5	19	−3

ᵖ Preliminary.   nss—Not shown separately.   *Less than $500,000.
¹ "Earnings" represents the foreign share in corporate or branch profits; "Income" is the amount distributed, after withholding taxes, as dividends, interest, or branch profits.
² "New investments" represents initial investments in U.S. companies or increase in equity capital of existing foreign-owned U.S. companies.
³ Includes market revaluations of securities held by insurance companies.
⁴ Included in "Insurance."

Short-term investments

In 1964, there was once again a very large gain in foreign holdings of short-term assets in the United States and of various obligations of the U.S. Government. These holdings rose by $3.2 billion in 1964 to a total of $31.9 billion. However, this was not accompanied, as in other recent years, by a sizable loss of U.S. monetary reserve assets. In the first half of 1965, by contrast, foreign holdings of liquid dollar assets dropped by about $1 billion, while U.S. monetary reserve assets were drawn down by $0.9 billion.

These dollar holdings by foreigners take a variety of forms, and included, at the end of 1964, $16.7 billion of deposits and other claims on U.S. banks, $11.2 billion of marketable debt of the U.S. Government, and an additional $3.2 billion of obligations of the U.S. Government arising mainly from special security issues or advance deposits by foreign governments.

Some $20.0 billion of these short-term dollar assets and U.S. Government obligations was reported to be held by foreign governments or intergovernmental organizations, $7.2 billion by foreign private banks, and $4.7 billion by other foreigners. However, these designations are based to a large extent on banking records, which often cannot identify the ultimate owner of the asset.

Table 15.—International Investment Position of the United States, Total 1950, by Area, 1963–64

[Millions of dollars]

Type of Investment	Total 1950	Total 1963 r	Total 1964 p	Western Europe 1963 r	Western Europe 1964 p	Canada 1963 r	Canada 1964 p	Latin American Republics 1963 r	Latin American Republics 1964 p	Other foreign countries 1963 r	Other foreign countries 1964 p	International institutions and unallocated 1963 r	International institutions and unallocated 1964 p
U.S. assets and investments abroad, total	31,539	88,301	98,720	24,825	27,801	21,712	24,596	15,727	17,335	21,127	24,211	4,910	4,777
Gold stock (not included in total)	22,820	15,596	15,471										
Private investments	19,004	66,513	75,419	17,000	19,529	21,706	24,591	12,352	13,798	12,647	14,598	2,808	2,903
Long-term	17,488	58,330	64,731	15,343	17,484	20,316	22,597	10,386	11,218	9,478	10,529	2,807	2,903
Direct	11,788	40,686	44,343	10,340	12,067	13,044	13,820	8,662	8,932	6,907	7,661	¹ 1,733	¹ 1,863
Foreign dollar bonds	1,692	7,335	8,218	781	779	3,835	4,474	359	556	1,286	1,369	1,074	1,040
Other foreign bonds ²	1,466	819	978	60	30	640	710	24	167	60	71		
Foreign corporate stocks	1,175	5,145	5,270	2,319	2,065	2,461	2,948	65	67	300	190		
Banking claims	390	³ 2,830	4,051	1,081	1,699	³ 90	³ 106	965	1,197	694	1,049		(x)
Other	977	1,515	³ 1,871	762	844	246	539	311	299	196	189		
Short-term assets and claims	1,516	8,183	10,688	1,657	2,045	1,390	1,994	1,966	2,580	3,169	4,069	1	(x)
Reported by banks	886	5,887	⁴ 7,846	923	1,210	638	913	1,589	2,126	2,737	3,597		(x)
Other	630	2,296	2,842	734	835	752	1,081	377	454	432	472	1	(x)
U.S. Government credits and claims	12,535	21,788	23,301	7,825	8,272	6	5	3,375	3,537	8,480	9,613	2,102	1,874
Long-term credits ⁶	10,768	17,149	18,772	7,029	7,356			3,134	3,298	5,944	7,018	1,042	1,100
Repayable in dollars ⁷	n.a.	13,162	13,971	5,992	6,199			2,872	2,972	3,256	3,700	1,042	1,100
Repayable in foreign currencies, etc.⁸	n.a.	3,987	4,801	1,037	1,157			262	326	2,688	3,318		
Foreign currencies and short-term claims	322	3,392	3,328	587	488	3	2	241	239	2,536	2,594	25	5
IMF gold tranche position and monetary authorities' holdings of convertible currencies	1,445	1,247	1,201	209	428	3	3			1		1,035	769
Foreign assets and investments in the United States, total	17,635	51,486	56,842	29,856	33,363	7,772	8,304	4,792	5,461	6,129	6,976	2,937	2,738
Long-term	7,997	22,791	24,979	16,237	17,726	3,882	4,187	1,393	1,686	1,095	1,168	184	212
Direct	3,391	7,944	8,363	5,491	5,491	2,183	2,284	112	134	158	126		
Corporate stocks	2,925	12,485	13,835	9,307	10,159	1,490	1,726	935	1,077	687	793	66	80
Corporate, State, and municipal bonds	181	702	922	460	663	(x)	(x)	77	80	48	49	117	130
Other	1,500	1,660	1,859	979	1,085	209	177	269	395	202	200	1	2
Short-term assets and U.S. Government obligations	9,638	28,695	31,863	13,619	15,637	3,890	4,117	3,399	3,775	5,034	5,808	2,753	2,526
By type:													
Private obligations	6,477	14,892	17,499	5,815	7,089	2,018	2,202	2,900	3,340	3,702	4,442	457	426
Reported by banks	5,751	14,157	16,688	5,415	6,656	1,937	2,117	2,786	3,226	3,562	4,263	457	426
Other	726	735	811	400	433	81	85	114	114	140	179	(x)	(x)
U.S. Government obligations	3,161	13,803	14,364	7,804	8,548	1,872	1,915	499	435	1,332	1,366	2,296	2,100
Bills and certificates	1,508	8,720	8,799	5,347	5,585	1,051	867	225	170	1,143	1,157	954	1,020
Marketable bonds and notes	1,470	⁹ 2,742	2,405	741	714	687	690	98	81	81	93	1,135	827
Nonmarketable bonds and notes		893	¹⁰ 1,440	768	1,111	125	¹⁰ 329						
Other ¹¹	183	1,448	1,720	948	1,138	9	29	176	184	108	⁴ 116	207	253
By holder:													
Foreign central banks and governments and international and regional institutions	n.a.	18,756	20,029	9,600	10,540	1,798	1,841	1,436	1,647	3,169	3,475	2,753	2,526
Foreign commercial banks ¹³	n.a.	5,713	7,179	2,360	3,274	1,668	1,836	377	404	1,308	1,665		
Other private holders and unallocated	n.a.	4,226	4,655	1,659	1,823	424	440	1,586	1,724	557	668	(x)	(x)

r Revised.   p Preliminary.   n.a. Not available.   (x) Negligible.

¹ Represents the estimated investment in shipping companies registered primarily in Panama and Liberia.
² Consists primarily of securities payable in foreign currencies, but includes some dollar obligations including prior to 1963 participations and loans made by the International Bank for Reconstruction and Development. Effective 1963 participations in IBRD loans are included under banking claims and "other" long term, according to country of obligor.
³ Excludes $200 million netted against a related inflow of U.S. direct investment capital.
⁴ New series. For detail see *Treasury Bulletin*, June 1965, p. 86.
⁵ Includes $254 million loaned to Canada in connection with Columbia River power development.
⁶ Excludes World War I debts that are not currently being serviced.
⁷ Includes indebtedness repayable in U.S. dollars, or optionally in foreign currencies when option rests with U.S. Government.

⁸ Includes indebtedness which the borrower may contractually, or at its option, repay with its currency, with a third country's currency, or by delivery of materials or transfer of services.
⁹ New series based on a Federal Reserve Board survey as of July 31, 1963. Data to reconcile the old and new series are not available.
¹⁰ Includes $204 million of nonmarketable bonds issued to the Government of Canada in connection with transactions under the Columbia River Treaty.
¹¹ Includes non-interest-bearing demand notes issued in payment of subscriptions to international and regional organizations (other than IMF), portfolio fund certificates sold abroad by Export-Import Bank, liabilities associated with Government grant and capital transactions (including restricted accounts), and advances for military exports and other Government sales.
¹³ As reported by U.S. banks; ultimate ownership is not identified.

FOREIGN INVESTMENTS, 1965-66

Samuel Pizer
and
Frederick Cutler

by SAMUEL PIZER and FREDERICK CUTLER

Foreign Investments, 1965-66

NET OUTFLOWS of U.S. private capital, which had reached a peak amount of $6.5 billion in 1964, receded to $3.7 billion in 1965. Although outflows in the first half of 1966 rose to a $4.0 billion rate, this increase reflected a carryover of $150 million of Canadian new issues originally scheduled for 1965 and a special outflow of $180 million for direct investments. Without these transactions, the annual rate in the first half of this year would have been somewhat under the 1965 rate.

In this article, the components of these capital flows are discussed in some detail, with special emphasis on the flows connected with direct investments abroad. In particular, a report is given on the latest projections by U.S. companies of the plant and equipment expenditures of foreign affiliates. These expenditures are financed in part by capital flows from the United States and by undistributed profits of the affiliates; both types of financing are covered in this article.

Data for other sources and uses of funds of foreign affiliates are now being processed and are scheduled for publication in the November issue of the SURVEY.

The most drastic shift in the makeup of private capital outflows has been the cessation of net lending by U.S. banks. Such outflows reached a peak of $2.5 billion in 1964, but were reversed to a net inflow of $0.1 billion in 1965, and $0.2 billion in the first half of 1966. Although the initial pressure for this reversal came from the application of foreign lending guidelines introduced in the Government's balance of payments program (which were announced in February 1965 and extended in December 1965), the overriding factor has been the intense domestic demand for bank loans. In the second quarter of 1966, there was a modest resumption of net foreign lending by banks, but this is probably only a temporary reversal of the recent trend.

American investments in foreign securities have been limited since July 1963 by the Interest Equalization Tax (IET) and by ceilings administered by the Federal Reserve Board on such investments by nonbanking financial institutions. New foreign issues sold to U.S. investors have remained sizable but have been confined largely to borrowers whose securities are exempt from the tax. New issues were at an annual rate of over $1.0 billion in the first half of 1966 even if the carryover from 1965 of $150 million of Canadian issues is excluded. The Canadian Government has compensated in part for the continued large-scale Canadian borrowing in

Table 1.—Plant and Equipment Expenditures of Direct Foreign Investments by Major Industries, 1960-67 [1]

[Millions of dollars]

Area and industry	Realized expenditures						Projected expenditures			
								1966		1967
	1960	1961	1962	1963	1964	1965	Projected in May–June 1965	Projected in Jan.–Feb. 1966	Projected in June 1966	Projected in June 1966
All areas, total	3,789	4,122	4,618	5,068	6,199	7,531	7,323	8,764	9,162	9,210
Mining and smelting	426	312	438	398	463	682	493	588	826	693
Petroleum	1,467	1,534	1,628	1,889	2,073	2,267	2,330	2,680	2,727	2,936
Manufacturing	1,397	1,782	2,042	2,251	3,007	3,893	3,809	4,786	4,797	4,790
Trade	196	222	253	266	328	351	396	416	478	495
Other industries	303	272	257	264	328	338	295	294	334	296
Canada, total	1,259	1,016	1,163	1,279	1,553	1,908	1,696	2,035	2,262	2,149
Mining and smelting	290	165	245	195	220	265	190	201	340	244
Petroleum	360	315	300	375	385	503	358	426	552	570
Manufacturing	384	385	458	535	771	952	964	1,201	1,171	1,147
Trade	60	39	55	71	80	84	72	84	84	85
Other industries	165	112	105	103	97	104	112	123	115	103
Latin America, total [2]	750	795	860	870	1,031	1,079	932	1,139	1,240	1,250
Mining and smelting	78	87	95	109	123	160	109	176	214	193
Petroleum	340	306	339	307	327	307	334	378	336	391
Manufacturing	211	254	286	308	413	446	336	443	511	505
Trade	31	41	41	43	50	65	54	70	78	76
Other industries	90	107	99	103	118	101	99	72	101	85
Europe, total	1,092	1,474	1,674	1,903	2,179	2,674	2,893	3,545	3,584	3,714
Mining and smelting	2	1	4	5	3	5	8	5	5	3
Petroleum	345	438	494	642	645	603	776	972	873	940
Manufacturing	650	906	1,024	1,107	1,328	1,873	1,855	2,323	2,406	2,467
Trade	83	116	129	118	160	158	221	213	261	266
Other industries	12	13	23	31	43	35	33	32	39	38
Other areas, total	688	837	921	1,016	1,436	1,869	1,802	2,045	2,077	2,096
Mining and smelting	56	59	94	89	117	252	186	206	267	253
Petroleum	422	475	495	565	716	854	862	904	966	1,035
Manufacturing	152	238	274	301	495	622	654	819	710	670
Trade	22	26	28	34	38	43	49	49	55	68
Other industries	36	40	30	27	70	98	51	67	79	70

NOTE.—Data for 1966 and 1967 are projected on the basis of company estimates. In this and subsequent tables, detail may not add to totals because of rounding.
1. Data for 1957–59 are shown on page 28 of the Survey of Current Business for September, 1965.
2. Includes "other Western Hemisphere."

NOTE.—This report was prepared in the International Investment Section of the Balance of Payments Division.

the United States by advance repatriations in the first half of this year of over $100 million of an outstanding Canadian Government issue.

Capital outflows for direct investment abroad—that is, to foreign business organizations in which U.S. investors have an equity interest of at least 10 percent—have accounted for a rising share of total private capital outflows.

Projections of Plant and Equipment Expenditures Abroad

U.S. firms report a steep rise in capital outlays by foreign affiliates in 1966
Further gains indicated for 1967

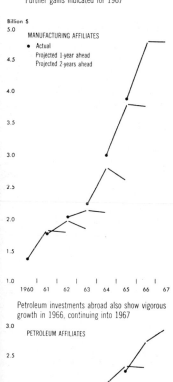

Petroleum investments abroad also show vigorous growth in 1966, continuing into 1967

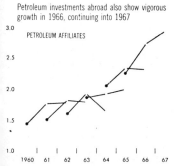

U.S. Department of Commerce, Office of Business Economics   66-9-8

In the 1960–63 period, such outflows amounted to 43 percent of the total, but they increased to nearly 90 percent in 1965 and appear to be headed for a similar share in 1966. In 1965, the aggregate outflows for direct investments was $3.3 billion, and in the first half of 1966, the annual rate was $3.2 billion. In both of these recent periods, there were large special outflows; in 1965, there were about $0.2 billion of outflows for refinancing that had no net effect on the balance of payments, and in the first half of 1966, there was an outflow estimated at $180 million that represented an exchange of U.S. securities for the shares of a foreign company. Also, American companies made use of financing raised abroad by U.S. affiliates established for the purpose of obtaining such financing. The amount of such foreign funds included in the figures for direct investment outflows was $60 million in 1965 and about $100 million in the first half of 1966. When all of these special transactions are eliminated, the direct-investment flow was $3.1 billion in 1965 and at an annual rate of $2.7 billion in the first half of 1966.

In the next section of this article, attention is focused on the major expansion now being carried out in the foreign production facilities of U.S. firms. Since in the past a large part of the financing of such expenditures has been provided by capital outflows from the United States, the moderation of such outflows so far this year indicates a major effort by the investing companies to comply with the request of the Government that they rely as much as possible on capital obtained abroad.

Foreign Plant and Equipment Expenditures

The latest set of reports, completed by major U.S. companies in June and July, shows that an extraordinarily strong rise in plant and equipment expenditures is underway this year. Projected outlays for 1966 were first estimated at $7.3 billion in the reports of June–July 1965; these were raised to $8.8 billion in a followup survey early in 1966 and are currently estimated at $9.2 billion. If this projection is real-

ized, it will amount to an advance of $1.6 billion, or 21 percent, above the record 1965 total.

The projection now being made for 1967 slightly exceeds the current 1966 projection. In the past these advance estimates have tended to be low—for example, in the early projections for 1965, the shortfall was 24 percent, and the present 1967 estimate, if realized, would also be about 25 percent above the first projection for 1966. Nevertheless, a bias of similar magnitude cannot be assumed for 1967, since tighter conditions in world capital markets may result in some postponement of investment plans.

Advances this year in capital outlays abroad are scheduled for virtually every industry and geographic area. Capital expenditures for manufacturing facilities are scheduled to rise 23 percent

Domestic and Foreign Capital Expenditures by U.S. Companies

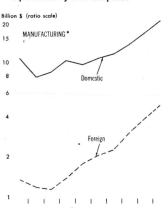

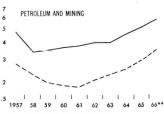

* Excludes primary iron and steel, and petroleum.
** Anticipated. Domestic investment includes actual outlays for 1st half.

U.S. Department of Commerce, Office of Business Economics   6-6-99

over last year, an increase of $0.9 billion, to a total of $4.8 billion. This is more than twice the investment rate only 3 years ago. Petroleum outlays this year are up by $460 million to $2.7 billion, for the first time exceeding the extraordinary high of 1957. Moreover, a further sizable advance has already been projected by the petroleum industry for 1967. Mining investments are also scheduled to rise to a new high in 1966, and the anticipation for 1967, although it suggests some decline from the 1966 record, is for a level substantially above that of earlier periods.

The latest set of projections for 1966 includes some notable shifts from those published in the March 1966 SURVEY. Capital outlays in the mining industry in 1966 have been raised by nearly $250 million, primarily because of decisions to increase investments in Canada, Peru, South Africa, and Australia. Projections for mining are subject to wide variation because of uncertainties about very large individual projects. For the petroleum industry, the current 1966 expectation is close to the March projection in the aggregate; however, within the total, large in-

creases in planned outlays in Canada and smaller gains in Africa and Asia are offset by reductions in expected outlays in Europe and Latin America. There seems to have been some shifting of outlays into 1967, especially in Europe; this may reflect efforts to contribute to the program to improve the balance of payments. In the aggregate, plans for manufacturing investments abroad in 1966 are also about the same now as in March, but here again there has been some shifting, with higher outlays now expected in Europe and Latin America, and cutbacks from earlier plans now indicated for Canada, Australia, and some countries in Africa and Asia.

Manufacturing investments

Capital expenditures by foreign affiliates in manufacturing are especially significant because of their size (over half of the total for all industries beginning in 1965), their rapid growth, and the interrelation of foreign producing activities and the merchandise trade of the United States. The extremely rapid rise of these foreign capital outlays is depicted in chart 8; and in chart 9, it can be seen that these outlays have outpaced domestic plant and equipment expenditures, even in the most recent period of rapid domestic expansion.

These 1966 projections would raise the share of foreign outlays in total capital expenditures of U.S. manufacturing firms to 22.6 percent (excluding certain industry groups not significant abroad).

Gains in the relative importance of foreign manufacturing investments since the early 1960's are especially noteworthy in view of the strong earnings record of domestic investment. As chart 10 indicates, the rate of return in domestic manufacturing investments has risen steadily, since the current business expansion started, from 10.2 percent in 1961 to 13.4 percent in 1964 and to a high of 15 percent in 1965. The return on European manufacturing investments of U.S. firms was much higher than U.S. rates until 1962, although it was declining rapidly. After

Table 2.—Plant and Equipment Expenditures of Direct Foreign Investments, by Country and Major Industry, 1964–67

[Millions of dollars]

	1964 r			1965			1966 p			1967 p		
	Mining and smelting	Petroleum	Manufacturing	Mining and smelting	Petroleum	Manufacturing	Mining and smelting	Petroleum	Manufacturing	Mining and smelting	Petroleum	Manufacturing
All areas, total	463	2,073	3,007	682	2,267	3,833	826	2,727	4,797	693	2,936	4,790
Canada	220	385	771	265	503	952	340	552	1,171	244	570	1,147
Latin American Republics, total	69	272	367	105	246	424	169	260	488	177	321	495
Argentina	(*)	12	90	(*)	15	101	(*)	11	114	(*)	22	107
Brazil	3	4	62	3	3	72	7	6	121	18	6	157
Chile	27	(*)	9	29	(*)	11	70	(*)	16	62	(*)	13
Colombia	(*)	58	24	(*)	35	26	(*)	36	22	(*)	47	23
Mexico	9	5	112	11	2	141	22	3	136	25	3	107
Peru	19	9	23	53	8	28	50	9	26	59	14	27
Venezuela	(*)	134	25	(*)	130	27	(*)	150	33	(*)	169	38
Other countries	1	(*)	22	3	(*)	17	8	(*)	21	4	(*)	24
Other Western Hemisphere	54	55	46	55	61	23	45	76	22	16	70	10
Europe, total	3	645	1,328	5	603	1,673	5	873	2,406	3	940	2,467
Common market, total	1	395	707	3	306	1,042	2	474	1,424	1	482	1,449
Belgium and Luxembourg		29	69		26	113		43	240		46	156
France	(**)	68	186	2	75	243	2	127	286	1	90	345
Germany	(**)	121	288	(**)	97	508	(**)	161	615	(**)	183	657
Italy	(**)	124	107	(**)	75	110	(**)	99	144	(**)	106	162
Netherlands		53	57		33	68		44	138		57	129
Other Europe, total	2	250	621	2	297	831	3	399	981	2	459	1,018
Denmark		20	6		21	6	(**)	35	13	(**)	61	8
Norway	(**)	10	13	(**)	12	16	(**)	19	20	(**)	32	24
Spain	(**)	25	42	(**)	6	77	(**)	42	89	(**)	20	107
Sweden		23	12		25	16		32	26		34	28
Switzerland		6	14		7	16		15	19		13	15
United Kingdom	(**)	126	511	(**)	177	653	(**)	220	758	(**)	250	801
Other countries	2	40	23	2	49	47	2	36	56	1	49	35
Africa, total	63	271	63	101	284	88	80	349	89	68	442	58
North Africa		191	1		176	2		187	2		259	3
East Africa		8	1		8	1		6	1		5	1
West Africa	19	47	16	27	72	40	23	124	59	29	143	22
Republic of South Africa	27	(*)	45	57	(*)	45	36	(*)	27	20	(*)	32
Other countries in Central and South Africa	17	(*)	(**)	17	(*)	(**)	21	(*)	(**)	19	(*)	(**)
Asia, total	3	280	219	4	430	292	3	500	311	3	462	378
Middle East		111	9		233	11	(**)	246	30	(**)	249	110
Far East, total	3	169	210	4	197	281	3	254	280	3	213	267
India		(*)	36		(*)	67		(*)	84		(*)	82
Japan		(*)	117		(*)	168		(*)	144		(*)	126
Philippine Republic	1	(*)	40	2	(*)	29	1	(*)	27	1	(*)	21
Other countries	2	(*)	17	2	(*)	17	2	(*)	25	2	(*)	39
Oceania, total	51	65	213	147	74	242	184	72	309	182	70	235
Australia	45	(*)	206	145	(*)	231	182	(*)	294	180	(*)	230
Other countries	6	(*)	7	2	(*)	11	2	(*)	15	2	(*)	5
International shipping		100			66			45			61	

*Included in area total.
**Less than $500,000.
r Revised.
p Projected on the basis of company estimates received in summer of 1966.

keeping pace with the domestic rate in 1963 and 1964, the European rate dropped in 1965 while the U.S. rate of return rose sharply. This has apparently had little or no effect as yet on the aggregate of capital outlays in Europe by manufacturing affiliates, perhaps because the European rate of return was still quite high at 13 percent, and the investing firms appear to expect a continued high rate of growth in European demand.

A breakdown of foreign manufacturing outlays into the principal industry groups is given in table 3. Outstanding growth is projected for the chemical industry, from outlays of $0.9 billion in 1965 to $1.2 billion in 1966 and $1.3 billion in 1967. This is the main industry for which, at this early date, significant gains are projected into next year. A similar pattern is evident for nonelectrical machinery, though the amounts are smaller. The transportation equipment industry reported that 1966 is a year of major expansion, but the lower outlays reported for 1967 may indicate a temporary saturation for this industry. For most other manufacturing industries, the 1966 figures represent the continuation of fairly regular advances in investment activity, and changes reported now for 1967 are comparatively small.

All major areas are sharing in the rise of manufacturing investments by U.S. firms, but by far the greatest increase is in the Common Market countries, where a scheduled gain of nearly 40 percent will bring total expenditures to $1.4 billion this year. Outlays in Belgium, Italy, and the Netherlands are now expected to advance more sharply than was indicated in the March reports. The United Kingdom is also scheduled to receive a rising amount of investment by U.S. firms into 1967, although 1966 expenditures appear to have been scaled down slightly. It remains to be seen whether the measures to protect the United Kingdom's balance of payments by tightening up domestic demand will alter these investment plans. A strong rise of 23 percent is scheduled for manufacturing investments in Canada in 1966, somewhat lower than Canadian estimates for all manufacturing outlays

in Canada. Latin American manufacturing investments by U.S. firms, especially for Brazil, show a moderate increase in 1966 to a level that will be sustained in 1967. The largest gain elsewhere is reported for Australia.

Table 3.—Plant and Equipment Expenditures Abroad by U.S. Manufacturing Companies, by Area and Major Industry, 1964-67

[Millions of dollars]

Areas and years	Total	Food products	Paper and allied products	Chemicals	Rubber products	Primary and fabricated metals	Machinery (excluding electrical)	Electrical machinery	Transportation equipment	Other industries
All areas, total:										
1964 r	3,007	159	180	619	109	303	414	223	726	273
1965	3,893	186	251	862	174	360	627	232	873	328
1966 p 1	4,797	205	271	1,159	188	463	765	265	1,119	362
1966 p 2	4,786	188	198	1,101	175	538	748	258	1,265	316
1967 p 1	4,790	223	273	1,316	167	336	838	280	982	375
Canada:										
1964 r	771	29	130	165	30	110	47	46	167	47
1965	952	42	180	225	29	73	67	47	224	65
1966 p 1	1,171	41	218	260	40	109	98	50	275	80
1966 p 2	1,201	41	124	314	33	148	98	72	283	89
1967 p 1	1,147	50	210	240	35	90	107	48	270	97
Latin America: 3										
1964 r	413	43	15	133	16	23	23	34	76	50
1965	446	39	17	151	28	35	28	27	73	48
1966 p 1	511	49	13	187	22	36	25	29	108	42
1966 p 2	443	48	14	150	24	31	24	30	81	42
1967 p 1	505	45	15	170	24	35	22	32	118	44
Europe:										
Common market:										
1964 r	707	26	11	121	26	78	184	46	161	55
1965	1,042	34	12	147	34	77	329	60	278	71
1966 p 1	1,425	36	17	295	49	73	393	70	394	98
1966 p 2	1,332	28	26	208	41	49	392	56	463	70
1967 p 1	1,450	40	15	381	52	66	474	79	255	88
Other Europe:										
1964 r	621	41	11	91	14	40	81	73	178	93
1965	831	49	13	174	39	80	117	64	180	115
1966 p 1	981	44	10	221	42	71	139	90	253	111
1966 p 2	991	32	14	229	40	76	122	75	312	90
1967 p 1	1,017	53	14	264	37	76	124	95	240	114
Other areas:										
1964 r	495	20	14	109	23	53	80	24	144	28
1965	622	22	29	165	43	95	85	35	138	30
1966 p 1	710	35	12	196	36	174	110	26	89	32
1966 p 2	819	39	20	200	38	233	112	25	126	25
1967 p 1	670	35	19	261	19	68	111	26	99	32

r Revised.
p Projected on the basis of company estimates.
1. Based on reports received in summer of 1966.
2. Based on reports received between December 15, 1965 and February 15, 1966.
3. Includes "other Western Hemisphere."

Table 4.—Domestic and Foreign Expenditures for Plant and Equipment in Selected Industries, 1965-66

[Millions of dollars]

Industry	Expenditures 1965						Expenditures 1966 p					
	Total	Domestic Amount	Domestic Percent	Foreign Amount	Foreign Percent	Percent of foreign to total	Total	Domestic Amount	Domestic Percent	Foreign Amount	Foreign Percent	Percent of foreign to total
Manufacturing, total for selected industries	16,002	12,437	100.0	3,565	100.0	22.3	19,637	15,202	100.0	4,435	100.0	22.6
Food products	1,426	1,240	10.0	186	5.2	13.0	1,645	1,440	9.5	205	4.6	12.5
Paper and allied products	1,371	1,120	9.0	251	7.0	18.3	1,731	1,460	9.6	271	6.1	15.7
Chemicals	3,452	2,590	20.8	862	24.2	25.0	4,119	2,960	19.5	1,159	26.1	28.1
Rubber products	514	340	2.7	174	4.9	33.9	618	430	2.8	188	4.2	30.4
Primary and fabricated metals	1,887	1 1,527	12.3	360	10.1	19.1	2,265	1 1,802	11.8	463	10.5	20.4
Machinery, except electrical	2,837	2,210	17.8	627	17.6	22.1	3,755	2,990	19.7	765	17.3	20.4
Electrical machinery	1,082	850	6.8	232	6.5	21.4	1,395	1,130	7.4	265	6.0	19.0
Transportation equipment	3,433	2,560	20.6	873	24.5	25.4	4,109	2,990	19.7	1,119	25.2	27.2
Mining and petroleum	8,069	5,120	.....	2,949	.....	36.5	9,463	5,910	.....	3,553	.....	37.5

p Projected on basis of company estimates.
1. Excludes primary iron and steel producers.

NOTE.—Foreign expenditures include acquisition of existing fixed assets, which are excluded from the domestic series.

Petroleum and mining investment

The petroleum industry is increasing its foreign capital expenditures sharply this year and has scheduled a further rise for 1967. Investment is advancing most rapidly in Europe, where expanded refinery and distribution facilities are being installed to handle the rapid growth in demand. Increased investments by the petroleum industry are also reported for North and West Africa. At the same time, steady though moderate increases in capital expenditures are underway in Canada, Latin America, and the Middle East.

As an indication of investment requirements it may be noted that production of crude oil abroad by U.S. companies rose 10.4 percent in 1965, primarily in the Middle East and North Africa, continuing the rapid pace of the past several years.

The resurgence of investments in

Table 5.—Value of Direct Investments Abroad ¹ by Selected Countries and Industries, at Yearend 1964 and 1965

Table 6.—Direct-Investment sidiary Earnings, by Selected

[Millions of dollars]

Line	Area and country	1964 r Total	1964 r Mining and smelting	1964 r Petroleum	1964 r Manufacturing	1964 r Public utilities	1964 r Trade	1964 r Other	1965 p Total	1965 p Mining and smelting	1965 p Petroleum	1965 p Manufacturing	1965 p Public utilities	1965 p Trade	1965 p Other	Net capital outflows 1964 r	1965 p Total	1965 p Mining and smelting	1965 p Petroleum	1965 p Manufacturing	1965 p Other
1	All areas. total	44,386	3,569	14,354	16,931	2,020	3,688	3,844	49,217	3,794	15,320	19,280	2,134	4,191	4,499	2,416	3,371	98	1,013	1,494	766
2	Canada	13,796	1,667	3,187	6,194	471	805	1,473	15,172	1,755	3,320	6,855	486	881	1,875	239	896	1	161	389	345
3	Latin American Republics, total.	8,894	1,104	3,102	2,341	568	947	832	9,371	1,114	3,034	2,741	596	1,034	852	143	171	-14	-80	214	50
4	Mexico	1,034	128	56	606	27	111	106	1,177	103	48	752	27	138	109	95	100	-32	-5	115	22
5	Panama	659	19	103	23	29	281	205	704	19	122	24	38	288	213	21	11	------	7	2	2
6	Other Central America and West Indies.	589	31	139	46	142	26	205	621	35	152	90	147	30	197	34	23	4	11	11	-3
7	Argentina	882	(*)	(*)	500	(*)	40	343	992	(*)	(*)	617	(*)	47	328	16	17	(*)	(*)	46	-29
8	Brazil	997	40	53	668	41	153	41	1,073	51	57	722	37	162	45	-36	-7	(*)	-5	2	-5
9	Chile	789	500	(*)	30	(*)	20	239	829	509	(*)	39	(*)	24	257	8	23	9	(*)	3	11
10	Colombia	508	(*)	255	148	30	53	22	527	(*)	269	160	29	49	20	28	11	(*)	13	6	-S
11	Peru	464	241	60	65	22	46	31	515	263	60	79	21	53	35	10	54	21	11	11	11
12	Venezuela	2,786	(*)	2,139	220	18	199	210	2,715	(*)	2,033	248	19	222	194	-53	-86	(*)	-98	15	-3
13	Other countries	186	7	67	33	21	18	38	219	8	89	40	21	21	40	17	25	1	21	4	(**)
14	Other Western Hemisphere.	1,311	250	488	166	47	89	271	1,437	310	500	199	45	91	291	124	89	57	-5	34	3
15	Europe, total	12,109	56	3,102	6,587	53	1,446	864	13,894	55	3,429	7,570	60	1,716	1,065	1,368	1,432	-1	372	732	328
16	Common Market, total.	5,426	13	1,523	3,139	45	528	178	6,254	16	1,617	3,688	46	658	229	807	814	(*)	135	543	135
17	Belgium and Luxembourg.	455	(**)	66	299	1	73	16	585	(**)	71	373	1	103	37	75	116	------	6	65	45
18	France	1,446	10	286	909	22	174	46	1,584	10	280	1,052	11	177	51	139	128	(*)	-8	131	3
19	Germany	2,082	(*)	577	1,326	5	117	57	2,417	(*)	610	1,547	12	170	77	276	353	(*)	52	249	52
20	Italy	850	(*)	350	389	2	72	37	972	(*)	401	446	2	80	39	207	143	(*)	71	67	6
21	Netherlands	593	(**)	244	216	16	92	25	698	(**)	252	270	17	127	31	110	74	------	15	28	31
22	Other Europe, total	6,683	43	1,579	3,448	8	918	687	7,639	39	1,811	3,881	11	1,058	836	561	618	(*)	236	189	193
23	Denmark	166	1	116	28	(**)	19	2	189	1	127	32	(**)	27	3	33	19	------	13	3	3
24	Norway	129	(*)	69	29	(**)	14	17	152	(*)	74	44	(**)	17	18	2	18	(*)	5	11	1
25	Spain	196	(*)	52	97	4	32	10	264	(*)	55	140	6	45	17	35	44	(d)	2	30	12
26	Sweden	260	(*)	157	45	(**)	49	8	305	(*)	170	60	(**)	67	8	32	45	------	21	10	14
27	Switzerland	948	(**)	50	158	(*)	344	395	1,116	(**)	60	177	(*)	397	482	217	154	------	60	2	92
28	United Kingdom	4,547	2	902	3,010	4	382	246	5,119	2	1,084	3,308	6	415	304	206	324	(**)	139	116	69
29	Other countries	438	26	233	80	-2	78	22	494	20	241	119	1	90	24	36	14	(*)	-5	17	2
30	Africa, total	1,685	358	883	227	2	91	123	1,904	361	1,020	292	(**)	114	117	141	160	-2	130	40	-8
31	Liberia	189	(*)	(*)	(*)	(*)	16	173	201	(*)	(*)	(*)	(*)	20	181	-7	7	(*)	(*)	(*)	7
32	Libya	492	(*)	(*)	(*)	(*)	3	399	424	(*)	(*)	(*)	(*)	4	420	70	17	(*)	(*)	(*)	17
33	Republic of South Africa	467	68	(*)	193	(**)	49	158	528	65	(*)	237	(**)	63	164	17	30	1	(*)	21	8
34	Other countries	628	199	357	34	6	23	9	751	204	453	54	(*)	27	13	61	105	-3	91	18	-1
35	Asia, total	3,112	34	2,054	556	55	225	187	3,611	37	2,384	673	61	253	203	221	438	1	353	56	29
36	Middle East	1,332	2	1,240	39	4	12	35	1,590	3	1,491	43	4	13	36	42	254	1	246	3	4
37	Far East, total	1,780	31	814	517	51	214	152	2,021	34	893	629	58	210	166	181	184	(**)	106	53	25
38	India	234	(*)	(*)	97	2	26	109	253	(*)	(*)	110	2	36	104	21	7	(*)	(*)	8	-1
39	Japan	598	(*)	(*)	207	2	60	329	676	(*)	(*)	274	2	62	337	78	21	(*)	(*)	21	(*)
40	Philippine Republic	473	(*)	(*)	131	42	69	230	529	(*)	(*)	153	40	77	259	37	31	(*)	(*)	13	18
41	Other countries	474	(*)	(*)	82	5	58	329	563	(*)	(*)	92	12	65	394	46	126	(*)	(*)	12	114
42	Oceania, total	1,593	100	453	860	2	85	94	1,811	162	499	950	2	103	95	98	142	56	41	28	17
43	Australia	1,475	100	(*)	810	(*)	59	506	1,677	161	(*)	895	(*)	74	547	125	133	55	(*)	24	54
44	Other countries	117	(**)	(*)	50	(*)	25	42	134	(**)	(*)	55	(*)	29	50	-27	9	(*)	1	4	4
45	International	1,885	------	1,064	------	821	------	------	2,017	------	1,133	------	884	------	------	80	43	------	41	------	2

r Revised.   p Preliminary.   *Combined in "Other industries."   **Less than $500,000.
1. The value of direct investments abroad was reduced in 1964 by $147 million, and in 1965 by $65 million, owing to valuation adjustments on companies' books, profits and losses on liquidations, or transfers to other investment categories. In particular, the value of direct investments in the public utilities industry in Brazil was reduced by $153 million as of the end of 1964 by a settlement with the Brazilian Government. The equivalent value was added to the total for U.S. private portfolio investments included in table 14. The value of investments in specific industries and countries is also affected by capital flows among foreign affiliates as shown in table 9.

mineral extraction reflects intense world demand for these products, coupled with the discovery of new resources. As table 2 shows, capital outlays abroad in mining and smelting (other than petroleum development) are now on a much larger scale than at any other time since 1957, when data were first collected. For Latin America, this represents a recovery to the levels of the 1950's and affects principally Chile, Peru, Mexico, and Brazil. Canada is also regaining the levels of earlier intensive investment activity in mining, with the development of copper, nickel, and potash now requiring large outlays. Substantial capital expenditures for mining are now appearing in Australia, where iron ore and bauxite resources are under development.

Capital outlays in the other industries are relatively stable, except for European trade and distribution where an

Capital Flows and Undistributed Sub-Countries, With Major Industries for 1965

Table 7.—Direct-Investment Earnings and Income,[2] by Selected Countries, with Major Industries for 1965

[Millions of dollars]

	Table 6—Continued						Table 7											
	Undistributed subsidiary earnings					Earnings						Income						Line
1964 r	1965 P					1964 r	1965 P					1964 r	1965 P					
	Total	Mining and smelting	Petroleum	Manufacturing	Other		Total	Mining and smelting	Petroleum	Manufacturing	Other		Total	Mining and smelting	Petroleum	Manufacturing	Other	
1,431	1,525	124	52	892	458	5,061	5,431	571	1,825	2,019	1,017	3,670	3,961	443	1,798	1,095	625	1
500	540	86	66	283	106	1,106	1,198	198	183	606	210	634	692	110	122	315	145	2
216	298	22	21	169	86	1,035	1,170	206	496	269	199	895	888	185	468	109	127	3
34	33	6	-3	25	5	92	100	15	1	62	21	61	73	8	3	42	19	4
26	42	----	13	2	26	68	77	(**)	14	5	58	43	37	----	1	4	33	5
9	11	----	2	4	5	36	38	10	5	5	19	29	30	10	4	2	15	6
29	87	(*)	(*)	65	22	91	133	(*)	(*)	84	48	64	50	(*)	(*)	21	29	7
59	84	(*)	8	53	23	58	102	(*)	10	64	28	20	5	(*)	2	13	5	8
13	17	(**)	(*)	5	12	81	83	57	(*)	6	20	73	69	(*)	56	1	13	9
11	4	(*)	-1	4	1	33	27	(*)	11	8	8	22	22	(*)	11	5	7	10
2	-6	(**)	-10	1	3	83	98	64	19	6	9	77	98	66	21	5	6	11
27	21	(*)	-2	12	11	547	504	(*)	405	29	70	521	485	(*)	408	17	59	12
6	5	(**)	1	-1	5	6	9	(**)	-1	-1	10	1	4	(**)	-2	(**)	6	13
34	39	3	7	9	19	149	161	85	24	21	30	116	126	82	18	15	12	14
408	381	-1	-51	294	138	1,110	1,161	8	-42	855	341	654	760	8	17	532	203	15
100	-3	(*)	-45	23	19	398	394	(*)	-32	362	63	275	365	(*)	18	305	43	16
14	16	(**)	-1	9	9	53	56	(**)	3	43	10	34	35	(**)	4	30	1	17
52	32	(*)	3	34	-5	82	79	(*)	13	65	1	27	42	(*)	9	28	5	18
18	-42	(*)	-18	-26	2	211	217	(*)	-17	207	27	178	236	(*)	8	205	23	19
-5	-33	(*)	-23	-14	3	19	-4	(*)	-22	7	11	23	28	(**)	-3	21	7	20
21	25	----	-6	21	10	33	46	----	-10	41	14	13	24	----		22	6	21
308	384	(*)	-5	271	118	712	767	(*)	-10	493	284	379	395	(*)	-1	227	169	22
(**)	3	----	-3	2	4	6	6	----	-3	4	6	8	5	----	1	2	2	23
3	5	----	(**)	3	4	7	6	(*)	-4	4	6	5	1	(*)	-4	1	3	24
4	15	(*)	2	9	5	11	25	(*)	3	12	10	7	10	(*)	1	3	5	25
4	-4	----	-8	4	(**)	20	15	----	-8	6	17	16	18	----		2	17	26
113	88	----	-5	15	78	151	153	----	-5	25	133	40	68	(**)		10	58	27
167	242	----	-1	220	23	473	498	----	-6	419	85	276	263	----	-4	201	62	28
17	34	(*)	10	18	6	44	65	(*)	14	22	28	26	31	(*)	4	4	22	29
42	47	4	7	20	15	346	380	61	240	42	37	301	332	55	233	21	22	30
-4	4	(*)	(*)	(*)	4	18	17	(*)	(*)	17	(*)	22	14	(*)	(*)	(*)	14	31
5	5	(*)	(*)	(*)	5	258	235	(*)	(*)	235	(*)	252	229	(*)			229	32
38	18	-4	(*)	17	5	87	101	(*)	34	29	38	46	77	(*)	35	20	23	33
3	20	8	5	3	4	-17	28	23	-8	4	9	-19	11	17	-13	2	6	34
74	60	3	-23	59	21	1,021	1,083	5	892	107	79	983	1,033	2	921	44	66	35
11	3	----	3	1	-1	813	826	----	816	5	4	836	822	----	813	4	5	36
63	58	3	-26	58	23	207	257	5	76	101	76	148	211	2	107	40	62	37
7	12	(*)	(*)	5	7	23	30	(*)	(*)	17	12	12	14	(*)		10	5	38
35	49	----	(*)	38	11	54	85	----	(*)	55	30	31	50	----	(*)	17	33	39
14	23	(*)	(*)	7	16	47	50	(*)	(*)	16	34	28	25	(*)	(*)	8	17	40
7	-27	(*)	(*)	8	-34	84	93	(*)	(*)	13	80	121		(*)	(*)	5	116	41
79	80	7	5	57	12	142	145	8	-6	119	24	59	62	1	-11	59	12	42
64	72	7	(*)	56	9	121	125	10	-6	108	7	54	52	3		50	-2	43
15	8	----	(*)	1	7	21	20	-2		11	11	10	10	-2		9	3	44
79	80	----	20	----	61	93	134	----	37	97	27	69	----		30	----	39	45

2. Income is the sum of dividends and interest, net *after* foreign withholding taxes, and branch profits; earnings is the sum of the U.S. share in the net earnings of subsidiaries and branch profits; undistributed subsidiary earnings is computed as the difference between the U.S. share of net earnings of subsidiaries and the U.S. share of gross dividends (dividends *before* deduction of withholding taxes).

Note.—Industry detail for revised country totals of tables 6 and 7 for the years 1963 and 1964 is available from the Balance of Payments Division of the Office of Business Economics.

increase is expected in 1966 and 1967. This projected rise reflects the expansion of wholesale and retail distributors as well as increased activity by some companies involved in renting equipment.

Capital Outflows and Earnings

Capital outflows from the United States for direct investment rose sharply from $2.4 billion in 1964 to $3.4 billion in 1965, and earnings retained abroad increased $0.1 billion. These sources of funds are an important part of the financing of the plant and equipment expenditures abroad described in the preceding section. This is illustrated in chart 11, which shows that the share of capital flows and undistributed profits in financing such expenditures has been well over 50 percent in manufacturing and close to 50 percent in the petroleum industry. These shares have not exhibited a distinct trend since 1961, but it now appears that they will decline in 1966, as U.S. companies cooperating in the program to improve

Table 8.—Net Capital Outflows to Manufacturing Affiliates Abroad, 1962–65, by Industry

[Millions of dollars]

Area and year	Manufacturing, total	Food products	Paper and allied products	Chemicals and allied products	Rubber products	Primary and fabricated metals	Machinery except electrical	Electrical machinery	Transportation equipment	Other industries
All areas, total:										
1962	711.7	42.6	5.2	99.3	31.4	65.9	85.7	60.1	225.1	96.2
1963	753.3	57.3	24.4	176.5	13.2	85.6	30.2	24.0	194.5	147.5
1964	1,030.3	74.8	9.1	298.7	2.1	69.8	117.9	45.8	207.1	204.9
1965	1,494.1	116.3	98.1	290.5	16.5	82.1	255.5	96.8	402.1	136.3
Canada:										
1962	11.8	−6.0	4.2	−25.5	−4.1	−1.1	27.9	11.8	−7.1	11.6
1963	119.6	5.5	12.2	18.4	2.6	6.2	24.0	3.8	37.4	9.5
1964	136.0	29.0	−8.6	28.2	−7.1	−3.9	15.3	11.6	48.4	23.0
1965	389.2	18.0	61.6	70.2	5.1	5.3	25.9	12.7	171.2	19.3
Latin America: [1]										
1962	133.3	1.6	−.3	39.4	−3.8	16.2	6.2	2.5	49.8	21.6
1963	150.0	31.6	4.4	48.8	−1.9	5.0	8.6	−7.5	17.1	43.8
1964	137.2	−9.2	2.1	73.6	8.5	7.9	9.5	−10.3	30.1	25.1
1965	248.5	50.5	18.6	84.1	−1.1	19.5	.4	10.5	38.1	27.9
Europe:										
1962	453.4	29.5	.5	64.4	34.3	26.5	49.6	40.3	156.4	52.1
1963	378.0	11.0	2.5	82.1	13.3	37.2	−12.5	28.5	132.9	83.1
1964	618.6	41.6	13.6	163.0	−.3	30.4	65.3	38.0	127.4	139.6
1965	732.3	41.5	12.8	92.6	2.6	59.8	209.1	55.9	175.5	82.6
Africa:										
1962	10.7	1.3	.2	.1	−.4	1.4	1.7	.2	3.9	2.2
1963	8.5	.7	.4	2.2	.2	2.1	2.3	1.1	−.9	.5
1964	18.6	2.5	.6	2.9	−.5	1.5	4.3	−.3	−3.1	.7
1965	39.7	1.2	2.6	2.4	1.0	17.3	7.3	(*)	7.2	.7
Asia:										
1962	30.4	1.3	.5	11.6	5.2	1.4	1.3	3.7	.2	5.2
1963	42.6	6.2	3.8	18.7	−.9	2.5	2.2	3.2	.9	6.2
1964	60.6	4.6	1.7	24.8	(*)	3.3	11.4	5.8	.3	8.7
1965	56.2	−1.4	2.0	25.8	−1.8	.9	6.6	15.3	1.5	7.3
Oceania:										
1962	72.2	15.0	.1	9.3	.2	21.5	−.9	1.7	21.9	3.5
1963	54.5	2.3	1.1	6.3	(*)	32.7	5.7	−5.0	7.0	4.5
1964	59.2	6.3	−.3	6.2	1.5	20.6	12.1	1.0	4.0	7.8
1965	28.2	6.5	.5	15.5	10.7	−20.7	6.2	2.4	8.6	−1.5

*Less than $50,000.
1. Includes "other Western Hemisphere."

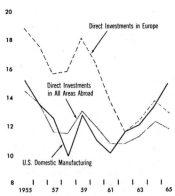

Return on Manufacturing Investments

Gains in domestic earnings rates in 1965 contrast with declines abroad

Percent

Direct Investments in Europe

Direct Investments in All Areas Abroad

U.S. Domestic Manufacturing

1955   57   59   61   63   65

NOTE.—Return on domestic manufacturing represents net income applied to net worth at the beginning of the year (First National City Bank of N.Y.). Return on direct manufacturing investments abroad and in Europe represents the U.S. share of net earnings for the year (see table 7) applied to book value of these investments at the beginning of the year. (See table 5.)

U.S. Department of Commerce, Office of Business Economics   66–9–10

the balance of payments shift their financing to foreign sources. However, there are several large changes in the capital outflow figures that do not correspond to changes in plant and equipment expenditures.

By far the largest rise in capital outflows in 1965 was for Canada, where they were up by nearly $0.7 billion. Of this, about $0.3 billion went into finance and trading affiliates, largely to refinance existing credits from the United States. About $0.4 billion of the increase was for the manufacturing and petroleum industries; this amount exceeded the total increase in plant and equipment expenditures of these industries. In the first half of 1966 direct-investment flows to Canada were considerably larger than in the first half of 1965, if allowance is made for over $100 million of refinancing that was included in the earlier figures.

The other major increase in 1965 direct-investment flows was to the Middle East, where the total rose by $0.2 billion. This corresponds in part

to larger capital expenditures and larger outlays for exploration and development, but it probably also reflects difficulties in financing increased working capital needs out of earnings that were leveling off.

Direct-investment flows to Europe were up only slightly from 1964 to 1965 and did not change significantly in the first half of 1966. Since Europe is the focal point of much of the investment activity discussed above, there has evidently been a significant effort to use foreign financing as much as possible. For instance, plant and equipment expenditures for manufacturing in Europe rose $550 million from 1964 to 1965, while capital outflows to this industry rose only about $100 million. Part of this foreign financing is obtained by special affiliates established by U.S. companies to raise funds for their direct investment activities. For such affiliates organized as U.S. corporations, estimates for borrowing abroad and the utilization of the funds obtained are as follows:

Foreign Funds Borrowed Through U.S. Affiliates

[Millions of dollars]

	Amount borrowed abroad (before discounts and commissions)	Amount used for direct investments	Amount retained at end of period [1]
1965	212	60	146
1966, Jan.–June [2]	318	97	365
Total	530	157	365

[1] After deduction of discounts and commissions; primarily held in short-term forms abroad.
[2] Excludes an estimated $180 million of convertible debentures issued in exchange for stock of a foreign company

These figures include some bank loans as well as debt securities issued, and the schedule of both the borrowing and the utilization of funds is somewhat imprecise. However, it is reasonably clear that of about $530 million borrowed through this channel to the end of June, only about $155 million was utilized for direct investments abroad and that a very large part of the remaining $365 million was being held in relatively liquid forms abroad, available for use as needed. Since these funds are held largely in the Euro-dollar market, the effects of the original borrowings on interest rates in Europe have been at least partially offset up to now by the reinvestment.

A breakdown of capital outflows by principal manufacturing product groups is given in table 8. This shows that the largest increases in 1965 outflows were in transportation equipment and non-electrical machinery, but that sizable increases also occurred in nearly all other product groups. Many of these gains reflect the rise in plant and equipment expenditures shown in table 3. In Canada, for instance, both sets of figures show large 1965 increases in paper and related products, chemicals, and transportation equipment. The gain in transportation equipment is probably related to the new treaty arrangements that are expected to lead to a greater volume of production of autos and parts in Canada.

In Europe, similar gains in both series are reported for 1965 in the nonelectrical machinery and transport equipment sectors. The former represents in part the acquisition of an interest in a large French company.

Earnings of direct investments

In 1965, the U.S. equity in the earnings of foreign affiliates rose 7.3 percent to $5.4 billion. However, this rate of increase was lower than that for the investment base (the book value of the U.S. investment in the affiliates), which rose 10 percent following a 9 percent rise in 1964. By the end of 1965 the book value was $49.2 billion as shown in table 5. Thus, the rate of return on investment declined, reversing the slow increase of recent years.

In 1965, the amount returned to the United States as dividends, interest, and branch profits rose sharply to nearly $4.0 billion (table 7). Since total earnings rose $0.4 billion while

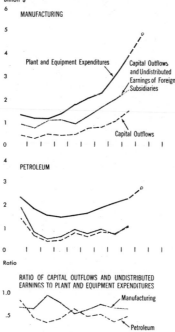

CHART 11

Comparison of Plant and Equipment Expenditures Abroad With U.S. Capital Outflows and Undistributed Earnings

Billion $

6   MANUFACTURING

Plant and Equipment Expenditures

Capital Outflows and Undistributed Earnings of Foreign Subsidiaries

Capital Outflows

PETROLEUM

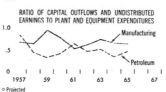

Ratio

RATIO OF CAPITAL OUTFLOWS AND UNDISTRIBUTED EARNINGS TO PLANT AND EQUIPMENT EXPENDITURES

Manufacturing

Petroleum

1957   59   61   63   65   67

o Projected

Note.—Capital outflows include amounts used to acquire existing enterprises or received from liquidations. However, an extraordinary $370 million acquisition in 1960 has been eliminated.

U.S. Department of Commerce, Office of Business Economics   66- 9-11

distributed profits rose $0.3 billion, the rise in undistributed profits over the 1964 amount was therefore relatively small.

Earnings of the manufacturing affiliates abroad advanced 9 percent to a new high of $2.0 billion in 1965. Sizable gains were reported in Canada, some Latin American countries, and the United Kingdom. However, earnings in the Common Market changed very little; a decline in Italy probably reflected a lag in the recovery of earnings from the lower rate of economic activity of the previous year. Dividends remitted from the Common Market nevertheless rose considerably, reflecting principally disbursements from Germany in advance of a change in the application of German taxes.

The petroleum industry scored virtually no gain in foreign earnings in 1965. The overall results for the industry reflect growing pressures of costs and taxes, while the ample supply of petroleum and products from many sources has resulted in highly competitive pricing practices. Minor gains were reported for Canada and Asia as well as for the international shipping affiliates. However, net losses were reported for Europe, reflecting a squeeze between the somewhat arbitrary prices that European refineries pay for crude oil and the competitive prices at which they must sell their products. In general, the regional distribution of earnings for the petroleum industry is affected by the use of partly nominal prices to allocate

Table 9.—Net Capital Flows Between Primary and Secondary Foreign Affiliates, 1961–65

[Millions of dollars; net inflows (−)]

	1961	1962	1963	1964 [r]	1965 [p]
Canada	4		−4	3	−8
Latin America	2	16	−1	−2	−3
Panama	10	13	14	12	8
Argentina	−6	−11	−14	−14	−5
Mexico	−4	11	−5	3	−5
Europe		−22	24	19	43
France	−15	−14	−5	−2	22
Germany	−8	−4	−20	−5	22
Italy	−25	−21	−9	−5	−9
Switzerland	60	48	105	60	77
United Kingdom	−6	−9	−4	(**)	−2
Other Europe	−6	−22	−13	−29	−22
Other Countries	−6	6	−19	−20	−32

[r] Revised
[p] Preliminary
** Less than $500,000.

income in vertically integrated enterprises.

Other industries showed generally higher earnings in 1965. Mining com-

Table 10.—Acquisitions and Sales by American Companies of Foreign Enterprises [1] by Area and Industry, 1964–65

[Millions of dollars]

Area and industry	1964			1965		
	Acquisitions	Sales	Net	Acquisitions	Sales	Net
All areas, total	431	106	328	369	90	279
Petroleum	11	29	−18	7	2	5
Manufacturing	339	16	323	268	46	222
Other industries	84	61	23	94	42	52
Canada, total	86	80	6	69	47	22
Petroleum	2	29	−27	4	2	2
Manufacturing	80	13	67	22	44	−22
Other industries	4	37	−33	42	(**)	42
Europe, total	324	3	321	258	2	256
Petroleum	8		8	3		3
Manufacturing	246	1	245	207	2	205
Other industries	70	2	68	48		48
Other areas, total	21	23	1	42	41	1
Petroleum	1		1			
Manufacturing	13	1	12	39		39
Other industries	10	22	−12	3	41	−38

[1] Includes acquisitions and sales of minority interests.
**Less than $500,000.

Table 11.—Direct-Investment Receipts of Royalties and Fees,[1] by Areas and Major Industries, 1964–65

[Millions of dollars]

Area and industry	1964 [r]	1955 [p]		
		Total	Royalties, license fees and rentals	Management fees and service charges
All areas, total	756	909	325	584
Petroleum	116	137	19	118
Manufacturing	479	568	253	315
Trade	58	74	28	46
Other industries	103	130	25	105
Canada, total	162	185	60	125
Petroleum	15	9	(**)	8
Manufacturing	125	144	51	93
Trade	9	12	4	9
Other industries	14	20	5	15
Latin America, total [2]	148	171	44	126
Petroleum	33	28	(**)	28
Manufacturing	64	79	30	49
Trade	17	23	9	14
Other industries	34	40	5	35
Europe: Common Market, total	150	174	93	81
Petroleum	8	16	1	16
Manufacturing	127	138	88	50
Trade	6	11	4	7
Other industries	9	9	1	8
Other Europe, total	155	195	76	119
Petroleum	8	13	1	12
Manufacturing	109	139	60	80
Trade	15	15	7	7
Other industries	23	28	7	21
Other areas, total	140	184	52	132
Petroleum	51	71	16	54
Manufacturing	55	67	24	43
Trade	11	14	4	10
Other industries	22	34	8	26

[p] Preliminary.
**Less than $500,000.
[r] Revised.
[1] Excludes foreign film rentals.
[2] Includes "other Western Hemisphere."

panies benefited from higher demand, and they raised earnings about 12 percent.

Royalties and fees

Payments of royalties and fees by foreign affiliates to their U.S. parent companies have become an increasingly important supplement to dividend remittances. In 1965, royalties and fees exceeded $900 million, nearly 20 percent above the 1964 amount. This was a faster rate of growth than in the year before. Gains in 1965 were widespread but were particularly large for the foreign manufacturing affiliates (table 11).

Foreign Investments in the United States

The principal feature of foreign investments in the United States since 1964 (other than changes in liquid dollar holdings) has been a continued net liquidation of U.S. corporate stocks, more than offset in the first half of 1966 by large additions to foreign holdings of deposits in U.S. banks with maturities of over 1 year and by purchases of various types of corporate and U.S. Government agency bonds. Flows of capital connected with foreign direct investments in the United States have been erratic and relatively small.

Net sales of corporate stocks rose to nearly $0.5 billion in 1965 and were over $0.1 billion in the first half of 1966. These represent mainly the reduction of holdings of the United Kingdom Government, but sales have also been recorded for other European countries. In contrast, Canadians have been net purchasers of U.S. equity securities, and in the second quarter of this year raised their net acquisitions to nearly $100 million.

For most of the period from 1962 to the early months of 1966, the U.S. market for corporate stocks was stronger than most foreign markets, but it failed to attract foreign investors. This contrasts with a persistent inflow for investment in these securities averaging $150 million per year in the 1951–62 period. It seems likely that the intensive demand in Europe for investment funds has diverted this

flow into European debt instruments or the Euro-dollar market.

In 1965 and the first half of 1966, purchases of U.S. bonds by foreigners were substantial, but this reflected rather special circumstances. In 1965, net purchases of U.S. corporate bonds by European countries (other than the United Kingdom, which was liquidating bonds acquired in 1964) amounted to about $150 million. However, that total includes purchases by foreigners of nearly $200 million of debentures and bonds issued by the newly organized U.S. financing affiliates of direct-investment companies, so that foreigners were apparently selling other U.S. corporate bonds. Some of the sales of U.S. equity securities by Europeans in 1965 mentioned above may also have been for the purpose of investing in these new issues. In the first half of 1966, European countries (other than the United Kingdom) purchased a net amount of $405 million of U.S. bonds. Since these purchases included about $475 million of securities issued by the special financing affiliates, there was evidently a continuing liquidation of other U.S. corporate bonds. Purchases of $187 million of U.S. bonds by international institutions in the first half were largely U.S. agency issues.

Another new development in 1965, which continued into 1966, was the acquisition by foreigners of long-term (over 1 year) certificates of deposit or other obligations of U.S. banks. These acquisitions amounted to a net of $230 million in 1965 and about $400 million in the first half of 1966 (excluding any United Kingdom transactions).

Direct investments in the United States

Despite certain sizable liquidations of direct investments in the United States, there was a net inflow of foreign capital of $71 million in 1965. The liquidations amounted to $77 million, and resulted primarily from the transfer to foreign affiliates of funds raised in the United States by a worldwide organization. However, this outflow was more than offset by $89 million of new investments, more than half from Canada. Also, intercompany transactions showed an inflow of about $60 million, the reverse of the 1964 experience when such transactions resulted in an outflow of the same amount, this reversal was accounted for largely by Japanese trading companies. A noteworthy development was an inflow of $40 million from Germany, primarily to finance distributing organizations.

The book value of foreign direct investments in the United States was $8.8 billion at the end of 1965, an increase of $450 million for the year (table 12). About 80 percent of the increase was accounted for by retained earnings.

Earnings in 1965 of these foreign-owned companies increased by $140 million, or almost 25 percent over the previous year, to a total of $735 million. Most of the gain was in manufacturing affiliates. Retained earnings increased only moderately for the year as most of the increase in earnings was paid out as dividends.

International Investment Position

The accumulated total of U.S. assets and investments abroad reached a record of over $106 billion by the end of 1965. The increase for the year was $7.0 billion. The book value of direct investments rose $4.8 billion—derived from capital outflows of nearly $3.4 billion and undistributed profits of $1.5 billion—to reach an accumulated total of $49.2 billion. Other long-term private investments abroad rose by $1.1 billion to $21.6 billion. This increase reflected capital outflows of a like amount; changes in market values were not significant. Of these portfolio investments, some $9.5 billion was in Canada and $5.2 billion in Europe. Short-term privately held foreign assets were reduced in 1965 because of the return flow of funds connected in large part with the application of the Govern-

ment's program to improve the balance of payments.

U.S. Government foreign credits and claims rose in 1965 by a net amount of $1.8 billion, to $25.1 billion. Most of the increase was in long-term credits (some repayable in foreign currencies) to less-developed countries. Holdings by the Government of reserve assets in the form of convertible foreign currencies and the IMF gold tranche rose by $443 million, reflecting mainly an additional subscription of $259 million to the IMF. On the other hand, the U.S. monetary gold stock diminished by $1.7 billion to $13.8 billion at the end of 1965.

Foreign assets and investments in the United States rose only about $2.0 billion in 1965, much less than in the previous year. This reflected pri-

Table 12.—Foreign Direct Investments in the United States, Selected Data, 1950, 1964 and 1965, by Country and Industry

[Millions of dollars]

	Value			Capital Flow						Earnings		
				1964			1965			1965		
	December 1950	December 1964	December 1965 ᵖ	Total	New Investments	Other	Total	New Investments	Other	Earnings	Income	Undistributed profits
Total	3,391	8,363	8,812	−5	71	−76	71	89	−18	736	392	358
By area:												
Canada	1,029	2,284	2,367	26	8	18	21	53	−32	195	154	58
United Kingdom	1,168	2,796	2,865	−36	33	−69	−52	11	−63	214	116	91
Other Europe	1,059	3,023	3,240	24	26	−2	38	19	19	285	91	195
Belgium	n.s.s.	175	198	8		8	16	1	15	8	3	7
France	n.s.s.	197	200	8	3	5	(*)	2	−2	9	4	5
Germany	n.s.s.	156	206	−5	5	−10	40	11	29	17	5	11
Italy	n.s.s.	82	88	−9	2	−11	8	3	5	(*)	1	−2
Netherlands	334	1,231	1,304	−6	4	−10	−33		−33	149	29	120
Sweden	n.s.s.	199	216	7	10	−3	7		7	14	4	10
Switzerland	348	896	938	24	2	22	4	2	2	77	40	37
Other countries	377	88	89	−3	(*)	−3	−4		−4	10	5	5
Japan	n.s.s.	72	119	−38	2	−40	33	2	31	40	28	14
Other countries	134	187	220	19	2	17	31	4	27	2	3	(*)
By industry:												
Petroleum	405	1,612	1,710	−55	1	−56	−63		−63	215	26	184
Manufacturing	1,138	3,213	3,465	59	45	14	119	68	51	303	176	129
Trade	n.s.s.	675	766	−65	4	−69	48	10	38	66	25	43
Insurance	³ 1,065	³ 2,181	³ 2,188	−1		−1	−1		−1	38	38	
Other Finance	(⁴)	(⁴)	(⁴)	34	5	29	−37	11	−48	107	108	6
Other industries	784	683	684	23	16	7	6	(*)	6	6	20	−5

ᵖ Preliminary.   n.s.s. Not shown separately.   *Less than $500,000.
1. "Earnings" represents the foreign share in corporate or branch profits; "Income" is the amounts distributed, after withholding taxes, as dividends, interest, or branch profits.
2. "New investments" represents initial investments in U.S. companies or increase in equity capital of existing foreign-owned U.S. companies.
3. Includes market revaluations of securities held by insurance companies.
4. Included in "Insurance."

Table 13.—Factors Affecting the U.S. Private Investment Position, 1964 and 1965

[Millions of dollars]

Type of investment	1964 ʳ	1965
U.S. private investments abroad:		
Total, beginning of year	66,513	75,820
Add: Capital outflow ¹	6,523	3,690
Reinvested earnings	1,431	1,525
Price changes and other adjustments	1,353	−93
Total, end of year	75,820	80,942
Direct investments:		
Value, beginning of year	40,686	44,386
Add: Capital outflow ¹	2,416	3,371
Reinvested earnings	1,431	1,525
Other adjustments ³	−147	−65
Value, end of year	44,386	49,217
Other long-term private investments abroad:		
Value, beginning of year	17,644	20,533
Add: Capital outflow ¹	1,961	1,080
Price changes	325	−9
Other adjustments	603	−20
Value, end of year	20,533	21,584
Short-term assets and claims:		
Value, beginning of year	8,183	10,901
Add: Capital outflow ¹	2,146	−761
Enlarged coverage of reports	572	1
Value, end of year	10,901	10,141
Foreign long-term investments in the United States:		
Direct investments:		
Value, beginning of year	7,944	8,363
Add: Capital inflow ¹	−5	71
Reinvested earnings	327	358
Other adjustments ³	97	20
Value, end of year	8,363	8,812
Other long-term investments:		
Value, beginning of year	14,847	16,616
Add: Capital inflow ¹	114	−238
Price changes	1,641	1,214
Other adjustments	14	4
Value, end of year	16,616	17,596

ʳ Revised.
1. Included in the balance of payments accounts.
2. For detail see note to table 5.
3. Mainly revaluations of securities held by affiliates of foreign insurance companies.

marily the reduction in the deficit in the U.S. balance of payments and the financing of a larger part of the remaining deficit through sales of gold. Foreign holdings of liquid dollar assets increased by only $133 million in 1965 as compared with a rise of $2.6 billion in 1964. Moreover, there was a sizable net sale of U.S. securities in 1965, representing largely the liquidation of British holdings. Price changes had added $1.6 billion to the market value of foreign holdings of U.S. securities in 1964 (table 13); in 1965, this gain was $1.2 billion.

Table 14.—International Investment Position of the United States, Total 1950, by Area, 1964–65

[Millions of dollars]

Type of investment	Total			Western Europe		Canada		Latin American Republics		Other foreign countries		International institutions and unallocated	
	1950	1964 r	1965 p	1964 r	1965 p	1964 r	1965 p	1964 r	1965 p	1964 r	1965 p	1964 r	1965 p
U.S. assets and investments abroad, total	31,539	99,119	106,065	27,875	29,594	24,844	25,995	17,325	18,207	24,276	27,140	4,799	5,129
Gold stock (not included in total)	22,820	15,471	[1]13,806	----	----	----	----	----	----	----	----	----	----
Private investments	19,004	75,820	80,942	19,602	21,164	24,839	25,987	13,789	14,387	14,665	16,238	2,925	3,166
Long-term	17,488	64,919	70,801	17,528	19,101	22,688	24,694	11,197	11,764	10,581	12,076	2,925	3,166
Direct	11,788	44,386	49,217	12,109	13,894	13,796	15,172	8,894	9,371	7,702	8,763	[2]1,885	[2]2,017
Foreign dollar bonds	1,692	8,218	9,126	779	823	4,474	5,096	555	550	1,370	1,508	1,040	1,149
Other foreign bonds [3]	1,466	978	1,050	30	80	710	736	167	163	71	71	----	----
Foreign corporate stocks	1,175	5,270	5,048	2,065	1,893	2,948	2,865	67	75	190	215	----	----
Banking claims	390	[4]4,085	[4]4,317	1,706	1,598	[4]127	[4]146	1,200	1,247	1,052	1,326	(*)	(*)
Other	977	[5]1,982	[5]2,043	839	813	633	679	314	358	196	193	----	----
Short-term assets and claims	1,516	10,901	10,141	2,074	2,063	2,151	1,293	2,592	2,623	4,084	4,162	(*)	(*)
Reported by banks	886	[6]7,957	[6]7,728	1,210	1,175	1,004	669	2,131	2,204	3,612	3,680	(*)	(*)
Other	630	2,944	2,413	864	888	1,147	624	461	419	472	482	(*)	(*)
U.S. Government credits and claims	12,535	23,299	25,123	8,273	8,430	5	8	3,536	3,820	9,611	10,902	1,874	1,963
Long-term credits [7]	10,768	18,777	20,318	7,354	7,403	----	----	3,298	3,679	7,025	8,141	1,100	1,095
Repayable in dollars [8]	n.a.	13,974	14,968	6,197	6,230	----	----	2,972	3,255	3,705	4,388	1,100	1,095
Repayable in foreign currencies, etc.[9]	n.a.	4,803	5,350	1,157	1,173	----	----	326	424	3,320	3,753	----	----
Foreign currencies and short-term claims	322	3,321	3,161	491	253	2	2	238	141	2,585	2,760	5	5
IMF gold tranche position and monetary authorities' holdings of convertible currencies	1,445	1,201	[1]1,644	428	774	3	6	----	----	1	1	769	863
Foreign assets and investments in the United States, total	17,635	56,883	58,932	33,367	34,149	8,307	8,169	5,462	6,034	7,008	7,905	2,739	2,675
Long-term	7,997	24,979	26,408	17,726	18,342	4,187	4,475	1,686	1,816	1,167	1,332	213	443
Direct	3,391	8,363	8,812	5,819	6,105	2,284	2,367	134	161	126	179	----	----
Corporate stocks	2,925	13,835	14,598	10,159	10,530	1,726	1,930	1,077	1,172	792	871	81	95
Corporate, State, and municipal bonds	181	922	916	663	654	(*)	(*)	80	77	49	47	130	138
Other	1,500	1,859	2,082	1,085	1,053	177	178	395	406	200	235	2	210
Short-term assets and U.S. Government obligations	9,638	31,904	32,524	15,641	15,807	4,120	3,694	3,776	4,218	5,841	6,573	2,526	2,232
By type: Private obligations	6,477	17,534	18,162	7,088	7,138	2,205	1,887	3,340	3,709	4,475	5,036	426	392
Reported by banks	5,751	16,718	17,195	6,652	6,584	2,117	1,778	3,226	3,599	4,297	4,842	426	392
Other	726	816	967	436	554	88	109	114	110	178	194	(*)	(*)
U.S. Government obligations	3,161	14,370	14,362	8,553	8,669	1,915	1,807	436	509	1,366	1,537	2,100	1,840
Bills and certificates	1,508	8,799	8,356	5,585	5,019	867	796	170	241	1,157	1,331	1,020	969
Marketable bonds and notes	1,470	[10]2,405	2,329	714	800	690	676	81	78	93	96	827	679
Nonmarketable bonds and notes		[11]1,440	[11]1,692	1,111	1,393	[11]329	[11]299	----	----	----	----	----	----
Other [12]	183	1,726	1,985	1,143	1,457	29	36	185	190	116	110	253	192
By holder: Foreign central banks and governments and international and regional institutions	n.a.	20,032	20,079	10,541	10,391	1,841	1,738	1,649	1,867	3,475	3,851	2,526	2,232
Foreign commercial banks [13]	2,100	7,303	7,419	3,339	3,498	1,848	1,541	408	409	1,708	1,971	(*)	(*)
Other private holders and unallocated	n.a.	4,569	5,026	1,761	1,918	431	415	1,719	1,942	658	751	(*)	(*)

r Revised.   p Preliminary.   n.a. Not available.   *Negligible.

1. Reflects payment of $259 million gold portion of increased U.S. subscription to the IMF in the second quarter of 1965.
2. Represents the estimated investment in shipping companies registed primarily in Panama and Liberia.
3. Consists primarily of securites payable in foreign currencies, but includes some dollar obligations including prior to 1963 participations and loans made by the International Bank for Reconstruction and Development. Effective 1963, participations in IBRD loans are included under banking claims and "other" long-term, according to country of obligor.
4. Excludes $200 million netted against a related inflow of U.S. direct investment capital.
5. Includes $254 million loaned to Canada in connection with Columbia River power development.
6. New series. For detail see Treasury Bulletin, August 1966, p. 99.
7. Excludes World War I debts that are not currently being serviced.
8. Includes indebtedness repayable in U.S. dollars, or optionally in foreign currencies when option rests with U.S. Government.
9. Includes indebtedness which the borrower may contractually, or at its option, repay with its currency, with a third country's currency, or by delivery of materials or transfer of services.
10. New series based on a Federal Reserve Board survey as of July 31, 1963. Data to reconcile the old and new series are not available.
11. Includes $204 million at end of 1964 and $174 million at end of 1965 of nonmarketable bonds issued to the Government of Canada in connection with transactions under the Columbia River Treaty.
12. Includes noninterest-bearing demand notes issued in payment of subscriptions to international and regional organizations (other than IMF), portfolio fund certificates sold abroad by Export-Import Bank, liabilities associated with Government grant and capital transactions (including restricted accounts), and advances for military exports and other Government sales. Effective 1965, includes liabilities of U.S. monetary authorities for gold deposited by and held for IMF.
13. As reported by U.S. banks; ultimate ownership is not identified.

INTERNATIONAL INVESTMENTS
OF THE UNITED STATES IN 1966

Walther Lederer
and
Frederick Cutler

By WALTHER LEDERER and FREDERICK CUTLER

International Investments of the United States in 1966

THIS article discusses the international investment position of the United States and, in more detail, the developments in direct investments. The review of plant and equipment expenditures by U.S. affiliates abroad that in the past has appeared with this article will be the subject of a separate press release and will be included in the October issue of the SURVEY. The 1966 data on direct investments are based on the regular quarterly surveys. A comprehensive survey of U.S. direct investments in 1966 has just been started, but the results will not be available for some time.

The International Investment Position

Total assets held abroad by United States residents and the Federal Government amounted to nearly $112 billion at the end of 1966. Total assets held by foreign residents in the United States were $60 billion. The rise in 1966 in U.S. assets abroad was about $5.6 billion, while foreign assets in the United States rose about $1.8 billion. (These figures are adjusted for differences in statistical coverage of the estimates for the two years presented in table 1). The net foreign asset position at the end of 1966 was about $51.5 billion, approximately $3.8 billion more than at the beginning of the year. Combining the change in U.S. official gold holdings, which declined by about $0.6 billion, with the changes in net foreign assets, the rise in net international assets of the United States was $3.2 billion.

In 1965 net foreign assets rose about $5.2 billion, but gold holdings dropped about $1.7 billion, so that the combined change was about $3.5 billion, roughly the same as in 1966.

The $3.2 billion rise in the net asset position in 1966 included a deterioration of $1.4 billion in the balance on reserve assets and liquid liabilities and a deterioration of $2.3 billion, if banking liabilities with an original maturity of one year or more are added. The balance on other assets and liabilities improved by $5.5 billion. Of this amount $4.2 billion resulted from capital transactions that are recorded in the balance of payments tabulations, and $1.4 billion from reinvested earnings (reinvested earnings of $1.7 billion by U.S. subsidiaries abroad less $0.3 billion by foreign subsidiaries in the United States). Declines in market values of securities reduced foreign assets in the United States by about

CHART 7

Return on Manufacturing Investments

Percent

NOTE.—Return on domestic manufacturing represents net income applied to net worth at the beginning of the year (First National City Bank of N.Y.). Return on direct manufacturing investments abroad and in Europe represents the U.S. share of net earnings for the year (see table 5) applied to book value of these investments at the beginning of the year. (See table 3)

U.S. Department of Commerce, Office of Business Economics   67-9-7

$1.8 billion, and U.S. assets abroad by about $0.8 billion, thus improving the net asset position of the United States by about $1 billion. On the other hand, U.S. Government assets were reduced by about $1 billion through devaluations of assets denominated in foreign currencies.

Relation to national wealth and income

The relative magnitudes of a country's external assets and liabilities must not be considered to be the equivalent to its "net worth," analogous to the net worth of a private enterprise. External assets are only a part of the total assets of a country; its net wealth consists of domestic and foreign assets, net of foreign liabilities. Only the change in this total is the proper measure of a country's success in raising its net wealth by producing more than it is consuming. No change in total wealth would take place if U.S.-owned assets located within our borders were exported and set up abroad, or if U.S.-owned assets located abroad were imported and set up here.

Although the choice of adding to capital assets located within the United States or to those located abroad does not affect the total wealth of the nation at the time the capital assets are created, it may have important longer run effects on domestic output and incomes, and these effects may vary considerably among different types of investments and under different economic circumstances.

In considering these effects, one among several factors is the difference in rates of capital income derived from domestic and foreign investments. In 1966, earnings on U.S. assets located abroad (including reinvested earnings of U.S. subsidiaries) were close to $8 billion or about 7.5 percent of the value of the assets at the beginning of the

39

year. Omitting U.S. Government credits and claims of $25.6 billion and the $600 million of income derived from them, the yield was slightly more than 8.5 percent. If about $1 billion of royalties and management fees obtained by U.S. corporations from their foreign affiliates are added to earnings, the yield on private investments was just under 10 percent.

However, taking account of the various categories of assets located abroad, the yield was not significantly different from that on domestic assets.

Earnings on direct investments abroad (before U.S. taxes) were about $5.76 billion or 11.7 percent of the invested capital; including receipts of royalties and fees the yield was about 13.75 percent. The comparable figures on direct investments in foreign manufacturing

Table 1.—International Investment Position of the United States at Yearend Total 1950, by Area, 1965–66

[Millions of dollars]

Type of investment	Total 1950	Total 1965 r	Total 1966 p	Western Europe 1965 r	Western Europe 1966 p	Canada 1965 r	Canada 1966 p	Latin American Republics 1965 r	Latin American Republics 1966 p	Other foreign countries 1965 r	Other foreign countries 1966 p	International organizations and unallocated 1965 r	International organizations and unallocated 1966 p
U.S. assets and investments abroad, total	31,539	106,174	111,874	29,688	32,187	26,041	27,529	18,241	19,387	27,108	28,207	5,096	4,564
Gold stock (not included in total)	22,820	¹13,806	13,235										
Private investments	19,004	81,051	86,235	21,258	23,353	26,033	27,519	14,421	15,183	16,206	17,037	3,133	3,143
Long-term	17,488	70,898	75,565	19,187	20,726	24,740	26,394	11,798	12,335	12,040	12,967	3,133	3,143
Direct	11,788	49,328	54,562	13,985	16,200	15,223	16,840	9,391	9,854	8,744	9,652	²1,985	²2,016
Foreign dollar bonds	1,692	9,115	9,512	822	790	5,091	5,503	561	560	1,493	1,532	1,148	1,127
Other foreign bonds ³	1,466	1,050	1,030	80	64	736	748	163	174	71	44		
Foreign corporate stocks	1,175	5,048	4,324	1,893	1,570	2,865	2,474	75	78	215	202	(*)	(*)
Banking claims	390	⁴4,317	⁵3,980	1,598	1,212	146	114	1,247	1,308	1,326	1,346	(*)	(*)
Other	977	⁵2,040	⁵2,157	809	890	679	715	361	361	191	191		
Short-term assets and claims	1,516	10,153	10,670	2,071	2,627	1,293	1,125	2,623	2,848	4,166	4,070	(*)	(*)
Reported by banks	886	⁶7,735	⁶7,911	1,175	1,361	669	608	2,204	2,398	3,687	3,544	(*)	(*)
Other	630	2,418	2,759	896	1,266	624	517	419	450	479	526	(*)	(*)
U.S. Government credits and claims	12,535	25,123	25,639	8,430	8,834	8	10	3,820	4,204	10,902	11,170	1,963	1,421
Long-term credits ⁷	10,768	20,318	21,182	7,403	7,308			3,679	4,094	8,141	8,690	1,095	1,090
Repayable in dollars ⁸	n.a.	14,968	15,999	6,230	6,120			3,255	3,585	4,388	5,204	1,095	1,090
Repayable in foreign currencies, etc.⁹	n.a.	5,350	5,183	1,173	1,188			424	509	3,753	3,486		
Foreign currencies and short-term claims	322	3,161	2,810	253	215	2	1	141	110	2,760	2,479	5	5
IMF gold tranche position and monetary authorities' holdings of convertible currencies	1,445	¹1,644	1,647	774	1,311	6	9			1	1	863	326
Foreign assets and investments in the United States, total	17,635	58,739	60,389	33,953	35,168	8,192	8,093	6,017	5,861	7,909	8,701	2,668	2,566
Long-term	7,997	26,374	27,000	18,304	17,851	4,498	4,539	1,811	1,939	1,325	1,878	436	793
Direct	3,391	8,797	9,054	6,076	6,273	2,388	2,439	161	177	172	165		
Corporate stocks	2,925	14,599	12,643	10,530	8,743	1,930	1,933	1,172	1,076	872	800	95	91
Corporate, U.S. Government agency, State, and municipal bonds	181	875	2,042	625	1,535	(*)	180	73	85	46	54	131	368
Other	1,500	2,103	3,261	1,073	1,300	180	167	405	601	235	859	210	334
Short-term assets and U.S. Government obligations	9,638	32,365	33,389	15,649	17,317	3,694	3,554	4,206	3,922	6,584	6,823	2,232	1,773
By type: Private obligations	6,477	18,163	20,796	7,139	9,713	1,887	2,042	3,700	3,691	5,045	5,061	392	289
Reported by banks	5,751	17,195	19,532	6,584	8,965	1,778	1,879	3,590	3,558	4,851	4,841	392	289
Other	726	968	1,264	555	748	109	163	110	133	194	220	(*)	(*)
U.S. Government obligations	3,161	14,202	12,593	8,510	7,604	1,807	1,512	506	231	1,539	1,762	1,840	1,484
Associated with Government grants and capital outflows ¹⁰		344	131					179	62	7	27	158	42
Associated with military sales contracts ¹⁰		1,575	1,916	1,450	1,705	35	52	5	2	85	157		
Associated with other specific transactions ¹⁰	183	198	186	4	3	174	145	6	3	14	35		
Nonmarketable, noncovertible securities not associated with specific transactions ¹¹		165	116	161	113	1				3	3		
Marketable or convertible bonds and notes	1,470	3,530	1,969	1,876	854	801	692	78	81	96	92	679	250
Bills and certificates	1,508	8,356	8,064	5,019	4,929	796	623	238	83	1,334	1,448	969	981
Gold deposits of IMF			34		211							34	211
By holder: Foreign central banks and governments and international and regional organizations	n.a.	19,919	17,921	10,233	9,317	1,738	1,386	1,863	1,343	3,853	4,102	2,232	1,773
Foreign commercial banks ¹²	2,100	7,419	9,932	3,498	5,875	1,541	1,709	409	454	1,971	1,894	(*)	(*)
Other private holders and unallocated	n.a.	5,027	5,536	1,918	2,125	415	459	1,934	2,125	760	827	(*)	(*)

r Revised. p Preliminary. n.a. Not available. *Negligible.
¹ Reflects payment of $259 million gold portion of increased U.S. subscription to the IMF in the second quarter of 1965.
² Represents the estimated investment in shipping companies registered primarily in Panama and Liberia.
³ Consists primarily of securities payable in foreign currencies, but includes some dollar obligations including prior to 1963 participations and loans made by the International Bank for Reconstruction and Development. Effective 1963, participations in IBRD loans are included under banking claims and "other" long-term, according to country of obligor.
⁴ Excludes $200 million netted against a related inflow of U.S. direct investment capital.
⁵ Includes $254 million loaned to Canada in connection with Columbia River power development.
⁶ New series. For detail see Treasury Bulletin, August, 1967, p. 89.
⁷ Excludes World War I debts that are not currently being serviced.
⁸ Includes indebtedness repayable in U.S. dollars, or optionally in foreign currencies when option rests with U.S. Government.
⁹ Includes indebtedness which the borrower may contractually, or at its option, repay with its currency, with a third country's currency, or by delivery of materials or transfer of services.
¹⁰ Corresponds to Section B, Table 5, p. 26.
¹¹ Corresponds to Section C, Table 5, p. 26.
¹² As reported by U.S. banks; ultimate ownership is not identified.

industries only were 10.9 percent and 14.3 percent respectively. In comparison, the rate of earnings after taxes on stockholders' equity in U.S. manufacturing enterprises (including their foreign affiliates) was estimated in FTC–SEC compilations at 13.4 percent for 1966.

Earnings in 1966 on private investments in foreign securities, bank and commercial credits, deposits and other foreign investments are estimated to have been about $1.6 billion, or roughly 5 percent of the $31.7 billion outstanding at the beginning of the year. This may have been slightly more than on comparable domestic assets, but the difference may reflect the higher risk and lower liquidity associated with foreign claims.

However, the effects of foreign investment on the national product and income cannot be judged only on the basis of profits and interest derived

Table 2.—Factors Affecting the U.S. Private Investment Position, 1965 and 1966

[Millions of dollars]

Type of investment	1965 ʳ	1966 ᵖ
U.S. private investments abroad:		
Total beginning of year	75,818	81,051
Add: Capital outflow ¹	3,743	4,217
Reinvested earnings	1,542	1,716
Price changes and other adjustments	−52	−749
Total, end of year	81,051	86,235
Direct investments:		
Value, beginning of year	44,384	49,328
Add: Capital outflow ¹	3,418	3,543
Reinvested earnings	1,542	1,716
Other adjustments	−16	−25
Value, end of year	49,328	54,562
Other long-term private investments abroad:		
Value, beginning of year	20,533	21,570
Add: Capital outflow ¹	1,078	261
Price changes	−11	−833
Other adjustments	−30	5
Value, end of year	21,570	21,003
Short-term assets and claims:		
Value, beginning of year	10,901	10,153
Add: Capital outflow ¹	−753	413
Enlarged coverage of reports.	5	104
Value, end of year	10,153	10,670
Foreign long-term investments in the United States:		
Direct investments:		
Value, beginning of year	8,363	8,797
Add: Capital inflow ¹	57	86
Reinvested earnings	357	339
Other adjustments ²	20	−168
Value, end of year	8,797	9,054
Other long-term investments:		
Value, beginning of year	16,616	17,578
Add: Capital inflow ¹	−124	2,078
Price changes	1,074	−1,687
Other adjustments	12	−23
Value, end of year	17,578	17,946

ʳ Revised.   ᵖ Preliminary.
¹ Included in the balance of payments accounts.
² Mainly revaluations of securities held by affiliates of foreign insurance companies.

from them. Investments usually result in new productive facilities and thus—for the country where they are located—in incomes through wages and salaries paid to those employed in these facilities, sometimes through purchases of locally produced materials, and through the payment of taxes. Such incomes derived from the investments usually exceed by a substantial margin the capital incomes derived from them. The extent to which these investments lead to an increment in total incomes and tax receipts in the capital importing countries will depend upon alternative opportunities for employment in these countries. Under conditions of full employment the net gains would be limited to the increase in productivity of the labor force and therefore would be smaller than when excess resources are available.

Likewise it cannot be assumed that locating an investment abroad necessarily results in a reduction of employment opportunities in the capital exporting countries. Some investments make it possible for U.S. exports, and thereby U.S. production and income, to be higher than they otherwise would be. Some foreign investments do not displace domestic investments, so that capital income derived from them is a net addition to total domestic incomes. Some foreign investments help to enlarge the supply of industrial materials without which domestic production could be seriously handicapped, and real domestic incomes adversely affected.

Relation to international liquidity

Just as the net international asset position (including official gold holdings) cannot be identified with a country's "net worth", so it cannot be considered as a measure of a country's international liquidity, i.e., its ability to meet foreign obligations, or to defend the exchange value of its currency. If international liquidity is measured by comparing the value of assets that could be sold to foreigners, relative to a country's foreign obligations, the assets should include also domestic assets (or shares in them), which in many instances may be more attractive to foreigners than some of the U.S.

assets located abroad. Using foreign assets alone would grossly understate this measure.

However, most of the privately owned assets, whether located within the country or abroad, are not in the form of monetary assets acceptable to foreigners in payment of U.S. obligations, nor are they available to U.S. authorities to be sold to foreigners in order to obtain such monetary assets. Indirect measures to induce sales to foreigners by their private owners have uncertain effects.

Problems of valuation

Another difficulty in using the net international asset position as a measure of a country's international liquidity is that the valuation of U.S. assets abroad and foreign assets in the United States does not necessarily represent the market values that would be realized if these assets were sold or otherwise liquidated. Many of the assets are not intended by their owners to be offered for sale and for many it would be difficult to find potential purchasers. In these cases it would be most difficult, therefore, to determine their market value. In general, that is likely to be more true for U.S. assets abroad than for foreign assets in the United States. At the end of 1966, about $8 billion of U.S. Government assets were foreign currency claims that with few exceptions can be used only for grants and loans and for meeting U.S. Government administrative expenditures in the countries issuing these currencies. Such administrative expenditures amounted to less than $300 million in 1966.

Direct investments at the end of 1966 comprised about $54.6 billion, or half of U.S. assets abroad, while foreign direct investments in the United States were valued at slightly over $9 billion, or about 15 percent of foreign assets in the United States. These valuations represent the cumulative amounts invested less liquidations and losses. They are neither capitalized earnings, nor current market values. The current market values of these assets cannot be estimated, but presumably they would depend upon the desire and financial resources of those who would want to acquire them, and the urgency of liquidation of those who own them.

The market value of such enterprises would be higher if the equity in them were divided into shares. The market values would be further increased if these shares were traded in well-established and relatively large capital markets. In view of the size of U.S. affiliates abroad relative to the amounts of capital available in foreign countries, it may be fair to assume that market values for U.S. direct investments abroad may be less favorable relative to the cumulative amount invested than might be expected for foreign direct investments in the United States.

Omitting foreign currency claims of the U.S. Government and direct investments, U.S. assets abroad at the end of 1966 were valued at $49.3 billion, while foreign assets in the United States were about $51.3 billion.

Of the $49.3 billion held by the United States abroad, $16 billion were U.S. Government loans payable in

Table 3.—Value of Direct Investments Abroad [1] by Selected Countries and Industries, at Year end 1965 and 1966

Table 4.—Direct-Investment Capital Out-Foreign Corporations,[2] by Selected

[Millions of dollars]

Line	Area and country	Table 3 1965 r Total	Mining and smelting	Petroleum	Manufacturing	Public utilities	Trade	Other	1966 p Total	Mining and smelting	Petroleum	Manufacturing	Public utilities	Trade	Other	Table 4 Net capital outflows 1965 r	1966 p Total	Mining and smelting	Petroleum	Manufacturing	Other
1	All areas, total	49,328	3,785	15,298	19,339	2,136	4,219	4,550	54,562	16,264	22,050	2,286	4,706	5,121	3,418	3,543	220	876	1,730	716
2	Canada	15,223	1,755	3,356	6,872	486	882	1,871	16,840	1,942	3,606	7,674	495	995	2,128	912	1,087	121	155	548	262
3	Latin American Republics, total	9,391	1,114	3,034	2,745	596	1,041	861	9,854	1,117	2,959	3,077	626	1,158	917	176	162	−24	−67	130	123
4	Mexico	1,182	104	48	756	27	138	110	1,244	108	42	797	29	153	115	99	16	−6	−5	7	19
5	Panama	724	19	130	24	36	293	221	793	19	154	28	44	317	232	20	30		15	2	12
6	Other Central America and West Indies	626	35	152	62	147	31	199	682	35	162	80	154	38	213	26	45	(**)	6	14	24
7	Argentina	992	(*)	(*)	617	(*)	47	327	1,031	(*)	(*)	652	(*)	44	335	16	−13	(*)	(*)	−10	−3
8	Brazil	1,074	51	57	723	37	162	45	1,246	58	69	846	38	182	53	23	85	(*)	1	66	19
9	Chile	829	509	(*)	39	(*)	24	257	844	494	(*)	51	(*)	32	207	23	−4	−14	(*)	6	4
10	Colombia	526	(*)	269	160	29	49	20	576	(*)	277	93	29	55	21	11	33	(*)	11	17	5
11	Peru	515	262	60	79	21	54	38	518	262	29	93	21	63	51	55	5	−9	−2	4	12
12	Venezuela	2,705	(*)	2,024	246	19	223	192	2,678	(*)	1,922	293	19	253	190	−93	−48	(*)	−101	24	29
13	Other countries	218	8	89	38	22	21	40	241	12	97	43	26	21	42	24	14	4	9	(**)	1
14	Other Western Hemisphere	1,445	310	512	200	45	91	287	1,619	364	579	235	48	87	306	95	114	52	32	28	2
15	Europe, total	13,985	54	3,427	7,606	60	1,730	1,107	16,200	54	3,977	8,879	67	1,928	1,294	1,479	1,805	1	634	899	271
16	Common Market, total	6,304	16	1,624	3,725	46	660	233	7,587	17	1,978	4,409	47	776	360	857	1,140	(*)	395	523	222
17	Belgium and Luxembourg	596	(**)	79	372	1	105	39	745	(**)	43	459	1	124	119	117	122		−33	61	94
18	France	1,609	10	281	1,076	14	178	50	1,758	10	288	1,194	14	192	60	152	93	(*)	5	68	20
19	Germany	2,431	(*)	617	1,555	17	170	77	3,077	(*)	906	1,848	13	217	93	359	614	(*)	314	237	63
20	Italy	982	(*)	409	451	2	80	40	1,148	(*)	474	535	1	89	49	158	150	(*)	71	72	7
21	Netherlands	686	(**)	238	270	17	127	33	858	(**)	267	373	18	155	46	71	161	(*)	38	85	38
22	Other Europe, total	7,681	39	1,803	3,882	14	1,069	874	8,613	37	1,999	4,470	20	1,152	934	622	665	(*)	239	376	50
23	Denmark	200	(*)	137	32	(**)	27	3	226	1	151	39	(**)	32	3	22	24	(**)	17	6	1
24	Norway	152	(*)	74	43	(**)	17	18	167	(*)	81	46	(**)	20	19	18	12	(*)	8	1	3
25	Spain	275	(*)	64	142	6	45	17	407	(*)	109	192	8	76	22	54	109	(*)	45	41	23
26	Sweden	315	(**)	179	60	(**)	67	8	369	(**)	198	90	(*)	72	*	47	58		23	27	8
27	Switzerland	1,120	(**)	15	177	1	410	517	1,210	(**)	42	211	1	430	526	151	33		35	12	−14
28	United Kingdom	5,123	2	1,093	3,306	6	413	304	5,652	3	1,167	3,714	8	412	349	317	384	(**)	105	262	16
29	Other countries	495	20	240	121	1	90	22	583	17	251	179	3	110	23	12	45	(*)	6	27	12
30	Africa, total	1,918	354	1,029	292	2	115	127	2,078	369	1,108	331	1	136	133	170	89	−4	70	17	7
31	Liberia	204	(*)	(*)	(*)	(*)	20	184	208	(*)	(*)	(*)	(*)	22	186	10	−8	(*)	(*)	(*)	−8
32	Libya	428	(*)	(*)	(*)	(*)	4	423	389	(*)	(*)	(*)	(*)	5	384	21	−42	(*)	(*)	(*)	−42
33	Republic of South Africa	529	65	126	237	(**)	63	38	601	73	140	271	(**)	76	41	31	21	(**)	(*)	14	8
34	Other countries	758	205	459	54	6	27	7	879	214	559	59	5	32	9	108	118	(**)	109	3	6
35	Asia, total	3,569	36	2,340	676	61	254	201	3,891	39	2,467	794	78	285	227	429	206	(**)	104	58	45
36	Middle East	1,536	2	1,436	44	4	13	36	1,671	3	1,560	51	4	16	38	245	121		112	4	5
37	Far East, total	2,033	34	904	631	58	241	165	2,219	37	907	743	74	269	190	183	85	(**)	−8	54	39
38	India	255	(*)	(*)	111	4	36	104	237	(*)	(*)	118	3	36	79	8	−10		(*)	5	−15
39	Japan	675	(*)	(*)	275	2	63	335	756		(*)	333	3	73	347	19	31		(*)	22	9
40	Philippine Republic	530	(*)	(*)	154	40	78	259	577	(*)	(*)	180	48	86	263	30	19	(*)	(*)	19	(**)
41	Other countries	573	(*)	(*)	92	12	65	404	650	(*)	(*)	112	20	73	444	126	44	(*)	(*)	7	37
42	Oceania, total	1,813	162	498	948	2	107	96	2,064	249	521	1,060	2	116	116	144	150	75	12	50	13
43	Australia	1,679	161	(*)	893	(*)	78	547	1,918	249	(*)	999	(*)	82	588	136	147	76	(*)	46	24
44	Other countries	134	−1	(*)	55	(*)	29	49	146	(**)	(*)	61	(*)	34	51	9	4	−1	(*)	4	1
45	International shipping companies incorporated abroad	1,985		1,101		884			2,016		1,047		968			12	−71		−64		−7

r Revised.　p Preliminary.　*Combined in "Other" industries.　**Less than $500,000.

[1] The value of investments in specified industries and countries is affected by capital flows among foreign affiliates as shown in table 8.

[2] Income is the sum of dividends and interest, net after foreign withholding taxes, received by, or credited to, the account of the U.S. owner, and branch profit after foreign taxes but before U.S. taxes; earnings is the sum of the U.S. share in the net earnings (or losses) of foreign corporations and branch profits after foreign taxes but before U.S. taxes; reinvested earnings

dollars, many of which have relatively long maturities.

Close to $15 billion were U.S. dollar bonds and other foreign securities, sold by foreigners and international organizations to U.S. investors. The valuations for the dollar bonds are based on quotations in U.S. markets; they do not

reflect the prices that could be obtained if they were sold abroad. The valuations of other foreign securities, mostly stocks, are estimated on the basis of price movements in foreign markets.

Market valuations depend, of course, on the amount of securities offered for sale relative to the demand for them.

Foreign securities not subject to the Interest Equalization Tax are sold in U.S. capital markets because our capital markets have larger capacities to absorb such new issues than can be expected of foreign markets. However, foreign markets for securities issued by public organizations and large international

flows and U.S. Share in Reinvested Earnings of Countries, With Major Industries for 1966

Table 5.—Direct-Investment Earnings and Income,[2] by Selected Countries, With Major Industries for 1966

[Millions of dollars]

Table 4 Continued						Table 5												
Reinvested earnings of foreign corporations						Earnings						Income						Line
1965 r	1966 p					1965 r	1966 p					1965 r	1966 p					
	Total	Mining and smelting	Petroleum	Manufacturing	Other		Total	Mining and smelting	Petroleum	Manufacturing	Other		Total	Mining and smelting	Petroleum	Manufacturing	Other	
1,542	1,716	130	100	975	511	5,460	5,680	660	1,859	2,098	1,063	3,963	4,045	524	1,778	1,118	625	1
540	539	67	89	274	109	1,209	1,240	191	196	633	221	703	766	120	114	362	170	2
306	299	28	−5	189	87	1,160	1,261	263	479	311	208	869	962	234	471	126	131	3
33	49	11	−2	36	4	96	109	19	1	71	19	70	60	7	2	37	14	4
48	47	....	14	2	31	80	85	....	14	6	66	34	43	....	2	5	36	5
11	8	....	3	2	4	38	52	9	6	7	30	29	46	9	4	5	27	6
87	61	(*)	(*)	49	12	133	128	(*)	(*)	79	49	50	67	(*)	(*)	32	36	7
84	85	(*)	11	57	17	101	122	(*)	17	81	24	19	33	(*)	4	22	6	8
17	16	−1	(*)	4	14	83	123	(*)	98	7	18	69	112	98	(*)	2	12	9
4	9	(*)	−2	10	1	26	36	(*)	99	16	1	22	24	(*)	18	6	(**)	10
−6	−7	8	−29	5	9	98	137	99	10	10	17	98	135	92	30	5	8	11
23	20	(*)	−1	19	2	497	456	(*)	384	31	41	475	438	(*)	385	13	40	12
5	10	(**)	−1	6	5	7	12	(**)	1	4	7	3	4	(**)	1	−1	3	13
39	41	3	8	9	21	160	185	96	32	26	30	126	148	93	26	20	10	14
388	434	−1	−77	366	145	1,176	1,155	10	−79	855	369	768	725	11	4	484	226	15
−3	105	(*)	−56	146	14	395	435	(*)	−39	413	60	366	316	(*)	17	253	46	16
16	13	(**)	−4	12	5	56	52	(**)	−2	37	16	35	35	(**)	(**)	24	12	17
32	50	(*)	3	48	−1	79	88	(*)	12	81	−5	42	36	(*)	8	32	−5	18
−42	17	(*)	−30	51	−5	217	208	(*)	−30	217	21	236	178	(*)	4	149	25	19
−33	9	(*)	−16	19	7	−4	39	(*)	−17	42	14	28	31	(*)	−1	25	7	20
25	16		−9	17	8	46	48		−3	37	15	25	35	....	6	23	7	21
391	329	(*)	−21	220	130	781	720	(*)	−40	442	318	402	409	(*)	−13	232	191	22
3	1	....	−3	1	3	6	5	....	−6	5	6	5	7	(**)	4	3	23	
5	3	(*)	−1	1	3	6	−1	(*)	−10	2	7	1	−3	(*)	−8	1	5	24
17	19	(*)	(**)	10	9	27	31	(*)	2	14	15	10	12	(*)	3	4	6	25
−4	−4		−5	3	−2	15	16		−5	5	16	18	20		(**)	2	18	26
91	85	(**)	−9	22	72	157	167	(**)	−9	27	148	68	82	(**)	6	8	77	27
242	190	(*)	−8	160	38	504	427	(*)	−25	359	94	270	251	(*)	−15	208	57	28
36	34	(*)	4	23	7	67	75	(*)	13	30	32	31	40	(*)	8	7	25	29
48	75	19	17	19	19	376	415	78	259	43	34	327	338	58	243	23	15	30
4	9	(*)	(*)	(*)	9	17	21	(*)	(*)	21	14	13	(*)	(*)	13	31		
5	4	(*)	(*)		4	232	270	(*)	(*)	270	226	266	(*)	(*)	266	32		
18	48	9	(*)	17	22	101	124	45	(*)	40	39	78	71	33	(*)	22	16	33
21	14	9	3	2	(**)	27	(**)	26	−32	3	3	9	−11	20	−34	1	3	34
61	111	3	29	56	23	1,099	1,124	4	930	109	80	1,039	1,010	1	905	47	56	35
3	13	....	12	2	(**)	840	876	....	863	6	7	836	863	....	852	4	7	36
58	98	3	18	54	23	259	248	4	68	103	73	203	147	1	54	43	49	37
12	−8	....	(*)	2	−10	30	3	....	(*)	8	−5	14	8	....	(*)	4	4	38
49	49	....	(*)	36	13	91	91	....	(*)	56	35	47	43	....	(*)	18	25	39
23	24	(*)	(*)	5	19	48	53	(*)	(*)	19	34	23	26	(*)	(*)	12	14	40
−27	32	(*)	(*)	11	21	91	102	(*)	(*)	20	81	119	70	(*)	(*)	9	61	41
80	97	12	10	62	13	146	166	18	2	121	25	62	67	6	−8	57	12	42
72	89	12	(*)	60	18	126	143	18	(*)	107	18	52	54	6	(*)	47	1	43
8	8	....	(*)	2	6	20	23	(**)	(*)	14	9	10	13	(**)	(*)	10	1	44
80	121	....	28	....	93	134	135	....	40	....	95	69	28	....	23	....	5	45

is computed as the difference between the U.S. share of net earnings (or losses) of foreign corporations and the U.S. share of gross dividends (dividends before deduction of withholding taxes).

NOTE.—In this and subsequent tables, detail may not add to totals because of rounding.

enterprises have grown considerably in the last years. What the market values of foreign securities would have been if U.S. purchases had been smaller and sales to foreigners higher cannot easily be estimated, but probably they would have been lower than those used in the valuations for the end of 1966.

In principle, similar considerations apply to foreign holdings of U.S. corporate securities, which were valued at $14.6 billion, or about the same as U.S. holdings of foreign securities. About $12.6 billion of the foreign holdings consisted of U.S. stocks. These stock holdings comprised, however, only about 2.6 percent of the market value of all stocks listed on the New York Stock Exchange in 1966. In view of this small share in the total market and the large turnover in the market, foreign sales would have to comprise a relatively large share of total foreign holdings to have major effects on their market value.

Liquidity of banking and commercial claims

The remainder of U.S. private assets abroad consists of claims reported by banks and commercial concerns. Most of the claims reported by banks are either medium-term or revolving loans with an unspecified maturity but classified as short term. About $8.6 billion or 72 percent of the bank-reported claims and $3.1 billion or 63 percent of the commercial claims were against countries in Latin America, Asia (including Japan), and Africa. Only about $3.8 billion of the short-term banking and commercial claims were against countries in Europe and against Canada where local capital resources and foreign exchange reserves are large enough to permit major liquidations of U.S. claims. The difficulties in achieving such liquidations may be illustrated by the experiences in 1965 and 1966.

In the last three quarters of 1965, following the introduction of the voluntary program to restrain capital outflow, and the application of the Interest Equalization Tax to long term bank loans, total claims on foreigners reported by U.S. banks fell by nearly $500 million, or about 4 percent of the amount outstanding at the end of

March. This decline approximately equaled the net increase in such claims during the first quarter of the year. In 1966, although these restrictions on new lending continued and, in addition, domestic credit became exceptionally tight, net liquidations declined to $250 million, or 2 percent of the amounts outstanding at the beginning of the year.

The experience with short-term foreign claims by commercial concerns on non-affiliated foreign residents including foreign banks was similar. During the first half of 1965, after the introduction of the voluntary program to improve the balance of payments, about $460 million of such claims, which totaled $2.9 billion at the beginning of that year, were liquidated. In the second half another $160 million were liquidated, but to a large extent were replenished by the reinvestment of $130 million in short-term foreign assets of funds obtained abroad through the sale by U.S. corporations of new securities to finance their direct investments abroad. In 1966, commercial holdings of short-term assets abroad increased again by $330 million, including about $140 million of funds obtained through the sale of securities.

In 1965 and 1966, liquidations of private assets held abroad, even with the cooperation of business, with the help of the Interest Equalization Tax, and with exceptionally tight credit conditions thus comprised only a relatively small part of total private assets held abroad. Furthermore, a large part of those assets that could more easily be liquidated, was sold early in that period, and net liquidations declined thereafter. Privately held assets abroad cannot be considered, therefore, a significant supplement to official reserve assets, which are at the disposal of Government authorities when needed to meet U.S. obligations abroad and to defend the exchange value of the dollar.

The official reserve assets at the end of last year totaled nearly $14.9 billion and consisted of about $1.3 billion of convertible currency holdings, about $300 million of gold tranche drawing rights on the IMF, and $13.2 billion of gold.

Liquidity of banking and Government liabilities

In contrast to banking claims, perhaps 90 percent of banking liabilities, which totaled about $21 billion at the end of 1966, have a very high degree of liquidity. These liabilities consist mainly of freely transferable demand deposits, time deposits, and privately issued open market papers with a maturity of less than one year held in trust accounts for foreigners. In many instances time deposits may be cashed before maturity although certain penalties may be incurred, and open market paper is widely traded. Time deposit certificates with an original maturity of one year or more are generally marketable, but also frequently provide the owners with the option to resell them to the issuing agency before maturity. Furthermore, a large part of the certificates outstanding at any one time actually mature in less than one year. These highly liquid funds serve as monetary media and reserve assets to foreign residents.

Exceptions to the high liquidity characteristic of banking liabilities to foreigners are deposits that are committed against outstanding letters of credit or that serve as compensating balances against bank loans. Data for these deposits are not available. Compensating balances may amount to between 10 and 20 percent of outstanding bank loans and acceptance credits, which totaled about $9.6 billion at the end of 1966.

U.S. Government liabilities of about $12.6 billion included about $10 billion of marketable or convertible securities and $0.2 billion of gold deposit obligations to the IMF. Because of the large market for these securities they also have a very high degree of liquidity, and therefore serve as a preferred investment of dollar reserve assets of foreign residents, particularly of foreign official agencies. At the end of 1966, total liquid liabilities and banking liabilities with an original maturity of one year or more that serve as foreign monetary and reserve assets amounted to about $30 billion, roughly half of all foreign assets in the United States.

The liquidity of these financial instruments refers primarily to the owners' facility in meeting U.S. dollar obligations. For foreign owners who have to meet their obligations in foreign currencies, liquidity of these instruments also requires that they be freely convertible into their own currencies with a minimum risk of variations in market or exchange values. Without that assurance their acceptance as an international medium of exchange and international reserve asset would be substantially reduced. The liquidity of these dollar instruments in terms of foreign currencies is, however, dependent upon the relation of the amounts held by foreigners to the amounts of reserves available to United States authorities. Changes in that relation are a function of the U.S. balance of payments and the partially related desire of foreigners to hold their reserves in liquid dollar funds or, alternatively, to exchange them against U.S. reserve assets, i.e., principally gold.

From the end of 1950 through 1966 liquid liabilities (without adjustment for committed deposits), and banking liabilities with an original maturity of one year or more to foreign residents and international organizations rose $24 billion, from $7.3 billion to about $31.3 billion. At the same time, U.S. official reserve assets declined from $22.8 billion to $14.9 billion or by $7.9 billion. The balance of these items changed, therefore, from net assets of $15.5 billion to net liabilities of $16.4 billion, a shift of about $32 billion.

Over the same time period, the balance of other assets and liabilities increased nearly $60 billion from net assets of $21.2 billion to net assets of $81.1 billion. This increase (aside from partly offsetting effects resulting from changes in market values of securities and losses on U.S. direct investments abroad) substantially exceeds the deterioration in the net position of the United States on official reserve assets, liquid liabilities and bank liabilities with an original maturity of one year or more. The problem of the balance of payments—which is reflected in the changes of the investment position—is, therefore, primarily a problem of international liquidity, but this problem is not substantially reduced by the rise to more than $80 billion in our net position in assets other than official reserves and liquid liabilities.

Geographic distribution

The balance of payments problem of the United States is also indicated by the geographic distribution of the foreign assets and liabilities. Although the worldwide net asset position of the United States was $51.5 billion, the net position with Western Europe was an excess of liabilities of nearly $3 billion. This is a large change from 1950, when the United States had net assets of $3.5 billion in Western Europe. The change from a net asset position to a net liability position occurred in the middle 1950's. From then until 1964 net liabilities increased to about $4.5 billion. The decline in net liabilities

Table 6.—Selected Data on Direct Investments Abroad, by Major Areas, 1960–66

[Millions of dollars]

	Book value at yearend					Net capital outflows					Earnings					Income				
	Total	Mining and smelting	Petroleum	Manufacturing	Other	Total	Mining and smelting	Petroleum	Manufacturing	Other	Total	Mining and smelting	Petroleum	Manufacturing	Other	Total	Mining and smelting	Petroleum	Manufacturing	Other
All areas, total:																				
1960	31,815	2,947	10,810	11,051	7,007	1,674	155	452	801	266	3,566	394	1,302	1,176	694	2,355	337	1,150	550	318
1961	34,667	3,044	12,190	11,997	7,436	1,599	70	793	462	274	3,815	362	1,476	1,203	774	2,768	297	1,336	722	413
1962	37,226	3,194	12,725	13,250	8,057	1,654	97	606	712	239	4,235	372	1,695	1,307	861	3,044	318	1,565	746	415
1963	40,686	3,369	13,652	14,937	8,728	1,976	85	828	774	289	4,587	388	1,824	1,541	834	3,129	321	1,715	656	437
1964	44,384	3,569	14,328	16,935	9,552	2,435	90	760	1,034	551	5,071	512	1,908	1,863	890	3,674	403	1,856	893	522
1965	49,328	3,785	15,298	19,339	10,906	3,418	88	977	1,525	828	5,460	571	1,830	2,022	1,037	3,963	442	1,799	1,094	628
1966	54,562	4,135	16,264	22,050	12,113	3,543	220	876	1,730	716	5,080	660	1,869	2,008	1,063	4,045	524	1,778	1,118	625
Canada:																				
1960	11,179	1,325	2,664	4,827	2,363	451	199	135	29	88	718	88	98	398	134	361	47	60	176	78
1961	11,602	1,367	2,828	5,076	2,331	302	9	100	117	76	726	96	114	360	156	464	51	78	213	122
1962	12,133	1,489	2,875	5,312	2,457	314	85	159	12	58	825	97	121	460	147	476	60	79	221	116
1963	13,044	1,549	3,134	5,761	2,600	365	7	188	120	50	948	127	149	525	147	455	80	80	192	103
1964	13,809	1,667	3,196	6,197	2,749	253	45	25	140	43	1,106	191	170	565	180	634	118	118	269	129
1965	15,223	1,755	3,356	6,872	3,240	912	1	179	395	337	1,209	198	183	606	222	703	110	122	315	156
1966	16,840	1,942	3,606	7,674	3,618	1,087	121	155	548	262	1,240	191	196	633	221	766	120	114	362	170
Latin America:[1]																				
1960	8,315	1,269	3,122	1,521	2,403	149	−60	24	125	60	970	224	370	147	229	719	234	331	64	90
1961	9,189	1,282	3,674	1,707	2,526	219	32	63	78	46	1,079	206	478	172	223	824	198	438	75	113
1962	9,474	1,271	3,642	1,944	2,617	29	−13	−67	133	−24	1,179	230	543	173	233	891	221	488	71	111
1963	9,891	1,303	3,636	2,213	2,739	235	24	5	150	56	1,125	219	532	171	203	956	210	544	70	132
1964	10,204	1,354	3,589	2,507	2,754	266	29	8	137	92	1,244	266	539	243	196	1,011	245	531	98	137
1965	10,836	1,424	3,546	2,945	2,921	271	43	−74	245	57	1,320	290	513	289	228	995	266	476	123	130
1966	11,473	1,481	3,538	3,312	3,142	276	28	−35	158	125	1,446	359	511	337	238	1,110	327	497	146	141
Western Europe:																				
1960	6,691	49	1,763	3,804	1,075	962	(**)	273	607	82	769	10	91	487	181	397	11	55	241	90
1961	7,742	48	2,152	4,255	1,287	724	(**)	376	233	115	837	8	63	530	236	486	9	47	326	104
1962	8,930	50	2,385	4,883	1,612	868	3	229	453	183	844	5	60	496	283	526	7	63	334	122
1963	10,340	55	2,776	5,634	1,875	924	1	362	395	166	996	4	67	627	298	507	6	73	305	123
1964	12,129	56	3,122	6,587	2,364	1,388	2	414	619	353	1,115	4	8	782	321	659	5	64	427	163
1965	13,985	54	3,427	7,606	2,898	1,479	−1	342	760	378	1,176	8	−41	859	350	768	8	17	532	211
1966	16,200	54	3,977	8,879	3,290	1,805	1	634	899	271	1,155	10	−79	855	369	725	11	4	484	226
Other areas:																				
1960	5,630	304	3,261	899	1,166	112	16	20	40	36	1,109	72	743	144	150	878	45	704	69	60
1961	6,134	347	3,536	959	1,292	354	29	254	34	37	1,173	52	821	141	159	994	39	773	108	74
1962	6,689	384	3,823	1,111	1,371	443	22	285	114	22	1,387	40	971	178	198	1,151	30	935	120	66
1963	7,411	462	4,106	1,329	1,514	452	53	273	109	17	1,518	38	1,076	218	186	1,211	25	1,018	89	79
1964	8,242	492	4,421	1,644	1,685	528	14	313	138	63	1,606	51	1,091	262	202	1,370	35	1,143	99	93
1965	9,284	552	4,969	1,916	1,847	756	45	530	125	56	1,755	75	1,175	268	237	1,497	58	1,184	124	131
1966	10,049	658	5,143	2,185	2,063	375	70	122	125	58	1,839	100	1,231	273	235	1,444	66	1,163	126	88

[1] Includes "other Western Hemisphere."   **Less than $500,000.

since 1964 was due largely to the drop in the market values of stocks, which affected foreign assets in the United States more than U.S. assets abroad. The change in the net position with Western Europe since 1950 reflects a substantially larger increase in net liabilities of the United States in liquid funds than in net U.S. assets in other investments.

The largest rise since 1950 in net U.S. assets abroad—$18.5 billion—was in Asia and Africa, which includes the oil-producing countries of the Middle East and North Africa as well as the countries receiving the largest share of Government assistance in that period. Next is Canada with an increase of about $15.3 billion, and then Latin America with a rise of just under $10 billion.

U.S. Direct Investments Abroad

Private capital outflows from the United States in 1966, net of funds bor-

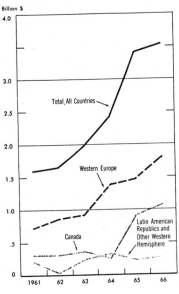

CHART 8

Capital Outflows for Direct Investment By Area

Billion $

Total, All Countries

Western Europe

Canada

Latin American Republics and Other Western Hemisphere

1961   62   63   64   65   66

U.S. Department of Commerce, Office of Business Economics   67-9-8

rowed abroad by U.S. corporations, amounted to $3.14 billion, about $230 million less than in 1965 and less than half of the $6.47 billion outflow in 1964. The very sharp decline in 1965 and the further reduction in 1966 can be attributed in part to the cooperation of banks and other business enterprises in the program to improve the balance of payments. Other factors contributing to these changes were the application of the Interest Equalization Tax to long-term bank loans, and the large increase in domestic capital requirements relative to the lending capacity of domestic financial organizations.

Outflows of capital for direct investments abroad (including funds that had been borrowed abroad by companies incorporated in the United States) rose from $3.4 billion in 1965 to $3.5 billion in 1966. (See table 6.) Funds borrowed abroad through the sale of securities by domestic subsidiaries of U.S. corporations specially organized to finance foreign investments (and in some instances by the parent companies themselves) and actually transferred to foreign affiliates amounted to about $50 million in 1965 and nearly $450 million in 1966. The total amounts borrowed by such means were about $190 million and $600 million in the two years; most of the amounts not transferred to foreign affiliates were left in foreign bank accounts or other short-term investments abroad.

In addition to borrowing funds abroad through security issues, U.S. corporations also obtained fund through loans from banks or other foreign sources.

These loans are included in the foreign liabilities reported by U.S. corporations to others than their own affiliates. In 1966 such liabilities increased by about $475 million, nearly $300 million more than in 1965 and $400 million more than in 1964. (See Balance of Payments Tables 1, 2, and 8, lines 54 and 55.) A large part of these funds has also been transferred to foreign affiliates of U.S. corporations, and is thus included in the figures for capital outflows for direct investments abroad.

Omitting funds borrowed abroad, the outflow of capital for direct invest-

ments in 1966 may have been between $2.8 and $2.9 billion, substantially less than the 1965 outflow of roughly $3.3 billion.

Growth of direct investments abroad

The latest data on plant and equipment expenditures by foreign affiliates indicate a continuing increase of actual or projected expenditures, but at a gradually declining rate of increase. The increase over the previous year was about 21 percent in 1965 and 17 percent in 1966. Projections for 1967 indicate a 12 percent rise, and for 1968, about 7 percent. These figures do not include the expansion of foreign investments through purchases of equity interests in existing enterprises, nor do they indicate capital requirements for other assets, such as inventories or credits on sales.

On the other hand, only a minor part of these capital requirements is usually met from the United States; a large part comes from the foreign affiliates themselves through the use of depreciation reserves and retained earnings; in addition foreign affiliates obtain large amounts from foreign lenders or investors.

For these reasons, there is not necessarily a close correlation between plant and equipment expenditures of the foreign affiliates and capital outflows for direct investments. Still, the relatively small increase in capital outflows in 1966 may already reflect the slower expansion of real investments last year. Preliminary figures for the first half of 1967 indicate that capital outflows for direct investments (including funds raised abroad by U.S. corporations, but disregarding the large liquidations in the second quarter) were at an annual rate of about $3 billion, slightly less than comparable figures for 1966.

Overall, United States companies invested $5.3 billion in foreign enterprises in 1966, raising the aggregate book value of these investments to $54.6 billion at year end. Most of that increase came from capital outflows of $3.5 billion. An additional $1.7 billion was added to these investments out of retained foreign earnings, about $175 million more than in the preceding year.

About 87 percent of all direct investment capital outflows went to developed countries as compared with about 75 percent in 1965. Increases in capital flows to Common Market countries and declines in outflows to the Middle East accounted for this shift. However, additions to the book value of direct investments in the developed areas accounted for only 77 percent of all such additions because the less developed countries accounted for a larger than proportionate share of the reinvested earnings of foreign subsidiaries and other affiliates incorporated abroad.

Investments in Europe

The cumulative value of direct investments in Western Europe was $16.2 billion at the end of 1966, about $2.2 billion or nearly 16 percent more than at the end of 1965 (table 3). The 1966 increase exceeded the $1.9 billion or 15.5 percent rise in the preceding year.

Investments in manufacturing industries increased about $1.3 billion in 1966, compared with $1 billion in 1965; those in the petroleum industry rose $550 million, compared with $325 million in the previous year. (Petrochemical and fertilizer plants are classified as manufacturing industries.)

The new investments in 1966 include about $200 million of acquisitions of equity interests in existing enterprises in manufacturing industries, and about the same amount in the petroleum industry. In 1965, acquisitions were about $260 million, nearly all of it in manufacturing.

Nearly half ($7.6 billion) of the total European investments at the end of 1966 was located in Common Market countries, including $3.1 billion in Germany. About 70 percent of the 1966 value of direct investments in the Common Market countries was placed there since the beginning of 1960; for Germany this percentage was even a little higher.

Investments in the United Kingdom were about $5.7 billion at the end of 1966, the largest for any single European country. These investments are older, however, than those in the

Common Market countries, with only 56 percent made during the 1960's.

Major assets are also held in Switzerland, particularly in trading and financial enterprises. To a certain extent these enterprises have their own investments outside of Switzerland, particularly in Common Market countries.

The $2.2 billion increase in direct investments in Europe in 1966 was financed through U.S. capital outflows of $1.8 billion (including funds borrowed abroad by the U.S. parent companies and their U.S. incorporated subsidiaries), and through the reinvestment of about $0.4 billion of the earnings of the affiliated European corporations (table 4). The relatively small amount of reinvested earnings reflects losses of nearly $80 million

on the books of European subsidiaries of American petroleum companies. These losses reflect in part the write-off of exploration expenditures and in part the manner in which earnings from the worldwide operations of the petroleum companies are distributed between producing and marketing areas. This distribution is strongly influenced by tax considerations in the various countries in which these companies operate. Capital investment by petroleum companies in Europe thus may have been financed through the reinvestment of earnings attributed to oil-producing countries. On the books of the parent companies and in the balance of payments tabulations, which are based on company reports, these transactions would appear as distributed income

Table 7.—Net Capital Outflows to Manufacturing Affiliates Abroad, 1962–66, by Industry

[Millions of dollars]

Area and year	Manu-factur-ing, total	Food products	Paper and allied products	Chemicals and allied products	Rubber products	Primary and fabricated metals	Machinery except electrical	Electrical machinery	Transportation equipment	Other industries
All areas, total:										
1962	711.7	42.6	5.2	99.3	31.4	65.9	85.7	60.1	225.1	96.2
1963	774.3	57.3	24.4	176.5	13.2	85.6	51.2	24.0	194.5	147.5
1964 r	1,034.3	74.8	9.1	302.7	2.1	69.8	117.9	45.8	207.1	204.9
1965 r	1,525.1	115.6	99.1	292.0	16.4	83.7	285.5	96.3	405.5	130.9
1966 p	1,730.3	109.3	150.5	492.3	19.5	130.5	220.8	113.4	314.0	180.0
Canada:										
1962	11.8	-6.0	4.2	-25.5	-4.1	-1.1	27.9	11.8	-7.1	11.6
1963	119.6	5.5	12.2	18.4	2.6	6.2	24.0	3.8	37.4	9.5
1964 r	140.0	29.0	-8.6	32.2	-7.1	-3.9	15.3	11.6	48.4	23.0
1965 r	394.7	17.7	62.5	70.0	5.1	6.5	27.4	12.7	173.2	19.8
1966 p	548.3	16.8	125.8	88.1	-1.4	23.6	30.5	6.8	241.8	16.3
Latin America: [1]										
1962	133.3	1.6	-.3	39.4	-3.8	16.2	6.2	2.5	49.8	21.6
1963	150.0	31.6	4.4	48.8	-1.9	5.0	8.6	-7.5	17.1	43.8
1964	137.2	-9.2	2.1	73.6	8.5	7.9	9.5	-10.3	30.1	25.1
1965 r	245.4	50.8	18.6	82.0	-1.1	19.5	.5	10.5	38.1	26.5
1966 p	158.4	8.6	4.5	94.4	5.3	12.8	12.2	8.7	-20.7	32.6
Europe:										
1962	453.4	29.5	.5	64.4	34.3	26.5	49.6	40.3	156.4	52.1
1963	395.0	11.0	2.5	82.1	13.3	37.2	4.5	28.5	132.9	83.1
1964	618.6	41.6	13.6	163.0	-.3	30.4	65.3	38.0	127.4	139.6
1965 r	760.5	40.8	12.8	97.0	2.4	60.2	239.6	53.4	176.0	78.3
1966 p	899.2	54.7	16.2	275.5	15.2	75.3	166.1	84.3	91.0	120.8
Africa:										
1962	10.7	1.3	.2	.1	-.4	1.4	1.7	.2	3.9	2.2
1963	8.5	.7	.4	2.2	.2	2.1	2.3	1.1	-.9	.5
1964	18.6	2.5	.6	2.9	-.5	1.5	4.3	-.3	-3.1	.7
1965 r	39.6	1.2	2.6	2.4	1.0	17.3	7.3	(**)	7.2	.5
1966 p	16.8	2.5	1.8	.6	-1.3	1.8	4.8	(**)	2.3	4.3
Asia:										
1962	30.4	1.3	.5	11.6	5.2	1.4	1.3	3.7	.2	5.2
1963	46.6	6.2	3.8	18.7	-.9	2.5	6.2	3.2	.9	6.2
1964	60.6	4.6	1.7	24.8	(**)	3.3	11.4	5.8	.3	8.7
1965 r	57.8	-1.2	2.0	25.1	-1.8	.9	6.5	17.4	1.5	7.4
1966 p	57.5	6.5	1.4	17.0	2.3	2.9	8.3	16.3	(**)	2.1
Oceania:										
1962	72.2	15.0	.1	9.3	.2	21.5	-.9	1.7	21.9	3.5
1963	54.5	2.3	1.1	6.3	(**)	32.7	5.7	-5.0	7.0	4.5
1964	59.2	6.3	-.3	6.2	1.5	20.6	12.1	1.0	4.0	7.8
1965 r	27.0	6.4	.5	15.5	10.7	-20.7	4.2	2.4	9.5	-1.6
1966 p	50.1	20.2	.8	16.0	-.6	14.1	-1.1	-2.7	-.5	3.9

r Revised.   p Preliminary.
**Less than $50,000.
1 Includes "other Western Hemisphere."

from the oil-producing countries and as capital outflows to the processing and marketing countries.

In manufacturing, trade and other industries, reinvested earnings of the European companies were about $500 million and accounted for nearly one third of the 1966 increase in the amount invested.

Other developed countries

United States investments in Canada rose at a record rate of $1.6 billion in 1966, about 13 percent more than in the year before. While capital outflows were at a high of $1.1 billion, reinvestment of earnings was unchanged from 1965. One-half of the new investment—about $800 million—was in manufacturing industries. The resource industries, petroleum and mining, absorbed $440 million to finance new projects and to expand production facilities of existing operations.

In other developed countries, United States investment increased $400 million in 1966; this was divided about evenly between funds obtained from parent companies and funds obtained from the reinvestment of foreign earnings. About $200 million was invested in manufacturing industries, and close to $100 million was spent for mining activities, primarily in the continuing build-up of production of iron ore producing facilities in Australia.

Less developed countries

Direct investments in less developed countries rose by $1.0 billion in 1966

Table 8.—Net Capital Flows Between Primary and Secondary Foreign Affiliates, 1961–66

[Millions of dollars; net inflows (−)]

Area and country	1961	1962	1963	1964	1965	1966 ᵖ
Canada	4		−4	3	−8	16
Latin America	2	16	−1	−2	−3	−24
Argentina	−6	−11	−14	−14	−5	4
Mexico	−4	11	−5	3	−5	2
Panama	10	13	14	12	8	7
Other Latin America	2	3	4	−3	−1	−37
Europe		−22	24	19	43	30
France	−15	−14	−5	−2	22	−6
Germany	−8	−4	−20	−5	−22	−16
Italy	−25	−21	−9	−5	−9	−7
Switzerland	60	48	105	60	77	28
United Kingdom	−6	−9	−4	(**)	−2	47
Other Europe	−6	−22	−43	−29	−22	−16
Other countries	−6	6	−19	−20	−32	−22

ᵖ Preliminary.
**Less than $500,000.

to a total of $18.1 billion at yearend. This increase was less than in 1965 when new investments amounted to $1.3 billion. The decline from 1965 in capital outflows from the United States was even larger, but was in part replaced by an increase in reinvested earnings.

Nearly $100 million of the decline in new investments is accounted for by non-recurrent capital outflows that were made in 1965 to acquire additional oil leases in the Persian Gulf area. In addition, last year some oil companies sold interests in their concessions in Libya to foreign enterprises; this resulted in return flows of capital to the United States. Another factor contributing to the decline was an increase from the previous year in the temporary return flow of capital to the parent companies to accumulate funds required to meet higher tax payments to oil producing countries.

About 60 percent of the new investment in 1966 in all of the less developed countries was in the Western Hemisphere. Outstanding investments in Venezuela, as in other recent years, declined because of return flows of capital from oil operations. These return flows do not imply a liquidation of United States investments in Venezuela, but rather an accumulation of reserves with the parent company to meet future exploration and capital expenditures. Investments in most other Western Hemisphere countries expanded, particularly in Brazil and the Caribbean area.

Capital outflows to manufacturing industries

In 1966, a record $1.7 billion of United States capital was invested in foreign manufacturing affiliates (table 7). This included close to $300 million used to acquire foreign enterprises or to buy additional equity interests from foreign holders. The change in capital outflows from 1965 differed among industries and areas. Capital outflows to the transportation equipment industry (including automobiles) was down in all areas except Canada, where the automotive trade agreement required investments to increase production of autos and parts. Other industries

to which capital flows from the United States were reduced included those producing nonelectrical machinery (primarily in Europe) and, to a lesser extent, food products.

Capital outflows to other manufacturing industries increased. Most important was a $180 million increase to the chemicals and allied products industry in Europe for investments for new construction of plants as well as funds to repay loans obtained abroad to acquire existing business firms. Investments in the paper and allied products industry doubled in Canada where United States companies have been spending large amounts in recent years to raise productive capacity for pulp, newsprint, and other products. The $50 million rise of capital outflows to "other industries" was concentrated largely in Europe and centered in the scientific instruments and equipment industries. The additional investment in primary and fabricated metals was limited mainly to the production and fabrication of aluminum products.

Earnings and incomes

Although the cumulative value of U.S. direct investments abroad increased 9 percent in 1964 and 11 percent in both 1965 and 1966, earnings in 1966 rose only 4 percent. Annual data from 1950 through 1966 are shown below:

Investment, Earnings, and Yields on U.S. Direct Investments Abroad

Year	Value of investment at start of year	Earnings	Yield
	(Billion dollars)		(Percent)
1966	49.3	5.68	11.5
1965	44.4	5.46	12.3
1964	40.7	5.07	12.5
1963	37.2	4.59	12.3
1962	34.7	4.24	12.2
1961	31.8	3.82	12.0
1960	29.8	3.57	12.0
1959	27.4	3.24	11.8
1958	25.4	3.01	11.9
1957	22.5	3.56	15.8
1956	19.4	3.30	17.0
1955	17.6	2.88	16.4
1954	16.3	2.40	14.7
1953	14.7	2.26	15.4
1952	13.0	2.33	17.9
1951	11.8	2.24	19.0
1950	10.7	1.77	16.5

However, the earnings on the foreign investments as measured for balance of payments purposes are not necessarily a complete measure of the income de-

Table 9.—Acquisitions and Sales by American Companies of Foreign Enterprises,[1] by Area and Industry, 1965–66

[Millions of dollars]

Area and industry	1965 Acquisitions	1965 Sales	1965 Net	1966 Acquisitions	1966 Sales	1966 Net
All areas, total	369	90	279	583	29	554
Petroleum	7	2	5	204	...	204
Manufacturing	268	46	222	314	25	289
Other industries	94	42	52	65	4	61
Canada, total	69	47	22	65	13	53
Petroleum	4	2	2	1	...	1
Manufacturing	22	44	−22	59	12	46
Other industries	42	(**)	42	6	1	5
Europe, total	258	2	256	427	4	423
Petroleum	3	...	3	202	...	202
Manufacturing	207	2	205	182	4	178
Other industries	48	...	48	43	(**)	43
Other areas, total	42	41	1	91	12	79
Petroleum	...	...	...	1	...	1
Manufacturing	39	...	39	74	9	65
Other industries	3	41	−38	16	3	13

[1] Includes acquisitions and sales of minority interests.
**Less than $500,000.

Table 10.—Direct-Investment Receipts of Royalties and Fees[1], by Areas and Major Industries, 1965–66

[Millions of dollars]

Area and industry	1965 [r] total	1966 [p] Total	1966 [p] Royalties, license fees and rentals	1966 [p] Management fees and service charges
All areas, total	924	1,045	362	683
Petroleum	138	127	12	116
Manufacturing	578	659	296	364
Trade	77	110	34	76
Other industries	131	148	20	127
Canada, total	185	215	55	159
Petroleum	9	15	(**)	15
Manufacturing	144	165	48	117
Trade	12	15	5	10
Other industries	20	20	2	18
Latin America, total [2]	174	176	50	126
Petroleum	29	24	1	24
Manufacturing	81	86	36	50
Trade	23	24	8	15
Other industries	40	42	4	37
Europe: Common Market, total	182	235	117	118
Petroleum	17	17	(**)	16
Manufacturing	144	176	108	68
Trade	12	29	7	22
Other industries	10	14	2	12
Other Europe, total	199	222	88	135
Petroleum	13	12	1	11
Manufacturing	142	158	73	85
Trade	16	23	9	15
Other industries	28	29	5	24
Other areas, total	184	196	52	144
Petroleum	71	59	9	50
Manufacturing	67	75	31	44
Trade	14	19	5	14
Other industries	33	43	7	36

[p] Preliminary.   [r] Revised.
**Less than $500,000.
[1] Excludes foreign film rentals.
[2] Includes "other Western Hemisphere."

Table 11.—Comparison of United States Direct-Investment Capital Flows and Transactions Covered Under the Balance of Payments Improvement Program

[Millions of dollars; outflows (−)]

Item	1965	1966
1. Balance of Payments, total, all countries	−3,418	−3,543
2. Reported in Balance of Payments Improvement Program	−2,655	−3,076
3. Difference (Line 1 less line 2)	−763	−467
4. Non-program items in balance of payments accounts, total (lines 5 through 9)	−516	−491
5. Financial institutions	−241	−146
6. Insurance	−30	−60
7. New issues sold to others than parent companies	−257	−302
8. Amortizations of issues held by others than parent companies	+66	+44
9. Other non-program flows	−54	−27
10. Difference due to coverage, errors and omissions (Line 3 less line 4)	−247	+24
Delaware company financing:		
11. Funds raised	191	594
12. Funds utilized	−52	−445

rived by American firms as a result of these investments. Such income can also accrue to U.S. parent companies through additional exports, imports at costs lower than the prices that would have to be paid to independent producers of the imported goods, receipts of royalties, management fees, and benefits resulting from the assumption of other costs, such as research and development expenditures, by foreign subsidiaries.

Even with these reservations, the figures shown in the tabulation suggest that in 1966 the yield of U.S. direct investments abroad declined substantially from the preceding year, and that it was less than in any other year of the 1950's or 1960's.

The disappointing earnings reflected a slowdown in business expansion in most of the industrial countries and also generally rising foreign taxes on natural resource industries. Yields on manufacturing investments were 10.9 percent as compared with 11.9 percent in the year before. Those on petroleum investments dropped from 12.8 percent in 1965 to 12.1 percent last year.

Earnings on manufacturing investments in Europe were $855 million, the same as in the preceding year, although investments at the beginning of 1966 were about $1 billion or nearly 15 percent higher than a year earlier. The average yields declined, therefore, from 13.0 percent in 1965 to 11.2 percent in 1966. Automobile companies and other firms in the transportation equipment industry experienced major declines in earnings, but companies in the machinery and, to a lesser extent, in the electrical equipment industry were also affected by relatively unfavorable business developments.

The combined effects of increased competition (resulting from a faster increase in the supply of oil products relative to demand) and of rising costs of crude oil (resulting from higher taxes paid to the oil producing countries) had an adverse effect on earnings of the petroleum industry in Europe.

In Canada, earnings on all investments increased only 2½ percent over 1965, while investments at the beginning of 1966 were 10 percent higher than a year earlier. Yields on manu-

facturing investments dropped from 9.8 percent in 1965 to 9.2 percent, and on mining and petroleum investments from 7.8 percent to 7.6 percent. The only group of industrialized countries in which earnings on U.S. direct investments had a significant rise was that comprising Australia, New Zealand and the Republic of South Africa.

Declining yields on investments were not limited to developed countries. Although earnings in less developed countries as a whole rose from $2.75 billion in 1965 to $2.9 billion in 1966, the rise was relatively less than the amount invested, and the yield declined from 17.3 to 17.0 percent. The decline was primarily in petroleum investments in the Middle East and Africa.

Of the $220 million rise in total earnings from 1965 to 1966, approximately $80 million was returned to U.S. parent companies in the form of dividends, interest, and branch profits (table 5). There was a rise in incomes from Canada, Latin America, and the Caribbean, and from the petroleum-producing countries in the Middle East and Africa, but incomes from Europe, particularly Germany and the United Kingdom, declined.

The decline in incomes received from Germany reflects extraordinary dividend distributions in the previous year. In anticipation of a change in the tax structure, dividend payments by U.S. subsidiaries were sharply increased in 1965, representing in part a distribution of previously retained earnings. In 1966, the division of earnings into dividends and retained earnings was about the same as in 1964.

Royalties and fees

In 1966, United States parent companies continued to receive an increasingly large proportion of their total receipts from foreign affiliates in the form of royalties and fees of various kinds (table 10). For a number of years these receipts have grown at a much faster rate than the receipts of other income from foreign affiliates. For example, in 1957, investment income (dividend, interest, and branch profits) and royalties and fees amounted to $2.5 billion, of which 10 percent was in the form of royalties and fees. By 1966, combined receipts had grown to $5.1 billion, of which more than 20 percent was represented by royalties and fees.

Gains in 1966 were concentrated in the manufacturing and trade industries.

Some decline in the receipt from petroleum affiliates was offset by a moderate rise in receipts from other industries. Since royalties and fees are largely responsive to increases in sales rather than to changes in net earnings, they should continue for some time to perform better than dividend income, which is affected by rising costs. Europe, from which 41 percent of royalties and fees were received by parent companies in 1965, accounted for about two-thirds of the growth of these items in 1966.

Portfolio Investments

Transactions by United States residents in foreign securities resulted in outflows of United States funds of $482 million in 1966 as compared with $758 million in 1965. During 1966, United States investors purchased about $1,210 million of newly issued foreign securities denominated in

United States dollars (foreign dollar bonds) out of some $1,321 million offered in the United States markets (table 12). Retirements of previously issued dollar bonds that had been purchased by U.S. investors amounted to $405 million. This amount included advance repayment by the Canadian government of bonds sold to U.S. investors in the fourth quarter of 1962 and the first quarter of 1963 to strengthen its U.S. dollar reserves, which had been reduced by the exchange crisis earlier in 1962. On balance, United States investors liquidated holdings in foreign denominated securities in the amount of $323 million last year.

Preliminary tabulations for the first half of 1967 show placement of foreign dollar bonds in the United States of $757 million, offset by redemptions and retirements of $230 million for a net of $527 million. With a net liquidation of foreign-denominated securities of $27 million, total net transactions in foreign securities were $500 million in the first half. The comparable total for net transactions in foreign securities in the first half of 1966 was $417 million.

During 1966 and the first half of 1967, the International Bank for Reconstruction and Development (IBRD) placed some $425 million in new issues in the United States. Considerable amounts of these placements are for future delivery and will be reflected in capital flow data in future periods. Most of the proceeds from these offerings was temporarily invested in securities of U.S. Government agencies.

The Middle East crisis in June of this year caused a sharp rise in the sale of Israel government securities in the United States. The increase in the volume of these securities sold in the United States market will probably extend into the second half of 1967 and will tend to raise the volume of foreign dollar bonds placed here above the level of 1966 transactions.

Foreign Direct Investments in the United States

Foreign direct investments in the United States rose by about $250 million in 1966 and reached a book

Table 12.—New Foreign Issues Placed In The United States,[1] 1965–June 1967

[Millions of dollars; before deducting discounts and commissions]

Areas	Gross amount sold			U.S. portion		
	Total	Publicly offered	Privately offered	Total	Publicly offered	Privately offered
1967 (January–June): ᵖ						
Total	824	571	253	760	539	221
Canada	534	305	229	500	302	198
Europe						
Australia, Republic of South Africa, New Zealand, and Japan						
Other countries [2]	164	140	24	156	133	23
International Bank [3]	126	126	---	104	104	---
1966 (July–December):						
Total	496	329	167	440	295	145
Canada	283	172	111	266	157	109
Europe	5	(*)	5	5	(*)	5
Australia, Republic of South Africa, New Zealand, and Japan	6	6	---	6	6	---
Other countries	117	66	51	89	58	31
International Bank [3]	85	85	---	74	74	---
1966 (January–June):						
Total	825	229	596	773	188	585
Canada	718	158	560	667	118	549
Europe	10	---	10	10	---	10
Australia, Republic of South Africa, New Zealand, and Japan						
Other countries	97	71	26	96	70	26
International Bank						
1965 (July–December):						
Total	619	184	435	562	157	405
Canada	390	50	340	373	50	323
Europe	95	15	80	73	5	68
Australia, Republic of South Africa, New Zealand, and Japan	20	20	---	18	18	---
Other countries	95	80	15	79	65	14
International Bank [3]	19	19	---	19	19	---
1965 (January–June):						
Total	698	401	297	637	344	293
Canada	339	54	285	334	53	281
Europe	30	30	---	11	11	---
Australia, Republic of South Africa, New Zealand, and Japan	43	43	---	37	37	---
Other countries	105	93	12	94	82	12
International Bank [3]	181	181	---	161	161	---

ᵖ Preliminary.   * Less than $500,000.
[1] Excludes issues offered in the United States but taken entirely by "foreigners."
[2] Includes an issue of the Inter-American Development Bank.
[3] May include "delayed deliveries."
NOTE.—The amounts shown for U.S. purchases exceed the figures used in the balance of payments accounts because the latter excludes discounts and commissions. The International Bank for Reconstruction and Development issues are reduced by the amount of delayed deliveries included in subsequent years.

value of $9.1 billion at the end of the year (table 13). The increase from 1965 was caused mainly by reinvested earnings of $340 million of United States subsidiaries of foreign parent firms, but it also included inflows of foreign capital of about $85 million. However, the value of these investments was adversely affected by other adjustments of $170 million, mainly a reduction in the value of securities held by foreign-owned insurance companies. If the effect of this valuation adjustment were eliminated, investments would have risen $425 million, about the same as the 1965 increase.

Of the more than $9 billion invested by foreigners in United States business enterprises, about $3.8 billion was held in manufacturing firms and more than $2 billion in financial and insurance firms. Canadian investors ranked first as owners of United States manufacturing companies controlled abroad, and British firms predominated in the finance and insurance groups. Petroleum investments were relatively unchanged at $1.7 billion.

Despite an increase in earnings of the U.S. companies, the amount available for reinvestment in 1966 was somewhat diminished because of an

increase in the rate of dividend distributions. More than one-half of the earnings of the U.S. affiliates was accounted for by the manufacturing group.

Net foreign capital inflows of $86 million were considerably reduced by the liquidation of an oil company owned by a Canadian parent firm for about $120 million. Capital inflows to manufacturing industries amounted to $111 million. About a third of this amount consisted of new investments by Germany.

Table 13.—Foreign Direct Investments in the United States, Selected Data, 1950, 1965, and 1966, by Country and Industry

[Millions of dollars]

	Value at yearend			Capital flow						Earnings,[1] income,[1] and undistributed profits					
				1965 ʳ			1966 ᵖ			1965 ʳ			1966 ᵖ		
	1950	1965 ʳ	1966 ᵖ	Total	New investments[2]	Other	Total	New investments[2]	Other	Earnings	Income	Undistributed profits	Earnings	Income	Undistributed profits
Total	3,391	8,797	9,054	57	100	−43	86	89	−3	642	298	358	695	371	339
By area:															
Canada	1,029	2,388	2,439	43	58	−15	2	25	−23	135	94	58	133	77	80
United Kingdom	1,168	2,852	2,864	−66	11	−77	23	18	5	214	116	91	234	125	102
Other Europe	1,059	3,224	3,409	23	26	−3	67	43	24	270	76	195	307	159	143
Belgium	n.s.s.	175	193	−7	1	−8	10		10	8	3	7	9	2	8
France	n.s.s.	200	215	(*)	2	−2	8	3	5	7	2	5	10	3	7
Germany	n.s.s.	209	247	43	14	29	28	36	−8	16	4	11	19	7	11
Italy	n.s.s.	87	87	7	3	4	1	1	(*)	−2		−2	1		1
Netherlands	334	1,304	1,402	−33		−33	20	3	17	147	26	120	153	73	78
Sweden	n.s.s.	215	217	6		6	−7	(*)	−7	13	3	10	18	7	10
Switzerland	348	940	949	6	6		7	(*)	7	71	34	37	89	64	23
Other countries	377	94	100	1		1	1		1	10	5	5	8	2	5
Japan	n.s.s.	118	103	33	2	31	−24	3	−27	22	10	14	14	7	8
Latin America	n.s.s.	161	177	27	4	23	14		14	3	3		4	2	2
Other countries	134	53	61	−3		−3	4	(*)	4	(*)		(*)	4		4
By industry:															
Petroleum	405	1,710	1,740	−63		−63	−94	1	−94	215	26	184	214	81	124
Manufacturing	1,138	3,478	3,789	132	75	57	111	47	64	303	176	129	357	159	200
Trade	n.s.s.	748	739	30	10	20	−39	9	−48	66	25	43	43	15	30
Insurance	³ 1,065	³ 2,169	³ 2,072	−20		−20	64		64	40	40		76	76	
Other finance	(⁴)	(⁴)	(⁴)	−37	11	−48	13	9	4	⁵ 11	⁵ 12	6	⁵ 7	⁵ 22	−5
Other industries	784	693	714	15	5	10	31	24	7	6	20	−5	−2	18	−10

ᵖ Preliminary.   ʳ Revised.   n.s.s. Not shown separately.   *Less than $500,000.
[1] "Earnings" represents the foreign share in corporate and branch profits; "Income" is the amount distributed, after withholding taxes, as dividends, interest and branch profits.
[2] "New investments" consist of the first reported capital inflow to establish a new company or operation in the U.S. and also inflows to acquire additional shares of existing companies.
[3] Includes market revaluations of securities held by insurance companies.
[4] Included in "Insurance."
[5] Earnings and income paid by agency banks in the U.S. to foreign home offices have been excluded from direct investment totals.

PLANT AND EQUIPMENT EXPENDITURES
BY FOREIGN AFFILIATES
OF U.S. CORPORATIONS, 1967-69

Plant and Equipment Expenditures by Foreign Affiliates of U.S. Corporations, 1967-69

Foreign affiliates of U.S. corporations have projected a 5 percent rise in plant and equipment expenditures for this year and a 4 percent advance for 1969. Actual expenditures rose 7 percent last year, a considerable slowdown from the experience of 1964–66.

PLANT and equipment expenditures by foreign affiliates of U.S. corporations are expected to rise 5 percent in the current year and an additional 4 percent in 1969. These increases follow a 7 percent rise in 1967 which brought total outlays in that year to $9.2 billion. The 1967 increase was slightly smaller than the rise projected last December and represents a significant slowdown from the 20 percent advance recorded in both 1964 and 1965 and the 16 percent rise in 1966.

These data are based on reports received by the Office of Business Economics in June and July of this year from about 500 major U.S. corporations with foreign affiliates. The sample results are adjusted to reflect foreign plant and equipment expenditures by all U.S. corporations.

The reports submitted by companies do not necessarily reflect the actual expenditures that are likely to be made. Experience over several years has shown, for instance, that midyear estimates for the same year are usually higher than the actual expenditures reported a year later, while those for the following year are usually lower. Therefore, year-to-year changes are computed by comparing the estimate for a given year with that made in the corresponding period of the preceding year, on the assumption that the estimates are based on similar types of information available to corporate officials responding to the questionnaires. For example, the 4 percent rise for 1969 is based on a compari-son of column A, 1969, of table 1, with column A, 1968.

Industry patterns

The slower overall growth in plant and equipment expenditures beginning in 1967 is attributable primarily to the leveling off of expenditures in manufacturing. Spending by manufacturers had risen about 30 percent in both 1964 and 1965, and 18 percent in 1966. However, no increase was recorded for 1967 and none is now projected for either 1968 or 1969.

Within manufacturing, two significant reversals of trend are suggested by the current data. The chemical industry is planning little increase in expenditures this year and a drop of almost 20 percent for 1969, after steady growth through 1967. In the transportation equipment industry, expenditures declined in 1967 and are expected to decrease again this year. For 1969, however, first estimates indicate a new surge in investment, much of it concentrated in Canada.

The petroleum industry, with a rise in expenditures of $0.5 billion or 19 percent in 1967, realized its largest gain on both a dollar and a percentage basis since 1957, when the plant and equipment expenditures survey was initiated. With the rise concentrated primarily in Europe, Africa, and the Far East,

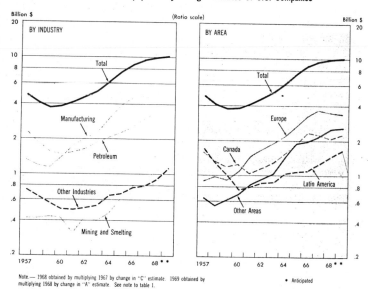

Expenditures for Plant and Equipment by Foreign Affiliates of U.S. Companies

Note.— 1968 obtained by multiplying 1967 by change in "C" estimate. 1969 obtained by multiplying 1968 by change in "A" estimate. See note to table 1.

* Anticipated

U.S. Department of Commerce, Office of Business Economics

petroleum affiliates accounted for better than four-fifths of the 1967 spending increase for all areas and industries. For 1968, outlays are expected to increase 9 percent while no further advance is presently planned for 1969.

The mining industry shows a consistently high growth rate in capital investment over the 3-year period covered by the current survey. The 14 percent rise in 1967, however, was well below the 1966 rate of advance and somewhat lower than previously projected. The

larger increases scheduled for 1968 and 1969 suggest that spending on some projects, initially planned for 1967, may have been delayed.

In other industries, including public utilities and trade, expenditures are expected to rise 25 percent in 1969 after steady but considerably smaller increases in 1967 and 1968.

Geographic patterns

Canada was the only major area in which foreign affiliates reduced capital expenditures in 1967, following a large

increase in 1966. The decline, concentrated almost entirely in manufacturing industries, is expected to continue at the same rate this year, but increased spending in all major industries is projected for 1969. Canada's share of total plant and equipment expenditures was a steady 25 percent during 1960–65 and rose to 27 percent in 1966. For 1967, its share was reduced to 24 percent, and if current estimates materialize, it will be at a new low of 21½ percent in both 1968 and 1969.

Table 1.—Estimates of Plant and Equipment Expenditures by Foreign Affiliates of U.S. Companies by Area and Industry—Summary of Surveys [1]

[Millions of dollars]

	1965 E	1966 A	1966 B	1966 C	1966 D	1966 E	1967 A	1967 B	1967 C	1967 D	1967 E	1968 A	1968 B	1968 C	1969 A
All areas, total	7,440	7,305	8,805	9,039	8,680	8,640	9,115	10,069	10,045	9,466	9,245	9,785	10,707	10,520	10,168
Mining and smelting	629	482	637	764	746	789	637	839	931	903	902	761	1,067	1,101	969
Petroleum	2,277	2,330	2,689	2,727	2,629	2,526	2,937	3,334	3,295	3,099	3,018	3,432	3,641	3,595	3,383
Manufacturing	3,884	3,832	4,796	4,793	4,553	4,583	4,803	5,098	5,035	4,709	4,513	4,853	5,200	4,963	4,894
Other industries	650	661	683	756	752	741	738	798	783	755	812	739	799	861	921
Canada, total	1,847	1,678	2,076	2,175	2,263	2,357	2,081	2,273	2,360	2,227	2,208	2,053	2,229	2,244	2,206
Mining and smelting	212	173	244	278	266	297	188	274	332	306	310	240	375	401	286
Petroleum	503	358	426	552	609	649	570	600	650	625	636	616	670	681	668
Manufacturing	944	963	1,199	1,143	1,156	1,174	1,132	1,163	1,122	1,064	998	963	933	893	991
Other industries	188	184	207	202	231	237	191	237	256	233	264	234	251	269	261
Latin America, total	1,073	933	1,140	1,238	1,105	1,092	1,250	1,431	1,441	1,339	1,258	1,601	1,923	1,715	1,791
Mining and smelting	160	110	176	214	211	229	193	288	208	287	292	335	454	412	490
Petroleum	307	334	378	336	282	268	391	366	380	368	301	475	491	426	433
Manufacturing	459	346	452	518	462	451	516	624	591	526	484	642	775	659	636
Other industries	147	144	134	171	150	143	150	156	172	159	181	150	204	218	233
Europe:															
Common market, total	1,418	1,611	1,959	1,993	1,928	1,853	2,024	2,215	2,216	2,093	2,136	2,193	2,235	2,077	2,105
Mining and smelting	2	1	2	2	2	3	1	4	2	3	3	1	3	3	3
Petroleum	306	406	534	474	476	434	482	623	582	528	583	565	528	490	526
Manufacturing	1,042	1,100	1,332	1,428	1,364	1,331	1,452	1,531	1,538	1,472	1,453	1,534	1,597	1,477	1,451
Other industries	68	104	92	89	86	85	90	88	93	90	97	92	107	108	126
Other Europe, total	1,222	1,282	1,586	1,562	1,417	1,400	1,667	1,764	1,755	1,630	1,501	1,621	1,697	1,726	1,752
Mining and smelting	2	7	4	3	6	4	2	8	4	4	5	6	6	7	4
Petroleum	297	371	438	309	397	344	459	583	558	542	466	473	538	563	521
Manufacturing	818	776	1,009	856	856	913	1,034	999	1,044	938	891	1,011	1,019	1,011	1,078
Other industries	106	129	135	164	158	141	173	175	149	147	139	131	135	145	150
Other areas, total	1,880	1,802	2,044	2,072	1,968	1,938	2,093	2,352	2,274	2,177	2,142	2,317	2,672	2,759	2,313
Mining and smelting	252	192	212	267	261	257	253	266	295	305	293	177	229	278	186
Petroleum	864	862	912	966	865	832	1,036	1,161	1,125	1,036	1,032	1,303	1,414	1,435	1,237
Manufacturing	621	648	804	708	714	714	669	782	741	710	687	704	877	924	738
Other industries	143	100	116	131	128	135	135	142	114	127	130	134	104	122	152

1. A. Estimated in June of previous year. B. Estimated in December of previous year. C. Estimated in June of current year. D. Estimated in December of current year. E. Actual—reported in June of following year.

Note.—Detail may not add to totals because of rounding.

Source: U.S. Department of Commerce, Office of Business Economics.

Table 1A.—Estimates of Plant and Equipment Expenditures by Foreign Affiliates of U.S. Corporations, by OFDI Schedule Area and Industry—Summary of Surveys

[Millions of dollars]

	1965														
All schedules, total [1]	5,595	5,627	6,729	6,864	6,417	6,282	7,034	7,796	7,686	7,240	7,037	7,733	8,479	8,276	7,962
Schedule A, total	1,743	1,471	1,840	1,992	1,807	1,787	1,951	2,194	2,212	2,056	1,994	2,465	2,724	2,582	2,733
Mining and smelting	209	140	214	261	250	271	244	332	351	332	337	375	489	455	521
Petroleum	638	645	693	708	591	574	785	790	838	736	699	1,075	1,003	1,006	1,020
Manufacturing	658	493	731	765	735	718	699	824	778	747	700	783	970	838	863
Other industries	238	194	202	259	231	225	223	249	245	242	258	231	262	283	329
Schedule B, total	2,026	2,175	2,416	2,306	2,139	2,124	2,450	2,699	2,660	2,523	2,355	2,504	2,918	2,992	2,571
Mining and smelting	147	154	165	184	188	185	182	201	219	234	222	119	171	212	133
Petroleum	714	798	835	801	754	692	891	1,068	1,021	1,000	942	1,002	1,243	1,256	988
Manufacturing	1,069	1,132	1,323	1,230	1,090	1,153	1,269	1,299	1,329	1,194	1,096	1,299	1,435	1,424	1,359
Other industries	96	91	93	92	107	94	109	110	91	95	95	83	69	100	92
Schedule C, total	1,826	1,981	2,473	2,566	2,471	2,371	2,633	2,903	2,814	2,661	2,688	2,764	2,837	2,702	2,658
Mining and smelting	62	16	15	41	42	36	23	23	30	32	33	32	33	33	28
Petroleum	422	529	735	666	675	612	692	856	787	739	742	738	726	652	710
Manufacturing	1,213	1,245	1,543	1,656	1,572	1,538	1,703	1,812	1,806	1,705	1,719	1,807	1,862	1,808	1,081
Other industries	129	192	181	203	183	185	215	212	202	185	194	191	217	209	239

See table 1 for other notes.
1 Does not include Canada.
For a listing of the countries in each schedule area, see Foreign Direct Investment Regula-

tions (15 CFR 1000.319; 33 F.R. 49) or reprints of the regulations dated July 20, 1968, Office of Foreign Direct Investments, U.S. Department of Commerce, Washington, D.C. 20230.

Source: U.S. Department of Commerce, Office of Business Economics.

Expenditures in Common Market countries rose 15 percent in 1967, well above the estimate made last December. However, outlays are expected to be reduced by about 5 percent in both 1968 and 1969. In other European countries, a significant expansion in the petroleum industry resulted in a 7 percent increase in total expenditures in 1967. After a small decline this year, spending in these countries is currently projected to increase again in 1969, at about the same rate as last year.

Led by rising investments in the mining industry, expenditures in Latin America are expected to increase substantially in both 1968 and 1969, following the 15 percent rise in 1967. Although the 1967 and 1968 advances are below the estimates made last December, Latin America's share of total plant and equipment expenditures is moving steadily upward, from 13 percent in 1966 to a projected 18 percent for 1969.

In all other areas, where a large share of U.S. investments is in the petroleum industry, outlays rose 11 percent in 1967. A further rise of 21 percent—well above previous estimates—is expected

for the current year. Total expenditures will change little in 1969, with reductions in petroleum offsetting increases in all other industries.

Impact on balance of payments

The impact of plant and equipment expenditures on the balance of payments is related directly to the method by which these expenditures are financed. The use of capital transfers from the U.S. parent or of retained earnings of the foreign affiliate has an adverse effect on the balance of payments through capital outflows from the United States and reductions in the repatriation of earnings on direct foreign investments. However, the affiliates have access to other funds besides these, principally their own depreciation reserves and funds borrowed abroad, whose use does not affect the balance of payments. Increasing reliance has been placed on foreign sources of funds in recent years. This is reflected in current data which indicate that a major share of the funds utilized for plant and equipment expenditures is not derived directly from retained earnings or capital transfers from the parent company. In 1967, for

example, plant and equipment expenditures were $9.2 billion while direct investment capital outflows from the United States were about $3.0 billion and earnings reinvested by the affiliates were about $1.6 billion. In addition, not all of the funds from these sources are used to finance plant and equipment outlays; some are used to purchase equities in existing foreign businesses and to meet working capital requirements.

Relationship to the foreign direct investment program

The estimates of plant and equipment expenditures reported in the current survey is of particular interest in relation to the mandatory controls under the foreign direct investment program. The objective of the program, announced on January 1, 1968, is a reduction in capital outflows and reinvested earnings in 1968 of at least $1 billion below the 1967 level. However, it should be clear that the program is designed not to control expenditures of foreign affiliated companies, but only to regulate the extent to which such expenditures may be financed with

Table 2.—Estimates of Plant and Equipment Expenditures by Foreign Manufacturing Affiliates of U.S. Companies by Area and Major Commodity—Summary of Surveys

[Millions of dollars]

	1965	1966					1967					1968			1969
	E	A	B	C	D	E	A	B	C	D	E	A	B	C	A
All areas, total	3,884	3,832	4,796	4,793	4,553	4,583	4,803	5,098	5,035	4,709	4,513	4,853	5,200	4,963	4,894
Chemicals	861	835	1,092	1,101	1,054	1,035	1,315	1,381	1,385	1,266	1,203	1,360	1,466	1,420	1,103
Machinery	882	925	1,033	1,057	1,044	1,044	1,150	1,205	1,198	1,149	1,083	1,212	1,256	1,204	1,298
Transportation equipment	873	1,067	1,265	1,119	1,018	966	982	989	949	852	797	819	906	817	1,018
Other manufacturing	1,267	1,005	1,406	1,456	1,436	1,537	1,356	1,523	1,504	1,439	1,429	1,461	1,572	1,523	1,475
Canada, total	944	963	1,199	1,143	1,156	1,174	1,132	1,163	1,122	1,064	998	963	933	893	991
Chemicals	225	300	314	260	230	221	240	213	239	194	168	254	205	180	207
Machinery	114	142	170	148	161	186	155	174	194	192	189	153	164	155	184
Transportation equipment	224	238	283	275	271	255	270	278	250	247	236	176	223	203	265
Other manufacturing	381	283	432	460	494	513	468	497	439	432	404	380	341	355	336
Latin America, total	459	346	452	518	462	451	516	624	591	526	484	642	775	659	636
Chemicals	151	101	150	187	166	143	170	213	166	160	138	213	237	177	200
Machinery	66	51	63	61	61	65	65	78	80	80	78	83	93	93	107
Transportation equipment	73	69	81	108	75	72	118	120	108	86	88	105	143	143	109
Other manufacturing	168	125	158	162	160	171	163	213	237	200	180	241	302	246	220
Europe:															
Common market, total	1,042	1,100	1,332	1,428	1,364	1,331	1,452	1,531	1,538	1,472	1,453	1,534	1,597	1,477	1,451
Chemicals	147	180	208	269	269	271	383	410	433	423	430	351	376	346	251
Machinery	389	416	448	462	459	441	553	565	571	536	508	619	626	594	594
Transportation equipment	278	362	463	394	389	373	255	261	253	252	245	245	256	211	267
Other manufacturing	228	143	214	273	248	245	261	295	281	262	270	319	339	326	340
Other Europe, total	818	776	1,009	996	856	913	1,034	999	1,044	938	891	1,011	1,019	1,011	1,078
Chemicals	174	140	229	221	163	187	264	239	252	206	210	226	232	269	168
Machinery	193	190	216	249	233	220	239	256	230	219	202	228	237	244	288
Transportation equipment	180	256	313	253	205	191	240	219	223	165	134	202	162	137	250
Other manufacturing	271	190	252	273	255	315	290	284	338	348	345	355	389	361	372
Other areas, total	621	648	804	708	711	714	669	782	741	710	687	704	877	924	738
Chemicals	164	114	191	194	226	213	258	305	295	288	257	317	416	447	278
Machinery	120	127	137	136	131	132	137	132	122	122	107	129	137	118	125
Transportation equipment	118	142	126	89	78	75	99	111	115	102	94	91	123	123	128
Other manufacturing	219	264	350	289	279	294	175	234	208	198	229	167	201	236	208

See table 1 for notes.

Source: U.S. Department of Commerce, Office of Business Economics.

funds provided by U.S. companies or with funds that would otherwise be repatriated to U.S. companies.

In the operation of the program, which is administered by the Office of Foreign Direct Investment (OFDI), foreign countries (except Canada, which has been exempted since March) are grouped into three schedule areas, A, B, and C. The degree of restriction of direct investment transactions is based on the classification of the country where the foreign affiliate is located. Transactions with affiliates located in the Schedule C countries, which include most of continental Western Europe and South Africa, are restricted most severely. They must be limited during 1968 to reinvested earnings and must not exceed 35 percent of the annual average of combined capital outflows and retained earnings with the affiliate in 1965 and 1966, and may be even less depending on the relation of repatriated to total earnings during the years 1964–66. For 1968, transactions with affiliates located in other developed areas (Schedule B) may equal 65 percent of the base-period average, and in the less developed countries (Schedule A), 110

Table 3.—Estimates of Plant and Equipment Expenditures by Foreign Affiliates of U.S. Companies, by Selected Country and Industry—
Summary of Surveys

[Millions of dollars]

	1965	1966					1967					1968			1969
	E	A	B	C	D	E	A	B	C	D	E	A	B	C	A
Manufacturing															
All areas, total	3,884	3,832	4,796	4,793	4,553	4,583	4,803	5,098	5,035	4,709	4,513	4,853	5,200	4,963	4,894
Canada, total	944	963	1,199	1,143	1,156	1,174	1,132	1,163	1,122	1,064	998	963	933	893	991
Latin America, total	459	346	452	518	462	451	516	624	591	526	484	642	775	659	636
Argentina	101	85	106	114	95	91	107	126	108	98	98	142	130	107	166
Brazil	78	73	91	124	109	100	160	185	164	161	131	183	242	216	175
Mexico	145	76	125	140	121	124	114	136	148	128	115	136	215	179	153
Other countries	135	112	130	140	137	136	135	177	171	139	140	181	188	157	142
Europe, total	1,860	1,876	2,341	2,421	2,220	2,243	2,485	2,529	2,582	2,410	2,344	2,544	2,616	2,488	2,528
Belgium and Luxembourg	113	118	185	222	191	186	156	205	216	217	201	217	178	171	109
France	243	225	294	286	273	288	348	341	377	375	378	396	453	438	416
Germany	508	535	627	638	622	581	657	643	546	518	534	589	577	505	589
Italy	110	110	115	144	128	125	162	162	180	160	141	179	220	201	209
Netherlands	68	113	108	138	150	151	129	180	220	202	199	152	169	161	127
United Kingdom	657	651	786	758	644	698	801	746	810	713	641	761	778	721	858
Other countries	160	124	223	238	212	214	232	252	233	225	250	250	241	291	220
Africa, total	88	91	106	89	83	94	58	80	90	66	76	62	70	83	42
Republic of South Africa	45	36	44	27	28	39	32	50	58	40	45	46	55	63	34
Other countries	43	55	62	62	55	55	26	30	32	26	31	16	15	20	8
Asia, total	291	219	338	310	347	327	377	422	393	402	399	388	498	547	455
Middle East	11	24	24	31	30	23	111	115	64	60	62	104	116	144	74
Far East	280	195	314	279	317	303	266	307	329	342	338	284	382	403	381
India	66	41	84	83	123	91	81	69	38	38	49	43	60	35	90
Japan	168	123	158	144	144	153	126	165	204	187	189	184	238	267	193
Other countries	46	31	71	52	50	59	60	74	87	118	99	57	84	101	98
Oceania, total	242	339	359	309	285	294	235	280	258	241	212	254	309	294	241
Australia	231	327	343	295	269	278	230	274	252	234	206	244	300	289	235
Other countries	11	12	16	15	15	15	5	6	6	7	6	11	9	5	6
Petroleum															
All areas, total	2,277	2,330	2,689	2,727	2,629	2,526	2,937	3,334	3,295	3,099	3,018	3,432	3,641	3,595	3,385
Canada, total	503	358	426	552	609	649	570	600	650	625	636	616	670	681	668
Latin America, total	307	334	378	336	282	268	391	366	380	368	301	475	491	426	433
Venezuela	130	166	175	150	128	101	169	147	150	126	103	224	235	185	217
Other Western Hemisphere	61	52	64	76	55	58	70	80	85	87	47	88	88	48	55
Other countries	116	116	139	110	99	109	152	139	145	155	151	163	168	193	161
Europe, total	603	776	972	873	873	778	940	1,206	1,140	1,070	1,049	1,038	1,066	1,052	1,047
Belgium and Luxembourg	26	20	26	43	38	41	46	42	55	55	101	34	32	35	31
France	75	99	125	127	123	96	90	130	72	54	61	103	85	79	95
Germany	97	98	221	161	163	172	183	251	280	243	251	205	159	145	208
Italy	75	77	99	99	113	87	106	101	102	93	93	119	111	112	114
Netherlands	33	112	64	44	40	39	57	100	72	83	78	104	140	118	77
United Kingdom	177	235	250	220	202	163	250	348	332	315	292	290	332	373	319
Other countries	120	135	187	179	194	180	208	234	227	227	173	183	207	190	217
Africa, total	284	350	322	349	287	289	412	469	450	427	395	544	616	566	399
Asia, total	440	377	482	500	459	425	463	511	527	466	456	463	521	620	527
Middle East	233	146	241	246	227	206	249	270	263	195	193	177	206	217	171
Far East	407	231	241	254	232	219	214	241	264	271	263	286	315	403	356
Oceania, total	74	76	83	72	78	69	70	107	72	74	80	131	150	130	18
International shipping	66	60	26	45	41	49	61	74	76	69	101	165	127	120	18

See table 1 for notes.

Source: U.S. Department of Commerce, Office of Business Economics.

percent of the base-period average. The moratorium on capital outflows applicable in Schedule C countries does not apply in Schedule A or B countries.

Plant and equipment expenditures by major industry and OFDI schedule area are presented in table 1a. Only the most recent projections in the table (1968 C and 1969 A) were made after the establishment of the mandatory program.

A comparison of 1968 projections made in December of last year (1968 B), before the mandatory controls were announced, with the current projections (1968 C) indicates that no significant changes in spending plans that might be ascribed to the new program have occurred. In Schedule C countries, where the mandatory controls should have had the most effect on expenditure plans, the expected changes in expenditures for 1968 were about the same in the surveys taken before and after announcement of the program. In Schedule B countries, the projected growth rates indicate upward revisions in overall expenditure plans after announcement of the program, contrary to what might have been expected. There was a reduction in the projected growth rate of expenditures in Schedule A countries. However, data on capital outflows during the first half of 1968 suggest that companies may not be fully utilizing the total direct investment allowable in this area. It may be inappropriate, therefore, to attribute the lower projected rate of increase in plant and equipment expenditures in Schedule A countries to the application of controls.

The slower growth of plant and equipment expenditures in 1968 reported in the current and previous surveys, as well as the moderate increase now projected for 1969, probably reflects basic changes in corporate investment plans that are not related to the current restrictions on capital flows. In many cases, there has been a shift from the larger investments required in earlier years to establish new productive facilities to the smaller outlays now needed for maintenance and expansion of existing plant and equipment. Many of these facilities are still relatively new, and current demand—at least in Canada and Europe—is expanding at a slower rate than it did several years earlier.

THE INTERNATIONAL INVESTMENT POSITION OF THE UNITED STATES IN 1967

Emil L. Nelson
and
Frederick Cutler

By EMIL L. NELSON AND FREDERICK CUTLER

The International Investment Position
of the United States in 1967

U.S. assets and investments in foreign countries increased by a sizable $10.5 billion during 1967 to reach a total of more than $122 billion. U.S. liabilities—foreign investments in the United States—rose by a substantial $9.2 billion to a total of almost $70 billion. The sharp deterioration of the current account surplus in the balance of payments last year, coupled with the large gain in our foreign investments, resulted in a substantial increase in our indebtedness to foreigners.

THIS article provides the review of information for the annual statistical foreign investments that in recent years has appeared in the September SURVEY. The discussion follows the sequence in which data are arranged in table I, which shows the international investment position of the United States. This position statement is a summary account of the assets held abroad by U.S. residents and of the U.S. liabilities to foreigners through their claims or titles to assets in the United States as of the end of 1967. The discussion of developments in the various categories of investments involves an analysis of capital transactions and related balance of payments flows during the period under review. Among the various types of assets and liabilities, the direct investment items are discussed in greatest detail, as has been customary in these articles.

Major changes in 1967

During 1967, U.S. assets and investments in foreign countries increased $10.5 billion to reach a total of $122.3 billion at yearend. This was the largest annual increase since the record rise of 1964, when our assets abroad rose

nearly $11 billion. In both years, outflows of private capital increased, especially in the final quarter, and the overall balance of payments situation worsened to such an extent that comprehensive changes were made in national policy for the succeeding year. Unlike 1964, the large increase in U.S. assets abroad last year was nearly matched by a $9.2 billion rise in our liabilities, so that our net foreign asset position in 1967 rose only $1.3 billion. After adjustment for the decrease of $1.2 billion in the gold stock,[1] our net position was almost unchanged

last year. In contrast, the increase in our net asset position (after adjustment for gold sales) was about $5.3 billion in 1964 and about $3.5 billion in 1965 and 1966.

Essentially this slowdown in the growth of the U.S. net asset position reflects the gradual erosion of the surplus on current account in the U.S.

1. Although the U.S. gold stock is an international asset, it has not been included in the position data of table 1 as part of the U.S. assets and investments abroad. However, since sales of gold to foreigners result in either increases in our foreign assets or decreases in our foreign liabilities, it is appropriate to take account of changes in the gold stock in the discussion of changes in net assets.

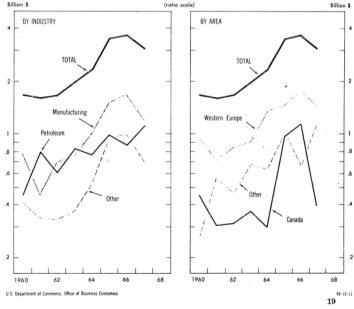

Capital Outflows for Direct Investment
By Industry Group and Major Area

U.S. Department of Commerce, Office of Business Economics

68-10-11

19

Table 1.—International Investment Position of the United States at Yearend

[Millions of dollars]

Type of investment	Total			Western Europe		Canada		Latin American Republics		Other foreign countries		International organizations and unallocated	
	1965ʳ	1966ʳ	1967ᵖ	1966ʳ	1967ᵖ	1966ʳ	1967ᵖ	1966ʳ	1967ᵖ	1966ʳ	1967ᵖ	1966ʳ	1967ᵖ
U.S. assets and investments abroad, total	106,270	111,840	122,292	32,039	35,378	27,705	29,368	19,287	20,748	28,249	31,691	4,560	5,107
Gold stock (not included in total)	¹13,806	13,235	12,065										
Private investments	81,147	86,321	93,287	23,342	25,279	27,693	29,330	15,102	16,172	17,045	19,028	3,139	3,478
Long-term	70,994	75,715	81,442	20,723	22,569	26,565	28,103	12,294	13,083	12,994	14,209	3,139	3,478
Direct	49,424	54,711	59,267	16,209	17,882	16,999	18,069	9,826	10,213	9,661	10,782	²2,016	²2,321
Foreign dollar bonds	9,115	9,513	9,666	790	712	5,503	5,492	547	597	1,550	1,708	1,123	1,157
Other foreign bonds ³	1,050	1,030	1,113	64	104	748	748	174	189	44	72		
Foreign corporate stocks	5,048	4,324	5,238	1,570	2,148	2,474	2,827	78	84	202	179	(*)	(*)
Banking claims ⁴	4,317	3,980	3,711	1,200	757	126	213	1,308	1,521	1,346	1,220	(*)	
Other ⁵	2,040	2,157	2,447	890	966	715	754	361	479	191	248		
Short-term assets and claims	10,153	10,606	11,845	2,619	2,710	1,128	1,227	2,808	3,089	4,051	4,819	(*)	(*)
Reported by banks	7,735	7,853	8,620	1,356	1,217	611	611	2,360	2,617	3,526	4,175	(*)	(*)
Other	2,418	2,753	3,225	1,263	1,493	517	616	448	472	525	644	(*)	(*)
U.S. Government credits and claims	25,123	25,519	29,005	8,697	10,099	12	38	4,185	4,576	11,204	12,663	1,421	1,629
Long-term credits ⁶	20,318	21,054	23,545	7,173	7,537		31	4,079	4,524	8,712	10,249	1,090	1,204
Repayable in dollars ⁷	14,968	15,981	17,978	6,090	6,468		31	3,569	3,971	5,232	6,304	1,090	1,204
Repayable in foreign currencies, etc.⁸	5,350	5,073	5,567	1,083	1,069			510	553	3,480	3,945		
Foreign currencies and short-term claims	3,161	2,818	2,695	213	221	3	4	106	52	2,491	2,413	5	5
IMF gold tranche position and monetary authorities, holdings of convertible currencies	¹1,644	1,647	2,765	1,311	2,341	9	3			1	1	326	420
Foreign assets and investments in the United States, total	58,739	60,410	69,613	35,170	40,955	8,093	9,305	5,861	6,536	8,720	10,274	2,566	2,543
Long-term	26,374	27,006	31,962	17,853	20,247	4,539	5,284	1,942	2,513	1,879	2,957	793	961
Direct	8,797	9,054	9,923	6,273	7,004	2,439	2,575	177	176	165	168		
Corporate stocks	14,599	12,043	15,511	8,743	10,512	1,933	2,539	1,076	1,271	800	1,068	91	121
Corporate, U.S. Government agency, State, and municipal bonds	875	2,042	2,159	1,535	1,440	(*)	(*)	85	96	54	181	368	442
Other	2,103	3,267	4,369	1,302	1,291	167	170	604	970	860	1,540	334	398
Short-term assets and U.S. Government obligations	32,365	33,404	37,651	17,317	20,708	3,554	4,021	3,919	4,023	6,841	7,317	1,773	1,582
Private obligations	18,163	20,799	22,901	9,713	10,835	2,042	2,683	3,691	3,840	5,064	5,323	289	220
Reported by banks	17,195	19,535	21,230	8,965	9,821	1,879	2,433	3,558	3,715	4,844	5,041	289	220
Other	968	1,264	1,671	748	1,014	163	250	133	125	220	282	(*)	(*)
U.S. Government obligations	14,202	12,605	14,750	7,604	9,873	1,512	1,338	228	183	1,777	1,994	1,484	1,362
Associated with Government grants and transactions increasing Government assets ⁹	344	139	54					61	32	36	22	42	
Associated with military sales contracts ¹⁰	1,575	1,021	1,985	1,704	1,789	52	30	(*)	5	165	161		
Associated with other specific transactions ¹¹	198	185	187	4	41	145	116	3	3	33	27		
Other nonmarketable liabilities including medium-term securities payable prior to maturity only under special conditions ¹²	165	116	585	113	363		200			3	22		
Marketable or convertible bonds and notes	3,530	1,969	2,381	854	1,347	692	716	81	41	92	109	250	168
Bills and certificates	8,356	8,064	9,325	4,929	6,333	623	276	83	102	1,448	1,653	981	961
Gold deposits of IMF	34	211	233									211	233
Memorandum items:													
Liabilities reflected in liquidity and official reserve transactions balances: ¹³													
To official agencies:													
Liquid (line 9)	16,206	14,666	16,710	7,488	9,872	1,189	996	1,129	1,116	3,849	3,693	1,011	1,033
Other (line 18)	616	1,375	2,687	396	587	144	314	175	451	660	1,335		
To commercial banks (line 10)¹⁴	7,419	9,936	11,088	5,875	6,206	1,709	2,076	454	473	1,898	2,333		
To other foreign residents and unallocated (line 11)	4,059	4,272	4,685	1,377	1,417	296	353	1,991	2,161	608	754		
To international and regional organizations (line 12)	1,431	905	686	8	6			148	108	29	23	720	549

ʳ Revised.   ᵖ Preliminary.   *Less than $500,000.

1. Reflects payment of $259 million gold portion of increased U.S. subscription to the IMF in the second quarter of 1965.
2. Represents the estimated investment in shipping companies registered primarily in Panama and Liberia.
3. Consists primarily of securities payable in foreign currencies, but includes some dollar obligations including prior to 1963 participations and loans made by the International Bank for Reconstruction and Development. Effective 1963, participations in IBRD loans are included under banking claims and "other long-term," according to country of obligor.
4. Excludes $200 million netted against a related inflow of U.S. direct investment capital.
5. Includes $254 million loaned to Canada in connection with Columbia River power development.
6. Excludes World War I debts that are not currently being serviced.
7. Includes indebtedness repayable in U.S. dollars, or optionally in foreign currencies or by delivery of materials or transfer of services, when option rests with U.S. Government.
8. Includes indebtedness which the borrower may contractually, or at its option, repay with its currency, with a third country's currency, or by delivery of materials or transfer of services.
9. Corresponds to balance of payments table 5, line B.7, Survey of Current Business, September, 1968, p. 35.
10. Corresponds to balance of payments table 5, line B.2, Survey of Current Business, September, 1968, p. 35.
11. Corresponds to balance of payments table 5, line B.13, Survey of Current Business, September, 1968, p. 35.
12. Corresponds to balance of payments table 5, line C.1, Survey of Current Business, September, 1968, p. 35.
13. Line numbers below correspond to those in balance of payments table 3, Survey of Current Business, September, 1968, p. 33.
14. As reported by U.S. banks; ultimate ownership is not identified.

Note: Differences between amounts outstanding and flows reported in balance of payments tables may not coincide due to changes in coverage, price changes, changes in valuation and other adjustments.

balance of payments. In 1967, the balance on goods, services, and unilateral transfers was only $1.7 billion, as compared with $5.6 billion in 1964, $4.1 billion in 1965, and $2.2 billion in 1966. This downward trend means that a growing proportion of our increased investment abroad had to be offset by increases in our indebtedness to foreigners.[2]

U.S. private investments abroad increased nearly $7.0 billion last year as compared with more than $9.0 billion in 1964. Some of the annual changes are caused by changes in the market value of previously held assets. Aside from the influences of such price changes, U.S. private investments rose about $8.0 billion in 1964, $5.3 billion in 1965, $6.0 billion in 1966, and $7.1 billion in 1967. Of the $7.1 billion advance last year, $1.6 billion was through reinvestment of earnings on direct investments abroad and $5.5 billion was in capital outflows.

U.S. Government claims on foreign countries increased $3.5 billion in 1967. Credits to developing countries and increases in outstanding loans of the Export-Import Bank accounted for most of the advance, but $1.1 billion of the total was the rise in foreign convertible currencies and the IMF gold tranche, which are included in U.S. official reserve assets.

The unusually large $9.2 billion rise in foreign holdings of assets in the United States included increases of $5.0 billion in long-term assets and $4.2 billion in short-term assets and U.S. Government obligations. The rise in holdings of long-term assets included an increase of $2.2 billion for price changes in previously held assets (mainly stocks) and one of $0.4 billion in reinvestment of earnings on foreign direct investments in the United States. Consequently, of the $5.0 billion increase in foreigners' long-term investments in 1967, less than half ($2.4 billion) was reflected in net U.S. balance of payments inflows.

2. The change in the U.S. net asset position during the year reflects, in addition to the balance of payments surplus on current account, (1) changes in the market value of outstanding securities and (2) earnings reinvested in subsidiaries. These two items are excluded from the U.S. balance of payments computations.

The rise of $4.2 billion in short-term claims and U.S. Government obligations included $3.5 billion in liquid liabilities to foreigners. This increase in liabilities was close to the official measure of the liquidity deficit in the balance of payments last year since total official reserve assets were practically unchanged. The decrease of $1.2 billion in the gold stock was almost fully offset by the $1.1 billion rise in other official reserve assets.

Direct Investments Abroad

At the end of 1967, nearly half of all U.S. investments abroad were direct investments, defined as U.S. ownership interest in foreign enterprises of at least 10 percent. The book value of direct investments was $59.3 billion (table 3), nearly double the amount at the beginning of this decade. Of this total, over 40 percent was in manufacturing affiliates, and both petroleum and all other industries had less than 30 percent each. At the end of 1960, petroleum investments were about equal with those in manufacturing; in the last 7 years, however, manufacturing has been the fastest growing category, accounting for almost half of the total growth in direct investments abroad.

An unprecedented increase occurred in private direct investment in the 1960's, reflecting the effects of earlier economic and political developments that created a new environment for international business. Rapid growth in foreign markets and important changes in international economic relations encouraged many more U.S. corporations to participate directly in foreign enterprises. The pattern of economic development and the technical proficiencies of American businesses have made Europe the favorite area and manufacturing the favorite type of investments. At the end of 1960, only one-fifth of U.S. direct investments were in Europe, and the European total was 20 percent less than in Latin America and 40 percent less than in Canada. By the end of 1967, direct investments in Europe had risen to 30 percent of all private direct investments abroad, and the European total had become 50 percent larger than investments in

Latin America and about equal to those in Canada.

Though interest in Europe appears undiminished, some unusual new developments in other areas have created a strong upsurge of activity in the last 3 or 4 years, particularly in the development of raw materials. Starting in the mid-1960's, there have been an increasing number of large-scale projects in mining and in the processing of raw materials.

CHART 12

Earnings of Foreign Affiliates

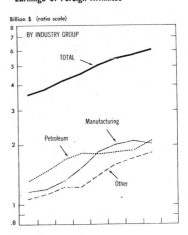

Billion $ (ratio scale)

BY INDUSTRY GROUP

TOTAL

Manufacturing

Petroleum

Other

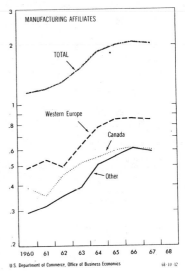

MANUFACTURING AFFILIATES

TOTAL

Western Europe

Canada

Other

1960   61   62   63   64   65   66   67   68

U.S. Department of Commerce, Office of Business Economics   68-10-12

The most notable are iron ore, copper, and bauxite mining and processing operations in Australia, Canada, Peru, West Africa, and other areas or countries. Additional projects to provide raw materials for the chemical industry were underway in several countries in Asia and Latin America. These include projects for sulfur extraction in petroleum and natural gas producing areas and for the production of basic chemicals, especially for agricultural fertilizers and petrochemicals.

Most of these mining ventures and some of the projects based on the processing of raw materials are designed primarily to supply markets in the more advanced foreign industrial nations. Unlike the petroleum industry, where the companies tend to integrate their operations from production to the retail market, the iron ore, coal, and other minerals produced in Australia, Peru, and other countries are designed mainly to supply raw material for foreign-owned corporations, especially in Japan.

Financing foreign operations

The annual increases in U.S. investments in foreign enterprises are the result of capital transfers from the U.S. owners to their foreign affiliates and the reinvestment in their share of earnings in the foreign operation. Table 2 indicates how the annual direct investment transactions accounted for the rise in the value of foreign investments during 1967 and the 2 preceding years. These increases in the value of foreign investment affect the U.S. balance of payments either directly through capital outflows or indirectly through the loss or postponement of income receipts that would have occurred if earnings were not retained abroad.

With the advent of the voluntary program in 1965, the U.S.-incorporated companies with affiliates operating abroad began borrowing funds in foreign capital markets and using the proceeds of such borrowings to finance investment in their affiliates. Initially, borrowing abroad by the U.S. company is a balance of payments inflow, and the liability to the foreign lender is reflected in table 1 as a foreign asset in the United States. When foreign-borrowed funds are transferred to a foreign affiliate, they are included in direct investment capital outflows, i.e., are reported with funds sent directly from the United States. There is no net effect on the balance of payments for that portion of the capital outflows representing the use of foreign-borrowed funds.

It is important to note that U.S. direct investment capital outflows and reinvested earnings are not the only sources of funds available to meet the total financial requirements of foreign affiliates. For established enterprises, internally generated depreciation reserves and locally borrowed funds may provide most of the financing required for ordinary working capital needs and the replacement of equipment. But in a rapidly expanding market the needs for expansion will be a significant part of a firm's total financing requirements, and long-term borrowing or equity financing by the parent company will probably be required.

Capital outflows

The total reduction in direct investment financing in 1967 was about $760 million of which $160 million was in reinvested earnings and $600 million in capital outflows. (Table 4.) The decline in capital outflows was due to reductions of over $0.5 billion in manufacturing and over $0.3 billion in "other" industry categories (table 6) partly offset by a rise of over $0.2 billion in petroleum. A majority of the industries within manufacturing showed declines in capital outflows from 1966 to 1967 (table 7).

While the downturn in capital outflows was the result of a variety of special factors, described below, general economic factors may have been involved. The economic slowdowns in major foreign countries in 1966 and the first half of 1967 may have caused a temporary reduction in the need for funds, especially if the buildup in inventories slowed down or was reversed. If exports to affiliates slowed down or declined, as seems evident from available data, the export credit component of capital outflows probably fell. The voluntary program of the Commerce Department may also have been a factor in the decline in capital outflows. The program had a clear impact on foreign borrowing by U.S. companies to finance their foreign investments, as noted above.

Developments in one year may not be indicative of changes in trend, but other data suggest some general tapering in the rate of expansion in U.S.-owned facilities abroad. Last year, plant and equipment expenditures by foreign affiliates increased only 7 percent, as compared with 16 percent in 1966 and 20 percent in each of the 2 preceding years.

The general economic influences discussed above and the changes in manufacturing were most evident in the industrialized areas. Capital outflows in 1967 were down nearly $750 million to Canada and about $370 million to Europe (chart 11). In addition, outflows to Latin America declined. These decreases were partially

Table 2.—Factors Affecting the U.S. Private Investment Position

[Millions of dollars]

Type of investment	1965	1966 r	1967
U.S. private investments abroad:			
Total, beginning of year	75,864	81,147	86,321
Add: Capital outflow [1]	3,794	4,297	5,504
Reinvested earnings	1,542	1,739	1,578
Price changes and other adjustments	−53	−862	−116
Total, end of year	81,147	86,321	93,287
Direct investments:			
Value, beginning of year	44,430	49,424	54,711
Add: Capital outflow [1]	3,468	3,623	3,020
Reinvested earnings	1,542	1,739	1,578
Other adjustments	−16	−75	−42
Value, end of year	49,424	54,711	59,267
Other long-term private investments abroad:			
Value, beginning of year	20,533	21,570	21,004
Add: Capital outflow [1]	1,079	256	1,270
Price changes	−11	−827	−204
Other adjustments	−31	5	105
Value, end of year	21,570	21,004	22,175
Short-term assets and claims:			
Value, beginning of year	10,901	10,153	10,606
Add: Capital outflow [1]	−753	418	1,214
Other adjustments	5	35	25
Value, end of year	10,153	10,606	11,845
Foreign long-term investments in the United States:			
Direct investments:			
Value, beginning of year	8,363	8,797	9,054
Add: Capital inflow [1]	57	86	251
Reinvested earnings	357	339	440
Other adjustments [2]	20	−168	178
Value, end of year	8,797	9,054	9,923
Other long-term investments:			
Value, beginning of year	16,616	17,577	17,952
Add: Capital inflow [1]	−125	2,070	2,094
Price changes	1,074	−1,687	2,022
Other adjustments	12	−8	−29
Value, end of year	17,577	17,952	22,039

r Revised.
[1] Included in the balance of payments accounts.
[2] Mainly revaluations of securities held by affiliates of foreign insurance companies.

offset by an increase of more than $200 million to Africa and Asia, due mainly to the oil industry, which also increased its outflows by some $210 million for investments in international shipping, which is not included in any of the area classifications. It should be noted that when earnings in branches (as distinct from subsidiaries) abroad are retained in the foreign operation, they are reported as capital outflows. This explains, in part, the 1967 rise in capital outflows in petroleum, where branch earnings in producing areas rose sharply.

It is always difficult, and for some purposes inappropriate, to select certain direct investment transactions for special treatment since every new investment is in some respect unique. But the changes in 1967 included a number of unusual developments that should not be ignored in analysis of overall changes. For example, the 1967 reduction in capital outflows included a large change in net acquisitions of existing properties (table 8). The amount for takeovers was $120 million less in 1967 than in 1966, and sales or liquidations of foreign affiliates were about $260 million more (reflecting mainly the liquidations discussed below in Canada and Latin America). Outflows in 1967 for the petroleum industry in the EEC countries were down by nearly $250 million, but a single takeover of a large European-owned company in 1966 inflated that year's outflows and accounted for much of the 1967 decline. This transaction, like some of the other direct investment capital outflow to Europe, was entirely offset by foreign acquisitions of bonds of U.S. companies.

The $750 million reduction in capital outflows to Canada involved a number of special developments. A sharp drop in sales to U.S. residents of bonds newly issued by U.S.-owned Canadian companies accounted for $210 million of the reduction (table 11). These bonds come under the exemption for Canada from the provisions of the IET (Interest Equalization Tax). When the Canadian issuing companies are U.S.-owned, the sales to the U.S. public are counted as part of the direct investment data.

Capital transactions for the Canadian transportation equipment industry reflect the impact of the United States-Canada Automotive Products Trade Agreement. Large investments to implement the agreement led to capital outflows averaging over $200 million in 1965 and 1966, but these shifted to a net inflow of $73 million in 1967. The outflows in 1966 also reflected $60 million in dividends that were paid but not transferred during the year and that were therefore included as an increase in current receivables due to the U.S. owners of the Canadian affiliates. The collection of these receivables early in 1967 reversed the capital outflow shown in 1966. Another capital inflow from Canada during 1967 resulted from a $33 million liquidation required in the settlement of an antitrust case in the food products industry (table 7).

In Latin America, the reported decline in the net outflow of funds for direct investment in 1967 (table 6) reflects two major liquidations. These arose through the transfer to local owners of majority shares of U.S. mining enterprises in Chile and Mexico. Together, these sales amounted to about $150 million,[3] and in addition to cash, the U.S. owners received foreign debt obligations of about $130 million.

Another unusual transaction—a capital inflow—distorted the 1967 data for the Latin America area shown in table 6. It reflected funds borrowed in Europe by finance companies incorporated in the Netherlands Antilles and subsequently transferred to U.S. parents. In the absence of this transaction and the special liquidations discussed above, the Latin American total in table 6 would have increased from capital outflows of $307 million in 1966 to about $450 million in 1967.

In Australia, a large refinancing transaction raised direct investment capital outflows in 1967 by $130 million and reduced credits extended to foreigners by U.S. financial institutions.

3. The liquidations are included as sales in table 8, and they are shown as capital inflows in table 4. The liquidations also affect the outstanding amounts of direct investment, which were adjusted to reflect the relevant changes in book values. The foreign debt instruments accepted by the U.S. owners increased other long-term private investments; consequently, the change in net U.S. private investments because of these transactions was relatively minor.

Direct investment earnings

Earnings from direct investments increased nearly 6 percent in 1967 to a total of $6 billion that was divided almost equally among manufacturing, petroleum, and all other industry groups. (Table 5.) The rate of increase was up from the 4 percent gain in 1966, but it was lower than in any previous year since 1958. Nearly all of the increase for 1967 reflected the 14 percent gain in petroleum earnings; mining and other industries also showed increases but manufacturing earnings declined about $2\frac{1}{2}$ percent. (Chart 12.) An 8 percent increase in the production of U.S. oil companies abroad accounted for the greater share of the gain in petroleum earnings, but changes in market conditions also contributed, especially after midyear when the Middle East conflict disrupted normal patterns of supply.

Although manufacturing earnings increased regularly prior to 1967, there was a definite slowing down in the growth of earnings in the last 3 years in spite of continuing increases in investment. Some of this slowdown reflects the slower pace of business expansion in industrialized areas.

Although 1967 earnings were down in Europe by about 2 percent, they rose in some industrialized countries. Canadian earnings were up over 7 percent because of increases in nonmanufacturing, particularly in mining, where new ventures started production last year. Other Eastern Hemisphere areas showed a gain in excess of 16

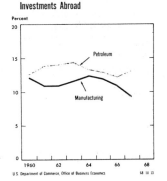

CHART 13

Rates of Return on U.S. Direct Investments Abroad

Percent

U.S. Department of Commerce, Office of Business Economics   68 10 13

Table 3.—Value of Direct Investments Abroad[1] by Selected Countries and Industries, at Yearend　　　　　　**Table 4.—Direct-Investment Capital Out-Foreign Corporations,[2]**

[Millions of dollars]

Line	Area and Country	1966 Total	1966 Mining and smelting	1966 Petroleum	1966 Manufacturing	1966 Public utilities	1966 Trade	1966 Other	1967 Total	1967 Mining and smelting	1967 Petroleum	1967 Manufacturing	1967 Public utilities	1967 Trade	1967 Other	Net outflow 1966	Net outflow 1967 Total	1967 Mining and smelting	1967 Petroleum	1967 Manufacturing	1967 Other
1	All areas, total	54,711	4,315	16,205	22,058	2,284	4,716	5,133	59,267	4,810	17,410	24,124	2,387	4,995	5,541	3,623	3,020	316	1,103	1,211	390
2	Canada	16,999	2,089	3,608	7,675	495	996	2,137	18,069	2,337	3,819	8,083	506	1,032	2,292	1,135	392	168	115	25	83
3	Latin American Republics, total	9,826	1,148	2,897	3,081	624	1,159	917	10,213	1,218	2,917	3,301	614	1,207	956	190	191	-1	-9	151	49
4	Mexico	1,248	108	42	802	29	152	114	1,342	100	43	890	27	166	115	19	-3	-67	(**)	57	7
5	Panama	792	19	153	28	44	317	231	804	19	158	33	44	326	223	28	6	....	-5	5	6
6	Other Central America and West Indies	683	35	162	82	154	38	213	756	34	184	104	155	43	237	47	61	-1	18	18	26
7	Argentina	1,035	(*)	(*)	656	(*)	44	335	1,080	(*)	(*)	677	(*)	53	350	-13	60	(*)	(*)	50	10
8	Brazil	1,247	58	69	846	38	183	53	1,326	68	79	891	32	195	62	87	38	(*)	-3	19	21
9	Chile	844	494	(*)	51	(*)	32	268	878	517	(*)	61	(*)	37	263	-4	23	17	(*)	7	-1
10	Colombia	571	(*)	277	190	29	54	21	610	(*)	309	192	28	56	26	28	31	(*)	29	(**)	3
11	Peru	548	291	29	93	22	63	51	605	340	38	98	22	54	53	34	65	43	16	7	-1
12	Venezuela	2,615	(*)	1,862	291	19	253	190	2,553	(*)	1,789	310	19	255	180	-50	-100	(*)	-74	-12	-15
13	Other countries	242	12	96	44	25	22	42	257	16	100	44	27	21	48	15	11	4	3	(**)	3
14	Other Western Hemisphere	1,622	367	578	236	48	87	306	1,708	431	585	271	51	92	278	117	26	63	-37	39	-39
15	Europe, total	16,209	54	3,981	8,876	67	1,933	1,297	17,882	61	4,404	9,781	78	2,055	1,504	1,809	1,442	7	526	670	239
16	Common Market, total	7,584	17	1,980	4,401	47	779	360	8,405	19	2,063	4,964	49	851	459	1,143	816	(*)	153	495	168
17	Belgium and Luxembourg	742	(**)	43	454	1	124	121	856	(**)	30	533	1	141	151	118	79	....	-6	50	35
18	France	1,758	10	288	1,201	14	187	58	1,904	10	302	1,312	14	194	71	93	138		20	80	37
19	Germany	3,077	(*)	907	1,839	13	225	93	3,487	(*)	1,047	2,064	14	259	103	620	447	(*)	166	226	56
20	Italy	1,148	(*)	475	534	1	88	48	1,242	(*)	486	592	1	98	66	150	107	(**)	35	58	14
21	Netherlands	859	(**)	267	372	18	155	47	917	(**)	197	463	18	161	78	162	45	(**)	-63	81	26
22	Other Europe, total	8,624	37	2,001	4,475	21	1,154	937	9,477	42	2,341	4,817	29	1,204	1,044	666	626	(*)	373	174	78
23	Denmark	226	1	151	39	(**)	32	3	273	1	188	45	(**)	36	3	24	50	(**)	41	9	1
24	Norway	167	(*)	81	46	(**)	20	19	183	(*)	90	49	(**)	24	20	12	11	(*)	9	1	1
25	Spain	408	(*)	109	192	8	76	23	480	(*)	90	257	10	94	27	109	70	(*)	-17	65	22
26	Sweden	370	(**)	198	90	(**)	74	8	438	(**)	250	97	(**)	83	8	60	70	(*)	58	5	7
27	Switzerland	1,211	(**)	42	212	1	431	526	1,332	(**)	16	280	1	430	605	33	39	(**)	-21	47	14
28	United Kingdom	5,657	3	1,169	3,716	8	411	350	6,101	2	1,429	3,877	12	411	372	381	342	(*)	286	36	20
29	Other countries	585	17	251	181	4	110	23	669	21	276	214	6	126	27	47	46	(*)	19	10	14
30	Africa, total	2,074	368	1,104	333	1	136	133	2,277	398	1,232	369	3	148	128	87	176	21	126	27	2
31	Liberia	207	(*)	(*)	(*)	(*)	22	185	173	(*)	(*)	(*)	(*)	23	150	-9	-27	(*)	(*)	(*)	-27
32	Libya	389	(*)	(*)	(*)	(*)	5	384	456	(*)	(*)	(*)	(*)	5	450	-43	55	(*)	(*)	(*)	55
33	Republic of South Africa	600	73	138	271	(**)	76	42	667	99	142	303	(**)	88	35	20	33	15	(*)	25	-6
34	Other countries	878	213	557	61	5	32	9	982	224	644	65	6	32	11	117	115	6	101	2	5
35	Asia, total	3,896	39	2,470	796	78	288	226	4,282	43	2,599	986	76	321	257	204	318	1	184	105	29
36	Middle East	1,669	3	1,557	51	4	17	38	1,748	3	1,607	59	6	19	54	118	150	....	134	4	12
37	Far East, total	2,227	37	913	745	74	271	188	2,533	40	992	927	69	303	202	86	168	1	50	100	17
38	India	243	(*)	(*)	119	3	37	84	266	(*)	(*)	125	2	39	100	-9	16	....	(*)	4	12
39	Japan	756	(*)	(*)	334	3	74	346	868	(*)	(*)	424	2	77	366	77	93	....	(*)	30	63
40	Philippine Republic	579	(*)	(*)	180	48	87	263	634	(*)	(*)	216	37	88	292	31	33	....	(*)	24	9
41	Other countries	649	(*)	(*)	111	20	73	444	765	(*)	(*)	162	28	99	477	19	26	....	(*)	42	-16
42	Oceania, total	2,069	251	521	1,061	2	116	118	2,515	322	591	1,332	2	139	127	152	326	57	50	195	25
43	Australia	1,923	251	(*)	1,000	2	82	588	2,354	320	(*)	1,258	2	101	673	148	324	55	(*)	191	78
44	Other countries	146	(**)	(*)	61	(**)	34	50	160	2	(*)	74	(**)	38	46	4	2	2	(*)	4	-3
45	International shipping	2,016	....	1,047	....	....	969	....	2,321	....	1,264	....	....	1,058	....	-71	149	....	147	....	2

' Revised. ᵖ Preliminary. *Combined in "Other" industries. **Less than $500,000.

1. The value of investments in specified industries and countries is affected by capital flows among foreign affiliates as shown in table 8.

2. Income is the sum of dividends and interest, net after foreign withholding taxes, received by, or credited to, the account of the U.S. owner, and branch profit after foreign taxes but before U.S. taxes; earnings is the sum of the U.S. share in net earnings (or losses) of foreign corporations and branch profits after foreign taxes but before U.S. taxes; reinvested earnings is computed as the difference between the U.S. share of net earnings (or losses) of foreign corporations and the U.S. share of gross dividends (dividends before deduction of withholding taxes).

NOTE.—In this and subsequent tables, detail may not add to totals because of rounding.

flows and U.S. Share in Reinvested Earnings of by Selected Countries

Table 5.—Direct-Investment Earnings and Income,¹ by Selected Countries

[Millions of dollars]

Table 4—Continued						Table 5												
Reinvested earnings of foreign corporations						Earnings						Income						Line
1966 r	1967 P					1966 r	1967 P					1966 r	1967 P					
	Total	Mining and smelting	Petroleum	Manufacturing	Other		Total	Mining and smelting	Petroleum	Manufacturing	Other		Total	Mining and smelting	Petroleum	Manufacturing	Other	
1,739	1,578	132	169	842	436	5,702	6,017	743	2,118	2,051	1,106	4,045	4,518	596	1,989	1,193	740	1
547	644	82	93	344	125	1,237	1,327	240	207	613	267	756	790	154	132	296	208	2
302	172	21	24	77	50	1,267	1,203	295	475	252	180	965	1,022	265	445	175	138	3
49	56	15	(**)	35	6	109	120	20	1	77	22	60	62	5	1	41	15	4
47	26	......	10	1	15	85	76	......	10	10	56	43	58	......	4	11	43	5
8	10	......	4	2	4	52	61	10	4	8	39	46	53	10	1	6	37	6
65	-3	(*)	(*)	-14	11	133	80	(*)	(*)	27	54	68	89	(*)	(*)	47	42	7
85	39	(*)	9	19	12	122	116	(*)	25	69	22	33	66	(*)	13	43	10	8
16	2	-4	(*)	4	2	123	150	135	(*)	7	8	112	143	129	(*)	3	11	9
9	8	(*)	3	3	2	36	15	(*)	3	8	4	24	6	(*)	-1	5	2	10
-7	-12	1	-7	-1	-5	137	90	72	11	3	4	135	103	72	18	3	9	11
19	41	(*)	1	28	12	457	484	(*)	380	44	60	440	435	(*)	374	15	47	12
10	5	(**)	1	(**)	4	12	10	......	5	(**)	5	4	6	(**)	5	(**)	2	13
41	39	2	23	-4	18	185	200	101	57	12	30	148	168	100	35	20	13	14
435	266	(**)	-89	251	104	1,161	1,139	6	-99	847	385	729	849	7	6	561	275	15
100	41	(*)	-56	101	-3	436	448	(*)	-24	424	48	321	398	(*)	35	310	52	16
14	21	(**)	-6	22	6	53	55	(**)	-2	39	17	35	32	......	1	18	14	17
50	4	(*)	-6	28	-17	88	59	(*)	7	71	-18	36	50	(*)	11	41	-2	18
11	-27	(*)	-27	12	-12	208	223	(*)	-20	229	13	183	241	(*)	16	200	24	19
9	23	(*)	-10	23	10	48	39	(*)	-10	46	15	31	28	(*)	-1	25	4	20
16	19	......	-7	16	10	48	61	......	1	39	22	35	46	......	8	27	12	21
335	225	(*)	-32	151	106	725	691	(*)	-75	422	344	408	452	(*)	-29	251	230	22
1	-5	......	-4	-3	2	5	-4	(**)	-8	-1	5	7	4	......	-1	3	3	23
3	5	(*)	(**)	2	3	-1	14	(*)	-13	4	9	-3	-5	(*)	-13	2	6	24
19	-2	(*)	(**)	-2	(**)	31	14	(*)	-1	5	9	12	16	(*)	(**)	7	9	25
-4	-5	......	-5	(**)	(**)	16	17	......	-5	5	17	20	23	......	(**)	5	18	26
86	114	......	-4	20	98	167	210	......	-10	39	182	81	99	......	-4	18	85	27
195	81	......	-29	111	-1	432	378	(**)	-53	340	92	251	274	(**)	-17	207	84	28
34	37	(*)	10	22	5	75	76	(*)	16	30	30	40	40	(*)	6	8	25	29
74	44	9	14	12	9	417	418	74	268	46	31	341	364	60	252	30	21	30
9	-5	(*)	(*)	(*)	-5	21	16	(*)	(*)	(*)	16	13	22	(*)	(*)	(*)	22	31
4	3	(*)	(*)	(*)	3	270	292	(*)	(*)	(*)	292	266	289	(*)	(*)	(*)	289	32
48	36	10	(*)	11	15	124	128	45	(*)	44	39	71	80	29	(*)	29	22	33
13	10	5	6	1	-2	2	-17	19	-45	2	6	-8	-26	15	-50	1	8	34
119	128	3	5	84	36	1,132	1,343	5	1,098	149	91	1,010	1,211	1	1,097	57	55	35
14	-14	......	-27	4	9	877	1,004	......	983	8	13	863	1,018	......	1,010	3	4	36
105	142	3	32	80	27	255	339	5	115	141	78	147	193	1	87	54	51	37
-3	7	......	(*)	2	5	8	20	......	(*)	12	8	8	11	......	(*)	8	3	38
49	79	......	(*)	61	17	91	123	......	(*)	85	37	43	46	......	(*)	22	24	39
26	30	(*)	(*)	9	20	55	61	(*)	(*)	27	34	26	26	(*)	(*)	14	12	40
32	27	(*)	(*)	8	19	102	136	(*)	(*)	17	118	70	110	(*)	(*)	10	100	41
100	117	14	17	78	8	169	171	21	-4	133	21	67	57	9	-19	54	13	42
92	104	14	(*)	68	22	146	151	20	(*)	119	11	54	50	8	(*)	51	-9	43
8	13	......	(*)	10	3	23	20	1	(*)	13	6	13	7	1	(*)	3	3	44
121	168	......	82	......	86	135	217	......	117	......	100	28	57	......	41	......	16	45

percent, due partly to the oil industry, and partly to other industries, especially in Japan and other Far East countries. In Latin America, the gains in petroleum earnings were insufficient to offset other declines, especially in manufacturing, and the total in Latin America decreased more than 3 percent.

All of the oil industry's 14 percent increase in earnings was realized outside of Europe. Total investments of the petroleum industry in Europe are greater than in Canada, Latin America, or the Middle East (table 3). But in each of the last 3 years, the European oil industry has shown net losses. This in part reflects accounting practices of the integrated petroleum companies; refining and marketing operations, which are important in Europe, generally do not show significant net earnings. Furthermore, in recent years, branch losses in exploration and devel-

opment, especially in the North Sea, have added to operating losses and thus have largely offset the dividends and other income receipts (table 6).

The yield on total U.S. direct investments abroad in 1967 (earnings related to the value of investment at the beginning of the year) fell to 11.0 percent for the third straight year of decrease. The peak return in the 1960's was the 12.5 percent earned in 1964. As chart 13 indicates, the yield on manufacturing investments fell steadily in the last 3 years. Petroleum industry yields also moved downward until the sudden increase in 1967. Although petroleum yields in 1964 were less than 1 percentage point above manufacturing yields, last year they were almost 4 percentage points higher. Aside from cyclical changes, the slower growth in total earnings may be explained as part of a long-term decline in the rates of

return on U.S. investments abroad.

Overall rates of return by area, especially in Europe, are frequently influenced by the accounting practices of the petroleum industry. However, the ratio of manufacturing earnings to investment has been higher in Europe than for total manufacturing, and during 1967, the yield on European manufacturing investments was considerably above those in Canada and Latin America. In Asia and Africa, the ratio was higher than in Europe, reflecting the exceedingly high rates of return in Japan and South Africa.

Direct investment income

Income receipts in the balance of payments, i.e., excluding reinvested earnings of subsidiaries, were $4.5 billion in 1967; this was a rise of 12 percent over 1966, twice the rate of increase in direct investment earnings. Consequently, the portion of earnings reinvested

Table 6.—Selected Data on Direct Investments Abroad, by Major Areas

[Millions of dollars]

	Book value at yearend					Net capital outflows					Earnings					Income				
	Total	Mining and smelting	Petroleum	Manufacturing	Other	Total	Mining and smelting	Petroleum	Manufacturing	Other	Total	Mining and smelting	Petroleum	Manufacturing	Other	Total	Mining and smelting	Petroleum	Manufacturing	Other
All areas, total:																				
1960	31,815	2,947	10,810	11,051	7,007	1,674	155	452	801	266	3,566	394	1,302	1,176	694	2,355	337	1,150	550	318
1961	34,667	3,044	12,190	11,997	7,436	1,599	70	793	462	274	3,815	362	1,476	1,203	774	2,768	297	1,336	722	413
1962	37,226	3,194	12,725	13,250	8,057	1,654	97	606	712	239	4,235	372	1,695	1,307	861	3,044	318	1,565	746	415
1963	40,686	3,369	13,652	14,937	8,728	1,976	85	828	774	289	4,587	388	1,824	1,541	834	3,129	321	1,715	656	437
1964	44,430	3,615	14,328	16,935	9,552	2,328	136	760	1,034	398	5,071	512	1,808	1,852	899	3,674	403	1,856	893	522
1965	49,424	3,881	15,298	19,339	10,906	3,468	138	977	1,525	828	5,460	571	1,830	2,022	1,037	3,963	442	1,799	1,094	628
1966	54,711	4,315	16,205	22,058	12,134	3,623	305	868	1,732	718	5,702	659	1,868	2,104	1,071	4,045	524	1,781	1,116	624
1967	59,267	4,810	17,410	24,124	12,924	3,020	316	1,103	1,211	390	6,017	743	2,118	2,051	1,106	4,518	596	1,989	1,193	740
Canada:																				
1960	11,179	1,325	2,664	4,827	2,363	451	199	135	29	88	718	88	98	398	134	361	47	60	176	78
1961	11,602	1,367	2,828	5,076	2,331	302	9	100	117	76	726	96	114	360	156	464	51	78	213	122
1962	12,133	1,489	2,875	5,312	2,457	314	85	159	12	58	825	97	121	460	147	476	60	79	221	116
1963	13,044	1,549	3,134	5,761	2,600	365	7	188	120	50	948	127	149	525	147	455	80	80	192	103
1964	13,855	1,713	3,196	6,198	2,748	298	91	25	140	42	1,106	191	170	565	180	634	118	118	269	129
1965	15,318	1,851	3,356	6,872	3,239	962	51	179	395	337	1,209	198	183	606	222	703	110	122	315	156
1966	16,999	2,089	3,608	7,675	3,628	1,135	172	154	549	260	1,237	191	196	628	222	756	120	112	354	170
1967	18,069	2,337	3,819	8,083	3,830	392	168	115	25	83	1,327	240	207	613	267	790	154	132	296	208
Latin America: [1]																				
1960	8,315	1,269	3,122	1,521	2,403	149	−60	24	125	60	970	224	370	147	229	719	234	331	64	90
1961	9,189	1,282	3,674	1,707	2,526	219	32	63	78	46	1,079	206	478	172	223	824	198	438	75	113
1962	9,474	1,271	3,642	1,944	2,617	29	−13	−67	133	−24	1,179	230	543	173	233	891	221	488	71	111
1963	9,891	1,303	3,636	2,213	2,739	235	24	5	150	56	1,125	219	532	171	203	956	210	544	70	132
1964	10,204	1,344	3,589	2,507	2,754	113	30	7	137	−61	1,244	266	539	243	196	1,011	245	531	98	137
1965	10,836	1,424	3,546	2,945	2,921	271	43	−74	245	57	1,320	290	513	289	228	995	266	476	123	130
1966	11,448	1,515	3,475	3,317	3,141	307	60	−37	159	125	1,452	359	512	342	239	1,113	327	499	147	140
1967	11,921	1,649	3,502	3,572	3,198	217	62	−46	190	10	1,403	396	532	264	210	1,190	365	480	195	151
Europe:																				
1960	6,691	49	1,763	3,804	1,075	962	(*)	273	607	82	769	10	91	487	181	397	11	55	241	90
1961	7,742	48	2,152	4,255	1,287	724	(*)	376	233	115	837	8	63	530	236	486	9	47	326	104
1962	8,930	50	2,385	4,883	1,612	868	3	229	453	183	844	5	60	496	283	526	7	63	334	122
1963	10,304	55	2,776	5,634	1,875	924	1	362	395	166	996	4	67	637	298	507	6	73	305	123
1964	12,129	56	3,122	6,587	2,364	1,388	2	414	619	353	1,115	4	8	782	321	659	5	64	427	163
1965	13,985	54	3,427	7,606	2,898	1,479	−1	342	760	378	1,176	8	−41	859	350	768	8	17	532	211
1966	16,209	54	3,981	8,876	3,298	1,809	1	636	896	276	1,161	10	−79	860	370	729	11	4	489	225
1967	17,882	61	4,404	9,781	3,636	1,442	7	526	670	239	1,139	6	−99	847	385	849	7	6	561	275
Other areas:																				
1960	5,630	304	3,261	899	1,166	112	16	20	40	36	1,109	72	743	144	150	878	45	704	69	60
1961	6,134	347	3,536	959	1,292	354	29	254	34	37	1,173	52	821	141	159	994	39	773	108	74
1962	6,689	384	3,823	1,111	1,371	443	22	285	114	22	1,387	40	971	178	198	1,151	30	935	120	66
1963	7,411	462	4,106	1,329	1,514	452	53	273	109	17	1,518	38	1,076	218	186	1,211	25	1,018	99	79
1964	8,242	492	4,421	1,643	1,686	529	13	314	138	64	1,606	51	1,091	262	202	1,370	35	1,143	99	83
1965	9,285	552	4,969	1,916	1,848	756	45	530	125	56	1,755	75	1,175	268	237	1,497	58	1,184	124	131
1966	10,055	657	5,141	2,190	2,067	372	72	115	128	57	1,852	99	1,239	274	240	1,447	66	1,166	126	89
1967	11,395	763	5,685	2,688	2,260	970	79	508	326	58	2,149	100	1,479	328	243	1,689	70	1,371	141	106

*Less than $500,000.   1. Includes "Other Western Hemisphere."

abroad by foreign-incorporated affiliates declined to 41 percent of the total in 1967 as compared with 46 percent in 1966. Uneasiness regarding certain currencies may have encouraged higher-than-normal dividend payments in some countries. However, there were several noteworthy cases of exceptional dividends that were clearly not associated with such considerations.

Income from mining was up strongly, reflecting initial income receipts from some major new ventures and higher receipts from Chile, which had been adversely affected by strikes in the copper industry in 1966. Income from petroleum was up roughly in line with the increase in earnings. Income from manufacturing affiliates rose 7 percent in spite of the overall decline in manufacturing earnings, with increases from Europe and Latin America offsetting a decline in income from Canada.

The changes in manufacturing income are closely related to large dividends from a few companies. The decline in income from Canada is related to the extraordinary volume of dividend payments in the transportation equipment industry (discussed above) that inflated 1966 income receipts. Large dividends were paid in 1967 by a subsidiary in an EEC country and immediately reinvested in the foreign affiliate. Consequently, they increase the income inflow and capital outflows in the same amounts.

Income receipts include interest income from affiliates, but net receipts for royalties, management fees, rentals, and similar charges are entered separately in the balance of payments accounts. The receipts of royalties from direct investments (table 10) are largely in manufacturing where patent rights and licensing arrangements are most common. Management fees and other service charges are more evenly distributed among industry groups. These receipts, which were $1.1 billion in 1967, have increased steadily for years, and will probably continue to expand with the growth of foreign operations. Since 1960, royalties and fees have risen about 16 percent annually as compared with 10 percent for income. However, in the last 2 years, the growth in these receipts has

slowed down; last year, they increased 11 percent, slightly less than income.

Other U.S. Investments Abroad

Aside from direct investments, there was a total of $63.0 billion of U.S. investments in foreign assets or other claims on foreigners at the end of 1967. These included $34.0 billion in private investments and $29.0 billion in U.S. Government claims. Claims relating to trade and other commercial and financial transactions accounted for about one-third of the total private assets, and most of the remainder was in long-term portfolio investments.

The balance of payments income on these private investments including the short-term claims, was about $1.7 billion in 1967.

Long-term investments

During 1967, private long-term assets other than direct investments increased $1.2 billion to a total of $22.2 billion at yearend. This gain was the result of price adjustments and net capital flows occurring in 1967, which are summarized in table 2. Adjustments for price movements in the U.S. portfolio holdings of all foreign securities included a net decline of $1 billion in the value of foreign-dollar bonds, largely offset by an $0.8 billion upward adjustment in the value of foreign stocks.

Portfolio transactions in 1967 accounted for most of the increase in these long-term assets since the other major item, banking claims, declined. U.S. purchases of newly issued foreign securities set a new record of $1.6

Table 7.—Net Capital Outflows to Manufacturing Affiliates Abroad by Industry

[Millions of dollars]

Area and year	Manufacturing total	Food products	Paper and allied products	Chemicals and allied products	Rubber products	Primary and fabricated metals	Machinery except electrical	Electrical machinery	Transportation equipment	Other industries
All areas, total:										
1963	774.3	57.3	24.4	176.5	13.2	85.6	51.2	24.0	194.5	147.5
1964	1,034.3	74.8	9.1	302.7	2.1	69.8	117.9	45.8	207.1	204.9
1965	1,525.1	115.6	99.1	292.0	16.4	83.7	285.5	96.3	405.5	130.9
1966r	1,732.0	107.6	147.9	503.4	19.0	134.4	214.9	117.5	317.3	170.0
1967	1,210.8	79.9	65.7	408.1	24.6	241.7	117.5	123.2	50.2	100.0
Canada:										
1963	119.6	5.5	12.2	18.4	2.6	6.2	24.0	3.8	37.4	9.5
1964	140.0	29.0	-8.6	32.2	-7.1	-3.9	15.3	11.6	48.4	23.0
1965	394.7	17.7	62.5	70.0	5.1	6.8	27.4	12.7	173.2	19.8
1966	549.3	16.8	125.8	90.1	-2.4	23.6	32.3	11.7	246.1	5.3
1967	25.1	-10.3	46.9	65.9	6.9	-23.7	2.9	8.7	-72.8	6
Latin America: [1]										
1963	150.0	31.6	4.4	48.8	-1.9	5.0	8.6	-7.5	17.1	43.8
1964	137.2	-9.2	2.1	73.6	8.5	7.9	9.5	-10.3	30.1	25.1
1965	245.4	50.8	18.6	83.0	-1.1	19.5	.5	10.5	38.1	26.5
1966	159.3	10.5	-.2	99.5	5.2	14.0	13.2	8.7	30.5	30.6
1967	189.6	11.4	2.9	82.5	5.8	33.0	17.5	1.3	-3.7	39.0
Europe:										
1963	395.0	11.0	2.5	82.1	13.3	37.2	4.5	28.5	132.9	83.1
1964	618.6	41.6	13.6	163.0	-.3	30.4	65.3	38.0	127.4	139.6
1965	760.5	40.8	12.8	97.0	2.4	60.2	239.6	53.4	176.0	78.3
1966	895.7	50.9	18.5	279.5	15.8	75.3	156.9	84.0	91.4	123.5
1967	669.6	62.5	10.3	191.8	1.8	100.6	65.0	108.3	81.5	47.7
Africa:										
1963	8.5	.7	.4	2.2	.2	2.1	2.3	1.1	-.9	.5
1964	18.6	2.5	.6	2.9	-.5	11.5	4.3	-.3	-3.1	.7
1965	39.6	1.2	2.6	2.4	1.0	17.3	7.3	(*)	7.2	.5
1966	18.7	2.5	1.8	.6	-1.3	3.7	4.8	(*)	2.3	4.3
1967	27.4	-.8	1.9	5.2	1.8	-2.7	3.5	.6	15.6	2.3
Asia:										
1963	46.6	6.2	3.8	18.7	-.9	2.5	6.2	3.2	.9	6.2
1964	60.6	4.6	1.7	24.8	(*)	3.3	11.4	5.8	.3	8.7
1965	57.8	-1.2	2.0	25.1	-1.8	.9	6.5	17.4	1.5	7.4
1966	58.0	6.6	1.3	17.7	2.3	3.7	8.3	15.9	.1	2.1
1967	104.6	11.4	1.9	55.0	.7	3.5	21.1	3.6	1.1	6.3
Oceania:										
1963	54.5	2.3	1.1	6.3	(*)	32.7	5.7	-5.0	7.0	4.5
1964	59.2	6.3	-.3	6.2	1.5	20.6	12.1	1.0	4.0	7.8
1965	27.0	6.4	.5	15.5	10.7	-20.7	4.2	2.4	9.5	-1.6
1966	51.0	20.2	.8	16.0	-.6	14.1	-.6	-2.7	-.5	4.3
1967	194.5	5.8	1.7	7.8	7.4	131.0	7.6	.6	28.5	4.1

r Revised.
* Less than $50,000.
1. Includes "Other Western Hemisphere".

billion last year. This increase was partly offset by redemptions of outstanding U.S. foreign-dollar bonds of nearly $0.5 billion. But there were also small net purchases of other securities, including outstanding stocks and bonds, for the first time since 1963, when the IET took effect. The net balance of payments transactions in foreign securities of all three types were $1.3 billion in 1967.

The outstanding volume of long-term bank loans declined again in 1967, providing a balance of payments inflow

Table 8.—Acquisitions and Sales by American Companies of Foreign Enterprises [1] by Area and Industry

[Millions of dollars]

Area and industry	1966			1967		
	Acquisitions	Sales	Net	Acquisitions	Sales	Net
All areas, total____	591	29	562	471	288	183
Petroleum_____	204	____	204	20	_____	20
Manufacturing.	321	25	296	330	105	225
Other industries____	66	4	62	121	183	-62
Canada, total____	67	13	54	112	38	74
Petroleum_____	1	_____	1	2	_____	2
Manufacturing.	60	12	48	39	38	1
Other industries____	7	1	6	71	_____	71
Europe, total_____	433	4	429	287	58	229
Petroleum_____	202	_____	202	12	_____	12
Manufacturing.	188	4	184	245	50	195
Other industries____	43	(*)	43	30	8	22
Other areas, total.	91	12	79	72	192	-120
Petroleum_____	1	_____	1	6	_____	6
Manufacturing.	74	9	65	46	17	29
Other industries____	16	3	13	20	175	-155

*Less than $500,000.
1. Includes acquisitions and sales of minority interests.

Table 9.—Net Capital Flows Between Primary and Secondary Foreign Affiliates

[Millions of dollars; net inflow (−)]

	1962	1963	1964	1965	1966	1967p
Canada_____	____	-4	3	-8	16	1
Latin America_____	16	-1	-2	-3	-24	1
Argentina_____	-11	-14	-14	-5	4	-1
Mexico_____	11	-5	3	-5	2	3
Panama_____	13	14	12	8	7	10
Other Latin America_____	2	4	-3	-1	-37	-11
Europe_____	-22	24	19	43	30	10
France_____	-14	-5	-2	22	-6	6
Germany_____	-4	-20	-5	-22	-16	-3
Italy_____	-21	-9	-5	-9	-7	13
Switzerland___	48	105	60	77	28	30
United Kingdom_	-9	-4	(*)	-2	47	-15
Other Europe_	-22	-43	-29	-22	-16	-21
Other countries___	6	-19	-20	-32	-22	-12

p Preliminary.
*Less than $500,000.

Since February 10, 1965, the IET has applied to nonexport loans with maturities over 1 year to developed countries other than Canada. Repayments on outstanding loans to these countries have not only exceeded their new loans but have also exceeded the net increases in long-term loans to areas exempt from the IET—Canada, Latin America, and other less developed countries. The original legislation gave the President authority to extend the IET to long-term bank lending, and this authority was invoked after the big upsurge in lending in 1964.

Prior to its application to long-term bank lending, the main purpose of the IET was to restrict purchases of new security issues by developed countries, and as table 11 indicates the IET was most effective in this area. In addition, U.S. purchases of outstanding foreign securities, other than from U.S. residents, were subject to the tax. Since the imposition of the tax in mid-1963, U.S. holdings in this category had been reduced each year until 1967, when there were net purchases of outstanding foreign stocks and bonds.

Purchases of outstanding foreign securities of all countries are subject to the IET, but there are important exemptions for new issues of international agencies, Canada, less developed countries, and, to a limited extent, Japan. Among the exempt areas, the the World Band accounted for much of the increase in new issues in 1967. It stepped up its borrowing in the United States to $246 million and has continued an unusually high rate of borrowing this year ($153 million in the first half of 1968). Developing nations also substantially increased their new issues, nearly doubling the 1966 level, but all of this increase was due to placements by the Israeli government. Its placements rose from a recent yearly average of $100 million to about $200 million in 1967, of which $150 million occurred in the second and third quarters, just after the Middle East crisis. Canada was by far the largest exempt borrower, with a record high of over $1.0 billion in new issues sold to U.S. residents, a 10 percent gain over 1966. The largest increase in these placements was in bonds guaranteed

by the Provincial governments of Canada. While Canadian Provinces also increased their borrowing in the Canadian capital market, the U.S. share of their total borrowings rose from about one-fifth in 1966 to over one-third in 1967. Similarly, although Canadian municipal authorities were reducing their borrowing activities in 1968, they increased their placements in the United States.

Short-term assets

Short-term claims on foreigners by U.S. banks and other private residents rose $1.2 billion to a total of nearly $12 billion at the end of 1967. After a modest rise in 1966, outstanding short-term bank loans to foreigners rose about $750 million to a total of $8.6 billion. The increase in credits extended to Japan accounted for about 80 percent of the total increase in bank credits.

Table 10.—Direct-Investment Receipts of Royalties and Fees,[1] by Areas and Major Industries

[Millions of dollars]

Area and industry	1966r	1967p		
		Total	Royalties, license fees, and rentals	Management fees and service charges
All areas, total_____	1,030	1,140	435	702
Petroleum_____	127	156	15	141
Manufacturing____	652	733	363	370
Trade_____	106	109	38	70
Other industries__	144	143	21	121
Canada, total_____	215	243	68	176
Petroleum_____	15	17	(*)	17
Manufacturing____	165	186	59	127
Trade_____	15	13	5	8
Other industries__	20	27	3	24
Latin America, total ²__	176	185	62	124
Petroleum_____	24	32	3	29
Manufacturing____	86	99	46	53
Trade_____	24	23	8	15
Other industries__	42	32	4	27
Europe: Common Market, total_____	224	235	142	93
Petroleum_____	17	18	(*)	18
Manufacturing____	169	177	131	45
Trade_____	27	27	9	18
Other industries__	11	14	2	11
Other Europe, total__	219	238	102	136
Petroleum_____	12	21	2	19
Manufacturing____	158	173	87	86
Trade_____	21	22	9	13
Other industries__	28	23	5	18
Other areas, total_____	196	238	64	174
Petroleum_____	59	68	10	58
Manufacturing____	75	99	40	59
Trade_____	19	24	7	17
Other industries__	43	48	7	41

p Preliminary.
r Revised.
*Less than $500,000.
1. Excludes foreign film rentals.
2. Includes "other Western Hemisphere".

Under the voluntary foreign credit restraint program, banks have been asked to limit the increase in their outstanding foreign credits and loans of various maturities relative to the amounts outstanding at the end of 1964. As part of their contribution toward meeting program goals—which in fact have been exceeded—the banks reduced their short-term claims on foreigners by some $250 million in the first 2 years of the program. In spite of the increase last year, banks were still well under their overall targets at the end of 1967. Under the program for 1968, in addition to the target ceiling on total bank lending, short-term credit outstanding to continental Western Europe is to be reduced by 40 percent of the amount outstanding on December 31, 1967.

Other private residents held a total of $3.2 billion in short-term foreign assets at the end of 1967. These holdings rose almost $0.5 billion in 1967 and more than $0.3 billion in 1966, but a significant part of these increases represented temporary deposits of the proceeds of foreign bond issues intended for direct investment purposes. These balances are exempt from the general regulation under the 1968 mandatory program on direct investment, which requires that other short-term assets held abroad not exceed the average level of such holdings in 1965 and 1966.

U.S. Government claims

U.S. Government assets held abroad (comprising long-term credits, foreign currency holdings and other assets, monetary holdings of convertible currencies, and the U.S. gold tranche in the IMF) rose $3.5 billion last year to reach $29 billion at yearend. Long-term U.S. Government assets were $23.5 billion of this total. Dollar-repayable assets, which accounted for $18 billion of the long-term assets, increased nearly $2 billion. Foreign Assistance Act credits to developing countries, many with maturities as long as 40 years, accounted for just over $1.0 billion of the increase and $6.5 billion of the total outstanding, while net disbursements of the Export-

Import Bank accounted for just over $0.7 billion of the increase and $4.5 billion of the total at yearend.

With few exceptions, the long-term credits repayable in foreign currencies and short-term claims of $2.7 billion in foreign currency holdings, (not included in official reserve assets) can be used only for grants and loans and for meeting U.S. Government administrative expenditures in the foreign country. Although changes in the programs for the distribution of farm products and changes in other foreign assistance legislation in the past several years have lowered the rate of accumulation of nonconvertible foreign currency claims, they still exceeded $8 billion at the end of 1967.

An additional $2.8 billion, or about 10 percent of the total U.S. Government claims, represented holdings of convertible currencies and the U.S. gold tranche in the IMF.

Foreign Investment in the United States

Total foreign investments in the United States of $69.6 billion at the end of last year were less than three-fifths as large as total U.S assets abroad. The $52.7 billion difference between U.S. foreign assets and liabilities could be attributed largely to the difference of $49.3 billion between the

amount of our direct investments abroad and foreigners' direct investments in the United States. Portfolio investments on both sides were almost equal, at about $22 billion each.

Although it follows that on a combined basis all other assets and liabilities were comparable in size, some of the entries on the liabilities side are very different in quality and purpose from similarly designated entries on the assets side. This is most readily apparent in comparing the foreign assets of the U.S. government—which are subject to the numerous constraints cited above—with its liabilities—which are largely in the form of liquid assets of foreign official agencies.

Direct investments

Although small in relation to our direct investments abroad, total investment by foreign companies in their U.S. affiliates approached $10 billion at the end of 1967. The increase of $0.9 billion in 1967 was much greater than the $0.3 billion increase in the preceding year. However, a considerable portion of the $0.6 billion difference between the two years reflected the revaluation of assets held by the U.S. affiliates. These assets, primarily stocks held by foreign-owned insurance companies in the United States, declined in value by about $0.2 billion in 1966 and increased about the same amount in 1967. This change in stock valuations

Table 11.—Newly Issued Foreign Securities to U.S. Residents

[Millions of dollars]

Issuer	1960	1961	1962	1963	1964	1965	1966	1967	1968 (Jan.-June)
Total [1]	554	523	1,076	1,250	1,063	1,206	1,210	1,619	724
Canada	221	237	458	693	700	709	922	1,007	452
Central government			125	125					72
Provincial government-guaranteed	82	22	70	283	332	244	341	601	221
Municipal authorities	100	26	71	32	163	54	141	160	82
Corporate issues	39	189	192	253	205	411	440	246	77
Japan	15	61	101	164		52	4	14	
International organizations	97	12	84		4	179	80	246	153
Less developed countries	171	113	180	104	323	170	189	352	119
Other developed countries	50	100	253	289	[1] 36	[2] 96	15		
Memorandum items:									
U.S. foreign direct investment subsidiaries, total [1]	14	75	76	41	67	188	302	45	223
In Canada	14	72	73	29	67	156	257	45	166
In less developed countries		3	3	11		19	32		57
In other developed countries				1		13	13		

1. New issues of U.S. direct investment subsidiaries are not included with portfolio issues but are recorded in the direct investment account.
2. Includes a $7 million placement exempt from IET.
3. Includes a $73 million placement exempt from IET.

conformed in general with the change in the level of all U.S. stock prices. Table 13 indicates total direct investments in major industries and the source of these investments by selected countries.

Direct investment capital inflows from abroad were $0.3 billion last year while reinvested earnings were $0.4 billion—two-thirds of the total earnings of foreign-owned subsidiaries in the United States. Capital inflows from foreign owners were $0.2 billion more than in 1966 and reinvested earnings $0.1 billion more. The increase in capital inflows was largely in inter-company accounts payable by U.S. companies to their foreign owners, but capital inflows for new investment, mostly stock ownership in U.S. companies, also increased. About a quarter of the new investments[4] in 1967 were inflows from Germany invested in U.S. chemical companies, and a similar por-

4. See footnote 2 to table 12 for a definition of new investment.

tion represented inflows from Switzerland invested in various types of manufacturing.

Earnings of foreign enterprises in the United States increased $0.1 billion of 15 percent in 1967, a development that ran counter to the experience for domestic corporations, whose overall earnings were lower in 1967 than the preceding year. The increase in total profits of U.S. subsidiaries in 1967 was reflected in a similar increase of reinvested earnings. Consequently, the outflow for dividend payments changed very little, and since other income payments also remained about the same, almost all of the $0.2 billion increase in the capital inflow represented a gain for the balance of payments in 1967.

In recognition of the potential balance of payments contributions through foreign direct investment in the United States, the Department of Commerce has strengthened its "Invest in the U.S." program. This program is designed to provide contacts between U.S companies and foreign investors for the purpose of promoting joint

ventures, licensing agreements, and other types of investment in the United States. The program seeks to attract foreign investment in new U.S. plants and licenses from foreign firms to manufacture in the United State products that are now being imported.

Foreign portfolio assets

The outstanding amount of foreign holdings of U S. securities other than Treasury obligations increased $3 billion in 1967, more than offsetting the $0.8 billion drop in value in 1966 and raising the total at the end of last year to $17.7 billion. Adjustments for price changes particularly in equities, accounted for $2 billion of the $3 billion gain in 1967, but unprecedented net purchases of U.S. stocks and bonds by foreigners also substantially increased the total outstanding investment.

The larger foreign interest in U.S. securities becomes more apparent when net liquidations of portfolio holdings by the British Government are excluded from changes in the total foreign portfolio account. After adjustment for

Table 12.—Foreign Direct Investments in the United States, Selected Data by Country and Industry

| | Value at yearend | | | Capital Flow | | | | | | Earnings,[1] income,[1] and undistributed profits | | | | | |
| | | | | 1966 | | | 1967 ᴾ | | | 1966 | | | 1967 ᴾ | | |
	1965	1966	1967 ᴾ	Total	New investments[2]	Other	Total	New investments[2]	Other	Earnings	Income	Undistributed profits	Earnings	Income	Undistributed profits
Total	8,797	9,054	9,923	86	89	-3	251	133	118	695	371	339	804	381	440
By area:															
Canada	2,388	2,439	2,575	2	25	-23	9	19	-10	133	77	80	146	84	80
United Kingdom	2,852	2,864	3,156	23	18	5	65	21	44	234	125	102	257	124	123
Other Europe	3,224	3,409	3,848	67	43	24	185	75	110	307	159	143	386	163	229
Belgium	175	193	228	10		10	18		18	9	2	8	23	9	17
France	200	215	265	8	3	5	26	2	24	10	3	7	26	12	16
Germany	209	247	318	28	36	-8	65	37	28	19	7	11	30	14	16
Italy	87	87	86	1	1	(*)	-8	2	-10	1		1	8	2	6
Netherlands	1,304	1,402	1,508	20	(*)	3	17	12	(*)	153	73	78	177	80	93
Sweden	215	217	239	-7	(*)	-7	3		3	18	7	10	14	7	7
Switzerland	940	949	1,096	7	(*)	7	63	34	29	89	64	23	102	36	71
Other countries	94	100	109	1		1	6		6	8	2	5	6	3	3
Japan	118	103	108	-24	3	-27	-2	18	-20	14	7	8	12	8	7
Latin America	161	177	176	14		14	-1		-1	4	2	2	(*)	(*)	(*)
Other countries	53	61	59	4	(*)	4	-5	(*)	-5	4		4	2	1	1
By industry:															
Petroleum	1,710	1,740	1,885	-94	1	-94	8	(*)	8	214	81	124	237	90	137
Manufacturing	3,478	3,789	4,181	111	47	64	138	84	54	357	159	200	380	132	255
Trade	748	739	848	-39	9	-48	67	21	46	43	15	30	70	28	42
Insurance	³2,169	³2,072	³2,193	64		64	36		36	76	76		85	85	
Other finance	(⁴)	(⁴)	(⁴)	13		13	4	-20	2	-22	⁵7	⁵22	-5	⁵23	⁵20	10
Other industries	693	714	816	31	24	7	22	26	-4	-2	18	-10	9	26	-4

ᴾ Preliminary. *Less than $500,000.
1. "Earnings" represents the foreign share in corporate and branch profits; "Income" is the amount distributed, after withholding taxes, as dividends, interest, and branch profits.
2. "New investments" consist of the first reported capital inflow to establish a new company or operation in the United States and also inflows to acquire additional shares of existing companies.

3. Includes market revaluations of securities held by insurance companies.
4. Included in "Insurance."
5. Earnings and income paid by agency banks in the United States to foreign home offices have been excluded from direct investment totals.

these liquidations, foreign net purchases of U.S. securities amounted to $0.2 billion in 1965, $1.0 billion in 1966 and $1.5 bill on in 1967.

A significant part of the increase in foreign holdings of U.S. securities, excluding Treasury issues, was the net purchase of bonds, which amounted to $0.3 billion in 1967. Excluding the net liquidations of a similar amount by the United Kingdom, net purchases were over $0.6 billion. A major portion of these purchases, approximately $0.4 billion, was the net proceeds of special bonds issued by U.S.-incorporated companies to raise funds for the financing of investment abroad.

In cooperating with the Commerce Department's voluntary program, U.S. corporations began placing issues on the international or Euro-bond market in mid-1965. (The quarterly amounts and types of these issues subsequently placed in each year are shown in table 14.) Although interest rates were significantly higher than in the United States, the companies placed a large number of these issues during early 1966 (chart 14). The Euro-bond market developed to absorb the growing volume of issues, but U.S. companies were forced to offer higher yields in order to compete for funds.

To avoid unduly high interest costs, the cooperating companies resorted to a variety of debt instruments to raise funds in the Euro-bond market. During periods of relatively moderate interest costs, as in early 1965 and again in 1967, special finance subsidiaries established by the U.S. companies placed primarily straight debt issues. When yields climbed, more intensive use was made of bonds con-

Table 13.—Value of Direct Investments in the United States by Major Industry and Country—End of 1967

[Millions of dollars]

	Total	Manu-facturing	Finance and insurance	Petroleum	Other
All areas	9,923	4,181	2,193	1,885	1,664
Canada	2,575	1,397	354	99	725
United Kingdom	3,156	1,009	1,189	612	346
Other Europe	3,848	1,660	569	1,160	459
Netherlands	1,508	388	41	1,021	57
Switzerland	1,096	744	309		43
Other	1,245	529	219	139	359
Other areas	343	113	79	15	134

vertible into the stock of the U.S. parent company. Rising U.S. stock prices made convertible bonds more attractive to the buyer and were an important factor in the switch to convertible issues. During the money squeeze of 1966, bond yields on straight debt issues rose to 6.5 percent. On the advice of underwriters, issues were postponed or reduced in size, so that the volume of placements fell in the second half of 1966. After conditions in the market relaxed, U.S. companies were induced to return to the market in 1967.

The announcement on January 1, 1968, of mandatory curbs on foreign direct investment transactions intensified borrowing by U.S. companies. This pushed up rates in the Euro-bond market to as high as 7 or 7.5 percent and led to a pronounced shift to the use of convertible issues during this period of high yields and rising U.S. stock prices (chart 14). In fact, in the first 9 months of 1968, convertible issues accounted for 85 percent of the $1.4 billion placed by U.S.-incorporated companies.

U.S. companies also raised funds on local capital markets abroad through issues denominated in the domestic currency of the market country. Although issues placed in certain countries have lower yields than other straight debt instruments, their use is restricted because they are normally subject to approval by national authorities.

The other major increase in foreign purchases of U.S. securities was in net purchases of U.S. stocks. If net liquidations of $0.1 billion by the United Kingdom government are eliminated, foreigners' net purchases in 1967 were more than $0.8 billion, an unprecedented increase over the $0.2 billion of net purchases in 1966. In the first half of 1968, foreign purchases were at an annual rate of $1.4 billion.

This increasing demand for U.S. stocks appears to have begun in Canada late in 1965 but did not start in Europe until late 1967. The increase in purchases generally appears to follow the upswings in the stock markets. Although there does not appear to be a close parallel between Canadian purchases of U.S. stocks and stock

price movements in this country and Canada, it is of interest that the average quarterly amount purchased during the 1967 bull market (about $55 million) was substantially above the 1960–65 quarterly average (about $10 million). European purchases of U.S. stocks since 1961 seem to have moved most often in the same direction as European stock prices. The recent upsurge in total foreign demand, while closely related to stock market developments abroad, was perhaps also stimulated by the simultaneous rise in U.S. stock prices. Furthermore, the increased activity by U.S. underwriters and other U.S. financial firms in European capital markets have made it possible to channel a rising share of the foreign demand for equity securities to U.S. stocks.

Other U.S. liabilities

Foreigners' holdings of short-term assets and other claims on the U.S. Government totaled $37.7 billion at the end of 1967. Of this amount, $33.2 billion were U.S. liquid liabilities as defined for the purpose of calculating the liquidity deficit in the U.S. balance of payments. The foreign liquid assets in table 1 include $21.2 billion in short-term liabilities of U.S. banks and $11.7 billion in U.S. Treasury obligations (marketable or convertible bonds and notes and bills and certificates). The remainder consists of U.S. liabilities to the International Mon-

Table 14.—Foreign Security Placements by U.S.-Incorporated Companies, by Type

[Millions of dollars]

Period	Straight debt: Payable in—			Convertible: Payable in—		Total [1]
	Dollars	Deutsche marks	Swiss francs	Dollars	Deutsche marks	
1965: Total	67	55		75		197
III	20					20
IV	47	55		75		177
1966: Total	161	56	10	182	190	600
I	55		10	120		185
II	51			62	180	293
III	10	25				35
IV	45	31			10	87
1967: Total	225	15	33	177		450
I	60		11	20		91
II	75	15	11	10		111
III	70		11	50		131
IV	20			97		117
1968: (9 months)	193	18	13	1,253		1,477
I	90			446		536
II	28	18		521		567
III	75		13	286		374

1. These amounts differ from balance of payments figures which are net of placement costs.

etary Fund, which are related to gold deposits in the United States.

In addition to these foreign holdings, officially defined as U.S. liquid liabilities, foreign governments and international organizations at the end of 1967 held $2.5 billion in near-liquid assets, included as "other long-term liabilities" in table 1. These near-liquid assets include investments in time deposits or certificates of deposit in U.S. banks. Consequently, at the end of 1967, there were $35.7 billion of liquid or near-liquid U.S. liabilities outstanding, more than half of the $69.6 billion of total foreign assets in the United States shown in table 1.

The remaining $33.9 billion of all other foreign assets in the United States on December 31, 1967, include the $27.6 billion of direct and portfolio investments discussed above. The balance of $6.3 billion consists of several items and includes $2.8 billion in miscellaneous government obligations and $3.5 billion in liabilities of corporations or other nonbank residents. The mis-

cellaneous government obligations are associated with a variety of military, foreign aid, and international financing agreements for special projects other than aid. The liabilities to foreigners by nonbanking concerns, especially the $1.7 billion of short-term liabilities, are probably associated mainly with trade, but in recent years, U.S. corporations have also arranged credits or loans with foreign banks to provide funds for a variety of uses abroad, including the financing of direct investment activities.

The distinctive features that differentiate liquid liabilities from other obligations are that they represent money or near-money, the latter consisting of instruments that can be immediately converted into monetary media with a minimum loss in value. The differentiation is related less to the maturity of the instruments than to the existence of a well-organized and broad market on which such assets can be sold. The use of the dollar as a reserve currency makes it very important to pay close attention to the liquid

liabilities that constitute monetary or near-monetary assets of other countries or that serve a special monetary role in international commercial and financial transactions.

The direct holdings of foreign official agencies accounted for over half of the $33.2 billion of liquid liabilities to foreigners at the end of 1967. Their holdings included over $9.7 billion of the $11.7 billion in U.S. Treasury obligations. The bulk of the other holdings by central banks, governments, and international monetary institutions were in the form of demand or short-term time deposits in U.S. banks. Dollar holdings by central banks and governments are the major foreign currencies component of the reserve assets of all countries.

Liquid liabilities to foreign commercial banks were about $11.1 billion at the end of 1967, of which about $8 billion were classified as demand deposits. It should be noted that in addition to demand deposits this classification includes all liabilities of U.S. banks to their foreign branches ($4.2 billion) and liabilities of agencies of foreign banks to their home offices. The oversea branches of U.S. banks have become increasingly active in the Euro-dollar market, aggressively bidding for deposits of foreign-owned dollars and using the balances for loan activity abroad and for deposit with head offices in the United States. Head office liabilities to branches were only about $1 billion, in 1964 but in mid-1968 they exceeded $6 billion.

The institutional arrangements that surround the Euro-dollar phenomenon are highly important in current money market operations in both Europe and the United States, and stability of the Euro-dollar market has become an important consideration in international monetary affairs. The supply of dollars in the Euro-dollar market is of vital interest in European monetary management. U.S. dollars (i.e., deposits in U.S. banks) are used extensively to make loans to finance international transactions both in trade and in a wide range of investment activities, and these transactions increase the scope for the employment of U.S. dollar assets held abroad.

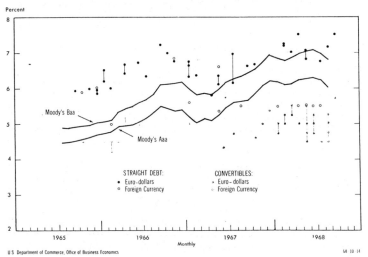

CHART 14

Yields on Individual Issues of Bonds Placed Abroad by U.S.- Incorporated Companies Compared With Average Yields on Corporate Bonds in the United States

U S Department of Commerce, Office of Business Economics   68 10 14

THE INTERNATIONAL INVESTMENT POSITION
OF THE UNITED STATES:

Developments in 1968

David T. Devlin
and
Frederick Cutler

By DAVID T. DEVLIN and FREDERICK CUTLER

The International Investment Position of the United States: Developments in 1968

The net international investment position of the United States showed virtually no change in 1968 as total U.S. international assets and total U.S. liabilities to foreigners both increased $11.4 billion. A very large increase in the value of nonliquid U.S. assets abroad—including a sharp rise in U.S. direct investment—was mostly offset by increased foreign purchases of U.S. stocks and bonds and other nonliquid inflows. Monetary reserves rose slightly more than liquid liabilities, with a small surplus in the balance of payments measured on the liquidity basis.

TOTAL international assets of the United States—including official reserve assets as well as investments abroad—rose $11,395 million in 1968, but total U.S. liabilities—foreign assets in the United States—rose $11,401 million. As a result, the net international investment position of the United States showed practically no change over the year, following the small $233 million increase in 1967. At yearend 1968, total assets exceeded total liabilities by $65.0 billion, virtually unchanged from the $64.8 billion position at yearend 1966.

This article first discusses the factors accounting for changes in the U.S. net international investment position: in particular, recorded balance of payments capital flows (equivalent to transfers of goods and services abroad net of unilateral transfers and adjusted for errors and omissions), reinvestment of direct investment earnings, and valuation changes in outstanding holdings.

After the change in the net position, is discussed the composition of the

shifts in assets and in liabilities is than analyzed, noting whether the changes are in liquid or nonliquid assets or liabilities. In addition, the change in the investment position is reconciled with balance of payments capital flows.

The flows of funds associated with U.S. direct investment abroad are discussed in considerable detail. Particular attention is given to changes in the value of U.S. direct investment abroad, to changes in other U.S. corporate foreign assets and liabilities, and to earnings, fees, and royalties associated with U.S. direct investment abroad. In 1968, the net flow associated with these items had an unusually favorable impact on the balance of payments—in spite of an acceleration in direct investments—as foreign earnings rose sharply and U.S. corporations financed a substantial part of their direct investments with funds borrowed abroad.

Changes in the Net International Position

As detailed in table 1, changes in the net investment position of the United States reflect three major factors. The first is net recorded balance of payments capital flows, which, in turn, must be equal to the balance on goods, services, and unilateral transfers adjusted for errors and omissions.[1] In effect, a surplus on these items allows an improvement in our investment position. The second is reinvested earnings of U.S. affiliates abroad minus reinvested earnings of foreign enterprises in the United States. Earnings of U.S. affiliates abroad not sent back to

[1] If errors and omissions in the balance of payments accounts could be identified, a part would presumably go into recorded capital flows and a part into recorded goods, services, and unilateral transfer accounts. The two accounts would then be equal in magnitude.

Table 1.—Factors Accounting for Changes in the Net International Investment Position of the United States

[Millions of dollars]

		Average			1966	1967	1968
		1951–55	1956–60	1961–65			
Balance on goods, services, and unilateral transfers (surplus (+))		−498	1,002	3,838	2,446	2,179	−349
Adjustment for: Errors and omissions (receipts (+))		300	173	−910	−489	−1,007	−642
Equals:	Net recorded balance of payments capital flows (outflow (+))	−197	1,175	2,927	1,956	1,172	−991
	Change in U.S. assets (increase (+))	1,002	3,283	5,097	5,276	8,024	8,286
	Change in U.S. liabilities (increase (−))	−1,199	−2,108	−2,170	−3,320	−6,852	−9,277
Plus:	Net reinvested earnings (increase (+))	670	990	1,072	1,400	1,158	1,654
Plus:	Changes in net valuation and other adjustments	−370	[1] −699	−636	43	−2,104	−670
	of which: Adjustments for statistical discrepancies	n.a.	n.a.	328	165	244	212
Equals:	Change in net international investment position of the United States	102	1,466	3,364	3,399	233	−6
	Change in U.S. assets (increase (+))	2,143	4,138	6,872	5,070	9,543	11,395
	Change in U.S. liabilities (increase (−))	−2,041	−2,673	−3,507	−1,671	−9,310	−11,401
Memorandum Item:	Net international investment position of the United States at end of period [2]	37,237	44,566	61,387	64,786	65,019	65,013

1. Includes an adjustment for direct investment in Cuba omitted from the data effective 1960.
2. The net position at the end of a given period is equal to the position at the end of the preceding period plus the total net change during the period.

NOTE.—Details may not add to totals because of rounding.
N.a. Not available.

NOTE.—Julius Freidlin, Nancy Keith, Russell Scholl, and Zalie Warner also made significant contributions.

23

Table 2.—International Investment Position of the United States at Yearend‡

[Millions of dollars]

Line	Type of investment	Total‡ 1950¹	1955¹	1960¹	1965¹	1967ʳ	1968ᵖ	Western Europe 1967ʳ	1968ᵖ	Canada 1967ʳ	1968ᵖ	Latin American Republics 1967ʳ	1968ᵖ	Other foreign countries 1967ʳ	1968ᵖ	International organizations and unallocated‡ 1967ʳ	1968ᵖ
1	Net International investment position of the U.S. (line 2 minus line 23)	36,727	37,237	44,566	61,387	65,019	65,013	−5,490	−8,278	20,099	20,704	14,259	15,060	21,507	22,730	14,644	14,797
2	U.S. assets and investments abroad, total‡	54,359	65,076	85,768	120,126	134,739	146,134	35,550	39,658	29,409	31,694	20,796	22,281	31,797	34,964	17,187	17,537
3	Private investments	19,004	29,136	49,430	81,197	93,603	101,900	25,410	28,124	29,371	31,679	16,216	17,077	19,113	20,922	3,493	4,098
4	Long-term	17,488	26,750	44,447	71,044	81,700	88,930	22,618	24,687	28,156	30,476	13,128	13,791	14,305	15,879	3,493	4,097
5	Direct	11,788	19,395	ʳ²31,865	ʳ49,474	59,486	64,756	17,926	19,386	18,097	19,488	10,265	11,010	10,862	12,167	³2,336	³2,705
6	Foreign dollar bonds	1,692	2,660	4,891	9,115	9,666	10,614	712	652	5,492	6,033	597	721	1,708	1,816	1,157	1,392
7	Other foreign bonds⁴	1,466	382	ʳ633	1,050	1,113	1,088	104	104	748	701	189	211	72	72		
8	Foreign corporate stocks	1,175	2,439	3,984	5,048	5,238	6,464	2,148	2,899	2,827	3,201	84	107	179	257	(*)	(*)
9	Banking claims	390	671	1,698	⁵4,317	⁵3,725	⁵3,367	757	527	227	228	1,521	1,346	1,220	1,266		
10	Other	977	1,203	1,376	⁵2,040	⁵2,472	⁵2,641	971	1,119	765	825	472	396	264	301		
11	Short-term assets and claims	1,516	2,386	4,983	10,153	11,903	12,970	2,792	3,437	1,215	1,203	3,088	3,286	4,808	5,043	(*)	1
12	Reported by banks	886	1,549	3,594	7,735	8,606	8,695	1,217	1,181	597	523	2,617	2,763	4,175	4,228	(*)	
13	Other	630	837	1,389	2,418	3,297	4,275	1,575	2,256	618	680	471	523	633	815	(*)	1
14	U.S. Government nonliquid credits and claims	11,090	13,143	16,979	23,479	26,306	28,524	7,799	8,011	35	11	4,580	5,204	12,683	14,041	1,209	1,257
15	Long-term credits⁷	10,768	12,420	14,087	20,318	23,643	25,940	7,585	7,805	31	4	4,528	5,174	10,295	11,705	1,204	1,252
16	Repayable in dollars⁸	n.a.	n.a.	n.a.	14,968	18,051	19,967	6,495	6,730	31	4	3,974	4,581	6,347	7,400	1,204	1,252
17	Repayable in foreign currencies, etc.⁹	n.a.	n.a.	n.a.	5,350	5,592	5,973	1,090	1,075			554	593	3,948	4,305		
18	Foreign currencies and other claims	322	723	2,892	3,161	2,663	2,584	214	206	4	7	52	30	2,388	2,336	5	5
19	Monetary reserve assets	24,265	22,797	19,359	15,450	14,830	15,710	2,341	3,523	3	4			1	1	12,485	12,182
20	Gold	22,820	21,753	17,804	¹⁰13,806	12,065	10,892									12,065	10,892
21	IMF gold tranche position	1,445	1,044	1,555	¹⁰863	420	1,290									420	1,290
22	Convertible currencies				781	2,345	3,528	2,341	3,523	3	4			1	1		
23	Foreign assets and investments in the United States, total	17,632	27,839	41,202	58,739	69,720	81,121	41,040	47,936	9,310	10,990	6,537	7,221	10,290	12,234	2,543	2,740
24	Long-term	7,997	13,408	18,418	26,374	32,011	40,267	20,248	26,037	5,284	6,172	2,517	2,749	2,995	4,204	967	1,105
25	Direct	3,391	5,076	6,910	8,797	9,923	10,815	7,004	7,750	2,575	2,659	176	164	168	242		
26	Corporate stocks	2,925	6,575	9,302	14,599	15,511	19,528	10,512	12,989	2,539	3,271	1,271	1,411	1,068	1,709	121	148
27	Corporate, U.S. Government agency, State, and municipal bonds	181	259	649	875	2,159	4,236	1,440	3,352	(*)	79	96	104	181	167	442	534
28	Other	1,500	1,408	1,557	2,103	4,418	5,688	1,292	1,946	170	163	974	1,070	1,578	2,086	404	423
29	Nonliquid short-term assets and U.S. Government obligations	825	900	1,235	3,250	4,590	7,237	3,296	4,591	601	1,638	165	164	528	844	(*)	(*)
30	Reported by U.S. private residents other than banks	726	734	964	968	1,778	2,531	1,103	1,753	255	277	125	132	295	369	(*)	(*)
31	Nonliquid U.S. Government obligations	99	166	271	2,282	2,812	4,706	2,193	2,838	346	1,361	40	32	233	475		
32	Associated with Government grants and transactions increasing Government assets (line B.7)¹¹		20	62	344	55	57		(*)			32	30	23	27		
33	Associated with military sales contracts (line B.2)¹¹	14	133	194	1,575	1,985	1,870	1,789	1,665	30	25	5	(*)	161	180		
34	Associated with other specific transactions (line B.13)¹¹	ʳ85	ʳ13	ʳ15	198	187	184	41	33	116	86	3	2	27	63		
35	Other nonmarketable medium-term securities payable prior to maturity only under special conditions (line C.1)¹¹				165	585	2,595	363	1,140	200	1,250			22	205		
36	Liquid assets	8,810	13,531	21,549	29,115	33,119	33,617	17,496	17,308	3,425	3,180	3,855	4,308	6,767	7,186	1,576	1,635
37	Private liabilities reported by banks	ʳ5,836	ʳ7,686	11,062	17,195	21,180	24,460	9,816	12,580	2,433	2,615	3,713	4,190	5,004	4,881	214	194
38	U.S. Treasury marketable or convertible bonds and notes	1,470	1,636	ʳ¹²2,326	3,530	2,381	¹²1,667	1,347	1,183	716	384	41	15	109	60	168	25
39	U.S. Treasury bills, certificates and other obligations	ʳ1,504	4,209	¹³8,161	8,356	9,325	7,260	6,333	3,545	276	181	101	103	1,654	2,245	961	1,186
40	Gold deposits of IMF				34	233	230									233	230
	Memorandum items:																
	Liabilities reflected in liquidity and official reserve transactions balances: Liquid liabilities (liquid assets of foreigners):																
41	To official agencies (line 9)¹⁴	n.a.	n.a.	¹³12,410	16,206	16,679	13,513	9,872	7,001	996	532	1,116	1,320	3,662	3,630	1,033	1,030
42	To commercial banks (line 10)¹⁴ ¹⁵	2,100	2,983	4,818	7,419	11,085	14,467	6,206	8,872	2,076	2,271	473	600	2,330	2,724		
43	To other foreign residents and unallocated (line 11)¹⁴	n.a.	n.a.	2,780	4,059	4,678	4,908	1,412	1,427	353	377	2,161	2,297	752	807		
44	To international and regional organizations (line 12)¹⁴	n.a.	n.a.	1,541	1,431	677	729	6	8			105	91	23	25	543	605
45	Certain nonliquid liabilities to foreign official agencies (line 18)¹⁴ ¹⁶	n.a.	n.a.	2	616	2,723	5,063	587	1,194	314	1,334	451	511	1,371	2,024		

(See page 25 for footnotes)

the United States as income (and not included in the current account) improve our investment position. The third factor is net changes in valuation of U.S. investments abroad and foreign investment in the United States (including adjustments in the various series for statistical discrepancies) which are also not included in the balance of payments accounts. Essentially, we improve our net investment position by transferring abroad real goods and services or by reinvesting foreign earnings abroad, but the position is also affected by valuation changes.

In almost every year since 1955 our net investment position has improved. The largest favorable factor has usually been a large surplus on goods, services, and unilateral transfers, partially offset in the 1960's by a negative adjustment for errors and omissions. Net earnings reinvested abroad show a rising favorable contribution to our net position. But valuation changes have usually been adverse to the United States.

During 1968, for the first time since the early 1950's, the U.S. balance on goods, services, and unilateral transfers turned adverse, mostly reflecting the $6.1 billion surge in merchandise imports. The errors and omissions adjustment remained negative and these two items reduced our net investment position almost $1.0 billion. This was an unfavorable shift of almost $4.0 billion from the average surplus that prevailed in the first half of the 1960's, and a deterioration of $2.2 billion from 1967. Net reinvested earnings, on the other hand, rose to over $1.6 billion in 1968, the highest level recorded. Net valuation changes in 1968 were adverse by some $0.7 billion. This mostly reflected a greater rise in the value of U.S. stocks held by foreigners (as U.S. stock prices rose) than the rise in the value of foreign

stocks held by U.S. residents. However, this valuation adjustment was much less adverse than the $2.1 billion adjustment in 1967. (In 1967, the value of foreign holdings of U.S. stocks rose even more, and the value of U.S. holdings of foreign bond issues showed a sharp fall.)

Since these factors almost exactly offset each other in 1968, the net international investment position of the United States showed practically no change, a sharp contrast with the very large improvements in our net position in the early 1960's. Most of the shift seems to have been associated with the parallel decline in our trade surplus.

While the net change in our investment position can be considered to be accounted for by the factors just described, capital flows, of course, may have a major impact on trade, services, and earnings. To this extent, the change in the net position is not determined independently of the capital flows. On the other hand, an outflow of capital from the United States does not necessarily result in a net change in the U.S. international investment position unless one of the factors mentioned also is influenced. U.S. purchases of foreign bonds increase interest receipts of the United States and thus improve the U.S. balance on goods and services. In this case, however, it is clear that the immediate improvement in the net position will be a small fraction of the initial outflow of capital. Likewise, U.S. direct investment abroad will increase U.S. earnings and may significantly encourage U.S. exports (at least in the short run), particularly if a new plant abroad requires U.S. equipment.

But setting aside the complex interdependence between capital flows and the current account items and earnings, if there is little or no net surplus from

trade, services, and transfers, retained earnings, or valuation changes, as was the case in 1967 and 1968, capital outflows from the United States (which increase certain assets abroad) must be financed by a rundown in other assets—possibly monetary reserves—or by a buildup in liabilities to foreigners—often liquid liabilities.

To analyze the external position of the United States, it is not enough to consider only the change in the net international investment position. Even when our net investment position improves, if the capital outflow is so great that there is a decline in monetary reserves, this adversely affects the U.S. balance of payments measured on the liquidity basis, as well as on the official reserve transactions basis. If there is an increase in liquid liabilities, this adversely affects the liquidity balance. The official reserves transaction balance is adversely affected if there is an increase in liquid or certain nonliquid liabilities to foreign monetary authorities.[2]

Increases in U.S. Assets and Liabilities

The $11.4 billion rise in U.S. international assets in 1968 reflected an $8.3 billion increase in private investments abroad, a $2.2 billion advance in nonliquid U.S. Government assets and a $0.9 billion increase in U.S. official reserves (tables 2 and 3). The 1968 increase in U.S. international assets was somewhat larger than in 1967, partly reflecting the fact that there was little change in monetary reserves in 1967. In addition, there was a greater increase in direct investments in 1968, as compared with the relatively

2. For further analysis of the meaning of our net international investment position see Lederer and Cutler, "International Investments of the United States in 1966," SURVEY OF CURRENT BUSINESS, September 1967, pp. 39–52.

ʳ Revised.   ᵖ Preliminary.   N.a. Not available.   *Less than $500,000 (±).   †Includes U.S. gold stock.

1. Unrevised except where indicated; otherwise the data are as published in the following: 1950, SURVEY, September 1967; 1955, *Balance of Payments Statistical Supplement, Revised Edition*, 1963; 1960, SURVEY, August 1962; and 1965, SURVEY, October 1968.
2. Data for Cuba omitted effective 1960; 1959 total for U.S. direct investment was $956 million (book value).
3. Represents the estimated investment in shipping companies registered primarily in Panama and Liberia.
4. Consists primarily of securities payable in foreign currencies.
5. Excludes $200 million netted against a related inflow of U.S. direct investment capital in 1961.
6. Includes $254 million loaned to Canada in connection with Columbia River power development in 1964.
7. Also includes paid-in capital subscriptions to international financial institutions (other than IMF) and outstanding amounts of miscellaneous claims which have been settled through international agreements to be payable to the U.S. Government over periods in excess of 1 year. Excludes World War I debts that are not currently being serviced.
8. Includes indebtedness repayable in U.S. dollars, or optionally in foreign currencies, or by delivery of materials or transfer of services, when option rests with U.S. Government.

9. Includes indebtedness which the borrower may contractually, or at its option, repay with its currency, with a third country's currency, or by delivery of materials or transfer of services.
10. Reflects payment of $259 million gold portion of increased U.S. subscription to the IMF in the second quarter of 1965.
11. Line numbers correspond to those in balance of payments table 5, SURVEY OF CURRENT BUSINESS, September 1969, p. 41.
12. Reflects new series on marketable Treasury bonds and notes.
13. Includes Treasury liabilities of $522 million to certain foreign military agencies, which were reflected in the liquidity balance but excluded from the official reserves transactions balance.
14. Line numbers correspond to those in balance of payments table 3, SURVEY OF CURRENT BUSINESS, September 1969, p. 38.
15. As reported by U.S. banks; ultimate ownership is not identified.
16. Portions of lines 28, 34, and 35 above.

NOTE.—Differences between amounts outstanding and flows reported in balance of payments tables may not coincide due to changes in coverage, price changes, changes in valuation and other adjustments.

Table 3.—Detailed Reconciliation of Changes in the International Investment Position of the United States and Balance of Payments Capital Flows

[Millions of dollars]

Lines in table 2	Type of investment (increase +)	1967^r	1968^p
1	Net international investment position of the United States (line 2 minus line 23)	233	-6
	of which: Balance of Payments capital flows	1,172	-991
	Other than capital flows	-946	984
2	U.S. assets and investments abroad, total	9,543	11,395
	of which: Capital flows	8,024	8,286
	Other than capital flows	1,518	3,109
3	Private investments	7,216	8,297
4	Long-term	5,919	7,230
5	Direct	4,709	5,270
	of which: Capital flows	3,154	3,025
	Reinvested earnings	1,508	2,142
	Other adjustments	-43	103
6-7	Foreign bonds	236	923
	of which: Capital flows	1,216	1,100
	Price changes	-1,068	-177
	Other adjustments	88	
8	Foreign corporate stocks	914	1,226
	of which: Capital flows	50	167
	Price changes	864	1,059
9-10	Banking and other claims	60	-189
	of which: Capital flows	26	-184
	Changes in coverage	34	
	Other adjustments		-5
11	Short-term assets and claims	1,297	1,067
	of which: Capital flows	1,209	1,049
	Changes in coverage	88	
	Other adjustments		18
14	U.S. Government nonliquid credits and claims	2,379	2,218
15	Long-term credits	2,560	2,297
	of which: Capital flows	2,631	2,321
	Losses on write-offs		-6
	Other adjustments	-71	-18
18	Foreign currencies and other claims	-181	-79
	of which: Capital flows	-209	-72
	Valuation changes	30	-13
	Other adjustments	-2	6
19	Monetary reserve assets	-52	880
23	Foreign assets and investments in the United States, total	9,310	11,401
	of which: Capital flows	6,852	9,277
	Other than capital flows	2,464	2,125
24	Long-term	5,005	8,256
25	Direct	869	892
	of which: Capital flows	251	319
	Reinvested earnings	440	488
	Other adjustments	178	85
26	Corporate stocks	2,868	4,017
	of which: Capital flows	701	2,083
	Price changes	2,221	1,934
	Other adjustments	-54	
27	Corporate, U.S. Government agency, State, and municipal bonds	117	2,077
	of which: Capital flows	316	2,277
	Price changes	-199	-200
28	Other	1,151	1,270
	of which: Capital flows	1,137	1,263
	Changes in coverage	14	
	Other adjustments		7
29	Nonliquid short-term assets and U.S. Government obligations	965	2,647
30	Reported by U.S. private residents other than banks	514	753
	of which: Capital flows	499	750
	Changes in coverage	15	
	Other adjustments		3
31	Nonliquid U.S. Government obligations	451	1,894
	of which: Capital flows	450	1,872
	Other adjustments	1	22
36	Liquid assets	3,340	498
	of which: Capital flows	3,492	712
	Changes in coverage	-152	-214

r Revised.   p Preliminary.

NOTE.—Details may not add to totals because of rounding.

low increase in 1967, as reinvested earnings rose sharply. U.S. investments in foreign dollar bonds also rose faster in 1968. Although recorded balance of payments outflows to purchase such bonds were roughly the same in both years, in 1967 the value of existing holdings of bonds fell sharply. In 1968, the fall in value was much smaller. Shifts in other long-term private accounts were mostly smaller and offsetting. Short-term bank reported claims rose much less in 1968 than in 1967, reflecting a tightening of the Credit Restraint Program, but other short-term claims rose faster in 1968 than in 1967, mostly reflecting the reinvestment abroad of part of the proceeds of increased foreign borrowing by U.S. corporations.

Of the $11.4 billion rise in foreign assets and investments in the United States (U.S. liabilities) in 1968, $8.3 billion was in long-term U.S. liabilities, $2.6 billion was in nonliquid short-term and U.S. Government obligations, and $0.5 billion was in liquid liabilities. Of the $9.3 billion rise in U.S. liabilities in 1967, only $5.0 billion was long-term, $1.0 billion was in nonliquid short-term and Government obligations, and $3.3 billion was in liquid liabilities. The large increase in long-term liabilities to foreigners in 1968 was primarily attributable to a surge in foreign purchases of U.S. stocks and of new Euro-bond issues of U.S. corporations. The sharp rise in foreign holdings of nonliquid U.S. Government obligations in 1968 reflected $2.0 billion of foreign official purchases of nonmarketable, nonconvertible, medium-term U.S. Treasury securities. (These near-liquid securities are technically not counted in the liquidity measure of the balance, but are counted in the official reserve transactions balance.)

Thus, although both in 1967 and in 1968 the net international investment position of the United States showed little change, the composition of the capital flows was quite different in the 2 years. In 1967, monetary reserve assets declined slightly and the $9.5 billion increase in U.S. assets abroad was only partly offset by the $6.0 billion increase in foreign holdings of non-

liquid U.S. assets. At the same time, there was a $3.3 billion increase in U.S. liquid liabilities to foreigners, with a deficit in the U.S. liquidity balance of about the same amount.

In 1968, on the other hand, monetary reserve assets rose and the increase in other U.S. assets abroad was greater than in 1967. But increased purchases of U.S. stocks and bonds by foreigners in 1968 resulted in a large part of the rise in U.S. assets being offset by inflows of nonliquid foreign capital. At the same time, there was a relatively small increase in liquid liabilities. Since monetary reserves increased slightly more than liquid liabilities (excluding adjustments for changes in coverage), the liquidity balance was in surplus.

U.S. Direct Investment Abroad

U.S. direct investment abroad increased by $5.3 billion in 1968, a considerably larger rise than in 1967 and about the same as the increase in 1966. In 1968, direct investments accounted for almost one-half of the gross rise in international assets of the United States, bringing the book value of U.S. direct investments abroad at yearend to $64.8 billion, equivalent to almost half of the calculated value of total U.S. international assets. In spite of the large increase in direct investment in 1968, the balance of payments capital outflow for direct investment, including the use of both U.S. funds and funds raised abroad, was somewhat lower than in 1967 and much below the outflows in 1965 and 1966 (table 4). The increase associated with reinvested earnings, on the other hand, was substantially more than reinvestments in earlier years.

To analyze the influence of direct investments on the U.S. balance of payments and on the net international investment position of the United States, one must look at a number of associated international transactions by U.S. corporations. In addition to the outflow of U.S. funds to finance direct investment, one is interested in how much U.S. corporations borrow abroad, either by new issues of securities or directly from foreign banks and others. Whether the proceeds of the borrowings are used to finance direct investments, are repatriated to the United States, or are left on deposit abroad for later utilization is also important. The use made of the earnings of foreign affiliates of the U.S. corporations must also be considered, particularly as to whether they are reinvested or are returned to the United States as income on direct investment. Fees and royalties from U.S. direct investment must also be counted. The calculation of the net flow resulting from these identifiable corporate transactions is detailed in table 4. Note that in this table, balance of payments signs are used and increases in U.S. claims abroad are therefore shown as minuses.

It must be emphasized, however, that the calculated net flow does not fully reflect all the influences on the balance of payments of U.S. corporate international transactions. The impact on U.S. exports and imports of U.S. direct investment abroad is not considered, for instance, although direct investments may have a substantial influence on both. Furthermore, large borrowings abroad by U.S. corporations may tend to reduce foreign purchases of other U.S. securities, such as stocks.

Such substitution effects cannot be measured. Whether the net impact of corporate transactions would be favorable or adverse after taking these effects into account is not known.

Besides these limitations, it might also be noted that we are restricting the analysis to transactions between U.S. corporations and foreigners. Thus, borrowing abroad by foreign affiliates of U.S. corporations and their internally generated depreciation reserves are excluded. The use of such funds, perhaps for plant and equipment expenditures or to increase working capital, is also excluded. While these flows have no net impact on the balance of payments or on the U.S. international investment position, nevertheless, a full analysis of U.S. corporate activity abroad would have to take them into account.

In 1968, the net flow of corporate funds associated with these identified transactions had a favorable impact on the U.S. balance of payments of $5.5 billion. This was some $2.7 billion higher than in 1967, and about $3.4 billion above the 1965–66 average. Offsetting the increase in direct investment, new issues of securities rose to $2.1 billion from about $0.5 billion in 1967. In addition, other borrowing

abroad by U.S. corporations (corporate liabilities other than new issues, which includes trade liabilities as well as financial borrowing) rose from under $0.5 billion in 1967 to $1.1 billion in 1968. To the extent that these funds were repatriated to the United States or used to finance the direct investment capital outflow (instead of U.S. funds), such borrowing had a favorable impact on the balance of payments, assuming that the direct investments would have been made in any case. In 1968, about $0.8 billion of the proceeds of new issues was used for direct investment as compared with $0.3 billion in 1967. Some of the proceeds of these borrowings, however, were invested abroad, mostly in the Euro-dollar market, pending their use in the foreign affiliates. About $1.0 billion of the proceeds of new issues was used this way in 1968; this accounted for most of the large increase in other corporate claims (which also includes trade credit). Such use of the proceeds neutralizes the favorable impact of the initial borrowing.

Another major change in 1968 was a $1.0 billion increase, to $7.1 billion, in adjusted earnings [3] on U.S. direct investment abroad. This increase in earnings was mostly associated with accelerated economic growth in Western Europe and elsewhere. Part of the earnings were repatriated to the United States as income on direct investment, which rose to $5.0 billion from $4.5 billion in 1967. The rest, as noted earlier, was used to finance part of the large increase in direct investment assets.

Increased fees and royalties from U.S. direct investments made a minor contribution to the improvement in the net flow in 1968. Note that the change in

Table 4.—Flows of Certain U.S. Corporate Funds—Changes in Foreign Assets and Liabilities, Adjusted Earnings, and Fees and Royalties

[Millions of dollars]

Debits (−), credits (+)	Total				Western Europe			
	1965	1966	1967	1968	1965	1966	1967	1968
Net flow	2,114	2,055	2,803	5,544	7	−119	393	2,960
Change in direct investment position	−4,994	−5,303	−4,709	−5,270	−1,856	−2,227	−1,714	−1,460
Balance of payments flows	−3,468	−3,639	−3,154	−3,025	−1,479	−1,813	−1,480	−995
Reinvested earnings	−1,542	−1,739	−1,598	−2,142	−408	−435	−269	−441
Other adjustments	16	75	43	−103	31	21	35	−24
Other corporate claims	368	−434	−590	−926	26	−444	−221	−725
Long-term	−88	−112	−281	−174	30	−79	−76	−149
Short-term [1]	456	−322	−309	−752	−4	−365	−145	−576
Corporate liabilities other than new issues of securities	136	459	448	1,102	119	371	325	1,100
Long-term	29	180	85	673	23	192	64	673
Short-term [1]	107	279	363	429	96	179	261	427
New issues of securities [2]	191	594	446	2,129	191	594	446	2,129
Of which: Used for direct investment	−52	−445	−278	−785	n.a.	n.a.	n.a.	n.a.
Deposited abroad (short-term corporate claims)	−139	−143	−96	−973	n.a.	n.a.	n.a.	n.a.
Adjusted earnings	5,505	5,784	6,115	7,127	1,176	1,165	1,119	1,337
Reinvested earnings	1,542	1,739	1,598	2,142	408	435	269	441
Income on U.S. direct investments abroad	3,963	4,045	4,517	4,985	768	730	850	916
Fees and royalties from U.S. direct investment	924	1,030	1,136	1,279	382	443	473	535
Offset to "other adjustments" in direct investment	−16	−75	−43	103	−31	−21	−35	24

N.a. Not available.
1. Excludes brokerage claims and liabilities.
2. New issues of securities sold abroad by U.S. corporations exclude securities issued by subsidiaries incorporated abroad and also exclude funds obtained abroad by U.S. corporations through bank loans and other credits. However, securities issued by subsidiaries incorporated in the Netherlands Antilles are treated as if they had been issued by U.S. corporations if the proceeds of such issues are transferred to U.S. parent companies.

3. Earnings, as normally defined in this article, are equal to reinvested earnings, plus income on U.S. direct investments abroad, minus interest income (since interest is included in the balance of payments entry for income on U.S. direct investments abroad but not in earnings), plus foreign withholding taxes on dividends paid by foreign affiliates (since withholding taxes, although included in earnings, are not transmitted to the United States as income). To analyze the balance of payments impact of earnings, a simple concept is useful: Adjusted earnings—used only in table 1 and in this section of the article—are defined as income on U.S. direct investments plus reinvested earnings. Thus, adjusted earnings equal earnings plus interest payments, minus foreign withholding taxes.

the direct investment position between yearends is partly due to "other adjustments." For particular countries or areas, this adjustment is made to take account of valuation changes in the book value of direct investments, as well as flows of funds due to transfers between directly owned foreign affiliates and indirectly owned firms. For the total of all countries, the second factor washes out so that the adjustment only reflects a change in valuation. These adjustments, however, do not affect the net flow since equal entries, with opposite signs, are included elsewhere in the table.

Most of the $2.7 billion improvement in the net flow in 1968 was probably associated with the Foreign Direct Investment Program which was tightened and made mandatory early in the year. Clearly, the increase in borrowing abroad by U.S. corporations and the use of the proceeds to finance direct investment was in large part due to the program. Furthermore, the program was most restrictive for Western Euro-

Table 5.—Value of Direct Investments Abroad [1] by Selected Countries and Industries, at Yearend

Table 6.—Direct Investment Capital Outflows Foreign Corporations,

[Millions of dollars]

Line	Area and country	T5 1967r Total	1967r Mining and smelting	1967r Petroleum	1967r Manufacturing	1967r Public utilities	1967r Trade	1967r Other	T5 1968p Total	1968p Mining and smelting	1968p Petroleum	1968p Manufacturing	1968p Public utilities	1968p Trade	1968p Other	T6 Net outflows 1967r	T6 1968p Total	1968p Mining and smelting	1968p Petroleum	1968p Manufacturing	1968p Other
1	All areas, total	59,486	4,876	17,404	24,167	2,393	5,010	5,636	64,756	5,370	18,835	26,354	2,672	5,266	6,258	3,154	3,025	383	1,181	905	556
2	Canada	18,097	2,342	3,819	8,095	506	1,038	2,298	19,488	2,636	4,088	8,546	599	1,115	2,505	403	594	194	163	9	228
3	Latin American Republics, total	10,265	1,277	2,903	3,305	621	1,297	952	11,010	1,402	2,976	3,699	627	1,249	1,057	184	461	119	59	211	73
4	Mexico	1,343	100	44	890	27	166	115	1,459	112	44	998	27	181	97	-4	55	5	-1	59	-8
5	Panama	801	19	158	33	46	326	218	922	19	176	58	53	340	276	3	75	......	10	20	46
6	Other Cent. Amer. & W.I.	758	34	184	105	155	43	238	795	33	198	121	147	45	251	62	27	-4	11	16	4
7	Argentina	1,082	(*)	(*)	678	(*)	53	351	1,148	(*)	(*)	729	(*)	57	362	62	28	(*)	(*)	18	10
8	Brazil	1,327	68	79	893	32	195	61	1,484	81	83	1,021	28	197	74	39	80	(*)	1	65	14
9	Chile	879	516	(*)	61	(*)	37	265	964	586	(*)	68	(*)	39	270	24	82	78	(*)	3	11
10	Colombia	597	(*)	294	192	29	56	26	629	(*)	324	193	29	58	25	20	31	(*)	28	4	-1
11	Peru	660	397	35	98	21	54	55	692	421	39	96	22	51	62	61	24	22	4	-2	(**)
12	Venezuela	2,555	(*)	1,793	311	19	253	180	2,620	(*)	1,780	376	18	255	190	-97	24	(*)	-9	31	2
13	Other countries	263	19	100	44	28	23	48	298	24	122	38	33	25	55	14	35	5	-3	2	11
14	Other Western Hemisphere	1,779	431	569	276	51	94	358	1,979	473	667	291	58	94	395	107	111	54	81	2	-27
15	Europe, total	17,926	61	4,423	9,798	78	2,060	1,507	19,386	61	4,640	10,778	94	2,126	1,688	1,480	995	-2	321	552	124
16	Common Market, total	8,444	19	2,086	4,976	49	853	461	8,992	19	2,149	5,373	54	848	549	852	425	(*)	135	233	58
17	Belgium & Luxembourg	867	(**)	30	542	1	142	151	963	(**)	14	583	1	159	205	90	60	......	-8	7	61
18	France	1,904	10	302	1,312	14	195	70	1,910	112	293	1,345	14	163	84	138	-21	(*)	-13	3	-11
19	Germany	3,486	(*)	1,047	2,064	14	258	103	3,774	(*)	1,104	2,273	18	264	115	447	236	(*)	89	133	13
20	Italy	1,246	(*)	486	595	1	98	66	1,272	(*)	479	664	3	107	28	107	122	(**)	12	9	8
21	Netherlands	942	(**)	221	463	18	161	79	1,073	(**)	259	557	18	157	82	70	122	(**)	55	80	-14
22	Other Europe, total	9,482	42	2,337	4,821	29	1,206	1,046	10,394	42	2,490	5,405	39	1,278	1,139	628	569	(*)	186	319	64
23	Denmark	273	1	188	45	(**)	36	3	204	1	111	48	(**)	41	3	50	-63	(**)	-68	2	3
24	Norway	183	(*)	90	49	(**)	24	20	200	(*)	101	51	(**)	26	22	11	11	(**)	6	2	3
25	Spain	480	(*)	93	257	10	94	27	587	(*)	140	306	13	100	28	70	111	(*)	45	61	5
26	Sweden	438	(*)	250	97	(**)	83	8	511	(*)	281	134	(**)	88	8	70	28	(*)	(*)	35	7
27	Switzerland	1,322	(**)	9	282	1	430	601	1,436	(**)	8	335	1	470	624	70	84	(**)	42	35	7
28	United Kingdom	6,113	2	1,432	3,878	12	411	379	6,703	2	1,562	4,257	20	417	445	137	28	(**)	1	38	-29
29	Other countries	673	21	276	214	6	129	27	753	19	288	274	6	137	28	353	375	(*)	153	152	70
30	Africa, total	2,273	400	1,219	370	3	151	131	2,673	387	1,567	400	4	163	152	175	308	-15	313	9	1
31	Liberia	174	(*)	(*)	(*)	(*)	22	152	174	(*)	(*)	(*)	(*)	24	150	-26	-11	(*)	(*)	(*)	-11
32	Libya	451	(*)	(*)	(*)	(*)	5	446	678	(*)	(*)	(*)	(*)	6	672	51	214	(*)	214	(**)	1
33	Republic of S. Africa	666	99	139	304	(**)	88	36	692	78	147	332	(**)	96	38	35	5	-14	(*)	14	5
34	Other countries	982	227	638	65	6	36	11	1,130	236	764	66	7	38	20	100	100	3	100	-4	1
35	Asia, total	4,289	42	2,600	988	76	321	261	4,693	44	2,800	1,138	88	355	269	325	234	1	162	49	22
36	Middle East	1,749	3	1,608	59	6	19	54	1,803	3	1,654	63	7	20	56	150	37	(**)	39	2	-4
37	Far East, total	2,540	40	992	929	69	303	208	2,891	42	1,146	1,075	82	334	213	174	197	1	123	47	26
38	India	267	(*)	(*)	125	2	39	101	281	(*)	(*)	131	1	41	107	17	7	(**)	(*)	4	3
39	Japan	870	......	(*)	425	2	77	366	1,048	......	(*)	521	3	98	426	34	77	......	(*)	10	67
40	Philippine Republic	639	(*)	(*)	216	39	87	296	668	(*)	(*)	237	39	88	303	30	21	(*)	(*)	21	-1
41	Other countries	765	(*)	(*)	162	27	99	477	894	(*)	(*)	185	38	107	564	93	92	(*)	(*)	11	80
42	Oceania, total	2,520	322	592	1,336	2	140	128	2,821	367	646	1,503	3	163	138	332	164	33	36	74	22
43	Australia	2,360	320	(*)	1,262	2	101	674	2,645	365	(*)	1,418	3	126	734	329	162	33	36	74	19
44	Other countries	160	2	(*)	74	(**)	38	46	175	2	(*)	85	1	37	51	3	2	(**)	(*)	-1	3
45	International shipping	2,336	......	1,279	......	1,057	......	......	2,705	......	1,451	......	1,200	......	54	150	158	......	46	......	112

r Revised.   p Preliminary.   *Combined in "other" industries.   **Less than $500,000.

1. The value of investments in specified industries and countries is affected by capital flows among foreign affiliates as shown in table 11.

2. Income is the sum of dividends and interest, net after foreign withholding taxes, received by, or credited to, the account of the U.S. owner, and branch profit after foreign taxes but before U.S. taxes. Earnings is the sum of the U.S. share in net earnings (or losses) of foreign corporations and branch profits after foreign taxes but before U.S. taxes. Reinvested earnings is computed as the difference between the U.S. share of net earnings (or

pean countries and, as is clear in table 4, most of the improvement in 1968 was concentrated in Western Europe. However, the figures to some extent overstate the Western European contribution in 1968. The improvement there was largely due to the fact that all of the new issues of securities were floated in Europe. Yet, a significant part of the funds used to purchase the new issues may have come ultimately from sources outside of Europe.

The $1.0 billion increase in earnings also made a significant contribution to the 1968 improvement in net corporate flows. Of course, to the extent that higher earnings resulted in larger direct investments, the rise in earnings did not contribute to the favorable shift. On the other hand, direct investment targets are sometimes set independently of earnings, and whether earnings or borrowed funds are used to finance the investment is a matter of corporate preference or negotiation with the Office of Foreign Direct Investment. (See the discussion of earnings below.)

and U.S. Share in Reinvested Earnings of by Selected Countries

Table 7.—Direct Investment Earnings and Income,[2] by Selected Countries

[Millions of dollars]

| Table 6—Continued | | | | | | Table 7 | | | | | | | | | | | | |
| Reinvested earnings of foreign corporations [2] | | | | | | Earnings | | | | | | Income | | | | | | Line |
1967r	Total	Mining and smelting	Petroleum	Manufacturing	Other	1967r	Total	Mining and smelting	Petroleum	Manufacturing	Other	1967r	Total	Mining and smelting	Petroleum	Manufacturing	Other	
1,598	2,142	126	239	1,246	531	6,034	7,010	789	2,466	2,514	1,242	4,518	4,985	645	2,288	1,275	776	1
644	762	102	107	407	147	1,327	1,478	285	243	672	278	790	849	180	160	306	203	2
181	297	7	25	181	84	1,208	1,367	294	478	389	206	1,022	1,063	275	452	206	131	3
57	63	7	2	50	5	121	132	17	3	95	17	62	67	9	1	45	12	4
26	47	(*)	9	2	35	76	101		10	17	74	58	62		5	17	41	5
11	9		3	(**)	6	66	61		12	5	3	46	53		2	4	42	6
−3	35	(*)	(*)	30	5	80	126	(*)	(*)	76	51	89	94	(*)	(*)	48	46	7
39	73	(*)	4	62	8	159	154	(*)	19	124	16	75	144	(*)	11	56	8	8
2	2	−8	(*)	4	7	150	154	(*)	7	143	14	143	144	(*)	131	2	11	9
7	1	(*)	2	−2	2	15	17	(*)	2	13	1	6	16	(*)	1	15	(**)	10
−4	9	(*)	1	(**)	6	91	108	(*)	85	10	9	103	99	(*)	83	4	3	11
39	56	(*)	6	37	13	484	490	(*)	387	54	49	435	430	(*)	380	15	35	12
7	(**)	1	(**)	−3	3	13	13	2	8	−4	6	14	6	1	9	(**)	4	13
29	59	1	17	13	28	190	219	98	57	19	45	168	169	99	41	10	19	14
269	442	2	−112	425	127	1,143	1,365	8	−134	1,038	453	849	915	6	4	587	318	15 S
41	101	(*)	−77	162	16	448	540	(*)	−51	499	92	398	438	(*)	34	331	73	16
21	26	(**)	−9	31	4	55	89	(**)	−4	47	46	32	57	(**)	17	40		17
4	20	(*)	−3	29	−11	59	91	(*)	17	89	−14	50	65	(*)	12	57	−4	18
−27	49	(*)	−32	76	4	223	258	(*)	−26	263	21	241	212	(*)	21	173	18	19
23	2	(*)	−18	12	8	50	45	(*)	−19	49	15	28	43	(**)	2	37	6	20
19	4		−21	14	11	61	56		−19	51	24	46	61		2	47	13	21
228	341	(*)	−35	263	112	695	825	(*)	−83	539	369	452	476	(*)	−30	256	251	22
−5	−6		−9	1	2	−4	−3		−14	4	7	4	7		−1	3	6	23
5	6	(*)	(**)	3	3	(**)	−1	(*)	−15	4	10	−5	−8	(*)	−16	2	6	24
−2	2	(*)	2	−5	5	−1	2	(*)	2	1	16	16		−1	6	12		25
−5	−11		−12	2	−1	14	19	(*)	−12	9	20	23	29	(**)		7	21	26
114	102		−4	24	83	210	205	(**)	−13	43	175	99	105		20	93	27	27
81	208		−21	212	18	378	506	(*)	−46	442	110	274	281	(**)	−12	209	84	28
40	39	(*)	9	27	2	79	83	(*)	16	35	32	40	46	(*)	7	8	30	29
46	71	2	15	20	33	421	671	69	501	42	58	364	583	63	483	21	17	30
−5	7	(*)	(*)	(*)	7	16	20	(*)	(*)	(*)	20	22	13	(*)	(*)	(*)	13	31
3	11	(*)	(*)	(*)	11	292	506	(*)	(*)	(*)	506	289	496	(*)	(*)	(*)	496	32
36	26	−7	(*)	16	17	128	120		31	37	52	80	74		32	19	23	33
12	26	6	5	5	10	−15	26	27	−22	6	15	−26	1	22	−27	1	5	34
129	183	(**)	44	105	34	1,343	1,473	(**)	1,182	199	92	1,211	1,282	(**)	1,143	84	55	35
−14	23		13	1	9	1,004	1,101		1,079	6	17	1,018	1,080		1,069	4	8	36
142	160	(**)	31	104	24	339	372	(**)	104	194	75	193	202	(**)	75	80	47	37
7	7		(*)	2	5	20	21		(*)	12	9	11	11		(*)	8	4	38
79	103		(*)	86	17	123	166		(*)	127	39	46	60		(*)	37	23	39
30	12	(*)	(*)	3	9	61	53	(*)	(*)	25	27	26	34	(*)	(*)	19	15	40
28	38	(*)	(*)	13	25	136	133	(*)	(*)	29	103	110	96	(*)	(*)	16	80	41
117	132	12	19	95	6	171	208	34	−5	154	24	57	85	23	−18	62	18	42
104	118	12	(*)	83	24	151	193	33	(*)	141	19	50	85	23	(*)	61	1	43
13	13		(*)	12	2	20	14	(**)	(*)	13	(**)	7	1	(**)	(*)	2	−1	44
183	196		124		72	232	229		144		86	57	38		22		16	45

losses) of foreign corporations and the U.S. share of gross dividends (dividends before deduction of withholding taxes). In order to reconcile the data in table 7 with reinvested earnings in table 6, the following formula applies (stated in millions of dollars for 1968): Earnings ($7,010) + interest ($395) equals income ($4,985) + withholding taxes ($278) + reinvested earnings ($2,142).

Country and industry distribution

The increase in the book value of direct investment (including both capital flows and reinvested earnings) in the developed countries of Canada, Europe, Republic of South Africa, Japan, Australia, and New Zealand totaled $3.4 billion in 1968. Manufacturing industries received 50 percent, petroleum 21 percent, mining 9 percent, and other industries (mainly trading and financial) 20 percent. The increase in Europe was lower than in 1967 but the increases in other developed countries were larger. The increase in investment in the developing countries of Latin America, Africa, and Asia totaled $1.5 billion. Manufacturing and petroleum affiliates each received about 33 percent, with mining investments receiving 13 percent and "other" 20

percent. The increase in direct investment in "International and unallocated" of $0.4 billion was mostly in shipping. In 1967 developed countries received $3.5 billion of the increase in direct investment and developing countries received about $0.8 billion of the $4.7 billion total increase (including "international"). The difference between the increases in investment in developing areas in 1968 and in 1967 was mostly due to higher 1968 investment in petroleum, banking, financial, and other service industries. (See tables 5–8 and chart 13.)

Manufacturing

The book value of direct investment in manufacturing enterprises rose $2.2 billion in 1968 and accounted for 40 percent of the $5.3 billion increase in

total direct investment during the year. This increase in manufacturing was about $0.1 billion higher than in 1967 but still below the 1965–66 increases. Some $1.2 billion of the increase represented reinvested earnings, up from $0.8 billion in 1967, and $0.9 billion was from capital outflows, down from $1.2 billion in 1967. Western Europe received about $1.0 billion of the 1968 increase in manufacturing investment compared with $0.9 billion in 1967. In the United Kingdom higher reinvested earnings and large acquisitions of several British firms in the tobacco and food manufacturing industries resulted in a particularly large increase in investment. In Germany the capital flow for direct investment dropped, but was partly offset by higher reinvested earnings. In Canada a higher ratio of reinvestment out of improved

Table 8.—Selected Data on Direct Investments Abroad, by Major Areas

[In millions of dollars]

	Book value at yearend				Net capital outflows					Earnings					Income				
	Total	Mining and smelting	Petroleum	Manufacturing	Other	Total	Mining and smelting	Petroleum	Manufacturing	Other	Total	Mining and smelting	Petroleum	Manufacturing	Other	Total	Mining and smelting	Petroleum	Manufacturing	Other
All areas, total:																				
1960	31,865	2,997	10,810	11,051	7,007	1,674	155	452	801	266	3,566	394	1,302	1,176	694	2,355	337	1,150	550	318
1961	34,717	3,094	12,190	11,997	7,436	1,599	70	793	462	274	3,815	362	1,476	1,203	774	2,768	297	1,336	722	413
1962	37,276	3,244	12,728	13,250	8,057	1,654	97	606	712	239	4,235	372	1,695	1,307	861	3,044	318	1,565	746	415
1963	40,736	3,419	13,652	14,937	8,728	1,976	85	828	774	289	4,587	388	1,824	1,541	834	3,129	321	1,715	656	437
1964	44,480	3,665	14,328	16,935	9,552	2,328	136	760	1,034	398	5,071	512	1,808	1,852	899	3,674	403	1,856	893	522
1965	49,474	3,981	15,298	19,339	10,906	3,468	138	977	1,525	828	5,460	571	1,830	2,022	1,037	3,963	442	1,799	1,094	628
1966	54,777	4,365	16,200	22,078	12,134	3,639	305	863	1,752	718	5,702	659	1,868	2,104	1,071	4,045	524	1,781	1,116	624
1967	59,486	4,876	17,404	24,167	13,039	3,154	330	1,097	1,229	499	6,034	746	2,120	2,055	1,112	4,518	596	1,989	1,193	740
1968	64,756	5,370	18,835	26,354	14,196	3,025	383	1,181	905	556	7,010	789	2,466	2,514	1,242	4,985	645	2,288	1,275	776
Canada:																				
1960	11,179	1,325	2,664	4,827	2,363	451	199	135	29	88	718	88	98	398	134	361	47	60	176	78
1961	11,602	1,367	2,828	5,076	2,331	302	9	100	117	76	726	96	114	360	156	464	51	78	213	122
1962	12,133	1,489	2,875	5,312	2,457	314	85	159	12	58	825	97	121	460	147	476	60	79	221	116
1963	13,044	1,549	3,134	5,761	2,600	365	7	188	120	50	948	127	149	525	147	455	80	80	192	103
1964	13,855	1,713	3,196	6,198	2,748	298	91	25	140	42	1,106	191	170	565	180	634	118	118	269	129
1965	15,318	1,851	3,356	6,872	3,239	962	51	179	395	337	1,209	198	183	606	222	703	110	122	315	156
1966	17,017	2,089	3,608	7,692	3,628	1,153	172	155	566	260	1,237	191	196	628	222	756	120	112	354	170
1967	18,097	2,342	3,819	8,095	3,842	403	173	115	20	95	1,327	240	207	613	267	790	154	132	296	208
1968	19,488	2,636	4,088	8,546	4,219	594	194	163	9	228	1,478	285	243	672	278	849	180	160	306	203
Latin America: [1]																				
1960	8,365	1,319	3,122	1,521	2,403	149	−60	24	125	60	970	224	370	147	229	719	234	331	64	90
1961	9,239	1,332	3,674	1,707	2,526	219	32	63	78	46	1,079	206	478	172	223	824	198	438	75	113
1962	9,524	1,321	3,642	1,944	2,617	29	−13	−67	133	−24	1,179	230	543	173	233	891	221	488	71	111
1963	9,941	1,353	3,636	2,213	2,739	235	24	5	150	56	1,125	219	532	171	203	956	210	544	70	132
1964	10,254	1,404	3,589	2,507	2,754	113	30	7	137	−61	1,244	266	539	243	196	1,011	245	531	98	137
1965	10,886	1,474	3,546	2,945	2,921	271	43	−74	245	57	1,320	290	513	289	228	995	266	476	123	130
1966	11,498	1,565	3,475	3,318	3,141	307	60	−37	160	125	1,452	359	512	342	239	1,113	327	499	147	140
1967	12,044	1,708	3,472	3,581	3,283	291	71	−66	194	92	1,398	397	519	269	213	1,190	365	480	195	151
1968	12,989	1,875	3,643	3,990	3,480	572	173	140	213	46	1,586	392	535	408	251	1,232	374	493	216	150
Europe:																				
1960	6,691	49	1,763	3,804	1,075	962	(*)	273	607	82	769	10	91	487	181	397	11	55	241	90
1961	7,742	48	2,152	4,255	1,287	724	(*)	376	233	115	837	8	63	530	236	486	9	47	326	104
1962	8,930	50	2,385	4,883	1,612	868	3	229	453	183	844	5	60	496	283	526	7	63	334	122
1963	10,340	55	2,776	5,634	1,875	924	1	362	395	166	996	4	67	627	298	507	6	73	305	123
1964	12,129	56	3,122	6,587	2,364	1,388	2	414	619	353	1,115	4	8	782	321	659	5	64	427	163
1965	13,985	54	3,427	7,606	2,898	1,479	−1	342	760	378	1,176	8	−41	859	350	768	8	17	532	211
1966	16,212	54	3,981	8,879	3,297	1,812	1	636	899	277	1,161	10	−79	860	370	729	11	4	489	225
1967	17,926	61	4,423	9,798	3,645	1,480	7	545	683	244	1,143	6	−99	847	388	849	7	6	561	275
1968	19,386	61	4,640	10,778	3,908	995	−2	321	552	124	1,365	8	−134	1,038	453	915	6	4	587	318
Other areas:																				
1960	5,630	304	3,261	899	1,166	112	16	20	40	36	1,109	72	743	144	150	878	45	704	69	60
1961	6,134	347	3,536	959	1,292	354	29	254	34	37	1,173	52	821	141	159	994	39	773	108	74
1962	6,689	384	3,823	1,111	1,371	443	22	285	114	22	1,387	40	971	178	198	1,151	30	935	120	66
1963	7,411	492	4,106	1,329	1,514	452	53	273	109	17	1,518	38	1,076	218	186	1,211	25	1,018	89	79
1964	8,242	492	4,421	1,643	1,686	529	13	314	138	64	1,606	51	1,091	262	202	1,370	35	1,143	99	93
1965	9,285	552	4,969	1,916	1,848	756	45	530	125	56	1,755	75	1,175	268	237	1,497	58	1,184	124	131
1966	10,051	658	5,136	2,190	2,067	366	72	110	128	57	1,852	99	1,239	274	240	1,447	66	1,166	126	89
1967	11,418	764	5,690	2,694	2,270	981	78	502	331	69	2,167	102	1,494	327	243	1,689	70	1,371	141	106
1968	12,892	798	6,464	3,041	2,589	864	19	557	132	157	2,581	103	1,822	395	260	1,988	86	1,630	167	106

*Less than $500,000.   1. Includes "other Western Hemisphere."

earnings added about $0.4 billion to manufacturing investments, moderately above 1967.

Direct investment in Latin American manufacturing affiliates also rose significantly faster in 1968 than in 1967 as plant and equipment expenditures accelerated, particularly in Argentina, Brazil, Mexico, and Venezuela. Reinvested earnings rose particularly fast, with larger net capital outflows as well. In Australia the rise in investment was slower than in 1967 because of completion or near completion of large plant expansions in the primary and fabricated metals industries. The rate of investment in manufacturing affiliates in African and Asian developing countries dropped by about 50 percent as expenditures for plant and equipment showed marked decreases from earlier years.

Petroleum

In the petroleum industry, the increase in book value of direct investment was $1.4 billion in 1968, as compared with $1.2 billion in 1967. Most of the new investment involved capital outflows. Reinvested earnings were about $0.2 billion, only slightly higher than in 1967. That reinvested earnings are such a small proportion of the increase in direct investments reflects the fact that a major part of petroleum investment abroad is organized in the form of wholly owned branches in which all increases in investment are counted as a capital outflow.

Investment in Canadian enterprises continued to grow by about $0.3 billion, as the need for refining, marketing and producing facilities attracted additional U.S. capital and encouraged further reinvestment. The book value of U.S. investment in Latin American petroleum enterprises had been on the decline since 1961 but during 1968 the trend was reversed. About $0.2 billion of additional investments were made in Colombia, Bolivia, Ecuador, Panama, and the "other Western Hemisphere" countries for refinery, pipelines and marketing facilities. Investment in European petroleum affiliates increased by more than $0.2 billion.

Intensive development of offshore oil and gas resources added to investment in the United Kingdom and other North Sea countries, while refining and distribution facilities (including pipelines) increased petroleum investments in Germany and the Netherlands.

Petroleum investments in Africa rose by over $0.3 billion. More than two-thirds of this was invested in Libya, with West African countries receiving most of the rest. Petroleum investment in the Middle East rose by less than $0.1 billion in 1968, about the same as in 1967, as exploration and development activity continued to shift to other areas, especially to Africa and Latin America. In the Far East, Japanese petroleum affiliates attracted substantial amounts of investment funds and the remainder was spent to meet the demand for new and enlarged refining and marketing facilities in other Far Eastern countries.

Mining and other

The book value of U.S. direct investment in foreign mining enterprises rose $0.5 billion in 1968, about the same increase as in the preceding year. Reinvested earnings were about $0.1 billion. The rest was capital outflows, but over $0.1 billion of this represented the placement with U.S. purchasers (other than the parent company) of a new debt issue of a publicly owned Canadian mining company whose voting stock was more than 50 percent held by U.S. residents. The value of U.S. direct investments in Latin American mining affiliates increased during 1968 by almost $0.2 billion. The increase was concentrated in Mexico, Brazil, Chile, and Peru. U.S. direct investment in Australian mining ventures showed a relatively small increase as construction of some of the new

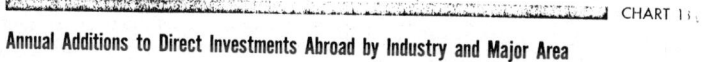

CHART 11

Annual Additions to Direct Investments Abroad by Industry and Major Area

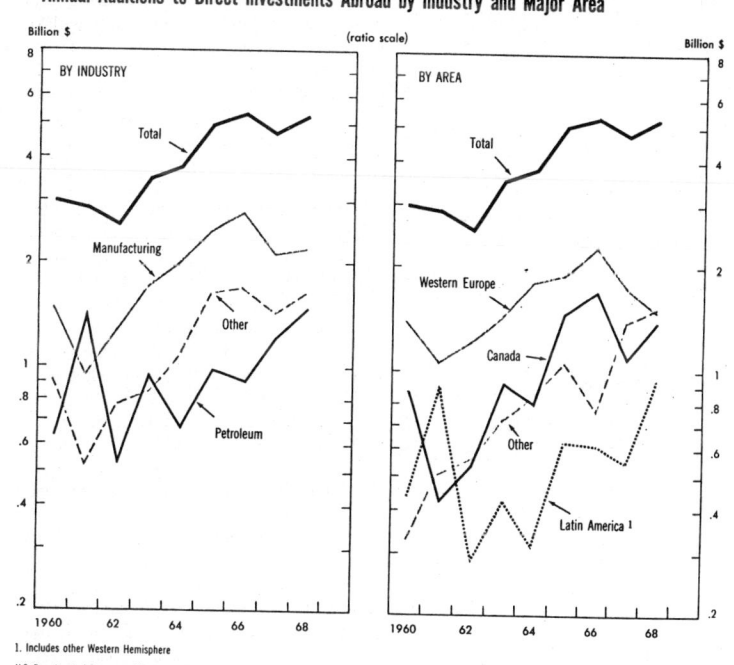

1. Includes other Western Hemisphere

U.S. Department of Commerce, Office of Business Economics

69-10-1

iron ore and bauxite mining projects were either completed or approaching completion.

U.S. direct investment in public utilities, trade and other industries increased during 1968 by over $1.1 billion, compared with only $0.9 billion in 1967. About one-half of this total reflects investments in the finance and service industries. Canada and Europe together received about two-thirds of

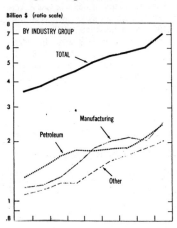

CHART 14

Earnings of Foreign Affiliates

Billion $ (ratio scale)

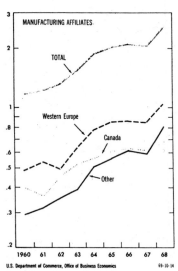

U.S. Department of Commerce, Office of Business Economics   69-10-14

these new investments reflecting acquisition and expansion of banking and other financial affiliates, as well as leasing and service facilities by computer and other heavy equipment firms. The primary reason for an increased investment in the public utility industry in Canada was the private placement of a $70 million debt issue of a U.S.-owned Canadian firm with U.S. investors other than its parent company.

Earnings

Earnings on U.S. direct investments abroad (not adjusted) in 1968 increased $1.0 billion to nearly $7.0 billion (table 7 and chart 14). As a result of the surge in earnings, the rate of return on all U.S. direct investments abroad recovered to almost 12 percent from the 1967 low of 11 percent, although it remained somewhat below the levels of the early 1960's (chart 15). The major explanation of the increase in both earnings and the rate of return was the widespread acceleration of economic growth abroad. Manufacturing and petroleum affiliates had particularly large increases in earnings and each accounted for about $2.5 billion of the total. Only mining affiliates, with earnings of $0.8 billion, showed a smaller increase than in 1967.

U.S. direct investments in Canada earned $1.5 billion in 1968, about $0.2 billion more than in 1967. Manufacturing contributed $0.7 billion of the total. Higher prices and increased sales raised the level of earnings for the paper and pulp industry. A large increase in exports of motor vehicles, parts, and accessories to the United States contributed to the steep rise in earnings for the Canadian transportation industry.

Earnings on U.S. investments in the Latin American republics totaled $1.4 billion in 1968, an increase of $0.2 billion over 1967. The manufacturing industry accounted for most of the increase. Unlike the other developing areas, Latin America had large increases in plant and equipment expenditures in manufacturing industries in the last few years, and this helped reverse the decline in earnings suffered in 1967. Manufacturing affiliates in

Argentina, Brazil, and Mexico had the largest gains.

Direct investments in Europe earned $1.4 billion in 1968, a $0.2 billion increase over 1967. Manufacturing affiliates, which account for the bulk of earnings, recovered from the business slowdown of 1967 and increased earnings by almost $0.2 billion. The petroleum industry in Europe had losses of over $0.1 billion, somewhat larger than the losses in 1967, as exploration and development expenditure in the North Sea increased. With the exception of France, all Common Market petroleum affiliates recorded losses from operations, in part reflecting the pricing arrangements by which international oil companies attribute earnings to production rather than marketing areas.

African affiliates earned $0.7 billion in 1968, a $0.3 billion increase over 1967. Petroleum accounted for $0.5 billion of total earnings and most of the increase reflected the unusually large

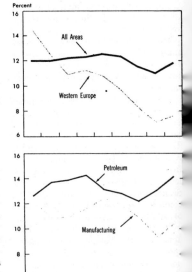

CHART 15

Rates of Return on U.S. Direct Investments Abroad

Percent

U.S. Department of Commerce, Office of Business Economics   69-10-

growth of oil and gas production, especially in Libya. New producing oil fields in other African countries also were beginning to show profits and were offsetting losses from continuing exploration and development expenditures.

Middle East direct investments, almost entirely petroleum, earned $1.1 billion in 1968, an increase of only $0.1 billion over 1967. The increase in 1967 was larger than in 1968 despite the adverse impact of the Middle East war in June 1967.

Direct investment income

About half of the $1.0 billion increase in earnings was allocated to income, which rose $0.5 billion to $5.0 billion in 1968. However, income receipts were smaller than they would have been (and

reinvested earnings higher) as a result of arrangements made by U.S. corporations with the Office of Foreign Direct Investments to substitute repatriation of funds held abroad (the proceeds of foreign borrowing) in place of income receipts.

Direct investment income from petroleum affiliates was nearly $2.3 billion, almost half of the total income in 1968. Most of the $0.3 billion rise in these income receipts reflected increased production and profits in African countries, primarily Libya. Petroleum income from Africa was still far below the $1.1 billion of receipts from more productive but older fields in Middle Eastern countries. Income from petroleum affiliates in Venezuela was practically unchanged at $0.4 billion.

Income receipts from manufacturing

affiliates in 1968 totaled nearly $1.3 billion. This was an increase of less than $0.1 billion over 1967, as most of the $0.5 billion rise in manufacturing earnings was reinvested. About $0.6 billion of the income came from Europe, $0.3 billion from Canada and $0.2 billion from Latin America.

U.S. Portfolio Investments Abroad

During 1968, the value of U.S. holdings of foreign bonds and stocks in-

Table 10.—Acquisitions and Sales by American Companies of Foreign Enterprises [1] by Area and Industry

[Millions of dollars]

Area and industry	1967			1968		
	Acquisitions	Sales	Net	Acquisitions	Sales	Net
All areas, total....	508	318	190	765	196	569
Petroleum......	22	......	22	32	7	25
Manufacturing.	365	135	230	625	138	487
Other industries......	121	183	−62	108	50	58
Canada, total.....	114	38	76	118	3	115
Petroleum......	2	......	2	8	......	8
Manufacturing.	41	38	3	89	(*)	89
Other industries......	71	......	71	21	2	19
Europe, total....	312	75	237	511	145	366
Petroleum......	12	......	12	4	1	3
Manufacturing.	270	67	203	460	127	333
Other industries......	30	8	22	47	16	31
Other areas, total.	82	205	−123	137	48	89
Petroleum......	8	......	8	20	6	14
Manufacturing.	54	30	24	76	11	65
Other industries......	20	175	−155	40	32	8

*Less than $500,000.
1. Includes acquisitions and sales of minority interests.

Table 9.—Net Capital Outflows to Manufacturing Affiliates Abroad by Industry

[Millions of dollars]

Area and year	Manufacturing total	Food products	Paper and allied products	Chemicals and allied products	Rubber products	Primary and fabricated metals	Machinery except electrical	Electrical machinery	Transportation equipment	Other industries
All areas total:										
1964..........	1,034.3	74.8	9.1	302.7	2.1	69.8	117.9	45.8	207.1	204.9
1965..........	1,525.1	115.6	99.1	292.0	16.4	83.7	285.5	96.3	405.5	130.9
1966..........	1,752.0	107.7	151.0	503.3	19.0	134.4	214.9	134.4	317.3	196.9
1967 ᴿ........	1,229.4	83.7	68.2	427.7	24.6	242.1	115.6	114.7	49.9	102.8
1968 ᴾ........	905.3	101.1	−7.4	277.5	10.0	151.6	70.0	−7.0	−2.3	311.8
Canada:										
1964..........	140.0	29.0	−8.6	32.2	−7.1	−3.9	15.3	11.6	48.4	23.0
1965..........	304.7	17.7	62.5	70.0	5.1	6.5	27.4	12.7	173.2	19.8
1966..........	566.0	16.8	125.8	90.0	−2.4	23.6	32.3	28.5	246.1	5.3
1967..........	19.8	−10.3	48.3	68.3	6.9	−23.4	1.9	.4	−73.0	.6
1968..........	8.7	20.6	−17.3	21.9	−7.5	29.3	.1	−.6	−103.8	66.0
Latin America: [1]										
1964..........	137.2	−9.2	2.1	73.6	8.5	7.9	9.5	−10.3	30.1	25.1
1965..........	245.4	50.8	18.6	82.0	−1.1	19.5	.5	10.5	38.1	26.5
1966..........	169.5	10.7	.2	90.5	5.2	14.0	13.2	8.7	−22.1	30.5
1967..........	193.7	12.3	2.8	84.9	5.8	33.5	17.3	1.3	−4.4	40.2
1968..........	213.3	9.9	−.6	47.8	.4	22.2	4.1	8.5	57.4	63.6
Europe:										
1964..........	618.6	41.6	13.6	163.0	−.3	30.4	65.3	38.0	127.4	139.6
1965..........	760.5	40.8	12.8	97.0	2.4	60.2	239.6	53.4	176.0	78.3
1966..........	898.7	50.9	21.5	279.5	15.8	75.3	156.9	84.0	91.4	123.5
1967..........	683.3	64.5	11.5	201.2	1.9	100.2	64.7	108.4	82.1	48.8
1968..........	551.7	54.0	9.9	154.1	5.0	89.8	67.8	−31.0	26.8	175.4
Africa:										
1964..........	18.6	2.5	.6	2.9	−.5	11.5	4.3	−.3	−3.1	.7
1965..........	39.6	1.2	2.6	2.4	1.0	17.3	7.3	(*)	7.2	.5
1966..........	18.7	2.5	1.8	.6	−1.3	3.7	4.8	(*)	2.3	4.2
1967..........	28.2	−.7	1.9	5.2	1.8	−2.7	4.2	.6	15.5	2.3
1968..........	9.3	1.7	−1.3	.4	7.3	−5.0	3.2	7.0	−2.7	−1.3
Asia:										
1964..........	60.6	4.6	1.7	24.8	(*)	3.3	11.4	5.8	.3	8.7
1965..........	57.8	−1.2	2.0	25.1	−1.8	.9	6.5	17.4	1.5	7.4
1966..........	58.0	6.6	1.3	17.7	2.3	3.7	8.3	15.9	.1	2.1
1967..........	106.0	12.2	2.0	55.2	.7	3.5	21.1	3.5	1.1	6.6
1968..........	48.7	6.8	2.0	27.8	−.2	2.4	−7.6	6.5	1.8	9.1
Oceania:										
1964..........	59.2	6.3	−.3	6.2	1.5	20.6	12.1	1.0	4.0	7.8
1965..........	27.0	6.4	.5	15.5	10.7	−20.7	4.2	2.4	9.5	−1.6
1966..........	51.0	20.2	.8	16.0	−.6	14.1	−.6	−2.7	−.5	4.3
1967..........	198.4	5.8	1.7	12.9	7.4	131.0	6.3	.6	28.5	4.1
1968..........	73.7	8.1	(*)	25.5	5.0	12.9	2.4	2.6	18.1	−1.0

ᴿ Revised.   ᴾ Preliminary.   *Less than $50,000.
1. Includes "other Western Hemisphere."

Table 11.—Net Capital Flows Between Primary and Secondary Foreign Affiliates

[Millions of dollars; net inflow (−)]

	1963	1964	1965	1966	1967	1968ᴾ
Canada............	−4	3	−8	16	1	−1
Latin America......	−1	−2	−3	−24	1	(*)
Argentina........	−14	−14	−5	4	−1	−3
Mexico..........	−5	3	−5	2	3	1
Panama..........	14	12	8	7	10	−2
Other Latin America......	4	−3	−1	−37	−11	4
Europe............	24	19	43	30	10	−5
France..........	−5	−2	22	−6	6	−3
Germany........	−20	−5	−22	−16	−3	−2
Italy............	−9	−5	−9	−7	13	8
Switzerland....	105	60	77	28	30	−11
United Kingdom..........	−4	(*)	−2	47	−15	4
Other Europe...	−43	−29	−22	−16	−21	−1
Other countries.....	−19	−20	−32	−22	−12	6

ᴾ Preliminary.
* Less than $500,000.

creased $2.2 billion to $18.2 billion, after the $1.2 billion increase in 1967 (table 3). Purchases of newly issued foreign securities totaled $1.7 billion in 1968 (table 13), up only slightly from the $1.6 billion of purchases in 1967. Almost all the new securities purchased were exempt from the Interest Equalization Tax. Purchases of new Canadian issues (including the first Government of Canada issue since 1963) amounted to nearly $1.0 billion, down slightly from 1967. New issues by international organizations, on the other hand, rose over $0.1 billion above the 1967 level. In the first half of 1969, particularly in the second quarter, new issues were at a slightly lower rate than in 1968, with Canadian issues somewhat higher and issues of international organizations somewhat lower.

Redemption of outstanding issues

totaled about $0.5 billion in 1968 and net purchases of outstanding securities were small. Thus, the balance of payments outflow for purchasing foreign securities totaled $1.3 billion. The remaining $0.9 billion increase in the value of U.S. investment in foreign securities reflected a $1.1 billion increase in the value of foreign stock holdings as foreign stock prices rose, and a $0.2 billion decline in the value of U.S. holdings of foreign bonds as interest rates abroad rose.

In 1967, the decline in value of outstanding U.S. foreign bond holdings was $1.1 billion. This decline, in combination with a smaller increase in the value of foreign stock holdings was the major reason the increase in U.S. portfolio investment was less than in 1968.

Foreign Direct Investment in the United States

The book value of foreign direct investments in the United States totaled $10.8 billion at yearend 1968, up $0.9 billion during the year (table 14). This was about the same increase as in 1967. The capital inflow in 1968 was $0.3 billion, and reinvested earnings totaled $0.5 billion, both higher than in 1967. Valuation adjustments—mostly on securities held by foreign-owned insurance companies—on the other hand, were somewhat less favorable in 1968.

The net capital inflow in 1968 resulted mainly from $0.4 billion of new foreign direct investments, i.e., the acquisition or establishment of companies. (Changes in intercompany accounts during the year were nominal.) About half of the new investment represented the purchase by an international petroleum company of additional stock in its U.S. subsidiary. In addition, with the approval of Japanese financial authorities, parent organizations in that country made additional equity investments of almost $0.1 billion in their U.S. trading subsidiaries, many times greater than in preceding years. These relatively large new investments in 1968 were partly offset by foreign liquidations of ownership in U.S. companies of over $0.1 billion. More than half of this amount was the sale of a single foreign-owned company to U.S. interests. (See table 15 for a breakdown by area and by industry of foreign direct investment at yearend 1968.)

Earnings from foreign direct investments in the United States in 1968 totaled $0.9 billion, 8 percent above the previous year. Companies in manufacturing and petroleum industries accounted for more than three-quarters of total earnings in 1968. More than 80 percent of earnings were concentrated in companies with owners in the United Kingdom, Canada, Netherlands, and Switzerland.

Table 12.—Direct Investment Receipts of Royalties and Fees,[1] by Areas and Major Industries

[Millions of dollars]

Area and industry	1967 [r]	1968 [p]		
		Total	Royalties, license fees, and rentals	Management fees and service charges
All areas, total	1,136	1,279	540	739
Petroleum	156	165	17	148
Manufacturing	728	823	449	374
Trade	110	112	43	69
Other industries	143	180	31	149
Canada, total	243	268	81	187
Petroleum	17	15	(*)	15
Manufacturing	186	202	73	130
Trade	13	16	6	10
Other industries	27	35	2	33
Latin America, total [2]	192	228	75	153
Petroleum	32	36	5	30
Manufacturing	105	119	56	63
Trade	24	27	9	18
Other industries	32	47	5	42
Europe: Common Market, total	235	281	178	103
Petroleum	18	23	(*)	23
Manufacturing	177	214	166	48
Trade	27	27	8	19
Other industries	14	16	3	13
Other Europe, total	238	255	128	126
Petroleum	21	20	2	18
Manufacturing	173	186	102	83
Trade	22	16	12	4
Other industries	23	33	12	21
Other areas, total	227	247	78	169
Petroleum	68	71	9	62
Manufacturing	88	102	51	50
Trade	24	25	8	18
Other industries	48	49	10	39

[p] Preliminary.   [r] Revised.   * Less than $500,000.
1. Excludes foreign film rentals.
2. Includes "Other Western Hemisphere."

Table 13.—Newly Issued Foreign Securities Sold to U.S. Residents
[Millions of dollars]

Issuer	1960	1961	1962	1963	1964	1965	1966	1967	1968	1969 (Jan.–June)
Total [1]	554	523	1,076	1,250	1,063	1,206	1,210	1,619	1,659	8
Canada	221	237	458	693	700	709	922	1,007	946	5
Central government			125	125					86	
Provincial government-guaranteed	82	22	70	283	332	244	341	601	508	2
Municipal authorities	100	26	71	32	163	54	141	160	101	
Corporate issues	39	189	192	253	205	411	440	246	251	2
Japan	15	61	101	164		52	4	14	3	
International organizations	97	12	84		4	179	80	246	390	1
Less developed countries	171	113	180	104	323	170	189	352	320	1
Other developed countries	50	100	253	289	2 36	3 96	15			
Memorandum items:										
U.S. direct investment enterprises total [1]	14	75	76	41	67	188	302	45	354	
In Canada	14	72	73	29	67	156	257	45	291	
In less developed countries		3	3	11			19	32	63	
In other developed countries				1		13	13			

1. New issues of U.S. direct investment enterprises placed with other than parent are not included with new issues [ ] are recorded in the direct investment account.
2. Includes a $7 million placement exempt from IET.
3. Includes a $73 million placement exempt from IET.

Income paid to foreign parents of U.S. companies was $0.4 billion in 1968. This was only slightly more than in 1967. Since 1968 earnings of U.S. subsidiaries were substantially higher than 1967, reinvested earnings in 1968 were correspondingly higher.

Foreign Portfolio Investment in the United States

In 1968, the value of foreign portfolio assets in the United States rose an extraordinary $6.1 billion and totaled $23.8 billion at yearend, when they comprised 29 percent of the calculated value of total U.S. liabilities to foreigners (tables 2 and 3). In addition to an increase of $1.7 billion in the value of outstanding securities, due primarily to appreciation in the value of U.S. equities, capital inflows amounted to an unprecedented $4.4 billion. (Foreign portfolio assets consist of holdings of U.S. corporate bonds and stocks, municipal and state bonds, and U.S. Government-backed agency bonds, but exclude

Treasury issues.) In 1967, the capital inflow was only $1.0 billion and the total rise in the value of foreign portfolio assets was only $3.0 billion.

Stock purchases

Foreign investors increased their net purchases of U.S. corporate stocks from $0.7 billion in 1967 to $2.1 billion during 1968. A good part of the increase was associated with the significant expansion of overseas activities by U.S. security dealers and investment funds, complemented by an apparent shift in European investor attitudes in favor of equity investments. The strong performance of the U.S. stock market was also a factor, although prices in European stock markets were rising at least as buoyantly. Unsettling political disturbances, such as the Middle East crisis, the invasion of Czechoslovakia, and the May strikes in France, also encouraged the inflow. In some European countries with large net purchases, special circumstances prevailed. For example, Germany was experiencing a

high rate of savings and simultaneously promoting capital outflows.

During the first half of 1969, however, foreign net purchases declined and by midyear became net sales. This decline was partly associated with the weak performance of the U.S. stock market, as well as anticipations of a slowdown of the U.S. economy with a consequent reduction in profits. In addition, high rates in the Euro-dollar market offered an attractive alternative investment.

Bond purchases

Through 1968, foreigners continued to add to their portfolio holdings of U.S. bonds (excluding Treasury issues). There was a net capital inflow of $2.3 billion, partially offset by a $0.2 billion reduction in the value of outstanding holdings as U.S. bond prices declined. The net increase of $2.1 billion raised foreign holdings of U.S. bonds to $4.2 billion at the end of 1968. International organizations, which had borrowed heavily in the U.S. bond market during the year, reinvested $0.1 billion of the

Table 14.—Foreign Direct Investments in the United States, Selected Data for 1966, 1967 and 1968, by Country and Industry

[Millions of dollars]

| | Value at yearend | | | Capital flow | | | | | | Earnings,[1] income,[1] and undistributed profits | | | | | |
| | | | | 1967 | | | 1968 ᵖ | | | 1967 | | | 1968 ᵖ | | |
	1966	1967	1968 ᵖ	Total	New invest-ments [2]	Other	Total	New invest-ments [2]	Other	Earnings	Income	Undistri-buted profits	Earnings	Income	Undistri-buted profits
Total	9,054	9,923	10,815	251	133	118	319	426	−107	804	381	440	868	388	488
By area:															
Canada	2,439	2,575	2,659	9	19	−10	−26	49	−75	146	84	80	152	64	102
United Kingdom	2,864	3,156	3,409	65	21	44	114	109	5	257	124	123	271	149	108
Other Europe	3,409	3,848	4,341	185	75	110	183	194	−11	386	163	229	416	159	263
Belgium	193	228	273	18		18	25		25	23	9	17	22	5	19
France	215	265	288	26	2	24	10	(*)	10	26	12	16	23	11	13
Germany	247	318	387	65	37	28	34	52	−18	30	14	16	43	7	35
Italy	87	86	92	−8	2	−10	2		2	8	2	6	5	1	4
Netherlands	1,402	1,508	1,750	12	(*)	12	141	138	3	177	80	93	192	87	102
Sweden	217	239	205	3		3	−74		−74	14	7	7	12	7	4
Switzerland	949	1,096	1,238	63	34	29	51	4	47	102	36	71	113	39	81
Other countries	100	109	108	6		6	−6		−6	6	3	3	6	2	5
Japan	103	108	181	−2	18	−20	60	74	−14	12	8	7	26	15	13
Latin America	177	176	164	−1		−1	−12		−12	(*)	(*)	(*)	(*)	(*)	(*)
Other countries	61	59	61	−5	(*)	−5	(*)	(*)	(*)	2	1	1ᵖ	3	1	2
By industry:															
Petroleum	1,740	1,885	2,261	8	(*)	8	231	212	19	237	90	137	263	109	143
Manufacturing	3,789	4,181	4,475	138	84	54	−23	81	−104	380	132	255	410	137	280
Trade	739	848	938	67	21	46	32	67	−35	70	28	42	81	25	57
Insurance	³ 2,072	³ 2,193	³ 2,305	36		36	5		5	85	85		73	73	
Other finance	(⁴)	(⁴)	(⁴)	−20	2	−22	47	60	−13	⁵ 23	⁵ 20	10	⁵ 38	⁵ 28	13
Other industries	714	816	836	22	26	−4	27	6	21	9	26	−4	3	16	−5

ᵖ Preliminary.   *Less than $500,000.

1. "Earnings" represents the foreign share in corporate and branch profits; "income" is the amount distributed, after withholding taxes, as dividends, interest, and branch profits. See footnote 2 on table 5 for an explanation of the relation between income, earnings, and undistributed profits.

2. "New investments" consists of the first reported capital inflow to establish or acquire a new company or operation in the United States and the cost of acquisition of additional shares of existing companies.

3. Includes market revaluations of securities held by insurance companies.

4. Included in "insurance."

5. Interest paid by agency banks in the United States to foreign home offices have been excluded from direct investment totals.

proceeds of their borrowings in U.S. agency bonds. However, the major portion of the increase was due to U.S. corporate bond placements abroad (table 16).

After World War II, foreigners made few purchases of U.S. corporate bonds until 1965 when the need for foreign funds due to voluntary restraints on capital outflows for U.S. direct investments abroad induced U.S. corporations to enter the emerging international capital market in Europe—the Euro-bond market. From midyear 1965 through 1967, U.S. corporations were able to raise over $1.2 billion by issuing various debt instruments in this relatively new market. In 1968, when the Direct Investment Program was tightened and made mandatory (as discussed in connection with direct investment abroad), U.S. corporations, in order to increase direct investments, sharply increased their foreign bond placements to an unprecedented $2.1 billion. This was nearly one-half the $4.7 billion of all new issues in the Euro-bond market in 1968.

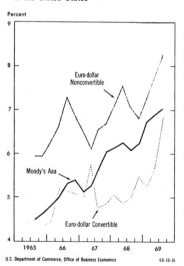

Interest Cost on Bonds Placed Abroad by U.S. Incorporated Companies Compared With Average Yields on Corporate Bonds in the United States

U.S. Department of Commerce, Office of Business Economics   69-10-16

To hold interest cost down and yet compete for available funds, over $1.5 billion of U.S. issues were convertible into common stock. Interest costs on such issues were 1 to 2 percent below nonconvertible issues in this market (see chart 16). The success of the convertible feature can be chiefly attributed to the good performance of the U.S. stock market during the year. Toward the end of 1968, interest rates on convertible issues moved up, partly reflecting the uncertainties in the U.S. stock market, and new issues of convertible bonds fell off.

At the same time, however, U.S. corporations increased placements in the low cost domestic bond market in Germany as authorities encouraged capital outflows. In 1968, these borrowings amounted to $0.3 billion of which about 90 percent occurred after August. Partly because of the strength of the German mark, interest costs there were as much as 1 to 1½ percent less than rates on nonconvertible dollar issues in the Euro-bond market. Placements by U.S. corporations were also somewhat higher in Switzerland (where interest rates were low) as the Swiss authorities somewhat relaxed their restrictions on foreign issues.

Because of certain tax considerations, U.S. corporations also established Netherland Antilles financial subsidiaries during the year to raise money in the Euro-bond market. Such securities usually have the guarantee of the parent and are often convertible into the stock of the U.S. company. These issues are considered net purchases of U.S. obligations only to the extent that the finance subsidiaries transfer the proceeds to the U.S. parent company.

In the first half of 1969, U.S. corporate Euro-bond issues declined, averaging $280 million a quarter compared to $550 million a quarter in 1968. Several factors explain the decline. Not the least is the high level of unutilized proceeds from earlier issues and the large leeway in quotas under the Direct Investment Program. In addition, the rates on Euro-bond issues rose sharply as European capital markets gradually tightened. Speculation that the mark would be revalued up-

ward also discouraged placements in Germany; mark issues dropped to $63 million in the first quarter of 1969 and zero in the following quarter. Another important factor was the increasing weakness of the U.S. stock market which reduced foreign demand for convertible issues. This was particularly noticeable in the second quarter of 1969 when only $90 million of such issues were placed.

Table 15.—Value of Foreign Direct Investments in the United States by Major Industry and Country—End of 1968

[Millions of dollars]

	Total	Manufacturing	Finance and insurance	Petroleum	Other
All areas	10,815	4,475	2,305	2,261	1,774
Canada	2,659	1,413	376	100	770
United Kingdom	3,409	1,076	1,239	749	345
Other Europe	4,341	1,865	616	1,397	463
Netherlands	1,750	426	54	1,215	55
Switzerland	1,238	863	331	....	44
Other Countries	1,353	576	231	182	364
Other areas	406	121	74	15	196

Table 16.—Foreign Security Placements by U.S.-Incorporated Companies, by Type

[Millions of dollars]

	Straight debt: Payable in—			Convertible: Payable in—			Total [1]
	Dollars	Deutsche marks	Swiss francs	Dollars	Deutsche marks	British sterling	
1965	67	55	.....	75	.....	.....	197
III	20	.....	.....	.....	.....	.....	20
IV	47	55	.....	75	.....	.....	177
1966	161	56	10	182	190	.....	599
I	55	.....	10	120	.....	.....	185
II	51	.....	.....	62	180	.....	293
III	10	25	.....	.....	.....	.....	35
IV	45	31	.....	.....	10	.....	86
1967	225	15	33	177	.....	.....	450
I	60	.....	11	20	.....	.....	91
II	75	15	11	10	.....	.....	111
III	70	.....	11	50	.....	.....	131
IV	20	.....	.....	97	.....	.....	117
1968	278	277	94	1,540	.....	.....	2,189
I	90	.....	12	494	.....	.....	596
II	15	19	41	526	.....	.....	601
III	75	110	14	406	.....	.....	605
IV	98	148	27	114	.....	.....	387
1969*	85	63	41	323	.....	44	556
I	85	63	27	232	.....	.....	407
II	.....	.....	14	91	.....	44	149

* Six-month total.
1. These amounts differ from balance of payments figures which are net of placement costs.

THE INTERNATIONAL INVESTMENT POSITION OF THE UNITED STATES:

Developments in 1969

David T. Devlin
and
George R. Kruer

By DAVID T. DEVLIN and GEORGE R. KRUER

The International Investment Position of the United States: Developments in 1969

The net international investment position of the United States improved by $1.5 billion in 1969 as total U.S. assets rose $11.1 billion and total liabilities rose only $9.6 billion. The rise in the value of U.S. direct investments abroad, including reinvested earnings, was $5.8 billion, slightly more than the rise in 1968. However, the net flow of corporate funds was slightly more favorable to the balance of payments than in 1968 because earnings on direct investments rose sharply The ratio of U.S. reserve assets to liabilities to foreign official agencies moved favorably, reflecting the 1969 surplus on the official reserve transactions balance; at the same time, the ratio of U.S. reserve assets to liquid liabilities continued to fall, reflecting the large liquidity deficit.

TOTAL international assets of the United States—including official reserve assets—rose $11,064 million in 1969 and U.S. liabilities to foreigners rose $9,542 million. As a result, the net international investment position improved by $1,522 million, which was substantially greater than the small improvement of only $152 million in 1968. At yearend 1969, total assets exceeded total liabilities by $67,046 million.

This article first considers the factors accounting for the recent changes in the U.S. net international investment position (table 1). The composition of the shifts in the total value of assets and liabilities from yearend to yearend is then discussed, noting the contribu-

NOTE.—Significant contributions were also made by Julius Freidlin, Russell Scholl and Zalie Warner.

tions of balance of payments flows, reinvested earnings, and valuation changes, as well as changes in coverage and statistical discrepancies (tables 2 and 3). In addition, the changing structure of the relation between the liquidity of U.S. assets and the liquidity of U.S. liabilities is analyzed (table 4 and chart 9).

A major part of the article is devoted to discussion of U.S. direct investment abroad and the flows associated with such investments. A summary is given in table 5 and detailed figures for 1969 are published here for the first time in tables 5 through 11. Foreign direct investment in the United States (tables 12 and 13) and portfolio investments (tables 14 and 15) are also discussed.

Changes in the Net International Position

Changes in the net international investment position of the United States reflect three major factors (table 1). The first is net recorded balance of payments capital flows, which must be equal to the current account (the balance on goods, services, and unilateral transfers) adjusted for errors and omissions.[1] In effect, a surplus on the current account adjusted for errors and omissions allows an improvement in our net investment position. The second is reinvested earnings of U.S. affiliates abroad minus reinvested earnings of foreign enterprises in the United States. Earnings of U.S. affiliates abroad not sent back to the United States as income (and thus not included in the current account) improve our invest-

[1]. If the errors and omissions in the balance of payments accounts could be identified, a part would presumably go into recorded capital flows and a part into recorded goods, services, and unilateral transfer accounts. The two accounts would then be equal.

ment position. The third factor is the net change in valuation of outstanding U.S. investments abroad and foreign investment in the United States (including adjustments in the various series for changes in coverage and statistical discrepancies); these are also not included in the balance of payments accounts. Essentially, we improve our net investment position by transferring abroad real goods and services or by reinvesting foreign earnings abroad, but the position is also affected by changes in valuation of outstanding assets and liabilities.

From the mid-1950's through 1966, we had a rather consistent rise in our net investment position, which largely reflected a strong trade balance and growing income on investments (and thus a surplus on the current account), as well as a moderate growth in reinvested earnings; these factors were only partly offset by adverse valuation adjustments. However, in 1967 (when the valuation adjustment was particularly adverse), and in 1968 (when the trade balance dropped sharply), the net investment position rose only nominally.

Our net position showed a $1.5 billion improvement in 1969. Net reinvested earnings amounted to $2.1 billion and, more importantly, there was an extremely favorable impact of over $3.0 billion due to valuation and price changes affecting outstanding portfolio holdings. (In 1968, valuation adjustments had been unfavorable.) As prices in the U.S. stock market declined in 1969, the value of outstanding U.S. stocks held by foreigners declined almost $3.0 billion, thus reducing U.S. liabilities to foreigners. In addition, rising long-term

21

interest rates in the United States reduced bond prices and the value of outstanding foreign holdings of U.S. bonds fell by almost another $1.0 billion. These shifts were only partly offset by a $1.0 billion decline in the value of outstanding foreign bonds held by U.S. residents which resulted from rising interest rates abroad. (Valuation adjustments to outstanding U.S. holdings of foreign stocks were small.)

On the other hand, the net investment position was adversely affected by the $3.7 billion net inflow of capital recorded in the balance of payments. This, in turn, reflected a $2.8 billion negative errors and omissions (a sharp deterioration from 1968) and a $0.9 billion deficit on current account ($0.5 billion more than in 1968). The deterioration in the current account largely reflected a sharp increase in payments to foreigners on their dollar holdings due mainly to the sharp rise in U.S. interest rates; there was little change in the trade balance.

There are reasons to believe that our investment position improved by more than the recorded amount in 1969. Available figures on Eurodollar market holdings suggest that a substantial part of the increased outflow from the United States on errors and omissions reflected flows of U.S. funds to the Eurodollar market. Such flows would increase U.S. assets abroad, but are not reflected in the recorded capital flows nor in the investment position. If rough allowance is made for such unrecorded flows to the Eurodollar market, it appears that the net investment position might have improved by perhaps as much as $3.0 billion, rather than $1.5 billion.

While the net change in our investment position can be considered to be accounted for by the factors just discussed (the current account adjusted for errors and omissions, reinvested earning and valuation adjustments), capital flows, of course, may have a major impact on trade, services, and earnings. To the extent this occurs, the change in the net investment position is not determined independently of capital flows. On the other hand, an outflow of capital from the United States does not necessarily result in a

net change in the U.S. international investment position unless one of the factors mentioned also is influenced. These questions were discussed more fully in the Investment Position article in the October 1969 SURVEY.

Changes in U.S. Assets and Liabilities

The composition of changes in assets and liabilities was quite different in 1969 than in 1968 (tables 2 and 3). The increase in U.S. nonliquid assets abroad was $9.8 billion in 1969, about $1.0 billion lower than in 1968. Outflows of capital recorded in the balance of payments were slightly lower in 1969. More importantly, price adjustment to the value of outstanding foreign securities held by U.S. residents was large and adverse in 1969 while it was favorable in 1968. This shift offset the favorable impact of an increase in reinvested earnings. As a result, the increase in assets due to factors other than capital flows was only $2,393 million in 1969, compared with $3,125 million in 1968.

The increase in U.S. nonliquid liabilities was only $1.2 billion in 1969, following a $11.0 billion increase in 1968. This $10 billion shift reflected a sharp fall in the inflow of nonliquid

funds from abroad as recorded in the balance of payments, and a large swing in price adjustments to foreign portfolio holdings in the United States, mostly reflecting the decline in prices of U.S. stocks.

The lower inflow of funds from abroad reflected smaller purchases of private U.S. securities by foreigners, and very large adverse shifts by foreign official agencies in their holdings of long-term time deposits at U.S. banks (table 2, line 33) and of "nonliquid" U.S. Treasury securities (table 2, line 37). These transactions by foreign official agencies are some of the "special financial transactions" which have distorted the liquidity balance in recent years.

Shifts in liquid assets and liabilities of the United States in 1968 and 1969 were even more striking. In the earlier year, U.S. liquid assets—i.e., U.S. monetary reserves—rose $880 million, while liquid liabilities rose only $495 million, producing a $385 million improvement in our net liquidity position. (The change in liquid liabilities included a $214 million adjustment for changes in coverage. Excluding this adjustment, the balance of payments flows were an $880 million increase in reserves and a $709 million increase in liquid liabilities. The difference is equal

Table 1.—Factors Accounting for Changes in the Net International Investment Position of the United States

[Millions of dollars]

Item	Average			1966 r	1967 r	1968 r	1969 p
	1951-55	1956-60	1961-65				
Balance on goods, services, and unilateral transfers (surplus (+))	-498	1,002	3,838	2,492	2,243	-336	-885
Adjustment for: Errors and omissions (receipts (+))	300	173	-910	-514	-1,088	-514	-2,841
Equals: Net recorded balance of payments capital flows (outflow (+))	-197	1,175	2,927	1,978	1,155	-848	-3,726
Change in U.S. assets (increase (+))	1,002	3,283	5,097	5,299	8,008	8,561	8,604
Change in U.S. liabilities (increase (-))	-1,199	-2,108	-2,170	-3,321	-6,853	-9,409	-12,330
Plus: Net reinvested earnings (increase (+))	670	990	1,072	1,400	1,158	1,687	2,101
Plus: Changes in net valuation and other adjustments	-370	1 -699	r -249	-10	-2,006	-687	3,147
of which: Changes in coverage and statistical discrepancies	n.a.	n.a.	n.a.	25	297	198	-188
Equals: Change in net international investment position of the United States	102	1,466	r 3,426	3,367	307	152	1,522
Change in U.S. assets (increase (+))	2,143	4,138	r 6,938	5,037	9,591	11,687	11,064
Change in U.S. liabilities (increase (-))	-2,041	-2,673	r -3,511	-1,670	-9,284	-11,535	-9,542
Addendum: Net international investment position of the United States at end of period 2	37,237	44,566	r 61,698	65,065	65,372	65,524	67,046

r Revised. p Preliminary. n.a. Not available.
1. Includes an adjustment for direct investment in Cuba omitted from the data effective 1960.
2. The net position at the end of a given period is equal to the position at the end of the preceding period plus the total net change during the period.

Table 2.—International Investment Position of the United States at Yearend‡

[Millions of dollars]

Line	Type of investment	Total‡				Western Europe		Canada		Japan		Latin American Republics and other Western Hemisphere		Other foreign countries		International organizations and unallocated‡	
		1960 [1]	1965 [1]	1968 ʳ	1969 ᵖ	1968 ʳ	1969 ᵖ	1968 ʳ	1969 ᵖ	1968 ʳ	1969 ᵖ	1968 ʳ	1969 ᵖ	1968 ʳ	1969 ᵖ	1968 ʳ	1969 ᵖ
1	NET INTERNATIONAL INVESTMENT POSITION OF THE UNITED STATES	44,556	61,698	65,524	67,046	−8,521	−14,090	20,800	22,550	1,453	1,591	16,100	16,863	20,881	23,232	14,812	16,898
2	U.S. assets abroad	85,768	120,457	146,772	157,836	39,721	41,373	31,810	34,323	5,732	6,469	24,923	26,261	27,034	29,542	17,552	19,867
3	Nonliquid	66,409	105,007	131,062	140,872	36,198	38,593	31,806	34,323	5,731	6,468	24,923	26,261	27,034	29,542	5,370	5,684
4	Private	49,430	81,528	102,519	1¹0,152	28,177	30,310	31,795	34,308	5,005	5,737	19,653	20,439	13,777	14,972	4,113	4,384
5	Long-term	44,447	71,375	89,529	96,029	24,738	26,721	30,581	32,600	1,682	2,110	16,103	16,946	12,314	13,266	4,112	4,384
6	Direct investments [2]	31,865	49,474	64,983	70,763	19,407	21,554	19,535	21,075	1,050	1,218	13,101	13,811	9,160	10,043	³ 2,731	³ 3,060
7	Foreign dollar bonds	4,891	9,115	10,565	10,579	652	583	5,995	6,110	309	265	721	688	1,507	1,609	1,381	1,324
8	Other foreign bonds	633	1,050	1,139	1,133	104	24	741	802	(*)	(*)	211	242	83	65		
9	Foreign corporate stocks	3,984	5,048	6,452	6,953	2,899	2,816	3,201	3,406	74	398	101	114	177	219		
10	Claims reported by U.S. banks	1,698	4,317	3,367	3,037	527	454	228	208	122	88	1,377	1,330	1,113	957		
11	Other [4]	1,376	ʳ 2,371	3,023	3,564	1,149	1,290	881	999	127	141	592	761	274	373		
12	Short-term	4,983	10,153	12,990	14,123	3,439	3,589	1,214	1,708	3,323	3,627	3,550	3,493	1,463	1,706	1	(*)
13	Claims reported by U.S. banks	3,594	7,735	8,711	9,606	1,181	1,418	533	826	3,114	3,372	2,889	2,805	994	1,185		(*)
14	Other [4]	1,389	2,418	4,279	4,517	2,258	2,171	681	882	209	255	661	688	469	521	1	(*)
15	U.S. Government	16,979	23,479	28,543	30,720	8,021	8,283	11	15	726	731	5,270	5,822	13,257	14,570	1,257	1,300
16	Long-term credits [5]	14,087	20,318	25,940	28,210	7,805	8,034	4	10	677	698	5,237	5,792	10,965	12,382	1,252	1,295
17	Repayable in dollars	N.A.	14,968	19,967	21,971	6,730	6,981	4	10	577	599	4,644	5,120	6,760	7,966	1,252	1,295
18	Other [6]	N.A.	5,350	5,973	6,239	1,075	1,053			100	99	593	672	4,205	4,415		
19	Foreign currencies and other claims	2,892	3,161	2,603	2,510	216	249	7	5	49	33	33	30	2,292	2,188	5	5
20	Liquid: U.S. monetary reserve assets	19,359	15,450	15,710	16,964	3,523	2,780	4	(*)	1	1					12,182	14,183
21	Gold	17,804	13,806	10,892	11,859											10,892	11,859
22	Convertible currencies		781	3,528	2,781	3,523	2,780	4	(*)	1	1						
23	IMF gold tranche position	1,555	863	1,290	2,324											1,290	2,324
24	U.S. liabilities to foreigners	41,202	58,759	81,248	90,790	48,242	55,463	11,010	11,773	4,279	4,878	8,823	9,398	6,153	6,310	2,740	2,969
25	Nonliquid	19,654	29,644	47,634	48,872	30,934	32,707	7,829	7,489	950	1,029	4,050	3,642	2,757	2,548	1,113	1,458
26	Private	19,382	27,362	42,890	43,945	28,056	29,500	6,468	6,327	939	996	4,015	3,595	2,299	2,069	1,113	1,458
27	Long-term	18,418	26,394	40,353	40,986	26,301	27,452	6,187	6,049	848	853	3,803	3,341	2,101	1,833	1,113	1,458
28	Direct investments	6,910	8,797	10,815	11,818	7,750	8,510	2,659	2,834	181	176	182	193	43	105		
29	Corporate and other bonds	649	875	4,214	4,800	3,366	3,770	69	87	(*)	(*)	149	141	96	63	534	739
30	Corporate stocks	9,302	14,599	19,551	18,140	13,186	12,106	3,285	2,950	9	10	2,364	2,156	559	758	148	160
31	Liabilities reported by U.S. banks	7	513	3,166	2,490	17	54	1	(*)	658	655	856	525	1,203	697	431	559
32	To private foreigners	7	393	825	983	6	54	N.S.S.	N.S.S.	N.S.S.	N.S.S.	345	316	N.S.S.	N.S.S.	431	559
33	To foreign official agencies		120	2,341	1,507	11		N.S.S.	N.S.S.	N.S.S.	N.S.S.	511	209	N.S.S.	N.S.S.		
34	Other [4]	1,550	ʳ 1,610	2,607	3,738	1,982	3,012	173	178	(*)	12	252	326	200	210		
35	Short-term	964	968	2,537	2,959	1,755	2,048	281	278	91	143	212	254	198	236	(*)	(*)
36	U.S. Government	272	2,282	4,744	4,927	2,878	3,207	1,361	1,162	11	33	35	47	458	479		
37	Certain liabilities to foreign official agencies [7]	2	496	2,723	2,645	1,029	1,251	1,334	1,129					359	265		
38	Other	271	1,786	2,021	2,282	1,849	1,956	27	33	11	33	35	47	99	214		
39	Liquid	21,549	29,115	33,614	41,918	17,308	22,756	3,181	4,284	3,329	3,849	4,773	5,756	3,396	ᵖ 3,762	1,627	1,511
40	To private foreigners [8]	9,139	12,909	20,103	28,907	10,307	16,897	2,649	3,789	N.S.S.	N.S.S.	3,405	4,062	N.S.S.	N.S.S.	597	492
41	To banks [9]	4,818	7,419	14,472	23,665	8,872	15,383	N.S.S.	N.S.S.	N.S.S.	N.S.S.	786	1,902	N.S.S.	N.S.S.		(*)
42	To others [9]	4,321	5,490	5,631	5,242	1,435	1,514	N.S.S.	N.S.S.	N.S.S.	N.S.S.	2,619	2,160	N.S.S.	N.S.S.	597	492
43	To foreign official agencies	12,410	16,206	13,511	13,011	7,001	5,859	532	495	N.S.S.	N.S.S.	1,368	1,694	N.S.S.	N.S.S.	1,030	1,019
44	Reported by U.S. banks	4,019	5,914	5,599	7,227	2,730	3,350	N.S.S.	N.S.S.	N.S.S.	N.S.S.	1,256	1,643	N.S.S.	N.S.S.	230	219
45	U.S. Treasury obligations	8,391	10,292	7,912	5,784	4,271	2,509	N.S.S.	N.S.S.	N.S.S.	N.S.S.	112	51	N.S.S.	N.S.S.	800	800
46	Addenda: Total liquid liabilities	21,549	29,115	33,614	41,918	17,308	22,756	3,181	4,284	3,329	3,849	4,773	5,756	3,396	3,762	1,627	1,511
47	Private, reported by U.S. banks	11,062	17,195	24,457	34,964	12,581	19,686	2,616	3,770	2,090	2,554	4,601	5,642	2,383	3,077	186	235
48	U.S. Treasury Marketable or convertible bonds and notes	¹0 2,326	3,530	¹0 1,667	1,517	1,183	1,086	384	272	9	61	30	33	36	33	25	32
49	U.S. Treasury bills, certificates, and other obligations	8,161	8,356	7,260	5,218	3,544	1,984	181	242	1,230	1,234	142	81	977	652	1,186	1,025
50	Gold deposits of IMF		34	230	219											230	219

ʳ Revised
ᵖ Preliminary.
N.A. Not available
*Less than $500,000 (±).
‡Includes U.S. gold stock.
N.S.S. Not shown separately.
1. Unrevised except where indicated; otherwise the data are as published in the SURVEY, October 1969.
2. Excludes data for Cuba after 1959.
3. For the most part represents the estimated investment in shipping companies registered primarily in Panama and Liberia.
4. These items mostly reflect transactions by U.S. nonbank residents as reported in lines 39, 40, 45, and 56 in balance of payments table 1, SURVEY, September 1970, page 36. However, the long-term position data given here include estimates for real estate, insurance, estates, and trusts, and prior to 1961, the short-term position data include an omissions estimate.
5. Also includes paid-in capital subscription to international financial institutions (other

than IMF) and outstanding amounts of miscellaneous claims which have been settled through international agreements to be payable to the U.S. Government over periods in excess of 1 year. Excludes World War I debts that are not currently being serviced.
6. Includes indebtedness which the borrower may contractually, or at its option, repay with its currency, with a third country's currency, or by delivery of materials or transfer of services.
7. Represents U.S. Government liabilities that are held in reserve assets of official monetary institutions. Also includes U.S. Government notes held by the Canadian Government in connection with the 1964 Colombia River power rights arrangements.
8. Includes liabilities to international and regional organizations.
9. As reported by U.S. banks: ultimate ownership is not identified.
10. A significant change in reporting coverage of the data occurred between this period and the preceding period.

NOTE.—Data for Japan are presented for the first time; the estimates are based on developments since 1946.

to the $171 million surplus in the liquidity balance recorded for 1968.)

In 1969, on the other hand, U.S. reserve assets rose $1,254 million, while liquid liabilities rose $8,304 million, producing a deterioration in our net liquidity position of $7,050 million. (Considering only balance of payments flows, the difference between the increase in reserves and the increase in liquid liabilities is $7,012 million, which

is equal to the recorded deficit in balance of payments on the liquidity basis for 1969.)

Liquidity structure

The evolution of the liquidity structure of U.S. assets and liabilities can be conveniently analyzed in terms of the ratios computed in table 4 and shown in chart 9. It must be recognized, however, that within each of the categories

of assets and liabilities used, the degree of liquidity of the various components is difficult to judge and can vary considerably. This difficulty increases when a number of categories are combined. Partly reflecting these considerations,

CHART 9

Liquidity Ratios: Outstanding U.S. Assets Abroad to Liabilities to Foreigners by Degree of Liquidity

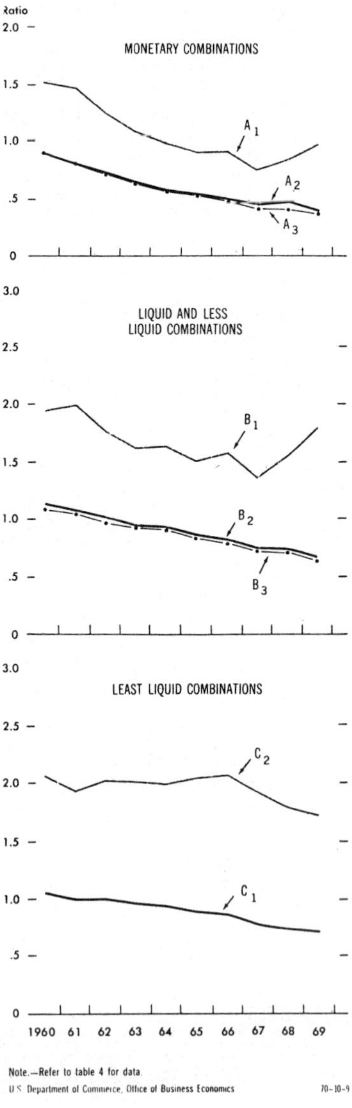

Note.—Refer to table 4 for data.
U.S. Department of Commerce, Office of Business Economics   70-10-9

Table 3.—Changes in the International Investment Position of the United States Reconciled with Balance of Payments Capital Flows

[Millions of dollars]

Lines in table 2	Net International Investment Position and U.S. Assets Abroad Item (Increase +)	1968 r	1969 p	Lines in table 2	U.S. Liabilities to Foreigners Item (increase +)	1968 r	1969 p
1	NET INTERNATIONAL INVESTMENT POSITION OF THE UNITED STATES	152	1,522				
	Balance of payments capital flows	−848	−3,726				
	Other than capital flows	1,000	5,248				
2	U.S. assets abroad	11,687	11,064	24	U.S. Liabilities to foreigners	11,535	9,542
	Capital flows	8,561	8,604		Capital flows	9,409	12,330
	Other than capital flows	3,125	2,460		Other than capital flows	2,125	−2,788
3	Nonliquid	10,807	9,810	25	Nonliquid	11,040	1,238
	Capital flows	7,681	7,417		Capital flows	8,700	4,131
	Other than capital flows	3,125	2,393		Other than capital flows	2,339	−2,893
4	Private	8,580	7,633	26	Private	9,105	1,055
5	Long-term	7,493	6,500	27	Long-term	8,346	633
6	Direct investments	5,492	5,780	28	Direct investments	892	1,003
	Capital flows	3,209	3,070		Capital flows	319	832
	Reinvested earnings	2,175	2,532		Reinvested earnings	488	431
	Valuation adjustments	108	178		Valuation adjustments	85	−260
7-8	Foreign bonds	925	8	29	Corporate and other bonds	2,093	586
	Capital flows	1,099	1,027		Capital flows	2,292	1,547
	Price changes	−174	−1,019		Price changes	−200	−961
9	Foreign corporate stocks	1,214	501	30	Corporate stocks	4,040	−1,411
	Capital flows	155	467		Capital flows	2,096	1,565
	Price changes	1,059	34		Price changes	1,944	−2,966
					Valuation adjustments		−10
10-11	Claims reported by U.S. banks and Other	−138	211	31-34	Liabilities reported by U.S. banks and Other	1,321	455
	Capital flows	−138	94		Capital flows	1,321	15
	Changes in coverage		117		Changes in coverage		440
12	Short-term	1,087	1,133		Short-term	759	422
	Capital flows	1,087	575	35	Capital flows	759	76
	Changes in coverage		558		Changes in coverage		346
15	U.S. Government	2,227	2,177	36	U.S. Government	1,935	183
16	Long-term credits	2,297	2,270	37	Certain liabilities to foreign official agencies	1,807	−78
	Capital flows	2,331	2,273		Capital flows	1,807	−162
	Losses on write-offs	−6	−3		Valuation adjustments		84
	Valuation adjustments	−29		38	Other	128	261
19	Foreign currencies and other claims	−70	−93		Capital flows	107	258
	Capital flows	−62	−89		Valuation adjustments		10
	Valuation adjustments	−14	−8		Statistical discrepancies	21	−7
	Statistical discrepancies	6	4	39	Liquid	495	8,304
20	Liquid: U.S. monetary reserve assets	880	1,254		Capital flows	709	8,199
	Capital flows	880	1,187		Other than capital flows	−214	105
	Other than capital flows		67	40	To private foreigners	3,663	8,804
21	Gold	−1,173	967	41	To banks	3,387	9,193
22	Convertible currencies	1,183	−747		Capital flows	3,387	9,217
	Capital flows	1,183	−814		Changes in coverage		−24
	Valuation adjustments		67	42	To others	276	−389
23	IMF gold tranche position	870	1,034		Capital flows	423	−501
					Changes in coverage	−147	112
				43	To foreign official agencies	−3,168	−500
				44	Reported by U.S. banks	−524	1,628
				45	U.S. Treasury obligations	−2,644	−2,128
					Capital flows	−2,577	−2,145
					Valuation adjustments		17
					Changes in coverage	−67	

Table 4.—Liquidity Ratios: Outstanding U.S. Assets to Liabilities to Foreigners by Degree of Liquidity

Refer to chart 9	Lines in table 2	Ratios	1960	1961	1962	1963	1964	1965	1966	1967	1968	1969
		MONETARY COMBINATIONS										
A_1	$\dfrac{20}{33,\ 37,\ 43}$	$\dfrac{\text{Reserves}}{\text{Liabilities to foreign official agencies}}$	1.56	1.49	1.25	1.10	1.00	0.92	0.93	0.76	0.85	0.99
A_2	$\dfrac{20}{39}$	$\dfrac{\text{Reserves}}{\text{All liquid liabilities}}$	.90	.80	.72	.64	.57	.53	.50	.45	.47	.40
A_3	$\dfrac{20}{33,\ 37,\ 39}$	$\dfrac{\text{Reserves}}{\text{All liquid liabilities and nonliquid liabilities to foreign official agencies}}$	.90	.80	.71	.63	.56	.52	.48	.41	.41	.37
		LIQUID AND LESS-LIQUID COMBINATIONS										
B_1	$\dfrac{20,\ 12}{33,\ 37,\ 43}$	$\dfrac{\text{Reserves and short-term private claims}}{\text{Liabilities to foreign official agencies}}$	1.96	2.00	1.78	1.63	1.65	1.52	1.59	1.38	1.55	1.81
B_2	$\dfrac{20,\ 12}{33,\ 37,\ 39}$	$\dfrac{\text{Reserves and short-term private claims}}{\text{All liquid liabilities and nonliquid liabilities to foreign official agencies}}$	1.13	1.08	1.01	.94	.93	.86	.82	.75	74	.67
B_3	$\dfrac{20,\ 12}{33,\ 35,\ 37,\ 39}$	$\dfrac{\text{Reserves and short-term private claims}}{\text{Liquid and near-liquid liabilities, excluding portfolio}}$	1.08	1.04	.97	.92	.91	.83	.79	.71	.70	.63
		LEAST LIQUID COMBINATIONS										
C_1	$\dfrac{20,\ 12,\ 7,\ 8,\ 9}{29,\ 30,\ 33,\ 35,\ 37,\ 39}$	$\dfrac{\text{Reserves, short-term private claims, and portfolio investment}}{\text{Liquid and near-liquid liabilities, including portfolio}}$	1.04	.99	1.00	.95	.93	.88	.86	.77	.72	.69
C_2	$\dfrac{2}{24}$	$\dfrac{\text{Total U.S. assets abroad}}{\text{Total U.S. liabilities to foreigners}}$	2.08	1.96	2.03	2.02	2.01	2.05	2.08	1.94	1.81	1.74

the assets and liabilities compared in the various ratios are not necessarily of equal liquidity.

The ratio of U.S. reserves to U.S. liabilities to foreign official agencies (ratio A_1) largely reflects the influence of the balance of payments as computed on the official reserve transactions basis. It is also influenced by the method of financing the official balance, i.e., whether it is financed by a change in U.S. reserves or an increase in liabilities. Reflecting the behavior of all ratios, when the ratio is greater than 1.0 (and reserves exceed liabilities, as from 1960 to 1963) a deficit of a given size will cause a greater reduction in the ratio if it is financed by an increase in liabilities than if it is financed by a decrease in reserves. When the ratio is 1.0 or less, a given loss of reserves has a greater adverse impact than an equal increase in liabilities. Of course, in judging the adequacy of U.S. reserves one must also take into account the absolute level of reserves and liabilities, as well as the ratios.

Reflecting the substantial deficits in the official settlements balance,

the A_1 ratio shows a consistent decline from 1960 through 1967, although it flattened in the mid-1960's when the balance temporarily improved. In 1968 and 1969, however, when the official balance was in substantial surplus, the ratio improved. At end 1969, it stood at about 1.0 (about the same as end 1964)—that is, U.S. reserves were equal to our liabilities to foreign official agencies. Of course, with the large official deficit in the first half of 1970, the ratio dropped significantly lower.

The ratio of U.S. reserves to all U.S. liquid liabilities (A_2) is similarly influenced by the liquidity deficit and whether it is financed by an increase in liabilities or a decline in reserves. This ratio has also shown a rather consistent decline reflecting the persistent deficits in the liquidity balance. At end 1969, the ratio was 0.4 (i.e., reserves were less than half of our liquid liabilities).

Including certain nonliquid liabilities to foreign official agencies (which reflect special financial transactions that are considered to distort the liquidity balance) with liquid liabilities and recomputing the ratio (ratio A_3), gives

essentially the same impression as the ratio of reserves to only liquid liabilities. However, the adjusted ratio is somewhat lower than the A_2 ratio reflecting the growth in holdings of nonliquid securities by foreign official agencies.

While U.S. reserves are the most highly liquid assets that are available to defend the value of the dollar, part of private short-term claims of banks and nonbanks can be considered sufficiently liquid to provide an offset to the liquid liabilities. Ratios B_1, B_2 and B_3 compare U.S. reserves plus short-term private claims to various combinations of liquid and less-liquid liabilities. The comparison with liabilities to foreign official agencies (B_1) indicates that such assets were about twice such liabilities in the early 1960's, declined to 1.38 in 1967 but then rose to 1.81 by end 1969. Not only is the level of the ratio consistently higher than the ratio of reserves alone to liabilities to official foreign agencies (A_1), but the deterioration from 1960 to 1969 is less pronounced. This indicates that the decline in U.S. reserves was to some extent offset by a buildup of generally less-liquid short-term private claims. Some of these claims, such as Eurodollar and money market holdings of banks and nonbanks, are quite liquid; others, such as trade credits, loans and brokers' claims are significantly less so.

The ratios of U.S. reserves and short-term private claims to liquid and less-liquid liabilities (B_2 and B_3) behave in a manner similar to the more monetary ratios computed in A_2 and A_3. However, the deterioration from 1960 to 1969 is not quite as strong, and the levels are somewhat more favorable. (Less liquid liabilities in ratio B_2 are the "nonliquid" liabilities to foreign official agencies. Less-liquid liabilites in ratio B_2 also include short-term private liabilities of nonbanks, such as brokers' liabilities, trade credits and loans from foreigners, a good part of which are probably not easily liquidated.)

Looking at a wider spectrum of assets and liabilities, in ratio C_1, U.S. portfolio assets are added to reserves and short-term private claims and compared with foreign portfolio assets in the United States, as well as with liquid and

other less-liquid liabilities (as used in ratio B_3). The impression is similar to that given by the more liquid combinations as A_3 and B_3; however, the deterioration is noticeably less pronounced. Of course, the value of portfolio holdings could decline sharply if either U.S. residents or foreigners attempted to liquify any substantial amounts of their holdings. This is one reason they cannot be considered as liquid as some of the other items discussed.

In general, it appears that there is a persistent tendency for the structure of U.S. assets to become relatively less liquid compared with the structure of U.S. liabilities. The proportion of liquid (or liquid and less-liquid) assets to total assets has tended to fall, while the proportion of liquid (or liquid and less-liquid) liabilities to total liabilities has shown relatively little change. For example, liquid liabilities plus nonliquid liabilities to foreign official agencies have persistently remained about one-half of total liabilities.

The ratio of total assets to total liabilities (C_2) is not intended to meas-

ure changes in the liquidity structure of our position. It focuses, instead, on the relative amount by which assets exceed liabilities, similar to the way the net international investment position focuses on the absolute difference between total assets and total liabilities. This ratio was about 2.0 in 1960, essentially remained at that level through 1966, and then declined in 1967 and 1968 as total assets and total liabilities both rose by about the same amount. Even in 1969, when there was a $1.5 billion improvement in the net international investment position, the improvement was not sufficient to prevent a further small decline in the ratio.

U.S. Direct Investments Abroad

The value of U.S. direct investments abroad increased by $5.8 billion in 1969, about $0.3 billion more than in 1968 (table 5). The 1969 increase brought the book value of such assets to $70.8 billion, or 45 percent of the value of all U.S. foreign assets. Capital outflows of $3.1 billion for direct investments abroad in 1969, which includes the use of both U.S. funds and funds raised abroad by U.S. corporations, were only marginally below the 1967 and 1968 level, but substantially below 1966 outflows of $3.7 billion. Reinvested earnings rose $357 million to $2.5 billion in 1969, but this was not as sharp an increase as that which occurred between 1967 and 1968.

A large number of international transactions must be examined in order to determine the balance of payments impact of U.S. direct investments abroad. These associated flows have have been combined with the explicit direct investment flows in table 5. Balance of payments signs are used and therefore increases in U.S. claims abroad are shown as minuses. (It should be noted that some of the accounts include items such as trade credits which are not related to direct investment.)

In addition to the outflow of direct investment funds, one needs to know how much is borrowed abroad by U.S. corporations, either directly from foreign banks and others, or by new issues

Table 5.—Flows of Certain U.S. Corporate Funds—Changes in Foreign Assets and Liabilities, Adjusted Earnings, and Fees and Royalties

[Millions of dollars]

Item, debits (—), credits (+)	Total					Western Europe				
	1965	1966 r	1967 r	1968 r	1969 p	1965	1966 r	1967 r	1968 r	1969 p
Net flow	2,114	2,033	2,821	5,311	5,578	7	—141	414	2,962	2,471
Change in direct investment position	—4,994	—5,325	—4,692	—5,492	—5,780	—1,856	—2,249	—1,670	—1,503	—2,147
Balance of payments flows	—3,468	—3,661	—3,137	—3,209	—3,070	—1,479	—1,834	—1,458	—1,001	—1,158
Reinvested earnings	—1,542	—1,739	—1,598	—2,175	—2,532	—408	—435	—269	—456	—845
Other adjustments	16	75	43	—108	—178	31	20	57	—46	—144
Other corporate claims	368	—434	—590	—992	—358	26	—444	—221	—738	180
Long-term	—88	—112	—281	—220	—424	30	—79	—76	—148	—131
Short-term [1]	456	—322	—309	—772	66	—4	—365	—145	—590	311
Corporate liabilities other than new issues of securities	136	459	448	1,149	969	119	371	325	1,141	806
Long-term	29	180	85	715	691	23	192	64	708	637
Short-term [1]	107	279	363	434	278	96	179	261	433	169
New issues of securities [2]	191	594	446	2,144	1,029	191	594	446	2,144	1,029
Of which: Used for direct investment Deposited abroad (short-term corporate claims)	—52	—445	—278	—785	—631	n.a.	n.a.	n.a.	n.a.	n.a.
	—139	—143	—96	—1,159	—187	n.a.	n.a.	n.a.	n.a.	n.a.
Adjusted earnings [3]	5,505	5,784	6,116	7,148	8,171	1,176	1,164	1,118	1,361	1,871
Reinvested earnings	1,542	1,739	1,598	2,175	2,532	408	435	269	456	845
Income on U.S. direct investments abroad	3,963	4,045	4,517	4,973	5,639	768	729	849	905	1,026
Fees and royalties from U.S. direct investment	924	1,030	1,136	1,246	1,369	382	443	473	511	588
Offset to "other adjustments" in direct investment	—16	—75	—43	108	178	—31	—20	—57	46	144

r Revised.   p Preliminary.   n.a. Not available.
1. Excludes brokerage claims and liabilities.
2. New issues of securities sold abroad by U.S. corporations exclude securities issued by subsidiaries incorporated abroad and also exclude funds obtained by U.S. corporations through bank loans and other credits. However, securities issued by subsidiaries incorporated in the Netherlands Antilles are treated as if they had been issued by U.S. corporations if the proceeds of such issues are transferred to U.S. parent companies.
3. For a discussion of this concept see the technical appendix.

of securities abroad. Furthermore, the various uses of the proceeds of borrowings—whether they are used to finance direct investments abroad at the time of borrowing, or are repatriated to the United States, or are left on deposit abroad for later utilization—have quite different impacts on the balance of payments. The disposition of the U.S. corporations' share of earnings of foreign affiliates—whether they are returned to the United States as income on direct investments or are reinvested abroad—has significant implications for the balance of payments, as does the amount of fees and royalties received by U.S. parents from their direct investments abroad. These effects are summarized in table 5. (As discussed in the Investment Position article in the October 1969 Survey there are a number of influences of U.S. corporate international transactions on the balance of payments which cannot be fully segregated and reflected in the table.)

The net flow of corporate funds in 1969 associated with the identifiable transactions had a favorable impact on the balance of payments of $5.6 billion, an improvement of $0.3 billion over 1968. (The $2.5 billion improvement between 1967 and 1968 was probably associated with the Foreign Direct Investment Program which was made mandatory at the beginning of 1968.)

In 1969, the change in the direct investment position was adverse by $288 million more than in 1968. This mostly reflected an increase in reinvested earnings as capital outflows showed a small improvement. Long-term corporate claims (other than direct investment) shifted adversely by $204 million in 1969; most of this shift was accounted for by the receipt of long-term notes as a result of the liquidation of a major U.S. direct investment in Latin America. The entries in this account and in the direct investment capital flows account due to the liquidation are mostly offsetting.

Borrowing abroad by corporations was down sharply in 1969; new issues of securities declined by $1.1 billion and other inflows from borrowing (as reflected in other corporate liabilities) declined by $180 million. Partly associ-

ated with the $1.3 billion adverse movement in borrowing was an improvement of $838 million in short-term claims. In 1968, when borrowing abroad was much higher, corporations left a substantial part of the funds borrowed on deposit abroad which caused a sharp increase in short-term claims. The net effect of the change in borrowing and in short-term claims was an adverse movement of $0.5 billion from 1968 to 1969.

The major improvement among all these accounts was in adjusted earnings on direct investments abroad, which increased by $1.0 billion to $8.2 billion in 1969. Income receipts accounted for $0.7 billion of the increase while the remainder was reinvested abroad. Fees and royalties showed a $123 million improvement between 1968 and 1969.

The $1.1 billion improvement in earnings and fees and royalties exceeded the adverse effects of the other flows by about $150 million; the remainder

of the overall improvement of $267 million came from the offset to the direct investment valuation adjustments.

Country and industry distribution of direct investment

The developed countries, which includes Canada, Western Europe, Australia, New Zealand, South Africa, and Japan accounted for $4.2 billion or 73 percent of the $5.8 billion growth in the book value of direct investments during 1969 (table 6, chart 10). In 1968, these areas accounted for $3.4 billion or 62 percent of the $5.5 billion total rise in direct investments. U.S. investment in Canadian affiliates increased by $1.5 billion during 1969, while investment in the European Economic Community (EEC) increased by $1.2 billion.

Investments in less developed countries rose over $1.2 billion last year, about $0.2 billion less than in 1968. The gain would have been about the

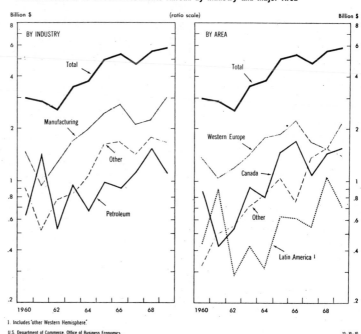

CHART 10

Annual Additions to Direct Investments Abroad by Industry and Major Area

1. Includes 'other Western Hemisphere.'

U.S. Department of Commerce, Office of Business Economics

70-10-10

same in both years except for the involuntary sales of majority interest in two mining enterprises to the Chilean Government and the sale of a public utility company to the Peruvian Government. Despite these sales, investment in the Latin American Republics increased by $0.6 billion. Direct investment in the international, unallocated category rose less than $0.3

billion in 1969, after rising $0.4 billion in 1968.

While the total value of U.S. direct investments abroad is not affected by valuation adjustments made as a result of capital flow between primary and secondary foreign affiliates, country values are adjusted as shown in table 7. And, although not shown in table 7, industry values are also affected.

Manufacturing. U.S. ownership in foreign manufacturing affiliates increased $3.0 billion during 1969 to almost $30.0 billion at yearend. In 1968, the increase was $2.2 billion. Last year's gain reflected reinvested earnings of $1.9 billion and capital outflows of $1.1 billion. Direct investments in manufacturing have shown the greatest increase in value of any industry since 1960 (table 9).

Table 6.—U.S. Foreign Direct Investments,

[Millions

Line	Area and country [2]	A.—Book value at yearend [1]												
		1968 [r]						1969 [p]						
		Total	Mining & smelting	Petro-leum	Manu-factur-ing	Trans-portation & utili-ties	Trade	Other	Total	Mining & smelt-ing	Petro-leum	Manu-factur-ing	Trans-portation & utili-ties	Trade	Other
1	All areas	64,983	5,435	18,887	26,414	2,672	5,280	6,295	70,763	5,635	19,985	29,450	2,676	5,832	7,184
2	Developed countries	43,500	3,145	9,922	21,716	699	3,608	4,410	47,701	3,315	10,447	24,282	722	4,043	4,892
3	Canada	19,535	2,638	4,094	8,568	599	1,123	2,513	21,075	2,764	4,359	9,389	629	1,221	2,713
4	Europe [3]	19,407	61	4,636	10,796	94	2,129	1,691	21,554	72	4,805	12,225	84	2,415	1,954
5	United Kingdom	6,694	2	1,563	4,243	20	420	446	7,158	2	1,563	4,555	16	455	566
6	European Economic Community	9,012	19	2,146	5,399	54	848	546	10,194	17	2,243	6,340	53	948	592
7	Belgium and Luxembourg	981	(*)	14	601	1	159	205	1,210	(*)	57	700	2	214	237
8	France	1,904	10	292	1,340	14	163	83	2,091	10	295	1,518	8	169	91
9	Germany	3,785	(**)	1,104	2,285	18	264	113	4,252	(**)	1,067	2,750	22	284	128
10	Italy	1,275	(**)	479	617	3	105	72	1,423	(**)	506	716	3	106	92
11	Netherlands	1,069	(*)	257	555	18	157	82	1,218	(*)	318	656	18	175	51
12	Other Western Europe	3,701	40	926	1,155	19	861	699	4,202	52	998	1,329	15	1,012	795
13	Denmark	204	1	111	48	(*)	41	3	309	1	197	58	(*)	49	4
14	Norway	201	(**)	101	52	(*)	26	21	223	(**)	103	62	(*)	34	24
15	Spain	582	(**)	135	306	13	100	29	577	(**)	116	295	8	120	38
16	Sweden	516	(*)	281	139	(*)	88	8	604	(*)	301	179	(*)	112	8
17	Switzerland	1,437	(*)	8	336	(*)	469	625	1,606	(*)	−30	380	1	541	714
18	Other [4]	761	19	292	275	6	137	32	883	24	308	356	6	155	33
19	Japan	1,050		405	522	3	99	21	1,218		447	639	5	101	25
20	Australia, New Zealand, and South Africa	3,508	446	787	1,830	3	257	185	3,854	479	836	2,029	4	306	200
21	Australia	2,652	365	(**)	1,412	3	124	748	2,936	395	(**)	1,567	4	156	814
22	New Zealand	160	(*)	(**)	85	(*)	37	37	163	−1	(**)	89	(*)	39	36
23	South Africa	696	81	148	333	(*)	96	39	755	84	158	374	(*)	112	28
24	Less developed countries	18,753	2,291	7,496	4,697	774	1,671	1,825	20,000	2,321	7,830	5,167	794	1,787	2,101
25	Latin American Republics and other Western Hemisphere	13,101	1,930	3,680	4,005	685	1,345	1,456	13,811	1,922	3,722	4,317	695	1,406	1,720
26	Latin American Republics	11,033	1,410	3,014	3,711	628	1,251	1,019	11,667	1,346	3,079	4,077	620	1,308	1,236
27	Mexico	1,466	112	44	1,003	27	180	101	1,631	136	35	1,108	28	191	133
28	Panama	919	19	214	58	53	340	235	1,071	19	239	90	56	345	322
29	Other Central America [5]	595	6	151	104	131	42	162	630	8	154	113	129	43	182
30	Argentina	1,156	(**)	(**)	730	(**)	57	369	1,244	(**)	(**)	789	(**)	68	387
31	Brazil	1,484	81	83	1,022	27	197	75	1,633	99	100	1,112	25	188	108
32	Chile	962	586	(**)	66	(**)	39	271	846	452	(**)	65	(**)	41	288
33	Colombia	632	(**)	323	195	29	58	26	684	(**)	342	220	29	63	30
34	Peru	692	421	(**)	96	22	51	101	704	443	(**)	97	(*)	59	106
35	Venezuela	2,627	(**)	1,780	382	18	258	188	2,668	(**)	1,771	416	18	276	186
36	Other [6]	499	52	169	56	50	29	143	554	50	190	67	55	33	159
37	Other Western Hemisphere [7]	2,068	519	667	293	58	94	436	2,144	576	643	270	74	98	484
38	Other Africa [8]	1,978	314	1,407	70	4	67	117	2,215	343	1,598	80	5	71	118
39	Liberia	174	(**)	(**)	(**)	(**)	24	150	172	(**)	(**)	(**)	(**)	24	148
40	Libya	662	(**)	(**)	(**)	(**)	6	656	775	(**)	(**)	(**)	(**)	6	769
41	Other	1,142	243	766	68	7	38	20	1,268	275	843	79	8	41	21
42	Middle East [8]	1,805	3	1,656	63	7	20	56	1,829	3	1,654	80	8	28	56
43	Other Asia and Pacific	1,869	44	753	559	78	239	196	2,145	53	856	660	86	282	207
44	India	281	(**)	(**)	132	1	41	106	294	(**)	(**)	143	1	44	105
45	Philippines	673	(**)	(**)	238	39	91	305	741	(**)	(**)	270	43	97	332
46	Other	915	(**)	(**)	190	37	107	581	1,110	(**)	(**)	247	42	140	680
47	International, unallocated	2,731		1,469		1,201	1	61	3,061		1,708		1,159	1	193

[r] Revised.　[p] Preliminary.　*Less than $500,000±.　**Combined in other industries.
1. The value of investments in specified industries and countries is affected by capital flows among foreign affiliates as shown in table 7.
2. Does not mean that all countries grouped in an "other" or regional category have U.S direct investment at any given time.
3. Direct investment statistics do not show any investments in Eastern Europe.
4. Includes Austria, Cyprus, Finland, Gibraltar, Greece, Greenland, Iceland, Ireland, Malta, Portugal, Turkey, and Yugoslavia.

The developed countries accounted for $2.6 billion of the 1969 increase in manufacturing, with Western Europe receiving about $1.4 billion. European machinery industries, electrical and nonelectrical, were major recipients of capital outflows for manufacturing direct investments in 1969 (table 10). Investment in German manufacturing affiliates rose nearly $0.5 billion, of which reinvested earnings contributed $0.3 billion. There were large flows of funds to German subsidiaries from parents early in the year, but after the mark revaluation and before the end of the year, most of the funds were returned to the United States. Common Market countries other than Germany had an increase in investment of nearly $0.5 billion, more than double the rise in 1968. In the United Kingdom investment was up $0.3 billion during 1969, with the bulk of the increase from reinvested earnings. Investment in manufacturing enterprises in "other Western Europe" increased by only $0.2 billion as losses incurred in the start up of new petrochemical and other manufacturing plants in Spain limited the growth in reinvested earnings.

Selected Data Items, Countries, and Industries

of dollars]

B.—Net capital outflows							C.—U.S. share in reinvested earnings of foreign corporations							D.—Earnings							E.—Income							Line
1968 r	1969 p						1968 r	1969 p						1968 r	1969 p						1968 r	1969 p						
Total	Total	Mining & smelting	Petroleum	Manufacturing	Other		Total	Total	Mining & smelting	Petroleum	Manufacturing	Other		Total	Total	Mining & smelting	Petroleum	Manufacturing	Other		Total	Total	Mining & smelting	Petroleum	Manufacturing	Other		
3,209	3,070	52	1,022	1,122	873		2,175	2,532	168	−59	1,901	522		7,022	7,955	844	2,494	3,185	1,432		4,973	5,639	664	2,635	1,325	1,014		1
1,873	1,993	75	432	909	578		1,491	2,083	96	−52	1,627	412		3,347	3,971	330	76	2,633	931		1,976	2,067	224	199	1,042	600		2
625	619	50	178	231	161		772	937	77	95	599	166		1,490	1,542	233	223	806	280		851	762	152	152	255	202		3
1,001	1,158	6	204	577	372		456	845	5	−198	820	218		1,369	1,855	10	−196	1,462	579		905	1,026	5	35	632	354		4
363	284	(**)	40	106	139		211	151	....	−41	169	24		503	488	(*)	−59	426	121		275	327	(*)	2	233	92		5
438	648	(**)	128	378	143		108	455	(**)	−147	549	53		543	888	(**)	−129	878	140		434	453	(**)	29	336	88		6
78	102		32	10	60		26	76		−24	70	29		89	135		−22	93	63		57	54		−3	24	33		7
−27	83	(**)	−1	74	9		20	84	(**)	3	82	−1		91	175	(**)	16	153	6		65	92	(**)	12	71	8		8
242	231	(**)	41	156	33		53	239	(**)	−77	300	16		258	467	(**)	−59	487	40		208	234	(**)	32	178	24		9
28	109	(**)	15	82	11		5	28	(**)	−35	51	12		49	70	(**)	−36	84	22		43	42	(**)	−1	34	10		10
118	123	(*)	40	55	28		4	28		−15	46	−4		56	41		−27	60	8		61	30		−12	30	12		11
200	226	(**)	36	93	97		136	239	(**)	−9	101	146		323	479	(**)	−8	159	328		196	246	(**)	4	63	179		12
−63	53	(*)	45	4	3		−6	4		−5	5	4		−3	11		−8	9	10		7	8		−2	4	6		13
12	9	(**)	3	4	2		6	13	(**)	−1	5	9		−1	9	(**)	−10	6	13		−8	−3	(**)	−8	1	5		14
106	−10	(**)	−18	5	4		3	7	(**)	−1	−11	18		19	22	(**)	−2	21	17		17	15	(**)	3	9	3		15
89	79		31	37	11		−11	11		−8	5	14		17	25		−8	12	21		29	17		(*)	9	8		16
12	43		−34	7	70		102	133		−3	46	89		205	291		−3	76	217		105	157		1	31	125		17
45	51	(**)	9	35	8		42	71	(**)	8	51	13		86	120	(**)	17	58	45		46	52	(**)	11	8	33		18
78	63		27	32	4		104	105		15	85	5		167	181		19	142	19		60	70		7	49	13		19
169	153	19	23	69	41		159	196	14	36	123	23		321	393	87	30	223	53		160	209	67	5	106	31		20
161	152	18	(**)	70	63		120	138	12	(**)	86	39		195	247	50	(**)	162	34		85	131	37	(**)	84	10		21
1	−5	(*)	−2	−2		12	9		(**)	6	3		14	19	(*)	7	12	7		2	10	(*)	4	6		22
6	6	1	(**)	1	3		26	50	2	(**)	31	17		111	127	36	(**)	48	43		74	68	29	(**)	16	22		23
1,146	760	−23	347	213	222		495	500	72	−7	273	162		3,444	3,747	513	2,287	552	395		2,948	3,273	439	2,298	284	253		24
677	345	−31	56	132	187		358	376	42	−15	225	123		1,574	1,634	449	462	457	266		1,218	1,277	404	472	237	164		25
477	271	−87	57	158	143		299	362	42	11	213	96		1,355	1,401	334	412	438	218		1,049	1,049	287	395	226	140		26
63	93	13	−11	49	42		63	69	11	1	52	4		132	141	18	4	104	15		67	74	6	2	54	12		27
72	84	(*)	21	12	52		47	55		5	19	−30		97	121		9	80	32		58	79		−4	14	62		28
24	36	2	3	11	20		6	−1		1	−2	(*)		39	26	3	1	25		35	29	3	−4	3	26		29
36	61	(**)	(**)	35	26		35	30	(**)	(**)	28	2		126	139	(**)	(**)	91	48		94	115	(**)	(**)	68	47		30
80	64	(**)	1	32	30		74	83	(**)	15	65	3		160	157	(**)	21	123	12		75	66	(**)	5	53	9		31
79	−137	−142	(**)	1	3		3	43	26	(**)	1	16		155	162	141	(**)	−3	24		144	114	108	(**)	−4	10		32
34	36	(**)	17	13	6		1	14	(**)	2	10	3		17	34	(**)	11	18	4		16	20	(**)	10	9	2		33
24	1	21	(**)	−2	−18		9	11	2	(**)	3	6		104	119	104	(**)	7	8		95	108	102	(**)	4	2		34
26	−20	(**)	−9	(*)	−11		56	61	(**)	2	33	26		490	465	(**)	334	57	74		430	401	(**)	329	23	48		35
40	53	−3	35	7	14		3	−3		1	−14	4		36	38	14	7	6	11		34	42	13	22	2	6		36
200	74	56	−1	−26	45		59	14	1	−26	12	28		219	233	116	50	19	48		169	228	116	78	10	24		37
302	169	(*)	170	4	−5		51	67	29	21	7	10		568	681	67	577	9	28		519	616	39	558	2	18		38
−8	−7	(**)	(**)	(**)	−7		5	3	(**)	(**)	(**)	3		20	17	(**)	(**)	(**)	17		15	15	(**)	(**)	(**)	15		39
203	107	(**)	(**)	(**)	107		11	6	(**)	(**)	(**)	6		506	611	(**)	(**)	(**)	611		496	606	(**)	(**)	(**)	600		40
106	69	3	57	4	5		35	58	29	20	7	2		42	52	57		−27	13	9		9	−4	28		−46	2	12		41
40	71	(*)	50	15	6		23	−40	(*)	−45	2	3		1,091	1,153	(*)	1,133	5	15		1,070	1,196		1,181	3	12		42
127	175	8	71	62	34		63	97	1	32	39	26		211	279	−3	115	81	86		141	184	−4	87	42	59		43
7	3			4	−1		7	10		(**)	7	3		21	27		(**)	21	7		11	14		(**)	11	2		44
24	41	(**)	(**)	24	17		15	26	(**)	(**)	6	19		55	65	(**)	(**)	24	41		34	38	(**)	(**)	16	22		45
96	131	(**)	(**)	34	97		41	61	(**)	(**)	25	37		135	187	(**)	(**)	36	151		95	133	(**)	(**)	14	119		46
191	316		243		73		188	−52		(*)		−52		231	237		132		106		48	298		137		161		47

5. Includes Costa Rica, El Salvador, Guatemala, Honduras, and Nicaragua.
6. Includes Bolivia, Dominican Republic, Ecuador, Haiti, Paraguay, and Uruguay.
7. Includes all of the Western Hemisphere except Canada and the 19 Latin American Republics included in line 26.

8. Includes United Arab Republic (Egypt) and all other countries in Africa except South Africa.
9. Includes Bahrain, Iran, Iraq, Israel, Jordan, Kuwait, Lebanon, Qatar, Saudi Arabia, Southern Yemen, Syria, Trucial States, Oman, and Yemen.

Table 7.—Net Capital Flows Between Primary and Secondary Foreign Affiliates

[Millions of dollars; net inflow (−)]

	1965	1966	1967	1968	1969 p
Canada	−8	16	1	−1	7
Europe	43	30	10	−5	2
France	22	−6	6	−3	−19
Germany	−22	−16	−3	−2	6
Italy	−9	−7	13	8	11
Switzerland	77	28	30	−11	6
United Kingdom	−2	47	−15	4	−28
Other	−22	−16	−21	−1	26
Latin American Republics and other Western Hemisphere	−8	−6	−20	6	−8
Argentina	−5	4	−1	−3	3
Mexico	−5	2	3	1	−1
Panama	8	7	10	−2	−13
Other	−6	−19	−32	10	3
Other countries	−27	−40	9	(*)	−1

p Preliminary.
* Less than $500,000±.

The value of manufacturing enterprises in the less developed countries increased by only $0.5 billion in 1969, with the bulk of the rise going to the Latin American Republics.

Petroleum. Investment in petroleum affiliates amounted to $20.0 billion at the end of 1969, an increase of $1.1 billion from 1968. This increase was significantly smaller than the $1.5 billion rise in 1968, and reflected smaller capital outflows and an adverse shift in reinvested earnings. During 1969, in fact, petroleum companies actually reported negative reinvested earnings of

Table 8.—Acquisitions and Sales by American Companies of Foreign Enterprises [1] by Area and Industry

[Millions of dollars]

Area and industry	1968			1969		
	Acquisitions	Sales	Net	Acquisitions	Sales	Net
All areas	800	220	580	805	163	642
Petroleum	33	11	22	31	(*)	31
Manufacturing	650	141	508	543	90	453
Other industries	117	68	49	231	73	158
Canada	137	.3	135	222	40	182
Petroleum	8		8	28		28
Manufacturing	100	(*)	100	142	27	114
Other industries	29	2	26	52	13	40
Europe	516	145	371	466	50	416
Petroleum	5	1	4	(*)	(*)	(*)
Manufacturing	464	127	336	329	37	292
Other industries	47	17	30	137	13	124
Other areas	147	72	75	116	73	43
Petroleum	20	10	10	2	(*)	2
Manufacturing	86	14	72	72	26	47
Other industries	41	49	−8	41	47	−6

* Less than $500,000.
1. Includes acquisitions and sales of minority interests.

$59 million, compared with positive reinvested earnings of over $0.2 billion in 1968. Disinvestment resulting from repatriating earnings in excess of current earnings was particularly noticeable in the case of certain tanker affiliates of oil companies and in the Middle East. The increase in book value of petroleum industry investments in the developed countries accounted for $525 million of last year's $1.5 bi'lion increase, while the less developed countries received $334 million; petroleum affiliates in the international, unallocated category (which is not included in either of the preceding two categories) accounted for the remaining $239 million.

The increase in book value of Canadian petroleum affiliates in 1969 was almost $0.3 billion, about the same as in 1968. The value of investments in European petroleum enterprises increased by less than $0.2 billion in 1969 as capital outflows dropped to $0.2 billion. Earnings were negative (more so than in 1968) which resulted in negative reinvestment of $0.2 billion; however this was largely offset by positive valuation adjustments.

The $334 million rise in book value of petroleum investments in less developed countries was less than half the 1968 increase. The increase in investment in African petroleum affiliates was limited by a large fourth quarter build up of accounts payable by U.S. companies to their producing branches, especially in Libya. Investment in Middle East petroleum enterprises was practically unchanged from 1968 as larger capital outflows for the year were offset by negative reinvested earnings.

The increase of investment in international tanker affiliates was slightly less than in 1968. The financing of new super tanker purchases attracted large capital outflows, but larger than usual dividend payments by several companies led to negligible reinvested earnings.

Mining and smelting. U.S. direct investment in foreign mining enterprises increased by $0.2 billion during 1969, much less than the rise in 1968. Reinvested earnings were the same each year, at about $150 million, while

capital outflows declined from $0.4 billion in 1968 to less than $0.1 billion in 1969. The involuntary sale of 51 percent ownership in two Chilean mining ventures reduced investment by over $0.2 billion. Even excluding these transactions the rise in investment would have been less than in 1968 due to the fact that some important investment projects in Australia were completed.

CHART 11

Earnings of Foreign Affiliates

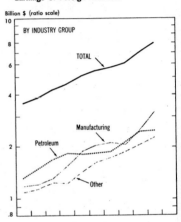

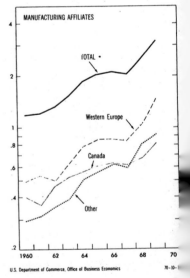

U.S. Department of Commerce, Office of Business Economics   70-10-

Transportation and public utilities. (Formerly public utilities; there has been no change in the composition of this category.) The $2.7 billion book value of U.S. investments in the transportation and public utilities industries at the end of 1969 was essentially unchanged from 1968, as a small capital outflow was offset by negative reinvested earnings. Capital outflows declined from 1968 to 1969; flows were enlarged in 1968 by security issues in

Table 9.—Selected Data on Direct Investments Abroad, by Major Areas

[Millions of dollars]

Area and year	Book value at yearend				Net capital outflows					Earnings					Income				
	Total	Mining & smelting	Petroleum	Manufacturing	Other	Total	Mining & smelting	Petroleum	Manufacturing	Other	Total	Mining & smelting	Petroleum	Manufacturing	Other	Total	Mining & smelting	Petroleum	Manufacturing	Other
All areas:																				
1960	31,865	2,997	10,810	11,051	7,007	1,674	155	452	801	266	3,566	394	1,302	1,176	694	2,355	337	1,150	550	318
1961	34,717	3,094	12,190	11,997	7,436	1,599	70	703	462	274	3,815	362	1,476	1,203	774	2,768	297	1,336	722	413
1962	37,276	3,244	12,725	13,250	8,057	1,654	97	606	712	239	4,235	372	1,695	1,307	861	3,044	318	1,565	746	415
1963	40,736	3,419	13,652	14,937	8,728	1,976	85	828	774	289	4,587	388	1,824	1,541	834	3,129	321	1,715	656	437
1964	44,480	3,665	14,328	16,935	9,552	2,328	136	760	1,034	398	5,071	512	1,808	1,852	899	3,674	403	1,856	893	522
1965	49,474	3,931	15,298	19,339	10,906	3,468	138	977	1,525	828	5,460	571	1,830	2,022	1,037	3,963	442	1,799	1,094	628
1966	54,799	4,365	16,222	22,078	12,134	3,661	305	885	1,752	718	5,702	659	1,868	2,104	1,071	4,045	524	1,781	1,116	624
1967	59,491	4,876	17,399	24,172	13,044	3,137	330	1,069	1,234	504	6,034	746	2,120	2,055	1,112	4,518	596	1,989	1,193	740
1968	64,983	5,435	18,887	26,414	14,248	3,209	440	1,231	945	592	7,022	795	2,449	2,519	1,259	4,973	644	2,271	1,265	793
1969	70,763	5,635	19,985	29,450	15,693	3,070	52	1,022	1,122	873	7,955	844	2,494	3,185	1,432	5,639	664	2,635	1,325	1,014
Canada:																				
1960	11,179	1,325	2,664	4,827	2,363	451	199	135	29	88	718	88	98	398	134	361	47	60	176	78
1961	11,602	1,367	2,828	5,076	2,331	302	9	100	117	76	726	96	114	360	156	464	51	78	213	122
1962	12,133	1,489	2,875	5,312	2,457	314	85	159	.12	58	825	97	121	460	147	476	60	79	221	116
1963	13,044	1,549	3,134	5,761	2,600	365	7	188	120	50	948	127	149	525	147	455	80	80	192	103
1964	13,855	1,713	3,196	6,198	2,748	298	91	25	140	42	1,106	191	170	565	180	634	118	118	269	129
1965	15,318	1,851	3,356	6,872	3,239	962	51	179	395	337	1,209	198	163	606	222	703	110	122	315	156
1966	17,017	2,089	3,608	7,692	3,628	1,153	172	155	566	260	1,237	191	196	628	222	756	120	112	354	170
1967	18,102	2,342	3,819	8,095	3,847	408	173	115	20	100	1,327	240	207	613	267	790	154	132	296	208
1968	19,535	2,638	4,094	8,568	4,235	625	195	169	26	236	1,490	275	243	672	300	851	169	160	301	221
1969	21,075	2,764	4,350	9,389	4,563	619	50	178	231	161	1,542	233	223	806	280	762	152	152	255	202
Europe:																				
1960	6,691	49	1,763	3,804	1,075	962	(*)	273	607	82	769	10	91	487	181	397	11	55	241	90
1961	7,742	48	2,152	4,255	1,287	724	(*)	376	233	115	837	8	63	530	236	486	9	47	326	104
1962	8,930	50	2,385	4,883	1,612	868	3	229	453	183	844	5	60	496	283	526	7	63	334	122
1963	10,340	55	2,776	5,634	1,875	924	1	362	395	166	948	4	67	627	298	507	6	73	305	123
1964	12,129	55	3,122	6,587	2,364	1,388	2	414	619	353	1,115	4	8	782	321	659	5	64	427	163
1965	13,985	54	3,427	7,606	2,808	1,479	–1	342	760	378	1,176	4	–41	859	350	768	8	17	532	211
1966	16,234	54	4,003	8,879	3,297	1,834	1	657	899	277	1,161	10	–79	860	370	729	11	4	489	225
1967	17,926	61	4,423	9,708	3,645	1,458	7	523	683	244	1,143	6	–99	847	388	849	7	6	561	275
1968	19,407	61	4,636	10,796	3,914	1,001	–2	317	562	123	1,369	8	–137	1,041	457	905	7	1	582	316
1969	21,554	72	4,805	12,225	4,453	1,158	6	204	577	372	1,855	10	–196	1,462	579	1,026	5	35	632	354
Japan:																				
1960	254	--------	125	91	38	18	--------	9	7	3	32	--------	14	8	10	15	--------	5	4	6
1961	302	--------	158	103	41	29	--------	23	7	–1	34	--------	13	10	11	15	--------	3	5	7
1962	373	--------	198	122	52	54	--------	41	9	4	33	--------	5	12	16	19	--------	7	4	9
1963	472	--------	260	145	67	68	--------	55	12	1	49	--------	11	28	10	21	--------	7	7	8
1964	598	--------	315	207	77	78	--------	51	23	4	59	--------	4	41	15	30	--------	8	8	14
1965	675	--------	321	275	79	19	--------	–3	21	2	91	--------	14	55	22	47	--------	9	17	21
1966	756	--------	331	334	91	32	--------	–1	22	11	91	--------	16	56	19	43	--------	8	18	17
1967	870	--------	347	425	98	34	--------	(*)	31	3	123	--------	21	85	16	46	--------	9	22	15
1968	1,050	--------	405	522	123	78	--------	46	11	21	167	--------	20	127	20	60	--------	8	37	15
1969	1,218	--------	447	639	132	63	--------	27	32	4	181	--------	19	142	19	70	--------	7	49	13
Australia, New Zealand, and South Africa:																				
1960	1,195	79	373	602	141	23	–6	–6	24	11	162	25	22	101	14	71	18	–1	45	8
1961	1,331	88	433	636	176	89	3	42	20	24	151	21	19	89	22	103	14	2	78	11
1962	1,539	107	483	742	206	127	7	24	79	16	196	20	28	129	20	107	13	–5	87	13
1963	1,783	145	527	881	229	109	12	26	61	9	226	21	20	155	29	97	13	3	65	16
1964	2,053	168	570	1,053	263	137	11	31	64	32	229	30	10	168	22	106	18	4	65	19
1965	2,334	227	616	1,185	305	175	57	43	48	27	246	42	11	157	36	140	36	6	79	19
1966	2,655	324	646	1,332	354	167	77	11	65	13	292	63	12	161	46	138	39	3	79	17
1967	3,172	419	720	1,640	394	364	70	48	223	23	299	66	18	176	38	138	38	–5	83	22
1968	3,508	446	787	1,830	445	171	22	40	83	26	320	64	18	192	46	161	55	–2	82	26
1969	3,854	479	836	2,029	510	153	19	23	69	41	393	87	30	223	53	209	67	5	106	31
Latin American Republics and other Western Hemisphere:																				
1960	8,365	1,319	3,122	1,521	2,403	149	–60	24	125	60	970	224	370	147	229	719	234	331	64	90
1961	9,239	1,332	3,674	1,707	2,526	219	32	63	78	46	1,079	206	478	172	223	824	198	438	75	113
1962	9,524	1,321	3,642	1,944	2,617	29	–13	–67	133	–24	1,179	230	543	173	233	891	221·	488	71·	111
1963	9,941	1,353	3,636	2,213	2,739	235	24	5	150	56	1,243	219	532	171	203	956	210	544	70	132
1964	10,254	1,404	3,589	2,507	2,754	113	30	7	137	–61	1,244	266	530	243	196	1,011	245	531	98	137
1965	10,886	1,474	3,546	2,945	2,921	271	43	–74	245	57	1,320	290	519	289	228	995	266	476	123	130
1966	11,498	1,565	3,475	3,318	3,141	307	60	–37	160	125	1,452	359	512	342	239	1,113	327	499	147	140
1967	12,049	1,709	3,473	3,586	3,282	296	71	–66	199	92	1,398	397	519	269	213	1,190	365	480	195	151
1968	13,101	1,930	3,680	4,005	3,486	677	227	177	222	50	1,574	392	531	408	243	1,218	374	489	216	139
1969	13,810	1,922	3,722	4,347	3,821	344	–31	56	132	187	1,634	449	462	457	266	1,277	404	472	237	164
Other areas:																				
1960	4,181	225	2,763	206	987	71	22	17	9	22	915	47	707	35	126	792	27	700	20	46
1961	4,501	259	2,945	220	1,075	236	26	181	7	14	988	31	789	42	127	876	25	768	25	56
1962	4,777	277	3,142	247	1,113	262	15	220	26	2	1,158	20	938	37	162	1,025	17	933	29	44
1963	5,156	317	3,319	303	1,218	275	41	192	36	7	1,243	17	1,045	35	147	1,093	12	1,008	17	55
1964	5,591	324	3,536	383	1,346	312	2	232	50	28	1,318	21	1,077	53	165	1,234	17	1,131	26	60
1965	6,276	325	4,032	456	1,464	562	–12	490	56	27	1,418	33	1,150	56	179	1,310	22	1,169	28	91
1966	6,640	334	4,159	524	1,622	167	–5	100	41	33	1,469	36	1,201	57	175	1,266	27	1,155	29	55
1967	7,372	346	4,617	629	1,779	578	9	448	77	43	1,745	36	1,455	66	189	1,505	32	1,367	36	69
1968	8,383	360	5,285	693	2,046	657	–1	482	40	136	2,102	55	1,774	79	194	1,777	41	1,614	48	74
1969	9,250	398	5,816	821	2,215	732	8	534	81	108	2,349	64	1,957	95	235	2,294	36	1,963	47	250

*Less than $500,000 (±).

the United States by a U.S.-owned Canadian gas transmission compay.

Negative reinvested earnings in 1969 were mostly the result of a large dividend payment by an international shipping company to the U.S. parent out of accumulated earnings of previous years.

Trade and other industries. U.S. direct investment in trade and "other" industries increased $1.4 billion last year, up from a rise of $0.9 billion in 1968. In developed countries the 1969 rise was $0.9 billion. Investment in European trade and "other" industries grew by over $0.5 billion; this was about double the 1968 increase and reflected the need for funds both to finance recievables and inventories of trading companies and for the acquisition of banking, financial and service companies. The book value of U.S. investment in trade and "other" industries in the less developed countries increased by $392 million with $325 million going to the Latin American Republics and other Western Hemisphere countries. In the less developed countries, U.S. investment in agricultural enterprises and trading companies accounted for about one-third of the increase while most of the remainder went to service and finance enterprises.

Earnings

Earnings (not adjusted) on U.S. direct investments abroad in 1969 were nearly $8.0 billion, up $0.9 billion over 1968 (table 6D, chart 11). U.S. equity in the earnings of affiliates in the less developed countries increased moderately to more than $3.7 billion in 1969, while earnings in the developed countries increased sharply to $4.0 billion. Earnings of the international, unallocated category were $0.2 billion in both years.

As a result of the continuing climb in earnings, the rate of return on all U.S. foreign direct investments rose to 13.0 percent in 1969, higher than any year in the 1960's during which the average annual yield was 12.6 percent (chart 12). For all industries combined, yields in the less developed countries were consistently higher than those in the developed countries. However, most of this difference reflected the structure

of the earnings distribution of petroleum affiliates; earnings in petroleum producing countries are consistently reported as higher than those in developed consuming countries. When rates of return on manufacturing are compared, yields in the two areas are about the same. In 1969, the rate of return on manufactuing investments was 12.7 percent in the less developed countries and 12.9 percent in the developed countries; for the decade, the annual average return on manufacturing investments in each area was 11.8 percent.

With the rise in the rate of return on manufacturing investments abroad to 12.8 percent in 1969, the rate of return of 12.6 percent on comparable domestic investments [2] was exceeded for the first

[2] Petroleum investments are excluded both from manufacturing abroad and from domestic manufacturing. While the rates of return are calculated somewhat differently (see chart 12), the comparison made is probably the most appropriate one.

time in a number of years. Over the past ten years yields on domestic investments averaged 12.4 percent, only slightly higher than the 11.8 percent average on direct investments abroad. Their movements over the years, however, have been significantly different, partly reflecting cyclical factors. Domestic yields were lower than yields abroad in the early 1960's reflecting lower profits associated with the domestic recession early in the decade. As the recovery progressed domestic yields surpassed those on foreign investments and reached a peak of 14.7 percent in 1966; during that year the return on foreign manufacturing investments was only 11.5 percent.

The gap was gradually closed during the next few years when economic expansion abroad was particularly strong. In 1969, the return on foreign investments continued to rise while

Table 10.—Net Capital Outflows to Manufacturing Affiliates by Industry
[Millions of dollars]

Area and year	Manufacturing total	Food products	Paper and allied products	Chemicals and allied products	Rubber products	Primary and fabricated metals	Machinery except electrical	Electrical machinery	Transportation equipment	Other industries
All areas:										
1965	1,525	116	99	292	16	84	286	96	405	131
1966	1,752	108	151	503	19	134	215	131	317	170
1967	1,234	84	68	428	25	242	116	115	1	108
1968r	945	100	-7	293	4	160	71	-2		326
1969p	1,122	124	-11	157	9	135	177	210	88	232
Canada:										
1965	395	18	63	70	5	7	27	13	173	20
1966	566	17	126	90	-2	24	32	-29	246	5
1967	20	-10	48	68	7	-24	2	(*)	-73	1
1968r	26	21	-16	21	-8	29	(*)	(*)	-91	70
1969p	231	52	-45	-2	9	15	51	61	38	53
Europe:										
1965	761	41	13	97	2	60	240	53	176	78
1966	899	51	22	280	16	75	157	84	91	124
1967	683	65	11	201	2	100	65	108	82	49
1968r	562	50	9	164	-1	95	68	-28	23	181
1969p	577	54	28	101	(*)	63	109	111	-2	112
Japan:										
1965	21	2	1	5	(*)	1	2	7	(*)	3
1966	22	(*)	1		(*)	1	4	12	(*)	3
1967	13	2	1	7		1	1	(*)		1
1968r	11	(*)	2	12	(*)	1	-10	2	(*)	4
1969p	32	(*)	(*)	8	(*)	11	-8	5	5	11
Australia, New Zealand and South Africa:										
1965	48	8	3	17	12	-20	11	2	17	-1
1966	65	23	3	17	-2	16	3	-3	2	7
1967	224	5	4	15	8	131	10	1	44	5
1968r	83	10	-1	25	6	18	6	10	10	-1
1969p	69	12	-1	18	-8	20	3	3	2	20
Latin American Republics and Other Western Hemisphere:										
1965	245	51	19	82	-1	20	1	10	38	27
1966	160	11	(*)	99	5	14	13	9	-22	30
1967	198	12	3	85	6	34	17	1	-4	45
1968r	222	12	-1	54	(*)	22	4	9	58	64
1969p	132	1	6	-4	1	24	21	10	44	29
Other areas:										
1965	55	-3	1	21	-2	16	5	11	1	4
1966	40	6	1	17	2	4	5	4	(*)	7
1967	95	10	1	50	2	(*)	21	4	2	7
1968r	40	7	(*)	16	6	-6	2	6	2	7
1969p	81	5	1	36	7	3	3	20	1	8

r Revised.   p Preliminary.   *Less than $500,000 (±).

domestic yields fell with the slowdown in domestic growth.

While these cyclical developments no doubt had a major influence on the rates, other factors were also important. New investments require a seasoning period before they reach their normal profitability. Since a larger portion of manufacturing investment abroad is new, compared with domestic manufacturing investment, this probably contributed to holding the average rate of return on investment abroad below domestic rates. Barring adverse cyclical developments or a surge in new investments, as the sizable amounts of new investments made abroad in the 1960's pass from the initial startup period—when costs are high and markets are being developed—to the "seasoned" stage, total earnings and the rate of return should tend to improve.

The increased earnings in 1969 prin- cipally reflected increases of $666 mil- lion in manufacturing industries and $172 million in "other" industries; mining and petroleum affiliates showed increases of less than $50 million.

Earnings of manufacturing affili- ates in Europe surged upward by 40 percent to $1,462 million, with Ger- many accounting for $224 million of the increase. Earnings of manufactur- ing affiliates in Germany were almost double the 1968 level, no doubt reflect- ing the strong growth there. In Canada, manufacturing was the only industry showing increased earnings in 1969 and accounted for $806 million of total earnings of $1,542 million.

The U.S. share of earnings of petro- leum affiliates in the developed coun- tries dropped from $144 million in 1968 to $76 million in 1969. This was due to higher costs for crude oil and products, mostly as the result of increased tanker costs, which eroded profits of refining and marketing affiliates. European pe- troleum affiliates suffered particularly high losses of $196 million in 1969, reflecting not only the higher tanker rates but also higher levels of explora- tion and development expenses in the North Sea offshore ventures. Earnings of petroleum affiliates in the less devel- oped countries increased by $126 million in 1969 despite a decline of $69 million in earnings in the Latin American Republics and other Western Hemi- sphere countries. Higher costs of pro- duction and large expenditures in Ecuador and Colombia, for developing producing fields and construction of pipelines and other facilities, were the major reasons for the decline in the latter area. Petroleum earnings in the other less developed countries increased by $195 million to $1,825 million in 1969, reflecting increased production. Even in these countries, however, earnings were constrained by higher taxes and other costs which were not matched by increases in prices for crude oil at the producing level.

Direct investment income

Income from direct investments amounted to $5.6 billion in 1969, an increase of over 13 percent from 1968; this was about equal to the percentage increase in earnings (table 6E). A disporportionately large share of the increased income—$250 million out of $666 million—was from affiliates in the international, unallocated category. This is largely the result of unusually large dividend payments by tanker affiliates of oil companies. Developed countries accounted for $91 million of the total increase in income and less developed countries $325 million.

Income includes net interest received on intercompany accounts and on the U.S. non-bank held portion of the for- eign affiliates long-term debt. Interest is not included in earnings because it is deducted by affiliates as an expense item. Income out of earnings amounted to $5.2 billion in 1969, up by $580 million from 1968; net interest received amounted to $481 million, an increase of $86 million from 1968 and double the 1965 level of $230 million. Not all of the increase in interest receipts represents

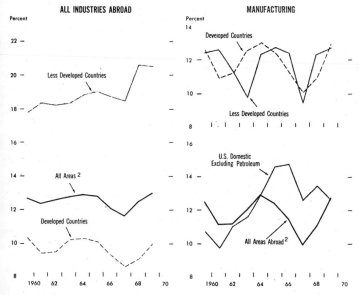

CHART 12

Rates of Return [1] on U.S. Direct Investments Abroad and Domestic Manufacturing Excluding Petroleum

1. Return on direct investments represents earnings plus interest (on intercompany accounts) applied to book value at beginning of year. Return on domestic manufacturing represents net income applied to net worth at beginning of year (as computed by First National City Bank of New York).
2. Data in the direct investments category "international, unallocated" is included in the figures for all areas but excluded from the figures for developed and less developed countries.

U.S. Department of Commerce, Office of Business Economics   70-10-12

a net gain to the U.S. balance of payments because U.S. companies have to meet interest charges for capital raised offshore which was relent to their foreign affiliates.

Most of the increase in income from manufacturing affiliates was the result of additional interest receipts as most of the $0.6 billion gain in earnings was reinvested and not returned to the U.S. as balance of payments income. Direct investment income receipts from petroleum affiliates increased about $0.4 billion in 1969 and the $2.6 billion remitted as income slightly exceeded 1969 earnings.

Direct investment royalties and fees

Royalties and fees received by U.S. corporations from foreign affiliates have grown sharply in recent years to nearly $1.4 billion in 1969 (table 11). These receipts from foreign affiliates represent charges to cover a portion of the funds spent by the U.S. firms for research and development of new products and processes, as well as an allocation of the administrative and other expenses incurred by parent companies on behalf of their foreign affiliates. Foreign manufacturing affiliates contributed about $0.9 billion, or 62 percent, of total receipts of royalties and fees, and European manufacturing affiliates accounted for over half of this total.

Foreign Direct Investments in the United States

During 1969 the value of foreign direct investments in the United States rose $1.0 billion to $11.8 billion at yearend, following a $0.9 billion rise in 1968 (tables 12 and 13). Capital inflows ($832 million) and reinvested earning ($431 million) tended to increase investments by $1,263 million in 1969, but this was partially offset by a $260 million downward adjustment in the value of assets held by foreign-owned U.S. companies, primarily securities held by insurance companies. In 1968, capital inflows were much smaller but valuation adjustments were favorable.

Capital inflows to the U.S. affiliates in 1969 reflected new investments of $538 million and other inflows—mostly shifts in intercompany accounts—of $294 million. New investments in manufacturing companies rose sharply while those in petroleum companies declined. In 1968 a foreign international petroleum company purchased more than $200 million of stock in its U.S. subsidiary and there was no similar transaction in 1969. The rise in new investments in manufacturing was fairly widespread, but investments by German parent companies in U.S. chemical affiliates were particularly large.

Capital inflows other than new investments showed a $400 million favorable swing from an outflow of $107 million in 1968. Of this shift, $310 million was due to an increase in the payables (liabilities) of U.S. companies to their foreign parents in 1969. During 1968 transactions on inter-company account had shown hardly any change. Besides the shifts on inter-company account, liquidation of direct investment assets in the United States resulted in outflows of only $17 million in 1969 compared with $108 million in 1968; this represented a favorable shift of $90 million.

Despite the increased investment in the United States during 1969, earnings of foreign-owned companies declined slightly from $868 million in 1968 to $834 million in 1969. This decline mainly reflected lower profits in the petroleum industry. Earnings of domestic corporations, including those in the petroleum industry, also fell in 1969.

Even though total earnings fell slightly, income paid to foreign parent organizations, primarily dividends on common stock, rose to $417 million in 1969 from $388 million in 1968. The lower earnings coupled with increased dividend payments resulted in reinvested earnings of only $431 million in 1969, down $57 million from 1968.

Table 11.—Direct Investment Receipts of Royalties and Fees,[1] by Areas and Major Industries

[Millions of dollars]

Area and industry	1964			1968 r			1969 p		
	Total	Royalties, license fees and rentals	Management fees and service charges	Total	Royalties, license fees and rentals	Management fees and service charges	Total	Royalties, license fees and rentals	Management fees and service charges
All areas	756	264	492	1,246	522	724	1,369	641	729
Petroleum	116	13	103	160	15	145	191	30	161
Manufacturing	479	210	269	801	435	366	853	510	343
Trade	58	22	36	112	43	69	131	76	56
Other Industries	103	19	84	174	29	145	194	25	169
Canada	162	41	121	261	77	184	268	92	176
Petroleum	15	(*)	15	15	(*)	15	19	1	19
Manufacturing	124	35	89	195	69	126	186	82	105
Trade	9	3	6	16	6	10	15	6	8
Other industries	14	3	11	34	1	33	48	4	44
Europe	306	147	159	511	294	217	588	381	207
Common Market	150	84	66	269	173	96	299	215	84
Petroleum	8	(*)	8	23	(*)	23	22	1	21
Manufacturing	127	79	48	206	161	45	241	194	47
Trade	6	4	2	27	8	19	22	16	6
Other industries	9	1	8	12	3	9	14	5	9
Other Europe (including United Kingdom)	155	13	93	242	121	121	289	165	123
Petroleum	8	1	8	20	2	18	26	3	23
Manufacturing	109	50	59	179	97	82	204	122	82
Trade	15	6	9	16	12	4	38	34	4
Other industries	23	6	17	27	10	17	21	6	15
Latin American Republics and other Western Hemisphere	148	36	112	226	73	153	239	74	165
Petroleum	32	2	30	33	3	30	39	7	32
Manufacturing	64	25	39	119	56	63	108	52	56
Trade	17	6	11	27	9	18	27	10	17
Other industries	34	2	32	47	5	42	64	5	59
Other areas	140	40	99	248	78	170	275	94	181
Petroleum	51	9	42	68	9	59	84	18	66
Manufacturing	55	21	34	101	51	50	114	61	53
Trade	11	4	7	26	8	18	29	9	20
Other industries	22	6	16	53	10	43	46	5	41

p Preliminary.   r Revised   * Less than $500,000   1. Excludes foreign film rentals.

U.S. Portfolio Investments Abroad

The market value of foreign stocks and bonds held by U.S. residents is estimated at $18.7 billion at yearend 1969, an increase of $0.5 billion during the year (table 2, lines, 7, 8, 9). Outflows of U.S. funds for purchases of such securities totaled $1.5 billion during the year, but rising interest rates and falling bond prices resulted in a $1.0 billion decline in the value of outstanding holdings.

U.S. holdings of foreign bonds remained unchanged from end 1968 to end 1969 at $11.7 billion. The reduction in value due to a sharp drop in bond prices was offset by net balance of payments outflows to acquire additional bonds amounting to $1.0 billion. Outflows of U.S. funds to purchase new foreign issues of bonds amounted to $1.5 billion and were down slightly from 1968; issues by the World Bank and by less developed countries declined, although new Canadian issues increased

(table 14). Inflows due to redemptions and to U.S. net sales of outstanding bonds amounted to $0.5 billion.

The market value of U.S. holdings of foreign stocks rose by nearly $0.5 billion to $7.0 billion at yearend 1969, largely due to $0.3 billion in net purchases of outstanding Japanese stocks plus $0.2 billion in purchases of new issues (included in table 14); nearly half of the new issues were Canadian oil stocks. Price changes had little impact on the value of outstanding holdings of foreign stocks.

The significant reduction in the Interest Equalization Tax in April 1969 apparently had little impact on foreign placements of securities in the United States, as nearly all new issues actually placed were exempt. Escalating domestic long-term interest rates during the year were an important factor in reducing foreign bond placements in 1969, particularly by the World Bank and less developed countries. In Canada, on the other hand, demand pressures were quite strong, which led to increases in local borrow-

ing and in placements in the United States.

In the first half of 1970 interest rates in the United States continued upward and foreign bond placements fell to $518 million. A significant drop in Canadian new issues, which was concentrated in the second quarter, accounted for most of the decline; this tendency was reinforced by somewhat more favorable borrowing conditions in Canada.

Foreign Portfolio Investments in the United States

After an extraordinary $6.1 billion increase in the market value of foreign portfolio assets in the United States in 1968, the value of such holdings declined by $0.8 billion in 1969 to $22.9 billion at yearend (table 2, lines 29 and 30). A $3.9 billion decline in the value of outstanding securities due to declining prices of both U.S. equities and bonds was only partly offset by $3.1 billion in capital inflows due to net purchases by

Table 12.—Foreign Direct Investments in the United States, Selected Data Items, Countries, and Industries
[Millions of dollars]

Area and industry	Book value at yearend			Net capital inflows						Earnings [1]		Income [1]		Reinvested earnings [1]	
				1968 ʳ			1969 ᵖ								
	1967	1968 ʳ	1969 ᵖ	Total	New invest-ments [2]	Other	Total	New invest-ments [2]	Other	1968 ʳ	1969 ᵖ	1968 ʳ	1969 ᵖ	1968 ʳ	1969 ᵖ
Total	9,923	10,815	11,818	319	426	107	832	538	294	868	834	388	417	488	431
By area:															
Canada	2,575	2,659	2,834	−26	49	−75	243	84	159	152	122	64	47	102	84
Europe	7,005	7,750	8,510	297	303	−6	550	359	191	687	658	308	348	371	318
United Kingdom	3,156	3,409	3,496	114	109	5	86	56	30	271	272	149	159	108	107
European Economic Community	2,405	2,790	3,306	212	190	22	363	244	−419	285	259	111	132	173	130
Belgium and Luxembourg	228	273	309	25		25	19		19	22	19	5	6	19	17
France	265	288	319	10	(*)	10	17	5	12	23	25	11	12	13	14
Germany	318	387	617	34	52	−18	204	134	70	43	22	7	10	35	13
Italy	86	92	95	2		2	−2		−2	5	8	1	3	4	5
Netherlands	1,508	1,750	1,966	141	138	3	125	105	20	192	185	87	101	102	81
Other Western Europe	1,444	1,551	1,708	−29	4	−33	101	59	42	131	127	48	57	90	81
Sweden	239	205	199	−74		−74	−9		−9	12	8	7	6	4	3
Switzerland	1,096	1,238	1,395	51	4	47	107	58	49	113	118	39	49	81	78
Other	109	108	114	−6		−6	3	1	2	6	1	2	2	5	(*)
Japan	108	181	176	60	74	−14	−34	25	−50	26	41	15	9	13	29
Latin American Republics and other Western Hemisphere	192	182	193	−10		−10	11	8	3	(ʳ*)	11	(*)	12	(*)	(*)
Other	43	43	105	−2	(*)	−2	62	62	(*)	3	2	1	1	2	(*)
By industry:															
Petroleum	1,885	2,261	2,493	231	212	19	142	15	127	263	219	109	124	143	90
Manufacturing	4,181	4,475	5,344	−23	81	−104	567	401	166	410	414	137	149	280	276
Trade	848	938	959	32	67	−35	−41	23	−64	81	88	25	21	57	62
Insurance	³2,193	³2,305	³2,189	5		5	66		66	73	75	73	75		
Other finance	(⁴)	(⁴)	(⁴)	47	60	−13	13	14	−1	⁵38	⁵44	⁵28	⁵36	13	14
Other	816	836	833	27	6	21	85	85		3	−6	16	12	−5	−11

ʳ Revised.   ᵖ Preliminary.   * Less than $500,000(±).

1. "Earnings" represents the foreign share in corporate and branch earnings; "income" is the amount distributed to foreign owners, after withholding taxes, as dividends, interest and branch profits. See technical appendix for an explanation of the relation between income, earnings, and reinvested earnings.
2. "New investments" consists of the first reported capital inflow to establish or acquire

a new company or operation in the United States and the cost of acquisition of additional shares of existing companies.
3. Includes market revaluations of securities held by insurance companies.
4. Included in "insurance."
5. Interest paid by agency banks in the United States to foreign home offices has been excluded from direct investment totals.

Table 13.—Value of Foreign Direct Investments in the United States by Major Industry and Country—End of 1969

[Millions of dollars]

	Total	Petroleum	Manufacturing	Insurance and other finance	Trade and other
All areas	11,818	2,493	5,344	2,189	1,792
Canada	2,834	132	1,644	325	733
Europe	8,510	2,322	3,530	1,766	892
United Kingdom	3,496	829	1,176	1,143	348
Netherlands	1,966	1,275	535	55	101
Switzerland	1,395		1,026	323	46
Other	1,653	218	793	245	397
Other areas	474	39	170	98	167

foreigners. In 1968, net purchases by foreigners accounted for $4.4 billion of the $6.1 billion increase in the value of foreign portfolio assets in the United States. At the end of 1969 foreigners held $18.1 billion of U.S. stocks and $4.8 billion of U.S. bonds.

Stocks

The value of foreign held U.S. stocks declined by $1.4 billion in 1969 as $1.6 billion of foreign net purchases of

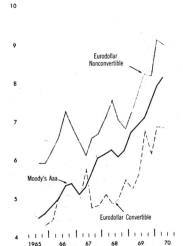

CHART 13

Yields on Bonds Placed Abroad by U.S. Incorporated Companies Compared With Yields on Corporate Bonds in the United States

Percent

Eurodollar Nonconvertible
Moody's Aaa
Eurodollar Convertible

1965 66 67 68 69 70

U.S. Department of Commerce, Office of Business Economics   70-10-13

corporate stock were more than offset by a $3.0 billion decline in stock values due to price changes. In contrast, in 1968, net purchases were higher at $2.1 billion, and the value of outstanding stock holdings appreciated by $2.0 billion. During 1968 when stock prices in the United States were rising, there was a broad foreign interest in equities, and foreign investment funds, which had been organized in the preceding years, made very large purchases. The size of the U.S. market particularly attracted the foreign investment funds because trading in large blocks of stock could be conducted without substantially affecting the price. In addition, unsettling political developments abroad, such as the invasion of Czechoslovakia and the strikes in France also encouraged purchases of U.S. stocks.

In 1969, the lower inflow was apparently related to the fact that U.S. stock prices turned downward at the same time that other foreign share prices, except those in the United Kingdom, performed well. Also, Eurodollar rates rose to 11 percent during 1969 and provided an attractive alter-

Table 14.—Newly Issued Foreign Securities Sold to U.S. Residents

[Millions of dollars]

Issuer	1967	1968	1969	1970 (Jan.-June)
Total [1]	1,619	1,703	1,667	533
Canada	1,007	949	1,270	387
Central government		86	16	
Provincial government-guaranteed	601	508	616	219
Municipal authorities	160	101	84	10
Corporate issues	246	254	554	158
Japan	14	3	9	
International organizations	246	390	164	49
Less developed countries	352	320	211	96
Other developed countries		41	14	2
Memorandum items:				
New issues of corporate stock included above	4	84	156	15
U.S. direct investment enterprises [1]	45	354	61	114
In Canada	45	291	61	114
In less developed countries		63		
In other developed countries				

1. New issues of U.S. direct investment enterprises placed with other than parent are not included with new issues but are recorded in the direct investment account.

native for funds that might otherwise have been invested in U.S. equities.

As U.S. stock prices dropped precipitously in the first half of 1970, foreigners made net sales of $0.2 billion. The fact that sales were so small relative to the $19.6 billion in outstanding holdings at the end of 1969 suggests a

Table 15.—Foreign Security Placements by U.S.-Incorporated Companies, by Type

[Millions of dollars]

	Straight debt: Payable in—				Convertible: Payable in—			Total [1]
	Dollars	Deutsche marks	Swiss francs	Other currencies	Dollars	Deutsche marks	Other currencies	
1965*	67	55			75			197
III	20							20
IV	47	55			75			177
1966	161	56	10		182	190		599
I	55		10		120			185
II	51				62	180		293
III	10	25						35
IV	45	31				10		86
1967	225	15	33		177			450
I	60		11		20			91
II	75	15	11		10			111
III	70		11		50			131
IV	20				97			117
1968	278	277	94		1,540			2,189
I	90		12		494			596
II	15	19	41		526			601
III	75	110	14		406			605
IV	98	148	27		114			387
1969	207	226	77		500		[2] 44	1,054
I	85	63	27		232		[2] 44	407
II			14		95			153
III	14	88	36		87			225
IV	108	75			86			269
1970*	286		28	[3] 32	80		[4] 8	434
I	106		14	[3] 15	22		[4] 8	165
II	180		14	[3] 17	58			269

* Six-month total.
1. These amounts differ from balance of payments figures which are net of placement costs.
2. Payable in British sterling.
3. Payable in Dutch guilders.
4. Payable in Swiss francs.

certain stability and long-term focus of foreign investments in U.S. equities.

Bonds

Foreign investments in U.S. bonds rose $0.6 billion in 1969, compared with $2.1 billion in 1968. Inflows of funds were $1.5 billion in 1969, down sharply from the $2.3 billion inflow in 1968. In addition, rising interest rates resulted in a $1.0 billion reduction in the value of outstanding holdings, compared with a reduction of only $0.2 billion in 1968.

The drop in foreign purchases of U.S. bonds largely reflected economic and institutional factors affecting U.S. corporate foreign borrowing. The large increase in new issues of securities sold abroad by U.S. corporations in recent years was partly in response to the Foreign Direct Investment Program. Under this program direct investments by U.S. companies which are financed by funds raised abroad are not subject to restriction. In 1968, when the program first became mandatory, U.S. corporations raised $2.1 billion from bond placements with foreign investors. In 1969, such issues fell, but they still amounted to $1.0 billion (table 15).

A sharp tightening in the Eurobond market and national capital markets abroad was probably a major factor in the 1969 decline in these issues (chart 13). In addition, the general weakness and uncertainty in U.S. stock markets made new bond issues convertible into U.S. stock at a fixed price much less attractive to foreigners; such offerings were reduced from $1.5 billion in 1968 to $0.5 billion in 1969 (table 15). The fact that U.S. corporations had nearly $1.0 billion of unused proceeds of earlier borrowing at end 1968, may have also discouraged further new issues in 1969.

U.S. corporations continued to establish Netherlands Antilles finance subsidiaries during the year as means for raising money in the Eurobond market. Tax considerations provided a major motive for establishing such subsidiaries. Security issues by these subsidiaries usually carry the guarantee of the U.S. parent company. For balance of payments purposes, these issues are considered net purchases of U.S. obligations by foreigners only to the extent that the finance subsidiaries transfer the proceeds to the U.S. parent. During 1969, $283 million of such proceeds were transferred to U.S. parents for either foreign or domestic use.

In the first half of 1970, international bond issues by U.S. corporations declined further from 1969. Convertible issues were still depressed, and the very tight market conditions encouraged U.S. borrowers employing straight debt to reduce maturities to medium-term 5-year notes. Also, floating rate instruments were utilized by two U.S. corporations, with the rate on the issues pegged to the 6 months Eurodollar interbank rate with a minimum rate clause. Such instruments are designed to avoid long-term commitments at record high interest rates.

In 1969, foreign transactions in outstanding securities (including U.S. Government agency bonds) somewhat offset the decline in new issues. The World Bank increased its net purchases of U.S. agency bonds by $0.2 billion to $0.3 billion. Furthermore, foreigners increased their purchases of other outstanding U.S. bonds from $30 million in 1968 to $182 million as U.S. bond yields moved substantially upward. In the first half of 1970, net purchases of agency bonds and of other outstanding U.S. bonds amounted to $188 million and $178 million, respectively.

Technical Note

The various direct investment earnings items, including those shown in tables 6C, D & E, are defined below and their derivation and relationship to each other are detailed.

Item and definition

1. Net earnings of foreign corporations: The U.S. parents' equity in the earnings of their foreign subsidiaries after provision for foreign income taxes, preferred dividends, and interest payments.

2. Net earnings of foreign branches: The earnings of foreign branches of U.S. companies after foreign income taxes, but before depletion charges and U.S. taxes. Included with net earnings of branches are the U.S. share in the net earnings of foreign partnerships, sole proprietorships and other types of foreign organizations. All branch earnings are as-

sumed to be repatriated to the United States and thus are balance of payments flow items. To the extent that branch earnings are left abroad they are implicitly entered as offsetting capital outflows.

3. Earnings: Net earnings of foreign corporations plus net earnings of foreign branches.

4. Gross dividends on common stock: Dividends paid out by foreign corporations before deduction of withholding taxes paid to foreign governments.

5. Foreign withholding tax: A tax withheld on the payment of dividends as distinguished from income taxes which are imposed on the earnings of a business. Taxes are also withheld by the payor on payments of interest and preferred dividends but both interest and preferred dividends are reported to the Balance of Payments Division on a net basis and, therefore, our data on withholding taxes relate only to those on common stock dividends.

6. Dividends: Dividends on common or voting stock only, net of foreign withholding taxes; dividends are included in income as balance of payments flow items.

7. Preferred dividends: Dividends received on preference or non-voting shares after deduction of any foreign withholding taxes. Preferred dividends are included in income as balance of payments flow items. Preferred dividends are treated like interest in these accounts even though on the foreign company's books they are not charged as an expense.

8. Interest: The net interest received on intercompany accounts or on long-term debt of foreign affiliates held by the parent or other nonbank U.S. investors, after deduction of any foreign withholding taxes. Interest is not included in earnings since it is deducted as an expense item by the foreign firm, but, it is included in income as a balance of payments flow item.

9. Income: The sum of dividends, preferred dividends, and interest received by or credited to the account of the U.S. owner—all net after foreign withholding taxes—plus branch earnings after foreign taxes; all before U.S. taxes.

10. Reinvested earnings: Net earnings of foreign corporations less gross dividends on common stock.

11. Adjusted earnings: The benefits of ownership accruing to a U.S. foreign direct investor after all foreign taxes, including withholding taxes, have been paid; this is comprised of (1) funds returned to the United States as income in the form of dividends, preferred dividends, branch profits, and interest, plus (2) funds left abroad to increase the investor's equity in the foreign enterprise as a reinvestment of earnings.

Derivation and relationship based on 1969 preliminary data

[Millions of dollars]

1. Net earnings of foreign corporations.	5,381	reported
2. Net earnings of foreign branches....	2,574	reported
3. Earnings.................	7,955	= 1+2
4. Gross dividends (on common stock).	2,849	= 5+6
5. Foreign withholding tax (on common stock).................	282	reported
6. Dividends (on common stock)......	2,567	= 4−5 (reported)
7. Preferred dividends...............	17	reported
8. Interest..................	481	reported
9. Income.................	5,639	= 2+6+7+8
10. Reinvested earnings..............	2,532	= 1−4 or 3−2−4
11. Adjusted earnings................	8,171	= 9+10 or 3+7+8−5.

PLANT AND EQUIPMENT EXPENDITURES BY FOREIGN AFFILIATES OF U.S. CORPORATIONS

Revised Estimates for 1970 and 1971

Howard Murad

By HOWARD MURAD

Plant and Equipment Expenditures by Foreign Affiliates of U.S. Corporations–Revised Estimates for 1970 and 1971

Foreign affiliates of U.S. corporations are provisionally estimated to have increased plant and equipment expenditures 22 percent in 1970 to a level of $13.2 billion, and are planning a 16-percent increase to $15.3 billion in 1971. The growth in both years is centered in spending by manufacturing affiliates in the developed areas.

PROPERTY, plant, and equipment expenditures by U.S. firms' foreign affiliates are provisionally estimated to have risen 22 percent in 1970 to a level of $13.2 billion. An increase of 16 percent is expected in 1971, with total outlays reaching $15.3 billion. The strength of spending growth in both years is primarily related to heavy expenditures by manufacturing affiliates in the developed countries, particularly in the European Economic Community.

These estimates are based on the semiannual survey taken by the Office of Business Economics in December 1970; the survey covered a sample of about 450 large U.S. corporations with approximately 4,500 foreign affiliates.

The current estimate of 1970 spending is significantly higher than the projection made 6 months earlier, when spending was expected to rise by only 16 percent to $12.5 billion. Petroleum affiliates now report a 3-percent rise in spending last year compared with the 4-percent reduction they projected 6 months earlier. The change is related primarily to accelerated tanker construction and stepped-up development of facilities in Europe and the Far East. In addition, manufacturers of transportation equipment

and machinery now estimate significantly higher spending than they indicated previously.

Spending in 1971 is $0.5 billion higher than previously projected, but the percentage increase in 1971 is slightly smaller because of the upward revision of the 1970 figure. The 1971 plans of petroleum affiliates have been raised substantially since the previous survey, while those of manufacturing affiliates, especially in Canada and Latin America have been reduced slightly.

In dollar terms, the growth of affiliates' spending from 1969 to 1971 is expected to be $4.5 billion, the largest 2-year increase since the initiation of

the survey in 1957. The high level of spending in 1970 was no doubt a factor in the large outflow of direct investment funds last year (reported in "The U.S. Balance of Payments: Fourth Quarter and Year 1970" elsewhere in this issue). The increase in plant and equipment expenditures planned for 1971, if realized, will also lead to large capital outflows, particularly with lower long-term interest rates in the United States. On the other hand, the use of foreign funds will be encouraged by the easing of conditions in the Eurobond market and by limitations on the use of U.S. funds set by the Office of Foreign Direct Investments (although the program was relaxed somewhat at year end).

CHART 13

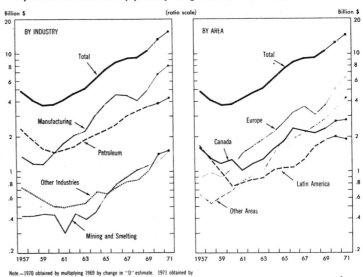

Expenditures for Plant and Equipment by Foreign Affiliates of U.S. Companies

Note.—1970 obtained by multiplying 1969 by change in "D" estimate. 1971 obtained by multiplying 1970 by change in "B" estimate. See note to table 2.

* Expected

U.S. Department of Commerce, Office of Business Economics

Industry pattern

Manufacturing affiliates are estimated to have increased expenditures by 39 percent to $6.9 billion in 1970. If current estimates are confirmed, these affiliates will have increased spending $1.9 billion, by far the largest yearly dollar gain for any industry in the history of the plant and equipment survey. While manufacturing in all major areas showed sizable increases, growth was particularly strong in the European Economic Community and Japan. Estimates for 1971 indicate an increase of 17 percent to a level of $8.1 billion, more than double the level in 1965. Manufacturing affiliates in Germany are planning a 55-percent increase.

Manufacturers of machinery show large percentage increases in both 1970 and 1971. They are estimated to have increased spending by 44 percent in 1970 to $1.9 billion and plan spending $2.6 billion in 1971, a 32-percent increase. Both years show sharp increases in spending by computer manufacturers in France, Germany, and Japan, countries where demand is being stimulated by the fast growth and increasing sophistication of business. However, not all of the increases registered by computer manufacturers represent actual expansion of plant capacity since these affiliates count as part of their capital expenditures the cost of machinery acquired or produced for leasing to others.

Manufacturers of transportation equipment are estimated to have spent $1.1 billion in 1970, 37 percent more than in 1969; the increase mainly reflected outlays by auto manufacturers in Canada and Germany. An increase of 22 percent is projected for 1971. Spending in Germany is again expected to rise steeply, while auto manufacturers in Canada plan to decrease spending.

Affiliates in the chemical industry reported a 22-percent increase in 1970 spending to a level of $1.4 billion, following a 9-percent decrease in 1969. Outlays rose in Germany, the Netherlands, Belgium, the United Kingdom, and Japan. In 1971 a modest 3-percent increase is planned, concentrated in Germany, the United Kingdom, and Spain.

Affiliates in the "other manufacturing" category increased spending by 48 percent in 1970 to $2.6 billion and plan a 12-percent increase to $2.9 billion in 1971. The sharp rise in 1970 was due largely to expenditures by primary and fabricated metals producers in Germany, the Netherlands, Australia, and the Middle East. The 1971 increase reflects expansion by primary and fabricated metals producers in the United Kingdom and Australia, and by miscellaneous manufacturers, primarily those producing photographic and photocopy equipment, in the United Kingdom and Canada.

Affiliates in the *petroleum* industry are estimated to have increased spending 3 percent in 1970 to $3.8 billion—the smallest percentage increase among the major industries. In 1971, however, they plan a 13-percent rise to $4.2 billion. Expenditures in Libya were reduced sharply in 1970, and further cuts are expected in 1971. The small net increase in total spending in 1970 is due to spending by affiliates in Italy, Japan, and other Far East countries. Substantial increases in 1971 are planned

Table 1.—Estimates of Plant and Equipment Expenditures by Foreign Affiliates of U.S. Corporations, Actual and Projected, by Percent Change and Amount [1]

Industry, area and schedule	(Percent change)								(Billions of dollars)									
	Actual				Current projection [2]		Prior projection [3]		Actual					Current projection [2]		Prior projection [3]		
	1966	1967	1968	1969 ʳ	1970	1971	1970	1971	1965	1966	1967	1968	1969 ʳ	1970	1971	1970	1971
Total	16	7	1	15	22	16	16	18	7.4	8.6	9.3	9.4	10.8	13.2	15.3	12.5	14.8
By industry																	
Mining and smelting	25	17	12	9	10	20	12	26	.6	.8	.9	1.0	1.1	1.2	1.5	1.3	1.5
Petroleum	11	19	10	10	3	13	−4	3	2.3	2.5	3.0	3.3	3.6	3.8	4.2	3.5	3.6
Manufacturing	18	−1	−7	18	39	17	32	26	3.9	4.6	4.5	4.2	5.0	6.9	8.1	6.5	8.3
Chemicals	21	16	0	−9	22	3	28	28	.9	1.0	1.2	1.2	1.1	1.4	1.4	1.4	1.8
Machinery	19	4	−7	32	44	32	38	36	.9	1.0	1.1	1.0	1.3	1.9	2.6	1.8	2.4
Transportation equipment	11	−18	−22	29	37	22	11	8	.9	1.0	.8	.6	.8	1.1	1.3	.9	1.0
Other manufacturing	21	−7	−6	27	48	12	40	30	1.3	1.5	1.4	1.3	1.7	2.6	2.9	2.4	3.1
Other industries	14	10	3	23	31	13	20	20	.7	.7	.8	.8	1.0	1.4	1.5	1.2	1.4
By area																	
Canada	28	−5	−5	10	18	2	16	7	1.8	2.4	2.2	2.1	2.3	2.7	2.8	2.7	2.9
Latin American Republics and other Western Hemisphere	2	17	29	12	7	−5	−1	10	1.1	1.1	1.3	1.6	1.9	2.0	1.9	1.9	2.0
Europe	23	12	−14	20	37	27	30	25	2.6	3.3	3.6	3.1	3.7	5.1	6.5	4.9	6.1
European Economic Community	31	15	−19	20	42	35	33	35	1.4	1.9	2.1	1.7	2.0	2.9	4.0	2.7	3.6
Other, including United Kingdom	15	8	−7	19	30	16	25	12	1.2	1.4	1.5	1.4	1.7	2.2	2.5	2.1	2.4
Other areas	3	9	17	15	20	24	10	21	1.9	1.9	2.1	2.5	2.9	3.4	4.2	3.1	3.8
By OFDI schedule																	
All schedules [4,5]	12	12	3	16	24	19	16	21	5.6	6.3	7.0	7.2	8.4	10.5	12.5	9.7	11.7
Schedule A	3	11	24	17	14	7	2	10	1.7	1.8	2.0	2.4	2.9	3.3	3.5	3.0	3.3
Schedule B	4	12	8	14	27	18	22	18	2.0	2.1	2.4	2.6	2.9	3.7	4.4	3.5	4.1
Schedule C	30	13	−16	18	33	33	26	33	1.8	2.4	2.7	2.2	2.6	3.5	4.7	3.3	4.4

ʳ Revised.
1. See notes to table 2 for derivation of 1970 and 1971 estimates.
2. Based on results of the survey taken in December 1970.
3. Based on results of the survey taken in June 1970, as published in September 1970; no adjustments have been made to reflect information received subsequent to publication.
4. Does not include Canada.

5. Beginning with 1970 Spain is classified in Schedule B; prior to 1970 it is classified in Schedule C. If Spain remained in Schedule C, the expected 1970 rise in expenditures by affiliates in Schedule C countries would have been 40 percent and spending would have totaled $3.7 billion instead of the $3.5 billion reported here; the increase in Schedule B countries would have been 21 percent while the amount would have been $3.5 billion.

for Indonesia, Japan, the Middle East, and the European Economic Community. However, a major portion of the increase is going into the expansion

of tanker operations, reflecting continuing uncertainty over the future of the Suez Canal and the increasing cost of leasing tankers.

Expenditures by affiliates engaged in *mining and smelting* are estimated to have increased spending by 10 percent last year and are expected to rise 20

Table 2.—Estimates of Plant and Equipment Expenditures by Foreign Affiliates of U.S. Corporations—Summary of Surveys [1]

[Millions of dollars]

Area and industry	1966 E	1967 E	1968 E	1969 D	1969 E	1970 A	1970 B	1970 C	1970 D	1971 A	1971 B
By area and major industry division											
All areas	**8,640**	**9,267**	**9,387**	**10,864**	**10,788**	**12,235**	**13,655**	**13,746**	**13,350**	**14,296**	**15,796**
Mining and smelting	789	920	1,035	1,172	1,132	1,016	1,283	1,350	1,294	1,280	1,534
Petroleum	2,526	3,000	3,311	3,789	3,640	4,112	4,167	4,046	3,916	4,228	4,693
Manufacturing	4,583	4,525	4,191	4,880	4,976	6,034	6,938	7,053	6,803	7,505	8,137
Other industries	741	823	850	1,023	1,039	1,073	1,266	1,296	1,338	1,282	1,432
Canada	**2,357**	**2,233**	**2,128**	**2,340**	**2,330**	**2,613**	**2,888**	**2,850**	**2,762**	**2,783**	**2,941**
Mining and smelting	297	332	340	347	340	321	409	429	402	400	536
Petroleum	649	636	669	686	629	783	754	742	738	679	691
Manufacturing	1,174	1,001	854	993	1,036	1,204	1,370	1,310	1,222	1,336	1,303
Other industries	237	264	265	314	326	306	355	370	401	368	411
Latin American Republics and other Western Hemisphere	**1,092**	**1,282**	**1,656**	**1,939**	**1,856**	**1,883**	**2,277**	**2,184**	**2,072**	**2,058**	**2,156**
Mining and smelting	229	288	456	510	497	386	502	489	448	419	388
Petroleum	268	306	405	533	501	570	639	594	583	528	620
Manufacturing	452	505	575	623	611	636	797	782	739	813	823
Other industries	143	183	220	273	247	291	338	318	301	298	325
Europe:											
Common market	**1,853**	**2,124**	**1,717**	**2,126**	**2,065**	**2,688**	**3,052**	**3,053**	**3,020**	**3,573**	**4,124**
Mining and smelting	3	3	3	3	3	4	6	3	3	3	3
Petroleum	434	582	401	518	472	615	662	594	565	681	808
Manufacturing	1,331	1,438	1,195	1,466	1,440	1,905	2,201	2,249	2,248	2,677	3,077
Other industries	85	100	118	139	149	163	183	207	199	211	232
Other Europe	**1,400**	**1,508**	**1,408**	**1,669**	**1,675**	**2,090**	**2,236**	**2,289**	**2,169**	**2,349**	**2,598**
Mining and smelting	4	5	7	9	8	9	6	8	8	8	15
Petroleum	344	463	450	423	404	524	540	451	424	526	594
Manufacturing	913	894	817	1,076	1,099	1,369	1,474	1,598	1,481	1,565	1,699
Other industries	141	146	134	162	164	189	215	232	256	250	290
Other areas	**1,938**	**2,121**	**2,477**	**2,790**	**2,862**	**2,961**	**3,202**	**3,370**	**3,333**	**3,534**	**3,982**
Mining and smelting	257	293	230	303	285	297	360	421	432	450	592
Petroleum	832	1,012	1,386	1,629	1,634	1,620	1,572	1,666	1,606	1,812	1,980
Manufacturing	714	687	749	722	791	920	1,095	1,114	1,113	1,115	1,235
Other industries	135	130	113	136	152	124	175	169	181	156	174
By area and major manufacturing industry											
All areas	**4,583**	**4,525**	**4,191**	**4,880**	**4,976**	**6,034**	**6,938**	**7,053**	**6,803**	**7,505**	**8,137**
Chemicals	1,040	1,210	1,208	1,109	1,118	1,259	1,525	1,513	1,354	1,566	1,570
Machinery	1,046	1,088	1,016	1,363	1,344	1,660	1,913	2,011	1,964	2,196	2,524
Transportation equipment	966	795	617	808	795	1,275	1,220	1,100	1,110	1,343	1,484
Other manufacturing	1,531	1,432	1,349	1,600	1,719	1,840	2,279	2,429	2,375	2,400	2,560
Canada	**1,174**	**1,001**	**854**	**993**	**1,036**	**1,204**	**1,370**	**1,310**	**1,222**	**1,336**	**1,303**
Chemicals	221	166	158	184	169	197	244	210	181	207	184
Machinery	186	190	144	193	222	221	238	252	209	273	282
Transportation equipment	255	234	194	207	211	368	321	271	312	258	210
Other manufacturing	513	411	358	409	434	418	567	576	520	598	626
Latin American Republics and other Western Hemisphere	**452**	**505**	**575**	**623**	**611**	**636**	**797**	**782**	**739**	**813**	**823**
Chemicals	143	150	179	203	198	148	203	208	176	176	196
Machinery	65	78	86	107	95	121	146	160	152	166	187
Transportation equipment	72	88	90	105	104	149	169	138	121	225	158
Other manufacturing	171	188	220	208	214	218	280	275	289	245	282
Europe:											
Common Market	**1,331**	**1,438**	**1,195**	**1,466**	**1,440**	**1,905**	**2,201**	**2,249**	**2,248**	**2,677**	**3,077**
Chemicals	275	427	313	293	288	362	482	465	431	519	561
Machinery	444	511	486	632	620	775	888	807	972	1,083	1,235
Transportation equipment	373	245	146	228	210	326	325	353	331	518	734
Other manufacturing	239	255	249	313	321	442	507	534	514	557	547
Other Europe	**913**	**894**	**817**	**1,076**	**1,099**	**1,369**	**1,474**	**1,598**	**1,481**	**1,565**	**1,699**
Chemicals	187	210	210	183	195	281	271	308	268	348	344
Machinery	220	202	203	280	261	342	402	424	362	431	481
Transportation equipment	191	134	86	173	180	273	257	218	227	210	240
Other manufacturing	315	349	318	440	464	472	545	648	624	576	635
Other areas	**714**	**687**	**749**	**722**	**791**	**920**	**1,095**	**1,114**	**1,113**	**1,115**	**1,235**
Chemicals	213	258	348	246	268	272	326	322	298	316	285
Machinery	132	107	98	151	146	200	240	277	269	242	.337
Transportation equipment	75	94	100	95	90	159	148	120	118	132	142
Other manufacturing	294	228	204	230	287	289	381	396	428	424	470

ʳ Revised.

1. A. Estimated in June of previous year. B. Estimated in December of previous year. C. Estimated in June of current year. D. Estimated in December of current year. E. Actual reported in June of following year. The most recent figures for 1970 and 1971 (columns 1970 (D) and 1971 (B) in tables 2–4) are not necessarily the best estimates of the actual expenditures likely to be made in these years. Better indications of year-to-year changes are likely to be obtained by comparing an estimate for a given year with that made in the corresponding

survey for the previous year—for example, 1970 (D) versus 1969 (D)—in order to adjust for systematic reporting bias. The "projections" for 1970 and 1971 in table 1 were derived on this basis. For 1970, the change in the (D) estimates (1970D/1969D) was applied to 1969E (actual) to obtain the 1970 adjusted estimate. For 1971, the change in the (B) estimate (1971B/1970B) was applied to the adjusted estimate for 1970. (For further discussion see the technical note on page 46 of the March 1969 issue of the SURVEY.)

Source: U.S. Department of Commerce, Office of Business Economics.

percent to $1.5 billion in 1971. The gains in both years are concentrated in Canada, Australia, and Indonesia, where many affiliates are developing nickel ore and bauxite deposits. Spending in Latin America shows sharp reductions in both years, which may be associated with the deterioration of the investment climate in countries that are traditional suppliers of ores.

Affiliates in the *"other industry"* category, which includes those engaged in trade, leasing and finance, are estimated to have increased outlays 31 percent in 1970 to $1.4 billion, and plan an increase of 13 percent in 1971 to $1.5 billion. Increases are especially large for affiliates in Canada, the United Kingdom, Spain, and the European Economic Community.

Geographic pattern

Largely as a result of spending by affiliates in the EEC countries, capital outlays in *Europe* are estimated to have increased 37 percent in 1970 to $5.1 billion, and are expected to increase by 27 percent this year to $6.5 billion. The increases in both 1970 and 1971 in the EEC reflect increased spending by manufacturing affiliates in Germany, the Netherlands, and France, as well as by affiliates engaged in petroleum refining in France, Germany, and Italy.

Increases in European countries outside the EEC are due to higher outlays by manufacturing affiliates, particularly in the United Kingdom and Spain. In 1971, development of oil sources in the North Sea is also contributing to the increase in outlays.

Spending by affiliates in *Latin America* increased 7 percent in 1970 to $2.0 billion, but is expected to total only $1.9 billion in 1971. The 1970 increase was attributable to spending by petroleum affiliates in Venezuela and manufacturing affiliates in Argentina and Mexico. Manufacturing affiliates—principally those in Brazil, Argentina and Mexico—expect to increase spending in 1971, but cuts are planned by affiliates in mining and smelting and in petroleum. A growing share of capital spending in Latin America is in manufacturing rather than in the extractive industries.

Spending in *Canada* is estimated to have increased 18 percent in 1970 to $2.7 billion and is expected to increase 2 percent to $2.8 billion in 1971. All major industry groups showed gains in 1970 with manufacturing showing the largest percentage and dollar increases. In 1971, however, manufacturing affiliates, particularly producers of transportation equipment, plan to reduce expenditures. Petroleum affiliates also expect spending to decline, but those in mining and

smelting and "other industries" expect gains.

Affiliates in *"other areas"* increased their expenditures by 20 percent in 1970 to $3.4 billion and plan to spend $4.2 billion in 1971, a 24-percent increase. There are noticeable increases in both years for manufacturers of machinery in Japan and of primary and fabricated metals in Australia and the Middle East. Affiliates in mining and smelting also show large increases.

Classified according to the country schedules established by the Office of Foreign Direct Investments, the largest increases in 1970 and 1971, in both dollar and percentage terms, are by affiliates in Schedule C countries (including most of continental Western Europe and South Africa) for which controls on capital outflows from the United States are strictest. These affiliates increased spending 33 percent last year to $3.5 billion, and expect a similar increase this year to $4.7 billion. Manufacturing and petroleum affiliates in the EEC show particularly large increases in both years. The aim of the investment controls under the OFDI program has, for the most part, been to limit use of U.S. funds for investments abroad, not to reduce expansion by foreign affiliates. To the extent that fixed asset investment can be financed by borrowing

Table 3.—Estimates of Plant and Equipment Expenditures by Foreign Affiliates of U.S. Corporations by OFDI Schedule Area and Industry—Summary of Surveys

[Millions of dollars]

Schedule	1966 E	1967 E	1968 E	1969 D	1969 E'	1970 A	1970 B	1970 C'	1970 D	1971 A'	1971 B
All schedule, total [1]	6,282	7,034	7,259	8,524	8,458	9,622	10,766	10,896	10,588	11,513	12,855
Schedule A	1,787	1,990	2,458	2,912	2,878	3,037	3,458	3,382	3,304	3,341	3,701
Mining and smelting	271	333	487	575	576	458	595	601	569	533	559
Petroleum	574	688	981	1,223	1,201	1,354	1,380	1,368	1,389	1,465	1,708
Manufacturing	718	714	705	772	768	866	1,055	1,012	957	985	1,025
Other industries	225	255	285	342	333	359	428	400	389	357	409
Schedule B [2]	2,124	2,374	2,560	2,916	2,928	3,364	3,673	3,832	3,706	3,933	4,333
Mining and smelting	185	222	187	223	183	200	241	276	285	315	393
Petroleum	692	935	1,116	1,182	1,163	1,199	1,205	1,165	1,062	1,190	1,265
Manufacturing	1,153	1,113	1,172	1,406	1,474	1,835	2,058	2,205	2,146	2,236	2,464
Other industries	94	104	85	104	108	130	169	185	213	192	210
Schedule C [2]	2,371	2,670	2,241	2,696	2,651	3,221	3,635	3,684	3,577	4,240	4,822
Mining and smelting	36	33	23	26	33	37	38	44	38	32	46
Petroleum	612	741	544	699	647	777	829	771	727	892	1,029
Manufacturing	1,538	1,697	1,459	1,709	1,698	2,127	2,454	2,526	2,484	2,948	3,345
Other industries	185	200	215	262	272	280	314	342	329	308	402

' Revised.
1. Does not include Canada. For a listing of the countries in each schedule area, see Foreign Direct Investments Regulation (15 CFR 1000.319 F.R. 49) or reprints of the regulation dated May 20, 1968, Office of Foreign Direct Investments, U.S. Department of Commerce, Washington, D.C. 20230.
2. Beginning with 1970, Spain is classified in Schedule B; prior to 1970 it is classified in Schedule C.

abroad, plant and equipment spending is not limited by the OFDI program.

Affiliates in Schedule B countries (including the United Kingdom, Japan, and Australia) increased spending 27 percent in 1970 to $3.7 billion and plan an 18-percent increase to $4.4 billion in 1971. Affiliates in Schedule A countries (including most of the less developed countries), for which controls on capital outflows are most lenient, show the smallest growth. Spending in these countries increased 14 percent in 1970 to $3.3 billion, and is expected to increase 7 percent to $3.5 billion in 1971.

Table 4.—Estimates of Plant and Equipment Expenditures by Foreign Manufacturing and Petroleum Affiliates of U.S. Corporations by Selected Country—Summary of Surveys

[Millions of dollars]

By area and major industry division	1966 E	1967 E	1968 E	1969 D	1969 E′	1970 A	1970 B	1970 C′	1970 D	1971 A′	1971 B
Manufacturing											
All areas	4,583	4,525	4,191	4,880	4,976	6,034	6,938	7,053	6,803	7,505	8,137
Canada	1,174	1,001	854	993	1,036	1,204	1,370	1,310	1,222	1,336	1,303
Latin American Republics and other Western Hemisphere	452	505	575	623	611	636	797	782	739	813	823
Argentina	91	100	71	107	95	140	169	172	152	162	149
Brazil	100	131	186	213	186	195	206	183	190	226	265
Mexico	126	133	182	161	170	160	220	221	230	210	233
Other	136	141	136	142	160	141	202	205	165	214	175
Europe	2,243	2,332	2,012	2,542	2,539	3,274	3,676	3,847	3,729	4,242	4,784
United Kingdom	698	643	582	834	858	1,079	1,131	1,225	1,152	1,194	1,338
European Economic Community	1,331	1,438	1,195	1,466	1,440	1,905	2,201	2,249	2,248	2,677	3,077
Belgium and Luxembourg	186	200	153	104	111	141	200	198	176	212	241
France	288	371	306	369	338	505	539	505	557	582	690
Germany	581	518	423	620	607	863	1,005	1,061	993	1,336	1,560
Italy	125	150	166	174	181	210	229	247	260	268	326
Netherlands	151	198	147	200	203	187	228	238	262	279	260
Other	214	251	235	242	241	290	344	373	329	370	361
Japan	153	190	227	262	268	306	413	428	429	453	531
Australia, New Zealand, and South Africa	332	256	295	270	306	381	403	384	358	437	432
Australia	278	208	240	235	258	322	347	331	313	361	365
New Zealand	15	6	4	5	6	9	10	8	7	11	15
South Africa	39	42	51	30	42	50	46	45	38	64	52
Other Africa	55	31	14	12	14	27	22	32	30	28	43
Middle East	23	62	111	55	73	31	40	87	123	66	82
Other Asia and Pacific	150	148	102	123	130	175	217	184	173	130	147
India	91	50	25	39	47	57	86	64	53	60	67
Other	59	98	77	84	83	118	131	120	120	71	80
Petroleum											
All areas	2,526	3,000	3,311	3,789	3,640	4,112	4,167	4,046	3,916	4,228	4,693
Canada	649	636	669	686	629	783	754	742	738	679	691
Latin American Republics and other Western Hemisphere	268	306	405	533	501	570	639	594	583	528	620
Venezuela	101	103	175	249	238	231	274	217	227	171	243
Other Latin American Republics	109	148	164	152	138	214	221	228	208	249	272
Other Western Hemisphere	58	55	66	132	125	125	144	150	147	108	104
Europe	778	1,045	851	941	876	1,139	1,202	1,045	988	1,208	1,401
United Kingdom	163	289	283	251	246	286	294	229	223	248	292
European Economic Community	434	582	401	518	472	615	662	594	565	681	808
Belgium and Luxembourg	40	101	71	61	31	126	142	109	79	120	160
France	96	61	62	78	86	93	90	95	111	110	131
Germany	172	251	100	162	154	170	158	140	139	196	220
Italy	87	93	86	121	111	156	171	164	156	167	209
Netherlands	39	77	82	96	91	70	101	87	80	88	89
Other	180	174	167	172	158	238	246	222	201	278	302
Japan	120	146	207	208	189	216	287	329	278	395	397
Australia, New Zealand, and South Africa	93	96	133	188	211	168	166	174	171	137	145
Other Africa	265	363	507	563	560	544	481	484	412	439	410
Middle East	206	191	185	151	154	180	140	154	147	162	234
Other Asia and Pacific	99	123	158	195	201	277	287	319	328	379	425
International shipping	49	94	196	324	320	235	211	206	270	300	369

′ Revised.

Source: U.S. Department of Commerce, Office of Business Economics.

PLANT AND EQUIPMENT EXPENDITURES BY FOREIGN AFFILIATES OF U.S. CORPORATIONS, 1970-72

Howard Murad

By HOWARD MURAD

Plant and Equipment Expenditures by Foreign Affiliates of U.S. Corporations, 1970-72

Foreign affiliates of U.S. corporations are planning to increase expenditures for plant and equipment 12 percent in 1971 to a total of $14.7 billion, to be followed by a 10 percent increase in 1972 to a total of $16.1 billion. These increases represent a considerable slowdown from the 21 percent growth rate registered in 1970.

EXPENDITURES for property, plant, and equipment by foreign affiliates of U.S. corporations are expected to total $14.7 billion in 1971, up 12 percent from the final 1970 estimate of $13.1 billion. First estimates for 1972 indicate an increase of 10 percent over 1971 to a total of $16.1 billion. (See chart 14, and table 1.)

These findings are based on the latest OBE semiannual survey of about 450 large U.S. firms, with approximately 4,800 foreign affiliates, taken in June 1971. The figures, therefore, reflect the economic environment prevailing at that time. The new economic program announced by the President in August, including the decision to allow the dollar to float against other currencies in foreign exchange markets, has clearly changed that environment.

Spending increased 21 percent from 1969 to 1970. Compared to that increase, the current estimate of 1971 spending shows a considerable slowdown in the rate of growth. The deceleration is centered in manufacturing, and probably reflects the general economic slowdown in Europe. On the other hand, expenditures in petroleum and mining and smelting show substantial increases. The expected growth of spending in 1972 reflects a recovery in manufacturing coupled with sharply reduced gains in petroleum and in mining and smelting.

The 1970 figures are final figures (the E report for that year), and the total differs only slightly from the estimate made 6 months earlier (the D report). The 1971 figures are based on the C reports and the 1972 figures on the A reports. As usual, table 1 gives 1971 and 1972 estimates adjusted to take account of systematic bias in the reports of planned spending. However, the bias adjustment procedure now used differs from that used previously, and allows, for the first time, publication of bias-adjusted projections in all the tables.

Industry pattern

Outlays by *manufacturing* affiliates (see table 2) are expected to show only small gains in 1971, the total rising 4 percent above 1970 to $6.8 billion. If current expectations for 1972 are realized, outlays will increase 13 percent to $7.6 billion. In both 1971 and 1972, affiliates plan to increase spending in all major areas except Canada. The

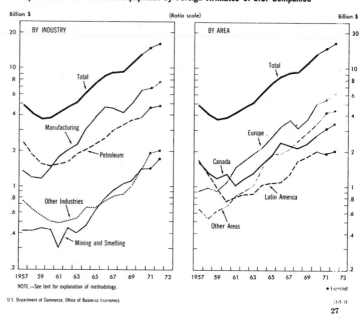

CHART 14

Expenditures for Plant and Equipment by Foreign Affiliates of U.S. Companies

NOTE.—See text for explanation of methodology.

U.S. Department of Commerce, Office of Business Economics

71-9-14

27

small size of the 1971 increase in part reflects reported delays of 1971 spending until 1972.

Within manufacturing, affiliates in the chemical industry plan little change in 1971 and 1972 from the $1.3 billion reached in 1970, with affiliates in Canada planning a decrease of 22 percent in 1971 and 9 percent in 1972. Affiliates in Europe plan an 11 percent increase in 1971 spending, but expect to reduce spending 6 percent in 1972. Both the increase in 1971 and the decrease in 1972 are due largely to the spending pattern of affiliates in the United Kingdom and Germany.

Affiliates engaged in machinery production plan relatively large increases. They plan to increase spending 7 percent in 1971 and 35 percent, to $2.8 billion, in 1972. In both years spending is expected to show especially strong growth in Canada, Latin America, the United Kingdom, and Japan. Largely reflecting spending in Germany, machinery producers in the EEC are projecting a small decrease in 1971, followed by a steep rise of 41 percent in 1972. (The cost of machinery acquired or produced by manufacturing affiliates

for leasing to others, a significant factor in the computer manufacturing industry abroad, is counted as part of affiliates' capital expenditure. Therefore, not all the growth registered in this area represents expansion of plant capacity.)

Manufacturers of transportation equipment expect spending to decline 6 percent in 1971 to $1.0 billion, reflecting substantial reductions in Canada and the United Kingdom. Investment is expected to pick up slightly in 1972, but to remain below the 1970 level.

All other manufacturing affiliates taken together expect to increase spending 6 percent in both 1971 and 1972, following an increase of 31 percent in 1970. Increases in 1971 are especially significant in Canada and the United Kingdom. In 1972, increases are particularly large in the United Kingdom, Germany, and Japan.

Affiliates in the *petroleum* industry (see table 3) estimate expenditures of $4.6 billion in 1971, up 22 percent from 1970. Increased expenditures are reported for nearly all major geographic areas, but are especially large for

tanker construction. The expected rise in 1972 is only 2 percent, concentrated in Canada, the Middle East, Japan, and those European countries affected by exploration in the North Sea (the United Kingdom, Norway, and the Netherlands). Major declines are reported elsewhere for 1972, particularly in Libya and Latin America.

Led by investment in Canada and Australia, affiliates in *mining and smelting* show the largest percentage increase of any major industry group in 1971, with spending rising 36 percent. The strength of the expected increase in both countries is more than enough to offset a 25 percent decline now seen for mining affiliates in Latin America. The sharp drop in Latin American spending is centered on reductions in Chile, where the government has nationalized some American holdings. The rise in spending by mining and smelting affiliates is much smaller in 1972. A large increase is expected in Canada and affiliates in Mexico and Central America also plan increases, but investment totals for Latin America are expected to remain far below the 1970 volume for that area.

Table 1.—Summary of Estimates of Plant and Equipment Expenditures by U.S. Corporations' Foreign Affiliates, by Percentage Change and Dollar Amount

| Industry, area, and schedule | Percent change | | | | | | | Billions of dollars | | | | | | | |
| | Actual | | | | | Projection | | Actual | | | | | | Projection | |
	1966	1967	1968	1969 r	1970	1971	1972	1965	1966	1967	1968	1969 r	1970	1971	1972
Total	16	7	1	15	21	12	10	7.4	8.6	9.3	9.4	10.8	13.1	14.7	16.1
By industry															
Mining and smelting	25	17	12	9	22	36	7	.6	.8	.9	1.0	1.1	1.4	1.9	2.0
Petroleum	11	19	10	10	5	22	2	2.3	2.5	3.0	3.3	3.6	3.8	4.6	4.7
Manufacturing	18	−1	−7	19	31	4	13	3.9	4.6	4.5	4.2	5.0	6.5	6.8	7.6
Chemicals	21	16	0	−9	16	1	−1	.9	1.0	1.2	1.2	1.1	1.3	1.3	1.3
Machinery	19	4	−7	32	43	7	35	.9	1.0	1.1	1.0	1.3	1.9	2.0	2.8
Transportation equipment	11	−18	−22	29	33	−6	3	.9	1.0	.8	.6	.8	1.1	1.0	1.0
Other manufacturing	21	−7	−6	27	31	6	6	1.3	1.5	1.4	1.3	1.7	2.2	2.4	2.5
Other industries	14	10	3	23	30	4	22	.7	.7	.8	.8	1.0	1.4	1.4	1.7
By area															
Canada	28	−5	−5	10	17	13	11	1.8	2.4	2.2	2.1	2.3	2.7	3.1	3.4
Latin American Republics and other Western Hemisphere	2	17	29	12	5	−2	6	1.1	1.1	1.3	1.6	1.8	2.0	1.9	2.0
Europe	23	12	−14	20	20	9	14	2.6	3.3	3.6	3.1	3.7	5.0	5.5	6.2
European Economic Community	31	15	−19	20	42	9	16	1.4	1.9	2.1	1.7	2.1	2.9	3.2	3.7
Other, including United Kingdom	15	8	−7	19	26	10	11	1.2	1.4	1.5	1.4	1.7	2.1	2.3	2.6
Other areas	3	9	17	15	17	24	6	1.9	1.9	2.1	2.5	2.9	3.4	4.2	4.4
By OFDI schedule															
All schedules 1, 2	12	12	3	16	22	12	9	5.6	6.3	7.0	7.2	8.4	10.3	11.6	12.7
Schedule A	3	11	24	17	11	16	8	1.7	1.8	2.0	2.4	2.9	3.2	3.7	4.0
Schedule B	4	12	8	14	24	12	4	2.0	2.1	2.4	2.6	2.9	3.6	4.1	4.2
Schedule C	30	13	−16	18	32	9	16	1.8	2.4	2.7	2.2	2.6	3.5	3.8	4.4

NOTE.—Projections are corrected for systematic bias; see text.

r Revised.

1. Does not include Canada.

2. Beginning with 1970 Spain is classified in Schedule B; prior to 1970 it is classified in Schedule C.

Source: U.S. Department of Commerce, Office of Business Economics.

Affiliates in other industries are expected to increase outlays 4 percent in 1971 (to $1.4 billion) and 22 percent in 1972 (to $1.7 billion). All major areas of the world showed increases in both years, except Canada, where a slight spending decrease is expected in 1971. Most of the planned growth in this aggregate group is related to expendi-

Table 2.—Estimates of Plant and Equipment Expenditures by U.S. Corporations' Foreign Manufacturing Affiliates, by Selected Country—Summary of Surveys

[Millions of dollars]

	Actual					Projection	
	1966	1967	1968	1969*	1970	1971	1972
All areas	4,583	4,525	4,191	4,976	6,524	6,751	7,642
Chemicals	1,040	1,210	1,208	1,118	1,294	1,310	1,303
Machinery	1,046	1,088	1,016	1,344	1,920	2,053	2,765
Transportation equipment	966	795	618	796	1,060	1,000	1,032
Other manufacturing	1,531	1,432	1,349	1,719	2,250	2,389	2,542
Canada	1,174	1,001	854	1,036	1,159	1,110	1,061
Chemicals	221	166	158	169	186	146	133
Machinery	186	190	144	222	212	259	318
Transportation equipment	255	234	194	211	289	173	183
Other manufacturing	513	411	358	434	472	532	427
Latin American Republics and Other Western Hemisphere	453	505	575	611	669	698	890
Chemicals	146	150	179	198	170	165	193
Machinery	65	78	86	95	141	176	215
Transportation equipment	71	88	90	104	112	116	204
Other manufacturing	171	188	220	214	246	241	278
Argentina	91	100	71	95	138	112	124
Chemicals	27	30	15	14	15	13	14
Machinery	11	18	16	23	45	41	56
Transportation equipment	33	34	22	40	49	31	29
Other manufacturing	20	18	18	18	29	27	25
Brazil	100	141	186	184	181	225	386
Chemicals	19	29	60	72	40	24	55
Machinery	30	35	40	40	56	85	110
Transportation equipment	20	34	51	39	31	51	144
Other manufacturing	32	33	35	33	54	65	77
Mexico	126	133	181	170	205	204	234
Chemicals	62	60	70	58	61	79	87
Machinery	14	17	17	22	28	36	38
Transportation equipment	6	8	5	14	26	20	23
Other manufacturing	44	48	89	76	90	69	86
Other	135	141	136	161	145	157	146
Chemicals	38	30	33	55	54	49	37
Machinery	11	8	12	9	12	14	11
Transportation equipment	12	13	13	11	6	14	8
Other manufacturing	74	90	78	86	73	80	90
Europe	2,244	2,332	2,012	2,539	3,614	3,846	4,427
Chemicals	462	636	524	483	676	749	705
Machinery	664	713	689	881	1,316	1,341	1,897
Transportation equipment	564	379	233	390	551	605	509
Other manufacturing	553	604	566	784	1,071	1,151	1,316
United Kingdom	698	643	582	858	1,093	1,198	1,292
Chemicals	115	127	111	126	175	186	140
Machinery	164	141	148	183	233	278	368
Transportation equipment	180	124	74	168	196	153	135
Other manufacturing	239	251	249	380	489	581	649
European Economic Community	1,331	1,438	1,195	1,440	2,191	2,323	2,775
Chemicals	275	427	314	288	418	481	493
Machinery	444	510	486	629	976	948	1,376
Transportation equipment	373	245	146	210	335	440	360
Other manufacturing	239	256	249	321	462	454	546
Belgium and Luxembourg	186	200	152	111	181	207	236
Chemicals	56	110	78	33	66	88	83
Machinery	24	46	42	30	38	38	73
Transportation equipment	60	23	5	4	7	13	13
Other manufacturing	46	21	27	43	70	68	67
France	288	371	307	338	547	574	708
Chemicals	31	50	28	30	40	39	55
Machinery	139	176	179	192	315	335	439
Transportation equipment	44	75	32	41	84	77	92
Other manufacturing	74	70	68	75	109	123	122
Germany	581	518	424	607	955	1044	1208
Chemicals	60	96	64	65	138	178	182
Machinery	191	184	166	273	409	381	568
Transportation equipment	267	142	106	159	237	338	238
Other manufacturing	63	96	88	110	171	147	220

	Actual					Projection	
	1966	1967	1968	1969*	1970	1971	1972
Europe—Continued							
Italy	125	150	165	181	279	260	376
Chemicals	26	34	39	20	39	32	44
Machinery	57	66	74	90	161	145	229
Transportation equipment	2	2	2	4	5	6	10
Other manufacturing	40	48	50	67	74	79	93
Netherlands	151	198	147	203	228	238	247
Chemicals	102	137	105	141	135	144	129
Machinery	32	38	26	35	53	51	67
Transportation equipment	1	2	1	1	2	6	7
Other manufacturing	16	21	15	26	38	37	44
Other	215	251	235	242	330	325	361
Chemicals	72	83	100	68	83	82	72
Machinery	56	61	54	78	107	115	153
Transportation equipment	11	10	12	12	20	12	14
Other manufacturing	76	98	69	83	120	116	121
Japan	153	190	227	268	374	460	638
Chemicals	55	81	128	108	110	157	197
Machinery	63	64	55	90	173	203	239
Transportation equipment	2	2	3	2	2	2	2
Other manufacturing	33	43	41	68	89	98	200
Australia, New Zealand, and South Africa	329	256	295	306	395	400	405
Chemicals	67	47	66	59	44	37	18
Machinery	47	28	32	35	51	57	66
Transportation equipment	72	86	96	86	105	102	131
Other manufacturing	142	95	101	126	196	204	190
Australia and New Zealand	289	214	244	264	335	327	307
Chemicals	57	33	57	52	38	25	9
Machinery	42	23	26	30	42	49	62
Transportation equipment	63	76	76	80	98	85	98
Other manufacturing	127	82	85	101	158	168	138
South Africa	40	42	52	42	60	73	98
Chemicals	10	14	10	7	6	12	9
Machinery	4	5	6	5	9	8	4
Transportation equipment	10	10	19	6	7	17	33
Other manufacturing	16	13	17	24	38	36	52
Other Africa	56	31	15	14	31	47	24
Chemicals	2	2	4	3	6	4	2
Machinery			1	*2	4	2	2
Transportation equipment			1	1	1	1	1
Other manufacturing	54	27	9	9	20	40	19
Middle East	23	62	111	73	126	27	29
Chemicals	18	50	103	63	50	2	6
Machinery	3	1	1	2	2	1	1
Transportation equipment							
Other manufacturing	3	11	7	8	74	24	22
Other Asia and Pacific	150	118	102	130	155	161	168
Chemicals	68	78	47	35	52	50	49
Machinery	22	14	8	18	21	14	27
Transportation equipment	1	5	1	2	1	1	2
Other manufacturing	59	52	46	75	81	99	90
India	91	50	26	47	66	90	85
Chemicals	44	28	11	11	23	25	24
Machinery	15	6	3	5	9	6	18
Transportation equipment							
Other manufacturing	31	16	12	31	34	59	43
Other	59	98	77	83	89	74	83
Chemicals	24	50	36	24	29	25	25
Machinery	7	8	5	13	12	8	9
Transportation equipment	1	5	1	1	1	1	2
Other manufacturing	28	36	35	45	47	40	47

* Revised.

NOTE.—Projections are corrected for systematic bias; see text.

Source: U.S. Department of Commerce, Office of Business Economics.

tures by affiliates engaged in trade, leasing, and services.

Geographic pattern

After a rise of 20 percent in 1970 to $5.0 billion, European affiliates are expected to increase spending 9 percent in 1971 and 14 percent in 1972 to $6.2 billion (table 1). The relatively small gain in 1971 reflects the moderate 6 percent increase by manufacturing affiliates in the European Economic Community; in 1972, these same affiliates are planning a 19 percent increase. Petroleum affiliates plan a 23 percent increase in 1971 and a 2 percent decrease in 1972. In both years,

the growth of spending in European countries outside the EEC is sparked by outlays of manufacturing affiliates in the United Kingdom and petroleum affiliates in the United Kingdom, Denmark, Norway, and Spain.

Spending by affiliates in Canada is expected to increase 13 percent in 1971 and 11 percent in 1972 to $3.4 billion, after increasing 17 percent in 1970. The increases in all 3 years are due largely to expenditures by affiliates in the extractive industries. Expenditures by mining and smelting affiliates are expected to rise 84 percent in 1971 and 11 percent in 1972. This heavy spending is connected with the development of iron

ore, nickel, and copper deposits. Manufacturing affiliates in Canada expect to reduce spending moderately in both 1971 and 1972.

Outlays in Latin America are expected to decrease 2 percent in 1971 but to rise 6 percent in 1972 to $2.0 billion. Continuing recent trends, mining and smelting affiliates are expecting to reduce spending in both years, but manufacturing firms are planning a 4 percent rise in 1971 and a 28 percent rise for 1972. Increases planned by manufacturers in Brazil and Mexico are especially large.

Affiliates in "other areas" are planning a 24 percent increase in 1971 to $4.2 billion, and a 6 percent increase to $4.4 billion in 1972. A large portion of the 1971 increase is due to spending by affiliates in mining and smelting and petroleum, which expect increases of 55 percent and 33 percent, respectively. The projected 1972 rise reflects increases in petroleum and manufacturing. The projected 1972 decrease in mining and smelting reflects reduced spending by affiliates in Australia, where large projects to develop nickel and bauxite deposits will be nearing completion.

Classified according to the country schedules established by the Office of Foreign Direct Investments, affiliates in Schedule C countries (including most of continental Western Europe and South Africa), for which controls on capital outflows from the United States are strictest, expect increases of 9 percent in 1971 and 16 percent in 1972, to $4.4 billion (table 1). While these rates of increase are considerably below the 32 percent reported in 1970, total spending by affiliates in Schedule C countries in 1972 will exceed totals for Schedules B and A for the first time since initiation of the control program in 1968. In both 1971 and 1972 the largest increases in the Schedule C aggregate are by manufacturing and petroleum affiliates.

The large expenditures projected by affiliates in Schedule C countries do not necessarily lead to an increase in the use of U.S. funds overseas, which the OFDI program is designed to limit. To the extent that investment needs can be financed by borrowing abroad,

Table 3.—Estimates of Plant and Equipment Expenditures by U.S. Corporations' Foreign Affiliates in the Petroleum and Mining and Smelting, and Other Industries (Except Manufacturing)—Summary of Surveys

[Millions of dollars]

By area and major industry division	Actual					Projection	
	1966	1967	1968	1969 ʳ	1970	1971	1972
Petroleum							
All areas	2,526	3,000	3,311	3,640	3,808	4,642	4,732
Canada	649	636	669	629	726	796	884
Latin American Republics and other Western Hemisphere	268	307	405	501	514	553	435
Venezuela	101	103	175	238	212	216	189
Other Latin American Republics	109	149	164	138	183	245	194
Other Western Hemisphere	58	55	66	125	119	92	52
Europe	778	1,045	851	876	974	1,145	1,187
United Kingdom	163	289	283	246	256	247	274
European Economic Community	434	582	401	472	546	671	659
Belgium and Luxembourg	40	101	71	31	71	133	41
France	96	61	62	86	107	96	119
Germany	172	251	100	154	128	177	208
Italy	87	93	86	111	166	187	195
Netherlands	39	77	82	91	74	78	95
Other	180	174	167	158	172	251	277
Japan	120	146	207	189	242	321	354
Australia, New Zealand, and South Africa	92	96	133	211	155	158	167
Other Africa	265	363	507	560	440	328	234
Middle East	206	191	185	154	141	230	345
Other Asia and Pacific	99	125	158	201	304	388	434
International shipping	49	94	196	319	312	699	670
Mining and Smelting							
All areas	790	920	1,035	1,132	1,384	1,885	2,010
Canada	297	332	340	340	413	762	889
Latin American Republics and other Western Hemisphere	229	288	456	497	477	359	386
Europe:							
European Economic Community	3	3	3	3	4	3	3
Other, including United Kingdom	4	5	7	7	12	18	12
Other areas	257	292	229	285	478	743	720
Other industries (except manufacturing)							
All areas	741	822	850	1,039	1,355	1,408	1,722
Canada	237	264	265	326	434	425	590
Latin American Republics and other Western Hemisphere	144	183	220	248	291	312	325
Europe:							
European Economic Community	85	100	118	149	188	192	251
Other, including United Kingdom	140	146	134	164	237	272	342
Other areas	135	129	113	152	205	207	214

NOTE: Projections are corrected for systematic bias: see text.

ʳ Revised.

Source: U.S. Department of Commerce, Office of Business Economics.

spending for plant and equipment is not limited by OFDI regulations.

Affiliates in Schedule B countries (including the United Kingdom, Japan, and Australia) except to increase spending 12 percent in 1971 and 4 percent in 1972 to $4.2 billion. Affiliates in Schedule A countries (including most of the less developed countries), for which controls on capital outflows are most lenient, show the largest growth in 1971—a rise of 16 percent. An increase of 8 percent to $4.0 billion is expected in 1972.

Note on methodology

The spending projections presented here were prepared with a revised method to eliminate—or at least reduce—any systematic bias in responses to the four expectations surveys taken for each year (in June and December of the preceding year and June and December of the year in question, i.e., A, B, C, and D reports). The revised method has two primary advantages over the old method. (For a complete discussion of the old method see the technical note on page 46 of the March 1969 issue of the SURVEY.) The first advantage of the new method is that it relies on experience over the last 5 years to adjust for possible bias in the current projection. The second advantage is that the method is applicable at disaggregated levels, thus making possible tabulation of cell data on a bias-adjusted basis.

The first step under the new method was to calculate, for the 1971 C and 1972 A reports separately, ratios of actual spending (the final E estimate) to the reported expectation, for each of the previous 5 years. No bias adjustment was made unless there was a deviation in the same direction in at least 4 of the 5 years. Also, no adjustment was made to items below $10 million. When an adjustment was necessary under these criteria, the median ratio of actual to expected spending in the 5-year period was applied as an adjustment factor.

The decision as to whether the first (A) and second (B) survey estimates for a given year need adjustment must be made without actual/expected ratios for the preceding year since there are no actual figures yet available for that year. In deriving the bias-adjusted 1972 data presented here, the years 1966–70 were used since actual data for 1971 are not available. In calculating bias adjustments for the third (C) and fourth (D) estimates of 1972 spending, the years 1967–71 will be used since final 1971 data will be available.

The tables published in this article were prepared by applying the "four out of five" rule at or below the lowest published country-industry data cell and then summing up to the published totals by industry and area.

A comparison of bias-adjusted projections derived under the old and the new methods indicates only minor differences for the 1971 C projection but major differences for the 1972 A projection:

	Million $		Percent change from preceding year	
	Old	New	Old	New
1971	14,830	14,686	14	12
1972	15,646	16,104	6	10

U.S. DIRECT INVESTMENTS ABROAD IN 1971

Julius N. Freidlin
and
Leonard A. Lupo

By JULIUS N. FREIDLIN and LEONARD A. LUPO

U.S. Direct Investments Abroad in 1971

THE value of U.S. direct investments abroad totaled $86.0 billion at yearend 1971, up $7.8 billion from yearend 1970 (table 2). The increase reflected both large capital outflows from the United States and large reinvestments of direct investment earnings (table 1). Particularly big increases in the value of investment were registered for manufacturing affiliates in the developed countries and for petroleum affiliates in other areas (table 2 and chart 8).

Direct investors' ownership benefits measured on the broad earnings basis totaled a record $12.6 billion in 1971

(table 3). The broad earnings basis sums the direct investors' receipts of dividends, interest, branch earnings, and royalties and fees from the affiliates plus the investors' share of affiliates' reinvested earnings. Manufacturing affiliates in developed countries contributed $4.1 billion to the $12.6 billion broad earnings total and petroleum affiliates in other areas contributed $3.6 billion. The total was up $1.7 billion from 1970, a record increase; the growth centered in petroleum affiliates in "other areas", which includes crude production affiliates in developing areas

and marketing and shipping affiliates in international.

Direct investment and U.S. corporate balance of payment flows

Table 1 shows both the identifiable direct investment transactions and the other identifiable transactions of U.S. corporations. Although the corporate data are not collected in a way that allows transactions associated with di-

NOTE.—Statistical material for this article was prepared under the general supervision of Richard L. Smith, with major assistance from Gregory G. Fouch.

CHART 8

Annual Additions to Direct Investments Abroad by Major Area and by Industry of Affiliate

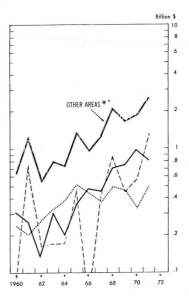

(Ratio scale)

Billion $

ALL AREAS
Manufacturing
Petroleum
Other Industries

DEVELOPED COUNTRIES

OTHER AREAS *

* Includes developing countries, and the international unallocated category.

U.S. Department of Commerce, Bureau of Economic Analysis

72-11-8

Table 1.—U.S. Balance of Payments Flows Related to Direct Investments Abroad and Other Corporate Transactions

[Millions of dollars]

Line	Item and balance of payments sign; debits (−), credits (+)	All areas			Developed countries			Other areas [1]			Change 1970–71		
		1969 r	1970 r	1971 p	1969 r	1970 r	1971 p	1969 r	1970 r	1971 p	All areas	Developed countries	Other areas
1	Net flow [2]	5,755	6,131	4,940	2,985	3,641	2,309	2,770	2,490	2,631	−1,191	−1,332	141
2	Change in corporate claims on foreigners	−6,966	−7,454	−8,959	−4,889	−5,116	−5,898	−2,076	−2,338	−3,060	−1,505	−782	−722
3	Change in direct investment position	−6,050	−7,145	−7,823	−4,386	−5,259	−5,201	−1,663	−1,886	−2,621	−678	57	−735
4	Balance of payments capital flows	−3,254	−4,400	−4,765	−2,129	−3,238	−2,824	−1,125	−1,162	−1,941	−365	414	−779
5	Reinvested earnings	−2,604	−2,948	−3,116	−2,134	−2,075	−2,375	−469	−874	−741	−168	−300	133
6	Adjustments [3]	−192	204	58	−123	54	−1	−69	150	60	−146	−55	−90
7	Change in other corporate claims	−916	−309	−1,136	−503	143	−697	−413	−452	−439	−827	−840	13
8	Long-term	−424	e −300	−109	−222	−96	−24	−202	−204	−85	191	72	119
9	Short-term: Liquid	371	351	−506	361	421	−379	10	−70	−127	−857	−800	−57
10	Nonliquid [4]	−301	−360	−521	−257	−182	−294	−44	−178	−227	−161	−112	−49
11	Adjustments [3]	−562			−385			−177					
12	Change in corporate liabilities to foreigners	2,128	3,364	1,635	1,959	3,044	1,368	169	320	267	−1,729	−1,676	−53
13	New issues of securities sold abroad by U.S. corporations	1,029	822	1,173	1,029	822	1,173				351	351	
14	Change in corporate liabilities other than new issues:	1,099	2,542	462	930	2,222	195	169	320	267	−2,080	−2,027	−53
15	Long-term	701	1,112	233	654	1,004	150	47	108	83	−879	−854	−25
16	Short-term [4]	293	987	−20	253	775	−204	40	212	184	−1,007	−979	−28
17	Adjustments [3]	105	443	249	23	443	249	82			−194	−194	
18	Direct investors' ownership benefits, broad earnings basis	9,944	10,868	12,571	5,430	6,210	7,087	4,513	4,658	5,484	1,703	877	826
19	Receipts of income on U.S. direct investments	7,340	7,920	9,455	3,296	4,135	4,712	4,044	3,784	4,743	1,535	577	959
20	Royalties and fees	1,682	1,919	2,169	1,212	1,403	1,599	469	515	570	250	196	55
21	Dividends and interest	3,084	3,550	4,156	1,856	2,402	2,637	1,228	1,148	1,519	606	235	371
22	Branch earnings	2,574	2,451	3,130	228	330	476	2,347	2,121	2,654	679	146	533
23	Reinvested earnings	2,604	2,948	3,116	2,134	2,075	2,375	469	874	741	168	300	−133
24	Offset to adjustments [3]	649	−647	−307	485	−497	−248	164	−150	−60	340	249	90

r Revised. p Preliminary.
1. Other areas includes developing countries and international, unallocated.
2. Lines 2+12+18+24.
3. These adjustments to the international investment position of the United States do not enter the balance of payments flow figures. The line 6 adjustment is for any difference between values realized by the U.S. reporter on sale or liquidation of the foreign affiliate, and the value of the reporter's equity as shown on the books of the foreign affiliate. The adjustments in lines 11 and 17 reflect changes in the value of outstanding amounts of other U.S. claims or liabilities, because of changes in price and in foreign currency values vis-a-vis the dollar; these lines also reflect adjustments for changes in coverage and for new benchmark surveys of assets and liabilities.
4. Excludes brokerage claims and liabilities.
5. Excludes funds obtained abroad by U.S. corporations through bank loans and other credits and also excludes securities issued by subsidiaries incorporated abroad. However, securities issued by finance subsidiaries incorporated in the Netherlands Antilles are treated as if they had been issued by U.S. corporations to the extent that the proceeds of such issues are transferred to U.S. parent companies.
6. Excludes an increase in U.S. corporate long-term claims of $286 million that was associated with increased foreign direct investment in the United States.

Table 2.—Additions to U.S. Direct Investment Position and Components of Financing, by Area and Industry: Amount and Change From Preceding Year

[Millions of dollars]

Line	Item and year	All areas				Developed countries				Other areas [1]			
		All industries	Petroleum	Manufacturing	Other	All industries	Petroleum	Manufacturing	Other	All industries	Petroleum	Manufacturing	Other
	Direct investment position:[2]												
1	Additions in 1971 p	7,823	2,544	3,215	2,065	5,201	1,231	2,717	1,253	2,621	1,313	496	812
2	Additions in 1970 r	7,145	1,832	2,734	2,579	5,259	1,261	2,399	1,599	1,886	571	335	980
3	Additions in 1969 r	6,050	995	3,113	1,942	4,386	541	2,652	1,193	1,663	454	461	48
4	Change, 1970–71	678	712	481	−514	−57	−30	319	−346	735	742	161	−167
5	Change, 1969–70	1,095	837	−379	637	872	720	−253	404	223	117	−125	32
	Net capital outflows from United States:[3]												
6	1971 p	4,765	1,940	1,468	1,357	2,824	956	1,225	644	1,941	983	243	715
7	1970 r	4,400	1,460	1,295	1,645	3,238	1,055	1,185	997	1,162	405	109	648
8	1969	3,254	919	1,160	1,175	2,129	447	955	727	1,125	471	206	448
9	Change, 1970–71	365	480	173	−288	−414	−99	40	−353	779	578	134	67
10	Change, 1969–70	1,146	541	135	470	1,109	608	230	270	37	−66	−97	200
	Reinvested earnings:[4]												
11	1971 p	3,116	616	1,785	716	2,375	266	1,508	602	741	350	277	114
12	1970 r	2,948	425	1,534	989	2,075	205	1,252	618	874	221	282	371
13	1969	2,604	−59	1,939	725	2,134	−52	1,665	522	469	−7	274	203
14	Change, 1970–71	168	191	251	−273	300	61	256	−16	−133	129	−5	−257
15	Change, 1969–70	344	484	−405	264	−59	257	−413	96	228	8		168
	Adjustments:[5]												
16	Change, 1970–71	146	42	55	50	55	7	22	26	90	35	32	24
17	Change, 1969–70	−396	−188	−109	−98	−177	−144	−69	36	−219	−44	−41	−135

r Revised. p Preliminary.
1. Includes developing countries and international, unallocated.
2. Lines 1, 2, and 3 correspond to appropriate column detail for line 3 in table 1.
3. Lines 6, 7, and 8 correspond to appropriate column detail for line 4 in table 1.
4. Lines 11, 12, and 13 correspond to appropriate column detail for line 5 in table 1.
5. Lines 16 and 17 correspond to appropriate column detail for line 6 in table 1.

rect investment to be separated from other corporate transactions, it is likely that much of the movement in these other corporate claims and liabilities is in fact associated with direct investment. It is for this reason that the data are brought together in table 1. The net flow shown in table 1 indicates the identifiable impact that all these transactions have on the U.S. balance of payments on the official reserve transactions basis. However, this figure is not coterminous with the balance of payments impact of direct investments. For one thing, some of the international transactions reported by U.S. corporations, such as trade credits, are in fact not associated with direct investment activities. Also, some of the important balance of payments effects of direct investment, such as exports and imports associated with direct investment and interest payments to foreign holders of U.S. corporate debt associated with direct investment, are not shown because adequate data on the role of U.S. direct investors in these accounts are lacking.

The identifiable U.S. corporate transactions shown in table 1 had a net favorable impact on the U.S. balance of payments of $4.9 billion in 1971 (line 1). This was $1.2 billion less than the comparable figure in 1970. Acceleration of direct investment in affiliates had an adverse impact of $0.7 billion on the

Table 3.—Alternative Measures of Return on U.S. Direct Investments Abroad, by Area and Industry

[Millions of dollars or percent]

Line	Item and year	All areas				Developed countries				Other areas [1]			
		All industries	Petroleum	Manufacturing	Other	All industries	Petroleum	Manufacturing	Other	All industries	Petroleum	Manufacturing	Other
	A. Branch earnings:												
1	1971 P	3,130	2,325	96	709	476	2	56	418	2,654	2,322	40	291
2	1970 r	2,451	1,731	82	638	330	−30	45	315	2,121	1,760	37	323
3	1969	2,574	1,781	72	721	228	−63	34	256	2,347	1,844	38	465
	B. Dividends:												
4	1971 P	3,534	969	1,611	953	2,153	182	1,370	601	1,381	787	241	352
5	1970 r	2,975	714	1,542	719	1,949	144	1,293	512	1,026	570	248	208
6	1969	2,583	739	1,051	794	1,465	168	851	446	1,118	571	199	348
	C. Foreign withholding taxes:												
7	1971 P	448	72	267	109	319	24	214	81	129	48	53	27
8	1970 r	416	65	257	93	298	23	206	69	118	43	51	24
9	1969	365	52	225	88	280	42	173	65	85	11	52	22
	D. Reinvested earnings:												
10	1971 P	3,116	616	1,785	716	2,375	266	1,508	602	741	350	277	114
11	1970 r	2,948	425	1,534	989	2,075	205	1,252	618	874	221	282	371
12	1969	2,604	−59	1,939	725	2,134	−52	1,665	522	469	−7	274	203
	E. Interest: [2]												
13	1971 P	622	166	233	223	484	135	194	156	138	31	39	68
14	1970 r	575	164	234	177	453	142	188	123	122	22	47	53
15	1969	501	117	213	171	391	96	168	126	110	20	45	44
	F. Royalties and fees:												
16	1971 P	2,169	259	1,116	794	1,599	125	957	516	570	134	158	278
17	1970 r	1,919	216	1,002	701	1,403	96	859	448	515	120	143	253
18	1969	1,682	195	868	619	1,212	87	737	389	469	107	132	231
	G. Measures of return, dollars: Earnings [3]												
19	1971 P	10,228	3,982	3,759	2,487	5,324	474	3,148	1,702	4,904	3,508	611	785
20	1970 r	8,789	2,935	3,416	2,439	4,652	342	2,797	1,514	4,137	2,593	619	925
21	1969	8,128	2,452	3,287	2,388	4,108	65	2,723	1,320	4,020	2,387	564	1,069
	Adjusted earnings [4]:												
22	1971 P	10,402	4,076	3,725	2,602	5,489	585	3,128	1,777	4,914	3,491	597	825
23	1970 r	8,949	3,034	3,392	2,523	4,807	461	2,779	1,568	4,143	2,573	614	955
24	1969	8,261	2,577	3,275	2,410	4,218	149	2,719	1,350	4,044	2,428	557	1,060
	Broad earnings [5]:												
25	1971 P	12,571	4,335	4,841	3,396	7,088	710	4,085	2,293	5,484	3,625	755	1,103
26	1970 r	10,868	3,250	4,394	3,224	6,210	557	3,638	2,016	4,658	2,693	757	1,208
27	1969	9,943	2,771	4,144	3,029	5,430	236	3,456	1,739	4,513	2,531	689	1,291
	Balance of payments income [6]:												
28	1971 P	9,455	3,719	3,056	2,680	4,712	444	2,577	1,691	4,743	3,275	478	989
29	1970 r	7,920	2,825	2,860	2,235	4,135	352	2,386	1,398	3,784	2,472	475	837
30	1969	7,339	2,831	2,205	2,305	3,296	288	1,791	1,217	4,044	2,512	415	1,088
	H. Measures of return, as a percent of direct investment position at beginning of year: Adjusted earnings:												
31	1971 P	13.3	18.8	11.5	14.4	10.3	5.0	11.7	16.1	19.6	34.9	10.9	8.6
32	1970 r	12.6	15.3	11.5	15.8	10.0	4.4	11.4	16.1	17.9	27.3	11.9	11.1
33	1969	12.7	13.6	12.4	12.2	9.7	1.5	12.5	11.4	18.8	27.1	11.9	13.5
	Broad earnings:												
34	1971 P	16.1	20.0	15.0	18.8	13.3	6.1	15.3	20.8	21.9	36.3	13.7	11.6
35	1970 r	15.3	13.0	14.9	20.2	13.0	5.3	14.9	20.7	20.1	28.6	14.7	14.1
36	1969	15.3	14.7	15.7	15.4	12.5	2.4	15.9	14.7	21.0	28.3	14.7	16.5
	Balance of payments income:												
37	1971 P	12.1	17.1	9.5	14.9	8.9	3.8	9.6	15.4	18.9	32.8	8.7	10.4
38	1970 r	11.1	14.2	9.7	14.0	8.6	3.4	9.8	14.4	16.3	26.2	9.2	9.8
39	1969	11.3	15.0	8.3	11.7	7.6	2.9	8.2	10.3	18.8	28.3	8.8	13.9

r Revised.   P Preliminary.
1. Includes developing countries and international, unallocated.
2. Includes preferred dividends, which in 1971 totaled $10 million.
3. Equals A+B+C+D.
4. Equals A+B+D+E.

5. Equals A+B+D+E+F.
6. Equals A+B+E+F.

NOTE.—For an explanation of the relation between earnings, reinvested earnings, foreign withholding taxes and interest, dividends, and branch earnings see the Technical Note.

Table 4.—Selected Data on U.S. Direct

[Millions

Area and year	Total, all industries					Mining and smelting				
	Book value at yearend [1]	Net capital outflows	Reinvested earnings [2]	Earnings	Interest dividends and branch earnings	Book value at yearend [1]	Net capital outflows	Reinvested earnings [2]	Earnings	Interest dividends and branch earnings
All areas:										
1964	44,480	2,328	1,431	5,071	3,674	3,665	136	105	512	403
1965	49,474	3,468	1,542	5,460	3,963	3,931	138	126	571	442
1966	54,799	3,661	1,739	5,702	4,045	4,365	305	129	659	524
1967	59,491	3,137	1,598	6,034	4,518	4,876	330	135	746	596
1968	64,983	3,209	2,175	7,022	4,973	5,435	440	123	795	644
1969	71,033	3,254	2,604	8,128	5,658	5,676	76	167	782	664
1970 r	78,178	4,400	2,948	8,789	6,001	6,168	383	111	675	553
1971 p	86,001	4,765	3,116	10,228	7,286	6,720	519	26	504	484
Canada:										
1964	13,855	298	500	1,106	634	1,713	91	73	191	118
1965	15,318	962	540	1,209	703	1,851	51	86	198	110
1966	17,017	1,153	547	1,237	756	2,089	172	67	191	120
1967	18,102	408	644	1,327	790	2,342	173	82	240	154
1968	19,535	625	772	1,490	851	2,638	195	103	275	169
1969	21,127	671	937	1,596	762	2,769	54	77	236	152
1970 r	22,790	908	787	1,586	944	2,989	149	70	250	175
1971 p	24,030	226	1,046	1,913	1,000	3,265	271	35	206	170
Europe:										
United Kingdom:										
1964	4,555	214	167	478	281	2	(**)	(**)	(**)	(**)
1965	5,123	317	242	504	270	2	(**)	(**)	(**)	(**)
1966	5,679	403	195	432	251	3	(**)	(**)	(**)	(**)
1967	6,113	331	81	378	274	2	(**)	(**)	(**)	(**)
1968	6,694	363	211	503	275	2	(**)	(**)	(**)	(**)
1969	7,190	316	151	502	332	2	(**)	(**)	(**)	(**)
1970 r	7,996	645	212	593	386	5	(**)	(**)	(**)	(**)
1971 p	8,941	646	297	757	472	8	(**)	(**)	(**)	(**)
European Economic Community:										
1964	5,421	802	100	398	275	13	(**)	(**)	(**)	(**)
1965	6,304	857	-3	395	366	16	(**)	(**)	(**)	(**)
1966	7,587	1,146	100	436	321	17	(**)	(**)	(**)	(**)
1967	8,444	852	41	448	398	19	(**)	(**)	(**)	(**)
1968	9,012	438	108	543	434	19	(**)	(**)	(**)	(**)
1969	10,255	660	503	945	460	17	(**)	(**)	(**)	(**)
1970 r	11,774	994	505	1,313	785	15	(**)	(**)	(**)	(**)
1971 p	13,574	1,305	497	1,389	886	13	(**)	(**)	(**)	(**)
Other Western Europe:										
1964	2,153	372	141	239	103	41	(**)	(**)	(**)	(**)
1965	2,558	305	149	277	132	37	(**)	(**)	(**)	(**)
1966	2,967	285	140	293	157	34	(**)	(**)	(**)	(**)
1967	3,369	275	147	317	178	40	(**)	(**)	(**)	(**)
1968	3,701	200	137	323	196	40	(**)	(**)	(**)	(**)
1969	4,206	233	239	479	246	52	(**)	(**)	(**)	(**)
1970 r	4,746	275	271	477	219	55	(**)	(**)	(**)	(**)
1971 p	5,106	131	215	507	300	57	(**)	(**)	(**)	(**)
Japan:										
1964	598	78	35	59	30					
1965	675	19	49	91	47					
1966	756	32	49	91	43					
1967	870	34	79	123	46					
1968	1,050	78	104	167	60					
1969	1,244	89	105	185	70					
1970 r	1,483	128	115	220	100					
1971 p	1,818	211	125	284	151					
Australia, New Zealand, and South Africa:										
1964	2,053	137	117	229	106	168	11	11	30	18
1965	2,334	175	98	246	140	227	57	3	42	36
1966	2,655	167	148	292	138	324	77	21	63	39
1967	3,172	364	152	299	138	419	70	14	66	38
1968	3,508	171	159	320	161	446	22	5	64	55
1969	3,865	160	199	401	214	479	20	13	86	68
1970 r	4,356	288	184	462	299	583	88	20	111	88
1971 p	4,876	304	196	474	304	718	105	15	86	74
Latin American Republics and other Western Hemisphere:										
1964	10,254	113	250	1,214	1,011	1,404	50	20	266	245
1965	10,886	271	345	1,529	995	1,474	43	25	290	266
1966	11,498	307	343	1,452	1,113	1,565	60	31	559	327
1967	12,049	296	211	1,398	1,190	1,709	71	24	397	365
1968	13,101	677	358	1,574	1,218	1,930	227	8	392	374
1969	13,858	375	376	1,646	1,277	1,958	-13	43	396	404
1970 r	14,760	568	442	1,482	1,057	2,071	130	-17	245	259
1971 p	15,763	668	373	1,467	1,124	2,116	58	-40	176	219
Other areas:										
1964	5,591	312	122	1,318	1,234	324	2	3	21	17
1965	6,276	562	123	1,418	1,310	325	-12	13	33	22
1966	6,640	167	216	1,469	1,266	334	-5	12	36	27
1967	7,372	578	244	1,745	1,505	546	9	4	36	32
1968	8,383	657	526	2,102	1,777	360	-1	15	55	41
1969	9,289	750	93	2,374	2,297	598	8	30	64	35
1970 r	10,274	594	432	2,655	2,212	451	18	34	61	28
1971 p	11,892	1,272	369	3,457	3,049	543	78	19	35	17

r Revised.   p Preliminary.   *Less than $500,000 (*).   **Included in other industries.

1. The value of investments in specified industries and countries is affected by capital flows among foreign affiliates shown in table 5.

2. Represents U.S. owners' share in the reinvested earnings of foreign corporations.

NOTE.—For an explanation of the relation between earnings, reinvested earnings, and interest, dividends, and branch earnings see the Technical Note.

of dollars]

Petroleum					Manufacturing					Other industries					Year
Book value at yearend [1]	Net capital outflows	Re-invested earnings [2]	Earn-ings	Interest dividends and branch earnings	Book value at yearend [1]	Net capital outflows	Re-invested earnings [2]	Earn-ings	Interest dividends and branch earnings	Book value at yearend [1]	Net capital outflows	Re-invested earnings [2]	Earn-ings	Interest dividends and branch earnings	
14,328	760	−35	1,803	1,856	16,935	1,034	934	1,852	893	9,552	398	427	899	522	1964
15,298	977	54	1,830	1,799	19,339	1,525	895	2,022	1,094	10,906	828	467	1,037	628	1965
16,222	885	106	1,868	1,781	22,078	1,752	983	2,104	1,116	12,134	718	520	1,071	624	1966
17,399	1,069	175	2,120	1,989	24,172	1,234	847	2,055	1,193	13,044	504	442	1,112	740	1967
18,887	1,231	239	2,449	2,271	26,414	945	1,261	2,519	1,265	14,248	592	541	1,259	793	1968
19,882	919	−59	2,452	2,638	29,527	1,160	1,939	3,287	1,337	15,948	1,099	557	1,606	1,020	1969
21,714	1,460	425	2,935	2,608	32,261	1,295	1,534	3,416	1,859	18,035	1,262	877	1,764	981	1970 r
24,258	1,940	616	3,982	3,459	35,475	1,468	1,785	3,759	1,941	19,549	837	689	1,983	1,402	1971 p
3,196	25	54	170	118	6,198	140	289	565	269	2,748	42	84	180	129	1964
3,356	179	66	183	122	6,872	395	283	606	315	3,239	337	106	222	156	1965
3,608	155	91	196	112	7,692	566	278	628	354	3,628	260	111	222	170	1966
3,819	115	93	207	132	8,095	20	344	613	296	3,847	100	125	267	208	1967
4,094	169	107	243	160	8,568	26	412	672	301	4,235	236	151	300	221	1968
4,361	179	95	242	152	9,406	248	599	833	255	4,591	190	166	285	202	1969
4,807	291	160	302	183	10,059	305	355	679	360	4,935	163	202	355	226	1970 r
5,134	69	252	371	149	10,537	−85	567	926	385	5,095	−29	192	410	296	1971 p
910	39	−20	44	28	3,011	116	164	360	200	632	60	22	74	54	1964
1,093	139	−1	−6	−4	3,306	111	220	419	204	723	66	23	91	70	1965
1,191	126	−8	−25	−15	3,716	259	165	364	208	769	18	38	94	57	1966
1,432	267	−29	−53	−17	3,878	38	111	340	207	802	27	−1	92	84	1967
1,563	154	−21	−49	−15	4,243	134	215	442	206	886	74	18	110	84	1968
1,577	53	−41	−59	3	4,567	117	169	440	236	1,043	145	24	122	92	1969
1,839	305	−41	−27	40	4,977	192	219	472	234	1,175	148	35	148	111	1970 r
2,192	300	54	70	46	5,421	252	199	485	270	1,321	94	45	203	157	1971 p
1,518	227	−60	−38	24	3,139	466	141	370	211	751	109	19	65	41	1964
1,624	140	−45	−32	18	3,725	576	23	362	305	939	141	19	64	43	1965
1,080	397	−56	−39	17	4,404	524	140	413	257	1,186	224	15	61	45	1966
2,086	176	−56	−24	35	4,976	505	101	424	310	1,363	171	−3	47	52	1967
2,146	132	−77	−51	34	5,399	253	167	502	329	1,448	53	18	91	71	1968
2,244	129	−147	−129	29	6,382	385	584	919	342	1,611	146	66	155	89	1969
2,523	233	38	25	8	7,177	464	367	1,060	655	2,059	296	100	229	122	1970 r
2,927	481	−87	−25	90	8,359	749	462	1,127	637	2,274	75	123	286	159	1971 p
694	148	−7	2	13	437	36	35	51	16	981	186	114	186	73	1964
710	63	−4	−3	5	576	74	54	77	23	1,234	169	98	203	106	1965
832	134	−13	−15	2	759	116	60	83	24	1,343	35	93	224	133	1966
905	80	−3	−22	−12	943	141	40	82	44	1,479	52	109	255	146	1967
926	31	−14	−37	−18	1,155	175	51	97	47	1,579	−4	98	263	167	1968
998	36	−9	−8	4	1,330	93	101	158	63	1,825	104	146	328	179	1969
1,104	114	−10	−24	−7	1,553	117	112	168	63	2,034	44	169	334	163	1970 r
1,083	(*)	−28	−38	−6	1,758	97	96	174	84	2,208	34	147	371	222	1971 p
315	51	−1	4	8	207	23	33	41	8	77	4	2	15	14	1964
321	−3	10	14	9	275	21	38	55	17	79	2	2	22	21	1965
331	−1	11	16	8	334	22	36	56	18	91	11	2	19	17	1966
347	(*)	15	21	9	425	31	61	85	22	98	3	3	16	15	1967
405	46	13	20	8	522	11	86	127	37	123	21	4	20	15	1968
447	27	15	19	7	646	39	85	146	49	150	23	5	20	13	1969
540	65	29	29	6	749	32	75	154	69	194	30	11	36	25	1970 r
637	78	24	29	11	959	118	87	193	92	222	15	14	63	49	1971 p
570	31	5	10	4	1,053	64	100	168	65	263	32	2	22	19	1964
616	43	3	11	6	1,185	48	75	157	79	305	27	17	36	19	1965
646	11	19	22	3	1,332	65	79	161	79	354	13	29	46	17	1966
720	48	22	18	−5	1,640	224	89	176	83	394	23	27	38	22	1967
787	40	23	18	−2	1,830	83	110	192	82	445	26	20	46	26	1968
837	24	36	....	5	2,035	72	126	227	108	514	44	24	87	33	1969
910	46	29	37	25	2,252	75	124	264	115	612	79	11	50	40	1970 r
981	28	52	68	29	2,449	94	98	241	153	728	78	31	76	48	1971 p
3,599	7	2	539	531	2,507	137	151	243	98	2,754	−61	77	196	137	1964
3,546	−74	30	513	476	2,945	245	178	289	123	2,921	57	111	228	130	1965
3,475	−37	2	512	409	3,318	160	202	342	147	3,141	125	108	259	140	1966
3,473	−66	38	519	480	3,586	199	78	269	195	3,282	92	70	213	151	1967
3,680	177	42	531	489	4,305	222	194	408	216	3,486	50	114	243	139	1968
5,722	56	−15	434	172	4,347	133	225	466	237	3,831	199	123	350	164	1969
3,938	160	68	417	345	4,621	104	228	514	280	4,131	174	162	306	173	1970 r
4,194	200	66	511	444	4,998	180	232	507	270	4,454	231	114	274	190	1971 p
3,536	232	−6	1,077	1,131	383	50	21	53	26	1,346	28	106	165	60	1964
4,032	490	−4	1,150	1,169	456	56	24	56	28	1,464	27	91	179	91	1965
4,159	100	59	1,201	1,155	524	40	22	57	29	1,622	33	123	175	55	1966
4,617	448	95	1,455	1,367	629	77	24	66	36	1,779	43	121	189	69	1967
5,285	482	166	1,774	1,614	693	40	26	79	48	2,046	136	119	194	74	1968
5,697	415	8	1,953	1,964	813	73	48	98	47	2,381	254	8	259	252	1969
6,053	245	153	2,176	2,007	874	5	54	105	52	2,895	326	192	313	125	1970 r
7,109	783	285	2,997	2,696	993	63	45	104	51	3,247	318	21	301	286	1971 p

year-to-year change (line 3), but most of the deterioration was in transactions with unaffiliated foreigners: corporate claims on unaffiliated foreigners shifted adversely by $0.8 billion (line 7), while borrowing abroad shifted adversely by $1.7 billion (line 12). A large part of the adverse shift in U.S. corporate capital accounts was offset by the record increase of $1.7 billion in direct investors' ownership benefits (line 18).

Overall, the $1.2 billion adverse shift from 1970 to 1971 reflected transactions with developed countries; transactions with other areas showed a slight improvement in net flows to the United States.

The 1971 deterioration may have been related to the international exchange crises, for both the increased direct investment capital outflow and the adverse swings in other U.S. corporate claims and liabilities were concentrated to an unusual degree in short-term accounts. For instance, among direct investment transactions, short-term capital outflows on intercompany accounts to incorporated foreign affiliates were $1.1 billion in 1971, compared with $0.7 billion in 1970. The adverse shifts in U.S. corporate capital transactions with unaffiliated foreigners were also concentrated in short-term accounts: short-term claims on foreigners increased sharply in 1971, compared with little change in 1970, and short-term liabilities decreased, compared with large increases in 1970. Some part of these shifts no doubt reflected a positioning of claims and liabilities in anticipation of a dollar devaluation. In addition, the exchange market uncertainties in 1971 probably made it more difficult than in prior years to arrange short-term foreign loans on attractive terms.

Factors other than the exchange market disruptions also influenced the 1971 deterioration in the net flow shown in table 1. For one thing, conditions in U.S. financial markets eased while conditions in some of the major foreign financial centers tightened, and both these developments would encourage outflows of U.S. funds to finance direct investment. Also, the 1970 and 1971 liberalizations of Foreign Direct Investment regulations possibly moderated the need to undertake new foreign borrowing as an offset to U.S. capital outflows for direct investment purposes.

In recent years, the rate of growth in direct investments has persistently exceeded that of other U.S. claims on foreigners. (See "The International Investment Position of the United States, Developments in 1971," in the October SURVEY.) At end-1971, the U.S. direct investment position accounted for nearly 48 percent of all foreign assets held by U.S. residents, up from 41 percent at end-1965. This increasing importance of direct investments is probably related to the structure of the U.S. balance of payments improvement programs. The programs allow larger U.S. capital outflows for direct investment purposes than would otherwise be permitted if the larger outflows are offset by eligible foreign borrowings—and the volume of eligible foreign borrowings has been large. In contrast, many other types of U.S. capital outflows, particularly for portfolio investments, are subject to the Interest Equalization Tax and many types of U.S. bank lending to foreigners are subject to the Voluntary Credit Restraint Program. Thus, the balance of payments improvement programs have probably been less restrictive of the growth in U.S. direct investments than of the growth in other U.S. claims on foreigners.

Growth in the U.S. direct investment position

By industry, the largest addition to the direct investment position in 1971 was, as usual, in manufacturing ($3.2 billion, see table 2). Continuing the trend of recent years, most of these manufacturing investments were in developed countries. The addition to U.S. direct investment in the petroleum industry was $2.5 billion, split about equally between developed countries and the "other areas" category (which includes developing countries as well as international operations such as shipping). Additions to U.S. direct investment in other industries totaled $2.1 billion.

The $7.8 billion addition to the U.S. direct investment position in 1971 represents a rapid $1.8 billion growth from 1969. This growth was mainly in investment in petroleum-related activities—production, transportation, refining, and marketing—as the addition to direct investment in petroleum affiliates accelerated from $1 billion in 1969 to $2.5 billion in 1971. This acceleration reflected continuing strong growth in foreign energy requirements and competition to secure and open new producing areas. Some of the growth in investment was in tankers and related port facilities, spurred by increased uncertainties in the Middle East that led the companies to adjust the amounts of crude produced in different areas and to change their transportation arrangements.

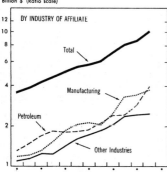

CHART 9

Earnings of Foreign Affiliates

Billion $ (Ratio scale)

BY INDUSTRY OF AFFILIATE

Total

Manufacturing

Petroleum

Other Industries

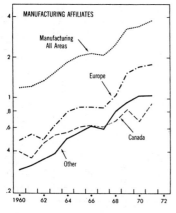

MANUFACTURING AFFILIATES

Manufacturing All Areas

Europe

Canada

Other

1960   62   64   66   68   70   72

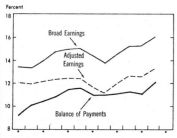

Rates of Return on U.S. Direct Investments Abroad

Alternative Measures of Return— All Foreign Affiliates [1]

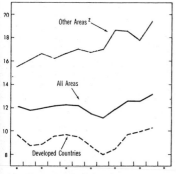

Adjusted Earnings by Major Area, All Foreign Affiliates

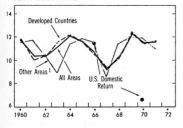

Manufacturing Affiliates' Adjusted Earnings Compared to Domestic Earnings of Parent Manufacturers [3]

1. Rates of return and alternative methods of computation are shown in table 3.

2. Includes developing countries and the international unallocated category.

3. U.S. domestic rate of return is the ratio of earnings from domestic operations to domestic net worth at the end of the year. These data are available for only 1966 and 1970. The rate of return of affiliates is the ratio of adjusted earnings to book value at the beginning of the year.

The U.S. domestic rate of return is calculated from a BEA sample of U.S. manufacturing firms which have foreign affiliates. The sample does not include all of the U.S. parents for which affiliate data are shown.

S. Department of Commerce, Bureau of Economic Analysis   72-11-10

Table 5.—Net Capital Flows Between Primary and Secondary Foreign Affiliates

[Millions of dollars]

Area and country (net inflow(−))	1967	1968	1969	1970	1971p
Canada	1	−1	7	1	−1
Europe	10	−5	2	18	38
France	6	−3	−19	11	15
Germany	−3	−2	6	8	3
Italy	13	8	11	9	14
Switzerland	30	−11	6	−1	5
United Kingdom	−15	4	−28	−1	2
Other	−21	−1	26	−8	−1
Latin American Republics and other Western Hemisphere	−20	6	−8	4	−47
Argentina	−1	−3	3	3	5
Mexico	3	1	−1	−5	4
Panama	10	−2	−13	1	−6
Other	−32	10	3	5	−50
Other countries	9	(*)	−1	−23	10

p Preliminary.
* Less than $500,000 (±).

The acceleration in additions to petroleum direct investment from 1969 to 1971 was split almost equally between developed countries and other areas, but the acceleration from 1969 to 1970 was almost entirely in developed countries while the acceleration from 1970 to 1971 was entirely in the "other areas."

Components of additions to direct investment

The two main components of the 1971 addition of $7.8 billion to the direct investment position (table 2) were net capital outflows from the United States ($4.8 billion) and the U.S. share in affiliates' reinvested earnings ($3.1 billion).

Reinvested earnings were less than 25 percent of the 1971 addition to direct investment in petroleum, but more than 50 percent of the addition to direct investment in manufacturing. This difference largely reflects the fact that almost all direct investment in crude petroleum production is in branches, reflecting the U.S. tax advantage attaching to the branch form of organization for extractive activities, while most foreign manufacturing affiliates are incorporated. Because of the way branch accounts are kept by the companies, the U.S. balance of payments accounts treat branch earnings as though they were entirely remitted to

the United States, and all additions to the net assets of foreign branches as U.S. capital outflows. As a result, no reinvested earnings figure is calculated for branches, but some of the net capital outflows to branches serve the same function as reinvested earnings do in the case of incorporated affiliates.

From 1969 to 1971, reinvested earnings grew from $2.6 billion to $3.1 billion, a 20 percent increase. This was less than half the rate of growth in net capital outflows, which went up from $3.3 billion to $4.8 billion, or 46 percent. The growth of reinvested earnings was slowed by a sharp increase in dividends remitted to U.S. parent companies, which bolstered the profit figures of the parents in a period when profits from domestic operations had deteriorated.

On the other hand, after mid-1970 U.S. corporations were rebuilding liquidity positions that had been run down in the preceding tight money period. This improvement facilitated

Table 6.—Acquisitions and Sales by American Companies of Foreign Enterprises,[1] by Area and Industry

[Millions of dollars]

Area and industry	1970r			1971p		
	Acquisitions	Sales	Net	Acquisitions	Sales	Net
All areas	855	157	698	650	188	462
Petroleum	4	10	*−6	34	7	27
Manufacturing	650	114	.536	550	127	423
Other industries	201	33	168	66	54	12
Canada	164	6	158	66	21	45
Petroleum	2		2	26	6	20
Manufacturing	108	3	105	30	2	28
Other industries	54	3	51	10	13	−3
Europe	567	56	511	412	112	300
Petroleum	2	8	−6	6	1	5
Manufacturing	472	42	430	360	98	262
Other industries	94	6	88	46	13	33
Other areas	123	94	28	172	56	116
Petroleum	(*)	2	−2	2		2
Manufacturing	70	68	2	160	27	133
Other industries	52	24	28	10	29	−19

r Revised.   p Preliminary.   * Less than $500,000 (±).
1 Acquisitions include partial and total purchases of voting securities of existing foreign corporations from foreign owners. Sales include partial and total sales of voting securities of foreign corporations by U.S. owners to foreign purchasers. Liquidations through the sale of assets, as distinct from sale of ownership interests, are not included. Changes in the share of ownership resulting from transactions between a parent and an affiliate—such as the purchase of treasury stock from an affiliate by a parent—are not included; only changes involving outside foreign owners or purchasers are included. Secondary foreign companies acquired or sold through primary foreign affiliates are not included.

the large increases in 1970 and 1971 in direct investment capital outflows. Those large increases may also have been facilitated by easing of Foreign Direct Investment regulations in 1970 and 1971.

Components of the return on U.S. direct investments

Table 3 gives alternative measures of the return on U.S. direct investments abroad, by major area and by major industry of the foreign affiliate. Panels A through F give the basic components used to calculate the various measures; panel G gives the dollar return on the basis of each of four measures; and panel H gives the percentage rates of return, calculated on the value of U.S.

Table 7A.—Preliminary 1971 Data on U.S. Direct Investment Abroad,

[Millions of

Line	Area and countries [3]	Total, all industries — Book value at year-end [1]	Net capital outflows	Reinvested earnings [2]	Earnings	Interest, dividends, and branch earnings	Mining and smelting — Book value at year-end [1]	Net capital outflows	Reinvested earnings [2]	Earnings	Interest, dividends, and branch earnings	Petroleum — Book value at year-end [1]	Net capital outflows	Reinvested earnings [2]	Earnings	Interest, dividends, and branch earnings
1	All areas	86,001	4,765	3,116	10,228	7,286	6,720	519	26	504	484	24,258	1,940	616	3,982	3,459
2	Developed countries	58,346	2,824	2,375	5,324	3,114	4,060	385	47	294	247	12,954	956	266	474	319
3	Canada	24,030	226	1,046	1,913	1,000	3,265	271	35	206	170	5,134	69	252	371	149
4	Europe [4]	27,621	2,083	1,009	2,652	1,659	78	9	−2	2		6,202	781	−61	7	130
5	United Kingdom	8,941	646	297	757	472	8	(**)	(**)	(**)	(**)	2,192	300	54	70	46
6	European Economic Community	13,574	1,305	497	1,389	886	13	(**)	(**)	(**)	(**)	2,927	481	−87	−25	90
7	Belgium and Luxembourg	1,815	167	122	221	99	(*)					117	61	−10		2
8	France	3,013	241	171	307	142	10	(**)	(**)	(**)	(**)	385	75	−5	17	21
9	Germany	5,214	474	145	640	476	(**)	(**)	(**)	(**)	(**)	1,300	92	7	(**)	21
10	Italy	1,860	330	−10	59	67	(**)	(**)	(**)	(**)	(**)	609	171	−72	−74	−2
11	Netherlands	1,672	94	69	161	102	(*)					516	82	−7	39	48
12	Other Western Europe	5,106	131	215	507	300	57	(**)	(**)	(**)	(**)	1,083	(*)	−28	−38	−6
13	Denmark	357	16	−20	−6	17	1					233	19		−23	2
14	Norway	282	4	8	1	−5	(**)	(**)	(**)	(**)	(**)	130	−3	−1	−17	−14
15	Spain	777	37	9	31	23	(**)	(**)	(**)	(**)	(**)	127	−6	−8	−8	1
16	Sweden	689	44	24	40	18	(*)					331	12			
17	Switzerland	1,884	−39	133	320	187	(*)					−83	−47	4	4	1
18	Other [5]	1,117	69	61	121	60	19	(**)	(**)	(**)	(**)	344	24	2	6	4
19	Japan	1,818	211	125	284	151						637	78	24	29	11
20	Australia, New Zealand and South Africa	4,876	304	196	474	304	718	105	15	86	74	981	28	52	68	29
21	Australia	3,704	244	136	340	236	602	95	13	50	53	(**)	(**)	(**)	(**)	(**)
22	New Zealand	200	11	14	26	11	8	(*)				(**)	(**)	(**)	(**)	(**)
23	South Africa	964	46	46	108	58	108	10	2	27	21	189	(**)	(**)	(**)	(**)
24	Developing countries	23,337	1,397	546	4,294	3,740	2,659	136	−21	210	236	9,163	718	135	3,047	2,883
25	Latin American Republics and other Western Hemisphere	15,763	668	373	1,467	1,124	2,116	58	−40	176	219	4,191	200	66	511	444
26	Latin American Republics	12,978	458	291	1,205	924	1,356	−1	−40	73	112	3,303	91	40	463	421
27	Mexico	1,840	52	−7	121	122	126	−12	−27	7	28	30	−3	(*)	4	3
28	Panama	1,461	138	77	138	73	19					286	17	9	9	(*)
29	Other Central America [6]	662	36	6	34	30	9	(*)		2	2	179	19	(*)	6	5
30	Argentina	1,350	50	14	78	67	(**)	(**)	(**)	(**)	(**)	(**)	(**)	(**)	(**)	(**)
31	Brazil	2,045	63	132	208	73	119	(**)	(**)	(**)	(**)	145	2	(**)	(**)	(**)
32	Chile	721	−18	−7	−5	11	452	−3	(*)	3	7	(**)	(**)	(**)	(**)	(**)
33	Colombia	745	56	15	63	47	(**)	1	(**)	(**)	(**)	345	10	1	31	30
34	Peru	688	8	1	44	38	415	−6		25	24	(**)	(**)	(**)	(**)	(**)
35	Venezuela	2,698	−59	48	498	447	(**)	(**)	(**)	(**)	(**)	1,634	−104		370	366
36	Other [7]	767	131	11	25	16	45	−2	(*)	12	12	685	127	7	9	−10
37	Other Western Hemisphere [8]	2,785	211	82	262	200	760	58		103	108	891	109	27	48	23
38	Other Africa [9]	2,869	174	98	577	481	386	19	17	32	15	2,095	115	72	515	444
39	Liberia	191	−7	11	17	6	(**)	(**)	(**)	(**)	(**)	(**)	(**)	(**)	(**)	(**)
40	Libya	1,044	33	(*)	409	410	(**)	(**)	(**)	(**)	(**)	(**)	(**)	(**)	(**)	(**)
41	Other	1,634	147	87	150	64	325	20	17	25	8	1,069	81	64	109	45
42	Middle East [10]	1,657	54	−9	1,876	1,888	3					1,465	48	−20	1,854	1,877
43	Other Asia and Pacific	3,048	501	85	374	247	155	59	(*)	2	2	1,410	355	16	167	118
44	India	329	16	8	40	27	(**)			(**)	(**)	(**)	(**)	(**)	(**)	(**)
45	Philippines	719	4	10	54	35	(**)	(**)	(**)	(**)	(**)	(**)	(**)	(**)	(**)	(**)
46	Other	2,000	481	64	280	185	(**)	(**)	(**)	(**)	(**)	(**)	(**)	(**)	(**)	(**)
47	International, unallocated	4,318	543	195	610	433						2,140	265	216	461	257

*Less than $500,000 (*) **Combined in other industries.

1. The value of investments in specified industries and countries is affected by capital flows among foreign affiliates shown in table 5.
2. Represents U.S. owners' share in the reinvested earnings of foreign corporations.
3. Does not mean that all countries grouped in an "other" or regional category have U.S. direct investment at any given time.
4. Direct investment statistics do not show any investments in Eastern Europe.

5. Includes Austria, Cyprus, Finland, Gibraltar, Greece, Greenland, Iceland, Ireland, Malta, Portugal, Turkey and Yugoslavia.
6. Includes Costa Rica, El Salvador, Guatemala, Honduras, and Nicaragua.
7. Includes Bolivia, Dominican Republic, Ecuador, Haiti, Paraguay, and Uruguay.
8. Includes all of the Western Hemisphere except Canada and the 19 Latin American Republics included in line 26.

direct investment at the beginning of the year, for three of the measures (it is not possible to calculate a rate of return for the "earnings" measure because data on the U.S. share in the net worth of the foreign affiliates were not collected for the years covered). Definition of the basic components (panels A through F) and explanation of the relationship among them are given in the Technical Note at the end of this article. The following paragraphs review the components one by one.

Net earnings of foreign branches in 1971 were $3.1 billion, an increase of $0.7 billion from 1970 (panel A). Petroleum branches in "other areas", which include most of the crude production affiliates and the marketing and shipping affiliates, accounted for the major part of these earnings.

The U.S. direct investors' receipts of common stock dividends from incorporated foreign affiliates were $3.5 billion in 1971, an increase of $0.6 billion from 1970 (panel B). Manufacturing affiliates in developed countries were the largest source of dividends. Foreign withholding taxes on common stock dividends in 1971 were $0.4 billion (panel C). These are taxes paid by incorporated affiliates to foreign governments in connection with common dividends paid to U.S. direct investors. These taxes are mainly paid to developed countries by manufacturing affiliates.

The U.S. direct investors' share of the reinvested earnings of incorporated affiliates was $3.1 billion in 1971, up from $2.9 billion in 1970 (panel D). Close to half of reinvested earnings were in manufacturing affiliates in developed countries. (The sum of reinvested earnings, dividends, and foreign withholding taxes equals the U.S. direct investors' share in earnings of incorporated foreign affiliates.)

Interest received by direct investors from affiliates in 1971 was $0.6 billion (panel E). Interest receipts have grown rapidly in recent years (they were only $0.2 billion in 1965) in part because of increases in interest rates. Interest, comprising receipts from all forms of foreign organization, comes mainly from affiliates in the developed countries.

Direct investment royalties and fees are net payments by foreign affiliates to U.S. direct investors for: (i) royalties, license fees, and rentals, which include parent company charges to cover a portion of expenses of research and development of new products and processes and rental fees for the use of tangible property; (ii) management fees and service charges, which represent an allocation of administrative and other expenses incurred by parent companies on behalf of their foreign affiliates.

Selected Data Items, Countries, and Industries

dollars]

Manufacturing					Other industries					Line
Book value at year-end [1]	Net capital outflows	Reinvested earnings [2]	Earnings	Interest, dividends, and branch earnings	Book value at year-end [1]	Net capital outflows	Reinvested earnings [2]	Earnings	Interest, dividends, and branch earnings	
35,475	1,468	1,785	3,759	1,941	19,549	837	689	1,983	1,402	1
29,483	1,225	1,508	3,148	1,620	11,848	259	554	1,408	927	2
10,537	-85	567	926	385	5,095	-29	192	410	296	3
15,538	1,098	756	1,785	990	5,803	195	316	859	539	4
5,421	252	199	485	270	1,321	94	45	203	157	5
8,359	749	462	1,127	637	2,274	75	123	286	159	6
1,015	75	92	125	35	683	31	41	96	62	7
2,167	162	129	226	102	451	4	47	64	19	8
3,307	361	127	576	402	607	20	10	64	53	9
1,001	147	53	112	57	250	12	10	22	13	10
870	4	60	88	41	285	8	15	34	13	11
1,758	97	96	174	84	2,208	34	147	371	222	12
66	(*)	(*)	3	3	57	-4	-20	14	12	13
74	....	4	6	2	77	8	5	12	7	14
419	29	-5	7	14	231	13	21	30	7	15
210	30	14	21	9	147	2	10	19	9	16
509	13	38	81	44	1,459	-5	92	235	142	17
481	24	44	56	13	273	21	15	60	44	18
959	118	87	193	92	222	15	14	63	49	19
2,449	94	98	244	153	728	78	31	76	48	20
1,846	53	76	191	125	1,255	99	47	89	58	21
114	6	10	17	7	87	6	4	8	4	22
489	35	13	35	22	178	1	31	47	15	23
5,991	243	277	611	321	5,523	301	156	425	300	24
4,998	180	232	507	270	4,454	231	114	274	190	25
4,708	189	216	466	245	3,611	178	76	204	147	26
1,272	57	17	94	76	412	9	3	16	15	27
144	-3	30	44	13	1,012	124	38	86	60	28
77	4	2	....	5	397	13	4	27	18	29
813	16	21	50	31	537	34	-7	29	36	30
1,409	48	112	171	58	372	13	20	37	15	31
50	-8	-6	-8	-1	219	-6	-1	(*)	5	32
256	36	11	28	15	144	9	3	4	2	33
92	4	(*)	10	9	181	10	1	8	5	34
516	28	27	63	34	548	16	21	65	47	35
80	6	2	7	4	257	(*)	2	11	10	36
290	-9	16	41	26	844	53	39	70	44	37
123	21	3	7	5	266	19	6	22	17	38
(**)	(**)	(**)	(**)	(**)	191	-7	11	17	6	39
(**)	(**)				1,044	33	(*)	409	410	40
121	21	3	7	5	118	25	3	9	7	41
92	2	5	7	3	98	5	6	14	9	42
779	40	37	90	44	704	46	33	114	83	43
169	5	6	24	15	160	11	2	16	12	44
258	(*)	9	24	11	461	4	5	30	24	45
352	35	22	43	18	1,648	446	42	237	167	46
....	....	....	....	....	2,178	278	-21	150	176	47

9. Includes United Arab Republic (Egypt) and all other countries in Africa except South Africa.

10. Includes Bahrain, Iran, Iraq, Israel, Jordan, Kuwait, Lebanon, Qatar, Saudi Arabia, Southern Yemen, Syria, Trucial States, Oman, and Yemen.

NOTE.—For an explanation of the relation between earnings, reinvested earnings, and interest, dividends, and branch earnings see the technical appendix.

These figures are net of any payments by U.S. parents to the foreign affiliates. Table 9 shows data on royalties and fees split between the two major categories listed under (i) and (ii). Payments of royalties and fees by foreign affiliates to U.S. residents other than their own parents are not included in the data on direct investment royalties and fees covered in this article.

Direct investment royalties and fees were $2.2 billion in 1971, up more than 13 percent from 1970 (panel F). Manufacturing affiliates in developed countries accounted for roughly three-fourths of the 1971 figure. Affiliates in the petroleum industry, as usual, reported only small payments of royalties and fees.

Table 7B.—Revised 1970 Data on U.S. Direct Investments Abroad,

[Millions of

Line	Area and country [3]	Total, all industries					Mining and smelting					Petroleum				
		Book value at year-end [1]	Net capital out-flows	Rein-vested earn-ings [2]	Earn-ings	Interest, divi-dends, and branch earn-ings	Book value at year-end [1]	Net capital out-flows	Rein-vested earn-ings [2]	Earn-ings	Interest, divi-dends, and branch earn-ings	Book value at year-end [1]	Net capital out-flows	Rein-vested earn-ings [2]	Earn-ings	Interest, divi-dends, and branch earn-ings
1	All areas	78,178	4,400	2,948	8,789	6,001	6,168	383	111	675	553	21,714	1,460	425	2,935	2,608
2	Developed countries	53,145	3,238	2,075	4,652	2,733	3,646	235	91	369	266	11,723	1,055	205	342	256
3	Canada	22,790	908	787	1,586	944	2,989	149	70	250	175	4,807	291	160	302	183
4	Europe [4]	24,516	1,914	988	2,384	1,390	75	−2	4	8		5,466	653	13	−26	42
5	United Kingdom	7,996	645	212	593	386	5	(**)	(**)	(**)	(**)	1,839	305	−41	−27	40
6	European Economic Community	11,774	994	505	1,313	785	15	(**)	(**)	(**)	(**)	2,523	233	38	25	8
7	Belgium and Luxembourg	1,529	175	95	174	73	(*)					65	1	−1		−3
8	France	2,590	332	147	239	100	10	(**)	(**)	(**)	(**)	319	29	−5	6	10
9	Germany	4,597	247	87	645	516	(**)	(**)	(**)	(**)	(**)	1,195	104	24	30	27
10	Italy	1,550	101	34	93	58	(**)	(**)	(**)	(**)	(**)	503	41	−45	−47	−1
11	Netherlands	1,508	139	143	163	37	(*)					441	58	65	36	−25
12	Other Western Europe	4,746	275	271	477	219	55	(**)	(**)	(**)	(**)	1,104	114	−10	−24	−7
13	Denmark	362	43	9	17	13	1					236	38		−1	3
14	Norway	268	34	10	4	−4	(**)	(**)	(**)	(**)	(**)	135	33	−1	−15	−11
15	Spain	737	119	17	32	17	(**)	(**)	(**)	(**)	(**)	140	28	−4	−2	1
16	Sweden	620	24	20	35	17	(*)					322	17			
17	Switzerland	1,777	6	167	307	139	(*)					−39	−15	5	5	1
18	Other [5]	981	50	48	83	37	23	(**)	(**)	(**)	(**)	310	12	−10	−12	−2
19	Japan	1,483	128	115	220	100						540	65	29	29	6
20	Australia, New Zealand, and South Africa	4,356	288	184	462	299	583	88	20	111	88	910	46	29	37	25
21	Australia	3,304	228	120	300	200	478	66	22	72	52	(**)	(**)	(**)	(**)	(**)
22	New Zealand	184	8	13	23	9	8	9				(**)	(**)	(**)	(**)	(**)
23	South Africa	868	52	49	139	80	96	15	−2	39	35	172	(**)	(**)	(**)	(**)
24	Developing countries	21,448	935	601	3,699	3,093	2,522	148	17	306	287	8,333	440	102	2,316	2,187
25	Latin American Republics and other Western Hemisphere.	14,760	568	442	1,482	1,057	2,071	130	−17	245	259	3,938	160	68	417	345
26	Latin American Republics	12,252	318	360	1,237	881	1,391	55	−17	145	156	3,173	38	40	368	323
27	Mexico	1,786	92	51	141	91	153	14	−1	6	5	33	−4	2	4	2
28	Panama	1,251	110	74	133	75	19					259	16	10	10	1
29	Other Central America [6]	624	21	3	22	21	10	2		2	3	160	5	1	−4	−5
30	Argentina	1,281	41	15	105	90	(**)	(**)	(**)	(**)	(**)	(**)	(**)	(**)	(**)	(**)
31	Brazil	1,847	102	106	209	92	131	(**)	(**)	(**)	(**)	118	1	17	32	11
32	Chile	748	−56	(*)	46	42	455	24	−20	21	34	(**)	(**)	(**)	(**)	(**)
33	Colombia	698	−6	16	45	29	(**)	(**)	(**)	(**)	(**)	334	−9	1	14	14
34	Peru	688	−44	22	76	53	427	−21		54	53	(**)	(**)	(**)	(**)	(**)
35	Venezuela	2,704	−5	63	428	363	(**)	(**)	(**)	(**)	(**)	1,735	−30		286	283
36	Other [7]	626	63	10	32	24	47	−2	−1	14	15	252	59	3	1	−1
37	Other Western Hemisphere [8]	2,508	250	82	245	176	679	74		100	103	765	92	29	50	22
38	Other Africa [9]	2,614	327	99	707	610	358	−17	33	62	29	1,914	300	48	600	553
39	Liberia	187	20	−5	16	21	(**)	(**)	(**)	(**)	(**)	(**)	(**)	(**)	(**)	(**)
40	Libya	1,012	230	12	564	552	(**)	(**)	(**)	(**)	(**)	930	66	43	45	3
41	Other	1,415	77	92	128	37	295	−12	33	58	25					
42	Middle East [10]	1,617	−166	−21	1,193	1,218	3					1,442	−161	−24	1,178	1,206
43	Other Asia and Pacific	2,457	206	80	317	208	91	35	(*)	−1	−1	1,039	141	9	121	84
44	India	305	11	−2	34	29	(**)					(**)	(**)	(**)	(**)	(**)
45	Philippines	701	−50	10	47	37	(**)	(**)	(**)	(**)	(**)	(**)	(**)	(**)	(**)	(**)
46	Other	1,450	245	71	235	142	(**)	(**)	(**)	(**)	(**)	(**)	(**)	(**)	(**)	(**)
47	International, unallocated	3,586	227	273	438	176						1,658	−35	119	277	165

*Less than $500,000 (±). **Combined in other industries.

1. The value of investments in specified industries and countries is affected by capital flows among foreign affiliates shown in table 5.
2. Represents U.S. owners' share in the reinvested earnings of foreign corporations.
3. Does not mean that all countries grouped in an "other" or regional category have U.S. direct investment at any given time.
4. Direct investment statistics do not show any investments in Eastern Europe.

5. Includes Austria, Cyprus, Finland, Gibraltar, Greece, Greenland, Iceland, Ireland Malta, Portugal, Turkey, and Yugoslavia.
6. Includes Costa Rica, El Salvador, Guatemala, Honduras, and Nicaragua.
7. Includes Bolivia, Dominican Republic, Ecuador, Haiti, Paraguay, and Uruguay.
8. Includes all of the Western Hemisphere except Canada and the 19 Latin American Republics included in line 26.

Alternative measures of return

Four measures of the dollar return on direct investment, reflecting alternative analytic viewpoints, obtained from different combinations of the components in panels A through F, are shown in panel G of table 3. Rates of return are shown in panel H and chart 10.

The U.S. share in *earnings* of the foreign affiliates gives a conventional measure of return from the viewpoint of the affiliates. This earnings measure sums branch earnings, dividends, withholding taxes, and reinvested earnings of incorporated foreign affiliates (panels A+B+C+D). Interest and royalties and fees are excluded because they are costs to the affiliates.

The U.S. share in earnings of foreign affiliates was $10.2 billion in 1971. The increase from 1970 was 16 percent, in line with the growth in 1968 and 1969; earnings growth in 1970 was 8 percent. The 1971 increase primarily reflected a rapid expansion in petroleum earnings, as increased production more than offset decreased profits per barrel caused by higher taxes and other costs. The increase in production resulted from growing demands for energy abroad along with a continuing shift away from coal. In 1971, for the first time in several years, earnings of petroleum affiliates exceeded earnings of manufacturing affiliates. The small increase in earnings of manufacturing affiliates mostly reflected increased earnings of Canadian transportation equipment affiliates, which had been depressed in 1970 by labor troubles. Otherwise, manufacturing earnings were held down in 1971 by slack economic conditions abroad. There was very little growth in aggregate earnings of the other industry groups in 1971, as an improvement in earnings of finance and insurance affiliates was offset by some deterioration in mining and smelting. Earnings of mining and smelting affiliates declined because of the Chilean nationalizations, strikes, and lower metal prices. Associated with these changes in the industry composition of earnings was a small decrease in the share of earnings accounted for by developed countries.

Adjusted earnings focuses on the return realized by the direct investor, rather than earnings from the point of view of the affiliates. It is equal to earnings plus interest less withholding taxes paid to foreign governments (panels A+B+D+E). Interest paid by affiliates to direct investors is part of adjusted earnings because loan capital is included in the value of direct investment; foreign withholding taxes on common dividends paid to direct investors are excluded because such

Selected Data Items, Countries, and Industries

dollars]

Manufacturing					Other industries					Line
Book value at year-end [1]	Net capital outflows	Reinvested earnings [2]	Earnings	Interest, dividends, and branch earnings	Book value at year-end [1]	Net capital outflows	Reinvested earnings [2]	Earnings	Interest, dividends, and branch earnings	
32,261	1,295	1,534	3,416	1,859	18,035	1,262	877	1,764	981	1
26,766	1,185	1,252	2,797	1,527	11,010	762	523	1,145	683	2
10,059	305	355	679	360	4,935	163	202	355	226	3
13,706	773	699	1,699	952	5,269	490	299	703	396	4
4,977	192	219	472	234	1,175	148	35	148	111	5
7,177	464	367	1,060	655	2,059	296	100	229	122	6
852	102	63	90	28	612	71	34	84	48	7
1,868	217	126	191	73	392	85	26	42	17	8
2,828	17	48	567	457	574	127	14	48	33	9
824	41	69	118	47	224	19	10	21	12	10
804	86	61	94	51	262	-5	17	33	11	11
1,553	117	112	168	63	2,034	44	169	334	163	12
66	6	2	4	3	59	-1	8	14	7	13
68		5	7	1	65	1	6	12	6	14
382	69	-1	8	12	215	22	22	26	4	15
165	5	8	13	7	133	1	12	22	10	16
459	22	56	83	28	1,357	-1	106	218	109	17
412	14	42	52	11	235	23	16	44	27	18
749	32	75	154	69	194	30	11	36	25	19
2,252	75	124	264	145	612	79	11	50	40	20
1,715	49	87	191	112	1,111	114	14	37	44	21
99	2	8	15	6	76	-3	4	7	3	22
438	23	29	58	27	162	15	22	43	18	23
5,495	109	282	619	332	5,098	238	200	458	287	24
4,621	104	228	514	280	4,131	174	162	306	173	25
4,336	106	212	475	256	3,353	89	125	249	147	26
1,199	60	37	110	72	401	21	11	21	12	27
117	-2	29	38	9	856	96	35	85	66	28
74	-6	-1		5	380	21	4	23	19	29
771	3	1	60	60	509	38	14	45	31	30
1,247	50	82	157	68	351	51	7	20	13	31
66	-2	3	1	-2	227	-78	17	24	10	32
235	-2	13	25	12	129	5	2	6	3	33
92	-8	6	11	4	169	-15	16	12	-4	34
462	11	39	65	25	506	14	24	77	55	35
73	2	4	7	3	255	4	4	10	7	36
285	-1	16	39	24	778	85	37	56	26	37
100	11	7	10	3	242	33	11	35	25	38
(**)	(**)	(**)	(**)	(**)	187	20	-5	16	21	39
(**)	(**)	(**)	(**)	(**)	1,012	230	12	564	552	40
99	11	7	10	3	91	11	9	14	5	41
85	1	3	5	2	87	-6	-1	10	10	42
690	-7	43	89	47	638	37	28	107	79	43
157	8	5	22	14	148	3	-7	13	15	44
251	-36	15	28	12	451	-14	-4	20	25	45
282	21	23	40	22	1,169	224	48	195	121	46
					1,928	262	154	161	11	47

9. Includes United Arab Republic (Egypt) and all other countries in Africa except South Africa.

10. Includes Bahrain, Iran, Iraq, Israel, Jordan, Kuwait, Lebanon, Qatar, Saudi Arabia, Southern Yemen, Syria, Trucial States, Oman, and Yemen.

NOTE.—For an explanation of the relation between earnings, reinvested earnings, and interest, dividends, and branch earnings see the technical appendix

taxes represent a reduction in benefits to direct investors. Royalties and fees are excluded as they are not included in the conventional concept of return on capital.

On the adjusted earnings basis, returns to U.S. direct investors were $10.4 billion in 1971, $1.5 billion more than in 1970. The adjusted earnings figures show roughly the same area and industry pattern as the earnings figures discussed above, with petroleum affiliates in "other areas" dominating the change from 1970 to 1971.

The $10.4 billion of adjusted earnings gave a rate of return of 13.3 percent on the U.S. direct investment position, up significantly from the rate of return in 1970 (panel H). The gain was largely in petroleum. The rate of return in

manufacturing was unchanged at 11.5 percent, while that for other industries fell from 1970 to 1971.

BEA has data for a special sample of 223 U.S. direct investors in manufacturing. These data permit comparison of the rate of return from foreign affiliates in manufacturing with the rate of return on domestic (U.S.) operations. The U.S. rates of return are available only for 1966 and 1970 and do not cover all the U.S. parents for which affiliate data are available. The U.S. rates of return are plotted as points in the third panel of chart 10.

For U.S. direct investments in foreign affiliates, the adjusted earnings measure approximates a return on net worth. The figures for direct investors' domestic operations are a measure of return on

domestic net worth: the U.S. income figure excludes fees and royalties, interest, and related receipts from the foreign affiliates, and the U.S. net worth figure excludes investments in the foreign affiliates. On this basis, the data for 1966 show a domestic rate of return in manufacturing of 11.5 percent, and an adjusted earnings rate of return of 10.7 percent on U.S. direct investments in foreign manufacturing affiliates; in 1970 the domestic rate of return was down to 6.7 percent, while the yield on the U.S. direct investments in the foreign affiliates had increased to 11.5 percent. It should be borne in mind that these comparisons are significantly affected by divergent domestic and foreign economic conditions in 1966 and 1970. In the United States,

Table 8.—Net Capital Outflows to Manufacturing Affiliates by Industry

[Millions of dollars]

Area and year	Manufacturing total	Food products	Paper and allied products	Chemicals and allied products	Rubber products	Primary and fabricated metals	Machinery except electrical	Electrical machinery	Transportation equipment	Other industries
All areas:										
1967	1,234	84	68	428	25	242	116	115	50	108
1968	945	100	-7	293	4	160	71	-2	1	326
1969	1,160	125	3	163	9	136	177	206	115	226
1970ʳ	1,295	134	111	78	44	191	205	178	193	158
1971ᵖ	1,468	204	52	327	....	24	302	115	252	192
Canada:										
1967	20	-10	48	68	7	-23	2	(*)	-73	1
1968	26	21	-16	21	-8	29	(*)	(*)	-91	70
1969	248	53	-35	2	8	16	49	59	38	58
1970ʳ	308	5	86	47	3	74	-39	-5	131	4
1971ᵖ	-85	26	17	81	-7	-20	21	-11	-241	49
Europe:										
1967	683	65	11	201	2	100	65	108	82	49
1968	562	50	9	164	-1	95	68	-28	23	181
1969	596	54	31	100	1	63	105	114	24	104
1970ʳ	773	90	23	-13	41	85	195	148*	50	154
1971ᵖ	1,098	144	32	187	-17	37	245	92	321	57
Japan:										
1967	31	2	1	8	(*)	1	18	-2	(*)	4
1968	11	(*)	2	12	(*)	1	-10	2	(*)	4
1969	39	(*)	1	9	(*)	10	-7	10	5	11
1970ʳ	32	3	-3	12	1	-4	8	1	8	5
1971ᵖ	118	11	(*)	11	(*)	3	-8	4	85	12
Australia, New Zealand, and South Africa:										
1967	224	5	4	15	8	131	10	1	44	5
1968	83	10	-1	25	6	18	6	10	10	-1
1969	72	12	-1	19	-8	20	4	3	2	21
1970ʳ	75	8	5	15	5	10	18	3	6	5
1971ᵖ	94	23	(*)	6	2	-6	17	24	21	7
Latin American Republics and other Western Hemisphere:										
1967	199	12	3	85	6	34	17	1	-4	45
1968	222	12	-1	54	(*)	22	4	9	58	64
1969	133	1	6	-4	7	24	24	10	45	26
1970ʳ	104	44	-1	24	-4	18	20	23	-3	-17
1971ᵖ	180	-5	1	33	10	2	24	....	64	51
Other areas:										
1967	77	10	2	50	2	(*)	4	5	1	5
1968	40	7	(*)	16	6	-6	2	6	2	7
1969	73	5	1	37	7	3	3	11	1	7
1970ʳ	6	-16	1	-7	-2	11	3	8	1	7
1971ᵖ	63	5	2	9	12	8	3	6	2	16

ʳRevised.   ᵖPreliminary.   *Less than $500,000 (±).

1966 was marked by strong pressures on industrial capacity while 1970 was marked by a recession. Abroad, 1966 tended to be a poor year relative to 1970.

The *broad earnings* measure is the most complete account of benefits received by direct investors from their foreign affiliates. The broad earnings measure is calculated by adding royalties and fees to adjusted earnings (panels A+B+D+E+F). Royalties and fees are included as representing a recovery of some of the research and development costs and administrative costs incurred by the U.S. parent company. Addition of 1971 royalties and fees of $2.2 billion to adjusted earnings gives a broad earnings figure of $12.6 billion, up from $10.9 billion in 1970. The $12.6 billion represents a

rate of return of 16.1 percent on the U.S. direct investment position; in 1970, the broad earnings rate of return was 15.3 percent. The increase centered in the petroleum industry. The broad earnings measure is concentrated in the developed countries more than the other measures, reflecting the importance of royalties and fees from manufacturing affiliates in those countries.

The *balance of payments income* measure is the Nation's identifiable return on direct investment as recorded in the U.S. balance of payments accounts. This measure equals broad earnings less reinvested earnings (panels A+B+E+F). Reinvested earnings are excluded because they are not now treated as a U.S. receipt in U.S. balance of payments accounting. (A revision of the U.S. balance of payments

accounting framework that would include reinvested earnings of incorporated affiliates as a U.S. receipt is being considered.)

From the balance of payments viewpoint, the return to the United States on direct investment was $9.5 billion in 1971. This gave a rate of return of 12.1 percent on the yearend 1970 value of U.S. direct investment of $78.2 billion, 1 percentage point higher than the 1970 rate of return. The rate varies considerably by area and by industry. Petroleum affiliates in the developed countries show a very low rate, while petroleum affiliates in other areas show a very high rate. This reflects the fact that transfers of oil to affiliates in consuming areas from affiliates in other areas are priced so as to show most of the petroleum firms' profits occurring

Table 9.—Direct Investment Receipts of Royalties and Fees,[1] by Area and Major Industry

[Millions of dollars]

Area and industry	1964 Total	1964 Royalties, license fees, and rentals	1964 Management fees and service charges	1969 Total	1969 Royalties, license fees, and rentals	1969 Management fees and service charges	1970 r Total	1970 r Royalties, license fees, and rentals	1970 r Management fees and service charges	1971 p Total	1971 p Royalties, license fees, and rentals	1971 p Management fees and service charges
All areas	1,013	521	492	1,682	943	739	1,919	1,092	826	2,169	1,235	934
Petroleum	116	13	103	195	34	161	216	34	82	259	31	228
Manufacturing	479	210	269	868	518	350	1,002	635	367	1,116	756	360
Trade	58	22	36	133	77	56	156	90	65	200	116	84
Foreign film rentals	257	257		288	288		299	299		295	295	
Other industries	103	19	84	198	26	172	247	35	212	300	38	262
Canada	190	68	121	302	126	176	357	165	192	397	186	211
Petroleum	15	(*)	15	20	1	19	17	1	16	20	1	19
Manufacturing	124	35	89	187	82	105	225	116	109	256	137	120
Trade	9	3	6	14	6	8	15	6	9	16	7	10
Foreign film rentals	27	27		34	34		37	37		37	37	
Other industries	14	3	11	47	3	44	63	6	57	67	4	63
Europe	2 416	2 257	159	709	499	211	810	568	242	936	654	283
European Economic Community	2 150	2 84	66	353	267	86	413	314	99	506	376	129
Petroleum	8	(*)	8	22	1	21	31	1	30	48	2	46
Manufacturing	127	79	48	249	200	49	287	237	50	325	290	34
Trade	6	4	2	24	17	7	30	21	9	53	27	26
Foreign film rentals	(2)	(2)		44	44		48	48		45	45	
Other industries	9	1	8	14	5	9	17	7	10	35	12	23
Other Europe, including United Kingdom	2 155	2 63	93	357	232	125	398	254	143	431	277	153
Petroleum	8	1	8	26	3	23	27	4	23	39	4	35
Manufacturing	109	50	59	206	123	83	229	139	90	235	150	85
Trade	15	6	9	38	34	4	41	39	2	47	52	-5
Foreign film rentals	(2)	(2)		65	65		63	63		64	64	
Other industries	23	6	17	22	7	15	37	8	29	47	8	39
Latin American Republics and other Western Hemisphere	192	80	112	302	133	169	318	143	175	336	158	178
Petroleum	32	2	30	41	9	32	38	6	32	40	4	36
Manufacturing	64	25	39	107	50	57	115	62	53	127	76	51
Trade	17	6	11	28	11	17	33	13	20	37	16	21
Foreign film rentals	44	44		57	57		54	54		54	54	
Other industries	35	3	32	69	6	63	78	7	70	78	8	70
Other areas	215	115	99	368	185	183	434	216	217	500	237	262
Petroleum	51	9	42	86	20	66	103	22	81	112	20	92
Manufacturing	55	21	34	119	63	56	145	80	65	173	103	70
Trade	11	4	7	29	9	20	37	12	25	54	13	41
Foreign film rentals	78	78		62	62		97	97		95	95	
Other industries	20	3	16	72	31	41	52	6	46	66	6	60

r Revised.   p Preliminary.   *Less than $500,000.
1. Table has been revised to include foreign film rentals received by companies from direct investment affiliates.

2. Breakdown of foreign film rentals for European Economic Community and other Europe not available; amount is included in Europe total.

in the "other areas" because of tax considerations and pricing agreements with the governments of producing countries. For both manufacturing and the "other industries" shown in table 3, the rate of return from affiliates in developed countries exceeded that from affiliates in other areas.

The three rates of return are plotted for the years 1960 through 1971 on chart 10. Over the period as a whole, all the rates of return tended to move up. The increase was sharpest on the balance of payments basis and slowest on the adjusted earnings basis. (Adjusted earnings excludes the fast-growing royalties and fees component.) On all three measures, the growth in the rate of return to the United States was interrupted in 1964 and 1965 by the impact of a slowdown in economic growth abroad, and the uptrend was not resumed until 1968. The rate of

return on the balance of payments basis was least affected, as growth in income transferred to the United States was maintained while the growth in reinvested earnings (which are not included in this measure) slowed.

The rate of return on U.S. direct investments was higher in 1971 than in 1970 on all three measures, mainly reflecting the large increases in the return from petroleum affiliates in producing areas. The rates of return from manufacturing affiliates in 1971 showed little change from 1970 as the effect of an increase in returns was about offset by the growth in the value of investments. The rates of return on manufacturing investments in 1971 remained higher in developed countries than in the other areas despite the economic slowdown in the developed areas.

interest and preferred dividends are reported to the BEA International Investment Division net of such taxes; therefore, our data on withholding taxes relate only to those on common stock dividends.

6. *Dividends:* Dividends on common or voting stock only, paid by foreign affiliates to U.S. parents, net of foreign withholding taxes (item 5); dividends are a balance of payments income flow item.

7. *Preferred dividends:* Dividends received by U.S. parents on preference or non-voting shares, after deduction of any foreign withholding taxes. Preferred dividends are a balance of payments income flow item. Preferred dividends are treated in the same way as interest in these accounts even though on the foreign company's books they are not charged as an expense.

8. *Interest:* Interest received on intercompany accounts or on long-term debt of foreign affiliates held by U.S. direct investors, after deduction of any foreign withholding taxes. Interest is not included in earnings (item 3) since it is deducted as an expense item by the foreign firm, but it is a balance of payments income flow item.

9. *Interest, dividends, and branch earnings:* The sum of dividends (item 6), preferred dividends (item 7), and interest received by or credited to the account of U.S. direct investors (item 8)—all net of foreign withholding taxes—plus branch earnings after foreign taxes (item 2); all before U.S. taxes.

10. *Reinvested earnings:* Net earnings of foreign corporations (item 1) less gross dividends on common stock (item 4).

Technical Note

THE various direct investment earnings items shown in tables 3, 4, 7A, and 7B are defined here and their derivation and relationship to each other are shown.

1. *Net earnings of foreign corporations:* The U.S. parents' share in the earnings of their foreign subsidiaries after provision for foreign income taxes, preferred dividends, and interest payments.

2. *Net earnings of foreign branches:* The earnings of foreign branches of U.S. companies after provision for foreign income taxes but before depletion charges or provisions for U.S. taxes. Included with net earnings of branches are the U.S. share in the net earnings of foreign partnerships, sole proprietorships, and other types of unincorporated foreign organizations. The total amount of net branch earnings is assumed to be repatriated to the

United States and is a balance of payments inflow. To the extent that branch earnings are in fact left abroad, they are implicitly entered in the U.S. balance of payments as capital outflows that offset the inflow of repatriated earnings.

3. *Earnings:* Net earnings of foreign corporations plus net earnings of foreign branches.

4. *Gross dividends on common stock:* Dividends on common stock paid out to U.S. parents by foreign corporations, before deduction of withholding taxes paid to foreign governments.

5. *Foreign withholding tax:* A tax on common stock dividends withheld by the payor at the time the dividends are paid; distinguished from an income tax, which is imposed on the earnings of a business. Taxes are also withheld by the payor on payments of interest and preferred dividends, but both

Derivation and Relationship Based on 1971 Preliminary Data

[Millions of dollars]

1. Net earnings of foreign corporations..	7,098	reported
2. Net earnings of foreign branches......	3,130	reported
3. Earnings..............................	10,228	=1+2
4. Gross dividends (on common stock)..	3,982	=5+6
5. Foreign withholding tax (on common stock dividends).....................	448	reported
6. Dividends (on common stock)........	3,534	reported
7. Preferred dividends..................	10	reported
8. Interest.............................	612	reported
9. Interest, dividends, and branch earnings.............................	7,286	=2+6+7+8
10. Reinvested earnings..................	3,116	=1−4 or 3−2−4

U.S. DIRECT INVESTMENT ABROAD
IN 1972

Leonard A. Lupo

By LEONARD A. LUPO

U.S. Direct Investment Abroad in 1972

THIS article presents estimates of the U.S. direct investment position abroad at yearend 1972 and the 1972 earnings and U.S. balance of payments income associated with it.[1]

The value of U.S. direct investment abroad amounted to $94.0 billion at yearend 1972, up $7.8 billion from yearend 1971 (tables 1 and 7). This 9 percent increase was in line with the average annual growth during the previous 5 years. In real terms, however, the growth rate probably was lower in 1972, if account were taken of effects of the December 1971 devaluation of the dollar and sharp price increases in 1972 in the United States and some major foreign countries.

The 1972 addition to the U.S. direct investment position abroad was almost as large as the record $8.0 billion increase in 1971, but the financing of the increase differed markedly. In 1972, reinvested earnings accounted for $4.5 billion of the increase while net capital outflows from the United States accounted for only $3.4 billion. In 1971, reinvested earnings were only $3.2 billion while net capital outflows ac-

1. The Technical Notes at the end of this article describe the derivation of the annual estimates from sample data, and define basic data items and terms. The previous article in this annual series, "U.S. Direct Investment Abroad in 1971," was published in the November 1972 SURVEY. This annual series of articles does not cover transactions of the foreign affiliates with foreigners, and does not present balance sheet or other accounts of the foreign affiliates. The most recent BEA data on foreign affiliate accounts is contained in the *Special Survey of U.S. Multinational Companies, 1970.* That Special Survey, which drew sample data from a small panel of reporters, is available from the National Technical Information Service, U.S. Department of Commerce, Springfield, Virginia 22151. Price $3.00. Quote Accession Number COM-72 11392 when ordering.

NOTE.—Julius N. Freidlin, Chief, Direct Investment Branch, International Investment Division, made major contributions to the analysis; Richard L. Smith and Gregory G. Fouch supervised preparation of the direct investment statistics with assistance from John W. Rutter.

counted for over $4.9 billion of the increase in the U.S. direct investment position. As a result of these changes, for the first time since 1955, reinvested earnings accounted for a larger share of the annual addition to the value of U.S. direct investment than did net capital outflows. Valuation and related adjustments, the remaining component in the change in the direct investment position, were relatively small in both years (table 2).

The big 1972 increase in reinvested earnings resulted from both an unusually large increase in the dollar value of earnings of incorporated foreign affiliates and a sharp decrease in the proportion of earnings paid out by them as dividends. Both developments were influenced by the 1971 dollar devaluation, which increased the dollar value of affiliates' foreign currency earnings, and reduced the amount of foreign currency earnings necessary to maintain normal growth of dollar remittances to the United States.

Direct investors' ownership benefits on the broad earnings basis—the most comprehensive measure of earnings available—sums the direct investors' receipts of dividends, interest, branch earnings, and royalties and fees from the affiliates plus the investors' share of affiliates' reinvested earnings. Broad earnings totaled $15.0 billion for 1972, up a record $2.3 billion from 1971. The broad earnings rate of return on the U.S. direct investment position moved up to 17.3 percent, also a record (table 12 and chart 13). Some of the increase in the rate of return reflected the fact that the value of the U.S. direct investment position essentially was not adjusted for changes in the foreign exchange

value of the U.S. dollar, while the dollar value of affiliates' foreign currency earnings was boosted by the dollar devaluation. As discussed in the Technical Notes, the data necessary for such adjustments to the direct investment position are available only in a benchmark year. In other years, such as 1972, the yearend position is essentially derived by adding the 1972 capital flows and reinvested earnings to the yearend 1971 position.

Direct investment and U.S. corporate balance of payments flows

Line 1 of table 1 sums the net impact of all identifiable U.S. corporate transactions with foreigners on the official reserve transactions balance in the U.S. balance of payments accounts. This figure should not be interpreted to be the balance of payments impact of U.S. direct investment. For one thing, U.S. corporate data, as now collected, do not allow all of the types of transactions associated with direct investment to be separated from other corporate transactions with foreigners, and some of the international transactions reported by U.S. corporations are in fact not associated with direct investment activities. Also, data are lacking on some of the important balance of payments effects of direct investment, such as exports and imports associated with direct investment and interest payments to foreign holders of U.S. corporate debt associated with direct investment.

Identifiable U.S. corporate transactions had a net favorable impact of $8.9 billion on the 1972 U.S. balance of payments, up $4.0 billion from 1971 (line 1). The main year-to-year improvements were an increase of over

$1.1 billion in corporate borrowing from unaffiliated foreigners (line 12), and an increase of $2.3 billion in direct investment earnings and related receipts from foreign affiliates (line 18). Statistical adjustments—including changes in valuation, changes in coverage, and statistical discrepancies—accounted for $0.3 billion of the improvement from 1971 (lines 6, 11, and 17), and the smaller growth in direct investment and other claims (line 2) accounted for another $0.3 billion of the improvement.

The $1.1 billion increase in net corporate borrowing from unaffiliated foreigners largely took the form of dollar-denominated bonds convertible into the stock of the U.S. parent. Sales of these bonds, concentrated in the first half of 1972, were facilitated by the attractive terms made possible by the better outlook in U.S. equity markets, as well as by increased confidence in the U.S. dollar at that time. In the second half of 1972, there was an increase in medium-term foreign bank

borrowings, a significant portion of which was in Japan. The heavy accumulation of dollars by the Japanese central bank, and their policy of depositing dollars in Japanese commercial banks, led to an easing of Japanese credit controls over the past year, with more attractive terms for foreign borrowers. As a result, Japan was for the first time a major source of funds for U.S. corporate borrowers.

The U.S. Government's Foreign Direct Investment Program (FDIP) has encouraged new foreign borrowing as a partial offset to U.S. capital outflows for direct investment purposes. In 1972, U.S. direct investors increased their foreign borrowing as described above, although borrowing of that magnitude probably was not necessary to maintain compliance with the FDIP. The increase in direct investors' foreign borrowing took place despite the improved domestic liquidity position of U.S. corporations and the generally lower costs of medium- and long-term credits in the United States relative to

costs of comparable credits abroad.

The $2.3 billion 1972 increase in direct investors' ownership benefits (line 18) reflected strong growth and rising prices in foreign countries, as well as the December 1971 dollar devaluation. However, the increase in income remitted to the United States was only $1.0 billion (line 19), less than 42 percent of the increase in total direct investors' ownership benefits; $1.4 billion of the increase in income remained abroad as reinvested earnings. During the previous 5 years, approximately 80 percent of the annual growth in direct investors' ownership benefits had been remitted to the United States.

Growth of direct investment

The $7.8 billion addition to the U.S. direct investment position in 1972 was only marginally less than the record 1971 addition (table 2). The decrease in the annual addition, the first since 1967, was mainly in the "other in-

CHART 11

Annual Additions to Direct Investment Abroad by Major Area and by Industry of Affiliate

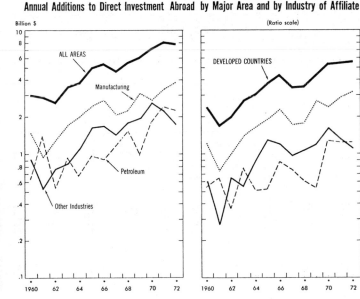

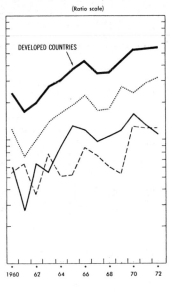

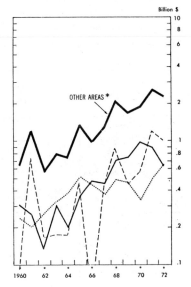

* Includes developing countries, and the international unallocated category.

U.S. Department of Commerce, Bureau of Economic Analysis

73-9-11

Table 1.—U.S. Balance of Payments Flows Related to Direct Investment Abroad and Other U.S. Corporate Transactions [1]

[Millions of dollars]

Line	Item and balance of payments sign; debits (−), credits (+)	All areas			Developed countries			Other areas[1]			Change: 1971–72 P		
		1970 r	1971 r	1972 P	1970 r	1971 r	1972 P	1970 r	1971 r	1972 P	All areas	Developed countries	Other areas
1	Net flow [3]	6,121	4,897	8,937	3,641	2,268	5,317	2,480	2,628	3,621	4,041	3,047	993
2	Change in corporate claims on foreigners	−7,454	−9,029	−8,762	−5,116	−6,019	−6,092	−2,338	−3,010	−2,670	267	−74	340
3	Addition to direct investment position	−7,145	−8,020	−7,834	−5,259	−5,427	−5,541	−1,886	−2,593	−2,293	186	−115	300
4	Balance of payments capital flows	−4,410	−4,943	−3,404	−3,238	−2,988	−1,897	−1,172	−1,955	−1,508	1,539	1,092	447
5	Reinvested earnings	−2,948	−3,157	−4,521	−2,075	−2,437	−3,668	−874	−720	−853	−1,365	−1,231	−134
6	Adjustments [4]	214	80	92	54	−1	23	160	81	69	12	25	−13
7	Change in other corporate claims	−309	−1,009	−928	143	−592	−551	−452	−417	−377	81	41	40
8	Long-term	[7] −300	−168	−202	−96	−93	−119	−204	−75	−83	−34	−26	−8
	Short-term:												
9	Liquid	351	−531	−492	421	−404	−263	−70	−127	−229	39	141	−102
10	Nonliquid [5]	−360	−496	−233	−182	−262	−168	−178	−234	−65	263	94	169
11	Adjustments [4]		186	−1		167	−1		19		−187	−168	−19
12	Change in corporate liabilities to foreigners	3,386	1,854	2,997	3,066	1,575	2,794	320	279	203	1,143	1,219	−76
13	New issues of securities sold abroad by U.S. corporations [6]	822	1,173	2,023	822	1,173	2,023				850	850	
14	Change in corporate liabilities other than new issues	2,564	681	974	2,244	402	771	320	279	203	293	369	−76
15	Long-term	1,112	384	694	1,004	289	624	108	95	70	310	335	−25
16	Short-term [5]	987	22	119	775	−162	−14	212	184	133	97	148	−51
17	Adjustments [4]	465	275	161	465	275	161				−114	−114	
18	Direct investors' ownership benefits, broad earnings basis	10,868	12,613	14,954	6,210	7,153	8,798	4,658	5,459	6,157	2,342	1,645	697
19	Receipts of income on U.S. direct investment	7,920	9,456	10,433	4,135	4,716	5,130	3,784	4,740	5,303	977	414	563
20	Royalties and fees	1,010	2,160	2,429	1,403	1,838	1,838	515	566	590	268	244	24
21	Dividends and interest	3,550	4,174	4,533	2,402	2,648	2,894	1,148	1,526	1,639	359	245	113
22	Branch earnings	2,451	3,121	3,471	330	473	397	2,121	2,648	3,074	350	−76	126
23	Reinvested earnings	2,948	3,157	4,521	2,075	2,437	3,668	874	720	853	1,365	1,231	134
24	Offset to adjustments [4]	−679	−541	−252	−519	−441	−183	−160	−100	−69	289	257	32

r Revised.   P Preliminary.   NOTE.—Detail may not add to totals because of rounding.
1. Excludes non-direct investment claims and liabilities of U.S. banking and brokerage institutions.
2. Other areas includes developing countries and international, unallocated.
3. Lines 2+12+18+24.
4. These adjustments to the international investment position of the United States do not enter the balance of payments flow figures. The line 6 adjustment is for any difference between values realized by the U.S. reporter on sale or liquidation of the foreign affiliate, and the value of the reporter's equity as shown on the books of the foreign affiliate. The adjustments in lines 11 and 17 reflect changes in the value of outstanding amounts of other U.S. claims or liabilities, because of changes in price and in foreign currency values vis-a-vis the dollar; these lines also

reflect adjustments for changes in coverage and for new benchmark surveys of assets and liabilities.
5. Excludes brokerage claims and liabilities.
6. Excludes funds obtained abroad by U.S. corporations through bank loans and other credits and also excludes securities issued by subsidiaries incorporated abroad. However, securities issued by finance subsidiaries incorporated in the Netherlands Antilles are treated as if they had been issued by U.S. corporations to the extent that the proceeds of such issues are transferred to U.S. parent companies.
7. Excludes an increase in U.S. corporate long-term claims of $286 million that was associated with increased foreign direct investment in the United States.

Table 2.—Addition to U.S. Direct Investment Position and Components of Financing, by Area and Industry: Amount and Change From Preceding Year

[Millions of dollars]

Line	Item and year	All areas				Developed countries				Other areas [1]			
		All industries	Petroleum	Manufacturing	Other	All industries	Petroleum	Manufacturing	Other	All industries	Petroleum	Manufacturing	Other
	Direct investment position: [2]												
1	Addition in 1972 P	7,834	2,247	3,847	1,740	5,541	1,242	3,192	1,107	2,293	1,005	654	633
2	Addition in 1971 r	8,020	2,438	3,371	2,210	5,427	1,235	2,867	1,325	2,593	1,203	504	886
3	Addition in 1970	7,145	1,832	2,734	2,579	5,259	1,261	2,399	1,599	1,886	571	335	980
4	Changes, 1971–1972	−186	−191	476	−470	115	7	325	−217	−300	−198	150	−253
5	Changes, 1970–1971	875	606	637	−369	168	−26	469	−275	706	632	168	−94
	Net capital outflows from United States: [3]												
6	1972 P	3,404	1,635	1,028	741	1,897	701	803	392	1,508	933	225	349
7	1971 r	4,943	1,950	1,556	1,436	2,988	976	1,319	694	1,955	975	238	742
8	1970	4,410	1,460	1,295	1,655	3,238	1,055	1,185	999	1,172	405	110	657
9	Changes, 1971–72	−1,539	−316	−528	−695	−1,092	−274	−515	−302	−447	−42	−13	−393
10	Changes, 1970–71	533	490	261	−219	−250	−79	134	−305	782	569	127	85
	Reinvested earnings: [4]												
11	1972 P	4,521	668	2,825	1,029	3,668	571	2,386	711	853	97	439	318
12	1971 r	3,157	500	1,854	803	2,437	251	1,565	621	720	249	289	182
13	1970	2,948	425	1,534	989	2,075	205	1,252	618	874	221	282	371
14	Changes, 1971–72	1,365	168	971	226	1,231	320	821	90	134	−152	150	136
15	Changes, 1970–71	208	74	320	−185	362	46	312	4	−154	28	7	−189
	Adjustments: [5]												
16	Changes, 1971–72	−12	−44	33		−25	−39	19	−5	13	−5	13	5
17	Changes, 1970–71	134	42	56	36	56	7	22	26	78	35	34	10

r Revised.   P Preliminary.   NOTE.—Detail may not add to totals because of rounding.
1. Includes developing countries and international, unallocated.
2. Lines 1, 2, and 3 correspond to appropriate column detail for line 3 in table 1.

3. Lines 6, 7, and 8 correspond to appropriate column detail for line 4 in table 1.
4. Lines 11, 12, and 13 correspond to appropriate column detail for line 5 in table 1.
5. Lines 16 and 17 correspond to appropriate column detail for line 6 in table 1.

Table 3.—Value of U.S. Direct Investment Abroad and of Foreign Direct Investment in the United States

	1960	1965	1970	1972ᵖ
	Billions of dollars			
Private nonliquid U.S. investment position abroad	49.3	79.8	117.8	144.8
Direct investment position	31.9	49.5	78.2	94.0
Other ¹	17.4	30.3	39.6	50.8
Private nonliquid foreign investment position in the United States	19.0	27.3	48.7	63.9
Direct investment position	6.9	8.8	13.3	14.4
Other ²	12.1	18.5	35.4	49.5
	Percent			
Direct investment position as percent of total private nonliquid investment position:				
U.S. investment abroad	65	62	66	65
Foreign investment in the United States	36	32	27	22

ᵖ Preliminary.
1. Excludes all U.S. Government claims and privately held U.S. liquid claims on foreign residents.
2. Excludes all U.S. Government liabilities to foreign residents and U.S. liabilities to foreign official agencies.

Source: Based on data published in "The International Investment Position of the United States," in the August 1973 SURVEY.

dustries" category (which includes mining and smelting, trade, banking and finance, public utilities, and agriculture) and, to a lesser extent, in petroleum. The net addition to direct investment in the "other industries" category was only $1.7 billion, well below the level of recent years; among the factors contributing to this slow-

Table 4.—Reinvested Earnings by and Net Capital Outflow to Incorporated Foreign Affiliates of U.S. Direct Investors

[Millions of dollars or ratios]

	Developed countries		Other areas	
	1971ʳ	1972ᵖ	1971ʳ	1972ᵖ
All industries:				
Total ¹	5,026	5,092	2,031	1,591
Reinvested earnings	2,437	3,668	720	853
Net U.S. capital outflows	2,589	1,424	1,311	738
Ratio, reinvested earnings to total	.48	.72	.35	.54
Of which, affiliates in manufacturing:				
Total ¹	2,850	3,133	510	642
Reinvested earnings	1,565	2,386	289	439
Net U.S. capital outflows	1,285	747	221	203
Ratio, reinvested earnings to total	.55	.76	.57	.68

ʳ Revised. ᵖ Preliminary.
1. Separate data for statistical and related adjustments, the remaining component of the addition to the U.S. direct investment position, are not available for incorporated foreign affiliates, so that the above total lines do not exactly measure the addition to U.S. direct investment. These adjustments (covering branches as well as incorporated affiliates) totaled $92 million in 1972, as given in line 6 of table 1.

down were a return of capital to the United States from some shipping and finance affiliates, and uncertainty over foreign investment policies of Andean Pact countries, where U.S. investment in the "other industries" category is sizable.

The 1972 addition to the U.S. direct investment position in petroleum, although large by historical standards, was less than the record 1971 addition. The continuing rapid growth reflected the response of U.S. petroleum companies to the exceptional worldwide demand for energy and petrochemicals. In particular, a large ongoing expansion of pipelines, port facilities, and liquid petroleum gas facilities required substantial investments.

The 1972 addition to the U.S. direct investment position in manufacturing was a record $3.8 billion, accounting for nearly half of the total growth in the U.S. direct investment position. In the previous five years, manufacturing had accounted for only 43 percent of the total addition to the U.S. direct investment position. Most of the 1972 addition to manufacturing investment was, as usual, in the developed countries.

By major area, the developed countries accounted for $5.5 billion, or 71 percent, of the 1972 addition to the U.S. direct investment position, compared with 67 percent in 1967. This change in shares over the 6-year period reflects a 9.8 percent compound annual growth rate in the U.S. direct investment position in the developed countries, compared with an 8.7 percent rate in "other areas." In each area investment in manufacturing grew faster, and investment in petroleum slower, than the all-industry average, despite a big 1969–71 acceleration in petroleum investment.

The growth in the U.S. direct investment position since 1960 has averaged 9.4 percent per year, generally in line with the growth in other private nonliquid U.S. investment abroad. During this period, the share of direct to total nonliquid U.S. investment abroad fluctuated in a fairly narrow band (see table 3), even though direct investors were less adversely affected than were other U.S. investors by provisions of

Table 5.—Dividend Payout Ratios of Incorporated Foreign Affiliates

[Millions of dollars or ratios]

	Developed countries		Other areas	
	1971ʳ	1972ᵖ	1971ʳ	1972ᵖ
All industries:				
Earnings ¹	4,941	6,407	2,238	2,508
Dividends ²	2,504	2,739	1,518	1,655
Ratio, dividends to earnings	.507	.428	.678	.660
Of which, affiliates in manufacturing:				
Earnings ¹	3,149	4,145	588	765
Dividends ²	1,584	1,759	299	326
Ratio, dividends to earnings	.503	.424	.509	.426

ʳRevised. ᵖPreliminary. Data are drawn from table 12.
1. The sum of dividends on common stock, foreign withholding taxes, and reinvested earnings.
2. Excludes preferred dividends.

U.S. balance of payments improvement programs created during the 1960's. The balance of payments programs allowed larger U.S. capital outflows for direct investment purposes than would otherwise be permitted, provided that the larger outflows were matched by foreign borrowings eligible as offsets to direct investment under the FDIP regulations. By yearend 1972, the volume of eligible foreign borrowings amounted to an estimated $15.0 billion. In contrast, many other types of U.S. capital outflows, particularly for portfolio investment, were subject to the Interest Equalization Tax and many types of U.S. bank lending to foreigners were subject to the Voluntary Credit Restraint Program; foreign borrowings were not treated as an offset for the U.S. capital outflows subject to these two payments measures. As a result, the balance of pay-

Table 6.—Direct Investment Net Capital Outflows by Type

[Millions of dollars]

	1970	1971ʳ	1972ᵖ
Balance of payments capital outflows (−)	−4,410	−4,943	−3,404
To incorporated foreign affiliates	−3,504	−3,898	−2,162
Short-term intercompany accounts	−691	−1,241	−216
Other	−2,813	−2,656	−1,946
To foreign branches ¹	−906	−1,045	−1,242

ʳ Revised.
ᵖ Preliminary.
NOTE.—Detail may not add to totals because of rounding.
1. Data on the term-structure of U.S. capital outflows to foreign branches are not available.

Table 7.—Selected Data on U.S. Direct

[Millions

Area and year	Total, all industries					Mining and smelting					Petroleum				
	Book value at year end¹	Net capital outflows	Reinvested earnings²	Earnings	Interest, dividends, and branch earnings	Book value at year end¹	Net capital outflows	Reinvested earnings²	Earnings	Interest, dividends, and branch earnings	Book value at year end¹	Net capital outflows	Reinvested earnings²	Earnings	Interest, dividends, and branch earnings
All areas:															
1965	49,474	3,468	1,542	5,460	3,963	3,931	138	126	571	442	15,298	977	54	1,830	1,799
1966	54,799	3,661	1,739	5,702	4,045	4,365	305	129	659	524	16,222	885	106	1,868	1,781
1967	59,491	3,137	1,598	6,034	4,518	4,876	330	135	746	596	17,399	1,069	175	2,120	1,989
1968	64,983	3,209	2,175	7,022	4,973	5,435	440	134	795	644	18,887	1,231	239	2,449	2,271
1969 ʳ	71,033	3,271	2,601	8,128	5,658	5,676	93	167	782	664	19,882	919	−59	2,452	2,638
1970 ʳ	78,178	4,410	2,948	8,789	6,001	6,168	393	111	675	553	21,714	1,460	425	2,935	2,608
1971 ʳ	86,198	4,943	3,157	10,299	7,295	6,685	510	23	499	482	24,152	1,950	500	3,856	3,442
1972 ᵖ	94,031	3,404	4,521	12,386	8,004	7,131	411	34	418	399	26,399	1,635	668	4,552	3,950
Canada:															
1965	15,318	962	540	1,209	703	1,851	51	86	198	110	3,356	179	66	183	122
1966	17,017	1,153	547	1,237	756	2,089	172	67	191	120	3,608	155	91	196	112
1967	18,102	408	644	1,327	790	2,342	173	82	240	154	3,819	115	93	207	132
1968	19,535	625	772	1,490	851	2,638	195	103	275	169	4,094	169	107	243	160
1969	21,127	671	937	1,596	762	2,769	54	77	236	152	4,361	179	95	242	152
1970	22,790	908	787	1,586	944	2,989	149	70	250	175	4,807	291	160	302	183
1971 ʳ	24,105	273	1,074	1,955	1,015	3,246	256	31	233	171	5,149	87	249	370	150
1972 ᵖ	25,784	380	1,367	2,236	984	3,490	240	6	139	131	5,311	−92	314	453	158
Europe:															
United Kingdom:															
1965	5,123	317	242	504	270	2	(**)	(**)	(**)	(**)	1,093	139	−1	−6	−4
1966	5,679	403	195	432	251	3	(**)	(**)	(**)	(**)	1,191	126	−8	−25	−15
1967	6,113	331	81	378	274	2	(**)	(**)	(**)	(**)	1,432	267	−29	−53	−17
1968	6,694	363	211	503	275	2	(**)	(**)	(**)	(**)	1,563	154	−21	−49	−15
1969	7,190	316	151	502	332	2	(**)	(**)	(**)	(**)	1,577	53	−41	−59	3
1970	7,996	645	212	593	386	5	(**)	(**)	(**)	(**)	1,839	305	−41	−27	40
1971 ʳ	9,007	685	324	779	469	9	(**)	(**)	(**)	(**)	2,176	290	−48	64	47
1972 ᵖ	9,509	−20	490	1,055	572	5	(**)	(**)	(**)	(**)	2,321	57	93	122	63
European Economic Community:															
1965	6,304	857	−3	395	366	16	(**)	(**)	(**)	(**)	1,624	140	−45	−32	18
1966	7,587	1,146	100	436	321	17	(**)	(**)	(**)	(**)	1,980	397	−56	−39	17
1967	8,444	852	41	448	398	19	(**)	(**)	(**)	(**)	2,086	176	−56	−24	35
1968	9,012	438	108	543	434	19	(**)	(**)	(**)	(**)	2,146	132	−77	−51	34
1969	10,255	660	503	945	460	17	(**)	(**)	(**)	(**)	2,244	129	−147	−129	29
1970	11,774	994	505	1,313	785	15	(**)	(**)	(**)	(**)	2,523	233	38	25	8
1971 ʳ	13,605	1,334	499	1,384	878	13	(**)	(**)	(**)	(**)	2,918	477	−93	−28	91
1972 ᵖ	15,745	1,069	1,062	1,910	861	10	(**)	(**)	(**)	(**)	3,494	470	93	40	−17
Other Western Europe:															
1965	2,558	305	149	277	132	37	(**)	(**)	(**)	(**)	710	63	−4	−3	5
1966	2,967	285	140	293	157	34	(**)	(**)	(**)	(**)	832	134	−13	−15	2
1967	3,369	275	147	317	178	40	(**)	(**)	(**)	(**)	905	80	−3	−22	−12
1968	3,701	200	137	323	196	40	(**)	(**)	(**)	(**)	926	31	−14	−37	−18
1969	4,206	233	239	479	246	52	(**)	(**)	(**)	(**)	998	36	−9	−8	4
1970	4,746	271	271	477	219	55	(**)	(**)	(**)	(**)	1,104	114	−10	−24	−7
1971 ʳ	5,127	150	218	533	300	57	(**)	(**)	(**)	(**)	1,098	15	−27	−38	−5
1972 ᵖ	5,461	24	333	719	387	64	(**)	(**)	(**)	(**)	1,177	100	−20	−45	−18
Japan:															
1965	675	19	49	91	47						321	−3	10	14	9
1966	756	32	49	91	43						331	−1	11	16	8
1967	870	34	79	123	46						347	(*)	15	21	9
1968	1,050	78	104	167	60						405	46	13	20	8
1969	1,244	89	105	185	70						447	27	15	19	7
1970	1,483	128	115	220	100						540	65	29	29	6
1971 ʳ	1,821	212	127	285	149						637	78	24	29	11
1972 ᵖ	2,222	200	171	345	163						796	89	47	51	9
Australia, New Zealand, and South Africa:															
1965	2,334	175	98	246	140	227	57	3	42	36	616	43	3	11	6
1966	2,655	167	148	292	138	324	77	21	63	39	646	11	19	22	3
1967	3,172	364	152	299	138	419	70	14	66	38	720	48	22	18	−5
1968	3,508	171	159	320	161	446	22	5	64	55	787	40	23	18	−2
1969	3,865	160	199	401	214	479	20	13	86	68	837	24	36	------	5
1970	4,356	288	184	462	229	583	88	20	111	88	910	46	29	37	25
1971 ʳ	4,904	333	195	479	310	716	105	13	84	74	980	29	50	68	31
1972 ᵖ	5,393	244	245	538	323	851	117	18	94	80	1,102	77	45	87	56
Latin American Republics and other Western Hemisphere:															
1965	10,886	271	345	1,320	995	1,474	43	25	290	266	3,546	−74	30	513	476
1966	11,498	307	343	1,452	1,113	1,565	60	31	359	327	3,475	−37	2	512	499
1967	12,049	296	211	1,398	1,190	1,709	71	24	397	365	3,473	−66	38	519	480
1968	13,101	677	358	1,574	1,218	1,930	227	8	392	374	3,680	177	42	531	489
1969 ʳ	13,858	392	376	1,646	1,277	1,958	30	43	396	404	3,722	56	−15	434	472
1970 ʳ	14,760	578	442	1,482	1,057	2,071	140	−17	245	259	3,938	160	68	417	345
1971 ʳ	15,789	691	399	1,500	1,130	2,097	59	−39	172	214	4,195	204	63	507	444
1972 ᵖ	16,644	279	600	1,532	962	2,082	−15	−1	158	171	4,267	28	46	295	246
Other areas:³															
1965	6,276	562	123	1,418	1,310	325	−12	13	33	22	4,032	490	−4	1,150	1,169
1966	6,640	167	216	1,469	1,266	334	−5	12	36	27	4,159	100	59	1,201	1,155
1967	7,372	578	214	1,745	1,505	346	9	4	36	32	4,617	448	95	1,455	1,367
1968	8,383	657	326	2,102	1,777	360	−1	15	55	41	5,285	482	166	1,774	1,614
1969 ʳ	9,289	750	93	2,374	2,297	398	8	30	64	35	5,697	415	8	1,553	1,964
1970 ʳ	10,794	594	432	2,655	2,212	451	18	34	61	28	6,053	245	153	2,176	2,007
1971 ʳ	11,838	1,265	321	3,385	3,044	548	79	22	36	17	6,999	770	186	2,883	2,674
1972 ᵖ	13,274	1,229	253	4,049	3,751	629	72	10	24	14	7,932	905	51	3,550	3,452

ʳ Revised.　　ᵖ Preliminary.　　*Less than $500,000 (±).　　**Included in other industries.

NOTE.—Detail may not add to totals because of rounding.

1. The value of investments in specified industries and countries is affected by capital flows among foreign affiliates as shown in the Technical Notes.
2. Represents U.S. owners' share in the reinvested earnings of foreign corporations.

Investment Abroad, by Major Area

of dollars]

Manufacturing					Other industries					Year
Book value at year end [1]	Net capital outflows	Reinvested earnings [2]	Earnings	Interest, dividends, and branch earnings	Book value at year end [1]	Net capital outflows	Reinvested earnings [2]	Earnings	Interest, dividends, and branch earnings	
19,339	1,525	895	2,022	1,094	10,906	828	467	1,037	628	1965
22,078	1,752	983	2,104	1,116	12,134	718	520	1,071	624	1966
24,172	1,234	847	2,055	1,193	13,044	504	442	1,122	740	1967
26,414	945	1,261	2,519	1,265	14,248	592	541	1,259	793	1968
29,527	1,160	1,939	3,287	1,337	15,948	1,099	557	1,606	1,020	1969 r
32,261	1,295	1,534	3,416	1,859	18,035	1,262	877	1,764	981	1970 r
35,632	1,556	1,854	3,834	1,950	19,728	927	780	2,111	1,422	1971 r
39,478	1,028	2,825	5,007	2,145	21,024	331	995	2,409	1,511	1972 p
6,872	395	283	606	315	3,239	337	106	222	156	1965
7,692	566	278	628	354	3,628	260	111	222	170	1966
8,095	20	344	613	296	3,847	100	125	267	208	1967
8,568	26	412	672	301	4,235	236	151	300	221	1968
9,406	248	599	833	255	4,591	190	166	285	202	1969
10,059	305	355	679	360	4,935	163	202	355	226	1970
10,590	-53	588	953	393	5,121	-18	206	428	300	1971 r
11,587	227	782	1,162	417	5,397	5	265	482	278	1972 p
3,306	111	220	419	204	723	66	23	91	70	1965
3,716	259	165	364	208	709	18	38	64	57	1966
3,878	38	111	340	207	802	27	-1	92	84	1967
4,243	134	215	442	206	886	74	18	110	84	1968
4,567	117	169	440	236	1,043	145	24	122	92	1969
4,977	192	219	472	234	1,175	148	35	148	111	1970
5,471	274	228	506	263	1,351	122	49	209	159	1971 r
5,827	-5	335	696	334	1,356	-71	62	237	175	1972 p
3,725	576	23	362	305	939	141	19	64	43	1965
4,404	524	140	413	257	1,186	224	15	61	45	1966
4,976	505	101	424	310	1,363	171	-3	47	52	1967
5,399	253	167	502	329	1,448	53	18	91	71	1968
6,382	385	584	919	342	1,611	146	66	155	89	1969
7,177	464	367	1,060	655	2,059	296	100	229	122	1970
8,381	769	463	1,123	631	2,294	89	128	289	156	1971 r
9,674	467	822	1,552	706	2,566	133	147	319	172	1972 p
576	74	54	77	23	1,234	169	98	203	106	1965
759	116	60	83	24	1,343	35	93	224	133	1966
943	141	40	82	44	1,479	52	109	255	146	1967
1,155	175	51	97	47	1,579	-4	98	263	167	1968
1,330	93	100	158	63	1,825	104	146	328	179	1969
1,553	117	112	168	63	2,034	44	169	334	163	1970
1,768	104	99	182	84	2,205	31	147	388	222	1971 r
1,961	12	201	297	98	2,260	-88	152	468	307	1972 p
275	21	38	55	17	79	2	2	22	21	1965
334	22	36	56	18	91	11	2	19	17	1966
425	31	61	85	22	98	3	3	16	15	1967
522	11	86	127	37	123	21	4	20	15	1968
646	39	85	146	49	150	23	5	20	13	1969
749	32	75	154	69	194	30	11	36	25	1970
962	120	88	193	91	223	15	15	63	47	1971 r
1,183	102	112	226	99	243	9	12	68	55	1972 p
1,185	48	75	157	79	305	27	17	36	19	1965
1,332	65	79	161	79	354	13	29	46	17	1966
1,640	224	89	176	83	394	23	27	38	22	1967
1,830	83	110	192	82	445	26	20	46	26	1968
2,035	72	126	227	108	514	44	24	87	33	1969
2,252	75	124	261	145	612	79	11	50	40	1970
2,461	105	99	249	157	747	95	33	78	48	1971 r
2,593	1	134	270	143	847	49	49	88	44	1972 p
2,945	245	178	289	123	2,921	57	111	228	130	1965
3,318	160	202	342	147	3,141	125	108	239	140	1966
3,586	199	78	269	195	3,282	92	70	213	151	1967
4,005	222	194	408	216	3,486	50	114	243	164	1968
4,347	133	225	466	280	3,831	199	123	350	173	1969
4,621	104	228	514	268	4,131	174	162	306	204	1970 r
4,999	172	240	514	281	4,499	255	135	308	264	1971 r
5,565	212	367	658	291	4,731	55	187	421	234	1972 p
456	56	24	56	28	1,464	27	91	179	91	1965
524	40	22	57	29	1,622	33	123	175	55	1966
629	77	24	66	36	1,779	43	121	189	69	1967
693	40	26	79	48	2,046	136	119	194	74	1968
813	73	48	98	47	2,381	254	8	259	252	1969
874	6	54	105	52	2,895	326	192	313	125	1970
1,001	65	49	114	62	3,291	350	65	351	291	1971 r
1,088	12	72	146	65	3,627	240	121	329	219	1972 p

3. Includes other Africa, Middle East, other Asia and Pacific, and international unallocated.

NOTE.—For an explanation of the relation between earnings, reinvested earnings, and interest, dividends, and branch earnings see the Technical Notes.

ments improvement programs have probably been less restrictive of the growth in U.S. direct investment than of the growth in other private nonliquid U.S. claims on foreigners.

In the case of foreign investment in the United States, by contrast, the growth rate of portfolio investment has persistently exceeded that of direct investment, and by yearend 1972 foreign direct investment in the United States accounted for only 22 percent of total nonliquid investment here by private foreigners.

The share of foreign direct investment in total private nonliquid foreign investment in the United States has declined steadily despite a number of institutional and economic changes since the mid-1960's which encouraged foreign direct investment here. (See "Foreign Direct Investment in the United States, 1962-71," in the February 1973 SURVEY.) However, other developments encouraged an even more rapid rise in foreign portfolio investment in the United States. These included the large volume of U.S. corporate borrowings from foreigners pursuant to the FDIP, favorable conditions in U.S. equity markets and the spread of U.S. brokerage houses abroad, which induced a rising volume of foreign portfolio investment in the United States.

Components of the addition to direct investment

The two main components comprising the $7.8 billion addition to the direct investment position in 1972 were: (i) $3.4 billion in net capital outflows from the United States, down $1.5 billion from the 1971 figure; and (ii) $4.5 billion in reinvested earnings of incorporated foreign affiliates, up $1.4 billion from the 1971 figure. The third component, valuation adjustments, was relatively small (table 2). The increase in reinvested earnings was mainly in developed countries, partly reflecting the relative importance of incorporated affiliates—principally in manufacturing—in these countries (see table 4).

Reinvested earnings were about 73 percent of the addition to direct investment in manufacturing in 1972 but less than 30 percent of the addition to direct investment in petroleum. This difference between the two industries largely reflects the fact that almost all direct investment in crude petroleum production in the developing countries is in branches, largely because U.S. tax advantages attach to the branch form of organization for extractive activities, while most manufacturing affiliates are incorporated. The U.S. balance of payments accounts treat branch earnings as though they were entirely remitted to the United States, with the entire addition to net assets of branches treated as a U.S. capital outflow. As a result, no reinvested earnings are calculated for branches, although some of the net capital outflow to branches serves the same function as do reinvested earnings of incorporated affiliates.

The 1972 increase in reinvested earnings resulted from: (i) an increase

Table 8A.—Preliminary 1972 Data on U.S. Direct Investment

[Millions

Line	Area and countries[3]	Total, all industries — Book value at year-end[1]	Net capital outflows	Reinvested earnings[2]	Earnings	Interest, dividends, and branch earnings	Mining and smelting — Book value at year-end[1]	Net capital outflows	Reinvested earnings[2]	Earnings	Interest, dividends, and branch earnings	Petroleum — Book value at year-end[1]	Net capital outflows	Reinvested earnings[2]	Earnings	Interest, dividends, and branch earnings
1	All areas	94,031	3,404	4,521	12,386	8,004	7,131	411	34	418	399	26,399	1,635	668	4,552	3,950
2	Developed countries	64,114	1,897	3,668	6,805	3,291	4,420	354	25	235	213	14,200	701	571	707	252
3	Canada	25,784	380	1,367	2,236	984	3,490	240	6	139	131	5,311	-92	314	453	158
4	Europe[4]	30,714	1,074	1,885	3,685	1,821	79	-2	(**)	(**)	(**)	6,992	627	165	117	28
5	United Kingdom	9,509	-20	490	1,055	572	5	(**)	(**)	(**)	(**)	2,321	57	93	122	63
6	European Economic Community	15,745	1,069	1,062	1,910	861	10	(**)	(**)	(**)	(**)	3,494	470	93	40	-17
7	Belgium and Luxembourg	2,130	134	158	245	92	(*)					181	97	-31	-28	2
8	France	3,432	156	252	422	172	7	(**)	(**)	(**)	(**)	472	19	16	31	15
9	Germany	6,262	658	381	902	497	(**)	(**)	(**)	(**)	(**)	1,689	297	73	74	28
10	Italy	1,978	43	68	147	80	(**)	(**)	(**)	(**)	(**)	503	-41	-60	-63	(*)
11	Netherlands	1,943	79	203	194	20	(*)					699	99	95	26	-61
12	Other Western Europe	5,461	24	333	719	387	64	(**)	(**)	(**)	(**)	1,177	100	-20	-45	-18
13	Denmark	377	21	-2	7	14	1					243	19	-9	-11	1
14	Norway	326	18	17	(*)	-13	(**)	(**)	(**)	(**)	(**)	154	12	1	-24	-22
15	Spain	903	66	62	99	36	(**)	(**)	(**)	(**)	(**)	155	21	1	4	3
16	Sweden	726	8	29	55	29	(*)					318	-1	-12	-13	(*)
17	Switzerland	1,911	-111	146	410	259	(*)					-3	78	2	2	2
18	Other[5]	1,218	22	82	149	63	20	(**)	(**)	(**)	(**)	311	-29	-2	-3	-2
19	Japan[11]	2,222	200	171	345	163						796	89	47	51	9
20	Australia, New Zealand and South Africa	5,393	244	245	538	323	851	117	18	94	80	1,102	77	45	87	56
21	Australia	4,121	207	184	401	252	707	94	13	68	61	(**)	(**)	(**)	(**)	(**)
22	New Zealand	247	12	25	37	11	8	(*)				(**)	(**)	(**)	(**)	(**)
23	South Africa	1,025	24	36	101	60	136	22	5	36	18	215	(**)	(**)	(**)	(**)
24	Developing countries	25,186	1,117	749	5,106	4,318	2,712	57	9	182	186	9,878	682	69	3,527	3,394
25	Latin American Republics and other Western Hemisphere	16,644	279	600	1,532	962	2,082	-15	-1	158	171	4,267	28	46	295	246
26	Latin American Republics	13,528	51	517	1,264	755	1,300	-46	-1	64	74	3,245	-76	47	277	225
27	Mexico	1,993	51	99	192	94	124	-11	7	9	2	32	(*)	2	4	2
28	Panama	1,423	-87	83	164	92	19					265	-7	10	10	(*)
29	Other Central America[6]	646	-26	9	32	25	15	6	(*)	3	3	159	-19	-1	-9	-9
30	Argentina	1,391	25	13	81	70	(**)	(**)	(**)	(**)	(**)	(**)	(**)	(**)	(**)	(**)
31	Brazil	2,490	193	224	312	80	136	(**)	(**)	(**)	(**)	169	(**)	(**)	(**)	(**)
32	Chile	621	-93	-5	-4	8	359	-92	(**)	(**)	(**)	(**)	(**)	(**)	(**)	(**)
33	Colombia	739	-21	16	42	24	(**)	(*)	(**)	(**)	(**)	327	-18	(*)	4	4
34	Peru	714	38	5	34	26	416	12	1	26	25	(**)	(**)	(**)	(**)	(**)
35	Venezuela	2,683	-65	58	393	329	(**)	(**)	(**)	(**)	(**)	1,546	-94	6	55	247
36	Other[7]	828	35	14	19	6	39	-7	1	11	10	424	35	7	-27	-33
37	Other Western Hemisphere[8]	3,116	228	83	268	207	782	31	(*)	94	98	1,022	104	-1	18	20
38	Other Africa[9]	3,086	123	96	582	489	425	24	10	24	13	2,254	88	74	527	454
39	Liberia	209	10	4	12	9	(**)	(**)	(**)	(**)	(**)	(**)	(**)	(**)	(**)	(**)
40	Libya	1,145	104	6	331	326	(**)	(**)	(**)	(**)	(**)	1,131	-11	(**)	72	202
41	Other	1,732	9	86	239	154	364	24	10	24	10	(**)	(**)	(**)	(**)	130
42	Middle East[10]	2,053	399	-8	2,452	2,463	5	3	(**)	(**)	(**)	1,807	371	-27	2,419	2,449
43	Other Asia and Pacific[11]	3,402	316	61	540	405	199	45	(*)	(*)	1	1,550	195	-25	287	246
44	India	335	-3	8	40	27	(**)	(**)	(**)	(**)	(**)	(**)	(**)	(**)	(**)	(**)
45	Philippines	707	13	-8	37	39	(**)					(**)	(**)	(**)	(**)	(**)
46	Other[11]	2,360	306	61	462	339	(**)	(**)	(**)	(**)	(**)	(**)	(**)	(**)	(**)	(**)
47	International, unallocated	4,733	391	104	476	395						2,321	251	28	318	304

*Less than $500,000 (±)   **Combined in other industries.

NOTE.—Detail may not add to totals because of rounding.

1. The value of investments in specified industries and countries is affected by capital flows among foreign affiliates as shown in the Technical Notes.
2. Represents U.S. owners' share in the reinvested earnings of foreign corporations.
3. Does not mean that all countries grouped in an "other" or regional category have U.S. direct investment at any given time.
4. Direct investment statistics do not show any investments in Eastern Europe.

5. Includes Austria, Cyprus, Finland, Gibraltar, Greece, Greenland, Iceland, Ireland, Malta, Portugal, Turkey and Yugoslavia.
6. Includes Costa Rica, El Salvador, Guatemala, Honduras, and Nicaragua.
7. Includes Bolivia, Dominican Republic, Ecuador, Haiti, Paraguay, and Uruguay.
8. Includes all of the Western Hemisphere except Canada and the 19 Latin American Republics included in line 26.
9. Includes United Arab Republic (Egypt) and all other countries in Africa except South Africa.

in the dollar value of earnings of incorporated foreign affiliates; and (ii) a sharp drop in the proportion of incorporated foreign affiliates' earnings paid out as dividends (see table 5). Dividends increased 9 percent last year, compared with a 14 percent average rate in the preceding 5 years.

There are several likely reasons, some of them temporary, for the decline in incorporated affiliates' payout ratios. First, exceptional earnings increases are usually not immediately reflected in increased dividends; management tends to raise dividends substantially only when convinced that the new

level can be maintained. Second, the devaluation reduced the amount of affiliates' foreign currency earnings needed to maintain normal growth of dollar remittances to the United States. Some continuing uncertainty with respect to the international monetary situation, and the effects of U.S. Government restrictions on dividend payments by the U.S. parent companies, probably also reduced the proportion of earnings remitted to the United States.

As the 1972 addition to the U.S. direct investment position was almost as large as the 1971 addition, the big 1972 increase in reinvested earnings was accompanied by a big decrease in net capital outflows from the United States, both in developed and in other areas (see table 4). For incorporated manufacturing affiliates in developed countries, reinvested earnings supplied approximately three-fourths of the 1972 addition to U.S. direct investment.

The 1972 decrease in direct investment net capital outflows from the United States was also influenced by other factors. Some of the decrease may have been related to increased confidence in the U.S. dollar, following the agreed devaluation of the dollar at the Smithsonian Conference of December 1971. The 1971 increase in net capital outflows to incorporated affiliates had been concentrated to an unusual degree in short-term accounts, and no doubt reflected some foreign exchange positioning in anticipation of a dollar devaluation rather than affiliate investment needs. In 1972, short-term capital outflows to incorporated affiliates were much lower than in the previous two years, suggesting that some of the affiliate investment needs in 1972 were met by an unwinding of the 1971 positioning (see table 6). Nearly half of the total decrease in net capital outflows from 1971 to 1972 was accounted for by capital reflows to the United States from affiliates in the United Kingdom (see table 7), apparently related to the sterling crises of 1972, and the associated expectations that sterling would depreciate. The reflows from the United Kingdom may also have been connected with cancella-

Abroad, Selected Data Items, Countries, and Industries

of dollars]

Manufacturing					Other industries					Line
Book value at year-end [1]	Net capital outflows	Reinvested earnings [2]	Earnings	Interest, dividends, and branch earnings	Book value at year-end [1]	Net capital outflows	Reinvested earnings [2]	Earnings	Interest, dividends, and branch earnings	
39,478	1,028	2,825	5,007	2,145	21,024	331	995	2,409	1,511	1
32,825	803	2,386	4,202	1,798	12,669	38	687	1,660	1,027	2
11,587	227	782	1,162	417	5,397	5	265	482	278	3
17,462	474	1,358	2,544	1,139	6,182	-25	362	1,024	654	4
5,827	-5	335	696	334	1,356	-71	62	237	175	5
9,674	467	822	1,552	706	2,566	133	147	319	172	6
1,172	18	131	172	43	777	19	58	101	46	7
2,482	106	193	320	128	521	31	43	72	29	8
3,827	253	290	749	446	746	108	18	79	59	9
1,166	35	117	183	64	309	49	11	27	16	10
1,027	54	92	128	60	217	-74	16	40	22	11
1,961	12	201	297	98	2,260	-88	152	468	307	12
63	-4	(*)	3	4	70	6	6	15	9	13
80	1	8	10	2	92	5	9	14	7	14
473	33	30	52	23	275	12	31	42	10	15
261	16	33	42	11	147	-7	8	26	18	16
534	-38	66	105	38	1,380	-151	78	303	218	17
550	4	64	84	20	337	47	21	67	45	18
1,183	102	112	226	99	243	9	12	68	55	19
2,593	1	134	270	143	847	49	49	88	44	20
1,981	16	109	216	116	1,432	97	63	117	75	21
131	3	13	19	5	108	8	12	18	5	22
481	-18	12	34	23	193	21	19	40	19	23
6,652	224	439	804	346	5,944	154	232	592	392	24
5,565	212	367	658	281	4,731	55	187	421	264	25
5,265	201	351	626	263	3,718	-28	120	298	194	26
1,385	42	78	151	72	451	21	12	28	18	27
162	-4	20	43	22	977	-76	53	111	70	28
110	31	4	9	5	362	-15	6	30	25	29
836	19	4	38	36	555	6	9	43	34	30
1,745	121	198	258	56	440	71	26	54	24	31
47	2	-3	-1	2	214	-2	-2	-3	6	32
262	-9	15	32	17	150	6	1	6	-4	33
90	-3	2	12	8	208	29	3	-4	-7	34
539	-2	30	74	39	599	31	22	64	43	35
89	4	4	9	5	276	4	2	25	24	36
299	11	16	33	18	1,013	82	68	123	70	37
124	-4	8	10	2	284	15	3	21	19	38
(**) (**)	(**)	(**)	(**)	(**)	209 1,145	10 104	4 6	12 331	9 326	39 40
122	-4	8	10	2	114	(*)	-4	3	11	41
104	7	5	8	3	137	19	14	25	11	42
860	10	58	128	60	793	66	28	125	98	43
177	1	8	28	17	158	-3	(*)	12	10	44
256	1	-2	18	15	451	12	-5	20	24	45
427	9	53	82	28	1,931	297	8	381	310	46
					2,413	140	76	157	91	47

10. Includes Bahrain, Iran, Iraq, Israel, Jordan, Kuwait, Lebanon, Qatar, Saudi Arabia, Southern Yemen, Syria, Trucial States, Oman, and Yemen.
11. Commencing with data for 1972, data for Okinawa is included with Japan instead of other Asia and Pacific.

NOTE.—For an explanation of the relation between earnings, reinvested earnings, and interest, dividends, and branch earnings see the Technical Notes.

tion of some planned U.S. investments there. Finally, foreign affiliates' plant and equipment expenditures were up only 2 percent in 1972, compared with a 14 percent increase in 1971,[2] and this

2. See "Plant and Equipment Expenditures of U.S.-Owned Foreign Affiliates: Revised Estimates for 1972 and 1973" in the March 1973 SURVEY.

possibly affected both reinvested earnings and net capital outflows.

Components of return on U.S. direct investment

Table 12 gives alternative measures of return on U.S. direct investment abroad, by major area and by major

industry of the foreign affiliate. Panels A through F give the basic components used to calculate the various measures; panel G gives the dollar return on the basis of each of four measures; and panel H gives the percentage rates of return for three of the measures, calculated on the value of U.S. direct

Table 8B.—Revised 1971 Data on U.S. Direct Investment

[Millions

Line	Area and countries [3]	Total, all industries					Mining and smelting					Petroleum				
		Book value at year-end [1]	Net capital outflows	Reinvested earnings [2]	Earnings	Interest, dividends, and branch earnings	Book value at year-end [1]	Net capital outflows	Reinvested earnings [2]	Earnings	Interest, dividends, and branch earnings	Book value at year-end [1]	Net capital outflows	Reinvested earnings [2]	Earnings	Interest, dividends, and branch earnings
1	All areas	86,198	4,943	3,157	10,299	7,295	6,685	510	23	499	482	24,152	1,950	500	3,856	3,442
2	Developed countries	58,571	2,988	2,437	5,414	3,122	4,041	371	41	290	250	12,958	976	251	465	324
3	Canada	24,105	273	1,074	1,955	1,015	3,246	256	31	203	171	5,149	87	249	370	150
4	Europe [4]	27,740	2,169	1,041	2,696	1,648	79	10	(**)	(**)	(**)	6,192	782	−72	−2	133
5	United Kingdom	9,007	685	324	779	469	9	(**)	(**)	(**)	(**)	2,176	290	48	64	47
6	European Economic Community	13,605	1,334	499	1,384	878	13	(**)	(**)	(**)	(**)	2,918	477	−93	−28	91
7	Belgium and Luxembourg	1,826	177	123	215	91	(*)		(*)			115	61	−12	−13	−5
8	France	3,020	246	172	307	141		10	(**)		(**)	387	77	−5	17	21
9	Germany	5,209	488	125	616	471	(**)	(**)	(**)	(**)	(**)	1,300	92	7	(**)	20
10	Italy	1,871	331	(*)	67	65	(**)	(**)	(**)	(**)	(**)	605	168	−72	−75	−2
11	Netherlands	1,679	92	78	179	110	(*)					510	79	−11	44	57
12	Other Western Europe	5,127	150	218	533	300	57	(**)	(**)	(**)	(**)	1,098	15	−27	−38	−5
13	Denmark	358	16	−20	−6	17	1					233	19	−22	−23	2
14	Norway	292	15	8	2	−4	(**)	(**)	(**)	(**)	(**)	141	7	−1	−16	−13
15	Spain	778	38	11	32	23	(**)	(**)	(**)	(**)	(**)	130	−3	−8	−6	1
16	Sweden	689	46	22	39	18	(*)					331	12	−3	−3	(*)
17	Switzerland	1,888	−31	129	336	186	(*)					−83	−47	4	4	1
18	Other [5]	1,122	67	68	129	61	19	(**)	(**)	(**)	(**)	346	26	2	6	4
19	Japan	1,821	212	127	285	149						637	78	24	29	11
20	Australia, New Zealand and South Africa	4,904	333	195	479	310	716	105	13	84	74	980	29	50	68	31
21	Australia	3,730	275	134	343	241	600	95	11	57	53	(**)	(**)	(**)	(**)	(**)
22	New Zealand	209	11	15	26	11	8					(**)	(**)	(**)	(**)	(**)
23	South Africa	965	47	46	109	59	108	10	2	27	21	189	(**)	(**)	(**)	(**)
24	Developing countries	23,358	1,411	575	4,324	3,739	2,644	138	−18	208	231	9,148	708	129	3,027	2,860
25	Latin American Republics and other Western Hemisphere	15,789	691	399	1,500	1,130	2,097	59	−39	172	214	4,195	204	63	507	444
26	Latin American Republics	12,982	435	317	1,239	929	1,345	−11	−40	69	107	3,276	66	37	461	421
27	Mexico	1,838	48	−5	123	123	127	−12	−27	7	28	30	−3	(*)	4	3
28	Panama	1,450	119	86	149	75	19		(*)			262	−5	7	7	(*)
29	Other Central America [6]	668	41	7	35	30	9	(*)		2	2	179	19	5	5	5
30	Argentina	1,353	50	18	80	66	(**)	(**)	(**)	(**)	(**)	(**)	(**)	(**)	(**)	(**)
31	Brazil	2,066	72	145	220	73	119	(**)	(**)	(**)	(**)	145	1	(**)	(**)	(**)
32	Chile	720	−18	−7	−10	2	452	−3	(**)	−1	2	(**)	(**)	(**)	(**)	(**)
33	Colombia	744	54	16	66	49	(**)	(**)	(**)	(**)	(**)	345	10	1	32	31
34	Peru	674	−4	(*)	44	40	402	−17	(**)	26	26	(**)	(**)	(**)	(**)	(**)
35	Venezuela	2,690	−66	47	497	446	(**)	(**)	(**)	(**)	(**)	1,633	−105	3	370	366
36	Other [7]	778	141	12	36	26	45	−2	(*)	12	12	383	126	6	−5	−10
37	Other Western Hemisphere [8]	2,807	256	81	262	200	751	71	(**)	103	107	918	138	26	47	23
38	Other Africa [9]	2,871	171	102	570	471	391	20	20	34	15	2,094	113	73	507	435
39	Liberia	195	−3	11	17	6	(**)	(**)	(**)	(**)	(**)	(**)	(**)	(**)	(**)	(**)
40	Libya	1,036	24	1	401	400	(**)	(**)	(**)	(**)	(**)	(**)	(**)	(**)	(**)	(**)
41	Other	1,641	151	90	152	64	330	22	20	27	8	1,074	85	64	107	46
42	Middle East [10]	1,661	59	−10	1,879	1,891	3					1,464	48	−20	1,856	1,879
43	Other Asia and Pacific [11]	3,036	490	84	375	247	154	59	2	2	2	1,396	344	13	157	103
44	India	329	16	8	41	27	(**)			(**)	(**)	(**)	(**)	(**)	(**)	(**)
45	Philippines	718	3	14	58	38	(**)	(**)	(**)	(**)	(**)	(**)	(**)	(**)	(**)	(**)
46	Other [11]	1,989	470	63	276	182	(**)	(**)	(**)	(**)	(**)	(**)	(**)	(**)	(**)	(**)
47	International, unallocated	4,270	545	145	561	434						2,045	266	119	364	257

*Less than $500,000 (±).   **Combined in other industries.
NOTE.—Detail may not add to totals because of rounding.
1. The value of investments in specified industries and countries is affected by capital flows among foreign affiliates as shown in the Technical Notes.
2. Represents U.S. owners' share in the reinvested earnings of foreign corporations.
3. Does not mean that all countries grouped in an "other" or regional category have U.S. direct investment at any given time.
4. Direct investment statistics do not show any investments in Eastern Europe

5. Includes Austria, Cyprus, Finland, Gibraltar, Greece, Greenland, Iceland, Ireland, Malta, Portugal, Turkey and Yugoslavia.
6. Includes Costa Rica, El Salvador, Guatemala, Honduras, and Nicaragua.
7. Includes Bolivia, Dominican Republic, Ecuador, Haiti, Paraguay, and Uruguay.
8. Includes all of the Western Hemisphere except Canada and the 19 Latin American Republics included in line 26.
9. Includes United Arab Republic (Egypt) and all other countries in Africa except South Africa.

investment at the beginning of the year. (It is not possible to calculate a rate of return for the fourth "earnings" measure because data on the appropriate base, the U.S. share in the net worth of the foreign affiliates, are not available.) Definitions of the basic components (panels A through F) and an

explanation of the relationship among them are given in the Technical Notes at the end of this article. The following paragraphs review the components one by one.

Net earnings of foreign branches in 1972 were $3.5 billion, an increase of $0.4 billion from 1971 (panel A).

Petroleum branches in "other areas", which include most of those engaged in crude petroleum production, accounted for most of the increase.

U.S. direct investors' receipts of common stock dividends from incorporated foreign affiliates were $3.9 billion in 1972, an increase of only $0.3 billion from 1971 (panel B). Manufacturing affiliates in developed countries were, as usual, the largest source of dividends. Foreign withholding taxes on common stock dividends in 1972 were $0.5 billion, little changed from the 1971 level (panel C). These are taxes paid by incorporated affiliates to foreign governments on common stock dividends to U.S. direct investors; amounts of such taxes vary with provisions of the tax treaties between the United States and individual foreign countries.

The U.S. direct investors' share of the reinvested earnings of incorporated affiliates was $4.5 billion in 1972, up from $3.2 billion in 1971 (panel D). Close to half of these reinvested earnings were in manufacturing affiliates in developed countries.

Interest received by direct investors from affiliates in 1972 was $0.7 billion (panel E). Interest, comprising receipts from all forms of foreign organization, comes mainly from affiliates in the developed countries.

Direct investment royalties and fees were $2.4 billion in 1972 (panel F). Manufacturing affiliates in developed countries accounted for nearly half of the 1972 figure. Affiliates in the petroleum industry, as usual, reported only small payments of royalties and fees. Details on fees and royalties are given in table 11.

Alternative measures of return

Four measures of the dollar return on direct investment, reflecting alternative analytic viewpoints, obtained from different combinations of the components in panels A through F, are shown in panel G of table 12. Three of these measures are expressed as rates of return in panel H and chart 13. As explained above, some of the 1972 increases in rates of return reflected the fact that the devaluation boosted the dollar value of affiliates'

Abroad, Selected Data Items, Countries, and Industries
of dollars]

	Manufacturing					Other industries				
Book value year-end[1]	Net capital outflows	Reinvested earnings[2]	Earnings	Interest, dividends, and branch earnings	Book value at year-end[1]	Net capital outflows	Reinvested earnings[2]	Earnings	Interest, dividends, and branch earnings	Line
35,632	1,556	1,854	3,834	1,950	19,728	927	780	2,111	1,422	1
29,633	1,319	1,565	3,206	1,620	11,939	323	580	1,452	927	2
10,590	-53	588	953	393	5,121	-18	206	428	300	3
15,620	1,146	790	1,811	978	5,849	232	324	887	537	4
5,471	274	228	506	263	1,351	122	49	209	159	5
8,381	769	463	1,123	631	2,294	89	128	289	156	6
1,015	74	93	127	35	695	42	42	102	61	7
2,174	168	130	226	101	448	1	47	64	19	8
3,295	369	108	553	399	613	27	10	63	52	9
1,014	153	60	118	56	252	11	12	24	12	10
882	4	72	100	41	288	9	17	35	12	11
1,768	104	99	182	84	2,205	31	147	388	222	12
66	(*)	(*)	3	3	58	-3	2	15	12	13
74	------	4	6	2	77	8	5	12	7	14
421	31	-4	8	15	229	10	23	30	7	15
212	33	14	21	9	146	1	11	21	9	16
512	19	35	83	43	1,459	-3	90	250	142	17
483	21	50	61	13	274	20	16	61	45	18
962	120	88	193	91	223	15	15	63	47	19
2,461	105	99	249	157	747	95	33	78	48	20
1,859	66	76	195	128	1,271	114	48	91	59	21
114	6	10	17	7	88	6	5	8	4	22
488	33	13	36	22	179	3	31	46	15	23
5,999	238	289	628	330	5,565	326	174	461	317	24
4,999	172	240	514	268	4,499	255	135	308	204	25
4,713	182	228	478	243	3,647	199	92	231	158	26
1,268	52	19	96	76	413	11	2	15	15	27
144	-3	30	44	13	1,026	128	49	98	62	28
78	5	2	7	5	402	17	4	21	17	29
813	16	22	51	32	539	34	-4	29	34	30
1,419	51	120	179	58	382	19	25	41	15	31
50	-8	-6	-8	-2	219	-7	(*)	-1	2	32
256	36	13	29	15	142	7	2	4	2	33
92	4	(*)	11	9	179	9	(*)	8	5	34
510	24	26	62	32	547	15	18	65	48	35
81	6	3	7	4	269	11	3	22	21	36
286	-9	12	35	24	852	56	43	77	46	37
123	21	3	8	5	264	17	6	21	16	38
(**)	(**)	(**)	(**)	(**)	195	-3	11	17	6	39
(**)	(**)	(**)	(**)	(**)	1,036	24	1	401	400	40
121	21	3	8	5	116	23	3	9	5	41
92	2	5	7	3	102	9	6	16	10	42
786	43	41	99	55	700	44	28	117	87	43
169	5	7	24	15	161	11	2	16	12	44
258	1	8	26	13	460	3	5	33	26	45
359	37	26	49	27	1,630	432	36	227	155	46
					2,225	278	25	197	177	47

10. Includes Bahrain, Iran, Iraq, Israel, Jordan, Kuwait, Lebanon, Qatar, Saudi Arabia, Southern Yemen, Syria, Trucial States, Oman, and Yemen.
11. Includes data for Okinawa.

NOTE.—For an explanation of the relation between earnings, reinvested earnings, and interest, dividends, and branch earnings see the Technical Notes.

foreign currency earnings, but the value of the U.S. direct investment position essentially was not adjusted for the December 1971 change in the foreign exchange value of the U.S. dollar.

The *U.S. share in earnings* of the foreign affiliates gives a conventional accounting measure of return from the viewpoint of the affiliates. This measure (panels A+B+C+D) sums branch earnings and earnings of incorporated affiliates; the latter are the sum of incorporated affiliates' dividends, withholding taxes, and reinvested earnings. Interest and royalties and fees are excluded because they are costs to the affiliates.

CHART 12

Earnings of Foreign Affiliates

Billion $ (Ratio scale)

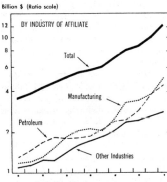

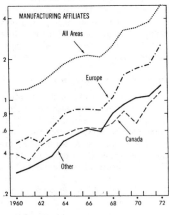

U.S. Department of Commerce, Bureau of Economic Analysis   73-9-12

The U.S. share in earnings of foreign affiliates was $12.4 billion in 1972, up 20 percent from 1971, following a 17 percent increase in 1971. The large 1972 increase was primarily in earnings of manufacturing affiliates in developed countries, reflecting the fact that the major change in the value of the dollar was with respect to the currencies of these countries. The 1971 increase, on the other hand, had primarily resulted from a rapid expansion in petroleum earnings, as increased petroleum production more than offset decreased profits per barrel caused by higher taxes and other costs. In 1972 as in 1971, there was very little growth in aggregate earnings of the "other industry" group.

Adjusted earnings focuses on the return realized by the direct investor, rather than on earnings from the point of view of the affiliates. It is equal to earnings plus interest less withholding taxes paid to foreign governments (panels A+B+D+E). Interest paid by affiliates to direct investors is part of adjusted earnings because loan capital is included in the value of direct investment; foreign withholding taxes on common dividends paid to direct investors are excluded because such taxes represent a reduction in benefits to direct investors. Royalties and fees are excluded as they are not a conventional component of return on capital.

On the adjusted earnings basis, returns to U.S. direct investors were $12.5 billion in 1972, $2.1 billion more than in 1971. The adjusted earnings figures show roughly the same area and industry pattern as the earnings figures discussed above, with manufacturing affiliates in developed areas dominating the change from 1971 to 1972.

The $12.5 billion of adjusted earnings gave a record rate of return of 14.5 percent on the U.S. direct investment position (panel H). Both manufacturing and petroleum showed strong gains, while the rate of return for other industries fell.

The *broad earnings* measure is the most complete account of benefits received by direct investors from their foreign affiliates. The broad earnings

measure is calculated by adding royalties and fees to adjusted earnings (panels A+B+D+E+F). Royalties and fees are included as representing a recovery of some of the research and development costs and administrative costs incurred by U.S. parent companies. Addition of 1972 royalties and fees of $2.4 billion to adjusted earnings gives a broad earnings figure of $15.0 billion, up from $12.6 billion in 1971. The $15.0 billion represents a rate of return of 17.3 percent on the U.S. direct investment position; in 1971, the broad earnings rate of return was 16.1 percent.

The *balance of payments income* measure is the Nation's identifiable return on direct investment as recorded in the U.S. balance of payments accounts. This measure equals broad earnings less reinvested earnings (panels A+B+E+F). Reinvested earnings are excluded because they are not now treated as an income receipt in U.S. balance of payments accounting. (A revision that would include reinvested

Table 9.—U.S. Direct Investors' Acquisitions From and Sales to Foreigners of Voting Stock in Primary Foreign Enterprises,[1] by Area and Industry

[Millions of dollars]

Area and industry	1971 [r]			1972 [p]		
	Acqui-si-tions	Sales	Net	Acqui-si-tions	Sales	Net
All areas	656	196	460	808	136	672
Petroleum	35	*9	26	38	10	28
Manufacturing	554	133	421	446	58	388
Other industries	67	54	13	324	68	256
Canada	67	21	46	52	29	23
Petroleum	26	6	20	18	5	13
Manufacturing	31	2	29	19	15	4
Other industries	10	13	−3	15	9	6
Europe	417	120	297	470	47	423
Petroleum	7	3	4	12		12
Manufacturing	363	104	259	298	32	266
Other industries	47	13	34	160	15	145
Other areas	172	56	116	286	60	226
Petroleum	2		2	8	5	3
Manufacturing	160	27	133	129	11	118
Other industries	10	29	−19	149	44	105

[r] Revised.   [p] Preliminary.
1. Acquisitions include partial and total purchases of voting securities of existing foreign corporations from foreign owners. Sales include partial and total sales of voting securities of foreign corporations by U.S. owners to foreign purchasers. Liquidations through the sale of assets, as distinct from sale of ownership interests, are not included. Changes in the share of ownership resulting from transactions between a parent and an affiliate—such as the purchase of treasury stock from an affiliate by a parent—are not included; only changes involving outside foreign owners or purchasers are included. Secondary foreign companies acquired or sold through primary foreign affiliates are not included.

SURVEY OF CURRENT BUSINESS

earnings in the payments accounting framework is being considered.)

From the balance of payments viewpoint, the return to the United States on direct investment was $10.4 billion in 1972. This gave a rate of return of 12.1 percent on the U.S. direct investment position, unchanged from the 1971 rate of return. The balance of payments measure of return was unchanged because the impact on earnings of the dollar devaluation and of the strong economic growth abroad went into reinvested earnings; other measures, which include reinvested earnings, showed large increases in the rate of return.

The balance of payments rate of return varies considerably by area and by industry. Petroleum affiliates in the developed countries show a low rate, while petroleum affiliates in other areas, mainly the developing countries, show a high rate of return. This reflects the fact that, because of tax considerations and pricing agreements with the governments of producing countries, transfers of oil from producing affiliates in developing countries to sales affiliates in other areas are priced so that most of the petroleum firms' profits appear in developing countries. For both manufacturing and the "other industries" shown in table 12, the rate of return from affiliates in developed countries exceeded that from affiliates in other areas.

The three rates of return are plotted for the years 1960 through 1972 on chart 13. Over the period as a whole, all the rates of return tended to move up. After the mid-1960's, when U.S. balance of payments improvement programs were strengthened, the balance of payments rate of return grew relatively slowly, while the other rates of return rose substantially.

TECHNICAL NOTES

A. Methodology

Annual data on U.S. direct investment abroad presented in this article were derived from a mandatory sample survey conducted by BEA covering the approximately 14,000 foreign affiliates of 1,200 U.S. direct investors. Data

Table 10.—Net Capital Outflows to Manufacturing Affiliates by Industry

[Millions of dollars]

Area and year	Total	Food products	Paper and allied products	Chemicals and allied products	Rubber products	Primary and fabricated metals	Machinery except electrical	Electrical machinery	Transportation equipment	Other
All areas:										
1968	945	100	−7	293	4	160	71	−2	1	326
1969	1,160	125	3	163	9	136	177	206	115	226
1970	1,295	134	111	78	44	194	205	178	193	158
1971 ʳ	1,556	206	44	365	1	21	307	117	267	229
1972 ᵖ	1,028	102	59	198	37	5	84	157	262	124
Canada:										
1968	26	21	−16	21	−8	29	(*)	(*)	−91	70
1969	248	53	−35	2	8	16	49	59	38	58
1970	305	5	86	47	3	74	−39	−5	131	4
1971 ʳ	−53	26	6	91	−7	−16	24	−14	−230	68
1972 ᵖ	227	−6	53	50	14	−33	35	−4	66	51
Europe:										
1968	562	50	9	164	−1	95	68	−28	23	181
1969	596	54	31	100	1	63	105	114	24	104
1970	773	90	23	−13	41	85	195	148	50	154
1971 ʳ	1,146	145	33	203	16	36	250	98	319	79
1972 ᵖ	474	55	−1	60	8	47	−19	135	150	40
Japan: [1]										
1968	11	(*)	2	12	(*)	1	−10	2	(*)	4
1969	39	(*)	1	9	(*)	10	−7	10	5	11
1970	32	3	−3	12	1	−4	8	1	8	5
1971 ʳ	120	11	(*)	11	(*)	3	−8	4	85	13
1972 ᵖ	102	19	(*)	23	(*)	(*)	37	2	1	19
Australia, New Zealand, and South Africa:										
1968	83	10	−1	25	6	18	6	10	10	−1
1969	72	12	−1	19	−8	20	4	3	2	21
1970	75	8	5	15	5	10	18	3	6	5
1971 ʳ	105	24	(*)	18	2	−10	17	22	26	6
1972 ᵖ	1	14	(*)	−5	(*)	−10	2	15	−23	8
Latin American Republics and other Western Hemisphere:										
1968	222	12	−1	54	(*)	22	4	9	58	64
1969	133	1	6	−4	1	24	24	10	45	26
1970	104	44	−1	24	−4	18	20	23	−3	−17
1971 ʳ	172	−5	3	33	10	−3	20	1	64	48
1972 ᵖ	212	15	6	63	6	6	30	23	67	−5
Other areas: [2]										
1968	40	7	(*)	16	6	−6	2	6	2	7
1969	73	5	1	37	7	3	3	11	1	7
1970	6	−16	1	−7	−2	11	3	8	1	7
1971 ʳ	65	5	2	9	12	10	3	6	2	15
1972 ᵖ	12	6	(*)	7	8	−6	−1	−15	(*)	12

ʳ Revised.   ᵖ Preliminary.   *Less than $500,000 (±).

NOTE.—Detail may not add to totals because of rounding.

1. Commencing with data for 1972, data for Okinawa is included with Japan instead of in other areas.
2. Includes other Africa, Middle East, other Asia and Pacific, and international, unallocated.

reported by this sample, with the exception of net capital outflows, were blown up, item by item, to obtain the estimates published in this article. Data for capital flows, the other main component of the annual addition to the U.S. direct investment position, were not blown up to a universe estimate, but were included essentially as reported; however, the sample data on capital flows were supplemented by additional capital flow data obtained from other U.S. residents. The sum of the resulting 1972 reinvested earnings and capital flow data, together with statical adjustments for valuation, coverage, and statistical discrepancies, were added to the estimated yearend 1971 U.S. direct investment position to ob

tain the estimated yearend 1972 position. The estimate of the yearend 1971 U.S. direct investment position had been obtained in the same way. The chain of estimates started after the year 1957, for which universe data were available from the 1957 benchmark survey of U.S. direct investors.

The blowup factors, based on the proportion that the annual sample formed of the 1957 benchmark survey data, were derived on the basis of an affiliate-by-affiliate matching process. Thus, for the matched panel, the ratio of the current year value of a data item to the preceding year value was computed. The resulting blowup factor then was applied to the universe estimate of the data item for the preceding

year; the resulting figure then was adjusted to compensate for any year-to-year additions or deletions of affiliates from the sample, to give the universe estimate for the current year.

As the 1957 benchmark is out of date, particularly with respect to country-industry detail, the universe estimates given in this article may be subject to a significant margin of error, especially for data cells at the lower levels of aggregation. New blowup factors based on the 1966 benchmark survey, the most recent survey of the universe of U.S. direct investors, are being prepared. These new factors will be the basis for a major revision of the annual direct investment data, scheduled for release in 1974.

Table 11.—Direct Investment Receipts of Royalties and Fees, by Area and Major Industry

[Millions of dollars]

Area and industry	1964			1970			1971 r			1972 p		
	Total	Royalties, license fees, and rentals	Management fees and service charges	Total	Royalties, license fees, and rentals	Management fees and service charges	Total	Royalties, license fees, and rentals	Management fees and service charges	Total	Royalties, license fees, and rentals	Management fees and service charges
All areas	1,013	521	492	1,919	1,092	826	2,160	1,237	923	2,429	1,468	961
Petroleum	116	13	103	216	34	182	258	32	226	276	26	249
Manufacturing	479	210	269	1,002	635	367	1,108	755	353	1,283	900	383
Trade	58	22	36	156	90	65	198	116	82	233	153	80
Foreign film rentals	257	257		299	299		296	296		339	339	
Other industries	103	19	84	247	35	212	300	37	263	297	49	248
Canada	190	68	121	357	165	192	389	186	203	434	200	234
Petroleum	15	(*)	15	17	1	16	20	1	20	22	1	21
Manufacturing	124	35	89	225	116	109	246	135	111	291	140	151
Trade	9	3	6	15	6	9	16	6	9	21	10	11
Foreign film rentals	27	27		37	37		39	39		39	39	
Other industries	14	3	11	63	6	57	68	5	64	61	9	52
Europe	1 416	1 257	159	810	568	242	936	655	282	1,094	828	266
European Economic Community	1 150	1 84	66	413	314	99	505	377	128	585	487	98
Petroleum	8	(*)	8	31	1	30	48	2	46	38	1	38
Manufacturing	127	79	48	287	237	50	325	290	34	389	373	16
Trade	6	4	2	30	21	9	53	28	25	66	41	25
Foreign film rentals	(²)	(²)		48	48		45	45		63	63	
Other industries	9	1	8	17	7	10	34	11	23	29	10	19
Other Europe, including United Kingdom	1 155	63	93	398	254	143	431	278	153	509	341	168
Petroleum	8	1	8	27	4	23	40	5	35	42	4	38
Manufacturing	109	50	59	229	139	90	235	150	85	269	183	86
Trade	15	6	9	41	39	2	47	52	-5	76	68	8
Foreign film rentals	(¹)	(¹)		63	63		64	64		75	75	
Other industries	23	6	17	37	8	29	46	7	38	47	11	36
Latin American Republics and other Western Hemisphere	192	80	112	318	143	175	335	157	176	326	154	172
Petroleum	32	2	30	38	6	32	40	4	36	40	4	35
Manufacturing	64	25	39	115	62	53	129	76	52	125	71	55
Trade	17	6	11	33	13	20	35	17	18	30	18	12
Foreign film rentals	44	44		54	54		54	54		54	54	
Other industries	35	3	32	78	7	70	77	7	70	76	7	69
Other areas ²	215	115	99	434	216	217	500	238	262	574	286	288
Petroleum	51	9	42	103	22	81	110	21	90	133	16	117
Manufacturing	55	21	34	145	80	65	174	103	70	210	134	76
Trade	11	4	7	37	12	25	47	13	34	40	16	24
Foreign film rentals	78	78		97	97		95	95		108	108	
Other industries	20	3	16	52	6	46	74	6	68	83	12	72

r Revised.   p Preliminary.   *Less than $500,000.

NOTE.—Detail may not add to totals because of rounding.
1. Breakdown of foreign film rentals for European Economic Community and other Europe

not available; amount is included in Europe total.
2. Includes Japan, Australia, New Zealand, South Africa, other Africa, Middle East, other Asia and Pacific, and international, unallocated.

The annual sample includes those U.S. residents having direct investment abroad amounting in the ag-

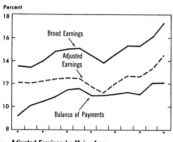

CHART 13

Rates of Return on U.S. Direct Investment Abroad

Alternative Measures of Return, All Foreign Affiliates [1]

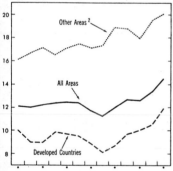

Adjusted Earnings by Major Area, All Foreign Affiliates

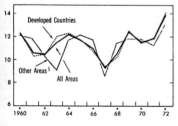

Manufacturing Affiliates' Adjusted Earnings by Major Area

1. Rates of return and alternative methods of computation are shown in table 12.

2. Includes developing countries, and the international, unallocated category.

U.S. Department of Commerce, Bureau of Economic Analysis   73-9-13

gregate to $2,000,000 or more, as measured on the books of their affiliated foreign enterprises. Such U.S. residents are required to file reports covering primary foreign affiliates in which they hold at least 10 percent of the voting stock, provided that the foreign affiliate has a book value of $25,000 or more. For secondary foreign affiliates, reports are required only if the percentage of the voting stock held is higher. Data on secondary affiliates are used to adjust the area-industry distribution of the U.S. direct investment position among foreign countries, so that the U.S. direct investment position in a secondary affiliate which is held through a primary affiliate appears in the country and industry of the secondary, rather than that of the primary. The value of the total U.S. direct investment position is not changed by these adjustments (see table below).

Net Capital Flows Between Primary and Secondary Foreign Affiliates

[Millions of dollars]

Area and country (net inflow (−) to country)	1972ᵖ
Net adjustment between primaries and secondaries..	0
Canada...	1
Europe...	−3
France..	−7
Germany...	10
Italy...	1
Switzerland.....................................	11
United Kingdom..................................	−14
Other...	−4
Latin American Republics and other Western Hemisphere..	5
Argentina.......................................	−1
Mexico..	2
Panama..	12
Other...	−8
Other countries...................................	−3

ᵖ Preliminary.

B. Earnings and related items

The derivation and relationship between various direct investment earnings items are given below.

1. Net earnings of foreign corporations: The U.S. parents' share in the earnings of their foreign subsidiaries after provision for foreign income taxes, preferred dividends, and interest payments, but before provision for U.S. taxes.

2. Net earnings of foreign branches: The earnings of foreign branches of U.S. companies after provision for foreign income taxes but before depletion charges or provisions for U.S.

taxes. Included with net earnings of branches are the U.S. share in the net earnings of foreign partnerships, sole proprietorships, and other types of unincorporated foreign organizations.

3. Earnings: Net earnings of foreign corporations plus net earnings of foreign branches.

4. Gross dividends on common stock: Dividends on common stock paid out to U.S. parents by foreign corporations, before deduction of withholding taxes paid to foreign governments.

5. Foreign withholding tax: A tax on common stock dividends withheld by the payor at the time the dividends are paid (distinguished from an income tax, which is imposed on the earnings of a business). Taxes are also withheld by the payor on payments of interest and preferred dividends, but both interest and preferred dividends are reported to the BEA International Investment Division on a net basis; therefore, BEA data on withholding taxes relate only to those on common stock dividends.

6. Dividends: Dividends on common or voting stock only, net of foreign withholding taxes (item 5); dividends are included in income as a balance of payments flow item.

7. Preferred dividends: Dividends received by U.S. parents on preferred or non-voting shares, after deduction of any foreign withholding taxes. Preferred dividends are included in income as a balance of payments flow item. Preferred dividends are treated in the same way as interest in these accounts even though on the foreign company's books preferred dividends are not charged as an expense, while interest is so charged.

8. Interest: Net interest received on intercompany accounts or on long-term debt of U.S.-owned foreign affiliates held by the parent or other nonbank U.S. investor, after deduction of any foreign withholding taxes. Interest is not included in earnings (item 3) since it is deducted as an expense item by the foreign firm, but it is a balance of payments income flow item.

9. Interest, dividends, and branch earnings: The sum of dividends (item 6), preferred dividends (item 7), and

interest received by or credited to the account of U.S. direct investors (item 8)—all net of foreign withholding taxes—plus branch earnings after foreign taxes (item 2); all before U.S. taxes.

10. Reinvested earnings: Net earnings of foreign corporations (item 1) less gross dividends on common stock (item 4).

Derivation and Relationship Based on 1972 Preliminary Data

[Millions of dollars]

1. Net earnings of foreign corporations ___ 8,915 reported.
2. Net earnings of foreign branches ___ 3,471 reported.
3. Earnings ___ 12,386=1+2.
4. Gross dividends (on common stock) ___ 4,394=5+6.
5. Foreign withholding tax (on common stock dividends) ___ 511 reported.
6. Dividends (on common stock) ___ 3,882 reported.
7. Preferred dividends ___ 10 reported.
8. Interest ___ 641 reported.
9. Interest, dividends, and branch earnings ___ 8,004=2+6+7+8.
10. Reinvested earnings ___ 4,521=1−4 or 3−2−4.

Table 12.—Alternative Measures of Return on U.S. Direct Investment Abroad, by Area and Industry

[Millions of dollars or percent]

Line	Item and year	All areas — All industries	Petroleum	Manufacturing	Other	Developed countries — All industries	Petroleum	Manufacturing	Other	Other areas [1] — All industries	Petroleum	Manufacturing	Other
	A. Branch earnings:												
1	1972 ᴾ	3,471	2,632	98	741	397	−56	58	396	3,074	2,688	40	346
2	1971 ʳ	3,121	2,301	98	722	473	−5	57	421	2,648	2,306	40	301
3	1970	2,451	1,731	82	638	330	−30	45	315	2,121	1,760	37	323
	B. Dividends:												
4	1972 ᴾ	3,882	1,144	1,790	948	2,390	165	1,523	702	1,493	979	267	246
5	1971 ʳ	3,549	978	1,612	959	2,161	194	1,365	602	1,389	784	248	357
6	1970	2,975	714	1,542	719	1,949	144	1,293	512	1,026	570	248	208
	C. Foreign withholding taxes:												
7	1972 ᴾ	511	108	295	108	349	27	236	86	162	81	59	22
8	1971 ʳ	472	76	270	126	343	25	219	98	129	52	51	27
9	1970	416	65	257	93	298	23	206	69	118	43	51	24
	D. Reinvested earnings:												
10	1972 ᴾ	4,521	668	2,825	1,029	3,668	571	2,386	711	853	97	439	318
11	1971 ʳ	3,157	500	1,854	803	2,437	251	1,565	621	720	249	289	182
12	1970	2,948	425	1,534	989	2,075	205	1,252	618	874	221	282	371
	E. Interest:[2]												
13	1972 ᴾ	651	173	257	220	504	143	218	143	147	30	39	77
14	1971 ʳ	625	163	240	223	488	135	198	155	137	27	42	68
15	1970	575	164	234	177	453	142	188	123	122	22	47	53
	F. Royalties and fees:												
16	1972 ᴾ	2,429	276	1,283	870	1,838	115	1,122	602	590	161	162	268
17	1971 ʳ	2,160	258	1,108	794	1,594	127	950	517	566	131	158	277
18	1970	1,919	216	1,002	701	1,403	96	859	448	515	120	143	253
	G. Measures of return, dollars: Earnings:[3]												
19	1972 ᴾ	12,386	4,552	5,007	2,827	6,805	707	4,202	1,895	5,581	3,845	804	932
20	1971 ʳ	10,299	3,856	3,834	2,610	5,414	465	3,206	1,743	4,885	3,391	628	867
21	1970	8,789	2,935	3,416	2,439	4,652	342	2,797	1,514	4,137	2,593	619	925
	Adjusted earnings:[4]												
22	1972 ᴾ	12,526	4,618	4,969	2,939	6,959	823	4,184	1,952	5,566	3,794	785	987
23	1971 ʳ	10,452	3,942	3,803	2,707	5,559	576	3,184	1,799	4,893	3,366	619	908
24	1970	8,949	3,034	3,392	2,523	4,807	461	2,779	1,568	4,143	2,573	614	955
	Broad earnings:[5]												
25	1972 ᴾ	14,954	4,893	6,253	3,808	8,798	938	5,305	2,554	6,156	3,955	947	1,254
26	1971 ʳ	12,613	4,200	4,912	3,501	7,153	703	4,135	2,316	5,459	3,497	777	1,185
27	1970	10,868	3,250	4,394	3,224	6,210	557	3,638	2,016	4,658	2,693	757	1,268
	Balance of payments income:[6]												
28	1972 ᴾ	10,433	4,225	3,428	2,779	5,130	367	2,920	1,843	5,303	3,858	508	937
29	1971 ʳ	9,456	3,700	3,058	2,697	4,716	452	2,570	1,695	4,740	3,249	488	1,003
30	1970	7,920	2,825	2,860	2,235	4,135	352	2,386	1,398	3,784	2,472	475	837
	H. Measures of return, as a percent of direct investment position at beginning of year: Adjusted earnings:												
31	1972 ᴾ	14.5	19.1	13.9	11.1	11.9	6.4	14.1	12.2	20.1	33.9	13.1	9.5
32	1971 ʳ	13.4	18.2	11.8	11.2	10.5	4.9	11.9	12.3	19.5	33.7	11.3	9.5
33	1970	12.6	15.3	11.5	11.7	10.0	4.4	11.4	12.0	17.9	27.3	11.9	11.1
	Broad earnings:												
34	1972 ᴾ	17.3	20.3	17.5	14.4	15.0	7.2	17.9	16.0	22.3	35.3	15.8	12.0
35	1971 ʳ	16.1	19.3	15.2	14.5	13.5	6.0	15.4	15.8	21.8	35.0	14.1	12.4
36	1970	15.3	16.3	14.9	14.9	13.0	5.3	14.9	15.4	20.1	28.6	14.7	14.1
	Balance of payments income:												
37	1972 ᴾ	12.1	17.5	9.6	10.5	8.8	2.8	9.9	11.5	19.2	34.5	8.5	9.0
38	1971 ʳ	12.1	17.0	9.5	11.1	8.9	3.9	9.6	11.6	18.9	32.5	8.9	10.5
39	1970	11.1	14.2	9.7	10.3	8.6	3.4	9.8	10.7	16.3	26.2	9.2	9.8

ʳ Revised. ᴾ Preliminary. NOTE.—Detail may not add to totals because of rounding.
1. Includes developing countries and international, unallocated.
2. Includes preferred dividends, which in 1972 totaled $10 million.
3. Equals A+B+C+D.
4. Equals A+B+D+E.
5. Equals A+B+D+E+F.
6. Equals A+B+E+F.

NOTE.—For an explanation of the relation between earnings, reinvested earnings, foreign withholding taxes and interest, dividends, and branch earnings see the Technical Notes.

EMPLOYMENT AND PAYROLL COSTS OF U.S. MULTINATIONAL COMPANIES

Thomas W. Kraseman
and
Betty L. Barker

By THOMAS W. KRASEMAN and BETTY L. BARKER

Employment and Payroll Costs of U.S. Multinational Companies

THIS article analyzes 1966 and 1970 employment and payroll cost data for a sample of 298 U.S. multinational companies (MNC's) responding to a special voluntary survey taken by the Bureau of Economic Analysis. The data reflect the employment and payroll costs of these 298 firms and their 5,237 majority-owned foreign affiliates (those owned 50 percent or more) in the actual circumstances of 1966 and 1970, i.e., given the existence of U.S. direct investment abroad. No attempt has been made to determine what the situation might have been with a different level or in the total absence of such investment. For example, the data show that the employment growth of U.S. parent companies exceeded that of all U.S. firms from 1966 to 1970 but do not indicate whether this growth would have been faster or slower if these companies' investments abroad had been smaller or nonexistent. The data presented here are no more than a starting point toward answers to the complex question of the effects of U.S. direct investment abroad on U.S. employment and wages.

Problems of comparability exist in the data used in this article, particularly in regard to industry classification. These problems have been resolved to the extent possible; where comparability could not be achieved, it is so indicated in the text.

After a brief description of the sample, the next two sections of this article review data on employment and payroll costs per employee in the United States, relating the U.S. parents in the sample to overall U.S. industry. The following two sections compare employment and payroll costs per employee of the foreign affiliates with those of their parent companies in the United States and to those of other firms in their foreign host countries. Some of the

major findings presented in these four sections are:

1. Employment in the United States of the 298 MNC's grew considerably faster from 1966 to 1970 than domestic employment of all U.S. firms in each of the three major industry groups examined—manufacturing, petroleum, and all other. Some of the growth in MNC employment may have been the result of mergers with and acquisitions of non-multinational companies since 1966. However, even after allowance is made for such mergers and acquisitions, MNC employment growth evidently exceeded that of all U.S. firms in the same industry.

For all industries combined, domestic employment of the 298 MNC's grew from 1966 to 1970 at a rate of 2.7 percent per year, compared with 1.8 percent for all U.S. firms. In individual industries, however, MNC employment growth generally exceeded the U.S. total for the industry by a much wider margin.

2. Comparisons of domestic payroll costs per employee of the MNC's and of all U.S. firms, by industry, show mixed results: costs of the MNC's were higher in some industries and lower in others. For all industries combined, payroll costs per employee of the MNC's were significantly above the national average, mainly because of the heavier weight in the MNC sample than in all U.S. private industry of manufacturing, where payroll costs per employee tend to be relatively high.

3. Employment abroad by the majority-owned foreign affiliates in 1970 was equal to one-third of the domestic employment of their U.S. parents. From 1966 to 1970, employment of these affiliates grew twice as fast as domestic employment of their 298 U.S. parents. In most individual industries as well,

growth in employment of the foreign affiliates was considerably faster than that of their U.S. parents. However, the growth of the parent companies was somewhat retarded by the 1970 business recession in the United States.

In most major foreign countries, employment of the foreign affiliates grew faster from 1966 to 1970 than total employment in the same country. Over this period, the rate of growth in employment of affiliates was 6.4 percent annually in developed countries and 1.9 percent in developing countries.

4. In every major industry and area, payroll costs per employee of the foreign affiliates were substantially below payroll costs per employee of the U.S. parents. However, available data for developed countries indicate that, at least in manufacturing, payroll costs per employee of the affiliates exceeded those for the industry as a whole in the same foreign country.

Payroll costs per employee of the foreign affiliates and of the U.S. parents both increased at about 6 percent per year from 1966 to 1970.

The sample data

The data on MNC employment and payroll costs used in this article were drawn primarily from the BEA special survey. The survey provides data on the number of employees and total payroll costs of the 298 U.S. parent companies in 1966 and 1970 and of their 5,237 majority-owned foreign affiliates in 1970. The 1966 employment and payroll data for the foreign affiliates in the sample were drawn from BEA's 1966 benchmark survey of the universe of all MNC's.[1] No attempt was made to

1. These data and other information on the domestic and international operations of U.S. multinational companies were released by BEA in a publication entitled *Special Survey of U.S. Multinational Companies, 1970*; it can be purchased from the National Technical Information Service, U.S. Department of Commerce, Springfield, Virginia 22151. Price $3. Quote accession number COM-72-11392 when ordering.

compute universe estimates for 1970.

For the foreign affiliates in the sample, the data on payroll costs were reported to BEA in U.S. dollars. The exchange rates used for conversion from foreign currencies to dollars were those normally used by the reporters in their own books. For the payroll cost data, these were probably the rates in effect at the time the affiliates' income statements were drawn, i.e., the end of the calendar year or the nearest fiscal year.

The relative importance of the sample of 298 firms in the MNC universe is suggested by a comparison of the sample with all 3,300 MNC's reporting in the 1966 benchmark survey. The 298 U.S. parent firms in the sample accounted for 29 percent of the U.S. assets of all MNC's in 1966, and their 5,237 majority-owned foreign affiliates held 55 percent of the assets and employed 62 percent of the workers of all majority-owned foreign affiliates in 1966.

In 1966, according to the benchmark survey data, the 298 parent firms in the sample included a significantly higher proportion of manufacturing and integrated petroleum companies—measured in terms of both numbers of firms and amount of assets—and a correspondingly lower proportion of firms of

other types, than the MNC universe. The reported U.S. assets of these 298 firms in 1966 were distributed 57 percent in manufacturing (excluding petroleum), 19 percent in petroleum, and 24 percent in other industries. The distribution of U.S. assets of all MNC's in 1966 was 34 percent in manufacturing (excluding petroleum), 9 percent in petroleum, and 57 percent in other industries. The reason for this difference is that the 1970 special survey focused on the larger nonfinancial MNC's, which tend to have a heavier concentration in manufacturing and petroleum than the total of MNC's.

Domestic Employment

Employment in the United States of the 298 parent companies in the MNC sample grew considerably faster from 1966 to 1970 than domestic employment of all U.S. firms in each of three major industry groups—manufacturing, petroleum, and all other—shown in table 1. In manufacturing, domestic employment of the MNC parents increased at an average of 1.9 percent per year, compared with 0.2 percent per year for all U.S. manufacturing firms. In two industries within manufacturing,

chemicals and transportation equipment, the growth rates for the sample and for the entire domestic industry were identical—2.2 and −1.7 percent per year, respectively. In all other manufacturing industries shown in table 1, the MNC employment growth rate from 1966 to 1970 exceeded the all-U.S. rate.

Domestic employment of MNC parents in the petroleum industry increased 2.2 percent per year while that of all U.S. petroleum firms declined slightly. In "other industries"—principally mining, trade, and other services—domestic employment of MNC's grew 5.6 percent per year, more than twice the growth rate for the comparable all-U.S. aggregate.

For all industries combined, the growth rate of domestic employment of the MNC sample was 2.7 percent annually from 1966 to 1970, compared with 1.8 percent for all U.S. private industry. This difference is considerably narrower than that in most of the component industries shown in table 1. The reason is the difference in industrial composition of the MNC sample as compared with all U.S. industry. The sample is more heavily weighted toward manufactur-

Table 1.—Employment of All U.S. Firms and of MNC's in Sample, by Industry [1]

Line	Industry [2]	U.S. firms						Majority-owned foreign affiliates of U.S. reporters											
		All U.S. firms			U.S. reporters in 1970 sample survey			All areas [3]			Developed areas			Developing areas		
		1966	1970	Average annual rate of growth, 1966–70	1966	1970	Average annual rate of growth, 1966–70	1966	1970	Average annual rate of growth, 1966–70	1966	1970	Average annual rate of growth, 1966–70	1966	1970	Average annual rate of growth, 1966–70
		(Thousands)		(Percent)	(Thousands)		(Percent)	(Thousands)		(Percent)	(Thousands)		(Percent)	(Thousands)		(Percent)
1	All private industry	57,259	61,486	1.8	7,968	8,851	2.7	2,412	2,970	5.3	1,797	2,300	6.4	599	647	1.9
2	Manufacturing	19,095	19,224	.2	5,885	6,335	1.9	1,704	2,156	6.1	1,408	1,747	5.5	297	409	8.3
3	Food products	1,779	1,784	.1	235	260	2.6	119	141	4.3	82	102	5.6	37	39	1.4
4	Chemicals and allied products	966	1,054	2.2	665	725	2.2	220	250	3.2	154	174	3.1	66	76	3.6
5	Primary and fabricated metals	2,702	2,698	0	709	724	.5	86	103	4.6	67	79	4.2	20	23	3.6
6	Machinery	3,831	3,906	.5	1,617	1,860	3.6	555	731	7.1	486	615	6.1	69	116	13.9
7	Transportation equipment	2,210	2,063	−1.7	1,681	1,568	−1.7	421	546	6.7	382	474	5.5	39	72	16.6
8	Other	7,607	7,719	.4	978	1,198	5.2	303	385	6.2	237	302	6.2	66	83	5.9
9	Petroleum [4]	486	480	−.2	479	522	2.2	296	271	−2.2	159	158	0	124	98	−5.7
10	Other industries	37,678	41,782	2.6	1,604	1,994	5.6	411	542	7.2	229	395	14.6	179	140	−6.0
11	Mining	349	357	.6	(D)	91	(D)	79	74	−1.6	28	45	12.6	51	29	−13.2
12	Trade	13,329	15,108	3.2	516	589	3.4	169	308	16.2	122	252	19.9	46	54	4.1
13	Other	24,000	26,317	2.3	(D)	1,314	(D)	163	161	(*)	79	98	5.5	82	58	−8.3

(D) Suppressed to avoid disclosure of data for individual reporters. (±).   *Less than 0.05 percent.

1. Employment of all U.S. firms is defined as the average number of full-time and part-time employees as calculated by BEA in conjunction with the annual national income and product accounts. These data are from SURVEY OF CURRENT BUSINESS, July 1970, page 39, and July 1973, page 41. Data for reporters in survey are from basic data table 1, line 22 and data for foreign affiliates are from basic data table set 3, line 23, from the *Special Survey of U.S. Multinational Companies, 1970.*
2. Data for all U.S. firms are classified by industry of the individual establishment. Data

for reporters in survey are classified by the major industry of the consolidated U.S. enterprise. Foreign affiliates are classified by industry of the foreign affiliate.
3. Data for affiliates classified as international are included in figures for all areas but excluded from figures for developed and developing areas.
4. The petroleum industry is defined on an integrated basis, the usual practice for direct investment statistics; data for all U.S. have been adjusted to this basis to the extent possible.

Source: U.S. Department of Commerce, Bureau of Economic Analysis, International Investment Division and National Income and Wealth Division.

ing, where domestic employment growth in 1966–70 was relatively slow; this slowed the growth in total domestic employment of the MNC's relatively more than it did that of all U.S. firms. If the distribution of employment among manufacturing, petroleum, and "other industries" had been the same for the 298 MNC's as for total U.S. private industry, domestic employment growth of the MNC's from 1966 to 1970 would have been 4.4 percent annually instead of 2.7 percent.

The slower-than-average growth in U.S. manufacturing employment from 1966 to 1970 was at least partly due to the fact that 1970 was a recession year in the United States, and the recession had a greater adverse impact on employment in manufacturing than in other industries.

Employment growth of the 298 MNC's in the sample from 1966 to 1970 stemmed partly from construction of new plants or expansion of domestic operations which were already in existence in 1966, and partly from the inclusion in the 1970 sample of reporters which were not direct investors abroad in 1966 or which were direct investors then but which had since merged with or acquired domestic companies which were not direct investors in 1966. Of the companies reporting in the 1970 survey, only a very small fraction were not themselves direct investors in 1966, but a considerable number had merged with or acquired companies which were not direct investors in 1966. There is little evidence to indicate how much of the 1966–70 domestic employment growth of the 298 companies reflects such mergers or acquisitions. However, another study suggests that mergers and acquisitions probably account for no more than one-fourth of the growth in employment of the 298 companies.[2]

The employment data for the 298 MNC's, broken down by industry, are not strictly comparable to those for all U.S. firms, since in the MNC data the entire consolidated domestic enterprise is classified in the industry of its major product, while in the national

totals each establishment within an enterprise is classified separately. Thus, if an enterprise had three establishments each producing a different product, its employment in the all-U.S. figures would be distributed among the three industries involved; in the MNC data, all of its employment would be shown in just one of the three industries—the one in which the consolidated enterprise had the largest sales.

There is no way to directly determine what effect the difference in classification systems has on the employment data. However, an indirect method of estimating the magnitude of the effect was attempted (see Appendix). The results indicate that classification problems, while fairly sizable in some individual industries, are probably not large enough to upset the major conclusion to be drawn from table 1—that employment was growing at a faster rate in the MNC's than in the United States as a whole in nearly every industry examined.

The petroleum industry presented especially difficult problems of comparability related to the establishment-enterprise classification problem. This is reflected in table 1, where domestic employment of the petroleum firms in the MNC sample is shown as slightly larger than the total for all U.S. petroleum firms in 1970. The discrepancy arises because, in the MNC data, the petroleum industry is defined on an integrated basis, including all stages of production—exploration and development, extraction, refining, transportation, and marketing—in a single industry category whereas in the data for all U.S. firms each of these operations is normally classified separately. For table 1, an attempt was made to construct data for the entire domestic industry on the same integrated basis as in the MNC sample. However, the all-U.S. employment data by industry that are used in this article, which were calculated by BEA in conjunction with its national income data,[3] are not

sufficiently detailed to permit this. Thus, the figures for all U.S. petroleum firms shown in table 1 include only crude petroleum and natural gas extraction, pipeline transportation, and petroleum refining; estimates for gasoline stations, petrochemicals, and tanker transportation were not available in the BEA data.

As noted earlier, the employment estimate for all U.S. petroleum firms in table 1 declined very slightly from 1966 to 1970. However, detailed employment data from the Bureau of Labor Statistics, which are not completely comparable to the data in table 1, indicate that employment in industrial organic chemicals (primarily petrochemicals) and gasoline service stations rose substantially from 1966 to 1970.[4] If the BLS data for these two industries were added to BLS data for the industries included in the U.S. petroleum industry in table 1, employment in the U.S. petroleum industry thus integrated would have risen at an annual rate of 1.8 percent—not far from the 2.2 percent rate for the petroleum companies in the MNC sample.

Domestic Payroll Costs

Comparisons of domestic payroll costs per employee of the 298 MNC's with those of all U.S. firms, by industry, give mixed results (table 2). For manufacturing as a whole, domestic payroll costs per employee of the MNC's were considerably above those of all U.S. firms in both 1966 and 1970. Within manufacturing, however, the MNC's in 1970 had lower payroll costs than the all-U.S. figure in three of the industries shown in table 2—foods, chemicals, and transportation equipment—but considerably higher payroll costs in the other three industries. In petroleum and mining, domestic payroll costs per employee of the MNC's were substantially below the all-U.S. figures, in trade they were about the same, while in other industries taken together they were higher.

---

2. See *Special Survey of U.S. Multinational Companies, 1970*, pages 9–10.

3. The BEA employment data are used in preference to employment estimates of the BLS because they agree conceptually with the annual payroll data for all U.S. firms used in this article. The BEA annual payroll data for all U.S. firms, in turn, are the most comparable definitionally to the payroll data of the MNC's in the special survey sample.

4. U.S. Department of Labor, Bureau of Labor Statistics, Bulletin 1312-9, *Employment and Earnings in the United States, 1909–72*, pp. 474 and 577.

For all industries combined, domestic payroll costs per employee of the MNC's exceeded the all-U.S. average in 1970 by $1,860 or nearly 25 percent. This substantial difference in the overall totals, compared with the mixed results for individual industries, at least partly reflects differences in industry composition between the MNC sample and all private U.S. industry: if the MNC employment total had the same industry distribution as all U.S. private employment, the difference in total payroll costs, although not for the individual industries comprising the totals, would largely disappear. Earnings of manufacturing employees are above the general average in both the MNC's and all U.S. firms; however, manufacturing accounted for nearly three-quarters of the employment of the 298 parents but for only about one-third of all U.S. private employment. Moreover, within manufacturing, the proportion of employment in the high-wage metal goods industries was considerably greater in the MNC's than in the United States as a whole.

After adjustment for problems of industry composition in the overall totals, differences in payroll costs between the MNC's and all U.S. firms, for some of the individual industries shown in table 2, still remain. These differences may result partly from the classification problem—the fact that MNC employment and payroll cost data are classified on the basis of the industry of the entire domestic enterprise, while the all-U.S. data are classified on the basis of each establishment. However, as discussed in the Appendix, this factor probably accounts for only a minor part of the differences, except perhaps in petroleum. The MNC data for the integrated petroleum industry include employees engaged in wholesale and retail distribution of oil and gasoline—activities paying much lower wages than extraction, transportation, and refining of petroleum, which are the only activities included in the data for all U.S. petroleum firms. However, no attempt has been made to estimate how much impact this factor may have.

A more important explanation for the differences between the MNC and

all-U.S. figures, by industry, probably lies in the fact that the industries shown in table 2 are quite broad and within each industry the MNC's can be engaged in very different types of activity from other U.S. firms, with very different levels of average pay. Within the chemical industry, for instance, data for all U.S. firms indicate that average cash weekly earnings of production workers in 1970 ranged from $190 in soaps and detergents down to $124 in fertilizers. In nonelectrical machinery, the range was from $168 in internal combustion engines to $125 in textile machinery.[5]

Finally, differences between payroll costs per employee between the MNC and all U.S. firms for individual industries may have resulted from the varying impact on these two groups of the many complex factors which affect wage rates, including, among others, technological efficiency, profitability, or the rate of expansion of the company. Since multinational companies tend to be among the largest, fastest growing,

5 Ibid. pp. 177-221 and 473-496.

Table 2.—Payroll Costs Per Employee of All U.S. Firms and MNC's in Sample, by Industry [1][2]

Line	Industry [3]	U.S. firms						Majority-owned foreign affiliates of U.S. reporters								
		All U.S. firms			U.S. reporters in 1970 sample survey			All areas [4]			Developed areas			Developing areas		
		1966	1970	Average annual rate of growth, 1966–70	1966	1970	Average annual rate of growth, 1966–70	1966	1970	Average annual rate of growth, 1966–70	1966	1970	Average annual rate of growth, 1966–70	1966	1970	Average annual rate of growth, 1966–70
		(Dollars)		(Percent)	(Dollars)		(Percent)	(Dollars)		(Percent)	(Dollars)		(Percent)	(Dollars)		(Percent)
1	All private industry	6,130	7,760	6.1	7,750	9,620	5.5	3,920	4,900	5.7	4,230	5,350	6.0	2,950	3,250	2.5
2	Manufacturing	7,490	9,340	5.7	8,290	10,300	5.6	3,820	4,820	6.0	4,120	5,290	6.5	2,400	2,810	4.0
3	Food products	6,800	8,590	6.0	6,740	8,160	4.9	3,210	3,780	4.2	3,760	4,350	3.8	2,030	2,280	3.0
4	Chemicals and allied products	9,040	11,380	5.9	8,460	10,420	5.4	3,690	4,940	7.6	4,190	5,650	7.8	2,520	3,320	7.2
5	Primary and fabricated metals	8,420	10,180	4.9	8,410	10,250	5.1	3,560	4,370	5.3	4,040	5,040	5.6	1,750	2,260	6.6
6	Machinery	8,010	10,050	5.8	8,260	10,760	6.9	3,770	4,870	6.6	4,010	5,330	7.4	2,070	2,440	4.2
7	Transportation equipment	9,790	12,500	6.3	8,820	11,120	6.0	4,260	5,250	5.4	4,350	5,520	6.1	3,410	3,510	.7
8	Other	6,140	7,730	5.9	7,580	8,910	4.1	3,710	4,520	5.1	4,070	5,040	5.5	2,420	2,640	2.1
9	Petroleum [5]	9,520	12,490	7.0	8,680	10,780	5.6	5,050	6,530	6.6	5,140	7,130	8.5	5,050	5,620	2.7
10	Other industries	5,390	6,980	6.7	5,530	7,140	6.6	3,500	4,390	5.8	4,350	4,880	2.9	2,400	2,900	4.8
11	Mining	8,050	10,530	6.9	(D)	9,840	(D)	3,700	5,320	9.6	4,610	6,910	10.7	3,200	2,860	−2.7
12	Trade	5,180	6,370	5.3	4,850	6,340	6.9	3,840	3,890	.3	4,250	4,080	−1.1	2,630	2,830	1.9
13	Other	5,470	7,270	7.4	(D)	7,320	(D)	3,070	4,900	12.4	4,420	6,020	8.0	1,780	2,930	13.3

(D) Suppressed to avoid disclosure of data for individual reporters.

1. For all U.S. firms, average payroll costs were calculated by dividing total compensation of employees in a given industry group by the average number of full-time and part-time employees in that industry group; data are from SURVEY OF CURRENT BUSINESS, July 1970, page 39, and July 1973, page 41. Data for reporters in survey were calculated from employment data in basic data table 1, line 22, and from data on total payroll costs in basic data table 1, line 23, of the *Special Survey of U.S. Multinational Companies, 1970*. Data for foreign affiliates were calculated from employment data in basic data table set 3, line 23, and from data on total payroll costs in basic data table set 3, line 24, of the *Special Survey*.

2. All data are rounded because the last digit of each figure was not significant.

3. In employee compensation data for all U.S. firms, the wage and salary component is classified by industry of the individual establishment whereas the supplementary benefits component is classified by major industry of the U.S. firm. Reporters in survey are classified by the major industry of the consolidated U.S. enterprise. Foreign affiliates are classified by industry of the foreign affiliate.

4. Data for affiliates classified as international are included in figures for all areas but excluded from figures for developed and developing areas.

5. The petroleum industry is defined on an integrated basis, the usual practice for direct investment statistics; data for all U.S. firms have been adjusted to this basis to the extent possible.

Source: U.S. Department of Commerce, Bureau of Economic Analysis, International Investment Division and National Income and Wealth Division.

and most technologically advanced firms in the United States, one might expect them to pay higher wages to their employees than other firms in the same industry. However, this is not the case for some of the individual industries shown in table 2, nor is it necessarily true for the all-industry totals if differences in industry composition between the MNC sample and all U.S. firms are taken into account.

Foreign Employment

Employment in the 5,237 majority-owned foreign affiliates of the 298 MNC's totaled 3 million in 1970 (table 1). Nearly three-quarters of the total was in manufacturing and most of the rest was in petroleum and trade—about 10 percent each. Within manufacturing, 34 percent was in machinery (electrical and nonelectrical), 25 percent in transportation equipment, and 12 percent in chemicals.[6]

Total foreign employment of the affiliates in the sample in 1970 was equal to one-third of their U.S. employment. Ratios of foreign to U.S. employment were highest in mining, at 81 percent, and in trade and petroleum, each almost 52 percent. The ratio in manufacturing was 34 percent.

Employment of the majority-owned foreign affiliates in the sample increased an average 5.3 percent annually from 1966 to 1970, double the growth rate of employment of the 298 parent companies in the United States. This reflects the much faster expansion in

---

6. A foreign affiliate is assigned to the industry in which its sales are most concentrated, even though it may have establishments operating in other industries. However, the incidence of multi-industry foreign affiliates is probably lower than that of multi-industry U.S. parents, because a much lesser degree of consolidation was permitted on the reporting forms for affiliates. Thus the affiliate data classified by industry are probably somewhat closer to being on an establishment basis than are the parent data. It should be noted that a foreign affiliate may be classified in an industry different from the industry in which its U.S. parent is classified. For example, table 1 shows employment in foreign affiliates which are themselves classified in manufacturing; it does not show employment in affiliates which, regardless of their own industry, have U.S. parents classified in manufacturing. If the foreign affiliate employment data were broken down by industry of the U.S. parents, the proportion of affiliate employment in manufacturing would be somewhat higher, the proportion in petroleum virtually unchanged, and the proportion in all other industries lower than shown in table 1. This reflects the fact that U.S. parent companies in manufacturing often have affiliates in the "other industries" category—primarily mining and trade—rather than in manufacturing.

the foreign operations of the MNC's than in their domestic operations during this period. For instance, the 1970 survey data indicate that plant and equipment expenditures in the United States by the 298 parent companies increased at an average annual rate of about 6 percent from 1966 to 1970, while data from a separate semiannual BEA survey indicate that plant and equipment expenditures abroad by the universe of all foreign affiliates increased at almost twice that rate. (Plant and equipment expenditure data for just the 5,237 majority-owned foreign affiliates in the 1970 survey sample are not available.)

Also contributing to the sharp difference in growth rates between the MNC parent companies and their foreign affiliates was the 1970 business recession in the United States, which had no counterpart in major foreign countries. While MNC data for 1969 are not available, total U.S. employment grew on the average by 2.5 percent annually from 1966 to 1969 and only 1.8 percent annually from 1966 to 1970; in manufacturing the average growth rates were 2 percent annually from 1966 to 1969 and only 0.4 percent from 1966 to 1970.

The 1966–70 growth rate of employment of foreign affiliates exceeded that of U.S. parent companies in nearly all major industries shown in table 1. Industries showing the largest differences were trade, with a 16.2 percent annual growth rate for affiliates compared to only 3.4 percent for U.S. parent companies; transportation equipment, with a 6.7 percent rate abroad and a moderate decline domestically; and primary and fabricated metals, with a 4.6 percent growth rate abroad and only slight growth domestically. The large differences in transportation equipment and metals manufacturing partly reflect the heavy adverse impact of the 1970 recession on domestic employment in durable goods manufacturing. At the opposite extreme, employment of foreign affiliates in petroleum declined about 2 percent annually while that of U.S. parent companies increased 2 percent annually. Employment of foreign mining affiliates also declined. It is not clear how much

of these reductions may have been due to expropriations by foreign governments or selloffs under pressure from foreign governments.

It should be noted that, in foreign countries, as in the United States, the growth in employment of the MNC sample from 1966 to 1970 partly reflected mergers with and acquisitions of other firms after 1966. The data do not indicate how much of the employment increase was attributable to such mergers and acquisitions.

The distribution of employment in the foreign affiliates, classified by major industry of the affiliates, is roughly in line with the distribution of domestic employment in the 298 U.S. parent firms, classified by major industry of the parent (table 3). The proportion of employment in manufacturing is virtually the same for parents and affiliates, both in total and in most of the component manufacturing industries; the proportion of employment in petroleum is greater, and in other non-manufacturing industries smaller, for the foreign affiliates than for the 298 U.S. parent firms, but the differences are not large.

By area, about four-fifths of the employment in the foreign affiliates of the 298 MNC's in 1970 was in developed countries. The major difference in the industrial composition of employment in developed versus developing countries was the greater importance of mining and petroleum in the latter. In 1970, these two industries accounted for 20 percent of the foreign affiliates' employment in developing areas, compared with only 9 percent in developed countries. Manufacturing, on the other hand, accounted for 76 percent of the affiliates' employment in developed countries, compared to 63 percent in developing areas. The share of affiliates' employment in trade was also larger in developed than in developing countries.

The average annual growth of employment in foreign affiliates from 1966 to 1970 was 6.4 percent in developed countries and 1.9 percent in developing countries (table 1). There were sharp declines in petroleum and mining employment in developing nations, and employment of trade affiliates increased only 4 percent per year in those nations compared to 20 percent per year in developed countries. On the other hand, employment in manufacturing affiliates grew 8.3 percent annually in the developing countries, compared to 5.5 percent in the developed areas. The growth of manufacturing employment in developing countries was especially strong in machinery and transportation equipment.

In most major foreign countries where the 298 MNC's were operating, employment in the foreign affiliates grew faster than total employment (including both government and private) in the same country (table 5). In the 6-nation European Economic Community, as it was constituted prior to 1973, total employment increased at an annual rate of 0.4 percent from 1966 to 1970 compared with a 6.7 percent rate for the MNC affiliates in those countries. Employment gains for the MNC affiliates were large everywhere in the EEC, but particularly in Belgium and the Netherlands. The very slow average employment rise in the EEC appears to be due mainly to tight supplies of labor—unemployment has been very low for much of the postwar period—combined with slow population growth. The surprisingly sharp gains of employment in MNC foreign affiliates in the face of tight labor supplies probably reflects the fact that the MNC's were situated in the most rapidly growing industries. In addition, some part of the expansion in foreign affiliates was probably due to acquisitions of existing firms as opposed to internal expansion, although data on this point are lacking.

In Europe outside the 6-nation EEC, employment growth of the affiliates was even faster—9.6 percent annually—while total employment remained virtually unchanged. In Australia and Japan, among the other major developed countries examined, employment of affiliates grew about 6 percent per year, compared with growth rates of only 2.9 and 1.5 percent a year, respectively, for total employment.

In manufacturing, the increase in employment of the affiliates from 1966 to 1970 was very rapid in every major European nation, ranging from 4.9

Table 3.—Industry Distribution of Employment of Sample MNC's

[Percent]

Industy	U.S. reporters in 1970 sample survey		Majority-owned foreign affiliates of U.S. reporters					
			All areas		Developed areas		Developing areas	
	1966	1970	1966	1970	1966	1970	1966	1970
All private industry	100.0	100.0	100.0	100.0	100.0	100.0	100.0	100.0
Manufacturing	73.9	71.6	70.6	72.6	78.4	76.0	49.6	63.2
Food products	2.9	2.9	4.9	4.7	4.6	4.4	6.2	6.0
Chemicals and allied products	8.3	8.2	9.1	8.4	8.6	7.6	11.0	11.7
Primary and fabricated metals	8.9	8.2	3.6	3.5	3.7	3.4	3.3	3.6
Machinery	20.3	21.0	23.0	24.6	27.0	26.7	11.5	17.9
Transportation equipment	21.1	17.7	17.5	18.4	21.3	20.6	6.5	11.1
Other	12.3	13.5	12.6	13.0	13.2	13.1	11.0	12.8
Petroleum	6.0	5.9	12.3	9.1	8.8	6.9	20.7	15.1
Other industries	20.1	22.5	17.0	18.2	12.7	17.2	30.0	21.6
Mining	(D)	1.0	3.3	2.5	1.6	2.0	8.5	4.5
Trade	6.5	6.6	7.0	10.4	6.8	11.0	7.7	8.3
Other	(D)	14.8	6.8	5.4	4.4	4.3	13.7	9.0

D Suppressed to avoid disclosure of data for individual reporters.

NOTE.—Calculated from data in table 1. Details may not add to totals because of rounding.

Source: U.S. Department of Commerce, Bureau of Economic Analysis, International Investment Division.

Table 4.—Employment and Payroll Costs Per Employee of MNC's in Sample, by Area [1]

Line	Area and industry	Employment			Payroll costs per employee [2]		
		1966	1970	Average annual rate of growth, 1966-70	1966	1970	Average annual rate of growth, 1966-70
		(Dollars)		(Percent)	(Dollars)		(Percent)
	All industries:						
1	United States	7,968	8,851	2.7	7,750	9,620	5.5
2	All foreign areas [3]	2,412	2,970	5.3	3,920	4,900	5.7
3	Developed areas	1,797	2,300	6.4	4,230	5,350	6.0
4	Canada	440	474	1.9	6,000	7,990	7.4
5	United Kingdom	420	587	8.7	3,460	3,760	2.2
6	European Economic Community Six	593	770	6.7	4,030	5,440	7.8
7	Other Europe	134	214	12.4	3,610	4,460	5.4
8	Japan	39	49	5.9	2,690	4,290	12.3
9	Australia, New Zealand, South Africa	171	206	4.8	3,170	4,580	9.6
10	Developing areas	599	647	1.9	2,950	3,250	2.5
11	Latin America	423	452	1.7	3,080	3,630	4.2
12	Other	177	196	2.6	2,630	2,370	-2.6
	Manufacturing: [4]						
13	United States	5,885	6,335	1.9	8,290	10,300	5.6
14	All foreign areas [3]	1,704	2,156	6.1	3,820	4,820	6.0
15	Developed areas	1,408	1,747	5.5	4,120	5,290	6.5
16	Canada	329	319	-.8	6,030	8,460	8.8
17	United Kingdom	367	444	4.9	3,410	3,940	3.7
18	European Economic Community Six	475	651	8.2	3,950	5,320	7.7
19	Other Europe	79	145	16.4	3,030	3,680	5.0
20	Japan	33	37	2.9	2,520	4,160	13.4
21	Australia, New Zealand, South Africa	125	151	4.8	2,900	4,240	10.0
22	Developing areas	297	409	8.3	2,400	2,810	4.0
23	Latin America	249	319	6.4	2,600	3,240	5.6
24	Other	48	90	17.0	1,350	1,290	-1.2

1. Employment of U.S. parent is from basic data table 1, line 22, and employment of foreign affiliates is from basic data table set 3, line 23, in the *Special Survey of U.S. Multinational Companies, 1970.* Average payroll costs of MNC's were calculated using these employment data and data on total payroll costs as shown in basic data table 1, line 23, for U.S. parents and basic data table set 3, line 24, for foreign affiliates, in the *Special Survey.*
2. Data on average payroll costs were rounded because the last digit of each figure was not significant.
3. Data for affiliates classified as international are included in figures for all foreign areas but excluded from figures for developed and developing areas.
4. U.S. reporters are classified by major industry of the consolidated U.S. enterprise; foreign affiliates are classified by industry of the foreign affiliate.

Source: U.S. Department of Commerce, Bureau of Economic Analysis, International Investment Division.

percent per year in the United Kingdom to 10.1 percent in Belgium and 16.6 percent in the Netherlands (table 6). These growth rates were substantially higher than those for each country's total manufacturing employment. This was also true in Australia, where employment of the manufacturing affiliates

Table 5.—Total Employment and Employment of Foreign Affiliates in Sample, Selected Countries, 1966 and 1970

Area	Total employment		Employment of foreign affiliates		Percent of foreign affiliates in total		Average annual rate of growth 1966–70	
	1966	1970	1966	1970	1966	1970	Total	Foreign affiliates
	(Thousands)				(Percent)			
EEC Six, total	73,062	74,278	593	770	0.8	1.0	0.4	6.7
Belgium	3,623	3,734	57	81	1.6	2.2	.8	9.2
France	19,684	20,410	145	178	.7	.9	.9	5.3
Germany	26,601	26,705	273	351	1.0	1.3	.1	6.5
Netherlands	4,413	4,567	33	52	.7	1.1	.9	12.0
Other EEC	18,741	18,862	85	108	.5	.6	.2	6.2
Other Europe, total	60,879	60,915	554	800	.9	1.3	(1)	9.6
United Kingdom	25,476	24,709	420	587	1.6	2.4	−.8	8.7
Selected major non-European developed countries:								
Australia	4,761	5,329	114	144	2.4	2.7	2.9	6.0
Canada	7,152	7,879	440	474	6.2	6.0	2.4	1.9
New Zealand	1,014	1,077	10	10	1.0	.9	1.5	0
Japan	47,210	50,150	39	49	.1	.1	1.5	5.9

1. Less than 0.05 percent. (±)

Sources: Employment estimates for individual countries are unpublished data furnished by U.S. Department of Labor, Bureau of Labor Statistics, Office of Productivity, Division of Foreign Labor Statistics and Trade. Employment data for foreign affiliates by country are unpublished data from U.S. Department of Commerce, Bureau of Economic Analysis, International Investment Division.

Table 6.—Total Manufacturing Employment and Employment of Manufacturing Foreign Affiliates in Sample, Selected Countries, 1966 and 1970

Area	Total manufacturing employment		Employment of manufacturing foreign affiliates		Percent of foreign affiliates in total		Average annual rate of growth, 1966–70	
	1966	1970	1966	1970	1966	1970	Total	Foreign affiliates
	(Thousands)				(Percent)			
EEC Six, total	23,811	24,746	475	651	2.0	2.6	1.0	8.2
Belgium	1,272	1,276	47	69	3.7	5.4	.1	10.1
France	5,433	5,551	118	148	2.2	2.7	.5	5.8
Germany	10,255	10,603	221	306	2.2	2.9	.8	8.5
Netherlands	1,326	1,318	20	37	1.5	2.8	−.2	16.6
Other EEC	5,525	5,998	68	91	1.2	1.5	2.1	7.6
Other Europe, total	19,119	19,096	446	590	2.3	3.1	(1)	7.2
United Kingdom	9,283	9,053	367	444	4.0	4.9	−.6	4.9
Selected major non-European developed countries:								
Australia	1,307	1,407	89	112	6.8	8.0	1.9	5.9
Canada	1,744	1,790	329	319	18.9	17.8	.7	−.8
New Zealand	278	304	5	5	1.8	1.6	2.3	.0
Japan	11,730	13,730	33	37	.3	.3	4.0	2.9

1. Less than 0.05 percent. (‡)

Sources: Employment estimates for individual countries are unpublished data furnished by U.S. Department of Labor, Bureau of Labor Statistics, Office of Productivity, Division of Foreign Labor Statistics and Trade. Employment data for foreign affiliates by country are unpublished data from U.S. Department of Commerce, Bureau of Economic Analysis, International Investment Division.

Table 7.—Payroll Costs Per Employee: Foreign Affiliates As a Percent of U.S. Parent Companies [1]

	All foreign areas		Developed areas		Developing areas	
	1966	1970	1966	1970	1966	1970
All private industry	50.6	50.9	54.6	55.6	38.1	33.8
Manufacturing	46.1	46.8	49.7	51.4	29.0	27.3
Food products	47.6	46.3	55.8	53.3	30.1	27.9
Chemicals and allied products	43.6	47.4	49.5	54.2	29.8	31.9
Primary and fabricated metals	42.3	42.6	48.0	49.2	20.8	22.0
Machinery	45.6	45.3	48.6	49.5	25.1	22.7
Transportation equipment	48.3	47.2	49.3	49.6	38.7	31.6
Other	48.9	50.7	53.7	56.6	31.9	29.6
Petroleum	58.2	60.6	59.2	66.1	58.2	52.1
Other industries	63.3	61.5	78.7	68.4	43.4	40.6
Mining	(D)	54.1	(D)	70.2	(D)	29.1
Trade	79.2	61.4	87.6	64.4	54.2	44.6
Other	(D)	66.9	(D)	82.2	(D)	40.0

(D) Suppressed to avoid disclosure of data for individual reporters.

1. Average payroll costs of foreign affiliates are classified by industry of foreign affiliate; average payroll costs of U.S. parents are classified by industry of consolidated domestic enterprise.

NOTE.—Percents are calculated from data in table 2.

Source: U.S. Department of Commerce, Bureau of Economic Analysis, International Investment Division.

grew at an annual rate of 5.9 percent, triple the growth rate for total Australian manufacturing. However, in most other major developed countries outside Europe, the growth rate of employment in manufacturing affiliates fell short of the corresponding national rate of increase. In Canada, employment of the manufacturing affiliates actually declined from 1966 to 1970 while total manufacturing employment expanded moderately.

Of the major developed countries examined, Canada had the heaviest concentration of employment by the foreign affiliates in the sample. Approximately 6 percent of total Canadian employment in 1970 was accounted for by these foreign affiliates. The figure was nearly 3 percent for Australia and about 1 percent both in the 6-nation EEC and in other Europe. It should be noted that the percentages cited here reflect only the majority-owned foreign affiliates of the 298 MNC's in the sample; the percentages could be considerably larger—perhaps as much as double in Canada and one-third higher in Europe—for the universe of all foreign affiliates.

The foreign affiliates of the 298 MNC's accounted for a considerably larger share of manufacturing employment than of total employment in every major country examined. The highest proportion was in Canada, where in 1970 nearly 18 percent of the manufacturing workers were employed by foreign affiliates in the MNC sample. The proportion was 8 percent in Australia and almost 5 percent in the United Kingdom and Belgium. The proportion in Japan was only 0.3 percent, mostly due to Japanese restrictions on entry by foreign firms. Again, these percentages reflect only the foreign affiliates in the sample and could be substantially higher for the universe of all foreign affiliates.

Payroll Costs of Foreign Affiliates

Payroll costs per employee were substantially lower in the foreign affiliates than in the 298 U.S. parents for every major industry and every major foreign area (tables 2 and 4). Payroll costs per employee of affiliates in Canada were the closest to those of the U.S. parent companies, but even here the gap was sizable. These differences are basically due to the generally lower wage levels in foreign countries, although in individual cases they may also reflect differences in the mix of high-wage versus low-wage industries in the averages. Another factor may be the greater proportion of higher-salaried executives employed by MNC's domestically than abroad. On the average, payroll costs per employee in 1970 were about half as large for the foreign affiliates as for the 298 U.S. parent firms, not only for the all-industry total but also for all manufacturing and for the component manufacturing industries (table 7). Outside of manufacturing, payroll costs per employee of the foreign affiliates averaged 61 percent of the level of parent firms in the same industry, with mining at 54 percent, petroleum and trade each at 61 percent, and other industries at 67 percent.

In interpreting the payroll cost data used here and elsewhere in this article, it must be kept in mind that lower (or higher) payroll costs per employee do not of themselves mean lower (or higher) labor costs per unit of output. Unit labor costs also depend on output per man-hour, and such data are not available at this time.

In developed countries, payroll costs per employee of the foreign affiliates were substantially higher, and thus closer to the average in U.S. parent firms, than in developing countries. Payroll costs per employee of foreign affiliates in developed countries averaged 56 percent of the level for U.S. parent firms in 1970, while in developing areas the figure was only 34 percent. In manufacturing, payroll costs per employee of affiliates in developed countries were 50 percent of the level for U.S. parent manufacturing firms, compared with 27 percent in developing countries. The smallest difference in payroll costs as between the developed and the developing countries was in the petroleum industry; in both groups of countries, affiliates in the petroleum industry had higher payroll costs per employee than in any other industry.

Payroll costs per employee of the foreign affiliates increased from 1966 to 1970 at an annual rate of 5.7 percent, virtually the same as the increase for the 298 U.S. parent firms and for all private U.S. industry (tables 2 and 4). Rates of increase varied substantially among major areas, but this may have partly reflected differences in industry mix. One surprising development was the actual decline of payroll costs per employee of affiliates in trade in the developed countries (table 2). This decline may have resulted from a proportionately larger expansion in retail operations, where wages are relatively low, than in wholesale operations in these countries. Although separate employment data for retail trade are not now available, employment in trade as a whole more than doubled from 1966 to 1970.

Available evidence indicates that payroll costs per employee of affiliates in manufacturing were significantly above the all-manufacturing averages in the same foreign country. While data problems may be especially serious here, the Bureau of Labor Statistics [7] was able to compile roughly comparable figures on compensation per employee in manufacturing for selected foreign countries. Comparison of these data with the BEA sample data indicates that in 1970, for example, foreign affiliates in manufacturing paid approximately $700 more per employee in the United Kingdom, $1,200 more in Canada, $1,000 more in Germany, $800 more in France, $1,300 more in Italy, and $1,700 more in Japan than the average for all manufacturing firms in the country. However, these comparisons may be considerably affected by differences in the industry mix of the foreign affiliates as compared with the nation as a whole.

[7]. U.S. Department of Labor, Bureau of Labor Statistics, Office of Productivity, Division of Foreign Labor Statistics and Trade.

Appendix

On an industry-by-industry basis, the domestic employment data for the 298 MNC's in the sample are not strictly comparable to the data for all U.S. firms because of unavoidable differences in industry classification between the two data sets. As indicated earlier, the domestic data for the MNC's are classified in the major industry of the entire consolidated U.S. enterprise, while the all-U.S. firm data are broken down by the industry of each individual establishment within the enterprise.

There is no direct way to determine the magnitude of the classification problems in the domestic employment data. However, rough estimates of the magnitude can be obtained

Table 8.—U.S. Reporters' Domestic Sales by Industry: Percentage in Dominant Industry and in Other Industries [1]

[Percent]

Industry	Sales in dominant industry	Sales in other specified industries	Sales in unspecified industries
Total	92.5	0	7.5
Manufacturing	85.5	4.7	9.8
Food products	78.4	12.5	9.1
Chemicals and allied products	62.3	27.0	10.7
Primary and fabricated metals	76.2	12.4	11.4
Machinery	62.9	23.1	14.0
Transportation equipment	82.2	12.6	5.2
Other	70.0	20.1	9.9
Petroleum	85.6	12.0	2.4
Other industries, total	87.1	9.8	3.1
Mining	55.7	38.0	6.3
Trade	88.3	9.7	2.0
Other	83.4	13.1	3.5

1. Based on unpublished data from the 1970 special survey.

Source: U.S. Department of Commerce, Bureau of Economic Analysis, International Investment Division

indirectly by taking sales data broken down by product, which was supplied by the 298 parent firms in the special survey, and then manipulating them to obtain estimates of employment broken down by product, using the procedure described below.

In the 1970 special survey, U.S. parent firms were asked to list their major products and to indicate the percent of their total sales in each product class. They were asked to account for at least 75 percent of their total sales in this way. Thus, a rough regrouping of sales—and then of employment, based on the regrouping of sales—by product becomes possible. The resulting employment figures by product class for the MNC's are then roughly comparable in terms of industry classification to the all-U.S. figures which are based on establishment reporting.

The steps for estimating employment from sales data were as follows:

1. For each MNC parent company, the sales total was distributed among the major industries shown in table 1, using the figures on percent of sales by product class reported by the firm.

2. The redistributed sales figures for each firm were then added up by industry, to give new industry sales totals. Since companies were not asked to classify more than 75 percent of their sales by industry, these totals necessarily omitted the portion of sales not classified. Table 8 shows the percentage of sales which were in the dominant MNC industry, the percentage of sales actually in other industries, and the percentage not specified by industry.

3. Average sales per employee by industry were computed, using the original MNC data on sales and employment. When these were compared with the amount of shipments per employee for the same industries from the Census Bureau's Annual Survey of Manufactures, they agreed very closely in nearly all cases.

4. The total of sales actually specified for each industry, as redistributed in step (2), were divided by the sales per employee from step (3), in order to obtain new estimates of employment redistributed by product class.

5. Because of the mechanics of the reweighting process, and because only those sales specified by industry could be

used, the new employment estimates by industry differed from the actual total of employment for all reporting MNC parent firms, which was 8,851,000 as shown in table 1. Therefore, it was necessary to "force" the new industry employment figures to equal this actual employment total. This was done by computing the percentage distribution of the new employment estimates by industry (using their own total) and applying this distribution to the 8,851,000 employment total. One effect of this step was to distribute the unspecified portion of sales (and hence of employment) in the same way as the specified portion.

Table 9 shows the end results of this estimating procedure. The first two columns show the effect of the redistribution of sales. In the redistribution process, a given industry both gained sales from, and lost sales to, other industries. In table 9, the losses and gains in each industry tend to balance out, and the revised distribution of sales does not differ markedly from the original distribution.

Table 9 also shows employment by industry as originally calculated and after the redistribution process. The differences in the original and redistributed employment are fairly large—both absolutely and in percentage terms—in machinery and in the miscellaneous "other" category. In most other industries, however, the differences are relatively small. None of the differences are large enough to upset the major conclusion that employment was growing faster in the MNC's than in the United States as a whole in nearly every industry examined.

It should be emphasized that the procedure described here is very rough, but does give an approximate idea of the magnitude of the differences resulting from use of the enterprise as against the establishment system of classification.

It should be noted that the mere fact that a given MNC industry included a large number of establishments (and hence employment) actually engaged in other industries is not in itself evidence of substantial bias in its employment trends. The degree of bias would depend, not simply on the amount of employment in establishments engaged in other industries, but also on the degree of difference in trend between these other industries and the dominant industry in which the MNC firms are classified. If the dominant industry and these "other" industries were expanding their employment at the same rate there would be no bias.

Table 9.—U.S. Reporters' Domestic Sales and Employment by Industry in 1970, as Originally Reported and as Redistributed

Industry	Sales		Employment			
	Original	Redistributed [1]	Original		Redistributed [2]	
	(Percent)	(Percent)	(Percent)	(Number)	(Percent)	(Number)
Total	100.0	100.0	100.0	8,851	100.0	8,851
Manufacturing	67.1	64.7	71.6	6,335	67.5	5,963
Food products	4.5	6.0	2.9	260	3.9	345
Chemicals and allied products	9.1	8.1	8.2	725	7.3	643
Primary and fabricated metals	7.3	7.9	8.2	724	8.9	785
Machinery	15.7	12.9	21.0	1,860	17.2	1,521
Transportation equipment	18.1	17.7	17.7	1,568	17.2	1,518
Other	12.5	12.1	13.5	1,198	13.0	1,151
Petroleum	15.4	14.6	5.9	522	5.6	493
Other industries	17.5	20.6	22.5	1,994	27.0	2,395
Mining	1.1	1.0	1.0	91	.9	80
Trade	7.2	7.7	6.7	589	7.1	624
Other	9.2	11.9	14.8	1,314	19.1	1,691

1. Redistributed according to percent of sales by industry supplied by reporting companies.
2. Obtained by dividing sales by employment in the original data to get sales per employee, and then sales per employee into the redistributed estimates of sales to get redistributed employment estimates.

Source: U.S. Department of Commerce, Bureau of Economic Analysis, International Investment Division.

PROPERTY, PLANT, AND EQUIPMENT EXPENDITURES BY MAJORITY-OWNED FOREIGN AFFILIATES OF U.S. COMPANIES:

Revised Estimates for 1966-72 and
Projections for 1973 and 1974

R. David Belli, Smith W. Allnutt,
and Howard Murad

By R. DAVID BELLI, SMITH W. ALLNUTT, AND HOWARD MURAD

Property, Plant, and Equipment Expenditures by Majority-Owned Foreign Affiliates of U.S. Companies:

Revised Estimates for 1966–72 and Projections for 1973 and 1974

THIS article presents revised estimates for 1966–72, revised projections for 1973, and BEA's first published projections for 1974 on property, plant, and equipment expenditures by majority-owned foreign affiliates of U.S. companies.

The revisions in the 1966–72 estimates result primarily from "benchmarking" reported sample data against the universe data from BEA's most recent census of U.S. direct investments abroad (covering the year 1966)[1], and several modifications to the method for deriving universe estimates from sample data. These changes also affected the 1973 and 1974 projections; in addition, part of the revision of the 1973 projections (compared to those published last spring) stemmed from actual changes in expectations and also from the use of a revised method of adjusting for bias in the reported expectations. The final data for 1972 and the projections for 1973 and 1974 presented in this article were gathered in the latest semiannual BEA survey, taken in June 1973.

As part of the revision process, the definition of the universe has been changed to include all primary and secondary foreign affiliates [2] in which U.S. ownership is at least 50 percent (majority-owned affiliates). Formerly, the universe was defined to include all primary foreign affiliates in which U.S. ownership was at least 25 percent. The

2. A primary foreign affiliate is a foreign business organization which is directly owned by a U.S. individual or organization. A secondary foreign affiliate is a foreign business organization which is indirectly owned by a U.S. individual or organization through another foreign affiliate.

net effect of the change in definition on the data series, by itself, was probably small since it resulted in both additions to and deletions from the universe; majority-owned secondary affiliates are now included in the universe while primary affiliates in which U.S. ownership is between 25 and 49 percent are now excluded.

NOTE.—The three authors were responsible for the first, second, and third major sections of the article, respectively. In addition, significant contributions were made by Juris E. Abolins and Ronald E. Reed to the preparation and presentation of these data and by Arnold A. Gilbert and Alan L. Tyson to the procedure for deriving universe estimates. The last named was also responsible for programing the estimating procedure.

1. Previously, all data for 1957–73 were benchmarked to the 1957 census of U.S. direct investments abroad.

Property, Plant, and Equipment Expenditures by Majority-Owned Foreign Affiliates of U.S. Companies

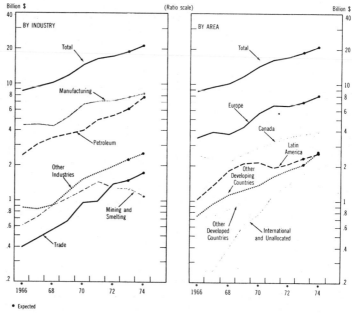

• Expected

U.S. Department of Commerce, Bureau of Economic Analysis

73-12-8

19

The remainder of the article is divided into three major sections. The first section presents a brief analysis of the revised data with particular emphasis on the projections for 1973 and 1974. (Industry and country detail is shown in tables 1 and 6A through 6I.) The second section describes the refined general method for deriving universe estimates from sample data in BEA's direct investment series. The last section outlines how that method was specifically applied to the property, plant, and equipment expenditures data, indicates the magnitude of the revisions, and describes the procedure for adjusting for reporting bias in the projected data.

Foreign Affiliate Expenditures

Property, plant, and equipment expenditures by majority-owned foreign affiliates of U.S. firms are expected to rise 11 percent in 1973 and 13 percent in 1974 to $21.4 billion (see table 1).

The expected increases in 1973 and 1974 are much larger than the gain of 5 percent in 1972, but in line with the 12 percent average annual rate of growth in the period 1966–72. (These are the years for which revised estimates of actual spending are available.)

Affiliates in the *petroleum* industry expect the strongest rise in capital spending in 1974—a 25 percent increase to $7.7 billion, following a 16 percent rise expected this year. In 1974, substantial increases are expected in most major oil producing areas except Latin America, with the largest gains expected in Indonesia and the North Sea area. In 1973, on the other hand, most of the projected increase is related to the expansion of tanker fleets by international shipping affiliates;

such spending is expected to fall slightly next year.

Since the estimates of 1973 and 1974 spending are based on the semiannual survey taken in June 1973, they do not reflect any impact of recent events in the Middle East. New estimates of 1973 and 1974 spending from the semiannual survey now being taken will be published in the March 1974 SURVEY OF CURRENT BUSINESS.

In the period 1966–72, expenditures by petroleum affiliates grew at an average rate of 14 percent per year, but the growth rate was quite uneven with exceptionally strong increases in 1967 and 1971. Of major importance in the 1966–72 period was the expansion of tanker fleets by U.S. oil firms through expenditures by their international shipping affiliates; outlays for that purpose rose from $0.1 billion in 1966 to $0.9 billion in 1972.

Expenditures in developing countries,

Table 1.—Estimates of Property, Plant, and Equipment Expenditures by Majority-Owned Foreign Affiliates of U.S. Companies, Actual and Projected, by Percent Change and Amount [1]

| | Percent change | | | | | | | | | Billions of dollars | | | | | | | | |
| | Actual | | | | | | | Projected [2] | | Actual | | | | | | | Projected [2] | |
	1967	1968	1969	1970	1971	1972	Average 1966–72	1973	1974	1966	1967	1968	1969	1970	1971	1972	1973	1974
Total	10	6	16	21	13	5	12	11	13	8.7	9.6	10.2	11.8	14.3	16.3	17.1	19.0	21.4
By industry																		
Mining and smelting	17	22	16	18	20	−15	12	1	−13	.6	.7	.9	1.0	1.2	1.5	1.2	1.3	1.1
Petroleum	24	14	7	6	26	8	14	16	25	2.4	3.0	3.5	3.7	3.9	5.0	5.4	6.2	7.7
Manufacturing	2	−4	20	29	6	0	8	9	7	4.4	4.5	4.3	5.2	6.7	7.1	7.1	7.7	8.3
Food products	7	−1	18	−7	−4	12	4	32	−10	.3	.3	.3	.4	.3	.3	.4	.5	.4
Paper and allied products	−34	1	5	43	62	12	10	−4	−15	.3	.2	.2	.2	.3	.5	.6	.6	.5
Chemicals and allied products	23	6	−3	17	6	−4	7	11	5	.9	1.1	1.2	1.1	1.3	1.4	1.3	1.5	1.6
Rubber products	−25	26	52	−3	3	78	17	−4	8	.2	.1	.2	.2	.2	.4	.4	.6	.6
Primary and fabricated metals	−12	1	24	68	18	−16	11	−8	−8	.4	.3	.3	.4	.7	.8	.7	.6	.6
Machinery (except electrical)	5	−10	35	43	12	−4	12	8	13	.9	.9	.8	1.1	1.6	1.8	1.7	1.9	2.1
Electrical machinery	19	1	33	33	2	14	16	45	3	.2	.3	.3	.4	.5	.5	.6	.8	.9
Transportation equipment	−7	−23	25	34	−15	−4	0	2	30	.9	.8	.6	.8	1.0	.9	.9	.9	1.1
Other manufacturing	8	5	35	16	−7	−7	8	7	19	.4	.4	.4	.5	.6	.6	.6	.6	.7
Trade	19	18	21	42	3	42	23	8	18	.4	.5	.6	.7	1.0	1.0	1.4	1.5	1.8
Other industries	−3	9	30	27	16	12	15	17	10	.9	.8	.9	1.2	1.5	1.8	2.0	2.3	2.5
By area																		
Developed countries	4	−3	16	28	14	2	10	8	12	6.7	7.0	6.8	7.8	10.0	11.5	11.7	12.6	14.2
Canada	−8	−5	15	16	11	12	6	4	6	2.5	2.3	2.2	2.5	2.9	3.2	3.6	3.7	4.0
Europe	13	−6	16	34	15	0	11	7	15	3.5	3.9	3.7	4.3	5.8	6.6	6.6	7.1	8.2
United Kingdom	13	0	7	35	12	−7	9	19	24	.9	1.0	1.0	1.1	1.5	1.7	1.6	1.9	2.3
European Economic Community (6) [3]	12	−14	28	37	18	1	12	2	7	2.1	2.3	2.0	2.5	3.5	4.1	4.1	4.2	4.5
Other Europe	20	17	−7	24	7	7	11	15	29	.5	.6	.7	.6	.8	.9	.9	1.1	1.4
Japan	30	39	18	35	21	1	24	34	26	.2	.2	.3	.3	.5	.6	.6	.8	1.0
Australia, New Zealand, and South Africa	−5	5	20	27	20	−10	9	8	7	.6	.5	.6	.7	.9	1.0	.9	1.0	1.1
Developing countries	30	29	12	6	2	9	14	10	21	1.8	2.3	3.0	3.3	3.5	3.6	4.0	4.4	5.3
Latin America	32	35	15	3	−9	5	12	12	10	1.0	1.4	1.8	2.1	2.2	2.0	2.1	2.3	2.6
Other Africa	31	35	8	−16	−12	−14	3	−7	14	.3	.4	.6	.5	.4	.4	.4	.4	.9
Middle East	21	13	−18	26	31	80	22	10	19	.2	.3	.3	.2	.3	.4	.7	.8	.9
Other Asia and Pacific	27	4	35	44	43	−4	23	14	52	.2	.3	.3	.4	.6	.8	.8	2.0	1.3
International and unallocated	2	58	54	23	52	18	33	44	−2	.3	.3	.4	.6	.8	1.2	1.4	2.0	2.0
Addendum:																		
European Economic Community (9) [4]								6	12								6.2	6.9

1. The property, plant, and equipment expenditures data series has been revised back to and including the year 1966 (see text for discussion).
2. Based on results of the survey taken in June, 1973. Spending projections are adjusted in order to eliminate—or at least reduce—any systematic bias in projected data (see text for discussion).

3. The "European Economic Community (6)" includes Belgium, France, Germany, Italy, Luxembourg, and the Netherlands.
4. The "European Economic Community (9)" includes the "European Economic Community (6)", the United Kingdom, Denmark, and Ireland.

primarily by affiliates engaged in exploration and production of crude oil, grew twice as fast from 1966 to 1972 as expenditures in developed areas. In the Middle East, petroleum outlays remained comparatively small until 1971 when a major expansion, centered in Saudi Arabia, began. Spending in the Far East and the Caribbean area was negligible in 1966 but grew substantially in subsequent years, while spending by the more mature petroleum affiliates in Venezuela and Middle Eastern countries except Saudi Arabia grew relatively slowly. Spending by petroleum affiliates in Europe increased an average of 9 percent per year, mainly to expand refinery capacity, while spending by Canadian affiliates rose very little.

Manufacturing affiliates expect to increase expenditures 9 percent this year and 7 percent in 1974, to $8.3 billion. In 1972 there was no change in their outlays. The planned increases in 1973 and 1974 are spread among both developed and less-developed countries. Strong increases are expected in both years in Japan and in several countries in Western Europe and Latin America. Canadian affiliates expect a substantial increase in 1973 but plan little growth next year.

Within manufacturing, expected changes in 1973 and 1974 are quite varied. Affiliates in the transportation equipment industry will lead growth in 1974 with a 30 percent increase, following little change in 1973 and declines in the preceding 2 years. Affiliates which manufacture food products, chemicals, and electrical machinery expect substantial increases this year to be followed by smaller gains or reductions in 1974. In both 1973 and 1974, affiliates in the non-electrical machinery industry plan large increases while affiliates which manufacture paper, concentrated in Canada, and primary and fabricated metals, expect reductions.

Expenditures by manufacturing affiliates rose at an average annual rate of only 8 percent from 1966 to 1972, the lowest rate among major industry groups. Most of the increase was in the 6-nation European Economic Community, as constituted prior to 1973, where spending grew at an average annual rate of 12 percent. In Japan, expenditures grew at twice that rate, but from a very small base of $0.1 billion in 1966. Outlays by relatively more mature affiliates in Canada and the United Kingdom grew at an average rate of only 4 percent per year.

Following a large drop in 1972, spending by affiliates in *mining and smelting* is expected to remain at the 1972 level this year but to fall substantially in 1974. Rising expenditures in Australia and Indonesia in 1973 and in Peru in 1974 are expected to offset large reductions in both years in Canada.

Expenditures by Canadian mining affiliates rose steadily from 1968 to 1970, then nearly doubled in 1971. The recent reductions of expenditures in Canada largely reflect completion of several large projects. Also, a substantial part of the estimated reduction for 1973 was due to the removal from both the sample and the universe of a large Canadian mining company in which many unrelated U.S. shareholders have an ownership interest. Such publicly-owned companies are treated as primary foreign affiliates if the aggregate U.S. ownership is greater than 50 percent. In 1973, the total U.S. equity participation in this Canadian company was below BEA's 50 percent cutoff.

Affiliates in *trade* expect to increase expenditures 18 percent in 1974 to $1.8 billion, following an increase of 8 percent this year. Particularly strong gains next year are expected in Canada and the United Kingdom.

The increases by trade affiliates this year and next are below the average annual increase of 23 percent from 1966 to 1972. Outlays were quite small in 1966 but growth through 1972 far outpaced that of all other major industry groups. With some notable exceptions, the major function of trade affiliates is to distribute the products of foreign manufacturing affiliates of the same U.S. parent company. Thus, expenditures by trade affiliates, like those by manufacturing affiliates, are concentrated heavily in developed countries. Their rapid expansion in the 1966–72 period to a large extent reflects previous and continuing overseas manufacturing investment by U.S. companies.

Affiliates in all *other industries* combined—including agriculture, public utilities, transportation, construction, finance, and services—expect a 17 percent increase in spending this year to be followed by a rise of 10 percent in 1974 to $2.5 billion. In 1973, the largest increase is expected in the United Kingdom, while Canadian affiliates will lead the growth next year. For the period 1966–72, expenditures by affiliates in this industry group grew at an average annual rate of 15 percent, slightly faster than the rate of growth for all industries combined.

A Procedure for Deriving Universe Estimates From Sample Survey Data

BEA's direct investment data series in non-census years are based on sample data which, in most of the series, are used to extrapolate universe data reported in a census (benchmark) year to derive universe estimates in subsequent years. All of the direct investment series are being revised because universe data from BEA's most recent direct investment census (1966) are now available. Also, for those series for which universe estimates in subsequent years are developed, as against just using the sample data as reported, the general procedure for deriving the universe estimates has been refined. This section of the article describes the revised general procedure and the next section discusses the specific application of this procedure to the series on foreign affiliate expenditures for property, plant, and equipment.

Procedure for estimating universe data

The earlier procedure for estimating a universe value for a given period from sample data for that period is to multiply the universe value in the prior period by the ratio of the sample's value in the current period to the sample's value in the prior period, and then add data reported by companies which are new to the universe in the current period (births). For the computation, the universe value in the prior period is reduced by the amount reported in that period for companies known to have since dropped out of the universe (deaths). The procedure is the conventional link-relative method, that is, the 1967 universe estimate is computed by applying the ratio of the 1967-to-1966 sample values to the 1966 benchmark universe value, then the 1968 universe estimate is computed by applying the ratio of the 1968-to-1967 sample values to the 1967 universe estimate and so on.

The formula previously used is:

$$U_t = \frac{S_t}{S_{t-1}}(U_{t-1} - Dr_{t-1}) + Br_t$$

where:

- $t-1$ = prior period
- t = current period, which is to be estimated
- U = universe data
- S = sample data for companies existing and reported in both periods
- Dr = data reported for deaths
- Br = data reported for births

The following refinements to this procedure have been made in conjunction with the benchmarking of the direct investment series to the 1966 census universe:

(1) Universe estimates are computed at four levels of aggregation—country-industry, country total, industry total, and grand total. The sum of all country-industry cells, all country total cells, and all industry total cells and the grand total can then be compared with each other in order to judge the validity of and to adjust, if necessary, the individual country-industry estimates. The published global universe estimate is the sum of the individual country-industry estimates after such adjustments.

(2) A procedure has been added for estimating data for total deaths and total births, i.e., including the values associated with unreported deaths and births.

(3) The procedure for adjustment to take account of cells for which reported samples are small has been standardized.

The second and third refinements are discussed below.

Total deaths and births

In the direct investment data series, affiliates which existed in the prior period but do not exist in the current period (deaths) report only in the prior period while affiliates which exist in the current period but did not exist in the prior period (births) report only in the current period. Data for such companies are not considered part of the sample data used to compute universe estimates, since the sample used is composed only of data of companies which report in both periods. In the formula previously used (cited above), data for deaths and births reported in the sample surveys were included as reported. This procedure has been modified in order to obtain an estimate of data for total births and deaths, including those which are not reported. This estimate is based on the assumption that the ratio of reported to total deaths or births is equal to the ratio of the sample plus reported deaths to the universe in the prior period. The total value of deaths—companies that were in the universe in the prior period but have since dropped out—is estimated by assuming that the ratio of the total value to the value of reported deaths is equal to the ratio of the universe value to the value of the sample (including data for firms that are known to have since died) in the prior period. Thus, for total deaths (D):

$$\frac{D_{t-1}}{Dr_{t-1}} = \frac{U_{t-1}}{S_{t-1} + Dr_{t-1}}$$

or:

$$D_{t-1} = \frac{U_{t-1}}{S_{t-1} + Dr_{t-1}} \cdot Dr_{t-1}$$

The total value of births—companies that have entered the universe since the prior period—is estimated in the same way:

$$B_t = \frac{U_{t-1}}{S_{t-1} + Dr_{t-1}} \cdot Br_t$$

The formula previously used, modified to include unreported births and deaths, becomes:

$$U_t = \frac{S_t}{S_{t-1}}\left[U_{t-1} - \left(\frac{U_{t-1}}{S_{t-1} + Dr_{t-1}} \cdot Dr_{t-1}\right)\right] + \left[\frac{U_{t-1}}{S_{t-1} + Dr_{t-1}} \cdot Br_t\right]$$

The reciprocal of the ratio

$$\left(\frac{U_{t-1}}{S_{t-1} + Dr_{t-1}}\right)$$

that is computed for each country-industry cell in order to blow up reported data for deaths and births is tested for adequacy of sample coverage. This test is the same as that described below in the discussion of small samples.

Small samples

At the country-industry cell level, the sample value of certain direct investment data items is quite small relative to the universe value in period $t-1$. In such cases, the change in the sample from period $t-1$ to period t does not necessarily reflect the change in the nonreported data in the cell. Therefore, the ratio of the sample (including reported deaths) to the universe for each country-industry cell is compared to a predetermined acceptable percentage. Denoting the acceptable percentage by Y, the criterion is that the computed ratio for each country-industry cell must be equal to or greater than Y:

$$\frac{S_{t-1} + Dr_{t-1}}{U_{t-1}} \geq Y$$

If the ratio in a given country-industry cell is less than Y, then the modified estimating formula is adjusted as follows (with the subscript i denoting industry):

(a) The ratio of the sample value in period t to the sample value in period $t-1$ is computed at the industry total level, rather than at the country-industry level:

$$\frac{Si_t}{Si_{t-1}}$$

and

(b) The ratio of the universe to the sample (including reported deaths) used to estimate total deaths and births is calculated with industry total data, rather than country-industry data:

$$\frac{Ui_{t-1}}{Si_{t-1} + Dri_{t-1}}$$

Table 2.—Differences Between Revised and Previously Published Universe Estimates of Property, Plant, and Equipment Expenditures by Majority-Owned Foreign Affiliates of U.S. Firms by Major Industry and Area, 1966–71

[Millions of dollars or percent]

	1966 Amount	As percent of revised universe	1967 Amount	As percent of revised universe	1968 Amount	As percent of revised universe	1969 Amount	As percent of revised universe	1970 Amount	As percent of revised universe	1971 Amount	As percent of revised universe
Total	85	1	289	3	765	8	1,030	9	1,332	9	1,436	9
By industry												
Mining and smelting	-169	-2	-191	-2	-142	-1	-93	-1	163	-1	-270	-2
Petroleum	-83	1	29	(*)	149	1	72	1	-149	-1	-194	1
Manufacturing	-186	-2	-44	(*)	133	1	221	2	219	2	268	2
Trade	8	(*)	38	(*)	107	1	126	1	231	2	154	1
Other industries	515	6	456	5	518	5	704	6	895	6	1,089	7
By area												
Canada	125	1	59	1	55	1	177	1	172	2	265	2
Latin America	-59	-1	83	1	189	2	260	2	233	2	118	1
Europe	219	3	301	3	588	6	566	5	793	6	840	5
Other areas	-199	-2	-154	-2	-66	-1	-128	(*)	134	1	213	1

(*) =Less than ±0.5 percent.

Source: U.S. Department of Commerce, Bureau of Economic Analysis, International Investment Division.

Since Y is held constant, the addition of the test for adequacy of sample coverage to the modified formula provides a standardized procedure for estimating universe totals where reported samples are small.

Table 4.—Revised Value of Property, Plant, and Equipment Expenditures by Affiliates in Sample and in Universe, and Sample as Percent of Universe, by Industry and Area, 1966

	Sample	Universe	Sample as percent of universe
	(Millions of dollars)		
Total	6,368	8,726	73
By industry			
Mining and smelting	522	621	84
Petroleum	2,011	2,443	82
Manufacturing	3,288	4,397	75
Food products	140	290	48
Paper and allied products	200	323	62
Chemicals	693	898	77
Rubber	101	161	63
Primary and fabricated metals	268	383	70
Machinery (except electrical)	741	883	84
Electrical machinery	151	237	64
Transportation equipment	803	870	92
Other	190	353	54
Trade	184	399	46
Other industries	364	865	42
By area			
Canada	1,818	2,482	73
Latin America	682	1,035	66
Europe	2,554	3,473	74
United Kingdom	725	919	79
European Economic Community (6)[1]	1,505	2,059	73
Other	324	495	65
Japan	143	159	90
Australia, New Zealand, and South Africa	451	574	79
Other areas	720	1,004	72

1. Includes France, Germany, Italy, Netherlands, Belgium, and Luxembourg only.

Source: U.S. Department of Commerce, Bureau of Economic Analysis, International Investment Division.

Estimation of Property, Plant, and Equipment Spending

The property, plant, and equipment series is the first to be benchmarked to the 1966 census of U.S. direct investment abroad and the first to which the modified procedure for computing universe estimates has been applied. Table 2 shows the differences between the new and old estimates of actual (not projected) spending for 1966 to 1971. The combined effect of the revisions has been to raise the level of total spending by affiliates above the previously published levels in each year. The upward revisions become larger each year, increasing from $85 million in 1966 to $1,436 million in 1971. In percentage terms, the difference between the old and new series ranges between 1 and 9 percent of the revised estimates.

Table 3.—Effect of New Method for Estimating Additions to and Liquidations From the Universe, 1967–1971

[Millions of dollars or percent]

Year	Total difference between revised and previously published data	Effect of estimating non-reported net additions	Effect of estimating non-reported net additions as percent of total difference
1967	289	81	28
1968	765	165	22
1969	1,030	333	32
1970	1,332	567	43
1971	1,436	807	56

Source: U.S. Department of Commerce, Bureau of Economic Analysis, International Investment Division.

Table 5.—Comparison of Projected Data Adjusted and Unadjusted for Bias and Percent Difference by Major Industry, 1973 and 1974

Industry	1973 Unadjusted	Adjusted	Percent difference	1974 Unadjusted	Adjusted	Percent difference
	(Millions of dollars)			(Millions of dollars)		
Total	20,797	18,995	-9	21,994	21,419	-3
Mining and smelting	1,368	1,261	-8	1,021	1,102	8
Petroleum	6,688	6,180	-8	7,846	7,707	-2
Manufacturing	8,807	7,743	-12	8,915	8,306	-7
Trade	1,547	1,505	-3	1,688	1,775	5
Other industries	2,386	2,306	-3	2,525	2,528	(*)

(*) =Less than ±0.5 percent.

Source: U.S. Department of Commerce, Bureau of Economic Analysis, International Investment Division.

By industry, the largest revisions were in the "other" category, mainly the hotel and construction industries. By area, the largest revisions were in Europe. In all other major industry or area categories shown in table 2, the difference between the old and new series never exceeds 2 percent of the revised estimate.

The estimating procedure now used is described in the preceding section of this article, and the differences between the current procedure and the one used previously for plant and equipment expenditures are discussed below. The most important modification is the new treatment of total births and deaths. Births have always been larger than deaths so that the failure to "inflate" the reported births and deaths to take account of nonreported cases resulted in net underestimation of property, plant and equipment expenditures abroad. The net amount involved for the unreported births and deaths in any one year was quite small—less than two percent of total expenditures.

Table 6A.—Estimates of Property, Plant, and Equipment Expenditures by Majority-Owned Foreign Affiliates of U.S. Companies for 1966, by Country and Industry [1]

[Millions of dollars]

Area or country	All industries	Mining and smelting	Petroleum	Manufacturing Total	Food products	Paper and allied products	Chemicals and allied products	Rubber products	Primary and fabricated metals	Machinery (except electrical)	Electrical machinery	Transportation equipment	Other manufacturing	Trade	Other industries
All countries	8,726	621	2,443	4,397	290	323	898	161	383	883	237	870	353	399	865
Developed countries	6,687	429	1,613	3,835	219	293	723	137	299	844	202	830	288	348	463
Canada	2,482	312	662	1,178	72	226	190	49	123	145	64	(D)	(D)	71	258
Europe	3,473	3	793	2,265	114	53	401	71	148	632	126	(D)	(D)	250	161
United Kingdom	919	0	174	666	29	4	101	25	50	188	37	(D)	(D)	40	38
European Economic Community (6)	2,059	(D)	481	1,375	62	35	247	29	64	408	69	354	106	161	(D)
Belgium and Luxembourg	279	0	(D)	223	4	6	39	12	8	(D)	6	(D)	19	11	(D)
France	452	0	(D)	286	17	4	28	7	9	121	16	(D)	(D)	11	(D)
Germany	857	0	228	567	22	8	71	6	27	162	24	(D)	(D)	67	8
Italy	266	(D)	89	154	11	13	19	2	14	61	21	1	10	53	(D)
Netherlands	204	0	41	145	8	4	89	2	5	(D)	2	1	(D)	15	4
Other Europe	495	(D)	138	224	24	14	53	17	34	36	20	6	20	49	(D)
Denmark	44	0	25	8	(D)	(D)	1	(D)	(D)	(D)	(D)	(D)	(*)	(D)	(D)
Ireland	17	(D)	5	11	3	0	1	(D)	1	(*)	(D)	0	4	(D)	(D)
Norway	32	(D)	10	14	(*)	(*)	1	(D)	0	1	(D)	0	(D)	(D)	(D)
Spain	130	0	26	67	17	8	24	3	4	2	(D)	2	(D)	17	20
Sweden	92	0	27	53	1	(D)	7	8	6	(D)	(D)	0	(D)	10	2
Switzerland	64	0	7	23	(D)	1	1	(*)	(D)	2	(D)	(D)	3	11	23
Other	116	(D)	38	47	1	3	(D)	(D)	(D)	(*)	5	2	7	6	(D)
Japan	159	0	50	99	2	(D)	35	(*)	(D)	(D)	3	(*)	2	6	4
Australia, New Zealand, and South Africa	574	114	108	293	30	(D)	96	(D)	27	(D)	8	73	16	21	38
Australia	464	109	82	234	(D)	7	90	(D)	24	10	6	56	13	12	27
New Zealand	27	(D)	(D)	14	(D)	(D)	1	1	1	0	1	(D)	1	3	5
South Africa	82	(D)	(D)	45	13	6	5	3	3	(D)	1	(D)	3	6	7
Developing countries	1,786	193	744	563	71	30	175	24	84	38	36	40	65	50	237
Latin America	1,035	178	253	392	59	27	120	19	30	30	18	39	51	43	169
Latin American Republics	854	128	196	365	58	(D)	106	(D)	30	29	18	39	49	41	123
Argentina	90	(D)	15	60	9	1	25	3	2	2	2	10	6	(D)	10
Brazil	119	2	6	91	11	(D)	17	4	8	14	6	(D)	13	7	13
Chile	84	(D)	2	8	3	(D)	2	0	(D)	0	(*)	1	(D)	1	(D)
Colombia	55	1	32	20	1	4	7	(D)	1	(*)	(*)	(D)	5	1	2
Mexico	131	9	1	100	11	4	35	3	11	12	6	7	11	10	10
Panama	16	0	(D)	1	1	0	(D)	0	0	0	0	0	0	1	(D)
Peru	116	54	19	28	9	(D)	9	(D)	1	(*)	(*)	(D)	1	1	11
Venezuela	164	(D)	96	37	5	3	5	2	(D)	(*)	(*)	(D)	10	(D)	17
Other Central America	43	1	9	13	4	(D)	(D)	1	1	0	1	0	1	3	18
Other and unallocated	36	(D)	(D)	7	3	0	2	0	1	(*)	0	1	1	1	10
Other Western Hemisphere	181	50	57	27	1	(D)	14	(D)	(*)	(*)	(*)	0	3	1	46
Bahamas	40	0	1	(D)	(*)	0	0	(D)	0	0	0	0	(D)	0	33
Bermuda	2	0	(*)	0	0	0	0	0	0	0	0	0	0	(*)	2
Jamaica	44	(D)	1	(D)	1	(D)	4	(D)	0	(*)	(D)	0	(D)	(D)	3
Other and unallocated	95	(D)	54	(D)	(*)	(D)	(D)	0	(*)	0	(D)	0	(*)	(*)	9
Other Africa	316	(D)	237	(D)	1	0	1	1	(D)	(*)	(D)	(*)	3	2	14
Liberia	11	(D)	(D)	(*)	0	0	(D)	(*)	0	0	0	0	0	(*)	5
Libya	111	(D)	110	(D)	0	0	0	0	0	0	0	0	0	(*)	(D)
Nigeria	78	(D)	68	4	(*)	0	1	0	(*)	(*)	(*)	0	1	(*)	(D)
Other and unallocated	116	4	(D)	(D)	1	0	(D)	1	(D)	(*)	(D)	(*)	(*)	3	2
Middle East	215	(D)	188	(D)	(*)	(D)	6	(D)	0	1	(D)	0	(*)	(*)	18
Iran	35	(D)	31	3	(*)	0	(D)	(D)	0	(D)	(D)	0	(*)	(*)	(D)
Other and unallocated	181	0	158	(D)	(*)	(D)	(D)	(D)	0	(D)	(D)	0	(*)	(*)	(D)
Other Asia and Pacific	220	5	65	108	11	(D)	48	(D)	(D)	8	17	1	10	5	36
India	28	0	(D)	(D)	(*)	0	3	(D)	(D)	7	(D)	1	(*)	0	(D)
Indonesia	(D)	0	(D)	0	0	0	0	0	0	0	0	0	0	0	(D)
Korea	(D)	0	0	(D)	0	0	(D)	0	0	0	(*)	0	1	(*)	(*)
Philippines	65	(D)	20	32	10	(D)	(D)	1	(*)	(*)	1	(D)	6	(D)	8
Other and unallocated	90	(D)	35	22	1	(*)	8	(D)	3	(*)	(D)	(D)	3	(D)	28
International and unallocated	253	----	86	----	----	----	----	----	----	----	----	----	----	1	165

*Less than $500,000.
D Suppressed to avoid disclosure of data for individual reporters.

1. The property, plant, and equipment expenditures data have been revised back to and including the year 1966 (see text for discussion).

However, the effect is cumulative and table 3 shows that by 1971, this procedural change accounted for 56 percent of the total difference between the revised and previously published series. The balance of the difference is the result of the bench-marking of the spending series to the 1966 census, including a change in the definition of the universe; the introduction of an adjustment for small samples; and the elimination of adjustments formerly made for extreme data movements. The specific contribution of each of these items to the total difference cannot be readily measured.

Benchmarking to the 1966 census

For purposes of computing the re-vised spending estimates presented in this article, the definition of the universe was changed to conform to that used for the spending data in the 1966 BEA census.[3] That census asked for data on expenditures for all primary

3. For a description of the census, see Bureau of Economic Analysis, *U.S. Direct Investments Abroad 1966. Part 1: Balance of Payments Data.*

Table 6B.—Estimates of Property, Plant, and Equipment Expenditures by Majority-Owned Foreign Affiliates of U.S. Companies for 1967, by Country and Industry [1]

[Millions of dollars]

Area or country	All indus-tries	Mining and smelt-ing	Petro-leum	Manufacturing										Trade	Other indus-tries
				Total	Food products	Paper and allied products	Chemi-cals and allied products	Rubber products	Primary and fabricated metals	Machin-ery (except electrical)	Electrical machin-ery	Transpor-tation equip-ment	Other manu-facturing		
All countries	9,557	729	3,030	4,482	310	212	1,104	121	337	924	282	808	383	475	841
Developed countries	6,978	444	1,896	3,795	224	166	842	103	274	879	243	736	327	411	432
Canada	2,292	316	609	1,060	72	97	144	33	83	166	79	274	112	84	223
Europe	3,932	4	1,093	2,359	119	62	599	63	160	647	152	379	178	303	173
United Kingdom	1,039	0	297	662	34	11	135	26	48	183	41	127	57	32	49
European Economic Community (6)	2,300	(D)	607	1,417	71	41	354	23	70	431	80	248	100	228	(D)
Belgium and Luxembourg	331	0	(D)	217	7	2	73	(D)	3	(D)	(D)	(D)	(D)	8	(D)
France	451	0	(D)	302	15	5	23	6	11	132	17	(D)	(D)	72	(D)
Germany	885	0	258	503	28	2	106	7	23	144	(D)	(D)	38	114	10
Italy	336	(D)	108	203	13	31	23	5	24	67	23	1	17	18	(D)
Netherlands	296	0	84	193	8	1	129	(D)	9	(D)	(D)	2	11	16	4
Other Europe	594	(D)	189	280	14	10	110	14	42	34	32	4	21	44	(D)
Denmark	50	(*)	(D)	8	(D)	(D)	(D)	(D)	0	(D)	(D)	(D)	1	2	(D)
Ireland	38	0	23	13	(D)	0	1	(D)	(D)	(*)	3	0	4	(D)	(D)
Norway	35	(D)	(D)	10	(*)	(*)	(*)	0	7	(D)	(D)	0	(D)	(D)	6
Spain	189	0	32	127	8	3	92	(D)	3	2	(D)	(D)	2	10	20
Sweden	112	0	42	55	(*)	(D)	(D)	9	6	(D)	(D)	0	1	14	2
Switzerland	59	0	7	19	(D)	1	1	(*)	(D)	(D)	(D)	(D)	5	14	19
Other	110	4	35	47	1	2	5	2	(D)	(*)	9	1	(D)	3	21
Japan	207	0	94	102	1	(D)	38	(D)	(*)	(D)	4	(*)	4	6	4
Australia, New Zealand, and South Africa	547	125	100	273	32	(D)	62	(D)	31	(D)	7	83	34	19	31
Australia	446	123	80	217	(D)	5	55	(D)	30	(D)	5	(D)	27	9	18
New Zealand	19	(D)	(D)	7	(D)	(D)	1	1	1	0	(*)	(D)	1	3	(D)
South Africa	82	(D)	(D)	49	15	2	6	3	1	3	1	12	6	7	(D)
Developing countries	2,319	285	1,029	687	86	46	262	18	62	45	39	72	56	64	255
Latin America	1,365	264	367	486	74	45	143	14	38	35	30	68	38	52	196
Latin American Republics	1,177	197	317	466	73	(D)	132	(D)	38	35	30	68	34	50	148
Argentina	184	(D)	41	99	10	1	36	1	2	2	3	38	6	(D)	26
Brazil	158	(D)	(D)	127	10	2	34	3	24	19	11	(D)	(D)	8	(D)
Chile	140	107	1	(D)	2	(D)	2	0	1	0	1	(D)	(D)	1	(D)
Colombia	72	1	43	25	2	2	14	1	(*)	(D)	1	(D)	4	(D)	(D)
Mexico	148	18	1	102	15	13	31	3	6	12	10	3	9	15	11
Panama	18	0	2	2	1	(D)	(*)	0	0	0	(*)	0	(D)	1	13
Peru	134	48	31	38	11	(D)	4	(D)	1	(*)	(*)	1	(*)	4	13
Venezuela	188	(D)	119	39	10	2	6	(D)	4	(D)	1	(D)	7	(D)	15
Other Central America	101	6	52	16	9	(*)	4	(D)	(*)	(D)	2	0	1	2	25
Other and unallocated	34	(D)	(D)	(D)	3	(*)	2	0	1	(D)	(*)	0	(D)	2	9
Other Western Hemisphere	188	67	50	21	1	(D)	12	(D)	(*)	(*)	(*)	0	4	2	48
Bahamas	37	0	2	(D)	(*)	0	(D)	0	0	0	0	0	(D)	(D)	30
Bermuda	2	0	(*)	0	0	0	0	0	0	0	0	0	0	0	2
Jamaica	39	(D)	2	(D)	1	(D)	4	(D)	0	(*)	(D)	0	1	(D)	10
Other and unallocated	110	(D)	46	(D)	(*)	(D)	(D)	(D)	0	0	(D)	0	(D)	1	6
Other Africa	414	12	360	26	1	0	2	(D)	(D)	(D)	(*)	(D)	4	2	14
Liberia	16	(D)	(D)	(D)	0	0	(D)	(D)	0	0	0	0	(D)	(*)	(D)
Libya	201	0	200	(D)	0	0	(D)	0	0	0	0	0	0	(D)	(D)
Nigeria	94	(D)	84	5	(*)	0	1	0	1	0	(D)	(D)	3	(D)	5
Other and unallocated	104	3	(D)	(D)	1	0	(D)	(D)	(D)	(D)	(D)	(D)	(D)	(D)	(D)
Middle East	260	(*)	197	53	(*)	(D)	51	(D)	0	(D)	(D)	0	(*)	(*)	9
Iran	105	(*)	56	47	(*)	0	45	(D)	0	(D)	(D)	0	(*)	0	2
Other and unallocated	155	0	141	6	(*)	(D)	6	(D)	0	(*)	(D)	0	(*)	1	7
Other Asia and Pacific	280	9	105	121	11	(D)	66	2	(D)	9	9	(D)	15	8	37
India	35	0	(D)	(D)	(*)	0	10	(*)	(D)	(D)	(D)	(*)	2	(*)	(D)
Indonesia	(D)	0	(D)	0	0	0	0	0	0	0	(D)	0	0	0	(D)
Korea	(D)	0	(D)	(D)	0	0	(D)	0	0	0	0	(D)	0	1	(D)
Philippines	61	(D)	18	28	8	(D)	(D)	2	(*)	(*)	(*)	(D)	5	(D)	12
Other and unallocated	147	(D)	55	54	2	(*)	33	(*)	(D)	5	5	(D)	7	(D)	24
International and unallocated	259	------	105	------	------	------	------	------	------	------	------	------	------	(*)	154

*Less than $500,000.
D Suppressed to avoid disclosure of data for individual reporters.

1. The property, plant, and equipment expenditures data have been revised back to and including the year 1966 (see text for discussion).

and secondary foreign affiliates in which U.S. ownership was at least 50 percent. In contrast, the universe covered by the unrevised spending series included all primary foreign affiliates in which U.S. ownership was at least 25 percent. Thus, while the new universe estimates for 1966 onward are based on data from the same sample surveys as used for the previously published estimates, only the data reported in those surveys for majority-owned foreign affiliates (MOFA's), both primary and secondary, are actually used in the new estimates.

In addition, each affiliate's industry and country classification from the 1966 census is now applied to that affiliate in subsequent years.[4] The industry classification of an affiliate was changed more often than the country classification. Most affected affiliates were reclassified from manufacturing to trade or other services.

[4]. These classifications will remain in effect until the next census is taken.

Table 6C.—Estimates of Property, Plant, and Equipment Expenditures by Majority-Owned Foreign Affiliates of U.S. Companies for 1968, by Country and Industry [1]

[Millions of dollars]

Area or country	All industries	Mining and smelting	Petroleum	Manufacturing Total	Food products	Paper and allied products	Chemicals and allied products	Rubber products	Primary and fabricated metals	Machinery (except electrical)	Electrical machinery	Transportation equipment	Other manufacturing	Trade	Other industries
All countries	10,152	893	3,460	4,323	308	215	1,167	152	342	827	284	624	404	560	916
Developed countries	6,757	467	1,931	3,467	240	135	828	112	267	777	243	543	321	491	400
Canada	2,183	360	622	857	78	47	130	47	80	110	76	198	92	135	209
Europe	3,712	7	1,015	2,200	133	80	550	59	166	609	150	255	197	331	160
United Kingdom	1,036	0	346	610	33	8	103	21	69	191	37	78	70	49	31
European Economic Community (6)	1,985	(D)	459	1,249	92	61	263	27	63	387	82	167	106	224	(D)
Belgium and Luxembourg	252	0	(D)	163	5	2	49	(D)	7	50	(D)	(D)	10	(D)	7
France	417	0	(D)	256	9	9	22	9	14	122	(D)	(D)	26	(D)	22
Germany	677	0	109	470	48	9	68	6	24	130	33	115	37	84	14
Italy	380	(D)	143	210	23	36	27	(D)	17	65	23	(D)	17	22	(D)
Netherlands	259	0	85	150	6	6	96	1	1	20	2	1	17	19	4
Other Europe	691	(D)	210	341	8	11	184	10	35	32	31	11	20	58	(D)
Denmark	43	0	29	3	1	(D)	(D)	(D)	0	(D)	(D)	(D)	(*)	(D)	(D)
Ireland	53	(D)	37	14	(D)	0	4	(D)	(D)	(*)	3	0	(D)	(D)	(D)
Norway	32	(D)	20	6	(*)	1	(*)	0	3	(D)	(D)	0	(D)	2	(D)
Spain	270	0	36	210	2	7	172	(D)	3	5	(D)	(D)	2	4	20
Sweden	118	0	47	55	1	1	3	4	20	24	2	0	1	15	2
Switzerland	79	0	6	21	(D)	(D)	3	(*)	(D)	2	(D)	(D)	5	30	21
Other	96	6	35	33	4	1	(D)	(D)	(D)	(*)	(D)	1	7	4	18
Japan	288	0	149	125	5	(D)	60	(D)	(D)	48	6	(*)	4	10	5
Australia, New Zealand, and South Africa	574	101	146	286	24	(D)	87	(D)	(D)	10	11	90	25	16	27
Australia	466	(D)	124	217	(D)	6	82	(D)	19	3	9	(D)	15	9	(D)
New Zealand	11	0	(D)	4	(D)	(D)	1	1	(*)	0	(*)	(D)	1	2	(D)
South Africa	97	(D)	(D)	65	13	(D)	4	3	(D)	7	2	21	13	5	(D)
Developing countries	2,986	425	1,300	856	68	80	340	40	76	51	40	80	82	68	335
Latin America	1,843	413	472	640	62	79	180	(D)	66	44	35	(D)	59	53	265
Latin American Republics	1,562	266	403	626	61	(D)	172	35	66	44	35	(D)	56	51	216
Argentina	159	(D)	42	72	5	1	17	3	8	4	3	23	8	17	(D)
Brazil	280	(D)	(D)	235	8	(D)	101	14	30	25	13	(D)	3	12	23
Chile	236	183	1	13	2	(D)	1	0	(D)	0	1	6	(*)	1	39
Colombia	78	1	53	23	2	1	8	2	(*)	(D)	1	(D)	4	(D)	(D)
Mexico	223	20	2	179	12	56	30	10	20	10	13	3	23	11	12
Panama	28	0	3	2	1	0	(*)	0	0	0	(*)	0	(*)	1	22
Peru	105	36	18	31	8	(D)	4	(D)	(D)	(*)	(*)	(D)	(*)	1	19
Venezuela	288	(D)	209	43	10	(D)	5	4	3	(*)	1	(D)	13	(D)	17
Other Central America	94	5	43	21	10	1	4	(D)	1	(D)	2	0	2	1	25
Other and unallocated	71	(D)	(D)	8	3	(*)	2	0	2	0	(*)	0	1	1	36
Other Western Hemisphere	281	147	69	13	1	(D)	8	(D)	(*)	(*)	(*)	0	3	2	49
Bahamas	40	0	3	(D)	(*)	0	(D)	0	0	0	0	0	(D)	(D)	34
Bermuda	2	0	(*)	0	0	0	0	0	0	0	0	0	0	(*)	2
Jamaica	121	(D)	1	6	(*)	(D)	4	(D)	0	(*)	0	0	1	(D)	5
Other and unallocated	118	(D)	66	(D)	(D)	(D)	(D)	0	(*)	0	(*)	0	(D)	2	8
Other Africa	558	10	520	11	1	0	2	(*)	(D)	(*)	(D)	0	4	2	16
Liberia	27	(D)	15	(*)	0	0	0	(*)	0	0	0	0	0	(*)	(D)
Libya	283	0	283	(D)	0	(D)	(D)	0	0	0	0	0	(D)	(D)	0
Nigeria	83	(D)	72	5	(*)	0	(D)	0	1	0	(*)	0	(D)	(D)	6
Other and unallocated	164	4	150	(D)	1	0	1	0	(D)	(*)	(D)	0	(D)	2	(D)
Middle East	295	(*)	167	114	(*)	(*)	(D)	(D)	0	1	(D)	0	(*)	4	10
Iran	154	(*)	44	(D)	(*)	0	(D)	(D)	(D)	(D)	(D)	0	(*)	(*)	(D)
Other and unallocated	141	0	123	(D)	(*)	(*)	5	(D)	0	(D)	0	0	(*)	4	(D)
Other Asia and Pacific	290	2	141	92	5	1	(D)	4	(D)	5	5	(D)	19	9	45
India	(D)	0	(D)	18	(*)	0	8	1	(D)	2	(D)	0	2	(*)	(D)
Indonesia	57	(D)	48	(D)	0	0	0	(D)	0	0	(D)	0	0	0	(D)
Korea	(D)	0	(D)	(D)	0	(D)	0	0	(D)	(D)	(*)	0	1	(D)	(D)
Philippines	46	0	17	16	3	(D)	2	2	(D)	(*)	(*)	(D)	(D)	2	11
Other and unallocated	127	(D)	36	54	1	(D)	35	(D)	1	3	3	(D)	10	(D)	26
International and unallocated	409	--------	229	--------	--------	--------	--------	--------	--------	--------	--------	--------	--------	(*)	180

*Less than $500,000.
D Suppressed to avoid disclosure of data for individual reporters.

1. The property, plant, and equipment expenditures data have been revised back to and including the year 1968 (see text for discussion).

The first step in the benchmarking process was to identify the MOFA's that were in both the sample in 1966 and the benchmark survey universe in 1966. For each such matched affiliate, if the plant and equipment expenditure data from the two surveys were within 10 percent of the data reported in the 1966 census, the census data were accepted as "correct." If they differed by more than 10 percent and if total expenditures by the affiliate were at least $50,000, the discrepancy was investigated further. Consultation with reporters resulted in some changes to the census data; however, more often the 1966 census data were accepted.

The final match showed that in 1966 the sample accounted for 73 percent of total property, plant, and equipment expenditures of all MOFA's (table 4). In terms of number of affiliates, the sample contained 5,800 MOFA's, 28 percent of all MOFA's.

Deriving universe estimates

Revised universe estimates have been

Table 6D.—Estimates of Property, Plant, and Equipment Expenditures by Majority-Owned Foreign Affiliates of U.S. Companies for 1969, by Country and Industry [1]

[Millions of dollars]

Area or country	All industries	Mining and smelting	Petroleum	Manufacturing Total	Food products	Paper and allied products	Chemicals and allied products	Rubber products	Primary and fabricated metals	Machinery (except electrical)	Electrical machinery	Transportation equipment	Other manufacturing	Trade	Other industries
All countries	11,818	1,039	3,712	5,197	362	226	1,129	231	425	1,120	377	780	547	675	1,194
Developed countries	7,839	547	1,919	4,275	278	176	847	165	343	1,054	307	685	422	584	512
Canada	2,508	421	564	1,111	80	81	155	49	106	218	86	229	107	155	257
Europe	4,304	5	992	2,707	164	81	551	105	206	746	195	376	281	380	220
United Kingdom	1,111	0	277	740	39	13	109	38	74	167	51	171	77	50	44
European Economic Community (6)	2,547	(D)	549	1,652	113	62	313	55	108	536	100	195	170	266	(D)
Belgium and Luxembourg	224	0	29	179	8	4	34	12	10	10	(D)	(D)	27	11	6
France	522	0	(D)	320	8	9	26	18	10	159	(D)	(D)	32	105	25
Germany	953	0	159	677	61	6	91	5	64	239	57	123	61	92	(D)
Italy	409	(D)	(D)	249	20	40	22	17	20	98	(D)	(D)	18	37	8
Netherlands	439	0	182	227	16	3	140	3	3	26	3	1	32	22	
Other Europe	645	(D)	166	316	11	6	129	11	25	44	44	10	35	64	(D)
Denmark	42	0	21	8	1		1	(D)	(D)	0	(D)	0	6	(D)	(D)
Ireland	31	(D)	(D)	24	(D)	0	(*)	(*)	0	2	(*)		(D)	(D)	5
Norway	38	(D)	19	12	(*)		(*)		7	(D)	(D)	(D)	(D)	1	23
Spain	227	0	41	157	3	2	108	6	4	16	21	2	2	6	(D)
Sweden	88	0	(D)	41	1	1	5	(*)	(D)	(D)	(D)	(D)	13	8	22
Switzerland	90	0	6	31	(D)		2	(D)	(D)	(D)	(D)	14		31	28
Other	128	3	41	42	2	2	2	2	(D)	(D)	(D)	14	1	(D)	14
Japan	340	0	135	188	5	(D)	77	(D)	(D)	77	16	(*)		8	12	5
Australia, New Zealand, and South Africa	686	122	228	270	29	(D)	64	(D)	(D)	11	10	80	26	37	30
Australia	567	(D)	189	220	(D)	7	59	(D)	30	7	8	73	19	20	(D)
New Zealand	14	0	(D)	5	(D)		1	1	(*)	(D)	(D)	(D)	1	4	(D)
South Africa	106	(D)	(D)	45	(D)	15	4	6	(D)	4	(D)	0	6	13	8
Developing Countries	3,349	492	1,424	922	85	50	281	66	82	66	70	96	126	91	421
Latin America	2,116	451	533	705	76	(D)	196	43	56	60	38	(D)	93	75	352
Latin American Republics	1,840	335	462	693	75	47	189	(D)	55	60	38	(D)	91	72	277
Argentina	202	(D)	47	105	8	1	13	5	5	11	5	44	11	(D)	34
Brazil	344	(D)	(*)	263	7	(D)	120	20	27	34	11	(D)	11	19	50
Chile	292	225	(*)	17	1	(D)	(D)	0	1	0	1	13	(*)	2	47
Colombia	72	1	43	25	6	2	5	(D)	(*)	12	(D)	0	6	2	(*)
Mexico	249	12	2	178	15	33	33	(D)	10	12	16	1	43	25	33
Panama	28	0	23	4	1	(D)	(D)	(D)	(D)	(D)	0	(*)	(*)	(D)	3
Venezuela	73	33	23	13	5	(D)	2	(D)	(D)	0	0	(*)	(*)	6	(D)
Peru	402	(D)	280	46	15	2	6	2	4	1	2	2	13	1	26
Other Central America	95	12	29	28	13	2	5	2	2	0	(D)	0	2	2	44
Other and unallocated	83	(D)	(D)	14	3	(*)	1	0	(D)	(D)	(*)	0	2	3	74
Other Western Hemisphere	277	116	71	12	1	(D)	7	(D)	(*)	(*)	(*)	0	(D)	(D)	57
Bahamas	70	0	10	(D)	(*)	0	0	0	0	0	0	0	0	(*)	2
Bermuda	2	0	(*)	0		0	0	(D)	0	0	(*)	0	0	(D)	(D)
Jamaica	111	95	3	(D)	(D)	(D)	(D)	4	(D)	0	(*)	(D)	0	(D)	(D)
Other and unallocated	93	22	58	2	(D)	(D)	(D)		0	0	(*)	(D)	0	(D)	(D)
Other Africa	600	22	552	10	2	0	2	(D)	(D)	0	0	0	5	2	15
Liberia	18	(D)	2	(D)	0	0	0	0	0	0	0	0	0	(*)	6
Libya	354	0	354	(D)	0	(D)	(D)	0	(*)	0	(*)	0	(D)	(*)	7
Nigeria	85	0	73	5	(*)	0	0	(D)	0	0	(D)	0	(D)	1	(D)
Other and unallocated	143	(D)	123	(D)	2	1	0	(D)	0	(D)	0	(D)	(D)	(D)	
Middle East	242	(*)	154	70	(*)	(*)	67	(D)	(D)	0	(D)	0	(*)	3	14
Iran	101	(*)	34	64	(*)	(*)	(D)	(D)	0	(D)	(D)	0	(*)	3	3
Other and unallocated	140	0	120	6	(*)	(D)	(D)	0	0	0	(*)		11		
Other Asia and Pacific	391	19	185	137	7	(D)	17	23	(D)	(D)	5	31	(D)	28	2	39
India	56	0	(D)	40	(*)	6	(D)	(D)	2	(D)	0	2	(D)	(D)	
Indonesia	81	1	71	(D)	0	0	(D)	0	0	(D)	0	1	(D)	(D)	
Korea	17	0	(D)	14	2	(D)	(D)	2	(*)	(*)	1	(D)	5	(D)	6
Philippines	40	(D)	17	73	4	(*)	6	13	(D)	2	23	(D)	20	(D)	29
Other and unallocated	197	(D)	69											(*)	261
International and unallocated	631	-----	370	-----	-----	-----	-----	-----	-----	-----	-----	-----	-----	-----	-----

*Less than $500,000.
D) Suppressed to avoid disclosure of data for individual reporters.

1. The property, plant, and equipment expenditures data have been revised back to and including the year 1966 (see text for discussion).

computed separately for 616 country-industry data cells (14 industries in each of 44 countries). Previously, estimates were made for 624 country-industry cells (16 industries in each of 39 countries). As outlined in the previous section of this article, estimates have now been made of unreported additions to and deletions

from the universe. Previously, additions and deletions were added or subtracted simply as reported, with no estimates for those unreported.

A standardized test for cells with small samples has now been applied, as described in the previous section of the article. Formerly, adjustment for inadequate coverage in cells where

the reported data were small relative to the universe was done manually without standard guidelines. For the plant and equipment series, the minimum acceptable sample-to-universe percentage coverage has been set at 25 percent, after comparing the results using this percentage with those using other percentages.

Table 6E.—Estimates of Property, Plant, and Equipment Expenditures by Majority-Owned Foreign Affiliates of U.S. Companies for 1970, by Country and Industry [1]

[Millions of dollars]

Area or country	All industries	Mining and smelting	Petroleum	Manufacturing										Trade	Other industries
				Total	Food products	Paper and allied products	Chemicals and allied products	Rubber products	Primary and fabricated metals	Machinery (except electrical)	Electrical machinery	Transportation equipment	Other manufacturing		
All countries	14,346	1,224	3,941	6,701	337	323	1,319	226	712	1,603	501	1,043	635	959	1,521
Developed countries	10,017	683	2,081	5,703	251	291	1,070	156	542	1,504	425	945	519	826	725
Canada	2,903	464	663	1,258	90	145	171	31	83	201	109	302	127	208	310
Europe	5,782	4	1,093	3,794	129	124	726	112	411	1,134	281	543	336	535	355
United Kingdom	1,502	0	328	1,021	37	20	157	19	174	257	56	189	113	82	71
European Economic Community (6)	3,480	(D)	599	2,379	79	97	419	87	204	816	165	337	173	366	(D)
Belgium and Luxembourg	387	0	(D)	299	7	12	77	21	19	(D)	17	(D)	46	16	(D)
France	800	0	(D)	498	(D)	12	35	35	6	241	34	(D)	49	145	(D)
Germany	1,269	0	130	963	32	5	136	(D)	120	(D)	34	214	49	140	36
Italy	801	(D)	180	373	(D)	59	41	23	36	142	71	(D)	13	31	(D)
Netherlands	423	0	131	246	13	9	130	(D)	23	39	10	(D)	16	34	12
Other Europe	799	(D)	167	394	12	6	150	5	33	61	60	17	50	88	(D)
Denmark	47	0	(D)	11	3	(D)	(D)	(D)	(D)	(*)	(D)	(D)	(*)	5	(D)
Ireland	43	0	(D)	38	(D)	0	22	(D)	2	(D)	3	(D)	7	(*)	(D)
Norway	59	(D)	27	24	(*)	(*)	1	0	17	(D)	(D)	0	(D)	(*)	5
Spain	245	(D)	42	157	1	1	110	(D)	2	12	(D)	14	1	(D)	37
Sweden	125	0	26	66	1	(*)	(D)	3	6	42	3	(D)	1	(D)	22
Switzerland	124	0	4	41	(D)	2	(D)	(*)	(D)	42	(D)	(D)	2	11	37
Other	155	2	45	57	3	(D)	3	(D)	(D)	3	22	1	20	42	32
Japan	459	0	157	279	11	7	81	(D)	(D)	(D)	19	(*)	9	17	6
Australia, New Zealand, and South Africa	873	215	168	371	21	14	93	(D)	(D)	(D)	17	100	48	65	54
Australia	700	204	138	292	(D)	13	87	(D)	(D)	(D)	12	90	19	35	32
New Zealand	24	(D)	(D)	6	(D)	(D)	(*)	1	1	0	(*)	(D)	1	7	4
South Africa	149	(D)	(D)	74	8	(D)	5	8	(D)	10	5	(D)	28	23	19
Developing countries	3,549	541	1,431	998	86	33	249	70	170	99	76	98	116	134	446
Latin America	2,176	454	583	688	78	25	157	(D)	79	92	47	(D)	76	94	355
Latin American Republics	1,828	320	473	675	78	(D)	148	35	79	91	(D)	(D)	74	90	269
Argentina	297	(D)	74	134	2	1	16	3	13	25	7	(D)	11	(D)	62
Brazil	290	(D)	(D)	226	12	(D)	73	19	32	49	(D)	(D)	10	20	27
Chile	282	222	(*)	(D)	(*)	(D)	1	2	(*)	1	1	(D)	3	2	(D)
Colombia	71	(*)	34	34	6	6	8	2	1	(D)	(D)	(D)	6	2	1
Mexico	228	(D)	(D)	177	19	8	38	6	24	12	24	15	30	25	18
Panama	33	0	(D)	(D)	1	(D)	(D)	0	0	0	(*)	0	(*)	2	(D)
Peru	75	37	22	7	3	(D)	2	(D)	(D)	0	(D)	(D)	(*)	2	7
Venezuela	365	(D)	244	51	17	2	5	3	6	(*)	2	3	13	(D)	22
Other Central America	104	(D)	32	28	14	(D)	3	(D)	3	0	3	0	(D)	1	(D)
Other and unallocated	83	(D)	(D)	6	3	(*)	(D)	(D)	0	(*)	(*)	0	1	2	30
Other Western Hemisphere	347	135	110	13	(*)	(*)	9	(D)	(*)	(*)	(D)	0	2	4	86
Bahamas	84	0	12	(D)	(*)	0	(D)	0	0	0	0	0	2	(D)	67
Bermuda	3	0	(*)	0	0	0	0	0	0	0	0	0	(D)	(D)	
Jamaica	131	(D)	7	6	(D)	0	0	4	0	0	(*)	0	(D)	(D)	(D)
Other and unallocated	129	(D)	91	(D)	(D)	(D)	(D)	0	(*)	(*)	0	0	(*)	3	11
Other Africa	507	15	441	(D)	1	(D)	(D)	(*)	(D)	0	(D)	0	4	(D)	31
Liberia	25	(D)	2	(*)	0	0	0	0	0	0	0	0	0	(*)	(D)
Libya	209	0	209	0	0	0	(D)	0	0	0	0	0	0	(*)	(D)
Nigeria	135	0	122	(D)	(*)	0	1	0	0	(*)	0	0	0	(D)	8
Other and unallocated	139	(D)	108	(D)	1	(D)	1	1	0	(*)	0	(D)	(D)	3	(D)
Middle East	305	0	145	(D)	(*)	(D)	(D)	(D)	(D)	1	(D)	0	(*)	(D)	20
Iran	85	0	30	(D)	(*)	(D)	(D)	(D)	(D)	(D)	(D)	0	(*)	(D)	4
Other and unallocated	220	0	114	(D)	(*)	(D)	6	(D)	(D)	(D)	0	0	(*)	(D)	17
Other Asia and Pacific	562	72	262	167	7	8	34	34	(D)	6	27	(D)	36	22	39
India	47	0	(D)	42	0	0	(D)	13	(D)	4	(D)	0	2	(*)	(D)
Indonesia	144	(D)	106	(D)	0	0	0	0	0	(*)	(*)	0	(D)	(*)	(D)
Korea	(D)	0	(D)	(D)	(D)	(D)	(D)	(D)	0	(D)	0	(D)	(D)	(D)	(D)
Philippines	(D)	(D)	28	14	2	(D)	1	(D)	(*)	(*)	(D)	(D)	5	5	9
Other and unallocated	277	42	109	82	5	6	8	13	(D)	2	20	(D)	16	28	28
International and unallocated	779	--------	429	--------										(*)	350

* Less than $500,000.
(D) Suppressed to avoid disclosure of data for individual reporters.

1. The property, plant, and equipment expenditures data have been revised back to and including the year 1966 (see text for discussion).

There is no longer any adjustment to eliminate the effect of extreme year-to-year change in the sample data used to calculate universe estimates. Formerly, an attempt was made to adjust for this type of movement, but the method was highly subjective and tests indicated that no adjustment yielded better results.

Bias adjustment of spending projections

As in the past, the data on projected spending presented in this article are adjusted so as to eliminate—or at least reduce—any systemic bias in the four projections obtained for each year (in June and December of the preceding year and June and December

of the year in question, i.e., A, B, C, and D projections).

For the C and D projections, the bias adjustment procedure involves calculating ratios of actual spending (the final, or E, estimate) to the comparable reported expectation for each of the previous 5 years. No bias adjustment is made unless there is

Table 6F.—Estimates of Property, Plant, and Equipment Expenditures by Majority-Owned Foreign Affiliates of U.S. Companies for 1971, by Country and Industry [1]

[Millions of dollars]

Area or country	All industries	Mining and smelting	Petroleum	Manufacturing Total	Food products	Paper and allied products	Chemicals and allied products	Rubber products	Primary and fabricated metals	Machinery (except electrical)	Electrical machinery	Transportation equipment	Other manufacturing	Trade	Other industries
All countries	16,280	1,465	4,959	7,106	324	524	1,397	232	840	1,794	513	889	593	984	1,766
Developed countries	11,464	1,138	2,450	6,216	246	460	1,237	160	661	1,679	443	820	510	802	858
Canada	3,215	827	698	1,153	87	283	154	19	44	222	108	164	70	174	363
Europe	6,646	5	1,406	4,260	132	156	910	124	489	1,209	291	548	402	562	414
United Kingdom	1,685	0	427	1,066	33	(D)	176	(D)	189	311	60	162	99	103	89
European Economic Community (6)	4,102	(D)	757	2,826	86	139	620	93	268	828	161	380	250	391	(D)
Belgium and Luxembourg	531	0	(D)	367	7	15	122	(D)	21	58	28	(D)	52	18	(D)
France	789	0	(D)	505	16	8	67	40	14	(D)	34	(D)	53	150	(D)
Germany	1,675	0	203	1,272	36	7	222	(D)	189	(D)	69	252	119	155	46
Italy	673	(D)	210	412	15	93	66	13	15	155	25	17	13	32	(D)
Netherlands	434	0	101	271	12	17	143	1	29	42	4	10	14	35	27
Other Europe	859	(D)	222	369	13	(D)	115	(D)	31	70	70	6	52	68	(D)
Denmark	54	0	23	5	2	(D)	(D)	(D)	(D)	(D)	(D)	(D)	(*)	(D)	(D)
Ireland	53	0	4	46	(D)	0	30	(D)	1	1	3	(D)	8	(D)	(D)
Norway	114	(D)	76	27	(*)	(D)	(*)	0	17	(D)	(D)	0	(D)	(D)	8
Spain	204	(*)	52	101	3	1	63	(D)	1	14	(D)	4	1	12	38
Sweden	131	0	25	83	2	(*)	(D)	5	10	46	4	(*)	(D)	10	13
Switzerland	118	0	5	41	(D)	2	5	(*)	2	5	(D)	1	19	21	50
Other	184	(D)	36	65	2	(D)	2	(D)	(D)	3	35	1	20	(D)	63
Japan	557	0	197	335	4	10	(D)	(D)	(*)	(D)	30	(*)	8	17	7
Australia, New Zealand, and South Africa	1,046	307	149	468	23	10	(D)	(D)	128	(D)	14	107	30	49	73
Australia	889	297	123	394	17	8	(D)	(*)	127	20	13	87	20	23	52
New Zealand	34	(D)	(D)	9	(D)	(D)	(D)	7	(D)	(D)	(D)	(D)	1	12	4
South Africa	123	(D)	(D)	65	(D)	(D)	(D)	13	(D)	(D)	(D)	(D)	9	13	16
Developing countries	3,633	327	1,740	890	78	65	161	72	178	115	70	69	82	183	493
Latin America	1,987	209	667	648	70	44	134	(D)	90	109	46	(D)	53	130	332
Latin American Republics	1,588	81	527	634	69	(D)	124	33	89	109	(D)	(D)	52	126	219
Argentina	243	3	57	93	4	10	16	2	12	15	10	17	7	32	58
Brazil	353	1	25	271	8	(D)	56	20	55	72	8	(D)	10	31	25
Chile	18	3	4	4	(*)	(D)	(D)	0	0	(D)	(D)	1	(D)	(*)	10
Colombia	84	(*)	(D)	37	4	9	9	4	(D)	(D)	2	(D)	5	6	(D)
Mexico	206	10	(*)	136	18	12	30	4	11	18	18	7	17	33	27
Panama	35	0	10	3	1	(D)	(D)	0	(D)	(D)	(*)	(*)	0	(D)	(D)
Peru	95	(D)	29	8	3	(D)	3	(D)	(D)	6	(D)	(*)	0	(D)	(D)
Venezuela	324	(D)	233	48	16	4	5	1	(D)	(*)	2	2	11	(D)	26
Other Central America	85	14	23	27	13	4	1	(D)	3	(D)	3	0	(D)	2	19
Other and unallocated	144	1	(D)	6	3	(*)	(D)	0	1	(D)	(*)	0	1	2	(D)
Other Western Hemisphere	398	128	140	14	1	(D)	10	(D)	1	(*)	(D)	0	1	4	113
Bahamas	112	0	15	4	(D)	0	(D)	0	0	0	0	0	11	(D)	92
Bermuda	3	0	(*)	0	0	0	0	0	0	0	0	0	0	(D)	(D)
Jamaica	128	(D)	6	8	(D)	0	5	(D)	(D)	(*)	0	0	1	(D)	5
Other and unallocated	155	(D)	119	2	(*)	(D)	(D)	0	(D)	(D)	0	(D)	3	(D)	(D)
Other Africa	444	14	366	(D)	3	(D)	3	(D)	(D)	0	(D)	0	3	(D)	27
Liberia	14	(D)	(D)	(*)	0	0	0	(*)	0	0	(*)	0	5	(*)	5
Libya	65	0	(D)	(D)	0	0	(D)	0	0	0	0	0	0	(*)	0
Nigeria	201	0	186	(D)	(*)	0	(D)	1	0	0	(*)	0	(D)	(D)	9
Other and unallocated	164	(D)	112	28	2	(D)	1	(D)	(D)	0	(D)	0	(D)	(D)	13
Middle East	401	0	251	(D)	(*)	(*)	7	(D)	(D)	(*)	(D)	0	(*)	(D)	71
Iran	48	0	42	1	(*)	0	(D)	(D)	0	0	(D)	0	0	(*)	4
Other and unallocated	353	0	208	(D)	(*)	(*)	17	0	(D)	(*)	0	0	(*)	(D)	66
Other Asia and Pacific	802	104	457	149	6	18	(D)	32	(D)	6	23	(D)	26	(D)	63
India	46	0	(D)	41	(D)	0	4	5	(D)	4	(*)	0	6	(*)	(D)
Indonesia	307	64	220	(D)	0	(D)	(D)	0	0	0	(*)	0	(D)	(D)	4
Korea	19	0	(D)	(D)	0	(*)	(D)	0	(D)	0	0	0	(D)	(D)	(D)
Philippines	57	(D)	(D)	18	3	(D)	(D)	(D)	(*)	(*)	(D)	(D)	5	2	11
Other and unallocated	373	(D)	196	65	(D)	(D)	6	19	(D)	1	17	(D)	12	(D)	47
International and unallocated	1,183	....	769	....	....	....	....	....	....	....	....	....	....	(*)	414

*Less than $500,000.
D Suppressed to avoid disclosure of data for individual reporters.

1. The property, plant, and equipment expenditures data have been revised back to and including the year 1966 (see text for discussion).

a deviation of projection from estimate in the same direction in at least 4 of the 5 years. Also, no adjustment is made to items below $10 million. When an adjustment is necessary under these criteria, the median ratio of actual to expected spending in the 5-year period is applied as an adjustment factor.

The decision as to whether the A and B projections for a given year need adjustment must be made without ratios of actual to expected spending for the preceding year since there are no actual figures yet available for that year. In deriving the bias-adjusted 1974 data (A projections) presented here, the years 1968–1972 were used since

actual data for 1973 are not available. This bias adjustment procedure is the same as that used in the past with two exceptions. First, the adjustment is calculated for all 616 country-industry cells. Previously, the adjustment was made in the same way but for only 138 consolidated data cells. Comparison of the data adjusted at these two levels of

Table 6G.—Estimates of Property, Plant, and Equipment Expenditures by Majority-Owned Foreign Affiliates of U.S. Companies for 1972, by Country and Industry [1]

[Millions of dollars]

Area or country	All indus-tries	Mining and smelt-ing	Petro-leum	Manufacturing										Trade	Other indus-tries
				Total	Food products	Paper and allied products	Chemi-cals and allied products	Rubber products	Primary and fabricated metals	Machin-ery (except electrical)	Electrical machin-ery	Transpor-tation equip-ment	Other manu-facturing		
All countries	17,088	1,249	5,350	7,123	364	586	1,349	413	702	1,716	586	855	552	1,395	1,972
Developed countries	11,728	965	2,507	6,023	279	526	1,159	224	578	1,599	492	697	469	1,228	1,005
Canada	3,596	719	804	1,452	90	281	325	65	61	209	121	213	86	222	400
Europe	6,628	5	1,365	3,830	156	219	648	148	472	1,130	328	391	337	906	523
United Kingdom	1,561	0	413	853	43	(D)	127	(D)	150	266	54	108	77	123	172
European Economic Community (6)	4,148	(D)	682	2,693	101	204	447	121	300	820	213	274	213	660	(D)
Belgium and Luxembourg	468	0	54	380	6	86	93	(D)	7	56	50	(D)	23	23	10
France	1,035	0	(D)	507	23	(D)	61	37	14	226	51	(D)	24	338	(D)
Germany	1,549	0	224	1,114	23	5	139	(D)	234	(D)	79	192	115	177	33
Italy	712	(D)	(D)	481	34	97	74	27	15	188	27	13	7	73	12
Netherlands	385	0	98	212	15	(D)	80	7	29	(D)	7	10	13	49	25
Other Europe	919	(D)	270	283	12	(D)	75	(D)	23	44	61	9	47	123	(D)
Denmark	65	0	23	7	3	(D)	(D)	(D)	(D)	2	(D)	(D)	(*)	(D)	(D)
Ireland	28	0	2	25	(D)	0	10	(D)	(*)	1	3	1	7	(D)	(D)
Norway	119	(D)	97	12	(*)	(D)	(*)	0	7	(D)	(D)	0	(D)	(D)	8
Spain	216	(*)	55	84	(D)	(D)	50	(D)	2	5	(D)	(D)	(D)	30	48
Sweden	114	0	27	54	1	(*)	(*)	5	13	(D)	4	(*)	2	27	6
Switzerland	146	0	6	42	(D)	(*)	6	1	2	5	(D)	1	18	28	69
Other	231	3	60	59	2	1	3	(D)	(D)	6	26	(D)	17	28	80
Japan	566	0	(D)	378	6	16	(D)	(D)	(*)	(D)	22	(*)	10	24	(D)
Australia, New Zealand, and South Africa	937	242	(D)	364	26	9	(D)	(D)	44	(D)	22	93	36	76	(D)
Australia	756	237	155	290	20	(D)	78	(D)	43	28	19	61	29	40	33
New Zealand	39	(D)	(D)	17	(D)	(D)	1	(D)	(D)	(D)	(D)	(D)	1	14	4
South Africa	142	(D)	24	57	(D)	1	11	5	(D)	6	(D)	(D)	6	22	(D)
Developing countries	3,966	284	1,910	1,099	85	61	189	189	125	117	94	157	83	167	507
Latin America	2,090	174	624	880	72	51	160	157	72	107	65	155	42	116	296
Latin American Republics	1,619	97	362	862	71	(D)	146	(D)	71	106	65	155	40	113	184
Argentina	150	2	25	66	5	3	21	3	5	3	6	15	5	16	41
Brazil	598	1	22	498	16	(D)	61	137	42	74	28	(D)	(D)	40	38
Chile	17	3	(*)	3	(*)	(D)	(D)	0	0	0	1	1	(D)	1	10
Colombia	85	(*)	31	48	6	(D)	10	8	(D)	(D)	(D)	(D)	4	5	(*)
Mexico	197	8	(*)	152	13	13	38	3	14	26	20	10	15	25	11
Panama	28	0	11	5	1	0	(D)	0	0	(*)	(*)	0	(D)	7	6
Peru	110	(D)	(D)	8	2	(D)	3	(D)	(D)	(*)	(*)	0	0	3	(D)
Venezuela	273	(D)	163	49	14	4	8	3	4	(*)	4	5	5	13	(D)
Other Central America	58	1	22	25	10	2	1	3	3	(*)	3	0	2	2	8
Other and unallocated	103	1	(D)	8	3	(*)	1	0	3	(*)	(*)	0	1	3	(D)
Other Western Hemisphere	471	77	262	18	1	(D)	13	(D)	1	(*)	(*)	0	2	3	112
Bahamas	213	0	114	6	(*)	0	(D)	0	0	0	0	0	(D)	(*)	93
Bermuda	2	0	(*)	0	0	0	0	0	0	0	0	0	0	(D)	(D)
Jamaica	68	(D)	5	9	(*)	(D)	6	0	(*)	(*)	(*)	0	(D)	(D)	4
Other and unallocated	188	(D)	143	3	(*)	(D)	(D)	0	0	0	0	0	(*)	3	4
Other Africa	384	15	313	31	4	(D)	5	(D)	(D)	0	(D)	(D)	4	5	20
Liberia	14	(D)	3	(D)	0	0	0	(D)	0	0	0	0	0	(*)	4
Libya	99	0	98	(D)	0	0	(D)	0	0	0	0	0	(D)	(D)	0
Nigeria	130	0	115	(D)	(*)	0	(D)	(*)	(*)	0	(*)	0	2	(D)	10
Other and unallocated	141	(D)	97	26	4	(D)	3	(D)	(D)	0	(D)	(D)	1	(D)	6
Middle East	722	0	590	45	(*)	(*)	9	(D)	(D)	(*)	(D)	0	(*)	23	65
Iran	96	0	(D)	(D)	(*)	0	(D)	(D)	(D)	(*)	(D)	0	(*)	(*)	4
Other and unallocated	626	0	(D)	(D)	(*)	(*)	(D)	0	(D)	(*)	0	0	(*)	22	61
Other Asia and Pacific	769	94	382	144	9	(D)	16	11	20	10	29	(D)	37	23	126
India	45	0	(D)	41	(D)	0	5	(D)	19	4	(D)	0	5	(*)	(D)
Indonesia	317	62	231	22	0	(D)	(D)	(D)	0	0	(D)	0	(D)	(D)	(D)
Korea	9	0	(D)	4	(D)	(*)	(D)	(D)	0	0	(D)	0	(D)	(D)	(D)
Philippines	50	0	19	18	5	(*)	3	(D)	(D)	(*)	(*)	(D)	5	4	9
Other and unallocated	349	32	123	59	3	(*)	5	2	(D)	5	19	(D)	22	19	115
International and unallocated	1,394		933											(*)	461

*Less than $500,000.
D Suppressed to avoid disclosure of data for individual reporters.

1. The property, plant, and equipment expenditures data have been revised back to and including the year 1966 (see text for discussion).

consolidation showed only slight differences because data for most major country-industry cells were adjusted separately at both levels.

Second, sample data are used to calculate the ratios over the 5-year period. Previously, the ratios were calculated from universe estimates. Use of the sample data was made necessary because revised universe estimates were not calculated for the projections, only for actual spending. A problem arises in using the sample data, however, because some reporters provide actual data but no projections. Since only data from reporters who give both actual and projected figures can be used to calculate the bias adjustment, the actual

Table 6H.—Estimates of Projected Property, Plant and Equipment Expenditures by Majority-Owned Foreign Affiliates of U.S. Companies for 1973, by Country and Industry [1]

[Millions of dollars]

Area or country	All industries	Mining and smelting	Petroleum	Manufacturing										Trade	Other industries
				Total	Food products	Paper and allied products	Chemicals and allied products	Rubber products	Primary and fabricated metals	Machinery (except electrical)	Electrical machinery	Transportation equipment	Other manufacturing		
All countries	18,995	1,261	6,180	7,743	479	564	1,493	395	649	1,851	849	873	589	1,505	2,306
Developed countries	12,628	881	2,762	6,515	336	523	1,257	253	508	1,701	714	729	494	1,250	1,221
Canada	3,741	534	878	1,659	131	240	448	83	58	204	175	218	103	253	417
Europe	7,123	3	1,506	4,071	167	263	614	155	411	1,223	483	424	332	845	697
United Kingdom	1,852	0	574	830	49	(D)	127	(D)	96	261	53	124	72	104	343
European Economic Community (6)	4,216	(D)	682	2,830	104	226	391	126	290	909	318	247	217	611	(D)
Belgium and Luxembourg	533	0	73	415	4	76	73	16	8	107	53	(D)	(D)	34	11
France	1,032	0	(D)	526	16	35	45	52	10	216	65	25	61	305	(D)
Germany	1,563	0	211	1,185	29	9	166	11	230	(D)	138	163	(D)	134	33
Italy	672	(D)	(D)	447	66	102	36	33	11	176	33	(D)	(D)	83	6
Netherlands	415	0	85	257	19	5	72	15	31	(D)	28	9	(D)	55	18
Other Europe	1,056	(D)	250	412	14	(D)	96	(D)	25	53	111	53	42	130	(D)
Denmark	53	0	19	8	(D)	(D)	(D)	(D)	(D)	1	(D)	(D)	(D)	(D)	(D)
Ireland	33	0	3	27	(D)	0	(D)	(*)	(D)	1	(D)	(D)	1	(D)	(D)
Norway	137	(D)	111	16	(*)	(D)	1	0	10	(D)	(D)	0	(D)	(D)	(D)
Spain	284	(*)	41	138	2	(D)	55	(D)	3	4	(D)	47	(D)	40	65
Sweden	111	0	18	63	1	1	(D)	7	7	(D)	3	(*)	2	25	5
Switzerland	219	0	8	84	(D)	(*)	8	1	3	6	(D)	3	25	38	88
Other	219	(D)	49	77	2	2	6	(D)	(D)	8	39	(D)	13	(D)	73
Japan	755	0	(D)	461	4	4	136	(D)	3	(D)	35	(*)	24	(D)	14
Australia, New Zealand, and South Africa	1,008	344	(D)	324	34	17	59	(D)	36	(D)	21	87	36	(D)	91
Australia	792	335	132	246	29	16	49	(D)	35	(D)	19	57	25	48	32
New Zealand	35	(D)	(D)	14	(D)	(D)	2	(D)	(D)	(D)	1	(D)	1	(D)	5
South Africa	181	(D)	(D)	65	(D)	(D)	8	9	(D)	(D)	2	(D)	9	13	54
Developing countries	4,367	380	1,981	1,228	143	41	236	142	142	150	135	144	95	255	522
Latin America	2,333	187	610	1,007	128	36	204	124	90	132	97	132	65	199	330
Latin American Republics	1,847	127	348	983	126	(D)	187	(D)	89	132	97	132	62	195	194
Argentina	168	3	20	90	7	4	19	3	7	6	5	32	7	29	27
Brazil	662	1	35	525	22	(D)	107	97	52	101	(D)	80	7	69	32
Chile	19	3	(*)	5	(*)	(*)	(D)	0	0	0	1	(D)	(D)	1	10
Colombia	65	(*)	21	38	6	(D)	7	(D)	(D)	(D)	2	(D)	2	5	1
Mexico	247	9	1	173	27	5	31	7	16	20	30	12	26	42	22
Panama	37	0	6	6	2	0	(D)	0	0	(D)	(D)	0	(D)	5	19
Peru	185	(D)	69	9	1	(D)	4	(D)	(D)	1	(D)	(*)	0	15	(D)
Venezuela	287	(D)	133	88	38	4	10	8	5	(*)	3	6	13	21	(D)
Other Central America	72	2	21	32	19	2	1	1	3	(*)	4	0	1	5	12
Other and unallocated	104	(D)	42	16	5	(*)	1	0	4	(*)	2	0	4	4	(D)
Other western hemisphere	486	60	262	24	2	(D)	17	(D)	1	(*)	(*)	0	2	4	137
Bahamas	196	0	75	7	(*)	0	(D)	0	0	0	0	0	0	(D)	114
Bermuda	(*)	0	(*)	0	0	0	0	0	0	0	0	0	(D)	(D)	(D)
Jamaica	45	(D)	5	13	0	2	0	8	(D)	(*)	(*)	0	(D)	(D)	7
Other and unallocated	245	(D)	182	4	(*)	(D)	(D)	0	(*)	(*)	0	(*)	0	2	(D)
Other Africa	359	14	287	24	5	(*)	5	(D)	(D)	0	(D)	(D)	1	7	27
Liberia	22	(D)	4	(*)	0	0	0	(*)	(D)	0	0	0	0	(*)	(D)
Libya	91	0	91	(D)	(D)	0	(D)	0	0	0	0	0	0	(D)	0
Nigeria	96	0	78	(D)	(*)	0	3	(D)	(*)	0	(*)	0	(D)	(D)	12
Other and unallocated	150	(D)	113	19	5	(*)	(*)	(D)	(D)	0	(D)	(D)	(D)	(D)	(D)
Middle East	796	0	683	33	1	(*)	4	(D)	(D)	(*)	(D)	0	(*)	25	55
Iran	79	0	(D)	(D)	(*)	0	(D)	(D)	0	(D)	(D)	0	0	(*)	(D)
Other and unallocated	718	0	(D)	(D)	1	(*)	(D)	(D)	0	(D)	(*)	0	(*)	25	(D)
Other Asia and Pacific	878	180	401	164	8	6	23	(D)	24	18	37	(D)	29	24	110
India	61	0	(D)	55	(*)	0	9	(D)	23	9	(D)	0	2	(D)	(*)
Indonesia	466	150	282	32	0	(D)	(D)	(D)	(D)	0	(D)	0	(D)	(D)	(D)
Korea	8	0	(D)	4	(D)	(*)	(D)	0	(D)	0	(*)	0	1	(*)	(D)
Philippines	57	0	17	25	(D)	(*)	2	3	(*)	(*)	1	(D)	4	6	9
Other and unallocated	285	29	92	48	2	(D)	9	(D)	(D)	8	21	(D)	(D)	17	98
International and unallocated	2,001	....	1,438	....	....	....	....	....	....	....	....	....	....	(*)	563
Addendum: European Economic Community (9)[2]	6,154	(D)	1,278	3,695	159	259	535	142	387	1,172	375	372	290	722	457

* Less than $500,000.
D Suppressed to avoid disclosure of data for individual reporters.
1. The property, plant, and equipment expenditures data have been revised back to and including the year 1966 (see text for discussion).

2. The "European Economic Community (9)" includes the "European Economic Community (6)", the United Kingdom, Denmark, and Ireland.

data which are usable are sometimes only a small portion of the total actual data of the sample. Thus, a test for adequacy of coverage was adopted. If in any year the actual data used are less than 25 percent of the total actual data reported, then no bias adjustment is made to the projection for that cell.

As a result of bias adjustment, projected total plant and equipment spending was reduced by 9 percent for 1973 and 3 percent for 1974 relative to the estimates before adjustment. The differences by major industry are shown in table 5.

Table 6I.—Estimates of Projected Property, Plant, and Equipment Expenditures by Majority-Owned Foreign Affiliates of U.S. Companies for 1974, by Country and Industry [1]

[Millions of dollars]

Area or country	All industries	Mining and smelting	Petroleum	Manufacturing										Trade	Other industries
				Total	Food products	Paper and allied products	Chemicals and allied products	Rubber products	Primary and fabricated metals	Machinery (except electrical)	Electrical machinery	Transportation equipment	Other manufacturing		
All countries	21,419	1,102	7,707	8,306	431	481	1,572	425	600	2,090	875	1,135	698	1,775	2,528
Developed countries	14,195	662	3,684	6,987	295	428	1,301	273	521	1,899	776	922	571	1,454	1,408
Canada	3,979	304	1,097	1,670	105	190	435	127	45	210	165	267	126	367	539
Europe	8,181	(D)	2,083	4,395	171	215	679	125	395	1,311	549	557	394	929	(D)
United Kingdom	2,296	0	769	1,017	46	57	117	23	100	232	61	201	114	156	354
European Economic Community (6)	4,824	(*)	889	2,910	106	151	462	92	206	1,024	328	302	239	613	113
Belgium and Luxembourg	585	0	150	392	4	39	81	(D)	25	91	34	(D)	51	31	12
France	1,062	0	(D)	683	20	27	65	(D)	11	(D)	71	17	69	271	(D)
Germany	1,736	0	291	1,251	38	4	213	5	121	401	184	194	92	161	33
Italy	672	(*)	153	425	23	78	40	(D)	6	(D)	27	(D)	7	90	5
Netherlands	470	0	(D)	259	20	4	63	(D)	45	(D)	13	27	20	60	(D)
Other Europe	1,360	(D)	426	469	20	7	100	10	23	56	159	54	42	160	(D)
Denmark	67	0	(D)	12	(D)	(D)	(D)	(D)	(D)	2	(D)	(D)	(*)	8	(D)
Ireland	29	0	(D)	20	(D)	0	(D)	(D)	(D)	1	(D)	(D)	1	(*)	(D)
Norway	268	(D)	237	15	(*)	(D)	1	0	7	(D)	(D)	0	(D)	2	(D)
Spain	356	(*)	71	154	2	(D)	57	(D)	3	4	(D)	47	(D)	50	81
Sweden	125	0	15	73	(D)	2	18	5	7	(D)	5	(*)	2	32	4
Switzerland	213	0	10	101	2	(*)	(D)	1	5	6	55	2	(D)	31	71
Other	303	1	59	94	3	2	9	(D)	(D)	9	49	(D)	14	37	111
Japan	955	0	280	575	4	4	151	(D)	12	(D)	41	(*)	11	85	14
Australia, New Zealand, and South Africa	1,081	(D)	223	346	15	19	37	(D)	69	(D)	22	98	40	73	(D)
Australia	881	347	180	277	(D)	18	27	(D)	68	16	20	82	32	43	35
New Zealand	35	(D)	(D)	12	(D)	(D)	1	(D)	1	(D)	(*)	(D)	2	14	5
South Africa	165	(D)	(D)	58	3	(D)	9	15	1	(D)	(D)	(D)	7	17	(D)
Developing countries	5,263	440	2,643	1,319	136	54	270	152	78	191	99	212	127	321	540
Latin America	2,571	288	622	1,066	120	44	232	129	43	176	69	182	72	232	363
Latin American Republics	2,039	204	334	1,046	119	(D)	217	(D)	42	176	69	182	70	229	226
Argentina	184	2	24	90	6	1	16	10	7	7	8	26	10	30	37
Brazil	734	1	36	567	20	(D)	118	99	20	135	35	(D)	(D)	85	45
Chile	20	3	(*)	5	0	(*)	(D)	0	0	0	(D)	(D)	(D)	1	11
Colombia	62	(*)	18	37	5	9	7	6	2	(D)	(D)	(D)	6	1	1
Mexico	308	8	1	215	34	12	57	6	5	29	16	33	22	57	26
Panama	22	0	6	4	2	0	(D)	0	0	(*)	1	0	(D)	6	6
Peru	260	(D)	78	10	2	2	(D)	4	(D)	(D)	(D)	(*)	0	4	(D)
Venezuela	291	16	134	80	34	3	9	4	3	(*)	(D)	4	20	34	27
Other Central America	59	2	17	26	13	1	1	(D)	1	(*)	4	0	2	3	10
Other and unallocated	98	(D)	18	11	4	(*)	1	0	1	0	(*)	0	5	2	(D)
Other Western Hemisphere	532	84	289	20	(*)	(D)	16	(D)	1	(*)	(*)	0	2	3	136
Bahamas	211	0	88	7	(D)	0	(D)	0	0	0	0	0	1	(*)	116
Bermuda	(*)	0	(*)	0	0	0	0	0	0	0	0	0	0	(D)	(D)
Jamaica	31	(D)	6	11	(D)	0	8	(D)	(*)	(*)	(*)	0	1	(D)	4
Other and unallocated	289	(D)	194	2	(*)	(D)	(D)	0	0	(*)	(*)	0	(*)	1	(D)
Other Africa	411	9	349	19	5	(*)	(D)	(D)	1	0	(D)	(D)	1	7	28
Liberia	22	(D)	5	(*)	0	0	0	(*)	0	0	0	0	0	(D)	10
Libya	106	0	105	(D)	0	0	(D)	0	0	0	0	0	0	(D)	c
Nigeria	148	0	130	(D)	(*)	0	(*)	3	(*)	(*)	(*)	0	1	(D)	13
Other and unallocated	135	(D)	108	13	5	(D)	(D)	(D)	1	0	(D)	(D)	(D)	(D)	6
Middle East	946	0	842	24	(*)	(*)	12	(D)	(D)	(*)	(D)	0	(*)	28	52
Iran	92	0	(D)	(D)	(*)	(*)	(D)	(D)	(D)	(*)	(D)	0	(*)	(*)	5
Other and unallocated	854	0	(D)	(D)	(*)	(*)	(*)	0	(D)	(*)	0	0	(*)	27	46
Other Asia and Pacific	1,336	144	830	210	11	10	(D)	20	(D)	24	15	29	(D)	53	97
India	64	0	9	55	0	0	9	(D)	24	5	(D)	0	2	(*)	(*)
Indonesia	919	120	751	(D)	0	4	3	(D)	0	(D)	0	0	1	0	(D)
Korea	9	0	(D)	(D)	(*)	(*)	(D)	0	(D)	(*)	(*)	(D)	(D)	5	10
Philippines	76	0	(D)	(D)	9	2	4	3	(*)	(*)	9	21	(D)	50	85
Other and unallocated	268	23	50	59	2	5	5	1	(D)	(D)	(D)	(D)	(D)	(*)	580
International and unallocated	1,960		1,380											(*)	580
Addendum: European Economic Community (9)[2]	6,916	(*)	1,692	3,959	164	(D)	586	115	373	1,259	393	506	354	777	489

*Less than $500,000.
D Suppressed to avoid disclosure of data for individual reporters.
1. The property plant, and equipment expenditures data have been revised back to and including the year 1966 (see text for discussion).
2. The "European Economic Community (9)" includes the "European Economic Community (6)," the United Kingdom, Denmark, and Ireland.

U.S. DIRECT INVESTMENT ABROAD
IN 1973

J[ulius] N. Freidlin
and
L[eonard] A. Lupo

By J. N. FREIDLIN and L. A. LUPO

U.S. Direct Investment Abroad in 1973

THIS article presents estimates of the U.S. direct investment position abroad at yearend 1973 and the associated earnings, balance of payments receipts, and net capital outflows during that year.[1] It also discusses the net impact on the U.S. balance of payments of identifiable U.S. corporate transactions, and examines various measures of return on U.S. direct investment abroad.

1. The Technical Notes at the end of this article describe the derivation of these estimates from sample data and define key terms. The previous article in this annual series, "U.S. Direct Investment Abroad in 1972," was published in the September 1973 SURVEY. The articles present changes in accounts of a U.S. direct investor with its own foreign affiliates; they do not present income statements or other accounts of the foreign affiliates. For example, *earnings* in this article refers to the U.S. direct investor's share in the earnings of its foreign affiliates, not to total earnings of its affiliates. The most recent BEA data on foreign affiliate accounts were published in the *Special Survey of U.S. Multinational Companies, 1970*. That special survey, which drew data for 1966 and 1970 from a small sample of reporters, is available from the National Technical Information Service, U.S. Department of Commerce, Springfield, Virginia 22151. Price $3.00. Quote Accession Number COM-72 11392 when ordering.

Highlights

The value of the U.S. direct investment position abroad was $107.3 billion at yearend 1973, an increase of $12.9 billion, or 14 percent, from 1972. The large addition comprised reinvested earnings of $8.1 billion, up 72 percent

NOTE.—Richard L. Smith and Gregory G. Fouch supervised preparation of the direct investment estimates with assistance from John W. Rutter and Ralph Kozlow.

CHART 2

Annual Additions to Direct Investment Abroad by Major Area and by Industry

(Ratio scale)

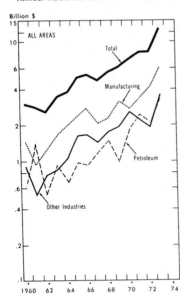
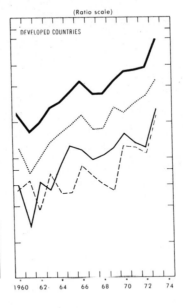
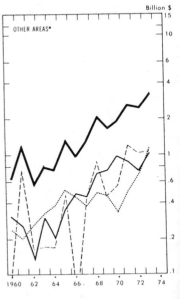

*Includes developing countries, international and unallocated.

U.S. Department of Commerce, Bureau of Economic Analysis

14-8-7

Table 1.—Addition to U.S. Direct Investment Position and Components of Financing

[Millions of dollars]

Line	Item, year, and change from previous year	All areas				Developed countries				Other areas [1]			
		All industries	Petroleum	Manufacturing	Other	All industries	Petroleum	Manufacturing	Other	All industries	Petroleum	Manufacturing	Other
	Direct investment position: [2]												
1	Addition in 1973 [p]	12,930	3,305	6,074	3,551	9,726	2,244	4,952	2,529	3,205	1,060	1,122	1,022
2	Addition in 1972 [r]	8,140	2,111	4,084	1,945	5,676	1,085	3,373	1,218	2,465	1,025	712	728
3	Change, 1972–73 [r]	4,790	1,194	1,990	1,606	4,050	1,159	1,579	1,311	740	35	410	294
4	Change, 1971–72	120	−327	713	−265	249	−150	506	−107	−128	−178	208	−158
	Net capital outflows: [3]												
5	1973 [p]	4,872	1,417	1,820	1,635	3,631	1,053	1,354	1,224	1,241	364	467	411
6	1972 [r]	3,517	1,603	1,100	815	1,988	693	832	464	1,529	910	267	351
7	Change, 1972–73	1,355	−186	721	820	1,642	360	522	760	−288	−547	199	60
8	Change, 1971–72	−1,426	−347	−456	−621	−1,000	−283	−487	−230	−426	−65	29	−391
	Reinvested earnings: [4]												
9	1973 [p]	8,124	1,927	4,408	1,788	6,147	1,166	3,741	1,240	1,977	761	668	548
10	1972 [r]	4,715	563	2,991	1,161	3,710	424	2,537	750	1,004	140	454	411
11	Change, 1972–73	3,409	1,364	1,418	627	2,437	742	1,204	491	973	621	214	137
12	Change, 1971–72	1,558	63	1,137	358	1,273	173	972	128	285	−109	165	229
	Adjustments: [5]												
13	Change, 1972–73	26	17	−149	158	−29	56	−145	61	55	−38	−3	97
14	Change, 1971–72	−12	−44	33	1	−24	−39	19	−5	12	−6	13	5

[r] Revised.   [p] Preliminary.
1. Includes developing countries, international and unallocated.
2. Lines 1 and 2 correspond to appropriate column detail for line 3 in table 2.
3. Lines 5 and 6 correspond to changes in the appropriate column detail for line 4 in table 2.
4. Lines 9 and 10 correspond to changes in the appropriate column detail for line 5 in table 2.
5. Lines 13 and 14 correspond to changes in the appropriate column detail for line 6 in table 2.
Note.—Details may not add to totals because of rounding.

Table 2.—Identifiable U.S. Corporate Transactions With Foreigners [1]

[Millions of dollars, balance of payments signs: debits (−), credits (+)]

Line	Item	All areas			Developed countries			Other areas [2]			Change, 1972–73		
		1971 [r]	1972 [r]	1973 [p]	1971 [r]	1972 [r]	1973 [p]	1971 [r]	1972 [r]	1973 [p]	All areas	Developed countries	Other areas
1	Net flow [3]	3,994	7,607	7,092	2,266	5,125	2,930	1,728	2,482	4,162	−515	−2,195	1,680
2	Change in corporate claims on foreigners	−9,037	−9,765	−15,649	−6,036	−6,640	−11,540	−3,001	−3,126	−4,109	−5,884	−4,900	−983
3	Addition to direct investment position	−8,020	−8,140	−12,930	−5,427	−5,676	−9,726	−2,593	−2,465	−3,204	−4,790	−4,050	−739
4	Net capital outflows	−4,943	−3,517	−4,872	−2,988	−1,988	−3,631	−1,955	−1,529	−1,241	−1,355	−1,643	288
5	Reinvested earnings	−3,157	−4,715	−8,124	−2,437	−3,710	−6,147	−720	−1,005	−1,977	−3,409	−2,437	−972
6	Valuation adjustment [4]	80	92	66	−1	23	52	81	69	14	−26	29	−55
7	Change in other corporate claims	−1,017	−1,625	−2,719	−600	−964	−1,814	−408	−661	−905	−1,094	−850	−244
8	Long-term [5]	−168	−253	−464	−98	−156	−276	−70	97	−188	−211	−120	−91
	Short-term:												
9	Liquid	−531	−505	−841	−404	−277	−565	−127	−228	−276	−336	−288	−48
10	Nonliquid [5]	−496	−214	−1,413	−266	−172	−972	−230	−42	−441	−1,199	−800	−399
11	Adjustments [4]	178	−653	−1	159	−359	−1	19	−294	....	652	358	294
12	Change in corporate liabilities to foreigners	1,846	3,580	2,207	1,564	3,224	1,671	282	356	536	−1,373	−1,553	180
13	New issues of securities sold abroad by U.S. corporations [6]	1,181	2,002	1,222	1,181	2,002	1,222	....	....	....	−780	−780	....
14	Change in corporate liabilities other than new issues	665	1,578	985	383	1,222	449	282	356	536	−593	−773	180
15	Long-term	384	594	264	289	561	118	95	33	146	−330	−443	113
16	Short-term [5]	22	160	943	−162	10	553	184	150	390	783	543	240
17	Adjustments [4]	259	824	−222	256	651	−222	3	173	....	−1,046	−873	−173
18	Direct investors' ownership benefits	11,702	14,055	20,377	7,152	8,856	12,628	4,550	5,200	7,749	6,322	3,772	2,549
19	Receipts on U.S. direct investments	8,545	9,340	12,253	4,715	5,146	6,481	3,830	4,195	5,772	2,913	1,335	1,577
20	Royalties and fees	2,160	2,415	2,838	1,594	1,816	2,182	566	600	656	423	366	56
21	Dividends and interest	4,174	4,548	5,327	2,648	2,899	3,637	1,526	1,649	1,690	779	738	41
22	Branch earnings [7]	2,211	2,377	4,088	473	431	662	1,738	1,946	3,426	1,711	231	1,480
23	Reinvested earnings	3,157	4,715	8,124	2,437	3,710	6,147	720	1,005	1,977	3,409	2,437	972
24	Offset to adjustments [4]	−517	−263	137	−414	−315	171	−103	52	−14	420	486	−66

[r] Revised.   [p] Preliminary.
1. Some balance of payments flows associated with U.S. corporate transactions are not separately identified in the U.S. balance of payments data and therefore are not reflected in the estimates given in this table. See text for further explanation. Claims and liabilities of U.S. banking and brokerage institutions are excluded.
2. Includes developing countries, international and unallocated.
3. Sum of lines 2+12+18+24.
4. These adjustments plus balance of payments flows are equal to the changes in the international investment position. Such adjustments do not enter the balance of payments flow figures. Line 24 is the sum of lines 6, 11, and 17, with sign reversed.
5. Excludes brokerage claims and liabilities.
6. Excludes funds obtained abroad by U.S. corporations through bank loans and other credits and also excludes securities issued by subsidiaries incorporated abroad. However, securities issued by finance subsidiaries incorporated in the Netherlands Antilles are treated as if they had been issued by U.S. corporations to the extent that the proceeds of such issues are transferred to U.S. parent companies.
7. Petroleum branch earnings have been revised as described in the Technical Notes.
Note.—Details may not add to totals because of rounding.

from 1972, and net capital outflows of $4.9 billion, up 39 percent. Valuation adjustments were small.

For the second consecutive year, re-invested earnings accounted for a larger share of the addition to the U.S. direct investment position in foreign-incorporated affiliates than did net capital outflows. This differs markedly from earlier experience, when net capital outflows usually exceeded reinvested earnings.[2]

The large increase in reinvested earnings resulted from an unusual increase in foreign-incorporated affiliate earnings and a sharp decrease in the proportion of their earnings paid out as dividends. Direct investors' earnings from their foreign-incorporated affiliates—comprising reinvested earnings, dividends, and foreign withhold-

---

2. None of the reinvested earnings stems from branch earnings because the U.S. balance of payments accounts treat branch earnings as entirely remitted to the United States. However, some U.S. income received from branches may be returned to them as a net capital outflow.

Table 3.—Dividend Payout Ratios of Foreign-Incorporated Affiliates

[Millions of dollars, or ratios]

Item and industry	All areas			Developed countries			Other areas [1]		
	1971	1972 r	1973 p	1971	1972 r	1973 p	1971	1972 r	1973 p
All industries:									
Earnings	7,178	9,109	13,407	4,941	6,449	9,669	2,238	2,660	3,738
Gross dividends	4,022	4,394	5,283	2,504	2,739	3,522	1,518	1,655	1,761
Ratio, gross dividends to earnings	.56	.48	.39	.51	.43	.36	.68	.62	.47
Petroleum:									
Earnings	1,554	1,811	3,239	470	616	1,507	1,085	1,196	1,733
Gross dividends	1,054	1,248	1,312	219	192	340	836	1,056	972
Ratio, gross dividends to earnings	.68	.69	.40	.47	.31	.23	.77	.88	.56
Manufacturing:									
Earnings	3,736	5,074	7,156	3,149	4,302	6,110	588	772	1,046
Gross dividends	1,882	2,083	2,748	1,584	1,765	2,369	299	318	379
Ratio, gross dividends to earnings	.50	.41	.38	.50	.41	.39	.51	.41	.36
Other:									
Earnings	1,888	2,223	3,011	1,322	1,531	2,052	566	693	959
Gross dividends	1,085	1,063	1,223	700	782	812	384	281	410
Ratio, gross dividends to earnings	.57	.48	.41	.53	.51	.40	.68	.41	.43

r Revised.   p Preliminary.
1. Includes developing countries, international and unallocated.
NOTE.—Details may not add to totals because of rounding.
Reported earnings are also equal to the sum of dividends, foreign withholding taxes, and reinvested earnings.
Estimates are drawn from table 12. Gross dividends exclude preferred dividends, but include foreign withholding taxes.

ing taxes—were $13.4 billion in 1973, a $4.3 billion or 47 percent increase over 1972. Almost 80 percent of this increase was reinvested as the overall dividend payout ratio of incorporated affiliates fell to 0.39 compared with 0.48 in 1972.

The growth in earnings probably stemmed from three factors: The February 1973 dollar devaluation, which

---

CHART 3

Adjusted Earnings by Major Area and by Industry[1]

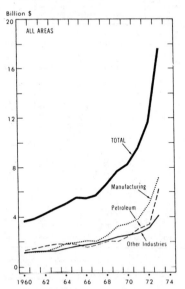
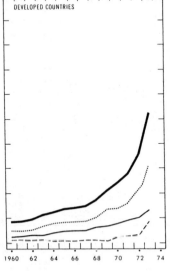
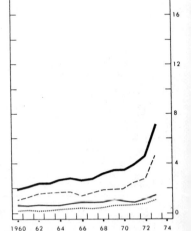

1. Adjusted earnings data are given in table 12.
2. Includes developing countries, international and unallocated.

SURVEY OF CURRENT BUSINESS

increased the value of affiliates' foreign currency earnings when translated into dollars; a high level of economic activity during most of the year, coupled with rapid price increases, which raised affiliates' book profits; and the petroleum supply situation, which had been tightening for some months prior to the fourth-quarter Arab production cutback, and which resulted in higher per-barrel product prices and higher profits of petroleum affiliates.

The decline in the payout ratio was partly attributable to the dollar devaluations, which reduced the portion of affiliates' foreign currency earnings needed to maintain their dollar remittances to U.S. direct investors. Also, the high rate of inflation raised costs of affiliates' investment projects, thereby increasing their requirements for financing, including reinvested earnings. Finally, some of the increase in affiliates' earnings represented exceptional book profits on inventories, again related to inflation. Part of these inventory profits may not have been regarded as available for distribution to stockholders.

The 1973 earnings of foreign branches, mainly in extractive industries, were $4.1 billion, up 72 percent from 1972. This increase resulted from the same factors as did the rise in earnings of incorporated affiliates. Combined earnings of branches and incorporated affiliates totaled $17.5 billion, a 52 percent increase over 1972.

Adjusted earnings were $17.5 billion in 1973, up $5.9 billion or 51 percent from 1972. This may be a more appropriate measure of return from the viewpoint of the direct investor than the conventional accounting concept of earnings used above. Adjusted earnings are defined as the sum of a direct investor's share in earnings of affiliates, plus interest receipts from affiliates, less foreign withholding taxes. Because interest receipts about offset foreign withholding taxes in 1973, the earnings and adjusted earnings totals were virtually identical. The adjusted earnings rate of return on U.S. direct investment was a record 17.4 percent, compared with the previous high of 12.9 percent in 1972.

Growth in U.S. Direct Investment Abroad

Table 1 and chart 2 show annual additions to the U.S. direct investment position by major area and industry categories.[3] There were record increases in

3. The annual addition estimates can be obtained in two ways: (i) by subtracting the book value (of the U.S. direct investment position abroad) at the end of one year from the book value at the end of the next year, using the estimates of book value in table 9; or (ii) by adding up the three components—net capital outflows, reinvested earnings, and valuation adjustments—of the annual addition. These three components are, respectively, lines 4, 5, and 6 of table 2.

Table 4.—Reinvested Earnings in and Net Capital Outflows to Foreign-Incorporated Affiliates

[Millions of dollars, or ratios]

Item and industry	All areas			Developed countries			Other areas [1]		
	1971	1972 r	1973 p	1971	1972 r	1973 p	1971	1972 r	1973 p
All industries:									
Total [2]	7,057	6,915	11,672	5,026	5,136	9,138	2,031	1,779	2,535
Reinvested earnings	3,157	4,715	8,124	2,437	3,710	6,147	720	1,005	1,977
Net capital outflows	3,900	2,201	3,548	2,589	1,426	2,991	1,311	774	558
Ratio, reinvested earnings to total	.45	.68	.70	.48	.72	.67	.35	.56	.78
Petroleum, total [3]	1,921	1,550	2,542	1,139	1,070	1,968	782	481	574
Reinvested earnings	500	563	1,027	251	424	1,166	249	140	761
Net capital outflows	1,421	987	615	888	646	802	533	341	−187
Ratio, reinvested earnings to total	.26	.36	.76	.22	.40	.59	.32	.29	
Manufacturing, total [2]	3,360	4,000	6,145	2,850	3,306	5,011	510	694	1,135
Reinvested earnings	1,854	2,991	4,408	1,565	2,537	3,741	289	454	668
Net capital outflows	1,506	1,009	1,736	1,285	769	1,270	221	240	467
Ratio, reinvested earnings to total	.55	.75	.72	.55	.77	.75	.57	.65	.59
Other, total [3]	1,774	1,367	2,985	1,036	762	2,158	738	604	826
Reinvested earnings	803	1,161	1,788	621	749	1,240	182	411	548
Net capital outflows	971	206	1,197	415	13	918	556	193	278
Ratio, reinvested earnings to total	.45	.85	.60	.60	.98	.57	.25	.68	.66

r Revised. p Preliminary.
1. Includes developing countries, international and unallocated.
2. Separate data for valuation adjustments, the remaining component of the addition to the U.S. direct investment position, are not available for foreign incorporated affiliates, so that the total lines do not exactly measure the addition to U.S direct investment. These adjustments (covering branches as well as incorporated affiliates) totaled $66 million in 1973, as given in line 6 of table 2.
NOTE.—Details may not add to totals because of rounding.

Table 5.—Net Capital Outflows by Industry, Area, and Type of Capital

[Millions of dollars, not seasonally adjusted]

Item	1971	1972 r	1973 p				
			Year	I	II	III	IV
Net capital outflows	4,943	3,517	4,872	2,445	943	510	974
To foreign-incorporated affiliates	3,898	2,201	3,548	1,858	321	719	650
Short-term intercompany accounts [1]	1,241	200	1,719	1,549	52	370	−190
Petroleum	822	668	516	346	−17	86	101
Manufacturing	296	−120	645	444	9	204	−72
Finance and insurance	13	−315	253	349	−36	101	−161
Other [2]	109	−33	305	347	96	−80	−58
Other [3]	2,656	2,001	1,829	371	270	348	841
Petroleum	599	319	99	152	−53	−55	56
Manufacturing	1,210	1,129	1,092	124	445	140	384
Finance and insurance	505	138	411	66	−10	164	192
Other [2]	344	416	228	30	−112	100	209
To branches [4]	1,045	1,317	1,324	587	622	−209	324
Petroleum	529	616	802	481	505	−321	137
Manufacturing	50	91	84	8	42	2	32
Finance and insurance	42	120	158	54	6	30	68
Other [2]	423	490	280	44	69	80	86
Of which, short-term intercompany accounts with developed areas [1]	720	−106	1,426	1,348	26	87	−35
Petroleum	417	427	599	401	−23	−79	301
Manufacturing	281	−109	448	402	−1	157	−111
Finance and insurance	−35	−300	160	301	−36	6	−111
Other [2]	59	−124	219	244	86	3	−114

r Revised. p Preliminary.
1. Calculated as the change in the amount outstanding from the beginning to the end of the accounting period. Each category reflects (i) transactions that result in net capital outflows from the United States, less (ii) conversions of outstanding short-term claims into long-term or equity claims, plus (iii) conversions of long-term claims or equity into short term. None of these conversions has a net effect on the balance of payments.
2. "Other" industries include all industries other than those listed, the major ones being mining and smelting, trade, agriculture, public utilities, and services.
3. "Other" types of capital outflows to foreign-incorporated affiliates reflect changes in long-term intercompany accounts; acquisition of capital stock of existing and newly established foreign companies in transactions with affiliated and unaffiliated foreigners; partial or total sales or liquidations of capital stock and other equity holdings; and verified transactions of nonreporters, which are not classified by type. This category includes transactions which result in net capital outflows plus conversions as described in footnote 1.
4. "Branches" include any unincorporated foreign affiliates. Detail on the term structure of this line is not available.

NOTE.—Details may not add to totals because of rounding.

1973 in each of the industry groups shown: petroleum, $3.3 billion, or 13 percent; in manufacturing, $6.1 billion, or 15 percent; and in the "other industries" category (mostly mining and smelting, trade, finance and insurance, public utilities, and agriculture), $3.6 billion, or 13 percent. Of the $12.9 billion total addition to the direct investment position, petroleum accounted for 26 percent, manufacturing for 47 percent, and "other industries" for 27 percent.

By area, developed countries accounted for $9.7 billion, or 75 percent of the total addition, a percentage which has been rising in recent years as the U.S. direct investment position in developed countries has grown faster than in other areas. The difference in the rate of growth reflects the greater weight of manufacturing in developed countries and the fact that, in each area, investment in manufacturing grew faster than the all-industry average.

Petroleum

Of the 1973 addition to petroleum direct investment, $2.2 billion was in developed countries, a 16 percent rise, resulting from the continuing response of U.S. petroleum companies to growing worldwide demand for energy and petrochemical feedstocks. Substantial expenditures were made to diversify sources of supply and accelerate development of new fields, as well as for terminals, refineries, and distribution facilities to help meet the increased petroleum demand. The additional investment was financed about equally by net capital outflows and by reinvested earnings.

Net capital outflows to the developed countries were also influenced by a shifting to the books of U.S. parent companies of trade receivables owed by petroleum affiliates in developed (mainly petroleum importing) countries to petroleum affiliates in developing (mainly petroleum exporting) countries. This shifting resulted in increased U.S. parents' claims on developed countries (a U.S. net capital outflow), offset by increased U.S. parents' liabilities to developed countries (a U.S. net capital inflow).

Petroleum reinvested earnings stemmed in part from higher petroleum prices and profits per-barrel, along with increased inventory profits.

The addition to petroleum investment in developing countries was $1.1 billion in 1973, about the same as in 1972. However, reinvested earnings replaced net capital outflows as the

Table 6.—Estimated Net Capital Outflows to Manufacturing Foreign Affiliates by Industry

[Millions of dollars]

Area and year	All manufacturing	Food products	Paper and allied products	Chemicals and allied products	Rubber products	Primary and fabricated metals	Machinery except electrical	Electrical machinery	Transportation equipment	Other
All areas:										
1969	1,160	125	3	163	9	136	177	206	115	226
1970	1,295	134	111	78	44	194	205	178	193	158
1971	1,556	206	44	365	1	21	307	117	267	229
1972 ʳ	1,100	116	59	200	34	18	72	174	285	141
1973 ᵖ	1,820	170	23	347	27	-12	267	230	459	310
Developed countries:										
Canada:										
1969	248	53	-35	2	8	16	49	59	38	58
1970	305	5	86	47	3	74	-39	-5	131	4
1971	-53	26	6	91	-7	-16	24	-14	-230	68
1972 ʳ	239	-5	54	52	14	-26	33	8	65	44
1973 ᵖ	102	8	-5	63	3	19	-7	7	43	-29
Europe:										
1969	596	54	31	100	1	63	105	114	24	104
1970	773	90	23	-13	41	85	195	148	50	154
1971	1,146	145	33	203	-16	36	250	98	319	79
1972 ʳ	493	58	-3	61	5	53	-26	139	145	61
1973 ᵖ	1,202	96	26	154	5	34	186	145	274	282
Japan:										
1969	39	(*)		9	(*)		10	-7	10	5	11
1970	32	3	-3	12		1	-4	8	1	8	5
1971	120	11	(*)	11	(*)		3	-8	4	85	13
1972 ʳ	102	19	(*)	21	(*)	(*)		36	3	2	21
1973 ᵖ	40	2	1	11		3	-4	15	4	-3	12
Australia, New Zealand, and South Africa:										
1969	72	12	-1	19	-8	20	4	3	2	21
1970	75	8	5	15	5	10	18	3	6	5
1971	105	24	(*)	18	2	-10	17	22	26	6
1972 ʳ	-2	13	1	-4	(*)	-10	(*)	15	-24	7
1973 ᵖ	10	16	2	22	2	-59	-4	-8	7	32
Other areas:										
Latin American Republics and other Western Hemisphere:										
1969	133	1	6	-4	1	24	24	10	45	26
1970	104	44	-1	24	-4	18	20	23	-3	-17
1971	172	-5	3	33	10	-3	20	1	64	48
1972 ʳ	232	25	6	64	6	6	30	24	74	-5
1973 ᵖ	345	37	(*)	80	4	-6	70	50	112	-2
Other: ¹²										
1969	73	5	1	37	7	3	3	11	1	7
1970	6	-16	1	-7	-2	11	3	8	2	7
1971	65	5	2	9	7	12	10	6	2	15
1972 ʳ	36	6	(*)	7	7	-6	-1	-14	24	13
1973 ᵖ	122	11	(*)	18	10	4	7	34	25	14

ʳ Revised.   ᵖ Preliminary.   * Less than $500,000 (±).
1. Commencing with 1972, estimates for Okinawa are included with Japan instead of other areas.

2. Includes other Africa, Middle East, other Asia and Pacific, international and unallocated.

NOTE.—Details may not add to totals because of rounding.

Table 7.—Net Acquisitions from Unaffiliated Foreigners of Voting Stock in Foreign-Incorporated Affiliates [1]

[Millions of dollars]

Item and area	1972 r				1973 p			
	All industries	Petroleum	Manufacturing	Other	All industries	Petroleum	Manufacturing	Other
All areas, net acquisitions	702	29	418	255	11	−87	154	−56
Acquisitions	854	39	492	323	626	11	419	196
Sales	152	10	74	68	615	98	265	252
Developed countries:								
Canada, net acquisitions	29	13	10	6	−1	1	−3	1
Acquisitions	60	18	27	15	26	6	12	8
Sales	31	5	17	9	27	5	15	7
Europe, net acquisitions	430	12	273	146	342	−60	241	161
Acquisitions	482	12	310	160	487	(*)	324	163
Sales	52	....	37	14	145	60	83	2
Other developed countries, net acquisitions	53	3	29	21	−128	4	−44	−87
Acquisitions	55	3	31	21	33	4	25	5
Sales	2	....	2	....	161	....	68	92
Other areas:								
Latin American Republics and other Western Hemisphere, net acquisitions	136	1	95	39	−24	−2	−27	4
Acquisitions	166	1	112	52	62	(*)	49	13
Sales	30	....	17	13	86	2	76	9
Other, net acquisitions [2]	54	−1	12	42	−179	−30	−14	−134
Acquisitions	92	4	12	75	17	2	9	7
Sales	38	5	....	33	196	32	23	141

r Revised.   p Preliminary.   * Less than $500,000 (±).

1. Net acquisitions are a component of net capital outflows to foreign-incorporated affiliates (table 5). Acquisitions include partial and total purchases of voting securities of existing foreign corporations from unaffiliated foreign owners. Sales include partial and total sales of voting securities of foreign corporations by U.S. owners to unaffiliated foreign purchasers. Liquidations through the sale of assets, as distinct from sale of ownership interests, are not included. Changes in the share of ownership resulting from transactions between a parent and an affiliate—such as the purchase of treasury stock from an affiliate by a parent—are not included; only changes involving outside foreign owners or purchasers are included. Secondary foreign companies acquired or sold through primary foreign affiliates are not included.

2. Includes other Africa, Middle East, other Asia and Pacific, international and unallocated.

NOTE.—Details may not add to totals because of rounding.

main source of funds. The 1973 drop in capital outflows was partially attributable to sales and liquidations of some U.S. petroleum-related investments in a few countries.[4] Net capital outflows to other developing countries to finance expansion in petroleum production and loading facilities were substantial.

Manufacturing

Most of the 1973 growth in the manufacturing direct investment position was accounted for by a $5.0 billion or 15 percent addition in developed countries, in response to strong demand and capacity pressures. Reinvested earnings financed most of the addition. Net capital outflows also increased, particularly to machinery and transportation equipment industries in the United Kingdom (tables 6 and 9).

There was a $0.6 billion increase in short-term debt owed by manufacturing affiliates in developed countries to their U.S. parents; the increase was concentrated in the first quarter, when foreign exchange market uncertainties were widespread (table 5).

The increase in net capital outflows to developed countries was tempered by increased direct investors' sales and decreased acquisitions of equity in

foreign enterprises in transactions with unaffiliated foreigners (table 7).

In developing countries, the addition to U.S. manufacturing direct investment was $1.1 billion or 15 percent, about equal to the manufacturing growth rate in developed countries.

Other industries

For the "other industries" group, the 1973 addition to the direct investment position in developed countries was $2.5 billion, with about equal contributions by net capital outflows and reinvested earnings. Net capital outflows, which were large relative to those in previous years, included sizable first-quarter short-term transactions by U.S.

Table 8.—U.S. Balance of Payments Income on Petroleum Direct Investment Abroad

[Millions of dollars, not seasonally adjusted]

Quarter	U.S. balance of payments income
1972 r:	
IV	953
1973 p:	
I	827
II	918
III	1,116
IV	1,464
1974 p:	
I	2,882

p Preliminary.   r Revised.

CHART 4

Rates of Return on U.S. Direct Investment Abroad

Alternative Rates of Return, All Areas [1]

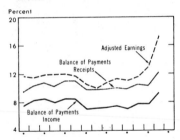

Adjusted Earnings Rate of Return by Major Area

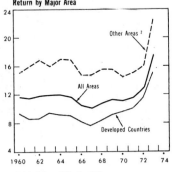

1. Rates of return and alternative methods of computation are shown in table 12.

2. Includes developing countries, international and unallocated.

U.S. Department of Commerce, Bureau of Economic Analysis   74-8-4

Table 9.—U.S. Direct Investment Abroad by Major Area,

[Millions of

Area and year	All industries					Mining and smelting					Petroleum				
	Book value at year end	Net capital outflows	Reinvested earnings[1]	Earnings	Balance of payments income[2]	Book value at year end	Net capital outflows	Reinvested earnings[1]	Earnings	Balance of payments income[2]	Book value at year end	Net capital outflows	Reinvested earnings[1]	Earnings	Balance of payments income[2]
All areas:															
1966	54,799	3,661	1,739	5,364	3,707	4,365	305	129	659	524	16,222	885	106	1,530	1,443
1967	59,491	3,137	1,598	5,650	4,133	4,876	330	135	746	596	17,399	1,069	175	1,736	1,604
1968	64,983	3,209	2,175	6,538	4,489	5,435	440	134	795	644	18,887	1,231	239	1,965	1,787
1969	71,033	3,271	2,604	7,544	5,074	5,676	93	167	782	664	19,882	919	−59	1,868	2,054
1970	78,178	4,410	2,948	8,118	5,330	6,168	393	111	675	553	21,714	1,460	425	2,264	1,937
1971	86,198	4,943	3,157	9,389	6,385	6,685	510	23	499	482	24,152	1,950	500	2,946	2,532
1972 r	94,337	3,517	4,715	11,485	6,925	7,110	382	41	419	305	26,263	1,603	563	3,311	2,826
1973 p	107,268	4,872	8,124	17,495	9,415	7,483	201	143	675	548	29,567	1,417	1,927	6,183	4,325
Canada:															
1966	17,017	1,153	547	1,237	756	2,089	172	67	191	120	3,608	155	91	196	112
1967	18,102	408	644	1,327	790	2,342	173	82	240	154	3,819	115	93	207	132
1968	19,535	625	772	1,490	851	2,638	195	103	275	169	4,094	169	107	243	160
1969	21,127	671	937	1,596	762	2,769	54	77	236	152	4,361	179	95	242	152
1970	22,790	908	787	1,586	944	2,989	149	70	250	175	4,807	291	160	302	183
1971	24,105	273	1,074	1,955	1,015	3,246	256	31	203	171	5,149	87	249	370	150
1972 r	25,771	350	1,384	2,251	989	3,455	210	------	133	130	5,301	−101	313	451	161
1973 p	28,055	540	1,846	2,846	1,126	3,735	190	91	230	149	5,864	89	476	670	219
Europe:[3]															
United Kingdom:															
1966	5,679	403	195	432	251	3	(**)	(**)	(**)	(**)	1,191	126	−8	−25	−15
1967	6,113	331	81	378	274	2	(**)	(**)	(**)	(**)	1,432	267	−29	−53	−17
1968	6,694	363	211	503	275	2	(**)	(**)	(**)	(**)	1,563	154	−21	−49	−15
1969	7,190	316	151	502	332	2	(**)	(**)	(**)	(**)	1,577	53	−41	−59	3
1970	7,996	645	212	593	386	5	(**)	(**)	(**)	(**)	1,839	305	−41	−27	40
1971	9,007	685	324	779	469	9	(**)	(**)	(**)	(**)	2,176	290	48	64	47
1972 r	9,582	35	508	1,086	583	5	(**)	(**)	(**)	(**)	2,312	59	82	110	62
1973 p	11,115	857	675	1,450	772	6	(**)	(**)	(**)	(**)	2,631	239	81	122	76
European Economic Community (6):[4]															
1966	7,587	1,146	100	436	321	17	(**)	(**)	(**)	(**)	1,980	397	−56	−39	17
1967	8,444	852	41	448	398	19	(**)	(**)	(**)	(**)	2,086	176	−56	−24	35
1968	9,012	438	108	543	434	19	(**)	(**)	(**)	(**)	2,146	132	−77	−51	34
1969	10,255	660	503	945	460	17	(**)	(**)	(**)	(**)	2,244	129	−147	−129	29
1970	11,774	994	505	1,313	785	15	(**)	(**)	(**)	(**)	2,523	233	38	25	8
1971	13,605	1,334	499	1,384	878	13	(**)	(**)	(**)	(**)	2,918	477	−93	−28	91
1972 r	15,720	1,087	1,020	1,866	859	9	(**)	(**)	(**)	(**)	3,363	475	−43	−96	−17
1973 p	19,294	1,695	1,909	3,188	1,265	11	(**)	(**)	(**)	(**)	4,393	702	318	416	151
Other Western Europe:															
1966	2,967	285	140	293	157	34	(**)	(**)	(**)	(**)	832	134	−13	−15	2
1967	3,369	275	147	317	178	40	(**)	(**)	(**)	(**)	905	80	−3	−22	−12
1968	3,701	200	137	323	196	40	(**)	(**)	(**)	(**)	926	31	−14	−37	−18
1969	4,206	233	239	479	246	52	(**)	(**)	(**)	(**)	998	36	−9	−8	4
1970	4,746	275	271	477	219	55	(**)	(**)	(**)	(**)	1,104	114	−10	−24	−7
1971	5,127	150	218	533	300	57	(**)	(**)	(**)	(**)	1,098	15	−27	−38	−5
1972 r	5,515	46	365	769	406	60	(**)	(**)	(**)	(**)	1,177	100	−21	−44	−17
1973 p	6,809	388	892	1,319	432	70	(**)	(**)	(**)	(**)	1,362	75	92	54	−21
Japan:[5]															
1966	756	32	49	91	43	------	------	------	------	------	331	−1	11	16	8
1967	870	34	79	123	46	------	------	------	------	------	347	(*)	15	21	9
1968	1,050	78	104	167	60	------	------	------	------	------	405	46	13	20	8
1969	1,244	89	105	185	70	------	------	------	------	------	447	27	15	19	7
1970	1,483	128	115	220	100	------	------	------	------	------	540	65	29	29	6
1971	1,821	212	127	285	149	------	------	------	------	------	637	78	24	29	11
1972 r	2,375	229	183	362	168	------	------	------	------	------	901	84	48	51	9
1973 p	2,733	36	311	548	222	------	------	------	------	------	922	−75	96	100	13
Australia, New Zealand, and South Africa:															
1966	2,655	167	148	292	138	324	77	21	63	39	646	11	19	22	3
1967	3,172	364	152	299	138	419	70	14	66	38	720	48	22	18	−5
1968	3,508	171	159	320	161	446	22	5	64	55	787	40	23	18	−2
1969	3,865	160	199	401	214	479	20	13	86	68	837	24	36	------	5
1970	4,356	288	184	462	299	583	88	20	111	88	910	46	29	37	25
1971	4,904	333	195	479	310	716	105	13	84	74	950	29	50	68	31
1972 r	5,395	241	250	546	326	847	117	13	89	80	1,100	75	45	87	56
1973 p	6,079	116	514	981	481	951	29	25	136	109	1,224	23	103	180	98
Latin American Republics and other Western Hemisphere:															
1966	11,498	307	343	1,452	1,113	1,565	60	31	359	327	3,475	−37	2	512	499
1967	12,049	296	211	1,398	1,190	1,709	71	24	397	365	3,473	−66	38	519	480
1968	13,101	677	358	1,574	1,218	1,930	227	8	392	374	3,680	177	42	531	489
1969	13,858	392	376	1,646	1,277	1,958	30	43	396	404	3,722	56	−15	434	472
1970	14,760	578	442	1,482	1,057	2,071	140	−17	245	259	3,938	160	68	417	345
1971	15,789	691	399	1,500	1,130	2,097	59	−39	172	214	4,195	204	63	507	444
1972 r	16,798	300	732	1,656	967	2,099	−15	16	175	171	4,292	28	71	303	243
1973 p	18,452	673	1,028	2,628	1,622	2,107	12	15	252	244	4,393	−59	208	858	643
Other areas:[6]															
1966	6,640	167	216	1,131	928	334	−5	12	36	27	4,159	100	59	863	817
1967	7,372	578	244	1,361	1,120	346	9	4	36	32	4,617	448	95	1,071	982
1968	8,383	657	326	1,618	1,293	360	−1	15	55	41	5,285	482	166	1,290	1,130
1969	9,289	750	93	1,790	1,713	398	8	30	64	35	5,697	415	85	1,369	1,380
1970	10,274	594	432	1,984	1,541	451	18	34	61	28	6,053	245	153	1,505	1,336
1971	11,835	1,265	321	2,475	2,134	548	79	22	36	17	6,999	770	186	1,973	1,764
1972 r	13,181	1,229	272	2,949	2,627	634	72	15	24	10	7,818	882	69	2,449	2,328
1973 p	14,731	569	949	4,536	3,495	602	−43	12	55	43	8,777	423	553	3,783	3,144
Addenda:															
European economic community (9):[7] 1973 p	31,257	2,601	2,727	4,770	2,035	18	(**)	(**)	(**)	(**)	7,365	979	432	544	208
Other Europe:[8] 1973 p	5,962	338	749	1,186	435	69	(**)	(**)	(**)	(**)	1,022	37	59	48	------

r Revised.   p Preliminary.   *Less than $500,000 (±).   **Combined in the "other industries" category to avoid disclosure of data for individual U.S. reporters.

1. Represents a U.S. reporter's share in the reinvested earnings of its foreign-incorporated affiliates.
2. Comprised of interest, dividends, and branch earnings. Petroleum branch earnings have been revised as described in the Technical Notes.
3. Direct investment statistics do not show any investment in Eastern Europe.
4. Includes Belgium, France, Germany, Italy, Luxemburg, and the Netherlands.

5. Commencing with 1972, estimates for Okinawa are included with Japan instead of other areas.
6. Includes other Africa, Middle East, other Asia and Pacific, international and unallocated.
7. Includes Denmark, Ireland, and the United Kingdom, in addition to the six countries listed in note 4 as members of the "European Economic Community (6)."
8. Excludes the "European Economic Community (9)" category.

Selected Items, 1966–73

dollars]

	Manufacturing					Other					
Book value at year end	Net capital outflows	Reinvested earnings[1]	Earnings	Balance of payments income[2]	Book value at year end	Net capital outflows	Reinvested earnings[1]	Earnings	Balance of payments income[2]	Year
22,078	1,752	983	2,104	1,116	12,134	718	520	1,071	624	1966
24,172	1,234	847	2,055	1,193	13,044	504	442	1,112	740	1967
26,414	945	1,261	2,519	1,265	14,248	592	541	1,259	793	1968
29,527	1,160	1,939	3,287	1,337	15,948	1,099	557	1,606	1,020	1969
32,261	1,295	1,534	3,416	1,859	18,035	1,262	877	1,764	981	1970
36,632	1,556	1,854	3,834	1,950	19,726	927	780	2,111	1,422	1971
39,716	1,160	2,991	5,172	2,144	21,249	433	1,118	2,583	1,560	1972r
45,791	1,820	4,408	7,286	2,757	24,137	1,434	1,645	3,351	1,785	1973p
7,692	566	278	628	354	3,628	260	111	222	170	1966
8,095	20	344	613	296	3,847	100	125	267	208	1967
8,568	26	412	672	301	4,325	236	151	300	221	1968
9,406	248	599	833	255	4,591	190	166	285	202	1969
10,059	305	355	679	360	4,935	163	202	355	226	1970
10,590	-53	588	953	393	5,121	-18	206	428	300	1971
11,639	239	822	1,209	426	5,378	3	250	458	271	1972r
12,635	102	1,010	1,524	535	5,821	159	269	422	222	1973p
3,716	259	165	364	208	769	18	38	94	57	1966
3,878	38	111	340	207	802	27	-1	92	84	1967
4,243	134	215	442	206	886	74	18	110	84	1968
4,567	117	169	440	236	1,043	145	24	122	92	1969
4,977	192	219	472	234	1,175	148	35	148	111	1970
5,471	274	228	506	263	1,351	122	49	209	159	1971
5,661	1	351	726	345	1,414	-25	74	250	176	1972r
6,827	494	475	945	437	1,651	124	119	384	258	1973p
4,404	524	140	413	257	1,186	224	15	61	45	1966
4,976	505	101	424	310	1,363	171	-3	47	52	1967
5,399	253	167	502	329	1,448	53	18	91	71	1968
6,382	385	584	919	342	1,611	146	66	155	89	1969
7,177	464	367	1,060	655	2,059	296	100	229	122	1970
8,381	769	463	1,123	631	2,294	89	128	289	156	1971
9,755	484	885	1,602	694	2,594	127	179	360	181	1972r
11,736	628	1,397	2,345	895	3,156	364	194	426	220	1973p
759	116	60	83	24	1,343	35	93	224	133	1966
943	141	40	82	44	1,479	52	109	255	145	1967
1,155	175	51	97	47	1,579	-4	98	263	167	1968
1,330	93	101	158	63	1,825	104	146	328	179	1969
1,553	117	112	168	63	2,034	44	169	334	163	1970
1,768	104	99	182	84	2,205	31	147	388	222	1971
1,975	7	221	315	97	2,303	-61	164	498	325	1972r
2,461	80	408	544	137	2,915	233	391	720	316	1973p
334	22	36	56	18	91	11	2	19	17	1966
425	31	61	85	22	98	3	3	16	15	1967
522	11	86	127	37	123	21	4	20	15	1968
646	39	85	146	49	150	23	5	20	13	1969
749	32	75	154	69	194	30	11	36	25	1970
962	120	88	193	91	223	15	15	63	47	1971
1,194	102	120	236	100	280	43	15	76	59	1972r
1,420	40	176	342	143	391	71	39	106	66	1973p
1,332	65	79	161	79	354	13	29	46	17	1966
1,640	224	89	176	83	394	23	27	38	22	1967
1,830	83	110	192	82	445	26	20	46	20	1968
2,035	72	126	227	108	514	44	24	87	33	1969
2,252	75	124	264	145	612	79	11	50	40	1970
2,461	105	99	249	157	747	95	33	78	48	1971
2,595	-2	138	276	146	854	51	54	95	44	1972r
2,883	10	275	481	200	1,021	55	111	184	74	1973p
3,318	160	202	342	147	3,141	125	108	239	140	1966
3,586	199	78	269	195	3,282	92	70	213	151	1967
4,005	222	194	408	216	3,486	50	114	243	139	1968
4,347	133	225	466	237	3,831	199	123	350	164	1969
4,621	104	228	514	280	4,131	174	162	306	173	1970
4,999	172	240	514	268	4,499	255	135	308	204	1971
5,597	232	381	663	272	4,809	55	265	515	280	1972r
6,460	345	525	860	319	5,492	376	280	658	416	1973p
524	40	22	57	29	1,622	33	123	175	55	1966
629	77	24	66	36	1,779	43	121	189	69	1967
693	40	26	79	48	2,046	136	119	194	74	1968
813	73	48	98	47	2,381	254	8	259	252	1969
874	6	54	105	52	2,895	326	192	313	125	1970
1,001	65	49	114	62	3,291	350	65	351	291	1971
1,111	37	74	146	64	3,617	237	115	330	226	1972r
1,371	122	143	244	91	3,982	67	241	454	217	1973p
18,962	1,126	1,966	3,388	1,337	4,912	496	330	839	491	1973p
2,061	76	314	447	132	2,809	225	375	691	303	1973p

NOTE.—Details may not add to totals because of rounding. For an explanation of the relations between earnings, reinvested earnings, and balance of payments income see the Technical Notes. Not all countries grouped in an "other" or regional category have U.S. direct investment at any given time.

direct investors with their finance affiliates (table 5). Net capital outflows to the developing countries were $0.4 billion (table 1) and would have been larger, except for selloffs of shipping and other affiliates totaling $0.3 billion (table 7).

U.S. Corporate Transactions With Foreigners

Table 2 gives the net impact on the U.S. balance of payments of identifiable U.S. corporate accounts with foreigners. It is not equivalent to the net impact of U.S. direct investment on the balance of payments for three reasons: (i) U.S. corporate data, as now collected, do not allow all transactions associated with direct investment to be separated from other corporate transactions with foreigners; (ii) data are lacking on interest payments to foreign holders of U.S. corporate debt associated with direct investment; and (iii) as explained in the Technical Notes, net capital outflows are sample data, rather than universe estimates.

The net inflow of funds to the United States resulting from U.S. corporate transactions with foreigners—including additions to the direct investment position, other capital account changes, and direct investor ownership benefits—was $6.9 billion, down $0.9 billion from the 1972 record. There was a $5.9 billion increase in corporate claims on foreigners and a $1.4 billion decrease in U.S. corporate borrowing from unaffiliated foreigners; these changes were largely offset by a $6.3 billion increase in direct investors' ownership benefits, comprising royalties and fees, dividends, interest, branch earnings, and reinvested earnings. Statistical adjustments were negligible.

There was a marked shift in the geographic origin of net corporate flows. The net flow to the United States from developed countries decreased $2.2 billion, to $2.9 billion, while the net flow from the "other areas" category (mostly developing countries) increased $1.7 billion, to $4.2 billion. There are several reasons for this change. First, exchange market disturbances in the first quarter mainly affected capital transactions with ed-

Table 10A.—Preliminary 1973 Estimates, U.S. Direct Investment

[Millions

Line	Area and country	All industries — Book value at year-end	Net capital outflows	Reinvested earnings [1]	Earnings	Balance of payments income [2]	Mining and smelting — Book value at year-end	Net capital outflows	Reinvested earnings [1]	Earnings	Balance of payments income [2]	Petroleum — Book value at year-end	Net capital outflows	Reinvested earnings [1]	Earnings	Balance of payments income [2]
1	All areas	107,268	4,872	8,124	17,495	9,415	7,483	201	143	675	548	29,567	1,417	1,927	6,183	4,325
2	Developed countries	74,084	3,631	6,147	10,330	4,299	4,774	232	116	369	261	16,397	1,053	1,166	1,542	537
3	Canada	28,055	540	1,846	2,846	1,126	3,735	190	91	230	149	5,864	89	476	670	219
4	Europe [3]	37,218	2,939	3,476	5,956	2,470	87	14	(**)	(**)	(**)	8,387	1,016	491	592	208
5	European Economic Community (9)	31,257	2,601	2,727	4,770	2,035	18	(**)	(**)	(**)	(**)	7,365	979	432	544	208
6	Belgium and Luxembourg	2,514	117	285	421	127	(*)		(*)	(**)		292	71	38	41	3
7	Denmark and Ireland	847	50	143	133	-3	1	(**)				340	38	33	6	-21
8	France	4,259	390	414	623	210	5	(**)	(**)	(**)	(**)	541	111	9	11	4
9	Germany	7,954	883	800	1,508	673	(**)	(**)	(**)	(**)	(**)	2,287	388	238	286	80
10	Italy	2,301	186	149	231	84	(**)	(**)	(**)	(**)	(**)	534	58	-18	-24	-4
11	Netherlands	2,266	119	261	405	171	1	(**)	(**)	(**)	(**)	739	74	51	102	68
12	United Kingdom	11,115	857	675	1,450	772	6	(**)	(**)	(**)	(**)	2,631	239	81	122	76
13	Other Western Europe	5,962	338	749	1,186	435	69	(**)	(**)	(**)	(**)	1,022	37	59	48	(*)
14	Norway	419	64	31	13	-11	(**)	(**)	(**)	(**)	(**)	216	51	9	-21	-24
15	Spain	1,017	-33	136	186	45	(**)	(**)	(**)	(**)	(**)	107	-55	-5	1	5
16	Sweden	846	63	60	93	37	(*)	(**)	(**)	(**)	(**)	364	24	19	19	2
17	Switzerland	2,593	200	440	706	260	(*)					21	12	8	9	4
18	Other [4]	1,086	44	82	189	104	22	(**)	(**)	(**)	(**)	314	5	27	41	12
19	Japan [5]	2,733	36	311	548	222						922	-75	96	100	13
20	Australia, New Zealand and South Africa.	6,079	116	514	981	481	951	29	25	136	109	1,224	23	103	180	98
21	Australia	4,526	7	329	689	380	785	16	16	100	83	(**)	(**)	(**)	(**)	(**)
22	New Zealand	313	29	38	58	20	8	(*)	(*)	(**)		(**)	(**)	(**)	(**)	(**)
23	South Africa	1,240	80	148	234	80	158	13	8	36	26	274	(**)	(**)	(**)	(**)
24	Developing countries [6]	27,867	1,198	1,510	6,538	4,932	2,709	-32	28	306	287	10,431	247	467	4,247	3,665
25	Latin American Republics and other Western Hemisphere	18,452	673	1,028	2,628	1,622	2,107	12	15	252	244	4,393	-59	208	858	643
26	Latin American Republics	14,797	376	794	2,089	1,287	1,342	28	15	156	146	3,067	-232	91	635	536
27	Mexico	2,249	52	162	275	109	128	-3	8	14	6	30	(*)	-2	4	5
28	Panama	1,665	(*)	204	292	102	19	(*)	(**)	(**)		344	16	53	53	(*)
29	Other Central America [6]	653	25	11	47	39	19	4		7	7	124	-11	-3	8	11
30	Argentina	1,407	9	-7	63	66	(**)	(**)	(**)	(**)	(**)	(**)	(**)	(**)	(**)	(**)
31	Brazil	3,199	343	355	448	84	180	(**)	(**)	(**)	(**)	104	-6	(**)	(**)	(**)
32	Chile	619	-3	2	1	1	359	(**)	(**)	(**)	(**)	(**)	(**)	(**)	(**)	(**)
33	Colombia	727	-26	29	53	24	(**)	(**)	(**)	(**)	(**)	277	-30	1	7	6
34	Peru	793	71	13	82	68	439	22	1	89	80	(**)	(**)	(**)	(**)	(**)
35	Venezuela	2,591	-98	-14	689	682	(**)	(**)	(**)	(**)	(**)	1,341	-205	-2	487	488
36	Other [7]	893	2	42	139	110	17	-6	1	12	11	412	-20	10	46	35
37	Other Western Hemisphere [8]	3,655	296	234	539	335	765	-16	(**)	95	98	1,326	173	117	223	107
38	Other Africa [9]	2,830	-427	177	618	446	397	-48	15	33	19	2,002	-391	145	548	406
39	Liberia	256	33	15	30	16	(**)	(**)	(**)	(**)	(**)	(**)	(**)	(**)	(**)	(**)
40	Libya	895	-252	3	284	281	(**)	(**)	(**)	(**)	(**)	(**)	(**)	(**)	(**)	(**)
41	Other	1,679	-208	159	304	148	338	-43	14	27	13	1,077	-189	140	258	120
42	Middle East [10]	2,682	588	108	2,277	2,172	5	(*)		(**)	(**)	2,377	513	99	2,242	2,146
43	Other Asia and Pacific [5]	3,903	365	198	1,014	692	199	5	-2	21	24	1,659	184	15	599	470
44	India	351	6	7	39	27	(**)			(**)	(**)	(**)	(**)	(**)	(**)	(**)
45	Philippines	711	4	21	65	37	(**)	(**)	(**)	(**)	(**)	(**)	(**)	(**)	(**)	(**)
46	Other [5]	2,841	354	169	910	628	(**)	(**)	(**)	(**)	(**)	(**)	(**)	(**)	(**)	(**)
47	International and unallocated	5,317	43	467	627	185						2,740	117	294	394	122
	Addenda: European Economic Community (6) [11]	19,296	1,694	1,909	3,162	1,266	11	(**)	(**)	(**)	(**)	4,394	702	318	446	152
	Other Europe [12]	6,808	388	892	1,299	432	71	(**)	(**)	(**)	(**)	1,362	75	92	106	-21

*Less than $500,000 (±).   **Combined in the "other industries" category to avoid disclosure of data for individual reporters.

1. Represents a U.S. reporter's share in reinvested earnings of its foreign incorporated affiliates.

2. Comprised of interest, dividends, and branch earnings. Petroleum branch earnings have been revised as described in the Technical Notes.

3. Direct investment statistics do not show any investment in Eastern Europe.

4. Includes Austria, Cyprus, Finland, Gibraltar, Greece, Iceland, Malta, Portugal, Turkey, and Yugoslavia.

5. Commencing with 1972, estimates for Okinawa are included with Japan instead of other Asia and Pacific.

6. Includes Costa Rica, El Salvador, Guatemala, Honduras, and Nicaragua.

7. Includes Bolivia, Dominican Republic, Ecuador, Haiti, Paraguay, and Uruguay.

8. Includes Western Hemisphere except Canada (line 3) and the 19 Latin American Republics (line 26).

9. Includes United Arab Republic (Egypt) and all other countries in Africa except South Africa.

10. Includes Bahrain, Iran, Israel, Jordan, Kuwait, Lebanon, Qatar, Saudi Arabia, South Yemen, Syria, Trucial States, Oman, and Yemen.

Abroad, Selected Items

of dollars]

Manufacturing					Other					Line
Book value at year-end	Net capital outflows	Reinvested earnings [1]	Earnings	Balance of payments income [2]	Book value at year-end	Net capital outflows	Reinvested earnings [1]	Earnings	Balance of payments income [2]	
45,791	1,820	4,408	7,286	2,757	24,427	1,434	1,645	3,351	1,785	1
37,960	1,354	3,741	6,181	2,348	14,954	992	1,124	2,238	1,153	2
12,635	102	1,010	1,524	535	5,821	159	269	422	222	3
21,023	1,202	2,280	3,835	1,469	7,722	707	704	1,530	794	4
18,962	1,126	1,966	3,388	1,337	4,912	496	330	839	491	5
1,376	58	162	267	100	846	−12	85	113	24	6
400	4	94	97	5	106	8	16	29	13	7
3,064	173	386	556	169	648	106	19	55	38	8
4,666	301	520	1,072	486	1,002	193	41	150	107	9
1,414	100	168	238	71	354	28	(*)	17	17	10
1,216	−4	161	212	69	311	48	49	91	34	11
6,827	494	475	945	437	1,651	125	119	384	258	12
2,061	76	314	447	132	2,809	225	375	691	303	13
93	5	8	14	6	111	8	14	20	6	14
563	1	92	120	26	348	21	49	65	14	15
290	9	27	43	18	192	30	14	31	18	16
737	50	152	218	66	1,834	138	279	479	190	17
378	10	35	52	16	372	29	19	96	75	18
1,420	40	176	342	143	391	71	39	106	66	19
2,883	10	275	481	200	1,021	55	111	184	74	20
2,165	−29	197	366	164	1,575	21	116	223	133	21
159	10	18	23	4	145	19	20	36	15	22
558	29	61	93	31	251	38	79	105	24	23
7,830	467	668	1,104	410	6,896	516	348	881	570	24
6,460	345	525	860	319	5,492	376	280	658	416	25
6,122	342	491	816	307	4,266	238	198	482	298	26
1,567	16	129	215	81	524	38	27	42	18	27
184	−7	33	53	18	1,118	−9	5	187	84	28
119	7	9	14	7	391	25	5	17	13	29
872	33	−1	34	37	536	−23	−6	28	30	30
2,213	230	274	332	54	612	118	81	113	31	31
44	−2	−1	(*)	1	217	−1	2	2	(*)	32
302	9	24	40	15	147	−6	4	7	3	33
96	5	5	13	6	258	44	7	−20	−27	34
619	36	16	96	71	631	72	−29	167	124	35
106	15	4	21	17	358	13	28	61	46	36
338	2	34	44	12	1,226	137	82	177	117	37
143	20	−1	4	5	288	−8	18	33	16	38
(**)	(**)	(**)	(**)	(**)	256	33	15	30	16	39
(**)	(**)	(**)	(**)	(**)	895	−252	3	284	281	40
142	19	−1	4	5	122	5	6	14	10	41
130	19	7	12	5	170	56	2	24	21	42
1,098	83	138	229	81	946	93	47	166	117	43
183	−1	5	24	16	168	8	3	15	12	44
267	16	9	31	16	445	−11	12	34	21	45
648	68	124	174	49	2,193	284	45	736	578	46
					2,577	−74	173	232	63	47
11,735	628	1,397	2,337	895	3,156	363	194	380	219	
2,461	80	408	543	137	2,915	233	391	649	316	

11. Includes Belgium, France, Germany, Italy, Luxembourg, and the Netherlands.
12. Excludes the "European Economic Community (6)" category.

NOTES.—Details may not add to totals because of rounding. For an explanation of the relations between earnings, reinvested earnings, and balance of payments income, see the Technical Notes. Not all countries grouped in an "other" or regional category have U.S. direct investment. Line numbers in table 10A do not match line numbers in table 10B because the change in composition of the European Economic Community necessitated changes in table 10A.

veloped countries, where most leading international financial centers are located. Second, corporate borrowing from unaffiliated foreigners in developed areas declined as rising interest rates made foreign loans less attractive or difficult to obtain or renew. Also, decreased dividend payout ratios inhibited growth in U.S. balance of payments income from developed countries, which account for about three-fourths of incorporated affiliates' earnings. In addition, earnings of petroleum-producing branches in developing countries were sharply higher. All of these branch earnings are credited as U.S. balance of payments income receipts; in contrast, only the dividends from incorporated affiliates are so credited.

Finally, increased demands for participation in U.S.-owned affiliates in extractive industries by a number of developing countries led some U.S. direct investors to reduce their capital positions. There were net capital inflows from petroleum affiliates in the Western Hemisphere and from mining and smelting affiliates in the developing countries. In addition there were instances of petroleum disinvestment in the Middle East, although total net capital outflows to finance expansion in petroleum there were substantial.

Return on U.S. Direct Investment

Table 12 presents alternative measures of the return on U.S. direct investment abroad and the components used in computing these measures. A comparison of the measures, as percentages of the direct investment position, is given in chart 4.[5]

Earnings gives a conventional accounting measure of return from the viewpoint of the affiliates. In 1973, these earnings were $17.5 billion, up 52 percent from 1972. The increase was widespread, covering all the area and industry groups shown.

The rise in petroleum earnings was

5. For each year, the denominator used to obtain these rates of return is the average of the beginning- and end-of-year direct investment position for that year. A percent rate of return is not given for the earnings measure, because data on an appropriate base, the U.S share in the net worth of the foreign affiliates, are not available.

Table 10B.—Revised 1972 Estimates, U.S.

[Millions]

Line	Area and country	All industries					Mining and smelting					Petroleum				
		Book value at year-end	Net capital outflows	Reinvested earnings[1]	Earnings	Balance of payments income[2]	Book value at year-end	Net capital outflows	Reinvested earnings[1]	Earnings	Balance of payments income[2]	Book value at year-end	Net capital outflows	Reinvested earnings[1]	Earnings	Balance of payments income[2]
1	All areas	94,337	3,517	4,715	11,485	6,925	7,110	382	41	419	395	26,263	1,603	563	3,311	2,826
2	Developed countries	64,359	1,988	3,710	6,880	3,331	4,376	325	10	220	213	14,152	693	424	559	255
3	Canada	25,771	350	1,384	2,251	989	3,455	210	(*)	133	130	5,301	−101	313	451	161
4	Europe [3]	30,817	1,168	1,892	3,721	1,847	74	−2	(**)	(**)	(**)	6,851	634	18	−30	28
5	United Kingdom	9,582	35	508	1,086	583	5	(**)	(**)	(**)	(**)	2,312	59	82	110	62
6	European Economic Community (6)	15,720	1,087	1,020	1,866	859	9	(**)	(**)	(**)	(**)	3,363	475	−43	−96	−17
7	Belgium and Luxembourg	2,143	143	161	246	89	(*)		(*)	(*)		184	101	−33	−30	2
8	France	3,443	160	259	430	173	6	(**)	(**)	(**)	(**)	421	19	14	29	15
9	Germany	6,260	650	386	905	495	(**)	(**)	(**)	(**)		1,650	296	35		28
10	Italy	1,989	53	70	147	79	(**)	(**)	(**)	(*)	(**)	494	−41	−69	−72	(*)
11	Netherlands	1,885	81	143	138	23	1		1			614	99	9	−60	−62
12	Other Western Europe	5,515	46	365	769	406	60	(**)	(**)	(**)	(**)	1,177	100	−21	−44	−17
13	Denmark	379	20	1	10	14	1					244	19	−8	−11	1
14	Norway	323	19	14	−3	−13	(**)	(**)	(**)	(**)	(**)	155	12	2	−23	−22
15	Spain	910	66	68	107	37	(**)	(**)	(**)	(**)	(**)	150	21	−4	(*)	3
16	Sweden	723	10	24	50	29	(*)					321	−1	−9	−9	(*)
17	Switzerland	1,951	−90	163	435	267	(*)					−1	78	4	4	2
18	Other [4]	1,229	21	94	170	73	20	(**)	(**)	(**)	(**)	308	−29	−5	−5	−2
19	Japan [5]	2,375	229	183	362	168						901	84	48	51	9
20	Australia, New Zealand and South Africa	5,395	241	250	546	326	847	117	13	89	80	1,100	75	45	87	56
21	Australia	4,123	209	185	405	255	703	94	8	63	61	(**)	(**)	(**)	(**)	(**)
22	New Zealand	245	11	25	36	11	8	(*)		(*)		(**)	(**)	(**)	(**)	(**)
23	South Africa	1,027	21	40	105	61	137	22	5	26	18	215	(**)	(**)	(**)	(**)
24	Developing countries [8]	25,235	1,134	894	4,110	3,195	2,733	57	32	199	181	9,774	658	97	2,410	2,265
25	Latin American Republics and other Western Hemisphere	16,798	300	732	1,656	967	2,099	−15	16	175	171	4,292	28	71	303	243
26	Latin American Republics	13,667	86	621	1,372	758	1,317	−46	16	81	74	3,246	−75	47	274	223
27	Mexico	2,025	75	108	197	91	124	−11	7	9	2	32	(*)	2	4	2
28	Panama	1,458	−81	113	210	108	19	(*)	(*)	(*)		269	−6	14	14	(*)
29	Other Central America [6]	638	−37	11	33	23	15	6		3	3	159	−19	−1	−10	−9
30	Argentina	1,403	26	24	89	68	(**)	(**)	(**)	(**)	(**)	(**)	(**)	(**)	(**)	(**)
31	Brazil	2,505	194	238	322	77	149	(**)	(**)	(**)	(**)	164	(*)	(**)	(**)	(**)
32	Chile	620	−93	−5	−4	7	359	−92	(**)	(**)	(**)	(**)	(**)	(*)	(**)	(**)
33	Colombia	737	−23	15	39	24	(**)	(**)	(**)	(**)	(**)	327	−18	(*)	3	3
34	Peru	712	37	4	33	26	416	12	1	26	25	(**)	(**)	(*)	(**)	(**)
35	Venezuela	2,700	−57	67	402	329	(**)	(**)	(**)	(**)	(**)	1,548	−92	6	254	246
36	Other [7]	868	44	47	50	5	39	−7	1	11	10	424	34	7	−27	−33
37	Other Western Hemisphere [8]	3,130	214	111	284	209	782	31	(*)	94	98	1,046	103	24	29	21
38	Other Africa [9]	3,091	126	99	504	410	432	24	18	26	9	2,254	87	75	454	381
39	Liberia	208	11	2	11	10	(**)	(**)	(**)	(**)	(**)	(**)	(**)	(**)	(**)	(**)
40	Libya	1,144	104	4	256	253	(**)	(**)	(**)	(**)	(**)	(**)	(**)	(**)	(**)	(**)
41	Other	1,739	11	92	237	147	369	24	16	21	6	1,132	−12	73	202	130
42	Middle East [10]	1,992	353	−22	1,391	1,418	5	3	(**)	(**)	(**)	1,767	343	−39	1,358	1,402
43	Other Asia and Pacific [5]	3,354	355	85	558	399	197	45	−2	−2	1	1,461	200	−10	294	239
44	India	337	−4	11	43	27	(**)		(**)	(**)	(**)	(**)	(**)	(**)	(**)	(**)
45	Philippines	698	6	−10	35	39	(**)	(**)	(**)	(**)	(**)	(**)	(**)	(**)	(**)	(**)
46	Other [5]	2,319	353	84	480	334	(**)	(**)	(**)	(**)	(**)	(**)	(**)	(**)	(**)	(**)
47	International and unallocated	4,743	395	111	496	400						2,336	252	43	343	306

* Less than $500,000 (±).   **Combined in the other industries category to avoid disclosure of data for individual reporters.

1. Represents a U.S. reporter's share in reinvested earnings of its foreign-incorporated affiliates.

2. Comprised of interest, dividends, and branch earnings. Petroleum branch earnings have been revised as described in the Technical Notes.

3. Direct investment statistics do not show any investment in Eastern Europe.

4. Includes Austria, Cyprus, Finland, Gibraltar, Greece, Greenland, Iceland, Ireland, Malta, Portugal, Turkey, and Yugoslavia.

5. Commencing with 1972, estimates for Okinawa are included with Japan instead of with other Asia and Pacific.

6. Includes Costa Rica, El Salvador, Guatemala, Honduras, and Nicaragua.

7. Includes Bolivia, Dominican Republic, Equador, Haiti, Paraguay, and Uruguay.

8. Includes Western Hemisphere except Canada (line 3) and the 19 Latin American Republics (line 26).

9. Includes United Arab Republic (Egypt) and all other countries in Africa except South Africa.

10. Includes Bahrain, Iran, Israel, Jordan, Kuwait, Lebanon, Qatar, Saudi Arabia, South Yemen, Syria, Trucial States, Oman, and Yemen.

Direct Investment Abroad, Selected Items

of dollars]

Manufacturing					Other					Line
Book value at year-end	Net capital outflows	Reinvested earnings [1]	Earnings	Balance of payments income [2]	Book value at year-end	Net capital outflows	Reinvested earnings [1]	Earnings	Balance of payments income [2]	
39,716	1,100	2,991	5,172	2,144	21,249	433	1,119	2,583	1,560	1
33,008	832	2,537	4,363	1,808	12,822	139	740	1,739	1,054	2
11,639	239	822	1,209	426	5,378	1	250	458	271	3
17,580	493	1,457	2,643	1,137	6,311	44	417	1,108	682	4
5,851	1	351	726	345	1,414	−25	74	250	176	5
9,755	484	885	1,602	694	2,594	128	179	360	181	6
1,182	23	135	175	42	777	19	59	101	45	7
2,493	113	197	324	128	523	28	48	77	30	8
3,855	257	314	764	402	755	97	38	140	65	9
1,173	36	124	187	63	322	58	16	31	16	10
1,052	56	115	151	59	218	−75	19	46	25	11
1,975	7	221	315	97	2,303	−61	164	498	325	12
66	−4	3	6	4	69	5	7	16	9	13
80	1	8	10	2	89	5	4	10	7	14
484	35	40	62	23	276	11	33	45	11	15
253	16	25	34	11	148	−6	8	26	18	16
529	−45	69	107	37	1,422	−122	90	324	227	17
563	4	77	97	20	338	46	22	78	54	18
1,194	102	120	236	100	280	43	15	76	59	19
2,595	−2	138	276	146	854	51	54	95	44	20
1,983	16	111	219	117	1,438	99	66	122	76	21
131	4	13	19	5	107	7	12	17	5	22
482	−21	14	37	23	193	20	21	42	19	23
6,708	267	454	809	336	6,020	151	311	692	413	24
5,597	232	380	663	272	4,809	55	266	515	280	25
5,296	222	362	627	253	3,808	−15	197	390	209	26
1,409	61	82	154	71	461	25	17	30	16	27
162	−4	20	42	20	1,008	−71	79	155	88	28
104	24	6	10	5	361	−47	6	30	23	29
839	21	4	37	35	564	5	20	53	33	30
1,745	122	197	253	1	446	72	41	69	25	31
46	1	−3	−1	16	214	−2	−2	−3	6	32
262	−9	15	31	8	148	5	(*)	5	5	33
89	−3	1	11	40	207	28	3	−4	−7	34
552	4	37	82	5	600	31	23	66	43	35
88	4	3	8		317	12	36	57	22	36
301	10	19	36	19	1,002	70	68	125	71	37
124	−3	7	7	1	283	17	(*)	17	19	38
(**)	(**)	(**)	(**)	(**)	208	11	2	11	10	39
(**)	(**)	(**)	(**)	(**)	1,144	104	4	256	253	40
122	−4	8	8	1	116	3	−4	6	11	41
104	7	5	8	3	116	(*)	11	25	13	42
883	33	62	131	60	812	77	36	135	100	43
180	(*)	11	31	17	157	−4	(*)	12	10	44
252	(*)	−6	15	15	445	6	−5	20	24	45
451	33	57	85	28	1,868	320	27	395	306	46
					2,407	143	68	153	93	47

NOTES.—Details may not add to totals because of rounding. For an explanation of the relations between earnings, reinvested earnings, and balance of payments income, see the Technical Notes. Not all countries grouped in an "other" or regional category have U.S. direct investment. Line numbers in table 10A do not match line numbers in table 10B because the change in composition of the European Economic Community necessitated changes in table 10A.

particularly steep, up 87 percent to $6.2 billion; large gains were recorded both in developed countries, where the main markets are located, and in developing countries, where most of the production for export occurs. (These earnings estimates may be revised.)[6]

Although the expansion in petroleum earnings was partly attributable to the effects on per-barrel profits of the fourth-quarter Arab production cutback, the supply situation—both for crude and for intermediate products—had been tightening for some months prior to the Arab action, because of previous restrictions on petroleum production imposed by some major producing countries and insufficient refining capacity. Also, there was a concurrent growth in U.S. demand, which led to an easing of restrictions on U.S. petroleum imports, and in demand in other major industrial countries. In the past, U.S. and foreign business upswings often were not in phase, so that rising U.S. demands could be met out of the temporary surplus in foreign refining capacity. Thus, the rise in petroleum earnings reflected basic supply and demand pressures throughout the year, in addition to the fourth quarter cutback. Some evidence as to the quarterly effects of these developments is given in table 8.

Adjusted earnings focuses on the return realized by investors, rather than on earnings from the viewpoint of affiliates. Interest is part of adjusted earnings because loans by an investor to its affiliates are included in direct investment; foreign withholding taxes are excluded because such taxes reduce benefits available to direct investors. The adjusted earnings figures are approximately the same in magnitude and area/industry pattern as the earnings figures, with by far the biggest percentage increases in petroleum.

The overall adjusted earnings rate of return was a record 17.5 percent in 1973, with each of the area and industry groups in table 3 showing strong gains.

6. See "U.S. Balance of Payments Developments: First Quarter 1974" in the June 1974 SURVEY.

However, these rates of return are somewhat overstated, because the value of the U.S. direct investment position— the denominator used to calculate the percentages—could not be adjusted upward for the December 1971 and February 1973 dollar devaluations, while the dollar value of affiliates' foreign currency earnings for 1972 and 1973 was boosted by these devaluations.[7]

Balance of payments income includes

Table 11.—Direct Investment Receipts of Fees and Royalties, by Area and Major Industry

[Millions of dollars]

Line	Area and industry	1970			1971			1972 r			1973 p		
		Total	Royalties, license fees, and rentals	Management fees and service charges	Total	Royalties, license fees, and rentals	Management fees and service charges	Total	Royalties, license fees, and rentals	Management fees and service charges	Total	Royalties, license fees, and rentals	Management fees and service charges
1	All areas	1,919	1,092	826	2,160	1,237	923	2,415	1,463	952	2,838	1,827	1,012
2	Petroleum	216	34	182	258	32	226	288	28	261	281	28	253
3	Manufacturing	1,002	635	367	1,108	755	353	1,250	896	354	1,570	1,164	406
4	Trade	156	90	65	198	116	82	238	152	86	263	196	67
5	Foreign film rentals	299	299		296	296		339	339		324	324	
6	Other	247	35	212	300	37	263	301	49	251	400	114	286
	Developed countries:												
7	Canada	357	165	192	389	186	203	420	200	220	478	226	252
8	Petroleum	17	1	16	20	1	20	22	1	21	27	1	25
9	Manufacturing	225	116	109	246	135	111	277	140	137	307	152	155
10	Trade	15	6	9	16	6	9	21	10	11	24	10	13
11	Foreign film rentals	37	37		39	39		39	39		38	38	
12	Other	63	6	57	68	5	64	61	9	52	83	24	58
13	Europe	810	568	242	936	655	282	1,089	824	265	1,308	1,055	253
14	European Economic Community (6)[1]	413	314	99	505	377	128	585	484	101	727	641	86
15	Petroleum	31	1	30	48	2	46	38	1	38	43	1	42
16	Manufacturing	287	237	50	325	290	34	388	371	17	526	512	14
17	Trade	30	21	9	53	28	25	66	39	27	55	43	12
18	Foreign film rentals	48	48		45	45		63	63		66	66	
19	Other	17	7	10	34	11	23	30	10	20	36	19	18
20	Other Europe, including United Kingdom	398	254	143	431	278	153	504	340	164	580	414	166
21	Petroleum	27	4	23	40	5	35	42	4	38	39	3	36
22	Manufacturing	229	139	90	235	150	85	267	182	85	320	223	97
23	Trade	41	39	2	47	52	−5	72	68	4	93	96	−3
24	Foreign film rentals	63	63		64	64		75	75		67	67	
25	Other	37	8	29	46	7	38	47	11	36	61	25	36
26	**Australia, New Zealand, South Africa, and Japan**	235	153	84	268	174	94	307	216	91	396	276	121
27	Petroleum	21	4	17	19	2	17	12	1	11	19	1	18
28	Manufacturing	117	68	50	144	91	53	170	120	50	226	166	59
29	Trade	11	9	2	12	10	2	13	12	1	31	23	8
30	Foreign film rentals	67	67		66	66		77	77		78	78	
31	Other	19	5	15	27	5	22	34	6	28	43	8	35
	Other areas:												
32	Latin American Republics and other Western Hemisphere	318	143	175	335	157	176	325	151	174	361	190	171
33	Petroleum	38	6	32	40	4	36	40	4	35	32	4	27
34	Manufacturing	115	62	53	129	76	52	121	68	53	135	85	49
35	Trade	33	13	20	35	17	18	34	18	16	32	19	13
36	Foreign film rentals	54	54		54	54		54	54		49	49	
37	Other	78	7	70	77	7	70	77	7	70	114	32	82
38	Other [2]	199	64	133	232	64	168	275	73	201	296	80	215
39	Petroleum	82	18	64	91	19	73	134	17	117	122	18	103
40	Manufacturing	28	12	15	30	12	17	27	15	12	57	25	31
41	Trade	26	3	23	35	3	32	31	4	27	27	4	23
42	Foreign film rentals	30	30		29	29		31	31		27	27	
43	Other	33	1	31	47	1	46	52	6	46	64	6	57
	Addenda:												
44	European Economic Community (9)[3]										1,118	902	216
45	Petroleum										73	3	70
46	Manufacturing										773	693	80
47	Trade										90	63	27
48	Foreign film rentals										107	107	
49	Other										75	36	39
50	Other Europe [4]										190	154	37
51	Petroleum										9	(*)	9
52	Manufacturing										74	43	31
53	Trade										59	77	−18
54	Foreign film rentals										26	26	
55	Other										23	8	15

r Revised.　p Preliminary.　*Less than $500,000(±).
1. Includes Belgium, France, Germany, Italy, Luxembourg and the Netherlands.
2. Includes other Africa, Middle East, other Asia and Pacific, international and unallocated.

3. Includes Denmark, Ireland, and the United Kingdom, in addition to the six countries listed in Note 1.
4. Excludes the "European Economic Community (9)" category.

NOTE.— Details may not add to totals because of rounding.

all identifiable income returns on direct investment recorded in the U.S. balance of payments accounts. This measure equals adjusted earnings less reinvested earnings. The latter are excluded be-

7. The data necessary to adjust for the effects of the dollar devaluations on the measurement of the direct investment position are not available to BEA.

cause they are not income receipts in the U.S. balance of payments accounts.

Balance of payments income on direct investment was $9.4 billion in 1973, up $2.5 billion or 36 percent from 1972. The changes in the balance of payments income measure of return are less than those in the earnings measure because most of the increase in incor-

porated affiliates' earnings is accounted for by reinvested earnings. The balance of payments income rate of return on the U.S. direct investment position was 9.3 percent in 1973, compared with 7.7 percent in 1972.

Almost all the increase in the balance of payments rate of return was from operations of petroleum affiliates, which

Table 12.—Alternative Measures of Return on U.S. Direct Investment Abroad

Line	Item and year	All areas				Developed countries				Other areas [1]			
		All industries	Petroleum	Manufacturing	Other	All industries	Petroleum	Manufacturing	Other	All industries	Petroleum	Manufacturing	Other
		Millions of dollars											
	A. Branch earnings: [r]												
1	1971	2,211	1,391	98	722	473	−5	57	421	1,738	1,396	40	301
2	1972 [p]	2,377	1,500	98	778	431	−57	61	427	1,946	1,557	37	351
3	1973 [p]	4,088	2,911	129	1,015	662	35	71	555	3,426	2,908	58	460
	B. Dividends:												
4	1971	3,549	978	1,612	959	2,161	194	1,365	602	1,389	784	248	357
5	1972 [r]	3,887	1,145	1,789	953	2,389	165	1,528	697	1,497	980	261	256
6	1973 [p]	4,593	1,129	2,364	1,100	3,071	297	2,053	721	1,522	832	311	379
	C. Foreign withholding taxes:												
7	1971	472	76	270	126	343	25	219	98	129	52	51	27
8	1972 [r]	507	103	295	110	349	27	237	85	158	76	57	25
9	1973 [p]	690	183	384	123	451	43	317	91	239	140	68	31
	D. Reinvested earnings:												
10	1971	3,157	500	1,854	803	2,437	251	1,565	621	720	249	289	182
11	1972 [r]	4,715	563	2,991	1,161	3,710	424	2,537	749	1,005	140	454	411
12	1973 [p]	8,124	1,927	4,408	1,788	6,147	1,166	3,741	1,240	1,977	761	668	548
	E. Interest: [2]												
13	1971	625	163	240	223	488	135	198	155	137	27	42	68
14	1972 [r]	662	181	257	223	510	147	220	144	152	35	37	80
15	1973 [p]	734	252	264	218	566	205	224	137	169	47	41	81
	F. Royalties and fees:												
16	1971	2,160	258	1,108	794	1,594	127	950	517	566	131	158	277
17	1972 [r]	2,415	288	1,250	877	1,815	115	1,102	598	600	173	148	279
18	1973 [p]	2,838	281	1,570	988	2,182	128	1,379	675	657	153	191	313
	G. Measures of return, dollars: Earnings: [3]												
19	1971	9,389	2,945	3,834	2,610	5,414	465	3,206	1,743	3,976	2,481	628	867
20	1972 [r]	11,485	3,311	5,172	3,002	6,880	559	4,363	1,958	4,606	2,753	809	1,044
21	1973 [p]	17,495	6,183	7,286	4,026	10,330	1,542	6,181	2,607	7,164	4,641	1,104	1,419
	Adjusted earnings: [4]												
22	1971	9,542	3,032	3,803	2,707	5,559	576	3,184	1,799	3,983	2,456	619	908
23	1972 [r]	11,640	3,390	5,135	3,115	7,040	678	4,345	2,017	4,599	2,711	790	1,099
24	1973 [p]	17,539	6,252	7,166	4,122	10,445	1,704	6,088	2,653	7,094	4,548	1,078	1,468
	Balance of payments income: [5]												
25	1971	6,385	2,532	1,950	1,904	3,122	324	1,620	1,178	3,264	2,207	330	726
26	1972 [r]	6,925	2,826	2,144	1,955	3,331	255	1,808	1,268	3,595	2,572	336	687
27	1973 [p]	9,415	4,325	2,757	2,334	4,299	537	2,348	1,414	5,117	3,787	410	920
	Balance of payments receipts: [6]												
28	1971	8,546	2,790	3,058	2,697	4,716	452	2,570	1,695	3,830	2,339	488	1,003
29	1972 [r]	9,340	3,115	3,394	2,832	5,146	370	2,910	1,866	4,195	2,745	484	966
30	1973 [p]	12,254	4,606	4,327	3,321	6,480	665	3,726	2,088	5,774	3,940	601	1,233
		Percent											
	H. Measures of return, as a percent of average of direct investment position at beginning- and end-of-year: [7] Adjusted earnings:												
31	1971	11.6	13.2	11.2	10.7	10.0	4.7	11.3	11.7	15.1	23.2	10.8	9.1
32	1972 [r]	12.9	13.4	13.6	11.4	11.5	5.0	13.9	12.2	16.0	23.3	12.4	10.2
33	1973 [p]	17.4	22.4	16.8	13.7	15.1	11.2	17.2	14.6	22.5	36.0	14.8	12.6
	Balance of payments income:												
34	1971	7.8	11.0	5.7	7.5	5.6	2.6	5.7	7.7	12.4	20.8	5.7	7.3
35	1972 [r]	7.7	11.2	5.7	7.1	5.4	1.9	5.8	7.6	12.5	22.1	5.3	6.4
36	1973 [p]	9.3	15.5	6.4	7.7	6.2	3.5	6.6	7.8	16.2	30.0	5.6	7.9
	Balance of payments receipts:												
37	1971	10.4	12.2	9.0	10.7	8.4	3.7	9.1	11.1	14.5	22.1	8.5	10.0
38	1972 [r]	10.3	12.4	9.0	10.3	8.4	2.7	9.3	11.2	14.6	23.6	7.6	8.9
39	1973 [p]	12.2	16.5	10.1	11.0	9.4	4.4	10.5	11.5	18.3	31.2	8.3	10.6

[r] Revised.   [p] Preliminary.
1. Includes developing countries, international and unallocated.
2. Includes preferred dividends, which in 1973 totaled $17 million.
3. Equals A+B+C+D.
4. Equals A+B+D+E.
5. Equals A+B+E.
6. Equals A+B+E+F.

7. The method of computation of the percentage rates of return differs from that in last year's article, which used beginning-of-year direct investment position figures as the denominator.

NOTE.—Details may not add to totals because of rounding. For an explanation of the relation between earnings, reinvested earnings, foreign withholding taxes, and interest, dividends, and branch earnings, see the Technical Notes. The definition of balance of payments income does not include royalties and fees and therefore differs from the definition given in last year's article. Petroleum branch earnings have been revised as described in the Technical Notes.

accounted for 46 percent of the U.S. direct investment balance of payments income and 60 percent of the increase in such income. Excluding petroleum, balance of payments income was $5.1 billion, a 7.0 percent rate of return, compared with 6.3 percent in 1972. The increase in the balance of payments rate of return excluding petroleum was smaller because most non-petroleum earnings come from incorporated affiliates, whose reinvested earnings are not part of U.S. balance of payments income. In contrast, branches account for nearly half of petroleum earnings abroad, and all branch earnings are included as income receipts in the U.S. balance of payments accounts.

The *balance of payments receipts* measure includes direct investment fees and royalties in addition to balance of payments income, and thus is a broader measure than balance of payments income.[8]

Balance of payments receipts were $12.3 billion, a 12.2 percent rate of return compared with the 9.3 percent balance of payments income rate of return. Much of the difference is attributable to manufacturing in developing countries, which accounted for roughly half of fee and royalty receipts.

Technical Notes

Methodology

Annual U.S. direct investment estimates are derived from a mandatory BEA sample survey covering approximately 16,000 foreign affiliates of 1,300 U.S. direct investors. Except for net capital outflows, data reported by this sample were expanded to obtain the universe estimates published in this article. Separate estimates were prepared for each reported item for 800 country-industry cells. The expansion factors were derived from an affiliate-by-affiliate match. For the matched affiliate panel, the expansion factors were the ratios of the current year values of the data items to the preceding year values. These ratios were applied to the universe estimates of the data items for the preceding year. The result was adjusted for any year-to-year changes in the sample from additions or deletions of affiliates, to give the current-year universe estimate.

Sample data on capital flows were not expanded to universe estimates but were supplemented by additional capital flow data obtained from public sources, as confirmed by the U.S. residents involved. The sum of the resulting 1973 reinvested earnings and capital flow estimates, together with valuation adjustments, were added to

the estimated yearend 1972 U.S. direct investment position to estimate the yearend 1973 position. The yearend 1972 and earlier figures were estimated in the same way, beginning with the universe data in the 1957 benchmark survey.

As the 1957 benchmark is out of date, the annual estimates in this article are subject to a significant margin of error. Revised estimates based on a 1966 benchmark survey are in preparation.

The reporters in the annual sample account for the bulk of the annual addition to the value of U.S. direct investment abroad. The sample includes those U.S. residents having aggregate direct investment abroad in branches or in foreign-incorporated affiliates, amounting to $2,000,000 or more, as measured on the books of the affiliated foreign enterprises.

Earnings

The definition of and relationship among direct investment earnings items, related items, and measures of return are as follows:

8. Terminology in this article differs from that in previous direct investment SURVEY articles, in which the term *balance of payments income* included fees and royalties. This change conforms to the current treatment in the U.S. balance of payments accounts, which list fees and royalties as payments for services rendered, rather than as income on direct investment.

1. *Net earnings of foreign-incorporated affiliates* are a U.S. direct investor's share in the earnings of its foreign-incorporated affiliates after provision for foreign income taxes and preferred dividends, but before provision for U.S. taxes.

2. *Net earnings of foreign branches* are earnings of foreign branches of U.S. direct investors after provision for foreign income taxes, but before depletion charges or provision for U.S. taxes. Also included is the U.S. share in the net earnings of other types of unincorporated foreign affiliates.

3. *Earnings* are net earnings of foreign-incorporated affiliates plus net earnings of foreign branches.

4. *Gross dividends* are dividends on common stock credited to a U.S. direct investor by its foreign-incorporated affiliates, before deduction of foreign withholding taxes.

5. *Foreign withholding taxes* are taxes on common stock dividends that are withheld by the foreign-resident payer at the time dividends are credited to a nonresident (as distinguished from an income tax on earnings). Taxes are also withheld by the payer on interest and preferred dividends, but such interest and preferred dividends are reported to BEA on a net basis; therefore, BEA estimates of withholding taxes relate only to common stock dividends.

6. *Dividends* are gross dividends on common stock less foreign withholding taxes.

7. *Preferred dividends* are dividends credited to a U.S. direct investor on its preferred or nonvoting shares in its foreign-incorporated affiliates, after deduction of foreign withholding taxes. Preferred dividends are treated in this article in the same way as interest, even though on a foreign affiliate's books preferred dividends are not charged as an expense, although interest is.

8. *Interest* is net interest on net intercompany accounts and long-term debt received by or credited to the U.S. direct investor or other nonbank U.S. investor on foreign affiliates, after deduction of foreign withholding taxes.

(*Continued on page 40*)

destination is largely due to the fact that these affiliates must be located near natural resources that they export to customers elsewhere. Unlike petroleum affiliates engaged in extraction, mining affiliates' sales to foreigners are mainly to unaffiliated rather than affiliated customers.

Affiliates engaged in trade made 68 percent of their sales locally in 1972, 28 percent were exported to third countries, and 4 percent were exported to the United States. The relatively greater importance of export sales to other foreign countries by trading affiliates, compared with manufacturing affiliates, is due to the fact that many trading affiliates act as international distributors for manufacturing affiliates of the same U.S. parent company.

Affiliates in all other industries, largely engaged in providing services, made 86 percent of their 1972 sales to local customers.

U.S. DIRECT INVESTMENT ABROAD IN 1974

Leonard A. Lupo
and
Julius N. Freidlin

BY LEONARD A. LUPO AND JULIUS N. FREIDLIN

U.S. Direct Investment Abroad in 1974

THIS article presents revised universe estimates of the U.S. direct investment position abroad at yearend, the return on the position, and associated U.S. balance of payments flows.[1] The series in this article were revised for 1966–73. The procedure by which universe estimates are prepared was refined, and the series were benchmarked to BEA's 1966 census of U.S. direct investment abroad. The previously published series for 1966–73 were benchmarked to BEA's 1957 census.[2]

Developments in 1974

Highlights

The U.S. direct investment position—the value of U.S. parents' net equity in and loans to foreign affiliates—increased 14.4 percent to $118.6 billion at yearend 1974 (charts 15 and 16). Of the $14.9 billion increase, net capital outflows and reinvested earnings accounted for $7.5 billion each, partly offset by a small negative valuation adjustment.

1. These estimates cover the accounts of U.S. direct investors (U.S. parents) with their foreign affiliates; they do not cover the accounts of the foreign affiliates. For example, dividends refer only to dividends distributed by the affiliates to their U.S. parents, not to all dividends distributed by the affiliates. The most recent universe estimates of affiliate accounts are given in *U.S. Direct Investment Abroad, 1966, Final Data*, Superintendent of Documents, U.S. Government Printing Office, Washington, D.C. 20402; price $5.15; specify catalog number C 56.109 when ordering.

2. Revised country/industry detail for 1973 and 1974 for selected series are given in this article. A forthcoming supplement will include country/industry detail for these and other direct investment series for 1966–74 and a description of the revisions to the series. For a copy of the supplement, write to the Bureau of Economic Analysis (BE–50), U.S. Department of Commerce, Washington, D.C. 20230.

NOTE.—Smith W. Allnutt III designed and supervised the benchmarking procedure. Robyn Hamilton, Ralph Kozlow, Ronald Reed, John Rutter, Richard L. Smith, Seiko Wakabayashi and Patricia C. Walker were importantly involved in the benchmarking or in the preparation of this article.

By industry, manufacturing affiliates accounted for $50.9 billion, or 43 percent, of the position; petroleum for $30.2 billion, or 25 percent; and "other industries"—where the positions in the finance and insurance, trade, and mining and smelting industries were the largest—for $37.5 billion, or 32 percent. By area, developed countries accounted for $82.8 billion, or 70 percent, of the position; developing countries for $28.5 billion, or 24 percent; and "international and unallocated" for $7.3 billion, or 6 percent.

Adjusted earnings—the return on the U.S. direct investment position—were $25.2 billion in 1974, up 48 percent from 1973 (chart 17).[3] Almost all of this increase was accounted for by earnings of unincorporated petroleum affiliates in the Middle East, and reflected higher production and higher prices. Adjusted earnings of manufacturing affiliates declined, as economic activity in most developed countries slowed markedly.

3. Adjusted earnings consists of U.S. parents' share in their foreign affiliates' earnings, less foreign withholding taxes on dividends paid to the parents by their affiliates, plus interest received from affiliates on intercompany accounts.

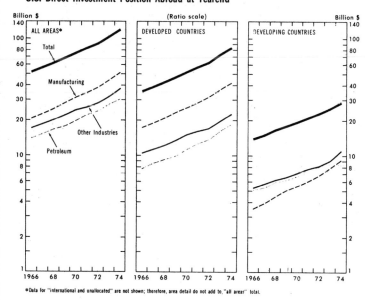

U.S. Direct Investment Position Abroad at Yearend

*Data for "international and unallocated" are not shown; therefore, area detail do not add to "all areas" total.

Balance of payments income from U.S. direct investment abroad rose from $8.8 billion in 1973 to $17.7 billion.[4] The increase was largely due to the surge in earnings of unincorporated petroleum affiliates. Balance of payments income from incorporated petroleum and other nonmanufacturing affiliates also increased, as dividend payout ratios and earnings rose. Income from manufacturing affiliates was virtually unchanged, as increased dividend payout ratios offset a decrease in earnings.

The 1974 addition to the direct investment position

By industry and area, the distribu-

4. Balance of payments income consists of U.S. parents' receipts of dividends from their foreign affiliates (after deducting foreign withholding taxes), interest received from affiliates on intercompany accounts, and earnings of unincorporated affiliates.

tion of the addition to the position last year changed significantly (table 1). By industry, petroleum affiliates accounted for 20 percent of the addition (compared with 25 percent in 1973), manufacturing affiliates for 44 percent (46 percent), and "other industries" for 37 percent (29 percent). Half of the "other industries" increase was in finance and insurance, as discussed below. By area, developed countries accounted for 71 percent of the addition (compared with 77 percent in 1973); the decline in the percentage was accounted for by European petroleum and manufacturing affiliates.

The components of additions to the position for incorporated affiliates differ from those for unincorporated affiliates. Additions for incorporated affiliates consist of reinvested earnings and net capital outflows, as shown in table 2.

Additions for unincorporated affiliates equal net capital outflows (table 3). No reinvested earnings are shown for unincorporated affiliates, as the U.S. balance of payments accounts treat such earnings as remitted to the United States. To the extent that earnings of unincorporated affiliates are reinvested, they are included (but not separately shown) in net capital outflows to such affiliates.

Addition to position of incorporated affiliates

Incorporated affiliates accounted for $13.4 billion, or 90 percent of the addition to the U.S. direct investment position in 1974. Reinvested earnings were $7.5 billion, down $0.6 billion from 1973; net capital outflows were $5.7 billion, up $2.0 billion; and there were small valuation adjustments.[5]

CHART 16

Annual Additions to Direct Investment Abroad

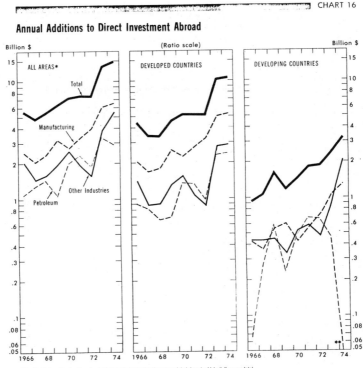

*Data for "international and unallocated" are not shown, therefore, area detail do not add to "all areas total.

**Petroleum addition in 1974 was reduction of $175 million.

U.S. Department of Commerce, Bureau of Economic Analysis

75-10-16

Reinvested earnings.—The decline in reinvested earnings in part reflected negative reinvested earnings of affiliates manufacturing transportation equipment in Europe and Latin America, as dividends exceeded earnings. Some of these affiliates increased dividends despite decreased earnings; others registered losses, mainly because of declines in auto sales.

Reinvested earnings of chemical affiliates rose, as their earnings increased and dividend payout ratios declined. These affiliates needed funds to finance exceptionally large plant and equipment expenditures in 1974,[6] and to finance

_____

5. The major valuation adjustments are capital gains and losses not carried through the affiliate's income account, and the difference between the market value and book value of transactions in the affiliate's equity shares by the U.S. parent with persons other than the affiliate.

6. "Property, Plant, and Equipment Expenditures by Majority Owned Foreign Affiliates of U.S. Companies: Projections for 1975 and 1976" in the September 1975 SURVEY OF CURRENT BUSINESS.

inventories of petroleum-based raw materials and intermediate products after the petroleum embargo. For all other industries combined, reinvested earnings were slightly lower than in 1973, as dividends increased somewhat more than earnings (table 4).

Despite their decline in 1974, reinvested earnings remained high. For the third successive year, they accounted for a larger share of the addition to the direct investment position than did net capital outflows. In earlier years the greater part of the addition usually had been financed by net capital outflows.

Several factors contributed to the relatively high level of reinvested earnings in 1974. As in the previous two years, the depreciation of the dollar against a number of leading currencies since 1971 increased the dollar value of affiliates' earnings in those currencies, and reduced the proportion

of such earnings needed to make dollar remittances to U.S. parents. Also, larger reinvested earnings were required by affiliates to finance inflated costs of their property, plant, and equipment expenditures from internal funds; external funds were either too costly or, in some cases, unavailable. Finally, because of the rapid inflation, a good part of affiliate earnings probably represented book profits on inventories, which were not available for payout as dividends.

Net capital outflows.—All of the $2.0 billion increase, to $5.7 billion, in net capital outflows was in short-term intercompany loans from U.S. parents to their foreign affiliates. Long-term intercompany loans were small, and net equity investment was $1.8 billion, about the same as in 1973 (table 3).

Some of the increase in short-term intercompany loans apparently was related to worldwide inflation, which

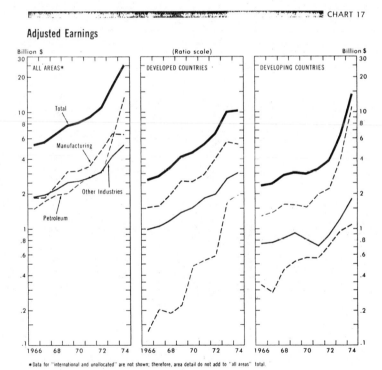

CHART 17

Adjusted Earnings

*Data for "international and unallocated" are not shown; therefore, area detail do not add to "all areas" total.

U.S. Department of Commerce, Bureau of Economic Analysis   75-10-17

Table 1.—U.S. Direct Investment Position Abroad, 1972–74

[Millions of dollars]

Area and industry	Position, yearend 1972	Addition in 1973				Position, yearend 1973	Addition in 1974				Position, yearend 1974
		Total	Net capital outflows[1]	Reinvested earnings	Valuation adjustments		Total	Net capital outflows[1]	Reinvested earnings	Valuation adjustments	
All areas	90,467	13,208	4,968	8,158	82	103,675	14,938	7,455	7,508	−26	118,613
Petroleum	23,974	3,339	1,442	1,925	−28	27,313	2,935	1,158	1,814	−37	30,248
Manufacturing	38,325	6,045	1,863	4,107	75	44,370	6,545	2,712	3,786	46	50,915
Other	28,168	3,824	1,663	2,126	35	31,992	5,458	3,585	1,907	−34	37,450
Developed countries	62,060	10,154	3,810	6,177	167	72,214	10,578	5,042	5,523	13	82,792
Petroleum	13,542	2,369	1,109	1,240	19	15,911	2,441	1,292	1,180	−30	18,352
Manufacturing	31,558	4,992	1,420	3,488	84	36,550	5,243	2,103	3,082	57	41,793
Other	16,959	2,794	1,280	1,449	64	19,753	2,894	1,647	1,261	−14	22,647
Canada	22,985	2,556	581	1,867	109	25,541	2,837	629	2,202	5	28,378
Petroleum	4,764	556	106	452	−2	5,320	396	−107	512	−9	5,716
Manufacturing	10,491	1,264	148	1,008	107	11,755	1,691	415	1,289	−13	13,446
Other	7,730	737	327	406	3	8,467	748	321	400	27	9,215
Europe	31,696	6,559	3,070	3,507	−17	38,255	6,250	3,563	2,721	−34	44,505
Petroleum	6,872	1,652	1,057	575	21	8,524	1,470	974	517	−21	9,994
Manufacturing	17,529	3,248	1,225	2,071	−48	20,777	2,988	1,515	1,448	26	23,765
Other	7,295	1,659	788	861	10	8,954	1,792	1,074	757	−39	10,746
Other developed	7,378	1,039	159	804	76	8,417	1,492	850	600	42	9,909
Petroleum	1,906	160	−53	213	(*)	2,066	576	425	151	(*)	2,642
Manufacturing	3,538	481	47	409	25	4,019	562	173	345	44	4,581
Other	1,934	398	165	182	51	2,332	354	252	105	−3	2,686
Developing countries	22,863	2,403	921	1,568	−85	25,266	3,213	1,718	1,558	−63	28,479
Petroleum	7,965	471	24	494	−47	8,436	−175	−592	423	−7	8,261
Manufacturing	6,767	1,053	443	619	−9	7,820	1,302	609	705	−11	9,122
Other	8,130	880	454	454	−29	9,010	2,087	1,701	430	−45	11,097
Latin America	14,897	1,587	654	991	−59	16,484	3,136	2,270	915	−48	19,620
Petroleum	2,979	64	−54	155	−37	3,043	514	421	85	8	3,557
Manufacturing	5,620	836	360	476	(*)	6,456	1,031	503	534	−8	7,487
Other	6,297	687	348	360	−22	6,984	1,592	1,346	295	−49	8,576
Other developing	7,966	816	266	576	−26	8,782	77	−552	643	−15	8,859
Petroleum	4,986	406	78	339	−10	5,392	−689	−1,013	338	−14	4,703
Manufacturing	1,147	215	83	143	−10	1,362	272	105	170	−4	1,634
Other	1,833	194	106	94	−7	2,027	494	356	135	3	2,521
International and unallocated	5,545	651	238	413	(*)	6,196	1,145	694	426	25	7,341

*. Less than $500,000 (±).
2. These estimates, by area, are in line 39 of table 9 in the U.S. balance of payments articles in the March, June, September, and December issues of the SURVEY.

NOTE.—Details may not add to totals because of rounding.

Table 2.—U.S. Direct Investment Position Abroad—Incorporated Affiliates, 1972–74

[Millions of dollars]

Area and industry	Position, yearend 1972	Addition in 1973				Position, yearend 1973	Addition in 1974				Position, yearend 1974
		Total	Net capital outflows	Reinvested earnings	Valuation adjustments		Total	Net capital outflows	Reinvested earnings	Valuation adjustments	
All areas	75,579	11,967	3,692	8,158	117	87,546	13,409	5,736	7,508	166	100,955
Petroleum	16,247	2,648	721	1,925	3	18,895	3,191	1,282	1,814	94	22,086
Manufacturing	37,414	5,965	1,779	4,107	79	43,379	6,426	2,595	3,786	45	49,805
Other	21,918	3,354	1,192	2,126	36	25,272	3,793	1,859	1,907	27	29,065
Developed countries	56,281	9,422	3,070	6,177	175	65,703	9,621	4,005	5,523	93	75,324
Petroleum	11,633	2,050	788	1,240	22	13,683	1,746	532	1,180	34	15,429
Manufacturing	31,131	4,925	1,350	3,488	88	36,056	5,172	2,032	3,082	58	41,228
Other	13,517	2,446	932	1,449	65	15,963	2,704	1,442	1,261	1	18,667
Canada	19,657	2,453	473	1,867	113	22,110	2,853	598	2,202	53	24,963
Petroleum	3,679	540	85	452	3	4,219	435	−117	512	39	4,654
Manufacturing	10,400	1,251	135	1,008	107	11,651	1,671	395	1,289	−13	13,322
Other	5,579	661	252	406	3	6,240	748	321	400	27	6,988
Europe	30,266	6,114	2,622	3,507	−14	36,380	5,287	2,568	2,721	−3	41,667
Petroleum	6,363	1,344	747	575	21	7,707	645	133	517	−5	8,352
Manufacturing	17,257	3,201	1,176	2,071	−45	20,458	2,951	1,477	1,448	27	23,400
Other	6,646	1,570	699	861	10	8,216	1,690	959	757	−25	9,906
Other developed	6,358	854	−25	804	75	7,212	1,482	838	600	43	8,694
Petroleum	1,591	166	−45	213	−2	1,757	667	516	151	0	2,424
Manufacturing	3,474	473	39	409	25	3,947	550	160	345	45	4,497
Other	1,293	215	−19	182	52	1,508	265	162	105	−1	1,773
Developing countries	14,097	1,986	476	1,568	−57	16,083	2,687	1,082	1,558	48	18,770
Petroleum	2,337	191	−284	494	−20	2,528	822	339	423	60	3,350
Manufacturing	6,284	1,038	429	619	−9	7,322	1,254	563	705	−13	8,576
Other	5,476	757	331	454	−29	6,233	611	179	430	1	6,844
Latin America	10,061	1,471	518	991	−39	11,532	1,872	910	915	48	13,404
Petroleum	759	−17	−155	155	−17	742	647	502	85	60	1,389
Manufacturing	5,189	828	353	476	(*)	6,017	1,001	473	534	−8	7,018
Other	4,114	659	320	360	−22	4,773	224	−66	295	−4	4,997
Other developing	4,035	516	−42	576	−18	4,551	815	172	643	(*)	5,366
Petroleum	1,578	208	−129	339	−2	1,786	175	−163	338	(*)	1,961
Manufacturing	1,095	209	76	143	−10	1,304	254	90	170	−6	1,558
Other	1,362	98	11	94	−7	1,460	387	246	135	6	1,847
International and unallocated	5,201	559	146	413	(*)	5,760	1,101	649	426	25	6,861

*. Less than $500,000 (±).

NOTE.—Details may not add to totals because of rounding.

Table 3.—Net Capital Outflows, 1973-74

[Millions of dollars]

Area and industry	1973							1974						
	Total	To incorporated affiliates					To unincorporated affiliates	Total	To incorporated affiliates					To unincorporated affiliates
		Total	Net equity	Net intercompany account					Total	Net equity	Net intercompany account			
				Total	Short-term	Long-term					Total	Short-term	Long-term	
All areas	4,968	3,692	1,882	1,810	1,724	86	1,276	7,455	5,736	1,793	3,943	3,705	238	1,719
Petroleum	1,442	721	227	495	578	-84	721	1,158	1,282	106	1,176	1,599	-423	-125
Manufacturing	1,863	1,779	975	804	698	107	84	2,712	2,595	940	1,655	1,389	266	117
Other	1,663	1,192	681	511	449	62	471	3,585	1,859	747	1,112	716	396	1,726
Developed countries	3,810	3,070	1,480	1,590	1,420	170	740	5,042	4,005	1,415	2,590	2,624	-34	1,037
Petroleum	1,109	788	229	558	606	-47	322	1,292	532	74	458	907	-449	760
Manufacturing	1,420	1,350	801	549	490	58	70	2,103	2,032	740	1,292	1,107	185	72
Other	1,280	932	450	483	324	159	348	1,647	1,442	601	841	610	230	206
Canada	581	473	133	339	62	278	108	629	598	191	408	248	160	5
Petroleum	106	85	8	77	-35	113	20	-107	-117	7	-124	-115	-9	10
Manufacturing	148	135	56	79	50	29	13	415	395	93	302	289	12	21
Other	327	252	69	183	47	136	75	321	321	90	230	73	157	1
Europe	3,070	2,622	1,372	1,250	1,373	-123	448	3,563	2,568	1,120	1,448	1,644	-196	395
Petroleum	1,057	747	216	532	745	-213	309	974	133	66	66	511	-445	841
Manufacturing	1,225	1,176	740	436	370	66	50	1,515	1,477	624	853	685	168	38
Other	788	699	417	282	258	24	89	1,074	959	430	529	448	81	116
Other developed	159	-25	-25	(*)	-15	15	184	850	838	104	734	732	2	12
Petroleum	-53	-45	6	-51	-104	53	-8	425	516	0	516	510	6	-91
Manufacturing	47	39	6	34	70	-36	8	173	160	23	137	133	4	33
Other	165	-19	-37	17	19	-1	184	252	162	81	82	89	-7	89
Developing countries	921	476	399	77	172	-95	445	1,718	1,082	308	774	526	248	637
Petroleum	24	-284	-21	-263	-174	-89	308	-592	339	9	330	304	26	-931
Manufacturing	443	429	173	256	207	49	14	609	563	200	364	283	81	45
Other	454	331	246	85	139	-54	123	1,701	179	99	80	-61	142	1,523
Latin America	654	518	364	154	132	22	136	2,270	910	227	683	515	168	1,360
Petroleum	-54	-155	-1	-154	-165	11	101	421	502	5	497	439	58	-81
Manufacturing	360	353	166	187	142	44	8	503	473	168	306	232	74	30
Other	348	320	199	121	154	-33	28	1,346	-66	54	-120	-157	37	1,412
Other developing	266	-42	35	-77	40	-117	308	-552	172	81	91	11	80	-724
Petroleum	78	-129	-20	-109	-9	-100	207	-1,013	-163	4	-167	-135	-32	-542
Manufacturing	83	76	7	69	65	4	6	105	90	32	58	50	7	16
Other	106	11	48	-37	-16	-21	95	356	246	45	201	96	105	116
International and unallocated	238	146	3	143	133	11	92	694	649	70	579	556	24	45

*Less than $500,000 (±).

NOTE.—Details may not add to totals because of rounding.

Table 4.—Dividend Payout Ratios of Incorporated Affiliates, 1973-74

[Millions of dollars, or ratio]

Area and industry	1973		1974		1973	1974
	Earnings	Gross dividends	Earnings	Gross dividends	Payout ratio (gross dividends/earnings)	
All areas	13,020	4,862	14,049	6,541	0.373	0.466
Petroleum	3,260	1,335	4,088	2,274	.410	.556
Manufacturing	6,584	2,477	6,279	2,493	.376	.397
Other	3,175	1,049	3,682	1,774	.330	.482
Developed countries	9,376	3,199	9,630	4,106	.341	.426
Petroleum	1,596	356	1,977	796	.223	.403
Manufacturing	5,638	2,150	5,278	2,196	.381	.416
Other	2,142	692	2,375	1,114	.323	.469
Canada	2,567	700	3,071	869	.273	.283
Petroleum	596	144	675	162	.242	.240
Manufacturing	1,441	432	1,774	484	.300	.273
Other	531	125	623	223	.235	.358
Europe	5,544	2,038	5,441	2,719	.368	.500
Petroleum	750	176	1,078	561	.235	.520
Manufacturing	3,464	1,393	2,887	1,439	.402	.498
Other	1,331	470	1,476	719	.353	.487
Other developed	1,265	461	1,118	518	.364	.463
Petroleum	250	38	224	74	.152	.330
Manufacturing	734	325	618	273	.443	.442
Other	280	98	276	171	.350	.620
Developing countries	3,014	1,446	3,613	2,055	.480	.569
Petroleum	1,334	840	1,701	1,278	.630	.751
Manufacturing	945	327	1,001	297	.346	.297
Other	735	280	912	482	.381	.529
Latin America	1,519	527	1,897	683	.347	.428
Petroleum	221	65	161	76	.294	.472
Manufacturing	730	254	767	232	.348	.303
Other	567	207	669	374	.365	.559
Other developing	1,495	918	2,016	1,373	.614	.681
Petroleum	1,112	773	1,539	1,201	.695	.780
Manufacturing	215	72	234	64	.335	.274
Other	167	73	243	108	.437	.444
International and unallocated	630	217	806	379	.344	.470

NOTE.—Details may not add to totals because of rounding.

boosted working capital requirements for carrying manufacturing inventories and trade receivables. Rebuilding of petroleum inventories, at sharply higher prices after the embargo, was another factor.

Virtually all the $1.8 billion in net equity investment resulted from transactions of U.S. parents with existing affiliates, largely those in manufacturing and in finance and insurance, particularly in Europe. Net equity investment resulting from transactions with unaffiliated foreigners was negligible, as equity acquisitions of $0.4 billion were offset by sales of about the same amount (table 5).

Another factor in the overall increase in net capital outflows to incorporated affiliates was the termination, early in 1974, of mandatory U.S. controls on direct investment abroad and the relaxation of some foreign regulations on capital inflows. U.S. controls had restricted financing of affiliates by U.S. parents with funds raised in the United States and had encouraged them to finance affiliates with funds raised abroad. With the end of the

Table 5.—Acquisitions From and Sales to Unaffiliated Foreigners of Voting Stock—Incorporated Affiliates, 1973–74 [1]

[Millions of dollars]

Area and industry	Acquisitions		Sales	
	1973	1974	1973	1974
All areas	666	370	627	399
Petroleum	12	2	99	36
Manufacturing	425	292	275	210
Other	229	76	253	152
Developed countries	575	306	343	254
Petroleum	10	1	65	27
Manufacturing	366	248	176	173
Other	198	57	102	53
Canada	26	85	27	54
Petroleum	6	1	5	(*)
Manufacturing	12	80	15	16
Other	8	4	7	38
Europe	517	186	156	175
Petroleum	(*)	0	60	27
Manufacturing	329	144	93	133
Other	187	42	3	15
Other developed	32	35	160	25
Petroleum	4	0	0	0
Manufacturing	25	23	68	24
Other	3	11	92	(*)
Developing countries	91	63	(D)	145
Petroleum	2	0	34	9
Manufacturing	59	44	99	36
Other	31	20	(D)	99
Latin America	70	55	85	76
Petroleum	(*)	0	2	0
Manufacturing	49	44	75	27
Other	21	11	8	49
Other developing	21	8	(D)	69
Petroleum	2	0	32	9
Manufacturing	10	0	24	9
Other	10	8	(D)	50
International and unallocated	0	0	(D)	(*)

*Less than $500,000.   D Suppressed to avoid disclosure of data of individual companies.

1. Acquisitions and sales are components of net capital flows to incorporated foreign affiliates.

Acquisitions include partial and total purchases of voting securities of existing foreign corporations from unaffiliated foreign owners. Sales include partial and total sales of voting securities of foreign corporations by U.S. owners to unaffiliated foreign purchasers. Liquidations through the sale of assets, as distinct from sale of ownership interests, are not included. Changes in the share of ownership resulting from transactions between a parent and an affiliate—such as the purchase of Treasury stock from an affiliate by a parent—are not included; only changes involving outside owners or purchasers are included.

NOTE.—Details may not add to totals because of rounding.

Table 6.—U.S. Corporate Foreign Borrowing and Claims Other Than Direct Investment [1]

[Millions of dollars]

Balance of payments sign (Credits +, debits −)	1973	1974
Corporate borrowing	2,424	1,472
New issues of securities sold abroad by U.S. Corporations [2]	1,222	116
Other long-term liabilities	332	−524
Short-term liabilities	870	1,880
Corporate claims	−2,579	−3,175

1. Excludes claims and liabilities of U.S. banking and brokerage institutions.

2. Includes proceeds from new issues of stock as well as bonds sold abroad by U.S. corporations. Excludes funds obtained abroad by U.S. corporations through bank loans and other credits and also excludes securities issued by subsidiaries incorporated abroad. However, securities issued by finance subsidiaries incorporated in the Netherlands Antilles are treated as if they had been issued by U.S. corporations to the extent that the proceeds of such issues are transferred to U.S. parent companies.

Source: Table C in "U.S. Balance of Payments Developments: First Quarter 1975," in the June 1975 SURVEY.

Table 7.—Adjusted Earnings Return on U.S. Direct Investment Abroad, 1973–74

Area and industry	Millions of dollars		Percent rate of return [1]	
	1973	1974	1973	1974
All areas	16,999	25,186	17.5	22.7
Petroleum	6,174	13,513	24.1	47.0
Manufacturing	6,579	6,422	15.9	13.5
Other	4,246	5,251	14.1	15.1
Developed countries	10,052	10,341	15.0	13.3
Petroleum	1,739	1,958	11.8	11.4
Manufacturing	5,607	5,337	16.5	13.6
Other	2,707	3,046	14.8	14.4
Canada	2,844	3,385	11.7	12.6
Petroleum	648	760	12.9	13.8
Manufacturing	1,450	1,786	13.0	14.2
Other	746	839	9.2	9.5
Europe	5,751	5,609	16.4	13.6
Petroleum	771	882	10.0	9.5
Manufacturing	3,429	2,929	17.9	13.2
Other	1,551	1,798	19.1	18.3
Other developed	1,458	1,347	18.5	14.7
Petroleum	320	316	16.1	13.4
Manufacturing	728	621	19.3	14.4
Other	410	409	19.2	16.3
Developing countries	6,297	14,023	26.2	52.2
Petroleum	4,089	11,135	49.9	133.4
Manufacturing	972	1,085	13.3	12.8
Other	1,235	1,803	14.4	17.9
Latin America	2,511	2,882	16.0	16.0
Petroleum	805	758	26.7	23.0
Manufacturing	751	841	12.4	12.1
Other	955	1,284	14.4	16.5
Other developing	3,785	11,141	45.2	126.3
Petroleum	3,284	10,377	63.3	205.6
Manufacturing	221	244	17.6	16.3
Other	280	519	14.5	22.8
International and unallocated	650	822	11.1	12.1

1. Adjusted earnings divided by the average of the beginning- and end-of-year direct investment positions.

NOTE.—Details may not add to totals because of rounding.

Table 9.—Adjusted Earnings and Related Items: Derivation and Relationship

[Millions of dollars]

	1974 amount and source
1. Earnings of incorporated affiliates	14,049 reported.
2. Earnings of unincorporated affiliates	11,091 reported.
3. Earnings	25,141 = 1+2.
4. Gross dividends (on common and preferred stock)	6,541 = 5 − 6.
5. Foreign withholding tax on dividends	691 derived.
6. Dividends	5,850 reported.
7. Interest	737 reported.
8. Reinvested earnings	7,508 = 1−4 or 10−9.
9. Balance of payments income	17,678 = 2+6+7 or 10−8.
10. Adjusted earnings	25,186 = 3−5+7 or 8+9.

NOTE.—Details may not add to totals because of rounding. "Reported" refers to universe estimates derived from reported sample data.

controls, there was less incentive for U.S. parents to borrow abroad; in 1974, foreign borrowing by U.S. corporations—most of which were U.S. parents—declined nearly $1.0 billion (table 6).

Addition to position of unincorporated affiliates

Unincorporated affiliates accounted for $1.5 billion, or 10 percent, of the

(Continued on page 64)

Table 8.—Balance of Payments Income on U.S. Direct Investment Abroad, 1973–74

[Millions of dollars]

Area and industry	1973				1974			
	Total [1]	Interest	Dividends	Earnings of unincorporated affiliates	Total [1]	Interest	Dividends	Earnings of unincorporated affiliates
All areas	8,841	612	4,309	3,920	17,678	737	5,850	11,091
Petroleum	4,249	207	1,174	2,868	11,699	260	2,014	9,425
Manufacturing	2,472	203	2,179	91	2,636	217	2,200	219
Other	2,120	202	956	962	3,343	260	1,636	1,447
Developed countries	3,875	438	2,838	599	4,817	503	3,674	640
Petroleum	499	152	317	30	778	194	724	−141
Manufacturing	2,119	168	1,898	53	2,255	168	1,945	142
Other	1,257	118	623	516	1,784	140	1,005	639
Canada	977	140	609	228	1,183	165	756	262
Petroleum	196	8	125	63	248	9	141	98
Manufacturing	442	57	376	9	497	58	421	18
Other	339	75	109	156	439	99	194	146
Europe	2,244	227	1,828	189	2,888	258	2,468	162
Petroleum	196	109	160	−72	365	144	520	−298
Manufacturing	1,358	95	1,239	24	1,482	94	1,286	101
Other	690	23	430	237	1,041	20	662	359
Other developed	654	71	401	183	746	80	450	216
Petroleum	107	35	33	39	165	42	64	60
Manufacturing	319	16	283	20	276	17	237	22
Other	228	20	85	123	305	22	149	134
Developing countries	4,729	148	1,255	3,326	12,465	193	1,797	10,476
Petroleum	3,595	35	718	2,842	10,712	32	1,090	9,590
Manufacturing	353	34	281	38	381	49	255	78
Other	781	79	257	445	1,373	112	453	808
Latin America	1,520	99	461	960	1,968	148	616	1,204
Petroleum	650	2	56	592	673	4	68	600
Manufacturing	275	30	217	29	307	41	197	68
Other	595	68	187	340	988	103	350	536
Other developing	3,209	49	794	2,366	10,498	44	1,181	9,272
Petroleum	2,945	33	661	2,251	10,039	28	1,021	8,990
Manufacturing	78	5	63	9	74	8	57	10
Other	186	10	70	106	384	9	103	273
International and unallocated	237	26	216	−5	396	42	378	−24

1. These estimates, by area, are in line 11 of table 9 in the U.S. balance of payments articles in the March, June, September, and December issues of the SURVEY.

NOTE. Details may not add to totals because of rounding.

Table 10.—Direct Investment Receipts of Fees and Royalties, 1973–74

[Millions of dollars]

Area and item [1][2]	1973 Total	Petroleum	Mfg. Total	Chemicals and allied products	Machinery	Transportation equipment	Other	Trade	Other	1974 Total	Petroleum	Mfg. Total	Chemicals and allied products	Machinery	Transportation equipment	Other	Trade	Other
All areas	2,513	251	1,552	326	608	145	473	139	571	3,023	286	1,855	404	702	203	545	178	705
Royalties & license fees	1,376	7	1,168	248	627	31	261	103	98	1,614	9	1,365	293	719	28	325	120	120
Other	1,138	245	384	78	-19	113	211	37	473	1,409	277	490	111	-16	175	220	57	586
Developed countries	1,949	111	1,366	279	574	132	381	113	359	2,360	128	1,662	347	670	190	454	138	432
Royalties & license fees	1,238	4	1,061	211	601	24	225	84	88	1,450	6	1,244	250	689	22	283	98	103
Other	711	106	304	68	-28	108	157	29	271	910	122	419	97	-19	169	172	40	329
Canada	416	25	298	41	74	90	94	21	71	525	27	388	51	86	147	105	29	80
Royalties & license fees	142	1	128	26	52	8	42	9	5	167	1	151	30	65	6	51	8	6
Other	274	24	170	15	22	82	52	12	67	358	26	237	21	21	141	54	21	74
Europe	1,180	70	848	199	398	28	223	71	190	1,420	85	1,005	240	465	31	269	86	245
Royalties & license fees	885	3	755	157	449	8	141	60	66	1,013	5	888	184	516	12	177	71	79
Other	295	67	93	42	-51	20	82	11	124	377	80	117	56	-51	19	92	15	166
European Economic Community (9)	1,028	62	760	183	369	25	193	59	138	1,231	75	918	221	434	29	234	66	173
Royalties & license fees	776	3	702	143	432	(D)	(D)	48	22	913	5	829	167	498	11	153	53	26
Other	252	59	67	40	-63	(D)	(D)	11	116	318	70	89	54	-64	18	82	13	146
United Kingdom	330	24	234	57	88	12	77	18	53	382	32	260	69	96	15	89	14	67
Royalties & license fees	198	2	178	40	90	(D)	(D)	14	3	230	3	210	49	103	5	53	13	3
Other	132	22	56	17	-2	(D)	(D)	4	50	152	28	59	20	-7	10	36	1	64
Belgium and Luxembourg	85	3	68	24	38	1	6	12	2	112	(D)	92	30	53	1	9	9	(D)
Royalties & license fees	57	0	47	14	28	1	5	8	2	76	1	65	18	36	(*)	10	9	2
Other	28	3	21	10	10	(*)	(*)	4	(*)	36	(D)	27	11	17	(*)	-1	(*)	(D)
France	176	13	132	24	62	4	43	7	24	197	15	119	26	66	4	53	10	23
Royalties & license fees	163	1	151	21	96	3	30	10	1	180	1	170	22	102	4	41	9	1
Other	13	12	-19	3	-34	(*)	12	-3	23	16	15	-21	3	-36	(*)	12	1	22
Germany	224	(D)	184	28	123	(D)	(D)	9	(D)	268	(D)	214	36	136	6	36	11	(D)
Royalties & license fees	193	(*)	181	25	143	(*)	14	7	4	225	(*)	209	27	162	1	20	9	6
Other	32	3	3	3	-20	(D)	(D)	2	(D)	42	(D)	5	10	-26	6	15	1	(D)
Italy	116	7	83	19	45	1	18	8	18	145	(D)	111	19	71	2	19	10	(D)
Royalties & license fees	84	(*)	77	15	(D)	(*)	(D)	5	1	99	(*)	92	13	68	1	10	5	1
Other	31	7	5	4	(D)	1	(D)	2	17	46	(D)	19	6	3	1	9	4	(D)
Netherlands	76	(D)	60	29	11	(D)	(D)	3	(D)	97	5	73	38	11	1	24	6	13
Royalties & license fees	66	0	62	26	(D)	(D)	(D)	3	2	84	(*)	77	34	26	(*)	16	5	2
Other	10	(D)	-2	3	(D)	(D)	(D)	(*)	(D)	13	5	-4	4	-15	1	7	1	11
Other [3]	21	1	8	3	1	(*)	4	2	11	31	1	10	4	1	(*)	5	7	13
Royalties & license fees	15	(*)	5	2	1	0	3	1	9	18	(*)	6	3	1	0	2	2	10
Other	6	1	2	1	1	(*)	1	1	2	12	1	4	1	(*)	(*)	3	5	3
Other	152	8	79	16	29	3	30	13	52	189	10	87	19	32	2	35	20	72
Royalties & license fees	109	(*)	53	14	17	(D)	(D)	12	44	130	1	59	17	18	(*)	24	18	53
Other	42	8	26	2	12	(D)	(D)	1	8	59	9	28	3	14	1	11	2	20
Japan	170	9	134	14	86	6	28	7	20	203	8	161	23	102	3	35	7	27
Royalties & license fees	139	(*)	131	12	89	6	24	7	1	157	(*)	148	17	96	3	32	8	1
Other	31	9	3	2	-3	(*)	5	(*)	20	46	8	13	5	5	(*)	3	-1	26
Australia, New Zealand, and South Africa	183	7	86	25	16	8	36	14	77	212	7	108	35	18	10	45	16	80
Royalties & license fees	72	(*)	48	17	12	1	18	8	17	84	(*)	57	20	12	1	24	10	17
Other	111	7	38	8	5	7	18	6	60	128	8	51	15	6	9	22	6	63
Developing countries	519	123	186	47	34	13	91	11	200	611	136	192	57	32	12	91	23	260
Royalties & license fees	131	2	107	37	26	7	37	13	10	156	3	121	43	29	7	42	16	16
Other	388	121	79	11	8	5	55	-2	190	455	134	71	15	2	6	48	7	243
Latin America	269	25	135	40	17	12	67	2	107	332	31	147	52	13	11	71	3	140
Royalties & license fees	102	1	81	30	13	7	31	11	9	110	1	91	35	15	6	34	11	8
Other	168	24	54	10	3	5	36	-9	99	216	29	55	16	-2	5	36	(*)	131
of which, Mexico	80	1	73	29	7	5	32	-5	11	95	1	85	38	6	6	36	-4	12
Royalties & license fees	55	(*)	51	23	8	4	16	3	1	66	(*)	59	25	9	4	20	5	1
Other	25	1	22	6	-1	1	16	-8	10	29	1	27	13	-4	1	16	-9	11
Other Africa	80	45	3	1	0	0	2	2	30	61	43	3	1	(*)	0	2	2	14
Royalties & license fees	(*)	(*)	1	(*)	(*)	0	(*)	(*)	-1	3	(*)	1	(*)	0	(*)		2	2
Other	80	45	2	(*)	(*)	0	2	1	31	59	43	2	(*)	(*)	0	2	2	12
Middle East	63	25	4	2	(*)	(*)	2	(*)	34	124	38	5	2	1	(*)	3	1	80
Royalties & license fees	3	(*)	2	1	1	(*)	(*)	(*)	(*)	7	(*)	3	1	1	(*)	1	(*)	4
Other	60	24	2	(*)	(*)	0	2	(*)	34	117	38	2	(*)	(*)	0	2	1	76
Other Asia and Pacific	108	28	44	5	17	1	20	6	29	94	24	37	3	18	1	15	7	26
Royalties & license fees	27	1	22	5	12	1	5	1	2	30	(*)	25	5	14	(*)	5	2	2
Other	81	27	22	(*)	5	1	15	5	27	64	24	12	-2	4	1	9	5	23
International and unallocated	46	17						16	12	52	22						17	14

*Less than $500,000 (±).   ᴰ Suppressed to avoid disclosure of data of individual companies.

1. These estimates, by area, are in line 7 of table 9 in the U.S. balance of payments articles in the March, June, September, and December issues of the SURVEY.

2. Royalties and license fees consists of payments for the sale or use of intangible property such as patents, processes, trademarks and copyrights; "other" consists of management fees, service charges, film and television tape rentals, and rentals for tangible property.

3. Other includes Denmark and Ireland.

NOTE.—Details may not add to totals because of rounding.

Table 11.—U.S. Direct Investment Abroad,

[Millions

Line	Area and industry	1966	1967	1968	1969	1970	1971	1972	1973	1974
		Direct investment position								
1	**All areas**	51,792	56,583	61,955	68,201	75,456	83,033	90,467	103,675	118,613
2	Petroleum	13,803	15,189	16,622	17,720	19,730	22,067	23,974	27,313	30,248
3	Manufacturing	20,740	22,803	25,160	28,332	31,049	34,359	38,325	44,370	50,915
4	Other	17,160	18,591	20,174	22,149	24,677	26,607	28,168	31,992	37,450
5	**Developed countries**	35,290	38,708	42,088	46,658	51,819	56,950	62,060	72,214	82,792
6	Petroleum	7,661	8,493	9,159	9,859	11,205	12,544	13,542	15,911	18,352
7	Manufacturing	17,214	18,912	20,721	23,285	25,572	28,320	31,558	36,550	41,793
8	Other	10,415	11,303	12,208	13,513	15,042	16,086	16,959	19,753	22,647
9	Canada	15,713	16,703	17,652	19,578	21,015	21,818	22,985	25,541	28,378
10	Petroleum	3,171	3,372	3,625	3,881	4,337	4,643	4,764	5,320	5,716
11	Manufacturing	6,697	7,059	7,535	8,404	8,971	9,504	10,491	11,755	13,446
12	Other	5,845	6,272	6,792	7,293	7,708	7,671	7,730	8,467	9,215
13	Europe	16,390	18,231	19,851	22,246	25,255	28,654	31,696	38,255	44,505
14	Petroleum	3,627	4,158	4,434	4,756	5,481	6,247	6,872	8,524	9,994
15	Manufacturing	8,906	9,867	10,940	12,372	13,819	15,628	17,529	20,777	23,765
16	Other	3,858	4,206	4,478	5,118	5,955	6,779	7,295	8,954	10,746
17	Other developed	3,187	3,774	4,284	4,834	5,549	6,478	7,378	8,417	9,909
18	Petroleum	863	963	1,100	1,223	1,387	1,654	1,906	2,066	2,642
19	Manufacturing	1,611	1,986	2,247	2,509	2,783	3,188	3,538	4,019	4,581
20	Other	712	824	938	1,102	1,379	1,636	1,931	2,332	2,686
21	**Developing countries**	13,866	14,928	16,545	17,735	19,168	20,992	22,863	25,266	28,479
22	Petroleum	5,651	5,312	5,900	6,140	6,620	7,300	7,965	8,436	8,261
23	Manufacturing	3,525	3,891	4,439	5,047	5,477	6,038	6,767	7,820	9,122
24	Other	5,290	5,725	6,206	6,548	7,072	7,654	8,130	9,010	11,097
25	Latin America	9,752	10,290	11,342	12,039	12,961	14,013	14,897	16,484	19,620
26	Petroleum	2,456	2,391	2,551	2,533	2,703	2,939	2,979	3,043	3,557
27	Manufacturing	2,973	3,238	3,723	4,202	4,541	4,995	5,620	6,456	7,487
28	Other	4,323	4,661	5,068	5,304	5,717	6,080	6,297	6,984	8,576
29	Other developing	4,114	4,638	5,202	5,695	6,207	6,979	7,966	8,782	8,859
30	Petroleum	2,595	2,921	3,348	3,607	3,917	4,361	4,986	5,392	4,703
31	Manufacturing	552	653	716	845	936	1,044	1,147	1,362	1,634
32	Other	967	1,064	1,138	1,244	1,354	1,574	1,833	2,027	2,521
33	**International and unallocated**	2,635	2,947	3,323	3,809	4,469	5,091	5,545	6,196	7,341
		Balance of payments income								
34	**All areas**	3,467	3,847	4,152	4,819	4,992	5,983	6,416	8,841	17,678
35	Petroleum	1,339	1,559	1,735	1,997	1,881	2,457	2,739	4,249	11,699
36	Manufacturing	950	1,018	1,055	1,126	1,605	1,696	1,910	2,472	2,636
37	Other	1,177	1,270	1,362	1,696	1,507	1,830	1,767	2,120	3,313
38	**Developed countries**	1,452	1,579	1,657	1,816	2,436	2,775	2,911	3,875	4,817
39	Petroleum	88	116	127	162	216	288	204	499	778
40	Manufacturing	818	850	851	920	1,357	1,437	1,621	2,119	2,255
41	Other	546	613	679	765	863	1,050	1,086	1,257	1,784
42	Canada	665	691	733	611	819	848	795	977	1,183
43	Petroleum	98	108	130	123	150	121	135	196	248
44	Manufacturing	280	231	224	178	278	311	351	412	497
45	Other	288	352	379	341	391	416	309	339	439
46	Europe	637	730	735	955	1,266	1,505	1,686	2,244	2,888
47	Petroleum	−16	5	−7	29	36	127	10	196	365
48	Manufacturing	453	526	520	602	901	922	1,084	1,358	1,482
49	Other	200	200	222	323	328	456	591	690	1,041
50	Other developed	151	157	190	251	351	422	430	654	746
51	Petroleum	6	3	4	10	29	40	59	107	165
52	Manufacturing	85	93	108	140	178	204	185	319	276
53	Other	59	62	78	101	144	178	185	228	305
54	**Developing countries**	1,916	2,171	2,430	2,652	2,340	2,712	3,079	4,729	12,465
55	Petroleum	1,229	1,382	1,580	1,684	1,496	1,895	2,213	3,595	10,712
56	Manufacturing	132	168	203	206	248	258	289	353	381
57	Other	584	621	646	762	596	559	576	781	1,373
58	Latin America	1,017	1,120	1,186	1,237	967	1,061	915	1,520	1,968
59	Petroleum	437	459	472	440	316	422	227	650	673
60	Manufacturing	108	141	164	171	205	208	236	275	307
61	Other	472	521	550	626	447	431	452	595	988
62	Other developing	929	1,051	1,244	1,415	1,372	1,651	2,164	3,209	10,498
63	Petroleum	793	923	1,108	1,244	1,180	1,473	1,987	2,945	10,039
64	Manufacturing	24	27	40	35	43	50	53	78	74
65	Other	113	100	96	136	149	128	124	186	384
66	**International and unallocated**	69	97	65	320	217	495	427	237	396

1. The data for 1966 are as reported in the 1966 census of U.S. direct investment abroad except for net capital outflows. Net capital outflows include census data only for companies which filed in both the 1966 sample survey and in the 1966 census.

NOTE.—Details may not add to totals because of rounding.

Selected Items, 1966–74 [1]

of dollars]

Net capital outflows / Reinvested earnings

1966	1967	1968	1969	1970	1971	1972	1973	1974	1966	1967	1968	1969	1970	1971	1972	1973	1974	Line
			Net capital outflows									Reinvested earnings						
3,625	3,073	2,880	3,190	4,281	4,738	3,530	4,968	7,455	1,791	1,757	2,440	2,830	3,176	3,176	4,532	8,158	7,508	1
787	1,102	1,174	924	1,492	1,940	1,613	1,442	1,158	156	206	248	29	575	421	356	1,925	1,814	2
1,611	1,224	946	1,210	1,263	1,564	1,163	1,863	2,712	918	845	1,357	1,987	1,528	1,796	2,830	4,107	3,786	3
1,227	746	760	1,056	1,527	1,234	754	1,663	3,585	717	707	836	814	1,073	959	1,346	2,126	1,907	4
3,064	2,198	1,627	2,044	3,071	2,895	1,989	3,810	5,042	1,206	1,266	1,699	2,344	2,141	2,538	3,692	6,177	5,523	5
743	736	505	487	1,083	1,097	648	1,109	1,292	45	90	64	62	270	254	390	1,240	1,180	6
1,374	960	638	924	1,106	1,280	840	1,420	2,103	719	729	1,116	1,665	1,206	1,499	2,396	3,488	3,082	7
948	502	393	633	883	518	501	1,280	1,647	442	447	519	616	665	785	906	1,449	1,261	8
965	372	384	582	763	64	376	581	629	627	650	834	1,002	699	1,023	1,379	1,867	2,202	9
113	106	147	152	301	73	−96	106	−107	85	91	108	111	159	234	276	452	512	10
439	11	−4	260	234	−39	227	149	415	285	334	442	610	339	574	770	1,008	1,289	11
433	255	241	170	228	29	245	327	321	257	224	285	280	201	214	333	406	400	12
1,835	1,435	984	1,197	1,894	2,209	1,139	3,070	3,563	414	423	617	1,054	1,136	1,215	1,891	3,607	2,721	13
593	574	358	261	676	822	588	1,057	974	−65	−42	−86	−103	49	−52	18	575	517	14
851	684	543	587	787	1,091	528	1,225	1,515	338	285	514	870	679	747	1,366	2,071	1,448	15
392	177	83	349	430	296	23	788	1,074	141	180	189	286	407	520	507	861	757	16
244	391	258	265	415	623	474	159	850	165	193	248	288	306	300	422	804	600	17
37	56	90	75	105	202	156	−53	425	25	41	42	54	62	71	96	213	151	18
84	265	99	76	85	228	85	47	173	96	110	161	185	187	178	259	409	345	19
124	70	70	114	225	193	233	165	252	44	43	44	50	57	51	67	182	105	20
499	757	1,151	798	984	1,302	1,132	921	1,718	427	297	480	420	601	557	795	1,568	1,558	21
−4	245	531	309	458	590	645	24	−592	68	33	51	−62	71	102	42	494	423	22
237	264	308	286	157	284	323	443	609	199	116	240	321	322	297	435	619	705	23
265	247	313	202	368	428	164	454	1,701	160	148	188	161	208	188	319	454	430	24
303	311	708	385	579	696	272	654	2,270	309	202	361	331	453	373	645	991	915	25
−107	−76	141	32	136	210	21	−54	421	23	11	19	−51	41	26	20	155	85	26
187	197	275	215	132	228	288	360	503	174	83	209	263	259	246	364	476	534	27
223	191	292	138	311	268	−37	348	1,346	113	108	132	118	153	101	262	360	295	28
196	446	444	412	405	606	860	266	−552	118	96	119	89	148	183	190	576	643	29
104	321	390	277	323	379	624	78	−1,013	45	22	32	−12	30	77	21	339	338	30
50	68	33	71	25	56	35	83	105	25	33	31	58	63	50	71	143	170	31
42	57	21	64	57	170	201	106	356	47	41	56	43	55	56	58	94	135	32
62	117	102	348	226	541	409	238	694	157	194	261	67	434	81	45	413	426	33

Adjusted earnings / Earnings

1966	1967	1968	1969	1970	1971	1972	1973	1974	1966	1967	1968	1969	1970	1971	1972	1973	1974	Line
			Adjusted earnings									Earnings						
5,259	5,605	6,592	7,649	8,169	9,159	10,949	16,999	25,186	5,231	5,522	6,486	7,485	8,023	9,002	10,800	16,940	25,141	34
1,496	1,765	1,983	2,026	2,456	2,878	6,174	6,128	13,513	1,482	1,751	1,963	1,996	2,405	2,835	3,063	6,128	13,513	35
1,868	1,863	2,411	3,113	3,133	3,492	4,740	6,579	6,422	1,909	1,860	2,395	3,071	3,141	3,517	4,761	6,674	6,498	36
1,895	1,977	2,198	2,510	2,580	2,790	3,113	4,246	5,251	1,840	1,912	2,128	2,418	2,477	2,649	2,976	4,137	5,129	37
2,660	2,845	3,357	4,190	4,577	5,313	6,603	10,052	10,341	2,665	2,792	3,277	4,065	4,458	5,181	6,465	9,975	10,270	38
133	206	−192	224	485	541	594	1,739	1,958	126	189	164	180	404	460	502	1,626	1,836	39
1,537	1,579	1,968	2,585	2,563	2,937	4,017	5,607	5,337	1,580	1,583	1,954	2,557	2,579	2,964	4,036	5,691	5,420	40
990	1,060	1,198	1,381	1,528	1,835	1,992	2,707	3,046	959	1,020	1,159	1,328	1,475	1,757	1,927	2,658	3,014	41
1,294	1,341	1,567	1,643	1,518	1,871	2,174	2,844	3,385	1,288	1,301	1,514	1,570	1,452	1,803	2,113	2,795	3,333	42
183	199	237	234	309	355	411	648	760	188	201	239	236	303	354	416	659	772	43
565	565	665	788	617	885	1,121	1,450	1,786	583	558	649	766	605	882	1,110	1,449	1,792	44
546	576	664	621	592	630	642	746	839	517	542	625	568	543	568	587	687	769	45
1,050	1,153	1,352	2,008	2,401	2,721	3,577	5,751	5,609	1,062	1,141	1,329	1,971	2,374	2,680	3,530	5,733	5,603	46
−81	−37	−93	−74	85	75	28	771	882	−90	−52	−116	−104	33	14	−47	678	780	47
791	811	1,033	1,473	1,581	1,670	2,451	3,429	2,929	809	817	1,033	1,466	1,605	1,693	2,478	3,487	2,988	48
341	379	412	610	735	976	1,098	1,551	1,798	342	376	412	609	736	972	1,098	1,568	1,835	49
316	351	408	539	658	722	852	1,458	1,347	315	351	435	523	632	697	823	1,447	1,334	50
31	43	47	64	91	111	155	320	316	28	40	41	49	67	92	133	290	284	51
181	203	269	325	366	381	445	728	621	187	208	272	324	369	389	448	754	640	52
104	105	122	150	201	229	252	410	409	100	103	122	150	196	217	242	403	410	53
2,373	2,469	2,909	3,072	2,941	3,269	3,874	6,297	14,023	2,352	2,452	2,889	3,044	2,926	3,264	3,888	6,339	14,089	54
1,297	1,415	1,632	1,622	1,567	1,997	2,255	4,089	11,135	1,297	1,424	1,641	1,640	1,601	2,047	2,327	4,176	11,291	55
331	284	444	528	570	555	724	972	1,085	330	277	441	515	562	554	725	983	1,078	56
744	769	834	923	805	717	895	1,235	1,803	725	751	807	889	763	663	836	1,180	1,720	57
1,326	1,322	1,546	1,568	1,421	1,434	1,560	2,511	2,882	1,306	1,297	1,519	1,526	1,375	1,384	1,509	2,479	2,801	58
460	470	492	389	357	447	247	805	758	461	472	494	393	359	447	248	813	761	59
282	224	373	434	464	455	600	751	841	278	215	366	419	454	452	599	759	835	60
584	628	682	744	600	532	713	955	1,284	567	611	659	715	562	485	662	997	1,205	61
1,047	1,147	1,363	1,504	1,521	1,834	2,314	3,785	11,141	1,045	1,154	1,370	1,517	1,551	1,880	2,379	3,861	11,268	62
838	946	1,140	1,232	1,210	1,550	2,008	3,284	10,377	836	952	1,147	1,247	1,242	1,599	2,079	3,363	10,525	63
49	60	70	93	106	100	124	221	244	51	62	75	95	106	192	175	224	243	64
160	141	152	179	205	184	182	280	519	158	140	148	175	201	175	174	273	515	65
226	291	326	387	650	577	472	650	822	215	278	319	376	639	557	448	625	782	66

Table 12.—U.S. Direct Investment Position Abroad at Yearend—1973

[Millions of dollars]

By country	All industries	Mining and smelting	Petroleum	Manufacturing Total	Food products	Chemicals and allied products	Primary and fabricated metals	Machinery	Transportation equipment	Other manufacturing	Transportation, communication, and public utilities	Trade	Finance and insurance	Other industries
All countries	103,675	6,038	27,313	44,370	3,781	8,415	2,971	11,811	7,544	9,848	2,837	9,313	9,726	4,079
Developed countries	72,214	3,773	15,911	36,550	3,042	6,488	2,295	10,259	6,469	7,997	839	6,784	6,107	2,250
Canada	25,541	2,666	5,320	11,755	1,102	1,767	779	2,325	2,249	3,532	665	1,606	2,752	778
Europe	38,255	56	8,524	20,777	1,577	3,814	1,368	6,743	3,514	3,757	136	4,519	3,065	1,178
United Kingdom	11,040	(D)	2,457	6,611	576	1,042	343	2,008	1,186	1,456	40	741	854	(D)
European Economic Community (6)	19,022	(D)	4,575	11,509	742	2,251	703	4,066	2,069	1,678	31	1,650	944	(D)
Belgium and Luxembourg	2,512	0	(D)	1,497	62	467	72	518	(D)	(D)	3	371	265	(D)
France	4,295	-1	639	2,946	186	453	119	1,011	481	693	4	(D)	130	(D)
Germany	7,650	-1	2,250	4,449	244	578	291	1,683	1,299	345	18	372	474	95
Italy	2,212	3	(D)	1,413	130	350	73	586	101	149	5	(D)	72	59
Netherlands	2,352	(D)	854	1,204	120	402	148	267	(D)	(D)	1	207	2	(D)
Other Europe	8,194	(D)	1,492	2,657	259	525	321	669	259	624	57	2,129	1,267	(D)
Denmark	514	1	334	72	(D)	12	5	(D)	(D)	(D)	1	(D)	1	(D)
Ireland	344	(*)	18	309	(D)	173	17	(D)	(D)	(D)	(*)	(D)	3	(D)
Norway	466	(D)	200	209	(*)	(D)	(D)	(D)	(*)	34	9	15	1	(D)
Spain	982	(D)	87	571	110	124	(D)	165	(D)	74	9	128	47	(D)
Sweden	859	0	(D)	429	(D)	31	30	236	(D)	103	4	72	8	(D)
Switzerland	3,814	0	79	702	68	73	53	100	(D)	(D)	2	1,716	1,105	211
Other	1,215	(D)	(D)	364	(D)	(D)	44	(D)	15	(D)	42	123	101	(D)
Japan	2,671	0	868	1,399	(D)	301	11	732	116	(D)	(D)	260	31	(D)
Australia, New Zealand, and South Africa	5,746	1,052	1,198	2,619	(D)	602	137	458	590	(D)	(D)	398	258	(D)
Australia	4,319	844	842	2,025	195	498	102	363	483	384	(D)	241	226	(D)
New Zealand	260	(D)	(D)	93	(D)	18	(*)	5	(D)	10	(*)	44	(D)	(D)
South Africa	1,167	(D)	(D)	501	69	85	35	91	(D)	(D)	1	113	(D)	45
Developing countries	25,266	2,265	8,436	7,820	739	1,927	676	1,552	1,075	1,851	652	2,010	2,309	1,774
Latin America	16,484	1,682	3,043	6,456	603	1,584	566	1,163	1,015	1,526	454	1,563	2,108	1,177
Latin American Republics	13,527	1,194	2,162	5,992	578	1,422	(D)	1,118	1,015	(D)	377	1,340	(D)	(D)
Argentina	1,144	44	141	781	65	171	(D)	124	218	(D)	1	54	61	(D)
Brazil	2,885	81	198	2,033	133	343	84	512	479	495	16	212	229	103
Chile	643	(D)	(D)	50	(*)	21	7	1	-5	23	131	28	(*)	16
Colombia	608	(D)	76	325	(D)	107	11	44	(D)	133	(D)	45	(D)	14
Mexico	2,379	85	10	1,798	169	503	162	359	212	396	31	305	61	88
Panama	1,549	1	(D)	89	(D)	73	(D)	2	(D)	(D)	42	375	699	(D)
Peru	859	466	149	164	42	29	15	6	22	47	-2	42	10	32
Venezuela	2,051	(D)	(D)	523	45	130	32	57	74	181	30	214	129	70
Other Central America	578	21	100	137	61	28	9	8	(*)	29	69	29	(D)	(D)
Other	832	5	361	91	41	19	12	7	(*)	23	47	35	175	108
Other Western Hemisphere	2,957	488	882	465	24	161	(D)	45	(*)	(D)	77	223	(D)	(D)
Bahamas	632	3	90	91	3	(D)	0	-2	0	(D)	11	(D)	255	(D)
Bermuda	504	0	91	(D)	6	(D)	0	(D)	(*)	2	(D)	(D)	1	29
Jamaica	618	(D)	29	214	10	10	(D)	2	0	(D)	(D)	5	9	25
Other	1,202	(D)	671	(D)	5	75	1	(D)	0	-5	18	30	(D)	52
Other Africa	2,376	408	1,589	143	16	25	56	1	(D)	(D)	35	57	34	109
Liberia	209	19	(D)	4	0	3	0	(*)	0	1	(D)	7	(D)	57
Libya	537	0	529	(*)	0	(*)	0	0	0	0	(*)	(D)	1	(D)
Nigeria	458	(*)	429	18	1	5	2	1	0	8	2	10	(*)	(*)
Other	1,171	388	(D)	124	15	17	55	(*)	(D)	(D)	(D)	(D)	(D)	(D)
Middle East	2,588	3	2,139	109	3	34	6	29	(D)	(D)	8	17	43	269
Iran	129	(*)	64	36	3	7	0	4	(D)	(D)	3	3	9	14
Other	2,459	3	2,075	73	(*)	27	6	25	(*)	15	5	14	34	255
Other Asia and Pacific	3,818	172	1,665	1,109	118	285	48	358	47	254	155	374	124	219
India	337	(*)	(D)	216	8	83	18	64	4	39	(*)	5	6	(D)
Indonesia	797	(D)	573	38	0	7	(D)	2	(*)	(D)	(D)	5	4	27
Philippines	656	(D)	118	295	87	84	-3	20	(D)	(D)	(D)	94	48	52
Other	2,028	11	(D)	561	22	110	(D)	272	(D)	96	114	273	65	(D)
International and unallocated	6,196		2,967								1,316	518	1,310	55
Addendum. European Economic Community (9)[1]	30,919	(D)	7,385	18,501	1,355	3,478	1,071	6,134	3,258	3,207	80	2,165	1,503	(D)

*Less than $500,000 (±).
DSuppressed to avoid disclosure of data of individual companies.
1. Consists of the "European Economic Community (6)," Denmark, Ireland, and the United Kingdom.

NOTE.—Details may not add to totals because of rounding.

Table 13.—U.S. Direct Investment Position Abroad at Yearend—1974

[Millions of dollars]

By country	All industries	Mining and smelting	Petroleum	Manufacturing							Transportation, communication, and public utilities	Trade	Finance and insurance	Other industries
				Total	Food products	Chemicals and allied products	Primary and fabricated metals	Machinery	Transportation equipment	Other manufacturing				
All countries	118,613	6,124	30,248	50,915	4,408	10,166	3,389	13,747	7,722	11,483	3,100	11,293	12,462	4,471
Developed countries	82,792	4,024	18,352	41,793	3,577	7,809	2,615	11,800	6,658	9,335	900	8,065	7,219	2,439
Canada	28,378	2,793	5,716	13,446	1,245	2,044	911	2,669	2,540	4,036	714	1,854	3,120	735
Europe	44,505	47	9,994	23,765	1,871	4,750	1,546	7,774	3,341	4,483	157	5,422	3,727	1,392
United Kingdom	12,461	(D)	2,915	7,201	684	1,232	393	2,130	1,132	1,630	60	825	1,049	(D)
European Economic Community (6)	21,741	(D)	4,847	13,337	898	2,829	797	4,820	1,902	2,091	39	2,008	1,157	(D)
Belgium and Luxembourg	2,878	0	371	1,817	76	670	76	583	(D)	(D)	3	430	199	55
France	4,886	−4	637	3,411	212	551	136	1,193	507	810	10	610	161	64
Germany	7,998	−1	2,038	4,804	320	667	333	1,943	1,102	431	15	445	607	99
Italy	2,769	5	634	1,764	138	399	90	773	107	235	10	227	75	76
Netherlands	3,209	(D)	1,168	1,541	152	542	163	329	(D)	(D)	1	295	115	(D)
Other Europe	10,303	(D)	2,231	3,227	289	690	356	824	307	763	59	2,589	1,521	(D)
Denmark	689	1	481	88	35	11	6	29	2	6	−1	74	1	45
Ireland	468	1	23	416	18	248	19	39	−2	94	(*)	22	4	3
Norway	710	(D)	393	248	(*)	(D)	142	(D)	(*)	40	(*)	17	2	(D)
Spain	1,354	(D)	210	735	126	156	63	214	68	108	10	168	60	(D)
Sweden	1,019	0	392	526	20	47	36	277	(D)	(D)	4	80	9	7
Switzerland	4,538	0	76	798	65	86	53	127	(D)	(D)	2	2,094	1,815	253
Other	1,525	3	656	416	24	(D)	36	(D)	12	130	43	135	130	141
Japan	3,337	0	1,368	1,533	88	336	16	787	129	178	31	275	58	72
Australia, New Zealand, and South Africa	6,572	1,184	1,274	3,048	373	670	142	569	648	637	−2	514	314	240
Australia	4,773	960	782	2,306	265	543	104	439	516	439	−2	307	2,2	149
New Zealand	342	(D)	(D)	117	27	25	1	8	(D)	(D)	(*)	52	5	41
South Africa	1,457	(D)	(D)	624	81	111	38	122	(D)	(D)	1	156	37	51
Developing countries	28,479	2,100	8,261	9,122	831	2,357	774	1,947	1,064	2,148	691	2,619	3,718	1,970
Latin America	19,620	1,439	3,557	7,487	679	1,951	639	1,458	980	1,779	474	1,987	3,410	1,266
Latin American Republics	14,704	1,037	2,036	6,996	652	1,784	(D)	1,395	980	(D)	308	1,713	1,480	1,043
Argentina	1,155	50	146	772	61	198	58	136	152	155	11	67	55	68
Brazil	3,658	84	243	2,502	161	451	107	685	489	622	18	350	282	164
Chile	600	343	(D)	43	(*)	17	8	(*)	−8	22	129	27	(*)	(D)
Colombia	629	17	58	375	18	147	13	51	4	143	15	53	94	16
Mexico	2,825	84	17	2,146	197	635	191	432	233	461	34	400	65	76
Panama	1,549	−1	55	115	6	94	1	7	−2	10	43	440	629	267
Peru	895	411	239	159	46	24	17	6	20	43	−2	52	9	30
Venezuela	1,772	21	659	609	54	145	40	67	90	208	31	245	125	87
Other Central America	681	22	(D)	174	64	50	(D)	4	1	(D)	68	41	53	(D)
Other	940	5	447	101	45	22	16	8	(*)	20	51	38	167	119
Other Western Hemisphere	4,916	402	1,521	491	27	167	(D)	63	(*)	(D)	76	273	1,930	223
Bahamas	721	4	175	87	3	(D)	0	−2	0	(D)	11	86	214	142
Bermuda	2,311	0	(D)	136	7	(D)	0	58	(*)	(D)	19	133	1,676	(D)
Jamaica	612	284	(D)	217	10	(D)	(D)	2	0	16	(D)	7	7	26
Other	1,272	114	992	50	7	39	1	5	0	−2	(D)	48	33	(D)
Other Africa	2,223	442	1,340	160	18	25	62	4	(D)	(D)	42	73	53	113
Liberia	258	19	103	2	0	3	0	(*)	0	(*)	31	7	34	61
Libya	542	0	534	(*)	0	(*)	0	0	0	0	(*)	2	1	5
Nigeria	238	(*)	209	20	1	6	2	2	0	8	2	14	(D)	(D)
Other	1,185	423	493	140	17	16	60	2	(D)	(D)	9	49	(D)	(D)
Middle East	2,129	3	1,618	130	4	48	7	35	(D)	(D)	12	38	70	259
Iran	−576	(*)	−622	50	3	17	1	5	(D)	(D)	3	5	13	−25
Other	2,705	3	2,240	80	(*)	31	6	29	(*)	13	8	33	57	284
Other Asia and Pacific	4,507	216	1,746	1,344	131	333	65	451	68	296	163	521	85	332
India	345	(*)	85	234	8	90	16	73	3	44	(*)	5	7	14
Indonesia	705	(D)	408	72	(*)	13	(D)	5	(*)	(D)	(D)	−1	6	35
Philippines	727	(D)	135	340	98	97	(*)	22	(D)	(D)	(D)	97	56	60
Other	2,729	22	1,118	699	24	133	(D)	351	(D)	110	132	420	115	223
International and unallocated	7,341		3,635								1,509	609	1,526	62
Addendum:														
European Economic Community (9) [1]	35,359	(D)	8,267	21,041	1,635	4,320	1,215	7,018	3,033	3,820	98	2,928	2,211	(D)

*Less than $500,000 (±).
D Suppressed to avoid disclosure of data of individual companies.
1. Consists of the "European Economic Community (6)," Denmark, Ireland, and the United Kingdom.

NOTE.—Details may not add to totals because of rounding.

Table 14.—Net Capital Outflows—1973

[Millions of dollars]

By country	All industries	Mining and smelting	Petroleum	Manufacturing Total	Food products	Chemicals and allied products	Primary and fabricated metals	Machinery	Transportation equipment	Other manufacturing	Transportation, communication, and public utilities	Trade	Finance and insurance	Other industries
All countries	4,968	220	1,442	1,863	189	354	54	357	495	414	-175	552	896	169
Developed countries	3,810	217	1,109	1,420	142	268	55	214	348	393	9	451	567	36
Canada	581	191	106	148	10	39	29	-27	45	52	4	-9	146	-5
Europe	3,070	9	1,057	1,225	115	194	48	272	296	300	1	370	384	23
United Kingdom	847	(D)	191	490	40	81	3	75	123	168	(D)	43	102	26
European Economic Community (6)	1,819	(D)	785	606	52	113	35	169	151	85	(D)	171	233	25
Belgium and Luxembourg	111	0	(D)	68	-1	8	-2	44	(*)	17	-1	45	-76	(D)
France	404	(*)	(D)	134	13	19	11	31	(D)	24	(D)	6	-43	(D)
Germany	920	0	403	305	17	91	9	46	48	(D)	(*)	(D)	203	(D)
Italy	197	(*)	(D)	103	13	18	10	48	(*)	3	2	-3	58	(D)
Netherlands	187	(D)	134	-5	8	-23	7	(*)			(D)	155	49	-27
Other Europe	403	(D)	81	129	23	(*)		10	28	22	48	(D)	(*)	-3
Denmark	50	(*)	(D)	13	(D)	(*)		(*)	(D)	(D)	(D)	1	(*)	-1
Ireland	3	1	(D)	-10	(D)	(D)	(D)	(D)	(*)	(D)		2	(*)	2
Norway	72	3	56	9	(*)	(*)		(D)	(*)	(D)	1	11	4	7
Spain	-31	1	-55	-1	2	-7	1		-1	8	(*)	18	(*)	(*)
Sweden	56	0	24	14	(D)	-4	(D)		8	2	(D)	101	51	-33
Switzerland	223	0	15	89	(D)	-1	(*)		4	46	(D)	15	-7	1
Other	37	(D)	3	15	(D)	1	(D)		(D)	(D)	(D)			
Japan	40	0	-75	41	2	16	-5	16	1	11	(D)	50	15	(D)
Australia, New Zealand, and South Africa	119	17	22	6	15	19	-16	-48	6	29	(D)	40	22	(D)
Australia	9	(D)	-3	-31	-3	12	-13	-42	(D)	-3	17	22	(D)	(D)
New Zealand	28	(*)	9	8	2	2	-4	1	(D)	(D)	(*)	4	(D)	(D)
South Africa	82	(D)	16	28	(D)	4	1	-7	(D)	(D)	(*)	14	2	(D)
Developing countries	921	3	24	443	46	86	-2	143	147	22	-25	103	236	136
Latin America	654	6	-54	360	35	108	-9	103	125	-2	-29	87	170	114
Latin American Republics	371	21	-199	338	29	95	-9	100	125	-3	-26	69	(D)	(*)
Argentina	7	(D)	(D)	26	(D)	8	(D)	-4	31	(*)	(*)	(D)	(D)	(*)
Brazil	346	28	-6	233	(D)	33	(D)	89	71	26	(*)	25	54	12
Chile	-3	(*)	(*)	-2	-1	-1	(*)	(*)	-1		(D)	1	1	1
Colombia	-26	1	-32	10	(*)	14	(*)	-3	-2	-4	3	7	5	(*)
Mexico	55	-4	-1	19	-1	18	-2	(D)	16	20	-10	21	6	12
Panama	9	1	30	-6	(D)	1	(D)	-1	(*)	(D)	(*)	4	-16	-6
Peru	81	22	56	2	1	20	-1	(*)	(*)	2	(*)	5	1	7
Venezuela	-124	(D)	(D)	35	2	3	-8	-2	5		(*)	-2	19	36
Other Central America	20	4	-12	8	4	1	-2	2	1	1	-1	5	(D)	(D)
Other	6	-6	-21	12	10		-2	(*)		0	4	(D)	(D)	(D)
Other Western Hemisphere	284	-15	145	22	6	13	(*)	3	0	1	-3	18	(D)	(D)
Bahamas	50	3	2	3	2	(*)	0	0	0	(*)	-3	(D)	23	(D)
Bermuda	40	0	(D)	(D)	1	(*)	(*)	(D)	0	(*)	-3	(D)	5	1
Jamaica	-9	-17	3	1	1	(*)	(*)	(D)	0	(*)	1	4	(D)	(D)
Other	203	(*)	(D)	(D)	2	(D)	(D)	(D)	0	(*)	(*)	-3	3	(D)
Other Africa	-655	-9	-627	-19	(D)	(D)	1	-1	(D)	(D)	(D)	-3	3	(D)
Liberia	33	(D)	(D)	1	0	0	0	0	0	1	(*)	(D)	(D)	-1
Libya	(D)	0	(D)	(*)	0	(*)	0	(*)	0	0	(*)	-2	(*)	4
Nigeria	(D)	0	(D)	3	(D)	1	(*)	1	0	2	1	1	(D)	(*)
Other	-15	(D)	(D)	-23	(D)	(D)	1	-1	(D)	(D)	(D)	(D)	(D)	(*)
Middle East	577	(*)	515	18	(D)	(D)	(*)	(*)	(D)	(D)	-1	10	16	19
Iran	-200	0	(D)	12	(D)	(D)	0	-1	(D)	(D)	(*)	(D)	4	5
Other	778	(*)	(D)	7	(*)	4	(*)	1	0	2	-1	(D)	11	14
Other Asia and Pacific	344	6	190	84	1	11	6	41	9	16	(D)	8	47	(D)
India	7	0	(D)	-1	1	-1	(*)	5	(*)	(*)	-7	(*)	1	(D)
Indonesia	211	(D)	(D)	8	0	1	(D)	1	(*)	(D)	(D)	-1	3	(D)
Philippines	5	(*)	-46	14	(*)	2	1	1	(D)	(D)	(D)	6	27	(D)
Other	121	(D)	50	63	-1	9	(D)	33	(D)	17	3	4	16	(D)
International and unallocated	238		309								-159	-2	92	-2
Addendum: European Economic Community (9) [1]	2,713	(D)	1,014	1,099	83	205	38	244	281	247	(D)	222	336	47

*Less than $500,000 (±).
D Suppressed to avoid disclosure of data of individual companies.
1. Consists of the "European Economic Community (6)," Denmark, Ireland, and the United Kingdom.

NOTE.—Details may not add to totals because of rounding.

Table 15.—Net Capital Outflows—1974

[Millions of dollars]

By country	All industries	Mining and smelting	Petroleum	Manufacturing Total	Food products	Chemicals and allied products	Primary and fabricated metals	Machinery	Transportation equipment	Other manufacturing	Transportation, communication, and public utilities	Trade	Finance and insurance	Other industries
All countries	7,455	−36	1,158	2,712	277	505	109	808	311	702	5	1,076	2,293	2⁴⁷
Developed countries	5,042	112	1,292	2,103	259	268	82	660	265	570	−8	679	780	84
Canada	629	46	−107	415	44	29	31	94	79	139	−15	65	241	−15
Europe	3,563	6	974	1,515	181	245	57	484	149	399	15	510	444	99
United Kingdom	364	(*)	339	399	54	58	27	138	27	95	7	29	77	13
European Economic Community (6)	1,536	(*)	97	873	123	147	37	300	27	241	7	287	215	57
Belgium and Luxembourg	249	0	(D)	141	11	98	−4	20	(D)	(D)	(*)	52	−33	(D)
France	386	−1	(D)	277	29	15	7	119	(D)	(D)	6	82	27	(D)
Germany	70	0	−338	211	48	−1	20	86	−20	78	−3	69	107	23
Italy	350	1	152	137	5	5	7	78	2	40	5	34	4	16
Netherlands	481	(*)	217	106	28	31	7	−3	(D)	(D)	−1	49	109	(*)
Other Europe	1,162	6	538	243	5	41	−7	46	96	63	1	194	152	29
Denmark	115	(*)	97	13	(D)	−5	(*)	(D)	(D)	(D)	−1	(D)	−1	(D)
Ireland	51	(*)	6	38	(D)	38	(*)	(D)	(D)	(D)		(*)	(D)	(D)
Norway	199	(D)	183	7	(*)	1	(D)	(D)	0	(*)	(*)	1	(*)	(D)
Spain	226	2	114	83	1	3	(D)	13	41	(D)	1	18	7	2
Sweden	65	0	(D)	25	(D)	−2		11	(D)	(D)	(*)	4	1	(D)
Switzerland	366	0	1	69	(*)	9	−2	3	(D)	(D)	(*)	149	122	24
Other	140	(D)	(D)	7	(D)	−4	(D)	(D)	(D)	(D)	1	7	22	(D)
Japan	464	0	424	15	(D)	−41	4	15	9	(D)	(D)	10	26	(D)
Australia, New Zealand, and South Africa	386	60	1	158	(D)	35	−11	66	28	(D)	(D)	94	69	(D)
Australia	173	51	−85	92	3	17	−9	49	17	16	(D)	53	58	(D)
New Zealand	60	1	(D)	11	(D)	5	(*)	1	−2	(D)	(*)	7	(D)	4
South Africa	153	8	(D)	55	(D)	13	−2	17	13	(D)	(*)	34	(D)	(D)
Developing countries	1,718	−148	−592	609	17	237	27	148	46	133	1	361	1,327	161
Latin America	2,270	−223	421	503	16	199	17	145	21	105	9	241	1,248	70
Latin American Republics	375	−136	−190	507	16	(D)	(D)	(D)	21	(D)	18	246	(D)	(D)
Argentina	17	1	(D)	14	2	14	(D)	2	(D)	(*)	(D)	10	1	(D)
Brazil	462	7	1	221	3	50	3	105	(D)	(D)	2	129	50	51
Chile	−61	(D)	2	−7	(D)	−4	1	(*)	−4	−1	1	1	(*)	(*)
Colombia	−11	(D)	−16	14	(D)	21	(*)	4	(D)	−1	(D)	9	(D)	(*)
Mexico	200	−25	3	162	2	79	8	30	17	25	1	62	6	−9
Panama	−135	−1	(D)	18	(D)	(D)	(*)	(D)	(D)	(D)	4	19	−149	(D)
Peru	110	−5	101	5	4	1	(*)	(*)	(*)	(*)		6	(*)	3
Venezuela	−367	(D)	(D)	40	2	2	3	3	21	9	−1	−2	−8	14
Other Central America	90	2	36	24	(*)	13	(D)	−1	1	(D)	−2	10	11	8
Other	70	(*)	(D)	16	4	4	3	(*)	0	5	1	2	(D)	10
Other Western Hemisphere	1,895	−86	611	−3	(*)	(D)	(D)	(D)	0	(D)	−8	−5	(D)	(D)
Bahamas	166	2	(D)	−6	(*)	−3	0	0	0	−2	−1	−8	5	(D)
Bermuda	1,725	0	(D)	(D)	(*)	(D)	0	−4	0	(D)	(D)	−7	(D)	(D)
Jamaica	−9	(D)	(D)	(*)	−1	(D)	(D)	(*)	0	(D)	(D)	1	−2	1
Other	14	(D)	(D)	(D)	1	(D)	0	(*)	0	1	(D)	9	(D)	−27
Other Africa	−364	(D)	−416	8	(*)	−2	−6	3	3	9	(D)	7	15	3
Liberia	32	(D)	(D)	3	0	0	0	0	0	3	(D)	(*)	(D)	4
Libya	4	0	3	(*)	0	(*)	0	0	0	(*)	(*)	(D)	0	(D)
Nigeria	(D)	0	(D)	1	(*)	1	(D)	(*)	0	(*)	(*)	−1	(D)	(D)
Other	(D)	30	(D)	5	(*)	−2	−5	3	3	6	(D)	(D)	1	(D)
Middle East	−487	(*)	−531	13	(*)	9	2	3	(*)	(*)	3	20	23	−15
Iran	−723	(*)	(D)	10	(*)	7	1	(*)	(*)	1	(*)	2	(D)	−39
Other	237	0	(D)	3	(*)	1	1	2	0	−1	3	18	(D)	24
Other Asia and Pacific	299	(D)	−65	84	1	31	14	−2	21	20	(D)	92	41	103
India	−7	0	(D)	1	(*)	(*)	(*)	3	(*)	(*)	(*)	(*)	(D)	(D)
Indonesia	−195	32	−260	26	(*)	6	(D)	1	0	(D)	(*)	−2	2	6
Philippines	30	(D)	11	16	(*)	6	2	1	(D)	(D)	(*)	−3	7	10
Other	470	11	(D)	40	1	19	(D)	−8	(D)	13	10	98	31	(D)
International and unallocated	694		458									13	36	186	2
Addendum:														
European Economic Community (9) [1]	2,567	1	538	1,323	182	238	64	441	59	340	13	331	292	63

*Less than $500,000 (±).
D Suppressed to avoid disclosure of data of individual companies.
1. Consists of the "European Econgic Community (6)," Denmark, Ireland, and the United Kingdom.

NOTE.—Details may not add to totals because of rounding.

Table 16.—Reinvested Earnings—1973

[Millions of dollars]

By country	All industries	Mining and smelting	Petroleum	Manufacturing							Transportation, communication, and public utilities	Trade	Finance and insurance	Other industries
				Total	Food products	Chemicals and allied products	Primary and fabricated metals	Machinery	Transportation equipment	Other manufacturing				
All countries	8,158	138	1,925	4,107	230	834	185	1,357	745	756	160	969	646	213
Developed countries	6,177	106	1,240	3,488	188	735	144	1,128	686	607	38	706	413	186
Canada	1,867	67	452	1,008	107	146	38	243	263	212	33	168	110	28
Europe	3,507	(*)	575	2,071	66	496	83	756	376	293	5	463	284	109
United Kingdom	562	(*)	81	350	26	91	5	90	52	87	(D)	41	43	(D)
European Economic Community (6)	1,884	(*)	338	1,366	17	317	52	577	264	139	(D)	100	80	(D)
Belgium and Luxembourg	309	0	41	185	4	80	8	60	4	29	(*)	26	55	3
France	399	-1	10	365	12	45	5	146	109	49	(*)	31	-1	-6
Germany	779	0	243	499	-9	64	28	249	140	27	(D)	23	24	(D)
Italy	151	1	-6	160	4	66	3	74	4	10	(*)	-10	5	1
Netherlands	247	(*)	50	157	6	63	8	48	7	25	(*)	31	-3	11
Other Europe	1,060	(*)	156	355	23	89	26	89	61	67	(D)	321	160	(D)
Denmark	56	0	(D)	8	4	3	1	4	-3	(*)	22	11	(*)	(D)
Ireland	79	0	(D)	76	1	52	1	1	-1	(D)	0	2	0	(D)
Norway	32	0	9	16	(*)	2	(D)	3	0	7	(*)	3	(*)	4
Spain	104	(*)	-5	62	16	9	10	26	-4	4	(*)	19	3	21
Sweden	44	0	15	30	-1	6	1	20	(*)	(D)	(*)	(*)	(*)	-2
Switzerland	583	0	1	122	(*)	5	5	22	(D)	6	(*)	285	146	30
Other	162	(*)	102	39	3	12	(D)	13	(D)		(D)	1	10	(D)
Japan	298	0	97	164	1	38	2	83	9	31	(*)	33	3	1
Australia, New Zealand, and South Africa	505	39	116	245	14	55	22	45	37	71	(*)	42	16	48
Australia	320	26	64	172	8	43	17	34	17	53	(*)	24	13	21
New Zealand	40	(*)	(D)	13	2	3	(*)	1	(D)	(D)	(*)	6	(*)	(D)
South Africa	145	12	(D)	60	4	9	4	10	(D)	(D)	0	11	3	(D)
Developing countries	1,568	32	494	619	42	99	41	229	59	149	23	194	181	24
Latin America	991	23	155	476	32	89	37	120	60	138	11	135	180	11
Latin American Republics	807	23	70	442	30	81	36	98	60	135	8	110	132	22
Argentina	4	5	(D)	1	-8	1	-1	3	-2	9	(*)	3	(D)	(*)
Brazil	356	7	40	259	18	21	14	67	60	79	1	12	26	11
Chile	4	-1	3	(*)	-1	(*)	(*)	0	0	1	(*)	(*)	(*)	-1
Colombia	23	1	(*)	20	3	5	1	3	(*)	7	1	22	3	-4
Mexico	170	9	(*)	138	15	43	14	26	15	1	2	54	77	(D)
Panama	190	(*)	(D)	7	2	2	(*)	1	(*)	1	1	5	(*)	2
Peru	12	2	-5	7	(*)			3	-3	9		10	15	-2
Venezuela	3	(*)	-16	-6	-2	(*)	6	3	1	9	2	10	15	-2
Other Central America	15	(*)	-3	14	4	(*)	(*)	2	(*)	1	(*)	1	2	(*)
Other	31	(*)	6	2	(*)	(*)	1	(*)	0	1	1	1	(D)	(*)
Other Western Hemisphere	184	(*)	86	34	2	8	(*)	21	0	3	4	25	48	-11
Bahamas	49	0	17	6	(*)	5	0	(*)	0	0	1	14	18	-7
Bermuda	98	0	(D)	22	1	(*)	0	21	0	(*)	3	9	(D)	-3
Jamaica	4	(*)	1	2	1	(*)	(*)	(*)	0	1	(*)	(*)	1	(*)
Other	33	0	(D)	4	2	3	(*)	(*)	0	1	1	1	(D)	-1
Other Africa	202	12	178	1	2	1	4	(*)	-2	-4	(D)	2	-2	(D)
Liberia	12	(D)	4	-1	0	(*)	0	0	0	-1	(D)	1	-2	3
Libya	(D)	0	(D)	0	0	0	0	0	0	0	0	(*)	0	(*)
Nigeria	(D)	0	(D)	(*)	1	(*)	(*)	(*)	0	-1	0	3	(*)	-4
Other	31	(D)	14	2	3	(*)	3		-1	-2	-1	(*)	-2	(*)	(D)
Middle East	98	0	90	6	1	2	(*)	2	-1	2	1	-2	1	(*)
Iran	17	0	(D)	2	1	2	0	(*)	-1	(*)	1	(D)	(*)	(*)
Other	81	0	(D)	4	(*)	(*)	(*)	2	(*)	2	(*)	(D)	1	1
Other Asia and Pacific	276	-3	71	135	7	7	1	108	1	12	(D)	59	2	(D)
India	5	(*)	1	4	(*)	1	(*)	2	(*)	1	(*)	(*)	(*)	(*)
Indonesia	22	(*)	(D)	3	0	(*)	(*)	1	0	3	(D)	-1	(*)	2
Philippines	20	(*)	2	11	7	2	(*)	1	-1	4	1	2	3	1
Other	229	-3	(D)	117	(*)	3	1	106	2	4	(*)	57	-1	(D)
International and unallocated	413		190								98	69	52	3
Addendum: European Economic Community (9)[1]	2,581	(*)	451	1,801	48	462	59	673	311	245	(D)	155	124	(D)

*Less than $500,000 (±).
D Suppressed to avoid disclosure of data of individual companies.
1. Consists of the "European Economic Community (6)," Denmark, Ireland, and the United Kingdom.

NOTE.—Details may not add to totals because of rounding.

Table 17.—Reinvested Earnings—1974

[Millions of dollars]

By country	All industries	Mining and smelting	Petroleum	Manufacturing Total	Food products	Chemicals and allied products	Primary and fabricated metals	Machinery	Transportation equipment	Other manufacturing	Transportation, communication, and public utilities	Trade	Finance and insurance	Other industries
All countries	7,508	185	1,814	3,786	346	1,173	291	1,130	−133	979	213	925	433	152
Developed countries	5,523	153	1,180	3,082	272	979	219	891	−77	798	51	625	324	109
Canada	2,202	82	512	1,289	99	248	102	250	212	379	44	185	127	−38
Europe	2,721	−2	517	1,448	111	659	102	554	−323	346	7	414	209	130
United Kingdom	528	(*)	119	173	54	116	23	−14	−83	77	4	54	109	70
European Economic Community (6)	1,214	−2	191	956	33	419	45	459	−193	193	2	84	−2	−14
Belgium and Luxembourg	111	0	−40	177	3	105	5	45	(D)	(D)	(*)	7	−37	4
France	202	−2	(D)	185	−4	83	(*)	69	(D)	(D)	(*)	4	4	−6
Germany	306	0	141	141	27	89	22	173	−179	9	1	14	29	−19
Italy	217	1	(D)	222	3	32	10	106	7	64	(*)	(D)	−2	(*)
Netherlands	379	(*)	97	231	4	109	7	66	1	44	1	39	4	7
Other Europe	979	−1	207	319	23	124	34	109	−48	76	(*)	276	102	75
Denmark	62	0	51	4	4	4	1	3	(D)	(D)	(*)	1	(*)	6
Ireland	70	(*)	−1	66	4	37	2	2	(D)	(D)		4	(*)	1
Norway	46	0	9	32	(*)	4	(D)	(D)	0	6	(*)	2	(*)	3
Spain	160	−1	13	80	15	28	11	36	(D)	(D)	(*)	22	6	29
Sweden	95	0	20	72	2	19	8	30	(*)	13	(*)	5	(*)	2
Switzerland	380	0	−4	28	−3	4	2	24	−9	8	(*)	238	88	31
Other	175	(*)	119	37	2	28	(D)	(D)	(D)	(D)	(*)	5	7	7
Japan	159	0	76	77	−12	31	(*)	42	4	11	(*)	5	1	1
Australia, New Zealand, and South Africa	441	74	75	268	74	41	16	45	30	63	(*)	22	−12	16
Australia	282	66	25	188	67	27	10	28	16	40	(*)	12	−12	3
New Zealand	23	(*)	(D)	13	(D)	1	(*)	2	(D)	1	0	1	(*)	(D)
South Africa	136	8	(D)	67	(D)	13	5	15	(D)	21	0	9	−1	(D)
Developing countries	1,558	32	423	705	74	194	72	240	−56	181	36	245	78	38
Latin America	915	27	85	534	59	169	57	141	−56	163	9	181	51	27
Latin American Republics	882	27	83	506	57	(D)	(D)	(D)	−56	163	4	127	117	20
Argentina	−8	5	(D)	−23	−7	13	3	10	(D)	(D)	−1	3	−9	(D)
Brazil	304	−4	44	241	25	58	20	61	(D)	(D)	1	9	4	10
Chile	9	−1	(D)	−1	−1	1	(*)	(*)	0	(*)	−1	−2	(*)	(D)
Colombia	39	(*)	(*)	38	2	20	2	3	(*)	12	(*)	−1	1	1
Mexico	245	25	5	185	26	54	22	41	4	37	2	32	−1	−3
Panama	135	(*)	3	8	2	(D)	(D)	(D)	(*)	2	−3	47	79	2
Peru	4	2	−2	−3	(*)	−6	2	1	−2	2	1	4	−1	4
Venezuela	88	(*)	−1	47	6	13	5	8	−4	19	2	32	4	3
Other Central America	14	(*)	(D)	13	4	9	2	−3	(*)	3	1	2	(D)	1
Other	53	1	(D)	1	(*)	(*)	2	(*)	0	−1	1	(*)	(D)	1
Other Western Hemisphere	33	(*)	3	29	3	(D)	(D)	(D)	0	1	5	55	−65	7
Bahamas	−77	0	(D)	2	(*)	3	0	(*)	0	−1	1	(D)	−46	−3
Bermuda	77	0	54	22	1	(D)	0	(D)	0		1	(D)	−23	(D)
Jamaica	7	(*)	(D)	3	1	1	(*)	(*)	0	1	(D)	(*)	1	(*)
Other	25	0	(D)	2	1	(D)	(D)	(D)	0	1	(D)	(*)	3	(D)
Other Africa	220	(D)	174	9	2	2	11	−1	−2	−4	(D)	9	3	1
Liberia	20	(D)	1	−4	0	(*)	0	0	0	−4	(D)	1	4	(*)
Libya	1	0	2	0	0	0	0	0	0	0	0	(*)	0	−1
Nigeria	(D)	0	(D)	2	(*)	1	(*)	(*)	0	(*)	0	4	(*)	−3
Other	(D)	6	(D)	11	2	1	11	−1	−2	(*)	(*)	4	(*)	5
Middle East	25	0	13	8	1	4	(*)	3	1	(*)	1	1	4	−2
Iran	19	0	(D)	3	1	2	0	1	1	−1	(*)	(*)	(D)	(*)
Other	6	0	(D)	5	(*)	2	(*)	2	(*)	1	1	1	(D)	−2
Other Asia and Pacific	398	(D)	152	153	12	19	3	96	1	22	(D)	54	20	12
India	15	(*)	−1	17	(*)	8	−2	6	(*)	6	(*)	(*)	(*)	(*)
Indonesia	104	(D)	95	8	0	1	(*)	1	0	6	(D)	(*)	(*)	1
Phillippines	45	(*)	11	29	11	6	1	1	1	9	−1	5	(*)	1
Other	234	(*)	48	100	(*)	5	5	88	(*)	2	8	50	19	11
International and unallocated	426	....	210								126	55	30	5
Addendum:														
European Economic Community (9)[1]	1,875	−2	360	1,198	95	576	70	450	−284	291	6	143	107	62

*Less than $500,000 (±).

D Suppressed to avoid disclosure of data of individual companies.

1. Consists of the "European Economic Community (6)," Denmark, Ireland, and the United Kingdom.

NOTE.—Details may not add to totals because of rounding.

Table 18.—Balance of Payments Income—1973

[Millions of dollars]

By country	All industries	Mining and smelting	Petroleum	Manufacturing							Transportation, communication, and public utilities	Trade	Finance and insurance	Other industries
				Total	Food products	Chemicals and allied products	Primary and fabricated metals	Machinery	Transportation equipment	Other manufacturing				
All countries	8,841	497	4,249	2,472	298	513	113	714	391	444	42	479	798	304
Developed countries	3,875	230	499	2,119	247	413	96	649	356	358	−2	298	499	232
Canada	977	134	196	442	26	75	43	71	108	118	(D)	26	120	(D)
Europe	2,244	2	196	1,358	158	273	42	478	206	201	−1	231	312	146
United Kingdom	716	−1	68	406	43	56	16	158	(D)	(D)	2	56	154	31
European Economic Community (6)	1,180	(*)	156	843	96	196	21	290	(D)	(D)	−3	68	89	26
Belgium and Luxembourg	116	0	1	102	6	32	1	36	(D)	(D)	(*)	2	10	1
France	187	0	4	151	7	39	4	54	5	42	−3	13	14	9
Germany	636	0	84	452	73	77	13	138	122	31	(*)	30	63	7
Italy	74	(*)	1	64	6	21	2	29	1	5	0	8	3	−2
Netherlands	166	0	66	75	4	28	2	33	1	8	(*)	15	−1	11
Other Europe	348	2	−28	109	19	21	5	31	(D)	(D)	(*)	107	69	89
Denmark	8	0	(D)	2	1	(*)	(*)	1	1	(*)	(*)	3	(*)	(D)
Ireland	−12	(*)	(D)	2	1	(*)	(*)	(*)	0	1	0	1	1	(D)
Norway	−14	0	−24	7	1	(*)	1	4	(*)	1	(*)	1	(*)	2
Spain	41	(*)	2	25	4	11	2	5	2	2	(*)	6	(*)	7
Sweden	29	0	2	22	1	2	(*)	15	(*)	4	(*)	4	(*)	(*)
Switzerland	195	0	(*)	38	(D)	5	1	4	(D)	11	(*)	72	57	28
Other	100	3	12	12	(D)	3	1	2	1	(D)	(*)	20	9	44
Japan	216	0	13	140	(D)	27	(*)	67	1	(D)	(D)	20	50	(D)
Australia, New Zealand, and South Africa	438	95	94	179	(D)	39	10	33	40	(D)	(*)	21	17	31
Australia	351	75	84	149	14	29	9	31	38	27	(*)	12	12	19
New Zealand	17	(*)	(D)	5	1	2	(*)	(*)	(*)	2	0	4	1	(n)
South Africa	70	20	(D)	26	(D)	8	1	2	2	(D)	0	6	4	(D)
Developing countries	4,729	267	3,595	353	51	99	17	65	35	86	16	139	287	72
Latin America	1,520	223	650	275	44	77	15	42	35	63	12	94	220	45
Latin American Republics	1,192	128	544	(D)	42	(D)	15	41	35	62	6	81	129	(D)
Argentina	67	(D)	13	(D)	3	(D)	6	(D)	(D)	6	(*)	(*)	(D)	5
Brazil	70	2	(D)	45	8	6	3	9	7	11	(*)	6	(D)	−4
Chile	2	1	(*)	(*)	(*)	(*)	(*)	0	(*)	(*)	(*)	2	(D)	(*)
Colombia	24	(*)	−5	17	1	8	(*)	2	(*)	7	(*)	9	(*)	(D)
Mexico	98	5	3	74	11	22	3	15	(*)	15	3	38	43	6
Panama	97	0	2	1	(*)	(*)	(*)	(*)	8	0	(*)	1	1	11
Peru	78	(D)	5	5	2	1	(*)	(*)	(*)	1	(*)	1	1	−1
Venezuela	621	(D)	484	75	8	18	1	(D)	(D)	20	(*)	21	9	(D)
Other Central America	38	(D)	(D)	6	2	1	(*)	(*)	(*)	1	(*)	1	2	10
Other	98	11	36	8	6	1	(*)	0	0	1	2	2	(D)	(D)
Other Western Hemisphere	328	96	105	(D)	2	(D)	0	(*)	0	(*)	6	13	91	(D)
Bahamas	80	0	2	(*)	1	(*)	0	(*)	0	0	2	2	70	4
Bermuda	8	0	0	(*)	(*)	(*)	0	(*)	0	0	(D)	1	1	(D)
Jamaica	79	(D)	2	(D)	1	(D)	0	(*)	0	(*)	3	1	3	(*)
Other	160	(D)	102	(D)		(D)	0	(*)	0	(*)	1	(D)	18	2
Other Africa	466	(D)	421	4	1	(*)	1	(*)	0	2	1	9	4	(D)
Liberia	14	7	(*)	(*)	0	(*)	0	0	0	(*)	(*)	0	3	3
Libya	294	0	294	0	0	0	0	0	0	0	0	(*)	0	(*)
Nigeria	82	0	80	1	0	(*)	0	0	0	(*)	0	(*)	0	1
Other	76	(D)	47	3	1	(*)	1	(*)	0	1	(*)	9	1	(D)
Middle East	2,089	0	2,065	5	(*)	1	(*)	2	0	2	(*)	2	7	9
Iran	409	0	406	3	0	(*)	0	1	0	2	(*)	(*)	(*)	(*)
Other	1,680	0	1,659	3	(*)	1	(*)	1	0	(*)	(*)	2	7	9
Other Asia and Pacific	655	(D)	460	69	6	21	1	21	(*)	19	3	33	56	(D)
India	22	0	6	13	1	5	(*)	4	(*)	2	0	(*)	2	1
Indonesia	476	(D)	444	2	0	1	0	1	0	(*)	0	(*)	6	(D)
Philippines	29	(*)	−4	14	4	2	(*)	(*)	(*)	8	4	6	7	3
Other	127	(*)	14	40	1	14	1	16	(*)	8	(*)	27	41	5
International and unallocated	237	....	155	....							28	41	12	(*)
Addendum:														
European Economic Community (9)[1]	1,892	−1	204	1,254	140	252	38	448	(D)	(D)	−1	127	245	65

*Less than $500,000 (±).
D Suppressed to avoid disclosure of data of individual companies.
1. Consists of the "European Economic Community (6)," Denmark, Ireland, and the United Kingdom.

NOTE.—Details may not add to totals because of rounding.

Table 19.—Balance of Payments Income—1974

[Millions of dollars]

By country	All industries	Mining and smelting	Petroleum	Manufacturing Total	Food products	Chemicals and allied products	Primary and fabricated metals	Machinery	Transportation equipment	Other manufacturing	Transportation, communication, and public utilities	Trade	Finance and insurance	Other industries
All countries	17,678	636	11,699	2,636	256	654	87	739	454	445	88	889	1,401	350
Developed countries	4,817	272	778	2,255	211	486	73	678	453	355	(*)	486	783	243
Canada	1,183	122	248	497	(D)	82	24	80	(D)	129	(D)	83	120	(D)
Europe	2,888	−8	365	1,482	108	347	36	513	294	184	(*)	356	581	111
United Kingdom	498	(*)	−47	280	25	55	7	126	12	55	2	43	207	13
European Economic Community (6)	1,681	(*)	420	984	59	233	25	347	217	104	−2	69	188	23
Belgium and Luxembourg	242	0	(D)	125	5	68	2	27	(D)	(D)	0	(D)	101	(*)
France	163	0	13	123	9	20	3	63	3	26	−2	15	9	4
Germany	831	0	(D)	551	37	56	14	190	(D)	(D)	(*)	(D)	68	8
Italy	61	(*)	(D)	100	4	43	3	43	(*)	6	0	(D)	12	(*)
Netherlands	384	0	279	86	3	46	2	24	2	8	(*)	12	−3	11
Other Europe	709	−7	−8	217	24	59	4	40	65	25	(*)	245	186	76
Denmark	5	0	−9	3	(*)	(D)	(*)	1	2	(D)	(*)	(D)	(*)	(D)
Ireland	24	(*)	−17	38	1	(D)	(*)	(*)	0	(D)	0	(D)	1	(D)
Norway	(*)	−2	−8	6	1	(*)	(*)	3	0	2	(*)	3	(*)	2
Spain	47	−1	4	20	5	12	2	6	2	2	(*)	6	1	7
Sweden	27	0	4	20	(*)	(D)	(*)	(D)	0	1	(*)	3	(*)	(*)
Switzerland	527	0	3	109	(D)	11	(*)	11	(D)	13	(*)	208	168	30
Other	80	−4	17	12	(D)	(D)	1	(D)	(D)	3	(*)	18	16	21
Japan	216	0	23	127	(D)	22	(*)	60	(D)	8	(D)	18	62	(D)
Australia, New Zealand, and South Africa	530	158	142	149	25	35	13	25	19	34	(*)	29	19	32
Australia	401	129	(D)	115	12	28	11	23	15	25	(*)	15	14	(D)
New Zealand	12	1	(*)	6	(D)	1	(*)	(*)	(D)	2	0	4	1	1
South Africa	117	28	(D)	29	(D)	6	1	2	(D)	7	0	10	5	(D)
Developing countries	12,465	363	10,712	381	45	168	14	62	1	90	8	310	605	86
Latin America	1,968	263	673	307	39	148	12	39	(*)	69	17	173	497	39
Latin American Republics	1,237	161	466	(D)	34	(D)	8	36	(*)	68	13	151	194	(D)
Argentina	66	(*)	21	22	3	5	(*)	4	3	7	(*)	4	20	(*)
Brazil	97	(D)	21	34	9	14	3	10	(D)	(D)	(*)	16	(D)	−4
Chile	7	4	0	1	1	1	(*)	0	(*)	(*)	(*)	1	1	−1
Colombia	60	−1	−8	21	1	10	(*)	2	(*)	7	1	(D)	(D)	−1
Mexico	110	10	3	74	12	21	3	15	8	15	(*)	12	4	7
Panama	162	0	(*)	(D)	(*)	(D)	(*)	1	0	(*)	7	79	71	(D)
Peru	29	51	−44	12	2	8	(*)	(*)	(*)	1	(*)	5	2	2
Venezuela	466	(D)	333	40	3	9	1	4	(D)	(D)	1	21	(D)	3
Other Central America	67	(D)	27	6	3	2	(*)	(*)	(*)	1	1	(D)	4	8
Other	173	(D)	114	4	1	2	(*)	(*)	0	1	3	3	15	(*)
Other Western Hemisphere	730	102	207	(D)	5	(D)	4	3	0	1	4	22	303	(D)
Bahamas	186	0	(D)	1	(*)	(*)	0	0	0	1	1	7	137	(D)
Bermuda	229	0	(D)	(D)	(*)	(D)	0	3	0	0	0	8	(D)	(*)
Jamaica	92	(D)	(D)	6	(*)	(*)	4	(*)	0	1	2	1	(*)	(*)
Other	223	(D)	(D)	(D)	4	(D)	0	(*)	0	(*)	1	6	(D)	(*)
Other Africa	793	(D)	743	2	1	−1	(*)	(*)	0	1	1	5	3	(D)
Liberia	28	(D)	5	(*)	0	(*)	0	0	0	(*)	(*)	0	2	(D)
Libya	359	0	356	0	0	0	0	0	0	0	0	(*)	0	2
Nigeria	346	0	346	(*)	0	0	0	(*)	0	(*)	0	(*)	0	−1
Other	60	10	37	1	1	−1	(*)	(*)	0	1	(*)	5	1	6
Middle East	8,482	0	8,434	6	(*)	1	(*)	1	0	3	(*)	7	17	17
Iran	661	0	657	2	(*)	(*)	(*)	0	(*)	1	(*)	(*)	(*)	2
Other	7,821	0	7,777	4	(*)	(*)	(*)	1	0	2	(*)	7	17	15
Other Asia and Pacific	1,223	(D)	862	66	5	20	1	22	2	17	−10	125	88	(D)
India	10	0	−2	8	1	4	(*)	2	(*)	1	0	(*)	3	(*)
Indonesia	989	(D)	897	3	0	(*)	(*)	1	0	1	2	1	(D)	(D)
Philippines	18	(*)	−30	13	3	2	(*)	(*)	(*)	8	1	9	(D)	(D)
Other	205	−5	−3	42	1	14	1	18	1	6	−13	115	(*)	9
International and unallocated	396	....	210	....							80	93	13	(*)
Addendum: European Economic Community (9) [1]	2,207	−1	347	1,305	85	320	32	474	231	163	(*)	118	396	42

*Less than $500,000 (±).
D Suppressed to avoid disclosure of data of individual companies.
1. Consists of the "European Economic Community (6)," Denmark, Ireland, and the United Kingdom.

NOTE.—Details may not add to totals because of rounding.

Table 20.—Adjusted Earnings—1973

[Millions of dollars]

By country	All industries	Mining and smelting	Petroleum	Manufacturing Total	Food products	Chemicals and allied products	Primary and fabricated metals	Machinery	Transportation equipment	Other manufacturing	Transportation, communication, and public utilities	Trade	Finance and insurance	Other industries
All countries	16,999	636	6,174	6,579	528	1,347	298	2,071	1,136	1,199	202	1,448	1,444	517
Developed countries	10,052	336	1,739	5,607	434	1,149	240	1,777	1,042	965	36	1,005	912	417
Canada	2,844	201	648	1,450	133	221	81	314	371	330	(D)	195	230	(D)
Europe	5,751	2	771	3,429	224	769	125	1,234	582	495	4	694	596	255
United Kingdom	1,278	-1	149	756	68	147	21	248	(D)	(D)	(D)	97	197	(D)
European Economic Community (6)	3,064	(*)	494	2,210	113	512	73	867	(D)	(D)	(D)	168	170	(D)
Belgium and Luxembourg	426	0	42	286	10	111	9	96	(D)	(D)	(*)	28	65	4
France	585	-1	14	516	19	83	9	200	114	91	-3	43	13	3
Germany	1,415	0	326	952	64	140	41	386	262	58	(D)	53	88	(D)
Italy	225	1	-4	224	10	87	5	104	5	14	(*)	-2	7	-1
Netherlands	413	(*)	116	231	10	91	9	81	8	33	(*)	46	-4	23
Other Europe	1,408	2	128	464	42	110	31	119	(D)	(D)	(D)	428	229	(D)
Denmark	64	0	(D)	11	4	3	1	5	-3		(*)	14	1	(D)
Ireland	67	(*)	(D)	78	2	52	1	1	-1	22	0	3	1	(D)
Norway	19	0	-14	23	1	3	(D)	7	(*)	(D)	(*)	4	(*)	6
Spain	146	(*)	-2	88	19	20	12	30	-2	8	(*)	26	4	31
Sweden	72	0	17	52	(*)	8	1	35	(*)	8	(*)	4	1	-2
Switzerland	779	0	1	160	(D)	11	6	26	(D)	(D)	(*)	357	203	58
Other	262	3	114	51	(D)	15	(D)	15	(D)	(D)	(D)	21	20	(D)
Japan	514	0	110	303	(D)	65	2	150	11	(D)	(D)	53	53	(D)
Australia, New Zealand, and South Africa	943	134	210	424	(D)	94	32	79	77	(D)	(*)	63	34	80
Australia	671	101	148	321	23	72	26	65	55	80	(*)	36	25	40
New Zealand	57	(*)	7	17	3	5	(*)	1	(D)	(D)	(*)	10	1	22
South Africa	215	32	54	86	(D)	17	5	13	(D)	(D)	0	17	8	18
Developing countries	6,297	299	4,089	972	94	198	58	294	95	234	40	333	468	96
Latin America	2,511	247	805	751	76	166	52	161	96	201	23	229	400	56
Latin American Republics	2,000	151	614	(D)	73	(D)	51	140	96	197	14	191	261	(D)
Argentina	71	(D)	(D)	(D)	-5	(D)	5	(D)	(D)	15	(*)	3	15	4
Brazil	426	9	(D)	304	26	28	18	76	67	90	1	19	(D)	7
Chile	6	1	3	(*)	-1	(*)	(*)	0	(*)	1	(*)	2	(*)	-1
Colombia	46	1	-4	37	3	13	1	5	(*)	14	1	3	(D)	(D)
Mexico	268	14	4	213	26	65	17	42	23	40	2	31	3	2
Panama	288	(*)	(D)	8	3	2	(*)	1	(*)	1	4	92	120	(D)
Peru	90	(D)	(D)	12	2	4	3	1	(*)	3	(*)	6	1	2
Venezuela	623	(D)	468	69	7	18	4	(D)	(*)	29	2	30	24	(D)
Other Central America	53	(D)	(D)	20	7	8	2	1	(*)	3	1	3	4	10
Other	129	11	42	10	6	1	2	(*)		1	4	3	(D)	(D)
Other Western Hemisphere	512	96	191	(D)	3	(D)	(*)	22	0	3	9	38	139	(D)
Bahamas	129	0	19	6	(*)	5	0	(*)	0	1	3	16	88	-3
Bermuda	106	0	(D)	22	1	(*)	0	21	0	(*)	3	(D)	(D)	(D)
Jamaica	83	(D)	2	(D)	2	(D)	(*)	(*)	0	1	3	1	4	1
Other	193	(D)	(D)	(D)	(*)	(D)	(*)	(*)	0	1	1	(D)	(D)	1
Other Africa	668	(D)	599	5	3	1	4	(*)	-2	-2	(D)	11	1	(D)
Liberia	26	(D)	4	-1	0	(*)	0	0	0	-1	(D)	1	1	6
Libya	(D)	0	(D)	0	0	0	0	0	0	0	0	(*)	0	(*)
Nigeria	(D)	0	(D)	1	(*)	1	(*)	(*)	0	-1	0	3	(*)	-3
Other	107	(D)	61	6	4	(*)	4	-1	-2	(*)	(*)	7	(*)	(D)
Middle East	2,187	0	2,155	11	1	3	(*)	4	-1	5	2	(*)	8	10
Iran	426	0	(D)	5	1	2	0	1	-1	2	1	(D)	(*)	(*)
Other	1,761	0	(D)	7	(*)	1	(*)	3	(*)	3	1	(D)	8	10
Other Asia and Pacific	931	(D)	530	204	13	28	2	129	1	31	(D)	92	58	(D)
India	27	(*)	7	17	1	6	(*)	6	(*)	3	(*)	(*)	2	1
Indonesia	499	(D)	(D)	5	0	1	(*)	2	0	4	(D)	(*)	6	(D)
Philippines	50	(*)	-2	25	11	4	1	-1	-1	12	4	8	10	4
Other	355	-3	(D)	157	1	17	2	122	2	12	(*)	81	40	(L)
International and unallocated	650		346								126	111	64	4
Addendum: European Economic Community (9) [1]	4,473	-1	656	3,054	188	713	97	1,121	(D)	(D)	(D)	282	368	(D)

*Less than $500,000 (±).
D Suppressed to avoid disclosure of data of individual companies.
1. Consists of the "European Economic Community (6)," Denmark, Ireland, and the United Kingdom.

NOTE.—Details may not add to totals because of rounding.

Table 21.—Adjusted Earnings—1974

[Millions of dollars]

By country	All industries	Mining and smelting	Petroleum	Manufacturing Total	Food products	Chemicals and allied products	Primary and fabricated metals	Machinery	Transportation equipment	Other manufacturing	Transportation, communication, and public utilities	Trade	Finance and insurance	Other industries
All countries	25,186	821	13,513	6,422	602	1,827	378	1,870	321	1,424	300	1,814	1,834	482
Developed countries	10,341	425	1,958	5,337	483	1,464	292	1,568	376	1,153	51	1,111	1,107	352
Canada	3,385	203	760	1,786	(D)	330	126	330	(D)	507	(D)	268	248	(D)
Europe	5,609	-10	882	2,929	218	1,005	137	1,068	-29	530	7	770	790	241
United Kingdom	1,026	(*)	72	453	79	171	30	112	-71	132	7	96	316	82
European Economic Community (6)	2,895	-2	611	1,940	92	652	69	806	25	297	(*)	152	185	8
Belgium and Luxembourg	353	0	(D)	302	8	174	7	71	-11	53	(*)	(D)	64	4
France	365	-2	(D)	308	5	103	3	132	(D)	(D)	-2	(D)	13	-2
Germany	1,137	0	(D)	692	64	145	36	363	(D)	(D)	(*)	(D)	97	-11
Italy	278	(*)	(D)	322	7	75	13	149	7	71	(*)	(D)	11	(*)
Netherlands	762	(*)	376	317	8	155	10	90	3	52	1	51	1	18
Other Europe	1,688	-8	199	536	47	183	38	150	17	101	(*)	521	288	151
Denmark	67	0	42	6	4	1	1	4	(D)	(D)	(*)	(D)	2	(D)
Ireland	94	(*)	-18	104	5	(D)	2	2	(D)	(D)	0	(D)	1	(D)
Norway	46	-2	1	38	1	4	(D)	(D)	(D)	8	(*)	4	(*)	5
Spain	197	-1	17	110	20	41	14	42	(D)	(D)	(*)	28	7	37
Sweden	123	0	24	92	2	(D)	8	(D)	(*)	14	(*)	8	1	-2
Switzerland	907	0	-1	137	(D)	15	3	36	(D)	21	(*)	446	250	70
Other	255	-4	136	49	(D)	(D)	(D)	(D)	(D)	(D)	(*)	23	23	28
Japan	376	0	99	204	(D)	53	1	102	(D)	19	(D)	23	62	(D)
Australia, New Zealand, and South Africa	971	232	217	417	99	76	28	69	49	96	(*)	50	7	47
Australia	683	195	(D)	303	80	55	21	51	31	65	(*)	27	2	(D)
New Zealand	35	1	(D)	19	(D)	2	(*)	2	(D)	3	0	4	1	(D)
South Africa	253	36	96	96	(D)	19	7	17	(D)	28	0	19	4	(D)
Developing countries	14,023	396	11,135	1,085	119	362	86	301	-55	271	44	556	684	124
Latin America	2,882	291	758	841	99	317	70	180	-56	232	26	354	548	65
Latin American Republics	2,119	188	549	(D)	91	(D)	(D)	(D)	-56	230	16	277	311	(D)
Argentina	58	5	(D)	-2	-4	18	4	13	(D)	(D)	(*)	7	11	(D)
Brazil	401	(D)	65	275	34	72	23	71	(D)	(D)	1	25	(D)	6
Chile	16	3	(D)	1	(*)	1	(*)	(*)	(*)	(*)	-1	-1	(*)	(D)
Colombia	99	-1	-8	58	2	30	2	5	(*)	19	1	(D)	3	(*)
Mexico	355	34	7	259	38	75	25	56	12	53	3	44	3	5
Panama	296	(*)	3	(D)	2	(D)	(D)	(D)	(*)	3	4	125	150	(D)
Peru	33	53	-46	9	2	3	2	1	-1	3	1	9	1	5
Venezuela	554	(D)	332	87	10	22	6	11	(D)	(D)	2	53	(D)	6
Other Central America	81	(D)	(D)	20	6	10	2	-3	(*)	4	2	(D)	(D)	9
Other	226	(D)	(D)	5	1	1	2	(*)	0	1	4	3	(D)	(D)
Other Western Hemisphere	763	102	209	(D)	8	(D)	(D)	(D)	0	-2	9	77	237	(D)
Bahamas	109	0	-39	3	1	3	0	(*)	0	-1	2	(D)	91	(D)
Bermuda	306	0	(D)	(D)	1	(D)	0	(D)	0	(*)	1	2	1	(*)
Jamaica	100	(D)	(D)	8	1	1	4	(*)	0	1	(D)	2	(D)	(D)
Other	248	(D)	170	(D)	5	(D)	(D)	(D)	0	1	(D)	6	(D)	(D)
Other Africa	1,013	(D)	917	11	3	2	11	-1	-2	-3	(D)	14	6	(D)
Liberia	49	(D)	5	-4	0	(*)	0	0	0	-4	(D)	1	6	(D)
Libya	360	0	359	0	0	0	0	0	0	0	(*)	(*)	0	1
Nigeria	(D)	0	(D)	2	(*)	1	(*)	(*)	0	(*)	0	4	(*)	-3
Other	(D)	16	(D)	13	3	1	11	-1	-2	1	(*)	9	1	11
Middle East	8,507	0	8,447	14	1	5	(*)	4	1	3	1	8	21	15
Iran	680	0	(D)	5	1	3	0	1	1	(*)	(*)	(*)	(D)	2
Other	7,826	0	(D)	9	(*)	2	(*)	3	(*)	3	1	8	(D)	13
Other Asia and Pacific	1,621	(D)	1,014	219	16	39	5	118	2	39	(D)	179	109	(D)
India	26	(*)	-3	25	1	11	-2	8	(*)	7	(*)	(*)	3	(*)
Indonesia	1,093	(D)	992	11	0	1	(*)	2	0	7	(D)	(*)	(D)	(D)
Philippines	63	(*)	-19	42	14	8	1	2	1	17	(*)	14	(D)	(D)
Other	439	-5	44	141	2	19	6	106	1	8	-5	165	79	20
International and unallocated	822	......	420	......	......	......	......	......	......	......	206	148	43	6
Addendum: European Economic Community (9) [1]	4,082	-3	707	2,504	180	896	102	924	-53	455	6	261	593	104

*Less than $500,000 (±).
D Suppressed to avoid disclosure of data of individual companies.
1. Consists of the "European Economic Community (6)," Denmark, Ireland, and the United Kingdom.

NOTE.—Details may not add to totals because of rounding.

Table 22.—Earnings—1973

[Millions of dollars]

By country	All indus-tries	Mining and smelt-ing	Petro-leum	Manufacturing							Trans-porta-tion, commu-nica-tion, and public utilities	Trade	Fi-nance and insur-ance	Other indus-tries
				Total	Food prod-ucts	Chemi-cals and allied prod-ucts	Primary and fabri-cated metals	Machin-ery	Trans-porta-tion equip-ment	Other manu-factur-ing				
All countries	16,940	617	6,128	6,674	548	1,353	302	2,117	1,150	1,204	190	1,447	1,378	505
Developed countries	9,975	326	1,626	5,691	453	1,149	243	1,825	1,057	963	34	1,010	869	418
Canada	2,795	197	659	1,449	134	218	85	317	380	316	49	194	177	71
Europe	5,733	2	678	3,487	234	766	127	1,270	587	503	2	702	608	253
United Kingdom	1,278	−1	123	780	68	149	22	263	102	176	4	104	193	75
European Economic Community (6)	3,056	(*)	442	2,244	123	508	74	887	415	236	−2	167	184	22
Belgium and Luxembourg	432	0	42	289	10	112	8	98	22	39	(*)	27	72	2
France	582	−1	12	517	19	84	9	201	113	91	−3	42	13	2
Germany	1,433	0	295	1,002	75	151	43	404	268	61	1	54	86	−5
Italy	223	1	−6	224	10	87	5	104	5	14	(*)	−2	7	−1
Netherlands	386	(*)	99	212	9	74	9	81	8	31	(*)	46	6	23
Other Europe	1,398	2	113	464	43	109	31	120	69	91	(*)	431	231	157
Denmark	57	0	(D)	10	4	3	1	5	−3	(*)	−1	13	1	(D)
Ireland	66	(*)	(D)	78	2	52	2	1	−1	22	0	3	1	(D)
Norway	12	0	−21	23	1	3	(D)	(D)	(*)	7	(*)	(D)	(*)	(D)
Spain	150	(*)	−2	91	20	21	12	31	−2	8	(*)	26	4	32
Sweden	69	0	15	52	−1	8	1	36	(*)	8	(*)	4	(*)	−2
Switzerland	783	0	1	160	12	11	6	26	(D)	(D)	(*)	359	207	56
Other	260	3	114	50	4	14	(D)	(D)	(D)	(D)	1	(D)	18	(D)
Japan	525	0	102	321	(D)	68	2	158	11	(D)	(D)	55	52	(D)
Australia, New Zealand, and South Africa	922	128	188	434	(D)	97	29	81	80	(D)	(D)	60	32	(D)
Australia	646	95	125	330	24	74	23	68	59	83	0	33	23	41
New Zealand	58	(*)	(D)	18	3	5	(*)	1	(D)	(D)	(D)	10	1	(D)
South Africa	218	33	(D)	86	(D)	18	5	13	(D)	25	0	17	8	(D)
Developing countries	6,339	291	4,176	983	96	204	59	292	92	241	34	328	445	83
Latin America	2,479	238	813	759	78	169	52	161	94	205	18	225	377	48
Latin American Republics	1,992	146	623	718	75	156	52	140	94	202	13	188	248	56
Argentina	73	−6	20	35	−5	14	5	6	(*)	15	(*)	2	18	4
Brazil	427	9	60	303	27	27	18	74	65	92	1	18	29	7
Chile	5	(*)	3	(*)	−1	(*)	(*)	0	0	1	(*)	2	(*)	−1
Colombia	47	1	−4	38	1	13	1	6	(*)	15	1	(D)	(D)	−1
Mexico	268	15	5	215	25	67	17	42	23	40	2	30	3	−1
Panama	273	(*)	(D)	8	3	2	(*)	1	(*)	1	4	91	106	(D)
Peru	90	(D)	−21	13	2	4	3	1	0	3	(*)	(D)	1	(D)
Venezuela	632	(D)	470	77	7	20	4	9	7	31	2	32	24	(D)
Other Central America	51	(D)	(D)	20	7	7	2	1	(*)	2	1	2	4	9
Other	128	11	43	10	6	1	1	(*)	0	1	3	3	(D)	(D)
Other Western Hemisphere	486	92	190	41	3	13	(*)	21	0	3	5	37	129	−8
Bahamas	124	0	19	6	(*)	5	0	(*)	0	1	2	15	88	−7
Bermuda	105	0	(D)	22	1	(*)	0	21	0	(*)	3	15	(D)	−3
Jamaica	76	(D)	2	3	2	(*)	(*)	(*)	0	1	(*)	1	(D)	1
Other	181	(D)	(D)	9	(*)	8	(*)	(*)	0	1	(*)	6	22	1
Other Africa	662	32	596	5	3	1	4	(*)	−2	−2	(D)	12	1	(D)
Liberia	24	(D)	4	−1	0	(*)	0	0	0	−1	(D)	1	1	5
Libya	330	0	330	0	0	0	0	0	0	0	0	(*)	0	(*)
Nigeria	202	0	203	1	(*)	1	(*)	(*)	−1	−1	0	3	(*)	−4
Other	105	(D)	60	5	3	(*)	4		−1	−2	(*)	(*)	8	(*)	(D)
Middle East	2,187	0	2,157	11	1	3	(*)	3	−1	5	1	(*)	8	9
Iran	423	0	417	5	1	2	0	1	−1	2	1	(*)	(*)	(*)
Other	1,764	0	1,739	6	(*)	1	(*)	2	(*)	3	1	1	8	9
Other Asia and Pacific	1,012	20	611	209	14	31	2	128	1	33	(D)	90	58	(D)
India	30	(*)	8	19	1	7	(*)	7	(*)	4	(*)	(*)	2	(D)
Indonesia	589	(D)	552	5	0	(*)	(*)	2	0	3	2	−1	6	(D)
Philippines	52	(*)	−3	28	11	4	1	−1	−1	14	4	9	10	4
Other	341	(D)	55	156	1	19	2	121	2	12	(D)	81	40	(D)
International and unallocated	625	....	326	....							122	110	64	4
Addendum: European Economic Community (9) [1]	4,458	−1	571	3,111	197	711	98	1,156	514	435	2	287	379	100

*Less than $500,000 (±).
D Suppressed to avoid disclosure of data of individual companies.
1. Consists of the "European Economic Community (6)," Denmark, Ireland, and the United Kingdom.

NOTE.—Details may not add to totals because of rounding.

Table 23.—Earnings—1974

[Millions of dollars]

By country	All industries	Mining and smelting	Petroleum	Manufacturing							Transportation, communication, and public utilities	Trade	Finance and insurance	Other industries
				Total	Food products	Chemicals and allied products	Primary and fabricated metals	Machinery	Transportation equipment	Other manufacturing				
All countries	25,141	794	13,513	6,498	608	1,837	375	1,908	350	1,420	287	1,795	1,773	480
Developed countries	10,270	418	1,836	5,420	490	1,469	289	1,613	409	1,149	47	1,117	1,068	364
Canada	3,333	197	772	1,792	146	328	127	333	363	495	64	266	183	59
Europe	5,603	-10	780	2,988	216	1,008	137	1,102	-10	535	(D)	779	818	(D)
United Kingdom	963	(*)	36	447	72	170	28	119	-78	135	(D)	99	294	(D)
European Economic Community (6)	2,954	-2	574	2,001	96	655	70	832	50	298	(D)	148	228	(D)
Belgium and Luxembourg	371	0	-39	305	8	177	7	72	(D)	(D)	(*)	16	85	3
France	355	-2	21	305	5	103	3	131	(*)	62	-2	23	13	-3
Germany	1,199	0	304	768	69	158	38	388	50	65	(*)	43	96	-12
Italy	271	(*)	-78	322	6	76	13	149	7	69	(*)	16	11	(*)
Netherlands	758	(*)	365	301	7	141	9	90	(D)	(D)	(D)	50	23	(D)
Other Europe	1,686	-8	169	540	49	183	38	151	18	102	(*)	532	296	157
Denmark	60	0	38	4	4	3	1	4	(D)	(D)	(*)	(D)	(*)	(D)
Ireland	95	(*)	-18	105	4	70	2	2	(D)	(D)	0	(D)	1	(D)
Norway	23	-2	-22	38	1	4	(D)	(D)	0	8	(*)	4	(*)	5
Spain	202	-1	17	113	21	42	14	43	(D)	(D)	(*)	29	7	38
Sweden	117	0	20	91	2	20	8	48	(*)	13	(*)	8	(*)	-2
Switzerland	933	0	-2	141	13	16	3	35	(D)	(D)	(*)	456	264	75
Other	255	-4	137	48	3	29	(D)	(D)	-3	15	(*)	23	23	28
Japan	383	0	88	219	(D)	56	(*)	108	7	(D)	(D)	25	62	(D)
Australia, New Zealand, and South Africa	951	232	196	421	(D)	78	25	71	49	(D)	0	47	6	51
Australia	654	194	99	306	80	57	18	52	32	67	0	24	(*)	31
New Zealand	35	1	(D)	18	3	2	(*)	2	(D)	(D)	0	5	1	(D)
South Africa	262	37	(D)	96	(D)	19	6	17	(D)	29	0	18	4	(D)
Developing countries	14,089	376	11,291	1,078	118	368	86	295	-59	271	40	531	663	111
Latin America	2,801	271	761	835	97	321	70	175	-60	231	21	330	528	55
Latin American Republics	2,069	175	556	721	89	243	(D)	(D)	-60	231	15	254	300	48
Argentina	55	5	40	-4	-4	18	4	13	(D)	(D)	(*)	6	12	-3
Brazil	405	2	70	275	35	72	23	67	-14	91	1	25	28	5
Chile	11	-1	(D)	1	(*)	1	(*)	(*)	0	(*)	(*)	-1	(*)	(D)
Colombia	99	-1	(D)	60	2	30	2	5	(*)	20	1	3	(D)	(*)
Mexico	348	36	8	257	36	77	25	56	(D)	(D)	2	39	3	2
Panama	288	(*)	3	13	2	7	(*)	3	(*)	2	4	127	140	1
Peru	28	45	-46	12	2	5	3	1	-2	3	1	9	1	6
Venezuela	533	(D)	332	85	9	22	(D)	(D)	3	35	2	38	13	(D)
Other Central America	78	(D)	22	18	6	10	2	-3	(*)	3	2	6	(D)	8
Other	223	16	123	5	1	1	2	(*)	0	1	3	3	52	21
Other Western Hemisphere	731	96	206	113	8	78	(D)	(D)	0	1	6	76	227	7
Bahamas	102	0	-39	2	(*)	3	0	(*)	0	-1	(D)	48	90	(D)
Bermuda	305	0	75	(D)	1	(D)	0	(D)	0	0	(*)	1	114	(D)
Jamaica	90	(D)	3	(D)	(D)	1	(D)	(*)	0	1	3	2	1	(*)
Other	235	(D)	167	19	(D)	(D)	(*)	(*)	0	1	(D)	5	22	(*)
Other Africa	1,010	(D)	915	10	3	1	11	-1	-2	-4	(D)	14	6	(D)
Liberia	47	(D)	5	-4	0	(*)	0	0	0	-4	(D)	1	6	(D)
Libya	360	0	358	0	0	0	0	0	0	0	0	(*)	0	1
Nigeria	493	0	491	2	(*)	1	(*)	(*)	0	(*)	0	4	(*)	-3
Other	110	16	60	12	3	1	11	-1	-2	(*)	(*)	9	1	11
Middle East	8,512	0	8,455	14	1	5	(*)	1	1	3	1	8	20	14
Iran	678	0	668	5	1	3	0	1	1	(*)	(*)	(*)	1	2
Other	7,834	0	7,786	8	(*)	2	(*)	3	(*)	3	1	8	19	12
Other Asia And Pacific	1,767	(D)	1,160	220	17	40	4	117	2	40	(D)	179	108	(D)
India	26	(*)	-3	25	1	11	-2	8	(*)	7	(*)	(*)	3	(*)
Indonesia	1,251	(D)	1,152	9	0	1	(*)	2	0	6	(D)	(*)	10	(D)
Philippines	70	(*)	-17	45	14	9	1	1	1	19	1	15	16	10
Other	420	-5	28	141	2	20	6	105	1	8	-5	164	78	19
International and unallocated	782		387								200	147	42	6
Addendum:														
European Economic Community (9) [1]	4,072	-3	630	2,557	176	898	102	957	-36	460	(D)	259	523	(D)

*Less than $500,000 (±).
D Suppressed to avoid disclosure of data of individual companies.
1. Consists of the "European Economic Community (6)," Denmark, Ireland, and the United Kingdom.

NOTE.—Details may not add to totals because of rounding.

(Continued from page 48)

addition to the U.S. direct investment position. This addition was in finance and insurance; the position in extractive industries decreased.

Net capital outflows were $1.7 billion (table 3) and there was a small negative valuation adjustment. Most of the outflows went to Latin American finance affiliates of U.S. petroleum parents. The net capital outflow resulted from a complicated shift in the area and industry distribution of trade receivables held by U.S. petroleum parents and their foreign affiliates. Essentially, U.S. parents: (i) reduced their trade receivables (claims) due from their incorporated petroleum distribution and marketing affiliates in petroleum importing areas (a U.S. net capital inflow); and (ii) increased claims on their unincorporated finance affiliates in Latin America (a U.S. net capital outflow). As a result, unincorporated finance affiliates, rather than U.S. parents, held the trade receivables due from affiliates in petroleum importing areas.

There were other large, and mostly offsetting, capital flows involving unincorporated petroleum affiliates. Substantial capital outflows to affiliates operating in the North Sea and other petroleum development areas, to finance development of new supply sources and to build terminals and distribution facilities, were offset by capital inflows from petroleum affiliates in established petroleum extraction areas.

Adjusted earnings

Adjusted earnings—the return on the U.S. direct investment position—were $25.2 billion, up 48 percent from 1973 (table 7). The adjusted earnings rate of

return, which is the ratio of adjusted earnings to the average of the beginning- and end-of-year direct investment positions—was a record 22.7 percent. This exceptional rate of return mainly reflected the earnings of petroleum affiliates, which accounted for 54 percent of total adjusted earnings in 1974 but only 26 percent of the average direct investment position. The adjusted earnings rate of return estimates were strongly affected by the very large adjusted earnings of an unincorporated petroleum affiliate in the Middle East, part of which ultimately accrue to the host country.[7] The rate of return for petroleum was 47 percent in 1974, up from 24 percent in 1973. Excluding the earnings accruing to the above mentioned affiliate's host country in both years, the 1974 rate of return for petroleum showed only a moderate rise. The area pattern of rates of return also was substantially affected by this special case.

Annual additions to the U.S. direct investment position were translated into dollars at foreign exchange rates prevailing when the additions were made; additions made in past years were not adjusted upward to take account of subsequent depreciations of the dollar, because the necessary data were not available. Accordingly, the rate of return—adjusted earnings divided by the direct investment position—is biased upwards.

Current-account balance of payments items

Two types of payments by foreign affiliates to U.S. parents are included

7. See "Foreign Direct Investment in the United States in 1973" in the August 1974 SURVEY OF CURRENT BUSINESS, Part II, and "Foreign Direct Investment in the United States in 1974" in this issue of the SURVEY.

in the current account of the U.S. balance of payments—income on direct investment, and fees and royalties.

Income was $17.7 billion, double the 1973 level (table 8). Petroleum affiliates accounted for $11.7 billion of the total; a substantial portion was accounted for by the previously-mentioned Middle East affiliate. The increased earnings reflected higher prices, higher crude production, and higher per-barrel profits, because tax and royalty rates in important producing countries were left essentially unchanged for most of 1974. However, late in the year, per-barrel profits were sharply curtailed by increased tax and royalty rates by host countries; reduced imports of petroleum by consuming countries—a result of high petroleum prices and the deepening recession—contributed to the decline in earnings.

Income from manufacturing affiliates increased slightly, despite a decrease in earnings, because their dividend payout increased; the increased payout apparently was related to their large earnings in the previous year.

Table 9 shows the derivation of adjusted earnings and their relationship to the various income items.

Fees and royalties were $3.0 billion in 1974, up $0.5 billion (table 10). Fees and royalties are not included in adjusted earnings or balance of payments income on direct investment because they are not returns on invested capital. They consist of payments for services rendered, including management fees and service charges, film and television rentals, rentals of tangible property, and payments for the sale or use of intangible property provided by U.S. parents to their affiliates.

AMERICAN BUSINESS ABROAD

Origins and Development
of the Multinational Corporation

An Arno Press Collection

Abrahams, Paul Philip. *The Foreign Expansion of American Finance and its Relationship to the Foreign Economic Policies of the United States, 1907-1921.* 1976

Adams, Frederick Upham. *Conquest of the Tropics:* The Story of the Creative Enterprises Conducted by the United Fruit Company. 1914

Arnold, Dean Alexander. *American Economic Enterprises in Korea, 1895-1939.* 1976

Bain, H. Foster and Thomas Thornton Read. *Ores and Industry in South America.* 1934

Brewster, Kingman, Jr. *Antitrust and American Business Abroad.* 1958

Callis, Helmut G. *Foreign Capital in Southeast Asia.* 1942

Crowther, Samuel. *The Romance and Rise of the American Tropics.* 1929

Davids, Jules. *American Political and Economic Penetration of Mexico, 1877-1920.* 1976

Davies, Robert Bruce. *Peacefully Working to Conquer the World:* Singer Sewing Machines in Foreign Markets, 1854-1920. 1976

de la Torre, Jose R., Jr. *Exports of Manufactured Goods from Developing Countries.* 1976

Dunn, Robert W. *American Foreign Investments.* 1926

Dunning, John H. *American Investment in British Manufacturing Industry.* 1958

Edelberg, Guillermo S. *The Procurement Practices of the Mexican Affiliates of Selected United States Automobile Firms.* 1976

Edwards, Corwin. *Economic and Political Aspects of International Cartels.* 1944

Elliott, William Yandell, Elizabeth S. May, J.W.F. Rowe, Alex Skelton, Donald H. Wallace. *International Control in the Non-Ferrous Metals.* 1937

Estimates of United States Direct Foreign Investment, 1929-1943 and 1947. 1976

Eysenbach, Mary Locke. *American Manufactured Exports, 1879-1914.* 1976

Gates, Theodore R., assisted by Fabian Linden. *Production Costs Here and Abroad.* 1958

Gordon, Wendell C. *The Expropriation of Foreign-Owned Property in Mexico.* 1941

Hufbauer, G. C. and F. M. Adler. *Overseas Manufacturing Investment and the Balance of Payments.* 1968

Lewis, Cleona, assisted by Karl T. Schlotterbeck. *America's Stake in International Investments.* 1938

McKenzie, F[red] A. *The American Invaders.* 1902

Moore, John Robert. *The Impact of Foreign Direct Investment on an Underdeveloped Economy: The Venezuelan* Case. 1976

National Planning Association. *The Creole Petroleum Corporation in Venezuela.* 1955

National Planning Association. *The Firestone Operations in Liberia.* 1956

National Planning Association. *The General Electric Company in Brazil.* 1961

National Planning Association. *Stanvac in Indonesia.* 1957

National Planning Association. *The United Fruit Company in Latin America.* 1958

Nordyke, James W. *International Finance and New York.* 1976

O'Connor, Harvey. *The Guggenheims.* 1937

Overlach, T[heodore] W. *Foreign Financial Control in China.* 1919

Pamphlets on American Business Abroad. 1976

Phelps, Clyde William. *The Foreign Expansion of American Banks.* 1927

Porter, Robert P. *Industrial Cuba.* 1899

Queen, George Sherman. *The United States and the Material Advance in Russia, 1881-1906.* 1976

Rippy, J. Fred. *The Capitalists and Colombia.* 1931

Southard, Frank A., Jr. *American Industry in Europe.* 1931

Staley, Eugene. *Raw Materials in Peace and War.* 1937

Statistics on American Business Abroad, 1950-1975. 1976

Stern, Siegfried. *The United States in International Banking.* 1952

U.S. Congress. House of Representatives. Committee on Foreign Affairs. *The Overseas Private Investment Corporation.* 1973

U.S. Congress. Senate. Special Committee Investigating Petroleum Resources. *American Petroleum Interests in Foreign Countries.* 1946

U.S. Dept. of Commerce. Office of Business Economics. *U.S. Business Investments in Foreign Countries.* 1960

U.S. Dept. of Commerce. Office of Business Economics. *U.S. Investments in the Latin American Economy.* [1957]

U.S. Dept. of Commerce and Labor. *Report of the Commissioner of Corporations on the Petroleum Industry:* Part III, Foreign Trade. 1909

U.S. Federal Trade Commission. *The International Petroleum Cartel.* 1952

Vanderlip, Frank A. *The American "Commercial Invasion" of Europe.* 1902

Winkler, Max. *Foreign Bonds, an Autopsy:* A Study of Defaults and Repudiations of Government Obligations. 1933

Yeoman, Wayne A. *Selection of Production Processes for the Manufacturing Subsidiaries of U.S.-Based Multinational Corporations.* 1976

Yudin, Elinor Barry. *Human Capital Migration, Direct Investment and the Transfer of Technology:* An Examination of Americans Privately Employed Overseas. 1976